New *Speaking Out* Videos on CD-ROM

OBSESSIVE-COMPULSIVE DISORDER

DAVE

"I tell myself, we're going to lock the door once today and leave ... it rarely happens."

HYPOCHONDRIASIS

HENRY

"I hear snickering in the background, 'Oh, it's him again.'"

POST TRAUMATIC STRESS DISORDER

SARA

"I would wake up 37 times a night for the slightest noise, thinking this crazy person was going to come in and do something to me."

MAJOR DEPRESSION

EVERETT

"You feel absolute worthlessness. You feel there is no hope for the future."

SOCIAL PHOBIA

STEVE

"I imagine that people are watching me. They are watching me stumble in my efforts...."

BULIMIA

JESSICA

"It started out with a diet for me ..."

HIV

JULIA

"HIV was the absolute prism through which I began to see the world ..."

BIPOLAR MOOD DISORDER WITH PSYCHOTIC FEATURES

ANN

"I felt very tense, like my mind was racing; that I was making unusual connections; that I couldn't sleep at night."

SCHIZOPHRENIA

LARRY

"My voices had gotten the most of me ..."

SCHIZOAFFECTIVE DISORDER

JOSH

"When I was first in the hospital, I thought I was in the middle of a massacre ..."

ADHD

JIMMY

"I think without it (medicine) I would be dreaming the whole entire day."

BORDERLINE PERSONALITY DISORDER

LIZ

"I have problems with anger management. In the past it has meant suicide attempts."

ALCOHOLISM

CHRIS

"The toughest thing I ever did was admitting that I had a problem."

AUTISM

XAVIER

"He is now talking, which was a blessing."

GENDER IDENTITY DISORDER

DENISE

"I didn't do it for the sexual purpose. It was just to be someone I always thought of myself as—to be the person I wanted to be."

Abnormal Psychology

Second Custom Edition for the
University of Illinois

THOMAS F. OLTMANNS
ROBERT E. EMERY

Taken from

Abnormal Psychology, Fifth Edition,
by Thomas F. Oltmanns and Robert E. Emery

PEARSON
Custom
Publishing

PEARSON
Prentice
Hall

Cover art: *Psych Heads* by Tom Rogers

Taken from:

Abnormal Psychology, Fifth Edition
by Thomas F. Oltmanns and Robert E. Emery
Copyright © 2007, 2004, 2001, 1998, 1995 by Pearson Education, Inc.
Published by Pearson Prentice Hall
Upper Saddle River, New Jersey 07458

This special edition published in cooperation with Pearson Custom Publishing.

Printed in the United States of America

10 9 8 7 6 5 4 3 2

ISBN 0-536-25935-6

2006500124

AL

Please visit our web site at *www.pearsoncustom.com*

PEARSON CUSTOM PUBLISHING
75 Arlington Street, Suite 300, Boston, MA 02116
A Pearson Education Company

Brief Contents

Contents

4 CLASSIFICATION AND ASSESSMENT OF ABNORMAL BEHAVIOR 92

5 MOOD DISORDERS AND SUICIDE   128

6 ANXIETY DISORDERS   174

7 ACUTE AND POSTTRAUMATIC STRESS DISORDERS, DISSOCIATIVE DISORDERS, AND SOMATOFORM DISORDERS   212

8 STRESS AND PHYSICAL HEALTH   250

9 PERSONALITY DISORDERS   278

10 EATING DISORDERS 316

16 PSYCHOLOGICAL DISORDERS OF CHILDHOOD 524

DSM-IV-TR TABLES

BOXES

CASE STUDIES

BRIEF CASE STUDIES

critical thinking **matters**

research methods

a closer look

getting help

PREFACE

◆◆

Emotional suffering touches all of our lives at some point in time. Psychological problems affect many of us directly and all of us indirectly—through our loved ones, friends, and the strangers whose troubled behavior we cannot ignore. Abnormal psychology is not about "them." Abnormal psychology is about all of us.

Abnormal psychology today also is about scientific inquiry. We once again bring both the science and the personal aspects of abnormal psychology to life in this fifth edition of our text. We answer pressing intellectual and human questions as accurately, sensitively, and completely as possible, given the pace of new discoveries. Throughout this book, we offer an engaging yet rigorous treatment of abnormal psychology, the latest research and theory, and the pressing needs of the people behind the disorders.

WHAT'S NEW IN THE FIFTH EDITION?

In this Fifth Edition of our text, we are excited to introduce two new features in every chapter called **Critical Thinking Matters** and **Getting Help,** as well as a new series of video interviews (that we helped to develop and edit) called **Speaking Out.** In addition, the Fifth Edition offers an engaging, streamlined presentation of psychological science including hundreds of updates based on the latest research.

Critical Thinking *Matters*

The new **Critical Thinking Matters** feature addresses a concern that instructors in abnormal psychology courses have told us about repeatedly, and it's one we wholeheartedly share: Students need to think critically about science and pseudoscience, especially in the Internet Age. Psychological disorders are frightening and burdensome to individuals, families, and society. Yet, any intellectually honest professional would admit that we simply do not have all the answers to many of the pressing questions posed to mental health experts. True, science is constantly moving forward as we uncover valuable new information about the causes and treatment of mental disorders. Some scientific leads prove to be misleading, however, and pseudoscientific misinformation (and outright charlatanism) abounds, especially on the Internet and in the popular media.

Critical thinking *matters* because psychological problems matter deeply to those who suffer and to their loved ones. Good research tells us—and them—which treatments work, and which ones don't, as well as what might cause mental illness, and what doesn't. Critical thinking *matters* because students in abnormal psychology surely will not remember all the details they learn in this course. In fact, they shouldn't focus exclusively on factual details, because the details will change with new scientific developments. If students can learn to think critically about abnormal psychology, the lesson will last a lifetime and be used repeatedly, not only in understanding psychological problems, but also in every area of life.

Our new **Critical Thinking Matters** features help students to *think* about science, about pseudoscience, and about themselves. For example, in Chapter 2 we address the belief, currently promoted widely on the Internet and in the popular media, that mercury in widely used measles/mumps/rubella (MMR) vaccinations in the 1990s caused an epidemic of autism (and perhaps a host of other psychological problems for children). **Critical Thinking Matters** outlines the concerns of the frightened public, but goes on to point out (1) the failure to find support for this fear in numerous, large scale scientific studies; (2) the scientific stance that the burden of proof lies with the proponents of any hypothesis, including speculations about MMR; and (3) the widely ignored fact that 10 of the original 13 authors who raised the theoretical possibility *publicly withdrew their speculation about autism and MMR in 2004.* (As we discuss in the text in Chapter 16, the apparent epidemic of autism very likely resulted from increased awareness of the disorder and loosened criteria for diagnosing autism.)

Our **Critical Thinking Matters** features also address important scientific and pseudoscientific issues about treatment. For example, our answer to the question, "Are all treatments equal?" is a resounding "No!" (Chapter 3), and we debunk treatments like "recovered memory therapy" (Chapter 7), facilitated communication (Chapter 15), and dozens of phony treatments for attention-deficit/hyperactivity disorder (Chapter 16). **Critical Thinking Matters** also gets personal, for example, by helping students to think critically about the media, body image, and eating disorders (Chapter 10) and resilience, not just risk, in response to stress (Chapter 8).

Getting Help

We also include a second key feature, **Getting Help,** in every chapter of this edition. (We introduced this feature in our fourth edition—and received enthusiastic reviews.) In **Getting Help,** we directly address students' personal concerns and begin to answer the sorts of questions that students often ask us privately after lecture. The **Getting Help** sections give responsible, empirically sound, and concrete guidance on such personal topics as:

- What treatments are likely to be most effective for particular disorders? (See Chapters 2, 6, 10, and 12)
- What can I do to help someone else? (See Chapters 5, 9, 10, and 16)
- How can I find the right therapist? (See Chapters 3, 5, and 12)
- Where can I get more reliable information from books, the Internet, or professionals in my community? (See Chapters 1, 5, 7, and 11)
- What self-help strategies can I try? (See Chapters 6, 11, and 12)

Students can also find research-based information on the effectiveness and efficacy of various treatments in Chapter 3, Treatment of Psychological Disorders, and in the Treatment headings near the end of every disorder chapter. We cover treatment generally at the beginning of the text but in detail in the context of each disorder, because different treatments are more or less effective for different psychological problems.

New *Speaking Out* Video Interviews

One of the best ways to understand the needs of the people behind the disorders is to hear their stories in their own words. We have worked in consultation with Prentice Hall and NKP Productions to produce a new video series called **Speaking Out: Interviews with People who Struggle with Psychological Disorders.** These sixteen new interviews give students a window into the lives of people who are not so different from anyone else, but who happen to struggle with disorders such as major depression, schizophrenia, OCD, anorexia nervosa, alcoholism, PTSD, hypochondriasis, borderline personality disorder, autism, ADHD, and others. We introduce students to each person in new **Video Cases** throughout the text, which ask students to view brief versions of the interviews on the CD-ROM found in each new copy of the fifth edition. The full versions of the interviews are available to instructors either on DVD or VHS, along with an Instructor's Video Guide.

We are especially proud of the **Speaking Out** videos and view them as a part of our text, not as a supplement, because we were intimately involved with their production. We screened potential video cases, helped to construct and guide the actual interviews, and gave detailed feedback on how to edit the films to make the disorders real for students and fit closely with the organization and themes in our fifth edition.

New Research

The unsolved mysteries of abnormal psychology challenge all of our intellectual and personal resources. In our fifth edition, we include the latest "clues" psychological scientists have unearthed in doing the detective work of research, including references to hundreds of new studies. But the measure of a leading-edge textbook is not merely the number of new references; it is the number of new studies the authors have reviewed and evaluated before deciding what to include and what to discard. For every new reference in this edition of our text, we have read many additional papers before selecting the one gem to include. Some of the updated research and perspectives in this edition includes:

- New information on the prevalence of mental disorders, especially in light of their impact on social adjustment and the global burden of disease (Chapter 1)
- Enhanced coverage of genetic and evolutionary perspectives on mental disorders (Chapter 2)
- Current controversies about science, pseudo-science, and cultural considerations in psychotherapy process and outcome research (Chapter 3)
- Revised discussion of the process of classification and the strengths and weaknesses of DSM-IV-TR, with an eye toward DSM-V (Chapter 4)
- New research on gene–environment interactions, focusing on stressful life events and the serotonin transporter gene (Chapter 5)
- Detailed consideration of whether a strep infection can trigger OCD in children (Chapter 6)
- Renewed interest in *resilience* in response to trauma—and new doubts about critical stress debriefing—in light of the lower than expected incidence of PTSD following September 11 (Chapter 7)
- New research on the growing interest in religious beliefs and coping with stress (Chapter 8)
- New evidence on the prevalence of personality disorders based on a national probability sample (Chapter 9)
- Evidence on eating and body image disorders among males, including steroid abuse (Chapter 10)
- New developments regarding genetics and the risk for alcoholism (Chapter 11)
- Questions about defining female sexual dysfunctions, and FDA consideration of testosterone patch for treatment of low sexual desire in women (Chapter 12)
- Coverage of new cognitive rehabilitation programs for the treatment of schizophrenia (Chapter 13)
- Discussion of the potential for the early diagnosis of Alzheimer's Disease (Chapter 14)
- Evidence and interpretation about the "epidemic of autism" (Chapter 15)
- Research and questions about the effectiveness and suicidal risk associated with antidepressants and adolescent depression (Chapter 16)
- New research on grief and bereavement, including the emerging construct of "psychological pain" (Chapter 17)
- New Supreme Court rulings about the right to refuse treatment, as well as the prohibition against capital punishment for juvenile offenders (Chapter 18)

THE GOLD STANDARD REMAINS UNCHANGED

We view integration as the gold standard of any forward-looking abnormal psychology text, and the gold standard remains unchanged in the fifth edition of our textbook. We see the most exciting and promising future for abnormal psychology in the integration of theoretical approaches, professional specialties, and science and practice, not in the old, fractured competition among "paradigms," a split between psychology and psychiatry, or the division between scientists and practitioners.

Integrated Understanding of Causes and Treatment

For much of the last century, abnormal psychology was dominated by theoretical paradigms, a circumstance that reminds us of the parable of the seven blind men and the elephant. One blind man grasps a tusk and concludes that an elephant is very much like a spear. Another feels a knee and decides an elephant is like a tree, and so on. Our goal from the first edition of **Abnormal Psychology** has been to show the reader the whole elephant. We do this through our unique *integrative systems approach*, in which we focus on what we know today rather than what we used to think. In every chapter, we consider the latest evidence on the *multiple* risk factors that contribute to psychological disorders, as well as the most effective psychological and biomedical treatments. Even if science cannot yet paint a picture of the whole elephant, we clearly tell the student what we know, what we don't know, and how psychologists think the pieces might fit together.

Pedagogy: Integrated Content and Method

We also continue to bring cohesion to abnormal psychology—and to the student—with pedagogy. Each disorder chapter unfolds in the same way, providing a coherent framework with a *consistent chapter outline*. We open with an Overview followed by one or two extended Case Studies. We then discuss Symptoms, Diagnosis, Frequency, Causes, and finally, Treatment (the same sections as in previous editions but with new, straightforward headings). Each chapter covers the key details of **DSM-IV-TR** throughout.

Abnormal psychology is not only about the latest research, but also about the methods psychologists use (and invent) in order to do scientific detective work. Unlike any other text in this field, we cover the scientific method by offering brief **Research Methods** features in every single chapter. Teaching methods in the context of content helps students appreciate the importance of scientific procedures and assumptions, makes learning research methods more manageable, and gives the text flexibility. By the end of the text, our unique approach allows us to cover research methods in *more* detail than we could reasonably cover in a single, detached chapter. Many of our students have told us that the typical research methods chapter seems dry, difficult, and—to our great disappointment—irrelevant. These problems never arise with our integrated, contextualized approach to research methods.

Abnormal psychology also is, of course, about real people with real problems. We bring the human, clinical side of abnormal psychology alive with detailed **Case Studies.** The **Case Studies** take the reader along the human journey of pain, triumph, frustration, and fresh starts that is abnormal psychology, and help students to think more deeply about psychological disorders, much as our own clinical experience enriches our understanding. (We both have been active clinicians as well as active researchers throughout our careers.) In extended cases near the beginning of each chapter, in briefer cases later, and in first-person accounts throughout, the student sees how ordinary lives are disrupted by psychological problems—and how effective treatment can rebuild shattered lives. The case studies also make the details and complexity of the science concrete, relevant, and essential to the "real world."

Sometimes a study or problem suggests a departure from current thinking or raises side issues that deserve to be examined in detail. We cover these emerging ideas in features we used to call **Further Thoughts** but we now simply identify with the topic at hand. One example of an emerging issue we discuss in this way is whether the female response to stress might be to "tend and befriend" rather than fight or flight (Chapter 8). Other topics include the common elements of suicide (Chapter 5), and a

system for classifying different types of rapists (Chapter 12).

SUPPLEMENTS

Print Supplements for Instructors

Instructor's Resource Manual (0-13-195057-6) Gordon Atlas of Alfred University has prepared an instructor's resource manual with notes and suggestions on how to integrate the new *Speaking Out* video segments into your course.

Test Item File (0-13-195058-4) Developed by Richard Cavasina of California University of Pennsylvania, this comprehensive test bank has been updated to include new questions on revised text material. It contains over 1,800 multiple choice, true/false, short answer, and essay questions. New to this edition's Test Item File is the Total Assessment Guide (T.A.G.), which organizes test questions by section and according to definitional, factual, conceptual, or applied questions.

PH Color Transparencies for Abnormal Psychology Series II (0-13-080451-7) This set of full-color transparencies includes illustrations, figures, and graphs from the text, as well as images from a variety of other sources.

Media and Online Resources for Instructors

NEW Video— Speaking Out: Interviews with People who Struggle with Psychological Disorders This new set of sixteen video segments allows students to see first-hand accounts of patients with various disorders. Filmed under the editorial direction of Tom Oltmanns and Robert Emery, the interviews were conducted by licensed clinicians and range in length from 10–25 minutes. These video segments are available on VHS cassettes or on DVD, and an Instructor's Resource Manual provides background notes and suggested discussion questions. Interviews include:

Everett—Major Depression
Sarah—Depression/Deliberate Self Harm
Ann—Bipolar Mood Disorder with Psychotic Features
Steve—Social Phobia (Social Anxiety Disorder)
Dave—Obsessive/Compulsive Disorder
Sara—PTSD
Henry—Hypochondriasis

Julia—Adjustment to Physical Illness/HIV Positive
Liz—Borderline Personality Disorder
Jessica—Anorexia Nervosa: Binge-Eating/Purging Type
Chris—Alcoholism
Larry—Schizophrenia
Josh—Schizoaffective Disorder
Xavier—Autism
Jimmy—Attention-Deficit/Hyperactivity Disorder (ADHD)
Denise—Gender Identity Disorder

Patients as Educators: Video Cases in Abnormal Psychology Created by James H. Scully, Jr., MD, and Alan M. Dahms, Ph.D., Colorado State University, this VHS tape includes a series of ten patient interviews illustrating a range of disorders. Each interview is preceded by a brief history of the patient and a synopsis of some major symptoms of the disorder, and ends with a summary and brief analysis.

ABCNEWS **ABC News Videos for Abnormal Psychology, Series III**
Qualified adopters can obtain this series consisting of segments from the *ABC Nightly News with Peter Jennings, Nightline, 20/20, Prime Time Live,* and *The Health Show.* The programs cover issues such as drugs and alcoholism, psychotherapy, autism, crime motivation, depression, and others. Contact your Prentice Hall representative for more details.

TestGen Testing Software (0-13-195067-3) Available on one dual-platform CD-ROM, this test generating software provides instructors "best in class" features in an easy to use program. Create tests using the TestGen Wizard and easily select questions with drag-and-drop or point-and-click functionality. Add or modify test questions using the built-in Question Editor and print tests in a variety of formats. The program comes with full technical support.

Prentice Hall Online Catalog Page (www.prenhall.com) This site is password-protected for instructors' use only, and allows you online access to all Prentice Hall Psychology supplements at any time. You'll find a multitude of resources—both text-specific and non-text-specific—for teaching abnormal psychology. From this site, you can download any of this text's key supplements, including the Instructor's Resource Manual, Test Item File, and PowerPoint presentations. Contact your local sales representative for the User ID and Password to access this site.

PowerPoint Presentations (www.prenhall.com/oltmanns) Presentations that highlight key points and include important tables, figures, and graphics from the text.

On-Line Course Management For instructors interested in using online course management, Prentice Hall offers fully customizable courses in BlackBoard and Course Compass to accompany this textbook. These online courses are preloaded with material for the fifth edition, including the test item file. Contact your local Prentice Hall representative or visit *www.prenhall.com/demo* for more information.

Student Supplements

NEW! *Speaking Out: Videos in Abnormal Psychology* **CD-ROM** With every new copy of the fifth edition, students will receive a CD-ROM containing video clips showing skilled clinicians interviewing real patients who have been diagnosed with various disorders. The CD-ROM includes sixteen segments from the new *Speaking Out* series and covers panic disorder, schizophrenia, anorexia nervosa, bipolar disorder, PTSD, major depression, autism, ADHD, borderline personality disorder, hypochondriasis, alcoholism, and others. Video Cases throughout the fifth edition indicate when students should go to the CD-ROM to view interviews that correspond to material in the text.

Companion Website (www.prenhall.com/oltmanns) All of the online resources on the fifth edition's Companion Website have been carefully created and selected to reinforce students' understanding of the concepts in the text. Students can take online quizzes and get immediate scoring and feedback, use interactive flashcards to test themselves on key terms, access PowerPoint presentations for each chapter, and link to related websites for more information on each chapter's topics.

 **Research Navigator™** *Research Navigator™* is an online resource that features three exclusive databases full of source material, including:

EBSCO's **ContentSelect™** Academic Journal Database, organized by subject. Each subject contains 50 to 100 of the leading academic journals by keyword, topic, or multiple topics. Articles include abstract and citation information and can be cut, pasted, e-mailed, or saved for later use.

The New York Times Search-by-Subject One Year Archive, organized by subject and searchable by keyword or multiple keywords. Instructors and students can view the full text of the article.
Best of the Web Link Library, organized by subject, offers editorially selected "best of the Web" sites. Link Libraries are continually scanned and kept up-to-date, providing the most relevant and accurate links for research assignments.

To see how this resource works, take a tour at *www.researchnavigator.com*, or ask your local Prentice Hall representative for more details.

Study Guide (0-13-195056-8) Michele Martin of Wesleyan College has created a study guide that includes numerous review and study questions and other learning aids to help reinforce students' understanding of the concepts covered in the text.

Current Directions in Abnormal Psychology Prentice Hall is pleased to continue to support the **American Psychological Society (APS)** reader series, **Current Directions in Psychological Science.** You can package the *Current Directions in Abnormal Psychology* reader for **free** with this text (ISBN 0-13-189579-6).

This reader contains selected articles from APS's journal *Current Directions in Psychological Science.* *Current Directions* was created as a means by which scientists could quickly and easily learn about new and significant research developments outside their major field of study. The journal's concise reviews span all of scientific psychology, and because of the journal's accessibility to audiences outside specialty areas, it is a natural fit for use in college courses. These readers offer a rich resource that connects students and scholars directly to leading scientists working in psychology today.

The American Psychological Society is the only association dedicated solely to advancing psychology as a science-based discipline. APS members include the field's most respected researchers and educators representing the full range of topics within psychological science. The Society is widely recognized as a leading voice for the science of psychology in Washington, and is focused on increasing public understanding and use of the knowledge generated by psychological research.

Abnormal Psychology Casebook: A New Perspective (0-13-093787-8) This text, by Andrew R. Getzfeld, uses clear, accessible language and explanations, and features real cases based on a variety of psychopathologies—all involving patients/clients from a wide variety of cultural, ethnic, racial, religious, social, and socioeconomic backgrounds—and all based on the author's own experiences as a practicing social worker and psychologist.

SafariX WebBook (0-13-195064-9) This new *Pearson Choice* offers students an online subscription to **Abnormal Psychology, Fifth Edition** at a 50% savings. With the SafariX WebBook, students can search the text, make notes online, print out reading assignments that incorporate lecture notes, and bookmark important passages. Ask your Prentice Hall representative for details, or visit www.safarix.com.

ACKNOWLEDGMENTS

Writing and revising this textbook is a never-ending task that fortunately is also a labor of love. This fifth edition is the culmination of years of effort, and is the product of many people's hard work. The first people we wish to thank for their important contributions to making this the text of the future, not of the past, are the following expert reviewers who have unselfishly offered us a great many helpful suggestions, both in this and in previous editions: John Dale Alden, III, Lipscomb University; John Allen, University of Arizona; Hal Arkowitz, University of Arizona; Gordon Atlas, Alfred University; Deanna Barch, Washington University; Thomas G. Bowers, Pennsylvania State University, Harrisburg; Gail Bruce-Sanford, University of Montana; Ann Calhoun-Seals, Belmont Abbey College; Caryn L. Carlson, University of Texas at Austin; Richard Cavasina, California University of Pennsylvania; Laurie Chassin, Arizona State University; Lee H. Coleman, Miami University of Ohio; Dean Cruess, University of Pennsylvania; Danielle Dick, Washington University; Juris G. Draguns, Pennsylvania State University; William Edmonston, Jr., Colgate University; Ronald Evans, Washburn University; John Foust, Parkland College; Alan Glaros, University of Missouri, Kansas City; Ian H. Gotlib, Stanford University; Irving Gottesman, University of Virginia; Mort Harmatz, University of Massachusetts; Marjorie L. Hatch, Southern Methodist University; Jennifer A. Haythornwaite, Johns Hopkins University; Holly Hazlett-Stevens, University of Nevada, Reno; Brant

P. Hasler, University of Arizona; Debra L. Hollister, Valencia Community College; Jennifer Jenkins, University of Toronto; Stuart Keeley, Bowling Green State University; Carolin Keutzer, University of Oregon; Mark H. Licht, Florida State University; Roger Loeb, University of Michigan, Dearborn; Carol Manning, University of Virginia; Richard D. McAnulty, University of North Carolina–Charlotte; Richard McFall, Indiana University; John Monahan, University of Virginia School of Law; Tracy L. Morris, West Virginia University; William O'Donohue, University of Nevada–Reno; Joseph J. Palladino, University of Southern Indiana; Demetrios Papageorgis, University of British Columbia; Ronald D. Pearse, Fairmont State College; Seth Pollak, University of Wisconsin; Melvyn G. Preisz, Oklahoma City University; Paul Rasmussen, Furman University; Rena Repetti, University of California, Los Angeles; Patricia H. Rosenberger, Colorado State University; Josh Searle-White, Allegheny College; Forrest Scogin, University of Alabama; Danny Shaw, University of Pittsburgh; Heather Shaw, American Institutes of Research; Janet Simons, Central Iowa Psychological Services; Patricia J. Slocum, College of DuPage; Darrell Smith, Tennessee State University; Cheryl Spinweber, University of California, San Diego; Bonnie Spring, The Chicago Medical School; Laura Stephenson, Washburn University; Eric Stice, University of Texas; Alexandra Stillman, Utah State University; Joanne Stohs, California State, Fullerton; Martha Storandt, Washington University; Milton E. Strauss, Case Western Reserve University; J. Kevin Thompson, University of South Florida; Robert H. Tipton, Virginia Commonwealth University; Douglas Whitman, Wayne State University; Michael Wierzbicki, Marquette University; Robert D. Zettle, Wichita State University; Ken Winters, University of Minnesota; and Eleanor Webber, Johnson State College.

We have been fortunate to work in stimulating academic environments that have fostered our interests in studying abnormal psychology and in teaching undergraduate students. We are particularly grateful to our colleagues at the University of Virginia: Eric Turkheimer, Irving Gottesman (now at University of Minnesota), Mavis Hetherington, John Monahan, Joseph Allen, Dan Wegner (now at Harvard), David Hill, Cedric Williams, and Peter Brunjes for extended and ongoing discussions of the issues that are considered in this book. More recently, Deanna Barch, Danielle Dick, Martha Storandt, and Randy Larsen (all in the Department of Psychology at Washington University) have added an important new perspective to our views regarding many important topics in this field. Close friends and colleagues at Indiana University have also served in this role, especially Richard McFall and Alexander Buchwald. Many undergraduate and graduate students who have taken our courses also have helped to shape the viewpoints that are expressed here. They are too numerous to identify individually, but we are grateful for the intellectual challenges and excitement that they have provided over the past several years.

Many other people have contributed to the text in important ways. Once again, Kimberly Carpenter Emery did extensive legal research for Chapter 18. Danielle Dick contributed substantial expertise regarding new developments in behavior genetics and gene identification methods. Martha Storandt and Carol Manning provided extensive consultation on issues related to dementia and other cognitive disorders. Jennifer Hill, Victoria Carter, and Nick Eaton provided important help with library research and manuscript preparation.

We also would like to express our deep appreciation to the Prentice Hall team who share our pride and excitement about this text, and who have worked long and hard to make it the very best text. Major contributors include: Jeff Marshall, Senior Acquisitions Editor; Stephanie Johnson, Sponsoring Editor; Jeannette Moyer, Senior Marketing Manager; Karen Berry, Production Editor at Pine Tree Composition; Maureen Richardson, Assistant Managing Editor; Joanne Hakim, Production Liaison; Leah Jewell, Editorial Director, Social Sciences; Rochelle Diogenes, Editor-in-Chief, Development; David Clevinger, Media Editor; Tricia Callahan, Editorial Assistant; Julie Tesser, Photo Researcher; Nancy Wells, Art Director; and Leslie Osher, Creative Design Director.

Finally, we want to express our gratitude to our families for their patience and support throughout our obsession with this text: Gail and Josh Oltmanns, and Sara, Billy, and Presley Baber; and Kimberly, Maggie, Julia, Bobby, Lucy, and John-John Emery. You remain our loving sources of motivation and inspiration.

—*Tom Oltmanns*
—*Bob Emery*

About the Authors

Thomas F. Oltmanns (top) is the Edgar James Swift Professor of Psychology in Arts and Sciences and Professor of Psychiatry at Washington University in St. Louis, where he is also Director of Clinical Training in Psychology. He received his B.A. from the University of Wisconsin and his Ph.D. from the State University of New York at Stony Brook. He was previously a faculty member in the psychology departments at Indiana University (1976 to 1986) and at the University of Virginia (1986 to 2003). He has served as Associate Editor of the *Journal of Abnormal Psychology* and as a member of several research review committees for the National Institutes of Health. He was elected president of the Society for a Science of Clinical Psychology in 1993 and twice received the "Outstanding Professor Award" from undergraduate psychology majors at UVa (in 1997 and 2002). He has written extensively about the role of cognitive and emotional factors in mental disorders such as schizophrenia and obsessive–compulsive disorder. His current research on the assessment of personality disorders is funded by NIMH. His previous books include *Schizophrenia* (1980), written with John Neale; *Delusional Beliefs* (1988), edited with Brendan Maher; and *Case Studies in Abnormal Psychology* (7th edition, 2006), written with Michele Martin.

Robert E. Emery (bottom) is Professor of Psychology, Director of the Center for Children, Families, and the Law, and an associate faculty member of the Institute of Law, Psychiatry, and Public Policy at the University of Virginia. He also served as Director of Clinical Training for nine years. He received a B.A. from Brown University in 1974 and a Ph.D. from SUNY at Stony Brook in 1982. His research focuses on family conflict, children's mental health, and associated legal issues, and he has authored over 100 scientific articles and book chapters. His awards include a "Citation Classic" from the Institute for Scientific Information, an Outstanding Research Publication Award from the American Associate for Marriage and Family Therapy, the Distinguished Researcher Award from the Association of Family and Conciliation Courts, and several awards and award nominations for his three books on divorce: *Marriage, Divorce and Children's Adjustment* (2nd ed., 1998, Sage Publications), *Renegotiating Family Relationships: Divorce, Child Custody, and Mediation* (1994, Guilford Press), and *The Truth about Children and Divorce: Dealing with the Emotions So You and Your Children Can Thrive* (2004, Viking). His current research is on genetically informed (twin) studies of the effects of major changes in family environments, including divorce, harsh parenting, early menarche, and teen pregnancy.

ABNORMAL PSYCHOLOGY

1

Examples and Definitions of Abnormal Behavior

© Jane Sterrett

CHAPTER OUTLINE

Recognizing the Presence of a Disorder
Defining Abnormal Behavior
Who Experiences Abnormal Behavior?
The Mental Health Professions
Psychopathology in Historical Context
Methods for the Scientific Study of Mental Disorders

◆◆

Mental disorders touch every realm of human experience; they are part of the human experience. They can disrupt the way we think, the way we feel, and the way we behave. They also affect relationships with other people. These problems often have a devastating impact on people's lives. In countries like the United States, mental disorders are the second leading cause of disease-related disability and mortality, ranking slightly behind cardiovascular conditions and slightly ahead of cancer (Lopez & Murray, 1998). The purpose of this book is to help you become familiar with the nature of these disorders and the various ways in which psychologists and other mental health professionals are advancing knowledge of their causes and treatment.

Many of us grow up thinking that mental disorders happen to a few unfortunate people. We don't expect them to happen to us or to those we love. In fact, mental disorders are very common. At least one out of every three people will experience a serious form of abnormal behavior, such as depression, alcoholism, or schizophrenia, at some point during his or her lifetime. When you add up the numbers of people who experience these problems firsthand as well as through relatives and close friends, you realize that, like other health problems, mental disorders affect all of us. That is why, throughout this book, we will try to help you understand not only the kind of disturbed behaviors and thinking that characterize particular disorders but the people to whom they occur and the circumstances that can foster them.

Most importantly, this book is about all of us, not "them"—anonymous people with whom we empathize but do not identify. Just as each of us will be affected by medical problems at some point during our lives, it is also likely that we, or someone we love, will have to cope with that aspect of the human experience known as a disorder of the mind.

OVERVIEW

The symptoms and signs of mental disorders, including such phenomena as depressed mood, panic attacks, and bizarre beliefs, are known as **psychopathology.** Literally translated, this term means "pathology of the mind." **Abnormal psychology** is the application of psychological science to the study of mental disorders.

In the first four chapters of this book, we will look at the field of abnormal psychology in general. We will look at the ways in which abnormal behaviors are broken down into categories of mental disorders that can be more clearly defined for diagnostic purposes, and how those behaviors are assessed. We will also discuss current ideas about the causes of these disorders and ways in which they can be treated.

This chapter will help you begin to understand the qualities that define behaviors and experiences as being abnormal. At what point does the diet that a girl follows in order to perform at her peak as a ballerina or gymnast become an eating disorder? When does grief following the end of a relationship become major depression? The line dividing normal from abnormal is not always clear. You will find that the issue is often one of degree rather the exact form or content of behavior.

The case studies in this chapter describe the experiences of two people whose behavior would be considered abnormal by mental health professionals. Our first case will introduce you to a person who suffered from one of the most obvious and disabling forms of mental disorder, known as schizophrenia. Kevin's life had been relatively unremarkable for many years. He had done well in school, was married, and held a good job. Unfortunately, over a period of several months, the fabric of his normal life began to fall apart. The transition wasn't obvious to either Kevin or his family, but it eventually became clear that he was having serious problems.

◆◆

CASE STUDY   A Husband's Paranoid Schizophrenia

Kevin and Joyce Warner (not their real names*) had been married for eight years when they sought help from a psychologist for their marital problems. Joyce was 34 years old, worked full time as a pediatric nurse, and was six months pregnant with her first child. Kevin, who was 35 years old, was finishing his third year working as a librarian at a local university. Joyce was extremely worried about what would happen if Kevin lost his job, especially in light of the baby's imminent arrival.

Although the Warners had come for couples therapy, the psychologist soon became concerned about certain eccentric aspects of Kevin's behavior. In the first session, Joyce described one recent event that had precipitated a major argument. One day, after eating lunch at work, Kevin had experienced sharp pains in his chest and had difficulty breathing. Fearful, he rushed to the emergency room at the hospital where Joyce worked. The physician who saw Kevin found nothing wrong with him, even after

extensive testing. She gave Kevin a few tranquilizers and sent him home to rest. When Joyce arrived home that evening, Kevin told her that he suspected that he had been poisoned at work by his supervisor. He still held this belief.

Kevin's belief about the alleged poisoning raised serious concern in the psychologist's mind about Kevin's mental health. He decided to interview Joyce alone so that he could ask more extensive questions about Kevin's behavior. Joyce realized that the poisoning idea was "crazy." She was not willing, however, to see it as evidence that Kevin had a mental disorder. Joyce had known Kevin for 15 years. As far as she knew, he had never held any strange beliefs before this time. Joyce said that Kevin had always been "a thoughtful and unusually sensitive guy." She did not attach a great deal of significance to Kevin's unusual belief. She was more preoccupied with the couple's present financial concerns and insisted that it was time for Kevin to "face reality."

Kevin's condition deteriorated noticeably over the next few weeks. He became extremely withdrawn, frequently sitting alone in a darkened room after dinner. On several occasions, he told her that he felt as if he had "lost pieces

of his thinking." It wasn't that his memory was failing, but rather he felt as though parts of his brain were shut off.

Kevin's problems at work also grew worse. His supervisor informed Kevin that his contract would definitely not be renewed. Joyce exploded when Kevin indifferently told her the bad news. His apparent lack of concern was especially annoying. She called Kevin's supervisor, who confirmed the news. He told her that Kevin was physically present at the library, but he was only completing a few hours of work each day. Kevin sometimes spent long periods of time just sitting at his desk and staring off into space and was sometimes heard mumbling softly to himself.

Kevin's speech was quite odd during the next therapy session. He would sometimes start to speak, drift off into silence, then reestablish eye contact with a bewildered smile and a shrug of his shoulders. He had apparently lost his train of thought completely. His answers to questions were often off the point, and when he did string together several sentences, their meaning was sometimes obscure. For example, at one point during the session, the psychologist asked Kevin if he planned to appeal his supervisor's decision. Kevin said,

---

*Throughout this text we use fictitious names to protect the identities of the people involved.

I'm feeling pressured, like I'm lost and can't quite get here. But I need more time to explore the deeper side. Like in art. What you see on the surface is much richer when you look closely. I'm like that. An intuitive person. I can't relate in a linear way, and when people expect that from me, I get confused.

Kevin's strange belief about poisoning continued to expand. The Warners received a letter from Kevin's mother, who lived in another city 200 miles away. She had become ill after going out for dinner one night and mentioned that she must have eaten something that made her sick. After reading the letter, Kevin became convinced that his supervisor had tried to poison his mother, too.

When questioned about this new incident, Kevin launched into a long, rambling story. He said that his supervisor was a Vietnam veteran, but he had refused to talk with Kevin about his years in the service. Kevin suspected that this was because the supervisor had been a member of army intelligence. Perhaps he still was a member of some secret organization. Kevin suggested that an agent from this organization had been sent by his supervisor to poison his mother. Kevin thought that he and Joyce were in danger. Kevin also had some concerns about Asians, but he would not specify these worries in more detail.

Kevin's bizarre beliefs and his disorganized behavior convinced the psychologist that he needed to be hospitalized. Joyce reluctantly agreed that this was the most appropriate course of action. She had run out of alternatives. Arrangements were made to have Kevin admitted to a private psychiatric facility, where the psychiatrist prescribed haloperidol (Haldol), a type of antipsychotic medication. Kevin seemed to respond positively to the drug, because he soon stopped talking about plots and poisoning—but he remained withdrawn and uncommunicative. After three weeks of treatment, Kevin's psychiatrist thought that he had improved significantly. Kevin was discharged from the hospital in time for the birth of their baby girl. Unfortunately, when the couple returned to consult with the psychologist, Kevin's adjustment was still a major concern. He did not talk with Joyce about the poisonings, but she noticed that he remained withdrawn and showed few emotions, even toward the baby.

When the psychologist questioned Kevin in detail, he admitted reluctantly that he still believed that he had been poisoned. Slowly, he revealed more of the plot. Immediately after admission to the hospital, Kevin had decided that his psychiatrist, who happened to be from Korea, could not be trusted. Kevin was sure that he, too, was working for army intelligence or perhaps for a counterintelligence operation. Kevin believed that he was being interrogated by this clever psychiatrist, so he had "played dumb." He did not discuss the suspected poisonings or the secret organization that had planned them. Whenever he could get away with it, Kevin simply pretended to take his medication. He thought that it was either poison or truth serum.

Kevin was admitted to a different psychiatric hospital soon after it became apparent that his paranoid beliefs had expanded. This time, he was given intramuscular injections of antipsychotic medication in order to be sure that the medicine was actually taken. Kevin improved considerably after several weeks in the hospital. He acknowledged that he had experienced paranoid thoughts. Although he still felt suspicious from time to time, wondering whether the plot had actually been real, he recognized that it could not really have happened, and he spent less and less time thinking about it.

◆◆◆

RECOGNIZING THE PRESENCE OF A DISORDER

Some mental disorders are so severe that the people who suffer from them are not aware of the implausibility of their beliefs. Schizophrenia is a form of **psychosis,** a general term that refers to several types of severe mental disorder in which the person is considered to be out of contact with reality. Kevin exhibited several psychotic symptoms. For example, Kevin's firm belief that he was being poisoned by his supervisor had no basis in reality. Other disorders, however, are more subtle variations on normal experience. We will shortly consider some of the guidelines that are applied in determining abnormality.

Mental disorders are typically defined by a set of characteristic features; one symptom by itself is seldom sufficient to make a diagnosis. A group of symptoms that appear together and are assumed to represent a specific type of disorder is referred to as a **syndrome.** Kevin's unrealistic and paranoid belief that he was being poisoned, his peculiar and occasionally difficult-to-understand patterns of speech, and his oddly unemotional responses are all symptoms of schizophrenia (see Chapter 13). Each symptom is taken to be a fallible, or imperfect, indicator of the presence of the disorder. The significance of any specific feature depends on whether the person also exhibits additional behaviors that are characteristic of a particular disorder.

The duration of a person's symptoms is also important. Mental disorders are defined in terms of *persistent* maladaptive behaviors. Many unusual behaviors and inexplicable experiences are short lived; if we ignore them, they go away. Unfortunately, some forms of problematic behavior are not transient, and they eventually interfere with the person's social and occupational functioning. In Kevin's case, he had become completely preoccupied with his suspicions about poison. Joyce tried for several weeks to ignore certain aspects of Kevin's behavior, especially his delusional beliefs. She didn't want to think about the possibility that his behavior was abnormal, and instead chose to explain his problems in terms of lack of maturity or lack of motivation. But as the problems accumulated, she finally decided to seek professional help. The magnitude of Kevin's

People with schizophrenia sometimes exhibit disorganized behavior, like this hospitalized woman.

Psychologists and other mental health professionals do not at present have laboratory tests that can be used to confirm definitively the presence of psychopathology because the processes that are responsible for mental disorders have not yet been discovered. Unlike specialists in other areas of medicine where many specific disease mechanisms have been discovered by advances in the biological sciences, psychologists and psychiatrists cannot test for the presence of a viral infection or a brain lesion or a genetic defect to confirm a diagnosis of mental disorder. Clinical psychologists must still depend on their observations of the person's behavior and descriptions of personal experience.

Is it possible to move beyond our current dependence on descriptive definitions of psychopathology? Will we someday have valid tests that can be used to establish independently the presence of a mental disorder? If we do, what form might these tests take? The answers to these questions are being sought in many kinds of research studies that will be discussed throughout this book.

Before we leave this section, we must also mention some other terms. You may be familiar with a variety of words that are commonly used in describing abnormal behavior. One term is *insanity*, which years ago referred to mental dysfunction, but today is a legal term that refers to judgments about whether a person should be held responsible for criminal behavior if he or she is also mentally disturbed (see Chapter 18). If Kevin had murdered his psychiatrist, for example, based on the delusional belief that the psychiatrist was trying to harm him, a court of law might consider whether Kevin should be held to be *not guilty by reason of insanity*.

Another old fashioned term that you may have heard is *nervous breakdown*. If we said that Kevin had "suffered a nervous breakdown," we would be indicating, in very general terms, that he had developed some sort of incapacitating but otherwise unspecified type of mental disorder. This expression does not convey any specific information about the nature of the person's problems. Some people might also say that Kevin was acting *crazy*. This is an informal, pejorative term that does not convey specific information and carries with it many unfortunate, unfounded, and negative implications. Mental health professionals refer to psychopathological conditions as mental disorders or abnormal behaviors. We will define these terms in the pages that follow.

problem was measured, in large part, by its persistence.

Impairment in the ability to perform social and occupational roles is another consideration in identifying the presence of a mental disorder. Delusional beliefs and disorganized speech typically lead to a profound disruption of relationships with other people. Like Kevin, people who experience these symptoms will obviously find the world to be a strange, puzzling, and perhaps alarming place. And they often elicit the same reactions in other people. Kevin's odd behavior and his inability to concentrate on his work had eventually cost him his job. His problems also had a negative impact on his relationship with his wife and his ability to help care for their daughter.

Kevin's situation raises several additional questions about abnormal behavior. One of the most difficult issues in the field centers on the processes by which mental disorders are identified. Once Kevin's problems came to the attention of a mental health professional, could he have been tested in some way to confirm the presence or absence of a mental disorder?

DEFINING ABNORMAL BEHAVIOR

Why do we consider Kevin's behavior to be abnormal? By what criteria do we decide whether a particular set of behaviors or emotional reactions should be viewed as a mental disorder? These are important questions because they determine, in many ways, how other people will respond to the person, as well as who will be responsible for providing help (if help is required). Many attempts have been made to define abnormal behavior, but none is entirely satisfactory. No one has been able to provide a consistent definition that easily accounts for all situations in which the concept is invoked (Frances, First, & Pincus, 1995; Kendell, 2002).

One approach to the definition of abnormal behavior places principal emphasis on the individual's experience of personal distress. We might say that abnormal behavior is defined in terms of subjective discomfort that leads the person to seek help from a mental health professional. This definition is fraught with problems, however. Kevin's case illustrates one of the major reasons that this approach does not work. Before his second hospitalization, Kevin was unable or unwilling to appreciate the extent of his problem or the impact his behavior had on other people. A psychologist would say that he did not have *insight* regarding his disorder. The discomfort was primarily experienced by Joyce, and she had attempted for many weeks to deny the nature of the problem. It would be useless to adopt a definition that considered Kevin's behavior to be abnormal only after he had been successfully treated.

Another approach is to define abnormal behavior in terms of statistical norms—how common or rare it is in the general population. By this definition, people with unusually high levels of anxiety or depression would be considered abnormal because their experience deviates from the expected norm. Kevin's paranoid beliefs would be defined as pathological because they are idiosyncratic. Mental disorders are, in fact, defined in terms of experiences that most people do not have.

This approach, however, does not specify how unusual the behavior must be before it is considered abnormal. Some conditions that are typically considered to be forms of psychopathology are extremely rare. For example, gender identity disorder, the belief that one is a member of the opposite sex trapped in the wrong body, affects less than one person out of every 30,000. In contrast, other disorders are much more common. In the United States, major depression affects one out of every 20 women, and alcoholism affects at least one out of every 10 men (Narrow, Rae, Robins, & Regier, 2002).

Another weakness of the statistical approach is that it does not distinguish between deviations that are harmful and those that are not. Many rare behaviors are not pathological. Some "abnormal" qualities have relatively little impact on a person's adjustment. Examples are being extremely pragmatic or unusually talkative. Other abnormal characteristics, such as exceptional intellectual, artistic, or athletic ability, may actually confer an advantage on the individual. For these reasons, the simple fact that a behavior is statistically rare cannot be used to define psychopathology.

What is the difference between normal and abnormal behavior?

Harmful Dysfunction

One useful approach to the definition of mental disorder has been proposed by Jerome Wakefield of Rutgers University (Wakefield, 1999). According to Wakefield, a condition should be considered a mental disorder if, and only if, it meets two criteria:

1. The condition results from the inability of some internal mechanism (mental or physical) to perform its natural function. In other words, something inside the person is not working properly. Examples of such mechanisms include those that regulate levels of emotion and those that distinguish between real auditory sensations and those that are imagined.

Andy Warhol was one of the most influential painters of the 20th century. His colleague, Jean-Michel Basquiat, was also an extremely promising artist. His dependence on heroin and his ultimately fatal overdose is one extreme example of the destructive and tragic effects of mental disorder.

2. The condition causes some harm to the person as judged by the standards of the person's culture. These negative consequences are measured in terms of the person's own subjective distress or difficulty performing expected social or occupational roles.

A mental disorder, therefore, is defined in terms of **harmful dysfunction.** This definition incorporates one element that is based as much as possible on an objective evaluation of performance. The natural function of cognitive and perceptual processes is to allow the person to perceive the world in ways that are shared with other people and to engage in rational thought and problem solving. The dysfunctions in mental disorders are assumed to be the product of disruptions of thought, feeling, communication, perception, and motivation.

In Kevin's case, the most apparent dysfunctions involved failures of mechanisms that are responsible for perception, thinking, and communication. Disruption of these systems was presumably responsible for his delusional beliefs and his disorganized speech. The natural function of cognitive and perceptual processes is to allow the person to perceive the world in ways that are shared with other people and to engage in rational thought and problem solving. The natural function of language abilities is to allow the person to communicate clearly with other people. Therefore, Kevin's abnormal behavior can be viewed as a pervasive dysfunction cutting across several mental mechanisms.

The harmful dysfunction view of mental disorder recognizes that every type of dysfunction does not lead to a disorder. Only dysfunctions that result in significant harm to the person are considered to be disorders. This is the second element of the definition. There are, for example, many types of physical dysfunction, such as albinism, reversal of heart position, and fused toes, that clearly represent a significant departure from the way that some biological process ordinarily functions. These conditions are not considered to be disorders, however, because they are not necessarily harmful to the person.

Kevin's dysfunctions were, in fact, harmful to his adjustment. They affected both his family relationships—his marriage to Joyce and his ability to function as a parent—and his performance at work. His social and occupational performances were clearly impaired. There are, of course, other types of harm that are also associated with mental disorders. These include subjective distress, such as high levels of anxiety or depression, as well as more tangible outcomes, such as suicide.

The definition of abnormal behavior presented in the official *Diagnostic and Statistical Manual of Mental Disorders*, published by the American Psychiatric Association and currently in its fourth revised edition—DSM-IV-TR (APA, 2000)—incorporates many of the factors that we have already discussed. This classification system is discussed in Chapter 4. This definition is summarized in Table 1–1, along with a number of conditions that are specifically excluded from the DSM-IV-TR definition of mental disorders.

The DSM-IV-TR definition places primary emphasis on the consequences of certain behavioral

---

TABLE 1–1   Summary of the DSM-IV-TR Definition of Mental Disorders

DEFINING CHARACTERISTICS

A behavioral or psychological syndrome (groups of associated features) that is associated with:

1. Present distress (painful symptoms), or
2. Disability (impairment in one or more important areas of functioning), or with
3. A significantly increased risk of suffering death, pain, disability, or an important loss of freedom

CONDITIONS EXCLUDED FROM CONSIDERATION

This syndrome or pattern must not be merely:

1. An expectable and culturally sanctioned response to a particular event (such as the death of a loved one)
2. Deviant behavior (such as the actions of political, religious, or sexual minorities)
3. Conflicts that are between the individual and society (such as voluntary efforts to express individuality)

syndromes. Accordingly, mental disorders are defined by clusters of persistent, maladaptive behaviors that are associated with personal distress, such as anxiety or depression, or with impairment in social functioning, such as job performance or personal relationships. The official definition, therefore, recognizes the concept of dysfunction, and it spells out ways in which the harmful consequences of the disorder might be identified.

The DSM-IV-TR definition excludes voluntary behaviors, as well as beliefs and actions that are shared by religious, political, or sexual minority groups (e.g., gays and lesbians). In the 1960s, for example, members of the Yippie Party intentionally engaged in disruptive behaviors, such as throwing money off the balcony at a stock exchange. Their purpose was to challenge traditional values. These were, in some ways, maladaptive behaviors that could have resulted in social impairment if those involved had been legally prosecuted. But they were not dysfunctions. They were intentional political gestures. It makes sense to try to distinguish between voluntary behaviors and mental disorders, but the boundaries between these different forms of behavior are difficult to draw. Educated discussions of these issues depend on the consideration of a number of important questions (see Critical Thinking *Matters* on page 10).

In actual practice, abnormal behavior is defined in terms of an official diagnostic system. Mental health, like medicine, is an applied rather than a theoretical field. It draws on knowledge from research in the psychological and biological sciences in an effort to help people whose behavior is disordered. Mental disorders are, in some respects, those problems with which mental health professionals attempt to deal. As their activities and explanatory concepts expand, so does the list of abnormal behaviors. The practical boundaries of abnormal behavior are defined by the list of disorders that are included in the official *Diagnostic and Statistical Manual of Mental Disorders.* The categories in that manual are listed inside the back cover of this book. The DSM-IV-TR thus provides another simplistic, though practical, answer to our question as to why Kevin's behavior would be considered abnormal: He would be considered to be exhibiting abnormal behavior because his experiences fit the description of schizophrenia, which is one of the officially recognized forms of mental disorder.

Culture and Diagnostic Practice

The process by which the *Diagnostic and Statistical Manual* is constructed and revised is necessarily influenced by cultural considerations. **Culture** is defined in terms of the values, beliefs, and practices that are shared by a specific community or group of people. These values and beliefs have a profound influence on opinions regarding the difference between normal and abnormal behavior (Lopez & Guarnaccia, 2000).

The impact of particular behaviors and experiences on a person's adjustment depends on the culture in which the person lives. To use Jerome Wakefield's (1992) terms, "only dysfunctions that are socially disvalued are disorders" (p. 384). Consider, for example, the DSM-IV–TR concept of female orgasmic disorder, which is defined in terms of the absence of orgasm accompanied by subjective distress or interpersonal difficulties that result from this disturbance (see Chapter 12). A woman who grew up in a society that discouraged female sexuality might not be distressed or impaired by the absence of orgasmic responses. According to DSM-IV–TR, she would not be considered to have a sexual problem. Therefore, this definition of abnormal behavior is not culturally universal and might lead us to consider a particular pattern of behavior to be abnormal in one society and not in another.

There have been many instances in which groups representing particular social values have brought pressure to bear on decisions shaping the diagnostic manual. The influence of cultural changes on psychiatric classification is perhaps nowhere better illustrated than in the case of homosexuality. In the first and second editions of the DSM, homosexuality was, by definition, a form of mental disorder, in spite of arguments expressed by scientists, who argued that homosexual behavior was not abnormal (see Chapter 12). Toward the end of the 1960s, as the gay and lesbian rights movement became more forceful and outspoken, its leaders challenged the assumption that homosexuality was pathological. They opposed the inclusion of homosexuality in the official diagnostic manual. After extended and sometimes heated

Video Case

Obsessive-Compulsive Disorder

DAVE

"I tell myself, we're going to lock the door once today and leave . . . it rarely happens."

On your CD-ROM menu, select "Anxiety Disorders" and click on "OCD: Dave." As you watch the video, ask yourself what impact Dave's compulsive checking might have on his level of adjustment. Is it harmful?

Some entertainers participate in bizarre or outrageous skits, as in the hit movie *Jackass*. The behaviors are shocking, but they are voluntary. Unless accompanied by other symptoms, they would ot be considered evidence of a mental disorder.

discussions, the board of trustees of the American Psychiatric Association agreed to remove homosexuality as a form of mental illness. They were impressed by numerous indications, in personal appeals as well as the research literature, that homosexuality, per se, was not invariably associated with impaired functioning. They decided that, in order to be considered a form of mental disorder, a condition ought to be associated with subjective distress or seriously impaired social or occupational functioning. The stage was set for these events by gradual shifts in society's attitudes toward sexual behavior (Bullough, 1976; Minton, 2002). As more and more people came to believe that reproduction was not the main purpose of sexual behavior, tolerance for greater variety in human sexuality grew. The revision of the DSM's system for describing sexual disorders was, therefore, the product of several forces, cultural as well as political.

In a more recent example, in the 1990s, feminist organizations expressed objections to the

IS SEXUAL ADDICTION A MEANINGFUL CONCEPT?

Stories about mental disorders appear frequently in the popular media. One topic that attracted a frenzy of media attention in 1998 was a concept that has been called "sexual addiction." Shortly after the public learned that President Clinton had had an illicit sexual affair with a young White House intern, newspapers, magazines, and television programs sought interviews with professional psychologists who offered their opinions regarding the President's behavior. Why would he risk his marriage, family, and career—some said the security of the nation—for a casual sexual relationship with someone on his staff?

Many experts responded by invoking the concept of mental disorder, specifically "sexual addiction" (some called it "sexual compulsion," and one even called it the "Clinton syndrome"). The symptoms of this disorder presumably include low self-esteem, insecurity, need for reassurance, and sensation seeking, to name only a few. One expert claimed that fully 20 percent of highly successful men suffer from sexual addiction.

Most of the stories failed to mention that sexual addiction does not appear in the official diagnostic manual. That, by itself, is not an insurmountable problem. Disorders have come and gone over the years, and it's possible that this one might turn out to be useful. Perhaps it will be included in the next edition. We shouldn't reject a new concept simply because it hasn't become part of the official classification system (or accept one on faith, simply because it has). The most important thing is that we *think critically* about the issues that are raised by invoking a concept like sexual addiction.

At the broadest possible level, we must ask ourselves "What *is* a mental disorder?" How is *disordered* behavior different from immoral behavior or illegal behavior? What is gained by adopting one perspective over another? Another important question is whether sexual addiction is more useful than other similar concepts. For example, narcissistic personality disorder includes many of the same features (such as lack of empathy, feelings of entitlement, and

a history of exploiting others). What evidence supports the value of one concept over another? Has the proposed disorder been defined in a specific way that can be used consistently by mental health professionals? On what basis do the experts claim to know how many people are affected by this condition?

Students who ask these kinds of questions are engaged in critical thinking, a process in which judgments and decisions are based on a careful analysis of the best available evidence. In order to consider these issues, you need to put aside your own subjective feelings and impressions, such as whether you find a particular kind of behavior disgusting, confusing, or frightening. It may also be necessary to disregard opinions expressed by authorities whom you respect (politicians, journalists, and talk-show hosts). Be skeptical. Ask questions. Consider the evidence from different points of view, and remember that some kinds of evidence are better than others.

possible inclusion of premenstrual dysphoric disorder in DSM-IV-TR. They were concerned about the implications of labeling women who have these problems as mentally ill (Caplan, 1995). In a compromise struck by APA's committee on DSM-IV-TR, premenstrual dysphoric disorder appears in an appendix for disorders recommended for further study. These deliberations are a reflection of the practical nature of the manual and of the health related professions. Value judgments are an inherent part of any attempt to define "disorder" (Sedgwick, 1981).

Many people think about culture primarily in terms of exotic patterns of behavior in distant lands. The decisions regarding homosexuality and premenstrual dysphoric disorder remind us that the values of our own culture play an intimate role in our definition of abnormal behavior. These issues also highlight the importance of cultural change. Culture is a dynamic process; it changes continuously as a result of the actions of individuals. To the extent that our definition of abnormal behavior is determined by cultural values and beliefs, we should expect that it will continue to evolve over time.

WHO EXPERIENCES ABNORMAL BEHAVIOR?

Having introduced many of the issues that are involved in the definition of abnormal behavior, we now turn to another clinical example. The woman in our second case study, Mary Childress, suffered from a serious eating disorder known as *bulimia nervosa*. Her problems raise additional questions about the definition of abnormal behavior.

As you are reading the case, ask yourself about the impact of Mary's eating disorder on her subjective experience and social adjustment. In what ways are these consequences similar to those seen in Kevin Warner's case? How are they different? This case also introduces another important concept associated with the way that we think about abnormal behavior: How can we identify the boundary between normal and abnormal behavior? Is there an obvious distinction between eating patterns that are considered to be part of a mental disorder and those that are not? Or is there a gradual progression from one end of a continuum to the other, with each step fading gradually into the next?

◆◆◆

CASE STUDY A College Student's Eating Disorder

Mary Childress was, in most respects, a typical 18-year-old sophomore at a large state university. She was popular with other students and a good student, in spite of the fact that she spent little time studying. Everything about Mary's life was relatively normal—except for her bingeing and purging.

Mary's eating patterns were wildly erratic. She preferred to skip breakfast entirely, and often missed lunch as well. By the middle of the afternoon, she could no longer ignore the hunger pangs. At that point, on two or three days out of the week, Mary would drive her car to the drive-in window of a fast-food restaurant. Her typical order included three or four double cheeseburgers, several orders of french fries, and a large milkshake (or maybe two). Then she binged, devouring all the food as she drove around town by herself. Later she would go to a private bathroom, where she wouldn't be seen by anyone, and purge the food from her stomach by vomiting. Afterward, she returned to her room, feeling angry, frustrated, and ashamed.

Mary was tall and weighed 110 pounds. She believed that her body was unattractive, especially her thighs and hips. She was extremely critical of herself and had worried about her weight for many years. Her weight fluctuated quite a bit, from a low of 97 pounds when she was a senior in high school to a high of 125 during her first year at the university. Her mother was a "full-figured" woman. Mary swore to herself at an early age that she would never let herself gain as much weight as her mother had.

Purging had originally seemed like an ideal solution to the problem of weight control. You could eat whatever you wanted and quickly get rid of it so you wouldn't get fat. Unfortunately, the vomiting became a vicious trap. Disgusted by her own behavior, Mary often promised herself that she would never binge and purge again, but she couldn't stop the cycle.

For the past year Mary had been vomiting at least once almost every day and occasionally as many as three or four times a day. The impulse to purge was very strong. Mary felt bloated after having only a bowl of cereal and a glass of orange juice. If she ate a sandwich and drank a diet soda, she began to ruminate about what she had eaten, thinking, "I've got to get rid of that!" Usually, before long, she found a bathroom and threw up. Her excessive binges were less frequent than the vomiting. Four or five times a week she experienced an overwhelming urge to eat forbidden foods, especially fast food. Her initial reaction was usually a short-lived attempt to resist the impulse. Then she would space out or "go into a zone," becoming only vaguely aware of what she was doing and feeling. In the midst of a serious binge, Mary felt completely helpless and unable to control herself.

There weren't any obvious physical signs that would alert someone to Mary's eating problems, but the vomiting had begun to wreak havoc with her body, especially her digestive system. She had suffered severe throat infections and frequent, intense stomach pains. Her dentist had noticed problems beginning to develop with her teeth and gums, undoubtedly a consequence of constant exposure to strong stomach acids.

Mary's eating problem started to develop when she was 15. She had been seriously involved in gymnastics for several years but eventually developed a knee condition that forced her to give up the sport. She gained a few pounds in the next month or two and decided to lose weight by dieting. Buoyed by unrealistic expectations about the immediate, positive benefits of a diet that she had seen advertised on television, Mary initially adhered rigidly to its recommended regimen. Six months later, after three of these fad diets had failed, she started throwing up as a way to control her intake of food.

Mary's problems persisted after she graduated from high school and began her college education. She felt guilty and ashamed about her eating problems. She was much too embarrassed to let anyone know what she was doing and would never eat more than a few mouthfuls of food in a public place like the dorm cafeteria. Her roommate, Julie, was from a small town on the other side of the state. They got along reasonably well, but Mary managed to conceal her bingeing and purging, thanks in large part to the fact that she was able to bring her own car to campus. The car allowed her to drive away from campus several times a week so that she could binge.

Mary's case illustrates many of the characteristic features of bulimia nervosa. As in Kevin's case, her behavior could be considered abnormal not only because it fit the criteria for one of the categories in DSM-IV-TR but also because she suffered from a dysfunction (in this case, of the mechanisms that regulate appetite) that was obviously harmful. The impact of the disorder was greatest in terms of her physical health: Eating disorders can be fatal if they are not properly treated because they affect so many vital organs of the body, including the heart and kidneys. Mary's social functioning and her academic performance were not yet seriously impaired. There are many different ways in which to measure the harmful effects of abnormal behavior.

Mary's case also illustrates the subjective pain that is associated with many types of abnormal behavior. In contrast to Kevin, Mary was acutely aware of her disorder. She was frustrated and unhappy. In an attempt to relieve this emotional distress, she entered psychological treatment. Unfortunately, painful emotions associated with mental disorders can also interfere with, or delay, the decision to look for professional help. Guilt, shame, and embarrassment often accompany psychological problems and sometimes make it difficult to confide in another person, even though the average therapist has seen such problems many times over.

Frequency in and Impact on Community Populations

Many important decisions about mental disorders are based on data regarding the frequency with which these disorders occur. At least 4 percent of college women would meet diagnostic criteria for bulimia nervosa (see Chapter 10). These data are a source of considerable concern, especially among those who are responsible for health services on college campuses.

Epidemiology is the scientific study of the frequency and distribution of disorders within a population (Gordis, 2004). Epidemiologists are concerned with questions such as whether the frequency of a disorder has increased or decreased during a particular period, whether it is more common in one geographic area than in another, and whether certain types of people—based on such factors as gender, race, and socioeconomic status—are at greater risk than other types for the development of the disorder. Health administrators

How thin is too thin? This young dancer suffers from an eating disorder. Some experts maintain that the differences between abnormal and normal behavior are essentially differences in degree, that is, quantitative differences.

often use such information to make decisions about the allocation of resources for professional training programs, treatment facilities, and research projects.

Two terms are particularly important in epidemiological research. **Incidence** refers to the number of new cases of a disorder that appear in a population during a specific period of time. **Prevalence** refers to the total number of active cases, both old and new, that are present in a population during a specific period of time. The *lifetime prevalence* of a disorder is the total proportion of people in a given population who have been affected by the disorder at some point during their lives. For example, the incidence of depression may rise in a given year, but the prevalence of that disorder in the general population may remain the same.

Prevalence and Gender Differences   How prevalent are the various forms of abnormal behavior? One large scale study, known as the Epidemiologic Catchment Area (ECA) Study, was conducted in the 1980s (Robins & Regier, 1991). Approximately 20,000 people were interviewed in five large metropolitan areas in the United States. Questions were asked pertaining to 30 of the major disorders listed in the DSM. The ECA study found that 32 percent of the people they interviewed received at least one *lifetime* diagnosis. This figure is much higher than many people expect, and it underscores the point that we made at the beginning of this chapter: All of us can expect to encounter the challenges of a mental disorder—either for ourselves or for someone we love—at some point during our lives.

Figure 1–1 lists some results from this study using one-year prevalence rates—the number of people with active symptoms during the 12 months prior to the interview. Notice that gender differences are found in many types of mental disorder: Anxiety disorders (phobias and panic) and depression are more common among women; alcoholism and antisocial personality are more common among men. Other conditions, like schizophrenia and bipolar mood disorder, appear with equal frequency in both women and men. Patterns of this sort raise interesting questions about possible causal mechanisms. What conditions would make women more vulnerable to one kind of disorder and men more vulnerable to another? There are many possibilities, including factors such as hormones, patterns of learning, and social pressures.

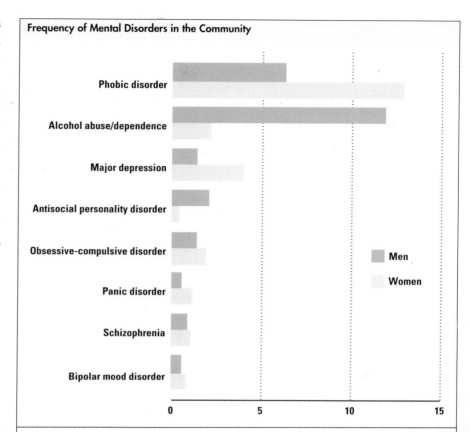

FIGURE 1–1: One-year prevalence rates for various mental disorders (ECA data).

Source: Adapted from L.N. Robins, B.Z. Locke, and D.A. Regier, 1991, An overview of psychiatric disorders in America. In L.N. Robins and D.A. Regier (Eds.), *Psychiatric Disorders in America: The Epidemiological Catchment Area Study*, pp. 328–366. New York: Free Press.

The ECA study found that mental disorders are experienced by many people at some point during their lives. This information is important, but epidemiologists agree that the figures include some people whose problems are not associated with substantial impairment in functioning. In other words, they are able to work around the disorder with only minimal disruption to their life—taking a train or bus, for example, if the person has a strong fear of flying. Overall prevalence rates for mental disorders would be somewhat lower (perhaps 20 percent of all adults) if we counted only those people whose symptoms were associated with significant distress or a disruption of social and occupational activities (Regier & Narrow, 2002).

Comorbidty and Disease Burden   Data from another, more recent epidemiological investigation—the National Cormorbidity Survey (NCS)—indicate that most severe disorders are concentrated in a much smaller segment of

Lee Robins, professor of sociology in psychiatry at Washington University, was the principal investigator in the ECA Study, which is one extensive base of information regarding the prevalence of mental disorders in the United States.

the population. Often these are people who simultaneously qualify for more than one diagnosis, such as major depression and alcoholism. The presence of more than one condition within the same period of time is known as **comorbidity** (or co-occurrence). Fourteen percent of the people in the NCS sample had three or more lifetime disorders, and 9 out of 10 people with a severe disorder fell into that highly comorbid group (Kessler & Zhao, 1999). These findings have shifted the emphasis of epidemiological studies from counting the absolute number of people who have any kind of mental disorder to measuring the functional impairment associated with these problems.

What impact do mental disorders have on people's lives?

Mental disorders are highly prevalent, but how do we measure the extent of their impact on people's lives? And how does that impact compare to the effects of other diseases? These are important questions when policymakers must establish priorities for various types of training, research, and health services.

Epidemiologists measure disease burden by combining two factors: mortality and disability. The common measure is based on time: lost years of healthy life, which might be caused by premature death (compared to the person's standard life expectancy) or living with a disability (weighted for severity). For purposes of comparison among different forms of disease and injury, the disability produced by major depression is considered to be equivalent to that associated with blindness or paraplegia. A psychotic disorder such as schizophrenia leads to disability that is comparable to that associated with quadriplegia.

The World Health Organization (WHO) sponsored an ambitious study called the Global Burden of Disease Study, which used these measures to evaluate and compare the impact of more than 100 forms of disease and injury throughout the world (Lopez & Murray, 1998; Murray & Lopez, 1997). Although mental disorders are responsible for only 1 percent of all deaths, they produce 47 percent of all disability in economically developed countries, like the United States, and 28 percent of all disability worldwide. The combined index (mortality plus disability) reveals that, as a combined category, mental disorders are the second leading source of disease burden in developed countries (see Figure 1–2). Investigators in the WHO study predict that, relative to other types of health problems, the burden of mental disorders will increase by the year 2020. These surprising results indicate strongly that mental disorders are one of the world's greatest health challenges.

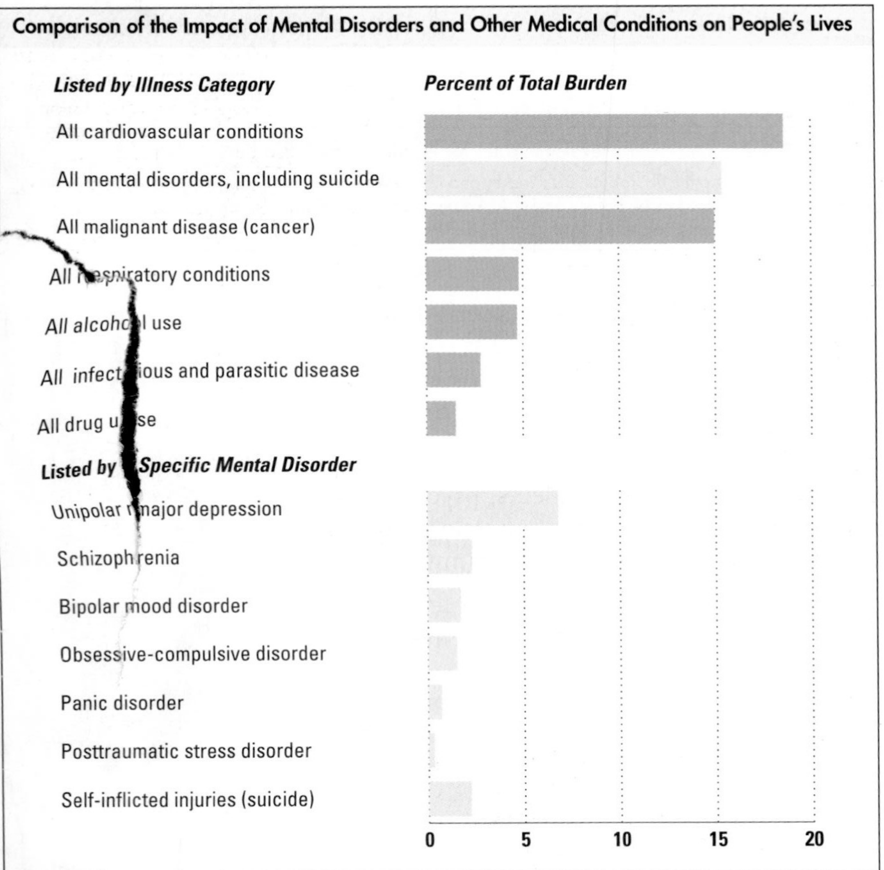

Cross-Cultural Comparisons

As the evidence regarding the global burden of disease clearly documents, mental disorders affect people all over the world. That does not mean, however, that the symptoms of psychopathology and the expression of emotional distress take the same form in all cultures. Epidemiological studies comparing the frequency of mental disorders in different cultures suggest that some disorders, like schizophrenia, show important consistencies in cross-cultural comparisons. They are found in virtually every culture that social scientists have studied.

Other disorders, like bulimia, are more specifically associated with cultural factors, as

Comparison of the Impact of Mental Disorders and Other Medical Conditions on People's Lives

Listed by Illness Category / *Percent of Total Burden*

- All cardiovascular conditions
- All mental disorders, including suicide
- All malignant disease (cancer)
- All respiratory conditions
- All alcohol use
- All infectious and parasitic disease
- All drug use

Listed by Specific Mental Disorder

- Unipolar major depression
- Schizophrenia
- Bipolar mood disorder
- Obsessive-compulsive disorder
- Panic disorder
- Posttraumatic stress disorder
- Self-inflicted injuries (suicide)

0   5   10   15   20

FIGURE 1–2: Disease burden in economically developed countries measured in disability-adjusted life years (DALYs).

Source: C.L. Murray, & A.D. Lopez (Eds.), 1996, *The Global Burden of Disease: A comprehensive assessment of mortality and disability from diseases, injuries, and risk factors in 1990 and projected to 2020.* Cambridge, MA: Harvard University Press.

revealed by comparisons of prevalence in different parts of the world and changes in prevalence over generations. Almost 90 percent of bulimic patients are women. Within the U.S., the incidence of bulimia is much higher among university women than among working women, and it is more common among younger women than among older women. The prevalence of bulimia is much higher in Western nations than in other parts of the world. Furthermore, the number of cases increased dramatically during the latter part of the twentieth century (Keel & Klump, 2003). These patterns suggest that holding particular sets of values related to eating and to women's appearance is an important ingredient in establishing risk for development of an eating disorder.

The strength and nature of the relationship between culture and psychopathology vary from one disorder to the next. Several general conclusions can be drawn from cross-cultural studies of psychopathology (Draguns & Tanaka-Matsumi, 2003), including the following points:

- All mental disorders are shaped, to some extent, by cultural factors.
- No mental disorders are entirely due to cultural or social factors.
- Psychotic disorders are less influenced by culture than are nonpsychotic disorders.
- The symptoms of certain disorders are more likely to vary across cultures than are the disorders themselves.

We will return to these points as we discuss specific disorders, such as depression, phobias, and alcoholism, throughout this book.

THE MENTAL HEALTH PROFESSIONS

People receive treatment for psychological problems in many different settings and from various kinds of service providers. The ECA study found that people receive mental health care from three general sources. Specialized mental health professionals, such as psychiatrists, psychologists, and social workers, treat fewer than half (40 percent) of those people who seek help for mental disorders (Manderscheid et al., 1999). Roughly one-third (34 percent) are treated by primary care physicians, who are most likely to prescribe

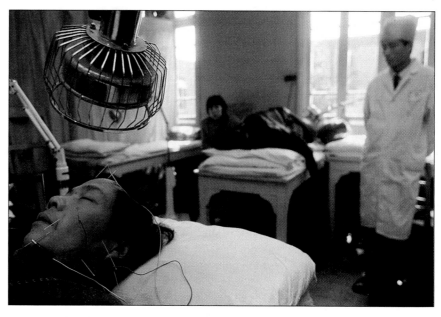

some form of medication. The remaining 26 percent of mental health services are delivered by social agencies and self-help groups, such as Alcoholics Anonymous.

Many forms of specialized training prepare people to provide professional assistance to those who suffer from mental disorders. Table 1–2 presents estimated numbers of different types of mental health professionals currently practicing in the United States. The overall number of professionals who provide mental health services expanded dramatically during the 1990s, with most of this growth occurring among nonphysicians (Scheffler, Ivey, & Garrett, 1998). Most of these professions require extensive clinical experience in addition to formal academic instruction. In order to provide direct services to clients, psychiatrists, psychologists, social workers, counselors, nurses, and marriage and family therapists must be licensed in their own specialties by state boards of examiners.

Psychiatry is the branch of medicine that is concerned with the study and treatment of mental disorders. Psychiatrists complete the normal sequence of coursework and internship training in a medical school (usually four years) before going on to receive specialized residency training (another four years) that is focused on abnormal behavior. By virtue of their medical training, psychiatrists are licensed to practice medicine and therefore are able to prescribe medication. Most psychiatrists are also trained in the use of psychosocial intervention.

Mental disorders are found in relatively similar numbers throughout the world, but approaches to treatment vary from one culture to the next. In China, acupuncture is used frequently to treat people who are depressed. Medication and psychotherapy are the most frequently used forms of treatment for depression in the U.S. and Europe.

Who provides help for people with mental disorders?

Clinical psychology is concerned with the application of psychological science to the assessment and treatment of mental disorders. A clinical psychologist typically completes five years of graduate study in a department of psychology, as well as a one-year internship, before receiving a doctoral degree. Clinical psychologists are trained in the use of psychological assessment procedures and in the use of psychotherapy. Within clinical psychology, there are two primary types of clinical training programs. One course of study, which leads to the Ph.D. (doctor of philosophy) degree, involves a traditional sequence of graduate training with major emphasis on research methods. The other approach, which culminates in a Psy.D. (doctor of psychology) degree, places greater emphasis on practical skills of assessment and treatment and does not require an independent research project for the dissertation. One can also obtain a Ph.D. degree in counseling psychology, a more applied field that focuses on training, assessment, and therapy.

Social work is a third profession that is concerned with helping people to achieve an effective level of psychosocial functioning (Duffy et al., 2002). Most practicing social workers have a master's degree in social work. In contrast to psychology and psychiatry, social work is based less on a body of scientific knowledge than on a commitment to action. Social work is practiced in a wide range of settings, from courts and prisons to schools and hospitals, as well as other social service agencies. The emphasis tends to be on social and cultural factors, such as the effects of poverty on the availability of educational and health services, rather than on individual differences in personality or psychopathology. Psychiatric social workers receive specialized training in the treatment of mental health problems.

Like social workers, professional counselors work in many different settings, ranging from schools and government agencies to mental health centers and private practice. Most are trained at the master's degree level, and the emphasis of their activity is also on providing direct service (U.S. Department of Labor, 1996). Marriage and family therapy (MFT) is a multidisciplinary field in which professionals are trained to provide psychotherapy. Most MFTs are trained at the master's level, and many hold a degree in social work, counseling, or psychology as well. Although the theoretical orientation is focused on couples and family issues, approximately half of the people treated by MFTs are seen in individual psychotherapy. Psychiatric nursing is a rapidly growing field. Training for this profession typically involves a bachelor's degree in nursing plus graduate level training (at least a master's degree) in the treatment of mental health problems.

Another approach to mental health services that is expanding rapidly in size and influence is psychosocial rehabilitation (PSR). Professionals in this area work in crisis, residential, and case management programs for people with severe forms of disorder, such as schizophrenia. PSR workers teach people practical, day-to-day skills that are necessary for living in the community, thereby reducing the need for long-term hospitalization and minimizing the level of disability experienced by their clients. Graduate training is not required for most PSR positions; three out of four people providing PSR services have either a high school education or a bachelor's degree.

It is difficult to say with certainty what the mental health professions will be like in the future. Boundaries between professions change as a function of progress in the development of therapeutic procedures, economic pressures, legislative action, and courtroom decisions. This has been particularly true in the field of mental health, where enormous changes have taken place over the past few decades (Scheffler, Ivey, & Garrett, 1998). Reform is currently being driven by the pervasive influence of managed care,

TABLE 1–2 Estimated Number of Clinically Trained Professionals Providing Mental Health Services in the United States

PROFESSION	NUMBER
Psychiatrists	40,900
Clinical psychologists	77,500
Social workers	194,600
Marriage and family therapists	47,100
Psychiatric nurses	16,600
Counselors	111,900
Psychosocial rehabilitation providers	100,000

Source: F.F. Duffy et al., Mental health practitioners and trainees. In R.W. Manderscheid and M.J. Henderson (Eds.), *Mental Health, United States, 2002.* Rockville, MD; U.S. Department of Health and Human Services, Chapter 21, Table 1 (go to www.mentalhealth.org/publications/allpubs/SMA04-3938).

which refers to the way that services are financed. For example, health insurance companies typically place restrictions on the types of services that will be reimbursed, as well as the specific professionals who can provide them. Managed care places a high priority on cost containment and the evaluation of treatment effectiveness. Legislative issues that determine the scope of clinical practice are also very important. Many psychologists are pursuing the right to prescribe medication (Robiner et al., 2003; Welsh, 2003). Decisions regarding this issue will also have a dramatic impact on the boundaries that separate the mental health professions. Ongoing conflicts over the increasing price of health care, priorities for treatment, and access to services suggest that debates over the rights and privileges of patients and their therapists will intensify in coming years.

One thing is certain about the future of the mental health professions: There will always be a demand for people who are trained to help those suffering from abnormal behavior. Many people experience mental disorders. Unfortunately, most of those who are in need do not get help. Among people in the United States who have an active mental disorder, only 20 percent received treatment for their problems (Kessler et al., 1994). Many factors may account for this fact. Some people who qualify for a diagnosis may not be so impaired as to seek treatment; others, as we shall see, may not recognize their disorder. In some cases, treatment may not be available, the person may not have the time or resources to obtain treatment, or the person may have tried treatments in the past that failed (see Getting Help, at the end of this chapter.)

PSYCHOPATHOLOGY IN HISTORICAL CONTEXT

Throughout history, many other societies have held very different views of the problems that we consider to be mental disorders. Before leaving this introductory chapter, we must begin to place contemporary approaches to psychopathology in historical perspective.

The search for explanations of the causes of abnormal behavior dates to ancient times, as do conflicting opinions about the etiology of emotional disorders. References to abnormal behavior

Clinical psychologists perform many roles. Some provide direct clinical services. Many are involved in research, teaching, and various administrative activities.

have been found in ancient accounts from Chinese, Hebrew, and Egyptian societies. Many of these records attribute abnormal behavior to the disfavor of the gods or the mischief of demons. In fact, abnormal behavior continues to be attributed to demons in some preliterate societies today.

The Greek Tradition in Medicine

More earthly and less supernatural accounts of the etiology of psychopathology can be traced to the Greek physician Hippocrates (460–377 B.C.), who ridiculed demonological accounts of illness and insanity. Instead, Hippocrates hypothesized that abnormal behavior, like other forms of disease, had natural causes. Health depended on maintaining a natural balance within the body, specifically a balance of four body fluids (which were also known as the four humors): blood, phlegm, black bile, and yellow bile. Hippocrates argued that various types of disorder, including psychopathology, resulted from either an excess or a deficiency of one of these four fluids. The specifics of Hippocrates' theories obviously have little value today, but his systematic attempt to uncover natural, biological explanations for all types of illness represented an enormously important departure from previous ways of thinking.

The Hippocratic perspective dominated medical thought in Western countries until the middle of the nineteenth century (Golub, 1994). People trained in the Hippocratic tradition viewed "disease" as a unitary concept. In other words,

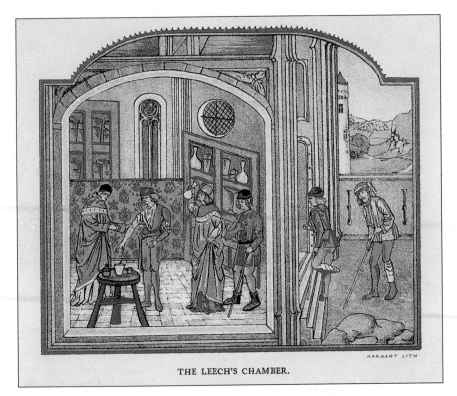

THE LEECH'S CHAMBER.

This 16-century illustration shows sick people going to the doctor who attempts to cure their problems by extracting blood from them using a leech. The rationale for such treatment procedures was to restore the proper balance of bodily fluids.

Dorothea Dix (1802–1887) *was an early advocate for the humane treatment of the mentally ill. Many mental institutions were built during the late 1800s due in large part to Dix's efforts.*

physicians (and others who were given responsibility for healing people who were disturbed or suffering) did not distinguish between mental disorders and other types of illness. All problems were considered to be the result of an imbalance of body fluids, and treatment procedures were designed in an attempt to restore the ideal balance. These were often called "heroic" treatments because they were drastic (and frequently painful) attempts to quickly reverse the course of an illness. They involved bloodletting (intentionally cutting the person to reduce the amount of blood in the body) and purging (the induction of vomiting), as well as the use of heat and cold. These practices continued to be part of standard medical treatments well into the nineteenth century (Starr, 1982).

The Creation of the Asylum

In Europe during the Middle Ages, "lunatics" and "idiots," as the mentally ill and mentally retarded were commonly called, aroused little interest and were given marginal care. Most people lived in rural settings and made their living through agricultural activities. Disturbed behavior was considered to be the responsibility of the family rather than the community or the state. Many people were kept at home by their families, and others

roamed freely as beggars. Mentally disturbed people who were violent or appeared dangerous often were imprisoned with criminals. Those who could not subsist on their own were placed in almshouses for the poor.

In the 1600s and 1700s, "insane asylums" were established to house the mentally disturbed. Several factors changed the way that society viewed people with mental disorders and reinforced the relatively new belief that the community as a whole should be responsible for their care (Grob, 1994). Perhaps most important was a change in economic, demographic, and social conditions. Consider, for example, the situation in the United States at the beginning of the nineteenth century. The period between 1790 and 1850 saw rapid population growth and the rise of large cities. The increased urbanization of the American population was accompanied by a shift from an agricultural to an industrial economy. Lunatic asylums—the original mental hospitals— were created to serve heavily populated cities and to assume responsibilities that had previously been performed by individual families.

Early asylums were little more than human warehouses, but as the nineteenth century began, the moral treatment movement led to improved conditions in at least some mental hospitals. Founded on a basic respect for human dignity and the belief that humanistic care would help to relieve mental illness, moral treatment reform efforts were instituted by leading mental health professionals of the day, such as Benjamin Rush in the United States, Phillipe Pinel in France, and William Tuke in England. Rather than simply confining mental patients, moral treatment offered support, care, and a degree of freedom. Belief in the importance of reason and the potential benefits of science played an important role in the moral treatment movement. In contrast to the fatalistic, supernatural explanations that had prevailed during the Middle Ages, these reformers touted an optimistic view, arguing that mental disorders could be treated successfully.

Many of the large mental institutions in the United States were built in the nineteenth century as a result of the philosophy of moral treatment. In the middle of the 1800s, the mental health advocate Dorothea Dix was a leader in this movement. Dix argued that treating the mentally ill in hospitals was both more humane and more economical than caring for them haphazardly in their communities, and she urged that special facilities be built to house mental patients. Dix and like-minded reformers were successful in their efforts. In 1830, there were only four public mental hospitals in the United States that housed a combined total of fewer than 200 patients. By 1880, there were 75 public mental hospitals, with a total population of more than 35,000 residents (Torrey, 1988).

The creation of large institutions for the treatment of mental patients led to the development of a new profession—psychiatry. By the middle of the 1800s, superintendents of asylums for the insane were almost always physicians who had experience in the care of people with severe mental disorders. The Association of Medical Superintendents of American Institutions for the Insane (AMSAII), which later became the American Psychiatric Association (APA), was founded in 1844. The large patient populations within these institutions provided an opportunity for these men to observe various types of psychopathology over an extended period of time. They soon began to publish their ideas regarding the causes of these conditions, and they also experimented with new treatment methods (Grob, 1994).

Worcester Lunatic Hospital: A Model Institution

In 1833, the state of Massachusetts opened a publicly supported asylum for lunatics, a term used at the time to describe people with mental disorders, in Worcester. Samuel Woodward, the asylum's first superintendent, also became the first president of the AMSAII. Woodward became very well known throughout the United States and Europe because of his claims that mental disorders could be cured just like other types of disease. We will describe this institution and its superintendent briefly because, in many ways, it became a model for psychiatric care on which other nineteenth-century hospitals were built.

Woodward's ideas about the causes of disorder represented a combination of physical and moral considerations. Moral factors focused on the person's lifestyle. Violations of "natural" or conventional behavior could presumably cause mental disorders. Judgments regarding the nature of these violations were based on the prevailing middle-class, Protestant standards that were held

The Massachusetts Lunatic Asylum (as it appeared in 1835) was the first large state mental institution in the United States.
From the collection of the Worcester Historical Museum, Worcester, Massachusetts.

by Woodward and his peers, who were almost invariably well educated, white males. After treating several hundred patients during his first 10 years at the Worcester asylum, Woodward argued that at least half of the cases could be traced to immoral behavior, improper living conditions, and exposure to unnatural stresses. Specific examples included intemperance (heavy drinking), masturbation, overwork, domestic difficulties, excessive ambition, faulty education, personal disappointment, marital problems, excessive religious enthusiasm, jealousy, and pride (Grob, 1994). The remaining cases were attributed to physical causes, such as poor health or a blow to the head.

Treatment at the Worcester Lunatic Hospital included a blend of physical and moral procedures. If mental disorders were often caused by improper behavior and difficult life circumstances, presumably they could be cured by moving the person to a more appropriate and therapeutic environment, the asylum. Moral treatment focused on efforts to reeducate the patient, fostering the development of self-control that would allow the person to return to a "healthy" lifestyle. Procedures included occupational therapy, religious exercises, and recreation. Mechanical restraints were employed only when considered necessary.

Moral treatments were combined with a mixture of physical procedures. These included standard heroic interventions, such as bleeding and purging, which the asylum superintendents had learned as part of their medical training. For example, some symptoms were thought to be produced by inflammation of the brain, and it

What was the rationale for moral treatment programs?

was believed that bleeding would restore the natural balance of fluids. Woodward and his colleagues also employed various kinds of drugs. Patients who were excited, agitated, or violent were often treated with opium or morphine. Depressed patients were given laxatives.

Woodward claimed that "no disease, of equal severity, can be treated with greater success than insanity, if the remedies are applied sufficiently early." He reported that the recovery rates at the Worcester hospital varied from 82 percent to 91 percent between 1833 and 1845. His reports were embraced and endorsed by other members of the young psychiatric profession. They fueled

enthusiasm for establishing more large public hospitals, thus aiding the efforts of Dorothea Dix and other advocates for public support of mental health treatment.

Lessons from the History of Psychopathology

The invention and expansion of public mental hospitals set in motion a process of systematic observation and scientific inquiry that led directly to our current system of mental health care. The creation of psychiatry as a professional group,

---

research methods

WHO MUST PROVIDE SCIENTIFIC EVIDENCE?

Scientists have established a basic and extremely important rule for making and testing any new hypothesis: The scientist who makes a new prediction must prove it to be true. Scientists are not obligated to disprove other researchers' assertions. Until a hypothesis is supported by empirical evidence, the community of scientists assumes that the new prediction is false.

The concepts of the experimental hypothesis and the null hypothesis are central to understanding this essential rule of science. An **experimental hypothesis** is any new prediction, such as the idea that eating chocolate can alleviate depression, made by an investigator. Researchers must adopt and state their experimental hypothesis in both correlational studies and experiments (discussed in Research Methods in Chapters 2 and 3). In all scientific research, the **null hypothesis** is the alternative to the experimental hypothesis. The null hypothesis always predicts that the experimental hypothesis is not true, for example, that eating chocolate does not make depressed people feel better. The rules of science dictate that scientists must assume that the null hypothesis holds until research contradicts it. That is, the burden of proof falls on the scientist who makes a new prediction, who offers an experimental hypothesis.

These rules of science are analogous to rules about the burden of proof that have been adopted in trial courts. In U.S. courtrooms, the law assumes that a defendant is innocent until proven guilty. Defendants do not need to prove

their innocence; rather, prosecutors need to prove the defendants' guilt. Thus the null hypothesis is analogous to the assumption of innocence, and the burden of proof in science falls on any scientist who challenges the null hypothesis, just as it falls on the prosecutor in a court trial.

These rules in science and in law serve important purposes. Both are conservative principles designed to protect the field from false assertions. Our legal philosophy is that "it is better to let 10 guilty people go free than to punish one innocent person." Scientists adopt a similar philosophy—that false "scientific evidence" is more dangerous than undetected knowledge. Because of these safeguards, we can be reasonably confident when an experimental hypothesis is supported or when a defendant is found guilty.

We can easily apply these concepts and rules to claims that were made for the effectiveness of treatment methods such as lobotomy. In this example, the experimental hypothesis is that severing the nerve fibers that connect the frontal lobes to other areas of the brain will result in a significant decrease in psychotic symptoms. The null hypothesis is that this treatment is no more effective than having no treatment at all. According to the rules of science, a clinician who claims to have discovered a new treatment must prove that it is true. Scientists are not obligated to prove that the assertion is false, because the null hypothesis holds until it is rejected.

The value of this conservative approach is obvious when we consider the needless

suffering and permanent neurological dysfunction that was ultimately inflicted upon thousands of patients who were given lobotomies or subjected to fevers and comas during the 1940s (Valenstein, 1986). Had surgeons assumed that lobotomies did not work, many patients' brains would have been left intact. Similar conclusions can be drawn about less invasive procedures, such as institutionalization, medication, and psychotherapy. These treatments are also associated with costs, which range from financial considerations—certainly important in today's health care environment—to the disappointment brought about by false hopes. In all these cases, clinicians who provide mental health services should be required to demonstrate scientifically that their treatment procedures are effective (Dawes, 1994; McFall, 2001).

There is one more similarity between the rules of science and the rules of the courtroom. Courtroom verdicts do not lead to a judgment that the defendant is "innocent," but only to a decision that she or he is "not guilty." In theory, the possibility remains that a defendant who is found "not guilty" did indeed commit a crime. Similarly, scientific research does not lead to the conclusion that the null hypothesis is true. Scientists never prove the null hypothesis; they only fail to reject it. The reason for this position is that the philosophy of knowledge, epistemology, tells us that it is impossible ever to prove that an experimental hypothesis is false in every circumstance.

TABLE 1-3	Somatic Treatments Introduced and Widely Employed in the 1920s and 1930s	
NAME	**PROCEDURE**	**ORIGINAL RATIONALE**
Fever therapy	Blood from people with malaria was injected into psychiatric patients so that they would develop a fever.	Observation that symptoms sometimes disappeared in patients who became ill with typhoid fever
Insulin coma therapy	Insulin was injected into psychiatric patients to lower the sugar content of the blood and induce a hypoglycemic state and deep coma.	Observed mental changes among some diabetic drug addicts who were treated with insulin
Lobotomy	A sharp knife was inserted through a hole that was bored in the patient's skull, severing nerve fibers connecting the frontal lobes to the rest of the brain.	Observation that the same surgical procedure with chimpanzees led to a reduction in the display of negative emotion during stress

Note: Lack of critical evaluation of these procedures is belied by the unusual honors bestowed upon their inventors. Julius Wagner-Jauregg, an Austrian psychiatrist, was awarded a Nobel Prize in 1927 for his work in developing fever therapy. Egaz Moniz, a Portuguese psychiatrist, was awarded a Nobel Prize in 1946 for introduction of the lobotomy.

committed to treating and understanding psychopathology, laid the foundation for expanded public concern and financial resources for solving the problems of mental disorders.

There are, of course, many aspects of nineteenth-century psychiatry that, in retrospect, seem to have been naive or misguided. To take only one example, it seems silly to have thought that masturbation would cause mental disorders. In fact, masturbation is now taught and encouraged as part of treatment for certain types of sexual dysfunction (see Chapter 12). The obvious cultural biases that influenced the etiological hypotheses of Woodward and his colleagues seem quite unreasonable today. But, of course, our own values and beliefs influence the ways in which we define, think about, and treat mental disorders. Mental disorders cannot be defined in a cultural vacuum or in a completely objective fashion. The best we can do is to be aware of the problem of bias and include a variety of cultural and social perspectives in thinking about and defining the issues (Manson, 1994).

The other lesson that we can learn from history involves the importance of scientific research. Viewed from the perspective of contemporary care, we can easily be skeptical of Samuel Woodward's claims regarding the phenomenal success of treatment at the Worcester asylum. No one today believes that 90 percent of seriously disturbed, psychotic patients can be cured by currently available forms of treatment. Therefore, it is preposterous to assume that such astounding success might have been achieved at the Worcester Lunatic Hospital. During the 19th century, physicians were not trained in scientific research methods. Their optimistic statements about treatment outcome were accepted, in large part, on the basis of their professional authority. Clearly, Woodward's enthusiastic assertions should have been evaluated with more stringent, scientific methods.

Unfortunately, the type of naive acceptance that met Woodward's idealistic claims has become a regrettable tradition. For the past 150 years, mental health professionals and the public alike have repeatedly embraced new treatment procedures that have been hailed as cures for mental disorders. Perhaps most notorious was a group of somatic (bodily) treatment procedures that was introduced during the 1920s and 1930s (Valenstein, 1986). They included inducing fever, insulin comas, and **lobotomy,** a crude form of brain surgery (see Table 1–3). These dramatic procedures, which have subsequently proved to be ineffective, were accepted with the same enthusiasm that greeted the invention of large public institutions in nineteenth-century America. Thousands of patients were subjected to these procedures, which remained widespread until the early 1950s, when more effective pharmacological treatments were discovered. The history of psychopathology teaches us that people who claim that a new form of treatment is effective should be expected to prove it scientifically (see Research Methods).

METHODS FOR THE SCIENTIFIC STUDY OF MENTAL DISORDERS

This book will provide you with an introduction to the scientific study of psychopathology. The application of science to questions regarding abnormal behavior carries with it the implicit assumption that these problems can be studied systematically and objectively. Such a systematic and objective study is the basis for finding order in the frequently chaotic and puzzling world of mental disorders. This order will eventually allow us to understand the processes by which abnormal behaviors are created and maintained.

Clinical scientists adopt an attitude of open minded skepticism, tempered by an appreciation for the research methods that are used to collect empirical data. They formulate specific hypotheses, test them, and then refine them based on the results of these tests. For example, suppose you formulated the hypothesis that people who are depressed will improve if they eat more than a certain amount of chocolate every day. This hypothesis could be tested in a number of ways, using the methods discussed throughout this book. In order to get the most from it, you may have to set aside—at least temporarily—personal beliefs that you have already acquired about mental disorders. Try to adopt an objective, skeptical attitude. We hope to pique your curiosity and share with you the satisfaction, as well as perhaps some of the frustration, of searching for answers to questions about complex behavior problems.

The Uses and Limitations of Case Studies

We have already presented one source of information regarding mental disorders: the **case study,** an in-depth look at the symptoms and circumstances surrounding one person's mental disturbance. For many people, our initial ideas about the nature and potential causes of abnormal behavior are shaped by personal experience with a close friend or family member who has struggled with a psychological disorder. We use a number of case studies in this book to illustrate the symptoms of psychopathology and to raise questions about their development. Therefore, we should consider the ways in which case studies can be helpful in the study of psychopathology, as well as some of their limitations.

A case study presents a description of the problems experienced by one particular person. Detailed case studies can provide an exhaustive catalog of the symptoms that the person displayed, the manner in which these symptoms emerged, the developmental and family history that preceded the onset of the disorder, and whatever response the person may have shown to treatment efforts. This material often forms the basis for hypotheses about the causes of a person's problems. For example, based on Mary's case, one might speculate that depression plays a role in eating disorders. Case studies are especially important sources of information about conditions that have not received much attention in the literature and for problems that are relatively unusual. Multiple personality disorder and transsexualism are examples of disorders that are so infrequent that it is difficult to find groups of patients for the purpose of research studies. Much of what we know about these conditions is based on descriptions of individual patients.

Case studies also have several drawbacks. The most obvious limitation of case studies is that they can be viewed from many different perspectives. Any case can be interpreted in several ways, and competing explanations may be equally plausible. Consider, for example, the life of Jane Addams, an extremely influential social activist during the early years of the twentieth

Many people lead successful lives and make important contributions to society in spite of their struggles with mental disorder. Jane Addams (1860–1935), who won the Nobel Peace Prize for her work in social justice, suffered through extended periods of profound depression as a young woman.

century. She founded a program to serve poor people in Chicago, promoted the assimilation of immigrants into middle-class life, and for these efforts was awarded the Nobel Peace Prize in 1931. As a young adult, Addams suffered through an eight-year period of profound depression. Some historians have argued that the foundation of her mood disorder was formed in a long-standing conflict with her father over her hopes to pursue a professional career—something that was discouraged among women at the time (Diliberto, 1999). His sudden death seemed to trigger the onset of her symptoms. Of course, many other factors might also have been involved. Her mother died when she was two years old. The impact of this tragic experience was intensified by subsequent losses, including the death of her older sister.

Heredity may also have played a role in the origins of Addams's depression. Her brother suffered from a mental disorder, including severe bouts of depression, and was treated at psychiatric hospitals throughout his adult life. Speculation of this sort is intriguing, particularly in the case of a woman who played such an important role in the history of the United States. But we must remember that case studies are not conclusive. Jane Addams's experience does not indicate conclusively whether the loss of a parent can increase a person's vulnerability to depression, and it does not prove that genetic factors are involved in the transmission of this disorder. These questions must be resolved through scientific investigation.

The other main limitation of case studies is that it is risky to draw general conclusions about a disorder from a single example. How can we know that this individual is representative of the disorder as a whole? Are his or her experiences typical for people with this disorder? Again, hypotheses generated on the basis of the single case must be tested in research with larger, more representative samples of patients.

Clinical Research Methods

The importance of the search for new information about mental disorders has inspired us to build another special feature into this textbook. Each chapter includes a Research Methods feature that explains one particular research issue in some detail. The Research Methods feature in this chapter, for example, is concerned

TABLE 1–4	List of Research Methods Featured in This Book
CHAPTER	**TOPIC**
1	Who Must Provide Scientific Evidence?
2	Correlations: Does Psychology Make You Smarter?
3	The Experimental Method: Does Therapy Work?
4	Reliability: Do Clinicians Agree?
5	Analogue Studies: Do Rats Get Depressed, and Why?
6	Statistical Significance: When Differences Matter
7	Retrospective Reports: Remembering the Past
8	Longitudinal Studies: Lives Over Time
9	Cross-Cultural Comparisons: The Importance of Context
10	Psychotherapy Placebos: Controlling for Expectations
11	Studies of People at Risk for Disorders
12	Hypothetical Constructs: What Is Sexual Arousal?
13	Comparison Groups: What Is Normal?
14	Finding Genes That Cause Behavioral Problems
15	Central Tendency and Variability: What Do IQ Scores Mean?
16	Samples: How to Select the People We Study
17	Heritability: Genes and the Environment
18	Base Rates and Prediction: Justice Blackmun's Error

with the null hypothesis, the need to consider not just that your hypothesis may be true, but also that it may be false. A list of the issues addressed in Research Methods throughout this textbook appears in Table 1–4. They are arranged to progress from some of the more basic research methods and issues, such as correlational and experimental designs, toward more complex issues, such as gene identification and heritability.

We decided to discuss methodological issues in small sections throughout the book, for two primary reasons. First, the problems raised by research methods are often complex and challenging. Some students find it difficult to digest and comprehend an entire chapter on research methods in one chunk, especially at the beginning of a book. Thus we have broken it down into more manageable bites. Second, and perhaps more important, the methods we discuss generally make more sense and are easier to understand when they are presented in the context of a clinical question they can help answer. Our discussions of research methods are, therefore, introduced while we are explaining contemporary views of particular clinical problems.

Research findings are not the end of the road, either. The fact that someone has managed to collect and present data on a particular topic does not mean that the data are useful. We want you to learn about the problems of designing and interpreting research studies so that you will become a more critical consumer of scientific evidence. If you do not have a background in research design or quantitative methods, the Research Methods features will familiarize you with the procedures that psychologists use to test their hypotheses. If you have already had an introductory course in methodology, they will show you how these problems are handled in research on abnormal behavior.

getting help

Many students take an abnormal psychology class, in part, to understand more about their own problems or the problems of friends or family members. If you are considering whether you want to get help for yourself or for someone you know, these Getting Help sections should give you a head start in finding good therapists and effective treatments.

Of course, psychology is not just about problems. If you are wondering if you need help, if you are just curious about the problems people can have, or even if you are skeptical or disinterested, you will definitely learn more about yourself and others from this course and studying psychology in general. That is what makes the subject so fascinating! But when the topic is abnormal psychology, you should be warned in advance about two risks.

The first is the "medical student's syndrome." As medical students learn about new illnesses, they often "develop" the symptoms of each successive disease they study. The same thing can happen when studying abnormal psychology. In fact, because many symptoms of emotional disorders share much in common with everyday experiences, students of abnormal psychology are even more likely to "discover" symptoms in themselves or others. ("Gee, I think maybe I have an anxiety disorder." "He is so self-absorbed; he has a personality disorder.") We all are frightened about experiencing illness and abnormality, and this fear can make us suggestible. So try to prepare yourself for bouts of the medical student's syndrome. And remember that it is normal to experience mild versions of many of the symptoms you will read about in this text.

Our second warning is much more serious. If you are genuinely concerned about your own problems or those of a loved one, you probably have or will consult various "self-help" resources—books, Web sites, or perhaps groups on or off line. Do not accept uncritically the treatment programs they may suggest. You probably know that not everything you hear or read is true, and psychological advice is no exception.

Misleading, inaccurate, or simply wrong information is a particular problem in abnormal psychology for three reasons. First, to be honest, as you will learn throughout this course, psychological scientists simply do not know the causes of or absolutely effective treatments for many emotional problems. Second, people who have emotional problems, and those who have loved ones who have emotional problems, often are desperate to find a cure. Third, some well meaning—and some unscrupulous—people will provide authoritative-sounding "answers" that really are theories, speculations, or distortions.

How can you know what information is accurate and what information is inaccurate? We have worked hard to bring you the most recent scientific information in this text. In addition to the detailed information we present in each chapter, we give you practical tips including recommended self-help books and Web sites in these Getting Help sections in each chapter. Two general resources you might want to explore now are Martin Seligman's book, *What You Can Change and What You Can't,* and the home page of the National Institute of Mental Health: www.nimh.nih.gov. But we don't want you to rely only on this text or other authorities. We want you to rely on your own critical thinking skills, especially when it comes to getting help for yourself or someone you care about. Remember this: There is an army of scientists out there trying to solve the problems of emotional disorders, because, like us, they want to help. Breakthrough treatments that really are breakthrough treatments will not be kept secret. They will be announced on the front page of newspapers, not in obscure books or remote Web sites.

SUMMARY

Mental disorders are quite common. At least one out of every three people will experience a serious form of abnormal behavior, such as depression, alcoholism, or schizophrenia, at some point during his or her lifetime. Just as each of us is likely to be affected by medical problems at some point, it is also not surprising that we, or someone we love, will have to cope with a disorder of the mind.

One of our goals in this chapter is to make you more familiar with certain symptoms of **psychopathology.** We have described two relatively common forms of mental disorder: schizophrenia and bulimia nervosa. Schizophrenia is a severe form of mental disorder, a **psychosis,** in which the person is out of touch with reality. Bulimia nervosa is an eating disorder that involves recurrent episodes in which the person cannot control what (or how much) he or she eats. These episodes of binge eating are followed by efforts to prevent weight gain, such as self-induced vomiting. These and many other types of mental disorder are described in greater detail in subsequent chapters of this book.

Mental disorders are defined in terms of typical signs and symptoms rather than identifiable causal factors. A group of symptoms that appear together and are assumed to represent a specific type of disorder is called a **syndrome.** There are no definitive psychological or biological tests that can be used to confirm the presence of psychopathology. At present, the diagnosis of mental disorders depends on observations of the person's behavior and descriptions of personal experience.

No one has been able to provide a universally accepted definition of abnormal behavior. Statistical infrequency and subjective distress cannot be used for this purpose because not all infrequent behaviors are pathological, and because some people who exhibit abnormal behaviors do not have insight into their conditions. One useful approach defines mental disorders in terms of **harmful dysfunction.** The official classification system, DSM-IV-TR, defines mental disorders as a group of persistent maladaptive behaviors that result in personal distress or impaired functioning.

Various forms of voluntary social deviance and efforts to express individuality are excluded from the DSM-IV-TR definition of mental disorders. Political and religious actions, and the beliefs on which they are based, are not considered to be forms of abnormal behavior, even when they seem unusual to many other people. We must recognize, however, that the process of defining psychopathology is still influenced by **culture.**

The scientific study of the frequency and distribution of disorders within a population is known as **epidemiology.** Some severe forms of abnormal behavior, such as schizophrenia, have been observed in virtually every society that has been studied by social scientists. There are also forms of psychopathology—including eating disorders—for which substantial cross cultural differences have been found. These epidemiological patterns may provide important clues that will help identify factors that influence the causes of mental disorders.

Some of the best information that is currently available on the epidemiology of mental disorders in the United States was collected in the Epidemiologic Catchment Area (ECA) Study. According to this study, the lifetime prevalence for at least one type of mental disorder was relatively high, with 32 percent of adults reporting at least one mental disorder at some point in their lives. The ECA study found significant gender differences for several types of mental disorder, including anxiety disorders, mood disorders, and alcoholism. Although a very large number of people experience a mental disorder at some time during their lives, most severe disorders are concentrated in a smaller segment of the population (14 percent) that is characterized by a high rate of **comorbidity.** The global burden of mental disorders is substantial. They are responsible for 47 percent of all disability in economically developed countries, like the United States, and 28 percent of all disability worldwide.

Many forms of specialized training prepare people to provide professional help to those who suffer from mental disorders. Psychiatry is a branch of medicine that is concerned with the study and treatment of mental disorders. A **psychiatrist** is licensed to practice medicine and is therefore able to prescribe medication. A **clinical psychologist** has received graduate training in the use of assessment procedures and psychotherapy. Most psychologists also have extensive knowledge regarding research methods, and their training prepares them for the integration of science and practice. Many other professions are also actively involved in the delivery of mental health services. These include social workers, professional counselors, and psychiatric nurses.

Throughout history, many societies have held different ideas about the problems that we consider to be mental disorders. Asylums were created in Europe and the United States during the 1600s and 1700s to house people who were mentally disturbed. Although the earliest asylums were little more than human warehouses, the moral treatment movement led to improved conditions in some mental hospitals. The existence of large institutions for mental patients led to the development of psychiatry as a profession. These physicians, who served as the superintendents of asylums, soon began to develop systems for describing, classifying, and treating people with various types of mental disorder. Their efforts led to the use of scientific methods to test these new ideas.

Scientific methods must be employed in the search for knowledge about mental disorders. A person who proposes a new theory about the causes of a form of psychopathology, or someone who advocates a new treatment procedure, should be expected to prove these claims with scientific evidence. The burden of proof falls on the clinical scientist who offers a new prediction, such as the claim that a particular kind of therapy is effective. In other words, the **null hypothesis** (the alternative to the **experimental hypothesis**) is assumed to be true until it is contradicted by systematic data. Individual **case studies** do not provide conclusive evidence about the causes of, or treatments for, mental disorders.

KEY TERMS

abnormal psychology   4
case study   22
clinical psychology   16
comorbidity   14

culture   9
epidemiology   12
experimental
 hypothesis   20

harmful dysfunction   8
incidence   13
lobotomy   21
null hypothesis   20

prevalence   13
psychiatry   15
psychopathology   4
psychosis   5

social work   16
syndrome   5

 Go to www.prenhall.com/oltmanns for online quizzes, interactive flash cards, powerpoint presentations, and chapter reviews.

2

Causes of
Abnormal Behavior

◆◆

What causes abnormal behavior? We all would like a clear answer to this question. People suffering from emotional problems—and their loved ones—may be desperate for one. True, some people quickly point the finger of blame at factors such as the trauma of abuse, poor parenting, or a "broken brain." But there is a big problem with these handy explanations: They are almost always wrong. The truth is that, with a few exceptions, the specific causes of emotional disorders remain a mystery. Doing the detective work is the job of psychological science. We discuss our best leads in this chapter, but you should know one important fact at the outset: A conspiracy of causes, not a lone culprit, is responsible for most cases of abnormal behavior.

OVERVIEW

You may be distressed to read that the cause, or *etiology*, of abnormal behavior remains a mystery. In fact, you may have read or heard some story in the popular media proclaiming "Case Solved!" about the cause of depression or some other emotional problem. Unfortunately, media accounts almost always reflect a misleading and oversimplifying rush to judgment. They pick one factor out of the lineup of causes because it makes a good, reassuring story.

Some scientists also claim to have solved the mystery of abnormal behavior. Throughout much of the twentieth century, many psychologists vowed allegiance to one of four broad theories purporting to explain the etiology of psychological disorders—the biological, psychodynamic, cognitive behavioral, and humanistic paradigms. A **paradigm** is a set of shared assumptions that includes both the substance of a theory and beliefs about how scientists should collect data and test the theory. Thus, the four paradigms disagreed not only about what causes abnormal behavior, but also about how to study it. Returning to our mystery metaphor, the paradigms not only picked different suspects out of the lineup, but they argued for different ways of proving guilt or innocence!

Most psychologists now recognize that abnormal behavior is caused by a combination of biological, psychological, and social factors (Hayes, 1992; Rutter & Rutter, 1993). Biological contributions to abnormal behavior range from

Twelve innocent students and one teacher were killed in a shooting rampage by two schoolmates in Columbine, Colorado. Such horrific events make us desperate to know, "Why?", but most abnormal behavior defies easy explanation.

imbalanced brain chemistry to genetic predispositions. Psychological contributions range from troubled emotions to distorted thinking. Social and cultural contributions range from conflict in family relationships to gender and racial bias. Because biological, psychological, and social factors all contribute to abnormal behavior, psychological scientists often refer to the **biopsychosocial model** when discussing integrated explanations of mental disorders.

In this chapter, we briefly review the four paradigms and explain how integrated approaches have emerged to replace them. We also outline a number of biological, psychological, and social factors that contribute to causing emotional problems. In later chapters, we return to these concepts when discussing specific psychological disorders. As we do in every chapter, we begin our investigation with a case study. Most cases, including the following one, come from our own therapy files.

CASE STUDY Meghan's Many Hardships

At the age of 14, Meghan B. attempted to end her life by taking approximately 20 Tylenol® capsules. Meghan took the pills after an explosive fight with her mother over Meghan's grades and a boy she was dating. Meghan was in her room when she impulsively took the pills, but shortly afterward she told her mother what she had done. Her parents rushed Meghan to the emergency room, where her vital signs were closely monitored. As the crisis was coming to an end, Meghan's parents agreed that she should be hospitalized to make sure that she was safe and to begin to treat her problems.

Meghan talked freely during the 30 days she spent on the adolescent unit of a private psychiatric hospital. Most of her complaints focused on her mother. Meghan insisted that her mother was always "in her face," telling her what to do and when and how to do it. Her father was "great," but he was too busy with his job as a chemical engineer to spend much time with her.

Meghan also had longstanding problems in school. She barely maintained a C average despite considerable efforts to do better.

Meghan said she didn't care about school, and her mother's insistence that she could do much better was a major source of conflict between them. Meghan also complained that she had few friends, either in or outside of school. She described her classmates as "straight," and said she had no interest in them. Meghan was obviously angry as she described her family, school, and friends, but she also seemed sad. She often denounced herself as "stupid," and she cried about being a "reject" when discussing why no friends, including her boyfriend, came to see her at the hospital.

Mrs. B. provided details on the history of Meghan's problems. Mr. and Mrs. B. could not have children of their own, and they adopted Meghan when she was 2 years old. According to the adoption agency, Meghan's birth mother was 16 years old when she had the baby. Meghan's biological mother was a drug user, and she haphazardly left the baby in the care of friends and relatives for weeks at a time. Little was known about Meghan's biological father except that he had had some trouble with the law, and Meghan's mother had known him only briefly.

When Meghan was 14 months old, her pediatrician reported her mother to a child abuse protection agency after noting bruises on Meghan's thighs and hips.

After a six-month legal investigation, Meghan's mother agreed to give her up for adoption. Meghan came to live with Mr. and Mrs. B. shortly thereafter.

Mrs. B. was eager to give Meghan all the love she had missed, and happily doted on her daughter. Mr. B. also was a loving father, but like Meghan, Mrs. B. noted that he was rarely at home. Everything seemed fine with Meghan until first grade, when teachers began to complain about her. She disrupted the classroom with her restlessness, and she did not complete her schoolwork. In second grade, a school psychologist suggested that Meghan was a "hyperactive" child who also had a learning disability, and her pediatrician recommended medication as a treatment. Mrs. B. was horrified by the thought of medication or of sending Meghan to a "resource room" for part of the school day. Instead, she decided to redouble her efforts at parenting.

Mrs. B. succeeded in getting Meghan through elementary school in reasonably good shape. Meghan's grades and classroom behavior remained acceptable as long as Mrs. B. consulted repeatedly with the school. Mrs. B. noted with bitterness, however, that the one problem that she could not solve was Meghan's friendships. The daughters of Mrs. B.'s friends and neighbors were well behaved and excellent students. Meghan did not fit in, and she never got invited to play with the other girls.

Mrs. B. was obviously sad when discussing Meghan's past, but she became agitated and angry when discussing the present. She was very concerned about Meghan, but she wondered out loud if the suicide attempt had been manipulative. Mrs. B. said that she had had major conflicts with Meghan ever since Meghan started middle school at the age of 12. Meghan would no longer work with her mother on her homework for the usual two hours each night. In addition, Meghan began arguing about everything from picking up her room to her boyfriend, an 18 year old whom Mrs. B. abhorred. Mrs. B. complained that she did not understand what had happened to her daughter. She clearly stated, however, that whatever it was, she would fix it.

What was causing Meghan's problems? Her case study suggests many plausible alternatives. Some difficulties seem to be a reaction to a mother whose attentiveness at age 8 seems intrusive at age 14. We also could trace some of her troubles to anger over her failures in school or to rejection by her peers. However, Meghan's problems seem bigger than this. Surely she was affected by the physical abuse, inconsistent love, and chaotic living arrangements during the first, critical years of her life, but could those distant events account for all of her current problems? What about biological contributions to Meghan's problems? Did her birth mother's drug abuse affect the developing fetus? Was Meghan a healthy, full term newborn? Given her biological parents' history of troubled behavior, could Meghan's problems be genetic? Unfortunately, we do not have ready answers to these questions, but we can tell you how psychological scientists are seeking to answer them.

BRIEF HISTORICAL PERSPECTIVE: TWENTIETH-CENTURY PARADIGMS

The search for explanations of the causes of abnormal behavior dates to ancient times. As we discussed in Chapter 1, many of the traditions begun by Hippocrates died away after the fall of the Roman Empire. Systematic, naturalistic accounts of mental illness were kept alive in Arab cultures (Grob, 1994), but the emphasis on objectivity and careful observation faded in Europe. The rudiments of the scientific method were rediscovered during the Renaissance (approximately 1300–1600 A.D.), but the scientific method was not applied to the study of abnormal behavior until much later. In fact, advances in the scientific understanding of abnormal behavior were not made until the nineteenth and early twentieth centuries, when three major events occurred. One was the discovery of the cause of general paresis, a severe mental disorder that has a deteriorating course and eventually ends in death. The second was the writing of Sigmund Freud, a thinker who had a profound influence not only on the field of abnormal psychology, but on Western society as a whole. The third was the creation of a new academic discipline called psychology.

The Biological Paradigm

The *biological paradigm* looks for biological abnormalities that might cause abnormal behavior. The roots of this approach can be traced to the discovery of the cause of *general paresis* (general paralysis), a severe physical and mental disorder that we now know is caused by *syphilis*, a sexually transmitted disease. In 1798, John Haslam distinguished general paresis from other forms of "lunacy" based on its symptoms, which include delusions of grandeur, cognitive impairment (dementia), and progressive paralysis. (General paresis also has an unremitting course and ends in death after many years.) The diagnosis inspired a search for the cause of the newly discovered disorder, but it took scientists more than 100 years to solve the mystery.

The breakthrough began with the recognition that many people with general paresis had contracted syphilis earlier in their lives. At first, however, researchers questioned whether syphilis alone caused general paresis. For example, one study conducted by Fournier in 1894 concluded that only 65 percent of paretic patients reported a history of syphilis. How could syphilis cause general paresis if a third of paretic patients never had contracted the sexually transmitted disease? But Kraft Ebbing demonstrated that Fournier's statistic was

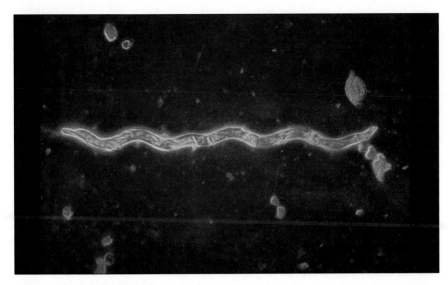

A microscopic image of the spirochete that causes syphilis and eventually causes general paresis if the syphilis goes untreated.

Sigmund Freud with his daughter, Anna.

patients proved that the infection had invaded and destroyed parts of the central nervous system. In 1910, Paul Ehrlich, a German microbiologist, developed arsphenamine, an arsenic-containing chemical that destroyed the spirochete and prevented general paresis. Unfortunately, the drug worked only if the patient was treated in the early stages of infection. Later, scientists learned that syphilis could be cured by another new discovery, penicillin—the first antibiotic. As a result, general paresis was virtually eliminated when antibiotics became widely available after the end of World War II.

The slow but dramatic discovery of the cause of general paresis gave great impetus to the search for biological causes for other mental disorders. The biological paradigm has successfully uncovered specific causes for some psychological disorders, particularly cognitive disorders (see Chapter 14) and forms of mental retardation (see Chapter 15). Despite dramatic increases in our understanding of the brain, however, the etiology of most mental illnesses defies straightforward biological explanation. Like heart disease and cancer, most mental disorders appear to be "lifestyle diseases" that result from the combination of biological, psychological, and social factors.

The Psychodynamic Paradigm

The *psychodynamic paradigm*, an outgrowth of the work and writings of Sigmund Freud (1856–1939), asserts that abnormal behavior is caused by unconscious mental conflicts that have roots in early childhood experience. Freud was trained as a neurologist, but experiences early in his career convinced him that abnormal behavior is caused by mental events that occur outside of conscious awareness.

Freud was trained in Paris by Jean Charcot (1825–1893), a neurologist who successfully used hypnosis to treat a disorder that used to be called *hysteria*. Hysteria is characterized by unusual physical symptoms; for example, "hysterical blindness" is the inability to see. The blindness is not caused by an organic impairment, and the afflicted individual may recover sight after resolving an emotional problem.

Freud observed that hysterical patients neither faked their symptoms, nor did they consciously associate them with emotional distress. Thus he suggested that their psychological conflicts were unconsciously "converted" into

wrong. When he attempted to inoculate paretic patients against syphilis three years later, none of Kraft Ebbing's patients became infected when exposed to a mild form of the disease. There could be only one explanation: *All* of them had been infected with syphilis previously.

After the turn of the twentieth century, the spirochete that causes syphilis was discovered. Postmortem examination of the brains of paretic physical symptoms. (In fact, these unusual problems are now called *conversion disorders*.) The peculiar problem of hysteria led Freud to believe that many memories, motivations, and protective psychological processes are unconscious, and this basic assumption was the impetus for his elaborate **psychoanalytic theory.** (The term *psychoanalytic theory* refers specifically to Freud's theorizing; the broader term *psychodynamic theory* includes not only Freudian theory but the revisions of his followers, which we discuss further in Chapter 3.)

Psychoanalytic theory divides the mind into three parts: the id, the ego, and the superego. The **id** is present at birth and houses biological drives, such as hunger, as well as two key psychological drives: sex and aggression. In Freudian theory, the id operates according to the *pleasure principle*—the impulses of the id seek immediate gratification and create discomfort or unrest until they are satisfied. Thus, in Freud's view, sexual or aggressive urges are akin to biological urges, like hunger.

The **ego** is the part of the personality that must deal with the realities of the world as it attempts to fulfill id impulses as well as perform other functions. Thus the ego operates on the *reality principle*. According to Freud, the ego begins to develop in the first year of life, and it continues to evolve, particularly during the preschool years. Unlike id impulses, which are primarily unconscious, much of the ego resides in conscious awareness.

The third part of the personality is the **superego,** which is roughly equivalent to the conscience. The superego contains societal standards of behavior, particularly rules that children learn from trying to be like their parents in their later preschool years. In Freud's view, societal rules are attempts to govern id impulses. As a result, he suggested that the three parts of the personality are often in conflict with one another. The ego must constantly mediate between the demands of the id and the prescriptions of the superego. According to Freud, conflict between the superego and the ego produces *moral anxiety*, whereas conflict between the id and the ego produces *neurotic anxiety*.

Freud suggested that the ego protects itself from anxiety by utilizing various **defense mechanisms,** unconscious self-deceptions that reduce conscious anxiety by distorting anxiety-producing memories, emotions, and impulses. For example, the defense of *projection* turns the tables psychologically. When you use projection, you project your own feelings on to someone else: "I'm not mad at you. You're mad at me!" A list of some of the more familiar defenses can be found in Table 2–1. Freud's profound influence is demonstrated by the fact that many defense mechanisms are a part of everyday language.

Freud viewed early childhood experiences, especially related to forbidden topics, as shaping personality and emotional health. In his theory of *psychosexual development*, in fact, Freud argued

Sigmund Freud (1856–1939) *developed psychoanalytic theory. Freud's approach has been criticized as being unscientific, but the influence of his ideas is unquestionable.*

TABLE 2–1	Some Freudian Defense Mechanisms
DENIAL	Insistence that an experience, memory, or need did not occur or does not exist. For example, you completely block a painful experience from your memory.
DISPLACEMENT	Feelings or actions are transferred from one person or object to another that is less threatening. For example, you kick your dog when you are upset with your boss.
PROJECTION	Attributing one's own feelings or thoughts to other people. For example, a husband argues that his wife is angry at him when, in fact, he is angry at her.
RATIONALIZATION	Intellectually justifying a feeling or event. For example, after not getting the offer, you decide that a job you applied for was not the one you really wanted.
REACTION FORMATION	Converting a painful or unacceptable feeling into its opposite. For example, you "hate" a former lover, but underneath it all you still really love that person.
REPRESSION	Suppressing threatening material from consciousness but without denial. For example, you "forget" about an embarrassing experience.
SUBLIMATION	Diverting id impulses into constructive and acceptable outlets. For example, you study hard to get good grades rather than giving in to desires for immediate pleasure.

that each stage of development is defined by a sexual conflict (see Table 2–5 on p. 56). The most important is the *Oedipal conflict*, which centers on boys' forbidden sexual desire for their mothers. Because these impulses are both overwhelming and impossible to fulfill, according to Freud, boys resolve the dilemma by adopting the actions and values of their mothers' spouse: They *identify* with their fathers. In Freud's view, girls face a similar dilemma, which he termed the *Electra complex*. Freud hypothesized that girls, unlike boys, do not desire their opposite gender parent sexually as much as they yearn for something their fathers have and they are "missing"—a penis. This is the Freudian notion of "penis envy."

It is not difficult to criticize these ideas as seeming far-fetched, overly sexualized, and blatantly sexist. We also can (and do) criticize psychoanalytic theory for being vague and untestable. Still, we recognize that Freud offered many innovative ideas. Some followers of psychoanalytic theory insist on interpreting Freud literally. We believe, however, that Freud would have criticized such literal interpretations, since he revised his ideas often during the course of his life. In this spirit, we prefer to view Freud's ideas as broad metaphors that can be valuable in the abstract, but not in the specific. Freud proposed many challenging concepts, and research supports some general aspects of his theorizing, for example, that much mental processing occurs outside of conscious awareness (Weston, 1998).

The Cognitive Behavioral Paradigm

The *cognitive behavioral paradigm* views abnormal behavior—and normal behavior—as a product of learning. Like the biological and psychodynamic paradigms, the foundations of the cognitive behavioral paradigm can be traced to the nineteenth century, specifically to 1879, when Wilhelm Wundt (1842–1920) began the science of psychology at the University of Leipzig. Wundt's substantive contributions to psychology were limited, but he made a profound and lasting contribution by introducing the scientific study of psychological phenomena, especially learning.

The two most prominent early contributors to learning theory and research were the Russian physiologist Ivan Pavlov (1849–1936) and the U.S. psychologist B. F. Skinner (1904–1990). These psychological scientists articulated, respectively, the principles of classical conditioning and operant conditioning—concepts that continue to be central to contemporary learning theory.

In his famous experiment, Pavlov (1928) rang a bell when he fed meat powder to dogs. After repeated trials, the sound of the bell alone elicited the salivation produced by the sight of food. This renowned experiment illustrates Pavlov's theory of classical conditioning. **Classical conditioning** is learning through association, and it involves four key components. There is an *unconditioned stimulus* (the meat powder), a stimulus that automatically produces the *unconditioned response* (salivation). A *conditioned stimulus* (the bell) is a neutral stimulus that, when repeatedly paired with an unconditioned stimulus, comes to produce a *conditioned response* (salivation). Finally, **extinction** occurs once a conditioned stimulus no longer is paired with an unconditioned stimulus. Eventually, the conditioned stimulus no longer elicits the conditioned response.

Skinner's (1953) principle of **operant conditioning** asserts that learned behavior is a function of its consequences. Specifically, behavior increases if it is rewarded, and it decreases if it is punished. In his numerous studies of rats and pigeons in the famous "Skinner box," Skinner identified four different, crucial consequences of behavior. *Positive reinforcement* is when the onset of a stimulus increases the frequency of behavior (for example, you get paid for your work). *Negative reinforcement* is when the cessation of a stimulus increases the frequency of behavior (you get up to turn off your alarm clock). *Punishment* is when the introduction of a stimulus decreases the frequency of behavior (you spend less money after your parents scold you); and *response cost* is when the removal of a stimulus decreases the frequency of behavior (you come home on time after getting grounded). *Extinction* results from ending the association between a behavior and its consequences, similar to the concept of extinction in classical conditioning.

The U.S. psychologist John B. Watson (1878–1958) was an influential proponent of applying learning theory to human behavior. Watson argued for *behaviorism*, suggesting that observable behavior was the only appropriate subject matter for the science of psychology, because thoughts and emotions cannot be

Psychologist B. F. Skinner (1904–1990) outlined the principles of operant conditioning. Skinner's determination to make psychology a science profoundly influenced the discipline in the twentieth century.

measured objectively. Subsequent research showed the importance of cognitive processes in learning, however, thus "cognitive" joined "behavioral" in the name of this paradigm. Cognitive behavior therapists generally have been more concerned with treatment than etiology, but a major assumption of the paradigm has been that much normal behavior—and abnormal behavior—is learned.

The Humanistic Paradigm

The *humanistic paradigm* argued that the essence of humanity is *free will*, the view that human behavior is not caused by either internal or external events, but by the choices we make voluntarily. In many respects, the humanistic paradigm was a reaction against *determinism*, the scientific view that human behavior is caused by potentially knowable factors (an assumption made by the other three paradigms). Because free will, by definition, is not predictably determined, it is impossible to conduct research on the causes of abnormal behavior within the humanistic paradigm. For this reason, the approach perhaps is best considered an alternative philosophy of human behavior, not as an alternative psychological theory. Major advocates of the humanistic paradigm included Abraham Maslow (1908–1970), Fritz Perls (1893–1970), and Carl Rogers (1902–1987).

The humanistic paradigm is also distinguished by its explicitly positive view of human behavior. Humanistic psychologists assume that human nature is inherently good, and blame dysfunctional, abnormal, or aggressive behavior on society, not on the individual (see Table 2–2). But we should inject a note of caution about the appealing term "humanistic": All psychologists

The android, Data, from *Star Trek: The Next Generation*, lacked free will (and emotion). Psychologists debate whether free will is a uniquely human quality—or an illusion.

are humanistic in the sense that their ultimate goal is to improve the human condition.

The Problem with Paradigms

The influential historian and philosopher Thomas Kuhn (1962) noted that the assumptions made by paradigms can both direct and misdirect scientists. Paradigms can tell us where and how to find answers to questions, but sometimes the apparent guidance can be a hindrance. The idea that a paradigm can be either enlightening or blinding

What is the problem with paradigms, particularly in searching for the cause of mental disorders?

TABLE 2–2	Comparison of Biological, Psychodynamic, Cognitive Behavioral, and Humanistic Paradigms			
TOPIC	**BIOLOGICAL**	**PSYCHODYNAMIC**	**COGNITIVE BEHAVIORAL**	**HUMANISTIC**
Inborn human nature	Competitive, but some altruism	Aggressive, sexual	Neutral—a blank slate	Basic goodness
Cause of abnormality	Genes, neurochemistry, physical damage	Early childhood experiences	Social learning	Frustrations of society
Type of treatment	Medication, other somatic therapies	Psychodynamic therapy	Cognitive behavior therapy	Nondirective therapy
Paradigmatic focus	Bodily functions and structures	Unconscious mind	Observable behavior	Free will

Water is more than the sum of two hydrogen atoms and one oxygen atom. According to systems theory, human behavior—both normal and abnormal—is greater than the sum of genes, emotion, and cognition.

can be illustrated by a brain teaser. Try to solve the following enigma, written by Lord Byron, before looking ahead for the answer:

> I'm not in earth, nor the sun,
> nor the moon.
> You may search all the sky—
> I'm not there.
> In the morning and evening—
> though not at noon,
> You may plainly perceive me,
> for like a balloon,
> I am suspended in air.
> Though disease may possess me,
> and sickness and pain,
> I am never in sorrow nor gloom;
> Though in wit and wisdom
> I equally reign
> I am the heart of all sin and have
> long lived in vain;
> Yet I ne'er shall be found in the tomb.

What is this poem about? The topic of this rhyme is not the soul or ghosts. It is not life or shadows, or a dozen other possibilities that may have occurred to you. Rather, the topic is the letter i (suspended in air, the heart of all sin). Why is the puzzle so difficult to solve? Because most people assume that the solution lies in the content of the poem, not in its form. This illustrates that the

assumptions made by a paradigm can act as blinders; they can lead us to overlook what otherwise might be obvious. However, paradigms also can open up new perspectives. For example, now that you have been able to adopt a new "paradigm"—to focus on the form, not the content of words—you can easily solve the following puzzle:

> The beginning of eternity, the end
> of time and space,
> The beginning of every end, the end
> of every place.

It is obvious that the answer is the letter e.

Like your initial approach to the brain teaser, the four paradigms make assumptions about the causes of abnormal psychology that can be too narrow. The biological paradigm can overemphasize the medical model, the analogy between physical and psychological illnesses. The psychodynamic paradigm can be unyielding in focusing on the past and the unconscious, even in the face of current life difficulties. The cognitive behavioral paradigm can be too literal, and overlook the rich social context of human behavior. Finally, the humanistic approach can be antiscientific, for reasons we have already discussed. In short, each paradigm has strengths—and weaknesses. As in the word puzzles, the trick is to know when to use what strategy.

SYSTEMS THEORY

Systems theory is an approach to integrating evidence on different contributions to abnormal behavior. The Austrian biologist and philosopher of science Ludwig von Bertalanffy (1901–1972) has been called the "father of systems theory" (Davidson, 1982), and the integrative approach has revolutionized many scientific disciplines including engineering, computer science, biology, and philosophy (Gottesman & Hanson, in press; Hinde, 1992; Richardson, 2000; von Bertalanffy, 1968). You can think of systems theory as a synonym for the biopsychosocial model, but systems theory also embraces several key concepts that deserve some elaboration.

Holism

A central principle of systems theory is holism, the idea that the whole is more than the sum of its parts. Holism is a familiar but important concept. A water molecule is more than the sum

CORRELATIONS: DOES PSYCHOLOGY MAKE YOU SMARTER?

The correlational study and *the experiment* (see Chapter 3) are two basic and essential methods of research. In a **correlational study,** the relation between two factors (their co-relation) is studied systematically. For example, you might hypothesize that psychology majors on your campus learn more about research methods than biology majors learn. To support this hypothesis, you might simply argue your point, or you could rely on case studies—"I know more research than my roommate, and she's a biology major!"

If you were to conduct a correlational study on the question, you would collect a large sample of both psychology and biology majors and compare them on an objective measure of knowledge of research methods. You would then use statistics to test whether research knowledge is correlated with academic major.

An important statistic for measuring how strongly two factors are related is the **correlation coefficient.** The correlation coefficient is a number that always ranges between −1.00 and +1.00. If all psychology majors got 100 percent correct on your test of research methods and all biology majors got 0 percent correct, the correlation between academic major and research knowledge would be 1.00. If all psychology and biology majors got 50 percent of the items correct, the correlation between major and knowledge would be zero. Two factors are more

strongly correlated when a correlation coefficient has a higher absolute value, regardless of whether the sign is positive or negative.

Positive correlations (from 0.01 to 1.00) indicate that, as one factor goes up, the other factor also goes up. For example, height and weight are positively correlated, as are years of education and employment income. Taller people weigh more; educated people earn more money. *Negative correlations* (from −1.00 to −0.01) indicate that, as one number gets bigger, the other number gets smaller. For example, population and open space are negatively correlated. As more people move into an area, the amount of open land diminishes.

In this chapter, we note a number of factors correlated with psychological problems. Levels of neurotransmitters in the brain are positively correlated with some emotional problems (they are elevated in comparison to normal), and they are negatively correlated with other types of emotional problems (they are depleted in comparison to normal). However, you should always remember that *correlation does not mean causation.*

Correlation *may* be a result of causation, but there are always two alternative explanations: reverse causality and third variables. We might want to conclude that X causes Y—that depleted neurotransmitters cause depression. However, the concept of **reverse causality**

indicates that causation could be operating in the opposite direction: Y could be causing X. Depression could be causing the depletion of neurotransmitters. The **third variable** problem indicates that a correlation between any two variables could be explained by their joint relation with some unmeasured factor— a third variable. For example, stress might cause both depression *and* the depletion of neurotransmitters.

Let us return to the study of psychology and biology majors to illustrate these issues further. If you found that psychology majors know more about research methods, can you conclude that majoring in psychology *causes* this result? No! People who know more about research methods to begin with might decide to become psychology majors (reverse causality). Or more intelligent people might both major in psychology and learn more about research methods (third variable).

As we discuss in Chapter 3, the experiment *does* allow scientists to determine cause and effect. However, it often is impractical or unethical to conduct experiments on psychological problems, while correlational studies can be conducted with far fewer practical or ethical concerns. Thus the correlational method has the weakness that correlation does not mean causation, but the strength that it can be used to study many real life circumstances.

---

of two hydrogen atoms and one oxygen atom. A human being is more than the sum of a nervous system, an organ system, a circulatory system, and so on. Similarly, abnormal psychology is more than the sum of inborn temperament, early childhood experiences, and learning history, or of nature and nurture.

Reductionism We can better appreciate the principle of holism if we contrast it with its scientific counterpoint, reductionism. **Reductionism** attempts to understand problems by focusing on smaller and smaller units, viewing the smallest possible unit as the true or ultimate cause. For example, when depression is linked with the depletion of certain chemicals in the brain, reductionists assume that brain chemistry is the cause of depression. Systems theory reminds us, however, that experiences such as having a negative view of the

world or living in a prejudiced society may cause the changes in brain chemistry that accompany depression (Cacioppo & Bernston, 1992; Valenstein, 1998). That is, the "chemical imbalance in the brain" may be a product of adverse life experiences (see Research Methods).

A far-out example may help you to understand system theory's concerns about reductionism. Assume for a moment that three Martian scientists are sent to Earth to discover what causes those metallic vehicles to speed, sometimes recklessly and sometimes slowly, across the planet's landmass. One Martian reports that the vehicles (called "automobiles," the ecologist discovers) move at different speeds based on the width of the black paths on which they are set, whether the paths are straight or curved, and the presence of a something called "radar traps." A second Martian, a psychologist, disagrees, noting that

How can two different explanations of the cause of mental disorders both be accurate at different levels of analysis?

the speed of automobiles is determined by the age, gender, and mood of the individual who sits inside them. The third scientist laughs at the other two. The Martian physicist notes that the speed of automobiles is caused by a chemical process that occurs inside an outdated machine, the internal combustion engine. The process involves oxygen, fuel, and heat, and results in mechanical energy.

Some lay people and some scientists seem to believe that ultimate causal explanations are most reductionistic accounts (Alessi, 1992; Uttal, 2001; Valenstein, 1998). The Martian example, however, shows the problems with blind reductionism. The most reductionistic, or *molecular*, explanation is no more (or less) accurate than the most general, or *molar*, one.

Levels of Analysis   The Martian example also illustrates an important point about ways of thinking about causality according to systems theory. Different psychologists focus on different—but not necessarily inconsistent—*levels of analysis* in trying to understand the causes of abnormal behavior (Hinde, 1992). Each level of analysis in the biopsychosocial model views abnormal behavior through a different "lens"; one is a microscope, another a

magnifying glass, and the third a telescope. One approach is not right, while the others are wrong. The lenses are just different, and each has value for different purposes.

Like Russian *matreska* dolls, accounts at different levels of analysis are nested one inside the other. In fact, we can distinguish all of the academic disciplines by their level of analysis and order them according to whether they are more molar or more molecular (Schwartz, 1982; see Table 2–3). Within psychology and across disciplines, systems theory strives to understand both the parts and the whole.

Causality

Human beings are not very patient with complicated explanations of causality. (You may feel this way yourself at this point.) Our orderly minds want to pinpoint a single causal culprit. We want to know *the* cause of cancer, *the* cause of heart disease, and *the* cause of mental illness.

But a question might help to unhinge you from this understandable human search for simplicity: What is *the* cause of automobile accidents? Of course, automobile accidents have many different causes: excessive speed, drunk drivers, slippery roads, and worn tires. We know it would be fruitless to search for *the* cause of automobile accidents. But much like the discovery of the cause of general paresis, we hope that scientists will discover *the* cause of every dreaded physical and mental disorder.

It is true that even complicated problems sometimes have a simple cause. Some car accidents are caused by a single factor such as faulty brakes or the driver's falling asleep at the wheel. Similarly, the cause of any one case of abnormal behavior occasionally can be located in one area of biological, psychological, or social functioning. More commonly, however, understanding the causes of psychological problems is like understanding the causes of car accidents. There is a conspiracy of causal influences, not a lone culprit.

Equifinality and Multifinality   This idea is formalized in the systems theory principle, *equifinality*, the view that there are many routes to the same destination (or disorder). In fact, we use the term *multiple pathways* as a synonym for equifinality. Both terms highlight that the same disorder may have several different causes.

Equifinality has a mirror concept, the principle of *multifinality*, which says that the same

TABLE 2–3	Ordering Academic Disciplines by Level of Analysis
LEVEL OF ANALYSIS	**ACADEMIC DISCIPLINE**
Beyond Earth	Astronomy
Supranational	Ecology, economics
National	Government, political science
Organizations	Organizational science
Groups	Sociology
Organisms	Psychology, ethology, zoology
Organs	Cardiology, neurology
Cells	Cellular biology
Biochemicals	Biochemistry
Chemicals	Chemistry, physical chemistry
Atoms	Physics
Subatomic particles	Subatomic physics
Abstract systems	Mathematics, philosophy

Source: Based on G.E. Schwartz, 1982. Testing the biopsychosocial model: The ultimate challenge facing behavioral medicine, *Journal of Consulting and Clinical Psychology, 50,* 1040–1053.

event can lead to different outcomes. For example, the principle of multifinality tells us that not all childhood experiences lead to the same adult outcomes. Not all abused children grow up with the same problems later in life. In fact, not all abused children *have* psychological problems as adults. Throughout the text, you will repeatedly see examples of the principle of multifinality, because the human psyche is indeed a very complex system.

Reciprocal Causality   **Reciprocal causality,** the idea that causality works in both directions, is another important if somewhat complicated systems theory concept (von Bertalanffy, 1968). Reciprocal causality is most easily understood when contrasted with *linear causality,* a scientific corollary of reductionism. According to linear causality, influences operate in one direction only: Parents cause their children to behave in a certain way, for example. In reality, however, children also change their parents' behavior through their independent actions and reactions to parenting (Bell, 1968; Maccoby, 1992). We must even think about the traditional operant conditioning experiment in terms of reciprocal causality (Skinner, 1956). Psychologists cause rats to press the bar in a Skinner box, but rats also cause scientists to feed them, as Skinner's own cartoon on this page illustrates.

The Diathesis-Stress Model   Because systems theory is complex, psychologists sometimes simplify their approach to understanding multiple influences on abnormal behavior by talking about the *diathesis-stress model.* A **diathesis** is a predisposition toward developing a disorder, for example, an inherited tendency toward depression. A **stress** is a difficult experience, for example, the loss of a loved one through an unexpected death. The diathesis-stress model suggests that mental disorders develop only when a stress is added on top of a predisposition; neither the diathesis nor the stress alone is sufficient to cause the disorder (Zuckerman, 1999).

Although it is a useful simplification, the diathesis-stress model does not imply that disorders are caused by the combination of only two risk factors, a diathesis and a stress. **Risk factors** are events or circumstances that are correlated with an increased likelihood or risk of a disorder and potentially contribute to causing the disorder. As we have noted, mental disorders appear to be produced by the combination of many different biological, psychological, and social risk factors.

Like car accidents, mental illnesses have many causes, not one.

Developmental Psychopathology

Because people change over time, knowledge of normal development is essential to understanding psychopathology. **Developmental psychopathology** is a new approach to abnormal psychology that emphasizes the importance of *developmental norms*—age-graded averages—to determine what constitutes abnormal behavior (Cicchetti & Cohen, 1995; Rutter & Garmezy, 1983). Developmental norms tell us that a full-blown temper tantrum is normal at 2 years of age, for example, but that kicking and screaming to get one's own way is abnormal at the age of 22. Development does not end at the age of 22, however, as predictable changes in both psychological and social experiences occur throughout adult life. Recognizing this, we devote an entire chapter (Chapter 17) to discussing the normal but psychologically trying changes that result from developmental transitions during adult life.

"Boy, have I got this guy conditioned! Every time I press the bar down he drops a piece of food."

We also discuss the development of abnormal behavior itself. Many psychological disorders follow unique developmental patterns. Sometimes there is a characteristic **premorbid history,** a pattern of behavior that precedes the onset of the disorder. A disorder may also have a predictable course, or **prognosis,** for the future. By discussing the premorbid adjustment and the course of different psychological disorders, we hope to present abnormal behavior as a moving picture of development and not just as a diagnostic snapshot.

We divide the remainder of this chapter into sections on biological, psychological, and social factors in the development of psychopathology. This material reviews basic information relevant to our more specific consideration of the causes of abnormal behavior in subsequent chapters.

BIOLOGICAL FACTORS

We begin our discussion of biological factors affecting mental functioning by considering the smallest anatomic unit within the nervous system, the neuron or nerve cell. Next, we consider the major brain structures and current knowledge of their primary behavioral functions. We then turn to psychophysiology, the effect of psychological experience on the

functioning of various body systems. Finally, we consider the broadest of all biological influences, the effect of genes on behavior.

In considering biological influences, it is helpful to note the distinction between the study of biological structures and of biological functions. The field of *anatomy* is concerned with the study of biological structures, and the field of *physiology* investigates biological functions. *Neuroanatomy* and *neurophysiology* are subspecialties within these broader fields that focus specifically on brain structures and brain functions. The study of neuroanatomy and neurophysiology is the domain of an exciting, multidisciplinary field of research called *neuroscience*.

The Neuron and Neurotransmitters

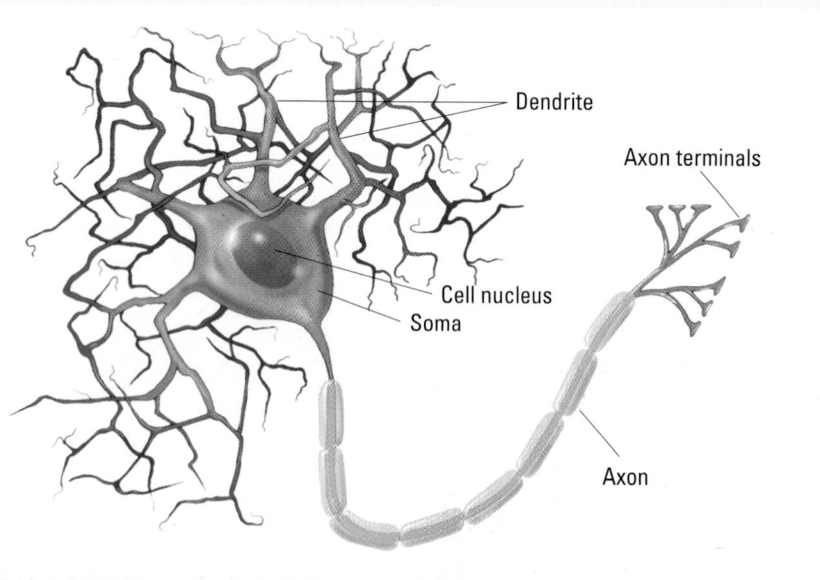

Billions of tiny nerve cells—**neurons**—form the basic building blocks of the brain. Each neuron has four major anatomic components: the soma, or cell body, the dendrites, the axon, and the axon terminal (see Figure 2–1). The *soma*—the cell body and largest part of the neuron—is where most of the neuron's metabolism and maintenance are controlled and performed. The *dendrites* branch out from the soma; they serve the primary function of receiving messages from other cells. The *axon* is the trunk of the neuron. Messages are transmitted down the axon toward other cells with which a given neuron communicates. Finally, the *axon terminal* is the end of the axon, where messages are sent out to other neurons (Barondes, 1993).

Scientists have made great strides in deciphering the processes involved in communication within and among neurons. Within each neuron, information is transmitted as a change in electrical potential that moves from the dendrites and cell body, along the axon, toward the axon terminal. The axon terminal is separated from other cells by a **synapse,** a small gap filled with fluid. Neurons typically have synapses with thousands of other cells (see Figure 2–2).

Unlike the electrical communication within a neuron, information is transmitted chemically across a synapse to other neurons. The axon terminal contains *vesicles* containing chemical substances called **neurotransmitters,** which are released into the synapse and are received at the **receptors** on the dendrites or soma of another neuron. Dozens of different chemical compounds serve as neurotransmitters in the brain, and the functions of particular neurotransmitters

The Neuron

Dendrite

Axon terminals

Cell nucleus

Soma

Axon

FIGURE 2–1: The anatomic structure of the neuron, or nerve cell.

Source: Figure 1.1, p. 6 from *Human Neuropsychology,* 2nd edition, by Brian Kolb and Ian Q. Whislaw. © 1980, 1985 by W.H. Freeman and Company. Reprinted by permission of W. H. Freeman and Company.

vary. Moreover, different receptor sites are more or less responsive to particular neurotransmitters.

Not all neurotransmitters cross the synapse and reach the receptors on another neuron. The process of **reuptake,** or reabsorption, captures some neurotransmitters in the synapse and returns the chemical substances to the axon terminal. The neurotransmitter then is reused in subsequent neural transmission.

In addition to the neurotransmitters, a second type of chemical affects communication in the brain. *Neuromodulators* are chemicals that may be released from neurons or from endocrine glands (which we discuss shortly). Neuromodulators can influence communication among many neurons by affecting the functioning of neurotransmitters (Ciaranello et al., 1995). Neuromodulators often affect regions of the brain that are quite distant from where they were released.

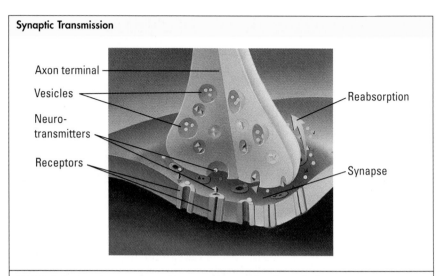

Synaptic Transmission

Axon terminal

Vesicles

Neuro-transmitters

Receptors

Reabsorption

Synapse

FIGURE 2–2: When an electrical nerve impulse reaches the end of a neuron, synaptic vesicles release neurotransmitters into the synapse. The chemical transmission between cells is complete when neurotransmitters travel to receptor sites on another neuron.

Source: Keith Kasnot, © National Geographic Image Collection.

Neurotransmitters and Psychopathology

Scientists have found that disruptions in the functioning of various neurotransmitters are present among some people with mental disorders. An oversupply of certain neurotransmitters is found in some mental disorders, an undersupply in other cases, and disturbances in reuptake in other psychological problems. In addition, the density and/or sensitivity of receptors has been implicated as playing a role in some forms of abnormal behavior.

Much research linking mental disorders with neurotransmitters has investigated how drugs alter brain chemistry and affect the symptoms of a disorder. For example, medications that alleviate some of the symptoms of schizophrenia are known to affect the availability of the neurotransmitter *dopamine* in the brains of animals. (Scientists cannot measure neurotransmitters in the living human brain, so neurotransmitter levels must be inferred either from animal studies or from indirect measures in humans.) This suggests that abnormalities in the dopamine system in the brain may be involved in schizophrenia. Other evidence links the availability of various neurotransmitters with depression, hyperactivity, posttraumatic stress disorder, and many other psychological problems. As we discuss in Mind-Body Dualism, however, the identification of biochemical differences definitely does not mean that these problems are caused by "a chemical imbalance in the brain," even though many people (including many mental health professionals) mistakenly leap to this conclusion.

Major Brain Structures

Neuroanatomists divide the brain into three subdivisions: the hindbrain, the midbrain, and the forebrain (see Figure 2–3). Basic bodily functions are regulated by the structures of the *hindbrain,* which include the medulla, pons, and cerebellum. The *medulla* controls various bodily functions involved in sustaining life, including heart rate, blood pressure, and respiration. The *pons* serves various functions in regulating stages of sleep. The *cerebellum* serves as a control center in helping to coordinate physical movements. The cerebellum receives information on body movements and integrates this feedback with directives from higher brain structures about desired actions. Few forms of abnormal behavior are identified with disturbances in the hindbrain, because the hindbrain's primary role is limited to supervising these basic physical functions (Matthysse & Pope, 1986).

The *midbrain* also is involved in the control of some motor activities, especially those related to fighting and sex. Much of the reticular activating system is located in the midbrain, although it extends into the pons and medulla as well. The *reticular activating system*

Why is the dualism between mind and body ultimately false?

The Healthy Brain

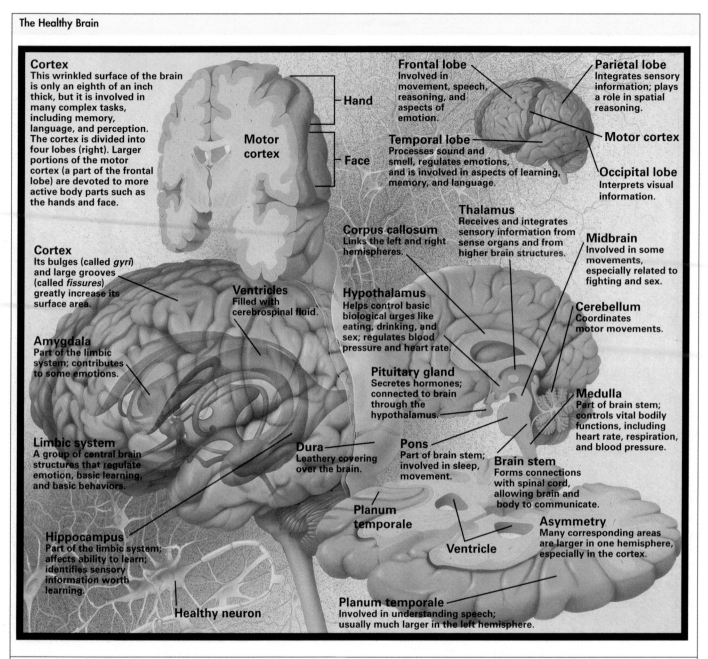

Cortex
This wrinkled surface of the brain is only an eighth of an inch thick, but it is involved in many complex tasks, including memory, language, and perception. The cortex is divided into four lobes (right). Larger portions of the motor cortex (a part of the frontal lobe) are devoted to more active body parts such as the hands and face.

Motor cortex

Hand

Face

Frontal lobe
Involved in movement, speech, reasoning, and aspects of emotion.

Temporal lobe
Processes sound and smell, regulates emotions, and is involved in aspects of learning, memory, and language.

Parietal lobe
Integrates sensory information; plays a role in spatial reasoning.

Motor cortex

Occipital lobe
Interprets visual information.

Cortex
Its bulges (called *gyri*) and large grooves (called *fissures*) greatly increase its surface area.

Corpus callosum
Links the left and right hemispheres.

Thalamus
Receives and integrates sensory information from sense organs and from higher brain structures.

Midbrain
Involved in some movements, especially related to fighting and sex.

Ventricles
Filled with cerebrospinal fluid.

Hypothalamus
Helps control basic biological urges like eating, drinking, and sex; regulates blood pressure and heart rate.

Cerebellum
Coordinates motor movements.

Amygdala
Part of the limbic system; contributes to some emotions.

Pituitary gland
Secretes hormones; connected to brain through the hypothalamus.

Medulla
Part of brain stem; controls vital bodily functions, including heart rate, respiration, and blood pressure.

Limbic system
A group of central brain structures that regulate emotion, basic learning, and basic behaviors.

Dura
Leathery covering over the brain.

Pons
Part of brain stem; involved in sleep, movement.

Brain stem
Forms connections with spinal cord, allowing brain and body to communicate.

Hippocampus
Part of the limbic system; affects ability to learn; identifies sensory information worth learning.

Planum temporale

Ventricle

Asymmetry
Many corresponding areas are larger in one hemisphere, especially in the cortex.

Healthy neuron

Planum temporale
Involved in understanding speech; usually much larger in the left hemisphere.

FIGURE 2–3: Scientists are only beginning to discover how the healthy brain performs its complex functions. You should view this complex figure as a rough road map that will be redrawn repeatedly. Like a roadmap, you should not try to memorize the figure, but use it as a guide. You will appreciate more and more detail as you return to examine it repeatedly. Despite the continuing mysteries, increasingly sophisticated tools have allowed researchers to identify more and more of the functions performed by different areas of the brain. For example, the four lobes of the brain's cortex play very different roles in thought, emotion, sensation, and motor movement (see top right of figure). Still, our incomplete knowledge of the healthy brain limits our understanding of brain abnormalities.

regulates sleeping and waking. Damage to areas of the midbrain can cause extreme disturbances in sexual behavior, aggressiveness, and sleep, but such abnormalities typically result from specific and unusual brain traumas or tumors (Matthysse & Pope, 1986).

Most of the human brain consists of the *fore-brain*. The forebrain evolved more recently than the hindbrain and midbrain and, therefore, is the site of most sensory, emotional, and cognitive processes. These higher mental processes of the forebrain are linked with the midbrain and hindbrain by the **limbic system.** The limbic system is made up of a variety of different brain structures that are central to the regulation of emotion and basic learning processes. Two of the

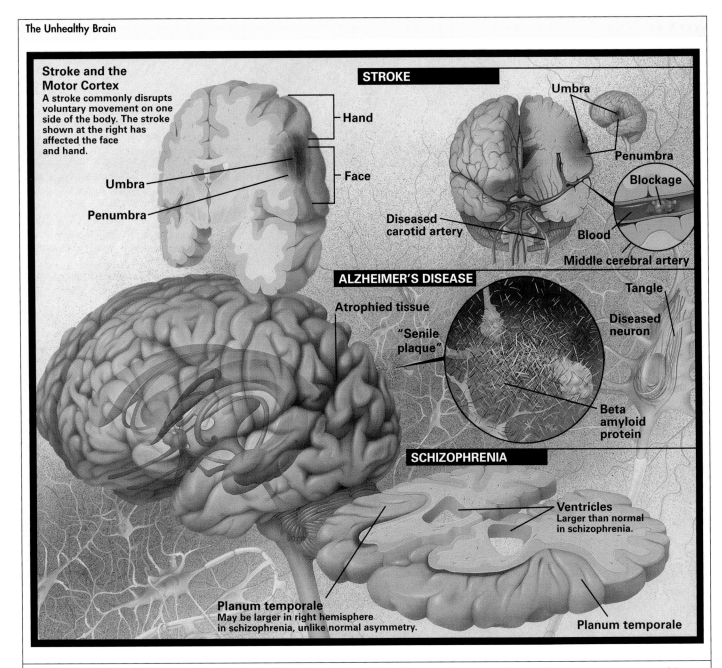

The Unhealthy Brain

Stroke and the Motor Cortex
A stroke commonly disrupts voluntary movement on one side of the body. The stroke shown at the right has affected the face and hand.

Umbra
Penumbra

Hand
Face

STROKE

Umbra
Penumbra
Blockage
Diseased carotid artery
Blood
Middle cerebral artery

ALZHEIMER'S DISEASE

Atrophied tissue
"Senile plaque"
Tangle
Diseased neuron
Beta amyloid protein

SCHIZOPHRENIA

Ventricles
Larger than normal in schizophrenia.

Planum temporale
May be larger in right hemisphere in schizophrenia, unlike normal asymmetry.

Planum temporale

Scientists have identified clear brain abnormalities only for some severe mental disorders. A stroke is caused by loss of blood supply to a region of the brain, and it kills off nearby cells (see Chapter 14.) Cells die rapidly near the center of the damaged tissue, the umbra. Cells die less rapidly in the periphery, the penumbra, and may be saved by future medical advances. Alzheimer's disease is a severe cognitive disorder associated with aging (see Chapter 14) that is characterized by atrophied brain tissue, "senile plaques" (caused by clumps of beta amyloid protein), and tangles of diseased or dead neurons. Schizophrenia is a very serious psychotic illness (see Chapter 13) that remains a mystery as a brain disorder, despite some promising leads. For example, among people with schizophrenia the ventricles often are enlarged, and asymmetries in the planum temporale may be reversed.

Source: Keith Kasnot, © National Geographic Image Collection.

most important components of the limbic system are the thalamus and the hypothalamus. The *thalamus* is involved in receiving and integrating sensory information from both the sense organs and higher brain structures. The **hypothalamus** also plays a role in sensation, but its more important functions are behavioral ones. The hypothalamus controls basic biological urges, such as eating, drinking, and sexual activity. Much of the functioning of the autonomic nervous system (which we discuss shortly) is also directed by the hypothalamus.

MIND–BODY DUALISM

There has been a "biological revolution" in our understanding of both abnormal and normal behavior. Neuroscientists continue to make exciting discoveries about brain functioning, and scientists constantly develop new medications that have more benefits and fewer side effects in treating certain mental disorders. The technical and practical advances are exciting, but the breakthroughs in neuroscience should not cloud our reasoning about the causes of abnormal behavior. In particular, we must not equate a neurophysiological *explanation* of a psychological disorder with the identification of a biological *abnormality*. We have already discussed our concerns about biological reductionism in this regard. Another potential problem stems from **dualism,** the philosophical view that the mind and body are somehow separable.

Dualism dates to the writings of the French philosopher René Descartes (1596–1650), who attempted to balance the dominant religious views of his times with emerging scientific reasoning. Descartes recognized the importance of studying human biology, but he wished to elevate human spirituality beyond that of other animals. In so doing, he argued that many human functions have biological explanations, but some human experiences have no somatic representation. Thus he argued for a distinction—a dualism—between mind and body.

Similar attempts to separate the psyche and the soma have clouded thinking for centuries. One contemporary dualism is that biological explanations may account for psychological abnormalities, but normal psychological experience is somehow independent of biology. Because of this persistent notion of dualism, biological explanations of psychological experience sometimes are erroneously equated with the identification of an abnormality. However, no aspect of the psychological world exists apart from the physical world. Just as a computer software program has an invisible electronic representation in the hardware of microchips, all psychological experience must have an underlying representation in the brain (Turkheimer, 1998; Valenstein, 1998). Even love must have a biochemical explanation, a fact that Calvin ponders in the accompanying cartoon. Love will still be love (we hope) even after scientists identify the "chemical imbalance in the brain" that explains it. The same logic applies to biochemical *explanations* of psychopathology, which cannot be automatically equated with biochemical *abnormalities*.

Calvin and Hobbes   by Bill Watterson

Cerebral Hemispheres

Most of the forebrain is composed of the two **cerebral hemispheres.** Many brain functions are **lateralized,** so that one hemisphere serves a specialized role as the site of specific cognitive and emotional activities. In general, the *left cerebral hemisphere* is involved in language and related functions, and the *right cerebral hemisphere* is involved in spatial organization and analysis. The lateralization and localization of certain brain functions often make it possible to pinpoint brain damage based solely on behavioral difficulties.

The two cerebral hemispheres are connected by the *corpus callosum,* which is involved in coordinating the different functions that are performed by the left and the right hemispheres of the brain. When we view a cross section of the forebrain, four connected chambers, or **ventricles,** become apparent. The ventricles are filled with cerebrospinal fluid, and they become enlarged in some psychological and neurological disorders.

The **cerebral cortex** is the uneven surface area of the brain that lies just underneath the skull. It is the site of the control and integration of sophisticated memory, sensory, and motor functions. The cerebral cortex is divided into four lobes (see Figure 2–3). The *frontal lobe,* located just behind the forehead, is involved in controlling a number of complex functions, including reasoning, planning, emotion, speech, and movement. The *parietal lobe,* located at the top and back of the head, receives and integrates sensory information and also plays a role in spatial reasoning. The *temporal lobe,* located beneath much of the frontal and parietal lobes, processes sound and smell, regulates emotions, and is involved in some aspects of learning, memory, and language. Finally, the *occipital lobe,* located behind the temporal lobe, receives and interprets visual information.

Major Brain Structures and Psychopathology   The brain is incredibly complex, and scientists are only beginning to understand the relations among various anatomic structures and functions. Because of the rudimentary knowledge we have about the brain, only obvious brain injuries and infections and the most severe mental disorders have clearly been linked with abnormalities in neuroanatomy. In most of these cases, brain damage is extensive. For example, during a *stroke*, blood vessels in the brain rupture, cutting off the supply of oxygen to parts of the brain and thereby killing surrounding brain tissue. This in turn disrupts the functioning of nearby healthy neurons because the brain cannot remove the dead tissue (see Figure 2–3). Tangles of neurons are found in patients with *Alzheimer's disease*, but the damage can be identified only during postmortem autopsies (see Figure 2–3). In patients with schizophrenia, the ventricles of the brain are enlarged, and asymmetries are also found in other brain structures (see Figure 2–3).

Still, research on the brain holds great promise. Scientists have made breakthroughs in observing the anatomic structure of the living brain and in recording some of its global physiological processes. These various imaging procedures are now being used to study psychological disorders ranging from schizophrenia to learning disabilities; they are discussed in Chapter 4, along with several methods of psychological assessment.

At present, the new brain imaging measures are more exciting technically than practically in terms of furthering our understanding of the etiology of psychopathology. Scientific advances frequently follow the development of new measures, however, and there is every reason to hope that advances in brain imaging will lead to improvements in understanding abnormalities in brain structure and function.

Psychophysiology

Psychophysiology is the study of changes in the functioning of the body that result from psychological experiences. Some of these physical reactions are familiar. A pounding heart, a flushed face, tears, sexual excitement, and numerous other reactions are psychophysiological responses. These and other psychophysiological responses reflect a person's psychological state, particularly the degree and perhaps the type of the individual's emotional arousal.

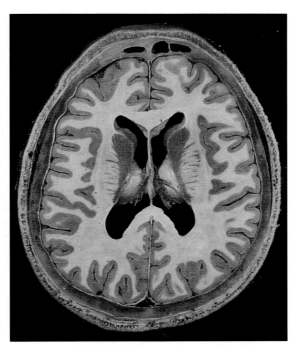

This cross-sectional image of the brain shows the ventricles, four connected chambers that are filled with cerebrospinal fluid.

Endocrine System   Psychophysiological arousal results from the activity of two different communication systems within the body, the endocrine system and the nervous system. The **endocrine system** is a collection of glands found at various locations throughout the body. Its major components include the ovaries or testes and the pituitary, thyroid, and adrenal glands (see Figure 2–4). Endocrine glands produce psychophysiological responses by releasing **hormones** into the bloodstream—chemical substances that affect the functioning of distant body systems and sometimes act as neuromodulators. The endocrine system regulates some aspects of normal development, particularly physical growth and sexual development. Parts of the endocrine system, particularly the adrenal glands, also are activated by stress and help prepare the body to respond to an emergency.

Certain abnormalities in the functioning of the endocrine system are known to cause psychological symptoms. For example, in *hyperthyroidism*, or *Graves' disease*, the thyroid gland secretes too much of the hormone thyroxin, causing restlessness, agitation, and anxiety. Recent research on depression also suggests that endocrine functioning sometimes may be involved in the etiology of this disorder.

Autonomic Nervous System   The more familiar and basic system of communication within the body is the *nervous system*. The human nervous system is divided into the *central nervous system*, which includes the brain and the spinal cord, and the peripheral nervous system. The *peripheral nervous system* includes all connections that stem from the central nervous system and innervate the body's muscles, sensory systems, and organs.

The peripheral nervous system itself has two subdivisions. The voluntary, *somatic nervous system* governs muscular control, and the involuntary, **autonomic nervous system** regulates the functions of various body organs, such as the heart and stomach. The somatic nervous system controls intentional or voluntary actions like scratching your nose. The autonomic nervous system is responsible for psychophysiological reactions—responses that occur with little or no conscious control.

The autonomic nervous system can be subdivided into two branches, the sympathetic and parasympathetic nervous systems. In general, the *sympathetic nervous system* controls activities associated with increased arousal and energy

expenditure, and the *parasympathetic nervous system* controls the slowing of arousal and energy conservation. Thus the two branches work somewhat in opposition to each other as a means of maintaining homeostasis.

Psychophysiology and Psychopathology Psychophysiological overarousal and underarousal both may contribute to abnormal behavior. For example, overactivity of the autonomic nervous system (a pounding heart and sweaty hands) has been linked with excessive anxiety. In contrast, chronic autonomic underarousal may explain some of the indifference to social rules and the failure to learn from punishment found in antisocial personality disorder. Psychophysiological assessment also is important, because it can be a useful way of objectively measuring reactions to psychological events, as we discuss in Chapter 4.

Behavior Genetics

Genes are ultramicroscopic units of DNA that carry information about heredity. Genes are located on **chromosomes,** chainlike structures found in the nucleus of cells. Humans normally have 23 pairs of chromosomes.

The field of *genetics* identifies specific genes and their hereditary functions, often by literally focusing at the level of molecules. Geneticists typically have training in biochemistry, not psychology. **Behavior genetics** is a much broader approach that studies genetic influences on the evolution and development of normal and abnormal behavior (McGuffin et al., 1994; Plomin, DeFries, & McClearn, 1990; Rutter et al., 2001). Behavior geneticists study various human characteristics, often in an attempt to discover if the behavior is more or less strongly affected by genes. However, many experts in genetics and behavior genetics are working together today in the hope of identifying specific genes involved in shaping normal and abnormal behavior (Plomin & Crabbe, 2000).

Some Basic Principles of Genetics One of the most important principles of genetics is the distinction between genotype and phenotype. A **genotype** is an individual's actual genetic structure. Advances in human genetics—the entire human genome has now been mapped—have allowed scientists to determine more and more aspects of genetic structure. Still, it is impossible to observe much of an individual's genotype directly.

The Endocrine System

Pineal body

Pituitary gland

Parathyroid gland

Thyroid gland

Thymus gland

(Stomach)

Adrenal glands

Pancreas

Kidney

Ovary (In female)

Testis (In male)

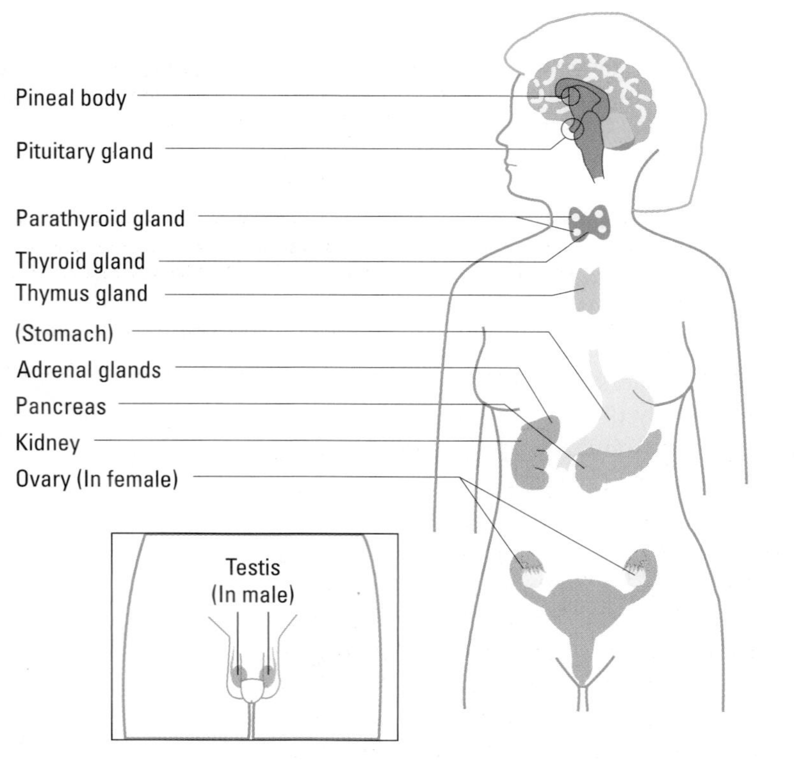

FIGURE 2–4: The glands that comprise the endocrine system, which affects physical and psychophysiological responses through the release of hormones into the bloodstream.

Source: John G. Seamon and Douglas T. Kenrick, 1994, *Psychology* (2nd ed.), p. 67. Upper Saddle River, NJ: Prentice Hall.

Instead, what we observe is the **phenotype,** the expression of a given genotype. It usually is impossible to infer a precise genotype from a given phenotype, because phenotypes, but not genotypes, are influenced by the environment. And different genotypes can produce similar phenotypes, as Austrian monk Gregor Mendel (1822–1884) discovered in his famous studies of garden peas.

Genes have alternative forms known as *alleles.* *Dominant/recessive inheritance* occurs when a trait is caused by a single or *autosomal* gene that has only two alleles (for example, A and *a*) and only one *locus,* a specific location on a chromosome. This is the pattern found in Mendel's peas. The gene for color had only two alleles, A (yellow, dominant) and *a* (green, recessive). Thus, three genotypes are possible: AA, *a*A (or A*a*), and *aa*. Because A is dominant over *a,* however, both AA and *a*A plants will have yellow color, while *aa* plants will be green. Thus, although three genotypes are possible, only two phenotypes are observed: yellow and green. Figure 2–5 shows the patterns of inheritance for dominant and recessive disorders.

Dominant/recessive inheritance causes some rare forms of mental retardation (Plomin, DeFries, & McClearn, 1990; Thapar et al., 1994), but most mental disorders are not caused by a single gene—if they have genetic causes at all. Instead, they are **polygenic,** that is, they are caused by more than one gene (Gottesman, 1991).

Polygenic inheritance has an important effect on the distribution of traits. In contrast to the categorically different phenotypes (for example, yellow versus green; see the top panel in Figure 2–6) produced by a single gene, polygenic inheritance produces characteristics that differ only by a matter of degree (for example, height). In fact, the distribution of a phenotype in the population begins to resemble the normal distribution as more genes are involved in determining the trait (see the bottom panel in Figure 2–6). Thus, when someone concludes that a polygenic mental disorder is "genetic," we must be cautious about what this means. It does *not* mean that the disorder is caused by dominant or recessive inheritance, nor does it tell us where to draw the line—the *threshold*—between normal and abnormal behavior (see Figure 2–7).

Family Incidence Studies   Behavior geneticists have developed important methods for studying broad, genetic contributions to behavior, including family incidence studies, twin studies, and adoption studies. Family incidence studies ask

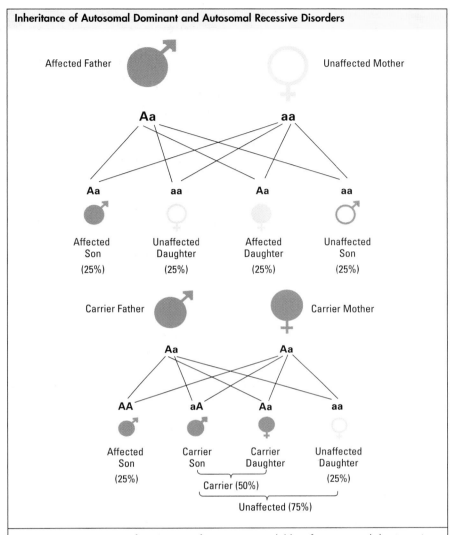

Inheritance of Autosomal Dominant and Autosomal Recessive Disorders

FIGURE 2–5: Patterns of transmission from parents to children for autosomal dominant (top figure) and autosomal recessive disorders (bottom figure). Note that the disorder is either present or absent for both patterns of inheritance.

Source: Based on S.V. Garaone, M.T. Tsuang, & D.W. Tsuang (1999). *Genetics of Mental Disorders.* New York: Guilford.

whether diseases "run in families." Investigators identify normal and ill **probands,** or index cases, and tabulate the frequency with which other members of their families suffer from the same disorder. If a higher prevalence of illness is found in families where there is an ill proband, this is consistent with genetic causation. The finding also is consistent with environmental causation, however, because families share environments as ell as genes. For this reason, no firm conclusions about the relative role of genes or the environment can be reached from family incidence studies alone.

Twin Studies   Studies of twins, in contrast, can provide strong evidence about genetic and

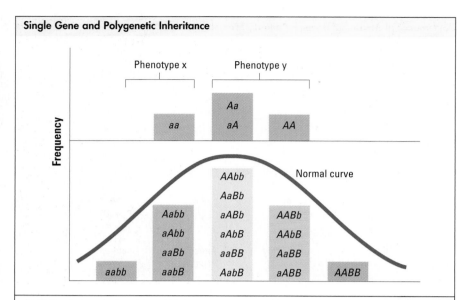

FIGURE 2–6: Single genes produce phenotypes that differ qualitatively, as illustrated in the top panel. Multiple genes produce phenotypes that differ quantitatively. As more genes are involved (only two in this illustration), the distribution of traits approximates the normal curve, as illustrated in the bottom panel.

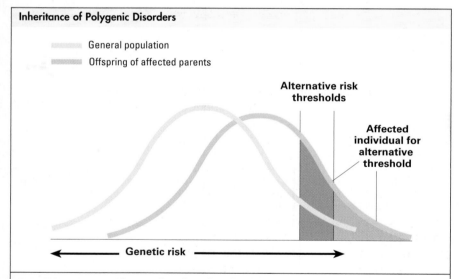

FIGURE 2–7: For polygenic disorders, the risk is higher for the offspring of affected (ill) parents, who inherit more of the multiple genes involved in the disorder. Still, the genetic risk varies widely in both the general and the affected population. Because the underlying characteristic is distributed continuously, there is no clear, objective place to mark the threshold of the disorder.

What differences between identical and fraternal twins show genetic (and environmental) contributions to mental disorders?

environmental contributions to a disorder. **Monozygotic (MZ) twins** are identical. One egg is fertilized by one sperm, and thus MZ twins have identical genotypes. **Dizygotic (DZ) twins** are fraternal. These twins are produced from two eggs and two sperm. Thus, like all siblings, DZ twins share an average of 50 percent of their genes, whereas MZ twins share 100

percent of their genes. Of course, most MZ and DZ twin pairs are raised in the same family. Thus MZ and DZ twins differ in their genetic similarity, but they are alike in their environmental experiences.

Comparisons between MZ and DZ twin pairs thus shed light on the genetic and environmental contributions to a disorder. The key comparison involves determining the **concordance rate** of the two sets of twins, specifically whether MZ twins are more alike than DZ twins are alike. A twin pair is concordant when both twins either have the same disorder or are free from the disorder, for example, both suffer from schizophrenia. The twin pair is discordant when one twin has the disorder but the other does not, for example, one twin has schizophrenia but the co-twin does not.

If we assume that the environmental effects on a disorder are the same for DZ twin pairs as they are for MZ twin pairs, then any differences between the concordance rates for MZ and DZ twins must be caused by genetics. If a disorder is purely genetic, for example, scientists should find a concordance rate of 100 percent for MZ twins (who are genetically identical) and 50 percent for DZ twins (who share half of the same genes on average) (see Table 2–4).

In contrast, similar concordance rates for MZ and DZ twins rule out genetic contributions and instead implicate environmental causes of a disorder. Environmental causes are implicated regardless of whether the concordance rates for MZ and DZ twins are both 0 percent, both 100 percent, or both anywhere in between. However, the level of concordance does provide information about the nature of the environmental contribution. *High* concordance rates for both MZ and DZ twins point to the etiological role of the **shared environment,** the experiences the two twins share in common, for example, growing up in poverty. When both MZ and DZ pairs have similarly high concordance rates, we know that genes do not explain the similarities. Instead, the common cause must be found in the environment shared by the twins. The shared environment would explain *all* of the variance in a trait if the concordance rate was 100 percent for both MZ and DZ twins (see Table 2–4).

Similar but *low* concordance rates for both MZ and DZ pairs point to the influence of the **nonshared environment,** the experiences that are unique to one twin, for example, being the favored child. In this case, genetic causes are again ruled out, and the importance of unique experiences is indicated by the fact that only one twin has a psychological disorder (Plomin, 1994). The nonshared environment would explain *all* of the variance in a trait if the concordance rate was 0 percent for both MZ and DZ twins (see Table 2–4). In real research, of course, nothing is perfect. However, twin studies provide useful estimates of the role played by genes, the shared environment, and the nonshared environment in studying a given disorder.

Evidence from twin studies often indicates that genes have a substantial influence on mental disorders. Somewhat surprising, behavior genetic research also indicates that many environmental influences appear to be nonshared (Harris, 1995, 1998). However, the logic of twin studies depends on the assumption that the environment affects DZ twins in the same way that it influences MZ twins. If MZ twins have more similar personalities than DZ twins, MZs may seek similar environments and get more similar responses from the environment. If so, then higher concordance rates for MZ twins might result from more similar environmental experiences and not from more similar genetic endowments.

Adoption Studies   For this reason, behavior genetic researchers also conduct adoption studies to examine genetic versus environmental contributions to the development of a disorder. In this research design, people who were adopted as infants are compared with their biological versus their adoptive relatives (usually their parents) in terms of concordance for a disorder. If concordance is higher for biological than for adoptive relatives, then genetic factors are involved, because adopted children share their biological relatives' genes but not their environment. On the other hand, if children are more similar to their adoptive than to their biological relatives, then environment must influence the characteristic, because adopted children share their adoptive relatives' environment but not their genes.

The logic of the adoption design might be clearer if we think about the case of the adopted girl, Meghan, from the beginning of this chapter. Genetic influences would be implicated if we found that Meghan (and other adopted children) developed problems similar to those found in their biological, but not among their adoptive, parents. On the other hand, environmental influences must be operating if Meghan and other adopted children developed problems (or strengths!) that were more similar to their adoptive than their biological parents.

A festival for twins. Monozygotic (MZ) twins are indentical; they develop from a single fertilized egg. Dizygotic (DZ) twins are fraternal; they develop from two different fertilized eggs.

Adoption studies have some potential problems, for example, the fact that adoption placement is selective. Still, you can be confident in the findings of behavior genetic researchers when adoption and twin studies produce similar results (Plomin, 1994).

Misinterpreting Behavior Genetics Findings
Behavior genetic research is powerful, but unfortunately, people often misinterpret it (Rutter, 1997; Turkheimer, 1998). One serious misinterpretation is that a psychological disorder is inevitable, even predestined, if it has a genetic component. This conclusion is wrong, in part because of polygenic inheritance. The probability of inheriting a disease is easily identified for simple dominant/recessive inheritance (see Figure 2–5). However, the chances of inheriting a polygenic disorder cannot be pinpointed, in part because there is no clear threshold separating normal and abnormal behavior (see

TABLE 2–4	Twin Studies: Implications of Different Findings	
CONCORDANCE	SUPPORTS INFLUENCE OF	CONCORDANCE FOR PERFECT CASE[1]
MZ > DZ	Genes	MZ = 100%; DZ = 50%
MZ = DZ; both high	Shared environment	MZ = 100%; DZ = 100%
MZ = DZ; both low	Nonshared environment	MZ = 0%; DZ = 0%

[1]The identified influence explains everything in the perfect case. Actual concordance rates almost always fall between these extremes, thus providing an index of the relative contributions of genes, the shared environment, and/or the nonshared environment.

Video Case

AUTISM

DR. KATHY PRATT

"There is still a tremendous amount of research being conducted to try to figure out exactly what the cause of autism is . . ."

Dr. Kathy Pratt on autism, see *Speaking Out: Case Studies in Abnormal Psychology.* Listen for her cautious tone in discussing causes, an uncertainty parents of children with autism understandably find frustrating.

Figure 2–7). And the concordance rates for various mental illness are almost always well below 100 percent for MZ twins, which is strong evidence that the *environment* contributes to the development— or prevention— of mental disorders (Faraone et al., 1999).

Behavior genetic findings also do not tell us what genetically influenced mechanism is at work. When we read that a disorder is "genetic," we tend to think there is "a gene" for depression, alcoholism, or hyperactivity; but is there? Think about this. Criminal behavior in adults also is genetic, as is divorce. For these two behaviors and many others—including political affiliation—concordance rates are notably higher for MZ than for DZ twins. But no one thinks (we hope) that

people have a "crime gene," a "divorce gene," or a "Republican gene." Behavior genetic studies do not tell us *how* genes are involved in behavior, or even precisely what characteristic is inherited, whether the outcome is depression or divorce. For criminal behavior, one hypothesized inherited mechanism is an underaroused autonomic nervous system. Perhaps people are genetically predisposed toward criminality if they are born less fearful and therefore less likely to learn from punishment. Perhaps; there are dozens of other possibilities. The point is that you need to think about behavior genetic research more deeply than simply concluding, "mental disorders are genetic."

You also are wrong if you think that genetic characteristics cannot be modified. For example, even in cases where mental retardation has a known genetic cause, environmental experiences such as dietary restrictions or rich, early intellectual stimulation can lead to substantial increases in IQ (Turkheimer, 1991). In short, the

---

critical thinking matters

DO VACCINATIONS CAUSE AUTISM?

In 1998, the highly reputable British journal *Lancet* published a study by Dr. Andrew Wakefield and a dozen co-authors (1998). In their paper, the authors speculated that the measles/mumps/rubella (MMR) vaccination might be responsible for 12 cases of autism they diagnosed. (*Autism* is a severe psychological disorder that begins very early in life and is marked by extreme problems with communication, social interaction and stereotyped behavior; see Chapter 15.) The researchers did not analyze their data scientifically, nor did they attempt to find children who were vaccinated but did not develop autism. In fact, a skeptical editorial was published together with the article and questioned its validity (Chen & DeStefano, 1998).

None of these limitations prevented a tsunami of concerns and assertions about childhood vaccinations causing autism. Warnings spread on television, radio, in print, and especially over the Internet. Many parents refused to vaccinate their children; others worried and debated what to do. Measles, mumps, and rubella are serious illnesses too, and the MMR vaccination works. The U.S. Congress held hearings. The National Institute of Health funded new research. Yet, as the National Institute of Child Health and Human Development wrote on

its Web site in July 2001 (and still left posted as of January 2005): "To date there is no conclusive evidence that any vaccine can cause autism."

If you are paranoid about vaccinations, you can read this appropriately cautious scientific statement, and focus on the "to date" and "conclusive" qualifications. Yet, science can *never* prove the negative. (Prove that those Martian scientists we discussed earlier did *not* write this text. *You* just can't see them!) This is why the burden of proof rests upon any scientist who offers a hypothesis. If we speculate that vaccinations cause autism—or Martians write textbooks, we need to prove the validity of our assertion. You do not need to prove us wrong. Until we can show that our hypothesis is true, the community of scientists assumes it is false.

It's fine to hypothesize, but it's more important to be skeptical—to doubt not only other people's theories but your own too. And with so much "scientific" information available on the Internet and elsewhere, it's important for you to be skeptical too, not only in psychology class but also in evaluating all kinds of information. We want you to think critically in abnormal psychology and in life.

So what new information is there about vaccinations and autism? Nothing is new, except

failure after failure to support Dr. Wakefield's speculation. For example, one Danish study of close to half a million children found no differences in the rate of autism between children who did and did not receive the MMR vaccine containing the supposed autism causing agent, *thimerosal* (Hviid et al., 2003). In fact, 10 of the original 13 co-authors of the 1998 study retracted their speculation in 2004: "We wish to make it clear that in this paper no causal link was established between MMR vaccine and autism, as the data were insufficient. However, the possibility of such a link was raised and consequent events have had major implications" (*New York Times*, March 4, 2004).

Misinformation still abounds even after public retractions and negative results for hundreds of thousands of children (versus speculations about 12). Do an Internet search, and you surely will find many vehement, if unscientific, arguments still asserting that MMR causes autism. We did. One site (that we will not name) said in January 2005, "The system's power to convince researchers to retract their initial findings is an amazing testimony to how corrupt it has become. Although MMR is not the cause of all cases of autism, it has clearly been linked to several cases I have come across." Critical thinking *matters*.

conclusion "It's genetic" does not mean, "It's inevitable" or "It's hopeless." Nature and nurture are not separate influences on behavior. Nature and nurture always work together (Li, 2003).

Genetics and Psychopathology   No doubt about it: Genes have very broad effects on abnormal—and normal—behavior. Genetic influences are important to recognize, but we are skeptical that specific genetic causes will be discovered for many mental disorders. Why? Remember that (1) most emotional problems, like most normal behaviors, appear to be polygenic; (2) behavior genetic findings fail to specify the mechanism of genetic influence; and (3) shared or nonshared environmental contributions to a disorder typically are found to be as large as genetic ones. In short, you should recognize pervasive genetic influences on behavior, but also think critically and beyond familiar models of dominant and recessive inheritance. In fact, you should be skeptical of anyone who claims to have found "the cause" of any mental disorder (see Critical Thinking *Matters*). Scientists have collared a single gene culprit responsible for a few, rare forms of mental disorder. However, we are unlikely to find a gene for depression, for eating disorders, or for most forms of psychopathology.

PSYCHOLOGICAL FACTORS

Genes influence *individual differences*, or how people are different from one another. Genes also help to determine *species-typical characteristics*—characteristics that people have in common as a part of human nature. Yet, we must begin our overview of psychological factors in emotional disorders on a humbling note: Psychology does not have a widely accepted theory of *personality*, the essential traits that, taken as a whole, describe human behavior. This is no small problem but a huge limitation, akin to chemistry without a periodic table of the elements or biology without a classification of living things. As a result, any listing of the psychological factors involved in mental disorders, including our own, is necessarily incomplete and likely to be controversial. Still, most psychological factors affecting mental health can be organized into one of the five categories: (1) human nature and temperament; (2) emotion; (3) learning and cognition; (4) our sense of self; and (5) human development.

Human Nature and Temperament

What are our basic psychological motivations—both those that we share with other animals and others that are uniquely human? Freud's answer to this question was that we have two basic drives, sex and aggression. In contrast, Watson suggested that we come into the world as blank slates—there is no human nature apart from our common experience. Today, psychologists are revisiting questions about the nature of human nature in a new, exciting, and controversial field of study called evolutionary psychology.

Evolutionary Psychology   Evolutionary psychology is the application of the principles of evolution to our understanding of the animal and human mind (Schmitt & Pilcher, 2004). Evolutionary psychologists assume that animal and human psychology, like animal and human anatomy, have evolved based on two broad evolutionary principles, natural selection and sexual selection.

Natural selection is the process through which successful inherited adaptations to environmental problems become more common over successive generations of offspring. The adaptation is selected by evolution, because it increases *inclusive fitness*, the reproductive success of those who have the adaptation, their offspring, and/or their kin. For example, the large human brain, with its particularly large cerebral cortex, presumably was selected across evolutionary history. The adaptations that a larger brain enabled (e.g., the use of tools for survival and

Evolution shapes behavior in animals and humans. Do humans compete for dominance, perhaps in more subtle ways than these stags compete?

How does the absence of an accepted theory of personality limit investigation into psychological factors in mental disorders?

The British psychiatrist John Bowlby (1907–1990) can be credited with developing attachment theory, a set of proposals about the importance of close caregiving relationships to children's psychological development.

weapons for defense) increased the survival and reproductive success of early humans with larger brains, as well as that of their offspring and kin.

Sexual selection improves inclusive fitness through increased access to mates and mating. Mating access can be increased by successful intrasexual competition, for example, a dominant male limits the mating opportunities of other males; or by successful *intersexual* selection, for example, a more brightly colored bird attracts more members of the opposite sex (Gaulin & McBurney, 2001; Larsen & Buss, 2002).

Evolutionary psychology seeks to understand how evolution shaped human behavior. Among other things, the approach actually seeks to answer the age-old question, What is human nature? As we have noted, psychologists do not agree about the nature of human nature, but two vital qualities that belong at the top of anyone's list are the need to form close relationships and the competition for dominance.

Attachment Theory   The theoretical writings of British psychiatrist John Bowlby (1907–1990) greatly influenced psychologists' views about the human need to form close relationships. Bowlby was trained in psychoanalysis, but he rejected Freudian theory and placed the need to form close relationships at the core of his view of development (Bowlby, 1969, 1982). The heart of Bowlby's theory was the observation that infants form **attachments** early in life—special and selective bonds with their caregivers.

Bowlby based his approach, known as *attachment theory*, on findings from *ethology*, the study of animal behavior. Ethologists have documented that close relationships develop between infants and caregivers in many species of

animals. In some species, selective relationships develop in the first hours or days of life, a process called *imprinting*, while human attachments are far more flexible and slow to develop. Still, human infants and toddlers, like many animal offspring, develop selective bonds to caregivers early in life, as you can readily observe by watching ducklings swimming behind a mother duck in the spring time or a toddler exploring the world in an irregular orbit around a parent. These bonds, together with toddlers' (and ducklings') displays of distress when they cannot readily find their caregivers—long and loud cries—keep infant and parent in close proximity. From an evolutionary standpoint, proximity has survival value, because parents protect their offspring from danger. Thus, attachment behavior is an inborn characteristic that is a product of natural selection.

Bowlby's writings were theoretical and clinical, but psychological scientists have found empirical support for many aspects of attachment theory. Research on the effects of *insecure* or *anxious attachments*—uncertain or ambivalent parent—child relationships that are a product of inconsistent and unresponsive parenting during the first year of life—is of particular relevance to the development of abnormal behavior (Ainsworth et al., 1978). Anxious attachments can make children mistrustful, dependent, and/or rejecting in subsequent relationships, a pattern that may continue into adult life. Critics argue that attachment difficulties can be overcome and call attention to the importance of relationships other than parenting (Rutter & Rutter, 1993), but as we discuss throughout the text, research shows that supportive relationships promote mental health throughout the life span.

Dominance   The development of attachments, or more generally of *affiliation* with other members of the same species, is one of the two broad categories of social behaviors studied by ethologists. The second is **dominance,** the hierarchical ordering of a social group into more and less privileged members (Sloman, Gardner, & Price, 1989). Dominance hierarchies are easily observed in human as well as other animal social groups, and from the perspective of evolutionary psychology, dominance competition is basic to sexual selection. Thus dominance is another prime candidate on our short list of species-typical human qualities.

A Japanese macaque monkey and her one-month-old baby. Strong bonds between infants and care givers are found across many species. Disruptions in human attachments may contribute to abnormal behavior.

In research on abnormal behavior, dominance is more of an implicit than explicit focus. For example, a strong internal sense of control and effectiveness is widely viewed as basic to positive mental health. And it is widely accepted that the best parents are *authoritative* (Maccoby & Martin, 1983), that is, they are both warmly responsive to children (thereby encouraging secure attachments) and firm in discipline (thereby maintaining parental authority).

Additional social motivations, as well as cognitive ones, belong on the list of basic human qualities. Still, we are confident that attachment and dominance will rank high on any final list. It is of interest to note that, in fact, Freud may have agreed with this view. Some contemporary psychodynamic theorists assert that Freud's basic drives of sex and aggression really are metaphors for the broader qualities of affiliation and dominance (Cameron & Rychlak, 1985).

Temperament   One of the most important areas of research on individual differences in personality is the study of **temperament,** characteristic styles of relating to the world. Psychologists long debated what elements make up the basic temperamental styles, but researchers apparently have reached consensus (Goldberg, 1993; Zuckerman, 1991). Based on extensive analyses of people's responses to structured questionnaires, researchers now agree on five dimensions. The "big five" dimensions of temperament and the opposite extremes that define them are: (1) openness to experience—imaginative and curious versus shallow and imperceptive; (2) conscientiousness—organized and reliable versus careless and negligent; (3) extraversion—active and talkative versus passive and reserved; (4) agreeableness—trusting and kind versus hostile and selfish; and (5) neuroticism—nervous and moody versus calm and pleasant. The acronym OCEAN, which uses the first letter of each term, will help you to remember "the big five."

Individual differences in temperament may play a role in a number of psychological disorders, especially personality disorders and child behavior problems. Still, you should view temperamental contributions to personality from a systems perspective. The critical issue is the *goodness of* fit between a child's biologically based temperament and the psychological and social environments. For example, a "difficult" temperament increases the risk for child behavior

problems, but parenting determines whether the difficult behavior grows worse or is controlled (Chess & Thomas, 1984).

Emotions

Emotions, internal feeling states, are essential to human experience and to our understanding of mental disorders. But we have hundreds of words for different feelings in the English language. What emotions are most essential? Researchers have used statistical analysis to reduce our lexicon of feelings to six basic emotions (National Advisory Mental Health Council, 1995):

- Love
- Joy
- Surprise

- Anger
- Sadness
- Fear

This list can be pared further into two categories, positive emotion (the left column) and negative emotion (the right column). Of course, negative emotions are most relevant to abnormal psychology, and we have separate chapters that focus primarily on sadness (Chapter 5) and fear (Chapter 6). We consider anger in relation to a number of disorders.

Emotions come to us without intention, effort, or desire, and as we have seen, emotions are controlled primarily by subcortical brain structures. Thus, our feelings are more "basic" or primitive than our thoughts, which are controlled by the cerebral cortex, a more recent product of evolution (Buck, 1999). Cognition can shape or modify emotion, but we cannot wholly control our feelings intellectually (Panksepp, 1988). This fact often becomes an issue in treating abnormal behavior, as people

Emotions often come to us without intention, effort, or desire, as illustrated by Halle Berry while accepting her Oscar for best actress for her role in *Monster's Ball.*

often want to but cannot easily change their emotions.

Learning and Cognition

Emotions, motivations, and temperamental styles can be modified, at least to some degree, by learning. Earlier, we discussed classical and operant conditioning, two modes of learning that are essential to the development of normal and abnormal behavior. We know, for example, that classical conditioning can create new fears, and antisocial behavior can be maintained by positive reinforcement.

Modeling A third learning mechanism described by the U.S. psychologist Albert Bandura of Stanford University (Bandura & Walters, 1963) is **modeling** or learning through imitation, a process that you surely have observed many times. A particular concern for the development of abnormal behavior is when parents or other important adults model dysfunctional behavior for children, for example, a parent with alcoholism.

Cognition and Social Cognition Cognitive psychologists study other, more complex learning mechanisms such as attention, information processing, and memory. In doing so, cognitive psychologists often draw analogies between human thinking and computers, but the "human computer" apparently is programmed in ways that make decision making more efficient but less objective (Kahneman, 2003). That is, we routinely make cognitive errors not because we reason wrongly, but because we use shorthand calculations that require little effort and typically are accurate enough—but sometimes are way off the mark.

Cognitive psychology has profoundly affected thinking about the cause of mental disorders, as has the parallel field of *social cognition*—the study of how humans process information about the social world. The important concept of attribution illustrates the cognitive approach. **Attributions** are perceived causes, that is, people's *beliefs* about cause–effect relations. Attributions reveal that people are "intuitive scientists." We routinely draw shorthand conclusions about causality instead of examining things scientifically. If your girlfriend gets mad at you for "ditching" her at a party, for example, you are unlikely to examine her feelings objectively.

Instead, you attribute her anger to some reasonable cause, perhaps her tendency to cling to you. Intuitive judgments are efficient because they require little cognitive effort, but research shows that attributions often are inaccurate (Nisbett & Wilson, 1977; Wilson, 2002).

Interestingly, one cognitive theory suggests that automatic and distorted perceptions of reality cause people to become depressed (Beck, Rush, Shaw, & Emery, 1979). For example, people prone to depression may conclude that they are inadequate based on a single unpleasant experience. A successful treatment based on this theory encourages depressed people to be more scientific and less intuitive in evaluating conclusions about themselves (see Chapter 5). One controversy, however, is whether depressed people actually see the world all too accurately. Perhaps non-depressed people are the ones who make routine cognitive errors by seeing the world, and themselves, in an unrealistically positive light (Taylor et al., 2003).

The Sense of Self

We share emotions and motivations with other animals, and we share some information-processing strategies with computers. Still, our sense of self seems to be uniquely human. The exact definition of our sense of self is elusive. This often is true personally and in various psychological theories.

One important and influential conceptualization is Erik Erikson's (1968) concept of **identity.** Erikson viewed identity as the product of the adolescent's struggle to answer the question "Who am I?" In his view, the conflict caused by this persistent question eventually produces an enduring identity, an integrated sense of individuality, wholeness, and continuity.

Other theorists have countered that we do not have one identity but many "selves." The psychologist George Kelly (1905–1966), for example, emphasized the identities linked with the different roles that people play in life. These include obvious roles like being a daughter, a student, and a friend, as well as less obvious roles, like being a "caretaker," a "jock," or "the quiet one." Kelly argued that people develop many different role identities, various senses of oneself that correspond with actual life roles.

The idea that children and adults must develop **self-control**—internal rules for guiding

Stanford University psychologist Albert Bandura (1925–) extensively studied modeling, the process of learning through imitation.

appropriate behavior—is an important concept in research on abnormal behavior. Self-control is learned through the process of *socialization*, wherein parents, teachers, and peers use discipline, praise, and their own example to teach children prosocial behavior and set limits on their antisocial behavior. Over time, these standards are *internalized*—that is, the external rules become internal regulations. The result is self-control (Maccoby, 1992).

Self-esteem, valuing one's abilities, is another important and much discussed aspect of our sense of self. Most of us want to view ourselves positively, and recent school programs have taken on the mission of raising children's self-esteem. Evidence indicates, however, that high self-esteem is more of a product of success than a cause of it, while raising self-esteem in isolation produces little if any benefit (Baumeister et al., 2003). Similarly, low self-esteem may result from psychological problems rather than causing them.

Stages of Development

Development, or how people grow and change, is of basic importance to normal and abnormal psychology. A key developmental concept is that psychological growth can be characterized by various **developmental stages**—periods of time marked by age and/or social tasks during which children or adults face common social and emotional challenges. Two prominent theories that divided development into stages are Freud's theory of psycho*sexual* development and Erikson's theory of psycho*social* development. As is evident in the name given to his theory, Freud highlighted the child's internal struggles with sexuality as marking the various stages of development. In contrast, Erikson emphasized social tasks and the conflicts involved in meeting the demands of the external world. Importantly and in contrast to Freud, Erikson also suggested that development does not end with adolescence; rather, he proposed that development continues throughout the life span.

The key tasks, ages, and defining events of these two stage theories are summarized in Table 2–5. In addition to noting differences between the theories, you should observe that both theorists use similar ages to denote the beginning and end of developmental stages of childhood. Other theorists also have suggested that key

Vincent van Gogh's self-portraits convey a haunting search for the sense of self. Vincent van Gogh (1853–1890). Self Portrait, 1889. Oil on canvas 65 × 54.5 cm. R.F. 1949–17. Musée d'Orsay, Paris, France. Erich Lessing/Art Resource, NY.

developmental transitions occur around the ages of 1, 6, and 12, as these ages are key times of change for children.

Developmental transitions mark the end of one developmental stage and the beginning of a new one, for example, the end of childhood and the beginning of adolescence. Developmental transitions often are a time of turmoil, as routine functioning changes and we are forced to learn new ways of thinking, feeling, and acting. In fact, we devote Chapter 17 to a discussion of difficult developmental transitions, because these times are emotionally challenging and often are linked to abnormal behavior.

SOCIAL FACTORS

The broadest perspective for understanding the causes of abnormal behavior is at the level of the social system. There is an almost endless number of potential social influences on behavior, including many aspects of interpersonal relationships, social institutions, and cultural values. Therefore we must be selective in reviewing social contributions to psychopathology. In this section we begin with a focus on relationships and then move on to a consideration of gender roles, ethnicity, poverty, and broad societal values.

TABLE 2–5	Freud's and Erikson's Stage Theories of Development						
AGE[1]	0–1½	1–3	2–6	5–12	11–20	18–30	25–70	65 ON
Freud	**Oral** Oral gratification through breastfeeding. Meeting one's own needs.	**Anal** Learning control over environment and inner needs through toilet training.	**Phallic** Sexual rivalry with opposite-gender parent. Oedipal conflicts, penis envy, identification.	**Latency** Not a stage, as psychosexual development is dormant during these ages.	**Genital** Mature sexuality and formation of mutual heterosexual relationships.			
Erikson	**Basic Trust vs. Basic Mistrust** Developing basic trust in self and others through feeding and caretaking.	**Autonomy vs. Shame and Doubt** Gaining a sense of competence through success in toileting and mastering environment.	**Initiative vs. Guilt** Gaining parental approval for initiative rather than guilt over inadequacy.	**Industry vs. Inferiority** Curiosity and eagerness to learn leads to a sense of competence or inadequacy.	**Identity vs. Role Confusion** Identity crisis is a struggle to answer question, "Who am I?"	**Intimacy vs. Self-absorption** Aloneness of young adult resolved by forming friendships and a lasting intimate relationship.	**Generativity vs. Stagnation** Success in work but especially in raising the next generation, or failure to be productive.	**Integrity vs. Despair** Satisfaction with the life one lived rather than despair over lost opportunities.

[1]Ages are approximate, as indicated by overlap in age ranges.

Social perspectives all emphasize that the development of psychopathology is a product of people's *social roles*, styles of behaving according to the expectations of the social situation. Much the way an actor assumes a role in a play, people play roles in their families and in society. In fact, *labeling theory* views emotional disorders themselves in terms of social roles (Rosenhan, 1973). According to labeling theory, abnormal behavior is created by social expectations; it is only what a given group or society deems to be abnormal. Labeling theory also suggests that people's actions conform to the expectations created by the label, a process termed the *self-fulfilling prophesy* (Rosenthal, 1966). For example, when an elementary school boy is labeled "a troublemaker," both he and his teachers may act in ways that make the label come true.

There is little doubt that expectations affect behavior. Still, labeling alone cannot somehow cause the severe hallucinations, delusions, and life disruptions that characterize severe disorders like schizophrenia, for example. The roles people play in life—including roles shaped by gender, race, social class, and culture—help to shape who they become, but psychopathology is much more than the expectations a label creates.

Relationships and Psychopathology

Much evidence links abnormal behavior with distressed or conflicted relationships. Anger and conflict in relationships are tied to a number of emotional disorders ranging from schizophrenia to conduct problems among children. Still, it often is impossible to determine if troubled relationships actually cause abnormal behavior. In many cases, it seems equally or more likely that relationship distress is the effect of an individual's emotional problems.

Marital Status and Psychopathology   The relationship between marital status and psychopathology is a good example of the cause–effect dilemma. The demographics of the U.S. family have changed greatly over the last few decades. Cohabitation before marriage is frequent, many children are born outside of marriage, and almost half of all marriages end in divorce (Cherlin, 1992). In part because of the uncertainty created by these rapid changes, researchers have frequently examined the psychological consequences of alternative family structures for children and for adults (Amato & Keith, 1991a, 1991b; Emery, 1994, 1999; Gotlib & McCabe, 1990; Whisman et al., 2000).

The findings of this large body of research indicate that marital status and psychological problems clearly are *correlated*. Somewhat more emotional problems are found among children and adults from divorced or never-married families than among people living in always-married families (Emery, 1999; Whisman, Sheldon, & Goering, 2000). Still, it is not clear that marital status *causes* the emotional problems. Alternative explanations include suggestions that common genetic factors cause both emotional disorders and marital disruption (McGue & Lykken, 1992), and that marital status can be a consequence, not a cause, of some psychological problems among adults (Gotlib & McCabe, 1990). Most likely, this is one more example of reciprocal causality. Marital status may cause psychopathology, but abnormal behavior also can create dysfunctional families.

Social Relationships In addition to relationships within the family, key relationships outside the family can also affect mental health. For example, research shows that a good relationship with an adult outside the family can shield children from the effects of troubled family circumstances (National Advisory Mental Health Council, 1995; Werner & Smith, 1992). Close relationships also help adults to cope with stress and maintain positive mental health (Reis, Collins, & Berscheid, 2000).

Research suggests that a few things are critical about **social support**—the emotional and practical assistance received from others. Significantly, one close relationship can provide as much support as being involved in many relationships. The greatest risk comes from having *no* social support. In addition, it is much worse to be actively rejected than to be neglected (Coie & Kupersmidt, 1983). Especially among children, it is far worse to be "liked least" than not to be "liked most" by your peers.

The association between abnormal behavior and the lack of supportive peer relationships may have several different causes. In some circumstances, peer rejection may be the cause of emotional difficulties. Being made an outcast surely can cause much distress. In other cases, the lack of a close relationship may be a consequence of psychopathology, as when a disturbed individual is extremely awkward in social relationships. Finally, social support may help people to cope more successfully with pre-existing emotional problems.

Gender and Gender Roles

Gender and **gender roles,** expectations regarding the appropriate behavior of males or females, can dramatically affect social relationships and social interaction. Boys and girls, men and women, are different. One common distinction argues that women are more *relational*, or oriented toward others, whereas men are more *instrumental*, or oriented toward action and achievement (Gilligan, 1982). Whether such differences really exist—and, if they do, what causes them—is open to debate. There is no doubt that some gender differences are determined by genetics and hormones, but there is also little doubt that socially prescribed gender roles exert a strong influence on our behavior (Maccoby, 1998).

Gender roles may influence the development, expression, or consequences of psychopathology. Some theorists have suggested, for example, that women's traditional roles foster dependency and helplessness, which accounts for the considerably higher rates of depression among women (Nolen-Hoeksema, 1990). Others have suggested that gender roles are not responsible for the etiology of abnormal behavior, but they do influence how psychopathology is expressed. According to this view, each gender may experience helplessness,

How might gender roles affect the development or expression of emotional problems?

Intimate relationships can be a source of great social support or emotional distress.

Socially prescribed gender roles exert a strong influence on our behavior and perhaps on the development, expression, and consequences of psychopathology.

but women are allowed to be depressed, whereas men's roles dictate that they "carry on" as if nothing were wrong. Instead of becoming depressed, men may express their inner turmoil by drinking or becoming physically ill.

Some people believe that *androgyny*—the possession of both "female" and "male" gender-role characteristics—is the answer to the problems associated with being either overly "feminine" or overly "masculine." Others believe that traditional gender roles should be embraced, not criticized. We cannot resolve such conflicting values, but we do repeatedly consider differences between men and women in the prevalence of psychological disorders. When appropriate, we interpret this evidence in terms of the roles played by men and women in U.S. society.

Prejudice and Poverty

Prejudice and poverty are broad social influences on psychological well being in the United States today. We consider these two factors together because they are so commonly linked in American life. In 2000, 10.3 percent of white families with children were living below the poverty level, compared with 24.9 percent of black families and 22.9 percent of Latino families. Race and poverty also are closely linked to marital status. Among married African American families with children, 6.3 percent lived in poverty, in comparison to 41.0 percent of families headed by a single mother. Among whites the comparable poverty rates were 5.8 percent married versus 27.5 percent single mother, and 16.9 percent married versus 41.4 percent single

mother for Hispanics (U.S. Census Bureau, 2002).

An increased risk for psychological disorders is associated with prejudice and poverty, although the separate consequences of race and poverty need to be disentangled (National Advisory Mental Health Council, 1995). Poverty is linked with many stressors, including gruesome ones (Evans, 2004). For example, one researcher found that 12 percent of school aged children living in a Washington, D.C., neighborhood reported having seen a dead body in the streets outside their homes (Richters, 1993). Poverty also increases exposure to chemical toxins, such as to the lead found in old, chipping paint and automotive exhaust fumes (Evans, 2004). When ingested at toxic levels, lead can cause damage to the central nervous system.

The conditions of poverty affect a disproportionate number of African Americans, but the experiences of American blacks and whites differ in many more ways than income. African Americans have endured a history of slavery and discrimination, and broad racial prejudices can undermine physical and mental health (Clark et al., 1999). Of course, African Americans are not the only targets of prejudice. For example, extensive evidence links the prejudice experienced by gays and lesbians to an increased risk for mental health problems (Meyer, 2003).

Societal Values

Broad social values also may influence the nature and development of abnormal behavior. For example, humanistic psychologists have questioned the conflict between the requirements for healthy psychological development and societal demands in our frenzied and competitive culture of materialism (Szasz, 1961). From this point of view, personal growth and genuine interpersonal relationships are frustrated by our frenzied pace and focus on "winning." Other people, however, find great value in the material, technological, and scientific gains that accompany industrialization. From this perspective, concerns about society's frustration of personal growth are, in fact, luxuries of the very success that commentators deride.

We do not attempt to address the "mental health" of American culture in this textbook. However, we do recognize the broad influences of society and culture on abnormal behavior. Our personal lives, our education, and even our science are deeply embedded within contemporary U.S. culture. The broad practices, beliefs, and values of our society play a role in defining abnormal behavior and in shaping the scientific enterprise that attempts to uncover the roots of psychopathology.

getting help

The problems that you study in this class can touch your life in a very personal way. At one time or another, you, someone in your family, or one of your close friends likely will experience a serious psychological problem. If so, we hope you will seek and find meaningful help. What can you do if you think you may want to get help?

A good place to start is to talk frankly with someone you trust—a friend, a family member, a mental health professional, maybe a professor. Taking this step can be difficult, but you surely will be relieved once you have opened up a little. In fact, this may be the end of your search for help. With the aid of a little perspective, you may be reassured that what you thought were "crazy" feelings or concerns really are pretty normal.

Normal? Yes. We mean it when we say that there is not a high wall dividing normal from abnormal behavior. Negative emotions are part of everyday life. Most of us experience mild to moderate levels of anxiety, sadness, and anger fairly often. In fact, these emotions often are adaptive. These feelings can energize us to cope with the challenges in our lives. So, maybe all you really need is the understanding and perspective of a caring friend or relative, or of an objective third party.

Recognizing where you are in your life also may help you to achieve a little perspective. The late teens and early twenties—the age of many people taking this class—is frequently a time of uncertainty and self-doubt. It is quite common for people at this point in their lives to question their goals, beliefs, values, friendships, sexuality, family relationships, and almost everything else. If this sounds like you, you may want to read ahead in Chapter 17, which discusses many of the challenges of the transition to adult life. You also may want to look at this chapter if you are a nontraditional student, because we also discuss many other common but trying developmental transitions throughout the adult life span. Times of change and challenge can be very exciting, but they also can be very distressing and lonely.

What should you do if you did not feel better after talking with someone you trust? We suggest that you consider consulting a mental health professional. This is a good next step whether you think you are suffering from a psychological problem, are not sure, or simply want help with some normal but distressing life experience. We know that there can be a stigma about consulting "a shrink," but we strongly believe that the stigma is wrong. Mental health problems are incredibly common, and a therapist, or maybe your family doctor, can offer you an informed perspective and some good treatment alternatives. We give suggestions about how to go about finding a reliable mental health professional in the Getting Help section of Chapter 3.

SUMMARY

The **biological, psychodynamic, cognitive behavioral,** and **humanistic** approaches to understanding the causes of abnormal behavior are alternative **paradigms,** and not just alternative theories. Biological approaches emphasize causes that occur "within the skin." Psychodynamic theory highlights unconscious processes and detailed case histories. Cognitive behavioral viewpoints focus on observable, learned behavior. Finally, the humanistic paradigm argues that behavior is not determined but, instead, is a product of free will.

None of these broad paradigms offers the "right" explanation of abnormal behavior, which is best understood in terms of the **biopsychosocial model,** the combination of different biological, psychological, and social factors. **Systems theory** is a way of integrating biological, psychological, and social contributions to abnormal behavior. Its central principle is **holism,** the idea that the whole is more than the sum of its parts—a scientific counterpoint to **reductionism.**

Biological factors in abnormal behavior begin with the **neuron,** or nerve cell. Communication between neurons occurs when the axon terminals release chemical substances called **neurotransmitters** into the **synapse** between nerve cells. Disrupted communication among neurons, particularly disruptions in the functioning of various neurotransmitters, is involved in several types of abnormal behavior, although you should be cautioned against mind–body dualism.

Neuroanatomists commonly divide the brain into three subdivisions: the hindbrain, the midbrain, and the forebrain. The forebrain is the location of most sensory, emotional, and cognitive processes. Most of the forebrain is composed of the two cerebral hemispheres, and many brain functions are lateralized, so that each hemisphere is the site of specific cognitive and emotional activities. Finally, the cerebral cortex is the uneven surface area of the brain that lies just underneath the skull. It is the site of the control and integration of sophisticated memory, sensory, and motor functions. Because of the rudimentary state of our knowledge about the brain, only the most severe mental disorders have been clearly linked with abnormalities in neuroanatomy. In most of these cases, brain damage is extensive and obvious.

Psychophysiology involves changes in the functioning of the body that result from psychological experiences. Psychophysiological arousal is caused by two different communication systems within the body: the **endocrine system** and the nervous system. Endocrine glands release **hormones** into the bloodstream that regulate some aspects of normal development as well as some responses to stress. The autonomic nervous system is the part of the central nervous system that is responsible for psychophysiological reactions. It has two branches, the sympathetic and the parasympathetic nervous systems. In general, the sympathetic nervous system controls arousal, and the parasympathetic nervous system controls energy conservation.

Behavior genetics is the study of genetic influences on the development of behavior. Most forms of abnormal behavior are **polygenic,** that is, they are caused by more than one **gene.** Comparisons of **monozygotic (MZ)** and **dizygotic (DZ)** twins can yield information about genetic contributions to behavior, as can adoption studies. The fact that a psychological disorder has a genetic component does not mean that the disorder will inevitably appear; genetically influenced behavior also is affected by the environment. Few single genes directly affect abnormal behavior; thus genetic effects probably occur at some more basic level—for example, by affecting psychophysiological arousal.

Psychology has not developed a list of its core components. Some promise toward this goal is offered by **evolutionary psychology,** the application of the principles of evolution to our understanding of the animal and human minds. Evolutionary psychologists assume that animal and human psychology have evolved based on natural selection and sexual selection. Two basic psychological motivations seen in humans and other animals are the formation of **attachments** and competition for **dominance. Emotion** drives these basic motivations. **Temperament** is an individual's characteristic style of relating to the world, and researchers agree on the "big five" dimensions of temperament.

Learning mechanisms include **classical conditioning, operant conditioning, modeling,** and human cognition, and they contribute to both normal and abnormal behavior. The sense of self is a uniquely human quality that also may play a role in causing emotional problems. The idea of **developmental stages** not only charts the course of normal development, against which abnormal behavior must be compared, but it highlights the important issue of developmental transitions.

Social roles influence the definition and development of psychopathology. Evidence links abnormal behavior with distressed or conflicted family relationships, and **social support** from people other than family members can be an important buffer against stress. **Gender roles** may influence the development, expression, or consequences of psychopathology. Race and poverty, which are often related, also are broad social influences on psychological well being in the United States today. Finally, there may be conflict between the demands of our competitive society and the requirements for healthy psychological development.

KEY TERMS

attachments   52
attributions   54
autonomic nervous
   system   46
behavior genetics   46
biopsychosocial
   model   30
cerebral cortex   44
cerebral hemispheres   44
chromosomes   46
classical conditioning   34
concordance rate   48
correlational study   37
correlation coefficient   37

defense mechanism   33
developmental
   psychopathology   39
developmental stages   55
diathesis   39
dizygotic (DZ) twins   48
dominance   52
dualism   44
ego   33
emotions   53
endocrine system   45
evolutionary
   psychology   51
extinction   34

gender roles   57
genes   46
genotype   46
hormones   45
hypothalamus   43
id   33
identity   54
lateralized   44
limbic system   42
modeling   54
monozygotic (MZ)
   twins   48
neurons   40
neurotransmitters   40

nonshared
   environment   48
operant conditioning   34
paradigm   29
phenotype   47
polygenic   47
premorbid history   40
probands   47
prognosis   40
psychoanalytic theory   33
psychophysiology   45
receptors   40
reciprocal causality   39
reductionism   37

reuptake   41
reverse causality   37
risk factors   39
self-control   54
shared environment   48
social support   57
stress   39
superego   33
synapse   40
systems theory   36
temperament   53
third variable   37
ventricles   44

Go to www.prenhall.com/oltmanns for online quizzes, interactive flash cards, PowerPoint presentations, and chapter reviews.

4

Classification and Assessment of Abnormal Behavior

◆◆◆

Imagine that you are a therapist who has begun to interview a new patient. She tells you that she has had trouble falling asleep for the past few weeks. She has become increasingly frustrated and depressed, in part because she is always so tired when she goes to work in the morning. Your job is to figure out how to help this woman. How serious is her problem? What else do you need to know? What questions should you ask and how should you collect the information? The process of gathering this information is called **assessment.** You will want to use data from your assessment to compare her experiences with those of other patients whom you have treated (or read about). Are there any similarities that might help you know what to expect in terms of the likely origins of her problems, how long they will last, and the kinds of treatment that might be most helpful? In order to make those comparisons, you will need a kind of psychological road map to guide your search for additional information. This road map is known as a *classification system*—a list of various types of problems and their associated symptoms. This chapter will describe the classification system that has been developed to describe various forms of abnormal behavior. It will also summarize the different kinds of assessment tools that psychologists use.

OVERVIEW

One important part of the assessment process is making a diagnostic decision based on the categories in the official classification system that describes mental disorders. **Diagnosis** refers to the identification or recognition of a disorder on the basis of its characteristic symptoms. In the field of mental health, a clinician assigns a diagnosis if the person's behavior meets the specific criteria for a particular type of disorder, such as schizophrenia or major depressive disorder. This decision is important because it tells the clinician that the person's problems are similar to those that have been experienced by some other people. The diagnosis enables the clinician to refer to the base of knowledge that has accumulated with regard to the disorder. For example, it will provide clues about associated symptoms and treatments that are most likely to be effective. To formulate a comprehensive treatment plan, the clinician utilizes the person's diagnosis plus many other types of information that we will discuss in this chapter.

In some fields, diagnosis refers to causal analysis. If your car doesn't start, you expect that your mechanic's "diagnosis" will explain the origins of the problem. Has the battery lost its charge? Is the fuel line blocked? Is the ignition switch dead? In this situation, the "diagnosis" leads directly to the problem's solution. In the field of psychopathology, assigning a diagnosis does not mean that we understand the etiology of the person's problem (see Chapter 2). Specific etiologies have not been identified for mental disorders. Psychologists can't "look under the hood" in the same way that a mechanic can examine a car. In the case of a mental disorder, assigning a diagnostic label simply identifies the nature of the problem without implying exactly how the problem came into existence.

Our consideration of the assessment enterprise and diagnostic issues will begin with an example from our own clinical experience. In the following pages we will describe Michael, a young man who found himself thinking and acting in ways that he could not seem to control. This case study illustrates the kinds of decisions that psychologists have to make about ways to collect and interpret information used in diagnosis and assessment.

◆◆

CASE STUDY   Obsessions, Compulsions, and Other Unusual Behaviors

Michael was an only child who lived with his mother and father. He was 16 years old, a little younger than most of the other boys in the eleventh grade, and he looked even younger. From an academic point of view, Michael was an average student, but he was not a typical teenager in terms of social behavior. He felt alienated from other boys, and he was extremely anxious when he talked to girls. He despised everything about school. His life at home was also unpleasant. Michael and his parents argued frequently, especially he and his father.

One awful incident summed up Michael's bitter feelings about school. As a sophomore, he decided to join the track team. Michael was clumsy and not athletic. When he worked out with the other long-distance runners, he soon became the brunt of their jokes. One day, a belligerent teammate forced Michael to take off his clothes and run naked to a shelter in the park. When he got there, Michael found an old pair of shorts, which he put on and wore back to the locker room. The experience was humiliating. Later that night, Michael started to worry about those shorts. Who had left them in the park? Were they dirty? Had he been exposed to some horrible disease? Michael quit the track team the next day, but he couldn't put the experience out of his mind.

In the following year, Michael became more and more consumed by anxiety. He was obsessed about "contamination," which he imagined to be spreading from his books and school clothes to the furniture and other objects in his house. When the clothes that he had worn to school rubbed against a chair or a wall at home, he felt as though that spot had become contaminated. He didn't believe this was literally true; it was more like a reminder by association. When he touched something that he had used at school, he was more likely to think of school. That triggered unpleasant thoughts and the negative emotions with which they were associated (anger, fear, sadness).

Michael tried in various ways to minimize the spread of contamination. For example, he took a shower and changed his clothes every evening at 6 o'clock immediately after he finished his homework.

After this "cleansing ritual" he was careful to avoid touching his books or dirty clothes as well as anything that they had touched.

If he bumped into one of the contaminated objects by accident, he went into the bathroom and washed his hands. Michael washed his hands 10 or 15 times in a typical evening. He paced back and forth watching television without sitting down so that he would not touch contaminated furniture.

Whenever he was not in school, Michael preferred to be alone at home, playing games on his computer. He did not enjoy sports, music, or outdoor activities. The only literature that interested him was fantasy and science fiction. *Dungeons and Dragons* was the only game that held his attention. He read extensively about the magical powers of fantastic characters and spent hours dreaming up new variations on themes described in books about this imaginary realm. When Michael talked about the *Dungeons and Dragons* characters and their adventures, his speech would sometimes become vague and difficult to follow. Other students at Michael's school shared his interest in *Dungeons and Dragons,* but he didn't want to play the game with them. Michael said he was different from the other students. He expressed contempt for other teenagers, as well as for the city in which he lived.

Michael and his parents had been working with a family therapist for more than two years. Although the level of interpersonal conflict in the family had been reduced, Michael's anxiety seemed to be getting worse. He had become even more isolated from other boys his own age, and had become quite suspicious about their motives. He often felt that they were talking about him, and that they were planning to do something else in order to humiliate him.

His worries about contamination had become almost unbearable to his parents, who were deeply confused and frustrated by his behavior. They knew that he was socially isolated and extremely unhappy. They believed that he would never be able to resume a more normal pattern of development until he gave up these "silly" ideas. Michael's fears disrupted his parents' own activities in several ways. They weren't allowed to touch him or his things after being in certain rooms of the house. His peculiar movements and persistent washing were troublesome to them. Michael's father usually worked at home, and he and Michael quarreled frequently, especially when Michael ran water in the bathroom next to his father's study.

Michael and his mother had always been very close. He was quite dependent on her, and she was devoted to him. They spent a lot of time together while his father was working. His mother had begun to find it difficult to be close to Michael. He shunned physical contact. When she touched him, he sometimes cringed and withdrew. Once in a while he would shriek, reminding her that she was contaminated by her contact with chairs and other objects like his laundry. Recently, Michael had also become aloof intellectually. His mother felt that he was shutting her out, as he seemed to withdraw further into his fantasy world of *Dungeons and Dragons* and his obsessive thoughts about contamination.

◆◆

After learning about Michael's problems, his worries about contamination, his efforts to avoid contamination, and his fear of being with other people, his therapist would be faced with several important decisions. One involves the level of analysis at which she should think about the problem. Is this primarily Michael's problem, or should she consider this problem in terms of all members of the family? One possibility is that Michael has a psychological disorder that is disrupting the life of his family. It may be the other way around, however. Perhaps the family system as a whole is dysfunctional, and Michael's problems are only one symptom of this dysfunction.

Another set of choices involves the type of data that his therapist will use to describe Michael's behavior. What kinds of information should be collected? The therapist can consider several sources of data. One is Michael's own report, which can be obtained in an interview or through the use of questionnaires. Another is the report of his parents. The therapist may also decide to employ psychological tests.

In conducting an assessment and arriving at a diagnosis, one question the therapist must ask is whether Michael's abnormal behavior is similar to problems that have been exhibited by other people. She would want to know if Michael's symptoms fall into a pattern that has been documented by many other mental health professionals. Rather than re-inventing the wheel each time a new patient walks into her office, the therapist can use a classification system to streamline the diagnostic process. The classification system serves as a common language among therapists, giving them a form of professional "shorthand" that enables them to discuss issues with colleagues. Because different disorders sometimes respond to different forms of treatment, the distinctions can be very important. In the next section we will review the development and modification of classification systems for abnormal behavior.

BASIC ISSUES IN CLASSIFICATION

A **classification system** is used to subdivide or organize a set of objects. The objects of classification can be inanimate things, such as CDs, rocks, or books; living organisms, such as plants, insects, or primates; or abstract concepts, such as numbers, religions, or historical periods. Formal classification systems are essential for the collection and communication of knowledge in all sciences and professions.

There are many ways to subdivide any given class of objects. Classification systems can be based on different principles (Bowker & Star, 1999). Some systems are based on descriptive similarities. For example, both a diamond and a ruby may be considered jewels because they are valuable stones. Other systems are based on less obvious characteristics, such as structural similarities. A diamond and a piece of coal, for example, may belong together because they are both made of carbon.

The point is simple: Classification systems can be based on various principles, and their value will depend primarily on the purpose for which they were developed. Different classification systems are not necessarily right or wrong; they are simply more or less useful. In the following section we will consider several fundamental principles that affect all attempts to develop a useful classification or typology of human behavior.

Categories versus Dimensions

Classification is often based on "yes or no" decisions (Hempel, 1961). After a category has been defined, an object is either a member of the category or it is not. A **categorical approach to classification** assumes that distinctions among members of different categories are qualitative. In other words, the differences reflect a difference in

Taxonomy is the science of arranging living organisms into groups. Humans and dolphins belong to the same "class" (mammals) because they share certain characteristics (are warm-blooded, nourish their young, and have body hair).

Why do we need a system to classify abnormal behaviors?

tasks. This process offers some advantages over categorical distinctions. For example, it allows scientists to record subtle distinctions that would be lost if they were forced to make all-or-none decisions.

From Description to Theory

The development of scientific classification systems typically proceeds in an orderly fashion over a period of several years. The initial stages, which focus on simple descriptions or observations, are followed by more advanced theoretical stages. At the latter point, greater emphasis is placed on scientific concepts that explain causal relationships among objects. In the study of many medical disorders, this progression begins with an emphasis on the description of specific symptoms that cluster together and follow a predictable course over time. The systematic collection of more information regarding this syndrome may then lead to the discovery of causal factors.

Clinical scientists hope that similar progress will be made in the field of psychopathology. Mental disorders are currently classified on the basis of their descriptive features or symptoms because specific causal mechanisms have not yet been discovered. While we may eventually develop a more sophisticated, theoretically based understanding of certain disorders, this does not necessarily mean we will ever know the precise causes of disorders. In fact, the most likely explanations for mental disorders involve complex interactions of psychological, biological, and social systems (see Chapter 2).

kind (quality) rather than a difference in amount (quantity). In the classification of living organisms, for example, we usually consider species to be qualitatively distinct; they are different kinds of living organisms. Human beings are different from other primates; an organism is either human or it is not. Many medical conditions are categorical. Infection is one clear example. A person is either infected with a particular virus, or he is not. It doesn't make sense to talk about whether someone is partially infected or almost infected.

Although categorically based classification systems are often useful, they are not the only kind of system that can be used to organize information systematically. As an alternative, scientists often employ a **dimensional approach to classification**—that is, one that describes the objects of classification in terms of continuous dimensions. Rather than assuming that an object either has or does not have a particular property, it may be useful to focus on a specific characteristic and determine how much of that characteristic the object exhibits. This kind of system is based on an ordered sequence or on quantitative measurements rather than on qualitative judgments.

For example, in the case of intellectual ability, psychologists have developed sophisticated measurement procedures. Rather than asking whether or not a particular person is intelligent (a "yes or no" judgment), the psychologist sets out to determine how much intelligence the person exhibits on a particular set of

CLASSIFYING ABNORMAL BEHAVIOR

We need a classification system for abnormal behavior for two primary reasons. First, a classification system is useful to clinicians, who must match their clients' problems with the form of intervention that is most likely to be effective. Second, a classification system must be used in the search for new knowledge. The history of medicine is filled with examples of problems that were recognized long before they could be treated successfully. The classification of a specific set of symptoms has often laid the foundation for research that eventually identified a cure or a way of preventing the disorder.

Brief Historical Perspective

Currently, two diagnostic systems for mental disorders are widely recognized. One—the *Diagnostic and Statistical Manual* (DSM)—is published by the American Psychiatric Association. The other—the *International Classification of Diseases* (ICD)—is published by the World Health Organization. Both systems were developed shortly after World War II, and both have been revised several times. Because the American diagnostic manual is now in its fourth edition, it is called DSM-IV-TR. The "TR" stands for "text revision" and refers to the fact that some of the background material provided in the manual was updated in 2000. The World Health Organization's manual is in its tenth edition and is therefore known as ICD-10.

During the 1950s and 1960s, psychiatric classification systems were widely criticized. One major criticism focused on the lack of consistency in diagnostic decisions (Nathan & Langenbucher, 2003). Independent clinicians frequently disagreed with one another about the use of diagnostic categories as they were listed in the first two editions of the American classification system, DSM-I and DSM-II. Objections were also raised from philosophical, sociological, and political points of view. For example, some critics charged that diagnostic categories in psychiatry would be more appropriately viewed as "problems in living" than as medical disorders (Szasz, 1960). Others were concerned about self-fulfilling prophesies. In other words, once a psychiatric label had been assigned, the person so labeled might be motivated to continue behaving in ways that were expected from someone who is mentally disturbed (see Labeling Theory on page 98). For all of these reasons, many mental health professionals paid less and less attention to the formal process of diagnosis during these years.

Renewed interest in the value of psychiatric classification grew steadily during the 1970s, culminating in the publication of the third edition of the DSM in 1980. This version of the manual represented a dramatic departure from previous systems. It was clearly a major turning point in the history of psychiatric classification (Jablensky, 1999; Sabshin, 1990). The committee that was responsible for developing DSM-III was chaired by Robert Spitzer, a psychiatrist at the New York State Psychiatric Institute. Spitzer and his colleagues made several bold changes in the manual. One broad consideration was their commitment to the production of a classification system that was based on clinical description rather than on theories of psychopathology that had not been empirically validated. This principle led to the elimination of some terms and categories that had been based on psychoanalytic concepts, like neurosis and hysteria (see Chapters 6 and 8). Other major changes included the introduction of a multiaxial system (described below) and the production of specific, detailed criterion sets for each disorder.

All these changes have been retained in both DSM-IV-TR and ICD-10, and are described in the following section. The two manuals are very similar in most respects. Deliberate attempts were made to coordinate the production of DSM-IV-TR and ICD-10. Most of the categories listed in the manuals are identical, and the criteria for specific disorders are usually similar.[1]

The DSM-IV-TR System

More than 200 specific diagnostic categories are described in DSM-IV-TR. These are arranged under 18 primary headings. A complete list appears on the inside covers of this book. Disorders that present similar kinds of symptoms are grouped together. For example, conditions that include a prominent display of anxiety are listed under "Anxiety Disorders," and conditions that involve a depressed mood are listed under "Mood Disorders."

The manual lists specific criteria for each diagnostic category. We can illustrate the ways in which these criteria are used by examining the diagnostic decisions that would be considered in Michael's case. The criteria for obsessive–compulsive disorder (OCD) are listed in Table 4–1 (p. 99). Michael would meet all of the criteria in "A" for both obsessions and compulsions. His repetitive hand-washing rituals were performed in response to obsessive thoughts regarding contamination. Consistent with criterion "B,"

Robert Spitzer, professor of psychiatry at Columbia University, chaired the committee that produced DSM-III. Spitzer's vision and forceful leadership helped the committee to accomplish one of the most important changes in psychiatric classification of ' twentieth century.

---

[1]There are some interesting differences between DSM-IV-TR and ICD-10. There are, for example, differences in the ways in which they subdivide mood disorders and personality disorders. The U.S. system also devotes more attention to eating disorders and sexual disorders, which appear to be less prevalent in other cultures (Andrews, Slade, & Peters, 1999; Kendell, 1991).

LABELING THEORY

What does it mean to be labeled with a psychiatric diagnosis? **Labeling theory** is a perspective on mental disorders that is primarily concerned with the social context in which abnormal behavior occurs and the ways in which other people respond to this behavior. It assigns relatively little importance to specific behaviors as symptoms of a disorder that resides within the person. Labeling theory is primarily concerned with the social factors that determine whether a person will be given a psychiatric diagnosis rather than the psychological or biological reasons for the abnormal behaviors (Link & Phelan, 1999). In other words, it is concerned with events that take place after a person has behaved in an unusual way rather than with factors that might explain the original appearance of the behavior itself.

Labeling theory is based on the assumption that it is useful to think of mental disorders as maladaptive social roles. The process of diagnostic labeling is the most important factor in establishing that role for a particular person (Scheff, 1966; 1999). The symptoms of mental disorders are viewed as violations of social expectations that most people take for granted: showing too much emotion, not showing enough emotion, or talking too much or in strange ways. A person who breaks these unwritten rules might be labeled as mentally disturbed.

According to labeling theory, the probability that a person will receive a diagnosis is determined by several factors. These include the severity of the unusual behavior and its visibility, as well as the tolerance level of the community. The most important considerations are the social status of the person who violates social expectations and the social distance between that person and mental health professionals. People from disadvantaged groups, such as racial and sexual minorities and women, are presumably more likely to be labeled than are white males.

The merits and limitations of labeling theory have been hotly debated, and the theory has inspired research on a number of important questions. Some studies have found that people from lower status groups, including racial [minorities], are indeed more likely to be assigned [diag]noses (Phelan & Link, 1999). On the [other hand, it] would also be an exaggeration to

say that the social status of the patient is the most important factor influencing the diagnostic process. In fact, clinicians' diagnostic decisions are determined primarily by the form and severity of the patient's symptoms rather than by such factors as gender, race, and social class (Farmer & Griffiths, 1992; Gove, 1990).

Another focus of the debate regarding labeling theory is the issue of **stigma** and the negative effects of labeling. Stigma refers to a stamp or label that sets the person apart from others, connects the person to undesirable features, and leads others to reject the person. Labeling theory notes that negative attitudes toward mental disorders prevent patients from obtaining jobs, finding housing, and forming new relationships. Various kinds of empirical evidence support the conclusion that a psychiatric label can have a harmful impact on a person's life. Negative attitudes are associated with many types of mental disorder, such as alcoholism, schizophrenia, and sexual disorders (Couture & Penn, 2003). When a person

becomes a psychiatric patient, the person expects to be devalued and discriminated against. These expectations cause the person to behave in strained and defensive ways, which may in turn cause others to reject him or her (Link et al., 1997).

Labeling theory has drawn needed attention to several important problems associated with the classification of mental disorders, but it does not provide an adequate explanation for abnormal behavior. It is clearly an exaggeration to think of mental disorders as nothing more than social roles. Many factors other than the reactions of other people contribute to the development and maintenance of abnormal behavior. Furthermore, a diagnosis of mental illness can have positive consequences, such as encouraging access to effective treatment. Many patients and their family members are relieved to learn that their problems are similar to those experienced by other people and that help may be available. The effects of diagnostic labeling are not always harmful.

Efforts to promote awareness of depression help to combat negative images of people with mental disorders.

T A B L E   4 – 1   **DSM-IV-TR Criteria for Obsessive–Compulsive Disorder**

A. Either obsessions or compulsions:

Obsessions as defined by (1), (2), (3), and (4):

1. Recurrent and persistent thoughts, impulses, or images that are experienced, at some time during the disturbance, as intrusive and inappropriate, and that cause marked anxiety or distress

2. The thoughts, impulses, or images are not simply excessive worries about real-life problems

3. The person attempts to ignore or suppress thoughts, impulses, or images or to neutralize them with some other thought or action

4. The person recognizes that the obsessional thoughts, impulses, or images are a product of his or her own mind (not imposed from without as in thought insertion)

Compulsions as defined by (1) and (2):

1. Repetitive behaviors (such as hand washing, ordering, checking) or mental acts (such as praying, counting, repeating words silently) that the person feels driven to perform in response to an obsession, or according to rules that must be applied rigidly

2. The behaviors or mental acts are aimed at preventing or reducing distress or preventing some dreaded event or situation; however, these behaviors or mental acts either are not connected in a realistic way with what they are designed to neutralize or prevent, or are clearly excessive

B. At some point during the course of the disorder, the person has recognized that the obsessions or compulsions are excessive or unreasonable.

C. The obsessions or compulsions cause marked distress; are time-consuming (take more than one hour a day); or significantly interfere with the person's normal routine, occupational (or academic) functioning, or usual social activities or relationships with others.

D. If another Axis I disorder is present, the content of the obsessions or compulsions is not restricted to it (for example, preoccupation with food in the presence of an Eating Disorder; preoccupation with drugs in the presence of a Substance Use Disorder; or guilty ruminations in the presence of Major Depressive Disorder).

Reprinted with permission from the *Diagnostic and Statistical Manual of Mental Disorders,* Fourth Edition, Text Revision. Copyright © 2000 by the American Psychiatric Association.

Michael admitted that these concerns were irrational. He also meets criterion "C" in that these rituals were time-consuming and interfered with his family's routine. His relationships with friends were severely limited because he refused to invite them to his house, fearing that they would spread contamination.

For various types of disorder, the duration of the problem is considered as well as the clinical picture. Criterion "C" for OCD specifies that the patient's compulsive rituals must take more than one hour each day to perform.

In addition to the inclusion criteria, symptoms that must be present, many disorders are also defined in terms of certain exclusion criteria. In other words, the diagnosis can be ruled out if certain conditions prevail. For example, in the case of OCD, the diagnosis would not be made if the symptoms occurred only during the course of another disorder, such as a person with alcoholism being preoccupied with thoughts of obtaining another drink (criterion "D").

The DSM-IV-TR employs a *multiaxial classification system;* that is, the person is rated on five separate axes. Each axis is concerned with a different domain of information. Two are concerned with diagnostic categories and the other three provide for the collection of additional relevant data. The rationale for this approach is that to manage individual cases, the clinician must consider several important factors besides specific symptoms. These supplementary factors include the environment in which the patient is living, aspects of the person's health that might affect psychological functions, and fluctuations in the overall level of the patient's adjustment. Table 4–2 lists the five specific axes from DSM-IV-TR.

The first two axes are concerned with clinical disorders that are defined largely in terms of symptomatic behaviors. Most diagnoses appear on Axis I, which includes conditions, such as OCD, schizophrenia, and mood disorders, that are the topics of most chapters in this text. Many of the diagnoses that are described on Axis I are characterized by episodic periods of psychological turmoil. Axis II is concerned with more stable, long-standing problems, such as personality disorders and mental retardation. The separation of disorders on Axis I and Axis II is designed to draw attention to long-standing conditions, such as a paranoid or dependent personality style, that might be overlooked in the presence of a more dramatic symptomatic picture, such as the hallucinations and delusions frequently found in schizophrenia. A person can be assigned more than one diagnosis on either Axis I or Axis II (or on both axes) if he or she meets criteria for more than one disorder.

Michael would receive a diagnosis of obsessive—compulsive disorder on Axis I, and these were, in fact, his most obvious symptoms. On Axis II, Michael would also be coded as meeting criteria for schizotypal personality disorder. This judgment depends on a consideration of his long-standing, relatively rigid patterns of interacting with other people and his inability to adjust to the changing requirements of different people and situations. For example, he was suspicious of other people's motives, he did not have any close friends in whom he could confide, and he was very anxious in social situations because he was afraid that other people might take advantage of him. These are important considerations for a therapist who wants to plan a treatment program for Michael, but they are relatively subtle considerations in comparison to the obsessions and compulsions, which were the primary source of conflict with his parents.

Axis III is concerned with general medical conditions that are outside the realm of psychopathology but may be relevant to either the etiology of the patient's abnormal behavior or the patient's treatment program. Examples include thyroid conditions, which may lead to symptoms of psychosis, and diabetes in children, which is sometimes associated with conduct disorders. The presence of chronic medical conditions does predict worse outcomes for certain kinds of mental disorders, especially depression (Saavedra et al., 2001). In Michael's case, there were no known physical disorders that were relevant to his psychological problems.

Axis IV is concerned with psychosocial and environmental problems that may affect the diagnosis or treatment of a mental disorder. The clinician is asked to indicate specific factors that are present in the person's life. The clinician is asked to record those problems that were present during the year prior to the current assessment. Problems that occurred prior to the previous year may be noted if the clinician is convinced that they made a significant contribution to the development of the person's current problems or if they have become a focus of treatment.

Michael's therapist noted the presence of three psychosocial problems: frequent arguments within the family, social isolation, and discord with classmates at school. Note that stressful circumstances may be the products as well as the causes of mental disorders. In Michael's case, for example, many of the family's arguments were precipitated by his hand-washing rituals. In deciding whether to list social stresses on Axis IV, psychologists need not determine whether the stresses primarily arose from or contributed to the condition. They are all listed if they are relevant to treatment planning, and these were all important considerations in Michael's case.

Finally, Axis V provides for a global rating of adaptive functioning. This rating is made on a

TABLE 4–2	Major Domains of Information in DSM-IV-TR
Axis I	Clinical Disorders and Other Conditions That May Be a Focus of Attention (includes all mental disorders in the manual except those listed on Axis II).
Axis II	Personality Disorders and Mental Retardation (includes all personality disorders and/or mental retardation. Clinician can also list maladaptive personality features, characteristic defense mechanisms, or coping styles).
Axis III	General Medical Conditions (includes medical problems that can cause symptoms of an Axis I or Axis II disorder or act as a psychological stressor).
Axis IV	Psychosocial and Environmental Problems (includes life events from the past year that may have an impact on diagnosis or treatment, such as divorce or unemployment).
Axis V	Global Assessment of Functioning (describes the person's level of psychological, social, and occupational functioning on a single scale from 1 to 100).

scale of 1 to 100, with higher numbers representing better levels of adjustment. The scale applies to psychological, social, and occupational functioning. Ratings are typically made for the person's current level of functioning. In some circumstances, the clinician might also consider the person's highest level of functioning during the past year. This information is considered useful because it draws attention to recent changes in the patient's condition and because it provides a balanced view of the patient's strengths as well as his or her weaknesses. Michael's psychologist assigned a rating of 50 for his current level of functioning. Michael was performing at an adequate level academically, but his social life was clearly impaired as a consequence of his rituals.

Culture and Classification

DSM-IV-TR addresses the relation between cultural issues and the diagnosis of psychopathology in two principal ways. First, the manual encourages clinicians to consider the influence of cultural factors in both the expression and recognition of symptoms of mental disorders. People express extreme emotions in ways that are shaped by the traditions of their families and other social groups to which they belong. Intense, public displays of anger or grief might be expected in one culture but considered signs of disturbance in another. Interpretations of emotional distress and other symptoms of disorder are influenced by the explanations that a person's culture assigns to such experiences. Religious beliefs, social roles, and sexual identities all play an important part in constructing meanings that are assigned to these phenomena (Tsai et al., 2001). The accuracy and utility of a clinical diagnosis depend on more than a simple count of the symptoms that appear to be present. They also hinge on the clinician's ability to consider the cultural context in which the problem appeared. This is a particularly challenging task when the clinician and the person with the problem do not share the same cultural background.

The diagnostic manual attempts to sensitize clinicians to cultural issues by including a glossary of **culture-bound syndromes.** These are patterns of erratic or unusual thinking and behavior that have been identified in diverse societies around the world and do not fit easily into the other diagnostic categories that are listed in the main body of DSM-IV-TR. They are

Axis IV calls for information about life events that may have an impact on diagnosis or treatment. This 7-year-old boy is drawing a picture of his friends who were killed by a bomb in Afghanistan.

called "culture-bound" because they have sometimes been considered to be unique to particular societies, particularly in non-Western or developing countries. Their appearance is easily recognized and understood to be a form of abnormal behavior by members of certain cultures, but they do not conform to typical patterns of mental disorder seen in the United States or Europe. Culture-bound syndromes have also been called *idioms of distress*. In other words, they represent a manner of expressing negative emotion that is unique to a particular culture and cannot be easily translated or understood in terms of its individual parts.

One syndrome of this type is a phenomenon known as *ataques de nervios*, which has been observed most extensively among people from Puerto Rico and other Caribbean countries (Guarnaccia et al., 1996). Descriptions of this experience include four dimensions, in which the essential theme is loss of control—an inability to interrupt the dramatic sequence of emotion and behavior. These dimensions include emotional expressions (an explosion of screaming and crying, coupled with overwhelming feelings of anxiety, depression, and anger), bodily sensations (including trembling, heart palpitations, weakness, fatigue, headache, and convulsions), actions and behaviors (dramatic, forceful gestures that include aggression toward others, suicidal thoughts or gestures, and trouble eating or sleeping), and alterations in consciousness (marked feelings of "not being one's usual self," accompanied by fainting, loss of consciousness, dizziness, and feelings of being outside of one's body).

The frequency and duration of ataques de nervios vary from one person to the next. An episode typically lasts less than an hour, but some last more than a day. When the ataque is over, often the person is unable to remember what occurred. The person may return quickly to his or her previous level of functioning, often feeling better or relieved.

Ataques are typically provoked by situations that disrupt or threaten the person's social world, especially the family. Many ataques occur shortly after the person learns unexpectedly that a close family member has died. Others result from an imminent divorce or after a serious conflict with a child. Women are primarily responsible for maintaining the integrity of the family in this culture, and they are also more likely than men to experience ataques de nervios. Puerto Rican women from poor and working-class families define themselves largely in terms of their success in building and maintaining a cohesive family life. When this social role is threatened, an ataque may result. This response to threat or conflict—an outburst of powerful, uncontrolled negative emotion—expresses suffering while simultaneously providing a means for coping with the threat. It serves to signal her distress to important other people and to rally needed sources of social support.

What is the relation between culture-bound syndromes and the formal categories listed in DSM-IV-TR? The answer is unclear and also varies from one syndrome to the next. Are they similar problems that are simply given different names in other cultures? Probably not, at least not in most instances (Guarnaccia & Rogler,

During an episode of *ataques de nervios,* the person experiences a loss of control of emotion and behavior. The experience can include feelings of "not being one's usual self" accompanied by fainting and dizziness.

1999). In some cases, people who exhibit behavior that would fit the definition of a culture-bound syndrome would also qualify for a DSM-IV-TR diagnosis, if they were diagnosed by a clinician trained in the use of that manual. But everyone who displays the culture-bound syndrome would not meet criteria for a DSM-IV-TR disorder, and of those who do, not all would receive the same DSM-IV-TR diagnosis.

The glossary on culture-bound syndromes has been praised as a significant advance toward integrating cultural considerations into the classification system (Lopez & Guarnaccia, 2000). It has also been criticized for its ambiguity. The most difficult conceptual issue involves the boundary between culture-bound syndromes and categories found elsewhere in the diagnostic manual. Some critics have argued that they should be fully integrated, without trying to establish a distinction (Hughes, 1998). Others have noted that if culturally unique disorders must be listed separately from other, "mainstream" conditions, then certain disorders now listed in the main body of the manual—especially eating disorders, such as bulimia—should actually be listed as culture-bound syndromes because they are found primarily among people living in Western or developed cultures (Keel & Klump, 2003). Popular images of women's ideal body shapes clearly play a major role in the etiology and expression of this disorder (see Chapter 10).

Thinking about this issue helps to place the more familiar categories in perspective and shows how our own culture has shaped our views of abnormal behavior. We must not be misled into thinking that culture only shapes conditions that appear to be exotic in faraway lands; culture shapes various facets of all disorders. Though it is imperfect, the glossary of culture-bound syndromes does serve to make clinicians more aware of the extent to which their own views of what is normal and abnormal have been shaped by the values and experiences of their own culture (Mezzich et al., 2001).

EVALUATING CLASSIFICATION SYSTEMS

The *Diagnostic and Statistical Manual* is an evolving document. An enormous effort was devoted to the revision process that resulted in the publication of DSM-IV in 1994. The work extended

RELIABILITY: DO CLINICIANS AGREE?

Several formal procedures have been developed to evaluate diagnostic reliability. Most studies of psychiatric diagnosis in the past 30 years have employed a measure known as **kappa.** Instead of measuring the simple proportion of agreement between clinicians, kappa indicates the proportion of agreement that occurred above and beyond that which would have occurred by chance. Negative values of kappa indicate that the rate of agreement was less than that which would have been expected by chance in this particular sample of people. Thus kappa of zero indicates chance agreement, and a kappa of 1.0 indicates perfect agreement between raters.

How should we interpret the kappa statistic? There is no easy answer to this question (Kirk & Kutchins, 1992). It would be unrealistic to expect perfect consistency, especially in view of the relatively modest reliability of other diagnostic decisions that are made in medical practice (Cameron & McGoogan, 1981; Koran, 1975). On the other hand, it isn't very encouraging simply to find that the level of agreement among clinicians is somewhat better than chance. We expect more than that from a diagnostic system, especially when it is used as a basis for treatment decisions. One convention suggests that kappa values of .70 or higher indicate relatively good agreement. Values of kappa below .40 are often interpreted as indicating poor agreement.

The reliability of many diagnostic categories has improved since the publication of DSM-III, in part, because of more detailed diagnostic criteria for specific disorders. Still, most studies also indicate that there is considerable room for improvement. The reliability of some diagnostic categories remains well below acceptable standards. Consider, for example, evidence from field trials that were conducted by the World Health Organization when ICD-10 was being prepared (Sartorius et al., 1993). Data were collected at more than 100 clinical centers in 39 countries around the world. Each person was interviewed separately by two clinicians who independently arrived at a diagnosis. Kappa values for several of the diagnostic categories are presented in Table 4–3.

The reliability data in Table 4–3 are organized according to major headings (such as anxiety disorders), which are then subdivided into more specific forms (such as obsessive–compulsive disorder). Note that kappa values for major headings are, in most cases, higher than those for specific subtypes. This pattern indicates that clinicians are more likely to agree on the general category into which an individual's problems fall than they are on the specific nature of those problems. To understand this process, imagine that you and a friend try to identify types of automobiles as they pass on the street. You might find it relatively easy to agree that a particular vehicle is a minivan, but you might have more trouble deciding whether it is the specific type of minivan made by Chrysler, Ford, or Toyota.

On the standard of .70 or higher, good agreement was found for many specific categories, especially obsessive–compulsive disorder, bipolar mood disorder, and paranoid schizophrenia. For some other categories, such as phobic disorder and depressive episode, diagnostic reliability was acceptable, while clearly leaving room for improvement. Reliability for generalized anxiety disorder was only fair, and the reliability for diagnosing personality disorders was very low. In the case of schizotypal personality disorder, for example, the kappa coefficient was only .37, a poor level of agreement. This evidence suggests that we should not accept uncritically the assumption that the diagnostic categories in DSM-IV-TR and ICD-10 are always used reliably (Kirk & Kutchins, 1992).

TABLE 4–3	Reliability for Diagnoses of Several Types of Mental Disorder
DISORDER	**KAPPA**
SCHIZOPHRENIC DISORDERS	**.82**
Paranoid schizophrenia	.73
Catatonic schizophrenia	.39
Hebephrenic schizophrenia	.43
ANXIETY DISORDERS	**.74**
Phobic disorder	.63
Obsessive–compulsive disorder	.81
Generalized anxiety disorder	.48
MOOD DISORDERS	**.77**
Manic episode	.69
Depressive episode	.66
Bipolar mood disorder	.81
PERSONALITY DISORDERS	**.47**
Schizotypal*	.37
Histrionic	.12
Dependent	.33
SUBSTANCE USE DISORDERS	**.80**
Alcohol dependence	.70
Opioid dependence	.77

*In ICD-10, schizotypal disorder is grouped with Schizophrenic Disorders rather than with Personality Disorders. We list it here for consistency with DSM-IV.

Source: Based on the World Health Organization's field trial for ICD-10 (see Sartorius et al., 1993).

over more than five years. Final decisions about the manual were made by the task force on DSM-IV, which was composed of 30 distinguished mental health professionals (26 psychiatrists and 4 psychologists). Work groups were appointed to examine each of the major diagnostic categories, such as anxiety disorders, mood disorders, and so on. The work groups made recommendations to the task force on the basis of reviews of the existing literature on the problem, new analyses performed on already collected sets of data, and large-scale, issue-focused field trials. The text revision, DSM-IV-TR, which provides updated presentations

Just as judges sometimes disagree in their assessment of evidence presented during a trial, psychologists and psychiatrists do not always agree on how various disorders should be diagnosed. Of course, both judges and mental health professionals attempt to be reliable (consistent) in their judgments.

What is the difference between reliability and validity?

regarding background information on each specific disorder, was published in 2000.

How can we evaluate a system like DSM-IV-TR? Is it a useful classification system? Utility can be measured in terms of two principal criteria: reliability and validity.

Reliability

Reliability refers to the consistency of measurements, including diagnostic decisions. If a diagnostic category is to be useful, it will have to be used consistently. One important form of reliability, known as inter-rater reliability, refers to agreement among clinicians. Suppose, for example, that two psychologists interview the same patient and that each psychologist independently assigns a diagnosis using DSM-IV-TR. If both psychologists decide that the patient fits the criteria for a major depressive disorder, they have used the definition of that category consistently. Of course, one or two cases would not provide a sufficient test of the reliability of a diagnostic category. The real question is whether the clinicians would agree with each other over a large series of patients. The process of collecting and interpreting information regarding the reliability of diagnosing mental disorders is discussed in Research Methods.

Validity

The ultimate issue in the evaluation of a diagnostic category is whether it is useful. By knowing that a person fits into a particular group or class, do we learn anything meaningful about that person? For example, if a person fits the diagnostic criteria for schizophrenia, is that person likely to improve when he or she is given antipsychotic medication? Or is that person likely to have a less satisfactory level of social adjustment in five years than a person who meets diagnostic criteria for bipolar mood disorder? Does the diagnosis tell us anything about the factors or circumstances that might have contributed to the onset of this problem? These questions are concerned with the validity of the diagnostic category. The term **validity** refers to the meaning or importance of a measurement—in this case, a diagnostic decision (Hempel, 1961; Kendell, 2002). Importance is not an all-or-none phenomenon; it is a quantitative issue. Diagnostic categories are more or less useful, and their validity (or utility) can be determined in several ways.

Validity is, in a sense, an index of the success that has been achieved in understanding the nature of a disorder. Have important facts been discovered? Systematic studies aimed at establishing the validity of a disorder often proceed in a sequence of phases (Robins & Guze, 1989), which are listed in Table 4–4. After a clinical description has been established, diagnostic categories are refined and validated through this process of scientific exploration.

The types of information generated by the research studies listed in Table 4–4 are associated with specific types of validity. It may be helpful to think of these types of validity in terms of their relationship in time with the appearance of symptoms of the disorder. *Etiological validity* is concerned with factors that contribute to the onset of the disorder. These are things that have happened in the past. Was the disorder regularly triggered by a specific set of events or circumstances? Did it run in families? The ultimate question with regard to etiological validity is whether there are any specific causal factors that are regularly, and perhaps uniquely, associated with this disorder. If we know that a person exhibits the symptoms of the disorder, do we in turn learn anything about the circumstances that originally led to the onset of the problem?

Concurrent validity is concerned with the present time and with correlations between the disorder and other symptoms, circumstances, and test procedures. Is the disorder currently associated with any other types of behavior, such as performance on psychological tests? Do precise measures of biological variables, such as brain structure and function, distinguish reliably between people who have the disorder and those who do not? Clinical studies that are aimed at developing a more precise description of a disorder also fall into this type of validity. For example, the data generated in the various DSM-IV-TR field trials contribute to the concurrent validity of the diagnostic categories with which they were concerned.

Predictive validity is concerned with the future and with the stability of the problem over time. Will it be persistent? If it is short lived, how long will an episode last? Will the disorder have a predictable outcome? Do people with this problem typically improve if they are given a specific type of medication or a particular form of psychotherapy? The overall utility or validity of a diagnostic category depends on the body of evidence that accumulates as scientists seek answers to these questions.

The list of categories included in DSM-IV-TR is based heavily on conventional clinical wisdom. Each time the manual is revised, new categories are added and old categories are dropped, presumably because they are not sufficiently useful. Up to the present time, clinicians have been more willing to include new categories than to drop old ones. It is difficult to know when we would decide that a particular diagnostic category is not valid. At what point in the accumulation of knowledge are clinical scientists willing to conclude that a category is of no use and to recommend that the search for more information should be abandoned? This is a difficult question that the authors of DSM-IV-TR have confronted, and it will become increasingly important in the production of future revisions.

Unresolved Questions

Several important issues will have to be addressed as more systematic information is collected about the diagnostic categories in DSM-IV-TR. As we saw in Chapter 1, one fundamental question that applies to every disorder involves the boundary between normal and abnormal behavior. The definitions that are included in the present version of the manual are often vague with regard to this threshold (Widiger & Clark, 2000). Many definitions rely on the requirement that a particular set of symptoms causes

"clinically significant distress or impairment in social or occupational functioning." Unfortunately, these concepts are not defined specifically. Clinicians must rely on their own subjective judgment to decide how distressed or how impaired a person must be by his or her symptoms in order to qualify for a diagnosis. These concepts are not defined in the manual, and measurement tools are not provided.

Cutoff points for the number of features that are required for a diagnosis also affect the boundary between normal and abnormal behavior. The cutoffs listed in DSM-IV-TR were often chosen with little empirical justification. Future research should determine optimal thresholds for each disorder. For example, in the case of schizotypal personality disorder, the present cutoff point is five out of nine features. Perhaps one of the features is unnecessary or redundant. In that case, the list could be shortened to eight criteria. Should one or more of the features be given special weight? Are they all equally important? These questions will have to be answered by investigators who explore the validity of each individual diagnostic category.

Specific time periods are also used in the definition of various disorders. The length of time is often based on a relatively arbitrary choice. For example, in the case of schizophrenia, DSM-IV-TR requires that the person exhibit symptoms for at least six months before the diagnosis can be made. An episode of major depression must last at least two weeks. A panic attack must develop abruptly and reach its peak within 10 minutes. The usefulness of these boundaries for the duration of symptoms and disorders is an important topic for future empirical studies.

TABLE 4–4   Types of Studies Used to Validate Clinical Syndromes
Identification and description of the syndrome, either by clinical intuition or by statistical analyses.
Demonstration of boundaries or "points of rarity" between related syndromes.
Follow-up studies establishing a distinctive course or outcome.
Therapeutic trials establishing a distinctive treatment response.
Family studies establishing that the syndrome "breeds true."
Demonstration of association with some more fundamental abnormality—psychological, biochemical, or molecular.

Source: Adapted from R.E. Kendell, 1989, Clinical validity, *Psychological Medicine, 19,* 47.

Problems and Limitations of the DSM-IV-TR System

Although DSM-IV-TR is a clear improvement over earlier versions of APA's classification system, the manual has been criticized extensively, often with good reason (Houts, 2001). Some clinicians have emphasized conceptual issues. They argue that the syndromes defined in DSM-IV-TR may not represent the most useful ways to think about psychological problems, either in terms of planning current treatments or in terms of designing programs of research. Widespread acceptance of DSM-IV-TR may hinder the consideration of promising alternative classification systems. For example, it might be better to focus on individual symptoms rather than on groups of symptoms.

These critics pose such questions as: Should we design treatments for people who exhibit distorted, negative ways of thinking about themselves, regardless of whether their symptoms happen to involve a mixture of depression, anxiety, or some other pattern of negative emotion or interpersonal conflict? The answer is: We don't know. It would certainly be premature to cut off consideration of these alternatives just because they address problems in a way that deviates from the official diagnostic manual. In our current state of uncertainty, diversity of opinion should be encouraged, particularly if it is grounded in

How could the DSM-IV-TR system be improved?

cautious skepticism and supported by rigorous scientific inquiry (Horwitz, 2002).

From an empirical point of view, DSM-IV-TR is hampered by a number of problems that suggest that it does not classify clinical problems into syndromes in the simplest and most beneficial way (Kendell, 2002; Widiger & Clark, 2000). One of the thorniest issues involves **comorbidity,** which is defined as the simultaneous appearance of two or more disorders in the same person. Comorbidity rates are very high for mental disorders as they are defined in the DSM system. For example, in the National Comorbidity Survey, among those people who qualified for at least one diagnosis at some point during their lifetime, 56 percent met the criteria for two or more disorders (Kessler, 1995). A small subgroup, 14 percent of the sample, actually met the diagnostic criteria for three or more lifetime disorders. That group of people accounted for almost 90 percent of the severe disorders in the study (Figure 4–1).

There are several ways to interpret comorbidity (Krueger, 2002). Some people may independently develop two separate conditions. In other cases, the presence of one disorder may lead to the onset of another. Unsuccessful attempts to struggle with prolonged alcohol dependence, for example, might lead a person to become depressed. Neither of these alternatives creates conceptual problems for DSM-IV-TR. Unfortunately, the very high rate of comorbidity suggests that these explanations account for a small proportion of overlap between categories.

The real problem associated with comorbidity arises when a person with a mixed pattern of symptoms, usually of a severe nature, simultaneously meets the criteria for more than one disorder. Consider, for example, a client who was treated by one of the authors of this text. This man experienced a large number of diffuse problems associated with anxiety, depression, and interpersonal difficulties. According to the DSM-IV-TR system, he would have met the criteria for major depressive disorder, generalized anxiety disorder, and obsessive–compulsive disorder, as well as three types of personality disorder listed on Axis II. It might be said, therefore, that he suffered from at least six types of mental disorder. But is that really helpful? Is it the best way to think about his problems? Would it be more accurate to say that he had a complicated set of interrelated problems that were associated

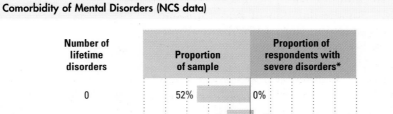

Comorbidity of Mental Disorders (NCS data)

Number of lifetime disorders	Proportion of sample	Proportion of respondents with severe disorders*
0	52%	0%
1	21%	3%
2	13%	8%
3 or more	14%	89%

FIGURE 4–1: Most severe* mental disorders are concentrated in a group of people (about one sixth of the population) who qualify for at least three lifetime disorders.

*"Severe disorders" were defined to include active mania, nonaffective psychosis, or active disorders of other types that either required hospitalization or created severe role impairment.
Source: R.C. Kessler et al., 1994, Lifetime and 12-month prevalence of DSM-III-R psychiatric disorders in the United States: Results from the National Comorbidity Survey, *Archives of General Psychiatry,* 51, 13. Copyright © 1994. Reprinted by permission of the American Medical Association.

with worrying, rumination, and the regulation of high levels of negative emotion, and that these problems constituted one complex and severe type of disorder?

The comorbidity issue is related to another limitation of DSM-IV-TR: the failure to make better use of information regarding the course of mental disorders over time. More than 100 years ago, when schizophrenia and bipolar mood disorder were originally described, the distinction between them was based heavily on observations regarding their long-term course. Unfortunately, most disorders listed in DSM-IV-TR are defined largely in terms of snapshots of symptoms at particular points in time. Diagnostic decisions are seldom based on a comprehensive analysis of the way that a person's problems evolve over time. If someone meets the criteria for more than one disorder, does it matter which one came first? Is there a predictable pattern in which certain disorders follow the onset of others? What is the nature of the connection between childhood disorders and adult problems? Our knowledge of mental disorders would be greatly enriched if greater emphasis were placed on questions regarding life-span development (Buka & Gilman, 2002).

All of these issues must be faced by clinicians when they use the DSM-IV-TR system. Attempts to provide solutions to these problems and limitations will ensure that the classification system will continue to be revised. As before, these changes will be driven by the interaction of clinical experience and empirical evidence.

BASIC ISSUES IN ASSESSMENT

Up to this point, we have discussed the development and use of classification systems. But we haven't talked about the way in which a psychologist might collect the information that is necessary to arrive at a diagnostic decision. Furthermore, we have looked at the problem only in relatively general terms. The diagnostic decision is one useful piece of information. It is not, however, a systematic picture of the specific person's situation. It is only a starting point. In the following section we extend our discussion to consider methods of collecting information. In so doing, we discuss a broad range of data that may be useful in understanding psychopathological behavior.

Purposes of Clinical Assessment

To appreciate the importance and complexity of assessment procedures, let's go back to the example of Michael. When Michael and his parents initially approached the psychologist, they were clearly upset. But the nature of the problem, in terms of Michael's behavior and the family as a whole, was not clearly defined. Before he could attempt to help this family, the psychologist had to collect more information. He needed to know more about the range and frequency of Michael's obsessions and compulsions, including when they began, how often he experienced these problems, and the factors that made them better or worse. He also needed to know whether there were other problems, such as depression or delusional beliefs, that might either explain these responses or interfere with their treatment. In addition, he had to learn how Michael got along with classmates, how he was doing in school, and how his parents responded when he behaved strangely. Was his behavior, at least in part, a response to environmental circumstances? How would the family support (or interfere with) the therapist's attempts to help him change? The psychologist needed to address Michael's current situation in terms of several different facets of his behavior.

Psychological assessment is the process of collecting and interpreting information that will be used to understand another person. Numerous data-gathering techniques can be used in this process. Several of these procedures are described in the following pages. We must remember, however, not to confuse the process of assessment with this list of techniques. Assessment procedures are tools that can be used in many ways. They cannot be used in an intellectual vacuum. Interviews can be used to collect all sorts of information for all sorts of reasons. Psychological tests can be interpreted in many different ways. The value of assessment procedures can be determined only in the context of a specific purpose.

Three primary goals guide most assessment procedures: making predictions, planning treatments, and evaluating treatments. The practical importance of predictions should be obvious: Many crucial decisions are based on psychologists' attempts to determine the probability of future events. Will a person engage in violent behavior? Can a person make rational decisions? Is a parent able to care for his or her children?

Assessment is also commonly used to evaluate the likelihood that a particular form of treatment will be helpful for a specific patient and to provide guideposts by which the effectiveness of treatment programs can be measured (Hayes, Nelson, & Jarrett, 1987). Different assessment procedures are likely to be employed for different purposes. Those that are useful in one situation may not be helpful in another.

Assumptions About Consistency of Behavior

Assessment involves the collection of specific samples of a person's behavior. These samples may include things that the person says during an interview, responses that the person makes on a psychological test, or things that the person does while being observed. None of these would be important if we assumed that they were isolated events. They are useful to the extent that they represent examples of the ways in which the person will feel or behave in other situations. Psychologists, therefore, must be concerned about the consistency of behavior across time and situations. They want to know if they can *generalize*, or draw inferences about the person's behavior in the natural environment on the basis of the samples of behavior that are obtained in their assessment. If the client is depressed at this moment, how did she feel one week ago, and how will she feel tomorrow? In other words, is this a persistent phenomenon, or is it a temporary state? If a child is anxious and unable to pay attention in the psychologist's office, will he also

exhibit these problems in his classroom? And how will he behave on the playground?

Psychologists typically seek out more than one source of information when conducting a formal assessment. Because we are trying to compose a broad, integrated picture of the person's adjustment, we must collect information from several sources and then attempt to integrate these data. Each piece of information may be considered to be one sample of the person's behavior. One way of evaluating the possible meaning or importance of this information is to consider the consistency across sources. Do the conclusions drawn on the basis of a diagnostic interview agree with those that are suggested by a psychological test? Do the psychologist's observations of the client's behavior and the client's self-report agree with observations that are reported by parents or teachers?

Evaluating the Usefulness of Assessment Procedures

The same criteria that are used to evaluate diagnostic categories are used to evaluate the usefulness of assessment procedures: reliability and validity. We have already discussed inter-rater reliability with regard to diagnostic decisions. In the case of assessment procedures, reliability can refer to various types of consistency. For example, the consistency of measurements over time is known as test–retest reliability. Will a person receive the same score if an assessment procedure is repeated at two different points in time? The internal consistency of items within a test is known as split-half reliability. If a test with many items measures a specific trait or ability, and if the items are divided in half, will the person's scores on the two halves agree with each other? Assessment procedures must be reliable if they are to be useful in either clinical practice or research.

The validity of an assessment procedure refers to its meaning or importance (Foster & Cone, 1995). Is the person's score on this test or procedure actually a reflection of the trait or ability that the test was designed to measure? And does the score tell us anything useful about the person's behavior in other situations? Knowing that the person has achieved a particular score on this evaluation, can we make meaningful predictions about the person's responses to other tests, or about his or her

Diagnostic interviews provide an opportunity to make detailed inquiries about a person's subjective experience while also observing his or her behavior.

Every assessment device has its own strengths and weaknesses. Each presents a somewhat different perspective on the person.

behavior in future situations? These are all questions about the validity of an assessment procedure. In general, the more consistent the information provided by different assessment procedures, the more valid each procedure is considered to be (see Critical Thinking *Matters*).

Cultural differences present an important challenge to the validity of assessment procedures. It is often difficult to understand the thoughts and behaviors of people from a cultural background that is different from our own. Measurement procedures that were constructed for one group may be misleading when they are applied to people from another culture. Language, religion, gender roles, beliefs about health and illness, and attitudes toward the family can all have an important impact on the ways in which psychological problems are experienced and expressed. These factors must be taken into consideration when psychologists collect information about the nature of a specific person's problems. Interviews, observational procedures, and personality tests must be carefully evaluated for cross-cultural validity (Padilla, 2001; Thomas, Turkheimer, & Oltmanns, 2000). Unfortunately,

this issue has often been overlooked in treatment planning and in psychopathology research. We should not assume that a questionnaire developed in one culture will necessarily be useful in another. Investigators must demonstrate empirically that it measures the same thing in both groups.

TYPES OF ASSESSMENT PROCEDURES

An enormous array of assessment tools is available to clinicians who are interested in treating or studying abnormal behavior. Many of these procedures are commonly employed in clinical practice, and they are also used in the process of research. The most useful assessment procedures are likely to vary from one problem to the next. Assessment procedures that are useful in evaluating the effectiveness of a drug treatment program for hospitalized depressed patients may be quite different from those used to predict the need for medication among hyperactive schoolchildren. Our purpose in the rest of this

SHOULD WE ALWAYS TRUST CLINICAL JUDGMENTS?

Lots of people believe that psychologists can read minds. Unfortunately, assessment procedures used by psychologists do not provide a magic window into the psyche. Many procedures have been developed to collect information about human behavior and clinical problems. Each has its own strengths and weaknesses. None is infallible.

If psychologists do make errors, why do people often accept the results of their assessments uncritically? In a classic essay, Paul Meehl (1973) described a problem that he called the *Barnum Effect,* after P.T. Barnum, the brilliant and shameless promoter who founded the circus called "The Greatest Show on Earth." The Barnum Effect refers to the practice of saying things about a specific person that are true of virtually all people. For example, imagine that the psychologist working with Michael had conducted a formal psychological assessment and concluded that Michael had ambivalent feelings about his parents, that he was sometimes lacking in self-confidence, or that his expectations were sometimes unrealistic. People often accept such vague or superficial statements as being meaningful comments about themselves, failing to understand that vague generalizations like these apply to almost everyone. Clearly psychological assessment

should be held to a higher standard. Diagnostic decisions and clinical judgments should contain meaningful, specific information.

What can we do to improve the validity of psychological assessments? One important step is to recognize their fallibility. Like everyone else, clinical psychologists are prone to a variety of cognitive biases and errors in decision making (Garb, 1998; Westen & Weinberger, 2004). Under conditions of uncertainty, they use mental short cuts to make clinical judgments. For example, they pay too much attention to information that confirms their initial impressions, and they tend to ignore information that is inconsistent with these impressions. They can be unduly influenced by vivid, individual cases that come readily to mind and sometimes fail to consider more important evidence based on data from large samples. The impact of these cognitive biases might be minimized if clinicians would deliberately consider alternative hypotheses (such as a diagnosis other than their first impression) and then consider evidence that would either support or disconfirm that possibility.

If you think about it for a moment, you probably will realize that these are common errors in human thinking, not just in assessments made by psychologists. As you study abnormal

psychology, you probably pay more attention to information that is consistent with your own ideas and are overly influenced by dramatic case studies. Critical thinking—careful, objective reasoning and evaluation—is the best safeguard against these tendencies for you and for professional psychologists.

Paul Meehl, Regents Professor Emeritus of Psychology at the University of Minnesota, is the only clinical psychologist ever elected to the National Academy of Science. His theory of schizophrenia has guided research efforts to discover signs of vulnerability to the disorder.

---

chapter is to outline a range of assessment procedures. This is a selective sampling of measures rather than an exhaustive review of assessment procedures.

We begin our discussion with measures that are typically concerned with psychological variables—characteristic traits and behaviors that are associated with abnormal behavior. From there, we move to a consideration of the assessment of social systems, such as families and institutional environments (schools and hospitals). The last section of this chapter is concerned with measures used in biological systems—the neurological and biochemical events that are associated with mental disorders. In many cases, the assessment of psychopathology is based on the combined use of measures that cover selective aspects of all of these systems.

At the end of each section is a quick summary of the advantages and limitations of each type of procedure. These summaries are intended only as general guides and not as definitive critiques. Please keep in mind our earlier comment: Each procedure is a tool that can be used for different purposes. The true value of the tool can be determined only in light of the specific purpose for which it is used.

ASSESSING PSYCHOLOGICAL SYSTEMS

"Person variables" are typically the first things that come to mind when we think about the assessment of psychopathology. What did the person do or say? How does the person feel about his or her current situation? What skills and abilities does the person possess, and are there any important cognitive or social deficits that should be taken into consideration? These questions about the individual person can be addressed through a number of procedures, including interviews, observations, and various types of self-report instruments and psychological tests.

Interviews

Often, the best way to find out about someone is to talk with that person directly. The clinical interview is the most commonly used procedure in psychological assessment. Most of the categories that are defined in DSM-IV-TR are based on information that can be collected in an interview. These data are typically supplemented by information that is obtained from official records (previous hospital admissions, school reports, court files) and interviews with other informants (for example, family members), but the clients' own direct descriptions of their problems are the primary basis for diagnostic decisions. Except for mental retardation, none of the diagnostic categories in DSM-IV-TR is defined in terms of psychological or biological tests.

Interviews provide an opportunity to ask people for their own descriptions of their problems. Many of the symptoms of psychopathology are subjective, and an interview can provide a detailed analysis of these problems. Consider, for example, Michael's problems with anxiety. The unrelenting fear and revulsion that he experienced at school were the central feature of his problem. His obsessive thoughts of contamination were private events that could only be known to the psychologist on the basis of Michael's self-report, which was quite compelling. His family could observe Michael's peculiar habits with regard to arranging his schoolbooks, changing his clothes, and washing his hands, but the significance of these behaviors to Michael was not immediately apparent without the knowledge that they were based on an attempt to control or neutralize his anxiety-provoking images of taunting classmates.

Interviews also allow clinicians to observe important features of a person's appearance and nonverbal behavior. In Michael's case, the psychologist noticed during the initial interview that the skin on Michael's hands and lower arms was red and chafed from excessive scrubbing. He was neatly dressed but seemed especially self-conscious about his hair and glasses, which he adjusted repeatedly. Michael was reluctant to make eye contact, and his speech was soft and hesitant. His obvious discomfort in this social situation was consistent with his own descriptions of the anxiety that he felt during interactions with peers. It was also interesting to note that Michael became visibly agitated when discussing particular subjects, such as the incident with his track team. At these points in the interview, he would fidget restlessly in his seat and clasp his arms closely around his sides. His speech became more rapid, and he began to stutter a bit. On one occasion, he found it impossible to sit still, and he began to pace quickly back and forth across the psychologist's office. These nonverbal aspects of Michael's behavior provided useful information about the nature of his distress.

Structured Interviews   Assessment interviews vary with regard to the amount of structure that is imposed by the clinician. Some are relatively open ended, or nondirective. In this type of interview, the clinician follows the train of thought supplied by the client. One goal of nondirective interviews is to help people clarify their subjective feelings and to provide general empathic support for whatever they may decide to do about their problems. In contrast to this open-ended style, some interviews follow a more specific question-and-answer format. Structured interviews, in which the clinician must ask each patient a specific list of detailed questions, are frequently employed for collecting information that will be used to make diagnostic decisions and to rate the extent to which a person is impaired by psychopathology.

Several different structured interviews have been developed for the purpose of making psychiatric diagnoses in large-scale epidemiological and cross-national studies (Segal, 1997). Investigators reasoned that the reliability of their

Video Case

DEPRESSION/DELIBERATE SELF HARM

SARAH

"I would be asked later 'well how did these cuts get here' and I would know that I had done it, but I wouldn't remember how I had done it or with what."

On your CD-ROM menu, select "Mood Disorders" and click on "Depression/ Deliberate Self Harm: Sarah." Notice how the interviewer uses a flexible sequence of questions to elicit a compelling description of the subjective experiences associated with Sarah's cutting behavior.

TABLE 4–5   Sample Items from the Structured Interview for DSM-IV Personality (SIDP-IV)

CLOSE RELATIONSHIPS

This part of the interview asks about your relationships with friends and family. Remember that I'm interested in the way you are when you are your usual self.

1. Criterion: Neither desires nor enjoys close relationships, including being part of a family
   "Do you have close relationships with friends or family?"
   (IF YES): "What do you enjoy about these relationships?"
   (IF NO): "Do you wish you had some close relationships?"

2. Criterion: Lacks close friends or confidants other than first-degree relatives
   "Not counting your immediate family, do you have close friends you can confide in?"

PERCEPTION OF OTHERS

The questions in this section ask about experiences you may have had with other people. Remember that I'm interested in knowing how you feel about these situations when you are your usual self, not during an episode of illness or hospitalization.

1. Criterion: Suspects, without sufficient basis, that others are exploiting, harming, or deceiving him or her
   "Have you had experiences where people who pretended to be your friends took advantage of you?"
   (IF YES): "What happened?"
   "How often has this happened?"
   "Are you good at spotting someone who is trying to deceive or con you?"
   (IF YES): "Examples?"

2. Criterion: Ideas of reference (excluding delusions of reference)
   "Have you ever found that people around you seem to be talking in general, but then you realize their comments are really meant for you?"
   (IF YES): "How do you know they're talking about you?"
   "Have you felt like someone in charge changed the rules specifically because of you, but they wouldn't admit it?"
   "Do you sometimes feel like strangers on the street are looking at you and talking about you?"
   (IF YES): "Why do you think they notice you in particular?"

Source: Reprinted with permission from the *Diagnostic and Statistical Manual of Mental Disorders,* Fourth Edition, Text Revision. Copyright © 2000 by the American Psychiatric Association..

diagnostic decisions would improve if they could ensure that clinicians always made a consistent effort to ask the same questions when they interviewed patients. Other forms of structured diagnostic interviews have been designed for use in the diagnosis of specific types of problems, such as personality disorders, anxiety disorders, dissociative disorders, and the behavior problems of children.

Structured interviews list a series of specific questions that lead to a detailed description of the person's behavior and experiences. As an example, consider the Structured Interview for DSM-IV-TR Personality Disorders (SIDP-IV; Pfohl, Blum, & Zimmerman, 1995), which could have been used as part of the assessment process in Michael's situation. The SIDP is a widely adopted semistructured interview that covers all of the DSM-IV-TR personality disorder

categories. Selected questions from the SIDP-IV are presented in Table 4–5. We have included in this table several of the questions that are specifically relevant to a diagnosis of schizotypal personality disorder.

Structured interview schedules provide a systematic framework for the collection of important diagnostic information, but they don't eliminate the need for an experienced clinician. If the interviewer is not able to establish a comfortable rapport with the client, then the interview might not elicit useful information. Furthermore, it is difficult to specify in advance all the questions that should be asked in a diagnostic interview. The client's responses to questions may require clarification. The interviewer must determine when it is necessary to probe further and in what ways to probe. Having lists of specific questions and clear definitions of diagnostic criteria will make the clinician's job easier, but clinical judgment remains an important ingredient in the diagnostic interview.

Advantages: The clinical interview is the primary tool employed by clinical psychologists in the assessment of psychopathology. Several features of interviews account for this popularity, including the following issues:

1. The interviewer can control the interaction and can probe further when necessary.
2. By observing the patient's nonverbal behavior, the interviewer can try to detect areas of resistance. In that sense, the validity of the information may be enhanced.
3. An interview can provide a lot of information in a short period of time. It can cover past events and many different settings.

Limitations: Several limitations in the use of clinical interviews as part of the assessment process must be kept in mind. These include the following considerations:

1. Some patients may be unable or unwilling to provide a rational account of their problems. This may be particularly true of young children, who have not developed verbal skills, as well as some psychotic and demented patients who are unable to speak coherently.
2. People may be reluctant to admit experiences that are embarrassing or frightening. They may feel that they should report to the interviewer only those feelings and behaviors that are socially desirable. Negative stereotypes about people with mental disorders interfere with an open and honest discussion of a person's problems.
3. Subjective factors play an important role in the interpretation of information provided in an interview. The person's responses to questions are not scored objectively, and there is always some variation in the format. The situation is not entirely structured and depends heavily on the training and experience of the interviewer.
4. Information provided by the client is necessarily filtered through the client's eyes. It is a subjective account and may be influenced or distorted by errors in memory and by selective perception.
5. Interviewers can influence their clients' accounts by the ways in which they phrase their questions and respond to the clients' responses.

Observational Procedures

In addition to the information that we gain from what people are willing to tell us during interviews, we can also learn a lot by watching their behavior. Observational skills play an important part in most assessment procedures. Sometimes the things that we observe confirm the person's self-report, and at other times the person's overt behavior appears to be at odds with what he or she says. A juvenile delinquent might express in words his regret at having injured a classmate, but his smile and the twinkle in his eye may raise doubts about the sincerity of his statement. In situations such as this, we must reconcile information that is obtained from different sources. The picture that emerges of another person's adjustment is greatly enriched when data collected from interviews are supplemented by observations of the person's behavior.

Observational procedures may be either informal or formal. Informal observations are primarily qualitative. The clinician observes the person's behavior and the environment in which it occurs without attempting to record the frequency or intensity of specific responses. Michael's case illustrates the value of informal observations in the natural environment. When

Why do clinical interviews sometimes provide limited or distorted results?

Direct observation can provide one of the most useful sources of information about a person's behavior. In this case, the children and their teacher are being observed from behind a one-way mirror in order to minimize reactivity, the effect that the observer's presence might have on their behavior.

the therapist visited Michael and his parents at their home, he learned that his ritualistic behaviors were more extreme than Michael had originally described. This was useful but not particularly surprising, as patients with OCD are often reluctant to describe in an interview the full extent of their compulsive behavior. The therapist also learned that the parents themselves were quite concerned with rules and order. Everything in their home was highly polished and in its place. This observation helped the therapist understand the extent to which Michael's parents might contribute to, or reinforce, his rigid adherence to a strict set of rules.

Although observations are often conducted in the natural environment, there are times when it is useful to observe the person's behavior in a situation that the psychologist can arrange and control. Sometimes it isn't possible to observe the person's behavior in the natural environment because the behavior in question occurs infrequently or at times when an observer cannot be present; at other times the environment is inaccessible; and sometimes the behavior that is of interest is inherently a private act. In these cases, the psychologist may arrange to observe the person's behavior in a situation that in some ways approximates the real environment. These artificial situations may also allow for more careful measurements of the person's problem than could be accomplished in a more complex situation.

In the case of obsessive—compulsive behavior, this approach might involve asking the person deliberately to touch an object that would ordinarily trigger ritualistic behaviors. The therapist might collect a set of objects that Michael would not want to touch, such as a school book, a pair of old track shorts, and the knob of a door leading to the laundry room. It would be useful to know specifically which objects he would touch, the degree of discomfort that he experienced when touching them, and the length of time that he was able to wait before washing his hands after touching these objects. This information could also be used as an index of change as treatment progressed.

Rating Scales Various types of procedures can be used to provide quantitative assessments of a person's behavior that are based on observations. One alternative is to use a **rating scale** in which the observer is asked to make judgments that place the person somewhere along a dimension.

For example, a clinician might observe a person's behavior for an extended period of time and then complete a set of ratings that are concerned with dimensions such as the extent to which the person exhibits compulsive ritualistic behaviors.

Ratings can also be made on the basis of information collected during an interview. The Yale-Brown Obsessive Compulsive Scale (Y-BOCS; Goodman et al., 1989; Woody, Steketee, & Chambless, 1995) is an example of an interview-based rating scale that is used extensively in the evaluation of people with problems like Michael's. Examples of items from the Y-BOCS are presented in Table 4–6. For each topic or set of questions, the interviewer is required to make a rating from 0 to 4, indicating the person's level of distress or impairment. The composite rating—the total across all the items in the scale—can be used as an index of the severity of the disorder.

Rating scales provide abstract descriptions of a person's behavior rather than a specific record of exactly what the person has done. They require social judgments on the part of the observer, who must compare this person's behavior with an ideal view of other people (Cairns & Green, 1979). How does this person compare to someone who has never experienced any difficulties in this particular area? How does the person compare to the most severely disturbed patients? The value of these judgments depends on the experience of the person who makes the ratings. They are useful to the extent that the observer is able to synthesize accurately the information that has been collected and then rate the frequency or severity of the problem relative to the behavior of other people.

Behavioral Coding Systems Another approach to quantifying observational data depends on recording the person's actual activities. Rather than making judgments about where the person falls on a particular dimension, **behavioral coding systems** focus on the frequency of specific behavioral events (Foster & Cone, 1986). This type of observation, therefore, requires fewer inferences on the part of the observer. Coding systems can be used with observations that are made in the person's natural environment as well as with those that are performed in artificial, or contrived, situations that are specifically designed to elicit the problem behavior under circumstances in which it can be observed precisely. In some cases, the observations are made directly by a therapist, and at other times the information is provided by people who have a better opportunity to see the person's behavior in the natural environment, including teachers, parents, spouse, and peers.

Some approaches to systematic observation can be relatively simple. Consider, once again, the case of Michael. After the psychologist had conducted several interviews with Michael and his family, he asked Michael's mother to participate in the assessment process by making detailed observations of his hand-washing over a period of several nights. The mother was given a set of forms—one for each day—that could be used to record each incident, the time at which it occurred, and the circumstances that preceded the washing. The day was divided into 30-minute intervals starting at 6:30 A.M., when Michael got out of bed, and ending at 10:30 P.M., when he usually went to sleep. On each line (one for each time interval), his mother indicated whether he had washed his hands, what had been going on just prior to washing, and how anxious (on a scale from 1 to 100) Michael felt at the time that he washed.

Some adult clients are able to complete this kind of record by keeping track of their own behavior—a procedure known as *self-monitoring*. In this case, Michael's mother was asked to help because she was considered a more accurate observer than Michael and because Michael did not want to touch the form that would be used to record these observations. He believed that it was contaminated because it had touched his school clothes, which he wore to the therapy session.

Two weeks of observations were examined prior to the start of Michael's treatment. They indicated several things, including the times of the day when Michael was most active with his washing rituals (between 6 and 9 P.M.) and those specific objects and areas in the house that were most likely to trigger a washing incident. This information helped the therapist to plan the treatment procedure, which would depend on approaching Michael's problem at the level that could most easily be handled and moving toward those situations that were the most difficult for him. The observations provided by Michael's mother were also used to mark his progress after treatment began.

Advantages: Observational measures, including rating scales and more detailed behavioral coding systems, can provide an extremely useful supplement to information that is typically collected in an interview format. Their advantage lies

TABLE 4–6   Sample Items from the Yale-Brown Obsessive–Compulsive Scale

TIME OCCUPIED BY OBSESSIVE THOUGHTS

How much of your time is occupied by obsessive thoughts?

0	None
1	Mild, less than 1 hour per day
2	Moderate, 1 to 3 hours per day
3	Severe, greater than 3 and up to 8 hours per day
4	Extreme, greater than 8 hours per day

INTERFERENCE DUE TO OBSESSIVE THOUGHTS

How much do your obsessive thoughts interfere with your social or work (or role) functioning? Is there anything that you don't do because of them?

0	None
1	Mild, slight interference, but overall performance not impaired
2	Moderate, definite interference, but still manageable
3	Severe, causes substantial impairment
4	Extreme, incapacitating

DISTRESS ASSOCIATED WITH OBSESSIVE THOUGHTS

How much distress do your obsessive thoughts cause you?

0	None
1	Mild, not too disturbing
2	Moderate, disturbing, but still manageable
3	Severe, very disturbing
4	Extreme, near constant and disabling distress

RESISTANCE AGAINST OBSESSIONS

How much of an effort do you make to resist the obsessive thoughts? How often do you try to disregard or turn your attention away from these thoughts as they enter your mind?

0	None
1	Mild, not too disturbing
2	Moderate, disturbing, but still manageable
3	Severe, very disturbing
4	Extreme, near constant and disabling distress

primarily in the fact that they can provide a more direct source of information than interviews can, because clinicians observe behavior directly rather than relying on patients' self-reports (Foster & Cone, 1986; Gottman, 1985). Specific types of observational measures have distinct advantages:

1. Rating scales are primarily useful as an over-all index of symptom severity or functional impairment.
2. Behavioral coding systems provide detailed information about the person's behavior in a particular situation.

Limitations: Observations are sometimes considered to be similar to photographs: They provide a more direct or realistic view of behavior than do people's recollections of their actions and feelings. But just as the quality of a photograph is influenced by the quality of the camera, the film, and the process that is used to develop it, the value of observational data depends on the procedures that are used to collect them (Nietzel, Bernstein, & Milich, 1994). Thus, observations have a number of limitations:

1. Observational procedures can be time-con-suming and therefore expensive. Raters usu-ally require extensive training before they can use a detailed behavioral coding system.
2. Observers can make errors. Their perception may be biased, just as the inferences of an interviewer may be biased. The reliability of ratings as well as behavioral coding must be monitored.
3. People may alter their behavior, either intentionally or unintentionally, when they know that they are being observed—a phenomenon known as **reactivity.** For example, a person who is asked to count the number of times that he washes his hands may wash less frequently than he does when he is not keeping track.
4. Observational measures tell us only about the particular situation that was selected to be observed. We don't know if the person will behave in a similar way elsewhere or at a different time, unless we extend the scope of our observations.
5. There are some aspects of psychopathology that cannot be observed by anyone other than the person who has the problem. This is especially true for subjective experiences, such as guilt or low self-esteem.

Personality Tests and Self-Report Inventories

Personality tests are another important source of information about an individual's adjustment. Tests provide an opportunity to collect samples of a person's behavior in a standardized situation. These samples of behavior presumably reflect underlying abilities or personality traits. In any psychological test, the person who is being tested is presented with some kind of standard stimuli. The stimuli may be specific questions that can be answered true or false. They might be problems that require solutions, or they can be completely ambiguous inkblots. Exactly the same stimuli are used every time that the test is given. In that way, the clinician can be sure that differences in performance can be interpreted as differences in abilities or traits rather than differences in the testing situation.

Personality Inventories Because of their structure, **personality inventories** are sometimes referred to as "objective tests." They consist of a series of straightforward statements; the person being tested is typically required to indicate whether each statement is true or false in relation to himself or herself. Several types of personality inventories are widely used. Some are designed to identify personality traits in a normal population, and others focus more specifically on psychological problems. We have chosen to focus on the most extensively used personality inventory—the Minnesota Multiphasic Personality Inventory (MMPI)—to illustrate the characteristics of these tests as assessment devices.

The original version of the MMPI was developed in the 1940s at the University of Minnesota by Starke Hathaway (1903–1984) and his colleagues. For the past 40 years, it has been the most widely used psychological test. Thousands of research articles have been published on the MMPI (Archer, 1992). The inventory was revised several years ago, and it is currently known as the MMPI-2 (Butcher, 2000; Greene, 2000).

The MMPI-2 is based on a series of more than 500 statements that cover topics ranging from physical complaints and psychological states to occupational preferences and social attitudes. Examples are statements such as, "I sometimes keep on at a thing until others lose their patience with me"; "My feelings are easily hurt"; and "There are persons who are trying to steal my thoughts and ideas." After reading each statement, the person is instructed to indicate whether it is true or false. Scoring of the MMPI-2 is objective. After the responses to all questions are totaled, the person receives a numerical score on each of 10 clinical scales as well as four validity scales.

Starke Hathaway, professor of psychology at the University of Minnesota, created the Minnesota Multiphasic Personality Inventory (MMPI), which has become the most widely employed objective test of personality.

TABLE 4–7   Clinical Scales for the MMPI

SCALE NUMBER	SCALE NAME	INTERPRETATION OF HIGH SCORES
1	Hypochondriasis	Excessive bodily concern; somatic symptoms
2	Depression	Depressed; pessimistic; irritable; demanding
3	Hysteria	Physical symptoms of functional origin; self-centered; demands attention
4	Psychopathic Deviate	Asocial or antisocial; rebellious; impulsive, poor judgment
5	Masculinity–Femininity	Male: aesthetic interests Female: assertive; competitive; self-confident
6	Paranoia	Suspicious, sensitive; resentful; rigid; may be frankly psychotic
7	Psychasthenia	Anxious; worried; obsessive; lacks self-confidence; problems in decision making
8	Schizophrenia	May have thinking disturbance, withdrawn; feels alienated and unaccepted
9	Hypomania	Excessive activity; lacks direction; low frustration tolerance; friendly
0	Social-Introversion	Socially introverted; shy; sensitive; overcontrolled; conforming

Before considering the possible clinical significance of a person's MMPI-2 profile, the psychologist will examine a number of validity scales, which reflect the patient's attitude toward the test and the openness and consistency with which the questions were answered. The L (Lie) Scale is sensitive to unsophisticated attempts to avoid answering in a frank and honest manner. For example, one statement on this scale says, "At times I feel like swearing." Although this is perhaps not an admirable trait, virtually all normal subjects indicate that the item is true. Subjects who indicate that the item is false (does not apply to them) receive 1 point on the L scale. Several responses of this sort would result in an elevated score on the scale and would indicate that the person's overall test results should not be interpreted as a true reflection of his or her feelings. Other validity scales reflect tendencies to exaggerate problems, carelessness in completing the questions, and unusual defensiveness.

If the profile is considered valid, the process of interpretation will be directed toward the 10 clinical scales, which are described in Table 4–7. Some of these scales carry rather obvious meaning, whereas others are associated with a more general or mixed pattern of symptoms. For example, Scale 2 (Depression) is a relatively straightforward index of degree of depression. Scale 7 (Psychasthenia), in contrast, is more complex and is based on items that measure

anxiety, insecurity, and excessive doubt. There are many different ways to obtain an elevated score on any of the clinical scales, because each scale is composed of many items. Even the more obvious scales can indicate several different types of problems. Therefore, the pattern of scale scores is more important than the elevation of any particular scale.

Rather than depending only on their own experience and clinical judgment, which may be subject to various sorts of bias and inconsistency, many clinicians analyze the results of a specific test on the basis of an explicit set of rules that are derived from empirical research (Greene, 2000). This is known as an **actuarial interpretation.** We can illustrate this process using Michael's profile. The profile is first described in terms of the pattern of scale scores, beginning with the highest and proceeding to the lowest. Those that are elevated above a scale score of 70 are most important, and interpretations are sometimes based on the "high-point pair." Following this procedure, Michael's profile could be coded as a 2–0; that is, his highest scores were on Scales 2 and 0. The clinician then looks up this specific configuration of scores in a kind of MMPI-2 "cookbook" to see what sort of descriptive characteristics apply. One cookbook offers the following statement about adolescents (mostly 14 and 15 years old) who fit the 2–0/0–2 code type:

Eighty-seven percent of the 2–0/0–2s express feelings of inferiority to their therapists. They say that they are not good-looking, that they are afraid to speak up in class, and that they feel awkward when they meet people or try to make a date (91 percent of high 2–0/0–2s). Their therapists see the 2–0/0–2s as anxious, fearful, timid, withdrawn, and inhibited. They are depressed, and very vulnerable to threat. The 2–0/0–2 adolescents are overcontrolled; they cannot let go, even when it would be appropriate for them to do so. They are afraid of emotional involvement with others and, in fact, seem to have little need for such affiliation. These adolescents are viewed by their psychotherapists as schizoid; they think and associate in unusual ways and spend a good deal of time in personal fantasy and daydreaming. They are serious young people who tend to anticipate problems and difficulties. Indeed, they are prone toward obsessional thinking and are compulsively meticulous. (Marks, Seeman, & Haller, 1974, p. 201)

Several comments must be made about this statement. First, nothing is certain. Actuarial descriptions are probability statements. They indicate that a certain proportion of the people who produce this pattern of scores will be associated with a certain characteristic or behavior. If 87 percent of the adolescents who produce this code type express feelings of inferiority, 13 percent do not. Many aspects of this description apply to Michael's current adjustment, but they don't all fit. The MMPI must be used in conjunction with other assessment procedures. The accuracy of actuarial statements can be verified through interviews with the person or through direct observations of his or her behavior.

What can a psychological test tell you that an interview cannot?

Advantages: The MMPI-2 has several advantages in comparison to interviews and observational procedures. In clinical practice, it is seldom used by itself, but, for the following reasons, it can serve as a useful supplement to other methods of collecting information.

1. The MMPI-2 provides information about the person's test-taking attitude, which alerts the clinician to the possibility that clients are careless, defensive, or exaggerating their problems.
2. The MMPI-2 covers a wide range of problems in a direct and efficient manner. It would take a clinician several hours to go over all of these topics using an interview format.

3. Because the MMPI-2 is scored objectively, the initial description of the person's adjustment is not influenced by the clinician's subjective impression of the client.
4. The MMPI-2 can be interpreted in an actuarial fashion, using extensive banks of information regarding people who respond to items in a particular way.

Limitations: The MMPI-2 also has a number of limitations. Some of its problems derive from the fact that it has been used for many years. When the MMPI-2 was developed in the late 1980s, its authors decided to maintain the same clinical scales (see Table 4–7). New standardization data were obtained, and some old-fashioned items were replaced, but the underlying structure of the MMPI-2 is still based on diagnostic concepts and dimensions of psychopathology that were used 40 years ago (Helmes & Reddon, 1993). More specific limitations of the MMPI-2 are listed below.

1. The test is not particularly sensitive to certain forms of psychopathology, especially those that have been added with the publication of DSM-III and DSM-IV-TR. These include certain types of anxiety disorders, personality disorders, and subtypes of mood disorders.
2. The test depends on the person's ability to read and respond to written statements. Some people cannot complete the rather extensive list of questions. These include many people who are acutely psychotic, intellectually impaired, or poorly educated.
3. Specific data are not always available for a particular profile. Many patients' test results do not meet criteria for a particular code type with which extensive data are associated. Therefore, actuarial interpretation is not really possible for these profiles.
4. Some studies have found that profile types are not stable over time. It is not clear whether this instability should be interpreted as lack of reliability or as sensitivity to change in the person's level of adjustment.

Other Self-Report Inventories   Sophisticated personality inventories like the MMPI-2 are not the only approach to the measurement of subjective psychological states. Many other questionnaires and checklists have been developed to collect information about adjustment problems, including subjective mood states such as depression and anxiety, patterns of obsessive thinking, and attitudes about drinking alcohol, eating, and sexual behavior. One example is the Beck Depression Inventory (BDI), which is used extensively in both clinical and research settings as an index of severity of depression.

The format of most self-report inventories is similar to that employed with objective personality tests like the MMPI-2. The primary difference is the range of topics covered by the instrument. Tests like the MMPI-2 are designed to measure several dimensions that are related to abnormal behavior, whereas a self-report inventory is aimed more specifically at a focal topic or at one aspect of the person's adjustment. Self-report inventories usually don't include validity scales, and they may not be standardized on large samples of normal subjects prior to their use in a clinical setting.

Self-report inventories offer many advantages as supplements to information that is collected during clinical interviews. They are an extremely efficient way to gather specific data regarding a wide range of topics. They can also be scored objectively and, therefore, provide a specific index that is frequently useful in measuring change from one period of time to the next—for example, before and after treatment.

Despite their many advantages, self-report inventories can lead to serious problems if they are used carelessly. The BDI, for example, was designed as an index of change. It can help clinicians identify a change in severity of a person's depression from one point in time to another. Unfortunately, many investigators and clinicians have erroneously used it for diagnostic purposes. It is a serious mistake to assume that anyone who appears to be depressed on the basis of a self-report inventory would necessarily be diagnosed as being depressed after a clinical interview. Self-report scales sometimes fail to identify patients who are considered depressed on the basis of a clinical interview. One reason for this discrepancy is the fact that some depressed patients consider themselves to be less depressed than they appear to a clinician when they are interviewed (Sayer et al., 1993).

Projective Personality Tests

In **projective tests,** the person is presented with a series of ambiguous stimuli. The best known projective test, introduced in 1921 by Hermann Rorschach (1884–1922), a Swiss psychiatrist, is based on the use of inkblots. The Rorschach test consists of a series of 10 inkblots. Five contain various shades of gray on a white background, and five contain elements of color. The person is asked to look at each card and indicate what it looks like or what it appears to be. There are, of course, no correct answers. The instructions are intentionally vague in order to avoid influencing the person's responses through subtle suggestions.

Projective techniques such as the Rorschach test were originally based on psychodynamic assumptions about the nature of personality and psychopathology. Considerable emphasis was placed on the importance of unconscious motivations—conflicts and impulses of which the person is largely unaware. In other words, people being tested presumably project hidden desires and conflicts when they try to describe or explain the cards. In so doing, they may reveal things about themselves of which they are not consciously aware or that they might not be willing to admit if they were asked directly. The cards are not designed or chosen to be realistic or representational; they presumably look like whatever the person wants them to look like.

Michael did not actually complete any projective personality tests. We can illustrate the way in which these tests might have been used in his case, however, by considering a man who had been given a diagnosis of obsessive–compulsive disorder on Axis I, as well as showing evidence of two types of personality disorder, dependent and schizotypal features. This patient was 22 years old, unemployed, and living with his mother. His father had died in an accident four years earlier. Like Michael, this man was bothered by intrusive thoughts of contamination, and he frequently engaged in compulsive washing (Hurt, Reznikoff, & Clarkin, 1991). His responses to the cards on the Rorschach frequently mentioned emotional distress ("a man screaming"), interpersonal conflict ("two women fighting over something"), and war ("two mushrooms of a nuclear bomb cloud"). He did not incorporate color into any of his responses to the cards.

The original procedures for scoring the Rorschach were largely impressionistic and placed considerable emphasis on the content of the person's response. Responses given in the example above might be taken to suggest a number of important themes. Aggression and violence are obvious possibilities. Perhaps the man was repressing feelings of hostility, as indicated by his frequent references to war and conflict. These themes were coupled with a guarded approach to emotional reactions, which is presumably reflected by his avoidance of color. The psychologist might have wondered whether the man felt guilty about something, such as his father's death. This kind of interpretation, which depends heavily on symbolism and clinical inference, provides intriguing material for the clinician to puzzle over. Unfortunately, the reliability and validity of this intuitive type of scoring procedure are very low (Wood, Nezworski, Lilienfeld, & Garb, 2003).

When we ponder the utility of these interpretations, we should also keep in mind the relative efficiency of projective testing procedures. Did the test tell us anything that we didn't already know or that we couldn't have learned in a more straightforward manner? The clinician might learn about a client's feelings of anger or guilt by using a clinical interview, which is often a more direct and efficient way of collecting information.

More recent approaches to the use of projective tests view the person's descriptions of the cards as a sample of his or her perceptual and cognitive styles. The psychologist John Exner has

developed an objective scoring procedure for the Rorschach that is based primarily on the form rather than the content of the subject's responses (Exner, 1993, 1999). According to Exner's system, interpretation of the test depends on the way in which the descriptions take into account the shapes and colors on the cards. Does the person see movement in the card? Does she focus on tiny details, or does she base her descriptions on global impressions of the entire form of the inkblot? These and many other considerations contribute to the overall interpretation of the Rorschach test. The reliability of this scoring system is better than would be achieved by informal, impressionistic procedures. The validity of the scores, however, remains open to question (Hunsley & Bailey, 2001).

There are many different types of projective tests. Some employ stimuli that are somewhat less ambiguous than the inkblots in the Rorschach. The Thematic Apperception Test (TAT), for example, consists of a series of drawings that depict human figures in various ambiguous situations. Most of the cards portray more than one person. The figures and their poses tend to elicit stories with themes of sadness and violence. The person is asked to describe the identities of the people in the cards and to make up a story about what is happening. These stories presumably reflect the person's own ways of perceiving reality.

Advantages: The advantages of projective tests center on the fact that the tests are interesting to give and interpret, and they sometimes provide a way to talk to people who are otherwise reluctant or unable to discuss their problems. Projective tests are more appealing to psychologists who adopt a psychodynamic view of personality and psychopathology because such tests are believed to reflect unconscious conflicts and motivations. Some specific advantages are listed below.

1. Some people may feel more comfortable talking in an unstructured situation than they would if they were required to participate in a structured interview or to complete the lengthy MMPI.
2. Projective tests can provide an interesting source of information regarding the person's unique view of the world, and they can be a useful supplement to information obtained with other assessment tools (Weiner, 2000).

THE FAR SIDE®   By GARY LARSON

© 1996 FarWorks, Inc. All Rights Reserved/Dist. by Creators Syndicate

The Far Side® by Gary Larson © 1996 FarWorks, Inc. All Rights Reserved. The Far Side® and the Larson® signature are registered trademarks of FarWorks, Inc. Used with permission.

"It's just a simple Rorschach inkblot test, Mr. Bromwell, so just calm down and tell me what each one suggests to you."

3. To whatever extent a person's relationships with other people are governed by unconscious cognitive and emotional events, projective tests may provide information that cannot be obtained through direct interviewing methods or observational procedures (Meyer & Archer, 2001; Stricker & Gold, 1999).

Limitations: There are many serious problems with the use of projective tests. The popularity of projective tests has declined considerably since the 1970s, even in clinical settings, primarily because research studies have found little evidence to support their reliability and validity (Wierzbicki, 1993; Wood et al., 2003).

1. Lack of standardization in administration and scoring is a serious problem, even though Exner's system for the Rorschach has made some improvements in that regard.
2. Little information is available on which to base comparisons to normal adults or children.
3. Some projective procedures, such as the Rorschach, can be very time-consuming, particularly if the person's responses are scored with a standardized procedure such as Exner's system.
4. The reliability of scoring and interpretation tends to be low.
5. Information regarding the validity of projective tests is primarily negative.

ASSESSING SOCIAL SYSTEMS

The same range of procedures that we have discussed for the assessment of person variables (psychological systems) can also be used to examine situation variables (social systems). For example, clinical interviews can be used to describe the client's family and social environments, both past and present. These are obviously important considerations in planning a treatment program.

In Michael's case, the psychologist was interested in Michael's social relationships with classmates as well as his interactions with his parents. His father indicated that he was quite concerned about Michael's problems and that he was willing to help as they planned a treatment procedure that would allow Michael to learn to cope more effectively with his obsessive thoughts

Projective tests require a person to respond to ambiguous stimuli. Here, a woman is taking the Thematic Apperception Test (TAT), in which she will be asked to make up a story about a series of drawings of people.

about contamination. Michael's mother also told the psychologist that arguments between Michael and his father often seemed to trigger an increase in the frequency of his compulsive washing rituals. This information convinced the psychologist that Michael's treatment should focus on improving his relationship with his father and not just on his compulsive washing. He made this decision knowing that family conflict and negative family attitudes have a negative impact on the results of treatment for obsessive–compulsive disorder (Leonard et al., 1993; Steketee, 1993).

Many self-report inventories, rating scales, and behavioral coding systems have been designed for the assessment of marital relationships and family systems. One popular self-report inventory is the Family Environment Scale (FES), which is composed of 90 true–false items and was designed to measure the social characteristics of families (Moos, 1990). Extensive testing with large numbers of families has been used to establish norms on the FES for distressed and nondistressed families. The FES has been used widely in clinical settings and in research studies. Unfortunately, evidence regarding test–retest reliability and the validity of the subscales is not impressive (Boyd et al., 1997; L'Abate & Bagarozzi, 1993).

Direct observations can also be used to assess the social climate within a family (Patterson, 1990). The Family Interaction Coding System (FICS) was developed by Gerald Patterson and John Reid, clinical psychologists at the Oregon Research Institute, to observe interactions between parents and children in their homes (Jones, Reid, & Patterson, 1975). A trained observer visits the family's home and collects information for at least 70 minutes just prior to lunch or dinner. Everyone in the family must be present during this time period, and they must stay in a two room area. For each five-minute block of time, the observer focuses on two members of the family and describes their behavior, using the coding system. The observer rotates his or her attention from one "target" to the next throughout the observation period.

Trained raters can achieve high levels of reliability with the FICS. In addition, a number of research studies have demonstrated that it is a valid measure of aggressive behaviors in children, as well as a useful way to assess the family context in which these behaviors occur. It can distinguish between the families of children with antisocial behavior or conduct disorders and nondisturbed families. The FICS is also sensitive to changes that occur during the course of family treatment (Grotevant & Carlson, 1989).

The main problem with the FICS is that it is expensive to train observers to use it, and the process of collecting data is very time-consuming. These problems stem from a focus of detailed elements of interaction. In order to avoid these limitations, some clinicians prefer to use observational systems that concentrate on more global aspects of family interaction (Alexander et al., 1995; Markman et al., 1995).

ASSESSING BIOLOGICAL SYSTEMS

Clinicians have developed a number of techniques for measuring the effects of biological systems on behavior. These techniques are seldom used in clinical practice (at least for the diagnosis of psychopathology), but they have been employed extensively in research settings, and it seems possible that they will one day become an important source of information on individual patients.

Psychophysiological Assessment

Changes in physiological response systems, such as heart rate, respiration rate, and skin conductance, can provide useful information regarding a person's psychological adjustment. The basic components of the human nervous system (reviewed in Chapter 2) include the central nervous system (CNS) and the peripheral nervous system (PNS). The PNS is divided into two parts: the somatic nervous system and the autonomic nervous system. The somatic nervous system is responsible for communication between the brain and external sense receptors, as well as regulation of voluntary muscle movements. The autonomic nervous system is responsible for body processes that occur without conscious awareness, such as heart rate. It maintains equilibrium in the internal environment.

The autonomic nervous system is highly reactive to environmental events and can provide useful information about a person's internal states, such as emotion (Keller, Hicks, & Miller, 2000). Recording procedures have been developed to measure variables such as respiration rate, heart rate, and skin conductance. As the person becomes aroused, activity levels change in these systems. Psychophysiological measures can, therefore, provide sensitive indices of the person's internal state.

It must be emphasized, however, that all of these measures do not act together. The concept of general arousal was abandoned many years ago (for example, see Lacey, 1967). If several physiological responses are measured at the same time, they may not all demonstrate the same strength, or even direction, of response. Moreover, physiological measures frequently disagree with the person's own subjective report. Therefore, as with other assessment procedures, physiological recordings should be used in conjunction with other measures. They represent supplements to, rather than substitutes for, the other types of measures that we have already considered.

Psychophysiological measurements have been used extensively in the assessment of anxiety disorders. Consider Michael's case. He was afraid to touch contaminated objects in his house. If he had been forced to do so, it is likely that his heart rate would have increased dramatically (Yartz & Hawk, 2001). Psychophysiological events of this sort can be monitored precisely. To the extent that the clinician might be in need of information that would confirm data from other sources (observation, self-report) or that could be used to measure changes in the person's response to particular stimuli in the environment, physiological measurements may be very useful.

Advantages: Physiological procedures are not used frequently in clinical settings, but they are used extensively in research on psychopathology. These tools have several advantages in comparison to other assessment procedures (Drobes, Stritzke, & Coffey, 2000).

1. Psychophysiological recording procedures do not depend on self-report and, therefore, may be less subject to voluntary control. People may be less able to make the assessment show what they want it to show.
2. Some of these measures can be obtained while the subject is sleeping or while the subject is actively engaged in some other activity.

Limitations: In addition to the fact that they require relatively sophisticated equipment and a technician who is trained in their use, physiological measures have a number of drawbacks.

1. The recording equipment and electrodes may be frightening or intimidating to some people. These emotional responses can skew results.
2. There are generally low correlations between different autonomic response systems. It is not wise to select arbitrarily one specific physiological measure, such as heart rate, and assume that it is a direct index of arousal.
3. Physiological reactivity and the stability of physiological response systems vary from person to person. The measures may be informative for some people but not for others.
4. Physiological responses can be influenced by many other factors. Some are person variables, such as age and medication, as well as psychological factors, such as being self-conscious or fearing loss of control (Anderson & McNeilly, 1991). Other important considerations are situational variables, such as extraneous noise and electrical activity.

Brain Imaging Techniques

The past two decades have seen a tremendous explosion of information and technology in the neurosciences. We now understand in considerable detail how neurons in the central nervous system communicate with one another, and scientists have invented sophisticated methods to create images of the living human brain (Bremner, 2005). Some of these procedures provide static pictures of various brain structures at rest, just as an X ray provides a photographic image of a bone or some other organ of the body. Studies of this type are typically concerned with the size of various parts of the brain. For example, many studies have compared the average size of the lateral ventricles—large chambers filled with cerebrospinal fluid—in

groups of patients with schizophrenia and normal comparison groups. Other methods can be used to create dynamic images of brain functions—reflecting the rate of activity in various parts of the brain—while a person is performing different tasks. These functional images allow scientists to examine which parts of the brain are involved in various kinds of events, such as perception, memory, language, and emotional experience. They may also allow us to learn whether specific areas or pathways in the brain are uniquely associated with specific types of mental disorders.

Precise measures of brain structure can be obtained with *magnetic resonance imaging* (MRI). In MRI, images are generated using a strong magnetic field rather than X rays (Posner & DiGirolamo, 2000). A large magnet in the scanner causes chemical elements in specific brain regions to emit distinctive radio signals. Both computerized tomography (CT) scanning and MRI can provide a static image of specific brain structures. MRI provides more detailed images than CT scans and is able to identify smaller parts of the brain. For this reason, and because it lends itself more easily to the creation of three-dimensional pictures of the brain, MRI has replaced CT scanning in most research facilities.

In addition to structural MRI, which provides a static view of brain structures, advances in the neurosciences have also produced techniques that create images of brain functions (Raichle, 2001). *Positron emission tomography* (PET) is one scanning technique that can be used to

Positron emission topography (PET scan) can provide useful images of dynamic brain functions. Areas that appear red or yellow indicate areas of the brain that are active (consuming the labeled glucose molecules), whereas those that are blue or green are relatively inactive. Different areas of the brain become active depending on whether the person is at rest or engaged in particular activities when the image is created.

This view of earth from space shows hot spots on the earth's surface at night, an indication of areas of heavier population. Imaging techniques like fMRI offer views of the brain that are similarly fascinating—and similarly lacking in resolution, detail, and meaning.

Brain Regions Associated with OCD

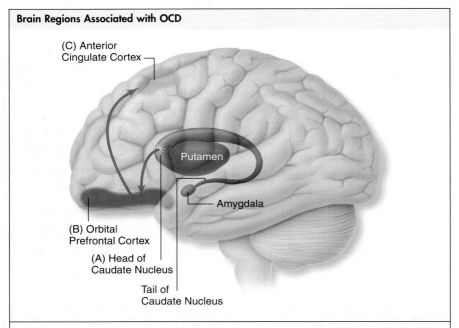

FIGURE 4–2: When a person with OCD experiences symptoms, an increase in neural activity is seen in the caudate (A), which triggers the urge to "do something," through the orbital prefrontal cortex (B), which gives the feeling that "something is wrong," and back through the anterior cingulated cortex (C), which keeps attention fixed on the feeling of unease.

Source: R. Carter, 1998, *Mapping the Mind.* Berkeley: University of California Press, illustrations by Malcolm Godwin. Copyright © 1998 by Moonrunner Design Ltd. Reprinted by permission of Malcolm Godwin, Moonrunner Design, Ltd.

(fMRI). When neurons are activated, their metabolism increases and they require increased blood flow to supply them with oxygen. The magnetic properties of blood change as a function of the level of oxygen that it is carrying. In fMRI, a series of images is acquired in rapid succession. Small differences in signal intensity from one image to the next provide a measure of moment-to-moment changes in the amount of oxygen in blood flowing to specific areas of the brain. While other functional imaging procedures such as PET are only able to measure activities that are sustained over a period of several minutes, fMRI is able to identify changes in brain activity that lasts less than a second (Huettel, Song, & McCarthy, 2004).

Functional brain imaging procedures have been used extensively to study possible neurological underpinnings of various types of mental disorder (Dougherty & Rauch, 2001). For example, in the case of obsessive–compulsive disorder (OCD), studies using PET and fMRI have suggested that symptoms of OCD are associated with multiple brain regions, including the caudate nucleus (one part of the basal ganglia, which are also illustrated in Figure 14–2), the orbital prefrontal cortex, and the anterior cingulate cortex (located on the medial surface of the frontal lobe). These pathways are illustrated in Figure 4–2. They seem to be overly active in people with OCD, especially when the person is confronted with stimuli that provoke his or her obsessions (Pujol et al., 2004; Szechtman & Woody, 2004).

These results are intriguing because they suggest that certain regions and circuits in the brain may somehow be associated with the presence of obsessive–compulsive symptoms. We must emphasize, however, that the results of such imaging procedure are not useful diagnostically with regard to an individual person. In other words, some people with OCD do not exhibit increased metabolism rates in the caudate or the anterior cingulate cortex, and some people who do not have OCD do show increased levels of activity in these brain regions.

Advantages: Brain imaging techniques provide detailed information regarding the structure of brain areas and activity levels in the brain that are associated with the performance of particular tasks. They have important uses, primarily as research tools:

1. In clinical practice, imaging techniques can be used to rule out various neurological

create functional brain images (Wahl, 2002). This procedure is much more expensive than the other imaging techniques because it requires a nuclear cyclotron to produce special radioactive elements. PET scans are capable of providing relatively detailed images of the brain. In addition, they can reflect changes in brain activity as the person responds to the demands of various tasks.

The newest and most exciting method of imaging brain functions involves *functional MRI* conditions that might explain behavioral or cognitive deficits. These include such conditions as brain tumors and vascular disease.

2. Procedures such as fMRI and PET can help research investigators explore the relation between brain functions and specific mental disorders. This type of information will be considered in several chapters later in this book.

Limitations: Brain imaging procedures are used extensively in the study and assessment of neurological disorders. In the field of psychopathology, they are currently research tools and have little clinical importance outside the assessment and treatment of disorders such as Alzheimer's disease (see Chapter 14). Some of the major limitations are listed below.

1. Norms have not been established for any of these measures. It is not possible to use brain imaging procedures for diagnostic purposes.

2. These procedures are relatively expensive—especially PET scans and fMRI—and some procedures must be used cautiously because the patient may be exposed to radioactive substances.

3. We should not assume that all cognitive processes, emotional experiences, or mental disorders are necessarily linked to activity (or the absence of activity) in a specific area of the brain. Scientists are still debating the extent to which these experiences are localized within the brain (Uttal, 2001).

Why are brain imaging procedures not used for the diagnosis of mental disorders?

---

getting help

Only one in five people who need treatment actually get it. There are several reasons for this unfortunate state of events. One is lack of information. If you don't recognize the presence of a serious problem, you won't seek help. You will get care more promptly and make better treatment choices if you understand your problems. One consideration is the extent to which your experiences resemble the formal diagnostic terms used by mental health professionals. Allen Frances, chairperson of the DSM-IV-TR Taskforce, and Michael First have written a useful book called, *Your Mental Health: A Layman's Guide to the Psychiatrist's Bible.* This primer for consumers of mental health services covers many types of adult and childhood disorders. Each chapter includes a concise, readable description of the typical symptoms and course of the disorder,

followed by a discussion designed to help you decide whether your problems warrant professional help ("Am I okay?"). Finally, the authors review treatment options and where to go for help for each of the problems.

Even after they recognize the presence of a serious problem, some people are reluctant to seek help; they fear there is a stigma attached to "mental problems" despite the fact that seeking therapy is now commonplace. Negative stereotypes regarding mental disorders persist. We hope that you will not allow these distorted views to delay or interfere with efforts to improve your life. If you have concerns about this issue, it may help to read about stigma and mental health, a problem that has been addressed by Rosalynn Carter, a leading advocate on behalf of people with mental disorders and wife of former president Jimmy Carter. Her book, *Helping Someone with Mental Illness,* contains an excellent

discussion of these issues. The Carter Center is actively involved in issues that affect public policies regarding mental disorders. The URL for their Web page is: www.cartercenter.org. It also contains information relevant to the struggle to correct biased and inaccurate views of people with mental disorders.

We can all help to eliminate discrimination against those who suffer from (or have recovered from) mental disorders. Advice for positive action is presented on several Web sites, including the National Mental Health Associations' "Stigma Watch" home page. This site includes, for example, a sample letter that can be mailed to legislators as well as instructions that encourage people to report media events that depict mental disorders in an unfair light. People will find it easier to seek help when they no longer need to worry about the potential effects of distorted, negative views of their problems.

SUMMARY

Formal **classification systems** for mental disorders have been developed in order to facilitate communication, research, and treatment planning. The current official system published by the American Psychiatric Association is the fourth edition of the *Diagnostic and Statistical Manual of Mental Disorders*, or DSM-IV-TR. It is based on a **categorical approach to classification** and typically employs specific inclusion and exclusion criteria to define each disorder. The categories that are defined in DSM-IV-TR are based primarily on descriptive principles rather than on theoretical knowledge regarding the etiology of the disorders. Five axes are included in this system. Axes I and II are employed for describing mental disorders (personality disorders and mental retardation on Axis II). The remaining three axes are concerned with supplementary information that may also be useful in treatment planning.

Cultural factors play an important role in both the expression and recognition of symptoms of mental disorders. The accuracy and utility of a clinical diagnosis depend on the clinician's ability to consider the cultural context in which the problem appeared. DSM-IV-TR includes a glossary of **culture-bound syndromes,** such as amok. These patterns of erratic or unusual thinking and behavior do not fit easily into the other categories that are listed in the main body of the diagnostic manual.

The usefulness of a classification system depends on several criteria, especially **reliability** and **validity.** The reliability of many categories in DSM seems to have improved with the introduction of specific inclusion criteria and exclusion criteria. Nevertheless, serious questions remain about this issue. The reliability of some categories, such as the personality disorders, is still marginal in many studies. Reliability is also likely to be diminished in clinical settings where clinicians are not experts in a particular disorder and reliability is not being monitored. The validity of most categories is still under active investigation.

The general process of collecting and interpreting information is called **assessment.** Many different assessment tools can be used to generate information systematically. Interviews, observations, and tests are among the most frequently used procedures. Assessments can be directed toward biological, psychological, and social systems. In many cases, information is collected and integrated across more than one system, but it is never possible to learn everything about a particular person. Choices have to be made, and some information must be excluded from the analysis.

Psychological systems are typically assessed using interviews, observations, or self-report inventories. Structured diagnostic interviews are used extensively in conjunction with the DSM-IV-TR classification system. They can also form the basis for ratings of the person's adjustment on a number of dimensions. Interviews can be used to collect additional information that is relevant to planning treatment. Their main advantage is their flexibility. Their primary limitation lies in the inability or unwillingness of some clients to provide a rational description of their own problems, as well as the subjective factors that influence the clinician's interpretation of data collected in an interview.

Psychological tests are also used in the assessment of psychological systems. **Personality inventories,** like the MMPI, offer several advantages as supplements to interviews and observations. They can be scored objectively, they often contain validity scales that reflect the person's attitude and test-taking set, and they can be interpreted in reference to well established standards for people with and without specific types of adjustment problems. Some psychologists use **projective personality tests,** like the Rorschach, to acquire information that might not be obtained from direct interviews or observations. Unfortunately, research studies have found little evidence to support the reliability and validity of projective tests. The continued use of these tests is, therefore, controversial.

Social systems, including marital relationships and families, can also be evaluated using interviews, observations, and self-report inventories. Although the instruments that are used for this purpose have not been developed as extensively as those that address psychological systems, they represent an important consideration in thinking about mental disorders and their treatment.

Many different tools are available for assessing biological systems related to mental disorders.

These include psychophysiological recording procedures, as well as brain imaging techniques, such as MRI and PET scans. Biological assessment procedures are used extensively in research studies. They do not have diagnostic value in clinical situations, except for the purpose of ruling out certain conditions, such as brain tumors and vascular disease.

KEY TERMS

actuarial
  interpretation   117
assessment   93
behavioral coding
  system   114
categorical approach
  to classification   95

classification system   95
comorbidity   106
culture-bound
  syndrome   101

diagnosis   93
dimensional approach
  to classification   96
kappa   103

labeling theory   98
personality inventories   116
projective tests   119
rating scale   114

reactivity   116
reliability   104
stigma   98
validity   104

 Go to www.prenhall.com/oltmanns for online quizzes, interactive flash cards, PowerPoint presentations, and chapter reviews.

5
Mood Disorders and Suicide

Sadness may be the price that we pay for attachments to other people. Losses are inevitable, and we all endure the pain that comes with them. Beyond relatively short-lived feelings of grief and sorrow, prolonged sadness can grow into something much more debilitating. Everyone's life contains the potential for despair. Some people manage to avoid it, but others become overwhelmed by it. When it reaches higher levels of intensity and begins to interfere with a person's ability to function and enjoy life, a low mood is known as clinical depression. In this chapter we will consider emotional disorders that involve prolonged periods of severe depression.

OVERVIEW

If one measures disability in terms of years lived with severe impairments, major depression is the leading cause of disability worldwide. The magnitude of the problem is truly staggering. Depression accounts for more than 10 percent of all disability (see Table 5–1). Experts predict that it will become an even greater problem by the year 2020 (Lopez & Murray, 1998; Wang, Simon, & Kessler, 2003). Younger generations are experiencing higher rates of depression than their predecessors, and those who become depressed are doing so at an earlier age (Andrade et al., 2003).

Psychopathologists use several terms to describe problems that are associated with emotional response systems. This language can become confusing because most of us already use these words in our everyday vocabulary.

Thus we must define these terms as they are used in psychopathology so that our discussion will be clear. **Emotion** refers to a state of arousal that is defined by subjective states of feeling, such as sadness, anger, and disgust. Emotions are often accompanied by physiological changes, such as changes in heart rate and respiration rate. **Affect** refers to the pattern of observable behaviors, such as facial expression, that are associated with these subjective feelings. People also express affect through the pitch of their voices and with their hand and body movements. **Mood** refers to a pervasive and sustained emotional response that, in its extreme form, can color the person's perception of the world (APA, 2000). The disorders discussed in this chapter are primarily associated with two specific moods: depression and elation.

TABLE 5–1	Leading Causes of Disability Worldwide (1990) as Measured by Years of Life Lived with a Disability (YLD)	
	TOTAL YLDS (MILLIONS)	PERCENT OF TOTAL
ALL CAUSES	472.7	
1. Unipolar major depression	50.8	10.7
2. Iron-deficiency anemia	22.0	4.7
3. Falls	22.0	4.6
4. Alcohol use	15.8	3.3
5. Chronic obstructive pulmonary disease	14.7	3.1
6. Bipolar mood disorder	14.1	3.0
7. Congenital anomalies	13.5	2.9
8. Osteoarthritis	13.3	2.8
9. Schizophrenia	12.1	2.6
10. Obsessive–compulsive disorders	10.2	2.2

Source: A.D. Lopez, & J.L. Murray, 1998, The global burden of disease, 1990–2020, *Nature Medicine, 4,* 1241–1243. Copyright © 1998 by Nature Publishing Group. Reprinted by permission of the publisher.

Depression can refer either to a mood or to a *clinical syndrome,* a combination of emotional, cognitive, and behavioral symptoms. The feelings associated with a **depressed mood** often include disappointment and despair. Although sadness is a universal experience, profound depression is not. No one has been able to identify the exact point at which "feeling down or blue" crosses a line and becomes depression. One experience shades gradually into the next. The transition has been described by Andrew Solomon (2001) in *The Noonday Demon,* an eloquent book in which he documents his own struggles with depression:

> Depression starts out insipid, fogs the days into a dull color, weakens ordinary actions until their clear shapes are obscured by the effort they require, leaves you tired and bored and self-obsessed—but you get through all that. Not happily, perhaps, but you can get through. No one has ever been able to define the collapse point that marks major depression, but when you get there, there's not much mistaking it. (p. 17)

People who are in a severely depressed mood describe the feeling as overwhelming, suffocating, or numbing. In the syndrome of depression, which is also called **clinical depression,** a depressed mood is accompanied by several other symptoms, such as fatigue, loss of energy, difficulty in sleeping, and changes in appetite. Clinical depression also involves a variety of changes in thinking and overt behavior.

The person may experience cognitive symptoms, such as extreme guilt, feelings of worthlessness, concentration problems, and thoughts of suicide. Behavioral symptoms may range from constant pacing and fidgeting to extreme inactivity. Throughout the rest of this chapter, we will use the term **depression** to refer to the clinical syndrome rather than the mood.

Mania, the flip side of depression, also involves a disturbance in mood that is accompanied by additional symptoms. **Euphoria,** or elated mood, is the opposite emotional state from a depressed mood. It is characterized by an exaggerated feeling of physical and emotional well-being (APA, 2000). Manic symptoms that frequently accompany an elated mood include inflated self-esteem, decreased need for sleep, distractibility, pressure to keep talking, and the subjective feeling of thoughts racing through the person's head faster than they can be spoken. Mania is, therefore, a syndrome in the same sense that clinical depression is a syndrome.

Mood disorders are defined in terms of *episodes*—discrete periods of time in which the person's behavior is dominated by either a depressed or manic mood. Unfortunately, most people with a mood disorder experience more than one episode. The following case studies illustrate the way that numerous symptoms combine to form syndromes that are used to define mood disorders. They also provide examples of the two primary types of mood disorders: (1) those in which the person experiences only episodes of depression, known as **unipolar mood disorder;** and (2) those in which the person experiences episodes of mania as well as depression, known as **bipolar mood disorder.** Episodes of depression are defined by the same symptoms, regardless of whether the person's disorder is unipolar or bipolar in nature. A small number of patients have only manic episodes with no evidence of depression; they are included in the bipolar category. Years ago, bipolar mood disorder was known as *manic–depressive disorder*. Although this term has been replaced in the official diagnostic manual, some clinicians still prefer to use it because it offers a more direct description of the patient's experience (Jamison, 1995).

CASE STUDY   An Attorney's Major Depressive Episode

"Life has lost its interest and meaning. I've failed at my job and failed in my relationships. I deserve to be alone."

Cathy was a 31-year-old attorney who had been promoted to the rank of partner the previous year and was considered one of the brightest, most promising young members of her firm. In spite of her apparent success, she was plagued by doubts about her own abilities and was convinced that she was unworthy of her promotion. Cathy decided to seek treatment because she was profoundly miserable. Beyond being depressed, she felt numb. She had been feeling unusually fatigued and irritable for several months, but her mood took a serious swing for the worse after one of the firm's clients, for whom Cathy was primarily responsible, decided to switch to another firm. Although the decision was clearly based on factors that were beyond her control, Cathy blamed herself. She interpreted this event as a reflection of her professional incompetence, in spite of the fact that virtually all of her other clients had praised her work and the senior partners in her firm had given her consistently positive reviews.

Cathy had always looked forward to going to the office, and she truly enjoyed her work. After she lost this client, however, going to work had seemed like an overwhelming burden. She found it impossible to concentrate and instead brooded about her own incompetence. Soon she started calling in sick. She began to spend her time sitting in bed staring at the television screen, without paying attention to any program, and she never left her apartment. She felt lethargic all the time, but she wasn't sleeping well. Her appetite disappeared. Her best friend tried repeatedly to get in touch with her, but Cathy wouldn't return her calls. She listened passively as her friend left messages on the answering machine. She just didn't feel like doing anything or talking to anyone.

Cathy considered her social life to be a disaster, and it didn't seem to be getting any better. She had been separated from her husband for 5 years, and her most recent boyfriend had started dating another woman. She had tried desperately for several weeks to force herself to be active, but eventually she stopped caring. The situation seemed completely hopeless. Although she had often gone to parties with other members of her law firm, she usually felt as though she didn't fit in. Everyone else seemed to be part of a couple, and Cathy was usually on her own. Other people didn't appreciate the depth of her loneliness. Sometimes it seemed to Cathy that she would be better off dead. She spent a good deal of time brooding about suicide, but she feared that if she tried to harm herself she might make things worse than they already were.

Cathy's problems would be classified as a unipolar mood disorder because she had experienced at least one episode of major depression and she had never had a manic episode. Her experience provides a framework in which we can discuss the difference between normal sadness and clinical depression. Some important considerations regarding this distinction are listed in Table 5–2. They include the extent to which the low mood remains consistent over an extended period of time as well as the inability to occasionally enjoy activities that would otherwise provide some relief from feeling down or blue. Distractions such as watching television or talking on the phone with a friend had lost their ability to make Cathy feel any better. Her mood had deteriorated shortly after one of her clients

TABLE 5–2	Important Considerations in Distinguishing Clinical Depression from Normal Sadness

1. The mood change is pervasive across situations and persistent over time. The person's mood does not improve, even temporarily, when he or she engages in activities that are usually experienced as pleasant.

2. The mood change may occur in the absence of any precipitating events, or it may be completely out of proportion to the person's circumstances.

3. The depressed mood is accompanied by impaired ability to function in usual social and occupational roles. Even simple activities become overwhelmingly difficult.

4. The change in mood is accompanied by a cluster of additional signs and symptoms, including cognitive, somatic, and behavioral features.

5. The nature or quality of the mood change may be different from that associated with normal sadness. It may feel "strange," like being engulfed by a black cloud or sunk in a dark hole.

switched to another firm. The intensity of her depression was clearly way out of proportion to the event that seemed to trigger it (departure of a client to another firm). She had withdrawn from other people and was no longer able to work or to participate in any kind of social activity. The onset of her depression was accompanied by a number of other symptoms, including feelings of guilt, lack of energy, and difficulty sleeping. Finally, the quality of her mood was more than just a feeling of sadness; she was so profoundly miserable that she felt numb. For all of these reasons,

What is the difference between clinical depression and a low mood?

Cathy's problems would fit the description of major depression.

Our next case illustrates the symptoms of mania, which often appear after a person has already experienced at least one episode of depression. People who experience episodes of both depression and mania are given a diagnosis of bipolar mood disorder. The symptoms of a full-blown manic episode are not subtle. People who are manic typically have terrible judgment and may get into considerable trouble as a result of their disorder. The central feature of mania is a persistently elevated or irritable mood that lasts for at least one week.

CASE STUDY Debbie's Manic Episode

"I am a psychic therapist, filled with the healing powers of the universe. I see things so clearly and deeply, and I must share this knowledge with everyone else."

Debbie, a 21-year-old single woman, was admitted to a psychiatric hospital in the midst of a manic episode. She had been in psychotherapy for depression for several months while she was in high school but had not received any type of treatment since then. After she completed two semesters at a community college, Debbie found a well-paying job in the advertising office of a local newspaper, where she had been working for 2 years.

Debbie's manic episode could be traced to experiences that began 3 or 4 months prior to her admission to the hospital. Debbie had been feeling unusually good for several weeks. At first she didn't think anything was wrong. In fact, her impression was quite the opposite. Everything seemed to be going right for her. Her energy level was up, and she felt a renewed confidence in herself and her relationships with other people, especially with her boyfriend, who had recently moved to a distant city. Debbie initially welcomed these feelings, especially because she had been so lethargic and also tended to be reserved with people.

One day when she was feeling particularly exhilarated, Debbie impulsively quit her job and went to visit her boyfriend. Giving up her job without careful consideration and with no prospect for alternative employment was the

first indication that Debbie's judgment was becoming impaired. Although she left home with only enough money to pay for her airplane ticket, she stayed for several weeks, mostly engaged in leisure activities. It was during this time that she started having trouble sleeping. The quality of her mood also began to change. It was less often cheerful and frequently irritable. She was extremely impatient and would become furious if her boyfriend disagreed with her. On one occasion, they had a loud and heated argument in the parking lot of his apartment complex. She took off her blouse and angrily refused to put it on again in spite of his demands and the presence of several interested bystanders. Shortly after the fight, she packed her clothes and hitchhiked back home.

After returning to her parents' home, Debbie argued with them almost continuously for several days. Her moods shifted constantly. One moment she would be bubbling with enthusiasm, gleefully throwing herself into new and exciting activities. If her plans were thwarted, she would fly into a rage. She phoned an exclusive tennis club to arrange for private lessons, which she obviously could not afford, especially now that she was unemployed. Her mother interrupted the call and canceled the lessons. Debbie left the house in a fury and set off to hitch a ride to the tennis club. She was picked up by two unknown men, who persuaded her to accompany them to a party rather than go to the club. By the time they arrived at the party, her mood was once again euphoric. She stayed at the party all

night and had intercourse with three men whom she had never met before.

The following day, Debbie borrowed money from a friend and took a train home. Another argument ensued when she arrived at home. Debbie struck her father and took the family car. Angry and frightened by her apparently irrational behavior, her parents phoned the police, who found her and brought her home. When another argument broke out, even more hostile than the first, the police took Debbie to their precinct office, where she was interviewed by a psychiatrist. Her attitude was flippant, and her language was abusive and obscene. On the basis of her clearly irrational and violent mood, as well as her marked impairment in judgment, the psychiatrist arranged for her to be committed to a psychiatric hospital.

Debbie's behavior on the ward was belligerent, provocative, and demanding. Although she hadn't slept a total of more than 4 hours in the previous 3 days, she claimed to be bursting with energy. She behaved seductively toward some of the male patients, sitting on their laps, kissing them, and occasionally unfastening her clothing. Although her speech was coherent, it was rapid and pressured. She expressed several grandiose ideas, including the boast that she was an Olympic swimmer and that she was a premed student in college. She had no insight into the severity of her mental condition. Failing to recognize that her judgment was impaired, she insisted that she had been brought to the ward so that she could help the other patients.

SYMPTOMS

The cases of Cathy and Debbie illustrate many of the most important symptoms and signs of mood disorders, which can be divided into four general areas: emotional symptoms, cognitive symptoms, somatic symptoms, and behavioral symptoms. Episodes of major depression and mania typically involve all four kinds of symptoms.

Emotional Symptoms

We all experience negative emotions, such as sadness, fear, and anger. These reactions usually last only a few moments, and they serve a useful purpose in our lives, particularly in our relationships with other people. Emotional reactions serve as signals to other people about our current feelings and needs. They also coordinate our responses to changes in the immediate environment.

Depressed, or **dysphoric** (unpleasant), mood is the most common and obvious symptom of depression. Most people who are depressed describe themselves as feeling utterly gloomy, dejected, or despondent. The severity of a depressed mood can reach painful and overwhelming proportions. Andrew Solomon (2001) has described the progression from sadness to severe depression in the following ways:

> I returned, not long ago, to a wood in which I had played as a child and saw an oak, a hundred years dignified, in whose shade I used to play with my brother. In twenty years, a huge vine had attached itself to this confident tree and had nearly smothered it. It was hard to say where the tree left off and the vine began. The vine had twisted itself so entirely around the scaffolding of tree branches that its leaves seemed from a distance to be the leaves of the tree; only up close could you see how few living oak branches were left. I empathized with that tree. My depression had grown on me as that vine had conquered the oak; it had been a sucking thing that had wrapped itself around me, ugly and more alive than I. (p. 18)

In contrast to the unpleasant feelings associated with clinical depression, manic patients like Debbie experience periods of inexplicable and unbounded joy known as euphoria. Debbie felt extremely optimistic and cheerful—"on top of the world"—in spite of the fact that her inappropriate behavior had made a shambles of her current life circumstances. In bipolar mood disorders, periods of elated mood tend to alternate with phases of depression.

Kay Jamison, professor of psychiatry at Johns Hopkins University School of Medicine, has written an eloquent and moving description of her own experiences with mania and depression.

> My manias, at least in their early and mild forms, were absolutely intoxicating states that gave rise to great personal pleasure, an incomparable flow of thoughts, and a ceaseless energy that allowed the translation of new ideas into papers and projects. (1995, pp. 5–6)

Unfortunately, as these feelings become more intense and prolonged, they can become ruinous. It may not be clear when the person's experience crosses the unmarked boundary between being productive and energetic to being out of control and self-destructive. Jamison described this subtle transition in the following way:

> There is a particular kind of pain, elation, loneliness, and terror involved in this kind of madness. When you're high it's tremendous. The ideas and feelings are fast and frequent like shooting stars, and you follow them until you find better and brighter ones. Shyness goes, the right words and gestures are suddenly there, the power to captivate others a felt certainty. There are interests found in uninteresting people. Sensuality is pervasive, and the desire to seduce and be seduced irresistible. Feelings of ease, intensity, power, well-being, financial omnipotence, and euphoria pervade one's marrow. But, somewhere, this changes. The fast ideas are far too fast, and there are far too many; overwhelming confusion

The quality of a depressed mood is often different from the sadness that might arise from an event such as the loss of a loved one. Some depressed people say that they feel like they are drowning or suffocating.

Manic episodes are sometimes associated with reckless and potentially self-destructive behaviors, including reckless driving.

replaces clarity. Memory goes. Humor and absorption on friends' faces are replaced by fear and concern. Everything previously moving with the grain is now against—you are irritable, angry, frightened, uncontrollable, and enmeshed totally in the blackest caves of the mind. (p. 67)

Many depressed and manic patients are irritable. Their anger may be directed either at themselves or at others, and frequently at both. Even when they are cheerful, people in a manic episode, like Debbie, are easily provoked to anger. Debbie became extremely argumentative and abusive, particularly when people challenged her grandiose statements about herself and her inappropriate judgment.

Anxiety is also common among people with mood disorders, just as depression is a common feature of some anxiety disorders (see Chapter 6). Two out of every three depressed patients also report feeling anxious (Rivas-Vasquez et al., 2004). People who are depressed are sometimes apprehensive, fearing that matters will become worse than they already are or that others will discover their inadequacy. They sometimes report that they are chronically tense and unable to relax.

Cognitive Symptoms

In addition to changes in the way people feel, mood disorders also involve changes in the way people think about themselves and their surroundings. People who are clinically depressed frequently note that their thinking is slowed down, that they have trouble concentrating, and that they are easily distracted. Cathy's ability to concentrate was so disturbed that she became unable to work. She had extreme difficulty making even the simplest decisions. After she started staying home, she sat in front of the television set but was unable to pay attention to the content of even the simplest programs.

Guilt and worthlessness are common preoccupations. Depressed patients blame themselves for things that have gone wrong, regardless of whether they are in fact responsible. They focus considerable attention on the most negative features of themselves, their environments, and the future—a combination known as the "depressive triad" (Beck, 1967).

In contrast to the cognitive slowness associated with depression, manic patients commonly report that their thoughts are speeded up. Ideas flash through their minds faster than they can articulate their thoughts. Manic patients can also be easily distracted, responding to seemingly random stimuli in a completely uninterpretable and incoherent fashion. Grandiosity and inflated self esteem are also characteristic features of mania.

Many people experience self-destructive ideas and impulses when they are depressed. Interest in suicide usually develops gradually and may begin with the vague sense that life is not worth living. Such feelings may follow directly from the overwhelming fatigue and loss of pleasure that typically accompany a seriously depressed mood. In addition, feelings of guilt and failure can lead depressed people to consider killing themselves. Over a period of time, depressed people may come to believe that they would be better off dead or that their family would function more successfully and happily without them. Preoccupation with such thoughts then leads to specific plans and may culminate in a suicide attempt.

Somatic Symptoms

The **somatic symptoms** of mood disorders are related to basic physiological or bodily functions. They include fatigue, aches and pains, and serious changes in appetite and sleep patterns. People, like Cathy, who are clinically depressed often report feeling tired all the time. The simplest tasks, which she had previously taken for granted, seemed to require an overwhelming effort. Taking a shower, brushing her teeth, and getting dressed in the morning became virtually impossible.

Sleeping problems are also common, particularly trouble getting to sleep. This disturbance frequently goes hand in hand with cognitive difficulties mentioned earlier. Worried about her endless problems and unable to relax, Cathy found that she would toss and turn for hours before finally falling asleep. Some people also report having difficulty staying asleep throughout the night, and they awaken 2 or more hours before the usual time. Early-morning waking is often associated with particularly severe depression. A less common symptom is for a depressed individual to spend more time sleeping than usual.

In the midst of a manic episode, a person is likely to experience a drastic reduction in the need for sleep. Some patients report that reduced sleep is one of the earliest signs of the onset of an episode. Although depressed patients typically feel exhausted when they cannot sleep, a person in a manic episode will probably be bursting with energy in spite of the lack of rest.

Depressed people frequently experience a change in appetite. Although some patients report that they eat more than usual, most reduce the amount that they eat; some may eat next to nothing. Food just doesn't taste good any more. Depressed people can also lose a great deal of weight, even without trying to diet.

People who are severely depressed commonly lose their interest in various types of activities that are otherwise sources of pleasure and fulfillment. One common example is a loss of sexual desire. Depressed people are less likely to initiate sexual activity, and they are less likely to enjoy sex if their partners can persuade them to participate.

Various ill-defined somatic complaints can also accompany mood disorders. Some patients complain of frequent headaches and muscular aches and pains. These concerns may develop into a preoccupation with bodily functions and fear of disease.

Behavioral Symptoms

The symptoms of mood disorders also include changes in the things that people do and the rate at which they do them. The term **psychomotor retardation** refers to several features of behavior that may accompany the onset of serious depression. The most obvious behavioral symptom of depression is slowed movement. Patients may walk and talk as if they are in slow motion. Others become completely immobile and may stop speaking altogether. Some depressed patients pause for very extended periods, perhaps several minutes, before answering a question.

In marked contrast to periods when they are depressed, manic patients are typically gregarious and energetic. Debbie's behavior provided many examples, even after her admission to the psychiatric hospital. Her flirtatious and provocative behavior on the ward was clearly inappropriate. She found it impossible to sit still for more than a moment or two. Virtually everything was interesting to her, and she was easily distracted, flitting from one idea or project to the next. Like other manic patients, Debbie was full of plans that were pursued in a rather indiscriminate fashion.

Other Problems Commonly Associated with Depression

Many people with mood disorders suffer from some clinical problems that are not typically considered symptoms of depression. Within the field of psychopathology, the simultaneous manifestation of a mood disorder and other syndromes is referred to as comorbidity, suggesting that the person exhibits symptoms of more than one underlying disorder.

Alcoholism and depression are clearly related phenomena. Many people who are depressed also drink heavily, and many people who are dependent on alcohol—approximately 40 percent—have experienced major depression at some point during their lives (Swendsen & Merikangas, 2000). The order of onset for the depression and alcoholism varies from one person to the next. Some people become depressed after they develop a drinking problem; others begin drinking after being depressed. There is also an association between these disorders within families. Alcohol abuse is common among the immediate families of patients with mood disorders. Eating disorders and anxiety disorders are also more common among first-degree relatives of depressed patients than among people in the general population.

Bereavement is part of normal human experience. A clinical diagnosis would not be made following the loss of a loved one unless symptoms persist for more than two months or include marked functional impairment.

DIAGNOSIS

Psychopathologists have proposed hundreds of systems for describing and classifying mood disorders. In the following section we will describe briefly some of the historical figures who played a prominent role in the development of classification systems (Berrios, 1992). This discussion should help place our description of the current diagnostic system, DSM-IV-TR, in perspective.

Brief Historical Perspective

Although written descriptions of clinical depression can be traced to ancient times, the first widely accepted classification system was proposed by the German physician Emil Kraepelin (1921). Kraepelin divided the major forms of mental disorder into two categories: *dementia praecox*, which we now know as schizophrenia (see Chapter 13), and *manic–depressive psychosis*. He based the distinction on age of onset, clinical symptoms, and the course of the disorder (its progress over time). The manic–depressive category included all depressive syndromes, regardless of whether the patients exhibited manic and depressive episodes or simply depression. In comparison to dementia praecox, manic–depression typically showed an episodic, recurrent course with a relatively good prognosis. Kraepelin observed that most manic–depressive patients returned to a normal level of functioning between episodes of depression or mania.

Are there different kinds of depression?

Despite the widespread acceptance and influence of Kraepelin's diagnostic system, many alternative approaches have been proposed. Two primary issues have been central in the debate regarding definitions of mood disorders. First, should these disorders be defined in a broad or a narrow fashion? A narrow approach to the definition of depression would focus on the most severely disturbed people—those whose depressed mood is entirely pervasive, completely debilitating, and associated with a wide range of additional symptoms. A broader approach to definition would include mild depression, which lies somewhere on the continuum between normal sadness and major depression.

The second issue concerns heterogeneity. All depressed patients do not have exactly the same set of symptoms, the same pattern of onset, or the same course over time. Some patients have manic episodes, whereas others experience only depression. Some exhibit psychotic symptoms, such as delusions and hallucinations, in addition to their symptoms of mood disorder; others do not. In some cases, the person's depression is apparently a reaction to specific life events, whereas in others the mood disorder seems to come out of nowhere. Are these qualitatively distinct forms of mood disorder, or are they different expressions of the same underlying problem? Is the distinction among the different types simply one of severity?

Contemporary Diagnostic Systems

The DSM-IV-TR approach to classifying mood disorders recognizes several subtypes of depression, placing special emphasis on the distinction between unipolar and bipolar disorders. The overall scheme, outlined in Table 5–3, includes two types of unipolar mood disorder and three types of bipolar mood disorder.

Unipolar Disorders The unipolar disorders include two specific types: major depressive disorder and dysthymia. In order to meet the criteria for major depressive disorder, a person must experience at least one major depressive episode in the absence of any history of manic episodes. Table 5–4 lists the DSM-IV-TR criteria for a major depressive episode. Although some people experience a single, isolated episode of major depression followed by complete recovery, most cases of unipolar depression follow an intermittent course with repeated episodes.

Dysthymia differs from major depression in terms of both severity and duration. Dysthymia represents a chronic mild depressive condition that has been present for many years. In order to fulfill DSM-IV-TR criteria for this disorder, the person must, over a period of at least 2 years, exhibit a depressed mood for most of the day on more days than not. Two or more of the following symptoms must also be present:

1. Poor appetite or overeating
2. Insomnia or hypersomnia
3. Low energy or fatigue
4. Low self-esteem
5. Poor concentration or difficulty making decisions
6. Feelings of hopelessness

These symptoms must not be absent for more than 2 months at a time during the 2-year period. If at any time during the initial 2 years the person met criteria for a major depressive episode, the diagnosis would be major depression rather than dysthymia. As in the case of major depressive disorder, the presence of a manic episode would rule out a diagnosis of dysthymia.

The distinction between major depressive disorder and dysthymia is somewhat artificial because both sets of symptoms are frequently seen in the same person. In such cases, rather than thinking of them as separate disorders, it is more appropriate to consider them as two aspects of the same disorder, which waxes and wanes over time. Some experts have argued that chronic depression is a single, broadly conceived disorder that can be expressed in many different combinations of symptoms over time (McCullough et al., 2003).

Bipolar Disorders   All three types of bipolar disorders involve manic or hypomanic episodes. Table 5–5 lists the DSM-IV criteria for a manic episode. The mood disturbance must be severe enough to interfere with occupational or social functioning. A person who has experienced at least one manic episode would be assigned a diagnosis of bipolar I disorder. The vast majority of patients with this disorder have episodes of major depression in addition to manic episodes.

Some patients experience episodes of increased energy that are not sufficiently severe to qualify as full-blown mania. These episodes are called **hypomania.** A person who has experienced

TABLE 5–3	DSM-IV-TR System for Classifying Mood Disorders

UNIPOLAR DISORDERS

Major Depressive Disorder
- One or more major depressive episodes
- No manic or unequivocal hypomanic episodes

Dysthymic Disorder
- Depressed mood for at least 2 years
- Never without these symptoms for more than 2 months during this period
- No major depressive episode during first 2 years

BIPOLAR DISORDERS

Bipolar I Disorder
- One or more manic episodes

Bipolar II Disorder
- One or more major depressive episodes
- At least one hypomanic episode
- No manic episodes

Cyclothymic Disorder
- Numerous periods with hypomanic symptoms and numerous periods with depressed mood for at least 2 years
- Never without these symptoms for more than 2 months during 2-year period
- No major depressive episodes
- No manic episode during first 2 years

Reprinted with permission from the *Diagnostic and Statistical Manual of Mental Disorders,* Fourth Edition, Text Revision. Copyright © 2000 by the American Psychiatric Association.

TABLE 5–4	Symptoms Listed in DSM-IV-TR for Major Depressive Episode

A. Five or more of the following symptoms have been present during the same 2-week period and represent a change from previous functioning; at least one of the symptoms is either (1) depressed mood, or (2) loss of interest or pleasure.

1. Depressed mood most of the day, nearly every day, as indicated either by subjective report (for example, feels sad or empty) or observation made by others (for example, appears tearful). Note: in children and adolescents, can be irritable mood.

2. Markedly diminished interest or pleasure in all, or almost all, activities most of the day, nearly every day.

3. Significant weight loss when not dieting or weight gain (for example, a change of more than 5 percent of body weight in a month), or decrease or increase in appetite nearly every day. Note: in children, consider failure to make expected weight gains.

4. Insomnia or hypersomnia nearly every day.

5. Psychomotor agitation or retardation nearly every day (observable by others).

6. Fatigue or loss of energy nearly every day.

7. Feelings of worthlessness or excessive or inappropriate guilt nearly every day (not merely self reproach or guilt about being sick).

8. Diminished ability to think or concentrate, or indecisiveness, nearly every day.

9. Recurrent thoughts of death (not just fear of dying), recurrent suicidal ideation without a specific plan, or a suicide attempt or a specific plan for committing suicide.

Reprinted with permission from the *Diagnostic and Statistical Manual of Mental Disorders,* Fourth Edition, Text Revision. Copyright © 2000 by the American Psychiatric Association.

TABLE 5-5 Symptoms Listed in DSM-IV-TR for Manic Episode

A. A distinct period of abnormally and persistently elevated, expansive, or irritable mood, lasting at least 1 week (or any duration if hospitalization is necessary).

B. During the period of mood disturbance, three or more of the following symptoms have persisted (four if the mood is only irritable) and have been present to a significant degree:

1. Inflated self esteem or grandiosity.

2. Decreased need for sleep—for example, feels rested after only 3 hours of sleep.

3. More talkative than usual, or pressure to keep talking.

4. Flight of ideas or subjective experience that thoughts are racing.

5. Distractibility—that is, attention too easily drawn to unimportant or irrelevant external stimuli.

6. Increase in goal directed activity (either socially, at work or school, or sexually) or psychomotor agitation.

7. Excessive involvement in pleasurable activities that have a high potential for painful consequences—for example, the person engages in unrestrained buying sprees, sexual indiscretions, or foolish business investments.

Reprinted with permission from the *Diagnostic and Statistical Manual of Mental Disorders, Fourth Edition, Text Revision.* Copyright © 2000 by the American Psychiatric Association.

at least one major depressive episode, at least one hypomanic episode, and no full-blown manic episodes would be assigned a diagnosis of *bipolar II disorder.* The symptoms used in DSM-IV-TR to identify a hypomanic episode are the same as those used for manic episode (at least three of the seven symptoms listed in Table 5–5). The differences between manic and hypomanic episodes involve duration and severity. The symptoms need to be present for a minimum of only 4 days to meet the threshold for a hypomanic episode (as opposed to 1 week for a manic episode). The mood change in a hypomanic episode must be noticeable to others, but the disturbance must not be severe enough to impair social or occupational functioning or to require hospitalization.

Cyclothymia is considered by DSM-IV-TR to be a chronic but less severe form of bipolar disorder. It is, therefore, the bipolar equivalent of dysthymia. In order to meet criteria for cyclothymia, the person must experience numerous hypomanic episodes and numerous periods of depression (or loss of interest or pleasure) during a period of 2 years. There must be no history of major depressive episodes and no clear evidence of a manic episode during the first 2 years of the disturbance.

Further Descriptions and Subtypes DSM-IV-TR includes several additional ways of describing subtypes of the mood disorders. These are based on two considerations: (1) more specific descriptions of symptoms that were present during the most recent episode of depression (known as *episode specifiers*) and (2) more extensive descriptions of the pattern that the disorder follows over time (known as *course specifiers*). These distinctions may provide a useful way to subdivide depressed patients, who certainly present a heterogenous set of problems. On the other hand, the validity of these subtypes is open to question, especially those based on episode specifiers. Long-term follow-up studies suggest that a patient's subtype diagnosis is likely to change over repeated episodes (Angst, Sellaro, & Merikangas, 2000).

One episode specifier allows the clinician to describe a major depressive episode as having melancholic features. **Melancholia** is a term that is used to describe a particularly severe type of depression. Some experts believe that melancholia represents a subtype of depression that is caused by different factors than those that are responsible for other forms of depression (Leventhal & Rehm, 2005). The presence of melancholic features may also indicate that the person is likely to have a good response to biological forms of treatment, such as antidepressant medication and electroconvulsive therapy (Schatzberg, 1999).

In order to meet the DSM-IV-TR criteria for melancholic features, a depressed patient must either (1) lose the feeling of pleasure associated with all, or almost all, activities or (2) lose the capacity to feel better—even temporarily—when something good happens. The person must also exhibit at least three of the following: (1) the depressed mood feels distinctly different from the depression a person would feel after the death of a loved one; (2) the depression is most often worst in the morning; (3) the person awakens early, at least 2 hours before usual; (4) marked psychomotor retardation or agitation; (5) significant loss of appetite or weight loss; and (6) excessive or inappropriate guilt.

Another episode specifier allows the clinician to indicate the presence of *psychotic features*—hallucinations or delusions—during the most recent episode of depression or mania. The psychotic features can be either consistent or inconsistent with the patient's mood. For example, if a depressed man reports hearing voices that tell him he is a worthless human being who deserves to suffer for his sins, the hallucinations would be considered "mood congruent psychotic features." Depressed patients who exhibit psychotic features are more likely to require hospitalization and treatment with a combination of antidepressant and antipsychotic medication (Parker et al., 1997).

Another episode specifier applies to women who become depressed or manic following pregnancy. A major depressive or manic episode can be specified as having a *postpartum onset* if it begins within 4 weeks after childbirth. Because the woman must meet the full criteria for an episode of major depression or mania, this category does not include minor periods of postpartum "blues," which are relatively common (Seyfried & Marcus, 2003).

The DSM-IV-TR course specifiers for mood disorders allow clinicians to describe further the pattern and sequence of episodes, as well as the person's adjustment between episodes. For example, the course of a bipolar disorder can be specified as *rapid cycling* if the person experiences at least four episodes of major depression, mania, or hypomania within a 12-month period. Patients whose disorder follows this problematic course are likely to show a poor response to treatment and are at greater risk than other types of bipolar patients to attempt suicide (Coryell et al., 2003).

A mood disorder (either unipolar or bipolar) is described as following a seasonal pattern if, over a period of time, there is a regular relationship between the onset of a person's episodes and particular times of the year. The most typical seasonal pattern is one in which the person becomes depressed in the fall or winter, followed by a full recovery in the following spring or summer.

Researchers refer to a mood disorder in which the onset of episodes is regularly associated with changes in seasons as **seasonal affective disorder.**[1] The episodes most commonly occur in winter, presumably in response to fewer hours of sunlight. Seasonal depression is usually characterized by somatic symptoms, such as overeating, carbohydrate craving, weight gain, fatigue, and sleeping more than usual. Among outpatients who have a history of at least three major depressive episodes, approximately one out of six will meet criteria for the seasonal pattern (Partonen & Magnusson, 2001). Most patients with seasonal affective disorder have a unipolar disorder, but many would meet criteria

---

[1]"Affect" and "mood" are sometimes used interchangeably in psychiatric terminology. Depression and mania were called "affective disorders" in DSM-III.

for bipolar II disorder. People in the latter group typically become depressed in the winter followed by a mood reversal to hypomania in the spring. Relatively few have bipolar I disorder (Oren & Rosenthal, 1992).

COURSE AND OUTCOME

To describe the typical course and outcome of mood disorders, it is useful to consider unipolar and bipolar disorders separately. Most studies point to clear-cut differences between these two conditions in terms of age of onset and prognosis (Perris, 1992).

Unipolar Disorders

Data regarding the onset and course of unipolar mood disorders must be viewed with some caution because virtually all studies have focused exclusively on the people who have sought treatment for their depression. Very little is

Video Case

BIPOLAR MOOD DISORDER WITH PSYCHOTIC FEATURES

ANN

"I felt very tense, like my mind was racing; that I was making unusual connections; that I couldn't sleep at night."

On your CD-ROM menu, select "Mood Disorders" and click on "Bipolar Mood Disorder with Psychotic Features: Ann." Although Ann's manic episodes were associated with increased productivity, they also led to serious occupational and social problems.

In a book about her struggle with postpartum depression, actress Brooke Shields described problems in forming a bond with her infant daughter.

known about untreated depressions. We do not know whether they become persistent problems; some may improve spontaneously in a short period of time.

People with unipolar mood disorders typically have their first episode in middle age; the average age of onset is in the mid-forties. The length of episodes varies widely. DSM-IV-TR sets the minimum duration at 2 weeks, but they can last much longer. In one large-scale follow-up study, 10 percent of the patients had depressive episodes that lasted more than 2 years (Thornicroft & Sartorius, 1993). Most unipolar patients will have at least two depressive episodes. The mean number of lifetime episodes is five or six.

The results of long-term follow-up studies of treated patients indicate that major depressive disorder is frequently a chronic and recurrent condition in which episodes of severe symptoms may alternate with periods of full or partial recovery (Thase, 2003). When a person's symptoms are diminished or improved, the disorder is considered to be in **remission,** or a period of recovery. **Relapse** is a return of active symptoms in a person who has recovered from a previous episode. These phases of the disorder are represented schematically in Figure 5–1.

Approximately half of all unipolar patients recover within 6 months of the beginning of an episode. The probability that a patient will recover from an episode decreases after 6 months, and 10 to 20 percent do not recover after 5 years. Among those who recover, 50 percent relapse within 3 years (Hart, Craighead, & Craighead, 2001). The risk of relapse goes down as the period of

remission increases. In other words, the longer the person remains free of depression, the better his or her chance of avoiding relapse.

Bipolar Disorders

Onset of bipolar mood disorders usually occurs between the ages of 28 and 33 years, which is younger than the average age of onset for unipolar disorders. The first episode is just as likely to be manic as depressive. The average duration of a manic episode runs between 2 and 3 months. The onset of a manic episode is not always sudden. Jamison noted, for example:

> I did not wake up one day to find myself mad. Life should be so simple. Rather, I gradually became aware that my life and mind were going at an ever faster and faster clip until finally, over the course of my first summer on the faculty, they both had spun wildly and absolutely out of control. But the acceleration from quick thought to chaos was a slow and beautifully seductive one. (p. 68)

The long-term course of bipolar disorders is most often episodic, and the prognosis is mixed (Angst, Sellaro, & Angst, 1998). Most patients have more than one episode, and bipolar patients tend to have more episodes than unipolar patients. The length of intervals between episodes is difficult to predict. The long-term prognosis is mixed for patients with bipolar mood disorder. Although some patients recover and function very well, others experience continued impairment. Several studies that have followed bipolar patients over periods of up to 10 years have found that 40 to 50 percent of patients are able to achieve a sustained recovery from the disorder. Many patients, however, remain chronically disabled. Rapid cycling patients are less likely to recover from an episode and are more likely to relapse after they do recover (Turvey et al., 1999).

FREQUENCY

Several studies provide detailed information regarding the frequency of mood disorders in various countries around the world (Kessler, 2002; Waraich et al., 2004). Some are based on information collected from nonclinical samples of men and women by investigators using structured diagnostic interviews. In other words, the people who participated in these

The Course of an Episode of Major Depression

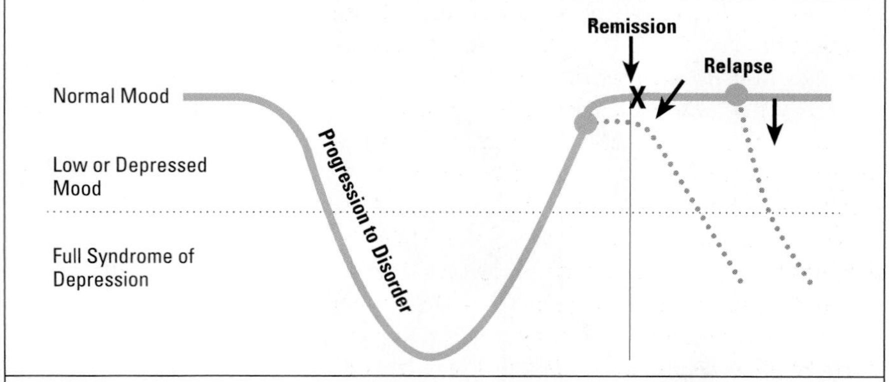

Normal Mood

Low or Depressed Mood

Full Syndrome of Depression

Progression to Disorder

Remission

Relapse

FIGURE 5–1: The phases leading into (and out of) an episode of depression.

Source: E. Frank, H.A. Swartz, & D.J. Kupfer, 2000. Interpersonal and social rhythm therapy: Managing the chaos of bipolar disorder, *Biological Psychiatry, 48,* 593–604. Copyright © 2000 by Society for Biological Psychiatry. Reprinted by permission of Elsevier, Ltd.

studies did not have to be in treatment at a hospital or clinic in order to be identified as being depressed. These studies are particularly important because large numbers of people experience serious depression without wanting or being able to seek professional help. Data based exclusively on treatment records would underestimate the magnitude of the problem.

Two of the largest studies were conducted in the United States. We have already described these studies briefly, in Chapter 1. One is the Epidemiologic Catchment Area (ECA) study, in which nearly 20,000 residents of five communities were interviewed (Robins & Regier, 1991). The other study, the National Comorbidity Survey (NCS), reports diagnostic information for a representative sample of 8,000 adults selected from the 48 contiguous states in the country (Kessler & Zhao, 1999).

Incidence and Prevalence

Unipolar depression is one of the most common forms of psychopathology. Among people who were interviewed for the ECA study, approximately 6 percent were suffering from a diagnosable mood disorder during a period of 6 months. Unipolar disorders are much more common than bipolar disorders. The ratio of unipolar to bipolar disorders is at least 5:1 (Smith & Weissman, 1992).

Lifetime risk for major depressive disorder was approximately 5 percent, averaged across sites in the ECA program (Weissman et al., 1991). The lifetime risk for dysthymia was approximately 3 percent, and the lifetime risk for bipolar I disorder was close to 1 percent. Almost half the people who met diagnostic criteria for dysthymia had also experienced an episode of major depression at some point in their lives. At each of the sites examined by Robins and her colleagues, the lifetime prevalence of all types of mood disorders combined (about 8 percent) ranked third behind substance use disorders (about 17 percent) and anxiety disorders (about 12 percent). The National Comorbidity Survey produced even higher figures for the lifetime prevalence of mood disorders (see Kessler et al., 1994). Therefore the prevalence estimates for mood disorders in the ECA study are probably conservative.

Because the ECA study identified a representative sample of community residents rather than patients already in treatment, it allows some insight regarding the proportion of depressed people who seek professional help for their problems. Slightly more than 30 percent of those people who met diagnostic criteria for a mood disorder made contact with a mental health professional during the 6 months prior to their interview. These data indicate that a substantial proportion of people who are clinically depressed do not receive professional treatment for their disorders. Finding ways to help these people represents an important challenge for psychologists and psychiatrists who treat mood disorders (Wittchen, Holsboer, & Jacobi, 2001).

Gender Differences

Women are two or three times more vulnerable to depression than men are (Nolen-Hoeksema, 2002). This pattern has been reported in study after study, using samples of treated patients as well as community surveys, and regardless of the assessment procedures employed. The increased prevalence of depression among women is apparently limited to unipolar disorders. In the ECA program, for example, the lifetime prevalence rates for major depression were 7 percent in women but only 2.6 percent in men. Relatively large gender differences were also observed for dysthymia, with lifetime prevalence rates of 4.1 percent in women and 2.2 percent in men. Gender differences were not observed, however, for bipolar mood disorders. The lifetime prevalence rates for bipolar I disorder were 0.9 percent for women and 0.7 percent for men (Weissman et al., 1991).

Some observers have suggested that the high rates for unipolar mood disorders in women reflect shortcomings in the data collection process. Women simply might be more likely than men to seek treatment or to be labeled as being depressed. Another argument holds that culturally determined sanctions make it more difficult for men to admit to subjective feelings of distress such as hopelessness and despair. None of these alternatives has been substantiated by empirical evidence. Research studies clearly indicate that the higher prevalence of depression among women is genuine. Possible explanations for this gender difference have focused on a variety of factors, including sex hormones, stressful life events, and childhood adversity as well as response styles that are associated with gender roles (Hankin &

Myrna Weissman, a professor of psychiatry at Columbia University, is one of the leading investigators in the study of the epidemiology of depression.

Video Case

MAJOR DEPRESSION

EVERETT

"You feel absolute worthlessness. You feel there is no hope for the future."

On your CD-ROM menu, select "Mood Disorders" and click on "Major Depression: Everett." Notice the importance and persistence of the negative way in which he views himself and his abilities.

Contrary to popular views, older people are actually less likely to be depressed than are younger people. Some subgroups of elderly people, however, are at high risk for depression.

Abramson, 2001; Kuehner, 2003). These issues are discussed later in this chapter.

Cross-Cultural Differences

Comparisons of emotional expression and emotional disorder across cultural boundaries encounter a number of methodological problems (see Research Methods in Chapter 9). One problem involves vocabulary. Each culture has its own ways of interpreting reality, including different styles of expressing or communicating symptoms of physical and emotional disorder. Words and concepts that are used to describe illness behaviors in one culture might not exist in other cultures. For example, some African cultures have only one word for both anger and sadness. Interesting adaptations are, therefore, required to translate questions that are supposed to tap experiences such as anxiety and depression. One investigation, which employed a British interview schedule that had been translated into Yoruba—a language spoken in Nigeria—used the phrase "the heart goes weak" to represent depression (Leff, 1988). Our own diagnostic categories have been developed within a specific cultural setting; they are not culture-free and are not necessarily any more reasonable than the ways in which other cultures describe and categorize their own behavioral and emotional disorders (Manson & Kleinman, 1998).

Cross-cultural differences have been confirmed by a number of research projects that have examined cultural variations in symptoms among depressed patients in different countries. These studies report comparable overall frequencies of mood disorders in various parts of the world, but the specific type of symptom expressed by the patients varies from one culture to the next. In Chinese patients, depression is more likely to be described in terms of somatic symptoms, such as sleeping problems, headaches, and loss of energy (Kleinman, 2004). Depressed patients in Europe and North America are more likely to express feelings of guilt and suicidal ideas (Kirmayer, 2001).

These cross-cultural comparisons suggest that, at its most basic level, clinical depression is a universal phenomenon that is not limited to Western or urban societies. They also indicate that a person's cultural experiences, including linguistic, educational, and social factors, may play an important role in shaping the manner in which he or she expresses and copes with the anguish of depression. Cross-cultural variations should also be kept in mind when clinicians attempt to identify central or defining features of depression. We will return to this point later in the chapter when we discuss the rationale behind studies that rely on animal models of depression.

Risk for Mood Disorders Across the Life Span

Age is an important consideration in the epidemiology of mood disorders. Some readers might expect that the prevalence of depression would be higher among older people than among younger people. This was, in fact, what many clinicians expected prior to large-scale epidemiological investigations, such as the ECA study. This belief may stem from the casual observation that many older people experience brief episodic states of acute unhappiness, often precipitated by changes in status (for example, retirement, relocation) and loss of significant others (for example, children moving away, deaths of friends and relatives). But brief episodes of sadness and grief are not the same thing as clinical depression.

Although many people mistakenly identify depression with the elderly, data from the ECA

project suggest that mood disorders actually are most frequent among young and middle-aged adults. Prevalence rates for major depressive episodes and dysthymia were significantly lower for people over the age of 65. The frequency of bipolar disorders was also low in the oldest age groups. These data are illustrated in Figure 5–2. Notice that rates of both major depression and bipolar I disorder are lowest in the oldest age group. When unipolar and bipolar mood disorders are combined to examine gender differences and age, the lowest rates are found in the oldest age group for both men and women.

Several explanations have been offered for this pattern. One interpretation is based on the fact that elderly people are more likely to experience memory impairments (see Chapter 14). People who are in their seventies and eighties may have more trouble remembering, and therefore may fail to report, episodes of depression that occurred several months before the research interview is conducted. Also, because mood disorders are associated with increased mortality (for example, suicide), many severely depressed people might not have survived into old age. These are both plausible hypotheses that may have influenced the results of the ECA study and related investigations. Nevertheless, the same pattern has been observed in several studies, and most investigators now believe that the effect is genuine: Clinical depression is less common among elderly people than it is among younger adults (Blazer, 2004; Wittchen, Knauper, & Kessler, 1994).

Finally, it should be noted that the frequency of depression is much higher among certain subgroups of elderly people. For example, the prevalence of depression is particularly high among those who are about to enter residential care facilities. Elderly people in nursing homes are more likely to be depressed in comparison to a random sample of elderly people living in the community (Zarate & Tohen, 1996).

The ECA findings on age and depression also raise another important question: Has the frequency of depression increased in recent years? The answer is apparently yes. People born after World War II seem to be more likely to develop mood disorders than were people from previous generations. In fact, several studies have reported a consistent trend toward higher lifetime rates of depression in successively younger generations (Lavori et al., 1987; Wittchen, Knauper, & Kessler, 1994). The average age of onset for clinical depression also seems to be lower in people

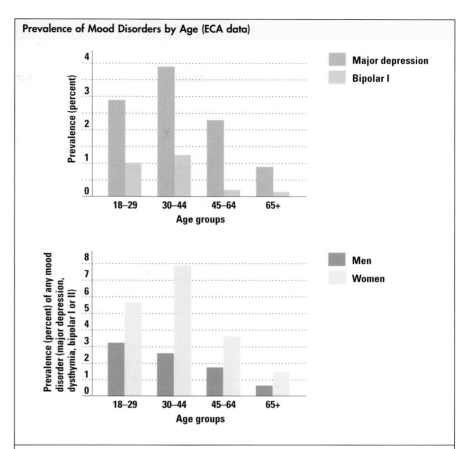

FIGURE 5–2: (top) Twelve-month prevalence for unipolar and bipolar mood disorders in different age groups. (bottom) Twelve-month prevalence for mood disorders in men and women in different age groups.

Source: M.M. Weissman, M.L. Bruce, P.J. Leaf, L.P. Florio, and C. Holzer, 1991. Affective disorders. In L.N. Robins and D.A. Regier (Eds.), *Psychiatric Disorders in America: The Epidemiologic Catchment Area Study.* New York: Free Press, p. 60. Copyright © 1991 by Lee N. Robins and Darrel A. Regier. Reprinted with the permission of The Free Press. All rights reserved.

who were born more recently. This kind of pattern is sometimes called a birth cohort trend.

CAUSES

In the next few pages we turn our attention to current speculation and knowledge about causes of mood disorders. Discussions of this topic must keep in mind the relatively high prevalence of these problems. Major depression is a severely disabling condition that affects at least 8 percent of the population, usually appearing during young adulthood when the person would be expected to be most active and productive. Why hasn't this problem been eliminated through the process of natural selection? Evolutionary theorists suggest

Are we more likely to experience depression as we get older?

that it is because, in addition to being painful and disruptive to a person's life, mild to moderate symptoms of depression may serve a useful purpose (Nesse, 1999; Price et al., 2004). This argument is focused on those situations in which depression represents a temporary response to circumstances in the person's environment. As we will see, many episodes of depression do seem to be triggered by stressful life events and harsh social circumstances. An evolutionary perspective would hold that the symptoms of depression—slowing down, loss of motivation, withdrawal from other people—may represent a response system that helps the person disengage from a situation that is not going well (McGuire & Troisi, 1998b). For example, someone who is involved in an unsuccessful marriage may eventually become depressed, withdraw, and reconsider the long-term benefits of investing further time and resources in a relationship that is likely to remain unrewarding. At low levels and over brief periods of time, depressed mood may help us refocus our motivations and it may help us to conserve and redirect our energy in response to experiences of loss and defeat. In that sense, we all have the capacity to become depressed.

Psychological explanations for mood disorders focus on individual differences, and they are primarily concerned with the most severe and disabling forms of depression. Why do some people develop major depression and others do not? What kinds of events are associated with a relatively drastic failure of the psychological and biological systems that regulate mood? A disorder that is as common as depression must have many causes rather than one. In Chapter 2, we discussed some general principles that are associated with systems theory. The principle of equifinality, which holds that there are many ways to reach the same outcome, clearly applies in the case of mood disorders.

Our consideration of etiological factors is organized around different levels of analysis. We will consider social, psychological, and biological mechanisms that are involved in the onset and maintenance of mood disorders. This organization should help you appreciate the complementary nature of these analyses. After we have considered the impact of stressful life events on mood, we will discuss psychological factors, such as cognitive biases, that shape a person's response to stress. Then we will review what is known about hormones and brain activities that coordinate our responses to environmental stressors. Biological mechanisms should not be viewed as an alternative to psychological or social explanations of depression. Rather, they help us understand at a microscopic level of analysis how our bodies perform important functions such as regulating emotion and responding to stressful events.

We will discuss evidence regarding unipolar and bipolar mood disorders separately, when it is appropriate. Most research on the etiology of bipolar mood disorders has focused on biological factors, especially genetics. There is also some recent evidence regarding the influence of stressful life events and the onset of manic episodes. Our discussion of psychological factors will focus exclusively on the etiology of unipolar depression because this topic has not been explored extensively with regard to bipolar disorders.

Social Factors

It should not be surprising that much of the literature on depression focuses on interpersonal loss and separation. From birth to death, our lives are intertwined with those of other people. We are fundamentally social organisms, and we feel sad when someone close to us dies. Similar feelings occasionally follow major disappointments, such as failure to win acceptance to the school of our choice or being fired from a job. In these cases, rather than losing other people, some clinicians have suggested that we may be losing "social roles" or ways in which we think about ourselves.

Various theories of depression have been built around a consideration of the impact of stressful life events. Beginning around the turn of the twentieth century, psychodynamic theories emphasized the central role played by interpersonal relationships and loss of significant others in setting the stage for depression as well as in bringing about a depressive episode (Freud, 1917/1961). Freud's theory laid the intellectual foundation for many subsequent studies of psychological and social factors in the development and maintenance of unipolar depression. He focused interest on the possibility that stressful life events, such as the death of a close friend or family member, may precipitate the onset of mood disorders. Freud was also interested in the observation that some people who become depressed are extremely dependent on other people for the maintenance of their self-esteem. This hypothesis anticipated subsequent studies of social skills in depression and the importance of interpersonal relationships over the course of mood disorders.

Stressful Life Events and Unipolar Disorders

Several investigations have explored the relationships between stressful life events and the development of unipolar mood disorders. Do people who become clinically depressed actually experience an increased number of stressful life events? The answer is yes. The experience of stressful life events is associated with an increased probability that a person will become depressed. This correlation has been demonstrated many times (Hammen, 2005; Monroe & Harkness, 2005).

Investigators have faced difficult methodological issues in order to interpret the strong relationship between stressful life events and the onset of depression. One particularly troublesome problem involves the direction of the relationship between life events and mood disorders. For example, being fired from a job might lead a person to become depressed. On the other hand, the onset of a depressive episode, with its associated difficulties in energy and concentration, could easily affect the person's job performance and lead to being fired. Therefore, if depressed people experience more stressful events, what is the direction of effect? Does failure lead to depression, or does depression lead to failure?

By using prospective research designs, in which subjects are followed over time, investigators have been able to address the question of cause and effect (see Research Methods in Chapter 8). Prospective studies have found that stressful life events are useful in predicting the subsequent onset of unipolar depression (Brown, 2002; Kendler, Karkowski, & Prescott, 1999). This evidence supports the argument that, in many cases, stressful life events contribute to (and are not merely consequences of) the onset of mood disorders.

Although many kinds of negative events are associated with depression, a special class of circumstances—those involving major losses of important people or roles—seems to play a crucial role in precipitating unipolar depression.

This conclusion is based, in large part, on a series of studies reported by George Brown, a sociologist, and Tirril Harris, a clinical psychologist, both at Guy's, King's, and St. Thomas' School of Medicine (University of London in England). Their studies have compared the living circumstances and life experiences of depressed and nondepressed women, regardless of whether they are receiving treatment for their problems. Brown and Harris (1978) found that "severe" events—those that are particularly threatening and have long-term consequences for the woman's adjustment—increase the probability that a woman will become depressed. On the other hand, the ordinary hassles and difficulties of everyday living (events that are not severe) do not seem to lead to the onset of depression (Monroe & Simons, 1991).

Severe events increase the probability of depression, but most women who experience a severe event do not become depressed. What is the difference between the circumstances of women who become depressed after a severe event and those who do not? Brown and his colleagues believe that depression is more likely to occur when severe life events are associated with feelings of humiliation, entrapment, and defeat (Brown, 1998; 2002). An example of a humiliating event would be a woman learning unexpectedly of her husband's long-standing infidelity. An example of an event fitting the entrapment theme would be a woman receiving official notification that her application to move out of appalling housing conditions had been denied. These data point to a particularly powerful relationship between the onset of depression and certain kinds of stressful life events. The likelihood that a woman will become depressed is especially high if she experiences a severe event that would be expected to lead to a sense of being devalued as a person or trapped with no way toward a brighter future (Kendler et al., 2003).

Comparisons among different populations can shed further light on the relation between severe life events and the etiology of depression. Brown (1998) repeated his study with women living in six different populations in Europe and Africa. Some of these are impoverished urban regions, such as a township in Harare, Zimbabwe, and others are rural. In each sample, Brown found that severe life events preceded the onset of most depressive episodes. He also found very large differences among these

George Brown has made important contributions to knowledge regarding the link between stressful life events and the onset of depression.

communities in terms of their overall prevalence of depression. These differences varied directly in proportion to the frequency with which their women experienced severe life events; communities with the highest rates of severe events produced the highest prevalence of major depression (see Figure 5–3). This pattern suggests that variations in the overall prevalence of depression are driven in large part by social factors that influence the frequency of stress in the community.

Social Factors and Bipolar Disorders   Most investigations of stressful life events have been concerned with unipolar depression. Less attention has been paid to bipolar mood disorders, but some have found that the weeks preceding the onset of a manic episode are marked by an increased frequency of stressful life events (Hlastala et al., 2000; Johnson & Kizer, 2002). The kinds of events that precede the onset of mania tend to be different from those that lead to depression. While the latter include primarily negative experiences involving loss and low self-esteem, the former include schedule-

disrupting events (such as loss of sleep) as well as goal attainment events. Some patients experience an increase in manic symptoms after they have achieved a significant goal toward which they had been working (Johnson et al., 2000). Examples of this kind of goal attainment event would be a major job promotion, being accepted to a competitive professional school program, or the blossoming of a new romantic relationship. These exhilarating experiences, coupled with the person's ongoing problems with emotion regulation, may contribute to a spiral of positive emotion and excess activity that culminates in a full-blown manic episode.

Aversive patterns of emotional expression and communication within the family can also have a negative impact on the adjustment of people with bipolar mood disorders. Longitudinal studies of bipolar patients have focused on the relation between frequency of relapse and the emotional climate within their families. Patients living with family members who are hostile toward or critical of the patient are more likely to relapse shortly after being discharged from the hospital (Miklowitz, Goldstein, & Neuchterlein, 1995). Furthermore, bipolar patients who have less social support are more likely to relapse (Cohen et al., 2004) and recover more slowly than patients with higher levels of social support (Johnson et al., 1999). Stressful life events can also delay recovery from an episode of depression in bipolar patients (Johnson & Miller, 1997). This evidence indicates that the course of bipolar mood disorder can be influenced by the social environment in which the person is living.

Psychological Factors

Severe events are clearly related to the onset of depression, but they do not provide a complete account of who will become depressed. Many people who do not become depressed also experience severe events. In the study reported by Brown and Harris (1978), only one out of every five women who reported a severe event in the preceding year became depressed. Presumably those who become depressed are somehow more vulnerable to the effects of stress. Several psychological factors may contribute to a person's vulnerability to stressful life events. In the following pages, we will consider two principal areas that have received attention in the research

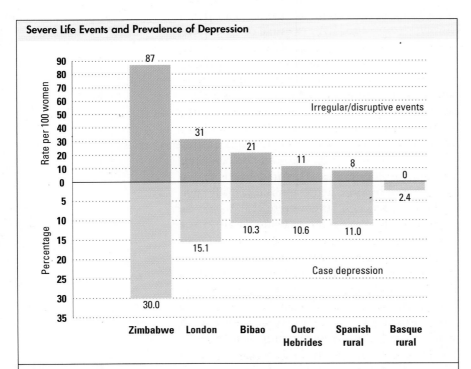

FIGURE 5–3: Yearly rate of irregular or disruptive severe events per 100 women in six populations and prevalence of cases of depression in the same year.

Source: Brown, G.W. (1998). Genetic and population perspectives on life events and depression. *Social Psychiatry and Psychiatric Epidemiology, 33,* 363–372. Copyright © 1998 by Springer-Verlag. Reprinted by permission of Springer-Verlag.

about negative or stressful experiences, the ways in which we actually respond to these events may also influence the probability that we will become depressed. In other words, it's not just how you think about an event or circumstance but the things that you actually do that will determine its eventual outcome. How does the depressed person cope with stressful events and respond to other people? What types of responses does the patient elicit from others? What are the extent and form of social resources that are available to help support the person during a crisis?

Some depressed people create difficult circumstances that increase the level of stress in their lives. In other words, the relationship between stressful life events and depression runs in both directions. Most of the research in this area has been done with female participants because women are more likely to be depressed than men. For example, in comparison to women who are not depressed and women with other medical disorders, unipolar depressed women generate higher levels of stress, especially in the context of interpersonal relationships (Coyne et al., 2002; Hammen, 2002; Harkness et al., 1999). Maladaptive tactics for coping with marital distress are important factors in this process. For example, when involved in a serious disagreement with a spouse, a depressed person might express escalating complaints and hostile, provocative comments rather than trying to work toward a solution to the conflict. This dynamic process leads to an escalation of stress. Negative life events, which are not caused by the person's own behavior, may contribute to the onset of depression. An example might be an economic recession that leads to the loss of a job, increased financial pressures within a family, and marital distress. One of the partners becomes depressed, and then that person may exacerbate the difficulty by behaving in a way that leads to even higher levels of stress and perhaps a further deterioration in his or her mood.

Social Relationships

The assumptions behind the interpersonal perspective on depression are very different from those incorporated in more cognitively oriented theories. For example, the cognitive perspective might argue that faulty processing of information leads those who are depressed to believe (erroneously) that their relationships with other people are inadequate. Interpersonal theorists suggest that depressed

Separation from a spouse during a war can be extremely stressful. Whether or not the person becomes depressed is influenced by cognitive events as well as interpersonal skills that are used to cope with this difficult situation.

people may actually behave in ways that have a genuinely negative effect on other people, thus alienating themselves from friends and family members (Coyne, 1999; Joiner, 2002).

The interpersonal perspective has produced some interesting findings regarding factors that contribute to depression. Several research studies have demonstrated that depressed people do indeed have a negative impact on other people's moods and on their nonverbal behavior (Joiner & Metalsky, 1995; Segrin & Abramson, 1994). In addition, depressed people have smaller and less supportive social networks than do people who are not depressed. They know fewer people, interact with them less often, and consider them to be less supportive. Family interactions are generally more negative and argumentative. Perhaps most importantly, these maladaptive patterns of interpersonal relationships are ongoing characteristics of the individual's behavior that persist into periods of symptomatic remission. They are not evident only during active episodes of major depression.

Response Styles and Gender

Another perspective on the development of depression has emphasized response styles, which represent a slightly different aspect of coping behavior. This approach has been developed in an effort to explain gender differences in the frequency of depression. The manner in which a person responds to the onset of a depressed mood seems to influence the duration and the severity of the mood (Nolen-Hoeksema, 1994, 2000). Two different response styles have been emphasized in this work. Some people respond to feelings of depression by turning their attention inward, contemplating the causes and implications of their sadness. This is called a *ruminative style*. Writing in a diary or talking extensively with a friend about how one feels are indications of a ruminative style. Other people employ a *distracting style* to divert themselves from their unpleasant mood. They work on hobbies, play sports, or otherwise become involved in activities that draw their attention away from symptoms of depression.

The first hypothesis of the response styles model is that people who engage in ruminative responses have longer and more severe episodes of depression than do people who engage in distracting responses. The second hypothesis is that women are more likely to employ a ruminative style in response to depression, whereas men are more likely to employ a distracting style. Because the ruminative style leads to episodes of greater duration and intensity, women are more susceptible to depression than are men.

Research evidence provides support for both of the response style hypotheses. A ruminative response style is relatively stable over time and tends to be associated with longer and more severely depressed moods. Furthermore, women are more likely than men to exhibit a ruminative coping style in response to the onset of a depressed mood. Prospective data indicate that people with a ruminative response style are more likely to experience the onset of a depressive episode than are people who employ a distracting style. Rumination also predicts the severity of the depressive episode (Just & Alloy, 1997; Nolen-Hoeksema, 2000).

Integration of Cognitive and Interpersonal Factors   The factors that we have considered in the preceding pages almost certainly work in combination rather than individually. We do not need to decide whether cognitive vulnerabilities are somehow more or less important than interpersonal behaviors because they are undoubtedly different sides of the same coin. The development of depression must be understood in terms of several stages: vulnerability, onset, and maintenance. Cognitive factors and interpersonal skills play an important role within each stage (Gotlib & Hammen, 1992; Alloy et al., 2004).

Vulnerability to depression is influenced by experiences during childhood, including events such as being repeatedly neglected or harshly criticized by parents. Negative ways of thinking

about the world and dysfunctional interpersonal skills are presumably learned early in life (Ingram & Ritter, 2000). As the child grows up, the combination of biased cognitive schemas and deficits in interpersonal skills then affects his or her social environment in several ways: It increases the likelihood that the person will enter problematic relationships; it diminishes the person's ability to resolve conflict after it occurs; and it minimizes the person's ability to solicit support and assistance from other people (Hammen & Garber, 2001).

The onset of depression is most often triggered by life events and circumstances. The stressful life events that precipitate an episode frequently grow out of difficult personal and family relationships. The impact of these experiences depends on the meanings that people assign to them. People become depressed when they interpret events in a way that diminishes their sense of self-worth. Persistent interpersonal and cognitive problems also serve to maintain a depressed mood over an extended period of time and help it escalate to clinical proportions.

Biological Factors

We have considered a number of social and psychological factors that contribute to the etiology of mood disorders. Biological factors are also influential in the regulation of mood. Various studies suggest that genetic factors are somehow involved in unipolar and bipolar disorders, that hormonal abnormalities are regularly associated with depression, and that depression is associated with abnormalities in the activation of specific regions of the brain.

Genetics   Genetic factors are clearly involved in the transmission of mood disorders (Sullivan, Neale, & Kendler, 2000). Studies that support this conclusion also suggest that bipolar disorders are much more heritable than unipolar disorders.

Family Studies   If the development of mood disorders is influenced by genetic factors, these disorders should be more common among the biological relatives of people who are depressed than they are among the general population. First-degree relatives (siblings, parents, and children) of patients with mood disorders should be more vulnerable to the disorder because they share 50 percent of their genes with an affected individual.

Peter Lewinsohn, whose model of depression inspired much of the research on interpersonal factors in depression. His longitudinal studies have contributed important information regarding the role of cognitive factors and social skills in the development of depression.

Several carefully controlled studies have confirmed this hypothesis. Family studies begin with the identification of an individual who has been diagnosed as having a mood disorder—the *proband*. Researchers obtain as much information as possible about the proband's relatives, through personal interviews, family informants, or mental health records. They use this information to decide whether each relative fits criteria for mood disorders. They can then compare the lifetime morbid risk among the patient's relatives with those figures already established for the general population.

Figure 5–4 presents a summary of data from several family studies of mood disorder. An interesting pattern distinguishes unipolar and bipolar mood disorders. Remember that the lifetime risk for major depressive disorder was approximately 5 percent in the ECA study, whereas the lifetime risk for bipolar disorder was approximately 1 percent. With these figures in mind, consider the frequency of disorder among the relatives of unipolar probands. The risk for bipolar disorder among their relatives is close to that seen in the general population, but the risk for unipolar disorder is almost double. Among the relatives of bipolar probands, the risk for both bipolar and unipolar disorder is much higher than that seen in the general population. The combined risk for both types of mood disorder is about 19 percent, almost double the combined risk of 10 percent found among the relatives of unipolar probands. Both types of mood disorder are, therefore, markedly familial. Family studies support the conclusion that bipolar mood disorders should be considered a separate type of mood disorder because the risk for bipolar disorder is elevated only among the families of probands who have bipolar disorders themselves (Winokur et al., 1995).

Twin Studies   The comparison of monozygotic (MZ) and dizygotic (DZ) twin pairs provides a more rigorous test of the possible influence of genetic factors (see Chapter 2). Several twin studies of mood disorders have reported higher concordance rates among MZ than among DZ twins (Bierut et al., 1999; McGuffin et al., 2003).

One classic study used national twin and psychiatric registers in Denmark to identify 110 pairs of same-sex twins in which at least one member was diagnosed as having a mood disorder (Bertelson et al., 1977). The concordance rates for bipolar disorders in MZ and DZ twins

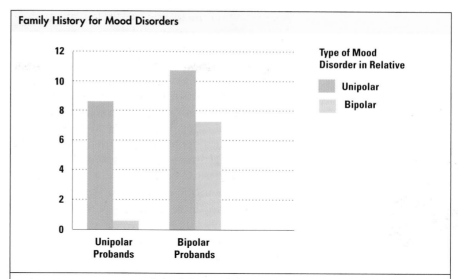

FIGURE 5–4: Average morbid risk for mood disorders in first-degree relatives of unipolar and bipolar patients. (Based on 7 studies of relatives of unipolar probands and 12 studies of relatives of bipolar probands.)

Source: R. Katz and P. McGuffin, 1993, The genetics of affective disorders. In D. Fowles (Ed.), *Progress in Experimental Personality and Psychotherapy Research.* New York: Springer. Copyright © 1993. Reprinted by permission of Springer Publishing Company, Inc., NY, 10036.

were .69 and .19, respectively. For unipolar disorders, concordance rates for MZ and DZ twins were .54 and .24, respectively. The fact that the concordance rates were significantly higher for MZ than for DZ twins indicates that genetic factors are involved in the transmission of both bipolar and unipolar mood disorders. The fact that the difference between the MZ and DZ rate was somewhat higher for bipolar than for unipolar disorders may suggest that genes play a more important role in bipolar disorders than in unipolar disorders. Similar patterns of MZ and DZ concordance rates have been reported subsequently from twin studies of mood disorders conducted in Sweden (Torgersen, 1986) and in England (McGuffin, Katz, Watkins, & Rutherford, 1996).

Twin studies also tell us that environmental factors influence the expression of a genetically determined vulnerability to depression. The best evidence for the influence of nongenetic factors is the concordance rates in MZ twins, which consistently fall short of 100 percent. If genes told the whole story, MZ twins would always be concordant. Mathematical analyses have been used to estimate the relative contributions of genetic and environmental events to the etiology of mood disorders. The results of these analyses are expressed in terms of *heritability*, which can range from 0 percent (meaning that genetic factors are not involved) to 100 percent (meaning that genetic factors alone are responsible for the development of the trait in question) (see Research Methods in Chapter 17). These analyses indicate that genetic factors are particularly influential in bipolar mood disorders, for which the heritability estimate is 80 percent. Genes and environment contribute about equally to the etiology of major depressive disorder, in which the heritability estimate is 52 percent. The genetic contribution may be relatively minor for dysthymia or neurotic depression, where the heritability estimate is only 10 percent (Katz & McGuffin, 1993).

Mode of Transmission and Linkage Studies The family and twin studies indicate that genetic factors play an important role in the development of mood disorders. They have not, however, established the operation of a particular mode of inheritance. It is difficult to identify specific genes involved in complex behavioral disorders because there is no straightforward pattern of inheritance. Most investigators view mood disorders as being polygenic—that is, they are influenced by several different genes—and each of these genes on its own only changes risk for the disorder by a small amount.

Several groups of investigators have searched for evidence of chromosomal linkage between the locus of a known gene and the locus for a gene that is responsible for mood disorders. Two loci are said to be linked when they occupy positions that are close together on the same chromosome. Linkage is usually detected by examining the degree of association between two or more traits within specific families (see Research Methods in Chapter 14).

Linkage studies of mood disorders have focused primarily on bipolar patients because genetic factors appear to be more influential in bipolar than in unipolar disorders. With the introduction of new gene-mapping techniques, our knowledge in this area is expanding dramatically. Unfortunately, most of the early results have been disappointing. Preliminary reports of linkage to regions on various chromosomes turned out to be erroneous. Findings from one laboratory often failed to replicate when they were tested by other investigators. More recently, the most consistent results across different studies have focused on chromosome 18. Genetic markers located in several different locations on chromosome 18 appear to be linked to the presence of bipolar mood disorder in certain families (McMahon et al., 2001; Souery et al., 2001).

The possibility of detecting linkage to known traits is very exciting. This knowledge might eventually enable mental health professionals to identify people who are vulnerable to a disorder before the onset of overt symptoms. At the same time, however, two important cautions must be kept in mind regarding the complexity of the search for causes of mood disorders. One problem involves genetic heterogeneity. Within the general population, there may be more than one locus that contributes to the development of depression. Mood disorders may be linked to one marker within a certain extended family and to an entirely different marker in another family. Second, we also know that the environment plays an important role in the development of mood disorders. The onset of a mood disorders is determined by a combination of genetic and environmental risk factors that the individual experiences.

Genetic Risk and Sensitivity to Stress How do genetic factors and stressful life events interact to bring about depression? The combined effects of genetic and environmental factors has been evaluated by incorporating the measurement of stressful life events into a standard twin design. One such study employed a large sample of female same-sex twins in a study of unipolar mood disorder (Kendler et al., 1995). The twins were divided into four groups, based on levels of genetic risk. They were also divided into those who had experienced a severe life event during the follow-up period and those who had not. The negative impact of severe events was much higher among those women who were also at greater genetic risk for unipolar depression. Therefore the effects of the environment and genetic factors are not independent. Genetic factors apparently control the person's sensitivity to environmental events.

A more recent and dramatic demonstration of this phenomenon was based on new genetic techniques that allow investigators to identify specific genes (Caspi et al., 2003). This investigation focused on the serotonin transporter (5-HTT) gene, which has been studied because several drugs that are used to treat depression have a direct impact on this particular neurotransmitter (see page 158). There are two alleles (long and short) for one particular region of the

5-HTT gene: The short allele ("s") is associated with reduced efficiency of neural transmission in serotonin pathways. People who are homozygous for the "s" allele of the 5-HTT gene are at a particularly high risk for becoming clinically depressed if they experience stressful life events (see Figure 5–5). In the absence of increased stress, the presence of this gene does not increase the person's risk for depression. Both factors seem to be necessary.

The Neuroendocrine System   Various kinds of central nervous system events are associated with the connection between stressful life events and major depression. In the following sections, we will consider evidence regarding hormones and specific regions of the brain. These are the biological phenomena that are closely associated with the social and psychological factors that we have described thus far. Cognitive and emotional events are implemented in these events (Miller & Keller, 2000). They are part of the process by which the brain communicates with the rest of the body and mobilizes activities in response to changes in the external environment.

The endocrine system plays an important role in regulating a person's response to stress. Endocrine glands, such as the pituitary, thyroid, and adrenal glands, are located at various sites throughout the body (see Figure 2–4). In response to signals from the brain, these glands secrete hormones into the bloodstream. One important pathway in the endocrine system that may be closely related to the etiology of mood disorders is called the *hypothalamic–pituitary–adrenal (HPA) axis*. When the person detects a threat in the environment, the hypothalamus signals the pituitary gland to secrete a hormone called ACTH, which in turn modulates secretion of hormones, such as cortisol, from the adrenal glands into the bloodstream. Increased levels of cortisol help the person to prepare to respond to the threat by increasing alertness and delivering more fuel to muscles while also decreasing interest in other activities that might interfere with self-protection (such as sleeping and eating). This system is illustrated in Figure 5–6.

Interest in the relation between mood disorders and the endocrine system was stimulated in part by descriptions of Cushing's syndrome, a disease associated with the adrenal glands that results in abnormally high concentrations of the hormone cortisol in the bloodstream (Sonino & Fava, 2001). Approximately half of all patients with Cushing's syndrome are also clinically depressed. After Cushing's syndrome is corrected, most patients also recover from their depression. This pattern suggests that abnormally high levels of cortisol may lead to the onset of depression (Plotsky et al., 1998).

An association between the HPA axis and depression is also indicated by evidence regarding the *dexamethasone suppression test* (DST), which has been used extensively to study endocrine dysfunction in patients with mood disorders (Nemeroff, 1998). Dexamethasone is a potent synthetic hormone. People who have taken a test dose of dexamethasone normally show a suppression of cortisol secretion because the hypothalamus is fooled into thinking that there is already enough cortisol circulating in the system. Some depressed people show a different response: Approximately half of depressed patients show a failure of suppression in response to the DST. After their symptoms have improved, most of these patients exhibit a normal response on the DST. This pattern is consistent with the hypothesis that a dysfunction of the HPA axis may be involved in the development or maintenance of clinical depression, at least for some people (Whybrow, 1997).

In what ways might endocrine problems be related to other etiological factors? Several

Why do some people become depressed after stressful life events while others do not?

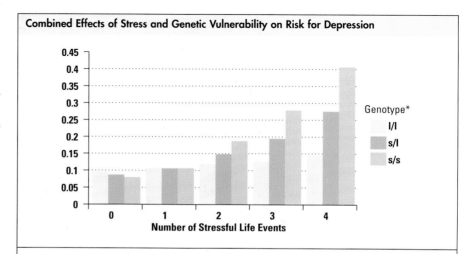

FIGURE 5–5: Probability of onset of major depressive episode as a function of genotype for the serotonin transporter gene.

*The short ("s") allele is associated with lower efficiency compared to the long ("l") allele.
Source: Caspi, A., Sugden, K., Moffitt, T. E., Taylor, A., Craig, I. W., Harrington, H., McClay, J., Mill, J., Martin, J., Braithwaite, A., & Poulton, R. (2003). Influence of life stress on depression: Moderation by a polymorphism in the 5-HTT gene. *Science, 301,* 386–389. Copyright © 2003 by American Association for the Advancement of Science. Reprinted by permission of the publisher.

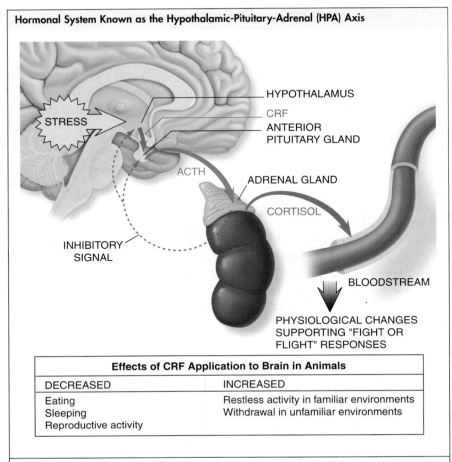

Hormonal System Known as the Hypothalamic-Pituitary-Adrenal (HPA) Axis

STRESS

HYPOTHALAMUS

CRF

ANTERIOR PITUITARY GLAND

ACTH

ADRENAL GLAND

CORTISOL

INHIBITORY SIGNAL

BLOODSTREAM

PHYSIOLOGICAL CHANGES SUPPORTING "FIGHT OR FLIGHT" RESPONSES

Effects of CRF Application to Brain in Animals	
DECREASED	INCREASED
Eating Sleeping Reproductive activity	Restless activity in familiar environments Withdrawal in unfamiliar environments

FIGURE 5-6: The hypothalamic-pituitary-adrenal axis is activated in response to stress.

Source: Adapted from C. Nemeroff, (1998). The neurobiology of depression. *Scientific American.*

possibilities exist. In terms of the specific link between the endocrine system and the central nervous system, overproduction of cortisol may lead to changes in brain structure and function. At a more general level, hormone regulation may provide a process through which stressful life events interact with a genetically determined predisposition to mood disorder. Stress causes the release of adrenal steroids, such as cortisol, and steroid hormones play an active role in regulating the expression of genes (Haskett, 1993).

Brain Imaging Studies The newest tools in the search for biological underpinnings of mood disorders are those that allow scientists to create detailed images of brain structures and to monitor ongoing brain functions in living patients (see Chapter 4 for a description of these procedures). The brain circuits that are involved in the experience and control of emotion are complex,

centering primarily on the limbic system and its connections to the prefrontal cortex and the anterior cingulate cortex. Brain imaging studies indicate that severe depression is often associated with abnormal patterns of activity as well as structural changes in various brain regions (Davidson et al., 2002). Some of these areas of the brain are illustrated in Figure 5–7. See Figure 2–3 for illustrations of the amygdala, hippocampus, and other structures involved in the limbic system.

Abnormal patterns of activation in regions of the prefrontal cortex (PFC) are often found in association with depression. This evidence has been collected using functional brain imaging procedures, such as PET and fMRI. Some areas show *decreased activity*, especially the dorsolateral prefrontal cortex on the left side of the brain. This area of the PFC is involved in planning that is guided by the anticipation of emotion. A person who has a deficit of this type might have motivational problems, such as an inability to work toward a pleasurable goal. Other areas of the PFC have been found to show *abnormally elevated* levels of activity in depressed people. These include the orbital PFC and the ventromedial PFC, areas of the brain that are important for determining a person's responses to reward and punishment. More specifically, the orbital PFC inhibits inappropriate behaviors and helps the person ignore immediate rewards while working toward long-term goals. The ventromedial PFC is involved in the experience of emotion and the process of assigning meaning to perceptions. Overactivity in these regions of the brain might be associated with the prolonged experience of negative emotion.

The anterior cingulate cortex (ACC) provides a connection between the functions of attention and emotion. It allows us to focus on subjective feelings and to consider the relation between our emotions and our behavior. For example, the ACC is activated when a person has been frustrated in the pursuit of a goal, or when he or she experiences an emotion, such as sadness, in a situation where it was not expected. People suffering from major depressive disorder typically show decreased activation of the ACC (Davidson et al., 2002). A reduction in ACC activity might be reflected in a failure to appreciate the maladaptive nature of prolonged negative emotions and a reduced ability to engage in more adaptive behaviors that might help to resolve the person's problems.

The amygdala (see Figure 5–7), almond-sized nuclei near the tip of the hippocampus on each side of the brain, appear to be an important part of the neural circuit involved in emotion (Whybrow, 1997). They are extensively connected to the hypothalamus. This system is responsible for monitoring the emotional significance of information that is processed by the brain and regulating social interactions. Functional imaging studies have identified elevated levels of resting blood flow and glucose metabolism in the amygdala among patients with major depressive disorder and bipolar mood disorder (Drevets, 2002). Higher metabolism rates are associated with more severe levels of depression. Patients who respond positively to treatment show a normalization of amygdala metabolism.

It is tempting to infer from this pattern that the increased activity reflected in images of the amygdala represents, at the neurochemical level of analysis, a reflection of the distorted cognitive functions that have been described by clinical psychologists in association with depression (Drevets & Raichle, 1998). Of course, this kind of speculation will need to be tested using more detailed research strategies in which specific cognitive processes are measured while brain activities are recorded in depressed and nondepressed people.

Neurotransmitters   Communication and coordination of information within and between areas of the brain depend on neurotransmitters, chemicals that bridge the gaps between individual neurons (see Chapter 2). Over the past several decades, scientists have gathered a great deal of information concerning the neurochemical underpinnings of depression and mania (McAllister-Williams, 2002; Whybrow, 1997). Our knowledge in this area began with the accidental discovery, during the 1950s, of several drugs that have the ability to alter people's moods. The development of antidepressant drugs stimulated research on several specific neurotransmitters that have been shown to be responsible for their effects. Most notable among these are serotonin, norepinephrine, and dopamine. Each neurotransmitter works in a broad set of pathways connecting fairly specific brain locations.

Serotonin is the chemical messenger that is enhanced by medications such as Prozac. It has a profound effect on a person's mood, with higher levels being associated with feelings of serenity and optimism. Serotonin also plays an important role in areas of the brain that regulate sleep and appetite. Serotonin pathways include connections involving the amygdala, the hypothalamus, and areas of the cortex. The beneficial effects of drugs like Prozac (see the section on treatment of depression) provide the most convincing evidence for the argument that some type of malfunction in serotonin pathways is involved in the etiology of depression.

We know that the relation between neurotransmitters and depression is complex, and the specific mechanisms are not well understood. There may be more than 100 different neurotransmitters in the central nervous system, and each neurotransmitter is associated with several types of postsynaptic receptors. It seems unlikely that a heterogeneous disorder like depression,

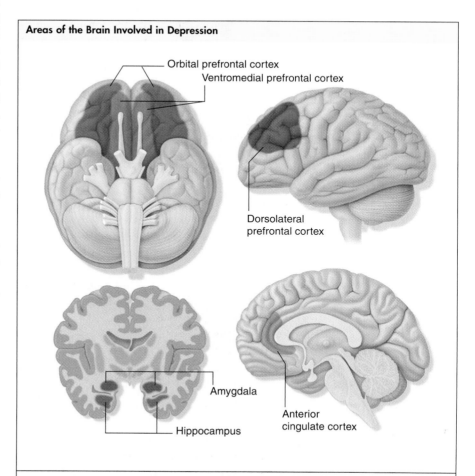

Areas of the Brain Involved in Depression

Orbital prefrontal cortex
Ventromedial prefrontal cortex
Dorsolateral prefrontal cortex
Amygdala
Hippocampus
Anterior cingulate cortex

FIGURE 5–7: Brain regions involved in emotion and mood disorders.
Source: After R.J. Davidson et al. (2002). Depression: Perspectives from affective neuroscience. *Annual Review of Psychology, 53,* p. 575.

which involves a dysregulation of many cognitive and emotional functions, will be linked to only one type of chemical messenger or only one loop in the brain's circuitry. Current theories tend to emphasize the interactive effects of several neurotransmitter systems, including serotonin, norepinephrine, dopamine, and neuropeptides (short chains of amino acids that exist in the brain and appear to modulate the activity of the classic neurotransmitters) (Stockmeier, 2003; Thase, Ripu, & Howland, 2002).

Why do some investigators study "depression" in animals?

Interaction of Social, Psychological, and Biological Factors

We have considered a variety of social, psychological, and biological factors that appear to be related to the etiology of mood disorders. How can these factors be combined or integrated? One type of research that illustrates this point has employed an animal model of depression (see Research Methods). When laboratory animals are exposed to uncontrollable stress (such as a 15-minute forced swim in cold water from which they cannot escape), they frequently exhibit behavioral symptoms that are similar to (yet obviously not the same as) those seen in depressed humans. The animals develop deficits in motor activity, sleep, and eating behaviors. This type of stress-induced depression in laboratory rats produces various temporary effects on neurotransmitters, including changes in the concentration of norepinephrine, serotonin, and dopamine in the specific regions of the limbic system and the frontal cortex. Rats that show these neurochemical consequences following exposure to stress exhibit signs of depression. If the neurotransmitters are not depleted, the rats do not appear to be depressed. Furthermore, administering antidepressant drugs to these animals has been shown to reverse or prevent the behavioral effects of uncontrollable stress. Selective breeding experiments have been able to produce subtypes of rats that differ in their response to behavioral challenges (such as the forced swim test), as well as in their response to antidepressant medication (Connor, Kelly, & Leonard, 1997; Weiss, Cierpial, & West, 1998).

This animal model illustrates the need to consider the interaction between biological and psychological phenomena. The data on stress-induced depression in rats suggest that neurochemical processes may be reactions to environmental events, such as uncontrollable stress in rats or severe life events in people. Psychological and biological explanations of depression are complementary views of the same process, differing primarily in terms of their level of analysis.

TREATMENT

Several procedures, both psychosocial and biological, have proved to be useful in the treatment of mood disorders. In the following pages we will examine some of the more prominent contemporary approaches to the treatment of unipolar and bipolar mood disorders, as well as the research evidence on their usefulness.

Unipolar Disorders

Most psychological approaches to the treatment of depression owe some debt to psychodynamic procedures and Freud's emphasis on the importance of interpersonal relationships. According to Freud's view, the primary goal of therapy should be to help the patient understand and express the hostility and frustration that are being directed against the self. These negative emotions are presumably rooted in dysfunctional relationships with other people. Freud

Rats wearing "water wings" in a forced swim test. One (left) shows vigorous motor activity while the other (right) shows passive behavior (floating without limb movement) that is considered an analogue for depression.

ANALOGUE STUDIES: DO RATS GET DEPRESSED, AND WHY?

Many questions about the etiology of psychopathology cannot be addressed using highly controlled laboratory studies with human subjects. For example, does prolonged exposure to uncontrollable stress cause anxiety disorders? This kind of issue has been addressed using correlational studies with people who have the disorders in question, but experiments on these issues cannot be done with human subjects. For important ethical reasons, investigators cannot randomly assign people to endure conditions that are hypothesized to produce full-blown disorders like clinical depression. The best alternative is often to study a condition that is similar, or analogous, to the clinical disorder in question. Investigations of this type are called **analogue studies** because they focus on behaviors that resemble mental disorders—or isolated features of mental disorders—that appear in the natural environment.

Many analogue studies depend on the use of animal models of psychopathology, which have provided important insights regarding the etiology of conditions such as anxiety, depression, and schizophrenia (Mineka & Zinbarg, 1991). In the 1960s, Harry Harlow's research demonstrated that rhesus monkey infants develop despair responses after separation from their mothers. The somatic symptoms exhibited by these monkeys—facial and vocal displays of sadness and dismay, social withdrawal, changes in appetite and sleep, and psychomotor retardation—were remarkably similar to many symptoms of clinical depression in humans.

This social separation model of depression has been used to explore several important variables that may be involved in mood disorders. For example, infant monkeys who have extensive experience with peers and other adults are less likely to become depressed following separation from their mothers. The skills that they learn through social exploration apparently allow them to cope more successfully with stress. The social separation model has also been used to explore neurochemical factors and mood disorders. Drug companies have used the model to evaluate the antidepressant effects of new drugs.

Some clinicians have argued that mental disorders like depression cannot be modeled in a laboratory setting, especially using animals as subjects. Cognitive symptoms—such as Beck's depressive triad—cannot be measured with animals. Do monkeys feel guilty? Can rats experience hopelessness or suicidal ideas? But these symptoms are not necessarily the most central features of the disorder. Cross-cultural studies have shown that in some non-Western societies somatic symptoms are the most prominent symptoms of depression. Many of these aspects of mood disorder are seen in animals. The value of any analogue study hinges, in large part, on the extent to which the analogue condition is similar to the actual clinical disorder. Some models are more compelling than others.

Analogue studies have one important advantage over other types of research design in psychopathology: They can employ an experimental procedure. Therefore the investigator can draw strong inferences about cause and effect. The main disadvantage of analogue studies involves the extent to which the results of a particular investigation can be generalized to situations outside the laboratory. If a particular set of circumstances produced a set of maladaptive behaviors in the laboratory, is it reasonable to assume that similar mechanisms produce the actual clinical disorder in the natural environment? In actual practice, questions about the etiology of disorders like depression will probably depend on converging evidence generated from the use of many different research designs.

---

also placed considerable emphasis on the apparently irrational beliefs that depressed people hold about themselves and their world. These cognitive factors are also emphasized by cognitive therapists.

Cognitive Therapy   Cognitive therapy has been developed and promoted by Aaron Beck and his colleagues (e.g., Beck et al., 1979; Clark, Beck, & Alford, 1999). His model assumes that emotional dysfunction is influenced by the negative ways in which people interpret events in their environments and the things that they say to themselves about those experiences. Based on the assumption that depression will be relieved if these maladaptive schemas are changed, cognitive therapists focus on helping their patients replace self-defeating thoughts with more rational self-statements.

A specific example may help illustrate this process. Consider the case of Cathy, the depressed attorney whom we introduced at the beginning of the chapter. Cathy focused a great deal of attention on relatively minor negative events at work, blaming herself for anything other than a perfect performance. Her therapist helped her to recognize that she was engaging in a pattern of cognitive distortion that Beck has labeled "selective abstraction." Taking a detail out of context, she would invariably ignore those aspects of her performance that refuted the conclusion that she was professionally incompetent. Her therapist helped her overcome these tendencies by teaching her to question her conclusions and to develop more objective ways of evaluating her experiences.

Cathy also tended to think about herself in absolute and unvarying terms. During the course of therapy, she learned to recognize this pattern and to substitute more flexible self-statements. Instead of saying to herself, "I am a hopeless introvert and will never be able to change,"

Aaron Beck has developed an influential cognitive theory of depression, emphasizing the importance of distorted ways of thinking about the self. He has pioneered the use of cognitive therapy for the treatment of depression.

she learned to substitute, "I am less comfortable in social situations than some other people, but I can learn to be more confident."

Although Beck's approach to treatment emphasizes the importance of cognitive events, it shares many features with behavioral approaches to intervention. Cognitive therapists are active and directive in their interactions with clients, and they focus most of their attention on their clients' current experience. They also assume that people have conscious access to cognitive events: Our thinking may not always be rational, but we can discuss private thoughts and feelings. Another important aspect of Beck's approach to treatment, and a characteristic that it shares with the behavioral perspective, is a serious commitment to the empirical evaluation of the efficacy of treatment programs. Several studies have found that cognitive therapy is effective in the treatment of nonpsychotic, unipolar depression (Sanderson & McGinn, 2001; Strunk & DeRubeis, 2001).

Interpersonal Therapy   Interpersonal therapy is another contemporary approach to the psychological treatment of depression (Klerman et al., 1984; Weissman, Markowitz, & Klerman, 2000). It is focused primarily on current relationships, especially those involving family members. The therapist helps the patient develop a better understanding of the interpersonal problems that presumably give rise to depression and attempts to improve the patient's relationships with other people by building communication and problem-solving skills. Therapy sessions often include nondirective discussions of social difficulties and unexpressed or unacknowledged negative emotions, as well as role playing to practice specific social skills.

Antidepressant Medications   The types of medication that are used most frequently in the treatment of unipolar mood disorders fall into four general categories: selective serotonin reuptake inhibitors (SSRIs), tricyclics (TCAs), monoamine oxidase inhibitors (MAO-Is), and "other," more recently developed drugs. Among patients who respond positively to antidepressant medication, improvement is typically evident within 4 to 6 weeks, and the current episode is often resolved within 12 weeks (DePaulo & Horvitz, 2002; Schulberg et al., 1999). Medication is usually continued for at least 6 to 12 months after the patient has entered remission in order to reduce the chance of relapse.

Selective Serotonin Reuptake Inhibitors   The **selective serotonin reuptake inhibitors (SSRIs)** were developed in the early 1980s and are now the most frequently used form of antidepressant medication, accounting for more than 80 percent of all prescriptions written for that purpose (Hirschfeld, 2001). Unlike the original forms of antidepressant medication, which were discovered by accident, SSRIs were synthesized in the laboratories of pharmaceutical companies on the basis of theoretical speculation regarding the role of serotonin in the etiology of mood disorders. There are many specific types of SSRIs (see Table 5–6). Controlled outcome studies indicate that Prozac and other SSRIs are about as effective as traditional forms of antidepressant medication (Kroenke et al., 2001; Masand & Gupta, 1999).

The SSRIs inhibit the reuptake of serotonin into the presynaptic nerve ending and thus promote neurotransmission in serotonin pathways by increasing the amount of serotonin in the synaptic cleft. They are called "selective" because they seem to have little if any effect on the uptake of norepinephrine and dopamine. Nevertheless, the SSRIs are not entirely selective, in the sense that some of them do block reuptake of other neurotransmitters. They also vary in the potency with which they block serotonin reuptake. Their effectiveness in treating

"I think the dosage needs adjusting. I'm not nearly as happy as the people in the ads."

depression does not seem to be directly related to either the extent to which a particular SSRI is selective with regard to serotonin or its potency in blocking serotonin reuptake (Healy, 1997).

The SSRIs are typically considered to be easier to use than other antidepressant drugs. They also have fewer side effects (such as constipation and drowsiness), and they are less dangerous in the event of an overdose. This does not mean, of course, that they are completely without side effects (see Critical Thinking *Matters* on page 160). Some patients experience nausea, headaches, and sleep disturbances, but these symptoms are usually mild and short term. The most troublesome side effects associated with SSRIs are sexual dysfunction and weight gain (Sussman & Ginsberg, 1998). The rate of decreased sexual desire and orgasmic dysfunction may be as high as 50 percent among both men and women taking SSRIs. Weight changes in response to SSRIs vary in relation to length of treatment. Many patients experience an initial weight loss, but most regain this weight after 6 months. Those who continue to take the medication may gain an average of 20 pounds.

Tricyclics   The **tricyclics (TCAs),** such as imipramine (Tofranil) and amitriptyline (Elavil), have been in relatively widespread use since the 1950s, but their use has declined since the introduction of the SSRIs because they have more side effects. Common reactions include blurred vision, constipation, drowsiness, and a drop in blood pressure. The TCAs affect brain functions by blocking the uptake of neurotransmitters (especially norepinephrine) from the synapse. Several controlled double-blind studies indicate that TCAs benefit many depressed patients, although improvements might not be evident until 2 or 3 weeks after the beginning of treatment (Friedman & Kocsis, 1996; Schatzberg, 1999). The several different kinds of tricyclic medication vary in potency and side effects, but they are generally equal in terms of effectiveness. Comparisons of TCAs and SSRIs indicate that they are approximately equal in terms of success rates, with positive responses being shown by 50 to 60 percent of depressed patients (Schulberg et al., 1999).

Monoamine Oxidase Inhibitors   The antidepressant effects of **monoamine oxidase inhibitors (MAO-Is),** such as phenelzine (Nardil), were discovered at about the same time as those of the tricyclic drugs. These drugs have not been used as

TABLE 5-6	Medications for Unipolar Mood Disorders	
DRUG CLASS	**GENERIC NAME (TRADE NAME)**	**MODE OF ACTION**
Selective serotonin Reuptake inhibitors (SSRI)	Fluoxetine (Prozac) Paroxetine (Paxil) Sertraline (Zoloft) Citalopram (Celexa) Fluvoxamine (Luvox)	Block 5-HT reuptake
Tricyclic antidepressants (TCA)	Amitriptyline (Elavil) Clomipramine (Anafranil) Imipramine (Tofranil)	Block reuptake of 5-HT and norepinephrine
Monoamine oxidase inhibitors (MAO-Is)	Phenelzine (Nardil)	Deactivate enzyme that breaks down monoamines
Other antidepressants	Trazodone (Desyrel)	Block 5-HT reuptake and block 5-HT receptors
	Buproprion (Wellbutrin)	Block norepinephrine and dopamine reuptake
	Venlafaxine (Effexor)	Block reuptake of 5-HT and norepinephrine

Note: 5-HT is serotonin.

extensively as tricyclics, however, primarily for two reasons. First, patients who use MAO-Is and also consume foods containing large amounts of the compound tyramine, such as cheese and chocolate, often develop high blood pressure. Second, some early empirical evaluations of antidepressant medications suggest that MAO-Is are not as effective as tricyclics.

More recent studies have shown that MAO inhibitors are indeed useful in the treatment of depressed patients (Friedman & Kocsis, 1996). They can be used safely when the patient avoids foods such as cheese, beer, and red wine. In addition, MAO-Is are now widely used in the treatment of certain anxiety disorders, especially agoraphobia and panic attacks (see Chapter 6).

The Efficacy of Psychotherapy and Medication
Considerable time and energy have been devoted to the evaluation of psychological and pharmacological treatments for depression. The bottom line in this lengthy debate—based on extensive reviews of the research literature—is that cognitive therapy and antidepressant medication are both effective forms of treatment for people who suffer from unipolar depression (Hollon, Thase, & Markowitz, 2002). This is true for people with major depressive disorder as well as dysthymia. In actual practice, many experts recommend treatment with a combination of psychotherapy and medication (Boland & Keller, 2001; Kupfer & Frank, 2001).

DO ANTIDEPRESSANT DRUGS CAUSE VIOLENT BEHAVIOR?

Extensive media attention has been devoted to the suggestion that some of the SSRIs can increase the risk of violent and suicidal behavior. Several dramatic cases have been discussed at great length. One example is Chris Pittman, who was found guilty in 2005 of killing his paternal grandparents with a shotgun when he was 12 years old. No one questioned the basic facts of the case. Pittman admitted that he blasted his grandparents with a shotgun while they were sleeping. He then set their house on fire and fled the area. After he was caught, his defense team mounted what some court observers called the *Zoloft defense,* claiming that the murders were triggered by the boy's reaction to antidepressant medication that he had been taking for several days before the murders (see Chapter 18 for a discussion of the insanity defense). Prosecutors argued, on the other hand, that he killed his grandparents because he was angry after they disciplined him for fighting with a younger student on the school bus earlier that day. In other words, his motivation did not involve a mental disorder or a reaction to medication. Pittman was tried as an adult, convicted by a jury, and sentenced to 30 years in prison.

Tragic public cases such as this one generate strong opinions on both sides. Magazines and Web sites are filled with warnings about the dangers of treating children and adolescents with SSRIs, some more extreme than others. Many psychiatrists have responded by

noting the beneficial effects that antidepressant medication can have for young people. Clearly parents should be warned about negative side-effects that are sometimes associated with drugs like Zoloft, but should they be frightened to the point that they avoid using one of the most effective forms of treatment for mood disorders? Critical thinking must prevail.

One important issue in this on-going debate is the need for empirical evidence. Do SSRIs cause a significant increase in the risk of violence and suicide? Millions of people take antidepressant medication. Many depressed people commit suicide, in spite of the best efforts to treat their condition. The fact that one person committed suicide or any other violent crime while taking a specific drug does not provide convincing evidence that the drug *caused* the person to engage in that behavior. The question is whether people taking Zoloft are more likely to be suicidal or violent than other (similarly) depressed people who are being given another form of treatment. The data do not point to an obvious link, but the issue has not been closed (Breggin, 2004; Dinan, 2000; Tardiff, Marzuk, & Leon, 2002). In the absence of better evidence, the U.S. Food and Drug Administration (FDA) now requires that a warning be printed on the label when Zoloft (and some other SSRIs) are prescribed for children, including the following statement:

"Families and caregivers of pediatric patients being treated with antidepressants . . .

should be alerted about the need to monitor patients for the emergence of agitation, irritability, unusual changes in behavior, and the other symptoms described above, as well as the emergence of suicidality."

The legal implications of these findings remain ambiguous. Most forms of antidepressant medication are capable of triggering manic episodes in people who are depressed (Goldberg & Truman, 2003), and the symptoms of mania sometimes include hostility and aggression. Does that mean that SSRIs can *cause* someone to become homicidal or suicidal? When people come out of a period of depression and their mood is lifting, they also experience an increase in energy. For many years, experts have recognized that this period of time can be especially dangerous for people who have harbored serious thoughts of violence. If they decide to act on those impulses, is it the pill's fault? Is the person no longer responsible for his or her behavior?

While the public does need to be warned about side-effects that can be associated with medication, it is also irresponsible to exaggerate or distort that evidence. People who are frightened do not make well-informed decisions. In fact, the risks of medication side effects must be balanced against the risks associated with failing to treat a potentially lethal condition such as depression. (Brent, 2004)

Recent efforts to evaluate and compare the effects of medication and psychotherapy have focused on the treatment of depression in primary care settings (Schulberg et al., 1999). Investigators have focused on patients in primary care because most depressed people who receive treatment are seen by their family physician rather than a mental health specialist. Special efforts are being made to increase family physicians' ability to recognize and treat mood disorders. Randomized trials indicate that medication and psychotherapy are approximately equivalent in primary care settings. For example, following 11 weeks of treatment, one study found that 64 percent of patients had recovered from an episode of depression, and the recovery rate was the same regardless of whether the

patients had been assigned to receive an SSRI or problem-solving therapy (Barrett et al., 2001). Both groups showed more improvement than patients who received a placebo treatment. Thus, either form of treatment is a reasonable choice for the initial treatment of unipolar depression.

Bipolar Disorders

Treatment of bipolar mood disorders has also focused on the combined use of medication and psychotherapy. A variety of mood stabilizing drugs are employed with bipolar patients. They are used to help people recover from episodes of mania and depression and also on a long-term maintenance basis to reduce the frequency of future episodes (Geddes et al., 2004). Antidepressant medications are sometimes used, usually in combination with a mood stabilizer, for the treatment of bipolar patients (Kupfer et al., 2001). Clinicians must be cautious, however, because antidepressants can sometimes trigger a switch from depression into a hypomanic or manic episode. We do not have extensive evidence regarding the effectiveness and safety of long-term antidepressant medication for bipolar disorders (Ghaemi et al., 2001).

Lithium   In 1949, the Australian psychiatrist John Cade discovered that the salt lithium carbonate was effective in treating bipolar mood disorders. An extensive literature indicates that lithium carbonate is an effective form of treatment in the alleviation of manic episodes, and it remains the first choice for treating bipolar disorders. It is also useful in the treatment of bipolar patients who are experiencing a depressive episode. Perhaps most importantly, bipolar patients who continue to take lithium between episodes are significantly less likely to experience a relapse (Bauer & Mitchner, 2004).

Unfortunately, there are also some limitations associated with the use of lithium. Many bipolar patients, perhaps 40 percent, do not improve when they take lithium (Mendlewicz, Souery, & Rivelli, 1999). Nonresponse is particularly common among rapid cycling patients, those who exhibit a mixture of manic and depressed symptoms, and those with comorbid alcohol abuse. Compliance with medication is also a frequent problem; at least half the people for whom lithium is prescribed either fail to take it regularly or stop taking it against their psychiatrist's advice. The main reasons that patients give for discontinuing lithium involve its negative side effects, including nausea, memory problems, weight gain, and impaired coordination.

Anticonvulsant Medications   Often, bipolar patients who do not respond to lithium are prescribed anticonvulsant drugs, particularly carbamazepine (Tegretol) or valproic acid (Depakene) (Walden et al., 1998). Outcome data suggest that slightly more than 50 percent of bipolar patients respond positively to these drugs. Like lithium, carbamazepine and valproic acid can be useful in reducing the frequency and severity of relapse, and they can be used to treat acute manic episodes. Valproic acid may be more effective than lithium for the treatment of rapid cycling bipolar patients and those with mixed symptoms of

mania and depression in a single episode (Gadde & Krishnan, 1997). Common side effects include gastrointestinal distress (nausea, vomiting, and diarrhea) and sedation.

Psychotherapy   Although medication is the most important method of treatment for bipolar disorders, psychotherapy can be an effective supplement to biological intervention. Both cognitive therapy and interpersonal therapy have been adapted for use with bipolar disorders. Cognitive therapy can address the patient's reactions to stressful life events as well as his or her reservations about taking medication (Craighead & Miklowitz, 2000).

A variation on interpersonal therapy, known as "interpersonal and social rhythm therapy" has been developed for use with bipolar patients (Frank, Swartz, & Kupfer, 2000). It is based on the recognition that a repeated episode of either mania or depression is often precipitated by one of the following factors: stressful life events, disruptions in social rhythms (the times of day in which the person works, sleeps, and so on), and failure to take medication. Special emphasis is placed on monitoring the interaction between symptoms (especially the onset of hypomanic or manic episodes) and social interactions. Therapists help patients learn to lead more orderly lives, especially with regard to sleep–wake cycles, and to resolve interpersonal problems effectively. Regulation of sleep and work patterns is also important. This therapy program is employed in combination with the long-term use of mood stabilizing medication.

Some preliminary evidence does suggest that the combination of psychotherapy and medication for the treatment of bipolar disorder may be more beneficial than medication alone, but the data are not conclusive (Jones, 2004). There is an obvious need for more extensive research on the effectiveness of various types of psychosocial treatment for bipolar mood disorders.

Electroconvulsive Therapy

The procedure known as electroconvulsive therapy (or ECT) has proved beneficial for many patients suffering from unipolar or bipolar mood disorders (see Chapter 3 for a review of the background of ECT). Electroconvulsive therapy is typically administered in an inpatient setting and consists of a series of treatments given three times a week for 2 to 7 weeks (Abrams, 2002; Fink,

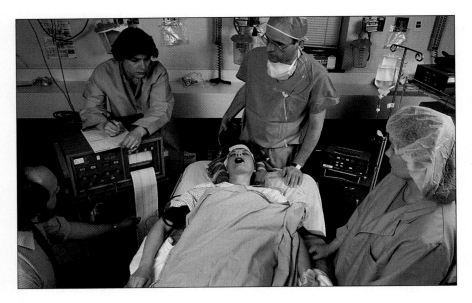

Electroconvulsive therapy is an effective form of treatment for severely depressed patients. It should be considered for people who do not improve with psychotherapy or antidepressant medication.

This man is receiving light therapy for the treatment of seasonal affective disorder.

the amount of postseizure memory impairment, but it may also be less effective (Kellner, 1997).

Although how ECT works remains largely a mystery (Nobler & Sackeim, 1998), empirical studies have demonstrated that it is an effective form of treatment for severely depressed patients (for example, Gagne et al., 2000). Reservations regarding the use of ECT center around widely publicized, although infrequent, cases of pervasive and persistent memory loss. Reviews of the research evidence indicate that ECT-induced changes in memory and other cognitive functions are almost always short-lived, and ECT does not induce loss of neurons or other changes in brain structure (Calev et al., 1995).

No one denies that ECT is an invasive procedure that should usually be reserved for patients who have been resistant to other forms of intervention, such as medication and cognitive therapy. Nevertheless, it remains a viable and legitimate alternative for some severely depressed patients, especially those who are so suicidal that they require constant supervision to prevent them from harming themselves. Rapid cycling bipolar patients and depressed patients with psychotic symptoms may also be more responsive to ECT than to medication (Fink, 2001). As always, the risks of treatment must be carefully weighed against those associated with allowing the disorder to follow its natural course.

2001). Many patients show a dramatic improvement after six to eight sessions, but some require more. In current clinical practice, muscle relaxants are always administered before a patient receives ECT. This procedure has eliminated bone fractures and dislocations that were unfortunate side effects of techniques used many years ago. The electrodes can be placed either bilaterally (on both sides of the head) or unilaterally (at the front and back of the skull on one side of the patient's head). Unilateral placement on the nondominant hemisphere (the right side of the head for right-handed people) may minimize

Seasonal Mood Disorders

The observation that changes in seasons can help bring on episodes of mood disorder leads to the relatively obvious implication that some patients might respond to manipulations of the natural environment. For centuries, physicians have prescribed changes in climate for their depressed clients (Wehr, 1989). The prominent French psychiatrist Jean Esquirol (1772–1840) reportedly advised a patient whose depression appeared when the days grew shorter to move from Belgium to Italy during the winter.

Modern light therapy was introduced in the 1980s (Rosenthal, 1998). Typical treatment involves exposure to bright (2,500 lux), broadspectrum light for 1 to 2 hours every day. The time of day during which the person is exposed to the light may not matter, but some patients respond best to early morning treatments. Some

patients also respond positively to shorter periods (30 minutes) of high-intensity (10,000 lux) light (Hill, 1992). This high-intensity light is roughly equivalent to the amount of light that would be generated by a 750-watt spotlight focused on a surface 1 square meter in area. The light source—most often a rectangular box containing fluorescent ceiling fixtures—must be placed close (90 cm) to the patient at eye level. Improvement in the person's mood is often seen within 2 to 5 days.

Outcome studies have found that light therapy is an effective form of treatment for seasonal affective disorder (Neuhaus & Rosenthal, 1997; Wesson & Levitt, 1998). The most difficult issue in evaluating this type of treatment has been to control for placebo effects. It is not possible to conduct a true double-blind study because patients know that they are being exposed to light, and they often believe that light will be helpful. One study used a comparison between treatment with a bright white light (supposedly the treatment that would be most effective) and treatment with a more dim red light (the placebo condition) (Wileman et al., 2001). Improvement rates were approximately equivalent in both groups, suggesting that light therapy might not be as effective as some clinicians have suggested. Nevertheless, the overall state of the research evidence is mixed, and many patients with seasonal affective disorders do respond well to light therapy. It is still considered by many clinicians to be a useful approach to this disorder. It is not exactly clear why or how light therapy works, but the process may help the body to normalize circadian rhythms, which regulate processes such as hormone secretion (Whybrow, 1997).

SUICIDE

BRIEF CASE STUDY

An Admiral's Suicide

Admiral Jeremy (Mike) Boorda was the highest-ranking officer in the U.S. Navy when, at the age of 56, he committed suicide (*Newsweek*, May 27, 1996). He was married and the father of four children. Boorda was the first person in the history of the navy to rise from the enlisted ranks to become chief of naval operations. Although his record of leadership was widely admired by both fellow officers and prominent politicians, he had recently been the subject of journalistic scrutiny. Questions had been raised about whether Boorda had legitimately earned two medals that he displayed on his uniform for several years (small Vs that are awarded to people who have shown valor in combat). These public symbols of heroism are a source of considerable status, especially among professional military people. Boorda had stopped wearing the medals after the issue was initially raised, but some members of the media had decided to pursue the issue further. On the morning of his death, Boorda was told that reporters from *Newsweek* magazine wanted to ask him some more questions about his justification for wearing these medals. He never met with them. Telling other officers that he was going home for lunch, Boorda went home and shot himself in the chest with a .38 revolver.

Why would such a successful person choose to end his own life? Suicide is an extremely personal, private, and complicated act. We may never know exactly why Admiral Boorda killed himself, but the circumstances surrounding his death are consistent with a number of facts about suicide. The highest rate of suicide in the United States is found among white males over the age of 50. Within this group, men who have been occupationally successful are more likely to commit suicide, especially if that success is threatened or lost. Notes that the admiral left for his wife and for navy personnel indicated that he could no longer face the public dishonor that might result from *Newsweek*'s investigation. Escape from psychological suffering is often a significant motive in suicide. Did Boorda commit suicide primarily to end his own subjective distress? Or was his death intended to avoid bringing disgrace to the navy, which had been plagued by other scandals in recent years? When he was appointed chief of naval operations, several months before his death, it had been hoped that he would restore morale and improve public confidence in the navy. The *Newsweek* probe threatened to negate all of those efforts. Did his death represent a personal sacrifice for the military service that he loved and to which he had devoted 40 years of his life? These difficult questions illustrate the challenges faced by clinicians, who must try to understand suicide so that they can more effectively prevent it.

Aides said that Admiral Boorda did not show any signs of being depressed, even on the morning that he died. Nor were there any indications of substance abuse or other mental disorders. In this respect, Boorda's situation was unusual. Although many people who commit suicide do not appear to be depressed, and psychopathology doesn't explain all suicidal behavior, there is undoubtedly a strong relationship between depression and self-destructive acts. The available evidence suggests that at least 50 percent of all suicides occur as a result of, or in the context of, a primary mood disorder (Jamison, 1999). Moreover, the risk of completed suicide is much higher among people who are clinically depressed than it is among people in the general population. Follow-up studies consistently indicate that 15 to 20 percent of all patients with mood disorders will eventually kill themselves (Clark & Goebel-Fabbri, 1999). Thus it seems reasonable to conclude that there is a relatively close link between suicide and depression.

Classification of Suicide

Common sense tells us that suicide takes many forms. DSM-IV-TR does not address this issue; rather, it lists *suicidal ideation* (thoughts of suicide) only as a symptom of mood disorders. Clinicians and social scientists have proposed a number of systems for classifying subtypes of suicide, based on speculation regarding different motives for ending one's own life. Therefore, in contrast to the principles that were followed in

Distinctions among Durkheim's types of suicide can be difficult to make. Do the motives of suicide bombers reflect a breakdown of social order? Or does their violent behavior represent a personal sacrifice for the sake of their society?

creating DSM-IV-TR, classification systems for suicide are based on causal theories rather than descriptive factors.

The most influential system for classifying suicide was originally proposed in 1897 by Emile Durkheim (1858–1917), a French sociologist who is one of the most important figures in the history of sociology (Coser, 1977). In order to appreciate the nature of this system, you must understand Durkheim's approach to studying social problems. Durkheim was interested in "social facts," such as religious groups and political parties, rather than the psychological or biological features of particular individuals. His scientific studies were aimed at clarifying the social context in which human problems appear, and they were based on the assumption that human passions and ambition are controlled by the moral and social structures of society. One of his most important scientific endeavors was a comparison of suicide rates among various religious and occupational groups.

In his book *Suicide*, Durkheim (1897/1951) argued that the rate of suicide within a group or a society would increase if levels of social integration and regulation are either excessively low or excessively high. He identified four different types of suicide, which are distinguished by the social circumstances in which the person is living:

- *Egoistic suicide* (diminished integration) occurs when people become relatively detached from society and when they feel that their existence is meaningless. Egoistic suicide is presumably more common among groups such as people who have been divorced and people who are suffering from mental disorders. The predominant emotions associated with egoistic suicide are depression and apathy.
- *Altruistic suicide* (excessive integration) occurs when the rules of the social group dictate that the person must sacrifice his or her own life for the sake of others. One example is the former practice in some Native American tribes of elderly persons voluntarily going off by themselves to die after they felt they had become a burden to others.
- *Anomic suicide* (diminished regulation) occurs following a sudden breakdown in social order or a disruption of the norms that govern people's behavior. Anomic suicide explains increased suicide rates that occur following an economic or political crisis or among people

who are adjusting to the unexpected loss of a social or occupational role. The typical feelings associated with anomie (a term coined by Durkheim, which literally means "without a name") are anger, disappointment, and exasperation.

- *Fatalistic suicide* (excessive regulation) occurs when the circumstances under which a person lives become unbearable. A slave, for example, might choose to commit suicide in order to escape from the horrible nature of his or her existence. This type of suicide was mentioned only briefly by Durkheim, who thought that it was extremely uncommon.

Durkheim believed that egoistic and anomic suicide were the most common types of suicide in Western industrial societies. Although he distinguished between these two dominant forms, he recognized that they were interconnected and could operate together. Some people may become victims of both diminished integration and ineffective regulation.

Durkheim's system for classifying types of suicide has remained influential, but it does have some limitations (Leenaars, 2004; Stack, 2004). For example, it does not explain why one person commits suicide while other members of the same group do not. All the people in the group are subject to the same social structures. Another problem with Durkheim's system is that the different types of suicide overlap and may, in some cases, be difficult to distinguish. If the system is used to describe individual cases of suicide, such as that of Admiral Boorda, would clinicians be likely to agree on these subtypes? We are not aware of any attempts to evaluate the reliability of such judgments, but it might be quite low.

Frequency of Suicide

In the United States and Canada, the annual rate of completed suicide across all age groups has averaged between 10 and 12 people per 100,000 population for several years (Goldsmith, 2001). More than 30,000 people in the United States kill themselves every year. Suicide rates vary as a function of many factors, including age, gender, and socioeconomic status (see Figure 5–8). The suicide rate among adolescents has increased alarmingly in recent decades (see Chapter 16). Between 1955 and 1980 (years in which "baby

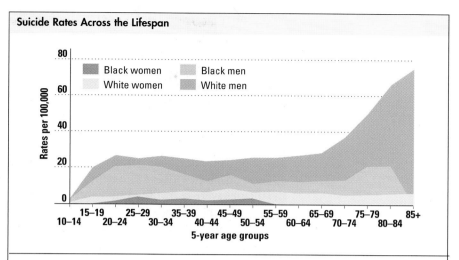

FIGURE 5–8: Suicide rates per 100,000 population by 5-year group, race, and gender, United States 1991.

Source: Moscicki, E.K., 1995, Epidemiology of suicidal behavior. *Suicide and Life-Threatening Behavior, 25,* 22–35. Copyright © 1995. Reprinted by permission of Guilford Publications, Inc.

boomers" became adults), the suicide rate tripled for young men between the ages of 15 and 24. The rate for young women in the same age range doubled during the same period (Garland & Zigler, 1993). Rates among other age groups have either fallen or remained steady. Suicide has become the third leading cause of death for people between the ages of 15 and 24, and it is the eighth leading cause of death in the general population (Moscicki, 1995).

Suicide attempts are much more common than are completed suicides. The ratio of attempts to completed suicides in the general population is approximately 10 to 1; among adolescents, the ratio is closer to 100 to 1 (Hendin, 1995). There are important gender differences in rates of attempted suicide versus rates of completed suicide. Females aged 15 to 19 years make three times as many suicide attempts as males. Completion rates, however, are four times higher among males (Tsuang, Simpson, & Fleming, 1992). The difference in fatalities may be due, in part, to the methods employed. Men and boys are more likely to use violent and lethal methods such as firearms and hanging, whereas women and girls are more likely to take an overdose of drugs, which may allow time for discovery and interventions by other people.

The risk of successful suicide is highest among older people. Suicide rates have increased dramatically among young adults in recent years, but the highest rates are still found among older people, especially older white men. Although suicide attempts are most common among younger people, with most being made by those younger than 30, the proportion of suicide attempts that end in death is particularly high among the elderly. It is not clear whether this pattern should be attributed to a difference in method or to decreased physical resilience. Rates of suicide in the United States—broken down by age, race, and gender—are illustrated in Figure 5–8. In 1991, more than 70 percent of all suicides were committed by white men, with the highest rate being among those over the age of 80. The pattern for women is somewhat different. Their risk for suicide increases steadily with age until midlife and then tends to level off.

Causes of Suicide

Many factors contribute to suicidal behavior. In the following discussion, we consider some of the variables that operate at the level of the individual person—psychological and biological considerations—and are associated with suicidal behavior. We also summarize some contemporary research on social factors that are related to suicide.

Psychological Factors Many experts have argued that psychological events lie at the core of suicidal behavior (Joiner, Brown, & Wingate, 2005). Social factors may set the stage for self-destructive acts, but events taking place within the person's mind are most immediately responsible for determining whether a particular individual will attempt to end his or her own life. Prominent among these events are intense emotional distress and hopelessness. An outline of several psychological variables that are commonly associated with suicide is presented in Common Elements of Suicide.

Why do some people decide to end their own lives?

Schneidman (1996) views suicide as an escape from unbearable psychological pain. According to his perspective, psychological pain is produced by prolonged frustration of psychological needs. Personality theorists have identified a number of fundamental human needs or motives (see Figure 2–7)—needs for achievement, esteem, belongingness, and safety. Frustration in meeting these needs can lead to prolonged and intense negative emotional states, such as shame, guilt, anger, and grief.

Most people who experience these emotions do not attempt suicide. But for some people, suicide appears to offer a solution or a way to end their intolerable distress.

Biological Factors Studies of the connection between neurotransmitters and suicide have focused primarily on reduced levels of serotonin, which might be related to poor impulse control as well as increased levels of violent and aggressive behavior (Joiner, Brown, & Wingate, 2005; Van Heeringen & Marusic, 2003). Analogue studies with animals have found that lesions resulting in serotonin dysfunction lead to increases in aggression and failure to inhibit responses that were previously punished. Difficulty in regulating serotonin systems has been found among people who attempted suicide, and it has also been found among people who have shown other types of violent and aggressive behavior, such as criminals convicted of murder (Garza-Trevino, 1994).

Serotonin dysfunction has also been linked to depressive disorders. It seems reasonable to wonder whether that connection might explain the findings regarding serotonin and suicide. People who attempt suicide may exhibit abnormal serotonin levels because they are depressed. That might be a reasonable interpretation for some of the data, but the results of other studies indicate that the link to suicide is more direct. Consider, for example, a follow-up study of 92 people who were hospitalized following a suicide attempt (Nordstrom et al., 1994). All of the participants met the criteria for a major depressive disorder. The investigators measured levels of a particular serotonin by-product, 5-HIAA (5-hydroxyindoleacetic acid), in each patient's cerebrospinal fluid (CSF) shortly after admission to the hospital. The patients were divided into two groups on the basis of these measurements: those below the median for CSF 5-HIAA and those above the median. In the first year after their attempted suicide, 11 of the 92 patients committed suicide, and 8 of the 11 who died were from the low CSF 5-HIAA group. This result suggests that biochemical measures might be useful for predicting risk for suicide within groups of depressed patients.

Twin studies and adoption studies have found that genetic factors are involved in the transmission of major mood disorders. Do genes contribute to the risk for suicide indirectly by increasing the risk for mental disorders, such as

COMMON ELEMENTS OF SUICIDE

Most people who kill themselves are suffering from some form of mental disorder, such as depression, substance dependence, or schizophrenia (Jamison, 1999). No single explanation can account for all self-destructive behavior. Edwin Schneidman (1996), a clinical psychologist who is a leading authority on suicide, described 10 characteristics commonly associated with completed suicide. Schneidman's list includes features that occur most frequently and may help us understand many cases of suicide:

1. The common purpose of suicide is to seek a solution. Suicide is not a pointless or random act. To people who think about ending their own lives, suicide represents an answer to an otherwise insoluble problem or a way out of some unbearable dilemma. It is a choice that is somehow preferable to another set of dreaded circumstances, emotional distress, or disability, which the person fears more than death. Attraction to suicide as a potential solution may be increased by a family history of similar behavior. If someone else whom the person admired or cared for has committed suicide, then the person is more likely to do so.

2. The common goal of suicide is cessation of consciousness. People who commit suicide seek the end of conscious experience, which to them has become an endless stream of distressing thoughts with which they are preoccupied. Suicide offers oblivion.

3. The common stimulus (or information input) in suicide is unbearable psychological pain. Excruciating negative emotions—including shame, guilt, anger, fear, and sadness—frequently serve as the foundation for self-destructive behavior. These emotions may arise from any number of sources.

4. The common stressor in suicide is frustrated psychological needs. People with high standards and expectations are especially vulnerable to ideas of suicide when progress toward these goals is suddenly frustrated. People who attribute failure or disappointment to their own shortcomings may come to view themselves as worthless, incompetent, or unlovable. Family turmoil is an especially important source of frustration to adolescents. Occupational and interpersonal difficulties frequently precipitate suicide among adults. For example, rates of suicide increase during periods of high unemployment (Yang, Stack, & Lester, 1992).

5. The common emotion in suicide is hopelessness-helplessness. A pervasive sense of hopelessness, defined in terms of pessimistic expectations about the future, is even more important than other forms of negative emotion, such as anger and depression, in predicting suicidal behavior (Weishaar & Beck, 1992). The suicidal person is convinced that absolutely nothing can be done to improve his or her situation; no one can help.

6. The common cognitive state in suicide is ambivalence. Most people who contemplate suicide, including those who eventually kill themselves, have ambivalent feelings about this decision. They are sincere in their desire to die, but they simultaneously wish that they could find another way out of their dilemma.

7. The common perceptual state in suicide is constriction. Suicidal thoughts and plans are frequently associated with a rigid and narrow pattern of cognitive activity that is analogous to tunnel vision. The suicidal person is temporarily unable or unwilling to engage in effective problem-solving behaviors and may see his or her options in extreme, all-or-nothing terms. As Schneidman points out, slogans such as "death before dishonor" may have a certain emotional appeal, but they do not provide a sensible basis for making decisions about how to lead one's life.

8. The common action in suicide is escape. Suicide provides a definitive way to escape from intolerable circumstances, which include painful self-awareness (Baumeister, 1990).

9. The common interpersonal act in suicide is communication of intention. One of the most harmful myths about suicide is the notion that people who really want to kill themselves don't talk about it. Most people who commit suicide have told other people about their plans. Many have made previous suicidal gestures. Schneidman estimates that in at least 80 percent of committed suicides, the people provide verbal or behavioral clues that indicate clearly their lethal intentions.

10. The common pattern in suicide is consistency of lifelong styles. During crises that precipitate suicidal thoughts, people generally employ the same coping responses that they have used throughout their lives. For example, people who have refused to ask for help in the past are likely to persist in that pattern, increasing their sense of isolation.

---

depression, schizophrenia, and substance abuse? Is there a more direct contribution of genetic factors to self-destructive behavior? The answer appears to be yes (Souery et al., 2003). One important investigation examined cases of depression and suicide in a group of large Amish families over a period of 100 years (Egeland & Sussex, 1985). Each family included at least one person who suffered from a mood disorder. Within this sample, there were 26 documented instances of suicide. The vast majority of the suicides (92 percent) occurred in people who had been diagnosed as having a mood disorder. Furthermore, most of the suicides occurred in a small subset of four families. The investigators suggested that this pattern might be best explained by the existence of a genetic factor that is associated with suicidal behavior, independent of risk for major depression. This factor might be associated with impulsive personality characteristics. Suicide appears to be an especially likely outcome when a person inherits a predisposition to both psychopathology and impulsive or violent behavior.

Social Factors Durkheim (1897/1951) believed that suicide rates had increased during the nineteenth century because of an erosion of the influence of traditional sources of social integration and regulation, such as the church and the family. Durkheim's own data and subsequent research by other investigators have provided support for the notion that social structures do represent one important consideration with regard to suicide (Stockard & O'Brien, 2002). For example, one study found that religious affiliation is significantly related to suicide rates; lowest rates were found among Catholics and Evangelical Baptists, whereas higher rates were found among mainstream Protestant denominations, such as Episcopalians, Presbyterians, and Lutherans (Pescosolido & Georgianna, 1989). This pattern can be explained in terms of social networks. People who belong to Catholic and conservative Protestant groups are more likely to participate in the various rituals and activities of the church community. These networks become an important source of emotional support during difficult times, protecting the person from the potential influence of self-destructive impulses.

Actress Margaux Hemingway killed herself in 1996 at the age of 41 by taking an overdose of a sedative. She was the fifth person in her family to commit suicide. Her grandfather, Ernest Hemingway, had committed suicide 35 years earlier.

Social policies regulating access to firearms, especially handguns, also have an effect on suicide rates. Guns are a particularly lethal method of suicide, accounting for more than 60 percent of the 30,000 deaths that occur in the United States each year (Hendin, 1995). In states with restrictive gun laws, the suicide rate usually drops, particularly among adolescents (Brent & Bridge, 2003). Of course, people who have definitely decided to end their own lives inevitably find a way to accomplish that goal, but many people who attempt suicide are ambivalent in their intent. Many attempts are made impulsively. Ready access to guns increases the chance that a person who does engage in an impulsive suicide attempt will die, because gunshot wounds are very likely to be fatal.

Prominent television and newspaper coverage of suicidal deaths, especially those of well-known celebrities, can have disastrous consequences by unintentionally encouraging other people to kill themselves (Martin, 1998). Young people are especially vulnerable to this effect, which is sometimes called contagious suicide or a suicide cluster. There was, for example, an increase in rates of suicide in both the United States and England in the months immediately after Marilyn Monroe committed suicide. Imitation of this sort may represent a misdirected attempt to lend meaning to a person's life through association with the death of a celebrity. It might also be inspired by the attention that results with increased media coverage that invariably follows in the wake of multiple or sequential suicides. Descriptions of someone else's death may simply reduce some people's resistance to impulsive action.

Treatment of Suicidal People

Efforts to avoid the tragic consequences of suicidal behavior can be organized at several levels. One approach would focus on social structures that affect an entire society. Durkheim's theory of suicide, for example, indicates that the social structure of a society influences suicide rates. The social factors that we have just considered suggest some changes that could be made in contemporary Western societies in an effort to reduce the frequency of suicide. For example, more restrictive gun control laws might minimize access to the most lethal method of self-destruction. More cautious reporting by the media of suicidal deaths might reduce the probability of cluster suicides. These are, of course, controversial decisions, in which many other considerations play an important role. The media, for example, are motivated to report stories in a way that will maximize their popularity with the public. And many people oppose gun control legislation for reasons that have nothing to do with suicide rates. Therefore it may be unrealistic to hope that these measures, aimed broadly at the level of an entire population, would be implemented widely. Most treatment programs that are concerned with suicidal behavior have been directed toward individual persons and their families.

Crisis Centers and Hot Lines Many communities have established crisis centers and telephone hot lines to provide support for people who are distraught and contemplating suicide. The purpose of these programs is typically viewed in terms of suicide prevention. Sponsored by various agencies, including community mental health centers, hospitals, and religious groups, these services are often staffed by nonprofessionals, frequently volunteers. They offer 24-hour-a-day access to people who have been trained to provide verbal support for those who are in the midst of a crisis and who may have nowhere else to turn. Rather than provide ongoing treatment, most crisis centers and hot lines help the person through the immediate crisis and then refer him or her to mental health professionals.

Public and professional enthusiasm for suicide prevention centers peaked during the 1960s and 1970s. Unfortunately, data that were reported in the 1970s and 1980s did not support optimistic claims that these centers were "saving lives." Empirical studies showed that suicide rates do not differ in comparisons of similar communities that either have or do not have suicide prevention programs. Availability of crisis centers and hot lines does not seem to reduce suicide rates in communities (Hendin, 1995; Lester, 2002).

Why don't hot lines reduce suicide rates? The challenges faced by these programs are enormous. Think about the characteristics of people who are driven to contemplate suicide. They are often socially isolated, feeling hopeless, and unable to consider alternative solutions. Many people with the most lethal suicidal

Elizabeth Shin was a 19 year-old student at MIT when she committed suicide. Her parents filed a lawsuit against the university, claiming that school officials could have prevented her death. This case involves several very difficult issues, including confidentiality (whether therapists can tell parents about such problems).

ideation will not call a hot line or visit a drop-in crisis center. In fact, most clients of suicide prevention centers are young women; most suicides are committed by elderly men. The primary problem faced by suicide prevention programs is this: The people who they are trying to serve are, by definition, very difficult to reach.

It might be hard to justify the continued existence of crisis centers and hot lines if they are viewed solely in terms of suicide prevention. Only a small proportion of people who call hot lines are seriously suicidal. Most are people who are experiencing serious difficulties and who need to talk to someone about those problems. The value of contact with these individuals should not be underestimated. Crisis centers and hot lines provide support and assistance to very large numbers of people in distress. These services are undoubtedly valuable in their own right, even if serious questions remain about their impact on suicide rates.

Psychotherapy Psychological interventions with people who are suicidal can take many forms. These include all the standard approaches to psychotherapy, such as cognitive, behavioral, psychoanalytic, and family therapy. These methods address underlying problems that have set the stage for the person's current problems. Additional treatment guidelines are also dictated by the threat of suicide. The following recommendations cover special considerations that are particularly important when clients have expressed a serious intent to harm themselves (adapted from Berman & Jobes, 1994):

1. *Reduce lethality.* The most important task is to reduce the person's experience of psychological pain, from which the person is seeking escape. At a more concrete level, this also involves reducing access to means that could be used to commit suicide, such as guns and pills.

2. *Negotiate agreements.* Therapists frequently ask clients who have threatened to kill themselves to sign a contract, in which the client agrees to postpone self-destructive behavior for at least a short period of time. This kind of written agreement typically includes the client's consent to contact the therapist directly before engaging in any lethal actions. Of course, these agreements can be broken, but they may provide brakes to inhibit impulsive actions. The process of negotiating the agreement can also help the clinician to determine the severity of the client's suicidal intentions.

3. *Provide support.* It is often useful to make concrete arrangements for social support during a suicidal crisis. Friends and family members are alerted and asked to be available so that the person is not alone. The presence of others allows the person to discuss his or her problems (if he or she chooses to do so) and also provides supervision that may inhibit dangerous behaviors.

4. *Replace tunnel vision with a broader perspective.* People who are seriously contemplating suicide are typically unable to consider alternative solutions to their problems. Death may strike others as an irrational choice, but to people contemplating suicide, in the midst of the crisis, it seems perfectly logical. The therapist

must help potential suicide victims develop or recover a more flexible and adaptive pattern of problem solving.

Medication   Treatment of mental disorders, especially depression and schizophrenia, is usually the most important element of intervention with suicidal clients. The use of various types of medication is often an important part of these treatment efforts. Antidepressant drugs are frequently given to patients who are clinically depressed, and antipsychotic medication is useful with those who meet the diagnostic criteria for schizophrenia (see Chapter 13).

Considerable attention has been devoted recently to the use of selective serotonin reuptake inhibitors (SSRIs), such as fluvoxamine (Luvox) and fluoxetine (Prozac), because of the link between suicide and serotonin disregulation. Extensive clinical reports suggest that the use of SSRIs in treating depression actually lowers suicide rates (Banki, 1995; Wagner, Zaborny, & Gray, 1994). It should also be noted, however, that placebo-controlled outcome studies have not addressed this specific question. Furthermore, cases have been reported in which treatment with SSRIs has been followed by the development of new suicidal ideation (King, Segman, & Anderson, 1994). This pattern suggests that the relation between serotonin and suicide is neither direct nor simple and that caution is warranted in the use of SSRIs in treating suicidal clients (see Critical Thinking *Matters*).

Involuntary Hospitalization   People who appear to be on the brink of committing suicide are often hospitalized, either with their permission or involuntarily (see Chapter 18 for a discussion of the legal issues involved in this process). The primary consideration in such cases is safety. In many cases, commitment to a hospital may be the best way to prevent people from harming themselves. The person's behavior can be monitored continuously, access to methods of harming oneself can be minimized (though perhaps not entirely eliminated), and various types of treatment can be provided by the hospital's professional staff.

getting help

The distinction between severe depression and the ups and downs of everyday life provides an important guide to the need for treatment. If you have been seriously depressed for several weeks and if depression is interfering with your ability to function, you should seek professional help. Fortunately, you have already taken the first step toward improvement. By reading this chapter, you can learn to recognize the symptoms of mood disorders.

Several effective forms of treatment are available for mood disorders. The first step in getting help is to find someone with whom you can talk. This might be your family physician, someone at your school's counseling center, or a therapist in private practice. It is important that you feel comfortable with the person you

choose and with the form of treatment that she or he will provide.

Depression is not uncommon, but people who are depressed often feel lonely and alienated. A number of good books may help make it easier for you to find the right treatment for yourself. Various forms of treatment, including antidepressant medication, are described in *Understanding Depression: What We Know and What You Can Do About It* (2002) by Raymond DePaulo. Self-help books may be useful to people whose depression has not reached severe proportions. The cognitive approach to therapy is described with exceptional clarity in *Feeling Good: The New Mood Therapy* (1999), by David Burns, a psychiatrist who has worked extensively with Aaron Beck. Helpful information regarding bipolar mood disorder can be found in *The Bipolar Disorder Survival Guide* (2002) by David Miklowitz.

People who are depressed need support and encouragement to seek treatment. Families and friends of depressed people find themselves in a very difficult and challenging situation. Mood disorders interfere with the person's ability to get along with other people and deplete his or her energy and motivation for seeking treatment. If they don't follow through with therapy or make noticeable improvements after several sessions, their friends can easily become discouraged or frustrated. Don't feel guilty if your efforts appear to go unrewarded. And don't blame the depressed person if he or she doesn't get better right away. Mood disorders are serious problems that require professional help. More detailed advice for families and friends can be found in a useful book titled *How to Survive When They're Depressed: Living and Coping with Depression Fallout* by Anne Sheffield (1999).

SUMMARY

Mood disorders are defined in terms of emotional, cognitive, behavioral, and **somatic symptoms.** In addition to a feeling of pervasive despair or gloom, people experiencing an episode of major **depression** are likely to show a variety of symptoms, such as diminished interest in their normal activities, changes in appetite and sleep, fatigue, and problems in concentration. In contrast, a person in a manic episode feels elated and energetic. Manic patients also exhibit related symptoms, such as inflated self-esteem, rapid speech, and poor judgment.

DSM-IV-TR lists two major categories of mood disorders. People with **unipolar mood disorders** experience only episodes of depression. People with **bipolar mood disorders** experience episodes of **mania,** which are most often interspersed with episodes of depression. There are two specific types of unipolar mood disorder in DSM-IV-TR. Major depressive disorder is diagnosed if the person has experienced at least one episode of major depression without any periods of mania. **Dysthymia** is a less severe, chronic form of depression in which the person

has been depressed for at least 2 years without a major depressive episode.

A person who has experienced at least one manic episode would receive a diagnosis of bipolar I disorder, regardless of whether he or she has ever had an episode of depression. One episode of major depression combined with evidence of at least one period of **hypomania** would qualify for a diagnosis of bipolar II disorder. **Cyclothymia** is a less severe, chronic form of bipolar mood disorder in which the person has experienced numerous periods of hypomania interspersed with periods of depressed mood.

The validity of the distinction between unipolar and bipolar mood disorders is supported by several types of evidence. Bipolar disorders tend to have an earlier age of onset and a worse prognosis than unipolar disorders.

Mood disorders are among the most common forms of psychopathology. Epidemiological studies have found that the lifetime risk for major depressive disorder is approximately 5 percent and the lifetime risk for dysthymic disorder is approximately 3 percent. Rates for both of these disorders are two or three times higher among women than among men. The lifetime risk for bipolar I disorder is close to 1 percent. Women and men are equally likely to develop bipolar mood disorder. The prevalence of depression appears to be increasing, with people born after World War II being more likely to become clinically depressed than people born in earlier generations.

The causes of mood disorders can be traced to the combined effects of social, psychological, and biological factors. Social factors include primarily the influence of stressful life events, especially severe losses that are associated with significant people or significant roles. Some studies show that people who are clinically depressed help to create some of the stressful events that they experience, especially those involving interpersonal relationships.

Two types of psychological factors play an important role in the development of mood disorders: cognitive responses to disappointment and failure and interpersonal skills. Cognitive theories are primarily concerned with the way in which depressed people experience a severe event. Beck's **schema** model places principal emphasis on cognitive distortions or the erroneous ways in which some people think about themselves and their environments. The **hopelessness** model holds that depression is associated with the expectation that desirable events will not occur or aversive events will occur regardless of what the person does. Furthermore, people will be more likely to become depressed if they attribute negative events to internal, stable, global factors.

Interpersonal theories focus on the ways in which individuals respond to people and events in their environments. Depressed people behave in ways that have a negative impact on other people. In this way they contribute to the stressful nature of their social environment. Coping behaviors may help to explain gender differences in the prevalence of unipolar depression. A ruminative style, in which the person's attention is turned inward, may be associated with longer and more severe episodes of depression. Women may be more likely than men to employ a ruminative style of response to the onset of a depressed mood.

Family and twin studies indicate that genetic factors play an important role in the etiology of both unipolar and bipolar mood disorders. They also indicate that genetic factors may play a stronger role in the development of bipolar than unipolar disorders. Genes may contribute to the development of depression directly through an effect on the central nervous system and indirectly by influencing the person's sensitivity to environmental events, such as severe stress. The mode of genetic transmission in mood disorders has not been identified. Linkage studies may help to find these pathways and could allow clinical scientists to identify individuals who are genetically predisposed to depression.

Neurochemical messengers in the brain also play a role in the regulation of mood and the etiology of mood disorders. Current thinking is focused on serotonin, norepinephrine, and dopamine, although many other neurotransmitter substances may also be involved in depression. Evidence regarding the long-term effects of antidepressant medications points to the importance of sensitivity and density of postsynaptic receptors as well as the interactive effects of multiple neurotransmitter systems.

Several types of psychological and biological treatment have been shown to be effective for mood disorders. Two types of psychotherapy, cognitive therapy and interpersonal therapy, are beneficial for unipolar and dysthymic patients. Three types of antidepressant medication are also useful in the treatment of major depressive disorder: **selective serotonin reuptake inhibitors, tricyclic antidepressants,** and **monoamine oxidase inhibitors.** Medication and psychotherapy are frequently used together. Outcome studies do not consistently favor either psychological or psychopharmacologic treatment.

Three other types of biological treatment are beneficial for specific types of mood disorder. Lithium carbonate and certain anticonvulsant drugs are useful for patients with bipolar mood disorders. Electroconvulsive therapy has been shown to be effective in the treatment of certain depressed patients, and it may be especially useful for patients who are severely suicidal or have failed to respond to other types of treatment. Light therapy seems to be effective for managing seasonal affective disorders.

People commit suicide for many different reasons. Most people who kill themselves are suffering some form of mental disorder, such as depression, substance abuse, or schizophrenia. For some people, suicide represents an escape from unbearable negative emotions or painful self awareness, which are often the result of frustrated psychological needs. Suicidal ideas are often accompanied by narrow patterns of perception and cognitive activity that make suicide seem like a reasonable solution to an otherwise unbearable dilemma. Serotonin dysfunction and genetic factors seem to contribute to the etiology of suicidal behavior. Social factors that have been studied in relation to suicide include religious affiliation, gun control laws, and media coverage of suicidal deaths. Efforts to prevent suicide include the use of hot lines and crisis centers, as well as the provision of psychotherapy and medication for people who are willing or able to seek professional treatment.

KEY TERMS

affect   129
analogue study   157
bipolar mood
   disorder   131
clinical depression   130
cyclothymia   138
depressed mood   130
depression   130

dysphoric   133
dysthymia   137
emotion   129
euphoria   130
hopelessness   148
hypomania   137
mania   130

melancholia   138
monoamine oxidase
   inhibitors (MAO-Is)   159
mood   129
mood disorders   130
psychomotor
   retardation   135

relapse   140
remission   140
schema   147
seasonal affective
   disorder   139
selective serotonin reuptake
   inhibitors (SSRIs)   158

somatic symptoms   134
tricyclics (TCAs)   159
unipolar mood
   disorder   131

 Go to www.prenhall.com/oltmanns for online quizzes, interactive flash cards, PowerPoint presentations, and chapter reviews.

6

Anxiety Disorders

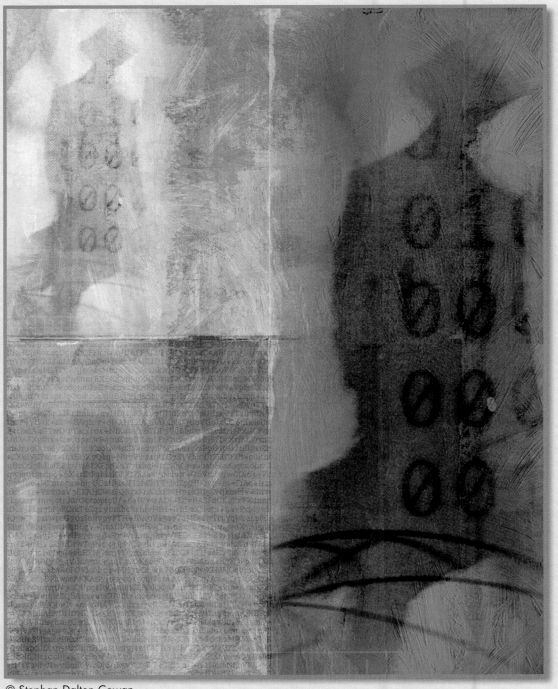

CHAPTER OUTLINE

Symptoms

Diagnosis

Frequency

Causes

Treatment

F ear and anxiety play important roles in all of our lives. Fear helps us avoid danger in our immediate environment. Have you ever jumped out of the street to avoid a car that was unexpectedly rushing toward you? Or run away from an animal with a menacing growl? The sudden burst of fear that you experienced allowed you to react immediately. Anxiety helps us anticipate and prepare for important events in the future. Remember when you called someone for the first time, performed at a musical recital, or spoke up in class? If you felt anxious in the time leading up to this event, you may have also noticed that your heart was pounding, your mouth was dry, and you were breathing faster. These are some of the physical signs of anxiety. Anxiety may be unpleasant, but it is often adaptive; we would have trouble organizing our lives if it was eliminated completely. Unfortunately, anxiety can also disrupt our lives. There are many ways in which anxiety can become maladaptive. It is often a question of degree rather than kind. We can worry too much, feel anxious too often, or be afraid at inappropriate times. In this chapter we will explore many of the important distinctions that psychologists make among phenomena such as fear, anxiety, worry, and panic. We will discuss the ways in which these experiences can become maladaptive and the ways in which the problems can be treated. In the next chapter, we will consider one other specific form of anxiety, known as posttraumatic stress disorder.

OVERVIEW

Taken together, the various forms of anxiety disorders—including phobias, obsessions, compulsions, and extreme worry—represent the most common type of abnormal behavior. The National Comorbidity Survey (NCS) found that 17 percent of adults in the U.S. population have at least one type of anxiety disorder in any given year (Kessler et al., 1995). This figure was higher than the 1-year prevalence rates that were observed for mood disorders (11 percent) and

substance use disorders (11 percent). Data from the NCS also indicate that the annual cost of anxiety disorders in the United States exceeded $42 billion in 1990 (Lepine, 2002). Anxiety disorders lead to significant social and occupational impairment (see Table 1–3).

Anxiety disorders share several important similarities with mood disorders. From a descriptive point of view, both categories are defined in terms of negative emotional responses. Feelings such as guilt, worry, and anger frequently accompany anxiety and depression. Many patients who are anxious are also depressed, and, similarly, many patients who are depressed are also anxious (Shankman & Klein, 2003).

The close relationship between symptoms of anxiety and those for depression suggests that these disorders may share common causal features. In fact, stressful life events seem to play a role in the onset of both depression and anxiety. Cognitive factors are also important in both types of problems. From a biological point of view, certain brain regions and a number of neurotransmitters are involved in the etiology of anxiety disorders as well as mood disorders (Shorter & Tyrer, 2003).

The following case study illustrates the kinds of symptoms that are included under the heading of anxiety disorders. You will probably notice the overlap among different features of anxiety disorders, including panic, worry, avoidance, and a variety of alarming physical sensations. This narrative was written by Johanna Schneller (1988), a freelance writer who has been treated for panic disorder. *Agoraphobia* refers to an exaggerated fear of being in situations from which escape might be difficult, such as being caught in a traffic jam on a bridge or in a tunnel.

◆◆◆◆◆◆◆◆◆◆◆◆◆◆◆◆◆◆◆◆◆◆◆◆◆◆◆◆◆◆◆◆◆◆◆◆◆◆◆

CASE STUDY   A Writer's Panic Disorder with Agoraphobia

My heart was really pounding now, and I felt short of breath, as if wheels were rolling across my chest. I was terrified of what was happening to me. Would I be able to get home?

"Three years have passed since my first panic attack struck, but even now I can close my eyes and see the small supermarket where it happened. I can feel the shoppers in their heavy coats jostling me with their plastic baskets, and once again my stomach starts to drop away.

"It was November. I had just moved to New York City and completed a long search for a job and an apartment. The air felt close in that checkout line, and black fuzz crept into the corners of my vision. Afraid of fainting, I began to count the number of shoppers ahead of me, then the number of purchases they had. The overhead lights seemed to grow brighter. The cash register made pinging sounds that hurt my ears. Even the edges of the checkout counter looked cold and sharp. Suddenly I became nauseated, dizzy. My vertigo intensified, separating me from everyone else in the store, as if I were looking up from underwater. And then I got hot, the kind of hot you feel when the blood seems to rush to your cheeks and drain from your head at the same time.

"My heart was really pounding now, and I felt short of breath, as if wheels were rolling across my chest. I was terrified of what was happening to me. Would I be able to get home? I tried to talk myself down, to convince myself that if I could just stay in line and act as if nothing was happening, these symptoms would go away. Then I decided I wasn't going to faint—I was going to start screaming. The distance to the door looked vast and the seconds were crawling by, but somehow I managed to stay in the checkout line, pay for my bag of groceries and get outside, where I sat on a bench, gulping air. The whole episode had taken ten minutes. I was exhausted.

"At home, I tried to analyze what had happened to me. The experience had been terrifying, but because I felt safe in my kitchen, I tried to laugh the whole thing off—really, it seemed ridiculous, freaking out in a supermarket. I decided it was an isolated incident; I was all right, and I was going to forget it ever happened.

"Two weeks later, as I sat in a movie theater, the uncomfortable buzz began to envelop me again. But the symptoms set in faster this time. I mumbled something to my friends about feeling sick as I clambered over them. It was minutes before I caught my breath, hours before I calmed down completely.

"A month full of scattered attacks passed before they started rolling in like Sunday evenings, at least once a week. I tried to find a pattern: They always hit in crowded places, places difficult to escape. My whole body felt threatened, primed to run during an attack. Ironically, my attacks were invisible to anyone near me unless they knew what to look for—clenched neck muscles, restless eyes, a shifting from foot to foot—and I was afraid to talk to anyone about them, to perhaps hear something I wouldn't want to hear. What if I had a brain tumor? And I was embarrassed, as if it were my fault that I felt out of control. But then one night I had an attack alone in my bed—the only place I had felt safe. I gave in and called a doctor.

"As the weeks passed and the attacks wore on, I began to think maybe I was crazy. I was having attacks in public so often I became afraid to leave my house. I had one on the subway while traveling to work almost every morning but, luckily, never panicked on the job. Instead, I usually lost control in situations where I most wanted to relax: on weekend trips, or while visiting friends. I felt responsible for ruining other people's good time. One attack occurred while I was in a tiny boat deep sea fishing with my family; another hit when I was on a weekend canoe trip with my boyfriend. I also suffered a terrifying attack while on my way to see friends, stuck in traffic, merging into a tunnel near Boston's Logan Airport, with no exit ramp or emergency lane in sight.

"I began declining offers I wanted to accept: all I could think was, 'What if I panic in the middle of nowhere?' The times I did force myself to go out, I sat near the doors of restaurants, in aisle seats at movie theaters, near the bathroom at parties. For some reason, I always felt safe in bathrooms, as if whatever happened to me there would at least be easy to clean up.

"On days when I didn't have an actual attack, I could feel one looming like a shadow over my shoulder; this impending panic was almost worse than the real thing. By remembering old episodes, I brought on new ones, and each seemed to pull me closer to a vision I had of my mind snapping cleanly in half, like a stalk of celery."

◆◆◆◆◆◆◆◆◆◆◆◆◆◆◆◆◆◆◆◆◆◆◆◆◆◆◆◆◆◆◆◆◆◆◆◆◆◆◆

Johanna's description of her problems raises a number of interesting questions, to which we will return later in the chapter. Was it just a coincidence that her first attack occurred shortly after the difficult experience of moving to a new city, starting a new job, and finding a new apartment? Could the stress of those experiences have contributed to the onset of her disorder? Was there a pattern to her attacks? Why did she feel safe in some situations and not in others? She mentions feeling out of control, as if she were responsible for her attacks. Could she really bring on another attack by remembering one from the past?

SYMPTOMS

People with anxiety disorders share a preoccupation with, or persistent avoidance of, thoughts or situations that provoke fear or anxiety. Anxiety disorders frequently have a negative impact on various aspects of a person's life. Johanna found that anxiety and its associated problems constrained both her ability to work and her social relationships. In spite of these problems, most people who knew Johanna probably did not know that she suffered from a mental disorder. In spite of the private terrors that she endured, she was able to carry on most aspects of her life.

In addition to these general considerations, the diagnosis of anxiety disorders depends on several specific types of symptoms, which we discuss in the following sections. We begin with the nature of anxiety, which should be distinguished from more discrete emotional responses, like fear and panic.

Anxiety

Like depression, the term *anxiety* can refer to either a mood or a syndrome. Here, we use the term to refer to a mood. Specific syndromes associated with anxiety disorders are discussed later in the chapter.

Anxious mood is often defined in contrast to the specific emotion of fear, which is more easily understood. **Fear** is experienced in the face of real, immediate danger. It usually builds quickly in intensity and helps organize the person's behavioral responses to threats from the environment (escaping or fighting back). Classic studies of fear among normal adults have often focused on people in combat situations, such as airplane crews during bombing missions over

Germany in World War II (Rachman, 1991). In contrast to fear, **anxiety** involves a more general or diffuse emotional reaction—beyond simple fear—that is out of proportion to threats from the environment (Barlow, 2001). Rather than being directed toward the person's present circumstances, anxiety is associated with the anticipation of future problems.

Anxiety can be adaptive at low levels, because it serves as a signal that the person must prepare for an upcoming event. When you think about final exams, for example, you may become somewhat anxious. That emotional response may help to initiate and sustain your efforts to study. In contrast, high levels of anxiety become incapacitating by disrupting concentration and performance.

A pervasively anxious mood is often associated with pessimistic thoughts and feelings ("If something bad happens, I probably won't be able to control it"). The person's attention turns inward, focusing on negative emotions and self-evaluation ("Now I'm so upset that I'll never be able to concentrate during the exam!") rather than on the organization or rehearsal of adaptive responses that might be useful in coping with negative events. Taken together, these factors can be used to define maladaptive anxiety, or what David Barlow, a psychologist at Boston University, has called *anxious apprehension*, which consists of (1) high levels of diffuse negative emotion, (2) a sense of uncontrollability, and

People react with strong negative emotions as they look toward the World Trade Center on September 11, 2001. Negative affect is a blend of several emotions, including fear, anger, sadness, and disgust.

Video Case

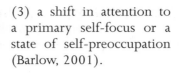

PANIC DISORDER

JERRY

"I couldn't be in one place, a movie or a church—things would be closing in on me, and I would have to get up and leave."

On your CD-ROM menu, select "Anxiety Disorders" and click on "Panic Disorder: Jerry." Pay careful attention to the description of his first panic attack, which occurred while he was driving a car on the interstate.

(3) a shift in attention to a primary self-focus or a state of self-preoccupation (Barlow, 2001).

Excessive Worry

Worrying is a cognitive activity that is associated with anxiety. In recent years psychologists have studied this phenomenon carefully because they consider it to be critical in the subclassification of anxiety disorders (DSM-IV-TR). **Worry** can be defined as a relatively uncontrollable sequence of negative, emotional thoughts that are concerned with possible future threats or danger. This sequence of worrisome thoughts is usually self-initiated or provoked by a specific experience or ongoing difficulties in the person's daily life. When excessive worriers are asked to describe their thoughts, they emphasize the predominance of verbal, linguistic material rather than images (Borkovec, Alcaine, & Behar, 2004). In other words, worriers are preoccupied with "self-talk" rather than unpleasant visual images.

Because everyone worries at least a little, you might wonder whether it is possible to distinguish between pathological and normal worry. The answer is yes, but there is not a clear line that divides the two kinds of experience. The distinction hinges on quantity—how often the person worries and about how many different topics the person worries. It also depends on the quality of worrisome thought. Excessive worriers are more likely than other people to report that the content of their thoughts is negative, that they have less control over the content and direction of their thoughts, and that in comparison to other adults, their worries are less realistic (Zebb & Beck, 1998).

Panic Attacks

A **panic attack** is a sudden, overwhelming experience of terror or fright, like the attack that was experienced by Johanna as she waited in the checkout line. Whereas anxiety involves a blend of several negative emotions, panic is more focused. Some clinicians think of panic as a normal fear response

Why is a panic attack sometimes called a "false alarm"?

that is triggered at an inappropriate time (Barlow, Brown, & Craske, 1994). In that sense, panic is a "false alarm." Descriptively, panic can be distinguished from anxiety in two other respects: It is more intense, and it has a sudden onset.

Panic attacks are defined largely in terms of a list of somatic or physical sensations, ranging from heart palpitations, sweating, and trembling to nausea, dizziness, and chills. Table 6–1 lists the DSM-IV-TR criteria for a panic attack. A person must experience at least 4 of these 13 symptoms in order for the experience to qualify as a full-blown panic attack. The symptoms must develop suddenly and reach a peak intensity within 10 minutes. The actual numbers and combinations of panic symptoms vary from one person to the next, and they may also change over time within the same person.

People undergoing a panic attack also report a number of cognitive symptoms. They may feel as though they are about to die, lose control, or go crazy. Some clinicians believe that the misinterpretation of bodily sensations lies at the core of panic disorder. Patients may interpret heart palpitations as evidence of an impending heart attack, or racing thoughts as evidence that they are about to lose their minds.

Panic attacks are further described in terms of the situations in which they occur, as well as the person's expectations about their occurrence. An attack is said to be expected, or *cued*, if it occurs only in the presence of a particular stimulus. For example, someone who is afraid of public speaking might have a cued panic attack if forced to give a speech in front of a large group of people. Unexpected panic attacks, like Johanna's experience in the grocery checkout line, appear without warning or expectation, as if "out of the blue."

Is there a typical pattern for panic attacks in the natural environment? In one descriptive study, panic disorder patients kept daily diaries describing panic experiences, and they also wore an ambulatory heart rate/physical activity recorder (Margraf et al., 1987). The average (mean) number of panic attacks among these patients was slightly less than one per day, but the number varied considerably across patients. Expected and unexpected panic attacks were experienced in roughly equivalent proportions. Unexpected attacks occurred most frequently at home, whereas situational attacks occurred most frequently in the car, usually while driving on freeways. The timing of unexpected attacks was evenly distributed across the day and night hours, with some occurring while the patient was asleep or trying to fall asleep. The results of this study and several others indicate that the symptoms and timing of panic attacks can vary widely from one patient to the next.

Phobias

In contrast to both diffuse anxiety, which represents a blend of negative emotions, and panic attacks, which are frequently unexpected, **phobias** are persistent, irrational, narrowly defined fears that are associated with a specific object or situation. Avoidance is an important component of the definition of phobias. A fear is not considered phobic unless the person avoids contact with the source of the fear or experiences intense anxiety in the presence of the stimulus. Phobias are also irrational or unreasonable. Avoiding only snakes that are poisonous or only guns that are loaded would not be considered phobic.

The most straightforward type of phobia involves fear of specific objects or situations. Different types of specific phobias have traditionally been named according to the Greek words for these objects. Examples of typical specific phobias include fear of heights (acrophobia), fear of enclosed spaces (claustrophobia), fear of small animals (zoophobia), fear of blood or injury, and fear of traveling on airplanes.

Some people experience marked fear when they are forced to engage in certain activities, such as public speaking, initiating a conversation, eating in restaurants, or using public rest rooms, which might involve being observed or evaluated by other people. Attempts to avoid these feared situations cause serious impairment in the person's social and occupational activities. For example, one young man who was treated by one of the authors of this text was afraid of urinating in public rest rooms. He planned his daily schedule with great care so that he would always be near a rest room with a locking door. Consequently, he was unable to attend movies or eat in restaurants unless they happened to have single-person rest rooms that he could lock from the inside.

The most complex and incapacitating form of phobic disorder is **agoraphobia,** which literally means "fear of the marketplace (or places of assembly)" and is usually described as fear of public spaces. The case of Johanna provides a brief description of the types of problems

THE FAR SIDE® BY GARY LARSON

The Far Side® by Gary Larson © 1990 FarWorks, Inc. All Rights Reserved. The Far Side® and the Larson® signature are registered trademarks of FarWorks, Inc. Used with permission.

© 1990 FarWorks, Inc. All Rights Reserved/Dist. by Creators Syndicate

Math phobic's nightmare

experienced by a person suffering from agoraphobia. The fear usually becomes more intense as the distance between the person and his or her familiar surroundings increases, or as avenues of escape are closed off. In that sense, agoraphobia

---

TABLE 6–1   Diagnostic Criteria for Panic Attack in DSM-IV-TR
A discrete period of intense fear or discomfort, in which four (or more) of the following symptoms developed abruptly and reached a peak within 10 minutes:

1. Palpitations, pounding heart, or accelerated heart rate
2. Sweating
3. Trembling or shaking
4. Sensations of shortness of breath or smothering
5. Feeling of choking
6. Chest pain or discomfort
7. Nausea or abdominal distress
8. Feeling dizzy, unsteady, lightheaded, or faint
9. Derealization (feelings of unreality) or depersonalization (being detached from oneself)
10. Fear of losing control or going crazy
11. Fear of dying
12. Paresthesias (numbness or tingling sensations)
13. Chills or hot flushes

Reprinted with permission from the *Diagnostic and Statistical Manual of Mental Disorders,* Fourth Edition, Text Revision. Copyright © 2000 by the American Psychiatric Association.

People with agoraphobia are afraid of crowded places from which they might not be able to escape. They also frequently experience panic attacks that are not cued by particular environmental circumstances.

Social phobias may involve prepared conditioning associated with faces that seem angry, critical, or rejecting.

is somewhat different from the other phobias because it is not so much a fear of being close to one specific object or situation (for example, animals, public speaking) as it is of being separated from signals associated with safety.

Typical situations that cause problems include crowded streets and shops, enclosed places like theaters and churches, traveling on public transportation, and driving an automobile on bridges, in tunnels, or on crowded expressways. In any of these situations, the presence of a trusted friend may help the person with agoraphobia feel more comfortable. In the most extreme form of the disorder, agoraphobic patients are unable to venture away from their own homes. Some people with agoraphobia are able to visit public places (for example, shopping malls, theaters), but may remain near exits or aisles so that their escape cannot be easily blocked.

The uncomfortable sensations experienced by people with agoraphobia are similar to those that have already been described for other anxiety disorders. They range from vague feelings of apprehension to specific physical sensations and full-blown panic attacks. People with agoraphobia are frequently afraid that they will experience an "attack" of these symptoms that will be either incapacitating or embarrassing, and that help will not be available to them. Many patients report that they are afraid of becoming dizzy, fainting, losing bladder or bowel control, or having heart problems. In some cases, previous experiences of this sort may have triggered persistent fear of repeated episodes.

Some clinicians have suggested that "fear of fear" is the central feature of agoraphobia (e.g., Goldstein & Chambless, 1978; Klein, 1981). The crucial event that triggers subsequent fears is often a terrifying, unexpected panic attack, which is why the two forms of anxiety disorder often occur in combination, as in Johanna's case. Following such an experience, the person may become acutely aware of all internal bodily sensations that may signal the onset of another attack. Fear of losing control of these internal experiences then leads, paradoxically, to a further increase in anxiety. This concept has been expanded to include fear of various strong emotions, including anger and depression as well as anxiety (Williams, Chambless, & Ahrens, 1997).

Obsessions and Compulsions

Obsessions are repetitive, unwanted, intrusive cognitive events that may take the form of thoughts or images or impulses. They intrude suddenly into consciousness and lead to an increase in subjective anxiety. Obsessive thinking can be distinguished from worry in two primary ways: (1) Obsessions are usually experienced as coming from "out of the blue," whereas worries are often triggered by problems in everyday living; and (2) the content of obsessions most often involves themes that are perceived as being socially unacceptable or horrific, such as sex, violence, and disease/contamination, whereas the content of worries tends to center around more acceptable, commonplace concerns, such as money and work (de Silva & Rachman, 2004).

Compulsions are repetitive behaviors or mental acts that are used to reduce anxiety.

Examples include checking many times to be sure that a door is locked or repeating a silent prayer over and over again. These actions are considered by the person who performs them to be senseless or irrational. The person attempts to resist performing the compulsion but cannot. The following case study illustrates many of the most common features of obsessions and compulsions.

◆◆

CASE STUDY Ed's Obsessive–Compulsive Disorder

Ed, a 38-year-old lawyer, lived with his wife, Phyllis. Most aspects of Ed's life were going well, except for the anxiety-provoking thoughts that lurked beneath his relatively easygoing exterior. One focus of Ed's anxiety was handwriting. He became so tense that his eyes hurt whenever he was forced to write. Feeling exhausted and overwhelmed, Ed avoided writing whenever possible. The problem seemed utterly ridiculous to him, but he couldn't rid himself of his obsessive thoughts.

Sinister meanings had somehow become linked in Ed's imagination to the way in which letters and numbers were formed. The worst letters were P and T (the first letters in "Phyllis" and in "Tim," his younger brother's name). "Improperly" formed letters reminded Ed of violent acts, especially decapitation and strangulation.

If the parts of a letter, such as the two lines in the letter T, were not connected, an image of a head that was not attached to its body might pop into his mind.

Closed loops reminded him of suffocation, like a person whose throat had been clamped shut. These images were associated with people whose names began with the malformed letter. As a result of these concerns, Ed's handwriting had become extremely awkward and difficult to read.

These writing problems made it very difficult for Ed to complete his work, especially when he was under time pressure. In one particularly upsetting incident, Ed was responsible for completing an important official form that had to be mailed that day. He came to a section in which he needed to write a capital P and became concerned that he hadn't done it properly. The loop seemed to be closed, which

meant that Phyllis might be strangled! He tore up the first copy and filled it out again. When it was finally done to his satisfaction, Ed sealed the form in an envelope and put it in the box for outgoing mail. After returning to his desk, he was suddenly overwhelmed by the feeling that he had indeed made a mistake with that P. If he allowed the form to be mailed, the evil image would be associated forever with his wife. Consumed by fear, Ed rushed back to the mailbox, tore up the envelope, and started a new form. Twenty minutes later, he had the form filled out and back in the mailbox. Then the cycle repeated itself. Each time, Ed became more distraught and frustrated, until he eventually felt that he was going to lose his mind.

In addition to his problems with writing, Ed was also afraid of axes. He would not touch an ax, or even get close to one. Any situation in which he could possibly encounter an ax made him extremely uncomfortable. He refused to shop in hardware stores because they sell axes, and he would not visit museums because their exhibits often contain artifacts such as medieval armor. His fear of axes was quite specific. Ed wasn't afraid of knives, guns, or swords.

One frightening experience seemed to trigger the pervasive anxiety that had plagued Ed for 20 years. When he was 17 years old, some friends persuaded Ed to try smoking marijuana. They told him that it would make him feel high—relaxed, sociable, and perhaps a bit giddy. Unfortunately, Ed didn't react to the drug in the same way that the others had. The physical effects seemed to be the same, but his psychological reaction was entirely different. After sharing two joints with his friends, Ed began to feel lightheaded. Then things around him began to seem unreal, as though he were watching himself and his friends in a movie. The intensity of these feelings escalated rapidly, and panic took over. Frightening thoughts

raced through his head. Was he losing his mind? When would it stop? This experience lasted about 2 hours.

The marijuana incident had an immediate and lasting impact. Ed became preoccupied with a fear of accidentally ingesting any kind of mind-altering drug, especially LSD. Every spot on his skin or clothing seemed as though it might be a microscopic quantity of this hallucinogen. He felt compelled to clean his hands and clothes repeatedly to avoid contamination. Intellectually, Ed knew that these concerns were silly. How could a tiny spot on his hand be LSD? It didn't make any sense, but he couldn't keep the thought out of his mind.

The most horrifying aspect of the drug experience was the sensation of being totally out of control of his actions and emotions. The fear of returning to that state haunted Ed. He struggled to resist impulses that he had never noticed before, such as the temptation to shout obscenities aloud in church. He also began to worry that he might hurt his younger brother. He resisted the impulses with all his might. He never acted on them, but they pervaded his consciousness and absorbed his mental energy.

The thoughts were so persistent and unshakable that Ed began to wonder if he might, in fact, be a pathological killer. Could he be as deranged and evil as Richard Speck, who had brutally murdered eight nurses in a Chicago apartment building in 1966? Ed spent many hours reading articles about Speck and other mass murderers. The number 8 came to have special meaning to him because of the number of Speck's victims. Over time, Ed's fears and worries became focused on numbers and letters. The violent images and impulses became a less prominent part of his everyday life, but the writing difficulties escalated proportionately.

◆◆

Ed's thoughts about violence and death illustrate the anxiety-provoking nature of obsessions. It is not just the intrusive quality of the thought but also the unwanted nature of the thought that makes it an obsession. Some scientists and artists, for example, have reported experiencing intrusive thoughts or inspirational ideas that appear in an unexpected, involuntary way, but these thoughts are not unwanted. Obsessions are unwelcome, anxiety-provoking thoughts. They are also nonsensical; they may seem silly or "crazy." In spite of the recognition that these thoughts do not make sense, the person with full blown obsessions is unable to ignore or dismiss them.

Examples of typical obsessive thoughts include the following: "Did I kill the old lady?" "Christ was a bastard!" "Am I a sexual pervert?" Examples of obsessive impulses include "I might expose my genitals in public," "I am about to shout obscenities in public," "I feel I might strangle a child." Obsessional images might include mutilated corpses, decomposing fetuses, or a family member being involved in a serious car accident. Although obsessive impulses are accompanied by a compelling sense of reality, obsessive people seldom act upon these impulses.

Most normal people experience obsessions in one form or another. Between 80 and 90 percent of normal subjects report having had intrusive, unacceptable thoughts or impulses that are similar in many ways to those experienced by patients being treated for obsessive–compulsive disorder (Rachman & de Silva, 1978; Salkovskis & Harrison, 1984). These include impulses to hurt other people, impulses to do something dangerous, and thoughts of accidents or disease. In contrast to the obsessions described by people who are not in treatment, those experienced by clinical patients occur more frequently, last longer, and are associated with higher levels of discomfort than normal obsessions. Clinical obsessions are also resisted more strongly, and patients report more difficulty dismissing their unwanted thoughts and impulses. Research evidence suggests that obsessions are relatively common, and that clinical obsessions differ from normal obsessions in degree rather than in nature. Similarities and continuities have also been observed between clinical compulsions and rituals that are commonly performed by people who do not qualify for a diagnosis of obsessive–compulsive disorder (Muris, Merckelbach, & Clavan, 1997).

Ed's constricted style of forming letters and his habitual pattern of going back to check and correct his writing illustrate the way in which compulsions are used to reduce anxiety. If he did not engage in these ritualistic behaviors, he would become extremely uncomfortable. His concern about someone being strangled or decapitated if the letters were not properly formed was not delusional, because he readily acknowledged that this was a "silly" idea. Nevertheless, he couldn't shake the obsessive idea that some dreadful event would occur if he was not excruciatingly careful about his writing. He felt as though he had to act, even though he knew that his obsessive thought was irrational. This paradox is extremely frustrating to obsessive–compulsive patients, and it is one of the most common and interesting aspects of the disorder.

Compulsions reduce anxiety, but they do not produce pleasure. Thus some behaviors, such as gambling and drug use, that people describe as being "compulsive" are not considered true compulsions according to this definition.

Although some clinicians have argued that compulsive rituals are associated with a complete loss of voluntary control, it is more accurate to view the problem in terms of *diminished control*. For example, Ed could occasionally manage to resist the urge to write in his compulsive style; the behavior was not totally automatic. But whenever he did not engage in this ritualistic behavior, his subjective level of distress increased dramatically, and within a short period of time he returned to the compulsive writing style.

The two most common forms of compulsive behavior are cleaning and checking. The case of Michael, presented in Chapter 4, provides an example of a person with compulsive cleaning rituals. Compulsive cleaning is often associated with an irrational fear of contamination, and in that respect it bears a strong resemblance to certain phobias (Rachman & Hodgson, 1980). There are passive as well as active features of compulsive cleaning. Compulsive cleaners, like Michael, go out of their way to avoid contact with dirt, germs, and other sources of contamination. Then, when they believe that they have come into contact with a source of contamination, they engage in ritualistic cleaning behavior, such as washing their hands, taking showers, cleaning kitchen counters, and so on. These rituals typically involve a large number of repetitions. Some people may wash their hands 50 times a day, taking several minutes to scrub their hands up to the elbow with industrial-strength cleanser. Others take showers that last 2 or 3 hours in which they wash each part of their body in a fixed order, needing to repeat the scrubbing motion an exact number of times.

Compulsive checking frequently represents an attempt to ensure the person's safety or the safety and health of a friend or family member. The person checks things, such as the stove or the lock on a door, over and over in an attempt to prevent the occurrence of an imagined unpleasant or disastrous event (for example, an accident, a burglary, or an assault).

DIAGNOSIS

To understand the way in which anxiety disorders are currently classified, we must briefly consider the ways in which they have been described in previous classification systems. This general set of emotional problems was the topic of considerable diagnostic controversy throughout the twentieth century and continues into the twenty-first.

Brief Historical Perspective

Anxiety and abnormal fears did not play a prominent role in the psychiatric classification systems that began to emerge in Europe during the second half of the nineteenth century (see Chapter 4). Anxiety disorders were probably left out of these descriptions because the authors were primarily superintendents of large asylums. Their patients were people who were psychotic (see Chapter 1) or so out of touch with reality that they could no longer reside in the larger community (Jablensky, 1985; Klerman, 1990a). People with anxiety problems seldom came to the attention of psychiatrists during the nineteenth century because very few cases of anxiety disorder require institutionalization.

Freud and his followers were responsible for some of the first extensive clinical descriptions of pathological anxiety states. Working primarily with patients who were not hospitalized, Freud had an opportunity to treat and study a variety of anxiety-related problems. He described cases of phobia, generalized anxiety, and obsessive–compulsive behavior. The form of specific symptoms (a phobia as compared to a compulsion) was

considered to be less important than the underlying causes, which were presumably similar.

Freud's psychological explanations for the origins of anxiety disorders were extremely influential throughout the twentieth century (Josephs, 1994). Freud focused primarily on the importance of mental conflicts and innate biological impulses (primarily sexual and aggressive instincts) in the etiology of anxiety (see Chapter 2). This perspective played a central role in the way that anxiety disorders were classified in early versions of the DSM. They were grouped with several other types of problems under the general heading of **neurosis,** a term used to describe persistent emotional disturbances, such as anxiety and depression, in which the person is aware of the nature of the problem. Neurotic disorders are distinguished from psychotic disorders, in which the person is often out of touch with reality and unaware of the nature of his or her problems (see Chapter 1).

The basic outline of Freud's theory of anxiety hinges on the notion that the person's ego can experience a small amount of anxiety as a signal indicating that an instinctual impulse that has previously been associated with punishment and disapproval is about to be acted on. This usually means that the person is going to do something aggressive or sexual that is considered inappropriate. Signal anxiety triggers the use of ego defenses—primarily repression—that prevent conscious recognition of the forbidden impulse, inhibit its expression, and thereby reduce the person's anxiety. When the system works as it should, anxiety is adaptive, and the person's behavior is regulated to conform with social expectations.

Unfortunately, people can still experience pathological levels of anxiety if the system is overwhelmed. Traumatic events or circumstances can lead to extreme levels of free-floating anxiety. The ego is then forced to resort to additional defensive maneuvers that can produce symptoms such as phobias and compulsions. The specific form of overt symptoms is determined by the defense mechanisms that are employed by the ego, but the underlying process is presumably the same across all of the anxiety neuroses.

Freud's conceptual model for the anxiety neuroses incorporated several important features, including the importance of biologically based impulses, learning experiences based on interactions with other people, and cognitive (or intrapsychic) events that play an important role in mediating between current and past experience. It was firmly grounded in Freud's observations of his own patients' experiences and the process of their treatment with psychoanalysis. Although it served as a useful stimulus to future clinicians and identified many important factors in the etiology of anxiety disorders, his model suffered from a number of weaknesses. Perhaps the major problem was that of measurement. Because Freud's ideas were based on unconscious mental processes that could not be measured directly, his theory of anxiety could not be tested empirically.

Contemporary Diagnostic Systems (DSM-IV-TR)

The DSM-IV-TR (APA, 2000) approach to classifying anxiety disorders is based primarily on descriptive features, rather than etiological hypotheses, and recognizes several specific subtypes. They include panic disorder, three types of phobic disorders, obsessive–compulsive disorder, and generalized anxiety disorder, as well as posttraumatic stress disorder (PTSD) and acute stress disorder. We will discuss PTSD and acute stress disorder in Chapter 7. The manual also describes problems with anxiety that appear in children, specifically separation anxiety disorder and school refusal. These problems will be discussed in Chapter 16.

Panic Disorder   To meet the diagnostic criteria for **panic disorder,** a person must experience recurrent, unexpected panic attacks. At least one of the attacks must have been followed by a period of 1 month or more in which the person has either persistent concern about having additional attacks, worry about the implications of the attack or its consequences, or a significant change in behavior related to the attacks. Panic disorder is divided into two subtypes, depending on the presence or absence of agoraphobia.

Agoraphobia   DSM-IV-TR defines agoraphobia in terms of anxiety about being in situations from which escape might be either difficult or embarrassing. This approach is based on the view that agoraphobia is typically a complication that follows upon the experience of panic attacks (Frances, First, & Pincus, 1995). Avoidance and distress are important elements of the definition. In order to meet the DSM-IV-TR criteria, the person must either avoid agoraphobic situations, such as traveling away from his or her own home; endure the experience with great distress; or insist on being accompanied by another person who can provide some comfort or security. In most cases, the person avoids a wide variety of situations rather than just one specific type of situation. People who fit this description of agoraphobia without meeting the criteria for panic disorder would be assigned a diagnosis of agoraphobia without history of panic disorder.

Specific Phobia   A *specific phobia* is defined in DSM-IV-TR as "a marked and persistent fear that is excessive or unreasonable, cued by the presence or anticipation of a specific object or situation." Frequently observed types of specific phobia include fear of heights, small animals (such as spiders, bugs, mice, snakes, or bats), tunnels or bridges, storms, illness and injury (including blood), being in a closed place (such as a very small room), and being on certain kinds of public transportation (such as airplanes, buses, or elevators). Exposure to the phobic stimulus must be followed by an immediate fear response. Furthermore, the person must appreciate the fact that the fear is excessive or unreasonable, and the person must avoid the phobic situation. DSM-IV-TR also provides a severity threshold: The avoidance or distress associated with the phobia must

Specific phobias are irrational fears associated with specific situations that the person avoids. Acrophobia is the name given to fear of heights.

interfere significantly with the person's normal activities or relationships with others.

Social Phobia The DSM-IV-TR definition of **social phobia** is almost identical to that for specific phobia, but it includes the additional element of performance. A person with a social phobia is afraid of (and avoids) social situations. These situations fall into two broad headings: doing something in front of unfamiliar people (performance anxiety) and interpersonal interactions (such as dating and parties). Fear of being humiliated or embarrassed presumably lies at the heart of the person's discomfort. Some people have a circumscribed form of social phobia that is focused on one particular type of situation. Examples include giving a speech, playing a musical instrument, urinating in a public rest room, or eating in a restaurant. For these people, the feared task could be completed easily if they were able to do it privately. In other cases, the fear is more generalized, and the person is intensely anxious in almost any situation that involves social interaction. This type of person might be described as being extremely shy. The extensive overlap between generalized social phobia and avoidant personality disorder (see Chapter 10) has created some confusion and has been the topic of numerous research studies (Hofmann, Heinrichs, & Moscovitch, 2004).

Generalized Anxiety Disorder Excessive anxiety and worry are the primary symptoms of **generalized anxiety disorder (GAD).** The person must have trouble controlling these worries, and the worries must lead to significant distress or impairment in occupational or social functioning. The worry must occur more days than not for a period of at least 6 months, and it must be about a number of different events or activities. In order to distinguish GAD from other forms of anxiety disorder, DSM-IV-TR notes that the person's worries should not be focused on having a panic attack (as in panic disorder), being embarrassed in public (as in social phobia), or being contaminated (as in obsessive–compulsive disorder). Finally, the person's worries and free-floating anxiety must be accompanied by at least three of the following symptoms: (1) restlessness or feeling keyed up or on edge, (2) being easily fatigued, (3) difficulty concentrating or mind going blank, (4) irritability, (5) muscle tension, and (6) sleep disturbance.

Generalized anxiety disorder remains one of the most controversial anxiety disorders, for several reasons. The diagnostic reliability of GAD is often substantially lower than that for other types of anxiety disorder (Chorpita, Brown, & Barlow, 1998). It also has the highest degree of overlap with the other anxiety disorders. The validity of GAD as a separate diagnostic category is, therefore, open to question. Some experts have suggested that it might be more useful to think of GAD as a trait or a vulnerability factor that sets the stage for later development of other specific types of anxiety disorder, such as panic disorder, social phobia, or obsessive–compulsive disorder (Brown, Barlow, & Liebowitz, 1994). On the other hand, findings have also been reported which indicate that GAD is an important, independent type of anxiety disorder (Kessler, Keller, & Wittchen, 2001). We will discuss some of this evidence in our consideration of genetic factors.

Obsessive–Compulsive Disorder DSM-IV-TR defines obsessive–compulsive disorder (OCD) in terms of the presence of either obsessions or compulsions. Most people who meet the criteria for this disorder actually exhibit both of these symptoms. The person must recognize that the obsessions or compulsions are excessive or unreasonable. The diagnostic manual specifies further that these thoughts must not be simply excessive worries about real problems. Intrusive thoughts about overdue bills, for example, would not qualify as obsessions. The DSM-IV-TR definition also requires that the person must attempt to ignore, suppress, or neutralize the unwanted thoughts or impulses.

The line of demarcation between compulsive rituals and normal behavior is often difficult to define. How many times should a person wash her hands in a day? How long should a shower last? Is it reasonable to check more than one time to be sure that the door is locked or the alarm clock is set? DSM-IV-TR has established an arbitrary threshold which holds that rituals become compulsive if they cause marked distress, take more than an hour per day to perform, or interfere with normal occupational and social functioning.

Video Case

SOCIAL PHOBIA

STEVE

"I imagine that people are watching me. They are watching me stumble in my efforts. . . ."

On your CD-ROM menu, select "Anxiety Disorders" and click on "Social Phobia: Steve." What is his worst fear when he is talking to another person at a party?

Obsessive thoughts about contamination can trigger ritualistic cleaning behaviors, including showers that can last for an hour or more.

"Lumpers" and "Splitters"

Experts who classify mental disorders can be described informally as belonging to one of two groups, "lumpers" and "splitters" (Mack, Forman, Brown, & Frances, 1994; Wittchen et al., 2001). Lumpers argue that anxiety is a generalized condition or set of symptoms without any special subdivisions. Splitters distinguish among a number of conditions, each of which is presumed to have its own etiology. During the first half of the twentieth century, psychiatrists tended to adopt a generalized position with regard to anxiety disorders (see Jablensky, 1985). In other words, they lumped together the various anxiety disorders. The DSM-IV-TR system splits them into many separate disorders.

Although it is currently not a popular position, a reasonable argument can still be made in favor of a more unified approach to the classification of anxiety disorders (Haslam, 2003; Nesse, 1999). Consider, for example, the cases of Ed in this chapter and Michael in Chapter 4. Both exhibited a relatively wide range of anxiety symptoms. The high rate of comorbidity among anxiety disorders suggests that these cases are not unusual. Should Ed be considered to have both a phobic disorder (fear of axes) and an obsessive–compulsive disorder? Or are these diverse symptoms best viewed as manifestations of the same anxiety disorder? These are questions

What is the expected long-term outcome for people with anxiety disorders?

about the validity of diagnostic categories (see Chapter 4). Decisions regarding the breadth or specificity of anxiety disorders will ultimately depend on evidence from many areas. Do phobias and OCD show distinct, separate patterns in family studies? Do they respond to different types of treatment? Can we distinguish between them in terms of typical patterns of onset and course? Definitive answers are not yet available. Future research efforts are needed to address these issues.

Course and Outcome

Anxiety disorders are often chronic conditions. Long-term follow-up studies focused on clinical populations indicate that many people continue to experience symptoms of anxiety and associated social and occupational impairment many years after their problems are initially recognized. On the other hand, some people do recover completely. The most general conclusion, therefore, is that the long-term outcome for anxiety disorders is mixed and somewhat unpredictable (Tyrer et al., 2004; Wittchen & Hoyer, 2001; Yonkers et al., 2003).

Consider, for example, the case of panic disorder. One long-term follow-up study examined patients 11 years after they were treated with medication. The investigators found that 67 percent of these patients did not have panic attacks during the year prior to the follow-up assessment, although half of the patients did continue to show at least moderate levels of phobic avoidance. Some of the patients had improved quickly and remained in a stable pattern of remission, but others followed an episodic pattern of periodic remission followed by relapse (Katschnig & Amering, 1998; Swoboda et al., 2003).

A 15-year longitudinal study of social phobia has reported that people who have an earlier age of onset often experience a more severe form of the disorder (Merikangas et al., 2002). In most cases, the person's symptoms were first evident during adolescence, and they remained quite stable over time. The participants in this study were young adults in a community sample rather than patients at a clinic; most did not receive treatment for their condition. The results indicate that the natural course of social phobia is often chronic in nature (Keller, 2003).

The long-term course of obsessive–compulsive disorder also follows a pattern of improvement mixed with some persistent symptoms. One remarkable study has reported outcome information for a sample of 144 patients with severe OCD who were assessed at two follow-up intervals: first about 5 years after they were initially treated at a psychiatric hospital and then again more than 40 years later (Skoog & Skoog, 1999). The data are interesting both because of the very long follow-up interval and because the patients were initially treated between 1947 and 1953, well before the introduction of modern pharmacological and psychological treatments for the disorder. The results are summarized in Figure 6–1. Slightly less than 30 percent of the patients were rated as being recovered at the first follow-up interval. By the time of the 40-year follow-up, almost 50 percent of the patients were considered to show either full recovery or recovery with subclinical symptoms. More than 80 percent of the patients showed improved levels of functioning if we also count people who continued to exhibit some clinical symptoms. Nevertheless, half of the patients in this sample exhibited symptoms of OCD for more than 30 years. This study shows that although many patients do improve, OCD is a chronic disorder for many people.

FREQUENCY

Some epidemiological studies focus exclusively on treated cases of a disorder, but that strategy can provide a distorted view of the distribution of the disorder within the general population. Many factors can influence whether a person decides to seek treatment. Some cases are less severe than others. Some people treat themselves without consulting a mental health professional. Some people are suspicious of medical facilities, and others are concerned about what people will think of them if they are treated for a mental disorder. Of course, people with agoraphobia are extremely reluctant to leave their homes for any reason. This issue has been a special problem in epidemiological studies of anxiety disorders. Only about 25 percent of people who qualify for a diagnosis of anxiety disorder ever seek psychological treatment. Therefore our estimates of the frequency and severity of these problems must be based on community surveys.

Prevalence

The National Comorbidity Survey (NCS), which included approximately 8,000 people aged 15 to 54 throughout the United States, found that anxiety disorders are more common than any other form of mental disorder (Horwath et al., 2002; Kessler et al., 1995). The same conclusion had been reached previously in the ECA study (see Table 1–2). Specific phobias are the most common type of anxiety disorder, with a 1-year prevalence of about 9 percent of the adult population (men and women combined). Social phobia is almost as common, with a 1-year prevalence of 8 percent. Agoraphobia without panic disorder and GAD both affect approximately 3 percent of the population, and 2 percent of adults meet the criteria for panic disorder in any given year. Obsessive–compulsive disorder affects another 2 percent of the population.

Comorbidity

The symptoms of various anxiety disorders overlap considerably. Many people who experience panic attacks develop phobic avoidance, and many people with obsessive thoughts would also be considered chronic worriers. One study found that 50 percent of people who met the criteria for one anxiety disorder also met the criteria for at least one other form of anxiety disorder or mood disorder (Brown & Barlow, 1992).

Both anxiety and depression are based on emotional distress, so it is not surprising that considerable overlap also exists between anxiety

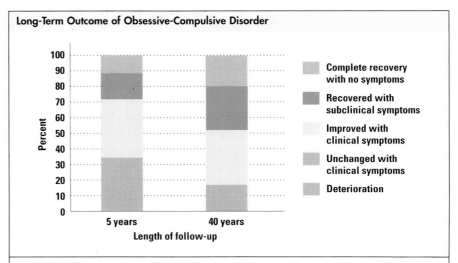

FIGURE 6–1: Changes in clinical severity for 144 patients with OCD measured 5 years and 40 years after hospitalization.

Source: G. Skoog & I. Skoog, 1999, A 40-year follow-up of patients with obsessive-compulsive disorder, *Archives of General Psychiatry, 56,* 121–127. Copyright © 1999. Reprinted by permission of American Medical Association.

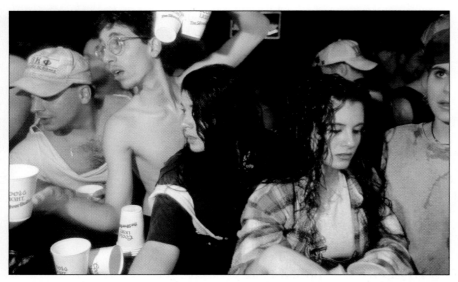

Heavy drinkers are more likely than other people to develop anxiety disorders, and people who are highly anxious are more likely to start to drink heavily.

disorders and mood disorders (Kessler et al., 1998; Regier et al., 1998). Approximately 60 percent of people who receive a primary diagnosis of major depression also qualify for a secondary diagnosis of some type of anxiety disorder. This extensive overlap raises interesting questions about the relation between these general diagnostic categories. Do people who meet the criteria for both depression and an anxiety disorder really suffer from two distinct syndromes? Or should we think about the existence of three types of disorder: "pure" anxiety disorders, "pure" mood disorders, and a third type of disorder that represents a mixture of anxiety and depression? Reasonable arguments have been made on both sides of this debate, which remains unresolved (Barlow & Campbell, 2000; Tyrer, 2001).

Substance dependence is another problem that is frequently associated with anxiety disorders. People who have an anxiety disorder are about three times more likely to have an alcohol use disorder than are people without an anxiety disorder (Grant et al., 2004). In situations such as these, questions of cause and effect are not clear. Did the person use alcohol in an attempt to reduce heightened anxiety, or did he or she become anxious after drinking excessively? Prospective studies conclude that it works both ways. One study found that among first-year college students, the presence of an anxiety disorder increased by four times the risk for later onset of heavy drinking problems. Conversely, the presence of alcohol dependence among first-year college students caused a similar increase in the probability that the person would later develop a new anxiety disorder (Kushner, Sher, & Erickson, 1999).

Gender Differences

There are significant gender differences in several types of anxiety disorders. Pertinent data from the National Comorbidity Survey are summarized in Table 6–2. The gender difference is particularly large for specific phobias, where women are three times as likely as men to experience the disorder. Women are about twice as likely as men to experience panic disorder, agoraphobia (without panic disorder), and generalized anxiety disorder. Social phobia is also more common among women than among men, but the difference is not as striking as it is for other types of phobia. The only type of anxiety disorder for which there does not appear to be a significant gender difference is OCD (Karno & Golding, 1991).

Among people who have anxiety disorder, relapse rates are also much higher for women than for men. For example, one follow-up study of patients with panic disorder found that women and men are equally likely to show an initial improvement in their condition. But among those patients who enter a period of remission, symptoms had returned within 3 years for 60 percent of women and only 40 percent of men (Yonkers et al., 2003).

The significant gender differences in the prevalence and course of anxiety disorders must be interpreted in the light of etiological theories, which are considered in the next section. Several explanations remain plausible. Psychological speculation has focused on such factors as gender differences in child-rearing practices or differences in the way in which men and women respond to stressful life events. Gender differences in hormone functions or neurotransmitter activities in the brain may also be responsible.

Anxiety Across the Life Span

Data from the ECA study indicate that the prevalence of anxiety disorders is lower among elderly men and women than it is among people in other age groups. Data from other studies support this conclusion (Blazer, 1997). This result is perhaps surprising, in light of the fact that many elderly people face problems associated with loneliness, increased dependency, declining physical and cognitive capacities, and changes in social and economic conditions. To explain this result, some scientists speculate that something about the aging process may reduce the probability that stressful or threatening life events will lead to the onset of an anxiety disorder (Flint, 1994).

Most elderly people with an anxiety disorder have had the symptoms for many years. It is relatively unusual for a person to develop a new case of panic disorder, specific phobia, social phobia, or obsessive–compulsive disorder at an advanced age. The only type of anxiety disorder that begins with any noticeable frequency in late life is agoraphobia (Barlow et al., 2003).

The diagnosis of anxiety disorders among elderly people is complicated by the need to consider factors such as medical illnesses and other physical impairments and limitations (Carmin, Pollard, & Gillock, 1999). Respiratory and cardiovascular problems may resemble the physiological symptoms of a panic attack. Hearing losses may lead to anxiety in interpersonal interactions. Subsequent avoidance might be inappropriately attributed to the onset of a social phobia. A frail elderly person who falls down on the street may become afraid to leave home alone, but this may be a reasonable concern rather than a symptom of agoraphobia. For reasons such as these, the diagnosis of anxiety disorders must be done with extra caution in elderly men and women.

Cross-Cultural Comparisons

The focus of typical anxiety complaints can vary dramatically across cultural boundaries. People in Western societies often experience anxiety in relation to their work performance, whereas in other societies people may be more concerned with family issues or religious experiences. In the Yoruba culture of Nigeria, for example, anxiety is frequently associated with fertility and the health of family members (Good & Kleinman, 1985).

Anxiety disorders have been observed in preliterate as well as Westernized cultures. Of course, the same descriptive and diagnostic terms are not used in every culture, but the basic psychological phenomena appear to be similar (Draguns & Tanaka-Matsumi, 2003). Cultural anthropologists have recognized many different culture-bound syndromes that, in some cases, bear striking resemblance to anxiety disorders listed in DSM-IV-TR. The following example of

"kayak angst" in an Inuit (Eskimo) hunter illustrates a similar point. The problem sounds a lot like panic disorder.

> Isak H., aged 34, [was a] hunter fisherman of mixed race from Nugatsiak. He had been quite well before. In 1939 he saw a kayak man drowned [sic] and was very much upset. In the summer of 1946, when he was paddling along in his kayak on a calm day with a soft backwash and bright sunshine he suddenly became terrified when looking down to the bottom of the sea. He seemed to feel the kayak filling with water, the point of the kayak being very distant and dim. His head felt queer and he took off his cap. His heart started beating rapidly and he trembled so violently that the kayak shook. Perspiration ran down his face, his heart seemed to turn over and his arms were heavy and numb. He made an effort to reach shore, he vomited, his bowels were loose and he had a strong desire to pass water. Next time he set out in his kayak the same symptoms occurred. He felt more and more terrified of crouching down in his kayak, and he finally gave up all attempts and stopped fishing by kayak. (Katschnig & Amering, 1990, pp. 77–78)

Very few epidemiological studies have attempted to collect cross-cultural data using standardized interviews and specific diagnostic criteria. One such study was conducted to evaluate specific drugs for the treatment of panic attacks (Cross-National Collaborative Panic Study, 1992). More than 1,000 patients were

TABLE 6–2 Gender Differences in the 12-Month Prevalence of Anxiety Disorders		
DISORDER	**WOMEN (%)**	**MEN (%)**
Any anxiety disorder	22.6	11.8
Panic disorder	3.2	1.3
Agoraphobia without panic disorder	3.8	1.7
Social phobia	9.1	6.6
Specific phobia	13.2	4.4
Generalized anxiety	4.3	2.0
Obsessive—compulsive disorder*	1.9	1.4

*Data on obsessive–compulsive disorder are from the Epidemiologic Catchment Area study (Karno & Golding, 1991) because the National Comorbidity Survey did not ask about obsessions and compulsions.

Source: R.C. Kessler, K.A. McGonagle, S. Zhao, C.B. Nelson, M. Hughes, S. Eshleman, H. Wittchen, & K.S. Kendler, 1994, Lifetime and 12-month prevalence of DSM-III-R psychiatric disorders in the United States: Results from the National Comorbidity Survey, *Archives of General Psychiatry,* 51, 8–19.

Isaac Marks a psychiatrist at the Institute of Psychiatry, University of London, is one of the world's leading authorities on the classification and treatment of anxiety disorders.

treated in 14 different countries in North America, Latin America, and Europe.

Several interesting findings emerged from this study. Panic disorder occurred in all the countries that were included in the study. Nevertheless, some important differences were found among panic patients from different regions. Choking or smothering and fear of dying were more common among patients from southern countries in both the Americas and in Europe. Phobic avoidance was much more common among panic patients seen at clinics in the United States and Canada—9 out of every 10 compared to patients seen at clinics in Latin American countries.

CAUSES

Now that we have discussed the various symptoms associated with anxiety disorders and their distribution within the population, we can consider the origins of these disorders. How do these problems develop? Going back to the cases that were presented at the beginning of the chapter, what might account for the onset of Johanna's panic attacks? Why would Ed find himself plagued by violent images and compelled to form letters in a meticulous fashion?

Is there a unique causal pathway for each type of anxiety disorder?

Adaptive and Maladaptive Fears

Current theories regarding the causes of anxiety disorders often focus on the evolutionary significance of anxiety and fear. These emotional response systems are clearly adaptive in many situations. They mobilize responses that help the person survive in the face of both immediate dangers and long-range threats. An evolutionary perspective helps to explain why human beings are vulnerable to anxiety disorders, which can be viewed as problems that arise in the regulation of these necessary response systems (Hoffmann, Moscovitch, & Heinrichs, 2004). The important question is not why we experience anxiety, but why it occasionally becomes maladaptive. When anxiety becomes excessive, or when intense fear is triggered at an inappropriate time or place, these response systems can become more harmful than helpful. In order to understand the development of anxiety

disorders, we must consider a variety of psychological and biological systems that have evolved for the purpose of triggering and controlling these alarm responses.

Should we expect to find unique causal pathways associated with each of the types of anxiety disorder listed in DSM-IV-TR? This seems unlikely, particularly in light of the extensive overlap among the various subtypes. Should we expect that all the different types of anxiety disorders are produced by the same causes? This also seems unlikely.

Isaac Marks and Randolph Nesse (1994) have proposed a broad evolutionary perspective for the causes of anxiety disorders that suggests a middle ground between these two extremes. They suggest that generalized forms of anxiety probably evolved to help the person prepare for threats that could not be identified clearly. More specific forms of anxiety and fear probably evolved to provide more effective responses to certain types of danger. For example, fear of heights is associated with a freezing of muscles rather than running away, which could lead to a fall. Social threats are more likely to provoke responses such as shyness and embarrassment that may increase acceptance by other people by making the individual seem less threatening. Each type of anxiety disorder can be viewed as the dysregulation of a mechanism that evolved to deal with a particular kind of danger. This model leads us to expect that the etiological pathways leading to various forms of anxiety disorders may be partially distinct but not completely independent.

Social Factors

Stressful life events, particularly those involving danger and interpersonal conflict, can trigger the onset of certain kinds of anxiety disorders. For example, various aspects of parent–child relationships may leave some people more vulnerable to the development of anxiety disorders when they become adults. Taken together, the evidence bearing on these issues helps explain the relationship between, and the overlap among, anxiety disorders and mood disorders.

Stressful Life Events Common sense might suggest that people who experience high stress levels are likely to develop negative emotional reactions, which can range from feeling "on edge" to the onset of full-blown panic attacks. In Chapter 5 we reviewed the literature concerning stressful life events and depression. As we have seen, the measurement of stressful events is a complex matter, and it is difficult to establish causal relations between stress and psychological disorders. Nevertheless, several investigations suggest that stressful life events can influence the onset of anxiety disorders as well as depression. Patients with anxiety disorders are more likely than other people to report having experienced a negative event in the months preceding the initial development of their symptoms (Kendler et al., 2003).

Why do some negative life events lead to depression while others lead to anxiety? The nature of the event may be an important factor in determining the type of mental disorder that appears (Updegraff & Taylor, 2000). People who develop an anxiety disorder are much more likely to have experienced an event involving danger (lack of security), whereas people who are depressed are more likely to have experienced a severe loss (lack of hope). Mixed cases frequently report both types of events (G. W. Brown, 1993; Rueter et al., 1999). In other words, different types of environmental stress may lead to different types of emotional symptoms. Those associated with insecurity, including severe disagreements with other people, and danger seem to be mostly closely associated with anxiety disorders. Interpersonal conflicts, such as serious arguments with a partner, parents, or close friends, seem to be especially common prior to the onset of agoraphobia (Franklin & Andrews, 1989).

Childhood Adversity   If recent dangers and conflicts can precipitate the full blown symptoms of an anxiety disorder, do past experiences—those that took place years ago—set the stage for this experience? Several research studies indicate that they can (Harkness & Wildes, 2002; Levitan et al., 2003). Studies of these phenomena focus on measures of childhood adversity. This concept includes women's recollections of parental indifference (being physically or emotionally neglected by their parents for an extended period of time) and physical abuse (being physically beaten or threatened with violence, usually in an attempt to control or punish the child).

One classic study included a community sample of approximately 400 working-class women (Brown & Harris, 1993). Twenty-five percent of these women met diagnostic criteria for at least one type of anxiety disorder. The relationship between childhood adversity and the presence of these anxiety disorders is illustrated in Figure 6–2. Women who were suffering from most types of anxiety disorder were more likely than women with no disorder to report having been exposed to parental indifference and physical abuse during childhood or adolescence. This pattern was particularly striking for the women with panic disorder. In contrast, women with specific phobias or only mild symptoms of agoraphobia could not be distinguished from the control group on the basis of childhood adversity. This result is consistent with the notion that somewhat different etiological pathways may be associated with specific phobias than with other, frequently more severe forms of anxiety disorder.

The evidence regarding childhood adversity and the later development of adult psychopathology points, once again, to similarities between depression and certain kinds of anxiety disorders. People who report parental neglect, abuse, and violence are more vulnerable to the development of both mood disorders and anxiety disorders (Kessler et al., 1997; Lara & Klein, 1999). Causal pathways are complex. There does not seem to be a direct connection between particular forms of adverse environmental events and specific types of mental disorder.

Attachment Relationships and Separation Anxiety   The evidence regarding childhood adversity is similar to another perspective on the origins of anxiety disorders that has been

Stressful life events that involve lack of personal security and serious danger—such as a flood—are often associated with the onset of anxiety disorders.

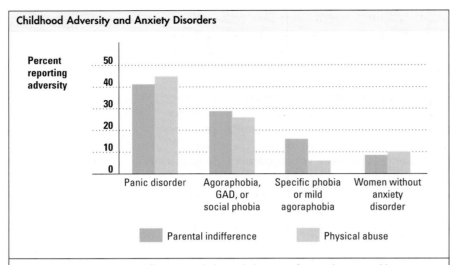

Childhood Adversity and Anxiety Disorders

FIGURE 6–2: Parental indifference and physical abuse are frequently reported by women who later develop panic disorder. They do not seem to be related to specific phobias.

Source: G.W. Brown and T.O. Harris, 1993, Aetiology of anxiety and depressive disorders in an inner-city population. 1. Early adversity, *Psychological Medicine, 23,* 141–154. Copyright © 1993 by Cambridge University Press. Reprinted by permission of the publisher.

concerned with the infant's attachment relationship with caretakers. Attachment theory (see Chapter 2) integrates the psychodynamic perspective with field observations of primate behavior and with laboratory research with human infants. According to the British psychiatrist John Bowlby (1973, 1980), anxiety is an innate response to separation, or the threat of separation, from the caretaker. Those infants who are insecurely attached to their parents are presumably more likely to develop anxiety disorders, especially agoraphobia, when they become adults.

Several studies have found that people with panic disorder and agoraphobia are more likely to report that they had problems associated with insecure attachment as children (Manicavasagar, Silove, & Hadzi-Pavlovic, 1998; Shear, 1996). Anxious attachment as infants may make these individuals more vulnerable, once they are adults, to the threats that are contained in interpersonal conflict, for example, loss of a loved one if a marriage dissolves. This hypothesis fits nicely with the observation that interpersonal conflict is a relatively frequent triggering event for the onset of agoraphobic symptoms. There is also an interesting connection between attachment styles and childhood adversity. People who report childhood adversities involving interpersonal trauma (assault, abuse, neglect) are more likely to be insecurely attached, and they are also more vulnerable to depression and anxiety (Mickelson, Kessler, & Shaver, 1997).

Attachment difficulties are not restricted to agoraphobia. Studies indicate that they also set the stage for other types of anxiety in adults, including generalized anxiety disorder (Cassidy & Mohr, 2001), and social phobia (Eng et al., 2001; Vertue, 2003). Of course, many anxiously attached children do not develop anxiety disorders when they grow up. The suggestion of a causal relationship between childhood attachments and adult anxiety disorders is intriguing, but the evidence supporting it will not be convincing until scientists conduct longitudinal studies to test this hypothesis. The same criticism obviously applies to research on childhood adversity. To test these hypotheses further, psychologists must conduct studies based on direct observations of parent–child relationships rather than on retrospective accounts of childhood behaviors, which are highly subjective and not always accurate or reliable.

Psychological Factors

Research suggests that stressful life events and childhood adversity contribute to the development of anxiety disorders. But what are the specific mechanisms that link these experiences to emotional difficulties, such as intense fears, panic attacks, and excessive worry? This question brings our discussion of causes to a different level of analysis. A number of psychological mechanisms undoubtedly play important roles in helping to shape the development and maintenance of anxiety disorders. They include learning processes and cognitive events.

Learning Processes and Phobias Since the 1920s, experimental psychologists working in laboratory settings have been interested in the possibility that specific fears might be learned through classical (or Pavlovian) conditioning (Ayres, 1998). The central mechanism in the classical conditioning process is the association between an unconditioned stimulus (US) and a conditioned stimulus (CS). The US is able to elicit a strong unconditioned emotional response (UR), such as fear. Examples of potential USs are painfully loud and unexpected noises, the sight of dangerous animals, and sudden, intense pain. According to psychologists' original views of the classical conditioning process, the CS could be any neutral stimulus that happened to be present when an intense fear reaction was provoked. Through the process of association, the CS would subsequently elicit a conditioned response (CR), which was similar in quality to the original UR (see Chapter 2). This explanation for the development of specific phobias fits easily with common sense as well as with clinical experience. Many intense, persistent, irrational fears seem to develop after the person has experienced a traumatic event (Merckelbach, Muris, & Schouten, 1996).

Preparedness Current views on the process by which fears are learned suggest that the process is guided by a *module*, or specialized circuit in the brain, that has been shaped by evolutionary pressures (Öhman & Mineka, 2001). Some psychologists have argued that the mind includes a very large number of prepared modules (specialized neural circuits) that serve particular adaptive functions, such as the recognition of faces and the perception of language (Pinker, 1997). These modules are designed to operate at maximal speed, are activated automatically, and perform without conscious awareness. They are also highly selective, in the sense that the module is particularly responsive to a narrow range of stimuli. Human beings seem to be prepared to develop intense, persistent fears only to a select set of objects or situations. Fear of these stimuli may have conferred a selective advantage upon those people—hundreds of thousands of years ago—who were able to develop fears and consequently avoid certain kinds of dangerous stimuli, such as heights, snakes, and storms. This is not to say that the fears are innate or present at birth, but rather that they can be learned and maintained very easily.

Many investigations have been conducted to test various facets of this **preparedness model** (Mineka & Öhman, 2002; Öhman & Mineka, 2001). The results of these studies support many features of the theory. For example, conditioned responses to fear-relevant stimuli (such as spiders and snakes) are more resistant to extinction than are those to fear-irrelevant stimuli (such as flowers). Furthermore, it is possible to develop conditioned fear responses after only one trial of learning.

The process of prepared conditioning may play an important role in the development of both social phobias and specific phobias. In specific phobias, the prepared stimuli are things like snakes, heights, storms, and small enclosed places. The prepared stimulus in social phobias might involve other people's faces. We are prepared to fear faces that appear angry, critical, or rejecting if they are directed toward us (Öhman, 1996). This process is presumably an evolutionary remnant of factors involved in establishing dominance hierarchies, which maintain social order among primates. Animals that are defeated in a dominance conflict are often allowed to remain as part of the group if they behave submissively. The responses of people with social phobias may be somewhat analogous, in the sense that they are afraid of directly facing, or being evaluated by, other people. When a performer makes eye contact with his or her audience, an association may develop very quickly between fear and angry or critical facial expressions.

Observational Learning We all learn many behaviors through imitation. Albert Bandura's early work on modeling, for example, demonstrated that children who observe a model hitting a doll are more likely to behave aggressively themselves when given the opportunity (see Chapter 2). Similar processes may also affect the development of intense fear, because some phobias develop in the absence of any direct experience with the feared object. People apparently learn to avoid certain stimuli if they observe other people showing a strong fear response to those stimuli (Poulton & Menzies, 2002). In other words, the traumatic event does not have to happen to you; it may be enough for you to witness a traumatic event happening to someone else or to watch someone else behave fearfully.

One series of intriguing experiments has combined observational learning with the preparedness formulation (e.g., Mineka & Cook, 1993). These studies focused on an animal model (see Research Methods in Chapter 5) of phobias: fear reactions among rhesus monkeys. Rhesus monkeys raised in their natural environment are markedly afraid of certain kinds of stimuli, such as snakes. Most monkeys reared in the laboratory do not initially react fearfully when they are presented with a toy snake. They quickly acquire this fear, however, after watching a monkey reared in the wild exhibit intense fear in the presence of snakes. The greater the fear exhibited by the wild monkey, the more intense the fears developed by the observer monkey. Further, live observation is not necessary. Monkeys can learn to fear snakes

How do "prepared modules" seem to guide the process of learning?"

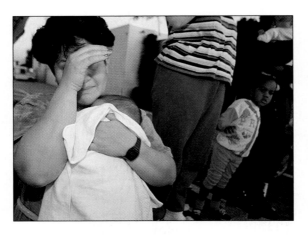

Vicarious learning can influence the development of strong fear responses. Children who observe adults demonstrating strong emotional responses may be more likely to develop phobias.

by watching videotapes of other monkeys exhibiting fear reactions.

Fear of snakes is clearly adaptive, because snakes represent a threat to rhesus monkeys in their natural environment. This could be seen as a prepared association. Will monkeys also learn to avoid nonthreatening and presumably unprepared stimuli if they observe a model reacting with intense fear? Is the association between fear and particular stimuli random, or is it selective? The data from these studies indicate that the relationship is, in fact, selective: Monkeys are prepared to learn to avoid fear-relevant stimuli (such as snakes and crocodiles) but are not prepared to learn to avoid fear-irrelevant stimuli (such as rabbits or kittens) (Cook & Mineka, 1991).

Learning experiences are clearly important in the origins of phobias, but their impact often depends on the existence of prepared associations between stimuli. Furthermore, vicarious learning is often as important as direct experience. The importance of the latter factor can be illustrated by considering the development of children's fears during the bombing of London in World War II. When civilian areas were subjected to prolonged and terrifying attacks, families sought safety in underground shelters. If intense fear could be conditioned to any originally neutral stimulus, most of the people subjected to this traumatic experience would develop specific phobic responses in association with whatever stimuli happened to be present during the worst moments of a raid (fear of tunnels, fear of the dark). In fact, it didn't work that way. Although people showed short-term emotional reactions, very few developed persistent, irrational phobic responses as a result of these terrifying experiences. Anecdotal evidence suggested that children were more likely to become

fearful if they had observed their parents exhibiting strong emotional responses during the raids (Rachman, 1990).

Cognitive Factors Up to this point, we have talked about the importance of life events and specific learning experiences—variables that can be measured outside the organism. But cognitive events also play an important role as mediators between experience and response. Perceptions, memory, and attention all influence the ways that we react to events in our environments. It is now widely accepted that these cognitive factors play a crucial role in the development and maintenance of various types of anxiety disorders. We will focus on four aspects of this literature: perception of controllability and predictability, catastrophic misinterpretation (panic attacks), attentional biases and shifts in the focus of attention, and thought suppression.

Perception of Control There is an important relationship between anxiety and the perception of control. People who believe that they are able to control events in their environment are less likely to show symptoms of anxiety than are people who believe that they are helpless. This is, of course, part of the reason that the events of September 11, 2001, were so terrifying. The attack on the World Trade Center in New York City was beyond the control of its victims, who were going about their everyday activities.

An extensive body of evidence supports the conclusion that people who believe that they are less able to control events in their environment are more likely to develop global forms of anxiety (Andrews, 1996), as well as various specific types of anxiety disorder (Mineka & Zinbarg, 1998). Laboratory research indicates that feelings of lack of control contribute to the onset of panic attacks among patients with panic disorder. The perception of uncontrollability has also been linked to the submissive behavior frequently seen among people with social phobias as well as the chronic worries of people with generalized anxiety disorder.

Catastrophic Misinterpretation A somewhat different type of cognitive dysfunction has been described by David Clark, a psychologist at Oxford University in England. According to this view, panic disorder may be caused by the *catastrophic misinterpretation* of bodily sensations or perceived threat (Clark, 1986b, 1999). Although panic attacks can be precipitated by external stimuli, they are usually triggered by internal stimuli, such as bodily sensations, thoughts, or images. On the basis of past experience, these stimuli initiate an anxious mood, which leads to a variety of physiological sensations that typically accompany negative emotional reactions (changes in heart rate, respiration rate, dizziness, and so on). Anxious mood is accompanied by a narrowing of the person's attentional focus and an increased awareness of bodily sensations.

The crucial stage comes next, when the person misinterprets the bodily sensation as a catastrophic event. For example, a person who believes that there is something wrong with his heart might misinterpret a slight acceleration in heart rate as being a sign that he is about to have a heart attack. He might say to himself, "My heart will stop and I'll die!" This reaction ensures the continued operation of this feedback loop, with the misinterpretation enhancing the person's sense of threat, and so on, until the process spirals out of control. Thus both cognitive misinterpretation and biological reactions associated with the perception of threat are necessary for a panic attack to occur.

The person's automatic, negative thoughts may also lead him to engage in behaviors that are expected to increase his safety, when in fact they are counterproductive. For example, some people believe that they should take deep breaths or monitor their heart rate if they become aroused. This is actually incorrect information, and the alleged safety behaviors can further exaggerate the person's fear response.

Many research studies have found that the subjective experience of body sensations is, in fact, closely associated with maladaptive or catastrophic thoughts among patients with panic disorder (McNally, 1994). Unfortunately, this connection does not provide strong evidence for a *causal* link between catastrophic thoughts and the onset of panic attacks for a variety of reasons (Roth, Wilhelm, & Pettit, 2005). One problem is the fact that catastrophic thoughts (such as fear of losing control and fear of dying) are, in fact, part of the definition of a panic attack (see Table 6–1). The theory is difficult to test (cannot be disproven) if there is no way to separate the measurement of catastrophic thoughts and the panic attack itself.

It is also clear that catastrophic misinterpretations cannot account for all instances of panic attacks. For example, patients with panic disorder sometimes experience panic attacks in their sleep (Craske & Rowe, 1997; Klein & Klein, 1989). How could that happen if the escalation to panic requires catastrophic misinterpretation of physical sensations, which presumably involves conscious cognitive processes? Clearly, other factors are also involved. One alternative explanation involves classical conditioning. The experience of an initial panic attack might lead to conditioned anxiety to cues associated with the first attack. These could be either internal bodily sensations or external stimuli. The conditioned anxiety might lower the person's threshold for subsequent panic attacks (Bouton, Mineka, & Barlow, 2001).

Attention to Threat and Biased Information Processing
Earlier in this chapter we discussed how worry involves negative thoughts and images that anticipate some possible future danger. In recent years, several lines of research have converged to clarify the basic cognitive mechanisms involved in worry. Experts now believe that attention plays a crucial role in the onset of this process. People who are prone to excessive worrying are unusually sensitive to cues that signal the existence of future threats (MacLeod et al., 2002; Mathews & Mackintosh, 2000; Williams, Mathews, & MacLeod, 1996). They attend vigilantly to even fleeting signs of danger, especially when they are under stress. At such times, the recognition of danger cues triggers a maladaptive, self-perpetuating cycle of cognitive processes that can quickly spin out of control.

The threatening information that is generated in this process is presumably encoded in

At first glance, this photo seems terrifying because the image looks like a shark. In fact, it's a dolphin, and once we know that, it seems less frightening. This is an example of the role played by cognitive factors in generating fear.

Thomas Borkovec, a clinical psychologist at Pennsylvania State University, has conducted extensive research on characteristics of uncontrollable worry and the treatment of anxiety disorders.

memory in the form of elaborate schemas, which are easily reactivated. In comparison with the depressed person, who is convinced that failure will definitely occur, the anxious person is afraid of failure that may occur as a future event, the outcome of which remains uncertain (Beck & Emery, 1985). The threat schemas of anxious people contain a high proportion of "what-if" questions, such as "What am I going to do if I don't do well in school this semester?" (Vasey & Borkovec, 1992).

Once attention has been drawn to threatening cues, the performance of adaptive, problem-solving behaviors is disrupted, and the worrying cycle launches into a repetitive sequence in which the person rehearses anticipated events and searches for ways to avoid them. The readily accessed network of threat-related schemas then activates an additional series of "what-if" questions that quickly leads to a dramatic increase in negative affect.

If worriers are preoccupied with the perception of threat cues and the rehearsal of dangerous scenarios but are unable to reach satisfactory solutions to their problems, why do they continue to engage in this vicious, maladaptive cycle? Thomas Borkovec, a clinical psychologist at Pennsylvania State University, and his students have studied the uncontrollable nature of the worry process. Two of Borkovec's conclusions are particularly important in explaining the self-perpetuating nature of worry: (1) Worry is an experience that is made up of "self-talk"—things that people say to themselves rather than visual images ("I'll never get all this work done!"). (2) Worry serves the function of avoiding unpleasant somatic activation through the suppression of imagery (Borkovec, Alcaine, & Behar, 2004). In other words, some people apparently continue to worry, even though it is not productive, because worrying is reinforced by an immediate (though temporary) reduction in uncomfortable physiological sensations.

Attentional mechanisms also seem to be involved in the etiology and maintenance of social phobias. People who are capable of performing a particular task when they are alone (in practice) cannot perform it in front of an audience. Barlow (2001) has argued that this deterioration in skill is caused by anxious apprehension, which is similar to Borkovec's description of the process of worrying. The cycle is illustrated in Figure 6–3. An increase in negative affect presumably triggers a shift toward self-focused attention ("Oh, no, I'm getting really upset") and activates cognitive biases and threat schemas ("What if I make a mistake?"). The person becomes distracted by these thoughts, and performance deteriorates. In a sense, the person's fearful expectations become a self-fulfilling prophesy.

Thought Suppression: Obsessive–Compulsive Disorder   The cognitive model of worry or anxious apprehension places primary emphasis on the role of attentional processes. Worrying is unproductive and self-defeating in large part because it is associated with a focus on self-evaluation (fear of failure) and negative emotional responses rather than on external aspects of the problem and active coping behaviors. We may be consciously aware of these processes and simultaneously be unable to inhibit them. The struggle to control our thoughts often leads to a process known as *thought suppression,* an active attempt to stop thinking about something.

It seems simple to say, "Stop worrying," but it is virtually impossible for some people to do so. In fact, recent evidence suggests that trying to rid one's mind of a distressing or unwanted

---

Anxious Apprehension and Social Phobia

ANXIETY-PROVOKING SITUATION

↓

NEGATIVE AFFECT
including sense of uncontrollability

DYSFUNCTIONAL PERFORMANCE

ATTENTIONAL SHIFT
to self-evaluative focus → FURTHER INCREASE IN AROUSAL

↓

COGNITIVE BIASES AND HYPERVIGILANCE
enhanced attention to threat cues

↓

ATTEMPTS TO COPE BY:

↓

AVOIDANCE
of situation

FIGURE 6–3: Processes involved in the generation of social anxiety.

Source: Adapted from D.H. Barlow, 2001, *Anxiety and its disorders,* 2nd ed. New York: Guilford, p. 65.

thought can have the unintended effect of making the thought more intrusive (Wegner, 1994). Thought suppression might actually increase, rather then decrease, the strong emotions associated with those thoughts. The bond between a thought and its associated emotion allows activation of one to result in the reinstatement of the other, a kind of dual pathway.

Obsessive–compulsive disorder may be related, in part, to the maladaptive consequences of attempts to suppress unwanted or threatening thoughts that the person has learned to see as being dangerous or forbidden (Abramowitz, Tolin, & Street, 2001; Purdon, 2004). Remember that obsessive thoughts are a common experience in the general population. They resemble "abnormal" obsessions in form and content. However, the obsessions of those in treatment for OCD are more intense and, perhaps most importantly, are more often strongly resisted and more difficult to dismiss. This resistance may be a key component in the association between emotional sensitivity and the development of troublesome obsessive thoughts. People who are vulnerable to the development of OCD apparently react strongly to events that trigger an emotional response (Oltmanns & Gibbs, 1995). These individuals become aware of their exaggerated reactivity and find it unpleasant. In an effort to control their reaction, they attempt to resist or suppress the emotion.

As a result of an individual's attempt to suppress strong emotion, a rebound effect may occur, culminating in a vicious cycle. Thoughts that are present during the instigation of such a cycle become robustly associated with the emotion and may become the content of an obsessive thought. This model may help to explain the episodic nature of obsessive–compulsive symptoms; relapse may be triggered by intense emotional episodes.

Biological Factors

Several pieces of evidence indicate that biological events play an important role in the development and maintenance of anxiety disorders. In the following pages we review the role of genetic factors and the use of chemicals to induce symptoms of panic. These factors undoubtedly interact with the social and psychological variables that we have considered in the preceding sections.

Genetic Factors   Some of the most useful information about the validity of anxiety disorders comes from studies aimed at identifying the influence of genetic factors. These data address the overlap, as well as the distinctions, among various types of anxiety disorder. They also shed additional light on the relationship between anxiety and depression.

Family Studies   Family studies of panic disorder raise interesting questions about subdivisions under the general heading of anxiety disorders (van den Heuvel et al., 2000). They indicate that the relatives of people with panic disorder show an elevated risk of panic disorder themselves but not an elevated risk of generalized anxiety disorder (see Figure 6–4). The same pattern holds for the relatives of people with generalized anxiety disorder: The relatives exhibit a high rate of GAD but not a high rate of panic disorder (Noyes et al., 1987; Skre et al., 1994). This evidence is consistent with the proposition that panic disorder and GAD are, indeed, etiologically separate disorders.

A family study of social phobia has demonstrated that the *generalized* form of this disorder (where the person is fearful in most types of social situations) is also familial in nature and etiologically distinct from other types of anxiety disorder. The investigators studied first-degree relatives of people who met the criteria for social phobia and had never had any other type of anxiety disorder (Fyer et al., 1993; Mannuzza et al., 1995). The probands (or "index cases") in

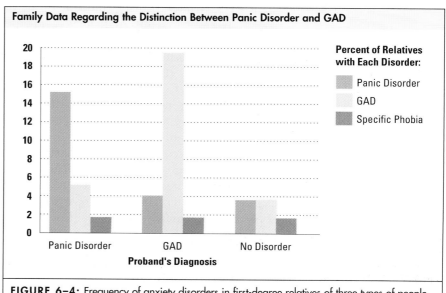

FIGURE 6–4: Frequency of anxiety disorders in first-degree relatives of three types of people.

TABLE 6-3	Twin Concordance Rates for Specific Anxiety Disorders		
DISORDER		**MZ**	**DZ**
Panic disorder		.24	.11
Agoraphobia		.23	.15
Social phobia		.24	.15
Animal phobia		.26	.11
Generalized anxiety disorder		.28	.17

Source: Data from the Virginia Twin Registry (Kendler et al., 1992a, 1992b).

the control group were people who had never had a mental disorder. The results indicated that the rate of social phobia was particularly high (16 percent) in the relatives of probands whose social phobia was generalized. In contrast, only 5 percent of the relatives in the control group met the diagnostic criteria for social phobia. Moreover, only 6 percent of the relatives of probands with nongeneralized social phobia (in which the person's fear is limited to one particular type of social situation, such as public speaking) had social phobia themselves. This pattern of results suggests that the nongeneralized form of social phobia is not influenced by genetic factors.

Data regarding obsessive–compulsive disorder suggest that a more general vulnerability to anxiety disorders is genetically transmitted through the family (Wolff et al., 2000). The predisposition can apparently be expressed in different ways, with OCD being only one of them. One study compared the frequency of mental disorders among relatives of patients with OCD to prevalence rates in relatives of people without a mental disorder (Black et al., 1992). The lifetime prevalence of OCD was roughly 2 percent in both groups, no higher than would be expected in the general population. There were significant differences between groups, however, with regard to other types of anxiety disorder. Thirty percent of the patients' relatives met the diagnostic criteria for at least one anxiety disorder, most often GAD. In comparison, only 17 percent of the relatives of the control subjects qualified for a diagnosis of some type of anxiety disorder. The relatives of the OCD probands apparently did not inherit a specific predisposition to this disorder, but they did inherit a more global tendency toward anxiety disorders. The

expression of that tendency is presumably influenced by subsequent experience.

The results of the family studies all point toward the potential influence of genetic factors in anxiety disorders. Most of the evidence also supports the validity of the DSM-IV-TR subtypes. Comparisons of panic and GAD support the movement toward separating these disorders in the diagnostic manual. The generalized form of social phobia also seems to be at least somewhat distinct from the other anxiety disorders. On the other hand, data regarding relatives of OCD probands are more consistent with the traditional preference in psychiatric classification for lumping anxiety disorders together.

Twin Studies Family studies do not prove the involvement of genes, because family members also share environmental factors (diet, culture, and so on). Twin studies provide a more stringent test of the genetic hypothesis (see Chapter 2). Kenneth Kendler, a psychiatrist at the Medical College of Virginia, and his colleagues have studied anxiety disorders in very large samples of male–male and female–female twin pairs (Kendler et al., 2001; Kendler, Neale, et al., 1992). The people who participated in this study were not psychiatric patients; they were living in the community and were identified through a statewide registry of twins. Diagnoses were assigned following structured diagnostic interviews conducted by the research team.

Table 6–3 summarizes the results of Kendler's study with regard to several types of anxiety disorder. For each type, concordance rates were significantly higher for MZ twins than for DZ twins. Nevertheless, the MZ concordance rates were also relatively low (in comparison to MZ concordance rates for bipolar mood disorders, for example). Anxiety disorders appear to be modestly heritable, with genetic factors accounting for between 20 and 30 percent of the variance in the transmission of GAD. (See Research Methods in Chapter 16 for a discussion of heritability.)

Kendler and his colleagues have examined the influence of both genetic and environmental factors on the etiology of several kinds of anxiety disorder, including panic disorder, GAD, and phobias in these samples of twins (Hettema, Neale, & Kendler, 2001; Hettema et al., 2005). Their analyses have led them to several important conclusions:

1. Genetic risk factors for these disorders are neither highly specific (a different set of

genes being associated with each disorder) nor highly nonspecific (one common set of genes causing vulnerability for all disorders).

2. Two genetic factors have been identified: one associated with GAD, panic disorder, and agoraphobia, and the other with specific phobias.

3. Environmental risk factors that would be *unique* to individuals also play an important role in the etiology of all anxiety disorders. Environmental factors that would be *shared* by all members of a family do not seem to play an important role for many people.

Neuroanatomy Laboratory studies of fear conditioning in animals have identified specific pathways in the brain that are responsible for detecting and organizing a response to danger (LeDoux, 2000; Öhman & Mineka, 2003). The amygdala plays a central role in these circuits, which represent the biological underpinnings of the evolved fear module that we discussed earlier in connection with classical conditioning and phobias (see page 193). Scientists have discovered these pathways by monitoring and manipulating brain activities in animals that are participating in studies using classical conditioning to pair an originally neutral stimulus (the CS) with an aversive stimulus (the US). The results of these studies tell us *where* emotional responses, such as fear and panic, are located in terms of brain regions. They also begin to explain *how* they are produced. That knowledge, coupled with data regarding social and psychological factors, will help us understand *why* people experience problems such as irrational fears and panic attacks.

The brain circuits involved in fear conditioning are illustrated in Figure 6–5. This drawing

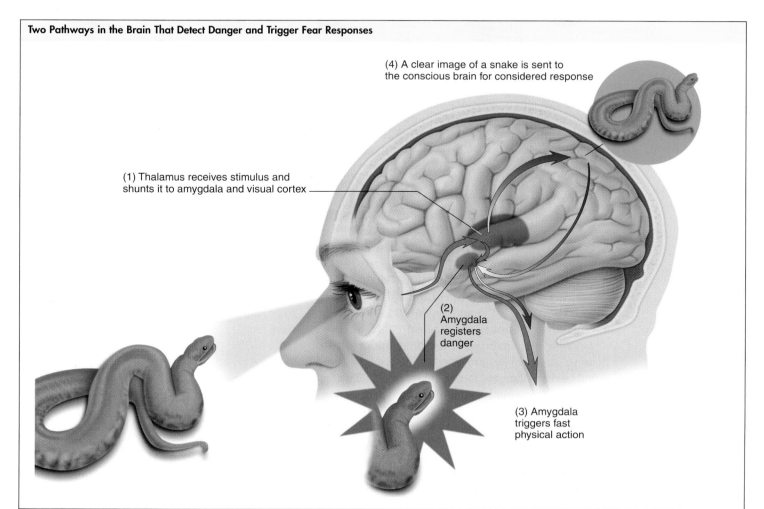

Two Pathways in the Brain That Detect Danger and Trigger Fear Responses

(4) A clear image of a snake is sent to the conscious brain for considered response

(1) Thalamus receives stimulus and shunts it to amygdala and visual cortex

(2) Amygdala registers danger

(3) Amygdala triggers fast physical action

FIGURE 6–5: (1) Evolved fear module, and (2) slower, indirect route through cortical processing areas.

Source: R. Carter, 1998, *Mapping the mind.* Berkeley; University of California Press, p. 96, illustrations by Malcolm Godwin. Copyright © 1998 by Moonrunner Design Ltd. Reprinted by permission of Malcolm Godwin, Moonrunner Design, Ltd.

uses the example of a person who has seen a dangerous snake (Carter, 1998). Sensory information is projected to the thalamus, and from there it is directed to other brain areas for processing. Emotional stimuli follow two primary pathways, both of which lead to the amygdala. The first pathway (the red arrow) might be called a "short cut," and represents the evolved fear module for conditioned fear. The message follows a direct connection between the thalamus and the amygdala, which is connected to the hypothalamus. Behavioral responses (such as the "fight or flight" response) are then activated and coordinated through projections from the hypothalamus to endocrine glands and the autonomic nervous system (see Chapter 2, as well as the discussion of the HPA axis in Chapter 5). Notice that this first pathway does not involve connections to cortical areas of the brain that might involve higher-level cognitive functions such as conscious memory or decision making. The amygdala does store unconscious, emotional memories—the kind that are generated through prepared learning.

A second, complementary path from the thalamus (the purple arrow) leads to the cortex and provides for a detailed, and comparatively slower, analysis of the information that has been detected. Using the example in Figure 6–5, information about the snake would be sent to the visual cortex. Once the pattern is recognized as a snake, the data would be integrated with additional information from memory about its emotional significance ("potentially dangerous"). This message would then be sent to the amygdala, which could, in turn, trigger an organized response to threat. This second pathway is longer and more complex than the first, and it will take longer to generate a response. The first pathway has presumably evolved because it is adaptive; it provides the organism with an alarm system that can be used to avoid immediate dangers in the environment. The fact that information can follow either path is consistent with the idea that some fear responses are "hard-wired" (easily learned, difficult to extinguish, and mediated by unconscious processes) while others are dependent on higher-level analyses that involved thinking and reasoning.

A word of caution must be added when we consider the functions of these specific neural pathways. The fact that they are involved in processing fearful reactions does not mean that the amygdala and associated structures are exclusively dedicated to this particular purpose. Studies with animals have shown that artificial stimulation of the amygdala can produce different effects, depending in large part on the environmental context in which the animal is stimulated (Kagan, 1998). Anger, disgust, and sexual arousal are all emotional states that are associated with activity in pathways connecting the thalamus, the amygdala, and their projections to other brain areas. Fear responses are, therefore, only one of the many kinds of behavior associated with these circuits.

The brain regions that have been identified in studies of fear conditioning seem to play an important role in both phobic disorders (Öhman & Mineka, 2001) and panic disorder (Ninan & Dunlop, 2005). In the case of panic disorder, the fear module may be triggered at an inappropriate time. The sensitivity of this pathway is not the same in all people, and it is presumably influenced by genetic factors as well as hormone levels. Social and psychological factors that affect the threshold of the fear module include stressful life events and the development of separation anxiety during childhood (which increases the rate of panic disorder when these children become adults). The subcortical pathway between the thalamus and the amygdala may be responsible for the misinterpretation of sensory information, which then triggers the hypothalamus and activates a variety of autonomic processes (dramatic increases in respiration rate, heart rate, and so on). Some investigators have also speculated that this brain circuit may be associated with the biased attention to threat cues that has been demonstrated in patients with generalized anxiety disorder (McNally, 1998; Stein et al., 2002).

Several other areas of the brain are also associated with anxiety and the symptoms of anxiety disorders. For example, the locus ceruleus, a small area located in the brain stem, has also been the focus of considerable emphasis in research on panic disorder. This area contains a large percentage of the brain's norepinephrine. Neural projections from the locus ceruleus extend to the cerebral cortex as well as various structures in the temporal lobes. Research with monkeys has demonstrated that the firing rate of neurons in the locus ceruleus increases dramatically when a

critical thinking matters

CAN A STREP INFECTION TRIGGER OCD IN CHILDREN?

New hypotheses about the causes of mental disorders are usually based on clinical observations. These ideas are then evaluated in research studies designed to test their validity. Sometimes the data support the new idea, and sometimes they don't. During this period of evaluation, clinicians and scientists find themselves in a period of uncertainty, with some people embracing what they consider to be an important advance in knowledge while others provide skeptical criticism. Both groups need to think critically about relevant evidence.

This state of affairs is currently illustrated by a controversial proposal regarding the development of OCD in children. Clinical scientists at the National Institute of Mental Health, headed by psychiatrist Susan Swedo, suggested that, in some cases, symptoms of OCD develop suddenly following a strep infection. According to their hypothesis, antibodies that are triggered by the infection attack nerve cells in the basal ganglia of the brain (see Figure 4–2 on page 124). Swedo and her colleagues created a new term to use in diagnosing children with OCD who have a sudden onset and also test positive for a strep infection. They call the disorder *Pediatric Autoimmune Neuropsychiatric Disorders Associated with Streptococcal Infection,* or PANDAS (Swedo & Grant, 2005). They

recommend that a throat culture be given to any child who shows a sudden onset of symptoms of OCD. Children who test positive for strep are put on long-term antibiotics which are claimed, in some cases, to produce "miraculous results" (Anderson, 1996).

Does the recognition of PANDAS represent a breakthrough discovery? Is it a valid diagnostic concept? Or is it a misguided hypothesis with potentially dangerous treatment implications? Reasonable people have taken both sides. The empirical evidence is certainly incomplete (Singer & Loiselle, 2003), and some would say it is weak (Kurlan, 2004). Swedo and her colleagues have indeed described several cases that fit their profile. One of their papers described 109 cases in which the parents described a rapid onset of OCD symptoms (Swedo et al., 1998). Among these, 50 tested positive for strep. That leaves 59 rapid-onset cases that must have been triggered by some other, unknown factor. But even in the cases that did test positive, the existence of a strep infection does not prove that it was *causally* related to the OCD.

"If 100 kids fall out of a tree and break their arms and we test them for strep, there's going to be a very high percentage of

children who have evidence of recent infection. That doesn't mean strep is the reason they fell out of a tree." (Shulman, quoted in Belkin, 2005).

Skeptics argue that, until more conclusive evidence is available to support the theory, we should assume that children who experience obsessions and compulsions are suffering from OCD, nothing more or less (Kurlan & Kaplan, 2004). Undue emphasis on the use of antibiotic treatment may lead parents to ignore more conventional treatments for the disorder, especially exposure and response prevention, which must still be considered the first line of defense for children and adults who experience this debilitating disorder. Clinicians should also consider potential problems associated with the use of antibiotics as a form of treatment for children with OCD. Risks include the possibility of developing drug allergies and the promotion of antibiotic resistance.

While PANDAS is an intriguing hypothesis, remember that the burden of proof lies with those who propose new diagnostic categories or causal theories. Until it has been supported by *strong* empirical evidence, which is not yet the case with regard to PANDAS, the community of scientists assumes that the new hypothesis is false.

---

monkey is frightened. Furthermore, electrical stimulation of the locus ceruleus triggers a strong fear response that resembles a panic attack (Goddard & Charney, 1997).

Finally, we should also mention the neurological foundations of OCD. The results of studies using brain imaging procedures with OCD patients do not overlap a great deal with findings for other types of anxiety disorder (Stein, 2000). As we discussed in Chapter 4, obsessions and compulsions are associated with multiple brain regions, including the basal ganglia (a system that includes the caudate nucleus and the putamen), the orbital prefrontal cortex, and the anterior cingulate cortex (see Figure 4–2 on page 124). These circuits are overly active in people with OCD, especially when the person is

confronted with stimuli that provoke his or her obsessions (Adler et al., 2000; Szechtman & Woody, 2004).

Neurochemistry *Pharmacological challenge procedures* have played an important role in exploring the neurochemistry of panic disorder. The logic behind this method is simple: If a particular brain mechanism is "challenged," or stressed, by the artificial administration of chemicals, and if that procedure leads to the onset of a panic attack, then the neurochemical process that mediates that effect may also be responsible for panic attacks that take place outside the laboratory. Pharmacological challenge procedures were inspired by a few clinical studies, reported in the 1940s and 1950s, which noted that patients with

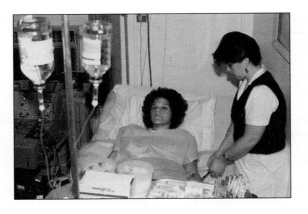

Clinical scientists have studied factors that influence the onset of panic attacks by using lactate infusion, which can elicit a full-blown panic attack among people who have panic disorder.

"anxiety neurosis" sometimes experienced an increase in subjective anxiety following vigorous physical exercise. This change in subjective symptoms appeared to be associated with an extremely rapid and excessive increase in lactic acid in the blood.[1]

To examine this phenomenon more closely, two psychiatrists decided to infuse lactate directly into anxiety disorder patients and a control group of people who did not have a psychological disorder (Pitts & McClure, 1967). Shortly after the lactate infusion began, 13 out of 14 of the anxiety patients experienced an anxiety attack, which they described as being similar to their typical symptoms. In contrast, only 2 of the 10 normal subjects reported an anxiety attack during lactate infusion.

Since this experiment was reported, a large number of studies have demonstrated that lactate infusions can provoke panic attacks in anywhere from 50 to 90 percent of patients with anxiety or panic disorders, as compared to only 0 to 25 percent of normal control subjects (Barlow, 2001). Unfortunately, the biological process through which this effect is produced is still unknown. Part of the problem is the lack of specificity of the provocative agents. Many other procedures have been found to induce panic in the laboratory. These include the infusion of different chemicals, such as caffeine, as well as the inhalation of air enriched with carbon dioxide. Various pharmacological challenge studies have suggested the influence of serotonin, norepinephrine, GABA, and dopamine in the production of panic attacks (Bourin et al., 1998). The general finding appears to be that several neurotransmitter systems are involved in the etiology of panic disorder. This conclusion also applies to other forms of anxiety disorder, such as GAD and social phobia (Ninan, 1999; Nutt, 2001; Pollack, 2001).

Panic induction procedures should also allow investigators to monitor brain activities that occur during a panic attack. Unfortunately, this is a difficult task for a number of reasons. The brain areas that appear to be most important in panic disorder, such as the amygdala and the locus ceruleus, are quite small and difficult to distinguish from adjacent structures. Distinguishing them requires imaging equipment that can produce very detailed pictures. Another problem involves the way in which patients may react to the brain imaging procedures, which can be anxiety-provoking because the person must be placed in a small constricted space and his or her movement restrained. People with panic disorder are more likely than others to hyperventilate in these circumstances, and hyperventilation can affect the resulting image. In spite of these problems, it seems likely that techniques such as PET and fMRI will be able to identify regions of the brain that are associated with the experience of panic attacks as well as other forms of anxiety. Studies using fMRI procedures do suggest that changes in the activity level of several brain areas, including the amygdala, anterior cingulate, and the orbitofrontal cortex, are found in people with panic disorder and other forms of anxiety (Bystritsky et al., 2001; Thomas et al., 2001).

TREATMENT

Anxiety disorders are one of the areas of psychopathology in which clinical psychologists and psychiatrists are best prepared to improve the level of their clients' functioning (see Getting Help). We begin by describing procedures that were used in an effort to help Ed, the person with obsessive–compulsive disorder whose problems were described at the beginning of this chapter.

---

[1]Lactic acid is formed during anaerobic respiration, the cellular respiration that occurs in the absence of oxygen. The respiratory and circulatory systems are usually able to support aerobic respiration when a person is resting. These systems become overloaded when skeletal muscles are used strenuously. Muscle fibers then need to depend on anaerobic respiration to generate energy (Hole, 1984). This process converts glucose to pyruvic acid. As the oxygen supply becomes depleted, pyruvic acid is converted to lactic acid, which accumulates in the bloodstream and is later converted back to glucose by the liver.

BRIEF CASE STUDY

Ed's Treatment

Ed's psychiatrist gave him a prescription for clomipramine (Anafranil), an antidepressant drug that is also used to treat people with severe obsessions. Weekly psychotherapy sessions continued as the dose was gradually increased. The medication had a beneficial impact after 4 weeks. Ed said that he had begun to feel as though he was trapped at the bottom of a well. After the medication, he no longer felt buried. His situation still wasn't great, but it no longer seemed hopeless or unbearable. He was also less intensely preoccupied by his obsessive violent images. They were still there, but they weren't as pressing. The drug had several annoying, though tolerable, side effects. His mouth felt dry, and he was occasionally a bit dizzy. He also noticed that he became tired more easily. Although Ed was no longer feeling seriously depressed, and the intensity of his obsessions was diminished, they had not disappeared, and he was now avoiding writing altogether.

Because the obsessions were still a problem, Ed's psychiatrist referred him to a psychologist who specialized in behavior therapy for anxiety disorders. He continued seeing the psychiatrist every other week for checks on his medication, which he continued to take. The new therapist told Ed that his fears of particular letters and numbers would be maintained as long as he avoided writing. Ed agreed to begin writing short essays every day, for a period of at least 30 minutes. The content could vary from day to day—anything that Ed felt like writing about—but he was encouraged to include the names of his wife and brother as often as possible. Furthermore, he was instructed to avoid his compulsive writing style, intentionally allowing the parts of letters to be separated or loops to be closed. At the beginning and end of each essay, Ed was required to record his anxiety level so that the therapist could monitor changes in his subjective discomfort. Over a period of 8 to 10 weeks, Ed's handwriting began to change. It was less of a struggle to get himself to write, and his handwriting became more legible.

The final aspect of behavioral treatment was concerned with his fear of axes. Ed and his therapist drew up a list of objects and situations related to axes, arranging them from those that were the least anxiety-provoking through those that were most frightening. They began with the least frightening. In their first exposure session, Ed agreed to meet with the psychologist while a relatively dull, wood-splitting maul was located in the adjoining room. Ed was initially quite anxious and distracted, but his anxiety diminished considerably before the end of their 2-hour meeting. Once that had been accomplished, the therapist helped him to confront progressively more difficult situations. These sessions were challenging and uncomfortable for Ed, but they allowed him to master his fears in an orderly fashion. By the end of the twelfth session of exposure, he was able to hold a sharp ax without fear.

Psychological Interventions

Psychoanalytic psychotherapy has been used to treat patients with anxiety disorders since Freud published his seminal papers at the turn of the twentieth century. The emphasis in this type of treatment is on fostering insight regarding the unconscious motives that presumably lie at the heart of the patient's symptoms, such as Ed's feelings about his brother. Although many therapists continue to employ this general strategy, it has not been shown to be effective in controlled outcome studies.

Systematic Desensitization and Interoceptive Exposure   Like psychoanalysis, behavior therapy was initially developed for the purpose of treating anxiety disorders, especially specific phobias. The first widely adopted procedure was known as systematic desensitization (see Chapter 3). In desensitization, the client is first taught progressive muscle relaxation. Then the therapist constructs a hierarchy of feared stimuli, beginning with those items that provoke only small amounts of fear and progressing through items that are most frightening. Then, while the client is in a relaxed state, he or she imagines the lowest item on the hierarchy. The item is presented repeatedly until the person no longer experiences an increase in anxiety when thinking about the object or situation. This process is repeated several times as the client moves systematically up the hierarchy, sequentially confronting images of stimuli that were originally rated as being more frightening.

In the years since systematic desensitization was originally proposed (Wolpe, 1958), many different variations on this procedure have been employed. The crucial feature of the treatment involves systematic maintained exposure to the feared stimulus (Mineka & Thomas, 1999; Rachman, 2002). Positive outcomes have been reported, regardless of the specific manner in which exposure is accomplished. Some evidence indicates that direct ("in vivo") exposure works better than imaginal exposure. A few prolonged exposures can be as effective as a larger sequence

Exposure treatments can be administered in imagination or in the person's natural environment. This tarantula is not dangerous, and it is used in desensitization for people with spider phobias.

Why is response prevention coupled with exposure in the treatment of OCD?

of brief exposures. Another variation on exposure procedures, known as flooding, begins with the most frightening stimuli rather than working up gradually from the bottom of the hierarchy. All of these variations on the basic procedure have been shown to be effective in the treatment of phobic disorders. Several research studies have demonstrated that exposure therapy leads to clinically meaningful improvement when compared to placebo treatments. Positive results are typically maintained several months after the end of treatment (Barlow, Raffa, & Cohen, 2002). Exposure is often accomplished in the presence of the therapist, but the treatment can be just as effective when the client directs his or her own systematic exposure in the natural environment.

The treatment of panic disorder often includes two specific forms of exposure. One, *situational exposure*, is used to treat agoraphobic avoidance (Hahlweg et al., 2001). In this procedure, the person repeatedly confronts the situations that have previously been avoided. These often include crowded public places, such as shopping malls and theaters, as well as certain forms of transportation, such as buses and trains. *Interoceptive exposure*, the other form of exposure, is aimed at reducing the person's fear of internal, bodily sensations that are frequently associated with the onset of a panic attack, such as increased heart and respiration rate and dizziness. The process is accomplished by having the person engage in standardized exercises that are known to produce such physical sensations. These may include spinning in a swivel chair, running in place, breathing through a narrow straw, or voluntary hyperventilation, depending on the type of sensation that the person fears and avoids. Outcome studies indicate that interoceptive exposure is one of the most important ingredients in the psychological treatment of panic disorder (Barlow et al., 2002; Meuret et al., 2005).

Exposure and Response Prevention The most effective form of psychological treatment for obsessive–compulsive disorder combines prolonged exposure to the situation that increases the person's anxiety with prevention of the person's typical compulsive response (Franklin & Foa, 2002; Marks, 1997). Neither component is effective by itself. The combination of exposure and response prevention is necessary because of the way in which people with obsessive–compulsive disorder use their compulsive rituals to reduce anxiety that is typically stimulated by the sudden appearance of an obsession. If the compulsive behavior is performed, exposure is effectively cut short.

Consider, for example, the treatment program employed with Ed. His obsessive thoughts and images, which centered around violence, were associated with handwriting. They were likely to pop into his mind when he noticed letters that were poorly formed. In an effort to control these thoughts, Ed wrote very carefully, and he corrected any letter that seemed a bit irregular. By the time he entered behavior therapy, Ed had avoided writing altogether for several months. The therapist arranged for him to begin writing short essays on a daily basis to be sure that he was exposed, for at least 30 minutes each day, to the situation that was most anxiety-provoking. He encouraged Ed to deliberately write letters that did not conform to his compulsive style. In their sessions, for example, Ed was also required to write long sequences of the letter T in which he deliberately failed to connect the two lines. He was not allowed to go back and correct this "mistake." The combination represents prolonged exposure to an anxiety-provoking stimulus and response prevention.

Controlled outcome studies indicate that this approach is effective with most OCD patients (Abramowitz, 1997). One review of 16 different outcome studies found that, after a few weeks of treatment with exposure and response prevention, the typical patient had shown improvements that were clinically important (see Research Methods). On the other hand, some patients (perhaps as many as 20 percent) do not respond positively to this form of treatment, and many continue to exhibit mild symptoms of the disorder after they have been successfully treated (Abramowitz, 1998).

Relaxation and Breathing Retraining   Behavior therapists have used relaxation procedures for many years. Relaxation training usually involves teaching the client alternately to tense and relax specific muscle groups while breathing slowly and deeply (Bernstein & Borkovec, 1973; Lehrer & Carr, 1997). This process is often described to the client as an active coping skill that can be learned through consistent practice and used to control anxiety and worry.

Outcome studies indicate that relaxation is a useful form of treatment for generalized anxiety disorder. Borkovec and his colleagues have compared applied relaxation and cognitive behavior therapy to nondirective psychotherapy for the treatment of patients with generalized anxiety disorder. Patients who received relaxation training and those who received cognitive therapy were more improved at the end of treatment

research methods

STATISTICAL SIGNIFICANCE: WHEN DIFFERENCES MATTER

Let's say that an outcome study reveals a statistical difference in the effectiveness of one form of treatment versus another form (or no treatment at all). Does this automatically mean that the difference is clinically significant? The answer is no. We can explain this point by using a hypothetical example. Imagine that you want to know whether exposure and response prevention are effective in the treatment of OCD. You could conduct a study, using an experimental design, in which 50 patients with OCD are randomly assigned to receive exposure and response prevention and another 50 patients—the control group—are not. The latter group might receive a placebo pill or nondirective supportive psychotherapy for purposes of comparison. Measures of obsessions and compulsions are collected before and after treatment for patients in both groups. Your hypothesis is that exposure treatment will lead to more improvement than will placebo or nondirective therapy. In contrast, the null hypothesis (see Research Methods in Chapter 1) holds that the two forms of treatment are not truly different. To conclude that exposure and response prevention is effective, you must reject the null hypothesis.

After collecting your data, you can use statistical tests to help you decide whether you can reject the null hypothesis. These tests assign a probability to that result, indicating how often we would find that result if there are not really differences between the two treatments.

Psychologists have adopted the .05 level, meaning that if a difference occurs only by chance, you would find this difference less than 5 times out of every 100 times you repeated this experiment. Differences that exceed the .05 level, therefore, are assumed to reflect real differences between the variables rather than mere chance. Such results are said to be *statistically significant.*

Statistical significance should not be equated with clinical importance (Jacobson & Truax, 1991). It is possible for an investigator to find statistically significant differences between groups (and therefore reject the null hypothesis) on the basis of relatively trivial changes in the patients' adjustment. Consider the hypothetical example outlined above and suppose that you measured outcome in terms of a questionnaire for obsessions and compulsions whose scores could range from 0 (no symptoms) to 100 (highest score possible). Let's also assume that the average person without OCD gets a score of 50 on this questionnaire and that a score of 70 or higher is typically considered to indicate the presence of problems that are associated with a disruption of the person's social and occupational functioning. Both groups have a mean rating of 90 on the scale prior to treatment. At the end of treatment, the mean rating for the exposure group has dropped to 75, and the mean for the control group is now 85. If you have included enough subjects, and depending on the amount of variation among scores within

each group, this difference might reach statistical significance. But is it clinically important? Probably not. The average patient in the exposure group still has a score above the cutoff for identifying meaningful levels of psychopathology and 25 points above the average for adults in the general population.

Clinical importance is sometimes measured in terms of the proportion of people in the treatment group whose outcome scores fall below a certain threshold of severity or within the range of scores that are produced by people without the disorder in question. In the case of OCD, people treated with exposure and response prevention do show levels of change that are considered clinically important as well as statistically significant (Abramowitz, 1998).

Clinical investigators should also consider the *kind* of changes that they expect to find as well as the *amount* of change. In addition to looking at changes in particular symptoms, such as a reduction in the frequency of compulsive behaviors, some clinical investigators also ask questions about the patient's quality of life (Gladis et al., 1999). These include an interest in the person's overall satisfaction as well as his or her ability to perform various social roles, at work, at school, or with friends and family. Therapists obviously hope that their patients will experience improvements in their overall quality of life and level of social adjustment when they are able to achieve a reduction in the severity of symptoms of mental disorders.

than those who received only nondirective therapy (Borkovec et al., 2002).

Breathing retraining is a procedure that involves education about the physiological effects of hyperventilation and practice in slow breathing techniques. It is often incorporated in treatments used for panic disorder (Barlow, 1997; Ley, 1999). This process is somewhat similar to relaxation in the sense that relaxation exercises also include instructions in breathing control. The person learns to control his or her breathing through repeated practice using the muscles of the diaphragm, rather than the chest, to take slow, deep breaths. Although breathing retraining appears to be a useful element in the treatment of panic disorder, the mechanisms involved are not entirely clear. A simple reduction in the frequency of hyperventilation is apparently not the main effect of breathing retraining. Some clinicians believe that the process works by enhancing relaxation or increasing the person's perception of control (Garssen, de Ruiter, & Van Dyck, 1992).

Cognitive Therapy Cognitive therapy is used extensively in the treatment of anxiety disorders. Cognitive treatment procedures for anxiety disorders have been developed by Aaron Beck (Beck, 1995; Beck & Emery, 1985) and Albert Ellis (1962, 1999). They are similar to those employed in the treatment of depression. Therapists help clients identify cognitions that are relevant to their problem; recognize the relation between these thoughts and maladaptive emotional responses (such as prolonged anxiety); examine the evidence that supports or contradicts these beliefs; and teach clients more useful ways of interpreting events in their environment (Schuyler, 1991).

In the case of anxiety disorders, cognitive therapy is usually accompanied by additional behavior therapy procedures. Barlow's approach to the treatment of panic disorder, for example, includes a cognitive component in addition to applied relaxation and exposure (Barlow, 1997). One aspect of the cognitive component involves an analysis of errors in the ways in which people think about situations in their lives. Typical examples of faulty logic include jumping to conclusions before considering all of the evidence, overgeneralizing ("That C in biology shows I'll never be a doctor"), all-or-none thinking (assuming that one mistake means total failure), and so on.

A second aspect of Barlow's cognitive component for panic patients is called *decatastrophizing*.

In this procedure, the therapist asks the client to imagine what would happen if his or her worst-case scenario actually happened. The same principles that are used in examining faulty logic are then applied to this situation. The therapist might say, "I don't think that you will fail the exam. But what would happen if you did fail the exam?" The client's initial reaction might be catastrophic ("I would die." "My parents would kill me." "I would flunk out of school."). Upon more careful analysis, however, the client might agree that these negative predictions actually represent gross exaggerations that are based on cognitive errors. Discussions in the therapy session are followed by extensive practice and homework assignments during the week. As one way of evaluating the accuracy of their own hypotheses, clients are encouraged to write down predictions that they make about specific situations and then keep track of the actual outcomes.

Several controlled outcome studies attest to the efficacy of cognitive therapy in the treatment of various types of anxiety disorder, including panic disorder, agoraphobia, social phobia, generalized anxiety disorder, and obsessive–compulsive disorder (Borkovec et al., 2002; Clark et al., 1999; Otto et al., 2004; Salkovskis, 1999).

Biological Interventions

Medication is the most effective and most commonly used biological approach to the treatment of anxiety disorders. Several types of drugs have been discovered to be useful. They are often used in conjunction with psychological treatment.

Antianxiety Medications The most frequently used types of minor tranquilizers are from the class of drugs known as benzodiazepines, which includes diazepam (Valium) and alprazolam (Xanax). These drugs reduce many symptoms of anxiety, especially vigilance and subjective somatic sensations, such as increased muscle tension, palpitations, increased perspiration, and gastrointestinal distress. They have relatively less effect on a person's tendency toward worry and rumination. Benzodiazepines were the most widely prescribed form of psychiatric medication until the 1990s.

Benzodiazepines bind to specific receptor sites in the brain that are ordinarily associated with a neurotransmitter known as gamma-aminobutyric acid (GABA). Benzodiazepines, which inhibit the activity of GABA neurons, are of two types, based on their rate of absorption and elimination from the body. Some, such as alprazolam and lorazepam (Ativan), are absorbed and eliminated quickly, whereas others, such as diazepam, are absorbed and eliminated slowly.

Benzodiazepines have been shown to be effective in the treatment of generalized anxiety disorders and social phobias (Ballenger, 2001; Federoff & Taylor, 2001). Drug effects are most consistently evident early in treatment. The long-term effects of benzodiazepines (beyond 6 months of treatment) are not well established (Mahe & Balogh, 2000). They are not typically beneficial for patients with specific phobias or obsessive–compulsive disorder. Certain high-potency benzodiazepines are also useful for treating panic disorder (Spiegel & Bruce, 1997). Alprazolam (Xanax) is considered by some psychiatrists to be the drug of choice for patients with this condition because it produces clinical improvement more quickly than antidepressants.

The results of most placebo-controlled outcome studies have been positive. The Cross-National Collaborative Panic Study (CNCPS), which was conducted in two phases, provides some of the best evidence in this regard. The first phase compared alprazolam to a placebo in 500 patients (Ballenger et al., 1988). Among the patients who received alprazolam, 30 percent were markedly improved after 8 weeks of treatment, and another 52 percent were moderately improved. Only 10 percent of the patients who received the placebo were markedly improved after treatment, and another 43 percent in this group were moderately improved.

The second phase of the CNCPS compared alprazolam, imipramine, and placebo treatment in a sample of 1,100 panic disorder patients. The investigators found that alprazolam and imipramine were equally effective in comparison to a placebo. Fewer patients dropped out of the alprazolam group, because the drug had fewer side effects than imipramine. Patients improved faster on alprazolam, but there were no differences between the two drugs after 6 to 8 weeks of treatment.

Many patients with panic disorder and agoraphobia relapse if they discontinue taking medication (Marks et al., 1993). Exposure may be a preferable form of treatment for patients with a diagnosis of panic disorder with agoraphobia

because of high relapse rates that have been observed after alprazolam is withdrawn.

Common side effects of benzodiazepines include sedation accompanied by mild psychomotor and cognitive impairments. These drugs can, for example, increase the risk of automobile accidents, because they interfere with motor skills. They can also lead to problems in attention and memory, especially among elderly patients.

The most serious adverse effect of benzodiazepines is their potential for addiction. Approximately 40 percent of people who use benzodiazepines for 6 months or more will exhibit symptoms of withdrawal if the medication is discontinued (Michelini et al., 1996). Withdrawal reactions include the reappearance of anxiety, somatic complaints, concentration problems, and sleep difficulties. They are most severe among patients who abruptly discontinue the use of benzodiazepines that are cleared quickly from the system, such as alprazolam. The risk for becoming dependent on benzodiazepines is greatest among people who have a history of abusing other substances, like alcohol.

Another class of antianxiety medication, known as the azapirones, includes drugs that work on entirely different neural pathways than the benzodiazepines (Cadieux, 1996). Rather than inhibiting the activity of GABA neurons, azapirones seem to act on serotonin transmission. The only azapirone in clinical use is known as buspirone (BuSpar). Placebo-controlled outcome studies indicate that buspirone is effective in the treatment of generalized anxiety disorder (Apter & Allen, 1999; Davidson et al., 1999). Some clinicians believe that buspirone is preferable to the benzodiazepines because it does not cause drowsiness and does not interact with the effects of alcohol. The disadvantage is that patients do not experience relief from severe anxiety symptoms as quickly with buspirone as they do with benzodiazepines.

Antidepressant Medications The selective serotonin reuptake inhibitors (SSRIs), discussed in Chapter 5, have become the preferred form of medication for treating almost all forms of anxiety disorder. These include drugs such as fluoxetine (Prozac), fluvoxamine (Luvox), sertaline (Zoloft), and paroxetine (Paxil). Reviews of controlled outcome studies indicate that they are at least as effective as other, more traditional forms of antidepressants in reducing symptoms of

Donald Klein, a psychiatrist at Columbia University, demonstrated that panic attacks could be treated successfully with antidepressant medication. His research led to the separate classification of panic disorder and generalized anxiety disorder.

various anxiety disorders (Davidson, 2001; Roy-Byrne & Cowley, 2002). They also have fewer unpleasant side effects, they are safer to use, and withdrawal reactions are less prominent when they are discontinued. Therefore, the SSRIs are now considered the first-line medication for treating panic disorder, social phobia, and obsessive–compulsive disorder (Zohar et al., 2000).

Imipramine (Tofranil), a tricyclic antidepressant medication, has been used for more than 40 years in the treatment of patients with panic disorder. A large number of double-blind, placebo-controlled studies indicate that it produces beneficial results (Jefferson, 1997; Mavissakalian & Ryan, 1998). Psychiatrists often prefer imipramine to antianxiety drugs for the treatment of panic disorder because patients are less likely to become dependent on the drug than they are to high-potency benzodiazepines like alprazolam.

Do psychological treatments have any advantages over medication for treatment of anxiety?

The tricyclic antidepressants are used less frequently than the SSRIs because they produce several unpleasant side effects, including weight gain, dry mouth, and overstimulation (sometimes referred to as an "amphetamine-like" response). Some of the side effects (like feeling jittery, nervous, lightheaded, and having trouble sleeping) are upsetting to patients because they resemble symptoms of anxiety. Side effects often lead patients to discontinue treatment prematurely. In one study of patients who received long term treatment with imipramine, 50 percent experienced distressing side effects, including 17 percent who found the effects intolerable (Noyes, Garvey, & Cook, 1989).

Clomipramine (Anafranil), another tricyclic antidepressant, has been used extensively in treating obsessive–compulsive disorder. Several placebo-controlled studies have shown clomipramine to be effective in treating OCD (Abramowitz, 1997; Kozak, Liebowitz, & Foa, 2000). One study found that more than 50 percent of the patients who received clomipramine improved to a level of normal functioning over a period of 10 weeks, compared to only 5 percent of the patients in a placebo group (Katz, DeVeaugh-Geiss, & Landau, 1990). Patients who continue to take the drug maintain the improvement, but relapse is common if medication is discontinued.

In actual practice, anxiety disorders are often treated with a combination of psychological and biological procedures. The selection of specific treatment components depends on the specific group of symptoms that the person exhibits. Table 6–4 summarizes various types of psychological treatment and specific types of medication that are effective with anxiety disorders. These are not the only types of treatment that are

TABLE 6–4 **Treatments of Choice for Anxiety Disorders**			
DISORDER	**MEDICATION**	**EXAMPLE**	**PSYCHOLOGICAL TREATMENT**
	Drug Class	*Generic Name (trade name)*	
Panic Disorder	SSRIs Benzodiazepines TCAs	Fluvoxamine (Luvox) Clonazepam (Klonopin) Imipramine (Tofranil)	Cognitive therapy Exposure (interoceptive) Breathing retraining
Agoraphobia	Benzodiazepines SSRIs TCAs	Lorazepam (Ativan) Sertraline (Zoloft) Imipramine (Tofranil)	Exposure (situational) Cognitive therapy
Generalized Anxiety Disorder	Benzodiazepines Azapirones	Alprazolam (Xanax) Buspirone (BuSpar)	Cognitive therapy Applied relaxation
Specific Phobias	Medication not usually recommended		Exposure *in vivo*
Social Phobia	SSRIs Benzodiazepines MAOIs	Paroxetine (Paxil) Clonazepam (Klonopin) Phenelzine (Nardil)	Exposure *in vivo* Cognitive therapy Social skills training
Obsessive–Compulsive Disorder	SSRIs TCAs	Fluoxetine (Prozac) Clomipramine (Anafranil)	Exposure plus response prevention Cognitive therapy

available, but they include those that have been subjected to empirical validation. The potential benefits and costs of combined treatment with medication and psychological procedures should be studied more carefully. Current evidence suggests that patients who receive both medication and psychotherapy may do better in the short run, but patients who receive only cognitive behavior therapy may do better in the long run because of difficulties that can be encountered when medication is discontinued (Otto et al., 2005).

---

getting help

 Most people suffering from anxiety disorders can be treated successfully. Several forms of intervention are beneficial, primarily behavior therapy, cognitive therapy, and medication. If you plan to work with a professional therapist, do some research before you begin working with a specific person. Read about treatments that have been evaluated empirically, and look for someone who uses one of these procedures. Some excellent Internet sites may help you find the best therapist for you. Patient-run organizations have established support groups in many communities and share information about treatment alternatives. One outstanding example is the Anxiety Disorders Association of America. The URL for its Web site is www.adaa.org. It includes a consumer's guide to treatment alternatives that is organized by specific types of anxiety disorders. More detailed information about obsessive–compulsive disorder and related problems can be obtained from the Obsessive Compulsive Foundation, a not-for-profit organization composed of people with OCD, their families, and professionals. Its Web address is www.ocfoundation.org.

Some people may be able to make improvements on their own with the advice of a useful self-help book. There are a lot of good alternatives to choose from in the area of anxiety disorders. We recommend two books that describe a combination of cognitive and behavioral approaches to treatment. *Triumph over Fear* (1995), by Jerilyn Ross and Rosalynn Carter, describes the successful experiences of people who have recovered from various types of anxiety disorders, including phobias, panic, and generalized anxiety disorder. Practical, self-help strategies are also summarized in *Overcoming Panic, Anxiety, and Phobias: New Strategies to Free Yourself from Worry and Fear* (1996), written by Shirley Babior and Carol Goldman. This book includes simple instructions in progressive muscle relaxation, cognitive techniques to master anxiety, and exposure procedures for overcoming avoidance. Finally, more specific information about dealing with obsessive–compulsive disorder can be found in *Stop Obsessing: How to Overcome Your Obsessions and Compulsions* (2001), by Edna Foa and Reid Wilson.

SUMMARY

Anxiety disorders are defined in terms of a preoccupation with, or persistent avoidance of, thoughts or situations that provoke **fear** or anxiety. **Anxiety** involves a diffuse emotional reaction that is associated with the anticipation of future problems and is out of proportion to threats from the environment. A pervasive anxious mood is typically associated with pessimistic thoughts and feelings. The person's attention may also turn inward, focusing on negative emotions and self-evaluation rather than on the organization or rehearsal of adaptive responses that might be useful in coping with negative events.

A **panic attack** is a sudden, overwhelming experience of terror or fright. Panic attacks are defined largely in terms of a list of somatic sensations, ranging from heart palpitations, sweating, and trembling to nausea, dizziness, and chills.

Phobias are persistent and irrational narrowly defined fears that are associated with avoidance of a specific object or situation. The most complex and incapacitating form of phobic disorder is **agoraphobia,** which is usually described as fear of public spaces. It is not so much a fear of being close to one specific object or situation as it is a fear of being separated from signals associated with safety.

Obsessions are repetitive, unwanted, intrusive cognitive events that may take the form of thoughts or images or impulses. They intrude suddenly into consciousness and lead to an increase in subjective anxiety. **Compulsions** are repetitive behaviors, considered by the person to be senseless or irrational, that reduce the anxiety associated with obsessions. The person attempts to resist but cannot. The two most common forms of compulsive behavior are cleaning and checking.

DSM-IV-TR recognizes several specific subtypes of anxiety disorders: **panic disorders** (with or without agoraphobia), phobic disorders (specific phobia, social phobia, and agoraphobia without panic attacks), obsessive–compulsive disorder, and generalized anxiety disorder, as well as posttraumatic stress disorder and acute stress disorder.

The NCS and ECA studies found that anxiety disorders are more common than any other form of mental disorder. Phobias are the most common type of anxiety disorder, with a 1-year prevalence of about 9 percent of the adult population, followed by social phobia (8 percent), generalized anxiety disorder (3 percent), obsessive–compulsive disorder (2 percent), and panic disorder (2 percent). Women are more likely than men to experience specific phobias, social phobias, agoraphobia, panic disorder, and generalized anxiety disorder. Gender differences are less marked in obsessive–compulsive disorder.

Stressful life events can influence the onset of anxiety disorders. Certain kinds of stresses may be differentially associated with particular types of emotional disorders: Severe events involving danger are most often associated with anxiety symptoms, while severe events involving loss are more often associated with depression. Among those people who have developed an anxiety disorder, interpersonal conflict is more characteristic of people with agoraphobia.

The learning model explained the development of phobic disorders in terms of classical conditioning, or the pairing of fear with originally neutral stimuli that happen to be present during a traumatic experience. A modified learning view, known as the **preparedness model,** is based on a recognition that there are biological constraints on the kinds of associations that members of a particular species are able to make. We may be prepared to develop intense, persistent fears only to a select set of objects or situations. People can apparently learn to avoid certain stimuli if they observe other people showing a strong fear response to those stimuli. Studies with infant monkeys support the preparedness model.

Cognitive theorists have argued that panic disorder is caused by the catastrophic misinterpretation of bodily sensations or perceived threat. This theory has the support of several research studies, but there are methodological problems associated with some of the studies. The cognitive theory of panic also has problems explaining some clinical observations regarding panic disorder, such as the fact that some patients experience panic attacks in their sleep.

People who are prone to excessive **worrying** are unusually sensitive to cues that signal the existence of future threats. The recognition of danger cues triggers a maladaptive, self-perpetuating cycle of cognitive processes that can quickly spin out of control. The threatening information that is generated in this process is presumably encoded in memory in the form of elaborate schemas that are easily reactivated. In comparison to the depressed person, who is convinced that failure will definitely occur, the anxious person is afraid of failure that may occur as a future event. Some people apparently continue to worry, even though it is not productive, because worrying is reinforced by an immediate (though temporary) reduction in uncomfortable physiological sensations.

Family studies support the separate classification of panic disorder and **generalized anxiety disorder.** An increased prevalence of panic disorder is found among the relatives of patients with panic disorder. Similarly, an increased prevalence of generalized anxiety is found among the relatives of patients with generalized anxiety disorder. In other words, the two disorders "breed true." This does not seem to be the case for obsessive–compulsive disorder, where patients' relatives show an increased risk for several types of anxiety disorder rather than a specific risk for OCD.

Twin studies indicate that genetic factors are involved in the etiology of several types of anxiety disorder, especially panic disorder. The evidence is inconsistent for generalized anxiety disorder. There appears to be a modest genetic influence on the development of phobic disorders. The influence of environmental events seems to be greatest in specific phobias.

Studies of fear conditioning in animals have identified specific pathways in the brain that are responsible for detecting and organizing a response to danger. The amygdala plays a central role in these circuits. Several other areas of the brain are also associated with anxiety and the symptoms of anxiety disorders. One example is the locus ceruleus, a small area located in the brain stem. Electrical stimulation of the locus ceruleus triggers a strong fear response that resembles a panic attack.

Pharmacological challenge studies have demonstrated that infusions of lactate and several other kinds of chemicals can provoke panic attacks, but the specific biological process through which this effect is produced is still unknown. Serotonin, norepinephrine, GABA, and dopamine are some of the neurotransmitters that are involved in the production of panic attacks. Many interacting neurotransmitter systems play a role in the etiology of anxiety disorders.

Several psychological approaches to the treatment of anxiety disorders have been shown to be effective. These include the use of exposure and flooding in the treatment of phobic disorders and prolonged exposure and response prevention in the treatment of obsessive–compulsive disorders. Various types of medication are also effective treatments for anxiety disorders. These include benzodiazepines for generalized anxiety disorder, and selective serotonin reuptake inhibitors for obsessive–compulsive disorder and panic disorder.

KEY TERMS

agoraphobia   179
anxiety   177
compulsions   181

fear   177
generalized anxiety
   disorder (GAD)   185

neurosis   183
obsessions   180
panic attack   178

panic disorder   184
phobias   179
preparedness model   193

social phobia   185
worry   178

Go to www.prenhall.com/oltmanns for online quizzes, interactive flash cards, PowerPoint presentations, and chapter reviews.

7

Acute and Posttraumatic Stress Disorders, Dissociative Disorders, and Somatoform Disorders

◆◆◆

Before September 11, 2001, the topics covered in this chapter may have seemed like intriguing curiosities. Now, they are very real, very personal, and uncomfortably close to home. A great many people experienced trauma on September 11, including the more than 100,000 people who directly witnessed the terrorist attacks on the World Trade Center and the Pentagon, and countless others who lost loved ones in the attacks. The experience of dissociation also became more personal in the days following September 11, as many people experienced a pervasive sense of unreality, or felt like robots going through the motions of life in a world that had changed dramatically. Other people, including many children, expressed their fear and anxiety through somatic symptoms such as stomachaches and concerns about their physical health.

OVERVIEW

This chapter is not about September 11, but we do consider some complicated issues relevant to an understanding of our emotional reactions to that terrible day. What are normal and abnormal reactions to trauma? What is the best way to address the incredible fear caused by trauma? Why do we feel numb in the aftermath of horror?

This last question brings us to an important topic that unites the three types of emotional disorder that we consider in this chapter. Vehement debates but few empirical studies focus on the relation between stress, anxiety, and **dissociation**—the disruption of the normally integrated mental processes involved in memory, consciousness, identity, or perception (APA, 2000; Spiegel & Cardena, 1991). The DSM-IV-TR classifies PTSD as an anxiety disorder. We prefer to consider PTSD in a separate chapter after anxiety disorders and before dissociative disorders, however, because PTSD is of unique importance and characterized by mixed symptoms of anxiety and dissociation.

Extreme examples of dissociation raise more vexing questions. Do problems like multiple personalities and the conversion of anxiety into dramatic physical symptoms prove that an important part of the human mind is unconscious? Or should we instead question the validity of some of these dramatic disorders rather

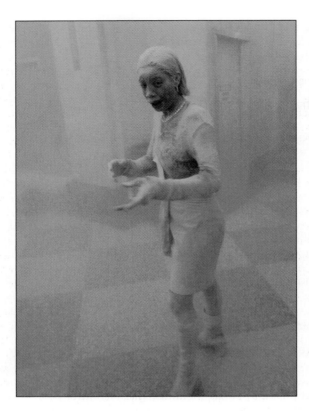

A traumatized woman takes shelter after being covered in dust from the collapsing World Trade Center towers. Over 100,000 people directly witnessed the September 11 attacks on the World Trade Center and the Pentagon.

than of our models of the mind? Because of the limited research, we must be cautious in attempting to answer these questions and skeptical in considering topics that are dramatic and often dramatized. At the same time, we cannot help but be captivated and challenged by unusual case studies of the disorders we discuss in this chapter. We begin by considering the less controversial and more adequately researched

problems of acute and posttraumatic stress disorders.

ACUTE AND POSTTRAUMATIC STRESS DISORDERS

Stress is an inevitable, and in some cases a desirable, fact of everyday life. Some stressors, however, are so catastrophic and horrifying that they can cause serious psychological harm. Such **traumatic stress** is defined in DSM-IV-TR as an event that involves actual or threatened death or serious injury to self or others and creates intense feelings of fear, helplessness, or horror. Examples of traumatic stressors include bombings, airplane crashes, rape, military combat, earthquakes, major fires, and devastating automobile wrecks.

Both survivors and witnesses are expected to be greatly distressed as a part of their normal response to traumatic stressors. For some victims, the trauma continues long after the event itself has ended. **Acute stress disorder (ASD)** occurs within 4 weeks after exposure to traumatic stress and is characterized by dissociative symptoms, reexperiencing of the event, avoidance of reminders of the trauma, and marked anxiety or arousal. **Posttraumatic stress disorder (PTSD)** also is defined by symptoms of reexperiencing, avoidance, and arousal, but in PTSD the symptoms either are longer lasting or have a delayed onset. The following case study illustrates the horrors and lasting trauma of sexual assault.

◆◆◆◆◆◆◆◆◆◆◆◆◆◆◆◆◆◆◆◆◆◆◆◆◆◆◆◆◆◆◆◆◆◆◆◆◆◆◆

CASE STUDY Sexual Assault and Stephanie's PTSD

One spring evening, Stephanie Cason, a bright, attractive, and well-adjusted 27-year-old graduate student, ran outside to investigate a major fire in another building in her apartment complex. While she was outside, Stephanie chatted amiably about the scene with a man who she assumed was a neighbor. After talking with a few other people, Stephanie returned to her apartment. The fire had caused a power outage, but Stephanie found her way upstairs and changed into her nightclothes. When she came back downstairs,

she found the very large man she had met outside standing in the shadows of her darkened apartment. Without saying a word, he raised a tire iron and struck Stephanie across the top of her head—repeatedly, until she fell to the floor and stopped screaming. Stephanie was cut deeply and stunned by the vicious blows, but she attempted to resist as the man began to grab at her breasts and rip at her clothes. He began to mutter obscenities and told Stephanie he wanted to have sex with her. All Stephanie could think was, "I'm going to be killed."

Somehow Stephanie remained strong enough to think keenly despite the shock of the assault and the blood pouring from her head. She decided she would "agree" to have sex with her assailant, but she told him that she needed to "freshen up" first. Eventually, Stephanie convinced him to let her go to clean up, and as soon as she reached her room, she shoved a bureau in front of the door and screamed frantically out the window for help. Her screams frightened her attacker and brought help to Stephanie. Later, she learned that one of the firefighters tackled and captured the assailant as he tried to run away from the apartment complex.

Stephanie saved herself from being raped, but she could not protect herself from the emotional fallout of her sexual assault. For days, eventually weeks, she felt intermittently terrified, dazed, and grateful to be alive. She replayed the horror of the evening in her mind repeatedly, and when she managed to fall asleep, she often was wakened by frightening nightmares. Stephanie was terrified to be alone, especially at night, but also at many times during the day. She relied on the unwavering support of her boyfriend and friends to stay nearby and help her cope.

Shortly after the assault, Stephanie sought help from a skilled clinical psychologist, but she fell into a depression despite the therapy. Antidepressant medication helped somewhat with her mood and lethargy, but for months after the trauma she was hypervigilant—constantly on the lookout for new threats; she had difficulty concentrating and experienced intermittent feelings of numbness or unreality. In addition, she frequently reexperienced the images and emotions surrounding the dreaded event. She was able to resume her studies after about 3 months, and within 6 or 8 months she

was working fairly regularly but with considerably less confidence and concentration than formerly. As the anniversary of her assault approached, Stephanie grew increasingly upset. The spring weather, usually a welcome change, reminded her of the terror of the previous spring. Her feelings of unreality returned, and she had flashbacks where she suddenly found herself reliving the dreaded night in her mind. The nightmares and her fears about being alone reappeared. As the dreaded date passed, her reactions eased slowly. After about 2 or 3 months, she was able to renew her normal life—as normal as her life could be—with fewer struggles than earlier.

Stephanie found it painful but also helpful to talk about her assault with friends and, over time, more publicly. After the passing of the 1-year anniversary, she actually gave a few lectures about her experiences to classes and to women's groups. Talking about the event gave her some relief, and more importantly, it gave her a sense that some good might come from her trauma. Stephanie also was willing and able to testify at the trial of her assailant, who was convicted and sent to prison for 20 years. Although she appeared strong in the courtroom, the trial renewed many of

Stephanie's symptoms of PTSD. She again relived the terror of the assault, avoided being alone at night, and became fearful and hypervigilant about potential dangers in her world.

Once the trial was finished and her assailant was sent to prison, Stephanie felt a degree of relief and resolution about the trauma. She also felt some satisfaction and pride in the strength it took to share her experiences with others. Still, she could not fully banish the demons of the traumatic sexual assault. She again experienced intensely distressing episodes of PTSD near the second and third anniversaries of the assault. And even at other times, Stephanie could unexpectedly fall victim to terror. For example, more than 3 years after the assault, her boyfriend (now her husband) silently entered her room after returning home unexpectedly one night. Frightened by his sudden appearance, Stephanie first screamed in terror, then sobbed in uncontrollable fear, and felt numb and unreal for several days afterwards.

Stephanie did not behave like a victim from the moment of the assault, throughout the trial, or in her public discussions of her trauma. But despite her admirable strength, Stephanie could not prevent or control the recurrent terror of PTSD brought on by a violent sexual assault.

◆◆

Symptoms of ASD and PTSD

As illustrated in Stephanie's terrifying experience, both acute and posttraumatic stress disorder are characterized by (1) reexperienced trauma; (2) marked avoidance of stimuli associated with the trauma; and (3) persistent arousal or increased anxiety. In addition, ASD is characterized by a fourth cluster of problems, dissociative symptoms. The dissociative symptoms were included in the diagnosis of ASD, but not PTSD, because dissociative symptoms are particularly likely to occur in the immediate aftermath of a trauma (Frances et al., 1995).

Reexperiencing   Like Stephanie, people who have been confronted with a traumatic stressor *reexperience* the event in a number of different ways. Some people experience repeated, distressing images or thoughts of the incident. For example, they visualize the trauma over and over, or they repeatedly question how they might have acted differently. Other people relive the trauma in horrifying dreams. Many people with ASD or PTSD have repeated and intrusive **flashbacks,** sudden memories during which the trauma is replayed

in images or thoughts—often at full emotional intensity. In rare cases, reexperiencing occurs as a *dissociative state*, and the person feels and acts as if the trauma actually were recurring in the moment. A combat veteran in a dissociative state might act as if he believes he is back in battle, and he may even take dangerous actions like gathering weapons or barricading himself in his residence. Typically, dissociative states are of short duration, but in unusual cases they can last for days.

Avoidance   Marked or persistent avoidance of stimuli associated with the trauma is another symptom of ASD and PTSD. Trauma victims may attempt to avoid thoughts or feelings related to the event, or, like Stephanie, they may avoid people, places, or activities that remind them of the trauma. In PTSD, the avoidance also may manifest itself as a general *numbing of responsiveness*. People suffering from PTSD often complain that they suffer from "emotional anesthesia"—their feelings seem dampened or even nonexistent. As a result, they frequently withdraw from others, particularly from close relationships.

Arousal or Anxiety   Despite their general withdrawal from feelings, people, and painful

Video Case

POST TRAUMATIC STRESS DISORDER

SARA

"I would wake up 37 times a night for the slightest noise, thinking this crazy person was going to come in and do something to me."

On your CD-ROM menu, select "Anxiety Disorders" and click on "Post Traumatic Stress Disorder: Sara." As you watch the video, listen for Sara's description of her PTSD symptoms: arousal, avoidance, and reexperiencing. Also consider ways in which the trauma of domestic violence is unique—for example, in the social isolation of the victim.

Following trauma, many people have intrusive flashbacks, sudden memories during which the trauma is replayed in images and thoughts often at full emotional intensity.

situations, people with ASD and PTSD also experience increased arousal and anxiety following the trauma, a symptom which predicts a worse prognosis when it is more severe (Schell et al., 2004). Examples of arousal and anxiety include Stephanie's hypervigilance in searching for dangers in her world, restlessness, agitation, and irritability. A number of people with PTSD or ASD also have an *exaggerated startle response*, excessive fear reactions to unexpected stimuli, such as loud noises. Symptoms of anxiety and arousal are the reason why traumatic stress disorders are grouped with the anxiety disorders in DSM-IV-TR.

Dissociative Symptoms   Acute stress disorder is characterized by explicit dissociative symptoms. Many people become less aware of their surroundings following a traumatic event. They report feeling dazed, and they may seem "spaced out" to other people. Other people experience *depersonalization*, feeling cut off from themselves or their environment. People with this symptom may report feeling like a robot or as if they were sleepwalking. *Derealization* is characterized by a marked sense of unreality about yourself or the world around you. Immediately after September 11, many people awoke wondering if the terrorist attacks had been only a nightmare—and the sense of unreality continued throughout the day. ASD also may be characterized by features of *dissociative amnesia*, specifically the inability to recall important aspects of the traumatic experience (Harvey, Bryant, & Dang, 1998).

DSM-IV-TR lists a sense of numbing or detachment from others as dissociative symptoms that characterize acute stress disorder. Note that a very similar symptom is listed as an indicator of avoidance, not dissociation, in the diagnosis of PTSD (see Table 7–1). This discrepancy in diagnostic criteria reflects some of the broader controversy about whether ASD and PTSD should be classified as dissociative or anxiety disorders (van der Kolk & McFarlane, 1996). In fact, research suggests that a subgroup of patients with PTSD dissociate, since they report low anxiety but exhibit high arousal on psychophysiological indicators (Griffin, Resick, & Mechanic, 1997).

Diagnosis of ASD and PTSD

Brief Historical Perspective   Maladaptive reactions to traumatic stress have long been of interest to the military, where "normal" performance is expected in the face of the trauma of combat. Historically, most of the military's concern has focused on battle dropout, that is, men who leave the field of action as a result of what has been called "shell shock" or "combat neurosis" (Frances et al., 1995). During the Vietnam War, however, battle dropout was less frequent than in earlier wars, but delayed reactions to combat were much more common (Figley, 1978). This change prompted much interest in PTSD, a condition first listed in the DSM in 1980 (DSM-III).

Contemporary Classification   The basic diagnostic criteria for PTSD—reexperiencing, avoidance, and arousal—have remained more or less the same in revisions of the DSM. However, two significant changes in the classification of traumatic stress disorders were made with the publication of DSM-IV in 1994: Acute stress disorder was included as a separate diagnostic category, and the definition of trauma was altered.

Acute Stress Disorder   The diagnostic criteria for ASD and PTSD are essentially the same. The two exceptions are that ASD explicitly includes dissociative symptoms and lasts no longer than 4 weeks (see Table 7–2), whereas PTSD continues for at least 1 month after a trauma or it has a delayed onset (see Table 7–1). Not surprisingly, many people suffer from ASD after experiencing trauma, and the presence of ASD may predict future PTSD (Harvey & Bryant, 1998, 1999). Still, some experts wonder whether ASD really describes *normal* reactions to trauma, and suggest that the diagnosis needs to be reformulated or dropped (Harvey & Bryant, 2002). The new classification was added to the DSM-IV without much research support. Why? The hope was that early intervention with ASD would prevent the development of PTSD. According to Allen Frances, the chair of the DSM-IV task force, "The diagnosis of acute stress disorder was included in DSM-IV because an ounce of prevention is worth a pound of cure" (Frances et al., 1995, p. 263).

What Defines Trauma?   Earlier versions of DSM defined trauma as an event "outside the range of usual human experience." Even before September 11, however, researchers discovered that, unfortunately, many traumatic stressors are a *common* part of human experience in the United States today (Frances et al., 1995). Thus DSM-IV-TR defines trauma as (1) the experience of an event involving actual or threatened death or serious injury to self or others and (2) a response of intense fear, helplessness, or horror in reaction to the event.

People often respond in similar ways to trauma, but different traumatic stressors also create unique psychological problems. Diagnosis and treatment must be sensitive to the unique consequences of a specific trauma (see The Trauma of Sexual Assault on page 219). Thus, researchers study both common and unique reactions to traumatic events including rape (Kilpatrick et al., 1989), child sexual abuse (Deblinger et al., 1989), spouse abuse (Astin et al., 1995), children's coping with residential fires (Jones & Ollendick, 2002), and torture (Basoglu et al., 1997).

Disaster and Emergency Workers   The psychological effects of exposure to natural or man-made disasters, like September 11 or the Oklahoma City bombing in 1995, also are of great concern. Estimates indicate that well over 100,000 people

---

TABLE 7–1   DSM-IV-TR Diagnostic Criteria for Posttraumatic Stress Disorder (PTSD)

A. The person has been exposed to a traumatic event in which both of the following were present:

1. The person experienced, witnessed, or was confronted with an event or events that involved actual or threatened death or serious injury, or a threat to the physical integrity of self or others.

2. The person's response involved intense fear, helplessness, or horror.

B. The traumatic event is persistently reexperienced in one (or more) of the following ways:

1. Recurrent and intrusive distressing recollections of the event including images, thoughts, or perceptions

2. Recurrent distressing dreams of the event

3. Acting or feeling as if the traumatic event were recurring

4. Intense psychological distress at exposure to internal or external cues that symbolize or resemble an aspect of the traumatic event

5. Physiologic reactivity upon exposure to internal or external cues that symbolize or resemble an aspect of the traumatic event

C. Persistent avoidance of stimuli associated with the trauma and numbing of general responsiveness (not present before the trauma), as indicated by three (or more) of the following:

1. Efforts to avoid thoughts, feelings, or conversations associated with the trauma

2. Efforts to avoid activities, places, or people that arouse recollections of the trauma

3. Inability to recall an important aspect of the trauma

4. Markedly diminished interest or participation in significant activities

5. Feeling of detachment or estrangement from others

6. Restricted range of affect

7. Sense of a foreshortened future

D. Persistent symptoms of increased arousal, as indicated by two (or more) of the following:

1. Difficulty falling or staying asleep

2. Irritability or outbursts of anger

3. Difficulty concentrating

4. Hypervigilance

5. Exaggerated startle response

E. Duration of the disturbance is more than 1 month

Specify if:

Acute: If duration of symptoms is less than 3 months

Chronic: If duration of symptoms is 3 months or more

Specify if:

With delayed onset: If onset of symptoms is at least 6 months after the stressor

Reprinted with permission from the *Diagnostic and Statistical Manual of Mental Disorders, Fourth Edition, Text Revision.* Copyright © 2000 by the American Psychiatric Association.

TABLE 7–2 DSM-IV-TR Diagnostic Criteria for Acute Stress Disorder (ASD)

A. The person has been exposed to a traumatic event in which both of the following were present:

  1. The person experienced, witnessed, or was confronted with an event or events that involved actual or threatened death or serious injury, or a threat to the physical integrity of self or others.

  2. The person's response involved intense fear, helplessness, or horror.

B. Either while experiencing or after experiencing the distressing event, the individual has three (or more) of the following dissociative symptoms:

  1. A subjective sense of numbing, detachment, or absence of emotional responsiveness

  2. A reduction in awareness of his or her surroundings (e.g., "being in a daze")

  3. Derealization

  4. Depersonalization

  5. Dissociative amnesia (i.e., the inability to recall an important aspect of the trauma)

C. The traumatic event is persistently reexperienced in at least one of the following ways: recurrent images, thoughts, dreams, illusions, flashback episodes, or a sense of reliving the experience; or distress on exposure to reminders of the traumatic event.

D. Marked avoidance of stimuli that arouse recollections of the trauma (e.g., thoughts, feelings, conversations, activities, places, people).

E. Marked symptoms of anxiety or increased arousal (e.g., difficulty sleeping, irritability, poor concentration, hypervigilance, exaggerated startle response, motor restlessness).

F. The disturbance causes clinically significant distress or impairment in social, occupational, or other important areas of functioning or impairs the individual's ability to pursue some necessary task, such as obtaining necessary assistance or mobilizing personal resources by telling family members about the traumatic experience.

G. The disturbance lasts for a minimum of 2 days and a maximum of 4 weeks and occurs within 4 weeks of the traumatic event.

Reprinted with permission from the *Diagnostic and Statistical Manual of Mental Disorders*, Fourth Edition, Text Revision. Copyright © 2000 by the American Psychiatric Association.

Likely reasons for the dramatic drop include our tremendous human resilience in coping, even in the face of trauma (Bonanno, 2004), and an outpouring of social support to and among New Yorkers (McNally et al., 2003).

September 11 also called attention to the trauma experienced by emergency workers. Firefighters, police, and paramedics must remain calm and effective in the face of trauma, but this does not make them immune to its aftereffects. It is, of course, important to note the strengths—and the heroism—of emergency workers in coping with trauma. *Hardiness*, a personal sense of commitment, control, and challenge in facing stress, predicts lower rates of PTSD (Sutker et al., 1995). In fact, a study of the Oklahoma City terrorist bombing found that firefighters suffered from PTSD at about half the rate of victims of the bombing (North et al., 2002). Still, the resilience expected of emergency personnel can create problems. Emergency workers need education about the potential psychological effects of trauma on *them*, opportunities to express troubling emotions, and, in some cases, specialized psychological help (Bryant & Harvey, 2000). Flexibility may be the key to successful emotional coping. Researchers found lower rates of PTSD among New York City college students who were better at enhancing *and* suppressing emotional expression following September 11 (Bonanno et al., 2004).

Comorbidity   Many people with PTSD also suffer from another mental disorder. Notably high levels of comorbidity are found for depression, other anxiety disorders, and substance abuse (Brady et al., 2004; Kessler et al., 1995), and it may be important to distinguish between trauma victims who internalize (e.g., get depressed) or externalize (e.g., become antisocial) (Miller et al., 2004). Other problems associated with PTSD include disturbing nightmares, physical symptoms like headaches and gastrointestinal problems, and troublesome emotions, particularly anger and grief, and relationship difficulties owing particularly to emotional numbing (Cook et al., 2004). Another important concern is increased suicide risk. One study found that 33 percent of rape survivors had thoughts of suicide, and 13 percent actually made a suicide attempt (Kilpatrick et al., 1992).

Differential diagnosis between ASD and PTSD and *adjustment disorder* is based on both the nature of the stressor and the type and severity of symptoms. Adjustment disorders (see Chapter 17) are caused by "normal" but painful

directly witnessed the attacks on the World Trade Center and the Pentagon, and based on past research, fully 35 percent may have developed PTSD (Yehuda, 2002). More directly, a random telephone survey of 1,008 residents living south of 110th Street in Manhattan found that, whether or not they directly witnessed the WTC attacks, 7.5 percent—equivalent to 67,000 people—suffered from PTSD 5 to 8 weeks later (Galea et al., 2002). Much more optimistically, the same research group found that a year and a half after the attacks the prevalence of PTSD among residents living south of 110th Street dropped to 1.7% (Galea et al., in press).

Are PTSD and ASD anxiety disorders, dissociative disorders, or a separate category of diagnosis?

stressors, such as losing a job, and they involve normal (if distressing) reactions to these events. Rather than being diagnosed as either an anxiety or a dissociative disorder, we anticipate that ASD, PTSD, and adjustment disorders will be grouped together in a new diagnostic category of stress-related mental disorders in future revisions of the DSM.

Frequency of Trauma, PTSD, and ASD

Early epidemiological studies suggested that PTSD was not a common psychological problem (e.g., Helzer, Robins, & McEvoy, 1987); however, more recent research documents that the incidence of PTSD is high. In fact, the National Comorbidity Survey found that nearly 8 percent of people living in the United States will experience PTSD at some point in their lives, including about 10 percent of women and 5 percent of men (Kessler et al., 1995).

What accounts for the increased incidence rates in more recent research? In large part, the increase is due to the recognition that traumatic stressors are common, not rare. In fact, a study of a random sample of 2,181 adults living in the Detroit area found that almost 90 percent of the participants had experienced at least one traumatic stressor in their lifetime. About 9 percent of participants developed PTSD following a trauma (Breslau et al., 1998; see Figure 7–1). Similarly rates of trauma and PTSD also are found in Mexico (Norris et al., 2003). Rape and assault clearly are among the very worst traumas, and they pose an especially high risk for PTSD (see Figure 7–1).

Other research also finds that women are especially likely to develop PTSD as a result of rape, while combat exposure is a major risk factor for PTSD among men (Breslau et al., 1991; Kessler et al., 1995; Prigerson et al., 2002). PSTD also is commonly found among crime victims (Kilpatrick & Acierno, 2003). Still, the single most common cause of PTSD is the sudden, unexpected death of a loved one. The risk for PTSD following the sudden death of a loved one is "only" about one in seven (Breslau et al., 1998). However, its high prevalence makes unexpected death a more widespread cause of PTSD (see Figure 7–1).

Trauma and PTSD Are Not Random   Good luck—or bad luck—can play an important role

---

THE TRAUMA OF SEXUAL ASSAULT

Like many other traumatic stressors, unfortunately sexual assault is not outside the realm of normal human experience in the United States today. Almost 10 percent of women report having been raped at least once in their lifetime, according to national surveys, and 12 percent report having been sexually molested (Kessler et al., 1995). Other evidence suggests a notably higher prevalence when the data include *acquaintance rapes,* assaults committed by people known to the victim (Goodman, Koss, & Russo, 1993).

Rape can be devastating physically, socially, and emotionally. Thirty-nine percent of rape victims are physically injured on parts of their bodies other than the genitals. A significant proportion of rape victims are infected with a sexually transmitted disease, and about 5 percent of rapes result in pregnancy (Goodman et al., 1993). Socially, sexual assault can undermine women's work, as well as their intimate relationships (Bryen et al., 1999).

Most victims of sexual assault show the symptoms of PTSD. Victims may reexperience the horrors of the assault; they may feel numbed in reacting to others, particularly sexual partners; they may avoid any potentially threatening situation; and they may maintain both autonomic hyperarousal and hypervigilance against possible victimization. Depression is also common. Sadness, crying, and withdrawal from others often are coupled with sleep and appetite disturbances. Loss of interest in sex, insecurities about sexual identity, sexual dysfunction, and negative feelings toward men also are common (Goodman et al., 1993).

Another frequent psychological problem is that many victims of sexual assault blame themselves, despite the fact that they are the victims. Women may wonder if they unwittingly encouraged their assailant, or they may chastise themselves for not being more cautious in avoiding dangerous circumstances. This irrational self-blame is abetted by cultural myths that women provoke rape or that they actually enjoy it. *Secondary victimization* is a growing concern, as insensitive legal, medical, and even mental health professionals can add to a rape victim's emotional burden rather than alleviating her distress. In fact, victims of acquaintance rape show increased symptoms of PTSD when they receive minimal community assistance and encounter victim-blaming behaviors from professionals who are supposed to help them (Campbell et al., 1999). Such findings may explain why as many as two-thirds of stranger rapes and four-fifths of acquaintance rapes are not reported to authorities.

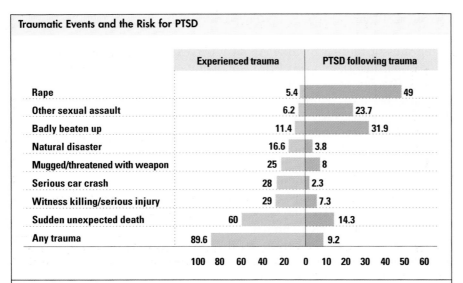

FIGURE 7–1: Bars to the left of center indicate the percentage of adults who had experienced each trauma among a representative sample of 2,181 adults aged 18 to 45 and living in the Detroit area. Bars to the right of center indicate the percentage of adults who developed PTSD after exposure to the particular trauma.

Note: The prevalence of rape as reported in this study was lower than that reported in other studies. We assume that this statistic reflects only more violent rapes.
Source: N. Breslau, R.C. Kessler, H.D. Chilcoat, L.R. Schultz, G.C. Davis, and P. Andreski, 1998, Traumatic and posttraumatic stress disorder in the community: The 1996 Detroit Area Survey of Trauma. *Archives of General Psychiatry, 55,* 626–632. Copyright © 1998. Reprinted by permission of American Medical Association.

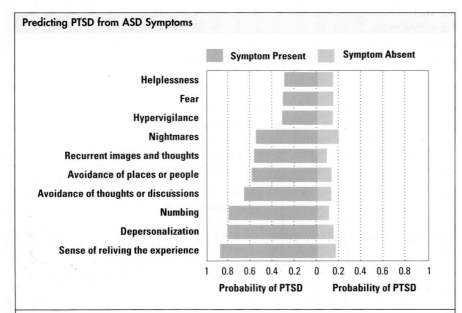

FIGURE 7–2: The presence of symptoms (e.g., hypervigilance) predicts future PTSD weakly, while other symptoms (e.g., numbing) are strong predictors. PTSD is unlikely when any symptom is absent.

Source: Adapted from R.A. Bryant & A.G. Harvey, 2000, *Acute stress disorder: A handbook of theory, assessment, and treatment.* Washington, D.C.: American Psychological Association, p. 31.

to exposure to events like September 11. In general, however, trauma does not occur completely at random. Because they engage in more risky behavior, men, young people in their late teens and early 20s, people with a history of conduct disorders, and extroverts all are more likely to experience trauma. People who are anxious or who have a family history of mental illness also experience more trauma, but the reasons for this are less clear. Finally, minorities and people with less education also are exposed to more traumatic stress, because they are more likely to live in dangerous environments.

The development of PTSD following a trauma also is not random. Those who are "neurotic"—anxious and easily upset—are more likely to develop PTSD after a trauma, as are people with a family or personal history of mental disorder. Women and minorities also are more likely to suffer from PTSD following a trauma, for reasons that have yet to be elaborated (Breslau et al., 1991; Breslau et al., 1995; Breslau et al., 1998).

Course and Outcome Researchers have found that people who suffer from ASD are more likely to develop PTSD subsequently (Bryant & Harvey, 2000). The prediction is far from perfect, however, and two caveats bear special scrutiny. First, people with *subclinical* ASD, that is, with symptoms that are not severe or pervasive enough to meet diagnostic criteria, nevertheless are at greater risk for PTSD than trauma victims with relatively few psychological symptoms (Harvey & Bryant, 1999). Second, the different symptoms of ASD are not equally good in predicting future PTSD. The presence of three symptoms—numbing, depersonalization, and a sense of reliving the experience—are the best predictors of PTSD (Bryant & Harvey, 2000; see Figure 7–2).

Other research shows how the symptoms of PTSD diminish gradually as time passes. The National Comorbidity Survey found that the symptoms of PTSD improved fairly rapidly during the first year, but more gradually over the next several years (see Figure 7–3). Symptoms diminished faster among people who received treatment, although this correlational finding does not prove that treatment caused the improvement. Regardless of whether they received treatment, over one-third of people who had suffered from PTSD continued to report symptoms of the disorder 10 years after the traumatic event (Kessler et al., 1995).

PTSD can be a chronic disorder. One study found continuing symptoms among many World War II prisoners of war—40 years after confinement. Only 30 percent of POWs who had suffered from PTSD (as diagnosed by retrospective report) were fully recovered, while 60 percent still had mild to moderate symptoms. Another 10 percent either showed no recovery or had a deteriorating course (Kluznik et al., 1986).

Causes of PTSD and ASD

By definition, traumatic stressors cause ASD and PTSD. Because not every traumatized person develops ASD or PTSD, however, trauma is a necessary but not a sufficient cause of the disorders. An extremely important task for researchers, therefore, is identifying factors that increase people's risk or resilience in the face of trauma.

Social Factors in ASD and PTSD Scientists studying social factors and the risk for PTSD have focused primarily on (1) the nature of the trauma and the individual's level of exposure to it and (2) the availability of social support following the trauma. Victims of trauma are more likely to develop PTSD when the trauma is more intense, life-threatening, and involves greater exposure. For example, victims of attempted rape are more likely to develop PTSD if the rape is completed; if they are physically injured during the assault; and if they perceive the sexual assault as life-threatening (Kilpatrick et al., 1989). Similarly, PTSD is more prevalent in Vietnam veterans who were wounded, who were involved in the deaths of noncombatants, or who witnessed atrocities (Koenen et al., 2003; Oei, Lim, & Hennessy, 1990). A study of PTSD following September 11 found a greater prevalence among people who lived south of Canal Street, close to the World Trade Center (Galea et al., 2002).

As with less severe stressors, social support after a trauma can play a crucial role in alleviating long-term psychological damage. A lack of social support is thought to have contributed to the high prevalence of PTSD found among Vietnam veterans (Oei, Lim, & Hennessy, 1990). Rather than being praised as heroes, returning veterans often were treated with disdain. This made it difficult for many veterans to find meaning in their sacrifices, and likely increased their risk for PTSD. People who had little social

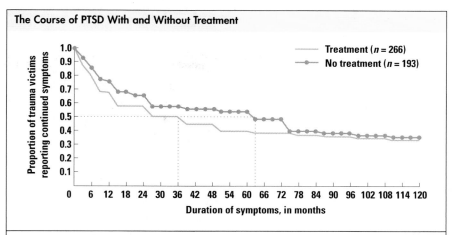

FIGURE 7–3: The symptoms of PTSD decline over time but persist for 10 years among one-third of people with the disorder. Treatment appears to hasten recovery, but this correlational finding may not mean causation.

Source: R.C. Kessler, A. Sonnega, E. Bromet, M. Hughes, and C.B. Nelson, 1995, Posttraumatic stress disorder in the National Comorbidity Survey, *Archives of General Psychiatry, 52,* 1057. Copyright © 1995. Reprinted by permission of American Medical Association.

support also were more likely to develop PTSD following September 11 (Galea et al., 2002).

A study of identical twins offers one of the strongest demonstrations of the importance of the environment in the etiology of PTSD. Among 715 MZ twin pairs who were discordant for military service in Southeast Asia during the Vietnam War era, the prevalence of PTSD was *nine times* higher for co-twins who served in Vietnam and experienced high levels of combat in comparison to their identical twin who did not serve (Goldberg et al., 1990).

Why do only some trauma victims suffer from PTSD?

Biological Factors in ASD and PTSD The same twin study provides some of the strongest evidence on biological factors in PTSD. In an analysis of more than 4,000 twin pairs, researchers found that MZ twins had a higher concordance rate than DZ twins for experiencing trauma, specifically exposure to combat. Following exposure to trauma, identical twins also had higher concordance rates for PTSD symptoms than did fraternal twins (True et al., 1993). Importantly, genetic contributions differed for various PTSD symptoms. Genes contributed most strongly to arousal/anxiety symptoms and least strongly to reexperiencing. Conversely, level of exposure to combat predicted symptoms of reexperiencing and avoidance but not arousal/anxiety (True et al., 1993).

What are some ways you could protect yourself from ASD or PTSD following a traumatic experience?

Rape crisis centers offer women support in dealing with sexual assault.

Edna Foa is a psychologist who has conducted extensive research on the etiology and treatment of PTSD.

Biological Effects of Exposure to Trauma A very different line of research focuses on the biological *consequences* of exposure to trauma and how these consequences may play a role in the maintenance of PTSD (Kaufman et al., 2004; Yehuda & McFarlane, 1995). People with PTSD show alterations in the functioning and perhaps even the structure of the amygdala and hippocampus, two biological findings consistent, respectively, with the experience of heightened fear reactivity and intrusive memories. Other evidence finds that PTSD is associated with increased levels of circulating norepinephrine and general psychophysiological arousal, for example, an increased resting heart rate (Yehuda, 2002). Together, the pattern of biological findings suggests that the sympathetic nervous system is aroused and the fear response is sensitized in PTSD.

The heightened reactivity may be due to the failure of the stress response system to shut down. As we discuss in Chapters 5 and 8, the *hypothalmic–pituitary–adrenal (HPA) axis* is an area of the brain known to be stimulated by normal stress. Normal stress increases the secretion of cortisol from the adrenal cortex. Surprisingly, however, people with PTSD show *lower* levels of cortisol availability. One possible explanation of this paradox is that cortisol serves the homeostatic function of shutting down biological systems that have been aroused by stress. This

suggests that the stress response system is activated but not turned off in PTSD (Yehuda, 2002).

Many brain systems surely are affected by trauma, at least temporarily. Still, it is not clear whether identified differences in brain function or structure reflect normal biological adaptations to stress, damage caused by trauma, or merely preexisting differences in the brain (Newport & Nemeroff, 2000; Pitman, 1997). In support of the last, all-important caution, one study of identical twins—including one Vietnam veteran with PTSD and his co-twin who neither served in Vietnam nor suffered from PTSD—found smaller than average hippocampus volume in the twin with PTSD *and* in his unaffected co-twin (Gilbertson et al., 2002). Even though neuroimaging gives us exciting new measurements, we still need to remember basic concerns about correlation and causation.

Psychological Factors in ASD and PTSD An early and important perspective on psychological contributions to PTSD focuses on two-factor theory. According to **two-factor theory,** classical conditioning *creates* fears when the terror inherent in trauma is paired with the cues associated with the traumatic event. Operant conditioning, in turn, *maintains* the fears (Keane, Zimering, & Caddell, 1985). Specifically, when fear-producing situations are avoided, the avoidance is negatively reinforced by the reduction of anxiety. For example, Stephanie's fears of being alone at night—when she was attacked—are easy to conceptualize as a result of classical conditioning. If she continued to avoid being alone at night, her symptoms would have been maintained by operant conditioning (reduced anxiety). Thus, Stephanie's courage in confronting her fears not only was admirable but also was a major step in easing her PTSD.

More recent psychological perspectives focus on individual differences in the risk for ASD and PTSD. In addition to preexisting mental health problems, research indicates that cognitive factors such as expectancies, preparedness, and control influence the risk for PTSD following a trauma. For example, pilots with prior crash training cope more successfully with helicopter crashes than pilots who have received no training, presumably because training increases preparedness (Shalev, 1996). The importance of preparedness and control also is supported by evidence that, despite greater physical suffering, political activists develop fewer psychological symptoms than nonactivists following torture

(Basoglu et al., 1997). On the other hand, negative appraisals—the rape victim who blames herself or driver who think he could have avoided an accident—are strongly tied to an increased risk for PTSD (Dunmore et al., 2001; Halligan et al., 2003; McNally et al., 2003).

Some theories suggest that dissociation is an unconscious defense that helps victims cope with trauma (Oei, Lim, & Hennessy, 1990). However, research indicates that dissociation is associated with more not less PTSD (Ehlers, Mayou, & Bryant, 1998; Griffin, Resick, & Mechanic, 1997; Harvey, Bryant, & Dang, 1998). Among a sample of Israeli war trauma victims, for example, more dissociation reported within 1 week following a trauma predicted *more* severe PTSD 6 months later (Shalev et al., 1996).

Dissociation may not be adaptive, but most theorists agree that victims of trauma must, over time, find a balance between gradually facing their painful emotions while not being overwhelmed by them. Psychologist Edna Foa, a leading PTSD researcher, has highlighted the importance of *emotional processing*, which involves facing fear, diminishing its intensity, and coming to some new understanding about the trauma and its consequences (Foa & Riggs, 1995; Foa & Street, 2001). According to Foa, three elements are essential for successful emotional processing. First, victims must allow themselves to be emotionally engaged with their traumatic memories. Second, victims need to find a way to articulate and organize their chaotic experience. Third, victims must learn how to develop a balanced view of the world—to come to believe that, despite the trauma, the world is not a terrible place (Foa & Riggs, 1995; Foa & Street, 2001; see Figure 7–4).

Integrating the experience of trauma with broader memories and beliefs involves the task of *meaning making*—finding some broader reason or higher value for enduring the trauma (Ehlers & Clark, 2000). Stephanie, for example, found meaning in her public speaking and by making people more aware of sexual assault, its prevention, and consequences.

Integration and Alternative Pathways   The combined evidence suggests alternative pathways can lead to ASD and PTSD. Anyone might develop ASD or PTSD given a critical level of exposure and a trauma of sufficient intensity. In other cases, a trauma may call attention to or exacerbate a pre-existing psychological disorder. In most cases,

however, trauma is a necessary but not sufficient cause of PTSD. The development of PTSD results from a combination of factors, including personality characteristics that predate the trauma, exposure during the trauma, and emotional processing and social support afterwards (Ozer et al., 2003; Ozer & Weiss, 2004).

Prevention and Treatment of ASD and PTSD

We know that trauma causes ASD and PTSD, and this leads to a very important question: Can we prevent the disorders with early intervention? Many experts hope that prevention is possible, and in this section, we consider emergency help designed to facilitate coping with trauma, treatments for ASD designed to prevent PTSD, and various treatments for PTSD.

How might biological, psychological, and social risk factors combine to cause PTSD?

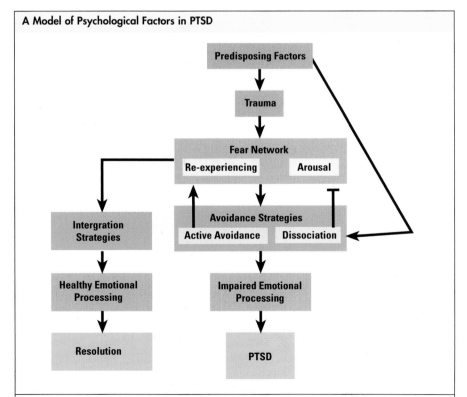

A Model of Psychological Factors in PTSD

FIGURE 7–4: Trauma victims may develop PTSD if they avoid their fears (which may be caused by dissociation or predisposing personality factors). In contrast, repeated attempts to integrate the trauma into one's experience—to find meaning in the horror—leads to healthy emotional processing and resolution.

Source: Adapted from: R.A. Bryant & A.G. Harvey, 2000, *Acute stress disorder: A handbook of theory, assessment, and treatment.* Washington, D.C. American Psychological Association, p. 38.

A medical worker comforts a distraught woman seeking treatment at a hospital following the collapse of the World Trade Center. Brief psychological treatments often are offered in the aftermath of trauma, but it is not clear if early intervention prevents ASD and PTSD.

Emergency Help for Trauma Victims The potential for preventing PTSD is so important that the Federal Emergency Management Agency, the government agency that deals with natural and man-made disasters, is required to provide special funding to community mental health centers during disasters. Emergency treatments range from intensive individual counseling sessions with hurricane victims to group discussions with children following an episode of school violence (Litz, 2004). Intervention approaches differ greatly, but offering immediate social support to trauma victims is a common goal of all early interventions (McNally et al., 2003; Raphael et al., 1996).

Perhaps the most widely used early intervention is **critical incident stress debriefing (CISD),** a single 1- to 5-hour group meeting offered within 1 to 3 days following a disaster. CISD is involves several phases where participants share their experiences and reactions, and group leaders offer education, assessment, and referral if necessary (Mitchell, 1982; Mitchell & Dyregrov, 1993). Many participants find CISD to be helpful, but some experts argue that CISD can be detrimental because it arouses too many emotions too soon after trauma (Shalev, in press). Not surprisingly, CISD is difficult to evaluate, since it is conducted in the midst of a crisis. Still, research to date provides no evidence that CISD prevents future PTSD (Bryant & Harvey, 2000; McNally et al., 2003). More systematic research is needed, especially on promising cognitive behavioral alternatives to CISD (Neuner et al., 2004).

Since World War I, interventions with soldiers who drop out of combat have been based on the three principles of offering (1) immediate treatment in the (2) proximity of the battlefield with

the (3) expectation of return to the front lines upon recovery. The effectiveness of these treatment principles was not studied systematically until a 1982 evaluation of the Israeli army during the Lebanon war. Results indicated that 60 percent of soldiers treated near the front recovered sufficiently to return to battle within 72 hours. Soldiers who expected to return to the front experienced lower rates of PTSD than did those who did not expect to return to battle. In addition, those soldiers who were treated on the front lines were less likely to develop PTSD subsequently when compared to soldiers who were treated in civilian facilities away from the battlefield (Oei, Lim, & Hennessy, 1990).

The trauma of combat and the structure of the military make generalization of these principles to other traumas difficult, but the goals are logical ones to modify to fit the unique circumstances of other traumas. Former Mayor Rudolph Giuliani followed these principles when, in the immediate aftermath of September 11, he regularly encouraged New Yorkers to grieve but also to go back to work, to go out, and to go on despite the horrors of the World Trade Center attacks. Such naturalistic efforts by community leaders may be more appealing, and perhaps as effective, as more artificial debriefings. Government agencies allocated over $150 million to pay for psychotherapy for New Yorkers in the wake of September 11, but $90 million remained unspent as of May 2003 (McNally et al., 2003).

Treatment of ASD Few studies of the treatment of ASD have been conducted, a circumstance that is not surprising given that the diagnosis was developed only recently. Nevertheless, some research indicates that structured interventions with ASD can lead to the prevention of future PTSD. Unlike CISD, these treatments last longer and target the select group of trauma victims who meet ASD diagnostic criteria. The empirically backed ASD treatments are based on the principles of cognitive behavior therapy (described shortly), although they are briefer, involving five $1\frac{1}{2}$ hour sessions (Bryant & Harvey, 2000; Bryant et al., in press).

Cognitive Behavior Therapy for PTSD Psychotherapists who specialize in PTSD suggest some general principles for the psychological treatment of the disorder. In the order in which they are likely to be addressed in therapy, these include (1) establishing a trusting therapeutic relationship,

(2) providing education about the process of coping with trauma, (3) stress-management training, (4) encouraging the reexperience of the trauma, and (5) integrating the traumatic event into the individual's experience (Scurfield, 1985).

Reexposure to the traumatic event is perhaps the least obvious, but most important, of these strategies (Frueh, Turner, & Beidel, 1995; Rothbaum & Foa, 1996). Therapeutic approaches differ in how reexposure is encouraged, yet all treatments require the reliving of trauma in some form. Depending on the client, the therapist, and the circumstances of the trauma, *prolonged exposure* might involve confronting feared situations *in vivo*, confronting fears in one's imagination, or recalling the trauma for extended periods of time. Prolonged exposure therapy typically includes additional cognitive behavior therapy components, for example, challenging automatic maladaptive thoughts that can result from the experience of trauma such as, "No one cares" or "The world is hopeless."

Mounting evidence supports the effectiveness of various cognitive behavioral treatments (Resick & Calhoun, 2001). A study of rape victims found that prolonged exposure, involving repeated reliving of the trauma over nine therapy sessions, produced more long-term reductions in PTSD symptoms than did three alternatives: (1) stress inoculation training (focusing on relaxation and stress management), (2) supportive counseling (which explicitly omitted exposure procedures), and (3) a wait list control group (Foa et al., 1991). Stress inoculation training produced more *short-term* benefits, but prolonged exposure was more effective in the long run. Reliving traumatic events is painful initially, and it may appear to impede progress. However, this painful reexperiencing may be exactly the right therapy (Foa et al., 2002). An important element in overcoming traumatic experience is confronting the experience in memory, in discussions, or, if practical and humane, in real life.

A related cognitive behavior therapy treatment, *imagery rehearsal therapy,* also can diminish recurrent nightmares, a troubling problem frequently associated with PTSD. Imagery rehearsal involves teaching clients that nightmares result from habit as well as trauma, and encouraging them to relive the nightmares while awake but to rewrite the nightmare script in any way they wish. Relatively brief group therapy not only reduces nightmares but improves sleep and also helps alleviate other symptoms of PTSD in

sexual assault survivors (Krakow et al., 2001). Other cognitive behavior therapy techniques that involve reliving and cognitively restructuring the traumatic experience also show promise in treating PTSD (Bryant et al., 2003; Resick et al., 2002).

EMDR   We should comment on one more exposure therapy for PTSD, *eye movement desensitization and reprocessing* (EMDR), a technique that has been greeted with considerable enthusiasm—and skepticism. Psychologist Francine Shapiro (1995) "discovered" that rapid back-and-forth eye movements reduced her own anxiety, and she soon applied the technique to her clients. She and her proponents have taught EMDR to thousands of practitioners, and case studies and limited research attest to the treatment's effectiveness, particularly in treating PTSD. However, many experts are skeptical of EMDR due to the lack of a theoretical basis for the treatment (Lohr et al., 1992). In fact, a recent meta-analysis concluded that EMDR can be an effective treatment—to the extent that it incorporates prolonged exposure. However, eye movements add nothing to the treatment's effectiveness (Davidson & Parker, 2001).

Antidepressant Medication   A recent consensus statement on the treatment of PTSD concluded that antidepressant medication and psychotherapy involving therapeutic reexposure are the two "first-line" therapies for PTSD (Ballenger et al., 2000). The recommendation of using antidepressants for PTSD is quite recent (Ledoux & Gorman, 2001). Their effectiveness likely is at least partially due to

Treatment of a traumatized soldier in Iraq.

the high comorbidity between PTSD and depression (Newport & Nemeroff, 2000). Traditional antianxiety medications, including the benzodiazepines, are not effective in treating PTSD.

DISSOCIATIVE DISORDERS

If the dissociative symptoms found in ASD and PTSD are dramatic, the symptoms of **dissociative disorders**—characterized by persistent, maladaptive disruptions in the integration of memory, consciousness, or identity—verge on the unbelievable. The person with a dissociative disorder may be unable to remember many details about the past; he or she may wander far from home and perhaps assume a

new identity; or two or more personalities may coexist within the same person. These apparently real but rare psychological problems raise probing questions not only about the disorders themselves but about the very nature of the human psyche.

Until recent years, dissociative disorders were of more interest to theorists and novelists than to psychological scientists. You may be familiar with dramatic portrayals for *multiple personality disorder*, as one of these disorders used to be called, in *Sybil* or the *The Three Faces of Eve*, both of which were widely read and made into popular motion pictures. Interest in dissociative disorders has grown among mental health professionals, but dissociative disorders are controversial and research is limited. We introduce these extraordinary problems in the following case study.

◆◆

CASE STUDY   Dissociative Fugue—Dallae's Journey

Dallae disappeared mysteriously during final exams during her junior year at a California university. Her roommate last saw Dallae when she was studying for her organic chemistry exam. Dallae had been agitated that night. She left her room several times and kept interrupting her roommate, who was cramming for the same exam. Dallae did not take the exam the next day. When she missed two more final exams, her roommate contacted the authorities.

At first, the police suspected foul play, because it did not seem likely that Dallae had left college on her own. None of her personal possessions were missing from her room; even her eyeglasses were still sitting on her desk. However, bank records indicated that Dallae withdrew all of her money from her bank account the day before the exam. Investigators also discovered that Dallae had been lying to her parents. She had told them that she had an A average in organic chemistry. In fact, she was failing the course, and she had not attended her laboratory section for almost 2 months.

When the local police failed to locate Dallae, they contacted the FBI. After a 4-week investigation, Dallae was located in a college town on the East Coast, where she was identified from a missing persons report. She had been brought to a hospital emergency room after she was found wandering on the streets.

At the time, she appeared confused and disoriented. She told the ER physician that her name was Dawn and that she had been living on the streets and sleeping in dormitory lounges. She said that she had just moved from the West Coast and had come to the town because she hoped eventually to attend the university. She gave a vague and sketchy account about other details of her life. For example, she could not say how she got to the East Coast.

Dallae allowed herself to be voluntarily admitted to the hospital's psychiatric unit. There she talked little and spent most of her time watching television. She told the staff that she was Vietnamese and had been adopted by American parents, but her stories continued to be vague and inconsistent. She said that she didn't remember things, but she did not seem greatly distressed by her memory impairment. A CAT scan and neuropsychological tests detected no physical abnormalities or deficits in short-term memory or motor functioning.

A hospital social worker contacted the local police about the disoriented young patient, and the police were able to identify Dallae from an FBI report. The social worker contacted Dallae's parents shortly thereafter, and her mother immediately flew east to see her. When her mother appeared at the hospital, Dallae did not recognize her. Her mother

was greatly distressed by Dallae's indifference, and she noted other puzzling oddities and inconsistencies. For one thing, Dallae was not Vietnamese, and she was not adopted. She had grown up with her married parents, who were Korean immigrants. Her mother also noted that although Dallae was right-handed, she used her left hand to write a note on the ward. Dallae's consistent use of her left hand was confirmed by the staff and by the neuropsychologist who had tested her.

Two nights after her mother arrived, Dallae's memories apparently returned. That night, she attempted suicide by slashing her wrists, but she was discovered by a hospital staff member, who quickly stopped the bleeding. Dallae was intermittently depressed and extremely agitated for the next several days, especially after seeing her mother. Although she would not talk at length, her conversation indicated that much of her memory was now intact, and she began writing with her right hand again.

During the next 2 weeks, Dallae gradually related details about her life to the psychologist who was treating her. Dallae had been a quiet and obedient girl all through her childhood. Dallae's parents worked very hard, and they had high ambitions for their three children. Dallae's older brother had an MBA and was a very successful young executive. Her older sister currently was editor of the law review at a prestigious law school. Ever since she was a young child, Dallae's parents had planned for her to become a doctor. In fact, all her life her parents had told friends and relatives that Dallae would be a doctor one day.

During discussions with her therapist, Dallae began to talk more freely. She noted that she had been terrified to tell her parents about her grades and her lack of interest in medicine, especially her father. Her father put endless pressure on Dallae to fulfill what she

saw as his dream. She cried at length when relating how he had struck her across the face during the previous Thanksgiving break, when she tried to tell him that she no longer wanted to study medicine.

After spending 6 weeks in the hospital, Dallae was released, and she returned to California with her parents. Her memory was intact at the time of the discharge, except that she continued to have no recollection of her trip across the country or of many of her days

living on the streets. She remained uncertain why she thought her name was Dawn, although she did mention being influenced by a television show she had seen about a Vietnamese child who had been adopted. At the time of Dallae's discharge, her depression had abated somewhat, and she was no longer actively suicidal. She reported being relieved at having told her mother about her feelings about medical school, but she remained very anxious about facing her father.

◆◆◆

Dallae suffered from *dissociative fugue*, a rare and unusual disorder characterized by sudden, unplanned travel, the inability to remember details about the past, and confusion about identity or the assumption of a new identity. Dissociative fugue typically follows a traumatic event. For example, it is sometimes observed among soldiers following a particularly gruesome battle. For Dallae, perhaps her poor grades could be considered traumatic, given her father's intense and constant pressure to succeed.

The travel in dissociative fugue is purposeful, despite the memory impairments. Dallae knew where she was going, and she could provide at least a vague explanation about why she was going there. Purposeful travel is the distinguishing symptom, but the core questions about fugue—and about all dissociative disorders—concern the split between conscious and unconscious psychological experience. How could Dallae be aware of the present but still be unaware of her past? Why didn't all her memories return after she saw her mother? Could she be faking part or all of her "illness"? Several key figures in the history of abnormal psychology have tried to answer such perplexing questions. In fact, attempts to explain these puzzling disorders resulted in some of the first theories about unconscious psychological processes and human awareness.

Hysteria and the Unconscious

Dissociative disorders (and somatoform disorders, which we discuss later in the chapter) once were viewed as expressions of hysteria. In Greek, *hystera* means "uterus," and the term **hysteria** reflects ancient speculation that these disorders were caused by frustrated sexual desires,

particularly the desire to have a baby. According to the theory, the uterus becomes detached from its normal location and moves about the body, causing a problem in the location where it eventually lodges. Variants of this somewhat sexist view continued throughout Western history, and as late as the nineteenth century many physicians erroneously believed that hysteria occurred only among women (Showalter, 1997).

Charcot, Freud, and Janet   New speculation about the etiology of hysteria emerged toward the end of the nineteenth century. Jean Charcot, who used hypnosis both to treat and to induce hysteria, was particularly influential. Charcot greatly influenced the thinking of Freud, who observed Charcot's hypnotic treatments early in his training. Charcot also had a strong influence on the work of Freud's contemporary and rival, Pierre Janet (1859–1947). Janet was a French philosophy professor who conducted psychological experiments on dissociation and who later trained as a physician in Charcot's clinic.

Both Janet and Freud were eager to explain and treat hysteria, and the problem led both of them to develop theories about unconscious mental processes. The two competitors differed sharply in their views. Janet saw dissociation as an abnormal process. To him, detachment from conscious awareness occurred only as a part of psychopathology. In contrast, Freud considered dissociation as a normal process, a routine means through which the ego defended itself against unacceptable unconscious thoughts. Freud saw dissociation and repression as similar processes, and, in fact, he often used the two terms interchangeably (Erdelyi, 1990; Perry & Laurence, 1984). Thus Freud viewed dissociative and somatoform disorders to be merely two of many expressions of unconscious conflict.

Pierre Janet (1859–1947) *conducted psychological experiments as a professor in Paris, and he later trained as a physician in Jean Charcot's clinic. Janet's views on dissociation were much more circumscribed than those of his rival, Sigmund Freud.*

The French neurologist Jean Charcot (1825–1893) demonstrating a case of hysteria at the Salpetiere, a famous hospital in Paris.

The two theorists criticized each other frequently. Janet thought that Freud greatly overstated the importance of the unconscious; Freud thought that Janet greatly underestimated it. Janet's work became increasingly obscure, however, as Freudian theory dominated the mental health professions throughout much of the twentieth century. As Freudian influences have declined in recent years, scholars have rediscovered Janet's contributions and his more narrow conception of dissociation and unconscious mental processes.

Cognitive Science and the Unconscious   Contemporary psychologists generally agree about two things. First, unconscious processes do exist, and they play a role in both normal and abnormal emotion and cognition (Epstein, 1994). The challenge of explaining unconscious mental processes is a real one in cognitive science, not merely a remnant of Freudian theory. For example, we are unaware of how we remember. We remember a forgotten event without knowing the strategy we used to access the memory.

Second, contemporary cognitive scientists continue to debate the importance of unconscious mental events. For example, one cognitive scientist has said that the unconscious mind is "dumb," not "smart" (Loftus & Klinger, 1992). From this perspective, unconscious mental processes are of limited importance in our mental life. Other experts suggest a more elaborate model of unconscious mental processes—for example, that we have two systems of information processing: a rational system and an emotionally driven experiential system (Epstein, 1994). The *rational system* involves abstract, logical knowledge that is adaptive for solving complex problems over time. The *experiential system* involves intuitive knowledge based on experience that is adaptive for responding to problems immediately without the delay of thought. The experiential system thus is emotional, powerful, and often illogical (Epstein, 1994). Rationally, we might know that airplanes are safer than automobiles, for example, but emotionally, we are more likely to fear airplanes—especially in the wake of September 11.

Whatever their theory, contemporary cognitive scientists insist that hypotheses about unconscious mental processes must be tested in research. In fact, scientists have created new research techniques to study unconscious processes, for example, the distinction between explicit and implicit memory. *Explicit memory* is the conscious recollection of a past event. **Implicit memory** is indicated by changes in behavior apparently based on a memory of a prior event but with no conscious remembering of the event (Schacter, 1987). To illustrate the distinction, consider the problem of *prosopagnosia*, an impairment of face recognition that sometimes follows specific forms of brain damage. Patients with prosopagnosia have no explicit memory for faces, that is, they are unable to recognize people they know. However, they demonstrate the normal preference for viewing faces that are familiar, even though they claim that the face is not familiar to them (Farah, O'Reilly, & Vecera, 1993). Apparently, patients have an *implicit memory* for familiar faces—that is, recognition occurs at some lower level of perception or consciousness. Such findings indicate a dissociation between conscious and unconscious cognitive processing.

Hypnosis: Altered State or Social Role?   The nature of **hypnosis,** in which subjects experience loss of control over their actions in response to suggestions from the hypnotist, is a topic of historical importance and contemporary debate about the unconscious mind. All agree that demonstrations of the power of hypnotic suggestion are impressive, and that different people are more or less susceptible to hypnosis. However, some experts assert that hypnosis is the dissociative experience of an altered state of consciousness. Others argue that hypnosis is merely a social role, where the subject voluntarily complies with suggestions due to social expectations and demands (Barnier, 2002; Kihlstrom, 1998b; Kirsch & Lynn, 1995, 1998; Woody &

Sadler, 1998). Beware of concluding that hypnosis must be real and powerful because you have seen it at work in a group demonstration. The trick that hypnotists use in this circumstance is to select only highly susceptible (or highly compliant!) participants for demonstration purposes.

Symptoms of Dissociative Disorders

Like many ordinary cognitive processes, the extraordinary symptoms of dissociative disorders apparently involve mental processing that occurs outside of conscious awareness. Extreme cases of dissociation include a split in the functioning of the individual's entire sense of self. In *dissociative identity disorder* (DID), two or more personalities coexist within a single individual, and one or both of the personalities may be unaware of the existence of the other. Unless we assume that the symptom is feigned, dissociative identity disorder demonstrates that the mind can function on multiple levels of consciousness.

Depersonalization is a less dramatic form of dissociation wherein people feel detached from themselves or their social or physical environment. Examples of depersonalization include feeling like a stranger in social interactions and out-of-body experiences—feelings of detachment from one's physical being, for example, the sensation of floating outside yourself and watching your actions as if you were another person.

Another dramatic example of dissociation is *amnesia*—the partial or complete loss of recall for particular events or for a particular period of time. Brain injury or disease can cause amnesia, but *psychogenic* (psychologically caused) amnesia results from traumatic stress or other emotional distress. Psychogenic amnesia may occur alone or in conjunction with other dissociative experiences. For example, in dissociative identity disorder one personality may not remember the actions, or even the existence, of another (Spiegel & Cardena, 1991).

Trauma and Dissociative Symptoms   It is widely accepted that fugue and psychogenic amnesia are usually precipitated by trauma, thus providing another link between dissociation and traumatic stress disorders. In these disorders, the trauma is clear and usually sudden, and in most cases, psychological functioning rapidly returns to normal. Much more controversial is the role that trauma might play in dissociative identity disorder (DID). Some researchers and clinicians argue that DID is linked with past, not present, trauma, particularly with chronic child physical or sexual abuse (Gleaves, 1996). Many psychological scientists are skeptical about this assertion, however, because information about childhood trauma is based solely on clients' reports—reports that may be distorted by many factors, including by a therapist's expectations (Kihlstrom, 2005. Lilienfeld et al., 1999). A related issue is the very controversial topic of **recovered memories,** dramatic recollections of long-ago traumatic experiences supposedly blocked from the conscious mind by dissociation (see Critical Thinking *Matters*).

Do you believe in the phenomena of recovered memories, dissociative identity disorder, hypnosis, and conversion reactions?

Diagnosis of Dissociative Disorders

Brief Historical Perspective   For centuries, theorists considered dissociative and somatoform disorders as alternative forms of hysteria. However, the descriptive approach to classification introduced in DSM-III (1980) led to the separation of dissociative and somatoform disorders into discrete diagnostic categories. The distinction is preserved in DSM-IV-TR (2000), because the symptoms of the two disorders differ greatly. Consistent with DSM-IV-TR, we review the two problems separately. We nevertheless discuss both problems in a single chapter because of their historical relationship and because both apparently involve unconscious processes.

Contemporary Classification   DSM-IV-TR distinguishes four major subtypes of dissociative disorders: dissociative fugue, dissociative amnesia, depersonalization disorder, and dissociative

Hypnotized college students reacting to the suggestion that they are on a beach in Hawaii. Performance hypnotists produce such dramatic effects by selecting only highly suggestible subjects for their demonstrations.

critical thinking matters

RECOVERED MEMORIES?

In 1990, George Franklin was convicted of the brutal murder of an 8-year-old girl. The crime occurred over 20 years earlier, and the major evidence was the "recovered memory" of Franklin's daughter Eileen. Eileen claimed she witnessed her father commit the rape and murder, but dissociation pushed the memory into her unconscious mind. Twenty years later, according to the daughter, the memory returned. Eileen provided both verifiable and inconsistent accounts of the horrifying event. She recalled a smashed ring on her friend's finger as she raised her hand to protect herself from a blow with a rock. Records corroborated the incident. On the other hand, Eileen changed her story about the time of day of the murder and whether her sister was riding in the van with them. Based solely on his daughter's testimony, George Franklin was convicted in 1990. However, his conviction was overturned in 1995, and he was released from prison. A U.S. District Court judge ruled that the lower court erred in excluding evidence that Eileen could have learned details of the 1969 murder from newspaper articles. The prosecutor decided not to retry the case when Eileen's sister revealed they both were hypnotized before the first trial—a fact Eileen lied about—and Eileen accused her father of a second murder but DNA evidence cleared him.

Was Eileen's memory accurate or fiction? Our concern about so-called recovered memories extends well beyond the Franklin case. As many as 25 percent of therapists say that recovering memories, particularly of sexual abuse, is an important part of therapy with female clients, and they use some dubious strategies to help their clients "remember" (Poole et al., 1995). Popular books also encourage people to search for (create?) memories that they do not recall, for example, in *The Courage to Heal,* the authors state:

> You may think you don't have memories, but often as you begin to talk about what you do remember, there emerges a constellation of feelings, reactions, and recollections that add up to substantial information. To say "I was abused," you don't need the kind of recall that would stand up in a court of law . . . Often the knowledge that you were abused starts with a tiny feeling, an intuition. It's important to trust that inner voice and work from there. Assume your feelings

are valid. So far, no one we've talked to thought she might have been abused and then later discovered that she hadn't been. (Bass & Davis, 1988, p. 22)

Despite the authors' claims, could such suggestions lead some people to create memories about events that never happened? Faced with accusations of past abuse, many parents say that misguided therapists are creating false memories, not helping troubled young adults. In fact, the term, *false memory syndrome,* was coined to account for the implanting of false beliefs (Kihlstrom, 1998a).

Are recovered memories examples of dissociation or of the power of suggestion? Determining the truth in the individual case may be impossible. Still, research clearly shows that memories, even of highly dramatic events, can be inaccurate (Loftus, 2003, 2004). In one study, researchers interviewed people the day after the space shuttle *Challenger* exploded, and detailed how participants learned of the tragedy. Three years later, they asked the same people to remember what they were doing, and about one-third reported vivid and grossly inaccurate memories (Neisser & Harsch, 1992). In another study, researchers created false memories of "sliming" a first or second grade teacher (putting Slime in the teacher's desk) among fully 65% of participants. The key to the deception was using actual school photos to help participants to "remember" (Lindsay et al., 2004).

Psychologist Elizabeth Loftus (2003, 2004), a memory researcher who has been an expert witness in many trials, clearly questions the validity of "recovered memories" from early in life, because few people can report *any* accurate memories before age 3 or 4. Even the most generous scientific claims date the very earliest accurate memories to no younger than 18 to 24 months (Howe, 2003).

The fact that people are especially likely to remember emotionally intense events is another reason to think critically about claims of recovered memories. Research does show that some documented victims of sexual abuse do not recall the experience many years later (Williams, 1994), but most do remember what happened (Goodman et al., 2003)—and many victims who do not remember were very young when they were abused. And, of course, documented cases of forgetting do not prove

that undocumented cases of remembering are accurate! Furthermore, research shows that people who report a history of child sexual abuse are *not* more likely to forget trauma-related material on laboratory tasks. However, people who report recovered memories of sexual abuse *are* more prone to develop false memories on laboratory measures. Studies on people who claim to have a recovered memory, but one that certainly is untrue—abduction by space aliens—also show that these people develop more false memories in the laboratory (McNally, 2003).

Scientific research does do not prove that memories of trauma are false (Gleaves et al., 2004). Still, the malleability of memory suggests many reasons for skepticism. One key question is whether some claims of recovered memories might be more accurate than others. For example, perhaps someone who claims to remember a trauma she once knew about, but had not thought about for years, is more accurate than someone who claims to have learned about a trauma for the first time through a recovered memory (McNally, 2003). The latter reports might be especially inaccurate when therapists have used dubious techniques to help victims "remember." Sadly, these people may be victims of their therapists, not of abuse.

Where were you when the World Trade Center towers collapsed? Researchers find that even powerful "flashbulb" memories of dramatic events often grow inaccurate over time.

identity disorder. **Dissociative fugue** is characterized by sudden and unexpected travel away from home, an inability to recall the past, and confusion about identity or the assumption of a new identity. The case of Dallae is an example of dissociative fugue.

Dissociative amnesia involves a sudden inability to recall extensive and important personal information that exceeds normal forgetfulness. The memory loss in dissociative amnesia is not attributable to substance abuse, head trauma, or a cognitive disorder, such as Alzheimer's disease. As with fugue, dissociative amnesia typically is characterized by a sudden onset in response to trauma or extreme stress and by an equally sudden recovery of memory. The most common form of amnesia in dissociative disorders is *selective amnesia*, in which patients do not lose their memory completely but instead are unable to remember only selected personal events and information, often events related to a traumatic experience. In one study of 25 patients in a dissociative disorders clinic, 76 percent had selective amnesia (Coons & Milstein, 1988, cited in Spiegel & Cardena, 1991). The following case study provides one dramatic account, based on an article written by David Grann for the *New York Times* (January 13, 2002).

BRIEF CASE STUDY

A New York City Firefighter's Amnesia for September 11

Kevin Shea, a firefighter for the Fire Department of New York, was one of the very few survivors rescued from the wreckage of the World Trade Center. On the evening of September 11, Shea was found buried under a pile of rubble, his thumb severed and his neck broken in three places. Fortunately, Shea was not paralyzed by his spinal injury, but, like his neck, Shea's memory was badly fractured.

Shea could remember his past and a few events from early on the day of September 11. For example, he could remember volunteering to help, even though he was off duty, and jumping on his firehouse's Engine 40 to rush downtown. As the engine approached the scene, he remembered seeing people falling from high floors of the towers. After this, however, Shea had no real memory of September 11, not until after he was hospitalized late in the day. For example, he had no

memory of either tower collapsing, even though he was there at the horrifying, chaotic scene.

Shea is a firefighter who deeply values bravery, and who lost every member of his engine in the WTC rescue attempt. He became desperate to learn that he survived despite trying to save others and not because he instead focused on saving himself. Through diligent efforts in the months after September 11, he was able to piece together some evidence about what happened that day. A few of the details he discovered brought back fragments of his memory. For example, when another firefighter reminded him that they had embraced in the command center of the south tower shortly before it collapsed, Shea remembered the event. However, other aspects of Shea's memory did not return. No memories returned when Shea met another firefighter who himself was injured while trying to rescue Shea. No memories returned when Shea talked with yet another injured firefighter who rode in an ambulance with him after the rescue. No memories returned even when Shea was shown a photo of himself lying injured, almost unconscious, in the street near the south tower, just moments before it collapsed.

It is unclear whether Shea suffered from dissociative amnesia due to the emotional trauma of the day, or whether his memory loss was caused by a blow to his head. Although by all accounts Kevin Shea was a hero, he could not convince himself of the truth of this assessment, because he could not remember how he acted during the WTC disaster on September 11.

Depersonalization disorder is a less dramatic problem that is characterized by severe and persistent feelings of being detached from oneself. Depersonalization experiences include such sensations as feeling as though you were in a dream or were floating above your body and observing yourself act. Occasional depersonalization experiences are normal and are reported by about half the population. In depersonalization disorder, however, such experiences are persistent or recurrent, and they cause marked personal distress. The onset of the disorder commonly follows a new or disturbing event, such as drug use. All depersonalization experiences are "as-if" feelings, not rigid, delusional beliefs. In fact, some experts question whether depersonalization should be considered a type of dissociative disorder. Unlike other dissociative disorders, depersonalization disorder involves only limited splitting between conscious and unconscious mental processes, and no memory loss occurs (Spiegel & Cardena, 1991).

To many people, the most fascinating subtype of dissociative disorder is **dissociative identity disorder (DID),** a condition also known as **multiple personality disorder.** This unusual mental disorder is characterized by the existence of two or more distinct personalities in a single individual. At least two of these personalities repeatedly take control of the person's behavior, and the individual's inability to recall information is too extensive to be explained by ordinary forgetfulness. The original personality especially is likely to have amnesia for subsequent personalities, which may or may not be aware of the "alternates" (Aldridge-Morris, 1989). Recent case histories have identified more and more alternate personalities in DID. The case of "Eve," published in 1957, identified 3 personalities; "Sybil" was reported to have 16 personalities in a 1973 best-seller (the veracity of which has been questioned; Rieber, 1999); and some more recent cases have claimed to have a 100, even 1,000, alters. Not surprisingly, such claims have generated more controversy about a diagnosis that already was controversial.

Kevin Shea, a firefighter for the FDNY, received numerous injuries, including a broken vertebrae, working as a rescue worker during the World Trade Center attacks. Shea also suffered from amnesia, perhaps as a result of a blow to the head or perhaps from emotional causes.

◆◆◆

BRIEF CASE STUDY
The Three Faces of Eve

Perhaps the best-known case history of multiple personality disorder was detailed in Thigpen and Cleckley's 1957 book, *The Three Faces of Eve,* which was made into a motion picture. Thigpen and Cleckley, two psychiatrists who treated the young woman, described the case of Eve White, a young mother with a troubled marriage who sought psychotherapy for severe headaches, feelings of inertia, and "blackouts." Eve White was seen for several therapy sessions and was hypnotized during this time as a treatment for her amnesia. Then, during what proved to be a remarkable session, Eve White became agitated and complained of hearing an imaginary voice. As Thigpen and Cleckley wrote, "After a tense moment of silence, her hands dropped. There was a quick, reckless smile and, in a bright voice that sparkled, she said, 'Hi there, Doc!'" (p. 137). Eve Black had emerged—a carefree and flirtatious personality who insisted upon being called "Miss" and who scorned Eve White, the wife and mother.

Therapy with Eve White, Eve Black, and a third, more calm and mature personality, Jane, lasted over a period of $2\frac{1}{2}$ years. Thigpen used hypnosis to bring out the different personalities in an attempt to understand and reconcile them with one another. He eventually adopted the goal of fading out the two Eves and allowing Jane to take control. Therapy appeared to be successful. According to the psychiatrists' account, treatment ended with one integrated personality in control. This personality was much like Jane, but she decided to call herself "Mrs. Evelyn White."

The end of therapy with Thigpen and Cleckley was not the end of therapy for "Eve." Eve, whose real name is Chris Sizemore, claims to have had a total of 22 different personalities, some of which developed before her treatment with Thigpen and Cleckley and some of which developed afterward. The personalities always occurred in groups of three, and they always included a wife/mother image, a party girl, and a more normal, intellectual personality (Sizemore & Pittillo, 1977). Sizemore has written several books about her life, and as a well-functioning, unified personality, she has become a spokesperson for mental health concerns. In her book, *A Mind of Her Own,* she offers the following observations on her personalities:

Among these twenty-two alters, ten were poets, seven were artists, and one had taught tailoring. Today, I paint and write, but I cannot sew. Yet these alters were not moods or the result of role-playing. They were entities that were totally separate from the personality I was born to be, and am today. They were so different that their tones of voice changed. What's more, their facial expressions, appetites, tastes in clothes, hand-writings, skills, and IQs were all different, too. (Sizemore, 1989, p. 9)

◆◆◆

The case of Chris Sizemore dramatically illustrates the characteristics of dissociative identity disorder. Sizemore's words also foreshadow controversies about the condition. Some professionals argue that dissociative identity disorder is nothing more than role playing; others assert that multiple personalities are very real and very common.

Frequency of Dissociative Disorders

The prevalence of dissociative disorders is difficult to establish. The conditions generally are considered to be extremely rare. For example, only about 200 case histories of dissociative identity disorder were reported in the entire world literature prior to 1980 (Greaves, 1980). However, a small but vocal group of professionals has argued that many patients suffering from dissociative disorders are misdiagnosed as having schizophrenia, borderline personality disorder, depression, panic disorder, or substance abuse (Gleaves, 1996; Ross, Norton, & Wozney, 1989). One study conducted in Manitoba, Canada claimed an unbelievably high prevalence: Over 10 percent of the general adult population suffers from a dissociative disorder—including 3 percent of adults with dissociative identity disorder (Ross, 1991). A later study by the same author claimed that 40 percent of hospitalized psychiatric patients met DSM-IV-TR criteria for the diagnosis of a dissociative disorder (Ross et al., 2002).

Clearly, either we missed millions of cases of dissociative disorders for decades, or some advocates are overzealous in defining dissociative disorders. Research suggests many reasons to disbelieve claims that dissociative disorders are both prevalent and overlooked (Kihlstrom, 2005; Waller & Ross, 1997): (1) Most cases of dissociative disorders are diagnosed by a handful of ardent advocates. (2) The frequency of the diagnosis of dissociative disorders in general and DID in particular increased rapidly after release of the very popular book and movie, *Sybil*. (3) The number of personalities claimed to

Chris Sizemore is "Eve," the patient from the book and movie *The Three Faces of Eve*. Sizemore is now cured and is an advocate for the mentally ill.

exist in cases of DID has grown rapidly, from a handful to 100 or more. (4) Dissociative disorders are rarely diagnosed outside of the United States and Canada; for example, only one unequivocal case of DID has been reported in Great Britain in the last 25 years (Casey, 2001). And (5) the symptoms of dissociation in the most commonly used instruments like the Dissociative Experiences Questionnaire are far less dramatic than those found in dissociative disorders (see Table 7–3). The strange but familiar feeling of déjà vu, for example, is widely considered to be an experience of dissociation (Brown, 2003).

Disorder or Role Enactment?   Some experts even doubt the very existence of dissociative identity disorder, arguing that DID is created by the power of suggestion (Mersky, 1992). The Canadian psychologist Nicholas Spanos (1942–1994) was a particularly outspoken critic, who argued that

TABLE 7–3   Sample Items from the Dissociative Experiences Questionnaire
• Some people find that sometimes they are listening to someone talk and they suddenly realize that they did not hear part or all of what was said.
• Some people have the experience of being in a familiar place but finding it strange and unfamiliar.
• Some people have the experience of finding themselves dressed in clothes that they don't remember putting on.
• Some people are told that they sometimes do not recognize friends or family members.
• Some people have the experience of feeling that their body does not seem to belong to them.
• Some people find that in one situation they may act so differently compared with another situation that they feel almost as if they were two different people.

Source: E.M. Bernstein and F.W. Putnam, 1986, Development, reliability, and validity of a dissociation scale, *Journal of Nervous & Mental Disease, 174,* 727–735. Copyright © 1986. Reprinted by permission of Lippincott Williams & Wilkins.

multiple personalities are caused by role playing. Spanos (1994) asserted that patients are influenced by their own and their therapists' goals and expectations about DID, and, like an actor who loses all perspective, they come to believe that the role is real.

Can one person can really have two different personalities?

To test his theory, Spanos and his colleagues conducted analogue experiments inspired by the case of Kenneth Bianchi, the infamous "Hillside Strangler." In 1979, Bianchi was charged with murdering two college women and was implicated in several other rape-murder cases where victims were left naked on the hillsides of Los Angeles. Considerable evidence supported Bianchi's guilt, but he reported frequent episodes of "blanking out," including an inability to remember events from the night that the murders were committed. At the request of his attorney, Bianchi was seen by a mental health expert, who hypnotized Bianchi and suggested to him, "I've talked a bit to Ken, but I think that perhaps there might be another part of Ken that I haven't talked to, another part that maybe feels somewhat differently from the part I've talked to. And I would like to communicate with that

Kenneth Bianchi, the convicted Hillside Strangler.

other part" (Watkins, 1984). Bianchi responded that he was not Ken but Steve. Steve knew of Ken, and he hated him. Steve also confessed to strangling "all of these girls."

Numerous experts who interviewed Bianchi disagreed about whether his apparent dissociative identity disorder was real or feigned. One of the experts was the psychologist and psychiatrist Martin Orne (1927–2000), an internationally recognized authority on hypnosis. Orne tested Bianchi by suggesting new symptoms to him. If Bianchi was faking, he might further the deception by developing the new symptoms. Orne suggested, for example, that if Bianchi really had dissociative identity disorder, he should have a third personality. Sure enough, a third personality, Billy, "emerged" when Bianchi was hypnotized (Orne, Dingers, & Orne, 1984). While hypnotized, Bianchi also followed Orne's suggestion to hallucinate that his attorney was in the room. Bianchi actually shook hands with the supposed hallucination—a very unusual behavior for someone under hypnosis. Orne concluded that Bianchi was indeed faking, and actually suffered from antisocial personality disorder (see Chapter 9). Bianchi's insanity defense failed, and he was found guilty of murder.

In testing his role theory, Spanos simulated procedures from the Bianchi case. In one study, undergraduate students played the role of the accused murderer and were randomly assigned to one of three conditions. In the "Bianchi" condition, the subjects were hypnotized, and the interviewer asked to communicate with their other part, just as Bianchi's interviewer had asked. Subjects assigned to the second, "hidden part" condition also were hypnotized, but this time it was suggested that hypnosis could get behind the "wall" that hid inner thoughts and feelings from awareness. In the final condition, there was no hypnosis, and subjects simply were told that personality included "walls" between hidden thoughts and feelings.

When subsequently asked, "Who are you?" by the interviewer in the mock murder case, 81 percent of the subjects in the Bianchi condition gave a name different from the one assigned to them in the role play, as did 70 percent of the subjects in the hidden part condition. In contrast, only 31 percent of the subjects in the no-hypnosis condition gave a new name (Spanos, Weekes, & Bertrand, 1985). In a subsequent study, hypnotized subjects also provided more "information" on exactly when in the past their alternate personalities had first emerged (Spanos et al., 1986).

These findings certainly raise the caution that the "symptoms" of DID can be induced by role playing and hypnosis (Lilienfeld et al., 1999). However, analogue studies cannot prove that role playing causes real cases of multiple personality (Gleaves, 1996). In fact, real patients show symptoms even on subtle measures where the "appropriate" answer is not obvious (Eich et al., 1997; Scroppo et al., 1998).

Given the current status of research, we reach some cautious conclusions. True dissociative disorders appear to be rare. Although some cases no doubt are misdiagnosed, a much greater problem is the creation of the diagnosis in the minds of clinicians and clients (Mersky, 1992; Piper, 1994; Showalter, 1997). At the same time, we do not doubt the existence of dissociative disorders.

Causes of Dissociative Disorders

Little systematic research has been conducted on the etiology of dissociative disorders; thus, theory and outright speculation dominate. One exception is the widely held view that the disorders often are precipitated by trauma.

Psychological Factors in Dissociative Disorders

As noted earlier, the onset of dissociative amnesia and fugue usually can be traced to a specific traumatic experience. Thus, there is little controversy about this etiological link. Much more dispute surrounds the purported association between trauma and DID. Many case studies suggest that multiple personalities develop in response to trauma, particularly the trauma of child abuse. In fact, some researchers have compiled large numbers of case studies from surveys of practitioners that support this view (Gleaves, 1996; Kluft, 1987; Putnam, Curoff, et al., 1986; Scroppo et al., 1998; see Table 7–4).

When interpreting these findings, however, you should note that studies of the long-term consequences of child physical or sexual abuse find little evidence of dissociation or, indeed, of other consistent forms of psychopathology (Emery & Laumann-Billings, 1998; Rind et al., 1998). And case studies are based on patients' memories and clinicians' evaluations. They are not objective assessments of the past. Researchers have many concerns about the validity of such *retrospective*

TABLE 7–4	Correlates of Dissociative Identity Disorder in Two Surveys of Clinicians	
ITEM	Ross[1] N = 236	Putnam[2] N = 100
Average age	30.8	35.8
Percentage of females	87.7%	92.0%
Average years of treatment before diagnosis	6.7	6.8
Average number of personalities	15.7	13.3
Opposite-sex personality present	62.6%	53.0%
Amnesia between personalities	94.9%	98.0%
Past suicide attempt	72.0%	71.0%
History of child physical abuse	74.9%	75.0%
History of child sexual abuse	79.2%	83.9%

[1]Based on data from C.A. Ross, G.R. Norton, and K. Wozney, 1989, Multiple personality disorder: An analysis of 236 cases, *Canadian Journal of Psychiatry, 34*, 413–418.

[2]Based on data from F.W. Putnam, J.J. Curoff, et al., 1986, The clinical phenomenology of multiple personality disorder: Review of 100 recent cases. *Journal of Clinical Psychiatry, 47*, 285–293.

reports—evaluations of the past from the vantage point of the present (see Research Methods on page 236). Memories may be selectively recalled, distorted, or even created to conform with a clinician's expectations (Kihlstrom, 2005).

If trauma is involved, how might it lead to the development of multiple personalities? One theory involves **state-dependent learning,** a process where learning that takes place in one state of affect or consciousness is best recalled in the same state of affect or consciousness (Bower, 1990). For example, when you are sad rather than happy, you more easily remember what happened when you were sad in the past. By extension, experiences that occur during a dissociated state may be most easily recalled within the same state of consciousness. Perhaps through the repeated experience of trauma, dissociation, and state-dependent learning, more complete and autonomous memories develop—ultimately leading to independent personalities (Braun, 1989).

Even if trauma contributes to dissociative disorders—and we are skeptical about trauma and DID, it clearly is not a sufficient cause. As we saw with ASD and PTSD, the vast majority of people who experience trauma do not develop a dissociative disorder. Thus, other factors must contribute to their development.

Biological Factors in Dissociative Disorders Very little evidence and not much more speculation addresses the role of biological factors in the etiology of dissociative disorders (Kihlstrom, 2005). One theorist has suggested a developmental disturbance in the orbital-frontal cortex, but this possibility has not been systemically investigated (Forrest, 2001). A preliminary twin study found no genetic contribution to dissociative symptoms, and suggested instead that the shared family environment was an important contributing cause (Waller & Ross, 1997).

Still, it is known that dissociative states or permanent dissociation can result from biological causes. Examples include the dramatic personality changes that sometimes accompany substance abuse and the amnesia found in cognitive disorders associated with aging. In DSM-IV-TR, a diagnosis of dissociative disorders is explicitly excluded if the dissociation occurs in conjunction with substance abuse or organic pathology. However, evidence that biological factors can produce dissociative symptoms is a reason to continue to search for biological contributions to dissociative disorders.

Social Factors in Dissociative Disorders A sociological view offers a very different perspective on the etiology of dissociative disorders. At least one theorist has suggested that dissociative disorders are produced by **iatrogenesis,** the manufacture of the dissociative disorders by their treatment. Mersky (1992) reviewed classic case histories of dissociative identity disorder and concluded that many "cases" were created by the expectations of therapists. Mersky does not doubt the pain experienced by the patients in these cases. He argues, however, that the patients developed multiple personalities in response to leading questions asked by their therapists. Like Spanos (1994), Mersky asserts that DID is little more than a social role. A twist on this reasoning is that perhaps highly hypnotizable people are convinced that they have a dissociative disorder because of their susceptibility to suggestion (Kihlstrom, Glisky, & Angiulo, 1994).

research methods

RETROSPECTIVE REPORTS: REMEMBERING THE PAST

The topic of recovered memories has created much recent controversy, but scientists have long been skeptical about the accuracy of people's reports about the past. In research methods, the concern is the reliability and validity of **retrospective reports**—current recollections of past experiences. When trying to demonstrate a relationship between current problems and childhood experiences, for example, researchers question the accuracy of the patient's reports of past difficulties. Concerns about retrospective reports are one of several reasons why investigators prefer prospective, longitudinal studies over retrospective research designs (see Research Methods in Chapter 8).

Concerns about retrospective reports focus on three particular issues in abnormal psychology (Brewin, Andrews, & Gotlib, 1993). First, normal memory often is inaccurate, particularly memory for events that occurred long ago and early in life. Second, memories of people with emotional problems may be particularly unreliable. Third, abnormal behavior may systematically bias memory; for example, memory processes may be "mood congruent." Depressed people may tend to remember sad experiences, anxious people may better recall fearful events, and so on.

Brewin, Andrews, and Gotlib (1993) revisited many of these concerns, but concluded that retrospective memories may be less flawed than some have suggested. The reviewers agreed that retrospective reports are often inaccurate. For example, only moderate correlations are found between children's and parents' reports about their past relationships, and, on average, children report more negative memories. At the same time, agreement between parents and children increases to an acceptable level for reports of specific, factual aspects of the past. Thus memory for specific, important events in the family may be fairly reliable and valid, but people may "rewrite" their histories with regard to more global and subjective experiences.

Brewin et al. (1993) also questioned the blanket assumption that psychopathology impairs memory. They found many flaws in research that supposedly demonstrated memory impairments for various psychological problems, and concluded that, except for serious mental illness, there is no evidence for memory impairments associated with anxiety or depression. In particular, depressed people do not erroneously recall more than their share of negative events about the past.

Brewin et al. (1993) urge that retrospective reports should not be dismissed out of hand. Psychologists have many reasons to prefer prospective, longitudinal research designs over retrospective methods, but longitudinal research is expensive to conduct. Retrospective reports of specific events may be sufficiently reliable and valid to justify using them as an initial, less expensive research method.

We believe that iatrogensis is the explanation for the virtual epidemic of DID cases diagnosed in the United States in recent years. However, evidence that DID can be diagnosed in the general population in Turkey (Akyuz et al., 1999), where there is no public awareness of the disorder, leads us to conclude that DID is a real but rare problem.

Treatment of Dissociative Disorders

Dating from the time of Janet and Freud, perhaps the central aspect of the treatment of dissociative disorders has been uncovering and recounting past traumatic events. It is presumed that if the trauma can be expressed and accepted, then the need for dissociation will disappear (Horevitz & Loewenstein, 1994). Many clinicians use hypnosis to help patients explore and relive traumatic events. However, no research supports the effectiveness of either abreaction, the emotional reliving of a past traumatic experience, or hypnosis as a treatment for dissociative disorders (Horevitz & Loewenstein, 1994). In fact, many skeptics are concerned that hypnosis can exacerbate or even create dissociative symptoms—or false memories of past abuse (Casey, 2001).

Whatever the approach, the goal of treatment for DID is not to have one personality triumph over the others. Rather, the objective is to reintegrate the different personalities into a whole (Coons & Bowman, 2001; Ellason & Ross, 1997). Integration is not unlike the far less difficult task we all face to reconcile the different roles we play into a coherent sense of self. Dallae, for example, needed to incorporate her parents' expectations for her career success with her own, independent desires, abilities, and acculturation experiences.

The goal of reintegration is considered to be more of a psychological than a pharmaceutical task (Horevitz & Loewenstein, 1994). Antianxiety, antidepressant, and antipsychotic medications may be used to treat dissociative disorders. The objective in prescribing these medications, however, is to reduce distress, not to cure the disorder.

At this time, no systematic research has been conducted on the effectiveness of any treatment for dissociative disorders, let alone on the comparison of alternative treatments (Kihlstrom, 2005; Maldonado et al., 2001). Advances in therapy await a more accurate description of the

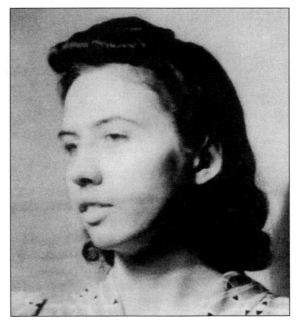

Shirley Mason Ardell, the real "Sybil." Her case spurred an explosion in the diagnosis of dissociative identity disorder, and in the number of diagnosed "alters," but actual therapy tapes suggest that her therapist may have implanted Sybil's 16 personalities.

disorders and, more generally, a better understanding of conscious and unconscious mental processes. In the meantime, treatments championed for dissociative disorders—and the accuracy of the diagnosis itself—should be viewed with a healthy dose of skepticism.

SOMATOFORM DISORDERS

In addition to dissociative disorders, hysteria included what we now know as **somatoform disorders**—problems characterized by unusual physical symptoms that occur in the absence of a known physical illness. There is no demonstrable physical cause for the symptoms of somatoform disorders. They are somatic (physical) in form only—thus their name.[1] We consider somatoform disorders together with dissociative disorders, because of their historical connection and because somatoform disorders involve a degree of dissociation. In some cases of somatoform disorder, the dissociation is relatively minor; in other cases, it is dramatic.

---

[1]The absence of demonstrable physical impairment distinguishes somatoform disorders for psychosomatic illnesses, stress-related physical disorders that do involve real, organic pathology (Chapter 8). In everyday language, we sometimes say, "His problems are psychosomatic" to indicate that an illness is "all in his head." However, somatoform disorders, not psychosomatic disorders, are the purely psychological problems.

Symptoms of Somatoform Disorders

All somatoform disorders involve complaints about physical symptoms, but somatoform disorders are not caused by physical impairments. There is nothing physically wrong with the patient, yet the symptoms are not feigned. The physical problem is very real in the mind, though not the body, of the person with a somatoform disorder.

The physical symptoms can take a number of different forms. In some dramatic cases, the symptom involves substantial impairment of a somatic system, particularly a sensory or muscular system. The patient will be unable to see, for example, or will report a paralysis in one arm. In other types of somatoform disorder, patients experience multiple physical symptoms rather than a single, substantial impairment. In these cases, patients usually have numerous, constantly evolving complaints about such problems as chronic pain, upset stomach, and dizziness. Finally, some types of somatoform disorder are defined by a preoccupation with a particular part of the body or with fears about a particular illness. The patient may constantly worry that he or she has contracted some deadly disease, for example, and the anxiety persists despite negative medical tests and clear reassurance by a physician.

Unnecessary Medical Treatment   People with somatoform disorders typically do not bring their problems to the attention of a mental health professional. Instead, they repeatedly consult their physicians about their "physical" problems (Bass et al., 2001; Looper & Kirmayer, 2002). This often leads to unnecessary medical treatment. In one study, patients with *somatization disorder* had seen a health care provider more than six times on average during the previous 6 months. In addition, 25 percent of people with somatization disorder had been hospitalized in the past year, compared with 12 percent of the general population (Swartz et al., 1987). People with *body dysmorphic disorder* also receive excessive medical care. Three-quarters of patients with the disorder seek medical treatment, primarily dermatologic or surgical, but the medical procedures produce little benefit (Phillips et al., 2001).

Patients with somatoform disorders often complain about realistic physical symptoms that are difficult to evaluate objectively. Thus physicians frequently do not recognize the psychological nature of the patients' problems, and they sometimes perform unnecessary medical procedures. For example, patients with somatoform disorders have surgery twice as often as people in the general population (Zoccolillo & Cloninger, 1986). In fact, some common surgical procedures are performed with startling frequency on patients with somatoform disorders. One research group concluded that, after discounting cancer surgeries, 27 percent of women undergoing a hysterectomy suffered from somatization disorder (Martin, Roberts, & Clayton, 1980).

Such data are distressing not only because of the risk to the patient but also because of the costs of unnecessary medical treatment. Estimates indicate that anywhere from 20 to 84 percent of patients who consult physicians do so for problems for which no organic cause can be found (Swartz et al., 1990). Such visits may account for as much as half of all ambulatory health care costs (Kellner, 1985). A variety of emotional problems can motivate people to consult their physicians, including the experience of trauma (Green et al., 1997), but much excessive health care utilization is specific to somatoform disorders. For example, patients with somatization disorder are three times more likely to consult physicians than are depressed patients (Morrison & Herbstein, 1988; Zoccolillo & Cloninger, 1986). In fact, health care expenditures for patients with somatization disorder are nine times the average annual per capita cost of medical treatment (Smith, Monson, & Ray, 1986).

Diagnosis of Somatoform Disorders

DSM-IV-TR lists five major subcategories of somatoform disorders: (1) conversion disorder, (2) somatization disorder, (3) hypochondriasis, (4) pain disorder, and (5) body dysmorphic disorder.

Conversion Disorder   The symptoms of **conversion disorder,** a classic type of somatoform disorder, often mimic those found in neurological diseases, and they can be dramatic. "Hysterical" blindness or "hysterical" paralysis are examples of conversion symptoms. Although conversion disorders often resemble neurological impairments, they sometimes can be distinguished from these disorders because they make no anatomic sense. The patient may complain about anesthesia (or pain) in a way that does not correspond with the innervation of the body. In some facial anesthesias, for example, numbness ends at the middle of the face; but the nerves involved in sensation do not divide the face into equal halves (see Figure 7–5).

The term *conversion disorder* accurately conveys the central assumption of the diagnosis—the idea that psychological conflicts are converted into physical symptoms. Conversion disorders captivated the attention of Charcot, Freud, and Janet and that led them to develop theories about dissociation and unconscious mental processes. The following case from Janet's writings illustrates his view of hysteria.

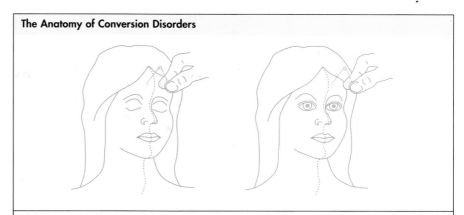

The Anatomy of Conversion Disorders

FIGURE 7–5: Conversion disorder symptoms may make no anatomical sense. As illustrated in this figure, pain insensitivity may be limited to one side of the face, but the nerves involved in pain sensation do not divide the face neatly in half.

Source: Adapted from D.M. Kaufman, 1985, *Clinical Neurology for Psychiatrists*, 2nd ed., p. 28. Orlando, FL. Grune & Stratton.

BRIEF CASE STUDY

Janet's Patient

A girl of nineteen years of age suffered, at the time of her monthly period, convulsive and delirious attacks which lasted several days. Menstruation began normally, but a few hours after the commencement of the flow the patient complained of feeling very cold and had a characteristic shivering; menstruation was immediately arrested and delirium ensued. In the interval of these attacks the patient had paroxysms of terror with the hallucination of blood spreading out before her, and also showed various permanent stigmata, among others anesthesia of the left side of the face with amaurosis of the left eye.

During a careful study of this patient's history, and particularly of the memories she had conserved of various experiences of her life, certain pertinent facts were ascertained. At the age of thirteen years she had attempted to arrest menstruation by plunging into a tub of cold water with resulting shivering and delirium; menstruation was immediately arrested and did not recur for several years; when it did reappear the disturbance I have just cited took place. Later on she had been terrified by seeing an old woman fall on the stairs and deluge the steps with her blood. At another time, when she was about nine years old, she had been obliged to sleep with a child whose face, on the left side, was covered with scabs, and during the whole night she had experienced a feeling of intense disgust and horror (Janet, 1914/1915, pp. 3–4).

This case describes symptoms that are consistent with conversion disorder. The numbness on the left side of the face of Janet's young patient is a clear example of a conversion symptom. At the same time, we wonder about other aspects of this classic case. The frightening hallucinations of blood might suggest another diagnosis, perhaps psychotic depression or schizophrenia, with the conversion symptom as a secondary aspect of the case. Differential diagnosis was poor during the time of Charcot, Janet, and Freud, and we think that this might explain why conversion disorders once were thought to be prevalent but are rare today. A hundred years ago, many problems that might be diagnosed accurately today as either physical or psychological maladies probably were misdiagnosed as conversion disorders.

Somatization Disorder   Today, a more common somatoform disorder is **somatization disorder,** characterized by a history of multiple somatic complaints in the absence of organic impairments. The extent of the health concerns in somatization disorder is apparent from a cursory examination of the DSM-IV-TR diagnostic criteria. In order to be diagnosed with somatization disorder, the patient must complain of at least eight physical symptoms. The complaints must involve multiple somatic systems, moreover, including symptoms of pain, gastrointestinal symptoms (for example, nausea and diarrhea), sexual symptoms (sexual dysfunction, menstrual difficulties), and pseudoneurologic symptoms (for example, double vision, numbness, or amnesia) (see Table 7–5).

Patients with somatization disorders sometimes present their symptoms in a *histrionic* manner—a vague but dramatic, self-centered, and seductive style. Patients also may exhibit *la belle indifference* ("beautiful indifference"), a flippant lack of concern about the physical symptoms. For example, a patient may list a long series of somatic complaints in an offhanded and cheerful manner. Although some experts view a histrionic style and la belle indifference as defining characteristics of somatization disorders, research indicates that they are found in only a minority of cases (Brown, 2004; Lipowski, 1988).

In contrast to stereotypes, somatization disorder is not more common among the aged, who consult health care professionals frequently because of chronic and real physical illnesses (National Institute of Mental Health, 1990). In fact, somatization disorder often begins in adolescence, and according to DSM-IV-TR criteria, it must have an onset prior to the age of 30. The problem is sometimes referred to as *Briquet's syndrome*, in recognition of the French physician Pierre Briquet, who was among the first to call attention to the multiple somatic complaints found in some "hysterias" (National Institute of Mental Health, 1990).

TABLE 7-5   DSM-IV-TR Diagnostic Criteria for Somatization Disorder

A. **A history of many physical complaints beginning before age 30 that occur over a period of several years and result in treatment being sought or significant impairment in social, occupational, or other important areas of functioning.**

B. **Each of the following criteria must have been met, with individual symptoms occurring at any time during the course of the disturbance.**

   1. Four pain symptoms: A history of pain related to at least four different sites or functions (for example, head, abdomen, back, joints, extremities, chest, rectum, during menstruation, or sexual intercourse, or during urination)

   2. Two gastrointestinal symptoms: A history of at least two gastrointestinal symptoms other than pain (for example, nausea, diarrhea, bloating, vomiting other than during pregnancy, or intolerance of several different foods)

   3. One sexual symptom: A history of at least one sexual or reproductive symptom other than pain (for example, sexual indifference, erectile or ejaculatory dysfunction, irregular menses, excessive menstrual bleeding, vomiting throughout pregnancy)

   4. One pseudoneurologic symptom: A history of at least one symptom or deficit suggesting a neurological disorder not limited to pain (conversion symptoms such as impaired coordination or balance, paralysis or localized weakness, difficulty swallowing or lump in throat, aphonia, urinary retention, hallucinations, loss of touch or pain sensation, double vision, blindness, deafness, seizures; dissociative symptoms such as amnesia; or loss of consciousness other than fainting)

Reprinted with permission from the *Diagnostic and Statistical Manual of Mental Disorders,* Fourth Edition, Text Revision. Copyright © 2000 by the American Psychiatric Association.

Hypochondriasis **Hypochondriasis** is a problem characterized by a fear or belief that one is suffering from a physical illness. Aspects of this mental disorder surely are familiar to you. The pejorative term *hypochondriac* is a part of everyday language. We all worry about our health, and even unrealistic worries sometimes are normal. Medical students often fear that they have contracted each new disease they encounter in their studies. Many students in abnormal psychology worry that each problem they read about is a perfect description of themselves.

Hypochondriasis is much more serious than these normal and fleeting worries. The preoccupation with fears of disease extends over long periods of time. The worries must last for at least 6 months according to DSM-IV-TR criteria. In addition, in hypochondriasis, a thorough medical evaluation or examination does not alleviate the fear of the disease. The person still worries that the illness may be emerging or that a test was overlooked. Still, the person with hypochondriasis is not delusional. For example, someone may worry excessively about contracting AIDS and therefore repeatedly go for blood tests. When faced with negative results, the person does not delusionally believe that he or she actually has contracted the illness. Instead, he persistently worries that the test was wrong or was taken too soon to detect the disease. Hypochondriasis is severe and preoccupying, and often leads to substantial impairment in life functioning.

Pain Disorder As its name implies, **pain disorder** is characterized by preoccupation with pain. Although there is no objective way to evaluate pain, psychological factors are judged to be significant in creating or intensifying the chronic pain in pain disorder. Complaints seem excessive and apparently are motivated at least in part by psychological factors. For example, some pain disorder patients may seem to relish the attention their illness brings to them. DSM-IV-TR distinguishes between pain disorder that occurs with associated problems in general medical conditions and pain disorder that appears in the absence of such problems. For example, low back pain that begins after a physical injury would be differentiated from back pain that cannot be traced to any physical cause.

As with hypochondriasis and somatization disorder, pain disorder can lead to the repeated, unnecessary use of medical treatments. People who experience chronic pain are at a particular risk for developing a dependence on minor tranquilizers or painkillers. The disorder also frequently disrupts social and occupational functioning.

Body Dysmorphic Disorder   **Body dysmorphic disorder** is a very different type of somatoform disorder in which the patient is preoccupied with some imagined defect in appearance. The preoccupation typically focuses on some facial feature, such as the nose or mouth, and in some cases may lead to repeated visits to a plastic surgeon. Preoccupation with the body part far exceeds normal worries about physical imperfections. The endless worry causes significant distress, and in extreme cases, it may interfere with work or social relationships.

U.S. researchers are just beginning to study body dysmorphic disorder, although the problem has received somewhat more attention among European and Asian mental health professional. One controversy is whether the diagnosis should be grouped with other somatoform disorders. In Japan and Korea, body dysmorphic disorder is classified as a type of social phobia (Phillips, 1991). The following brief case history illustrates this unusual type of somatoform disorder.

Some people suspect that Michael Jackson suffers from body dysmorphic disorder given his multiple plastic surgeries to change his appearance.

BRIEF CASE STUDY
Body Dysmorphic Disorder

 28-year-old single white man became preoccupied at the age of 18 with his minimally thinning hair. Despite reassurance from others that his hair loss was not noticeable, he worried about it for hours a day, becoming "deeply depressed," socially withdrawn, and unable to attend classes or do his schoolwork. Although he could acknowledge the excessiveness of his preoccupation, he was unable to stop it. He saw four dermatologists but was not comforted by their reassurances that his hair loss was minor and that treatment was unnecessary. The patient's preoccupation and subsequent depression have persisted for 10 years and have continued to interfere with his social life and work, to the extent that he avoids most social events and has been able to work only part time as a baker. He only recently sought psychiatric referral, at the insistence of his girlfriend, who said his symptoms were ruining their relationship (Phillips, 1991, pp. 1138–1139).

Malingering and Factitious Disorder   Somatoform disorders represent real *psychological* problems, even if the physical symptoms are not real. As such, somatoform disorders must be distinguished from **malingering,** pretending to have a somatoform disorder in order to achieve some external gain, such as a disability payment. Because there is no objective way to test for somatoform disorders, detecting malingering is extremely difficult. Besides searching for an obvious reason for feigning an illness, one clue to malingering can be when a patient presents symptoms that are more, not less, dramatic.

A related diagnostic concern is **factitious disorder,** a feigned condition that, unlike malingering, is motivated primarily by a desire to assume the sick role rather than by a desire for external gain. People with factitious disorder pretend to be ill or make themselves appear to be ill, for example, by taking drugs to produce a rapid heart rate. They will undergo extensive and often painful medical procedures in order to garner attention from health care professionals. A rare, repetitive pattern of factitious disorder is sometimes called *Munchausen syndrome,* named after Baron Karl Friedrich Hieronymus von Munchausen, an eighteenth-century writer known for his tendency to embellish the details of his life.

Frequency of Somatoform Disorders

No one knows how prevalent conversion disorders were during the time of Charcot, Janet, and Freud, but the literature of the period suggests that they were common (Shorter, 1992). Today, conversion disorders are rare, perhaps as infrequent as 50 cases per 100,000 population (Akagi & House, 2001). Ironically, the unusual disorders treated by Freud and Janet have been less enduring than the theories developed to explain them! The lower prevalence today may be a result of improved diagnostic practices—cases now are correctly diagnosed as real physical or psychological illnesses, or perhaps of Western society's greater acceptance of the expression of feelings (Shorter, 1992). A very different—and controversial—viewpoint is that conversion disorders *are* prevalent today, but they take the form of conditions like chronic fatigue syndrome, Gulf War syndrome, and similar puzzling maladies (Showalter, 1997).

Most other somatoform disorders also appear to be relatively rare. For example, one study found a 0.7 percent prevalence of body dysmorphic disorder (Otto et al., 2001).

Hypochondriasis also is quite rare, although less severe worrying about physical illness is quite common (Looper & Kirmayer, 2001). The lifetime prevalence of somatization disorder in the United States is only 0.13 percent (Swartz et al., 1990). However, like hypochondriacal worrying, physical complaints that do not meet all of the diagnostic criteria for somatization disorder are very common (Ladwig et al., 2001). In one study, 11.6 percent of people suffered from four to six physical symptoms with no identifiable organic cause (fewer than the eight required for the diagnosis of somatization disorder) (Swartz et al., 1990). Indeed, a new diagnostic category, *multisomatoform disorder*, which requires only three physical symptoms—but chronic ones—has been proposed and likely will be included in DSM-V (Kroenke et al., 1997).

Gender, SES, and Culture   With the exception of hypochondriasis, all other forms of somatoform disorder are more common among women. This is particularly true of somatization disorder, which may be as much as 10 times more common among women than men (Swartz et al., 1990). Why women? Some feminist writers attribute women's hysteria during the time of Freud and Janet to the sexual repression of the Victorian era. Today's disproportionate prevalence among women often is blamed on widespread sexual abuse. Feminist Elaine Showalter (1997) criticizes both of these views. Instead, she argues, "Women still suffer from hysterical symptoms not because we are essentially irrational or because we're all victims of abuse but because, like men, we are human beings who will convert feelings into symptoms when we are unable to speak" (p. 207).

In addition to gender, socioeconomic status and culture are thought to contribute to somatization disorder. In the United States, somatization is more common among lower socioeconomic groups and people with less than a high school education. It is four times more common among African Americans than among Americans of European heritage, and considerably higher in Puerto Rico than on the U.S. mainland (Canino, Bird, et al., 1987). However, expected differences between industrialized and nonindustrialized countries were not found in a study sponsored by the World Health Organization (see Figure 7–6). The one notable cultural difference was the high prevalence of somatization in Latin America

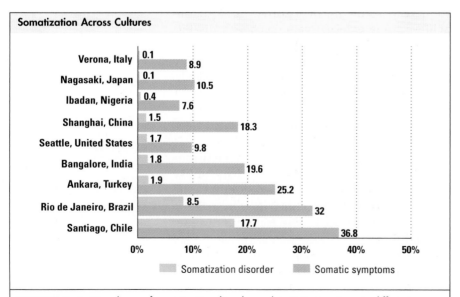

Somatization Across Cultures

Location	Somatization disorder	Somatic symptoms
Verona, Italy	0.1	8.9
Nagasaki, Japan	0.1	10.5
Ibadan, Nigeria	0.4	7.6
Shanghai, China	1.5	18.3
Seattle, United States	1.7	9.8
Bangalore, India	1.8	19.6
Ankara, Turkey	1.9	25.2
Rio de Janeiro, Brazil	8.5	32
Santiago, Chile	17.7	36.8

FIGURE 7–6: Prevalence of somatization disorder and somatic symptoms in different countries. Somatization is not more common in nonindustrialized countries, contrary to common assumptions.

Note: Somatization disorder was based on ICD-10 diagnosis; somatic symptoms included a minimum for 4 for men and 6 for women.

Source: O. Gureje, G.E. Simon, T.B. Ustun, & D.P. Goldberg, 1997, Somatization in cross cultural perspective: A World Health Organization study in primary care. *American Journal of Psychiatry, 154,* 989–995. Copyright © 1997. Reprinted by permission of the American Psychiatric Association.

(Gureje et al., 1997). Some speculate that this is due to a Latin view of emotional expression as a sign of weakness, while others hypothesize that it is due to the stigma associated with mental illness.

Comorbidity   Somatoform disorders typically occur with other psychological problems, particularly depression and anxiety (Guerje et al., 1997; Otto et al., 2001; Smith et al., 2005). The link between depression and somatoform disorders has several possible explanations. Either condition may cause the other, or both could be caused by a third variable, such as life stress. One possibility that primary care physicians must consider carefully is that some patients may express depression indirectly through their somatic complaints (Lipowski, 1988).

As with depression, there are several possible explanations for the comorbidity between somatoform disorders and anxiety, including similarities in the defining symptoms. A particular concern is the accurate, differential diagnosis of panic disorder. Some symptoms of panic, such as dizziness, numbness, and fears about dying, may be dismissed by physicians, or they may be misdiagnosed as either hypochondriasis or somatization disorder (Lipowski, 1988).

Finally, somatization disorder has frequently been linked with antisocial personality disorder, a lifelong pattern of irresponsible behavior that involves habitual violations of social rules. The two disorders do not typically co-occur in the same individual, but they often are found in different members of the same family (Lilienfeld, 1992). Because antisocial personality disorder is far more common among men, while somatoform disorders have the opposite pattern, some have speculated that the two problems are flip sides of the same coin. Antisocial personality disorder may be the male expression of high negative emotion and the absence of inhibition, whereas somatization disorder is the female expression of the same characteristics (Lilienfeld, 1992).

Causes of Somatoform Disorders

Despite their historical significance, until very recently little systematic research has been conducted on somatoform disorders. Some sound scientific evidence is finally being gathered, and

we can integrate emerging findings with some theoretical considerations within the context of the biopsychosocial model.

Biological Factors—The Perils of Diagnosis by Exclusion   An obvious—and potentially critical—biological consideration in somatoform disorders is the possibility of misdiagnosis. A patient may be incorrectly diagnosed as suffering from a somatoform disorder when, in fact, he or she actually has a real physical illness that is undetected or is perhaps unknown. The diagnosis of a somatoform disorder requires that no organic cause of the symptom can be identified. This is very different from the positive identification of a psychological cause of the symptom.

Because mental health professionals cannot demonstrate psychological causes of physical symptoms objectively and unequivocally, the identification of somatoform disorders involves a process called *diagnosis by exclusion*. The physical complaint is assumed to be a part of a somatoform disorder only when various known physical causes are excluded or ruled out. Indeed, many experts refer to somatoform disorders as "medically unexplained syndromes" (Looper & Kirmayer, 2002; Smith et al., 2005). The possibility always remains, however, that an incipient somatic disease has been overlooked. Some of the problems with diagnosis by exclusion can be appreciated by way of analogy. Consider the difference in certainty between two police lineups, one in which a victim positively identifies a criminal—"That's him!"—versus a second in

Diagnosis by exclusion is like trying to identify the culprit by ruling out the other suspects in a lineup. The real criminal may not be in the lineup, and in diagnosis by exclusion, the real disease may not have been detected.

which an identification is made by ruling out alternatives—"It isn't him or him or him, so it must be that one."

The possibility of misdiagnosis is more than a theoretical concern. Follow-up studies of patients diagnosed as suffering from conversion disorders indicate that somatic illnesses are later detected in some cases (Shalev & Munitz, 1986). Typically, a neurological disease such as epilepsy or multiple sclerosis is the eventual diagnosis. In one classic study, fully a quarter of patients diagnosed as having a conversion symptom later developed a neurological disease (Slater, 1965). Fortunately, recent research has found a much smaller percentage (5 percent or less) of undetected physical illnesses when following up cases of somatoform disorder several years later (Crimlisk et al., 1998; Schuepbach et al., 2002). We attribute the new findings to the improved detection of real physical illnesses, and again wonder how many of the "hysteria" cases treated by Charcot, Freud, and Janet would be diagnosed as real physical conditions today.

Are some physical symptoms really signs of emotional troubles?

Psychological Factors—Imagined or Real Trauma

Initially, both Freud and Janet assumed that conversion disorders were caused by a traumatic experience. According to their reasoning, trauma overwhelmed normal coping efforts, and unconscious coping processes were called into action as a result. However, Freud later questioned the accuracy of his patients' reports of traumatic sexual abuse. Instead, he decided that their memories of trauma were fantasized, not real. This conclusion led him to develop his theory of childhood sexuality (Freud, 1924/1962).

Thus, Freud came to believe that dissociation and other intrapsychic defenses protected individuals from their unacceptable sexual impulses, not from their intolerable memories (Freud, 1924/1962). In his view, conversion symptoms were expressions of intolerable unconscious psychological conflicts. In Freudian terminology, this is the *primary gain* of the symptom. Ironically, some contemporary theorists have noted that, unfortunately, childhood sexual abuse is all too common, and they have suggested that Freud's initial position may have been the accurate one.

Recent evidence does suggest that the onset of somatization is triggered by traumatic stress, but not necessarily sexual abuse. Increased somatoform pain disorder was found among 418 tortured Bhutanese refugees living in camps in Nepal, in comparison to 392 refugees in the same camps who were not tortured (Van Ommeren et al., 2001). Exposure to dead bodies, another gruesome experience, also has been tied to increased somatic symptoms. A study of 358 people who worked in the mortuary during the Gulf War found an increase in somatization from before to after the experience. Somatic symptoms included faintness, pains in the chest, nausea, trouble breathing, hot or cold spells, numbness, and feeling weak. Importantly, somatization increased more among workers with greater exposure to death (see Figure 7–7). Although it is not clear why trauma leads to increased somatization, likely contributors include an increased awareness of one's own body, the somatic consequences of stress, and the expression of psychological distress through complaints about somatic symptoms.

Freud also suggested that hysterical symptoms could produce **secondary gain**, for example, avoiding work or responsibility or to gain attention and sympathy. This view has more support than Freud's ideas about primary gain, although cognitive behavior therapists call this

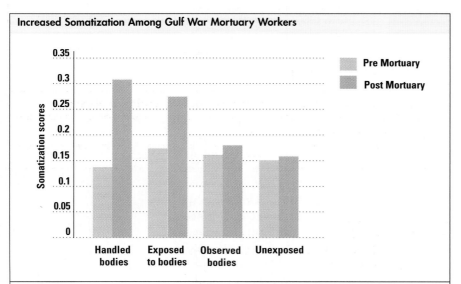

Increased Somatization Among Gulf War Mortuary Workers

Somatization scores (y-axis: 0, 0.05, 0.1, 0.15, 0.2, 0.25, 0.3, 0.35)

Legend: Pre Mortuary / Post Mortuary

Categories: Handled bodies, Exposed to bodies, Observed bodies, Unexposed

FIGURE 7–7: Somatic complaints, including faintness, chest pains, nausea, trouble breathing, hot or cold spells, numbness, and feeling weak, increased from before to after exposure to dead among Gulf War mortuary workers. Workers exposed more directly to death showed a more notable increase in somatization.

Source: J.E. McCarroll, R.J. Ursano, C.S. Fullerton, X. Liu, & A. Lundy, 2002, Somatic symptoms in Gulf War mortuary workers. *Psychosomatic Medicine, 64,* 29–33. Copyright © 2002. Reprinted by permission of Lippincott Williams & Wilkins.

process *reinforcement*, not secondary gain. In addition to positive reinforcement (extra attention) or negative reinforcement (avoidance of work), *learning the sick role* through modeling may be a part of the etiology of somatoform disorders (Lipowski, 1988). Cognitive tendencies also may contribute, especially (1) a tendency to amplify somatic symptoms (Brown, 2004; Kirmayer, Robbins, & Paris, 1994); (2) *alexithymia*—a deficit in one's capacity to recognize and express the emotions signaled by physiological arousal (Bankier et al., 2001); (3) the misattribution of normal somatic symptoms (Brown, 2004; Rief, Hiller, & Margraf, 1998); and (4) memory biases (Pauli & Alpers, 2002). Figure 7–8 summarizes how these and other factors may contribute to the development of somatoform disorders.

Social Factors in Somatoform Disorders   Social and cultural theorists offer a straightforward explanation of the physical symptoms of somatization disorder, hypochondriasis, and pain disorder. Patients with these disorders are experiencing some sort of underlying psychological distress. However, they describe their problems as physical symptoms and, to some extent, experience them that way because of limited insight and/or the lack of social tolerance of psychological complaints. A simple analogy for this theorizing is a child who complains about an upset stomach, not about fear of failure, before giving a piano recital. Presumably, increased psychological sophistication in the West explains the decrease in somatoform disorders over the course of the last century (Shorter, 1992). As noted earlier, however, somatoform disorders apparently are not more prevalent in nonindustrialized than industrialized countries (see Figure 7–6).

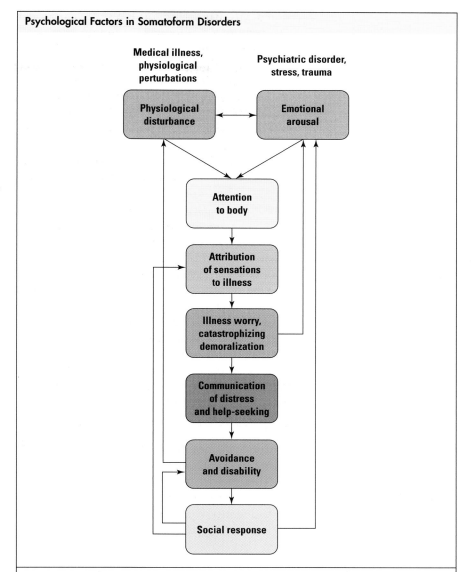

Psychological Factors in Somatoform Disorders

FIGURE 7–8: Minor physical symptoms may develop into a somatoform disorder when combined with stress, excessive attention to physical symptoms, misattributions, and other psychological tendencies and social reactions.

Source: Adapted from K.J. Looper & L.J. Kirmayer (2002). Behavioral medicine approaches to somatoform disorders. *Journal of Consulting and Clinical Psychology, 70,* 810–827.

Treatment of Somatoform Disorders

Charcot, Janet, and Freud encouraged their patients to recall and recount psychologically painful events as a way of treating conversion disorders. In the century or more since their techniques were developed, however, no systematic research was conducted on any "cathartic" therapies for somatoform disorders. In fact, very little research was conducted on any treatment. Fortunately, this is changing and accumulating evidence indicates that cognitive behavior therapy is effective in reducing physical symptoms in somatization disorder (Kroenke & Swindle, 2000), hypochondriasis (Clark et al., 1998), and body dysmorphic disorder (Rosen, Reiter, & Orosan, 1995).

The most extensive studies of cognitive behavioral treatments focus on pain disorders. Operant approaches to chronic pain attempt to alter contingencies that reward "pain behavior" and the sick role. The goal is to reward successful coping and life adaptation instead (Fordyce, 1976). Cognitive behavior therapy also uses cognitive restructuring to address the emotional and cognitive components of pain. Research demonstrates the effectiveness of both variations on behavior therapy in treating chronic lower back pain (Blanchard, 1994).

Recent evidence also indicates that antidepressants may be helpful in treating somatoform disorders. SSRIs have been shown to produce more improvement in comparison to placebo for body dysmorphic disorder (Phillips et al., 2002), and pain disorder (Fishbain et al., 1998). In fact, both medications and cognitive behavior therapies that are effective in treating depression and anxiety often also are treatments that work for somatoform disorders, perhaps because the problems often are comorbid (Looper & Kirmayer, 2002; Simon, 2002).

One reason for the limited research on the psychological treatment of somatoform disorders is that primary care physicians treat most of these patients (Bass et al., 2001). Patients with somatoform disorders typically consult physicians about their ailments, and they often insist that their problems are physical despite negative test results. Such patients are likely to refuse a referral to a mental health professional. Thus primary care physicians often must learn how to manage hypochondriasis, somatization disorder, and related problems in the medical setting.

This can be a difficult task. Primary care physicians may become frustrated by their failure to identify a clear physical problem or may be unsympathetic toward "hypochondriacs" when they have so many patients with "real" problems. Not surprisingly, such reactions can weaken the physician–patient relationship, a consequence that can intensify the problem. In fact, the major recommendation for the medical management of patients with somatization disorder is to establish a strong and consistent physician–patient relationship. Physicians are urged to schedule routine appointments with these patients every month or two and to conduct brief medical exams during this time (National Institute of Mental Health, 1990). This approach not only provides consistent emotional support and medical reassurance, but it helps to eliminate the iatrogenic effects of the somatization disorder by reducing unnecessary medical procedures. A physician who is familiar with a patient with somatization disorder is more likely to recognize the psychological origin of the physical complaints and is less likely to order unnecessary medical tests or treatment procedures. In fact, at least one study has documented the effectiveness of this management approach (Smith, Monson, & Ray, 1986).

Whatever the approach to treatment, it is essential for the physician to convey a sense of concern about patients' complaints. Patients who do not receive this empathy are likely to ignore the physician's advice and simply recruit a new, more understanding physician (National Institute of Mental Health, 1990). This means that referrals to a mental health professional must be made with care. In addition, the mental health professional might need to coordinate treatment with the referring physician and perhaps offer treatment in a medical setting (Bass et al., 2001).

getting help

The disorders discussed in this chapter are fascinating, and the controversies about them are intellectually exciting—unless you or someone you know is suffering from PTSD or a dissociative or somatoform disorder. In this case, the unusual symptoms of these disorders can be extremely frightening, the lack of acceptance can be isolating, and the controversy surrounding the disorders can seem callous, manipulative, or both.

The controversies and limited scientific information make it difficult to make clear recommendations for getting help. However, you can review the treatment sections of the three categories of disorder to get some specifics on the best approaches based on current research. These treatments generally involve some type of cognitive behavior therapy and/or antidepressant medication.

We also can readily offer a strong suggestion: If you have been the victim of trauma, for example, rape, abuse, or disaster, or a victim or witness of some other form of violence, talk to someone about it. You may find it difficult to trust anyone, but trying to "forget about it" is exactly the wrong thing to do. Confronting fear, embarrassment, or others' lack of understanding is far better than keeping it all inside. If you are not willing to consider therapy, start by confiding in a friend, a family member, even a stranger.

We are particularly concerned about the trauma of rape, including acquaintance rape, an all-too-frequent occurrence among college students. If you or someone you know has been raped, the first step may be to get to a hospital emergency room or to call the police. You also may want to contact a rape crisis center in your area. The Rape Abuse and Incest Network National hot line, (800)-656-4673, can provide you with the telephone number of the rape crisis center closest to you. You also may want to visit its Web site. A good self-help book on rape is *Free of the Shadows: Recovering from Sexual Violence,* by Caren Adams and Jennifer Fay.

There are many other resources available for victims of rape, disasters like September 11, and other types of trauma. If you are surfing the Web for information, we suggest that you begin your Internet exploration with the National Institute of Mental Health. You will find much helpful information there, as well as links to other useful Web sites.

Another reason why we recommend that you begin with the NIMH Web site is that you need to be extremely cautious about information on and potential treatments for PTSD and dissociative and somatoform disorders. The controversies discussed in this chapter are not just theoretical ones. There are many self-help resources—and professionals—who claim that one side or the other of a given controversy is fact, not theory or opinion. We urge you to be wary if a professional or resource fails to acknowledge the uncertain state of scientific information and the range of opinion about such things as the long-term consequences of childhood trauma, the prevalence of multiple personality disorder, or the nature of recovered memories. A dramatic illustration of the havoc that can be created by those who are supposed to help can be found in the book *Remembering Satan,* Lawrence Wright's journalistic account of the consequences of one episode of false "recovered memories" of satanic ritual abuse.

SUMMARY

To some extent, all the intriguing disorders we consider in this chapter involve **dissociation,** the disruption of the normally integrated mental processes involved in memory or consciousness. Many of the disorders also are known or hypothesized to be reactions to **traumatic stress,** exposure to some event that involves actual or threatened death or serious injury to self or others and creates intense fear, helplessness, or horror. Sources of traumatic stress include rape, combat, experiencing or witnessing violence, and natural or man made disasters.

Acute stress disorder (ASD) is a short-term reaction to trauma that is characterized by symptoms of dissociation, reexperiencing, avoidance, and increased anxiety or arousal. **Posttraumatic stress disorder (PTSD)** is characterized by very similar symptoms—reexperiencing, numbed responsiveness or avoidance, and increased autonomic arousal—but the symptoms either last for longer than 1 month or have a delayed onset. Trauma may be reexperienced as a **flashback**—a dissociative state in which the person relives the trauma in the moment. The diminished responsiveness sometimes is called emotional anesthesia. The increased arousal in ASD or PTSD may include excessive fear, anxiety, or irritability, as well as general psychophysiological arousal.

Epidemiological studies show that trauma is distressingly common and often leads to PTSD, especially rape for women and combat exposure for men. More symptoms of ASD predict later PTSD, and the nature and level of exposure to a traumatic event, as well as social support after the occurrence of the trauma, are crucial to long-term adjustment. By definition, trauma is the central cause of PTSD, but other factors contribute to its etiology. Genetic factors increase the risk both for experiencing trauma and for developing PTSD following trauma. Key psychological contributions include **two-factor theory,** a combination of classical and operant conditioning, and **emotional processing,** which involves facing fear, diminishing its intensity, and coming to some new understanding about the trauma and its consequences.

Early intervention holds the hope of easing the pain of trauma, but data are lacking on the effectiveness of **critical incident stress debriefing** and other early interventions. Promising evidence suggests that treating acute stress disorder may reduce PTSD. Prolonged exposure is perhaps the least obvious but most important strategy for treatment for PTSD, which has a chronic course in about one-third of cases.

Dissociative disorders are characterized by persistent, maladaptive disruptions in the integration of memory, consciousness, or identity. **Somatoform disorders** are identified by unusual physical symptoms that occur in the absence of a known physical illness. Memories become inaccessible in dissociative disorders; psychological distress is converted into physical symptoms in somatoform disorders. Thus these unusual emotional problems involve unconscious processes by definition, and they challenge psychological theorists to explain those psychological events that occur outside of awareness. Both Freud and Janet developed their influential theories about unconscious processes when attempting to explain these disorders.

Dissociative disorders include **dissociative fugue,** characterized by sudden and unexpected travel away from home, an inability to recall the past, and confusion about identity or the assumption of a new identity; **dissociative amnesia,** a sudden inability to recall extensive and important personal information that exceeds normal forgetfulness; **depersonalization disorder,** a less dramatic problem characterized by severe and persistent feelings of being detached from oneself; and **dissociative identity disorder (DID),** also known as **multiple personality disorder,** characterized by the existence of two or more distinct personalities in a single individual.

Although some suggest otherwise, dissociative disorders are rare. Some evidence links the conditions with traumatic experiences, particularly with child abuse, but we must be very cautious in drawing inferences from purported **recovered memories** of past abuse, the sudden remembering of long forgotten traumatic experiences. Evidence is weak or nonexistent on other factors that may contribute to the development of dissociative disorders. Similarly, there is no systematic research on the treatment of dissociative disorders, although clinical tradition emphasizes reliving trauma as a way of reintegrating experience.

The term **conversion disorder** accurately conveys the central assumption of the diagnosis—the idea that psychological conflicts are converted into physical symptoms. **Somatization disorder** is characterized by a history of multiple, somatic complaints in the absence of organic impairments. **Hypochondriasis** is characterized by a fear or belief that the individual is suffering from a physical illness. **Pain disorder** is characterized by preoccupation with pain. Although there is no objective way to evaluate pain, psychological factors are judged to be significant in creating or exacerbating the chronic pain in pain disorder. In **body dysmorphic disorder** the patient is preoccupied with some imagined defect in appearance—a preoccupation that typically focuses on some facial feature, such as the nose or mouth.

True somatoform disorders are rare, although complaints about unexplained medical conditions are common and represent a significant proportion of medical care. Until recently, the etiology of somatoform disorders has not been the subject of much research. Etiological concerns include the possible misdiagnosis of incipient neurological diseases as somatoform disorders; the experience of trauma; secondary gain or reinforcement for the sick role; cognitive factors, such as a tendency to amplify somatic symptoms; and alexithymia—a deficit in the individual's capacity to recognize and express the emotions signaled by physiological arousal. Cultural influences on somatoform disorders may be less prominent than previously thought. Cognitive behavior therapy and antidepressant medications are emerging as useful treatments for somatoform disorders, which also may require supportive medical management.

KEY TERMS

Go to www.prenhall.com/oltmanns for online quizzes, interactive flash cards, PowerPoint presentations, and chapter reviews.

8

Stress and Physical Health

CHAPTER OUTLINE

Defining Stress

Symptoms of Stress

Diagnosis of Stress and Physical Illness

The Role of Psychological Factors in Some Familiar Illnesses

Cardiovascular Disease

◆◆

How do you feel when you are "stressed out"? Different people feel jittery, tired, down, preoccupied, vigilant, defeated, angry, sick, or just plain lousy. How do you cope? Some people try to eliminate stress by solving the problem; others calm themselves by writing (Sloan & Marx, 2004) or talking about the stress; and still other people distract themselves in healthy ways (exercise) or unhealthy ones (smoking, alcohol, or overeating). What are the consequences of stress and different ways of coping with it? Can stress *really* make you sick? How?

OVERVIEW

Scientists define **stress** as any challenging event that requires physiological, cognitive, or behavioral adaptation. Stress may involve minor, daily hassles, like taking an exam, or major events, such as going through a divorce. As we saw in Chapter 7, *traumatic stress* involves actual or threatened death or serious injury to oneself or others and a reaction of intense fear, helplessness, or horror. This chapter is about more normal stress, how we cope with it, and how stress affects our physical health.

Scientists once thought that stress contributed only to a few physical diseases, like ulcers, migraine headaches, hypertension (high blood pressure), asthma, and other *psychosomatic disorders*,[1] a term indicating that a disease is a product of both the *psyche* (mind) and the *soma*

Students taking the SAT exam. Stress is a fact of life.

(body). Today, the term "psychosomatic disorder" is old-fashioned. Medical scientists now view *every* physical illness—from colds to cancer to AIDS—as a product of the interaction between the mind and body. Thus, there is no longer a list of "psychosomatic disorders" in the DSM-IV-TR or elsewhere.

---

[1]In everyday language, we sometimes use the term *psychosomatic* to imply that an illness is imagined or not real. Unlike conversion disorders (Chapter 7), psychosomatic disorders involve very real physical damage or dysfunction.

Theories of the etiology of physical illnesses have adopted, and in many ways have promoted, the systems approach. This holistic view of health and disease has brought about major changes in medicine. Of particular note is the rapid development of **behavioral medicine,** a multidisciplinary field that includes both medical and mental health professionals who investigate psychological factors in the symptoms, cause, and treatment of physical illnesses. Psychologists who specialize in behavioral medicine often are called *health psychologists.*

Learning more adaptive ways of **coping,** responses aimed at diminishing the burden of stress, can limit the recurrence or improve the course of many physical illnesses (Lazarus, 2000; Snyder, 1999). In order to promote health,

specialists in behavioral medicine therefore study and encourage healthy coping thorough stress management, proper diet, regular exercise, and avoidance of tobacco use. In treating diseases, behavioral medicine includes interventions such as educating parents of chronically ill children, teaching patients strategies for coping with chronic pain, and even running support groups for people with terminal cancer.

In this chapter we discuss innovations in behavioral medicine, and review evidence on the link between stress and some physical illnesses. In order to illustrate the challenges in studying stress, we also include an extended discussion of the number one killer in the United States today, cardiovascular disease. We begin with a case study from our files.

CASE STUDY Bob Carter's Heart Attack

One Thursday afternoon, Bob Carter, a salesman for a beer and liquor wholesaler, was completing his route, calling on customers. Throughout the morning, he had felt a familiar discomfort in his chest and left arm. As had been happening on occasion for at least a year, that morning he experienced a few fleeting but sharp pains in the center and left side of his chest. This was followed by a dull ache in his chest and left shoulder and a feeling of congestion in the same areas. Breathing deeply made the pain worse, but Bob could manage it as long as he took shallow breaths. He continued on his route, alternately vowing to see a doctor soon and cursing his aging body.

After grabbing a hamburger for lunch, Bob called on a customer who was behind in his payments. At first, Bob shared a cigarette with the customer and chatted with him in a friendly way. He was a salesman, after all. Soon it was time to pressure him about the bill. As Bob raised his voice in anger, a crushing pain returned to his chest and radiated down his left arm. This was much worse than anything he had experienced before. The pain was so intense that Bob was unable to continue speaking. He slumped forward against the table, but with his right arm he waved away any attempt to help him. After sitting still for about 10 minutes, Bob was able to drag himself to his car and drive to his home 30 miles away. When his wife saw him shuffle into the

house looking haggard and in obvious pain, she called for an ambulance. The Carters soon discovered that Bob had suffered a *myocardial infarction* (a heart attack).

Bob was 49 years old at the time. His home life was happy, but it also put a lot of pressures on him. His 24-year-old daughter was living at home while her husband was serving in combat duty overseas. Naturally, the entire family was anxious about the son-in-law's well-being. More stress came from Bob's 21-year-old daughter, who had just graduated from college and was getting married in 3 weeks. Finally, Bob's 19-year-old son was home from his first year of college, full of rebellion and ideas that challenged Bob's authority. There was no shortage of family stress.

Bob also put plenty of stress on himself. A former high school athlete, he had always been competitive and hard-driving. He wanted to be the best at whatever he did, and right now his goal was to be the best salesman in his company. Bob used his charm, humor, and some not-so-gentle pressure to sell his products, and it worked. But once he had become the best salesman in his wholesaling company, Bob wanted to be the best salesman for the producers whose products he sold. No matter what he accomplished, Bob drove himself hard to meet a new goal.

Bob maintained his drive and competitiveness from his youthful days as a star athlete,

but he had not maintained his physical condition. The only exercise he got was playing golf, and he usually rode in a cart instead of walking the course. He was at least 30 pounds overweight, smoked a pack and a half of cigarettes a day, ate a lot of fatty red meat, and drank heavily. Bob was a good candidate for a heart attack.

Bob recuperated quickly in the hospital. He was tired and in considerable pain for a couple of days, but he was telling jokes before the end of a week. His cardiologist explained what had happened and gave Bob a stern lecture about changing his lifestyle. He wanted Bob to quit smoking, lose weight, cut down on his drinking, and gradually work himself back into shape with a careful program of exercise. He urged Bob to slow down at work and told him to quit worrying about his children—they were old enough to take care of themselves.

To underscore these messages, the cardiologist asked a psychologist from the hospital's behavioral medicine unit to consult with Bob. The psychologist reviewed information on coronary risk with Bob and gave him several pamphlets to read on risk factors. The psychologist also explained that the hospital ran several programs that might interest Bob after discharge. These included workshops on stress management, weight reduction groups, and exercise classes. The fees for these programs were minimal, because the hospital ran them as a community service. The psychologist asked Bob if he had other concerns that he wanted to discuss, but Bob said there were none. The psychologist suggested that some issues might come up in the future. Cardiac patients and their families sometimes had trouble adjusting to the sudden reminder of the patient's mortality. Bob thanked the psychologist for the information but waved off the offer of assistance much as he had waved off help in the middle of his heart attack.

Bob was discharged from the hospital 10 days after being admitted. Against his doctor's advice, he walked his daughter down the aisle at her wedding the following weekend, and he was back to work within a month. At his 6-week checkup, Bob admitted to his cardiologist that he was smoking again. His weight was unchanged, and his exercise and drinking were only a "little better." When the cardiologist chastised Bob for not following medical advice, Bob promised to renew his efforts. He belied his commitment, however, by commenting that giving up these small pleasures might not make him live any longer, it would just seem that way. Clearly, one heart attack was not going to get Bob Carter to slow down.

◆◆

The case of Bob Carter illustrates how stress can contribute to coronary heart disease, but it also raises a number of questions about the link. What is the physiological mechanism that transforms psychological stress into coronary risk? Is stress the problem, or is the real culprit the unhealthy behaviors that result from stress—smoking, drinking, and overeating? What is the role of personality in stress? Can someone like Bob change his lifestyle, and if so, does this lower the risk for future heart attacks? We consider these and related questions in this chapter. First, though, we need to consider more carefully exactly what we mean by "stress."

DEFINING STRESS

We define *stress* as a challenging event that requires physiological, cognitive, or behavioral adaptation. However, we need to examine this definition closely. Is stress the event itself? Some people would relax after becoming the top salesman, but Bob Carter viewed this achievement as another challenge. Perhaps stress should be defined in terms of the individual's reactions to an event. However, our theories indicate that stress causes adverse reactions. Defining stress in terms of these reactions runs the risk of becoming an exercise in circular logic. In fact, scientists continue to debate whether stress is best defined as a life event itself or an *appraisal* of life events, the event plus the individual's reaction to it.

Stress as a Life Event

Researchers often define stress as a life event—a difficult circumstance regardless of the individual's reaction to it. For example, Holmes and Rahe's (1967) Social Readjustment Rating Scale (SRRS) assigned stress values to life events based on the judgments of a large group of normal adults. The SRRS views stressors that produce more *life change units* as causing more stress (see Table 8–1).

Researchers consistently link stress ratings on the SRRS and similar instruments to a variety of physical illnesses (Miller, 1989). Critics note, however, that stress checklists (1) rely on retrospective reports; (2) contain stressors that do not apply to people of different ages and ethnic backgrounds (Contrada et al., 2001) (Is the SRRS a good measure of college student stress?); (3) treat both positive and negative events as stressors (Would you equate getting married with getting fired?); (4) fail to distinguish between short-lived and chronic stressors; and (5) most importantly, treat the same event as causing the same amount of stress for everyone, when, for example, getting pregnant is much more stressful for an unwed teenager than for a married couple in their thirties.

Dohrenwend and colleagues (1990) demonstrated how the same stressor does have different meanings for different people. For example, an assault caused a *large* change for nearly 20 percent of the respondents in this study, but it caused *no* change for the same percentage of people (see Table 8–2). Because of this variability, many experts believe stress must be defined by the combination of an event plus each individual's reaction to it.

Stress as Appraisal of Life Events

Perhaps the most influential advocate of this position is Richard Lazarus (1966), who defined stress by the individual's *appraisal* of a challenging life event. According to this view, an impending exam, for example, causes you stress when your knowledge is inadequate, but not when you feel confident about the subject matter. Your *primary appraisal* is your evaluation of the challenge,

TABLE 8-1   Change Caused by Different Life Events

LIFE EVENT	LIFE CHANGE UNITS	LIFE EVENT	LIFE CHANGE UNITS
Death of one's spouse	100	Son or daughter leaving home	29
Divorce	73	Trouble with in-laws	29
Marital separation	65	Outstanding personal achievement	28
Jail term	63	Wife beginning or stopping work	26
Death of a close family member	63	Beginning or ending school	26
Personal injury or illness	53	Change in living conditions	25
Marriage	50	Revision of personal habits	24
Being fired at work	47	Trouble with one's boss	23
Marital reconciliation	45	Change in work hours or conditions	20
Retirement	45	Change in residence	20
Change in the health of a family member	44	Change in schools	20
Pregnancy	40	Change in recreation	19
Sex difficulties	39	Change in church activities	19
Gain of a new family member	39	Change in social activities	18
Business readjustment	39	Mortgage or loan of less than $10,000	17
Change in one's financial state	38	Change in sleeping habits	16
Death of a close friend	37	Change in number of family get-togethers	15
Change to a different line of work	36	Change in eating habits	15
Change in number of arguments with one's spouse	35	Vacation	13
Mortgage over $10,000	31	Christmas	12
Foreclosure of a mortgage or loan	30	Minor violations of the law	11
Change in responsibilities at work	29		

The SRRS rates different stressors as causing more or less life change for people. More difficult stressors have a higher number of "life change units."

Source: Reprinted with permission from T.H. Holmes and R.H. Rahe. The Social Readjustment Rating Scale, *Journal of Psychosomatic Research,* 11, © 1967, Pergamon Press. Copyright © 1967 by Elsevier, Inc. Reprinted by permission of Elsevier, Ltd.

TABLE 8-2   Different Reactions to the Same Life Event

TYPE OF EVENT	PERCENTAGE OF SUBJECTS REPORTING EACH AMOUNT OF CHANGE			
	LARGE	MODERATE	LITTLE	NONE
Serious physical illness	47.2%	27.8%	8.3%	16.7%
Relations with mate got worse	41.2	47.1	0.0	11.8
Relative died (not child/spouse)	8.3	8.3	29.2	54.2
Close friend died	5.3	15.8	29.8	49.1
Financial loss (not work related)	16.3	44.2	18.6	20.9
Assaulted	18.5	22.2	40.7	18.5
Broke up with a friend	0.0	26.1	37.0	37.0
Laid off	13.3	63.3	13.3	10.0
Had trouble with a boss	17.5	35.0	32.5	15.0
Got involved in a court case	9.5	9.5	28.6	52.4

Source: Adapted from B.P. Dohrenwend et al., 1990, Measuring life events: The problem of variability within event categories, *Stress Medicine,* 6, 182.

threat, or harm posed by a particular event. Your *secondary appraisal* is your assessment of your abilities and resources for coping with that event (Lazarus & Folkman, 1984). Thus, even if you believe your knowledge is inadequate, the impending exam will cause less stress if you have the time and the ability to study adequately.

The appraisal approach recognizes that the same event is more or less stressful for different people, but runs the risk of being an exercise in circular logic. What is stress? Stress is an event that causes us to feel threatened and overwhelmed. What causes us to feel threatened and overwhelmed? Stress. Logically, such a definition would be a *tautology*, a redundant statement that means nothing. We agree that stress is best defined as a life event and its individual challenge. Because of the potential tautology, however, researchers must carefully distinguish independent variables (stressors) from hypothesized dependent variables (adverse outcomes on page 256).

SYMPTOMS OF STRESS

Stress is a part of life. In fact, stress is an *adaptive* response to many aspects of living. If you had no stress response, you would not be motivated to jump out of the way of a cement truck barreling down on you, let alone to study for your exams!

The renowned American physiologist Walter Cannon (1871–1945), one of the first and foremost stress researchers, recognized the adaptive, evolutionary aspects of stress. Cannon (1935) viewed stress as the activation of the **fight or flight response,** the reaction you witness when a cat is surprised by a barking dog. The cat can either flee to safety or turn to scratch at the dog. The fight or flight response has obvious survival value. Cannon observed, however, that fight or flight is a *maladaptive* reaction to much stress in the modern world such as being reprimanded by your boss or giving a speech before a large audience. In other words, the human environment may have evolved more rapidly than our physiological reactions to it. (Some psychologists think that fight or flight is a *male* reaction to stress. See Tend and Befriend on page 256.)

Psychophysiological Responses to Stress

Physiologically, the fight or flight response activates your *sympathetic nervous system:* Your heart and respiration rates increase, blood pressure rises,

your pupils dilate, blood sugar levels elevate, and your blood flow is redirected in preparation for muscular activity (Baum et al., 1987; Koranyi, 1989). These physiological reactions heighten your attention, provide energy for quick action, and prepare your body for injury (Sapolsky, 1992, 2003). This physiological reaction is adaptive if a truck is headed your way, and presumably it also was an adaptive response to many threats over the course of human evolution. When your boss is yelling—or you worry that your boss *might* yell—the response only leaves your body racing and you feeling nervous and agitated.

Adrenal Hormones   How does the stress response work physiologically? When a perceived threat registers in the cortex, it signals the *amygdala,* the brain structure primarily responsible for activating the stress response, which in turn secretes *corticotrophin-releasing factor* (CRF). CRF stimulates the brainstem to activate the sympathetic nervous system. In response to the sympathetic arousal, the *adrenal glands* release two key hormones. One is *epinephrine* (commonly known as *adrenaline*), which acts as a neuromodulator, and leads to the release of *norepinephrine* and *epinephrine* into the bloodstream (see Figure 8–1). This familiar "rush of adrenaline" further activates the sympathetic nervous system.

The second key adrenal hormone is **cortisol,** often called the "stress hormone" because its release is so closely linked with stress. Cortisol has a less rapid action than adrenaline, yet it

Why must psychologists worry about circular reasoning when defining stress as an event plus a response?

Even welcome life events, like graduation or marriage, can be stressful.

TEND AND BEFRIEND:
THE FEMALE ALTERNATIVE TO FIGHT OR FLIGHT?

Health psychologist Shelly Taylor and her colleagues (2000) suggest that fight or flight may be a particularly *male* response to stress. Females, particularly primate females, may be more likely to respond to stress with a pattern that these theorists term **tend and befriend.** *Tending* involves caring for offspring in a way that protects them from harm. *Befriending* is responding to threat with social affiliation, thereby reducing the risk of physical danger and encouraging the exchange of resources.

Taylor and her colleagues (2000) conceptualize the origin of tend and befriend, like fight or flight, in terms of evolutionary psychology. They hypothesize that the inclusive fitness of a female's genes is increased by caretaking and blending into the environment in response to threat. They argue that social affiliation

provides both the safety of numbers and the opportunity to share resources during times of hardship. Attachment is the mechanism hypothesized to modulate tending and befriending, but Taylor focuses on the benefits of attachment for the caretaker rather than the infant. She argues that evolution might have selected for caretaking tendencies in adult females.

Taylor et al. (2000) provide specific neuroendocrine hypotheses as well as a broader evolutionary conceptualization of tending and befriending. They suggest that female aggression, unlike aggression in males, may not be mediated by sympathetic arousal modulated by *testosterone* (the male sex hormone), thereby limiting the female's fight response. In turn, flight tendencies might be countered by the release of *oxytocin* by the pituitary and modulated by the female sex hormone, *estrogen,*

resulting in the activation of the parasympathetic nervous system, which has a calming effect.

Taylor and her colleagues (2000) acknowledge that their ideas are speculative, but their novel theorizing suggests many creative directions for new research, for example, including more females in studies of stress. Prior to 1995, 83 percent of the participants in laboratory studies of stress were males. Critics might suggest that the biologically based views of female–male differences are sexist, but Taylor is careful to acknowledge cultural influences on gender roles. She and her coworkers also remind us that biology is not destiny. Finally, they speculate that tending and befriending may also be a response in the *male* repertoire, but a less prominent one than fight or flight.

How does the body prepare for fight or flight and why is this maladaptive in the face of stress today?

Walter Cannon

(1871–1945) *was one of the first scientists to conduct systematic research on stress. Cannon focused on the emergency response, the body's physiological preparation for fight or flight.*

functions quickly to help the body make repairs in response to injury or infection. One function of cortisol is "containment" of pathogens in the body—the same function performed by the exogenous steroids that you may take for inflammation and skin irritation. Like externally administered steroids, however, cortisol can promote healing in the short run, but an excess of cortisol can harm the body by damaging the hippocampus, causing muscular atrophy, and producing hypertension (Sapolsky, 1992; Song & Leonard, 2000; Yehuda, 2002).

Immune System Responses The release of cortisol and CRF also cause *immunosuppression,* the decreased production of immune agents. In fact, research in this area has spawned new field of study, **psychoneuroimmunology (PNI),** the investigation of the relation between stress and immune function (Adler, 2001; Song & Leonard, 2000). PNI research shows that particularly vulnerable to stress are T *cells,* one of the two major types of *lymphocytes,* white blood cells that fight off *antigens,* foreign substances like bacteria that invade the body. Decreased T cell production makes the body more susceptible to infectious diseases during times of stress (Adler, 2001; Song & Leonard, 2000).

Why would stress inhibit immune function? From an evolutionary perspective, *heightened* immune functioning might seem to better prepare the body for the infection that may follow injury. Maier, Watkins, and Fleshner (1994) note, however, that the immune response creates inflammation, maintains fever, and intensifies pain—all of which impair immediate action. In fact, the immune system acts as something of a sense organ, telling the brain when the body is functioning poorly and setting off a collection of cognitive, emotional, and behavioral changes—sickness (Maier & Watkins, 1998). Thus, inhibited immune function may be an adaptive short-term reaction to stress even though it is maladaptive in the long run.

Recent evidence suggests that stress may both inhibit and enhance immune functioning. Short-term stressors and physical threats *enhance* certain immune responses, particularly aspects of immune functioning that respond quickly, require little energy, and may contain infection due to an injury. However, stress impairs other aspects of immune function, particularly actions that drain energy from the fight or flight response, and chronic stressors and losses (as opposed to threats) also create immunosuppression (Segerstrom & Miller, 2004). Like this more differentiated immune response, recent evidence

The Physiology of the Stress Response

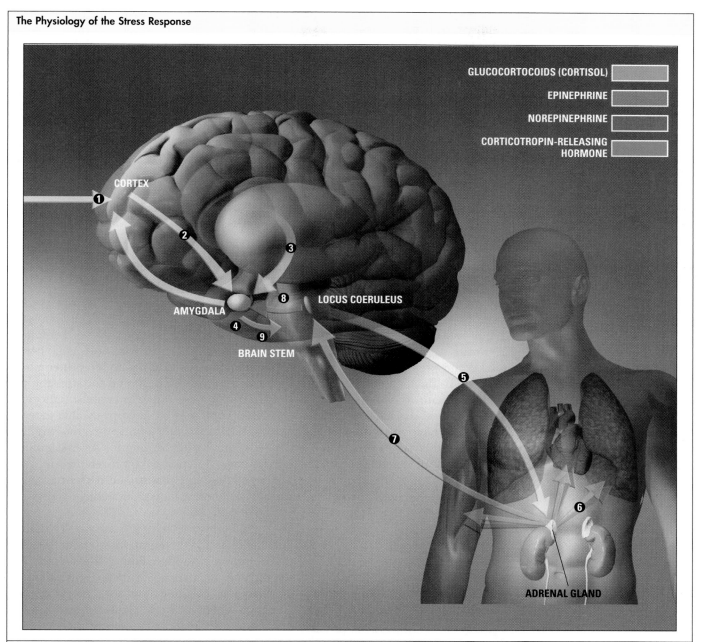

FIGURE 8–1: Stress pathways are diverse and involve many regions of the brain in feedback loops that can sometimes greatly amplify a response. The process—simplified somewhat in this diagram—begins when an actual or perceived threat activates the sensory and higher reasoning centers in the cortex (1). The cortex then sends a message to the amygdala, the principal mediator of the stress response (2). Separately, a preconscious signal may precipitate activity in the amygdala (3). The amygdala releases corticotropin-releasing hormone, which stimulates the brain stem (4) to activate the sympathetic nervous system via the spinal cord (5). In response, the adrenal glands produce the stress hormone epinephrine; a different pathway simultaneously triggers the adrenals to release glucocorticoids. The two types of hormones act on the muscle, heart and lungs to prepare the body for "fight or flight" (6). If the stress becomes chronic, glucocorticoids induce the locus coeruleus (7) to release norepinephrine that communicates with the amygdala (8), leading to the production of more CRH (9)—and to ongoing reactivation of stress pathways.

Source: R. Sapolsky (2003). *Taming stress. Scientific American,* 286, p. 89, figures by Alfred Kamajian. Reproduced by permission of Alfred Kamajian.

Hans Selye (1907–1982) *was a physiologist and prolific stress researcher. Selye's concept of the general adaptation syndrome continues to influence contemporary research on the stress response.*

also suggests that different stressors also set off different cortisol responses (Dickerson & Kemeny, 2004).

Illness and Chronic Stress When repeated over time, your physiological reactions to stress can leave you susceptible to illness. Cannon (1935) hypothesized this occurs because intense or chronic stress overwhelms the body's **homeostasis** (a term he coined), the tendency to return to a steady state of normal functioning. He suggested that, over time, the prolonged arousal of the sympathetic nervous system eventually damages the body, because it no longer returns to its normal resting state.

Canadian physiologist Hans Selye (1907–1982), another very influential stress researcher, offered a different hypothesis based on his concept of the **general adaptation syndrome (GAS).** Seyle's GAS consists of three stages: alarm, resistance, and exhaustion (see Figure 8–2). The stage of *alarm* occurs first and involves the mobilization of the body in reaction to threat. The stage of *resistance* comes next and is a period of time during which the body is physiologically activated and prepared to respond to the threat. *Exhaustion* is the final stage, and it occurs if the body's resources are depleted by chronic stress. Selye viewed the stage of exhaustion as the key in the development of physical illness from stress. At this stage, the body is damaged by continuous, failed attempts to reactivate the GAS (Selye, 1956).

Although similar, Selye's theory differs from Cannon's in important ways. An analogy for

Cannon's theory is a car in which the engine continues to race instead of idling down after running fast. In contrast, an analogy for Selye's theory is a car that has run out of gas and is damaged because stress keeps turning the key, trying repeatedly and unsuccessfully to restart the engine.

Stress may create physical illness in both ways, but a third mechanism may be as important. Because the stress response uses so much energy, the body may not be able to perform many routine functions, such as storing energy or repairing injuries (Sapolsky, 1992). The result is greater susceptibility to illness. An automotive analogy for this third model is car running constantly at such high speeds that the cooling and lubricant systems cannot keep up, making a breakdown likely.

Coping

In good ways, and in bad, we have many potential ways to cope with stress. Two general coping strategies are problem-focused and emotion-focused coping (Lazarus & Folkman, 1984). **Problem-focused coping** involves attempts to change a stressor. If your job is too stressful, you can look for a new one. In contrast, **emotion-focused coping** is an attempt to alter internal distress. Before taking a big exam, you might sit quietly and breathe deeply for several minutes. Forgiveness is another approach to emotion-focus coping, one that has been shown to have health-promoting effects (Witvliet, Ludwig, & Vander Laan, 2001).

Culturally, Americans tend to fix things rather than accept them, while other societies (for example, Asian cultures) focus more on acceptance than change. Either way, we all face a problem in deciding how to cope: It is often unclear what will work. Consider, for example, if you are stressed out by poor grades in a difficult class. Should you redouble your efforts, drop the course, or accept that this is not your best subject? Problem-focused coping can help you conquer stress, but failed attempts at problem-focused coping *increase* rather than decrease distress. For some of life's challenges, we must change our reactions, because we cannot change our lives. In short, there is much truth in Reinhold Niebuhr's (1951) "Serenity Prayer":

> God, give us the serenity to accept what cannot be changed;

A white blood cell (microphage) reaches out to capture a bacterium.

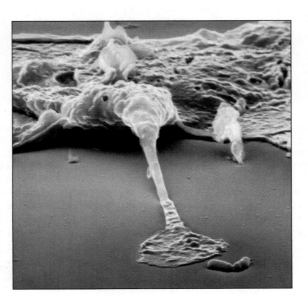

Give us the courage to change what
  should be changed;
Give us the wisdom to distinguish one
  from the other.

Predictability and Control   Events *are* less stressful when we are better prepared to cope with them. Studies of animals and humans show that *predictability* and *control* can dramatically reduce stress. For example, rats have smaller physiological responses to shocks that are signaled by the flash of a light than to unsignaled shocks of the same magnitude (Sapolsky, 1992). The predictability apparently allows the animals (and humans too) to begin to cope even before the onset of a stressor. The signaled shock elicits a response that is similar to (but weaker than) the response to the actual stressor. However, the signal also decreases negative responding to the shock itself (Baum et al., 1987).

The importance of control also can be demonstrated in animal research. Rats have a smaller stress response when they can stop a shock by pressing a bar in comparison to rats exposed to exactly the same shock but who have no control (Sapolsky, 1992). Even the *illusion* of control can help to alleviate stress in humans. However, the perception of control can increase stress when people believe they can exercise control but fail to do so, or when they lose control over a formerly controllable stressor (Mineka & Kihlstrom, 1978). In short, control alleviates stress when it can be exercised or even when it is illusory, but failed attempts at control intensify stress.

Outlets for Frustration   Research also indicates that responding with physical activity reduces physiological reactions to stress. The effort does not necessarily need to involve problem-focused coping, because the activity need not be directed at the stressor itself but may include other *outlets for frustration*. For example, rats secrete less cortisol if they can attack another rat or run on a running wheel after being given an electric shock (Sapolsky, 1992).

Repression   *Repression* is one form of emotion-focused coping that can be maladaptive physically (Cramer, 2000; Somerfield & McCrae, 2000). People who do not acknowledge their experience of anxiety show exaggerated psychophysiological reactions to stress such as increased heart rate and blood pressure (Schwartz, 1989). Psychophysiological reactions to stress also are greater for "defensive deniers"—people who report positive

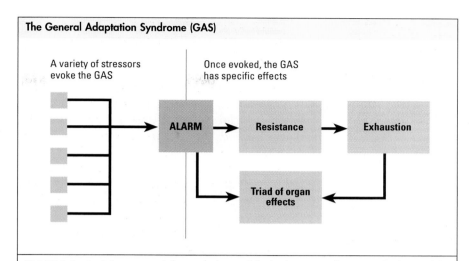

FIGURE 8-2: Selye assumed that stress harmed the body most at the stage of exhaustion.
Source: Adapted from A. Baum, L.M. Davidson, J.E. Singer, and S.W. Street, 1987, *Stress as a psychophysiological response.* In A. Baum and J.E. Singer (Eds.), Handbook of Psychology and Health. Stress, vol. 5, p. 4. Hillsdale, NJ: Erlbaum.

mental health but whom clinicians judge to have emotional problems (Shedler, Mayman, & Manis, 1993). Other research indicates that when people are encouraged to recount very stressful experiences, they show reductions in various psychophysiological indicators of the stress response (Pennebaker, 1990; Petrie et al., 1995). Bob Carter is one example of a repressor who kept his feeling bottled up. He "swallowed" a lot of his anger, and this probably had adverse physiological effects, increasing his blood pressure and putting him at greater risk for a heart attack.

Optimism   Optimism is a basic key to effective coping. People with an optimistic coping style have a positive attitude toward dealing with stress, even when it cannot be changed, while pessimists are defeated from the outset (see Table 8–3). Positive thinking is linked with better health habits and less illness in general, and for those with heart disease,

Calvin and Hobbes
by Bill Watterson

Air traffic controllers perform a job with high demands, limited control, and lives at stake, a recipe for stress.

Is stress always bad?

AIDS, and other serious physical illnesses (Carver & Scheier, 1999; Kubzansky et al., 2001; Shatte et al., 1999). Stress is taxing, but less so if we approach stress optimistically (Folkman & Moskowitz, 2000; see Critical Thinking *Matters*).

Religion   For many people, religious and philosophical beliefs are essential to coping with stress. Surprisingly, psychologists have only recently begun to study religious coping (Hill & Paragament, 2003). Emerging evidence demonstrates the health value of religious practices, for example, mortality risk is lower among those who attend church services, probably as a result of improved health behavior (Powell, Shahabi, & Thoresen, 2003).

New research also is shattering some misconceptions about religious coping. For example, a recent study of 200 Latinos with arthritis found that greater religious coping predicted improved psychological well-being. Some view religious beliefs as promoting acceptance of one's lot in life, but in this study religious coping predicted *active*, not passive, coping efforts. Active coping, in turn, predicted lower levels of pain and depression (Abraído-Lanza, Vásquez, & Echeverría, 2004). The religious beliefs of these Latino arthritis suffers apparently helped them to gain control *with* God, not to accept control *by* God (Pargament & Park, 1995).

Health Behavior

Stress may also cause illness indirectly by disrupting healthy behavior (Cohen & Williamson, 1991). **Health behavior** is action that promotes good health, including positive efforts like eating, sleeping, and exercising adequately and avoiding unhealthy activities such as cigarette smoking, excessive alcohol consumption, and drug use. As in the case of Bob Carter, poor health habits, and not stress per se, may be responsible for much of the relation between stress and illness (Bogg & Roberts, 2004). In considering the tremendous importance of health behavior, think about the fact that basic health behaviors—personal hygiene, sanitation, and an adequate diet—are more responsible for our vastly increased health and life expectancy than are scientific advances like the discovery of penicillin (Ray, 2004; see Figure 8–3).

Following Medical Advice   Stress may also be related to the very important health behavior of following medical advice, something that as many as 93 percent of all patients fail to do fully (Taylor, 1990). This is a particular problem for illnesses like hypertension (high blood pressure) that usually have no obvious symptoms. In such cases patients may discontinue their medication because it produces no noticeable relief, even though it may be controlling a dangerous underlying condition. Stressors such as family conflict also can interfere with adherence to treatments that *do* have clear symptoms. For example, children with insulin-dependent diabetes are less likely to adhere to medical recommendations concerning exercise, diet, and testing blood sugars

TABLE 8-3 Coping Tendencies of Optimists and Pessimists	
OPTIMISTS	**PESSIMISTS**
Information seeking	Suppression of thoughts
Active coping and planning	Giving up
Positive reframing	Self-distraction
Seeking benefit	Cognitive avoidance
Use of humor	Focus on distress
Acceptance	Overt denial

From C.S. Carver & M.F. Scheier, 1999, Optimism. In C.R. Snyder (Ed.), *Coping: The Psychology of What Works*, p. 194. New York: Oxford University Press. Used by permission of Oxford University Press, Inc.

when family conflict is high (Miller-Johnson et al., 1994).

Illness Behavior   *Illness behavior*—behaving as if you are sick—also appears to be stress related. Considerable research indicates that increased stress is correlated with such illness behaviors as making more frequent office visits to physicians or allowing chronic pain to interfere with everyday activities (Taylor, 1990). Effective coping with chronic illness involves some ignoring of physical discomfort and living life as normally as possible.

Social Support   Finally, the fact that many people consult physicians for psychological rather than physical concerns underscores the value of *social support* in coping with stress. Social support not only can encourage positive health behavior, but research shows that social support can have direct, physiological benefits. For example, stressed monkeys exhibit less immunosuppression when they interact more often with other monkeys (Cohen et al., 1992), and stressed rabbits develop clogged arteries more slowly if they

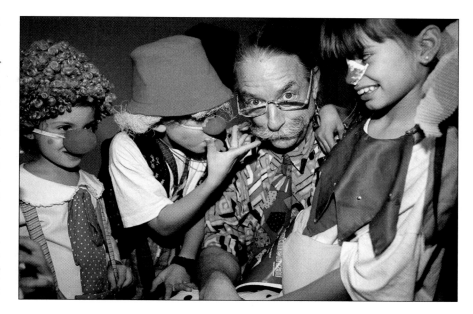

affiliate with other rabbits (McCabe et al., 2002). Increased social support also predicts improved immune, cardiovascular, and endocrine functioning in humans (Schneiderman et al., 2004; Uchino, Cacioppo, & Kiecolt-Glaser, 1996). And it may be better to give than to receive. Providing

The real-life Patch Adams inspired the film in which Robin Williams played the title role. Adams was a rebellious medical student in the 1960s who wanted to provide holistic care and instill optimism in his patients.

critical thinking matters

RESILIENCE

Our popular culture, and the tone of much psychological research, tells us that stress is always bad, something to be avoided. Stress will make us tense, irritable, and unhappy. Stress will make us sick.

As we have seen, stress can make us more susceptible to illness, but a little critical thinking leads us to ask: Are we really *so* vulnerable to stress? After all, humans evolved in stressful, often dangerous environments. Evolution *must* have selected for successful strategies for coping with stress, not crumbling in the face of it. And stress is a part of everyday life, often a good part—a challenge. We typically expect to rise to the challenge of a sporting event, a difficult class, even a crisis in our lives. Does it make sense that humans are so fragile?

The answer is "No" according to proponents of the recent *positive psychology* movement, an approach that highlights human psychological strengths (Linley & Joseph, 2005). Focusing on our positive qualities,

psychologists increasingly recognize pervasive human **resilience,** the ability to cope successfully with the challenges of life, including very stressful ones. The resilience perspective notes that most people overcome even traumatic stressors. Most people do *not* develop PTSD or ASD following a trauma; most people who have lost a loved one are *not* overcome by depression in their bereavement (Bonanno, 2004).

To be sure, successful coping is not the same as the absence of inner distress (Litz, 2005). One study found, for example, that among resilient young people whose parents divorced—college students doing well in school and free from emotional problems—nearly half reported they had a harder childhood than most other kids. Almost one-third agreed that they sometimes wondered if their father even loved them (Laumann-Billings & Emery, 2000). These young people bounced back from the stress of their parents divorce, but the bounce apparently still hurt.

Even successful coping can be painful, but pain is not the same as pathology. In fact, not only are most people resilient, but some people grow—they get stronger—as a result of facing the challenge of stress (Linley & Joseph, 2005). Bicyclist Lance Armstrong's battle with cancer only spurred him on to win after win in the Tour de France, for example.

Psychologists do not yet understand all that resilience entails. Resilience lies partly within the individual—for example, our hardiness; resilience is defined, in part, by the nature, duration, and intensity of stress; and part of resilience is attributable to the supports available in the environment (Roisman, 2005). Whatever resilience is, it is a quality that most people seem to possess in most circumstance. Stress can make us weaker, or it can make us stronger. While chronic, uncontrollable stress can break us down, most ordinary people facing ordinary stressors find their strength.

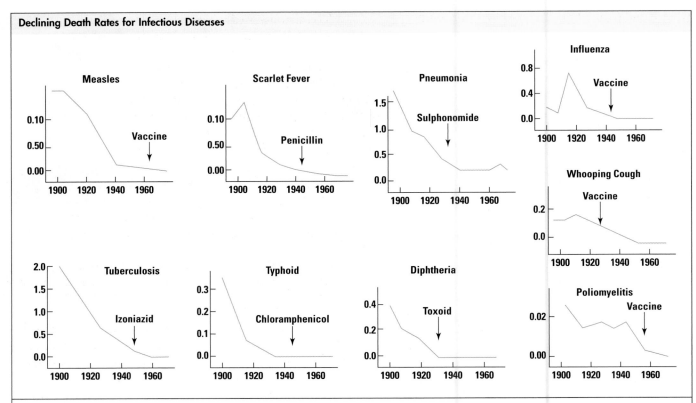

FIGURE 8–3: Annual death rates per 1,000 population for nine infectious diseases in relation to timing of discoveries of drugs that demonstrably cure or prevent them. The pattern strongly suggests that improved public health since 1900—prevention of the conditions that lead to infection—accounts for most of the decline in death.

Source: From "Medical Measures and the Decline of Mortality," by J. B. McKinlay and S. M. McKinlay, in *The Sociology of Health and Illness: Critical Perspectives* (p. 25), by P. Conrad & R. Kern (Eds.), 1981, New York: St. Martin's Press. Copyright © 2000 by Worth Publishers. Reprinted by permission of the publisher.

social support promotes good health at least as much as receiving it does (Brown et al., 2003).

Of all potential sources of social support—or conflict—a good marriage may be most critical to physical health (Kiecolt-Glaser & Newton, 2001). In one fascinating study, 90 newly married couples were admitted to a hospital research ward where they engaged in a 30-minute discussion of marital problems. Partners who were more hostile or negative during the interaction showed greater immunosuppression over the next 24 hours in comparison to newlyweds who had more positive conversations (Kiecolt-Glaser et al., 1993). Blood pressure also remained elevated longer following hostile interactions than following friendly interactions.

A follow-up study brought the results full circle: Couples who divorced in the subsequent 10 years had epinephrine levels that had been 34 percent higher during their newlywed conflicts. A conflicted marriage is bad for your health, and too much stress is bad for your marriage (Kiecolt-Glaser et al., 2003).

Illness as a Cause of Stress

Stress can cause illness, but illness also causes stress. For example, consider the effects of the diagnosis of insulin-dependent diabetes on a 10-year-old boy and his family. In order to maintain a normal range of blood sugars, the child and his parents must frequently test his blood sugars, adjust to giving and receiving one, two, or three injections of insulin daily, and carefully monitor exercise and diet because of their profound effect on blood sugars. In addition, the child and his family must somehow cope with the stigma of being "different." Finally, they have to learn to cope with the possibility of his suffering profound, long-term side effects from hyperglycemia (high blood sugars), including kidney dysfunction or blindness. As these considerations suggest, helping children, adults, and families cope with chronic illness is another important role of experts in behavioral medicine.

DIAGNOSIS OF STRESS AND PHYSICAL ILLNESS

How do psychologists classify stress and identify stress related illnesses? As you might guess, the classification of stress is difficult and often controversial.

Brief Historical Perspective

Historically, the only physical illnesses thought to be affected by stress were a few psychosomatic disorders, such as ulcers and asthma. The field of psychosomatic medicine was dominated by psychoanalytic psychiatrists who endorsed the idea that specific personality types caused specific psychosomatic diseases. These theorists attempted to classify psychosomatic illnesses according to the unique personality type that caused it. For example, Franz Alexander (1950), one of the most influential of the theorists, wrote:

> The crucial finding in ulcer patients is the frustration (external or internal) of passive, dependent, and love-demanding desires that cannot be gratified in normal relationships. Onset of illness occurs when the intensity of the patient's unsatisfied dependent cravings increases either because of external deprivation or because the patient defends against his cravings by assuming increased responsibilities. (Alexander, French, & Pollock, 1968, p. 16)

Contemporary Approaches

Research does not support the idea that personality is directly related to psychosomatic symptoms, and contemporary approaches also reject the view that only certain physical illnesses are affected by stress. DSM-IV-TR does not include a list of psychosomatic disorders. Instead, virtually any physical illness can be coded on Axis III, *general medical conditions*. When a physical illness is the focus of treatment, the diagnosis of *psychological factors affecting medical condition* is used on Axis I (see Table 8–4). The diagnosis may be used for various psychological factors, including not only mental disorders but also psychological symptoms, personality traits, maladaptive health behaviors, or stress-related physiological responses.

DSM-IV-TR also has a separate axis for coding stressors, Axis IV, psychosocial and environmental problems. Earlier versions of DSM asked clinicians to rate the amount of stress using an approach similar to the SRRS, but this proved to be an unreliable method (Skodol et al., 1990). Now DSM-IV-TR simply asks clinicians to rate the presence or absence of difficulties within various categories of life events (see Table 8–5).

TABLE 8-4	DSM-IV-TR Diagnostic Criteria for Psychological Factors Affecting Medical Condition

A. A general medical condition (coded on Axis III) is present.

B. Psychological factors adversely affect the general medical condition in one of the following ways:

1. The factors have influenced the course of the general medical condition as shown by a close temporal association between the psychological factors and the development or exacerbation, or delayed recovery from, the general medical condition.
2. The factors interfere with the treatment of the general medical condition.
3. The factors constitute additional health risks for the individual.
4. Stress-related physiological responses precipitate or exacerbate symptoms of the general medical condition.

Reprinted with permission from the *Diagnostic and Statistical Manual of Mental Disorders*, Fourth Edition, Text Revision. Copyright © 2000 by the American Psychiatric Association.

TABLE 8-5	DSM-IV-TR Categories of Psychosocial and Environmental Problems

CATEGORY	EXAMPLES
Problems with primary support group	Death of a family member, family health problems, divorce, sexual abuse, inadequate discipline, family discord, birth of a sibling
Problems related to the social environment	Death or loss of a friend, social isolation, discrimination, adjustment to life cycle transition
Educational problems	Illiteracy, academic problems, discord with teacher, inadequate school environment
Occupational problems	Unemployment, stressful work schedule, job change, discord with boss
Housing problems	Homelessness, unsafe neighborhood, discord with neighbors
Economic problems	Extreme poverty, inadequate finances
Problems with access to health care services	Inadequate health care services, inadequate health insurance
Problems related to interaction with the legal system/crime	Arrest, litigation, incarceration, victim of crime
Other psychosocial problems	Exposure to disasters, war, discord with non-family caregivers

Reprinted with permission from the *Diagnostic and Statistical Manual of Mental Disorders*, Fourth Edition, Text Revision. Copyright © 2000 by the American Psychiatric Association

THE ROLE OF PSYCHOLOGICAL FACTORS IN SOME FAMILIAR ILLNESSES

Why is stress and health behavior critical to cancer and AIDS?

At the beginning of the twentieth century, infectious diseases, specifically influenza, pneumonia, and tuberculosis, were the most common causes of death in the United States (Taylor, 1995). Thanks to advances in medical science, and especially in public health, far fewer people die of infectious diseases at the beginning of the twenty-first century (see Figure 8–4). Today, most of the leading causes of death are *lifestyle diseases* that are affected in many ways by stress and health behavior (Human Capital Initiative, 1996).

In the following sections we briefly review evidence on stress and lifestyle factors in the etiology, course, and treatment of cancer, HIV infection, chronic pain, and sleep disorders. After this, we consider the relation between stress and today's number one killer, cardiovascular disease, in some detail.

Cancer

Cancer is the second leading cause of mortality in the United States today, accounting for 23 percent of all deaths. In contrast to the declining rate of death due to heart disease, moreover, cancer deaths have risen by 20 percent over the last 30 years (American Cancer Society, 1994). At first glance, cancer would seem to be the paramount example of a purely biological illness, but the importance of psychological factors becomes apparent upon closer examination. For example, our health behavior such as cigarette smoking contributes to the extent to which we are exposed to various *carcinogens*, cancer-causing agents.

Psychological factors also are at least modestly associated with the course of cancer (McKenna et al., 1999). Not surprisingly, cancer patients often are anxious or depressed, and their negative emotions can lead to increases in negative health behavior such as alcohol consumption and decreases in positive health behavior such as exercise. PTSD among cancer patients also is quite common (Kangas, Henry, & Bryant, 2005). These outcomes are important, because cancer patients who are more emotionally expressive have fewer medical appointments, better quality of life, and better health status (Stanton et al., 2000). The absence of social support also can undermine compliance with unpleasant but vitally important medical treatments for cancer (Anderson, Kiecolt-Glaser, & Glaser, 1994). In facing the specter of cancer, the encouragement and physical assistance of family and friends can boost patients' resolve to bear treatment side effects such as hair loss and intense nausea, and partners' specific reactions to breast cancer and its treatment predict relationship quality a year later (Wimberly et al., 2005).

Some research also indicates that stress may *directly* affect the course of cancer. In animal analogue studies, for example, rats exposed to inescapable shock are less able to reject implanted cancer tumors than rats exposed to escapable shock or no stress at all (Visintainer, Seligman, & Volpicelli, 1982). Adverse effects on the immune system may explain how stress may exacerbate the course of cancer. Immunity plays an important

The 15 Leading Causes of Death in the United States in 2000

The 15 Leading Causes of Death in the United States in 2000 (y-axis, 0 to 800,000)

Categories (x-axis): Heart disease, Cancer, Stroke, Chronic lung disease, Unintentional injuries, Diabetes, Influenza and pneumonia, Alzheimer's disease, Kidney disease, Septicemia, Suicide, Chronic liver disease/cirrhosis, Hypertension, Pneumonitis due to solids/fluids, Homicide

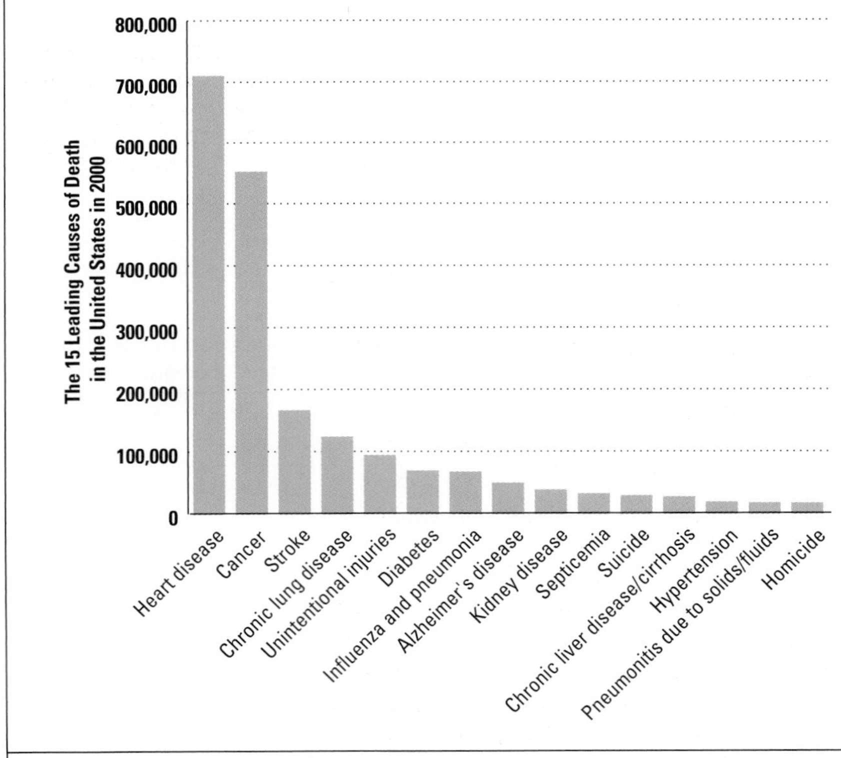

FIGURE 8–4: Stress and health behavior play a central role in most of the major causes of death in the United States today.

Source: A.M. Minino & B.L. Smith, 2001, Deaths: Preliminary data for 2000. *National Vital Statistic Report, 49*, no. 12. Hyattsville, MD: National Center for Health Studies.

role in limiting the spread of cancerous tumors, and immunosuppression due to stress may disrupt this protective function (Anderson et al., 1994).

A cause and effect relationship between stress and the course of cancer also has been implied by some exciting treatment research. Various psychological treatments have been offered to cancer patients in an attempt to improve their quality of life. The type of intervention varies widely, but treatments often include a structured, self-help group. Many of these interventions are successful in improving the quality of life among cancer patients, and a few appear to have had beneficial *physical* effects (Anderson et al., 1994). For example, one study found that 6 years after treatment, significantly fewer patients who participated in a support group died (9 percent) in comparison to patients who received no psychosocial treatment (29 percent) (Fawzy et al., 1993).

Any number of factors may explain this striking outcome, including lower stress, increased social support, and improved health behavior. We must be cautious not to overinterpret the result, however, especially since a recent study of 235 women with breast cancer found that support groups led to decreased reports of pain and psychological symptoms but did not affect survival rates (Goodwin et al., 2001). Still, it is strictly that psychological factors contribute to the course of one of our most dreaded physical illnesses.

A support group for cancer survivors.

Basketball superstar Ervin (Magic) Johnson became a spokesman for increasing awareness of HIV and AIDS after he tested HIV positive.

Acquired Immune Deficiency Syndrome (AIDS)

Acquired immune deficiency syndrome (AIDS) is caused by the **human immunodeficiency virus (HIV),** which attacks the immune system and leaves the patient susceptible to infection, neurological complications, and cancers that rarely affect those with normal immune function. However, people who are HIV positive vary widely in how rapidly they develop AIDS. Some people develop AIDS within months after HIV infection, whereas others remain symptom-free for 10 years or more.

HIV and AIDS have reached epidemic proportions throughout the world, with a notably high prevalence in Africa. In the United States, 729,326 cases of AIDS had been reported to the Centers for Disease Control and Prevention (CDC) as of June 30, 2000 (CDC, 2000). Furthermore, the CDC has estimated that 200,000 people in the United States

have HIV but are unaware of their infection (Karon et al., 1996). In 1981, AIDS was diagnosed for the first time; in 1996, it was the eighth leading cause of death in the United States (Peters et al., 1998). Fortunately, however, death due to AIDS has declined rapidly since the middle of the 1990s due to treatments that do not cure the illness but do promote a longer, healthier life. As a result, AIDS no longer is among the 15 leading causes of death in the United States (Minino & Smith, 2001).

Behavioral factors play a critical role in the transmission of AIDS. Scientists have yet to determine precisely how HIV is transmitted, but researchers have isolated a number of high-risk behaviors. Contact with bodily fluids, particularly blood and semen, is very risky, and transmission often occurs during anal sex between homosexual men and heterosexual vaginal intercourse. The use of condoms greatly reduces the risk of the sexual transmission of HIV. Other behaviors that increase

Video Case

HIV

JULIA

"HIV was the absolute prism through which I began to see the world..."

On your CD-ROM menu, select "Stress and Illness" and click on "HIV: Julia." As you watch the video, pay attention to the critical role health behavior plays in illness. Also, consider how HIV made Julia stronger, not weaker.

Teaching relaxation and guided imagery are two components of many pain management programs.

the risk for HIV infection include sharing hypodermic needles; also, an infected mother can transmit the infection to her unborn child (U.S. Department of Health and Human Services, 1993).

According to the CDC, approximately 40,000 new HIV infections occurred in the United States in 1998. Of these, 60 percent of men were infected through homosexual sex, 25 percent through injection drug use, and 15 percent through heterosexual sex. Of newly infected men, 50 percent were black, 30 percent white, and 20 percent Hispanic. Of new infections among women, 75 percent were infected through heterosexual sex and 25 percent through injection drug use. Of newly infected women, 64 percent were black, 18 percent white, and 18 percent Hispanic (CDC, 1999b).

Scientists and policymakers have launched large-scale media campaigns to educate the public about HIV and AIDS and to change risky behavior. How effective are these programs? Evidence indicates that although the public has become much more knowledgeable about AIDS, changing behavior is very difficult. For example, practices such as condom use are now more widely followed, but unprotected sex is still very common even among members of high-risk groups (Taylor, 1995).

Recent evidence has linked increased stress with a more rapid progression of HIV, and the availability of social support is associated with a more gradual onset of symptoms (Evans et al., 1997; Leserman et al., 1999). Support groups lower distress among treated patients, although, unlike cancer, no benefits for longevity have been found. Broader social support also is extremely important to the AIDS patient's social and psychological well-being. Unfortunately, misunderstanding and fear cause many people, including many health professionals, to distance themselves from AIDS rather than offering understanding, acceptance, and support.

Pain Management

Pain is a part of many acute injuries and illnesses, and pain often serves the useful functions of alerting people to a problem and motivating them to seek treatment. Pain is not always adaptive, however. In many cases, pain is not a signal of an underlying condition that can be treated. Problematic pain can take the form of recurrent acute pain, such as headaches, or pain can be chronic, for example, lower back problems.

Pain can take a huge toll on the sufferer, family members, and financial resources. And the adverse personal, social, and economic consequences of pain are important to society, because pain is pervasive. Some estimates indicate that as many as 90 million people in the United States suffer from recurrent or chronic pain (Taylor, 1995).

Pain is subjective, and this makes it difficult to evaluate or compare patients' reports about the extent or nature of their pain. Evaluation is especially difficult when pain is not associated with an identifiable injury or illness, as is commonly the case with headaches and lower back pain. Some evidence links reports of increased pain with depression and anxiety (Keefe et al., 2001), and conversely, higher levels of positive affect predict lower levels of reported pain (Zautra, Johnson, & Davis, 2005). People who are anxious or depressed may be more sensitive to pain, less able to cope with it, and more willing to complain than are people who have similar levels of suffering (Pincus & Morley, 2001).

Psychologists have tried a number of treatments to reduce pain. Many experts view emotion or insight-focused psychotherapy as counterproductive and potentially damaging

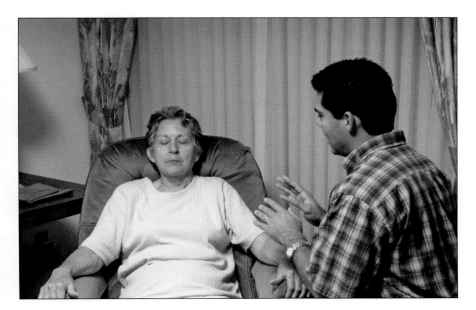

(Keefe et al., 2001). More direct treatments include hypnosis, biofeedback, relaxation training, and cognitive therapy. Researchers report a degree of success with each of these approaches, but pain reduction typically is modest (Patterson, 2004). As a result, most current efforts focus on the *pain management*, not pain reduction. The goal of pain management is to help people to cope with pain in a way that minimizes its impact on their lives, even if the pain cannot be eliminated or controlled entirely. Such programs typically include education about pain and its consequences, pain control methods such as relaxation or exercise, attempts to change maladaptive expectations about pain, and social interventions with families or support groups.

Researchers have found that pain management programs are successful in treating a wide variety of problems, including headaches, lower back pain, and facial pain. Following treatment, patients report greater satisfaction with their life and relationships, improved employment status, and less reliance on medication. Moreover, patients commonly report that their pain has lessened once they are better able to function in their lives (Taylor, 1995). It is not clear whether improved life functioning actually reduces pain or just reduces patients' awareness of discomfort. In either case, however, these positive results offer strong justification for using behavioral medicine in the treatment of chronic pain.

Sleep Disorders

Mental health professionals typically were concerned with sleep disturbances only as a symptom of some other mental disorder, such as depression or anxiety, but this circumstance is changing. In 1994, DSM first included a diagnostic category for **primary sleep disorder,** a condition where the difficulty in sleeping is the principal complaint. Two types of primary sleep disorders are listed in DSM-IV-TR. *Dyssomnias* are difficulties in the amount, quality, or timing of sleep. *Parasomnias* are characterized by abnormal events that occur during sleep, for example, nightmares.

The dyssomnias include primary insomnia, primary hypersomnia, narcolepsy, breathing-related sleep disorder, and circadian rhythm sleep disorder. *Primary insomnia* involves difficulties initiating or maintaining sleep, or poor quality of sleeping (e.g., restless sleep), that last for at least

a month and significantly impair life functioning. Primary insomnia is a common problem, although its exact prevalence is unknown, and it typically is precipitated by stress. Fortunately, effective treatments have been developed for insomnia that involve stimulus control (only staying in bed during sleep) and resetting circadian rhythms by going to bed and getting up at set times, as well as not napping, regardless of the length of sleep (Bastein et al., 2004; Bootzin, 2000). *Primary hypersomnia* is excessive sleepiness characterized by prolonged or daytime sleep, lasting at least a month and significantly interfering with life functioning. Primary hypersomnia is similar to *narcolepsy*, irresistible attacks of refreshing sleep, lasting at least 3 months. However, narcolepsy also is characterized by the sudden loss of muscle tone for brief periods of time (usually following intense emotion) and/or intrusive periods of dreaming just before awakening. The "sleep-attacks" in narcolepsy are also less resistible than is the general desire to sleep in primary hypersomnia (APA, 2000).

Breathing-related sleep disorder involves the disruption in sleep due to breathing problems such as *sleep apnea*, the temporary obstruction of the respiratory airway. People with sleep apnea typically snore loudly due to an airway that is partially obstructed as a result of obesity or other conditions. Sleep apnea patients will stop breathing for 20 to 30 seconds when the obstruction becomes complete, and this is followed by gasping, body movements, or even louder snoring. Not surprisingly, sleep apnea disrupts not only the patients' sleep but also the

Nightmares and other sleep disorders are common problems, but scientists only recently have begun to study sleep disorders systematically.

sleep of others in their vicinity. *Circadian rhythm sleep disorder* is a mismatch between the patients' 24-hour sleeping patterns and their 24-hour life demands that causes significant life distress. The disorder is found more commonly among adolescents and people who work night shifts (APA, 2000).

The parasomnias include nightmare disorder, sleep terror disorder, and sleepwalking disorder. People with *nightmare disorder* are frequently awakened by terrifying dreams. *Sleep terror disorder* also involves abrupt awakening from sleep, typically with a scream, but it differs from nightmare disorder in important respects. People with nightmare disorder recall their dreams and quickly orient to being awake; people with sleep terror disorder recall little of their dreams, show intense autonomic arousal, and are difficult to soothe. Moreover, a person with sleep terror typically returns to sleep fairly quickly and recalls little, if anything, about the episode the following morning.

Finally, *sleepwalking disorder* involves rising from the bed during sleep and walking about in a generally unresponsive state. In extreme cases, the person may use the bathroom, talk (with a minimum of meaningful dialogue), eat, or even run in a frantic attempt to escape some threat. Upon awakening, however, the person cannot remember the episode. Occasional episodes of sleepwalking are fairly common, especially among children. Like all sleep disorders, sleepwalking disorder tends to be diagnosed only if it

Over half of all victims of sudden death following myocardial infarction (heart attack) have no previous history of treatment for CHD.

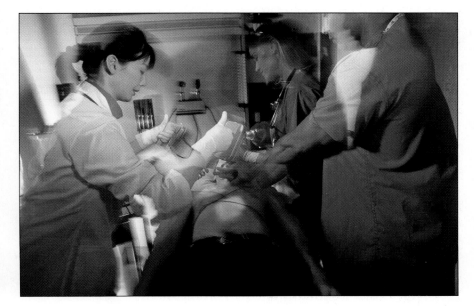

causes significant distress or impairs the person's ability to function (APA, 2000).

CARDIOVASCULAR DISEASE

The number-one killer in the United States today is cardiovascular disease, and we focus on this disease as a means of more deeply exploring stress research and treatment. **Cardiovascular disease (CVD)** is a group of disorders that affect the heart and circulatory system. The most important of these illnesses are **hypertension** (high blood pressure) and **coronary heart disease (CHD)**. The most deadly and well-known form of coronary heart disease is **myocardial infarction (MI)**, commonly called a heart attack. Hypertension increases the risk for CHD, as well as for other serious disorders, such as stroke.

Cardiovascular disorders are the leading cause of mortality not only in the United States, where they account for over one-third of all deaths (Minino & Smith, 2001), but also in most industrialized countries. About two-thirds of the deaths due to cardiovascular disorders are caused by coronary heart disease. Mortality due to CHD is of particular concern because victims of the disease tend to be relatively young. About half of all Americans with CHD and about a quarter of all stroke victims are under the age of 65 (Jenkins, 1988).

An individual's risk for developing CVD, and particularly CHD, is associated with a number of health behaviors, including weight, diet, exercise, and cigarette smoking. In addition to health behavior, personality styles, behavior patterns, and forms of emotional expression appear to contribute directly to the development of CVD (Rozanski, Blumenthal, & Kaplan, 1999).

Symptoms of Hypertension and CHD

Hypertension is often referred to as the "silent killer" because it produces no obvious symptoms. For this reason, high blood pressure often goes undetected, and routine blood pressure monitoring is extremely important. The measurement of blood pressure includes two readings. *Systolic* blood pressure is the highest pressure that the blood exerts against the arteries. This occurs when the heart is pumping blood. *Diastolic* blood pressure is the lowest amount of pressure that the blood creates against the arteries. This occurs between heartbeats. Generally, hypertension is defined by a systolic reading above 140 and/or a diastolic reading above 90 when measured while the patient is in a relaxed state.

The most notable symptom of CHD is chest pain. Typically, the pain is centralized in the middle of the chest, and it often extends through the left shoulder and down the left arm. In less severe forms of the disorder, the pain is mild, or it may be sharp but brief. The pain of myocardial infarction typically is so intense, however, that it is crippling. In fact, two-thirds of all deaths from CHD occur within 24 hours of a coronary event (Kamarck & Jennings, 1991). In over half of these sudden deaths, the victim received no previous treatment for CHD, an indication that either there were no warning symptoms or the symptoms were mild enough to have been ignored. Research using portable electrocardiogram monitoring and diary recordings indicates that patients are unaware of many episodes of inadequate oxygen supply to the heart (Krantz et al., 1993; Schneiderman, Chesney, & Krantz, 1989).

Diagnosis of CVD

Myocardial infarction and angina pectoris are the two major forms of coronary heart disease. *Angina pectoris* involves intermittent chest pains that are usually brought on by some form of exertion. Attacks of angina do not damage the heart, but the chest pain can be a sign of underlying pathology that puts the patient at risk for a myocardial infarction. MI (heart attack) does involve damage to the heart, and as noted, it often causes *sudden cardiac death*, which is usually defined as death within 24 hours of a coronary episode.

Hypertension can be primary or secondary. *Secondary hypertension* results from a known problem such as a diagnosed kidney or endocrine disorder. It is called secondary hypertension because the high blood pressure is secondary to—that is, a consequence of—the principal physical disorder. Primary or **essential hypertension** is the major concern of behavioral medicine and health psychology. In the case of essential hypertension, the high blood pressure is the principal disorder. There is no single, identifiable cause of essential hypertension, which accounts for approximately 85 percent of all cases of high blood pressure.

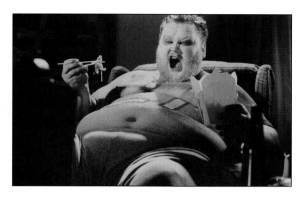

Heart disease is a lifestyle illness. Obesity, lack of exercise, and a fatty diet all are risk factors for CHD.

Instead, multiple physical and behavioral risk factors contribute to the elevated blood pressure.

Frequency of CVD

Cardiovascular disease has been the leading killer in the United States since the 1920s, but recent changes are encouraging. The rate of death due to CVD has declined by 25 percent or more in the United States, Japan, and many Western European countries. At the same time, mortality rates attributed to CVD have increased in many Eastern European countries. Some but not all of these trends are attributable to changes in diet, cigarette smoking, and blood pressure (Jenkins, 1988). Another part of the explanation may be increased awareness of the negative effects of stress in the West—and the increased industrialization and increased stress in Eastern Europe.

Why is coronary heart disease called a "lifestyle disease"?

Risk Factors for CHD   Epidemiological studies have identified several risk indicators for CHD. Men are twice as likely to suffer from CHD as are women, and sex differences are even greater with more severe forms of the disorder. Age is another major risk factor. For men, risk for CHD increases in a linear fashion with increasing age after 40. For women, risk for CHD accelerates more slowly until they reach menopause and increases sharply afterwards. Rates of CHD also are higher among low-income groups, a finding that likely accounts for the higher rates of CHD among black than among white Americans. Finally, a positive family history is also linked to an increased risk for CHD, due at least in part to genetic factors (Jenkins, 1988).

Behavior and CHD   In addition to these background factors, several health behaviors have been linked to CHD. Hypertension increases the risk for CHD by a factor of 2 to 4. The risk for CHD also is two to three times greater among those who smoke a pack or more of cigarettes a day. Obesity, a fatty diet, elevated serum cholesterol levels, heavy alcohol consumption, and lack of exercise also increase the risk for CHD. Specific risk ratios are difficult to identify for each of these factors, however, because weight, diet, cholesterol, alcohol consumption, and exercise all are closely interrelated (Jenkins, 1988).

CHD also is associated with psychological characteristics, including depression (Frasure-Smith & Lespérance, 2005; Rozanski et al., 1999). However, researchers are still sorting out how much specific psychological factors increase risk. For example, in 1981, the National Heart, Lung, and Blood Institute officially concluded that the *Type A behavior pattern* (a competitive, driven personality) increased the risk for CHD. However, recent research has challenged this conclusion, as we discuss shortly.

Risk Factors for Hypertension About 30 percent of all U.S. adults suffer from hypertension, and many of the same risk factors that predict CHD also predict high blood pressure, including genetic factors, a high-salt diet, health behavior, and lifestyle factors. Hypertension is more common in industrialized countries; and in the United States, high blood pressure is found with greater frequency among men, African Americans, low-income groups, and people exposed to high levels of chronic life stress. Although many of these risk factors are interrelated, they appear to have independent effects in increasing the prevalence of hypertension. For example, one study found that hypertension was twice as common among blacks as whites, but among black men who lived in high-stress neighborhoods, the risk was four times as great (Roberts & Rowland, 1981).

Causes of CVD

Biological Factors in CVD The immediate cause of CHD is the deprivation of oxygen to the heart muscle. No permanent damage is caused by the temporary oxygen deprivation (*myocardial ischemia*) that accompanies angina pectoris, but part of the heart muscle dies in cases of myocardial infarction. Oxygen deprivation can be caused by temporarily increased oxygen demands on the heart, for example, as a result of exercise. More

problematic is when atherosclerosis causes the gradual deprivation of the flow of blood (and the oxygen it carries) to the heart. *Atherosclerosis* is the thickening of the coronary artery wall that occurs as a result of the accumulation of blood lipids (fats) with age, and which also may be caused by inflamation resulting from stress (Black & Garbutt, 2002). The most dangerous circumstance is when oxygen deprivation is sudden, as occurs in a *coronary occlusion*. Coronary occlusions result either from arteries that are completely blocked by fatty deposits or from blood clots that make their way to the heart muscle.

The immediate biological causes of hypertension are less well understood, as are the more distant biological causes of both hypertension and CHD. As we noted, a positive family history is a risk factor for both hypertension and CHD, and most experts interpret this as a genetic contribution. However, research using animal models of CVD suggests that heritable risk interacts with environmental risk. For example, rats prone to develop hypertension do so only when exposed to salty diets or environmental stress (Schneiderman, Chesney, & Krantz, 1989).

Psychological Factors in CVD The most important of the known psychological contributions to CVD are the wide variety of health behaviors that (1) have a well-documented association with heart disease; (2) decrease the risk for CVD when they are modified; and (3) often are difficult to change. Improved health behavior—including avoiding or quitting smoking, maintaining a proper weight, following a low-cholesterol diet, exercising frequently, monitoring blood pressure regularly, and taking antihypertensive medication as prescribed—can reduce the risk of heart disease.

Stress also contributes to CVD, in two different ways. First, stress taxes the cardiovascular system through increased heart rate and blood pressure and can precipitate immediate symptoms or broader episodes of CHD. A dramatic example of the immediate effects of stress was observed during the Los Angeles earthquake of 1994. Cardiac deaths on the day of the earthquake rose to 24, from an average of 4.6 the preceding week (Leor, Poole, & Kloner, 1996). Second, over the long run, the heart may be damaged by constant stress. We consider four areas that this can happen: cardiovascular reactivity to stress, actual exposure to life stress, characteristic styles of responding to stress, and depression and anxiety (Krantz et al., 1988; Rozanski et al., 1999).

Cardiovascular Reactivity to Stress   Increased blood pressure and heart rate are normal reactions to stress, but researchers have long observed that different people exhibit different *cardiovascular reactivity to stress*—greater or lesser increases in blood pressure and heart rate—when exposed to stress in the laboratory. Are people who show greater cardiovascular reactivity to stress more likely to develop CVD?

Yes. In a study of patients with coronary artery disease, patients who reacted to mental stress in the laboratory with greater myocardial ischemia (oxygen deprivation to the heart) had a higher rate of fatal and nonfatal cardiac events over the next 5 years in comparison to their less reactive counterparts. In fact, mental stress was a better predictor of subsequent cardiac events than was physical stress (exercise testing) (Jiang et al., 1996).

Life Stressors and CVD: Job Strain   A high-level cardiovascular reactivity will have little effect on an individual if she experiences little stress. Because people are exposed to different stressors, real-life stress must also be considered in the equation that predicts CVD. Research shows that exposure to chronic stress increases risk for cardiovascular disease (Krantz et al., 1988; Schneiderman et al., 2004). For example, increased rates of coronary heart disease are found among people with high-stress occupations. What appears to be most damaging is *job strain*, a situation that pairs high psychological demands with a low degree of decisional control (Karasek et al., 1982). A waitress has relatively high demands and low control, for instance, whereas a forest ranger has relatively few demands and a high degree of control. Figure 8–5 portrays a number of occupations and how they vary in terms of psychological demands and decisional control.

Several studies have found a relationship between job strain and CHD (Krantz et al., 1988; Rozanski et al., 1999). For example, among women who participated in the Framingham Heart Study—a major longitudinal study of the development of coronary heart disease—the risk for CHD was one and one-half times higher among those who had high job strain based on objective evaluations of their occupations (see Research Methods on page 272). The risk was three times higher among women whose self-reports indicated high job strain (LaCroix & Haynes, 1987).

Such strains are not limited to employment, but include work that is performed in other life

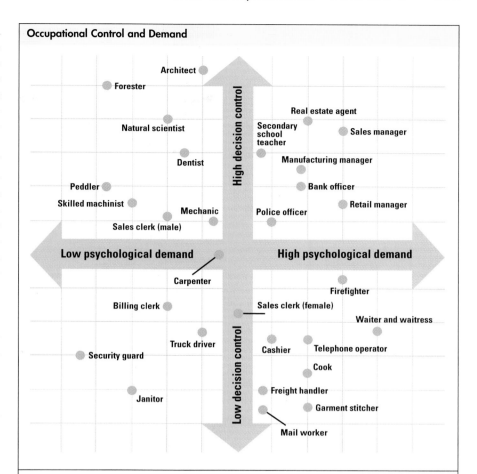

FIGURE 8–5: Occupations classified according to the degree of demand and control that are associated with them. Jobs with low control and high demands cause more job strain and increased cardiovascular risk.

Source: From R.A. Karasek, 1988. Cited in D.S. Krantz, R.J. Contrada, D.R. Hill, and E. Friedler, Environmental stress and biobehavioral antecedents of coronary heart disease, *Journal of Consulting and Clinical Psychology,* 56, 334.

roles. In an earlier analysis of women in the Framingham study, women who were employed for more than half of their adult lives were no more likely to develop CHD than were homemakers. However, working women with children were more likely to suffer from heart disease. In fact, the risk for CHD increased with the number of children for working women but not for homemakers (Haynes & Feinleib, 1980). This finding echoes the dilemma of contemporary women (and men) who feel strains not only within their occupation but also among their various family roles.

Type A Behavior and Hostility   Characteristic styles of responding to stress may also increase the risk for CVD, particularly the **Type A behavior pattern**—a competitive, hostile, urgent, impatient, and achievement-striving style of responding to

research methods

LONGITUDINAL STUDIES: LIVES OVER TIME

A **longitudinal study** involves studying people repeatedly over time. The approach contrasts with the **cross-sectional study** in which people are studied at only one time point. One goal of a longitudinal study can be to learn whether the effects of an experiment (such as a treatment outcome study) grow smaller, perhaps stronger, or stay the same over time. When a longitudinal study involves a correlational design, a common goal is to determine whether hypothesized causes come before their assumed effects. We know that causes must precede effects in time. The bat must be swung before the ball can be hit over the fence. If we can demonstrate that stress comes before heart disease in longitudinal research, this helps scientists to rule out the alternative interpretation (reverse causality), that the illness caused the stress.

Of course, a major liability of a longitudinal study is higher cost. It is much less expensive to study stress and heart disease at one point in time than to assess stress now and CHD as it develops over the next 10 years. One way around the expense is to use a *retrospective study* (sometimes called a follow-back study). In this research design, scientists look backward in time either by asking people to recall past events or by examining records from the past. The retrospective method is less expensive, but it is of limited value because of distorted memories and limited records (see Research Methods in Chapter 7).

The **prospective design** (sometimes called a follow-forward study) is a more effective but more expensive alternative. In prospective research, supposed causes are assessed in the present, and subjects are then followed longitudinally to see if the hypothesized effects develop over time. Using the follow-up method, scientists can assess a range of predictions more thoroughly and more objectively than in follow-back studies.

Researchers use both retrospective and prospective methods in studying health and illness and abnormal psychology in general. When you learn that a finding was supported in prospective longitudinal research, you can have greater confidence in the investigator's hypothesis about causality than if the research were cross-sectional. Remember, however, that correlation does not mean causation, even in a longitudinal study. It remains possible that the supposed "cause" and the "effect" both result from some third variable. For example, a researcher might find that Type A behavior measured at one point in time predicts CHD several years later. But chronic job stress may cause both the Type A behavior and the heart disease. Scientists need many studies utilizing many different types of research methods in order to establish causation. And you need to understand the strengths and weaknesses of research methods in order to be an informed consumer of scientific information.

These stock traders illustrate the Type A behavior pattern. Type A is a personality style characterized by competitiveness, hostility, urgency, impatience, and achievement striving in response to challenge.

challenge. As originally identified by cardiologists Meyer Friedman and Ray Rosenman (1959), the *Type A* individual is a "superachiever" who, like Bob Carter, knows no obstacle to success and who may sacrifice everything for the sake of achievement (Jenkins, 1988). *Type B* individuals, in contrast, are more calm and content.

The National Blood, Heart, and Lung Institute concluded in 1981 that Type A was a risk factor for CHD, independent of other risks, for example, diet. This official sanction stimulated a great deal of additional research, but many studies conducted since 1980 have failed to support earlier findings (Rozanski et al., 1999). One explanation may be that research methods contribute to the conflicting findings. Observation of behavior is important, as prediction is better when Type A is assessed from a structured interview (during which the interviewer provoked Type A behavior) rather than self-report (Miller et al., 1991). Also, *hostility* predicts future heart disease better than other aspects of Type A behavior or the pattern as a whole (Miller et al., 1996; Smith & Ruiz, 2002). A Finnish investigation found that three items reliably predicted death among men who had a history of CHD or hypertension: ease with which anger was aroused, argumentativeness, and irritability (Koskenvuo et al., 1988).

Depression and Anxiety   Depression is three times more common among patients with CHD than in the general population, and depression doubles the risk for future cardiac events (Frasure-Smith & Lespérance, 2005; Rozanski et al., 1999). Still, researchers have yet to untangle to what extent depression is a reaction to heart disease, as it certainly can be, versus a contributor to coronary risk (and if the latter, what physiological mechanism increases risk). A recent, randomized intervention study of over 2,400 depressed or isolated heart attack patients only raised further questions about the causal link between depression and CHD. Cognitive behavior therapy, sometimes combined with antidepressant medication, alleviated depression somewhat, but the treatment group had no better coronary outcome than untreated controls (ENRICHD, 2003).

Anxiety seems to be associated with one crucial aspect of CHD: sudden cardiac death (Rozanski et al., 1999). *Heart-focused anxiety*, preoccupation with heart and chest sensations, is another important concern (Eifert, Zvolensky, & Lejuez, 2000).

Social Factors in CVD   Social factors can influence the risk for CVD in many ways. Friends and family members can encourage a healthy—or an unhealthy—lifestyle (Pennix et al., 1997). Interpersonal conflict can create the anger and hostility that can increase the risk for coronary heart disease, whereas a spouse's confidence in coping with heart disease predicts patients' increases survival over 4 years (Rohrbaugh, Shoham, Coyne, et al., 2004). Economic resources, being married, and/or having a close confidant all predict a more positive prognosis among patients with coronary artery disease (R. B. Williams et al., 1992). Finally, societal values, such as attitudes about health behaviors like smoking and cultural norms about competition in the workplace also can affect the risk for CVD.

Recognizing the importance of interpersonal and societal influences, many efforts have been directed toward structuring the *social ecology*—the interrelations between the individual and the social world—to promote health (Stokols, 1992). As a child, you were exposed to many of these efforts, such as antismoking campaigns or the awards given in school for physical fitness. Good health is commonly promoted in the media, and more employers also are encouraging positive health behavior. Do these broad-scale efforts work? We address this question shortly.

Integration and Alternative Pathways   CVD is an excellent example of the value of the systems approach. For the purpose of integration, we return to the analogy between the functioning of the cardiovascular system and an automobile. Some cars are built for high performance, some for economy. Some are defective when they leave the factory. Whatever its original condition, a car's state of repair is affected by how it is driven and how it is maintained. Similarly, CVD is caused by a combination of genetic makeup, an occasional structural defect, maintenance in the form of health behavior, and how hard the heart is driven by stress, depression, coping, and societal standards.

Much progress has been made in identifying biological, psychological, and social risk factors for CVD. An important goal for future research is to integrate knowledge across risk factors (Kop, 1999). Numerous questions need to be addressed. For example, how do we distinguish the effects of stress as an immediate, precipitating cause of CHD from its cumulative effects on health over long periods of time? To what extent are the risks associated with stress caused by poor health behavior and not by stress itself? What protects those individuals who do not become ill, even when they are exposed to multiple risk factors?

Prevention and Treatment of CVD

Several medications known as *antihypertensives* are effective treatments for reducing high blood pressure. Other drugs, called *beta blockers*, reduce the risk of myocardial infarction or sudden coronary death following a cardiac episode (Johnston, 1989). Still other biomedical interventions reduce the risk factors associated with CVD. For example, serum cholesterol can be lowered with medication. Because many of the risk factors for CVD are linked with health behavior, it may be possible to prevent heart disease with psychological intervention (Rozanski et al., 1999).

Primary Prevention   As we noted, numerous public service advertisements attempt to prevent CVD by encouraging people to quit smoking, eat well, exercise, monitor their blood pressure, and otherwise improve their health behavior. Few of these familiar efforts have been evaluated systematically, although researchers have conducted

A graphic health warning on a pack of cigarettes sold in Canada. In 2000, the Canadian government approved such warnings, the first country in the world to take such an aggressive anti-smoking stance.

a handful of careful studies. One of the most important studies took place in three small California communities near Stanford University (Farquhar et al., 1977). Media campaigns designed to improve knowledge and change behavior were offered in two towns that formed the experimental groups, whereas no intervention was given in one town that was used as a control group. The media campaigns were supplemented with face-to-face interviews in one of the two towns receiving the intervention.

Findings indicated that the media campaigns increased the public's knowledge about CHD, particularly in the community where face-to-face interviews took place. Did this increased knowledge lead to changes in behavior? The answer appears to be yes—up to a point. People in the experimental communities improved their diet and lowered their serum cholesterol, but they made only minor changes in smoking (Farquhar et al., 1977). The study could not determine whether the interventions helped reduce the incidence of heart disease. Recall, however, that the rates of CVD have declined in Western countries as health behavior has improved. Increasing public awareness can slowly improve health behavior and eventually may lower the risk of heart disease.

How effective are attempts at the primary and secondary prevention of coronary heart disease?

Secondary Prevention The treatment of essential hypertension is one of the most important attempts at the secondary prevention of CHD. Treatments of hypertension fall into two categories. One focuses on improving health behavior, and the other emphasizes **stress management,** attempts to teach more effective coping skills.

Improvements in health behavior—including weight reduction, decreased alcohol consumption, and reduced intake of dietary salt—can help lower blood pressure. For many patients these behavioral changes eliminate the need for taking antihypertensive medication (Johnston, 1989). What is not clear, however, is how to get people to make these changes. Psychological intervention is minimally effective, in part because many attempts to change health behavior are weak or poorly constructed. For example, physicians may simply encourage their patients to lose weight or give them educational pamphlets to read. More intensive treatments appear to be more effective (Dusseldorp et al., 1999).

The major form of stress management used to treat hypertension is behavior therapy, particularly relaxation training and biofeedback. **Biofeedback** uses laboratory equipment to monitor physiological processes that generally occur outside conscious awareness and to provide the patient with conscious feedback about these processes. Blood pressure may be displayed on a video screen, for example, so that increases or decreases are readily apparent to the patient.

Biofeedback tries to teach to control the functions of their autonomic nervous system. During biofeedback, the patient can experiment with various coping strategies, for example, imagining lying on a beach, and observe whether the techniques are successful in lowering heart rate or blood pressure. This is an innovation conceptually and practically, because the functions of the autonomic nervous system traditionally have been viewed as uncontrollable, as conveyed by the term *autonomic*.

Both relaxation training and biofeedback produce reliable, reductions in blood pressure. Unfortunately, the reductions are small, often temporary, and considerably less than those produced by antihypertensive medications (Andrews et al., 1984). Overall, stress management appears to improve quality of life but has little effect on disease (Claar & Blumenthal, 2003). Biofeedback is a particularly dubious treatment, one that some well-respected investigators suggest should be abandoned as a treatment for hypertension (Johnston, 1989).

The Trials of Hypertension Prevention (TOHP) is an important ongoing study of whether stress management and health behavior interventions succeed in lowering high blood pressure (TOHP Collaborative Research Group, 1992). In this investigation, more than 2,000 women and men with hypertension were randomly assigned to one of seven different treatments. Treatments included three lifestyle interventions—weight reduction, sodium (salt) reduction, and stress management—plus four nutritional supplement conditions. Group meetings were held over several weeks for the three lifestyle interventions. In the nutrition conditions, the patient's ordinary diet was supplemented with dietary agents hypothesized to lower blood pressure: either calcium, magnesium, potassium, or fish oil. Results from Phase I of the study indicated that only the weight reduction and the salt reduction programs were successful in lowering blood pressure over a follow-up period of up to 1½ years. Neither stress management nor any of the dietary supplements produced beneficial effects. Findings from Phase II of the TOHP underscored the importance of weight loss, as even a modest reduction in weight lowered produced clinically significant reductions in blood pressure (Stevens et al., 2001).

The Multiple Risk Factor Intervention Trial (MRFIT) is another important investigation, of over 12,000 men at risk for CHD who were assigned at random to intervention and control groups. Carefully developed intervention programs, including both education and social support, produced improved health behavior, including reduced smoking and lower serum cholesterol. However, the men randomly assigned to the treatment groups did not have a lower incidence of heart disease during the 7 years following intervention (MRFIT, 1982). An encouraging interpretation of this discouraging outcome is that men in the control group also improved their health behavior. The control group had a lower disease rate than expected based on their risk indicators, and the study was conducted during a time when the public's concern with health increased dramatically.

Tertiary Prevention Tertiary prevention of CHD targets patients who have already had a cardiac event, typically a myocardial infarction. The hope is to reduce the incidence of recurrence of the illness. Exercise programs are probably the most common treatment recommended for cardiac patients, but evidence of their effectiveness is limited (Johnston, 1989). The most effective programs are individualized for each patient (Frasure-Smith & Prince, 1985). One patient may benefit from a smoking reduction program, a second by a stress reduction workshop, and a third by exercise classes. Handing out educational pamphlets or delivering stern lectures in the physician's office does little to alter health behavior. Successful programs are both highly structured and carefully tailored to the individual (Blanchard, 1992).

Some of the most optimistic evidence on the treatment of CHD comes from studies of interventions designed to alter the Type A behavior pattern (Friedman et al., 1986), a somewhat surprising circumstance given the controversies about the risk research on Type A. Intervention with Type A individuals following myocardial infarction is multifaceted. For example, it includes **role playing**—improvisational play acting—to teach patients how to respond to stressful interactions with reduced hostility. In role playing, cardiac patients act out their usual responses to such situations as dealing with a bothersome subordinate, and the therapist models alternative, less hostile means of responding to the frustration. In subsequent role plays, the patients try out the new way of coping. Cognitive therapy designed to alter faulty

Manuel Lujan, former U.S. Secretary of the Interior, works out as part of his heart rehabilitation program following his fourth heart attack.

thought patterns also is a part of the intervention with Type A cardiac patients (Thoresen & Powell, 1992). At some level, for example, Bob Carter probably believed that he must be the best at everything he did in life. One goal of cognitive therapy is to help patients like Bob to develop beliefs and goals that are more realistic—and healthy.

Studies also suggest that Type A behavior can be modified, and this may reduce the subsequent risk for CHD (Nunes, Frank, & Kornfeld, 1987; Thoresen & Powell, 1992). One study of nearly 600 patients found that stress management training reduced the annual incidence of cardiac events by almost 50 percent in comparison to 300 patients who received standard medical care (Friedman et al., 1986). Importantly, subjects who showed the greatest reduction in Type A behavior were four times less likely to experience a myocardial infarction during the following 2 years.

As a final note, we should mention that some valuable treatments focus on the effects of heart disease on life stress rather than the other way around. Cardiac patients and their families can be helped to cope more effectively with the social and psychological consequences of having a heart attack, including depression, anxiety, restricted activities, and changes in sexuality, marriage, and family relationships (Johnston, 1985). Since depression is a risk factor for future cardiac illness (Carney et al., 1995), such interventions may, in turn, help to improve the patient's physical health. The link between stress and physical health clearly is a reciprocal one.

---

getting help

 Stressed out? We all are at times—when we face exams, have to deal with difficult relationships, or just have too much to do and not enough time to do it.

If there is too much stress in your life, a helpful first step is to analyze it. One great way to begin is to write about the situations that stress you out, your responses, and your attempts at coping. You could start a journal; you could write someone a letter (that you may or may not mail); or you could just jot down a few notes. Writing can help you get some things off your chest—and off your mind—but it can also help you to sort things out. Writing takes thoughts and feelings from the inside and puts them out there, in the world, where you can look at them. Sometimes just putting your thoughts into words

can help: "Whew! I don't have to think about that anymore!" Another benefit is that you can always go back and read what you wrote and correct and organize your thoughts and feelings. An engaging, research-based account of the benefits of writing is James Pennebaker's *Opening Up: The Healing Power of Expressing Emotions.*

Another way to analyze stress in your life is to complete some stress-rating forms. You can find one commonly used form in Table 8–1 (page 254), or you can complete a stress rating measure online. A quick Internet search will pull up several sites that allow you to complete stress rating measures. Some are designed specifically for college students.

What about coping with stress? If your usual strategies aren't working, a useful resource about relaxation is Herbert Benson's

book, *The Relaxation Response.* Exercise is another healthy coping technique. If you have troubling physical symptoms linked with stress, you should consult your family physician. A mental health professional may be more appropriate to contact if your stress responses are emotional.

Finally, if you are suffering from the stress of having a physical illness and want to know about the latest research, the place to start on line is the home page of the National Institutes of Health (NIH). If your illness is chronic, particularly difficult, or rare, you might find it helpful to communicate online with others who suffer from the same disease. Because there are so many resources on the Internet, most search engines contain a category specifically for "health." As you browse, remember to be skeptical and cautious in evaluating information.

SUMMARY

Scientists now view every physical illness as a product of the interaction between the psyche and soma, mind and body. This holistic view has influenced both psychology and medicine, as is evidenced by the rapid development of **behavioral medicine,** a multidisciplinary field

that investigates psychological factors in physical illness.

Stress is a challenging event that requires physiological, cognitive, or behavioral adaptation, but scientists disagree about precisely how stress is best defined. Stress activates the **fight or**

flight response, a reaction to threat characterized by intense arousal of the sympathetic nervous system. In response, the *adrenal glands* release two key hormones, epinephrine (adrenaline), which leads to the familiar "rush of adrenaline," and **cortisol** (the "stress hormone") which helps the body make repairs similar to steroids (and which, like steroids, also can be harmful). Research on **psychoneuroimmunology (PNI)** shows that stress also can impair aspects of the functioning of the immune system.

Coping with stress may involve **problem-focused coping,** an attempt to change the stressor, or **emotion-focused coping,** an attempt to alter distress internally. Predictability and control are other key cognitive evaluations that can greatly facilitate coping, as are having outlets for frustration and **optimism.** Psychologists surely have underestimated people's **resilience** in coping with stress. Stress can cause **health behavior,** including fewer positive actions (e.g., exercise) or more negative actions (e.g., alcohol consumption). Illness behavior, behaving as if you were sick, also is stress related.

Lifestyle is central to the top causes of death in the United States today. Behavior contributes to cancer through exposure to some carcinogens, health behavior, social support in coping with the illness, and perhaps through effects on immune functioning. **Acquired immune deficiency syndrome (AIDS)** is caused by the **human immunodeficiency virus (HIV),** which is transmitted through risky behaviors, such as unprotected sex and shared hypodermic needles. Psychologists also work to help people cope with chronic pain, most notably through pain management programs. More attention also is being paid to **primary sleep disorders.**

The number-one killer in the United States today is **cardiovascular disease (CVD)** disorders that affect the heart and circulatory system. Cardiovascular diseases include **essential hypertension** (high blood pressure) and **coronary heart disease (CHD),** particularly **myocardial infarction (MI),** or heart attack. Several health behaviors have been linked to CVD. Psychological factors contributing to CVD include **cardiovascular reactivity,** responses to stressors presented in a laboratory; chronic stressors in real life (e.g., job strain); the hostility that is part of the **Type A behavior pattern;** and depression and anxiety. The primary prevention of CHD includes attempts to encourage people to improve their health behavior. The treatment of hypertension through improved health behavior, or **stress management,** is one of the more important attempts at the secondary prevention of CHD. Tertiary prevention of CHD targets patients who have already had a cardiac event, for example, attempting to modify their Type A behavior.

KEY TERMS

Go to www.prenhall.com/oltmanns for online quizzes, interactive flash cards, PowerPoint presentations, and chapter reviews.

9
Personality Disorders

CHAPTER OUTLINE

◆◆◆

People are social organisms. Reproduction and survival depend on successful, cooperative interactions with other people. We form social alliances for many purposes, such as raising families, doing our jobs, and living in a community. We also compete with others, and in some cases we have to protect ourselves from others. These relationships are governed by a variety of psychological mechanisms that, taken together, constitute our personalities. **Personality** refers to enduring patterns of thinking and behavior that define the person and distinguish him or her from other people. Included in these patterns are ways of expressing emotion as well as patterns of thinking about ourselves and other people. For the most part, personality serves as the glue that anchors and facilitates interactions with other people. But it can also go awry. When enduring patterns of behavior and emotion bring the person into repeated conflict with others, and when they prevent the person from maintaining close relationships with others, an individual's personality may be considered disordered.

Of course, the dividing line between eccentricity and personality pathology is difficult to define. We all have our quirks and idiosyncrasies, and there are many different ways to manage relationships with other people. For example, it is often helpful to be skeptical of the things that other people do and say. When does a tendency to be suspicious of other people's motives cross the line into paranoia? Self-confidence is another admirable quality, but it can lead to problems if it escalates into full-blown grandiosity. In many ways, the distinctions among healthy traits, eccentricity, and personality pathology depend on the person's ability to adapt to the demands of different situations. Variety and flexibility in interpersonal behavior are undoubtedly helpful. People with personality disorders can make their own social problems worse (often unwittingly) by persistently responding in ways that do not suit the social challenges that they face.

OVERVIEW

Personality disorders are considered separately from other forms of psychopathology in DSM-IV-TR. Most clinical disorders are listed on Axis I, whereas the personality disorders are listed on Axis II. All of the personality disorders are based on exaggerated personality traits that are frequently disturbing or annoying to other people. For example, in the first case study of this chapter, you will meet a young man whose consistently impulsive and deceitful behavior brought him into repeated conflicts with other people and with legal authorities.

In order to qualify for a personality disorder diagnosis in DSM-IV-TR, a person must fit the *general definition* of personality disorder (which applies to all 10 subtypes) and must also meet the *specific criteria* for a particular type of personality disorder. The specific criteria consist of a list of traits and behaviors that characterize the disorder. The general definition of **personality disorder** presented in DSM-IV-TR emphasizes the duration of the pattern and the social impairment associated with the traits in question. The problems must be part of "an enduring pattern of inner experience and behavior that deviates markedly from the expectations of the individual's culture" (APA, 2000). The pattern must be evident in two or more of the following domains: cognition (such as ways of thinking about the self and other people), emotional responses, interpersonal functioning, or impulse control. This pattern of maladaptive experience and behavior must also be:

What is the difference between being eccentric and having a personality disorder?

- Inflexible and pervasive across a broad range of personal and social situations

- The source of clinically significant distress or impairment in social, occupational, or other important areas of functioning
- Stable and of long duration, with an onset that can be traced back at least to adolescence or early adulthood

The concept of social dysfunction plays an important role in the definition of personality disorders. It provides a large part of the justification for defining these problems as mental disorders. If the personality characteristics identified in DSM-IV-TR criterion sets typically interfere with the person's ability to get along with other people and perform social roles, they become more than just a collection of eccentric traits or peculiar habits. They can then be viewed as a form of harmful dysfunction (Wakefield, 1999; see Chapter 1). In fact, most of the clusters of pathological personality traits that are described on Axis II do lead to impaired social functioning or occupational impairment (Oltmanns, Melley, & Turkheimer, 2002; Zanarini et al., 2005).

Personality disorders are among the most controversial categories in the diagnostic system for mental disorders (Kendell, 2002; Potter, 2004). They are difficult to identify reliably, their etiology is poorly understood, and there is relatively little evidence to indicate that they can be treated successfully. There are some discrepancies between DSM-IV-TR and ICD-10, its European counterpart, in their descriptions of these problems. For example, one type of personality disorder in the U.S. system, narcissistic, is not included in ICD-10. For all of these reasons, you should think critically about the validity of these categories.

Although they are difficult to define and measure, personality disorders are also crucial concepts in the field of psychopathology. Several observations support this argument. First, personality disorders are associated with significant social and occupational impairment. They disrupt interpersonal relationships in families and in the workplace. They also play an important role in many cases of marital violence (Holtzworth-Munroe et al., 2000). Second, the presence of pathological personality traits during adolescence is associated with an increased risk for the subsequent development of other mental disorders (Johnson et al., 1999; Krueger, 1999). Negative emotionality (high neuroticism) often predicts the later onset of major depression or an anxiety disorder. Impulsivity and antisocial personality

Since 1981, this successful artist has painted more than 1,500 self-portraits. He says he will never paint anything other than his own image because it is the only subject that holds his interest. Self-absorption is one central feature of narcissistic personality disorder.

increase the person's risk for alcoholism. Third, in some cases, personality disorders actually represent the beginning stages of the onset of a more serious form of psychopathology. Paranoid and schizoid personality disorders, for example, sometimes precede the onset of schizophrenic disorders. Finally, the presence of a comorbid personality disorder can interfere with the treatment of a disorder such as depression (Mulder, 2002).

The following cases illustrate several of the most important features of personality disorders.

Our first case is an example of antisocial personality disorder, which is defined in terms of a pervasive and persistent disregard for, and frequent violation of, the rights of other people. This 21-year-old man was described by Hervey Cleckley (1976) in his classic treatise on this topic. The man had been referred to Cleckley by his parents and his lawyer after his most recent arrest for stealing. The parents hoped that their son might avoid a long prison sentence if Cleckley decided that he was suffering from a mental disorder.

CASE STUDY A Car Thief's Antisocial Personality Disorder

Tom looks and is in robust physical health. His manner and appearance are pleasing. In his face a prospective employer would be likely to see strong indications of character as well as high incentive and ability. He is well informed, alert, and entirely at ease, exhibiting a confidence in himself that the observer is likely to consider amply justified. This does not look like the sort of man who will fail or flounder about in the tasks of life, but like someone incompatible with all such thoughts.

[In childhood, Tom] appeared to be a reliable and manly fellow but could never be counted upon to keep at any task or to give a straight account of any situation. He was frequently truant from school. No advice or persuasion [deterred] him [from] his acts, despite his excellent response in all discussions. Though he was generously provided for, he stole some of his father's chickens from time to time, selling them at stores downtown. Pieces of table silver would be missed. These were sometimes recovered from those to whom he had sold them for a pittance or swapped them for odds and ends which seemed to hold no particular interest or value for him. He resented and seemed eager to avoid punishment, but no modification in his behavior resulted from it. He did not seem wild or particularly impulsive, a victim of high temper or uncontrollable drives. There was nothing to indicate he was subject to unusually strong temptations, lured by definite plans for high adventure and exciting revolt.

He lied so plausibly and with such utter equanimity devised such ingenious alibis or simply denied all responsibility with such convincing appearances of candor that for many years his real career was poorly estimated.

Among typical exploits with which he is credited stand these: prankish defecation into the stringed intricacies of the school piano, the removal from his uncle's automobile of a carburetor for which he got 75 cents, and the selling of his father's overcoat to a passing buyer of scrap materials.

At 14 or 15 years of age, having learned to drive, Tom began to steal automobiles with some regularity. Often his intention seemed less that of theft than of heedless misappropriation. A neighbor or friend of the family, going to the garage or to where the car was parked outside an office building, would find it missing. Sometimes the patient would leave the stolen vehicle within a few blocks or miles of the owner, sometimes out on the road

He lied so plausibly and with such utter equanimity that for many years his real career was poorly estimated.

where the gasoline had given out. After he had tried to sell a stolen car, his father consulted advisors and, on the theory that he might have some specific craving for automobiles, bought one for him as a therapeutic measure. On one occasion while out driving, he deliberately parked his own car and, leaving it, stole an inferior model which he left slightly damaged on the outskirts of a village some miles away.

Private physicians, scoutmasters, and social workers were consulted. They talked and worked with him, but to no avail. Listing the deeds for which he became ever more notable does not give an adequate picture of the situation. He did not every day or every week bring attention to himself by major acts of mischief or destructiveness. He was usually polite, often

considerate in small, appealing ways, and always seemed to have learned his lesson after detection and punishment. He was clever and learned easily. During intervals in which his attendance was regular, he impressed his teachers as outstanding in ability. Some charm and apparent modesty, as well as his very convincing way of seeming sincere and to have taken resolutions that would count, kept not only the parents but all who encountered him clinging to hope. Teachers, scoutmasters, the school principal, and others recognized that in some very important respects he differed from the ordinary bad or wayward youth. (They) made special efforts to help him and to give him new opportunities to reform or readjust.

When he drove a stolen automobile across a state line, he came in contact with federal authorities. In view of his youth and the wonderful impression he made, he was put on probation. Soon afterward he took another automobile and again left it in the adjoining state. It was a very obvious situation. The consequences could not have been entirely overlooked by a person of his excellent shrewdness. He admitted that the considerable risks of getting caught had occurred to him but felt he had a chance to avoid detection and would take it. No unusual and powerful motive or any special aim could be brought out as an explanation.

Tom was sent to a federal institution in a distant state where a well-organized program of rehabilitation and guidance was available. He soon impressed authorities at this place with his attitude and in the way he discussed his past mistakes and plans for a different future. He seemed to merit parole status precociously and this was awarded him. It was not long before he began stealing again and thereby lost his freedom (Cleckley, 1976, pp. 64–67).

Notice that the fundamental features of Tom's problems were clearly evident by early adolescence, and they were exhibited consistently over an extended period of time. The stable, long-standing nature of personality disorders is one of their most characteristic features. In this way, they are distinguished from many other forms of abnormal behavior that are episodic in nature.

This case is an excellent example of the senseless nature of the illegal and immoral acts committed by people who meet the diagnostic criteria for antisocial personality disorder. Another puzzling feature of this disorder is the person's apparent lack of remorse and the inability to learn from experience that accompanies such a history of delinquent behavior. It is difficult to understand why someone would behave in this manner. Mental health professionals appeal to the notion of personality disorder to help them understand these irrational behaviors.

The case of Tom also illustrates some other important features of personality disorders. Most other forms of mental disorder, such as anxiety disorders and mood disorders, are ego-dystonic; that is, people with these disorders are distressed by their symptoms and uncomfortable with their situations. Personality disorders are usually ego-syntonic—the ideas or impulses with which they are associated are acceptable to the person. People with personality disorders frequently do not see themselves as being disturbed. We might also say that they do not have insight into the nature of their own problems. Tom did not believe that his repeated antisocial behavior represented a problem. The other people for whom he created problems were suffering, but he was not. Many forms of personality disorder are defined primarily in terms of the problems that these people create for others rather than in terms of their own subjective distress.

The ego-syntonic nature of many forms of personality disorder raises important questions about the limitations of self-report measures—interviews and questionnaires—for their assessment. Many people with personality disorders are unable to view themselves realistically and are unaware of the effect that their behavior has on others. Therefore, assessments based exclusively on self-report may have limited validity (Klein, 2003; Oltmanns & Turkheimer, 2006). They may underestimate the frequency and severity of certain aspects of personality pathology, particularly those problems associated with narcissism. The development of alternative assessment methods, such as collecting information from peers, family members, or mental health professionals remains an important challenge for future research studies (Westen & Arkowitz-Westen, 1998).

SYMPTOMS

The specific symptoms that are used to define personality disorders represent maladaptive variations in several of the building blocks of personality (see Chapter 2). These include motives, cognitive perspectives regarding the self and others, temperament and personality traits. We have organized our description of typical symptoms around these issues, which run through the broad mixture of specific symptoms that define the 10 types of personality disorder included in DSM-IV-TR.

Social Motivation

The concept of a motive refers to a person's desires and goals (Emmons, 1997). Motives (either conscious or unconscious) describe the way that the person would like things to be, and they help to explain *why* people behave in a particular fashion. For example, a man might have neglected to return a telephone call because he wanted to be alone (rather than because he forgot that someone had called). Two of the most important motives in understanding human personality are *affiliation*—the desire for close relationships with other people—and *power*—the desire for impact, prestige, or dominance (Winter et al., 1998). Individual differences with regard to these motives have an important influence on a person's health and adjustment.

Many of the symptoms of personality disorders can be described in terms of maladaptive variations with regard to needs for affiliation and power. One particularly important issue is the absence of motivation for affiliation. While most people enjoy spending time with other people and want to develop intimate relationships with friends and family members, some people do not. They prefer isolation. Severely diminished or absent motivation for social relationships is one pervasive theme that serves to define certain kinds of personality disorder.

Exaggerated motivation for power (and achievement) also contributes to the picture that describes personality disorders. For example, some people are preoccupied with a need for admiration and the praise of others. They think of themselves as privileged people and insist on special treatment. In some cases, excessive devotion to work and professional accomplishment can lead a person to ignore friends and family members as well as the pursuit of leisure activities. This lack of balance can have a serious disruptive effect on the person's social adjustment.

Cognitive Perspectives Regarding Self and Others

Our social world also depends on mental processes that determine knowledge of ourselves and other people (Baumeister, 1997; Kihlstrom & Hastie, 1997). Distortions of these mechanisms are associated with personality disorders. For example, one central issue involves our image of ourselves. When you are able to maintain a realistic and stable image of yourself, you can plan, negotiate, and evaluate your relationships with other people. Knowing (and having confidence in) your own values and opinions is a necessary prerequisite for making independent decisions without the assistance or reassurance of others. Self-image is also intimately connected to mood states. If you vacillate back and forth between unrealistically positive and negative views of yourself, your mood will swing dramatically. You may also need constant reassurance from others and be too dependent on their opinions as a means of maintaining your own self-esteem. We have to be able to evaluate our own importance. Of course, it's useful to think of yourself in positive terms (and many maintain a positive "halo"), but extreme grandiosity can be disruptive. Perhaps even more damaging is a pattern in which people see themselves as socially inept or inferior to other people.

When we misperceive the intentions and motives and abilities of other people, our relationships can be severely disturbed. Paranoid beliefs are one example. Some people believe, without good reason, that other people are

"You want only happiness, Douglas. I want wealth, power, fame, and happiness."

exploiting, deceiving, or otherwise trying to harm them. Unreasonable fears of being abandoned, criticized, or rejected are also examples of distorted perception of others' intentions. Working effectively in a group of people also requires realistic appraisal of the talents and abilities of others. In order to cooperate with other people, we must be able to appreciate their competence. People with personality disorders run into problems because they misperceive other people in many different ways (as being either threatening, or uncaring, or incompetent).

Many elements of social interaction also depend on being able to evaluate the nature of our relationships with other people and then to make accurate judgments about appropriate and inappropriate behaviors. A successful relationship with a sexual partner involves knowing when intimacy is expected and when it should be avoided. Some people with personality disorders experience persistent problems in social distance (either becoming too intimate or maintaining too much distance from others). Finally, another important element of interpersonal perception is the ability to empathize with others—to anticipate and decipher their emotional reactions and use that knowledge to guide our own behavior. Deficits in the ability to understand the emotions of other people represent one of the core features of personality disorders.

Temperament and Personality Traits

If motivation helps to explain *why* people behave in certain ways, temperament and personality traits describe *how* they behave. *Temperament* refers to a person's most basic, characteristic styles of relating to the world, especially those styles that are evident during the first year of life (Caspi & Roberts, 1999; Mervielde et al., 2005). Definitions of temperament typically include dimensions such as activity level and emotional reactivity (see Chapter 2). These factors vary considerably in level or degree from one infant to the next and have important implications for later development, such as social and academic adjustment when the child eventually enters school. For example, children who demonstrate a "lack of control" when they are very young are much more likely than their peers to experience problems with hyperactivity, distractibility, and conduct disorder when they are adolescents (Caspi et al., 1995). Young children who are extremely shy are more likely to be anxious and socially inhibited in subsequent years (Eisenberg et al., 1998) (see Chapter 16).

Experts disagree about the basic dimensions of temperament and personality. Some theories are relatively simple, using only three or four dimensions. Others are more complicated and consider as many as 30 or 40 traits. One point of view that has come to be widely accepted is known as the five factor model of personality (Digman, 2002; Trull & McCrae, 2002). The basic traits (also known as domains) included in this model have already been summarized in Chapter 2. They are neuroticism, extraversion, openness to experience, agreeableness, and conscientiousness. Each of the five principal domains can be subdivided into six more specific elements or facets (see Table 9–1). Taken as a whole, the five-factor model provides a relatively comprehensive description of any person's behavior.

Many personality disorders are defined in terms of maladaptive variations on the kinds of traits listed in Table 9–1 (Widiger & Simonsen, 2005). Problems may arise in association with extreme variations in either direction (high or low). Dramatically elevated levels of anger–hostility, impulsiveness, and excitement seeking are

particularly important, as are extremely low levels of trust, compliance, and tendermindedness. Although some forms of personality disorder are associated with high levels of anxiousness and vulnerability, people with antisocial personality disorder frequently exhibit unusually low levels of anxiety and concern about danger. We return to these dimensions in the next section of this chapter.

Context and Personality

Two important qualifications must be made about the development and persistence of individual differences in temperament and personality. First, these differences may not be evident in all situations. Some important personality features may be expressed only under certain challenging circumstances that require or facilitate a particular response. For example, Tom did not always appear to be impulsive and irresponsible. He was usually polite when he was with adults, and he went through intervals in which he followed rules and attended school regularly.

The second qualification involves the consequences of exhibiting particular traits. Social circumstances frequently determine whether a specific pattern of behavior will be assigned a positive or negative meaning by other people. Difficult temperament, for example, may serve an adaptive function when it is beneficial for an infant to be demanding and highly visible—for example, during a famine or while living in a large institution. On the other hand, in some circumstances, difficult temperament can be associated with an increased risk for certain psychiatric and learning disorders.

Consider the traits that Tom exhibited, especially impulsivity and lack of fear. These characteristics might be maladaptive under normal circumstances, but they could be useful—indeed, admirable—in certain extraordinary settings. War is one extreme example. People in combat situations have to act quickly and decisively, often at great risk to their own physical health. A disregard for personal safety might be adaptive under these circumstances. Tom's ability to lie in a calm and convincing fashion was another interesting trait. Again, this might have been a valuable adaptive skill if Tom had been an espionage agent. The meanings that are assigned to particular traits depend on the environment in which they are observed.

Thomas Widiger, Professor of Psychology at the University of Kentucky, is a leading expert on personality disorders and an advocate for the use of the Five Factor Model to describe pathological personality features.

TABLE 9-1	Domains and Facets of the Five-Factor Model of Personality	
	PEOPLE WITH HIGH SCORES ARE:	PEOPLE WITH LOW SCORES ARE:
Neuroticism		
Anxiousness	extremely nervous	lack appropriate anxiety
Anger–Hostility	hypersensitive; easily angered	unable to express anger
Depressiveness	continually depressed	unable to appreciate losses
Self-Consciousness	very easily embarrassed	indifferent to opinions of others
Impulsiveness	extremely impulsive	restrained or restricted; dull
Vulnerability	easily overwhelmed by stress	oblivious to danger
Extraversion		
Warmth	inappropriately affectionate	can't develop intimate relations
Gregariousness	unable to tolerate being alone	socially isolated
Assertiveness	domineering, pushy	resigned and ineffective
Activity	driven; frantic; distractible	sedentary and passive
Excitement-Seeking	reckless, careless	dull; monotonous
Positive Emotions	giddy; lose control of emotions	solemn; unable to enjoy things
Openness to Experience		
Fantasy	preoccupied with daydreams	imagination tends to be sterile
Aesthetics	obsessed with unusual interests	don't appreciate culture or art
Feelings	governed by strong emotionality	seldom have strong feelings
Actions	unpredictable	avoid change; stick to routine
Ideas	preoccupied with strange ideas	reject new ideas
Values	lack guiding belief systems	dogmatic and closed minded
Agreeableness		
Trust	gullible	paranoid and suspicious
Straightforwardness	too self-disclosing	dishonest and manipulative
Altruism	often exploited or victimized	no regard for rights of others
Compliance	acquiescent; docile; submissive	argumentative; defiant
Modesty	meek and self-denigrating	conceited; arrogant; pompous
Tender-Mindedness	overwhelmed by others' pain	callous; coldhearted; ruthless
Conscientiousness		
Competence	overly perfectionistic	lax; incapable or work
Order	preoccupied with rules, order	disorganized; sloppy
Dutifulness	places duty above morality	not dependable; unreliable
Achievement Striving	workaholic	aimless; no clear goals
Self-Discipline	single-minded pursuit of goals	hedonistic; self-indulgent
Deliberation	ruminate to excess	makes careless decisions

Source: Adapted from T.A. Widiger, P.T. Costa, Jr., & R.R. McCrae (2002). A proposal for Axis II: Diagnosing personality disorders using the five-factor model. In P.T. Costa, Jr., & T.A. Widiger (Eds.), *Personality Disorders and the Five-Factor Model of Personality,* 2nd ed, pp. 431–456. Washington, DC: American Psychological Association.

DIAGNOSIS

The authors of DSM-IV-TR have organized ten specific forms of personality disorder into three clusters on the basis of broadly defined characteristics. The specific disorders in each cluster are listed in Table 9–2. In the following pages we give brief descriptions of these personality disorder subtypes. These descriptions provide an overview that will be useful when we review the epidemiology of personality disorders. Later in the chapter we describe in considerably more detail four disorders that are relatively frequent and have been studied extensively: schizotypal, borderline, antisocial, and dependent personality disorders.

TABLE 9-2	Personality Disorders Listed in DSM-IV-TR
Cluster A includes people who often appear odd or eccentric	
Paranoid	Distrust and suspiciousness of others.
Schizoid	Detachment from social relationships and restricted range of expression of emotions.
Schizotypal	Discomfort with close relationships; cognitive and perceptual distortions; eccentricities of behavior.
Cluster B includes people who often appear dramatic, emotional, or erratic	
Antisocial	Disregard for and frequent violation of the rights of others.
Borderline	Instability of interpersonal relationships, self-image, emotions, and control over impulses.
Histrionic	Excessive emotionality and attention seeking.
Narcissistic	Grandiosity, need for admiration, and lack of empathy.
Cluster C includes people who often appear anxious or fearful	
Avoidant	Social inhibition, feelings of inadequacy, and hypersensitivity to negative evaluation.
Dependent	Excessive need to be taken care of, leading to submissive and clinging behavior.
Obsessive–compulsive	Preoccupation with orderliness and perfectionism at the expense of flexibility.

Cluster A: Paranoid, Schizoid, and Schizotypal Personality Disorders

Cluster A includes three disorders: paranoid, schizoid, and schizotypal forms of personality disorder. The behavior of people who fit the subtypes in this cluster is typically odd, eccentric, or asocial. All three types share similarity with the symptoms of schizophrenia (see Chapter 13). One implicit assumption in the DSM-IV-TR system is that these types of personality disorder may represent behavioral traits or interpersonal styles that precede the onset of full-blown psychosis. Because of their close association with schizophrenia, they are sometimes called *schizophrenia spectrum disorders*.

Paranoid personality disorder is characterized by the pervasive tendency to be inappropriately suspicious of other people's motives and behaviors. People who fit the description for this disorder are constantly on guard. They expect that other people are trying to harm them, and they take extraordinary precautions to avoid being exploited or injured. Although we can all benefit from being cautious and skeptical, paranoid thinking is much more than that. The pattern is so

stable and wide-ranging that it interferes with the person's social and occupational adjustment. People who are paranoid are completely inflexible in the way that they view the motives of other people, and they are unable to choose situations in which they can trust other people (see Critical Thinking *Matters*).

Because paranoid people do not trust anyone, they have trouble maintaining relationships with friends and family members. They frequently overreact in response to minor or ambiguous events to which they attribute hidden meaning. When they overreact, people with paranoid personality disorder often behave aggressively or antagonistically. These actions can easily create a self-fulfilling prophesy. In other words, thinking (incorrectly) that he or she is being attacked by others, the paranoid person strikes. The other person is, naturally, surprised, annoyed, and perhaps frightened by this behavior, and begins to treat the paranoid person with concern and caution. This response serves to confirm the original suspicions of the paranoid individual, who does not comprehend how his or her own behavior affects others.

Paranoid personality disorder must be distinguished from psychotic disorders, such as schizophrenia and delusional disorder. The pervasive suspicions of people with paranoid personality disorder do not reach delusional proportions. In other words, they are not sufficiently severe to be considered obviously false and clearly preposterous. In actual practice, this distinction is sometimes quite subtle and difficult to make.

Schizoid personality disorder is defined in terms of a pervasive pattern of indifference to other people, coupled with a diminished range of emotional experience and expression. These people are loners; they prefer social isolation to interactions with friends or family. Other people see them as being cold and aloof. By their own report, they do not experience strong subjective emotions, such as sadness, anger, or happiness.

Schizotypal personality disorder centers around peculiar patterns of behavior rather than on the emotional restriction and social withdrawal that are associated with schizoid personality disorder. Many of these peculiar behaviors take the form of perceptual and cognitive disturbance. People with this disorder may report bizarre fantasies and unusual perceptual experiences. Their speech may be slightly difficult to follow because they use words in an odd way or because they express themselves in a vague or disjointed manner. Their affective expressions may be constricted in range, as in schizoid personality disorder, or they may be silly and inappropriate.

In spite of their odd or unusual behaviors, people with schizotypal personality disorder are not psychotic or out of touch with reality. Their bizarre fantasies are not delusional, and their unusual perceptual experiences are not sufficiently real or compelling to be considered hallucinations.

Cluster B: Antisocial, Borderline, Histrionic, and Narcissistic Personality Disorders

Cluster B includes antisocial, borderline, histrionic, and narcissistic personality disorders. According to DSM-IV-TR, these disorders are characterized by dramatic, emotional, or erratic behavior, and all are associated with marked difficulty in sustaining interpersonal relationships. The rationale for grouping these disorders together is less compelling than that for Cluster A. In particular, antisocial personality disorder clearly involves something more than just a dramatic style or erratic behavior.

Antisocial personality disorder is defined in terms of a persistent pattern of irresponsible and antisocial behavior that begins during childhood or adolescence and continues into the adult years. The case study of Tom, with which we opened this chapter, illustrates this pattern of behavior. The DSM-IV-TR definition is based on features that, beginning in childhood, indicate a pervasive pattern of disregard for, and violation of, the rights of others. Once the person has become an adult, these difficulties include persistent failure to perform responsibilities that are associated with occupational and family roles. Conflict with others, including physical fights, is also common. These people are irritable and aggressive with their spouses and children as well as with people outside the home. They are impulsive, reckless, and irresponsible.

critical thinking matters

DO YOU HAVE TO BE PARANOID TO SURVIVE?

Andrew Grove, chairman of the board of Intel Corporation, has written a popular book about business management titled, *Only the Paranoid Survive.* He argues that successful corporate leaders must be vigilant; they have to anticipate negative events in the business world as well as future problems with their competitors. Grove's title raises an interesting point about the nature of personality disorders. Their definition does reflect a tension between adaptive personality traits and more extreme, maladaptive ways of thinking about oneself and other people. It can be useful to be suspicious, vigilant, skeptical, or even jealous (in some circumstances), but we should not confuse these traits with paranoid thought. By promoting an informal and misleading use of the word "paranoia," Grove's title does the field of psychopathology a disservice. In order to make progress toward understanding the nature of mental disorders, we have to be precise in our use of terms.

How can we distinguish between a cautious approach to the motives of other people and pathological paranoia? The difference depends, in part, on emotional reactions—such as irritability and hostility—that are associated with chronic suspicion and vigilance (Frances, First, & Pincus, 1995). Because they believe that others are causing problems for them, paranoid people are angry (Clifton, Turkheimer, & Oltmanns, 2004). Paranoid people can also become anxious and withdrawn. Their fear is based on the conviction that others intend to cause them harm, and they try to protect themselves by avoiding other people. The exaggerated negative emotions that accompany paranoid thinking are not likely to foster survival in the business world or in other social circumstances.

Another way to distinguish between normal suspicions and paranoia involves the amount of time that the person spends thinking about threats posed by other people. While most people become suspicious from time to time, paranoid people are *preoccupied* with the notion that others are out to get them. They are unable to think otherwise (Shapiro, 1965). Paranoid people are also impaired in their ability to consider information from another person's point of view. Most of us are able to seek and consider another person's perception or interpretation of uncertain events; paranoid people cannot. For all of these reasons, paranoia will promote failure rather than survival in the business world.

One of the most important elements of critical thinking involves the careful definition of terms. Sloppy talk leads to sloppy thinking. People who suggest that "a little paranoia can be useful" or "only the paranoid survive" are engaging in a misleading use of terms. It is clearly useful to be skeptical and cautious when considering the motives of other people. But the rigid and maladaptive patterns of thought that are characteristic of paranoid personality disorder are clearly pathological. The failure to appreciate the complexity and extent of these phenomena represents a distraction from, rather than a contribution to, serious scholarship.

Ted Bundy was executed in 1989 for killing at least 22 women. He was charming, intelligent, and self-assured.

In what ways are borderline and narcissistic personality disorders similar?

We have all read newspaper accounts of famous examples of antisocial personality disorder. These often include people who have committed horrendous acts of violence against other people, including genocidal war crimes and serial murders. You should not be misled, however, into thinking that only serious criminals meet the criteria for this disorder. Many other forms of persistently callous and exploitative behavior could lead to this diagnosis.

Borderline personality disorder is a diffuse category whose essential feature is a pervasive pattern of instability in mood and interpersonal relationships. People with this disorder find it very difficult to be alone. They form intense, unstable relationships with other people and are often seen by others as being manipulative. Their mood may shift rapidly and inexplicably from depression to anger to anxiety over a pattern of several hours. Intense anger is common and may be accompanied by temper tantrums, physical assault, or suicidal threats and gestures.

Many clinicians consider identity disturbance to be the diagnostic hallmark of borderline personality disorder. People with this disturbance presumably have great difficulty maintaining an integrated image of themselves that simultaneously incorporates their positive and negative features. Therefore, they alternate between thinking of themselves in unrealistically positive terms and then unrealistically negative terms at different moments in time. When they are focused on their own negative features,

they have a deflated view of themselves and may become seriously depressed. They frequently express uncertainty about such issues as personal values, sexual preferences, and career alternatives. Chronic feelings of emptiness and boredom may also be present.

BRIEF CASE STUDY
Borderline Personality Disorder

A single woman of 35 had worked with four (therapists) over a period of 11 years, before the last of these referred her to me. Since Beatrice had graduated from college at age 22, she had seemed to circulate in a holding pattern. She saw herself as an executive-to-be in the corporate world, but in actuality had held just a few entry-level jobs, and those only briefly. Once or twice she quit in a huff because the job was "not interesting enough" or because "they weren't promoting me fast enough." She had no distinct career goals, nor had she taken any special courses to prepare herself for some particular path. The work problem did not pose a threat to her well-being, since she lived off a large trust fund that her family had set up for her.

On the relational side her situation was not much better. Beatrice had never been "serious" with anyone and had little interest in men apart from their ability to pay compliments on her appearance. Her self-image was contradictory: she alternated between seeing herself as "model pretty" or else ugly. While buying an ice cream, she would feel devastated if the counterman did not make eyes at her; if he did, she would feel "insulted."

She had no hobbies or sustaining interests and found evenings with nothing to do intolerable. On such evenings she would usually engage her mother in long phone conversations (her parents lived in a different city), demanding that her mother come and visit. If this were not possible, she would slam the phone down, only to then call her mother back half an hour later to apologize.

During the time I worked with Beatrice, her most noticeable personality traits were those of anger, argumentativeness, scornfulness, irritability, and vanity. Her intensity and demandingness made her troublesome in her family; her parents and siblings were mostly good-natured and got on well when she was not in their midst (Stone, 1993, pp. 250–251).

Histrionic personality disorder is characterized by a pervasive pattern of excessive emotionality and attention seeking behavior. People with this disorder thrive on being the center of attention. They want the spotlight on them at all times. They are self-centered, vain, and demanding, and they constantly seek approval from others. When interacting with other people, their behavior is often inappropriately sexually seductive or provocative. Their emotions tend to be shallow and may vacillate erratically. They frequently react to situations with inappropriate exaggeration.

The concept of histrionic personality disorder overlaps extensively with other types of personality disorder, especially borderline personality disorder. People with both disorders are intensely emotional and manipulative. Unlike people with borderline personality disorder, however, people with histrionic personality disorder have an essentially intact sense of their own identity and a better capacity for stable relationships with other people.

There may also be an etiological link between histrionic and antisocial personality disorders. Both may reflect a common, underlying tendency toward lack of inhibition. People with both types of disorder form shallow, intense relationships with others, and they can be extremely manipulative. Family history studies indicate that this predisposition to disinhibition may be expressed as histrionic personality disorder in women and as antisocial personality disorder in men (Cale & Lilienfeld, 2002; Pfohl, 1995).

The essential feature of **narcissistic personality disorder** is a pervasive pattern of grandiosity, need for admiration, and inability to empathize with other people. Narcissistic people have a greatly exaggerated sense of their own importance. They are preoccupied with their own achievements and abilities. Because they consider themselves to be very special, they cannot empathize with the feelings of other people and are often seen as being arrogant or haughty.

There is a considerable amount of overlap between narcissistic personality disorder and borderline personality disorder. Both types of people feel that other people should recognize their needs and do special favors for them. They may also react with anger if they are criticized. The distinction between these disorders hinges on the inflated sense of self-importance that is found in narcissistic personality disorder and the deflated or devalued sense of self found in borderline personality disorder (Ronningstam & Gunderson, 1991).

Cluster C: Avoidant, Dependent, and Obsessive–Compulsive Personality Disorders

Cluster C includes avoidant, dependent, and obsessive–compulsive personality disorders. The common element in all three disorders is presumably anxiety or fearfulness. This description fits most easily with the avoidant and dependent types. In contrast, obsessive–compulsive personality disorder is more accurately described in terms of preoccupation with rules and with lack of emotional warmth than in terms of anxiety.

Avoidant personality disorder is characterized by a pervasive pattern of social discomfort, fear of negative evaluation, and timidity. People with this disorder tend to be socially isolated when outside their own family circle because they are afraid of criticism. Unlike people with schizoid personality disorder, they want to be liked by others, but they are extremely shy—easily hurt by even minimal signs of disapproval from other people. Thus they avoid social and occupational activities that require significant contact with other people.

Avoidant personality disorder is often indistinguishable from generalized social phobia (see Chapter 6). In fact, some experts have argued that they are probably two different ways of defining the same condition (Frances, First, &

Video Case

BORDERLINE PERSONALITY DISORDER

LIZ

"I have problems with anger management. In the past it has meant suicide attempts."

On your CD-ROM menu, select "Personality Disorders" and click on "Borderline PD: Liz." Pay careful attention to the description of her thoughts immediately prior to her suicide attempt.

Pincus, 1995). Others have argued that people with avoidant personality disorder have more trouble than people with social phobia in relating to other people (Millon & Martinez, 1995). People with avoidant personality disorder are presumably more socially withdrawn and have very few close relationships because they are so shy. People with social phobia may have a lot of friends, but they are afraid of performing in front of them. This distinction is relatively clear when social phobia is defined narrowly in terms of a particular kind of situation, such as public speaking. It is much more difficult to make if the social phobia becomes more generalized.

The essential feature of **dependent personality disorder** is a pervasive pattern of submissive and clinging behavior. People with this disorder are afraid of separating from other people on whom they are dependent for advice and reassurance. Often unable to make everyday decisions on their own, they feel anxious and helpless when they are alone. Like people with avoidant personality disorder, they are easily hurt by criticism, extremely sensitive to disapproval, and lacking in self confidence. One difference between avoidant and dependent personality disorders involves the point in a relationship at which they experience the most difficulty. People who are avoidant have trouble initiating a relationship (because they are fearful). People who are dependent have trouble being alone or separating from other people with whom they already have a close relationship. For example, a

person with dependent personality disorder might be extremely reluctant to leave home in order to attend college.

Obsessive–compulsive personality disorder (OCPD) is defined by a pervasive pattern of orderliness, perfectionism, and mental and interpersonal control, at the expense of flexibility, openness, and efficiency. People with this disorder set ambitious standards for their own performance that frequently are so high as to be unattainable. Many would be described as "workaholics." In other words, they are so devoted to work that they ignore friends, family members, and leisure activities. They are so preoccupied with details and rules that they lose sight of the main point of an activity or project. Intellectual endeavors are favored over feelings and emotional experience. These people are excessively conscientious, moralistic, and judgmental, and they tend to be intolerant of emotional behavior in other people.

The central features of this disorder may involve a marked need for control and lack of tolerance for uncertainty (Gibbs, South, & Oltmanns, 2003). At modest levels, these traits can represent an adaptive coping style, particularly in the face of the demands of our complex, technological society. Very high levels of these characteristics begin to interfere with a person's social and occupational adjustment. For example, people with OCPD find it difficult to delegate responsibilities to others, and their perfectionism makes it extremely difficult for them to finish projects within established deadlines.

Obsessive–compulsive personality disorder should not be confused with obsessive–compulsive disorder (OCD), a type of anxiety disorder (see Chapter 6). A pattern of intrusive, unwanted thoughts accompanied by ritualistic behaviors is used to define OCD. The definition of obsessive–compulsive personality disorder, in contrast, is concerned with personality traits, such as excessively high levels of conscientiousness. Traditional psychodynamic theory has maintained that obsessive–compulsive personality disorder often precedes the onset of OCD, in much the same way that schizotypal personality disorder is presumably an early manifestation of the predisposition to schizophrenia. Research evidence is ambiguous on the issue (Nestadt et al., 1991). In fact, people who meet the criteria for obsessive–compulsive personality disorder seem to be at risk for various kinds of anxiety

"And this is my pocket."

disorders, including generalized anxiety disorder and panic disorder as well as OCD. Obsessive–compulsive personality disorder may be more closely related to the form of OCD that involves checking rituals than to the form of OCD that involves washing and cleaning rituals (Gibbs & Oltmanns, 1995).

A Dimensional Perspective on Personality Disorders

DSM-IV-TR treats personality disorders as discrete categories, and it assumes that there are sharp boundaries between normal and abnormal personalities. In fact, there are a lot of people with serious personality problems who do not fit the official DSM-IV-TR subtypes. Another frequent complaint about the description of personality disorders is the considerable overlap among categories. Many patients meet the criteria for more than one type (Grant et al., 2005). It is cumbersome to list multiple diagnoses, especially when the clinician is already asked to list problems on both Axis I and Axis II. In fact, many clinicians are reluctant to make more than one diagnosis on Axis II; consequently, much information is frequently left out.

For these reasons, many experts favor the development of an alternative classification system for PDs, one that would be based on a dimensional view of personality pathology (Widiger & Simonsen, 2005). A dimensional system might provide a more complete description of each person, and it would be more useful with patients who fall on the boundaries between different types of personality disorder. It could also be easier to use than the DSM-IV-TR approach. One proposal is to use the five-factor model as the basic structure for a comprehensive description of personality problems (First et al., 2002; Lynam & Widiger, 2001). This approach would require the clinician to consider information regarding the 30 personality facets listed in Table 9–1. This system would be economical compared to making a judgment regarding the presence of at least 80 PD features in DSM-IV-TR (approximately 8 features for each of the 10 PD categories). An example of a description based on the five-factor dimensional approach to PDs is provided in the following brief case study.

♦♦♦

BRIEF CASE STUDY

Narcissism from the Perspective of the Five-Factor Model

Patricia was a 41-year-old married woman who presented at an outpatient mental health clinic complaining of interpersonal difficulties at work and recurring bouts of depression. [She] reported a long history of banking jobs in which she had experienced interpersonal discord. Shortly before her entrance into treatment, Patricia was demoted from a supervisory capacity at her current job because of her inability to interact effectively with those she was supposed to supervise. She described herself as always feeling out of place with her coworkers and indicated that most of them failed to adequately appreciate her skill or the amount of time she put in at work. She reported that she was beginning to think that perhaps she had something to do with their apparent dislike of her. However, even during the initial treatment sessions, her descriptions of her past and current job situations quickly and inevitably reverted to defensive statements concerning others' mistreatment and lack of appreciation of her. Despite her stated goal of changing her own behavior to be better liked, it quickly became clear that her actual wish was to cause her coworkers and supervisors to realize her superiority and to treat her accordingly.

Patricia often made condescending remarks about coworkers working under her, indicating that they were inferior to her in intelligence and abilities and thus had little or nothing to offer her. Patricia pretended to have a back injury as an excuse to avoid sales work, thus forcing the other employees to do this less pleasant job

Anger and hostility are important symptoms of several forms of personality disorder, including paranoid, antisocial, borderline, and narcissistic PDs.

while she was given more prestigious loan accounts. [She] also reported one incident in which a friend had agreed to meet her for dinner but was late because her child was ill. Patricia was highly offended and irritated by what she referred to as her friend's "lack of consideration" in being late. She felt no compassion for her friend or the child.

Patricia's tendency toward suspiciousness was exemplified by her belief that others did not like her and conspired against her to make her job harder (e.g., by "purposely" failing to get necessary paperwork to her on time). Finally, her uncooperativeness was illustrated by her tendency not to follow instructions at work and to refuse to cooperate with her husband at home. For example, although her boss had asked Patricia not to stay at the bank after hours because of security considerations, she often stayed late to work, saying that the boss's request was "stupid and restrictive."

Patricia described herself as both depressed and anxious. She also tended to become enraged when criticized or "treated badly." Although Patricia denied feelings of humiliation and insecurity, when criticized [she] would blush and either defensively make excuses for her behavior or negate the criticism ("She's just envious of me because I'm smarter than she is").

Other people seldom called or visited with her to talk about their problems; when they did, she responded with intellectual advice usually delivered in a condescending manner, such as, "When you're older, you'll understand better how things are." Her solitary nature in having few friends and keeping to herself at work may in fact have resulted in part from actual rebuffs from others in response to her antagonistic behavior.

Finally, Patricia perceived herself as accomplished, persistent, and strongly committed to the highest standards of conduct. These impressions may indicate a classic narcissistic inflation of self-image, especially given that she was, even by her own report, having considerable difficulties at work (Corbitt, 2002, pp. 294–297).

This woman's interpersonal difficulties could be succinctly described in terms of a combination of low agreeableness (trust, modesty, altruism, and compliance), low extraversion (warmth and gregariousness), high neuroticism (anger–hostility, anxiousness, and depression), and high conscientiousness (competence, dutifulness, and achievement striving). Based on DSM-IV-TR, she would meet the criteria for narcissistic personality disorder. If the categorical approach were used, however, a complete description of her personality problems would also require that the clinician note the presence of some

How are normal personality traits related to personality disorders?

features of paranoid PD (such as unjustified doubts about the loyalty of coworkers; reacting with rage to perceived attacks on her character or reputation) and obsessive–compulsive PD (excessive devotion to work to the exclusion of leisure activities and friendships), even though she did not exhibit enough features of these other disorders to meet their diagnostic threshold. A dimensional approach like the one illustrated in this case may eventually replace the 10 PD categories on Axis II when the next version of DSM is published.

FREQUENCY

Personality disorders are generally considered to be one of the most common forms of psychopathology, but it is difficult to provide research evidence to support that claim. Only antisocial personality disorder has been studied extensively. The other personality disorders have not been included in large-scale epidemiological studies, such as the Epidemiologic Catchment Area study and the National Comorbidity Survey. Problems and inconsistencies associated with reliance on self-report measures make the problem of establishing prevalence rates even more complicated.

Prevalence in Community and Clinical Samples

How many people in the general population would meet the criteria for at least one personality disorder if they were given a diagnostic interview? In studies that have examined community based samples of adults, the overall lifetime prevalence for having at least one Axis II disorder (any type) varies between 10 and 14 percent (Samuels et al., 2002; Torgersen, Kringlen, & Cramer, 2001).

Evidence regarding the prevalence of specific types of personality disorder in community samples is summarized in Figure 9–1. This figure presents summary data that have been averaged across a number of studies (Mattia & Zimmerman, 2001). Among community samples, the highest prevalence rates are found for obsessive–compulsive personality disorder. The other types vary in prevalence between 1 and 2 percent of the population. The most obvious exception is narcissistic personality disorder, which appears to be the least common form, affecting only 0.2 percent of the population.

Investigators have identified very few cases of narcissistic personality disorder when they have interviewed people in community samples (as opposed to clinic settings). The fact that almost no one endorses narcissistic symptoms does not necessarily mean, however, that the disorder does not occur. Rather, it seems possible that people who experience these features do not recognize the nature of their own problems or are unwilling to admit them. Self-report measures, such as questionnaires and interviews, may not be effective instruments for assessing narcissistic personality disorder. More accurate information might be obtained from other people who know the person well and can report examples of grandiosity, exploitation, or lack of empathy (Oltmanns & Turkheimer, 2006).

The most precise information that is available regarding the prevalence of personality disorders in community samples is concerned specifically with the antisocial type (Moran, 1999). In both the ECA study and NCS, structured interviews relating to this disorder were conducted with several thousand participants. The overall lifetime prevalence rate for antisocial personality disorder (men and women combined) was 3 percent in both the NCS and ECA studies.

Notice that the prevalence rates for ASPD from the ECA and NCS studies are higher than the rate reported in Figure 9–1, which reflects an average across several studies. Some studies have found rates that are much lower than those of the ECA and NCS reports. One rigorous investigation of 11,000 people in Taiwan found that only 0.2 percent met the criteria for antisocial personality disorder (Compton et al., 1991). This result might be taken to indicate that antisocial personality disorder is more common in our individualistic society than it is in a society that places greater emphasis on collectivism. But this is only one interpretation. More information is clearly needed before strong conclusions can be drawn.

One final issue regarding prevalence rates involves comorbidity. There is considerable overlap among categories in the personality disorders. At least 50 percent of people who meet the diagnostic criteria for one personality disorder also meet the criteria for another disorder (Grant et al., 2005). To some extent, this overlap is due to the fact that similar symptoms are used to define more than one disorder. For example,

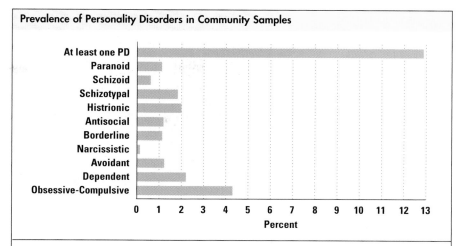

FIGURE 9–1: Estimates of the prevalence of personality disorders.
Source: J.I. Mattia & M. Zimmerman (2001). Epidemiology. In W.J. Livesley (Ed.), *Handbook of Personality Disorders: Theory, Research, and Treatment.* New York: Guilford. Copyright © 2001. Reprinted by permission of Guilford Publications, Inc.

impulsive and reckless behaviors are part of the definition of both antisocial and borderline PDs. Social withdrawal is used to define schizoid, schizotypal, and avoidant PD.

There is also extensive overlap between personality disorders and disorders that are diagnosed on Axis I of DSM-IV-TR. Approximately 75 percent of people who qualify for a diagnosis on Axis II also meet criteria for a syndrome such as major depression, substance dependence, or an anxiety disorder (Dolan-Sewell, Krueger, & Shea, 2001). This overlap may also be viewed from the other direction: Many people who are treated for a mental disorder listed on Axis I, such as depression or alcoholism, would also meet the criteria for a personality disorder (Thomas et al., 1999). Borderline personality disorder appears to be the most common personality disorder among patients treated at mental health facilities (both inpatient and outpatient settings). Averaged across studies, the evidence suggests that this disorder is found among slightly more than 30 percent of all patients who are treated for psychological disorders (Lyons, 1995). Rates are especially high among those who have been hospitalized, but the specific figures vary considerably from one study to the next.

Gender Differences

The overall prevalence of personality disorders is approximately equal in men and women (Weissman, 1993). There are, however, consistent gender differences with regard to at least one

Vivien Leigh won Academy Awards for her performances as Scarlett O'Hara in *Gone with the Wind* (1940) and Blanche Du Bois in *A Streetcar Named Desire* (1952). Both characters exhibit blends of histrionic and narcissistic features that fit stereotyped views of female personality traits.

specific disorder: Antisocial personality disorder is unquestionably much more common among men than among women. The ECA study found rates of 4.5 percent for men and 0.8 percent for women (Robins, Tipp, & Przybeck, 1991). The NCS reported rates of 5.8 percent for men and 1.2 percent for women (Kessler et al., 1994). Thus antisocial personality disorder is actually an alarmingly common problem among adult males in the United States.

Epidemiological evidence regarding gender differences for the other types of personality disorder is much more ambiguous. Very few community based studies have been done using standardized interviews as a basis for diagnosis. In one community sample of more than 3,400 adults, the prevalence of histrionic personality disorder was found to be 2.2 percent in both men and women (Nestadt et al., 1990). Almost nothing is known about the extent of potential gender differences for the other types of personality disorder. Borderline personality disorder and dependent personality disorder may be somewhat more prevalent among women than men, but the evidence is not strong (Skodol & Bender, 2003). There has been some speculation that paranoid and obsessive–compulsive personality disorders may be somewhat more common among men than women (Bernstein, Useda, & Siever, 1995).

Gender Bias and Diagnosis   One of the controversies that has surrounded the diagnosis of personality disorders involves the issue of gender bias (Widiger, 1998). Critics contend that the definitions of some categories are based on sex role stereotypes and therefore are inherently sexist. The dependent type, for example, might be viewed as a reflection of certain traditionally feminine traits, such as being unassertive or putting the needs of others ahead of one's own. It has been suggested that DSM-IV-TR arbitrarily labels these traits as maladaptive. Traditionally masculine traits, such as being unable to identify and express a wide range of emotions, are presumably not mentioned in the manual. This practice arbitrarily assigns responsibility for interpersonal difficulties to the women themselves. Therefore these definitions may turn traditional sex role behaviors into "disorders" and minimize the extent to which women may simply be trying to cope with unreasonable or oppressive environmental circumstances, including discrimination and sexual abuse (Caplan, 1995; Jordan, 2004).

This argument leads to a number of interesting and important questions. One is concerned with the presence of bias within the criterion sets themselves. If the criteria for certain categories are based on stereotypes of feminine traits, is it relatively easy for a woman to meet the criteria for that diagnosis even if she is not experiencing significant distress or impairment in other areas of her life? The answer to that question is, tentatively, no (Funtowicz & Widiger, 1999). In other words, the threshold for assigning a diagnosis of personality disorder does not appear to be lower for those types that are based largely on traits that might be considered traditionally feminine (dependent, histrionic, borderline) than for those that are based on traits that might be considered traditionally masculine (antisocial, paranoid, compulsive).

A second question is concerned with the possibility of gender bias in the ways that clinicians assign diagnoses to their clients, regardless of whether the criteria themselves are biased. Are clinicians more likely to assign diagnoses such as dependent and borderline personality disorder to a woman than to a man, if both people exhibit the same set of symptoms? The answer to this question is, tentatively, yes. One study found that both male and female mental health professionals were significantly (though not overwhelmingly) more likely to describe a person as exhibiting symptoms of borderline personality disorder if that person were female rather than male (Becker & Lamb, 1994).

Stability of Personality Disorders over Time

Temporal stability is one of the most important assumptions about personality disorders. Evidence for the assumption that personality disorders appear during adolescence and persist into adulthood has, until recently, been limited primarily to antisocial personality disorder. A classic follow-up study by Lee Robins (1966) began with a large set of records describing young children treated for adjustment problems at a clinic during the 1920s. Robins was able to locate and interview almost all of these people, who by then were adults. The best predictor of an adult diagnosis of antisocial personality was conduct disorder in childhood. The people who were most likely to be considered antisocial as adults were boys who had been referred to the clinic on the basis of serious theft or aggressive behavior; who exhibited such behaviors across a variety of situations; and whose antisocial behaviors created conflict with adults outside their own homes. More than half of the boys who exhibited these characteristics were given a diagnosis of antisocial personality disorder as adults.

Another longitudinal study has collected information regarding the prevalence and stability of personality disorders among adolescents (Bernstein et al., 1993). This investigation is particularly important because it did not depend solely on subjects who had been referred for psychological treatment and because it was concerned with the full range of personality disorders. The rate of personality disorders was relatively high in this sample: Seventeen percent of the adolescents received a diagnosis of at least one personality disorder. Categorically defined diagnoses were not particularly stable; fewer than half of the adolescents who originally qualified for a personality disorder diagnosis met the same criteria 2 years later. Nevertheless, many of the study participants continued to exhibit similar problems over the next 8 years. Viewed from a dimensional perspective, the maladaptive traits that represent the core features of the disorders remained relatively stable between adolescence and young adulthood (Crawford, Cohen, & Brook, 2001).

Several studies have examined the stability of personality disorders among people who have received professional treatment for their problems, especially those who have been hospitalized for schizotypal or borderline disorders. Many patients who have been treated for these problems are still significantly impaired several years later, but the disorders are not uniformly stable (Grilo et al., 2004; Stone, 2001). Recovery rates are relatively high among patients with a diagnosis of borderline personality disorder. If patients who were initially treated during their early twenties are followed up when they are in their forties and fifties, only about one person in four would still qualify for a diagnosis of borderline personality disorder. The long-term prognosis is less optimistic for schizotypal and schizoid personality disorders. People with these diagnoses are likely to remain socially isolated and occupationally impaired (Seivewright et al., 2002).

Which personality disorders are least likely to change as a person gets older?

Culture and Personality

In DSM-IV-TR, personality disorders are defined in terms of behavior that "deviates markedly from the expectations of the individual's culture." In setting this guideline, the authors of DSM-IV-TR recognized that judgments regarding appropriate behavior vary considerably from one society to the next. Some cultures encourage restrained or subtle displays of emotion, whereas others promote visible, public displays of anger, grief, and other emotional responses. Behavior that seems highly dramatic or extraverted (histrionic) in the former cultures might create a very different impression in the latter cultures. Cultures also differ in the extent to which they value individualism (the pursuit

Is this young Afghan woman more extraverted than the others? Is she a risk-taker? It is impossible to make these personality judgments without more knowledge of the culture in which she lives. She may be unveiled because she is younger than the other women, or because she is not married.

of personal goals) as opposed to collectivism (sharing and self-sacrifice for the good of the group) (Triandis, 1994). Someone who seems exceedingly self-centered and egotistical in a collectivist society, such as Japan, might appear to be normal in an individualistic society like the United States.

The personality disorders may be more closely tied to cultural expectations than any other kind of mental disorder (Alarcon, Foulks, & Vakkur, 1998). Some studies have compared the prevalence and symptoms of personality disorders in different countries, and the data suggest that similar problems do exist in cultures outside the United States and Western Europe (Pinto et al., 2000; Yang et al., 2000). Nevertheless, much more information is needed before we can be confident that the DSM-IV-TR system for describing personality disorders is valid in other societies. Two questions are particularly important:

1. In other cultures, what are the personality traits that lead to marked interpersonal difficulties and social or occupational impairment? Are they different from those that have been identified for our own culture?

research methods

CROSS-CULTURAL COMPARISONS: THE IMPORTANCE OF CONTEXT

Over the past 25 years, psychologists have begun to adopt a broader focus in their consideration of human behavior, including mental disorders. This means paying more attention to cultural diversity in the samples used in research studies.

At the broadest level, culture is a system of meanings that determines the ways in which people think about themselves and their environments. It shapes their most basic view of reality. Consider, for example, the process of bereavement following the death of a close relative. In some Native American cultures, people learn to expect to hear the spirit of the dead person calling to them from the afterworld (Kleinman, 1988). This is a common experience for people in these cultures. It resembles auditory hallucinations (perceptual experiences in the absence of external stimulation) that are seen in people with psychotic disorders. But among some Native American peoples, hearing voices from the dead is a "normative" or common response; it is not a sign of dysfunction. Perhaps most importantly, this type of experience is not regularly associated with social or occupational impairment. It would be a mistake, therefore, to consider these experiences to be symptoms of a mental disorder.

Cross-cultural psychology is the scientific study of ways that human behavior and mental processes are influenced by social and cultural factors (Ho, 1994; Lonner & Malpass, 1994). This field includes the study of ethnic differences (among cultural groups living in close proximity within a single nation). Comparison is a fundamental element of any cross-cultural study. Cross-cultural psychologists examine ways in which human behaviors are different, as well as ways in which they are similar, from one culture to the next.

Cross-cultural comparisons are relevant to the study of psychopathology in many ways. One way involves epidemiology—comparisons of the prevalence of disorders across cultures. Investigations aimed at etiological mechanisms, including biological, psychological, and social variables, can also be extremely informative when viewed in cross-cultural perspective. For example, we know that negative patterns of thinking are correlated with depressed mood in middle-class Americans. Is the same relationship found among people living in rural China? Virtually any study of psychopathology would provide useful information if it were replicated in different cultures.

The valuable process of making cross-cultural comparisons can actually be quite difficult. Several complex issues must be faced by investigators who want to study psychopathology in cross-cultural perspective:

1. *Identifying meaningful groups:* The first step in making cross-cultural comparisons is the selection of participants who are representative members of different cultures. This may be a relatively straightforward process if the comparison is to be made between two small, homogeneous groups such as two isolated rural villages in two very different countries (say, Peru and Zimbabwe). The situation becomes much more complex if the investigator's goal is to compare ethnic groups within a large, multicultural society such as the United States. Hispanic Americans, for example, include people whose cultural backgrounds can be traced to many different Spanish-speaking homelands with very different cultural traditions, such as Puerto Rico, Mexico, and Cuba. Even greater cultural diversity is found among various Native American peoples. How do we determine which people share a common culture? What is the cultural "unit," and how do we find its boundaries?

2. *Selecting equivalent measurement procedures:* Comparison between groups can be valid only if equivalent measurement procedures are used in both cultures (or in all groups). Participants in different cultures often speak different languages (or different dialects). Questionnaires and psychological tests must be cross validated to ensure that they measure the same concepts in different cultures.

3. *Considering causal explanations:* Suppose that investigators identify a reliable difference between people in two different cultures. They must now decide how to interpret this difference. Is it, in fact, due to cultural variables? Or would the differences disappear if other variables, such as poverty, education, and age, were held constant between the two groups?

4. *Avoiding culturally biased interpretations:* Investigators, who are often middle class and white, must interpret the results of cross-cultural research cautiously. In particular, scientists must not interpret differences between cultures or ethnic groups as being indicative of deficits in minority groups or non-Western cultures. Some cross-cultural psychologists have suggested that it is more important to study developmental processes within cultures or ethnic groups than to compare outcomes between groups.

2. Are the diagnostic criteria that are used to define personality disorder syndromes in DSM-IV-TR (and ICD-10) meaningful in other cultures?

Cross-cultural studies that are designed to address these issues must confront a number of difficult methodological problems (see Research Methods).

Within a particular society, the experiences of people from cultural and ethnic minorities should also be considered carefully before diagnostic decisions are made. Phenomena associated with paranoid personality disorder, including strong feelings of suspicion, alienation, and distrust, illustrate this issue. People who belong to minority groups (and those who are recent immigrants from a different culture) are more likely than members of the majority or dominant culture to hold realistic concerns about potential victimization and exploitation. For example, black Americans may develop and express mild paranoid tendencies as a way of adapting to ongoing experiences of oppression (Whaley, 1998). Clinicians may erroneously diagnose these conditions as paranoid personality disorder if they do not recognize or understand the cultural experiences in which they are formed. In this particular case, it is obviously important for the clinician to consider the person's attitudes and beliefs regarding members of his or her own family or peer group, as well as the person's feelings about the community as a whole.

People with schizotypal PD tend to be loners, and many have social anxiety that can be traced to distrust of other people.

these are people who exhibit most, if not all, of the features of the disorder. You should not infer from these descriptions that everyone who meets the criteria for these disorders would represent this type of typical case. Remember, also, that many people simultaneously meet the criteria for more than one personality disorder; these cases are relatively simple examples. The following case illustrates some of the most important features of schizotypal personality disorder (SPD).

SCHIZOTYPAL PERSONALITY DISORDER (SPD)

Now that we have reviewed some of the important general issues for the entire set of personality disorders, we consider four specific types of disorder in more detail. We have decided to focus on schizotypal, borderline, and antisocial types because they have been the subject of extended research and debate in the scientific literature. We will also discuss dependent personality disorder to illustrate current thinking about one of the Cluster C disorders, even though this disorder has not been studied as extensively as the other three categories.

We begin each of the four sections with a brief case study. We have chosen cases that are prototypes for each disorder. In other words,

BRIEF CASE STUDY

Schizotypal Personality Disorder

Sandra, when she first came for treatment at the age of 27, presented with marked anxiety in social situations and in getting along with coworkers, eccentric behavior, and paranoid ideas. She had no close female friends and only one male friend, and though the latter was a sexual relationship, she revealed almost nothing to him about her past. She had many strange beliefs involving astrology, foods, and medicines.

Sandra had only one friend during her adolescence: someone who shared her faddishness about foods and her beliefs in astrology. Girls excluded her from their school clubs. She never understood why they rejected her, though it is probable that they considered her "weird" because of her inability to make small talk, and her voice pattern: a flat, high-pitched, stilted-sounding monotone that made her come across as mannered and insincere. Added to this peculiarity of speech was her tendency to skip from topic to topic abruptly, giving equal emphasis to each, such that it was difficult to distinguish the trivial from the important. From a therapeutic standpoint, this was particularly bedeviling, since it strained one's intuitive capacities to the uttermost just to figure out what was really bothering her or what was the "main theme" on any particular day.

Her empathic skills were very limited, leading her to comment at times that she found people and their motives completely puzzling: "I can't connect up with them. If they invite me to lunch with them, I can't seem to join in the conversation or else I say the wrong thing, so after a while they don't invite me anymore and I eat by myself." If a teaching supervisor wore a dour expression walking down the hall, Sandra assumed the supervisor was dissatisfied with her work, even though it might be a person who was not even assigned to her department. She tended to be surly and "superior" sounding when asking for vacation requests and the like—and often didn't get what she wanted because of having alienated the people whose favor she needed. This reinforced her notion that the world was pretty much against her.

Though considered a knowledgeable teacher, she had no charm or patience with the children and was eventually given a semi-administrative job where little interaction with others was necessary. With boyfriends, she was comfortable about having sex, but made such fussy and endless-seeming preparations (such as doing her fingernails in the bathroom for half an hour) that the men lost the mood and usually ended the relationship after a few months.

More striking than her empathic difficulties was a curious inability to grasp what one might call the statistics of everyday life. Travel was a great burden, since she felt it necessary to plan for all possible contingencies. She once went to (France) on an August vacation packing her winter overcoat, because, as she reminded me, "There was a cold spell there in the '50s and it could happen again." Furthermore, she sent a packet of clothes on ahead to the hotel because, "What if my baggage got stolen?" She had great difficulty, in other words, aligning her behavior in harmony with the expectable, in contrast with the remotely possible—all thinkable events being in her mind equally probable (Stone, 1993, pp. 179–180).

The concept of schizotypal personality disorder is closely tied to the history of schizophrenia as a diagnostic entity (Gottesman, 1987). The term was originally coined as an abbreviation for *schizophrenic phenotype*. These maladaptive personality traits are presumably seen among people who possess the genotype that makes them vulnerable to schizophrenia. The symptoms of schizotypal personality disorder represent early manifestations of the predisposition to develop the full-blown disorder. It has been recognized for many years that a fairly large proportion of the family members of schizophrenic patients exhibit strange or unusual behaviors that are similar to, but milder in form than, the disturbance shown by the patient.

Symptoms

The DSM-IV-TR criteria for schizotypal personality disorder are listed in Table 9–3. These criteria represent a blend of those characteristics that have been reported among the relatives of schizophrenic patients and those symptoms that seem to characterize nonpsychotic patients with schizophrenic-like disorders (Siever, Bernstein, & Silverman, 1995). In addition to social detachment, emphasis is placed on eccentricity and cognitive or perceptual distortions.

People who meet the criteria for schizotypal personality disorder frequently meet the criteria for additional Axis II disorders. There is considerable overlap between schizotypal personality disorder and other personality disorders in Cluster A (paranoid and schizoid), as well as with avoidant personality disorder. This finding is not particularly surprising, given the conceptual origins of the schizotypal category. There is also quite a bit of overlap between schizotypal personality disorder and borderline personality disorder.

Causes

Most of the interest in the etiology of schizotypal personality disorder has focused on the importance of genetic factors. Is schizotypal personality disorder genetically related to schizophrenia? Family and adoption studies indicate that the answer is yes (Appels et al., 2004; Battaglia & Torgersen, 1996). Twin studies have examined genetic contributions to schizotypal personality disorder from a dimensional perspective in which schizotypal personality traits are measured with questionnaires. This evidence also points to a significant genetic contribution (Linney et al., 2003).

The first degree relatives of schizophrenic patients are considerably more likely than people in the general population to exhibit schizotypal personality disorder. One large study of this type, the Roscommon Family Study, was conducted in a rural county in western Ireland. The investigators interviewed more than 1,700 parents and siblings of three groups of probands: 300 schizophrenic patients, 100 patients with major mood disorders, and 150 people with no history of psychiatric disorder (Kendler et al., 1993). Some of the results of this study are summarized in Figure 9–2 (see page 300).

The most striking finding was an increased prevalence of schizotypal personality disorder (6.9 percent) among the relatives of the schizophrenic patients. Prevalence rates for paranoid and avoidant personality disorder were also significantly higher among the relatives of the schizophrenic patients. Kendler and his colleagues did not find increased rates of these personality disorders among the relatives of people with mood disorders. These results suggest that these disorders, especially schizotypal personality disorder, are genetically related to schizophrenia. The diagnostic specificity of this finding remains open to question; some studies have reported that schizotypal personality disorder is found with increased frequency among the children of parents with mood disorders (Erlenmeyer-Kimling et al., 1995).

Treatment

Two important considerations complicate the treatment of people with personality disorders in general and SPD in particular, and make it difficult to evaluate the effectiveness of various forms of intervention. One consideration involves the ego-syntonic nature of many personality disorders (discussed earlier). Many people with these disorders do not seek treatment for their problems because they do not see their own behavior as being the source of distress (Ewing, Falk, & Otto, 1996). A related difficulty involves premature termination: A relatively high proportion of personality disorder patients drop out of treatment before it is completed.

When people with personality disorders appear at hospitals or clinics, it is often because they are also suffering from another type of mental disorder, such as depression or substance abuse. This comorbidity is the second consideration that complicates treatment. "Pure forms" of personality disorder are relatively rare. There is tremendous overlap between specific personality disorder

---

TABLE 9–3   DSM-IV-TR Criteria for Schizotypal Personality Disorder

A. A pervasive pattern of social and interpersonal deficits marked by acute discomfort with, and reduced capacity for, close relationships as well as by cognitive or perceptual distortions and eccentricities of behavior, beginning by early adulthood and present in a variety of contexts, as indicated by five (or more) of the following:

1. Ideas of reference (excluding delusions of reference).
2. Odd beliefs or magical thinking that influences behavior and is inconsistent with subcultural norms (such as superstitiousness, belief in clairvoyance, or telepathy).
3. Unusual perceptual experiences, including bodily illusions.
4. Odd thinking and speech (vague, circumstantial, metaphorical, overelaborate, or stereotyped).
5. Suspiciousness or paranoid ideation.
6. Inappropriate or constricted affect.*
7. Behavior or appearance that is odd, eccentric, or peculiar.
8. Lack of close friends or confidants other than first-degree relatives.
9. Excessive social anxiety that does not diminish with familiarity and tends to be associated with paranoid fears rather than with negative judgments about self.

B. Does not occur exclusively during the course of Schizophrenia, a Mood Disorder with Psychotic Features, another Psychotic Disorder, or a Pervasive Developmental Disorder.

---

*Inappropriate affect refers to emotional responses that appear to be inconsistent with the social context—for example, uncontrollable giggling at a wake or funeral. Constricted affect refers to the absence of emotional responsiveness, such as lack of facial expressions. See Chapter 13 for a more detailed discussion.

Reprinted with permission from the *Diagnostic and Statistical Manual of Mental Disorders, Fourth Edition, Text Revision.* Copyright © 2000 by the American Psychiatric Association.

---

categories and other forms of abnormal behavior, including disorders that would be listed on both Axis I and Axis II. Treatment is seldom aimed at problem behaviors that are associated with only one type of personality disorder, and the efficacy of treatment is, therefore, difficult to evaluate.

The literature regarding treatment of schizotypal personality disorder, like that dealing with its causes, mirrors efforts aimed at schizophrenia. A few studies have focused on the possible treatment value of antipsychotic drugs, which are effective with many schizophrenic patients. Some studies have found that low doses of antipsychotic medication are beneficial in alleviating cognitive problems and social anxiety in patients who have received a diagnosis of schizotypal personality disorder (Koenigsberg et al., 2003). There is also some indication that patients with schizotypal personality disorder may respond positively to antidepressant medications, including SSRIs. In

Why are personality disorders so difficult to treat?

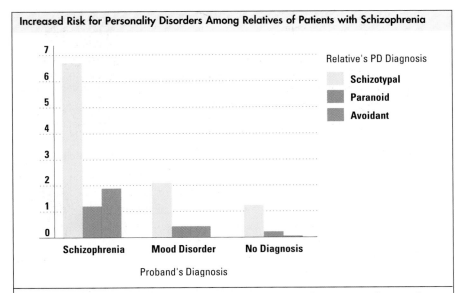

FIGURE 9-2: Familial relationship between schizophrenia and three types of personality disorder.

Source: K.S. Kendler, M. McGuire, A.M. Gruenberg, A. O'Hare, J. Spellman, D. Walsh (1993). The Roscommon Family Study. III. Schizophrenia-related personality disorders in relatives. *Archives of General Psychiatry, 50,* 781–788. Copyright © 1993. Reprinted by permission of American Medical Association.

general, the therapeutic effects of medication are positive, but they tend to be modest.

Clinical experience seems to suggest that these patients do not respond well to insight oriented psychotherapy, in part because they do not see themselves as having psychological problems and also because they are so uncomfortable with close personal relationships. Some clinicians have suggested that a supportive, educational approach that is focused on fostering basic social skills may be beneficial if the goals of treatment are modest (Crits-Christoph, 1998; Gabbard, 2000). Unfortunately, controlled studies of psychological forms of treatment with schizotypal personality disorder have not been reported.

BORDERLINE PERSONALITY DISORDER (BPD)

Borderline personality disorder is one of the most perplexing, most disabling, and most frequently treated forms of personality disorder. Because of the severity of their problems, people with BPD are more likely to come into clinics seeking treatment. Experts on psychiatric classification have discussed the possibility that this diagnostic category might be moved to Axis I when DSM-V is written in the next few years (with a different name, such as "emotion dysregulation disorder").

Of course, no one knows for certain what will happen when the manual is revised. The following case illustrates many of the features associated with this disorder.

BRIEF CASE STUDY

Borderline Personality Disorder

Barbara, a single woman of 24, sought treatment with me shortly after discharge from a hospital, where she had spent three weeks because of depression, panic attacks, and a suicide gesture. This had been her seventh hospitalization—all of them brief, and all for similar symptoms—since age 17. Cheerful and cooperative as a young girl, she underwent a radical change of personality at the time of her menarche. Thereafter, she became irascible, rebellious, moody, and demanding.

For a time she was anorexic; later on, bulimic (maintaining her normal weight by vomiting). Schoolwork deteriorated, and she took up with a wild crowd, abusing marijuana and other drugs and engaging in promiscuous sex. At one point she ran away from home with a boyfriend, and didn't return for three months.

She quit high school with one year to go. Her life became even more chaotic; she scratched her wrists on a number of occasions, and consorted with abusive men who would use her sexually and then beat her up.

By the time I began working with Barbara, she had been abusing alcohol for about a year, and had also become addicted to benzodiazepines. Her proneness to panic-level anxiety now took the form of agoraphobia, necessitating her being accompanied by a parent to her therapy sessions. Premenstrually, her irritability rose to fever pitch: she would strike her parents with her fists, sometimes necessitating help from the police. She would then threaten to kill herself.

Lacking any hobbies or interests, apart from dancing, she was bored to distraction at home, yet afraid to venture out. Nothing gave her any pleasure except glitzy clothes (which her agoraphobia rendered irrelevant).

For a few weeks Barbara dated a man from her neighborhood, and although she was able to leave the house if she were with him, she used the opportunity in a self-destructive way, going to wild nightclubs and provoking him with demands to the point where he drove her only halfway home, pushing her out of the car, so that she had to hitchhike home at 2 A.M. This precipitated a suicide attempt with a variety of medications (Stone, 1993, pp. 248–249).

The intellectual heritage of borderline personality disorder (BPD) is quite diverse, and it is more difficult to trace than that of schizotypal personality disorder. It is, in fact, rather confusing. Several traditions are important, and in some cases they represent conflicting points of view (Leichtman, 1989).

Otto Kernberg (1967, 1975), a psychiatrist at Cornell University, has developed an explanation of borderline personality that is based on psychodynamic theory. According to Kernberg, borderline personality is not a specific syndrome. Rather, it refers to a set of personality features or deficiencies that can be found in individuals with various disorders. In Kernberg's model, the common characteristic of people diagnosed with borderline personality is faulty development of ego structure. Another common feature of people with borderline disorder is *splitting*—the tendency to see people and events alternately as entirely good or entirely bad. Thus a man with borderline personality might perceive his wife as almost perfect at some times and as highly flawed at other times. The tendency toward splitting helps explain the broad mood swings and unstable relationships associated with borderline personalities.

Kernberg's emphasis on a broadly defined level of pathology, rather than on discrete clinical symptoms, resulted in a relatively expansive definition of borderline personality. Viewed from this perspective, borderline disorder can encompass a great many types of abnormal behavior, including paranoid, schizoid, and cyclothymic personality disorders, impulse control disorders (see Impulse Control Disorders on page 302), substance use disorders, and various types of mood disorder.

In an effort to foster research on borderline disorders, these psychodynamic views regarding personality organization were translated into more reliable, descriptive terms by several prominent clinicians. John Gunderson (1984, 1994), a psychiatrist at Harvard University, identified a number of descriptive characteristics that are commonly associated with Kernberg's concept of borderline personality. Gunderson and his colleagues developed a structured interview that would allow clinicians to diagnose the condition reliably and served as the basis for the current definition of BPD in DSM-IV-TR.

Symptoms

The DSM-IV-TR criteria for borderline personality disorder are presented in Table 9–4. The overriding characteristic of borderline personality disorder is a pervasive pattern of instability in self-image, in interpersonal relationships, and in mood.

> To be borderline means to lack grounding emotionally and to exist from moment to moment without any sense of continuity, predictability, or meaning. Life is experienced in fragments, more like a series of snapshots than a moving picture. It is a series of discrete points of experience that fail to flow together smoothly or to create an integrated whole. (Moskovitz, 1996, pp. 5–6)

Borderline personality disorder overlaps with several other categories on Axis II, including the histrionic, narcissistic, paranoid, dependent, and avoidant types. There is also a significant amount of overlap between borderline personality disorder and Axis I disorders, especially depression (Trull, 1995). Many patients with other types of impulse control problems, such as substance dependence and eating disorders, also qualify for a diagnosis of borderline personality disorder.

Follow-up studies suggest many similarities between borderline personality disorder and mood disorders. In many cases, the symptoms of BPD are evident before the onset of major depression. For example, one study focused on a group of 100 outpatients with a diagnosis of borderline personality disorder (Akiskal, 1992). During follow-up, 29 percent of the sample

John Gunderson, a psychiatrist at Harvard University, has played a central role in the development of diagnostic criteria for borderline personality disorder.

TABLE 9–4   DSM-IV-TR Criteria for Borderline Personality Disorder

A. **A pervasive pattern of instability of interpersonal relationships, self-image, and affects, and marked impulsivity beginning by early adulthood and present in a variety of contexts, as indicated by five (or more) of the following:**

1. Frantic efforts to avoid real or imagined abandonment.

2. A pattern of unstable and intense interpersonal relationships characterized by alternating between extremes of idealization and devaluation.

3. Identity disturbance: markedly and persistently unstable self image or sense of self.

4. Impulsiveness in at least two areas that are potentially self-damaging (for example, spending, sex, substance abuse, reckless driving, binge eating).

5. Recurrent suicidal behavior, gestures, or threats, or self-mutilating behavior.

6. Affective instability due to a marked reactivity of mood (such as intense episodic dysphoria, irritability, or anxiety usually lasting a few hours and only rarely more than a few days).

7. Chronic feelings of emptiness.

8. Inappropriate, intense anger or difficulty controlling anger (for example, frequent displays of temper, constant anger, recurrent physical fights).

9. Transient, stress related paranoid ideation or severe dissociative symptoms.

IMPULSE CONTROL DISORDERS

Failure to control harmful impulses is associated with several of the disorders listed in DSM-IV-TR. People who meet the criteria for borderline personality disorder and antisocial personality disorder engage in various types of impulsive, maladaptive behaviors (most often self-mutilation in the case of BPD, and theft and aggression in the case of ASPD). People in the midst of a manic episode frequently become excessively involved in pleasurable activities that can have painful consequences, such as unrestrained buying or sexual indiscretions. These are examples of impulse control problems that appear as part of a more broadly defined syndrome or mental disorder.

DSM-IV-TR includes several additional problems under a heading called **impulse control disorders.** They are coded on Axis I rather than Axis II. Relatively little is known about these problems (Hollander & Rosen, 2000; Hucker, 1997). They are defined in terms of persistent, clinically significant impulsive behaviors that are not better explained by other disorders in DSM-IV-TR. They include the following:

- *Intermittent explosive disorder:* Aggressive behaviors resulting in serious assaultive acts or destruction of property. The level of aggression is grossly out of proportion to any precipitating psychosocial stressors (McElroy, 1999).
- *Kleptomania:* Stealing objects that are not needed for personal use or for their financial value. The theft is not motivated by anger or vengeance (Presta et al., 2002).
- *Pyromania:* Deliberate and purposeful setting of fires, accompanied by fascination with or attraction to fire and things that are associated with it. The behavior is not motivated by financial considerations (as in arson), social or political ideology, anger, vengeance, or delusional beliefs (Geller, McDermeit, & Brown, 1997).
- *Trichotillomania:* Pulling out one's own hair, resulting in noticeable hair loss as well as significant distress or impairment in social or occupational functioning (O'Sullivan et al., 2000).
- *Pathological gambling:* Repeated maladaptive gambling that is associated with other

problems, such as repeated, unsuccessful efforts to stop gambling, restlessness or irritability when trying to stop gambling, lying to family members and friends to conceal the extent of gambling, and committing crimes to finance gambling (Sharpe, 2002).

In most cases, the impulsive behavior is preceded by increasing tension and followed by a feeling of pleasure, gratification, or relief. The motivation for these impulsive behaviors is, therefore, somewhat different than the motivation for compulsive behavior (see Chapter 6). Impulsive and compulsive behaviors can be difficult to distinguish, as both are repetitious and difficult to resist. The primary difference is that the original goal for impulsive behavior is to experience pleasure, and the original goal for compulsive behavior is to avoid anxiety (Frances, First, & Pincus, 1995).

The most frequent type of impulse control disorder is pathological gambling. The lifetime prevalence of pathological gambling in the United States is approximately 2 or 3 percent of the population and seems to be increasing with the spread of legalized gambling (Shaffer, Hall, & Bilt, 1999; Welte et al., 2001). Men are more likely than women to become pathological gamblers. They tend to be intelligent, well educated, competitive people who enjoy the challenges and risks involved in betting. Substance use disorders (see Chapter 11) and antisocial personality disorder are commonly associated with pathological gambling. Evidence from twin studies suggests that impulsivity represents a common form of vulnerability to all of three types of disorder, and this predisposition is influenced by genetic factors (Slutske et al., 2000; Slutske et al., 2001).

Most gambling is not associated with a mental disorder. Social gambling is a form of recreation that is accepted in most cultures. Professional gambling is an occupation pursued by people whose gambling is highly disciplined. Pathological gambling, in contrast, is out of control, takes over the person's life, and leads to horrendous financial and interpersonal consequences.

The tragic life of Art Schlichter provides a vivid illustration of the devastating impact that

persistent, uncontrolled, impulsive gambling can have on a person and his family (Keteyian, 1986; Valente, 1996). Schlichter, an All-American quarterback at Ohio State University, was the first player drafted by the National Football League in 1982. He had been gambling since high school, but the problem became worse after he started playing professional football. His career was disappointing. As the pressures mounted, so did his gambling debts, which eventually reached $1 million. He was cut from several teams in the National Football League and the Canadian Football League, and was ultimately banned from the NFL for betting on professional games. He entered treatment for his compulsive gambling on several occasions, but the results were unsuccessful and his repeated promises to stop gambling went unfulfilled. Schlichter has been arrested and jailed on several occasions for charges that include forgery, theft, and bank fraud. In 2001, he was sentenced to 6 years in prison for violating the terms of his probation. Schlichter's promising football career was ruined, and his young family was torn apart by his uncontrolled gambling.

The impulse control disorders occupy an interesting and controversial niche in DSM-IV-TR. The implication of impulse control disorders is that people who repeatedly engage in dangerous, illegal, or destructive behaviors must have a mental disorder. If they do not, why do they do these things? Unfortunately, this reasoning quickly becomes circular. Why does he gamble recklessly? Because he has a mental disorder. How do you know he has a mental disorder? Because he gambles recklessly. This logical dilemma is particularly evident in the case of impulse control disorders because these problem behaviors do not appear as part of a broader syndrome in which other symptoms of disorder are also present. In other words, the problem behavior is the disorder. Until we can step outside this loop, validating the utility of the diagnostic concept by reference to other psychological or biological response systems, we are left with an unsatisfying approach to the definition of these problems.

developed severe depression. Another longitudinal study of patients who were discharged from a private psychiatric hospital is also interesting in this regard. In a sample of patients with a pure diagnosis of borderline personality disorder (that is, those who did not receive any other diagnosis on Axis I or II), 23 percent developed major depressive episodes during the course of the 15-year follow-up (McGlashan, 1986).

Causes

Genetic factors do not seem to play a central role in the etiology of borderline personality disorder when it is viewed in terms of the syndrome that is defined in DSM-IV-TR (Torgersen, 1994). It is premature to conclude that genes are irrelevant to the development of this set of problems because the fundamental personality traits that serve to define the disorder, such as neuroticism and impulsivity, are influenced by genetic factors (Skodol et al., 2002; Nigg & Goldsmith, 1994). Nevertheless, most of the discussion regarding causes of borderline personality disorder has focused on environmental events.

Some investigators have argued that borderline patients suffer from the negative consequences of parental loss or neglect during childhood (Davis & Akiskal, 1986). This model is supported by studies of the families of borderline patients and by comparisons with the literature on social development in monkeys that examined the effects of separating infants from their mothers. Studies of patients with borderline personality disorder do point toward the influence of widespread problematic relationships with their parents. Separation appears to be only one aspect of this complicated picture. Adolescent girls with borderline personality disorder report pervasive lack of supervision, frequent witnessing of domestic violence, and being subjected to inappropriate behavior by their parents and other adults, including verbal, physical, and sexual abuse (Helgeland & Torgersen, 2004; Pally, 2002). The extent and severity of abuse vary widely across individuals. Many patients describe multiple forms of abuse by more than one person.

The association between borderline personality disorder and the patients' recollections of childhood maltreatment raises an important question about the direction of this relationship: Does childhood abuse lead to borderline personality

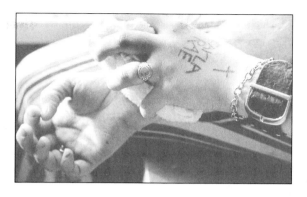

Some people with borderline personality disorder engage in recurrent suicidal gestures of self-mutilating behavior.

disorder? Or are people with borderline personality disorder simply more likely to remember that they were abused by their parents, due to biased reporting?

Longitudinal data from a study of adolescents in upstate New York provide important evidence on this point (Johnson et al., 1999). Rather than relying exclusively on self-report measures, the investigators obtained data on child maltreatment from the New York State Central Registry for Child Abuse. Maltreatment included documented cases of physical abuse, sexual abuse, and childhood neglect. People with documented evidence of childhood abuse and neglect were four times more likely than those who had not been mistreated to develop symptoms of personality disorders as young adults. Strongest connections were found for Cluster B disorders (see Figure 9–3 on page 304). Physical abuse was most closely associated with subsequent antisocial personality disorder; sexual abuse with borderline personality disorder; and childhood neglect with antisocial, borderline, narcissistic, and avoidant personality disorder. These data support the argument that maladaptive patterns of parenting and family relationships increase the probability that a person will develop certain types of personality disorder.

Treatment

Given that the concept of borderline personality disorder is rooted in psychodynamic theory, it should not be surprising that many clinicians have advocated the use of psychotherapy for the treatment of these conditions. In psychodynamic therapy, the *transference relationship*, defined as the way in which the patient behaves toward the therapist and which is believed to reflect early primary relationships, is used to increase patients' ability to experience themselves and

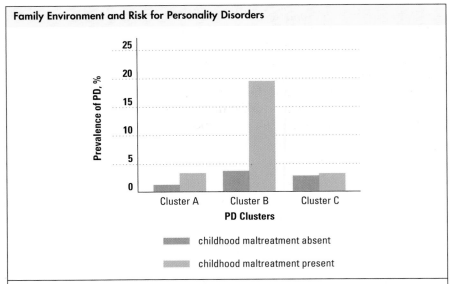

Family Environment and Risk for Personality Disorders

childhood maltreatment absent

childhood maltreatment present

FIGURE 9–3: Associations between childhood maltreatment and risk for early adulthood personality disorders.

Source: J.G. Cohen., J. Brown., E.M. Smailes, D.P. Bernstein. (1999). Childhood maltreatment increases risk for personality disorders during early adulthood. *Archives of General Psychiatry, 56,* 600–606. Copyright © 1999. Reprinted by permission of American Medical Association.

Linehan's approach to treatment, the term refers to strategies that are employed by the therapist in order to help the person appreciate and balance apparently contradictory needs to accept things as they are (such as intense negative emotions) and to work toward changing patterns of thinking and behavior that contribute to problems in the regulation of emotions. Emphasis is placed on learning to be more comfortable with strong emotions, such as anger, sadness, and fear, and learning to think in a more integrated way that accepts both good and bad features of the self and other people. Traditional behavioral and cognitive techniques, such as skill training, exposure, and problem solving, are also employed to help the patient improve interpersonal relationships, tolerate distress, and regulate emotional responses. Finally, considerable emphasis is placed on the therapist's acceptance of patients, including their frequently demanding, manipulative, and contradictory behaviors. This factor is important, because borderline patients are extremely sensitive to even the most subtle signs of criticism or rejection by other people.

One controlled study of dialectical behavior therapy produced encouraging results with regard to some aspects of the patients' behavior (Linehan et al., 1994, 1999). All of the patients in this study were women who met diagnostic criteria for BPD and also had a previous history of suicide attempts or deliberate self-harm. Patients were randomly assigned to receive either DBT or treatment as usual, which was essentially any form of treatment that was available within the community. The adjustment of patients in both groups was measured after 1 year of treatment and over a 1 year period following termination. One of the most important results involved the dropout rate. Almost 60 percent of the patients in the treatment as usual group terminated prematurely, whereas the rate in the DBT group was only 17 percent. The patients who received DBT also showed a significant reduction in the frequency and severity of suicide attempts, spent fewer days in psychiatric hospitals over the course of the study, and rated themselves higher on a measure of social adjustment. The groups did not differ, however, on other important measures, such as level of depression and hopelessness.

other people in a more realistic and integrated way (Clarkin et al., 2001; Gabbard, 2000).

As we have said, personality disorders have traditionally been considered to be hard to treat from a psychological perspective, and borderline conditions are among the most difficult. Close personal relationships form the foundation of psychological intervention, and it is specifically in the area of establishing and maintaining such relationships that borderline patients experience their greatest difficulty (see Getting Help on page 313). Their persistent alternation between overidealization and devaluation leads to frequent rage toward the therapist and can become a significant deterrent to progress in therapy. Not surprisingly, between one-half and two-thirds of all patients with borderline personality disorder discontinue treatment, against their therapists' advice, within the first several weeks of treatment (Kelly et al., 1992).

One promising approach to psychotherapy with borderline patients, called *dialectical behavior therapy* (DBT), has been developed and evaluated by Marsha Linehan (1993; Linehan et al., 2001), a clinical psychologist at the University of Washington. This procedure combines the use of broadly based behavioral strategies with the more general principles of supportive psychotherapy. In philosophy, the term *dialectics* refers to a process of reasoning that places opposite or contradictory ideas side by side. In

Positive results have also been reported in more recent studies in which women with BPD were randomly assigned to either dialectical behavior therapy or treatment as usual. Outcome measures indicated that women who were treated with dialectical behavior therapy experienced more improvement than women in the control groups with regard to symptoms such as depression and hopelessness (Bohus et al., 2004; Koons et al., 2001; Verheul et al., 2003).

In general, these studies suggest that DBT is a promising form of treatment for people with borderline personality disorder. It should be noted, however, that the sample sizes in these studies are quite small. Important methodological questions have been raised about the outcome results, including the possible influence of the allegiance effect (see Research Methods in Chapter 10). DBT has become one of the most popular and rapidly expanding forms of psychological treatment, and it has begun to be used in treating other problems that involve impulsive behavior, such as substance use disorders and binge eating disorders (Robins & Chapman, 2004). Enthusiasm for the therapeutic value of DBT will undoubtedly lead to more rigorous evaluations of its effectiveness in clinical settings.

Psychotropic medication is also used frequently in the treatment of borderline patients. Unfortunately, no disorder-specific drug has been found. Psychiatrists employ the entire spectrum of psychoactive medication with borderline patients, from antipsychotics and antidepressants to lithium and anticonvulsants (Koenigsberg, Woo-Ming & Siever, 2002; Zanarini & Frankenburg, 2001). Different types of drugs are recommended to treat individual symptoms, such as impulsive aggression, emotional instability, and transient paranoid thinking, but there is no systematic proof that a specific drug is effective for any of the borderline features.

ANTISOCIAL PERSONALITY DISORDER (ASPD)

Antisocial personality disorder (ASPD) has been studied more thoroughly and for a longer period of time than any of the other personality disorders (Blashfield & McElroy, 1989). One case study involving this disorder was presented at the beginning of this chapter. Tom, the man in that case, illustrated the pattern of repeated antisocial behavior that is associated with the disorder. Emotional and interpersonal problems also play an important role in the definition of antisocial personality disorder. The following case, written by Robert Hare, a clinical psychologist at the University of British Columbia, illustrates the egocentricity that is a central feature of the disorder. It also demonstrates the stunning lack of concern that such people have for the impact of their behavior on other people, especially those who are close to them.

BRIEF CASE STUDY

Antisocial Personality Disorder

Terry is 21, the second of three boys born into a wealthy and highly respected family. His older brother is a doctor, and his younger brother is a scholarship student in his second year of college. Terry is a first-time offender, serving 2 years for a series of robberies committed a year ago.

By all accounts, his family life was stable, his parents were warm and loving, and his opportunities for success were enormous. His brothers were honest and hardworking, whereas he simply "floated through life, taking whatever was offered." His parents' hopes and expectations were less important to him than having a good time. Still, they supported him emotionally and financially through an adolescence marked by wildness, testing the limits, and repeated brushes with the law—speeding, reckless driving, drunkenness—but no formal convictions. By age 20 he had fathered two children and was heavily involved in gambling and drugs. When he could no longer obtain money from his family he turned to robbing banks, and he was soon caught and sent to prison. "I wouldn't be here if my parents had come across when I needed them," he said. "What kind of parents would let their son rot in a place like this?" Asked about his children, he replied, "I've never seen them. I think they were given up for adoption. How the hell should I know!" (Hare, 1993, p. 167).

The contrast between Terry's willingness to blame his problems on his parents and his apparent inability to accept responsibility for his own children is striking. It illustrates clearly the callous indifference and shallow emotional experience of the person with antisocial personality disorder.

Current views of antisocial personality disorder have been greatly influenced by two specific books. These books have inspired two different approaches to the definition of the disorder itself. The first book, *The Mask of Sanity*, was written by

Hervey Cleckley, a psychiatrist at the University of Georgia, and was originally published in 1941. It includes numerous case examples of impulsive, self-centered, pleasure seeking people who seemed to be completely lacking in certain primary emotions, such as anxiety, shame, and guilt. Cleckley used the term **psychopathy** to describe this disorder. According to Cleckley's definition, the psychopath is a person who is intelligent and superficially charming but is also chronically deceitful, unreliable, and incapable of learning from experience. This diagnostic approach places principal emphasis on emotional deficits and personality traits. Unfortunately, Cleckley's definition was difficult to use reliably because it contained such elusive features as "incapacity for love" and "failure to learn from experience."

The second book that influenced the concept of antisocial personality disorder was a report by Lee Robins of her follow-up study of children who had been treated many years earlier at a child guidance clinic. The book, *Deviant Children Grown Up* (1966), demonstrated that certain forms of conduct disorder that were evident during

What is the difference between antisocial personality disorder and psychopathy?

Andrew Fastow, former Enron chief financial officer, is now serving a 10-year prison sentence for fraud. Grandiosity, deceit, manipulativeness, and lack of remorse are traits associated with the "white collar psychopath."

childhood, especially among boys, were reliable predictors of other forms of antisocial behavior when these same people became adults. The diagnostic approach inspired by this research study was adopted by DSM-III (APA, 1980). It places principal emphasis on observable behaviors and repeated conflict with authorities, including failure to conform to social norms with respect to lawful behavior. This approach can be used with greater reliability than psychopathy because it is focused on concrete consequences of the disorder, which are often documented by legal records, rather than subjectively defined emotional deficits, such as lack of empathy.

Psychopathy and ASPD are two different attempts to define the same disorder. Yet they are sufficiently different that they certainly do not identify the same people, and they are no longer used interchangeably. Critics argued that DSM-III had blurred the distinction between antisocial personality and criminality. Cleckley's approach had been relatively clear on this point; all criminals are not psychopaths, and all psychopaths are not criminals. The DSM-III definition made it difficult to diagnose antisocial personality disorder in a person who did not already have a criminal record, such as an egocentric, manipulative, and callous businessperson. It also moved in the direction of including a much larger proportion of criminals within the boundaries of antisocial personality disorder (Hart & Hare, 1997). The true meaning of the concept might have been sacrificed in DSM-III for the sake of improved reliability.

Symptoms

Table 9–5 lists the DSM-IV-TR criteria for antisocial personality disorder. One prominent feature in this definition is the required presence of symptoms of conduct disorder (see Chapter 16) prior to the age of 15, which reflects the impact of Robins's work. The definition also requires the presence of at least three out of seven signs of irresponsible and antisocial behavior after the age of 15. One of these criteria, "lack of remorse," did not appear in DSM-III but was one of Cleckley's original criteria. Its inclusion in DSM-IV-TR clearly signals an attempt to move the definition back toward the original concept.

Some investigators and clinicians prefer the concept of psychopathy to the DSM-IV-TR definition of antisocial personality. Robert Hare has developed a systematic approach to the assessment of psychopathy, known as the Psychopathy Checklist (PCL), that is based largely on Cleckley's original description of the disorder. The PCL includes two major factors (groups of symptoms): (1) emotional/interpersonal traits and (2) social deviance associated with an unstable or antisocial lifestyle. Key symptoms for both factors are summarized in Table 9–6 on page 308. The major difference between this definition of psychopathy and the DSM-IV-TR definition of antisocial personality disorder involves the list of emotional and interpersonal traits (although DSM-IV-TR does include being deceitful and failure to experience remorse). Extensive research with the PCL indicates that, contrary to previous experience with Cleckley's criteria, the emotional and interpersonal traits can be used reliably (Hart & Hare, 1997).

The ultimate resolution of this prolonged dispute over the best definition of antisocial personality disorder will depend on systematic comparisons of the two approaches (Lilienfeld, 1994; Skilling et al., 2002). This situation is a classic example of studying the validity of a diagnostic concept (see Chapter 4). How different are these definitions? Which definition is most useful in predicting events such as repeated antisocial behavior following release from prison? The field trial that was conducted when DSM-IV-TR was being prepared was one large-scale effort of this type (Widiger et al., 1996). That project did not find any major differences in validity between the DSM-based definition of antisocial personality disorder and a PCL-based definition of psychopathy.

Antisocial Behavior over the Life Span

Not everyone who engages in antisocial behavior does so consistently throughout his or her lifetime. Terrie Moffitt, a clinical psychologist at the University of London, has proposed that there are two primary forms of antisocial behavior: transient and nontransient. Moffitt (1993, 1997) considers adolescence-limited antisocial behavior to be a common form of social behavior that is often adaptive and that disappears by the time the person reaches adulthood. This type presumably accounts for most antisocial behavior, and it is unrelated to antisocial personality disorder.

A small proportion of antisocial individuals, mostly males, engage in antisocial behavior at all ages. Moffitt calls this type

| TABLE 9–5 | DSM-IV-TR Criteria for Antisocial Personality Disorder |

A. There is a pervasive pattern of disregard for and violation of the rights of others occurring since age 15, as indicated by three (or more) of the following:

1. Failure to conform to social norms with respect to lawful behavior as indicated by repeatedly performing acts that are grounds for arrest.
2. Deceitfulness, as indicated by repeated lying, use of aliases, or conning others for personal profit or pleasure.
3. Impulsivity or failure to plan ahead.
4. Irritability and aggressiveness, as indicated by repeated physical fights or assaults.
5. Reckless disregard for safety of self or others.
6. Consistent irresponsibility, as indicated by repeated failure to sustain consistent work behavior or honor financial obligations.
7. Lack of remorse, as indicated by being indifferent to or rationalizing having hurt, mistreated, or stolen from another.

B. The individual is at least 18 years old.

C. Evidence of Conduct Disorder with onset before age 15.

Reprinted with permission from the *Diagnostic and Statistical Manual of Mental Disorders, Fourth Edition, Text Revision.* Copyright © 2000 by the American Psychiatric Association.

life-course-persistent antisocial behavior. The specific form of these problems may vary from one age level to the next:

> Biting and hitting at age 4, shoplifting and truancy at age 10, selling drugs and stealing cars at age 16, robbery and rape at age 22, and fraud and child abuse at age 30. The underlying disposition remains the same, but its expression changes form as new social opportunities arise at different points in development. (Moffitt, 1993, p. 679)

Follow-up studies suggest that in some ways psychopaths tend to "burn out" when they reach 40 or 45 years of age. These changes are most evident for the impulsive, socially deviant kinds of behavior that are represented in the second factor on Hare's Psychopathy Checklist (Harpur & Hare, 1994). Indeed, older psychopaths are less likely to exhibit a pathological "need for excitement" or to engage in impulsive, criminal behaviors. In contrast to this pattern, personality traits associated with the emotional–interpersonal factor on the PCL, such as deceitfulness, callousness, and lack of empathy, do not become less conspicuous over time. These are apparently more stable features of the disorder.

It is not clear whether the age-related decline in social deviance represents a change in personality structure (improved impulse control and diminished sensation seeking). Moffitt's theory suggests that, as psychopaths grow older,

Robert Hare, a psychologist at the University of British Columbia, is a leading expert on psychopathy. He developed the Psychopathy Checklist, which has become the standard assessment instrument for this disorder.

they may find new outlets for their aggression, impulsive behavior, and callous disregard for others. For example, they might resort to fraud or child abuse, for which they are less likely to get caught.

Causes

Psychologists have studied etiological factors associated with psychopathy and antisocial personality disorder more extensively than for any of the other personality disorders. Research studies on this topic fall into three general areas. One is concerned with the biological underpinnings of the disorder, especially the possible influence of genetic factors. The second focus of investigation is social factors. The relationship between familial conflict and the development of antisocial behavior in children falls under this general heading. The third group of studies has addressed the nature of the psychological factors that might explain the apparent inability of people with antisocial personality disorder to learn from experience.

Biological Factors   Several investigators have used twin and adoption methods to study the contributions of genetic and environmental factors to the development of antisocial personality disorder and of criminal behavior more generally. The adoption strategy is based on the study of adoptees: people who were separated from their biological parents at an early age and raised by adoptive families (see Chapter 2). Several adoption studies have found that the development of antisocial behavior is determined by an interaction between genetic factors and adverse environmental circumstances (Rhee &

Waldman, 2002). In other words, both types of influence are important. The highest rates of conduct disorder and antisocial behavior are found among the offspring of antisocial biological parents who are raised in an adverse adoptive environment.

Consider, for example, the results of one particularly informative study that was conducted by Remi Cadoret, a psychiatrist at the University of Iowa, and several colleagues (Cadoret et al., 1995; Yates, Cadoret, & Troughton, 1999). The investigators studied men and women who had been separated at birth from biological parents with antisocial personality disorder. This target group was compared to a control group of people who had been separated at birth from biological parents with no history of psychopathology. The offspring and their adoptive parents were interviewed to assess symptoms of conduct disorder, aggression, and antisocial behavior in the offspring. The adversity of the adoptive home environment was measured in terms of the total number of problems that were present, including severe marital difficulties, drug abuse, or criminal activity.

The results of the study by Cadoret and his colleagues indicated that people who were raised in more difficult adoptive homes were more likely to engage in various types of aggressive and antisocial behavior as children and as adults. Further analyses revealed that the harmful effects of an unfavorable environment were more pronounced in the target group than in the control group. In other words, offspring of antisocial parents were much more likely to exhibit symptoms of conduct disorder (truancy, school expulsion, lying, and stealing) as children and exaggerated aggressive behavior as adolescents if they were raised in an adverse adoptive home environment. Being raised in an adverse home environment did not significantly increase the probability of conduct disorder, aggression, or antisocial behavior among offspring in the control group. Thus antisocial behavior appeared to result from the interaction of genetic and environmental factors.

Social Factors   Adoption studies indicate that genetic factors interact with environmental events to produce patterns of antisocial and criminal behavior. The combination of a genetic predisposition toward antisocial behavior and environmental adversity is particularly harmful. What kinds of events might be involved in this process? Obvious candidates include physical abuse and

TABLE 9–6 Key Symptoms of Psychopathy	
EMOTIONAL/INTERPERSONAL TRAITS	**SOCIAL DEVIANCE (ANTISOCIAL LIFESTYLE)**
Glib and superficial	Impulsive
Egocentric and grandiose	Poor behavior controls
Lack of remorse or guilt	Need for excitement
Lack of empathy	Lack of responsibility
Deceitful and manipulative	Early behavior problems
Shallow emotions	Adult antisocial behavior

Source: R.D. Hare (1991). Without Conscience: The Disturbing World of the Psychopaths Among Us. New York: Pocket Books. Reprinted by permission of Pocket Books.

childhood neglect, as indicated by the longitudinal study of adolescents and their families (Johnson et al., 1999).

How can the interaction between genetic factors and family processes be explained? Moffitt's explanation for the etiology of life course persistent antisocial behavior depends on the influence of multiple, interacting systems. One pathway involves the concept of children's temperament and the effect that their characteristic response styles may have on parental behavior. Children with a "difficult" temperament—that is, those whose response style is characterized by high levels of negative emotion or excessive activity—may be especially irritating to their parents and caretakers (Bates, Wachs, & Emde, 1994). They may be clumsy, overactive, inattentive, irritable, or impulsive. Their resistance to disciplinary efforts may discourage adults from maintaining persistent strategies in this regard. This type of child may be most likely to evoke maladaptive reactions from parents who are poorly equipped to deal with the challenges presented by this kind of behavior. Parents may be driven either to use unusually harsh punishments or to abandon any attempt at discipline. This interaction between the child and the social environment fosters the development of poorly controlled behavior. Antisocial behavior is perpetuated when the person selects friends who share similar antisocial interests and problems.

After a pattern of antisocial behavior has been established during childhood, many factors lock the person into further antisocial activities. Moffitt's theory emphasizes two sources of continuity. The first is a limited range of behavioral skills. The person does not learn social skills that would allow him or her to pursue more appropriate responses than behaviors such as lying, cheating, and stealing. Once the opportunity to develop these skills is lost during childhood, they may never be learned. The second source of continuity involves the results of antisocial behavior during childhood and adolescence. The person becomes progressively ensnared by the aftermath of earlier choices. Many possible consequences of antisocial behavior, including being addicted to drugs, becoming a teenaged parent, dropping out of school, and having a criminal record, can narrow the person's options.

Psychological Factors Adoption, twin, and family studies provide clues to the types of etiological factors that may cause antisocial personality

Antisocial behavior can be perpetuated when the person selects friends who share similar antisocial interests and problems.

disorder. Another series of studies, beginning in the 1950s and extending to the present, has been concerned with the psychological mechanisms that may mediate this type of behavior. These investigations have attempted to explain several characteristic features of psychopathy—such as lack of anxiety, impulsivity, and failure to learn from experience—using various types of laboratory tasks.

Subjects in the laboratory tasks are typically asked to learn a sequence of responses in order either to receive a reward or avoid an aversive consequence, such as electric shock or loss of money. Although the overall accuracy of psychopaths' performance on these tasks is generally equivalent to that of nonpsychopathic subjects, their behavior sometimes appears to be unaffected by the anticipation of punishment (Lykken, 1957; Newman & Wallace, 1993).

Two primary hypotheses have been advanced to explain the poor performance of psychopaths on these tasks. One point of view is based on Cleckley's argument that psychopaths are emotionally impoverished. Their lack of anxiety and fear is particularly striking. Research support for this hypothesis is based in large part on an examination of physiological responses while subjects are performing laboratory tasks. One particularly compelling line of investigation involves the examination of the eye blink startle reflex. People blink their eyes involuntarily when they are startled by a loud, unexpected burst of noise. For most people, the magnitude of this response is increased if, at the time they are startled, they are engaged in an ongoing task that elicits fear or some other negative emotional state (such as viewing frightening or disgusting stimuli). The magnitude of the startle response is decreased if the person is engaged in a task that elicits positive emotion. Psychopaths' startle responses follow a pattern different from those observed in normal subjects (Herpertz et al., 2001; Patrick & Zempolich, 1998); they do not show the exaggerated startle response that is indicative of fear in the presence of aversive stimuli. This emotional deficit may explain why psychopaths are relatively insensitive to, or able to ignore, the effects of punishment (Hare, 1993).

The other hypothesis holds that psychopaths have difficulty shifting or reallocating their attention to consider the possible negative consequences of their behavior. Evidence for this explanation is based in large part on the observation that psychopaths respond normally to punishment in some situations but not in others. This is especially evident in mixed-incentive situations, in which the person's behavior might be either rewarded or punished. Psychopaths are preoccupied with the potential for a successful outcome. They will continue gambling when the stakes are high, even when the odds are badly against them. And they will pursue a potential sexual encounter, even when the other person is trying to discourage their interest. They fail to inhibit inappropriate behavior because they are less able than other people to stop and consider the meaning of important signals that their behavior might lead to punishment (Newman, Schmitt, & Voss, 1997; Patterson & Newman, 1993).

Critics of this line of research have noted some problems with existing psychological explanations for the psychopath's behavior. One limitation is the implicit assumption that most people conform to social regulations and ethical principles because of anxiety or fear of punishment. The heart of this criticism seems to lie in a disagreement regarding the relative importance of Cleckley's criteria for psychopathy. It might be argued that the most crucial features are not low anxiety and failure to learn from experience, but lack of shame and pathological egocentricity. According to this perspective, the psychopath is simply a person who has chosen, for whatever reason, to behave in a persistently selfish manner that ignores the feelings and rights of other people. "Rather than moral judgment being driven by anxiety, anxiety is driven by moral judgment" (Levenson, 1992).

Treatment

People with antisocial personalities seldom seek professional mental health services unless they are forced into treatment by the legal system. When they do seek treatment, the general consensus among clinicians is that it is seldom effective. This widely held impression is based, in part, on the traits that are used to define the disorder; like people with borderline personality disorder, people with antisocial personality disorder are typically unable to establish intimate, trusting relationships, which obviously form the basis for any treatment program.

The research literature regarding the treatment of antisocial personality disorder is sparse (Salekin, 2002). Very few studies have identified cases using official diagnostic criteria for antisocial personality disorder. Most of the programs that have been evaluated have focused on juvenile delinquents, adults who have been imprisoned, or people otherwise referred by the criminal justice system. Outcome is often measured in terms of the frequency of repeated criminal offenses rather than in terms of changes in behaviors more directly linked to the personality traits that define the core of antisocial personality. The high rate of alcoholism and other forms of substance dependence in this population is another problem that complicates planning and evaluating treatment programs aimed specifically at the personality disorder itself.

Although no form of intervention has proved to be effective for antisocial personality disorder, psychological interventions that are directed toward specific features of the disorder might be useful. Examples are behavioral procedures that were originally designed for anger management and deviant sexual behaviors (Reid & Gacono, 2000; Sanderlin, 2001). Behavioral treatments can apparently produce temporary changes in behavior while the person is closely supervised, but they may not generalize to other settings (Rice & Harris, 1997).

DEPENDENT PERSONALITY DISORDER (DPD)

Dependent personality disorder (DPD) is listed in the third cluster of Axis II in DSM-IV-TR, along with avoidant and obsessive–compulsive personality disorders. Cluster C includes descriptions of various types of people who are anxious or fearful. Those who meet the criteria for DPD assume a submissive role in relationships with other people. They require an extraordinary level of reassurance and support, clinging to others who will take care of them. The following case study illustrates many of the most important features of this disorder.

BRIEF CASE STUDY

Dependent Personality Disorder

The patient, Mrs. S., was a 48-year-old married, Caucasian female. [She] reported numerous decision-making situations which provoke anxiety and attempts to seek reassurance. For example, buying food in the supermarket, deciding what to make for dinner, and buying furniture all provoked anxiety and led Mrs. S. to seek reassurance from her husband. Further, Mrs. S. reported feeling anxious when her husband was not there to reassure her (such as when he was away and Mrs. S. was responsible for trimming the garden bushes and lawn). Finally the patient related numerous anxiety-provoking instances in which decisions she made were initially approved of by an authority figure (such as her husband or physician) and then criticized by an important other (such as after following the instructions of her physician, she was criticized for doing so by a friend).

During school years, Mrs. S. always wanted to be part of the "group," but she felt uncomfortable because no one would assure her explicitly that she "fit in." Moreover, her high school advisor noted on Mrs. S.'s record that she "lacked initiative."

When the patient went to college, she studied nursing because "a lot of people my age went into nursing." When the time came to choose between a university-based or hospital-based program, she relied largely on her mother's advice.

The patient's first job as a nurse went rather smoothly because her supervisors were readily available. Unfortunately, her second position did not work out well. Apparently, Mrs. S. had trouble adjusting because she did not have "supportive" supervisors. She left this position after a short time.

Mrs. S. did not have much of a dating history. Her husband was her first and only lover. She was greatly attracted to him because he was "very forceful" and an "independent decision maker" (Turkat & Carlson, 1984, pp. 156–157).

Dependent personality disorder was introduced as a separate type of mental disorder in DSM-III (APA, 1980). Before then, the concept of dependency was viewed primarily as a personality trait rather than a mental disorder in its own right. It was considered to be a vulnerability factor that increased the person's risk for other types of mental disorder, particularly depression (Bornstein, 1998).

Freud proposed that dependent interpersonal relationships set the stage for later onset of depression (see Chapter 5). Contemporary investigators are still very much interested in that hypothesis. The term sociotropy is sometimes used to refer to dependency in that context. According to one version of this theory, people who are dependent, or sociotropic, may be particularly likely to become depressed if they experience a stressful event that is interpersonal in nature. Longitudinal studies suggest that a dependent or sociotropic interpersonal style does predict the later onset of depression (Davila, 2001; Mazure et al., 2000).

How is dependent personality disorder related to depression?

Symptoms

The DSM-IV-TR criteria for dependent personality disorder are listed in Table 9–7. These criteria reflect two underlying components: preference for affiliation and fear of criticism and rejection (Horowitz, 2004; Livesley, 1995). Preference for affiliation reflects the motivation to remain close to other people who will provide security and comfort. Fear of criticism and rejection reflects a

TABLE 9–7 DSM-IV-TR Criteria for Dependent Personality Disorder
A. A pervasive and excessive need to be taken care of that leads to submissive and clinging behavior and fears of separation, beginning by early adulthood and present in a variety of contexts, as indicated by five (or more) of the following:
1. Has difficulty making everyday decisions without an excessive amount of advice and reassurance from others.
2. Needs others to assume responsibility for most major areas of his or her life.
3. Has difficulty expressing disagreement with others because of fear of loss of support or approval (does not include realistic fears of retribution).
4. Has difficulty initiating projects or doing things on his or her own (because of lack of self-confidence in judgment or abilities rather than a lack of motivation or energy).
5. Goes to excessive lengths to obtain nurturance and support from others, to the point of volunteering to do things that are unpleasant.
6. Feels uncomfortable or helpless when alone because of exaggerated fears of being unable to care for himself or herself.
7. Urgently seeks another relationship as a source of care and support when a close relationship ends.
8. Is unrealistically preoccupied with fears of being left to take care of himself or herself.

Reprinted with permission from the *Diagnostic and Statistical Manual of Mental Disorders, Fourth Edition, Text Revision.* Copyright © 2000 by the American Psychiatric Association.

lack of self-confidence and includes actions aimed at eliciting help and approval from others.

Dependent personality disorder overlaps with several other categories listed on Axis II of DSM-IV-TR. The greatest overlap is with borderline personality disorder (Reich, 1996). People with both types of personality disorder are fearful of being abandoned by other people. The reactions that they show are quite different, however. People with BPD become enraged and manipulative when they think they are being abandoned, whereas people with DPD respond with clinging and submissive behaviors (Hirschfeld, Shea, & Weise, 1995).

Causes

Relatively little research has been conducted on the etiology of dependent personality disorder as a separate form of mental disorder. There is, however, a substantial body of evidence concerned with the development of dependency as a personality trait. We must, therefore, use this evidence to draw inferences about pathways leading to dependent personality disorder. The available evidence points toward the importance of social and psychological factors in the development of extreme dependency. Genetic factors seem to play a relatively minor role (Nigg & Goldsmith, 1994).

Overprotective, authoritarian parents are likely to foster the development of dependency in their children (Baker, Capron, & Azorlosa, 1996; Bornstein, 1996). This conclusion is supported by the results of many different types of empirical research. It is also consistent with several different psychological theories that emphasize the importance of parent–child relationships in the formation and maintenance of dependent personality traits. For example, according to attachment theory (Ainsworth, 1989), children have a basic need to form a secure attachment to adults who will care for them (see Chapter 2). Those who are anxiously or insecurely attached as children are likely to become highly dependent during adolescence and adulthood. The process through which this pattern develops presumably involves the child's expectations about the availability of the parent. Children who have little confidence that attachment figures will be easily accessible and responsive when they need something may attempt to remain unusually close to those people, thus behaving in a clinging and dependent manner.

Treatment

There is virtually no literature on the outcome of treatment for dependent personality disorder. Therefore we cannot say whether any therapeutic procedures have been shown to be effective with this type of problem. People with this disorder may be less likely to seek treatment than people with other types of mental disorder. When they enter therapy, it is often because they also have other problems, such as depression, an anxiety disorder, or a substance use disorder. Whatever information is available on the treatment of this disorder is based on theoretical speculation and clinical experience (rather than empirical research).

Psychodynamic therapists have written most extensively about the treatment of dependent personality disorder. The primary goal in their approach is to help the person recognize the dependent pattern and the negative impact that it has on his or her relationships. Unfortunately, insight into the self-defeating nature of exceedingly dependent relationships may not be sufficient to allow the person to change his or her behavior. Behavior therapists (Goldfried & Davison, 1994) and interpersonal therapists (Benjamin, 1996) emphasize the need to teach skills in assertive communication. The client must learn to communicate feelings (both positive and negative) and desires accurately. The goal is to help the person develop interpersonal skills that will allow him or her to be more independent and self-reliant.

Cognitive therapy may also be beneficial in the treatment of dependent personality disorder. Problem-solving strategies, coupled with regular practice in making decisions, may foster independence and decrease the client's need to depend on other people for reassurance and support in routine situations. Cognitive therapy also addresses irrational or catastrophic self-statements about the potential consequences of behaving more independently or of ending a relationship (Beck, Freeman, & Davis, 2004; Crits-Christoph, 1998).

Psychopharmacology is not typically used as a specific treatment for dependent personality disorder. When medication is employed with such clients, it is usually aimed at the treatment of comorbid Axis I disorders, such as depression, agoraphobia, and panic disorder (Links, Heslegrave, & Villella, 1998).

getting help

As we mention in this chapter, most people who would meet the diagnostic criteria for a personality disorder do not enter treatment, at least not voluntarily. Although their interpersonal problems are pervasive and deeply ingrained, they are reluctant or completely unable to see the active role that they play in maintaining their own misfortunes (regardless of their origins). The pejorative way in which personality disorders are sometimes portrayed may make some people reluctant to acknowledge that they have a personality disorder. We prefer to discuss these problems in terms of personality limitations or maladaptive response styles. No one is perfect. Being able to recognize your own weaknesses is a sign that you are open-minded and willing to change. This is the first important step toward improvement.

It also helps to have a little compassion for yourself, along with the determination to work toward a lasting change in the way you relate to the people and events of your life. *Lost in the Mirror: An Inside Look at Borderline Personality Disorder*, by Richard Moskovitz, provides an insightful and sympathetic guide to the painful emotional experiences associated with borderline personality disorder. It also illustrates ways in which these symptoms affect the lives of patients, their families, and their friends.

If you are interested in help because you have to deal with someone who you think may have a personality disorder, you probably feel confused, frustrated, and angry. You may also feel extremely guilty if you blame yourself for problems in the relationship or for the other person's unhappiness. This may be especially true if you are involved in a romantic relationship or must work closely with someone who might meet the criteria for a PD. Fortunately, it is often possible to adapt to such interactions. Several self-help guides provide advice about getting along with difficult people. One good example is *Fatal Flaws: Navigating Destructive Relationships with People with Disorders of Personality and Character* (Yudofsky, 2005). Most recommend that you begin by learning about the predictable nature of the other person's style. Recognize the presence of personality weaknesses and learn how to adapt to them. You must also accept the limits of your own ability to control the other person or to get him or her to change.

Sometimes the only solution is to end the relationship. At their most extreme, people with personality disorders cannot form reciprocal, mutually satisfying relationships with other people. This is particularly true in the case of antisocial personality disorder. Some unscrupulous people repeatedly abuse, exploit, and cheat others. We all may run across such people from time to time, and we need to learn how to protect ourselves. Robert Hare, an expert on psychopathy, concludes his book, *Without Conscience*, with a brief "survival guide" that may help you minimize your risk. He notes, for example, that we should be aware of the symptoms and interpersonal characteristics of psychopathy. We should be cautious in high-risk situations, and know our own weaknesses. Hare's advice may be extremely helpful to someone who finds himself or herself trapped in a relationship with someone who is a psychopath. In fact, you may want to speak to a therapist or counselor to figure out why you have become involved in such an unequal, nonreciprocal relationship.

SUMMARY

Personality disorders are defined in terms of rigid, inflexible, maladaptive ways of perceiving and responding to oneself and one's environment that lead to social or occupational problems or subjective distress. This pattern must be pervasive across a broad range of situations, and it must be stable and of long duration. Among the hallmark features of personality disorders are major problems in interpersonal relationships. Many of the traits and symptoms that are associated with these problems are egosyntonic. In other words, many people with personality disorders do not see themselves as being disturbed.

Personality disorders are controversial for a number of reasons, including their low diagnostic reliability, the tremendous overlap among specific personality disorder categories, and the relative absence of effective forms of treatment. They are presumably defined in terms of behaviors that deviate markedly from the expectations of the person's culture. Unfortunately, little information is currently available to indicate whether the DSM-IV-TR system for personality disorders will be useful in societies other than the United States, Canada, and Western Europe.

Many systems have been proposed to describe the fundamental dimensions of human personality. One that has become very popular is the five-factor model, which includes the basic traits of neuroticism, extraversion, openness to experience, agreeableness, and conscientiousness. Extreme variations in any of these traits—being either pathologically high or low—can be associated with personality disorders.

DSM-IV-TR lists 10 types of personality disorder, arranged in 3 clusters. There is considerable overlap among and between these types. Cluster A includes **paranoid, schizoid,** and **schizotypal personality disorders.** These categories generally refer to people who are seen as being odd or eccentric. Cluster B includes **antisocial, borderline,**

histrionic, and **narcissistic personality disorders.** People who fit into this cluster are generally seen as being dramatic, unpredictable, and overly emotional. Cluster C includes **avoidant, dependent, and obsessive–compulsive personality disorders.** The common element in these disorders is presumably anxiety or fearfulness.

Dimensional approaches to the description of personality disorder provide an interesting alternative to this categorical system. These procedures rate a person on a number of traits, such as those included in the five-factor model. Dimensional classification systems have the advantage of being better able to account for similarities and differences among people with various combinations of personality traits.

The lifetime prevalence of personality disorders among adults in the general population is between 10 and 14 percent. The overall lifetime prevalence rate for antisocial personality disorder (men and women combined) was approximately 3 percent in the ECA and NCS studies, with rates being at least four times higher in men than in women. The NCS and ECA studies did not ask questions about the other specific types of personality disorder. Borderline personality disorder is the most frequently diagnosed form of personality disorder among people seeking mental health services (both inpatients and outpatients).

The disorders listed in Cluster A, especially schizoid and schizotypal personality disorders, have been viewed as possible antecedents or subclinical forms of schizophrenia. They are defined largely in terms of minor symptoms that resemble the hallucinations and delusions seen in the full blown disorder, as well as peculiar behaviors that have been observed among the first degree relatives of schizophrenic patients. Research on the etiology of schizotypal personality disorder has focused primarily on studies of its genetic relationship to schizophrenia.

The most important features of borderline personality disorder revolve around a pervasive pattern of instability in self image, in interpersonal relationships, and in mood. Some investigators believe that borderline personality disorder is an extremely heterogeneous category that should be further subdivided. Research regarding the etiology of borderline personality disorder has focused on two primary areas. One involves the impact of chaotic and abusive families. The other is concerned with the premature separation of children from their parents. Both sets of factors presumably can lead to problems in emotional regulation.

Psychopathy and antisocial personality disorder are two different attempts to define the same disorder. The DSM-IV-TR definition of ASPD places primary emphasis on social deviance in adulthood (repeated lying, physical assaults, reckless and irresponsible behavior). The concept of psychopathy places greater emphasis on emotional and interpersonal deficits, such as lack of remorse, lack of empathy, and shallow emotions. Adoption studies indicate that the etiology of antisocial behavior is determined by an interaction between genetic factors and adverse environmental circumstances. Laboratory studies of people who meet the criteria for psychopathy have focused on two hypotheses. One suggests that psychopaths are emotionally impoverished. The other holds that psychopaths have difficulty shifting their attention in order to avoid punishment.

Treatment procedures for people with personality disorders are especially difficult to design and evaluate, for three principal reasons. First, people with these disorders frequently don't have insight into the nature of their problems. Thus they are unlikely to seek treatment, and if they do, they frequently terminate prematurely. Second, pure forms of personality disorder are relatively rare. Most people with a personality disorder who are in treatment also exhibit comorbid forms of personality disorder and/or comorbid Axis I disorders, such as depression or drug addiction. Third, people with a personality disorder have difficulty establishing and maintaining meaningful, stable interpersonal relationships of the sort that are required for psychotherapy.

Treatment for schizotypal and borderline personality disorders often involves the use of antipsychotic medication or antidepressant medication. A few controlled studies indicate that these drugs can be beneficial. Long-term outcome tends to be better for patients with borderline than schizotypal personality disorder. Various types of psychological intervention, including psychodynamic procedures as well as dialectical behavior therapy, have frequently been employed with borderline patients. People with antisocial personality disorder seldom seek treatment voluntarily. When they do, the general consensus among clinicians is that it is seldom effective.

KEY TERMS

antisocial personality
  disorder   287
avoidant personality
  disorder   289
borderline personality
  disorder   288
cross-cultural
  psychology   296

dependent personality
  disorder   290
histrionic personality
  disorder   288
impulse control
  disorders   302

narcissistic personality
  disorder   289
obsessive–compulsive
  personality
  disorder   290

paranoid personality
  disorder   286
personality   279
personality disorder   280
psychopathy   306

schizoid personality
  disorder   286
schizotypal personality
  disorder   286

 Go to www.prenhall.com/oltmanns for online quizzes, interactive flash cards, PowerPoint presentations, and chapter reviews.

10

Eating Disorders

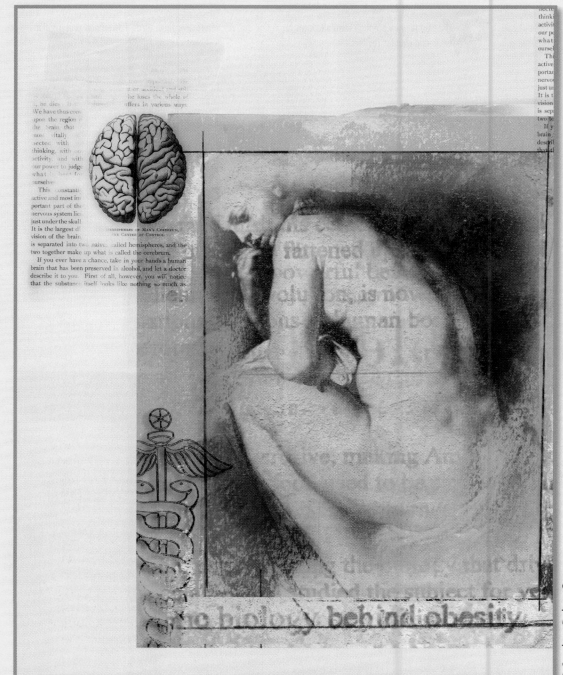

CHAPTER OUTLINE

◆◆

Popular culture in the United States is obsessed with physical appearance. We are told that "beauty is only skin deep," but the entertainment, cosmetic, fashion, and diet industries are eager to convince young people that "looks are everything." Perfect men are handsome, muscular, and successful. Perfect women are beautiful and thin—extremely thin. In fact, women's thinness is equated with beauty, fitness, success, and ultimately with happiness. Given our national obsession with appearance, diet, and weight, we should not be surprised that many people, especially young women, become obsessed to the point of developing eating disorders.

OVERVIEW

Eating disorders are severe disturbances in eating behavior that result from the sufferer's obsessive fear of gaining weight. Some experts have suggested that "dieting disorder" is a more accurate term, because dread of weight gain and obsession with weight loss are central features of eating disorders (Beumont, Garner, & Touyz, 1994). DSM-IV-TR lists two major types of eating disorders: anorexia nervosa and bulimia nervosa. The most obvious characteristic of **anorexia nervosa** is extreme emaciation, or more technically, the refusal to maintain a minimally normal body weight. The term *anorexia* literally means "loss of appetite," but this is a misnomer. People with anorexia nervosa *are* hungry, yet they starve themselves nevertheless. Some unfortunate victims literally starve themselves to death.

Bulimia nervosa is characterized by repeated episodes of binge eating, followed by inappropriate compensatory behaviors such as self-induced vomiting, misuse of laxatives, or excessive exercise. The literal meaning of the term *bulimia* is "ox appetite," meaning "hungry enough to eat an ox," but people with bulimia nervosa typically have a normal appetite and maintain a normal weight. In fact, most sufferers view their binge eating as a failure of control, not as an indulgence of their hunger. People with bulimia nervosa usually are ashamed and secretive about their binge eating and purging.

Both anorexia and bulimia are about 10 times more common among females than males, and they develop most commonly among women in their teens and early twenties. The

The images of women portrayed in advertising and the popular media contribute to the development of eating disorders.

increased incidence among young people reflects both the intense focus on young women's physical appearance and the difficulties many adolescent girls have in adjusting to the rapid changes in body shape and weight that begin with puberty (Hsu, 1990). According to the National Centers for Disease Control and Prevention, at any point in time 44 percent of high school females are attempting to lose weight compared with 15 percent of males. (Many adolescent boys want to *gain* weight in order to look bigger and stronger [Serdula et al., 1993]). A national survey found that almost half of American women have a negative body image, particularly concerning their waist, hips, and/or thighs (Cash & Henry, 1995; see Figure 10–1). European American and Latina women report higher rates of body dissatisfaction than African Americans (Bay-Cheng et al., 2002), with dissatisfaction increasing from the 1980s to the 1990s among white women (Cash et al., 2004). Fortunately, levels of body dissatisfaction declined between the 1990s and 2001 among both European American and African American women, perhaps indicating a growing resistance to the popular media's culture of thinness (Cash et al., 2004).

In this chapter, we discuss the symptoms of anorexia nervosa separately from those of bulimia nervosa, because they differ considerably. We combine the two disorders when reviewing diagnosis, frequency, and causes, however, because they share many developmental similarities. For example, many people with anorexia nervosa also binge and purge on occasion; many people with bulimia nervosa have a history of anorexia nervosa. When considering treatment, we again discuss the two disorders separately, reflecting the important differences in the focus and effectiveness of therapy for each disorder (Keel et al., 2000). We begin with a case study.

CASE STUDY   Serrita's Anorexia

Serrita was an attractive, well-dressed, and polite 15-year-old high school sophomore who was living in a friendly joint-custody arrangement. She spent alternating weeks living with each of her successful, middle-class parents. Serrita was an excellent student who her mother described as a "sweet girl who never gave me an ounce of worry—until now." When she was first seen by a clinical psychologist for the treatment of anorexia nervosa, Serrita was 5 feet 2 inches tall and weighed 81 pounds. Serrita's gaunt appearance was painfully obvious to anyone else who looked at her. Despite her constant scrutiny of her own body, however, Serrita firmly denied that she was too thin. Instead, she asserted that she looked "almost right." She was still on a diet, and every day she carefully inspected her stomach, thighs, hips, arms, and face for any signs of fat. Although Serrita was generally pleased with the image she saw in her bathroom mirror, she remained deathly afraid of gaining weight. She monitored her food intake with incredible detail, and she could recite every item of food she had consumed recently, as well as discuss its caloric and fat content.

Serrita began her diet 9 months earlier after visiting her family doctor, who told her that she could stand to lose a pound or two. At the time, Serrita weighed 108 pounds, a normal weight for her age, height, and body type. Serrita claimed that the doctor's comment motivated her to begin a diet, and she also wanted to look more attractive. Serrita wanted to look like the women in her favorite magazines, but she felt that she wasn't the "cute, all-American girl"—she saw herself as too short, too dark, and her features as too sharp. Serrita secretly hoped that having a "great body" would compensate for her perceived inadequacies.

Serrita's diet began normally enough. She read extensively about food, weight, and diet, and quickly lost the 6 pounds she wanted to lose. Without really planning to do so, Serrita simply continued her diet. She developed the habit of scouring her image in the mirror, and she invariably found some spot that was just a bit "too fat." As a result, she continually set a new goal to lose another couple of pounds. She weighed herself constantly and said that the bathroom scale became her "best friend." Her friends and family compliments soon turned into worried warnings, but privately Serrita was exhilarated by their comments. To her, the concerned remarks only proved that her diet was working.

Serrita's diet was extreme and rigid, and she adhered obsessively to a routine. Breakfast consisted of one slice of dry wheat toast and a small glass of orange juice. Lunch was either an apple or a small salad without dressing. In between meals, Serrita drank several diet colas, which helped control her constant, gnawing appetite. Dinner typically was a family meal whether Serrita was at her mom's or her dad's house. During these meals, Serrita picked at whatever she was served. Sometimes her parents would plead with her to eat more, and Serrita would eat a bit to appease them. On occasion, perhaps once a week, Serrita forced herself to vomit after dinner, because she felt that she had been made to eat too much.

Serrita's parents eventually became so concerned about her weight loss that they made her go to see her family physician. The physician also was very concerned about Serrita's low weight, and she discovered that Serrita had not menstruated in over 6 months. The physician raised the possibility that Serrita was suffering from anorexia nervosa. She immediately made a referral to a psychologist as well as to a nutritionist, who, the physician hoped, would correct Serrita's extreme views about dieting.

In talking with the psychologist, Serrita agreed that she understood why everyone was concerned about her health. She knew about anorexia nervosa, which she realized was a serious problem. Serrita even hinted that she knew that she was suffering from anorexia nervosa. Nevertheless, Serrita steadfastly denied that she needed to gain weight. Although she was happy to talk with the psychologist, she was not prepared to change her eating habits. Serrita was deathly afraid that eating even a little more would cause her to "lose control" and "turn into a blimp." Perhaps more importantly, she was *proud* of her mastery of her hunger. She was not about to give up the control she had fought so hard to obtain.

SYMPTOMS OF ANOREXIA

Serrita showed all the classic symptoms of anorexia nervosa: extreme emaciation, a disturbed perception of her body, an intense fear of gaining weight, and, in women, the cessation of menstruation. Serrita also exhibited a number of problems that are commonly associated with anorexia nervosa but are not defining symptoms: obsessive preoccupation with food, occasional purging, and a "successful" struggle for control over persistent hunger. Finally, Serrita did not suffer from a few important problems that are sometimes associated with anorexia nervosa, particularly mood disturbance, sexual difficulties, a lack of impulse control, and medical problems secondary to the weight loss.

Refusal to Maintain a Normal Weight

The most obvious and most dangerous symptom of anorexia nervosa is a *refusal to maintain a minimally normal body weight*. Like Serrita, anorexia nervosa often begins with a diet to lose just a few pounds. The young woman weighs near her healthy body weight, and she decides to lose a little weight, perhaps to fit into some new clothes. The diet goes awry, however, and losing weight eventually becomes the key focus. Weight

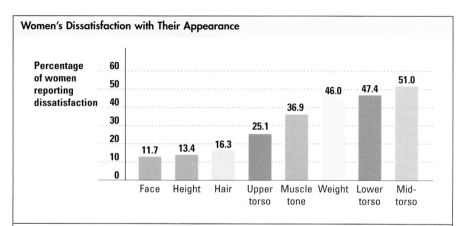

FIGURE 10-1: Percentage of females reporting that they were "very or mostly dissatisfied" with specific physical attributes in a national sample of women aged 18 to 70 interviewed in 1993.

Source: T.F. Cash and P.E. Henry, 1995, Women's body images: The results of a national survey in the U.S.A., *Sex Roles,* 33, 19–28. Copyright © 1995. Reprinted by permission of Springer Science and Business Media.

falls well below the normal range, and often plummets to dangerously low levels.

DSM-IV-TR contains no formal cutoff as to how thin is too thin, but suggests 85 percent of expected body weight as a rough guideline. The *body mass index*,[1] a calculation derived from weight and height, is another useful way to determine whether or not someone is significantly underweight. Both DSM-IV-TR and the body mass cutoffs represent weights well beyond "thin" and into the realm of "emaciated," but weight loss often is more extreme: The average victim of anorexia loses 25 to 30 percent of normal body weight (Hsu, 1990). Unlike Serrita, who was fortunate in this sense, some people with anorexia nervosa are not treated until their weight loss becomes life threatening. In fact, about 10 percent of people with anorexia nervosa are estimated to die of starvation, suicide, or medical complications stemming from their extreme weight loss (APA, 2000; Hsu, 1995).

Disturbance in Evaluating Weight or Shape

In what ways do people with anorexia nervosa show a disturbance in evaluating their weight and shape?

A second defining symptom of anorexia nervosa is a perceptual, cognitive, or affective disturbance in evaluating one's weight and shape. Like Serrita, many individuals steadfastly *deny problems with their weight.* Even when confronted with their own withered image in a mirror, some people with anorexia nervosa nevertheless insist that their weight is not a problem.

Other people with the disorder suffer from *a disturbance in the way body weight or shape is experienced.* Sometimes this may include a **distorted body image,** an inaccurate perception of body size and shape. One early study found that young women with anorexia nervosa overestimated the size of various body parts in comparison to a normal control group (Slade & Russell, 1973). The

following excerpt, which we received anonymously from a student, illustrates the symptom.

> I'll try to explain how a person with an eating disorder sees a distorted image of herself. It's almost like she sees herself as bloated—of course she sees herself, she recognizes herself, but as bigger than usual. Also, the skinnier she gets, the more she notices fat deposits around the waist, under the arms, etc., because the more fat is lost, the more attention is drawn to the little bit of fat that still exists. Also, it's the point of reference in the background that may sometimes be distorted. She looks in the bathroom mirror and thinks, "Did I take up that much space against this wall yesterday?" (Anonymous, 1999)

Not all people with anorexia nervosa suffer from a distorted body image, and many people without the disorder inaccurately estimate the size of their body (Garfinkel, Kennedy, & Kaplan, 1995; Thompson, 1996). Still, all people with the disorder are *unduly influenced by their body weight or shape in self-evaluation.* Experts agree that, whatever its specific form, a defining characteristic of anorexia nervosa is a disturbance in the way one's body or weight is perceived or evaluated. People with anorexia nervosa do not recognize their emaciation for what it is.

Fear of Gaining Weight

An *intense fear of becoming fat* is a third central characteristic of anorexia. The fear of gaining weight presents particular problems for treatment. A therapist's encouragement to eat more can terrify someone who fears that relaxing control, even just a little, will lead to a total loss of control. Ironically, the fear of gaining weight is not soothed by the tremendous weight loss. In fact, the fear may grow more intense as the individual loses more weight (APA, 2000).

Cessation of Menstruation

Amenorrhea, the absence of at least three consecutive menstrual cycles, is the fourth and final defining symptom of anorexia nervosa in females. The amenorrhea has led to speculation about the role of sexuality and sexual maturation in causing anorexia nervosa. However, the amenorrhea typically is a *reaction* to the physiological

---

[1]You can calculate your body mass index as follows: (1) Multiply your weight in pounds by 700; (2) divide this number by your height in inches; (3) divide this second number by your height in inches. You can interpret the resulting number according to the body mass index: Under 16 = extremely underweight; 16–18 = significantly underweight; 20–25 = healthy weight; 27–30 = overweight; 30–40 = significantly overweight; over 40 = extremely overweight.

changes produced by anorexia nervosa, specifically a low level of estrogen secretion, and not a symptom that precedes the disorder (APA, 2000). Sexual disinterest is also a common reaction to severe weight loss (Keys et al., 1950). In any case, the presence or absence of menstruation fails to differentiate between women who meet other diagnostic criteria (Herzog & Delinsky, 2001).

Medical Complications

Anorexia nervosa can cause a number of medical complications. People with anorexia commonly complain about constipation, abdominal pain, intolerance to cold, and lethargy. Some of these complaints stem from the effects of semistarvation on blood pressure and body temperature, both of which may fall below normal. In addition, the skin can become dry and cracked, and some people develop *lanugo*, a fine, downy hair, on their face or trunk of their body. Broader medical difficulties may include anemia, infertility, impaired kidney functioning, cardiovascular difficulties, dental erosion, and osteopenia (bone loss) (Pomeroy, 1996). A particularly dangerous medication complication is an *electrolyte imbalance*, a disturbance in the levels of potassium, sodium, calcium, and other vital elements found in bodily fluids. Electrolyte imbalance can lead to cardiac arrest or kidney failure. Anorexia nervosa may begin with the seemingly harmless desire to be a bit thinner, but the eating disorder can lead to serious health problems, including death.

Struggle for Control

Some people with eating disorders act impulsively, but clinical accounts and some research suggest that more are conforming and controlling. People with anorexia nervosa often take great pride in their self-denial, feeling like masters of control. Some theorists speculate that the disorder actually develops out of a desperate sense of having no control. Excessively compliant "good girls" may find that obsessively regulating their diet allows them to be in charge of at least one area of their lives (Bruch, 1982).

Caraline, 28 years old, told a reporter, "I'm not telling you how much I weigh because I'm ashamed I don't weigh less." She later died of complications due to anorexia nervosa.

Olympic-class gymnast Christy Heinrich with her boyfriend in 1993. After a 5-year struggle with anorexia nervosa, she died of multiple organ failure in 1994. She weighed less than 50 pounds at the time.

Conscientious objectors who became subjects in a study of semistarvation during World War II. Many of the men developed symptoms similar to those found in anorexia nervosa.

Comorbid Psychological Disorders

Anorexia nervosa may be associated with other psychological problems, particularly obsessive–compulsive disorder (Kasvikis et al., 1986), obsessive–compulsive personality disorder (Gillberg, Rastam, & Gillberg, 1995), and depression (Braun, Sunday, & Halmi, 1994). In many

cases, however, these comorbid psychological problems may be reactions to anorexia, not causes of it.

People with anorexia nervosa are obsessed with food and diet, and they often follow compulsive rituals in regard to eating. However, a unique study found that obsessive–compulsive behavior can result from starvation rather than cause it. In this study, 32 World War II conscientious objectors fulfilled their military obligation by voluntarily undergoing semistarvation for 24 weeks. (The researchers wanted to learn about the effects of starvation on military personnel in the field.) As the men reduced their food intake and lost more and more weight, they developed extensive obsessions about food and compulsive eating rituals. For many of the men, in fact, the obsessions and compulsions continued long after they returned to their normal weight (Keys et al., 1950). Obsessive–compulsive personality disorder may sometimes contribute to anorexia nervosa, but some obsessive–compulsive *behavior* may be a reaction to starvation.

Most people with anorexia nervosa also show symptoms of mild depression, such as sad mood, irritability, insomnia, social withdrawal, and diminished interest in sex (Braun, Sunday, & Halmi, 1994). Like obsessive–compulsive behavior, however, depression is a common secondary reaction to starvation. Mood disturbances sometimes play a role in the development of anorexia nervosa, but depression can also be a reaction to the eating disorder (Cooper, 1995; Hsu, 1990).

Finally, anorexia often co-occurs with the symptoms of bulimia (see Figure 10–2). In some cases, purging follows episodes of binge eating. In other cases, purging may be a means of further controlling eating that already is dramatically restricted. People with anorexia nervosa who do *not* binge eat or purge generally are better adjusted on measures of their mental health—for example, they have lower rates of depression (Braun, Sunday, & Halmi, 1994).

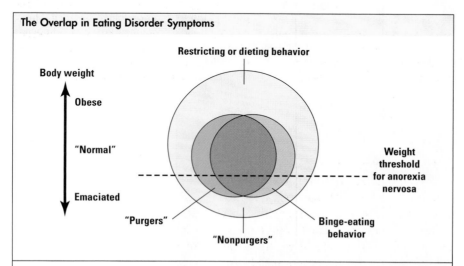

The Overlap in Eating Disorder Symptoms

FIGURE 10–2: Illustration of the relationship between binge eating, purging, and extreme dieting in eating disorders. All three problematic eating behaviors can be found among people with different body weights.

Source: D.M. Garner, M.V. Garner, and L.W. Rosen, 1993, Anorexia nervosa "restrictors" who purge: Implication for subtyping anorexia nervosa, *International Journal of Eating Disorders,* 13, 182. Copyright © 1993 by Wiley Periodicals, Inc., a Wiley Company. Reprinted by permission of John Wiley & Sons, Inc.

SYMPTOMS OF BULIMIA

Bulimia nervosa and anorexia nervosa, although different, share similarities. One connection is that many people with bulimia nervosa have a history of anorexia nervosa, as in the following case study.

CASE STUDY   Michelle's Secret

Michelle was a sophomore at a state university when she first sought help for a humiliating problem. Several times a week, she fell into an episode of uncontrollable binge eating followed by self-induced vomiting. Michelle had enough control to limit her binge eating to times when her roommate was away. But when Michelle was alone and feeling bad—the episodes usually occurred on "bad days," of which Michelle had many—she would buy a half-gallon of ice cream and perhaps a bag of cookies, and bring the food back to her room, where she secretly gorged herself. The binge brought her some comfort when she first started eating, but by the time she was finished, she felt physically uncomfortable, sickened by her lack of control, and terrified of gaining weight. To compensate, she would walk across the street to an empty bathroom in the psychology department. There, she forced herself to vomit by sticking her finger down her throat.

The vomiting brought relief from the physical discomfort and fear of gaining weight, but it did not relieve her shame. Michelle was disgusted by her actions, but she could not stop herself. In fact, the pattern of binge eating and purging had been going on for most of the school year. Michelle decided to seek treatment only when a friend from her psychology class discovered her purging in the bathroom. The friend also had a history of bulimia nervosa, but she had gotten her eating under control. She convinced Michelle to try therapy.

Michelle's eating problems began when she was in high school. She had studied ballet since she was 8 years old, and with the stern encouragement of her instructor she had struggled to maintain her willowy figure as she became an adolescent. At first she dieted openly, but her parents constantly criticized her inadequate eating. In order to appease them, Michelle occasionally would eat a normal meal but force herself to vomit shortly afterwards. When she was a junior in high school, Michelle's parents confronted her and brought her to a psychologist, who treated her for anorexia nervosa. She was 5 feet 6 inches tall at the time, but she weighed only 95 pounds. Michelle was furious and refused to talk in any depth with the therapist. She allowed herself to gain a few pounds—to about 105—only to convince her parents that she did not need treatment.

Michelle's weight eventually stabilized between 105 and 110 pounds—enough of a gain that her parents allowed her to stop therapy. Even though she was very thin, Michelle continued to plan her diet with great care. She avoided fat with a vengeance. She counted every calorie at every meal every day, and had not eaten even a lick of ice cream in years. Throughout college, she starved herself all week so she could eat normally on dates during the weekend. Occasionally, she forced herself to vomit after eating too much, but she did not see this as a big problem. Until the previous summer, she had maintained her weight near her goal of 105 pounds. Over the summer, however, Michelle relaxed her diet as she "partied" with old friends. She gained about 15 pounds, a healthy weight for her height and body type. When she returned to college, however, Michelle grew disgusted with her appearance and fearful of gaining even more weight.

Michelle tried to lose weight, but she met with little success. She started to purge more frequently in a desperate attempt to lose weight, but she soon found herself binge eating more frequently, too. Michelle was extremely frustrated by her "lack of self-control." Although she now recognized her past problems with anorexia nervosa, Michelle openly longed for the discipline she had once achieved over her hunger and diet.

By all outward appearances, Michelle was a bright, attractive, successful, and happy young woman. Nevertheless, she admitted to her new therapist that she felt like a failure and a "fake." She longed to have a long-term dating relationship, but although she dated a lot, she had never had a real boyfriend. She also was intensely if privately competitive with her girlfriends. She wanted to be more beautiful and intelligent than other girls, but she inevitably felt inferior to one classmate or another. She was determined at least to be thinner than her girlfriends, but she felt that she had lost all control over this goal. Michelle also was furious with her parents. Their constant questions about her well-being caused her to feel angry and resentful instead of loved and supported. Michelle said that they asked all the right questions, but cared more about the family's image than about Michelle as a person. Michelle pretended to be happy and normal, but inside she felt as though she was going to explode. Secretly, she was miserable.

Michelle's frequent struggles with binge eating and purging, her sense of lost control during a binge, and her undue focus on her weight and figure are the core symptoms that define bulimia nervosa. Depression also is commonly associated with the disorder, as it was for Michelle.

Binge Eating

Binge eating is defined in DSM-IV-TR as eating an amount of food in a fixed period of time, for example, less than 2 hours, that is clearly larger than most people would eat under similar circumstances. There have been some attempts to define a binge more objectively, such as eating more than 1,000 calories, or subjectively, such as based on the individual's appraisal. Variations in normal eating complicate these alternative definitions, however. Eating a very large number of calories may be normal under certain circumstances and having two cookies may be considered a "binge" by other people. Thus the present DSM-IV-TR definition relies on a clinician's judgment about normal eating patterns (Garfinkel, Kennedy, & Kaplan, 1995).

Physical fitness offers many benefits, but some people exercise excessively to compensate for binge eating.

Sadly, many of the inappropriate eating behaviors that are symptoms of bulimia nervosa border on being statistically normal—and clearly unhealthy—in our food- and weight-obsessed society. Over 35 percent of people report occasional binge eating. Distressingly large numbers of people also report that they fast (29 percent) and use self-induced vomiting (8 percent) or laxatives (over 5 percent) in an attempt to compensate for their eating (Fairburn & Beglin, 1990).

Binges may be planned in advance, or they may begin spontaneously. In either case, binges typically are secret. Most people with bulimia nervosa are ashamed of their eating problems and often go to elaborate efforts to conceal their binge eating. During a binge, the individual typically eats very rapidly and soon feels uncomfortably full. Although the types of foods that are consumed can vary widely, the person often selects ice cream, cookies, or other foods that are high in calories. Foods also may be selected for smooth texture to make vomiting easier, one reason why ice cream is a popular binge food.

Binge eating is commonly triggered by an unhappy mood, which may begin with an interpersonal conflict, self-criticism about weight or appearance, or intense hunger following a period of fasting. The binge initially is comforting and alleviates some unhappy feelings, but physical discomfort and fear of gaining weight soon override the positive aspects of binge eating (Garfinkel, Kennedy, & Kaplan, 1995).

A key feature of binge eating is a sense of lack of control during a binge. Some individuals experience a binge as a "feeding frenzy," where they lose all control and eat compulsively and rapidly. Others describe a dissociative experience, as if they were watching themselves gorge. But the lack of control is not absolute. For example, people with bulimia can stop a binge if they are interrupted unexpectedly. In fact, as the disorder progresses, some people feel more in control during a binge, but unable to stop the broader cycle of binge eating and compensatory behavior.

Inappropriate Compensatory Behavior

Almost all people with bulimia nervosa engage in **purging,** designed to eliminate the consumed food from the body. The most common form of purging is self-induced vomiting; as many as 90 percent of people with bulimia nervosa engage in this behavior (APA, 2000). Vomiting brings immediate relief from physical discomfort, and reduces morbid fears of gaining weight. Other less common forms of purging include the misuse of laxatives, diuretics (which increase the frequency of urination), and, most rarely, enemas. Ironically, purging has only limited effectiveness in reducing caloric intake. Vomiting prevents the absorption of only about half the calories consumed during a binge, and laxatives, diuretics, and enemas have few lasting effects on calories or weight (Kaye et al., 1993).

Inappropriate compensatory behaviors other than purging include extreme exercise or rigid fasting following a binge. The extent to which these actions actually compensate for binge eating also is questionable, given what we know about the body's biological regulation of weight (Brownell & Fairburn, 1995).

Excessive Emphasis on Weight and Shape

People with bulimia nervosa place *excessive emphasis on body shape and weight* in evaluating themselves, a symptom shared in common with anorexia nervosa (see Table 10–1). Their self-esteem, and much of their daily routine, center around weight and diet. Some people with bulimia nervosa are exhilarated by positive comments or interest in their appearance, but their esteem plummets if a negative comment is made or if someone else draws more attention. Other people with the disorder constantly criticize their appearance, and the struggle with binge eating and purging only adds to their self-denigration. In either case, the individual's sense of self is linked too closely to appearance instead of personality, relationships, or achievements.

Comorbid Psychological Disorders

Depression is common among individuals with bulimia nervosa, especially those who self induce vomiting (APA, 2000). Some individuals become depressed prior to developing the eating disorder, and the bulimia may be a reaction to the depression in some of these cases. In many instances, however, depression begins at the same time as or follows the onset of bulimia nervosa (Braun, Sunday, & Halmi, 1994). In such circumstances, the depression is likely to be a reaction to the bulimia. In fact, depression often lifts following successful treatment of bulimia nervosa (Mitchell et al., 1990). Whether depression is an effect or cause of bulimia, eating disturbances are more severe and social impairment is greater when the two problems are comorbid (Stice & Fairburn, 2003).

Other disorders that may co-occur with bulimia nervosa include anxiety disorders, personality disorders (particularly borderline personality disorder), and substance abuse, particularly excessive use of alcohol and/or stimulants. Although each of these psychological difficulties presents special challenges in treating bulimia, the comorbidity with depression is most common and most significant (Brewerton et al., 1995).

Medical Complications

A number of medical complications can result from bulimia nervosa. Repeated vomiting can erode dental enamel, particularly on the front teeth, and in severe cases teeth can become chipped and ragged looking. Repeated vomiting can also produce a gag reflex that is triggered too easily and perhaps unintentionally. One consequence of the sensitized gag reflex—one that is just beginning to be reported in the scientific literature—is *rumination*: the regurgitation and

Video Case

BULIMIA

JESSICA

"It started out with a diet for me . . ."

On your CD-ROM menu, select "Eating Disorders" and click on "Bulimia: Jessica." As you watch the video, listen for Jessica's struggles with appearance and weight and how they were magnified—sometimes very directly—by her efforts to pursue a career in the performing arts.

What are some similarities and differences between anorexia and bulimia?

TABLE 10–1	Anorexia Nervosa and Bulimia Nervosa: Key Differences and Similarities	
ISSUE	**ANOREXIA NERVOSA**	**BULIMIA NERVOSA**
	Differences	
Eating/weight	Extreme diet; below minimally normal weight	Binge eating/compensatory behavior; normal weight
View of disorder	Denial of anorexia; proud of "diet"	Aware of problem; secretive/ashamed of bulimia
Feelings of control	Comforted by rigid self-control	Distressed by lack of control
	Similarities	
Self-evaluation	Unduly influenced by body weight/shape	Unduly influenced by body weight/shape
Comorbidity of AN/BN	Some cases of AN also binge and purge	Many cases of BN have history of AN
SES, age, gender	Prevalent among high SES, young, female	Prevalent among high SES, young, female

The late Princess Diana publicly acknowledged her battles with bulimia nervosa.

rechewing of food (Parry-Jones, 1994). Another possible medical complication is the enlargement of the salivary glands, a consequence that has the ironic effect of making the sufferer's face appear puffy. As in anorexia nervosa, potentially serious medical complications can result from electrolyte imbalances. Finally, rupture of the esophagus or stomach has been reported in rare cases, sometimes leading to death (Pomeroy, 1996).

DIAGNOSIS OF EATING DISORDERS

Brief Historical Perspective

Isolated cases of eating disorders have been reported throughout history. In fact, the term *anorexia nervosa* was coined in 1874 by a British physician, Sir William Withey Gull (1816–1890). Still, the history of professional concern with the disorders is very brief. References to eating disorders were rare in the literature prior to 1960, and the disorders have received scientific attention only in recent decades (Fairburn & Brownell, 2002; Striegel-Moore & Smolak, 2001). In fact, the term *bulimia nervosa* was used for the first time only in 1979 (Russell, 1979).

The diagnoses of anorexia nervosa and bulimia nervosa first appeared in DSM in 1980 (DSM-III). Although the diagnostic criteria have changed somewhat, the same eating behaviors remain as the central features of these disorders. The only major change was the creation of a separate diagnostic category for eating disorders. They previously had been listed as a subtype of the Disorders Usually First Diagnosed in Infancy, Childhood, or Adolescence, because most eating disorders begin during the teenage years. The new, separate grouping reflects the fact that eating disorders can begin during adult life.

Contemporary Classification

Anorexia Nervosa DSM-IV-TR lists two types of eating disorders: anorexia nervosa and bulimia nervosa. Anorexia nervosa is defined by four symptoms described earlier (see Table 10–2). DSM-IV-TR also includes two subtypes of anorexia nervosa. The *restricting type* includes people who rarely engage in binge eating or purging. In contrast, the *binge eating/purging type* is defined by regular binge eating and purging during the course of the disorder. People with the binge-eating/purging type make up approximately half of those people with anorexia nervosa, and some evidence indicates that they weigh more before their anorexia, are more impulsive, and have more personality disorders than pure restrictors (Agras, 1987; Garfinkel, Kennedy, & Kaplan, 1995).

What about people with anorexia nervosa who purge but do not binge? Should they be considered the restricting type or the binge-eating/purging type? Evidence suggests that purging, not binge eating, is the key. In a study comparing 116 pure restrictors with both binge purge (N = 190) and purge only (N = 74) participants, both of the groups who purged were older, had a longer history of anorexia nervosa, had more obesity in their families, were more impulsive, and suffered from more psychopathology in comparison to the pure restrictors (Garner, Garner, & Rosen, 1993). Thus it is appropriate that DSM-IV-TR defines the binge-eating/purging subtype in terms of *either* binge eating or purging (see Table 10–2).

However, a recent longitudinal study of 51 women with the restricting type and 85 women with the binge-eating/purging type raises questions about the subtypes. The researchers found no differences between the subtypes in impulsivity, and at an 8-year follow-up, 62 percent of the former restrictors met diagnostic criteria for binge-eating/purging, and only 12 percent of the restrictors reported that they had never regularly engaged in binge eating and purging (Eddy et al., 2002). Anorexia is a key distinction from bulimia, but the binge-purge subtype may be less important than formally thought.

Bulimia Nervosa   Bulimia nervosa is defined by five symptoms described earlier (see Table 10–3) and also is divided into two subtypes in DSM-IV-TR. The *purging type* is characterized by the regular use of self-induced vomiting or the misuse of laxatives, diuretics, or enemas. The individual with the *nonpurging type* of bulimia nervosa does not regularly purge but instead attempts to compensate for binge eating with fasting or excessive exercise. The purging subtype of bulimia nervosa is more common and is associated with more frequent binge eating, more psychopathology (particularly depression), and more family dysfunction, including parental discord and child sexual abuse (Garfinkel, Lin, & Goering, 1996; McCann et al., 1991).

Binge Eating Disorder and Obesity   There has been some debate about whether other eating problems should be included in the DSM-IV-TR list of eating disorders. **Binge eating disorder** is one problem that was given extensive consideration. In fact, provisional diagnostic criteria for binge eating disorder are included in an appendix of DSM-IV-TR for diagnostic categories requiring further study. The proposed disorder involves episodes of binge eating much like those found in bulimia nervosa but without compensatory behavior.

Research has demonstrated that binge eating is associated with a number of psychological and physical difficulties other than anorexia nervosa and bulimia nervosa (Fairburn & Wilson, 1993). Among these problems is **obesity,** or excess body fat, a circumstance that roughly corresponds with a body weight 20 percent *above* the expected weight. A cutoff of 40 percent above normal is a rough marker of severe overweight (Brownell, 1995). As with binge eating, the DSM-IV-TR committee considered classifying obesity as an eating disorder, but too little information was available to justify this move (Garfinkel, Kennedy, & Kaplan, 1995). Calling

TABLE 10–2   DSM-IV-TR Diagnostic Criteria for Anorexia Nervosa
A. Refusal to maintain body weight at or above a minimally normal weight for age and height (e.g., weight loss leading to maintenance of body weight less than 85 percent of that expected; or failure to make expected weight gain during period of growth, leading to body weight less than 85 percent of that expected).
B. Intense fear of gaining weight or becoming fat, even though underweight.
C. Disturbance in the way in which one's weight or shape is experienced, undue influence of body weight or shape on self-evaluation, or denial of the seriousness of the current low body weight.
D. In postmenarcheal females, amenorrhea, that is, the absence of at least three consecutive menstrual cycles.

Specify type:

Restricting type: During the current episode, the person has not regularly engaged in binge eating or purging behavior.

Binge-eating/purging type: During the current episode, the person has regularly engaged in binge eating or purging behavior.

Reprinted with permission from the *Diagnostic and Statistical Manual of Mental Disorders,* Fourth Edition, Text Revision. Copyright © 2000 by the American Psychiatric Association.

TABLE 10–3   DSM-IV-TR Diagnostic Criteria for Bulimia Nervosa
A. Recurrent episodes of binge eating. An episode of binge eating is characterized by both of the following:
1. Eating, in a discrete period of time (e.g., within any 2-hour period), an amount of food that is definitely larger than most people would eat during a similar period of time and under similar circumstances.
2. A sense of lack of control over eating during the episode (e.g., a feeling that one cannot stop eating or control what or how much one is eating).
B. Recurrent inappropriate compensatory behavior in order to prevent weight gain, such as self-induced vomiting; misuse of laxatives, diuretics, enemas, or other medications; fasting; or excessive exercise.
C. The binge eating and inappropriate compensatory behaviors both occur, on average, at least twice a week for 3 months.
D. Self-evaluation is unduly influenced by body shape and weight.
E. The disturbance does not occur exclusively during episodes of anorexia nervosa.

Specify type:

Purging type: During the current episode, the person has regularly engaged in self-induced vomiting or the misuse of laxatives, diuretics, or enemas.

Nonpurging type: During the current episode, the person has used other inappropriate compensatory behaviors, such as fasting or excessive exercise, but has not regularly engaged in self-induced vomiting or the misuse of laxatives, diuretics, or enemas.

Reprinted with permission from the *Diagnostic and Statistical Manual of Mental Disorders,* Fourth Edition, Text Revision. Copyright © 2000 by the American Psychiatric Association.

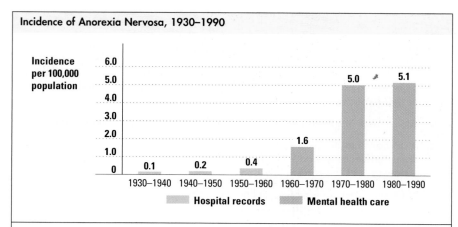

FIGURE 10-3: Anorexia nervosa has increased dramatically in recent decades. This figure portrays the annual incidence per 100,000 people in the general population based on data pooled from studies of hospital records and outpatient mental health care. Considerably higher rates are found among population subgroups, particularly young women.

Source: H.W. Hoek, 1995, The distribution of eating disorders. In K.D. Brownell and C.G. Fairbanks (Eds.), *Eating Disorders and Obesity: A Comprehensive Handbook,* p. 209. New York: Guilford. Copyright © 1995. Reprinted by permission of Guilford Publications, Inc.

obesity a "mental disorder" is controversial, especially given the high prevalence of overweight individuals in the United States and throughout the world. In fact, some professionals question our society's constant focus on dieting and our castigation of obese people. Obesity is not just a lack of "willpower," as biological factors contribute substantially to body shape and weight (Brownell & Rodin, 1994).

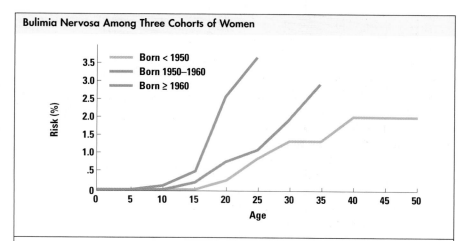

FIGURE 10-4: The lifetime cumulative risk for developing bulimia nervosa is far greater for women born after 1960 than for women born before 1950. The risk for developing the disorder decreases with age, at least among the earlier birth cohort. Later birth cohorts have not yet moved through the entire age of risk.

Source: K.S. Kendler, C. MacLean, M. Neale, R. Kessler, A. Heath, and L. Evans, 1991, The genetic epidemiology of bulimia nervosa, *American Journal of Psychiatry,* 148, 1631. Copyright © 1991. Reprinted by permission of American Psychiatric Association.

FREQUENCY OF EATING DISORDERS

Estimates of the epidemiology of anorexia and bulimia vary, but it is clear that the prevalence of both disorders has increased dramatically since the 1960s and 1970s (Hoek, 1995; Kendler et al., 1991; Lucas et al., 1999). Figure 10–3 illustrates the surge in the number of new cases of anorexia nervosa based on one investigator's compilation of evidence from a number of different studies (Hoek, 1995). According to this summary, the annual *incidence,* the number of new cases each year, of anorexia nervosa rose from 1 case per million people in 1930–1940 to over 50 cases per million people in 1980–1990. Figure 10–3 also suggests that anorexia nervosa is rare in the general population. It is far more common among certain segments of the population, however, particularly among young women. DSM-IV-TR indicates that lifetime prevalence of anorexia nervosa is 0.5 among females, a figure that is consistent with other estimates (Hoek, 1995). Anorexia nervosa also occurs among males, but it is about 10 times more common among women than men.

Recent decades also seem to have witnessed a torrent of new cases of bulimia nervosa. Changes in the incidence of bulimia nervosa are difficult to document, however, because the diagnostic term was introduced only in 1979. In an attempt to demonstrate the striking increase in bulimia nervosa over time, investigators, therefore, have examined cohort effects in prevalence rates. A **cohort** is a group that shares some feature in common, for example, year of birth; thus **cohort effects** are differences that distinguish one cohort from another.

Figure 10–4 portrays birth cohort effects in lifetime prevalence rates of bulimia nervosa among a large sample of American women who were born either before 1950, between 1950 and 1959, or in 1960 or after. The figure clearly indicates substantial cohort effects. The lifetime prevalence of bulimia nervosa was far greater among the cohort of women born after 1960 than it was for the cohort of women born before 1950. The risk for women born between 1950 and 1959 was intermediate between these two extremes (Kendler et al., 1991). Thus the recent surge of cases of bulimia nervosa is not due to a general increase among all women but instead results from a flood of cases—some say an epidemic—among women born after 1960.

Figure 10–4 also shows that the risk of developing the disorder declines with increasing age, at least among older cohorts. It remains to be seen whether the flattening of the risk curve with age will be repeated with younger cohorts of women.

Bulimia nervosa is far more common than anorexia nervosa (Fairburn, Hay, & Welch, 1993; Hoek, 1995). According to DSM-IV-TR, bulimia nervosa occurs among 1 to 3 percent of women, a rate that is two to six times the number of cases of anorexia nervosa. Moreover, the prevalence of subclinical bulimia—occasional binge eating and/or purging—is far greater than the number of cases that meet DSM-IV-TR criteria for bulimia nervosa. Finally, we should note again the considerable overlap between anorexia nervosa and bulimia nervosa. About 50 percent of all people with anorexia nervosa engage in episodes of binge eating and purging (Agras, 1987; Garfinkel, Kennedy, & Kaplan, 1995), and perhaps 15 percent of cases of bulimia nervosa have a history of anorexia nervosa (Sullivan, 2002).

Standards of Beauty

Both anorexia and bulimia nervosa are approximately 10 times more common among women than among men. Many scientists believe that this huge difference is explained by gender roles and standards of beauty (Hsu, 1990; Striegel-Moore, 1995). Popular attitudes about women in the United States tell us that "looks are everything," and thinness is essential to good looks. In contrast, young men are valued as much for their achievements as for their appearance, and, the ideal body type for men is considerably larger than for women (Hsu, 1990; Striegel-Moore, 1995; see Critical Thinking *Matters* on page 330). In fact, women are much more likely than men to have a negative body image, and that disparity has been growing over time (Feingold & Mazzella, 1998).

The growing prevalence of eating disorders may be explained by changing standards of beauty. Marilyn Monroe, the movie idol of the 1950s, is chunky by today's standards. *Playboy* centerfolds and Miss America Beauty Pageant

Model Kate Moss. Contemporary images of women place a premium on slimness and suggest that women should be judged by their appearance. Both of these messages apparently contribute to the etiology of eating disorders.

contestants—cultural icons but dubious role models for young women—prove how our ideals of beauty have changed. Between 1959 and 1988, their ratio of weight to height declined dramatically. In fact, 69 percent of *Playboy* centerfolds and 60 percent of Miss America contestants meet one diagnostic criterion for anorexia nervosa: Their body weight is at least 15 percent below expected weight for their height. The body shapes of these idealized women also have changed over time. Average bust and hip sizes have decreased, while waist sizes have increased slightly (Garner et al., 1980; Wiseman et al., 1992).

Standards of beauty are relative, not absolute. Today, eating disorders are much more common in North America, Western Europe, and Japan and other industrialized Asian countries; bulimia may be completely culture bound (Keel & Klump, 2003). In other cultures, women who are more

How do society's standards of beauty contribute to eating disorders?

THE PRESSURE TO BE THIN

Critical thinking matters in evaluating psychological research and in being a skeptic about unsubstantiated claims about the causes and treatment of emotional problems. Critical thinking also matters in everyday life. Consider how young women (and men) embrace standards of beauty based on the images of women in the media, and, in turn, apply fashion model standards to themselves and others.

The images are everywhere. Super-thin models routinely grace the cover and inside of fashion magazines. The average fashion model is 5' 11" and 117 pounds; the average woman in the U.S. is 5' 4" and 140 pounds. Television and movie actresses are not only talented and beautiful but exceptionally thin. Cameron Diaz and Julia Roberts, for example, both meet the body mass index requirement for anorexia nervosa (Owen & Laurel-Seller, 2000). Advertisements in all kinds of media for all kinds of products use images of sexy, beautiful, and very thin women, images that often are altered not only to erase facial blemishes but to lengthen legs or otherwise distort body shape. Even girls' dolls are unrealistically thin and beautiful. The ubiquitous Barbie Doll has a shape that translates into 39–18–33 figure in human equivalents. (A real-life GI Joe would have a 55" chest and a 27" bicep.)

The pressure to be thin greatly affects women who make their careers as actresses, models, and singers. The dubious "who's who" of women in the popular media who have *publicly admitted* to having an eating disorder (often in an attempt to encourage healthier body images among the girls and young women who admire them) includes: actresses Mary-Kate Olsen and Courtney Thorne-Smith; fashion model Carre Otis; singers Paul Abdul and Victoria Beckham (Posh Spice of the Spice Girls); and the Playboy models, the Barbi Twins.

Psychological studies repeatedly show that exposure to images of super-thin women increases body image dissatisfaction among girls and young women (Halliwell & Dittmar, 2004). Yet, young women face contradictory messages when parents or others tell them, "Beauty is only skin deep." For one, both extensive psychological research and everyday experience repeatedly tell us that attractiveness *does* matter, not only to romantic attraction (although men prefer a more curvaceous figure than women *think* they like), but also appearance matters in the evaluations of same-gender peers, teachers, employers, and on and on. And even as public health advocates battle the culture of thinness, other public health officials tell young

people—rightly—to be careful about what they eat, do not to eat too much, and try to lose weight. In fact, obesity is a much more prevalent public health problem than eating disorders. In the U.S., one out of every two adults and 20% of children are overweight, and obesity is associated with a great many health risks (Heinberg et al., 2001).

So where does critical thinking come in? Critical thinking is all about being reasonable and thinking for yourself. Appearance does matter, but few of us, female or male, can hope to look like models or movie stars. After all, these professionals literally are one in a million (or a billion). The stars of popular media devote much of their life to their appearance, and they *still* need the help of makeup, camera angles, creative fashions, and various electronic "corrections." Health matters too, and exercise is a great way to promote health, maintain an attractive physical appearance, and remember that your body is good for something other than being looked at. And most of us are more impressed by what someone does, by who they are, than what they look like. Remembering this is a useful reminder when we start to think critically—instead of using critical thinking—in evaluating our own weight and shape.

---

rounded are considered to be more beautiful (Hsu, 1990; Striegel-Moore, 1995). In Third World countries, where food is scarce, wealth is positively correlated with body weight. Being larger is a symbol of beauty and success. In industrialized nations, where food is plentiful, wealth is negatively correlated with weight (Hsu, 1989). As the Western saying goes, "You can never be too rich or too thin."

Age of Onset

Both anorexia and bulimia nervosa typically begin in late adolescence or early adulthood. A significant minority of cases of anorexia nervosa begin during early adolescence, particularly as girls approach puberty. The adolescent onset of eating disorders has provoked much

speculation about their etiology. Certain characteristics of adolescence have been hypothesized to cause eating disorders; these include hormonal changes (Garfinkel & Garner, 1982), autonomy struggles (Minuchin, Rosman, & Baker, 1978), and problems with sexuality (Coovert, Kinder, & Thompson, 1989). Other theorists have noted that the young adolescent girl is the most idealized cultural image of beauty (Hsu, 1990; Striegel-Moore, 1995). The natural and normal changes in body shape and weight offer a more simple explanation of the adolescent onset. Weight gain is normal during adolescence, but the addition of a few pounds can trouble a young woman focused on the numbers on her scale. Furthermore, breast and hip development not only change body shape, but they affect self-image, social interaction, and the fit of familiar clothes.

CAUSES OF EATING DISORDERS

The culture of thinness clearly contributes to the high rate of eating disorders today. However, other social, psychological, and biological risk factors play a role in eating disorders, because not every young woman suffers from these problems.

Social Factors

Standards of beauty and the premium placed on young women's appearance contribute to causing eating disorders. This conclusion is supported by epidemiological evidence and other research documenting that:

- Eating disorders are far more common among young women than young men (Hoek, 1995; Hsu, 1990).
- The prevalence of eating disorders in the United States has risen, as the image of the ideal woman has increasingly emphasized extreme thinness (Garner et al., 1980; Hoek, 1995; Kendler et al., 1991; Wiseman et al., 1992).
- Eating disorders are even more common among young women working in fields that emphasize weight and appearance, such as models, ballet dancers, and gymnasts (Bryne, 2002).
- Young women are particularly likely to develop eating disorders during adolescence and young adult life, an age during which our culture places a particular emphasis on appearance, beauty, and thinness (Hoek, 2002; Hsu, 1990).
- Eating disturbances are more common among young women who report greater exposure to popular media, endorse more gender-role stereotypes, or internalize societal standards about appearance (Heinberg, Thompson, & Stormer, 1995; Stice et al., 1994).
- Eating disorders are considerably more common among middle- and upper-class whites, who are especially likely to equate thinness with beauty in women. Eating disorders also may be increasing among well-to-do African Americans, who increasingly hold to the thinness ideal (Hsu, 1990; Thompson, 1996; Wildes, Emery, & Simons, 2001).
- Eating disorders are far more prevalent in industrialized societies, where thinness is the ideal, than in nonindustrialized societies,

Actress Mary Kate Olsen admitted battling with anorexia nervosa. Actresses and models face strong pressures to be perfectly beautiful and perfectly thin. They can create unrealistic standards for themselves—and for their fans.

where a more rounded body type is preferred (Hsu, 1990).
- The prevalence of eating disorders is higher among Arab and Asian women who are living or studying in Western countries than among women living in their native country (Hoek, 2002).

Rounded bodies once were the Western ideal of beauty for women, as illustrated in *Turkish Bath* painted by Jean Auguste Dominique Ingres in 1859–1863 (Louvre, Paris).

EATING DISORDERS IN MALES

What do psychologists know about eating disorders among males? Our culture clearly values different body types for males than for females. Adolescent boys often want to be bigger and stronger, not slimmer. Women rate themselves as being thin only when they are below 90 percent of their ideal body weight. In contrast, men see themselves as thin even when they weigh as much as 105 percent of their expected weight (Anderson, 2002). Surveys indicate that the majority of females want to lose weight, but males are about equally divided between those who want to lose weight and those who want to gain weight.

In fact, some experts argue that pressures to be strong and muscular have created a new eating disorder among males. The problem, sometimes called "reverse anorexia" or the "Adonis complex," is characterized by excessive emphasis on extreme muscularity and often accompanied by the abuse of anabolic steroids (Anderson, 2002; Ricciardelli & McCabe, 2004). You may recall that baseball slugger Mark McGuire was taking Androstenedione ("Andro," an over-the-counter steroid hormone)

when he broke the record for most home runs in a single season. McGuire's popularity and success apparently contributed to growing steroid use among young males in the U.S., where 3–12 percent of teenage boys have tried steroids (Ricciardelli & McCabe, 2004).

More realistic expectations about thinness surely contribute to the lower prevalence of anorexia and bulimia among males. However, men with these eating disorders are less likely to seek treatment than are women, perhaps because they are less likely to recognize the problem or feel more stigmatized because of it (Woodside et al., 2001). Men with anorexia or bulimia deviate far from male norms, and this can lead to rejection and stigmatization by other men, therapists, and even females with eating disorders. The stigma of being a man with an eating disorder also alters one common symptom of anorexia nervosa. Females with anorexia nervosa typically view their appearance positively, perhaps even with a degree of pride. In contrast, anorexia nervosa is much more likely to have a negative effect on the self esteem of a male, because weight and/or eating struggles are "unmanly," that is, different

from the cultural image of the ideal male (Andersen, 1995).

Anorexia and bulimia are more common among certain subgroups of males than in the general population. Male wrestlers have a particularly high prevalence of bulimia, a result of the intense pressure to "make weight"—to weigh below the weight cutoffs used to group competitors in a wrestling match. Eating disorders also are more common among gay than heterosexual men, an interesting finding since gay men place more emphasis on appearance (Carlat, Camargo, & Herzog, 1997; Russell & Keel, 2002).

Other aspects of eating disorders are similar for males and females. For both men and women, the disorders typically begin during adolescence or young adulthood. Other than the exceptions we have noted, similar factors also predict a risk for developing eating disorders in both females and males, including "reverse anorexia" (Ricciardelli & McCabe, 2004). Whether the ideal image is unrealistically thin or unrealistically muscular, cultural stereotypes about appearance can be risky for both males and females who internalize them.

Mark McGuire took androstenedione ("andro"), an over-the-counter steroid hormone, when he broke the single season home run record. Many teenage boys take steroids to build their bodies, a trend some consider to be a new eating disorder.

Billy Bob Thornton dieted for a movie role, but his weight loss got out of control prompting speculation that he suffered from anorexia nervosa.

Together, these facts make it clear that adolescent girls and young women are at risk for developing eating disorders, in part because they attempt to shape themselves, quite literally, to fit the image of the ideally proportioned, thin woman (see Eating Disorders in Males). We should note, however, that the culture of thinness plays a stronger role in the development of bulimia than anorexia. Cases of anorexia nervosa are found in the historical literature, occur in nonwestern cultures, and appear to have increased less than cases of bulimia nervosa in response to cultural ideals of thinness (Keel & Klump, 2003).

Of course, not every woman in the United States develops either eating disorder. Other stressors must interact with culture to produce eating disorders (Polivy & Herman, 2002). The individual's *internalization* of the ideal of thinness is one basic influence (Thompson & Stice, 2001). Several lines of work support the importance of internalization, including level of exposure to the media. In one study, ninth- and tenth-grade high school girls received a free subscription to *Seventeen* magazine at random. One year later, those who received the magazine reported increased negative affect, but only if their body image was more negative and they felt more pressure to be thin when the study began (Stice, Spangler, & Agras, 2001). Some girls apparently are more vulnerable to the media's "thin" message, while others are inoculated at least to some degree.

Troubled Family Relationships   Troubled family relationships may be another factor that increases vulnerability (Fairburn et al., 1997). Researchers have documented family problems in a number of studies, but the typical patterns differ for anorexia nervosa and bulimia nervosa. Young people with bulimia nervosa report considerable conflict and rejection in their families, difficulties that also may contribute to their depression. In contrast, young people with anorexia generally perceive their families as cohesive and nonconflictual (Fornari et al., 1999; Vandereycken, 1995).

Although the families of young people with anorexia nervosa appear to be well functioning, some theorists see the families as being too close—as *enmeshed families*, families whose members are overly involved in one another's lives. According to the enmeshment hypothesis, young people with anorexia nervosa are obsessed with controlling their eating, because

eating is the *only* thing they can control in their intrusive families (Minuchin et al., 1978). Yet it is not clear whether intrusive parental concern is a cause or an effect of the eating disorder. Parents of an adolescent with anorexia nervosa may become "enmeshed" as a worried reaction to their daughter's obviously emaciated appearance, not as a cause of it. In any case, family power struggles over eating often become one focus of the treatment of anorexia nervosa (Polivy & Herman, 2002).

Child sexual abuse is another family difficulty that might contribute to the development of eating disorders. However, sexual abuse does not appear to play a *specific* role in the development of eating disorders. Instead, sexual abuse may increase the risk for a variety of psychological problems, including, but not limited to, eating disorders. Women with eating disorders are more likely than normal controls to report a history of sexual abuse, but are no more likely to report a history of sexual abuse than are women who suffer from other psychological problems (Palmer, 1995; Welch & Fairburn, 1996).

Finally, we should note that there are many direct ways in which parents may influence children toward developing eating disorders. Many parents struggle with diet and thinness themselves, and they are models of preoccupation for their children; other parents directly encourage their children to be extra thin as a part of the general push to compete with their peers (Vandereycken, 2002).

Psychological Factors

Researchers have hypothesized about many psychological factors contributing to eating disorders. Here we highlight four of the most important: control issues, depression/dysphoria, body image dissatisfaction, and reactions to dietary restraint.

A Struggle for Perfection and Control   One of the first and most prolific clinical observers of eating disorders was Hilde Bruch (1904–1984), a physician who fled her native Germany in 1933 to escape the Nazi regime and subsequently settled and studied psychiatry in the United States. Bruch viewed a struggle for control as the central psychological issue in the development of eating disorders (Bruch, 1982). Bruch observed that

How are eating disorders similar and different among males and females?

Psychiatrist Hilde Bruch (1904–1984) was an early and prolific clinical observer who viewed the young woman's struggle for control as a central issue in the development of eating disorders.

girls with eating disorders seem to be exceptionally "good"—conforming and eager to please. She suggested that these exceptionally "good girls" give up too much of the normal adolescent struggle for autonomy and, instead, attempt to please others, particularly their parents. Bruch thus viewed their obsessive efforts to control eating and weight as a way that overly compliant "good girls" control themselves further. At the same time, she also saw their dieting as an attempt to wrest at least a little control from their parents—control over what they eat. In this *struggle for control*, young people with anorexia nervosa "succeed" and take considerable pride in their extreme self-control. In contrast, people with bulimia nervosa continually strive—and fail—to gain complete control over eating and weight. The success or failure of control, in turn, may explain the denial that characterizes anorexia nervosa and the humiliation that accompanies bulimia nervosa.

Perfectionism is another term for the endless pursuit of control described by Bruch. Perfectionists set unrealistically high standards, are self critical, and demand a nearly flawless performance from themselves. Research demonstrates that young women with eating disorders endorse perfectionist goals both about eating and weight and about general expectations for themselves (Bastiani et al., 1995; Garner, Olmstead, & Polivy, 1983).

Young people with eating disorders may also try to control their own emotions excessively, perhaps as a result of their constant attempt to please others instead of themselves (Bruch, 1982). The result may be a lack of **introceptive awareness**—recognition of internal cues, including various emotional states as well as hunger. People with eating disorders may be more tuned in to how they look than how they feel—sad, angry, or happy, or even whether they are hungry (Viken et al., 2002). In fact, a large study of the development of eating disorders found that lack of introceptive awareness predicted the development of eating disorders 2 years in the future (Leon et al., 1993; Leon et al., 1995).

Depression, Low Self-Esteem, and Dysphoria

Depression is commonly comorbid with eating disorders, particularly bulimia nervosa. Researchers

have found an increased prevalence of depression not only among people with eating disorders but also among the members of their families (Strober, 1995). Research also shows that antidepressant medications reduce some symptoms of bulimia nervosa (Mitchell, Raymond, & Specker, 1993). Bulimia thus appears to be a reaction to depression in some cases.

In other cases, however, depression may instead be a reaction to bulimia nervosa and especially to anorexia nervosa (Hsu, 1990; Polivy & Herman, 2002). Depression improves markedly following successful group psychotherapy for bulimia (Mitchell et al., 1990), and in one large study, depression failed to predict either concurrent or future eating disorders (Leon et al., 1995). Another study of anorexia nervosa found considerable depression at the time of the original diagnosis but not at a 6-year follow-up (Rastam, Gillberg, & Gillberg, 1995). Thus depression may contribute to the development of eating disorders in some cases, but in most eating disorders, depression appears to be a secondary problem and not the primary issue (Stice & Agras, 1999).

Still, some experts suggest that depressive *symptoms*, and not necessarily clinical depression, play a role in the onset of eating disorders. Low self-esteem is a particular concern (Fairburn et al., 1997). In particular, women with eating disorders may be preoccupied with their *social self*, how they present themselves in public and how other people perceive and evaluate them (Jones, 1985; Striegel-Moore, Silberstein, & Rodin, 1993). Women with bulimia nervosa or a negative body image report more public self-consciousness, social anxiety, and perceived fraudulence (Striegel-Moore, Silberstein, & Rodin, 1993). They also show increases in self-criticism and deterioration in mood following negative social interactions (Steiger et al., 1999). In short, people with eating disorders often depend on others for self-esteem.

Depressive symptoms also clearly play a role in maintaining problematic eating behaviors. *Dysphoria* or negative mood states commonly trigger episodes of binge eating in bulimia nervosa and in the binge-eating/purging subtype of anorexia nervosa (Steiger et al., 1999). The dysphoria may be brought on by social criticism or conflict, dissatisfaction with eating and diet, or an ongoing depressive episode. In summary, although most cases of clinical depression appear to be reactions to eating disorders,

How do "control issues" differ in anorexia and bulimia?

In what different ways do depression and depressive symptoms contribute to eating disorders?

depression, low self-esteem, and periods of dysphoria can contribute to the onset or maintenance of eating disorders.

Negative Body Image *A negative body image,* a highly critical evaluation of one's weight and shape, has long been thought to contribute to the development of eating disorders (Polivy & Herman, 2002). Psychologists have used a number of techniques to evaluate a negative body image, including self-report measures, calipers or other devices used to directly estimate the size of various body parts, and schematic figures such as the ones in Figure 10–5 (Thompson, 1996).

Early studies focused on a *distorted body image,* a perceptual inaccuracy in judging one's size, particularly in cases of anorexia nervosa. Current research focuses on *dissatisfaction* with body image, a negative evaluation of one's body that includes cognitive and affective elements and not just perceptual distortions. One way to assess a negative body image is to compare people's ratings of their "current" and "ideal" size by asking them to pick from the schematics in Figure 10–5. Several longitudinal studies have found negative evaluations of weight, shape, and appearance to predict the subsequent development of disordered eating (Attie & Brooks-Gunn, 1989; Cattarin & Thompson, 1994; Striegel-Moore, Silberstein, & Rodin, 1989). A negative body image may be a particular problem when combined with other risk factors, including perfectionism and low self-esteem (Vohs et al., 1999).

Dietary Restraint Some symptoms of eating disorders may be effects of *dietary restraint,* that is, direct consequences of restricted eating (Heatherton & Polivy, 1992; Herman & Polivy, 1988). This is ironic, because many of the "out-of-control" symptoms of eating disorders appear to be caused by inappropriate efforts to control eating! These symptoms include binge eating, preoccupation with food, and perhaps out-of-control feelings of hunger.

Inappropriate dieting is hypothesized to contribute directly to subsequent binge eating. According to this view, an overly restrictive diet increases hunger, frustration, and lack of attention to internal cues, all of which make binge eating more likely. In addition, "quick-fix" diets rarely work, and dieters are likely to be left with a sense of failure, disappointment, and self-criticism. The negative affect, in turn, may make further binge eating likely and further lowers

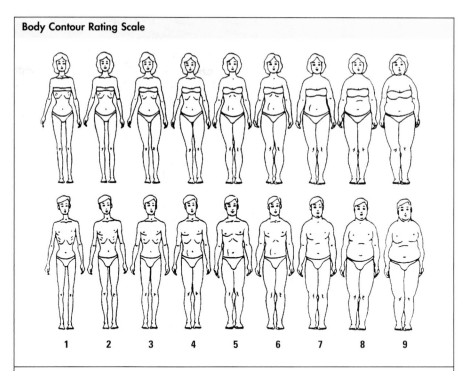

Body Contour Rating Scale

1 2 3 4 5 6 7 8 9

FIGURE 10–5: These schematic figures are used in research to assess differences between real and ideal body image. People pick two figures, their current and their ideal shape. The discrepancy between the ratings is an index of negative body image.

Source: J.K. Thompson, 1996, Assessing body image disturbance: Measures, methodology, and implementation. In J.K. Thompson (Ed.), *Body Image, Eating Disorders, and Obesity,* p. 79. Washington, DC: American Psychological Association. Copyright © 1996. Reprinted by permission of the author.340

self-esteem (Heatherton & Polivy, 1992; Herman & Polivy, 1988).

Despite the intuitive appeal of the dietary restraint view, contrary evidence comes from a randomized trial of normal weight women randomly assigned to a low calorie diet. Dieting women both lost weight and *decreased* binge eating 18 weeks later (Presnell & Stice, 2003). Perhaps dietary restraint increases binge eating

Many women with eating disorders have a distorted body image, as illustrated by this young woman examining her figure in a mirror that gives the illusion of fatness.

Societal values that emphasize women's thinness, beauty, and appearance over agency contribute to eating disorders. Venus and Serena Williams, here celebrating their gold medal in doubles tennis at the Sydney Olympics, are fit, attractive, and extremely capable role models who may help to offset those values.

under different circumstances, or it may be that, in past research, dieting has been linked to binge eating only because it served as a proxy for general concerns about food and weight.

Dietary restraint also may directly cause some of the symptoms of anorexia nervosa. The military studies of semistarvation conducted during World War II found that, during refeeding, many men felt intense, uncontrollable hunger, even after eating a considerable amount of food (Keys et al., 1950). Perhaps a similar reaction explains some of the intense fear of losing control and gaining weight found in anorexia nervosa. The bottom line is that some symptoms of eating disorders may result from the body's rebellion against a severely restricted diet.

Biological Factors

Weight regulation is a result of the interplay among behavior (e.g., energy expenditure, eating), peripheral physiological activity (e.g., digestion, metabolism), and central physiological activity (e.g., neurotransmitter release) (Blundell, 1995). The body strives to maintain weight around certain **weight set points,** fixed weights or small ranges of weight. The process is very much like the way a thermostat regulates heating and cooling to maintain air temperature at a given setting. Thus, if weight declines, hunger increases and food consumption goes up (Keesey, 1995). There is a slowing of the *metabolic rate,* the rate at which the body expends energy, and movement toward *hyperlipogenesis,* the storage of abnormally large amounts of fat in fat cells throughout the body (Brownell & Fairburn, 1995). All of these reactions have obvious survival value and are likely products of evolution. The body does not distinguish between intentional attempts to lose weight and potential starvation. Thus some aspects of eating disorders are a result of the individual's struggle against their own biology.

Other evidence suggests that genetic factors contribute to eating disorders. An extensive twin study of bulimia nervosa found a concordance rate of 23 percent for MZ twins and 9 percent for DZ twins (Kendler et al., 1991). Higher MZ than DZ concordance rates for dysfunctional eating attitudes have also been reported (Klump, McGue, & Iacono, 2000; Rutherford et al., 1993). A recent study compared MZ twins *discordant* for bulimia nervosa, and found that affected twins were more anxious as children. Ill twins currently showed more obsessive–compulsive symptoms and lower feelings of mastery, optimism, and self-esteem in comparison to their identical twin without an eating disorder (Bulik, Wade, & Kendler, 2000). These symptoms may have contributed to the development of the eating disorders, but with the exception of childhood anxiety, the differences also may have been consequences, not causes, of bulimia nervosa.

MZ–DZ twin differences in early disorders could be explained by several different heritable mechanisms. It is unlikely that eating disorders are directly inherited, especially given the historically recent surge in prevalence rates. Rather, genetics may influence some personality characteristic that, in turn, increases the risk for bulimia nervosa (Strober and Bulik, 2002). Or a certain body type may be inherited (Bouchard, 2002), and this may account for the higher concordance rates found among MZ twins, but only when combined with cultural expectations about thinness—and with individual concerns about living up to these expectations. Genes clearly affect weight and body type, but we cannot mindlessly conclude that eating disorders are "genetic."

Finally, several neurophysiological measures are correlated with eating disorders, including elevations in endogenous opioids, low levels of serotonin, and diminished neuroendocrine functioning (Yates, 1990). Most of these differences in brain functioning, however, appear to be effects of eating disorders and not causes of them. In extremely rare cases, eating disorders have been linked with a specific biological abnormality, such as a hormonal disturbance or a lesion in the *hypothalamus*, the area of the brain that regulates routine biological functions, including appetite.

Integration and Alternative Pathways

Social and cultural values that emphasize thinness, beauty, and appearance over agency are the starting point in understanding eating disorders, particularly among young women. Most young women in the United States today are concerned with weight and shape, but only a minority develop an eating disorder. Risk factors that combine with cultural attitudes to produce eating disorders include direct familial and social pressures to be thin, a negative body image, dietary restraint, and genetic influences on body weight and shape (Jacobi et al., 2004; Stice, 2001, 2002). Less obvious risk factors include preoccupation with external evaluation, lack of introceptive awareness, and excessive conformity and self-control.

Research on the etiology of eating disorders underscores the importance of *equifinality*. There are many pathways to developing an eating disorder. Some women are naturally thin, but their perfectionism drives them to become even thinner. Other women may have a more rounded body type determined by genetics, and as a result of contemporary standards of beauty, they struggle, and repeatedly fail, to mold their body into something it was never meant to be. For some people, an eating disorder is an expression of depression. Others may develop an eating disorder because they focus on outward appearances instead of internal values. Clearly, eating disorders are best understood in terms of a systems approach (Halmi, 1997).

A key issue that remains unresolved is why some women develop anorexia nervosa and others develop bulimia nervosa. Many social, psychological, and biological factors in the development of the two disorders are similar. Future research should determine what causes some young women to master their appetite—and become emaciated as a result—or what causes other women to continually struggle with frequent binge eating and compensatory behavior.

TREATMENT OF ANOREXIA NERVOSA

The treatments for anorexia nervosa and bulimia nervosa differ in approach and effectiveness; therefore, we consider them separately. The treatment of anorexia nervosa usually focuses on two goals. The first goal is to help the patient gain at least a minimal amount of weight. If weight loss is severe, the patient may be treated in an inpatient setting (Keel et al., in press), where clinicians may use coercive methods or introduce strict behavior therapy programs in which rewards such as social activities are made contingent on weight gain. Hospitalization also may be needed to prevent suicide, to address severe depression or medical complications, or to remove the patient temporarily

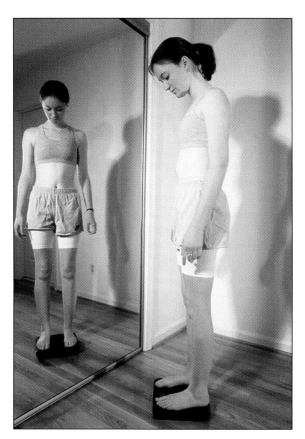

In treating anorexia nervosa, the first goal is establishing a safer, more normal body weight.

from a dysfunctional social circumstance (Garner & Needleman, 1996).

The second goal in treating anorexia nervosa is more general—to address the broader difficulties that may have caused or are maintaining the disorder. Many different forms of treatment may be used to achieve this goal. The clinical literature commonly advocates family therapy. There are many different forms of family therapy, but perhaps the most common is *structural family therapy*, which views parents' interference with adolescent autonomy—and avoidance of their own disagreements—as the central problems in anorexia nervosa. Structural family therapists attempt to redefine the eating disorder as an interpersonal problem, to get the young person with anorexia nervosa out of the sick role, and to encourage parents to confront their own conflicts directly and not through their children (Minuchin, Rosman, & Baker, 1978). Some evidence indicates that family therapy for anorexia nervosa is more effective than treating the client individually, at least when the client is an adolescent (Robin et al., 1999; Russell et al., 1987).

Clinicians have also tried a number of different individual therapies for anorexia nervosa. Three approaches of note are (1) Bruch's (1982) modified psychodynamic therapy designed to increase introceptive awareness and correct distorted perceptions of self; (2) cognitive behavioral approaches that aim to alter the belief that "weight, shape, or thinness can serve as the sole or predominant referent for inferring personal value or self-worth" (Garner & Bemis, 1982, p. 142); and (3) *feminist therapies*, which encourage young women to pursue their own values rather than blindly adopting prescribed social roles (Fallon, Katzman, & Wooley, 1994). There is currently little, if any, evidence to show that any of these treatments is effective. Similarly, medications such as antidepressants seem to offer little relief for victims of anorexia nervosa (Vitousek, 2002).

Keep in mind, however, that the three approaches to individual therapy share the common goal of basing self-esteem more on internal standards and less on external evaluations. Working toward this end is a logical goal in treating and, we believe, in preventing anorexia nervosa. If you are concerned about your own body image or eating habits, or if you are concerned about those of a friend, the Getting Help section at the end of this chapter provides some general information and resources in addition to the treatment options outlined below.

Course and Outcome of Anorexia Nervosa

Evidence on the course and outcome of anorexia nervosa demonstrates that contemporary treatments are not very effective. At posttreatment follow-up assessments, 50 to 60 percent of patients have a weight within the normal range, 10 to 20 percent remain significantly below their healthy body weight, and the remainder are intermediate in weight (Hsu, 1990; Steinhausen, 1996). Perhaps as many as 10 percent starve themselves to death or die of related complications, including suicide.

Although important, weight gain is not the only measure of the course of anorexia nervosa. In fact, more than half of women with a history of anorexia nervosa continue to have difficulties with eating, notwithstanding gains in weight. Menstruation returns along with weight gain for most women, but many continue to be preoccupied with diet, weight, and body shape. Moreover, people may also develop new problems with social life, depression, or bulimia, as a result of their perfectionism, reliance on external evaluation, or continued struggles with body image (Hsu, 1990). Predictors of a better prognosis include an early age of onset, conflict-free parent–child relationships, early treatment, less weight loss, and the absence of binge eating and purging (Steinhausen, 1996). The following account, written by a young woman after her long and, finally, successful struggle with anorexia nervosa, illustrates some of the continuing problems:

I do not have a story that ends with a miraculous recovery, and I would be suspicious of anyone who claimed that they had completely gotten over an eating disorder. I continue to struggle with worries about food and my body. I exercise every day without fail. I am prone to stress fractures and will most likely encounter early osteoporosis due to the irreversible effects of starvation on my bones. I am lucky that I will be able to have children someday, though many long-term anorexics are never able to. Despite these lingering effects of the disorder, they pale in comparison to what I consider to be the most detrimental of all. When I look back on those six or so years, it sickens me to realize how much of life I missed. I allowed my obsession with my weight to take over my life. (Zorn, 1998, p. 21)

TREATMENT OF BULIMIA NERVOSA

In recent years, researchers have developed several effective approaches to treating bulimia nervosa. The most effective treatments include antidepressant medication, cognitive behavior therapy, and interpersonal psychotherapy.

Antidepressant Medications

All classes of antidepressant medications are somewhat effective in treating bulimia nervosa; however, medication alone is not the treatment of choice. Binge eating and compensatory behavior improve only among a minority of people treated with antidepressants, and relapse is common when medication is stopped (Walsh, 1995). Most importantly, research shows that, alone or perhaps in combination with medication, psychotherapy is an important component of treatment (Agras et al., 1992; Mitchell et al., 1990; Walsh et al., 1997; Wilson et al., 1999). One exception may be treating bulimia in a primary care setting, where most patients fail to complete self-help cognitive behavior therapy programs and more follow through with antidepressant medication (Walsh et al., 2004).

Cognitive Behavior Therapy

The most thoroughly researched psychotherapy for bulimia nervosa is cognitive behavior therapy. As developed by the British psychiatrist Christopher Fairburn, the cognitive behavioral approach views bulimia as stemming from several maladaptive tendencies, including an excessive emphasis on weight and shape in determining self-esteem; perfectionism; and dichotomous "black or white" thinking (Fairburn, 1996). Fairburn's cognitive behavioral treatment includes three stages. First, the therapist uses education and behavioral strategies to normalize eating patterns. The goal is to restore more normal eating and end the cycle where extreme dietary restraint leads to binge eating and, in turn, to purging. Second, the therapist addresses the client's broader, dysfunctional beliefs about self, appearance, and dieting. Techniques include a variation of Beck's cognitive therapy to address perfectionism or depression, and individual problems such as poor impulse control or troubled relationships also may be addressed at this stage. Third, the therapist attempts to consolidate gains and prepare the client for expected relapses in the future. Key goals at this final stage of treatment are to develop realistic expectations about eating, weight concerns, and binge eating, as well as clear strategies for coping with relapses in advance (Fairburn, 2002).

Overall, cognitive behavior therapy leads to a 70 to 80 percent reduction in binge eating and purging across people in treatment. Between one-third and one-half of all clients are able to cease the bulimic pattern completely, and the majority of individuals maintain these gains at 6-month to 1-year follow-up (Agras et al., 2000; Fairburn et al., 1993). Cognitive behavior therapy also may be effective in group therapy (Mitchell et al., 1990) and self-help formats (Carter & Fairburn, 1998), although individual therapy is more effective (Thompson-Brenner et al., 2003).

What alternative approaches are most effective for treating bulimia?

Interpersonal Psychotherapy

Interpersonal psychotherapy, which was originally developed for the treatment of depression, also may be an effective treatment for bulimia nervosa. This is surprising because interpersonal therapy does not address eating disorders directly but instead focuses on difficulties in close relationships. Interpersonal therapy for bulimia initially was studied as a placebo control treatment in a study of cognitive behavior therapy. Fairburn and colleagues (1991, 1993) planned to evaluate whether cognitive behavior therapy had specific treatment effects above and beyond the general benefits of receiving psychotherapy. The investigators chose interpersonal therapy as a credible placebo treatment because interpersonal problems often are associated with bulimia nervosa. However, they hypothesized that cognitive behavior therapy would outperform the interpersonal approach. The study also included a third condition, a behavior therapy alone group, which essentially was cognitive behavior therapy without the cognitive elements.

When Fairburn and his colleagues (1991) evaluated outcome shortly after treatment, they found that cognitive behavior therapy was more effective than interpersonal therapy in changing dieting behavior, self-induced vomiting, and attitudes about weight and shape. Cognitive behavior therapy also was more effective than behavior therapy alone when attitude change was the outcome

British psychiatrist *Christopher Fairburn* is internationally recognized for his development of effective cognitive behavior therapy treatments for bulimia nervosa. Fairburn's surprising results also have identified interpersonal therapy as a second line treatment for bulimia nervosa.

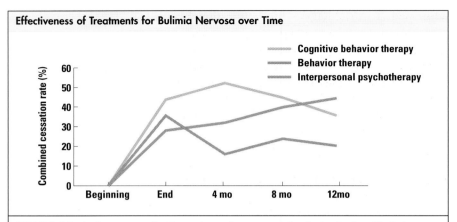

Effectiveness of Treatments for Bulimia Nervosa over Time

Cognitive behavior therapy
Behavior therapy
Interpersonal psychotherapy

FIGURE 10–6: Percentage of patients who no longer purged or had episodes of bulimia according to objective or subjective reports. Note the decline for the behavior therapy group and continued improvement for the interpersonal therapy group over the 1-year follow-up interval.

Source: C.G. Fairburn, R. Jones, R.C. Peveler, R.A. Hope, and M. O'Connor, 1993, Psycotherapy and bulimia nervosa: Longer-term effects of interpersonal psychotherapy, behavior therapy, and cognitive behavior therapy, *Archives of General Psychiatry, 50,* 423. Copyright © 1993. Reprinted by permission of American Medical Association.

measure; however, the results of the two behavioral treatments were similar in other respects.

A very different picture emerged at 12-month follow-up (Fairburn et al., 1993) (see Figure 10–6). The improvements brought about by behavior therapy alone deteriorated over time, and a large number of patients dropped out of this group, perhaps reflecting their dissatisfaction with the treatment. In comparison, the improvements in the cognitive behavior therapy group remained fairly stable. Most surprising, members of the interpersonal therapy group *continued to improve* in the 12 months following the end of treatment. At 1-year follow-up, in fact, the improvements for interpersonal therapy equaled the improvements for cognitive behavior therapy and outdistanced the behavior therapy alone group.

The continued improvement for the interpersonal therapy group was surprising and

PSYCHOTHERAPY PLACEBOS: CONTROLLING FOR EXPECTATIONS

research methods

A placebo is a treatment that contains no active ingredients for the disorder being treated. A *placebo control group* is a group of people who receive only a placebo treatment in an outcome study. Scientists must include placebos and placebo control groups in treatment outcome research, because the mere expectation of change can produce many psychological and physical benefits. New treatments work, in part, because the client and the therapist expect them to work.

Medication placebos are easily administered. Physicians give patients a pill that looks like the real medication but contains no active chemical ingredients. Psychotherapy placebos are much more challenging. How can we create a psychological treatment that contains no active ingredients but increases the client's and the therapist's expectations for change just as much as the real treatment?

One approach psychologists use is to offer an established, alternative therapy, but one not designed to treat the disorder being studied. In their study of bulimia nervosa, Fairburn et al. (1993) thought interpersonal therapy was a reasonable placebo psychotherapy. The investigators believed that interpersonal therapy contained no "active ingredients" for treating bulimia nervosa, but thought clients' therapists would view it as legitimate.

But this does not fully resolve the problem of creating a psychotherapy placebo. Researchers typically "believe" in their new treatment—otherwise they would not be studying it. Evidence on the *allegiance effect* shows that the *therapist's* beliefs help make a treatment work. The allegiance effect tells us that cognitive behavior therapy should have been more successful in the Fairburn et al. (1993) study, because the investigators were cognitive behavior therapists. In fact, we are particularly impressed by the results for interpersonal therapy in this study, because interpersonal therapy overcame the allegiance effect in this study and in a replication (Agras et al., 2000).

What research methods control for the influence of the experimenter's expectations on outcome? In drug research, scientists use the *double-blind study,* where neither the patient nor the therapist knows whether the patient is receiving an active treatment or a placebo. Unfortunately, "real" and placebo psychotherapies are transparent to therapists, making it impossible to conduct double-blind studies of psychotherapy. An alternative approach is to include a pill placebo, a method that also can facilitate comparisons between studies of the effectiveness of drugs and psychotherapy (Klein, 1996). This is a positive step, but even pill placebo effects are not always easy to

interpret. For example, medications are more effective when they produce more side effects (Greenberg et al., 1994). There are at least two possible reasons for this. More side effects may increase the patient's expectations for change, because they make the drug seem powerful. Or even in a double-blind study, clinicians may be able to determine whether patients are receiving the real medication or a placebo based on the side effects.

Another way of addressing the allegiance effect in psychotherapy outcome research is to have investigators who hold *opposing allegiances* participate in the same study. Cognitive behavior therapy is offered by cognitive behavior therapists, interpersonal therapists deliver interpersonal therapy, and so on. This overcomes the allegiance effect, but creates a new problem: Because the same therapists cannot deliver the different treatments, effects due to the individual therapists are uncontrolled.

In the absence of a perfect psychotherapy placebo, two conclusions seem clear. First, we must recognize that the expectations of clients, therapists, and experimenters can influence the findings of therapy outcome research. Second, we are particularly impressed when, contrary to expectations, a placebo psychotherapy is as effective as the "real thing."

impressive, for at least two reasons. First, the interpersonal treatments explicitly excluded direct discussions of eating, diet, and related topics. Second, the investigators had lower expectations for the interpersonal therapy group, and the *allegiance effect* often influences treatment outcome (see Research Methods). A recent, larger study replicated the results of this investigation, although cognitive behavior therapy again produced more rapid improvement (Agras et al., 2000). Cognitive behavior therapy clearly is the first-line treatment for bulimia nervosa, but interpersonal therapy and antidepressant medication may be useful supplemental or alternative treatments.

Course and Outcome of Bulimia Nervosa

Bulimia nervosa also has a persistent course, although the outcome is more positive than for anorexia nervosa, especially with treatment (Herzog et al., 1999; Sullivan, 2002; Thomson-Brenner et al., 2003). Without treatment, one third to one half of women with bulimia have an eating disorder 5 years later, many continuing to meet diagnostic criteria for bulimia nervosa (Fairburn et al., 2003). Following treatment, in contrast, about half of clients are free of all symptoms, about one in five continue to meet the diagnostic criteria for bulimia nervosa, and the remainder have occasional relapses or subclinical levels of binge eating and compensatory behavior (Keel et al., 2002). Most clients manage to maintain a weight that is generally in the normal range, and—in contrast to anorexia nervosa—mortality is rare (Keel & Mitchell, 1997). Comorbid psychological disorders also tend to improve with improvements in bulimia nervosa (Hsu, 1995; Keel & Mitchell, 1997). Predictors of continued binge eating include a longer duration, greater emphasis on shape and weight, childhood obesity, poorer social adjustment, and persistent compensatory behavior (Fairburn et al., 2003).

PREVENTION OF EATING DISORDERS

Can eating disorders be prevented? This question is of huge importance, especially given the pervasive body dissatisfaction and disordered eating found among women today. Until recently, the results of prevention research were discouraging.

Few, if any, benefits were produced by first-generation prevention efforts, which focused on education about the adverse effects of eating disorders, or by second-generation initiatives offering education about resisting the culture of thinness. As reviewed in a recent meta-analysis by Eric Stice and Heather Shaw (2004), however, a third generation of prevention research shows promise for reducing disordered eating.

What efforts are most effective at prevention? Surprising, the content of effective programs appears to matter less than the style of delivery. Whether a prevention program focuses on promoting healthy weight control, a critical view of the thin ideal, increasing self-esteem, or stress management matters less than whether it: (1) targets at-risk individuals instead of an unselected

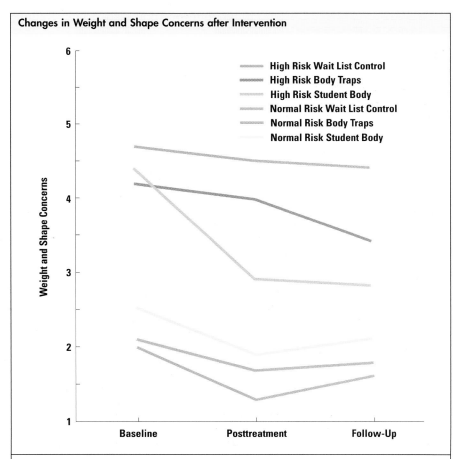

FIGURE 10–7: Participants who completed the Internet-based Student Body (SB) program improved significantly in their eating attitudes in comparison to a Wait List Control (WLC) group. Among SB participants at high risk, concerns about weight and shape improved significantly more than among the classroom-based Body Traps (BT) group. BT did not differ from WLC on any measure at any time.

Source: Adapted from A.A. Celio et al., 2000, Reducing risk factors for eating disorders: Comparison of an Internet and a classroom-delivered psychoeducational program. *Journal of Consulting and Clinical Psychology, 68,* 650–657.

group; (2) involves an interactive component rather than being purely didactic; (3) includes more than one session; and (4) is directed toward women (exclusively) in their late teens or older (Stice & Shaw, 2004). More successful programs also may be covert, that is, their stated goal is to increase acceptance of one's body rather than reduce disordered eating, a strategy that may get around defensiveness about body image.

One such successful prevention effort involved 76 female undergraduates who responded to flyers but did not have an eating disorder (Celio et al., 2000). Investigators assigned the women at random to either: (1) Student Bodies (SB), an 8-week program involving required on line exercises, group discussion, reading about health, weight, and eating, all of which was supplemented by three face-to-face meetings; (2) Body Traps (BT), an 8-week classroom program involving weekly 2-hour lectures and group discussions on similar topics to SB; and (3) a Wait List Control (WLC) group. At the 2-month and 6-month follow-up assessments, SB improved significantly more than the WLC group on measures of weight and shape concerns, but BT did not differ from either group. In addition, women at high risk (due to high levels of body dissatisfaction) improved more in SB than in either BT or WLC (see Figure 10–7 on page 341). The homework assignments, and the more private and perhaps more engaging use of the internet, probably determined SB's success (Celio et al., 2000).

Psychologists and society clearly have a long way to go to help women, and men, find the right balance between eating too little and too much, being obsessed with appearance, and being lax about health. Still, the results of a new generation of prevention research are an encouraging step in the right direction.

---

getting help

 Eating disorders are very common, so it is likely that you or someone close to you may be struggling with eating issues. What can help?

One step is to get more information, but you need to be careful. Some self-help books and Web sites on eating disorders offer misleading or inaccurate information. One Web site that we recommend is the home page of the National Eating Disorders Awareness Association, a nonprofit organization dedicated to increasing the awareness and prevention of eating disorders. The Web page of the National Institute of Mental Health also contains helpful information about eating disorders. An excellent self-help book is *Overcoming Binge Eating*, by Christopher Fairburn, whose treatment research is discussed in this chapter. *Living with*

Anorexia and Bulimia, by James Moorey, is another good book that deals with a broader range of eating issues.

If you are seriously concerned about your own eating, weight, or body shape, you should talk with a professional. Colleges and universities often have special information and treatments for eating disorders. Call your student health service for information and referral. If no student health resources are available to you, another option is to talk with your family physician. You should have a physical exam to explore possible medical complications caused by your abnormal eating, and your physician also should know of mental health professionals who specialize in eating disorders. As indicated by the research we review in this chapter, some of the treatment options you should consider and discuss include cognitive behavior therapy,

the most strongly supported treatment alternative; interpersonal therapy; family therapy; and antidepressant medication. Hospitalization may be another option, but only for very serious problems like severe weight loss.

If you are concerned about a friend's eating, you should make a plan and talk to her or him. Bring some information on local resources for treating eating disorders. And be prepared to listen as well as to talk! Your friend probably has not confided about his or her problems with many people. If your friend denies a problem, there is no point in arguing. You have done your job by raising the issue. It will be up to him or her to admit to the problem and get help. A good resource before and after talking with a friend is *Surviving an Eating Disorder: Strategies for Friends and Families,* by Michele Siegel, Judith Brisman, and Margot Weinshel.

SUMMARY

Eating disorders are severe disturbances in eating behavior that result from the sufferer's obsessive fear of gaining weight. DSM-IV-TR lists two major subtypes of eating disorders: anorexia nervosa and bulimia nervosa. The defining symptoms of **anorexia nervosa** include extreme emaciation, a disturbed perception of one's body, an intense fear of gaining weight, and the cessation of menstruation (in women). People with anorexia nervosa are preoccupied with food, revel in their control over eating, and may have mood disturbances, sexual difficulties, lack of impulse control, and medical problems secondary to the weight loss. The defining symptoms of **bulimia nervosa** are **binge eating** and compensatory behavior (**purging** or excessive exercise), a sense of lost control during a binge, and undue focus on weight and shape. Depression is commonly associated with bulimia nervosa; substance abuse and personality disorders are to a much lesser degree.

DSM-IV-TR includes two subtypes of anorexia nervosa. The restricting type includes people who rarely engage in binge eating or purging behavior, whereas the binge eating/purging type is characterized by regular binge eating and purging. Bulimia nervosa also is divided into two subtypes. The purging type is characterized by the regular use of self-induced vomiting or the misuse of laxatives, diuretics, or enemas. The nonpurging type compensates for binge eating with fasting or excessive exercise. There has been debate about adding to the DSM-IV-TR list of eating disorders. **Binge eating disorder** is included in a special appendix. **Obesity** has been considered for inclusion, but rejected.

The prevalence of both anorexia nervosa and bulimia nervosa has increased dramatically in recent years, particularly among young women. Both anorexia and bulimia nervosa are approximately 10 times more common among women than among men, and many scientists blame our society's gender roles and standards of beauty for encouraging eating disorders. Standards of beauty and pubertal changes in body shape and weight also may account for the onset of eating disorders during adolescence and early adulthood.

Adolescent girls and young women are at risk for developing eating disorders, in part, because they attempt to shape themselves to fit the image of the ideal woman. The emphasis on appearances also lessens the value of other roles filled by girls and women. To a lesser extent, family relationships also may influence eating disorders. Four of the most prominent psychological factors in the development of eating disorders are issues of control and perfectionism, dysphoria combined with a lack of **introceptive awareness,** body image dissatisfaction, and reactions to dietary restraint. Biological contributions include the body's attempts to maintain **weight set points,** genetic influences on body weight and shape, and in rare cases a dysfunction of the hypothalamus.

Treatments for anorexia nervosa and bulimia nervosa differ in approach and effectiveness. Anorexia nervosa may require inpatient treatment with the initial goal of gaining weight, even through the use of coercive methods if necessary. Following treatment, 50 to 60 percent of people with anorexia nervosa have a normal weight, and 10 to 20 percent have weights well below normal (the remainder are in between these two groups). About 10 percent of people with the disorder die of starvation, suicide, or medical complications. Changing long-term eating patterns and attitudes in anorexia nervosa is difficult, and no clearly effective psychological treatment or medication has been identified for the disorder.

Treatments for bulimia nervosa are more promising, particularly cognitive behavior therapy, and to a lesser extent, interpersonal psychotherapy and antidepressant medication. About half of clients with bulimia nervosa are free of all symptoms following treatment, about one in five continues to meet the diagnostic criteria, and the remainder have occasional relapses or subclinical levels of binge eating and compensatory behavior. Weight is generally in the normal range, and comorbid psychological disorders appear to improve with improvements in bulimia nervosa. Finally, recent research provides hope for the prevention of disordered eating, with a focused, active, and targeted delivery apparently more important than the content of the prevention program.

KEY TERMS

Go to www.prenhall.com/oltmanns for online quizzes, interactive flash cards, PowerPoint presentations, and chapter reviews.

11

Substance Use Disorders

© Jane Sterrett/theispot.com

CHAPTER OUTLINE

Symptoms

Diagnosis

Frequency

Causes

Treatment

The abuse of alcohol and other drugs is one of the most serious problems facing our society today. It is likely that you or someone close to you will be affected by the substance use issues outlined in this chapter. Alcohol and drug problems receive a great deal of attention in the popular media, as illustrated by actor Robert Downey, Jr.'s, repeated struggles with cocaine addiction and the drug related suicide of Kurt Cobain, leader of the rock group Nirvana. Research efforts, treatment priorities, and national publicity have all helped transform national attitudes about the abuse of chemical substances. The picture of the drug addict as a homeless derelict whose personality defects and lack of motivation are largely responsible for the problem is being replaced by a new view in which substance abuse is seen as a chronic mental disorder that affects people from all walks of life (Leshner, 1997).

OVERVIEW

The costs of substance abuse are astronomical. According to the Global Burden of Disease Study, alcohol use was the fourth leading cause of disability worldwide in 1990. Cirrhosis of the liver, which is frequently the result of chronic alcoholism, is a leading cause of death in the United States. In addition, alcohol plays a prominent role in many suicides, homicides, and motor vehicle accidents. The rate of deaths attributable to the use of tobacco is growing rapidly, particularly in developing countries, where 50 percent of adult men are regular smokers. By the year 2020, tobacco is expected to kill between 8 million and 9 million people annually worldwide, more than any single disease, including AIDS (Lopez & Murray, 1998).

DSM-IV-TR uses two terms to describe substance use disorders, and these terms reflect different levels of severity. **Substance dependence,** the more severe of the two forms, refers to a pattern of repeated self-administration that often results in tolerance, the need for increased amounts of the drug to achieve intoxication; withdrawal, unpleasant physical and psychological effects that the person experiences when he or she tries to stop taking the drug; and compulsive drug-taking behavior. **Substance abuse** describes a more broadly conceived, less severe pattern of drug use that is defined in terms of interference with the person's ability to fulfill major role obligations at work or at home, the recurrent use of a drug in dangerous situations, and repeated legal difficulties associated with drug use.

Addiction is another, older term that is often used to describe problems such as alcoholism.

The term has been replaced in official terminology by the term substance dependence, with which it is synonymous, but it is still used informally by many lay people.

A **drug of abuse,** sometimes called a *psychoactive substance,* is a chemical substance that alters a person's mood, level of perception, or brain functioning (Schuckit, 1999a). All drugs of abuse can be used to increase a person's psychological comfort level (make one feel "high") or to alter levels of consciousness. The list of chemicals on which people can become dependent is long and seems to be growing longer. It includes drugs that are legally available, whether over the counter or by prescription only, as well as many that are illegal (see Table 11–1).

Depressants of the central nervous system (CNS) include alcohol as well as types of medication that are used to help people sleep, called *hypnotics,* and those for relieving anxiety, known as *sedatives* or *anxiolytics.* The CNS stimulants include illegal drugs like amphetamine and cocaine, as well as nicotine and caffeine. The opiates, also called *narcotic analgesics,* can be used clinically to decrease pain. The *cannabinoids,* such as marijuana,

produce euphoria and an altered sense of time. At higher doses, they may produce hallucinations. People with a substance use disorder frequently abuse several types of drugs; this condition is known as **polysubstance abuse.**

One basic question we must address is whether we should view each type of addiction as a unique problem. Experts who answer yes to this question point out that each class of abused substance seems to affect the body in distinct ways. For example, when taken orally, some opiates can be used for long periods of time without leading to significant organ damage (Jaffe & Jaffe, 1999). Chronic use of alcohol and tobacco, on the other hand, can have a devastating impact on a person's physical health.

Despite these differences, the various forms of substance abuse share many common elements. All forms of abuse represent an inherent conflict between immediate pleasure and longer term harmful consequences. The psychological and biochemical effects on the user are often similar, as are the negative consequences for both social and occupational behaviors. The reasons for initial experimentation with a drug, the factors that influence the transition to dependence, and the processes that lead to relapse after initial efforts to change are all similar in many respects. For these reasons, many clinicians and researchers have moved toward a view of substance abuse that emphasizes common causes, behaviors, and consequences (Marlatt et al., 1988). In fact, DSM-IV-TR employs a single set of diagnostic criteria that defines dependence for all types of drugs.

The variety of problems associated with substance use disorders can be illustrated using a case study of alcohol dependence. Ernest Hemingway (1899–1961), a Nobel Prize–winning writer, was severely dependent on alcohol for many years. The following paragraphs, quoted from an article by Paul Johnson (1989), describe the progression of Hemingway's drinking and the problems that it created. They illustrate many typical features of substance dependence, as well as the devastating impact that alcohol can have on various organs of the body. Johnson's description also raises a number of interesting questions about the etiology of this disorder. Most men and women consume alcoholic beverages at some point during their lives. Why do some people become dependent on alcohol while others do not? What factors influence the transition from social drinking to abuse?

TABLE 11–1	Commonly Abused Drugs	
CLASS	**EXAMPLES**	**BRAND NAMES AND STREET NAMES**
CNS Depressants	Alcohol	beer, wine, liquor
	Barbiturates	*barbs,* Amytal, Nembutal, Seconal
	Benzodiazepines	*roofies, tanks,* Xanax, Valium, Halcion
	Methaqualone	*quaalude, ludes*
CNS Stimulants	Amphetamine	*black beauties, crosses, hearts*
	Cocaine	*blow, coke, crack, flake, rocks, snow*
	Methamphetamine	*crank, crystal, glass, ice, speed*
	Nicotine	cigars, cigarettes, smokeless tobacco
	Caffeine	coffee, tea, soft drinks
Opiates	Heroin	*horse, smack, H, junk, skag*
	Opium	laudanum, paregoric, dover's powder
	Morphine	Roxanol, Duramorph
	Methadone	Amidone, Dolophine, Methadose
	Codeine	Tylenol w/Codeine, Robitussin A-C
Cannabinoids	Marijuana	*grass, herb, pot, reefer, smoke, weed*
	Hashish	*hash*
Hallucinogens	LSD	*acid, microdot*
	Mescaline	*buttons, cactus, mesc, peyote*
	Psilocybin	*magic, mushroom, purple passion*
	Phencyclidine	PCP, *angel dust, boat, hog, love boat*
	MDMA	*ecstasy, XTC, Adam*

Note: Street names for drugs appear in italics.

◆◆

CASE STUDY Ernest Hemingway's Alcohol Dependence

Hemingway began to drink as a teenager, the local blacksmith secretly supplying him with strong cider. His mother noted his habit and always feared he would become an alcoholic. In Italy he progressed to wine, then had his first hard liquor at the officers' club in Milan. His wound [from World War I] and an unhappy love affair provoked heavy drinking: In the hospital, his wardrobe was found to be full of empty cognac bottles, an ominous sign. In Paris in the 1920s, he bought Beaune by the gallon at a wine cooperative, and would and did drink five or six bottles of red at a meal. He taught Scott Fitzgerald to drink wine direct from the bottle, which, he said, was like "a girl going swimming without her swimming suit." In New York he was "cockeyed," he said, for "several days" after signing his contract for *The Sun Also Rises*, probably his first prolonged bout.

Hemingway particularly liked to drink with women, as this seemed to him, vicariously, to signify his mother's approval. Hadley [the first of his four wives] drank a lot with him, and wrote: "I still cherish, you know, the remark you made that you almost worshipped me as a drinker." The same disastrous role was played by his pretty 1930s companion in Havana, Jane Mason, with whom he drank gin followed by champagne chasers and huge jars of iced daiquiris; it was indeed in Cuba in this decade that his drinking first got completely out of hand. One bartender there said he could "drink more martinis than any man I have ever seen." On safari, he was seen sneaking out of his tent at 5 A.M. to get a drink. His brother Leicester said that, by the end of the 1930s, at Key West, he was drinking seventeen Scotch-and-sodas a day, and often taking a bottle of champagne to bed with him at night.

At this period, his liver for the first time began to cause him acute pain. He was told by his doctor to give up alcohol completely, and indeed tried to limit his consumption to three whiskeys before dinner. But that did not last.

During World War II his drinking mounted steadily and by the mid-1940s he was reportedly pouring gin into his tea at breakfast. A.E. Hotchner, interviewing him for *Cosmopolitan* in 1948, said he dispatched seven double-size Papa Doubles (the Havana drink named after him, a mixture of rum, grapefruit and maraschino), and when he left for dinner took an eighth with him for the drive. And on top of all, there was constant whiskey: His son Patrick said his father got through a quart of whiskey a day for the last 20 years of his life.

Hemingway's ability to hold his liquor was remarkable. Lillian Ross, who wrote his profile for the *New Yorker*, does not seem to have noticed he was drunk a lot of the time he talked to her. Denis Zaphior said of his last safari: "I suppose he was drunk the whole time but seldom showed it." He also demonstrated an unusual ability to cut down his drinking or even to eliminate it altogether for brief periods, and this, in addition to his strong physique, enabled him to survive.

But despite his physique, his alcoholism had a direct impact on his health, beginning with his damaged liver in the late 1930s. By 1959, following his last big drinking bout in Spain, he was experiencing both kidney and liver trouble and possibly hemochromatosis (cirrhosis, bronzed skin, diabetes), edema of the ankles, cramps, chronic insomnia, blood-clotting and high blood uremia, as well as his skin complaints. He was impotent and prematurely aged. Even so, he was still on his feet, still alive; and the thought had become unbearable to him. His father had committed suicide because of his fear of mortal illness. Hemingway feared that his illnesses were not mortal: On July 2, 1961, after various unsuccessful treatments for depression and paranoia, he got hold of his best English double-barreled shotgun, put two canisters in it, and blew away his entire cranial vault.

Why did Hemingway long for death [and why did he drink]? He felt he was failing his art. Hemingway had many grievous faults, but there was one thing he did not lack: artistic integrity. It shines like a beacon through his whole life. He set himself the task of creating a new way of writing English, and fiction, and he succeeded. It was one of the salient events in the history of our language and is now an inescapable part of it. He devoted to this task immense resources of creative skill, energy, and patience. That in itself was difficult. But far more difficult, as he discovered, was to maintain the high creative standards he had set himself. This became apparent to him in the mid-1930s, and added to his habitual depression. From then on his few successful stories were aberrations in a long downward slide.

If Hemingway had been less of an artist, it might not have mattered to him as a man. He would simply have written and published inferior novels, as many writers do. But he knew when he wrote below his best, and the knowledge was intolerable to him. He sought the help of alcohol, even in working hours. He was first observed with a drink, a "Rum St. James," in front of him while writing in the 1920s. This custom, rare at first, became intermittent, then invariable. By the 1940s, he was said to wake at 4:30 A.M. [He] "usually starts drinking right away and writes standing up, with a pencil in one hand and a drink in another." The effect on his work was exactly as might be expected, disastrous. Hemingway began to produce large quantities of unpublishable material, or material he felt did not reach the minimum standard he set himself. Some was published nonetheless, and was seen to be inferior, even a parody of his earlier work. There were one or two exceptions, notably *The Old Man and the Sea* (1952), which won him the Nobel Prize, though there was an element of self-parody in that, too. But the general level was low, and falling, and Hemingway's awareness of his inability to recapture his genius, let alone develop it, accelerated the spinning circle of depression and drink (Johnson, 1989, pp. 58–59).

◆◆

SYMPTOMS

Substance use disorders are associated with a host of problems, many of which are illustrated in the life of Ernest Hemingway. Nevertheless, substance dependence is difficult to define. Alcoholism is one important example. George Vaillant (1995), a psychiatrist at Dartmouth Medical School and the author of an important longitudinal study of alcoholic men, notes that it is difficult to say that one specific problem or set of problems represents the core features of this disorder:

> Not only is there no single symptom that defines alcoholism, but often it is not who is drinking but who is watching that defines a symptom. A drinker may worry that he has an alcohol problem because of his impotence. His wife may drag him to an alcohol clinic because he slapped her during a blackout. Once he is at the clinic, the doctor calls him an alcoholic because of his abnormal liver-function tests. Later society labels him a drunk because of a second episode of driving while intoxicated. (p. 24)

The number of problems that a person encounters seems to provide the most useful distinction between people who are dependent on a substance and those who are not. These problems can be sorted loosely into two general areas: (1) patterns of pathological consumption, including psychological and physiological dependence; and (2) consequences that follow a prolonged pattern of abuse, including social and occupational impairment, legal and financial difficulties, and deteriorating medical condition.

It might seem that the actual amount of a drug of abuse that a person consumes would be the best indication of the existence of a problem. Hemingway, for example, clearly consumed enormous quantities of alcohol over a period of many years. The average person with an alcohol use disorder does drink more frequently and in larger quantities than the average person without an alcohol use disorder (Dawson, 2000). Nevertheless, the amount of a drug that a specific person consumes is not a good way to define substance use disorders, because people vary significantly in the amount of any given drug they can consume. Factors such as age, gender, activity level, and overall physical health influence a person's ability to metabolize various kinds of drugs. For example, some people can drink a lot without developing problems; others drink relatively little and have difficulties.

The Concept of Substance Dependence

Many psychological features or problems are associated with dependence on chemical substances. One such feature involves *craving*. This word is frequently used to describe a forceful urge to use drugs, but the relationship between craving and drug use is actually very complex (Sayette et al., 2000). People who are dependent on drugs often say that they take the drug to control how they are feeling. They need it to relieve negative mood states or to avoid withdrawal symptoms from previous episodes. They may feel compelled to take the drug as a way to prepare for certain activities, such as public speaking, writing, or sex. Some clinicians refer to this condition as **psychological dependence.**

One useful index of craving is the amount of time that the person spends planning to take the drug. Is access to drugs or alcohol a constant preoccupation? If the person is invited to a party or is planning to eat at a restaurant, does he or she always inquire about the availability of alcoholic drinks? If the person is going to spend a few days at the beach in a neighboring state, will he or she worry more about whether liquor stores will be closed on weekends or holidays than about having enough food, clothes, or recreational equipment?

As the problem progresses, it is not unusual for the person who abuses drugs to try to stop. In the case of alcoholism, for example, it is possible for even heavy drinkers to abstain for at least short periods of time. Most clinicians and researchers agree that diminished control over

"Excuse me, Reverend, but what, exactly, do you have to do to get a drink around here?"

drinking is a crucial feature of the disorder (Walters, 1999). Some experts have described this issue as "freedom of choice." When a person first experiments with the use of alcohol, his or her behavior is clearly voluntary; the person is not compelled to drink. After drinking heavily for a long period of time, most people with a drinking disorder try to stop. Unfortunately, efforts at self-control are typically short-lived and usually fail.

Tolerance and Withdrawal   Two particularly important features of substance dependence are the phenomena known as tolerance and withdrawal. These symptoms are usually interpreted as evidence of *physiological dependence*. **Tolerance** refers to the process through which the nervous system becomes less sensitive to the effects of alcohol or any other drug of abuse. For example, a person who has been regularly exposed to alcohol will need to drink increased quantities to achieve the same subjective effect ("buzz," "high," or level of intoxication).

The development of drug tolerance seems to be the result of three separate mechanisms (Julien, 2001). Two are pharmacological and the third is behavioral. *Metabolic tolerance* develops when repeated exposure to a drug causes the person's liver to produce more enzymes that are used to metabolize, that is, break down, the drug. The drug, therefore, is metabolized more quickly and the person has to take increasing larger doses in order to maintain the same level in his or her body. *Pharmacodynamic tolerance* occurs when receptors in the brain (see Figure 2–2 on page 41) adapt to continued presence of the drug. The neuron may adapt by reducing the number of receptors or by reducing their sensitivity to the drug. This process is known as *down regulation*. The third process involved in drug tolerance involves *behavioral conditioning mechanisms* (Siegel, 2001). Cues that are regularly associated with the administration of a drug begin to function as conditioned stimuli and elicit a conditioned response that is opposite in direction to the natural effect of the drug. As this compensatory response increases in strength, it competes with the drug response so that larger amounts of the drug must be taken to achieve the same effect.

Some drugs are much more likely than others to produce a buildup of tolerance (APA, 2000). The most substantial tolerance effects are found among heavy users of opioids, such as heroin, and CNS stimulants, such as amphetamine and cocaine. Pronounced tolerance is also found among people who use alcohol and nicotine. The evidence is unclear regarding tolerance effects and prolonged use of marijuana and hashish. Most people who use cannabinoids are not aware of tolerance effects, but these effects have been demonstrated in animal studies. Hallucinogens (LSD) and phencyclidine (PCP) may not lead to the development of tolerance.

What evidence is needed to show that a drug is addictive?

Withdrawal refers to the symptoms experienced when a person stops using a drug. The symptom can go on for several days. For example, alcohol is a CNS depressant, and the heavy drinker's system becomes accustomed to functioning in a chronically depressed state. When the person stops drinking, the system begins to rebound within several hours, producing many unpleasant side effects—hand tremors, sweating, nausea, anxiety, and insomnia. The most serious forms of withdrawal include convulsions and visual, tactile, or auditory hallucinations. Some people develop delirium, a sudden disturbance of consciousness that is accompanied by changes in cognitive processes such as lack of awareness of the environment or inability to sustain attention (see Chapter 14). This syndrome is called *alcohol withdrawal delirium* in DSM-IV-TR (more traditionally known as *delirium tremens*, or DTs) if it is induced by withdrawal from alcohol.

The symptoms of withdrawal vary considerably for different kinds of substances. Table 11–2 compares various drugs of abuse in terms of withdrawal and other related characteristics. Unpleasant reactions are most evident during withdrawal from alcohol, opioids, and the general class of sedatives, hypnotics, and anxiolytics (such as Valium and Xanax). Withdrawal symptoms are also associated with stimulants, such as amphetamine, cocaine, and nicotine, though they are sometimes less pronounced than those associated with alcohol and opioids.

Withdrawal symptoms are not often seen after repeated use of cannabis or hallucinogens, and they have not been demonstrated with phencyclidine. Caffeine is the most widely used psychoactive substance in the world. We all know people who crave coffee, especially in the morning. And some heavy coffee users experience severe headaches when they stop drinking caffeine (Nehlig, 1999). You may be surprised

TABLE 11-2	Comparison of Various Psychoactive Substances			
SUBSTANCE	**CAN PRODUCE DEPENDENCE**	**CAN PRODUCE INTOXICATION**	**ASSOCIATED WITHDRAWAL**	**CAN PRODUCE DEMENTIA**
Alcohol	yes	yes	yes	yes
Amphetamines	yes	yes	yes	no
Caffeine	no	yes	no	no
Marijuana/hashish	yes	yes	no	no
Cocaine	yes	yes	yes	no
Hallucinogens	yes	yes	no	no
Inhalants	yes	yes	no	yes
Nicotine	yes	no	yes	no
Opiates	yes	yes	yes	no
Phencyclidine (PCP)	yes	yes	no	no
Sedatives, hypnotics, and anxiolytics	yes	yes	yes	yes

Reprinted with permission from the *Diagnostic and Statistical Manual of Mental Disorders,* Fourth Edition, Text Revision. Copyright © 2000 by the American Psychiatric Association.

to see in Table 11–2 that, according to DSM-IV-TR, the use of caffeine is not considered to lead to dependence or withdrawal symptoms. The authors of DSM-IV-TR acknowledged these symptoms, but they decided that the symptoms did not cause clinically significant distress and impairment and, therefore, should not be included in the manual as a type of mental disorder.

All these problems serve to emphasize the fact that symptoms of substance use disorders fall along a continuum. It is convenient to consider these problems in terms of qualitative distinctions: people who can control their drinking and those who cannot; people who crave alcohol and those who do not; people who have developed a tolerance to the drug and those who have not; and so on. In fact, there are no clear dividing lines on any of these dimensions. Drug use disorders lie on a continuum of severity (Bucholz et al., 1996). For this reason it is extremely difficult to define the nature of substance dependence disorders.

People can become dependent on many different kinds of drugs. Although patterns of dependence are similar in some ways for all drugs, each type of drug also has some unique features. In the next few pages we briefly review some of the most important classes of drugs. For

each group, we will describe short-term effects on physiology and behavior, as well as the consequences of long-term abuse. Unless otherwise specified, these descriptions are based on information presented by William McKim (2000) in his textbook on drugs and behavior.

Alcohol

Alcohol affects virtually every organ and system in the body (Tabakoff & Hoffman, 1999). After alcohol has been ingested, it is absorbed through membranes in the stomach, small intestine, and colon. The rate at which it is absorbed is influenced by many variables, including the concentration of alcohol in the beverage (for example, distilled spirits are absorbed more rapidly than beer or wine), the volume and rate of consumption, and the presence of food in the digestive system. After it is absorbed, alcohol is distributed to all the body's organ systems. Almost all the alcohol that a person consumes is eventually broken down or metabolized in the liver. The rate at which alcohol is metabolized varies from person to person, but the average person can metabolize about 1 ounce of 90-proof liquor or 12 ounces of beer per hour (Nathan, 1993). If the person's consumption rate exceeds this metabolic limit, then blood alcohol levels will rise.

Short-Term Effects Blood alcohol levels are measured in terms of the amount of alcohol per unit of blood. A "drink" is considered to be 12 ounces of beer, 4 ounces of wine, or 1 ounce of 86-proof whiskey. The average 160-pound man who consumes 5 drinks in 1 hour will have a blood alcohol level of 100 milligrams (mg) per 100 milliliters (ml) of blood, or 100 mg percent (Kowalski, 1998). There is a strong correlation between blood alcohol levels and CNS intoxicating effects. According to DSM-IV-TR, the symptoms of alcohol intoxication include slurred speech, lack of coordination, an unsteady gait, nystagmus (involuntary to-and-fro movement of the eyeballs induced when the person looks upward or to the side), impaired attention or memory, and stupor or coma.

In most states, the legal limit of alcohol concentration for driving is 100 mg percent. Some state legislatures have lowered this limit to 80 mg percent, because slowed reaction times and interference with other driving skills may occur at lower blood alcohol levels (Mejeur, 1999). People with levels of 150 to 300 mg percent will almost always act intoxicated. Neurological and respiration complications begin to appear at higher levels. There is an extreme risk of coma leading to toxic death when blood alcohol levels go above 400 mg percent.

Long-Term Consequences   The prolonged use and abuse of alcohol can have a devastating impact on many areas of a person's life. The disruption of relationships with family and friends can be especially painful. The impact of Hemingway's drinking on his writing career and his family life is clearly evident. Most critics agree that his literary accomplishments were confined primarily to the early stages of his career, before his alcoholism began to interfere with his ability to write. Drinking also took its toll on his marriages, which were characterized by frequent and occasionally furious conflict in public and by repeated episodes of verbal and physical abuse in private (Johnson, 1989). Also, the heavy use of alcohol by a pregnant woman can cause damage to her fetus (see Chapter 15).

Many people who abuse alcohol experience blackouts. In some cases, abusers may continue to function without passing out, but they will be unable to remember their behavior. An example is the person who drives home drunk from a party and in the morning finds a dent in the car bumper but can't remember how it got there. Sometimes problem drinkers will be told by a friend about how they behaved at the previous night's party, but they cannot remember what they did.

Regular heavy use of alcohol is also likely to interfere with job performance. Coworkers and supervisors may complain. Attendance at work may become sporadic. Eventually the heavy drinker may be suspended or fired. Related to job performance is the problem of financial difficulties. Losing one's job is clearly detrimental to one's financial stability, as are the costs of divorce, health care, liquor, and so on.

Many heavy drinkers encounter problems with legal authorities. These problems may include arrests for drunken driving and public intoxication, as well as charges of spouse and child abuse. Many forms of violent behavior are more likely to be committed when a person has been drinking.

On a biological level, prolonged exposure to high levels of alcohol can disrupt the functions of several important organ systems, especially the liver, pancreas, gastrointestinal system, cardiovascular system, and endocrine system. The symptoms of alcoholism include many secondary health problems, such as cirrhosis of the liver, heart problems (in part, the result of being overweight), and various forms of cancer, as well as severe and persistent forms of dementia and memory impairment or amnestic disorders, such as Korsakoff's syndrome (see Chapter 14). Alcoholism is also associated with nutritional disturbances of many types, because chronic abusers often drink instead of eating balanced meals. In fact, over an extended period of time, alcohol dependence has more negative health consequences than does abuse of any other drug, with the exception of nicotine.

The misuse of alcohol leads to an enormous number of severe injuries and premature deaths in every region of the world (Murray & Lopez, 1997). The specific impact of alcohol varies among geographic regions, in part because of differences in the age structure of different populations. Deaths that result from alcohol-related injuries are much more common among young men, while deaths from alcohol-related diseases are responsible for more deaths among older men (see Figure 11–1 on page 352).

Video Case
ALCOHOLISM

CHRIS

"The toughest thing I ever did was admitting that I had a problem."

On your CD-ROM menu, select "Substance Use Disorders" and click on "Alcoholism: Chris." How was Chris's pattern of drinking different from that of his friends?

The negative consequences of alcohol dependence typically include a devastating impact on social relationships and work performance.

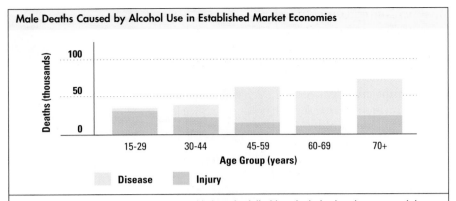

Male Deaths Caused by Alcohol Use in Established Market Economies

FIGURE 11–1: Young men are more likely to be killed by alcohol-related injuries, while older men often die as a result of alcohol-related disease.

Source: C.J.L. Murray & A.D. Lopez (1997). Global mortality, disability, and the contribution of risk factors: Global burden of disease study. *Lancet, 349,* 1436–1442. Copyright © 1997. Reprinted by permission of Elsevier, Ltd.

Nicotine

Nicotine is the active ingredient in tobacco, which is its only natural source. Nicotine is almost never taken in its pure form because it can be toxic. Very high doses have extremely unpleasant effects. Controlled doses are easier to achieve by smoking or chewing tobacco, which provides a diluted concentration of nicotine. Another way of ingesting nicotine is to inhale snuff (powdered tobacco) into the nostrils. When tobacco smoke is inhaled, nicotine is absorbed into the blood through the mucous membranes of the lungs. This route of administration results in the highest concentrations of nicotine because it is carried directly from the lungs to the heart and from there to the brain.

Short-Term Effects The effects of nicotine on the peripheral nervous system (see Chapter 2) include increases in heart rate and blood pressure. In the central nervous system, nicotine has pervasive effects on a number of neurotransmitter systems (Houezec, 1998). It stimulates the release of norepinephrine from several sites, producing CNS arousal. Nicotine also causes the release of dopamine and norepinephrine in the mesolimbic dopamine pathway, also known as the reward system of the brain. The serotonin system, which also mediates the effects of antidepressant medication, is influenced by nicotine. In fact, some people have suggested that nicotine mimics the effects of antidepressant drugs.

Nicotine has a complex influence on subjective mood states. Many people say that they smoke because it makes them feel more relaxed.

Some believe that it helps them control their subjective response to stress. This phenomenon is somewhat paradoxical in light of the fact that nicotine leads to increased arousal of the sympathetic nervous system. Various explanations may account for this apparent inconsistency. One involves differences in dosage levels; low doses of nicotine may lead to increased arousal while higher doses lead to relaxation. Another alternative involves withdrawal. Regular smokers may feel relaxed when they smoke a cigarette because it relieves unpleasant symptoms of withdrawal.

Long-Term Consequences Nicotine is one of the most harmful and deadly addicting drugs. Considerable evidence points to the development of both tolerance and withdrawal symptoms among people who regularly smoke or chew tobacco. The physiological symptoms of withdrawal from nicotine include drowsiness, lightheadedness, headache, muscle tremors, and nausea. People who are attempting to quit smoking typically experience sleeping problems, weight gain, concentration difficulties, and mood swings ranging from anxiety to anger and depression (Piasecki, Fiore, & Baker, 1998). From a psychological point of view, withdrawal from nicotine is just as difficult as withdrawal from heroin. Many people report that these symptoms disappear after a few months, but some have serious cravings for several years after they quit.

People who smoke tobacco increase their risk of developing many fatal diseases, including heart disease, lung disease (bronchitis and emphysema), and various types of cancer (Kozlowski et al., 2001). Eighty percent of all deaths caused by lung cancer can be attributed to smoking tobacco. More than 3.5 million people in the world die prematurely each year as a result of tobacco. Large numbers of people are also killed or injured in fires caused by careless smoking. Women who smoke are also more likely to experience fertility problems. Babies born to mothers who smoked during pregnancy are also likely to weigh less than those born to mothers who do not smoke, and they may be more vulnerable to certain types of birth defects.

Amphetamine and Cocaine

Members of the class of drugs known as **psychomotor stimulants** produce their effects by simulating the actions of certain neurotransmitters, specifically epinephrine, norepinephrine, dopamine, and serotonin (as discussed later in this chapter). Cocaine is a naturally occurring stimulant drug that is extracted from the leaf of a small tree that grows at high elevations, as in the Andes Mountains. The amphetamines (such as dexedrine and methamphetamine) are produced synthetically.

The stimulants can be taken orally, injected, or inhaled. It is easier to maintain a constant blood level when the drugs are taken orally. They are absorbed more slowly through the digestive system, and their effects are less potent. More dramatic effects are achieved by injecting the drug or sniffing it. Cocaine can also be smoked, using various procedures that have been popularized in the past several years. Some people employ a particularly dangerous procedure called "freebasing," in which the drug is heated and its vapors are inhaled. Many people have been seriously burned when these highly combustible chemicals are accidentally ignited.

Short-Term Effects

Cocaine and amphetamines are called stimulants because they activate the sympathetic nervous system (Constable, 2004). They increase heart rate and blood pressure and dilate the blood vessels and the air passages of the lungs. Stimulants also suppress the appetite and prevent sleep. These effects have been among the reasons for the popularity and frequent abuse of stimulants. They have been used, for example, by truck drivers who want to stay awake on long trips and by students who want to stay awake to study for exams. Unfortunately, in addition to their addicting properties, large doses of amphetamines can also lead to dizziness, confusion, and panic states, which clearly interfere with activities such as driving and studying.

Many people use (and abuse) stimulants because they induce a positive mood state. When they are injected, amphetamines and cocaine produce very similar subjective effects, but the effects of cocaine do not last as long. Low doses of amphetamines make people feel more confident, friendly, and energetic. At higher doses, the person is likely to experience a brief, intense feeling of euphoria. The rushes associated with snorting or injecting cocaine are frequently described in sexual terms. Although many people believe that cocaine enhances sexual arousal and pleasure, most of the evidence suggests that prolonged use leads to sexual dysfunction (Jaffe, 1995). Tolerance develops quickly to the euphoric effects of stimulant drugs. The feelings of exhilaration and well-being are typically followed, several hours later, by the onset of lethargy and a mildly depressed or irritable mood.

Acute overdoses of stimulant drugs can result in irregular heartbeat, convulsions, coma, and death. The highly publicized overdose deaths of several prominent athletes, such as that of All-American basketball star Len Bias in 1986, indicate that the intense cardiovascular effects of cocaine can be fatal, even among people who are otherwise strong and healthy. Individual differences in sensitivity to the subjective effects of cocaine may play a role in cocaine-related deaths. In other words, people who are resistant to cocaine-induced euphoria may consume unusually large quantities of the drug while trying to achieve the rush that others have described.

Long-Term Consequences

High doses of amphetamines and cocaine can lead to the onset of psychosis. The risk of a psychotic reaction seems to increase with repeated exposure to the drug (Bolla, Cadet, & London, 1998). This syndrome can appear in people who have no prior history of mental disorder, and it usually disappears a few days after the drug has been cleared. Stimulants can also increase the severity of symptoms among people who had already developed

What are the long-term consequences of abusing psychomotor stimulants?

Singer Whitney Houston has experienced many legal, occupational, and personal problems as a consequence of her abuse of cocaine, alcohol, and other drugs.

some type of psychotic condition. The symptoms of amphetamine psychosis include auditory and visual hallucinations, as well as delusions of persecution and grandeur.

As with other forms of addiction, the most devastating effects of stimulant drugs frequently center around the disruption of occupational and social roles. The compulsion to continue taking cocaine can lead to physical exhaustion and financial ruin. People who are dependent on cocaine must spend enormous amounts of money to support their habit. They may have to sell important assets, such as their homes and cars, in order to finance extended binges. Some people become involved in a variety of criminal activities in order to raise enough money to purchase drugs.

Prolonged use of amphetamines has also been linked to an increase in violent behavior, but it is not clear whether this phenomenon is due to the drug itself or to the lifestyles with which it is frequently associated. Some violence might be related to a drug-induced increase in paranoia and hostility. Statistics concerning drugs and violent crime are very difficult to interpret. The direct effects of the drug on human behavior are confounded with various economic and social factors that are associated with buying, selling, and using an expensive, illegal drug like cocaine.

People who discontinue taking stimulant drugs do not typically experience severe withdrawal symptoms. The most common reaction is depression. Long-term exposure to high doses of amphetamine can lead to a profound state of clinical depression, which is often accompanied by ideas of suicide.

Opiates

The **opiates** (sometimes called opioids) are drugs that have properties similar to those of opium. The natural source of opium is a poppy with a white flower. The main active ingredients in opium are morphine and codeine, both of which are widely used in medicine, particularly to relieve pain. They are available legally only by prescription in the United States. In Canada, small quantities of codeine are available without a prescription in over-the-counter painkillers and cough medicines. Heroin is a synthetic opiate that is made by modifying the morphine molecule. It was originally marketed as an alternative

to morphine when physicians believed, erroneously, that heroin is not addictive.

The opiates can be taken orally, injected, or inhaled. Opium is sometimes eaten or smoked. When morphine is used as a painkiller, it is taken orally so that it is absorbed slowly through the digestive system. People who use morphine for subjective effects most often inject the drug because it leads more quickly to high concentrations in brain tissue. Heroin can be injected, inhaled through the nose in the form of snuff, or smoked and inhaled through a pipe or tube.

Short-Term Effects The opiates can induce a state of dreamlike euphoria, which may be accompanied by increased sensitivity in hearing and vision. People who inject morphine or heroin also experience a rush—a brief, intense feeling of pleasure that is sometimes described as being like an orgasm in the entire body.

Laboratory studies of mood indicate that the positive, emotional effects of opiates do not last. They are soon replaced by long-term negative changes in mood and emotion. These unpleasant experiences are relieved for 30 to 60 minutes after each new injection of the drug, but they eventually color most of the rest of the person's waking experience.

The opiates can induce nausea and vomiting among novice users, constrict the pupils of the eye, and disrupt the coordination of the digestive system. Continued use of opiates decreases the level of sex hormones in both women and men, resulting in reduced sex drive and impaired fertility.

Some people mix cocaine and opiates into a mixture known as a *speedball* to enhance these subjective feelings. The following brief case describes the preparation of this combination of drugs and one heroin addict's immediate reaction to the injection of a speedball.

◆◆◆

BRIEF CASE STUDY

Feelings After Injecting Heroin

He pushes the plunger on the syringe, squirting water into the heroin powder, then strikes a match and waves it just under the metal lid. The liquid bubbles and the heroin quickly dissolves with very little heat required. *That's good,* he thinks. Sometimes the dope is so good it needs hardly any fire to dissolve it. Next, he shakes in a couple of small rocks of cocaine from the foil wrapper and is impressed that they vanish immediately in the solution. He swirls the liquid around, rips open the filter from one of his Marlboros, and uses the white fibers as a strainer through which to draw the liquid speedball into the syringe. He carefully places the loaded syringe between his teeth. He rolls up his sleeve, removes his belt with one hand, and takes a seat on the edge of the toilet. He wraps the belt tight around his right arm and hopes he can get a clean hit on one of the veins he watches come up. *There, I'll go there.*

The needle point feels sharp going in, which is good; it means he's got an unused needle. When he pulls back on the plunger a little stream of blood slithers up into the syringe, discoloring the slightly yellow liquid. He loosens the belt, careful not to dislodge the needle from the vein, takes a breath, and slowly pushes the liquid into his arm. He pulls the needle out and dabs with his finger at the drop of blood left behind on his arm. As he does this he feels the freeze in his arm from the cocaine. His arm feels numb. Then it reaches his stomach and mouth. His heart races. He tastes the medicinal flavor just as the first wave of rushes is reaching his brain. His stomach heaves. His scalp tingles and he gets a little scared at first—the wave of sensation is stronger than usual. He fights the urge to vomit, the heroin kicks in and the nausea retreats as the warm, heroin heat replaces the heart-thumping freeze caused by the cocaine. His heart starts to slow down, or so it seems. A quiet, hollow siren rages in his head. The familiar beads of perspiration crowd each other on his forehead, and one drops onto his arm when he bends over to begin cleaning everything up. He puts away his paraphernalia, threads his belt into his pants, and sits down again. *Good stuff, very good,* he thinks as he nods for a second.

Back on Houston Street now, he decides to have a cup of espresso in a little coffee shop he comes upon. Sitting back at a table with a view of the street, he savors the thick hot coffee, lights a cigarette, and blows the smoke to the ceiling. *Nothing hurts,* he thinks. The lousy job that he needs to hold onto, the flak he catches from his wife, the fact that he is turning forty and doesn't have anything to show for his life—none of it fazes him, but he still thinks about it. A spotty work history, no college, and rent that is three weeks late don't matter right now. He feels warm, loose, and sexy. Was the waitress's smile a flirt or was she smiling because she caught him nodding? Doesn't matter. He smiles back and thinks maybe he can buy his wife a gold-plated necklace instead of the real one. It will look just like the one she pointed out anyway.

And that was what he did (Fernandez, 1998, pp. 72–73).

High doses of opiates can lead to a comatose state, severely depressed breathing, and convulsions. The number of people admitted to hospital emergency rooms for treatment of heroin overdoses increased substantially during the 1990s. Between 3,000 and 4,000 people die from accidental overdoses of heroin in the United States each year (Leland, 1996).

Long-Term Consequences   The effects of opiates on occupational performance and health depend in large part on the amount of drugs that the person takes. At high doses, people who are addicted to opiates become chronically lethargic and lose their motivation to remain productive. At low doses, some people who use opiates for an extended period of time can remain healthy and work productively in spite of their addiction. This functioning is, of course, dependent on the person having easy and relatively inexpensive access to opiates. One possibility is being maintained by a physician on methadone, a synthetic opiate that is sometimes used therapeutically as an alternative to heroin.

People who are addicted to opiates become preoccupied with finding and using the drug, in order to experience the rush and to avoid withdrawal symptoms. Tolerance develops rather quickly, and the person's daily dose increases regularly until it eventually levels off and remains steady. Many of the severe health consequences of opiate use are the result of the lifestyle of the addict rather than the drug itself. The enormous expenses and difficulties associated with obtaining illegal opiates almost invariably consume all the person's resources. The person typically neglects housing, nutrition, and health care in the search for another fix. Heroin addicts are much more likely than other people in the general population to die from AIDS, violence, and suicide.

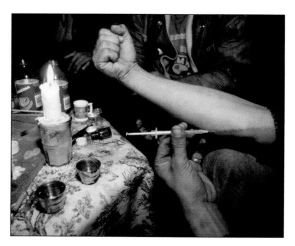

The positive, emotional effects of opiates do not last. They are soon replaced by long-term negative changes in mood and emotion.

Barbiturates and Benzodiazepines

The families of drugs known as barbiturates and benzodiazepines are also known informally as tranquilizers, hypnotics, and sedatives. *Tranquilizers* are used to decrease anxiety or agitation. *Hypnotics* are used to help people sleep. *Sedative* is a more general term that describes drugs that calm people or reduce excitement (other than the relief of anxiety). The **barbiturates,** such as phenobarbital (Nembutal) and amobarbital (Amytal), were used for a variety of purposes, including the treatment of chronic anxiety. The **benzodiazepines,** which include diazepam (Valium) and alprazolam (Xanax), have replaced the barbiturates in the treatment of anxiety disorders, in large part because of their lower potential for producing a lethal overdose.

Short-Term Effects   Sedatives and hypnotics can lead to a state of intoxication that is identical to that associated with alcohol. It is characterized by impaired judgment, slowness of speech, lack of coordination, a narrowed range of attention, and disinhibition of sexual and aggressive impulses. Intravenous use of barbiturates can lead quickly to a pleasant, warm, drowsy feeling that is similar to the experience achieved when taking opiates. The benzodiazepines can sometimes lead to an increase in hostile and aggressive behavior. Some clinicians call this a "rage reaction" or aggressive dyscontrol.

Long-Term Consequences   People who abruptly stop taking high doses of benzodiazepines may experience symptoms that are sometimes called a *discontinuance syndrome.* These symptoms can include a return—and, in some cases, a worsening—of the original anxiety symptoms, if the medication was being used to treat an anxiety disorder. The person may also develop new symptoms that are directly associated with drug withdrawal. These include irritability, paranoia, sleep disturbance, agitation, muscle tension, restlessness, and perceptual disturbances. Withdrawal symptoms are less likely to occur if the medication is discontinued gradually rather than abruptly.

Cannabis

Marijuana and hashish are derived from the hemp plant, *Cannabis sativa.* The most common active ingredient in cannabis is a compound called delta-9-tetrahydro-cannabinol (THC). Because every part of the plant contains THC, cannabis can be prepared for consumption in several ways. **Marijuana** refers to the dried leaves and flowers, which can be smoked in a cigarette or pipe. It can also be baked in brownies and ingested orally. **Hashish** refers to the dried resin from the top of the female cannabis plant. It can be smoked or eaten after being baked in cookies or brownies.

Oral administration of cannabis material leads to slow and incomplete absorption. Therefore the dose must be two or three times larger to achieve the same subjective effect as when it is smoked. Most of the drug is metabolized in the liver.

Short-Term Effects   The subjective effects of marijuana are almost always pleasant. "Getting high" on marijuana refers to a pervasive sense of well-being and happiness. Laboratory research has shown that marijuana can have variable effects on a person's mood. Many people begin to feel happy, but some become anxious and paranoid. The mood of other people seems to be especially important. After smoking marijuana, a person's mood may become more easily influenced by how other people are behaving.

Cannabis intoxication is often accompanied by *temporal disintegration*, a condition in which people have trouble retaining and organizing information, even over relatively short periods of time. Conversations may become disjointed because the drug interferes with the people's ability to recall what they have said or planned to say. Lapses in attention and concentration problems are frequent.

Long-Term Consequences   The issue of the addictive properties of cannabis remains controversial (Fortgang, 1999; Onaivi, 2003). Some tolerance effects to THC have been observed in laboratory animals. Tolerance effects in humans remain ambiguous. Most evidence suggests that people do not develop tolerance to THC unless they are exposed to high doses over an extended period of time. Some people actually report that they become more sensitive (rather than less sensitive) to the effects of marijuana after repeated use. This phenomenon is called *reverse tolerance.* Although reverse tolerance has been reported casually by frequent users, it has not been demonstrated in a laboratory situation, where dosage levels can be carefully controlled.

Withdrawal symptoms are unlikely to develop among occasional smokers of marijuana. People who have been exposed to continuous, high doses of THC may experience withdrawal symptoms, such as irritability, restlessness, and insomnia.

Prolonged heavy use of marijuana may lead to certain types of performance deficits on neuropsychological tests, especially those involving sustained attention, learning, and decision making (Pope & Yurgelun-Todd, 1996). These effects should be interpreted cautiously. Follow-up studies of adults who used cannabis over a period of several years did not find evidence of cognitive decline associated with the drug (Lyketsos et al., 1999).

Hallucinogens and Related Drugs

Drugs that are called **hallucinogens** cause people to experience hallucinations. Although many other types of drugs can lead to hallucinations at toxic levels, hallucinogens cause hallucinations at relatively low doses. There are many different types of hallucinogens, and they have very different neurophysiological effects. The molecular structure of many hallucinogens is similar to the molecular structure of various neurotransmitters, such as serotonin and norepinephrine. The most common hallucinogen is a synthetic drug called LSD (D-lysergic acid diethylamide), which bears a strong chemical resemblance to serotonin. It achieves its effect by interacting with certain types of serotonin receptors in the brain. *Psilocybin* is another type of hallucinogen whose chemical structure resembles that of serotonin. It is found in different types of mushrooms, which grow primarily in the southern United States and Mexico. Mescaline is a type of hallucinogen that resembles norepinephrine. It is the active ingredient in a small, spineless cactus called peyote. Mescaline and psilocybin have been used in religious ceremonies by various Native American peoples for many centuries.

MDMA (methylene-dioxy-methamphetamine, also known as ecstasy) is one of several synthetic amphetamine derivates. It could be classified as a stimulant but most texts list it as a type of hallucinogen (Julien, 2001). MDMA is also known as a "club drug" because it is popular among people who attend "raves" and dance clubs (LSD and methamphetamine are also known as club drugs). MDMA is usually taken as

a tablet, but the powder form can be inhaled or injected. Within half an hour of ingesting MDMA orally, the person begins to experience an enhanced mood state and a feeling of well-being that often lasts several hours. Although it does not produce vivid hallucinations, MDMA does lead to changes in perceptual experiences, such as distortions in the sense of time and space, as well as increased sensory awareness. It also produces changes in blood pressure and can interfere with the body's ability to regulate its temperature.

Phencyclidine (PCP) is another synthetic drug that is often classified with the hallucinogens, although its effects are very different than those associated with LSD and mescaline. It was originally developed as a painkiller. Small doses of PCP lead to relaxation, warmth, and numbness. At higher doses, PCP can induce psychotic behavior, including delusional thinking, catatonic motor behavior, manic excitement, and sudden mood changes. The drug is typically sold in a crystallized form that can be sprinkled on leaves, such as tobacco, marijuana, or parsley, and then smoked. Some people snort it or inject it after dissolving the crystals in water.

Short-Term Effects   The effects of hallucinogenic drugs are difficult to study empirically because they are based primarily in subjective experience. They typically induce vivid, and occasionally spectacular, visual images. During the early phase of this drug experience, the images often take the form of colorful geometric patterns. The later phase is more likely to be filled with meaningful

MDMA is known as a "club drug" because it is popular among people who attend "raves" and dance clubs. It causes changes in perceptual experiences, such as distortions in the sense of time and space, as well as increased sensory awareness.

images of people, animals, and places. The images may change rapidly, and they sometimes follow an explosive pattern of movement.

Although these hallucinatory experiences are usually pleasant, they are occasionally frightening. "Bad trips" are a decidedly unpleasant experience that can lead to panic attacks and the fear of losing one's mind. People can usually be talked through this process by constantly reminding them that the experience is drug-induced and will be over soon.

Most hallucinogens are not particularly toxic. People do not die from taking an overdose of LSD, psilocybin, or mescaline. However, PCP is much more toxic. High doses can lead to coma, convulsions, respiratory arrest, and brain hemorrhage. MDMA (Ecstasy) can damage serotonin neurons on a permanent basis, and it has been associated with some fatalities (Gold et al., 2001).

Long-Term Consequences The use of hallucinogens follows a different pattern than that associated with most other drugs. Hallucinogens, with the possible exception of PCP, are used sporadically and on special occasions rather than continuously. If these drugs are taken repeatedly within 2 or 3 days, their effects disappear. Most people do not increase their use of hallucinogens over time. People who stop taking hallucinogens after continued use do not experience problems; there seem to be no withdrawal symptoms associated with the hallucinogens that resemble serotonin and norepinephrine. The perceptual effects of hallucinogenic drugs almost always wear off after several hours. There are cases, however, in which these drugs have induced persistent psychotic behavior. Most experts interpret these examples as an indication that the drug experience can trigger the onset of psychosis in people who were already vulnerable to that type of disorder. As genes involved in the predisposition toward psychosis are identified, it will become possible to test this hypothesis.

Some people who have taken hallucinogens experience *flashbacks*—brief visual aftereffects that can occur at unpredictable intervals long after the drug has been cleared from the person's body. Scientists do not understand the mechanisms that are responsible for flashbacks. Flashbacks may be more likely to occur when the person is under stress or after the person has used another drug, such as marijuana.

DIAGNOSIS

The problems that we have reviewed indicate that substance dependence represents an extremely diverse set of problems. Everyone—clinicians and researchers, as well as those who abuse drugs and their families—seems to recognize the existence of a serious psychological disorder. But does it have a core? What is the best way to define it? In the following pages we briefly review some of the ways in which alcoholism and drug abuse have been defined. We must begin with the recognition that alcoholism and other types of addiction have not always been viewed as medical conditions that require treatment (Walters, 1999).

Brief History of Legal and Illegal Substances

One of the most widely recognized facts about alcohol consumption is that drinking patterns vary tremendously from one culture to the next and, within the same culture, from one point in time to another. Public attitudes toward the consumption of alcohol have changed dramatically during the course of U.S. history. For example, heavy drinking was not generally considered to be a serious problem in colonial times (Levine, 1978). In fact, it seemed to be an integral part of daily life. The average amount of alcohol consumed per person each year was much higher in those days than it is today. A typical American in the eighteenth century drank approximately 4 gallons of alcohol a year; the corresponding figure for our own society is about 2.5 gallons (Fingarette, 1988). Drunkenness was not considered to be either socially deviant or symptomatic of medical illness.

Public attitudes toward alcohol changed dramatically in the United States during the first half of the nineteenth century. Members of the temperance movement preached against the consumption of alcohol in any form. Temperance workers ardently believed that anyone who drank alcohol would become a drunkard. Their arguments were largely moral and religious rather than medical or scientific, and many of their publications included essays on the personality weaknesses that were associated with such morally reprehensible behaviors (Levine, 1978). The temperance movement was, in fact, able to persuade many thousands of people to abandon the consumption of alcohol.

The movement finally succeeded in banning the manufacture and sale of alcoholic beverages when Congress approved the Eighteenth Amendment to the Constitution in 1919. During the following years, known as the Prohibition era, the average consumption of alcohol fell substantially, and the incidence of associated medical illnesses, such as cirrhosis of the liver, also declined. Nevertheless, these laws were extremely difficult to enforce, and Prohibition was repealed in 1933.

DSM-IV-TR

As we noted at the beginning of this chapter, DSM-IV-TR divides addictions into two categories: substance abuse and substance dependence, with the latter being the more severe and advanced form of disorder. This distinction is based, in part, on the recognition that many people who suffer serious impairment from substance abuse do not progress to the level of dependence (Bucholz, 1999). The manual lists 11 types of drugs that can lead to problems of abuse and dependence (refer to Table 11–2). Rather than including separate definitions of dependence and abuse for each class of substance, the manual provides one generic set of criteria for substance dependence and another for substance abuse. These criterion sets can be applied to any type of drug.

The DSM-IV-TR criteria for substance dependence are presented in Table 11–3 on page 360. Tolerance and withdrawal are listed along with five other problems that describe a pattern of compulsive use and loss of control. The person has to exhibit at least three of the seven criteria for a diagnosis of substance dependence to be made. Tolerance and withdrawal are not required for the person to meet this definition of dependence. Their importance is recognized with a subtype designation. If there is evidence of either tolerance or withdrawal (or both), the additional specification of *physiological dependence* is made. Symptoms of withdrawal seem to be more important than symptoms of tolerance in this regard. People with a history of physiological dependence report more severe drug-related problems, greater intensity of exposure to drugs, and more comorbid conditions such as anxiety and depression (Schuckit et al., 1998a, 1998b).

Despite control efforts, alcohol was still available from illegal sources throughout the Prohibition years.

This approach to the definition of substance dependence is convenient because it points to a unified view of addiction. However, it also has some disadvantages. Perhaps most important is the fact that the use of a single definition of dependence may conceal differences between the kinds of problems that are associated with various classes of drugs (Frances, First, & Pincus, 1995). For example, dependence on opiates almost always involves physiological symptoms of tolerance and withdrawal, whereas dependence on cannabis or hallucinogens almost never does.

Substance abuse is defined in terms of harmful consequences that appear in the absence of tolerance, withdrawal, or a pattern of compulsive use (dependence). The DSM-IV-TR definition of substance abuse is presented in Table 11–4 on page 361. One difficult issue in defining this condition involves the identification of a boundary between substance abuse and the recreational use of drugs. The diagnostic manual emphasizes the terms *recurrent* and *maladaptive pattern* for this purpose. The problem must be persistent before this diagnosis would be considered. Someone involved in a single drug-related incident would not meet the criteria for this disorder, regardless of how serious the incident might have been (Frances, First, & Pincus, 1995).

Important questions have been raised about the validity of the DSM-IV-TR substance abuse

Where is the boundary between substance abuse and recreational drug use?

George Vaillant, Professor of Psychiatry at Harvard Medical School, has found that the lives of alcoholic men follow an unpredictable, episodic course in which periods of abstinence are often followed by relapse.

category, especially with regard to alcoholism (Winters et al., 1999). Many people who receive a diagnosis of alcohol abuse do so on the basis of a single symptom—hazardous use—which usually involves driving while intoxicated. This is certainly a grave problem with enormous negative consequences, but it is not clear whether this form of maladaptive behavior should be considered a mental disorder if it occurs in the absence of other symptoms of alcohol abuse. Perhaps the drunk driver would be better viewed as a person who has persistently chosen, for whatever reason, to engage in reckless and illegal behavior that ignores the safety of other people. One group of investigators has recommended that the alcohol abuse category be retained but with the stipulation that people cannot meet the criteria for this disorder if the diagnosis is based only on driving after drinking (Hasin et al., 1999).

Proposed Subtypes

DSM-IV-TR does not recognize any systems for subtyping substance dependence, other than the presence or absence of physiological symptoms (tolerance or withdrawal). Nevertheless, procedures for subdividing alcoholism have been employed extensively in research studies (Bucholz et al., 1996; Sher, 1991). One currently influential system was proposed by

Robert Cloninger, a psychiatrist at Washington University in St. Louis (Cloninger, Sigvardsson, & Bohman, 1996).

Cloninger suggested that there are two prototypical varieties of alcoholism. According to this system, Type 1 alcoholism is characterized by a somewhat later onset, prominent psychological dependence (loss-of-control drinking), and the absence of antisocial personality traits. It is found in both men and women. Type 2 alcoholism, which is found almost exclusively among men, typically has an earlier onset and is associated with the co-occurrence of persistent antisocial behaviors. This proposed distinction has been useful in many research studies. On the other hand, the difference between Type 1 and Type 2 alcoholism may be more quantitative than qualitative in nature (Vaillant, 1994).

Course and Outcome

It is impossible to specify a typical course for substance dependence, especially alcoholism. Age of onset varies widely, ranging from childhood and early adolescence throughout the life span. Although we can roughly identify stages that intervene between initial exposure to a drug and the eventual onset of tolerance and dependence, the timing with which a person moves through these phases can vary enormously. The best available information regarding the course

---

TABLE 11–3   DSM-IV-TR Criteria for Substance Dependence

A. A maladaptive pattern of substance use, leading to clinically significant impairment or distress, as manifested by three (or more) of the following, occurring at any time in the same 12-month period:

1. Tolerance, as defined by either of the following:
   a. A need for markedly increased amounts of the substance to achieve intoxication or desired effect.
   b. Markedly diminished effect with continued use of the same amount of the substance.
2. Withdrawal, as manifested by either of the following:
   a. The characteristic withdrawal syndrome for the substance (criteria sets for withdrawal are listed separately for specific substances).
   b. The same (or a closely related) substance is taken to relieve or avoid withdrawal symptoms.
3. The substance is often taken in larger amounts or over a longer period than was intended.
4. There is a persistent desire or unsuccessful efforts to cut down or control substance use.
5. A great deal of time is spent in activities necessary to obtain the substance (for example, visiting multiple doctors or driving long distances), use the substance (for example, chain-smoking), or recover from its effects.
6. Important social, occupational, or recreational activities are given up or reduced because of substance use.
7. The substance use is continued despite knowledge of having a persistent or recurrent physical or psychological problem that is likely to have been caused or exacerbated by the substance (for example, current cocaine use despite recognition of cocaine-induced depression, or continued drinking despite recognition that an ulcer was made worse by alcohol consumption).

Reprinted with permission from the *Diagnostic and Statistical Manual of Mental Disorders,* Fourth Edition, Text Revision. Copyright © 2000 by the American Psychiatric Association.

of substance use disorders comes from the study of alcoholism. The specific course of this problem varies considerably from one person to the next. The only thing that seems to be certain is that periods of heavy use alternate with periods of relative abstinence, however short-lived they may be (Finney, Moos, & Timko, 1999; Schuckit et al., 2002).

In an effort to examine the natural history of alcoholism, George Vaillant (1996; 2003) studied the lives of 456 inner city adolescents from Boston and 268 former undergraduate students from Harvard University. Initial information was collected in 1940, when the participants were adolescents. Follow-up information was collected every other year by questionnaire and every fifth year by physical examination. The college group has been followed until 70 years of age, and the core city group has been followed to age 60. At some point during their lives, 21 percent of the college men and 35 percent of the core city men met diagnostic criteria for alcohol abuse, which Vaillant defined as the presence of four or more problems in such areas as employer complaints, marital and family difficulties, medical complications, and legal problems.

As expected, the mortality rate was higher among men who abused alcohol than among those who did not. Heart disease and cancer were twice as common among the alcohol abusers, perhaps in part because they were also more likely to be heavy cigarette smokers.

Most of the alcoholic men went through repeated cycles of abstinence followed by relapse. The life course of alcohol abuse could be charted most clearly for 121 of the core city men who abused alcohol and remained in the study until age 60 and 46 college men who abused alcohol and remained in the study until age 70. These data are illustrated in Figure 11–2. In the graphs in Figure 11–2, abstinence is defined as less than one drink per month for more than a year. Social drinking refers to problem-free drinking for 10 years or more. Controlled drinking is more than one drink per month for at least 2 years with no reported problem. The main differences between the groups were that the core city men began abusing alcohol at an earlier age, and they were also more likely than the college men eventually to achieve stable abstinence. The average age of onset of alcohol abuse was 40 years for the college men and 29 years for the core city men.

TABLE 11–4   DSM-IV-TR Criteria for Substance Abuse

A. A maladaptive pattern of substance use leading to clinically significant impairment or distress, as manifested by one (or more) of the following, occurring within a 12-month period:

1. Recurrent substance use resulting in a failure to fulfill major role obligations at work, school, or home.

2. Recurrent substance use in situations in which it is physically hazardous.

3. Recurrent substance-related legal problems.

4. Continued substance use despite having persistent or recurrent social or interpersonal problems caused or exacerbated by the effects of the substance.

B. The symptoms have never met the criteria of substance dependence for this class of substance.

Reprinted with permission from the *Diagnostic and Statistical Manual of Mental Disorders,* Fourth Edition, Text Revision. Copyright © 2000 by the American Psychiatric Association.

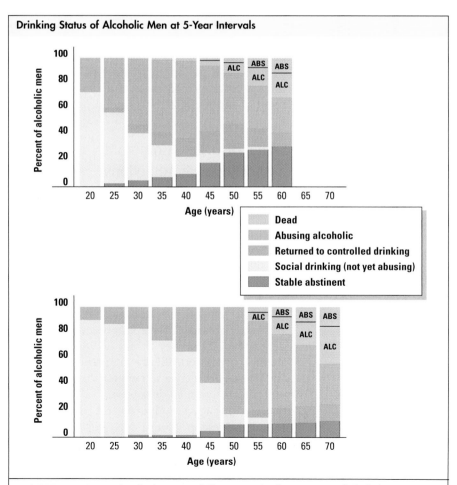

FIGURE 11–2: Results of a long-term follow-up study of two groups of alcoholics: 121 core city men (top) and 46 college men (bottom). The core city men began abusing alcohol at a younger age and were more likely to achieve stable abstinence by age 60.

Source: G.E. Vaillant (1996). A long-term follow-up of male alcohol abuse. *Archives of General Psychiatry, 53,* 243–249. Copyright © 1996. Reprinted by permission of American Medical Association.

Many men spent the previous 20 years alternating between periods of controlled drinking and alcohol abuse. The proportion of men who continued to abuse alcohol went down after the age of 40. The proportion of alcoholic men in both groups who became completely abstinent went up slowly but consistently during the follow-up period. The longer a man remained abstinent, the greater the probability that he would continue to be abstinent. Vaillant's data indicated that relapse to alcohol abuse was unlikely among men who were able to remain abstinent for at least 6 years.

Many important questions remain to be answered about the relapse process. Is there a "safe point" that separates a period of high risk for relapse from a period of more stable change? Vaillant's data suggest that the 6-year mark may be important for men who abuse alcohol. Will this suggestion be replicated in other studies? And does it generalize to other drugs? Do relapse rates stabilize over time? Is an addicted person more likely to succeed on a later attempt to quit than on an early attempt? Answers to these questions will be useful in the development of more effective treatment programs.

Other Disorders Commonly Associated with Addictions

People with substance use disorders often exhibit other forms of mental disorder as well. Most prominent among these are antisocial personality disorder (ASPD), mood disorders, and anxiety disorders (Kushner, Sher, & Erickson, 1999; Merikangas et al., 1998a). Conduct disorder (the childhood manifestation of ASPD) is strongly related to concurrent alcohol use in adolescence and the subsequent development of alcohol dependence (Crowley et al., 1998). ASPD and alcohol/drug dependence frequently co-occur, and there is evidence to suggest that they represent alternative manifestations of a general predisposition toward behavioral disinhibition (Kendler, Prescott, Myers, & Neale, 2003).

The complexity of the association between substance use disorders and mood/anxiety disorders makes them difficult to untangle. In some cases, prolonged heavy drinking or use of psychoactive drugs can result in feelings of depression and anxiety. The more the person drinks or uses drugs, the more guilty the person feels about his or her inability to control the problem.

In addition, continued use of alcohol and drugs often leads to greater conflict with family members, coworkers, and other people. Sometimes the depression and anxiety precede the onset of the substance use problem. In fact, some people seem to use alcohol and drugs initially in a futile attempt to self-medicate for these other conditions. Ultimately, the drugs make things worse.

FREQUENCY

Drug-related problems are found in most countries. There are interesting variations, however, in patterns of use for specific types of drugs. The use of specific drugs is determined, in part, by their availability. For example, opium is used most heavily in Southeast Asia and in some Middle Eastern countries, where the opium poppy is cultivated. Cocaine is used frequently in certain countries of South America where coca trees grow; it is also imported into North America, particularly the United States. Use of cannabis is widespread around the world, in part because the plants can grow in many different climates. In contrast, in Japan, where the amount of land available for cultivation is severely limited, the largest drug problem involves amphetamine, a synthetic drug.

The fact that people in some regions are frequent drug users does not necessarily imply that a particular population will have a high rate of substance dependence. Culture shapes people's choices about the use of drugs and the ways in which they are used. It influences such factors as the amount of a drug that is typically ingested, the route of administration, and the person's beliefs about drug effects (Heath, 1999; Westermeyer, 1999). These considerations, in turn, influence the probability that serious problems will develop. Consider, for example, the Indians of South America who produce coca for market. They have traditionally used the leaves as medicines and in religious ceremonies. They also roll the leaves into a ball that can be tucked in the cheek and sucked for an extended period of time. This form of use relieves cold, hunger, and thirst. It does not produce the severe dependence problems that are associated with the use of refined cocaine, a much more potent drug that can be sniffed or injected.

When we consider the epidemiology of drug addiction, we must keep in mind the distinction between use and dependence. Many people who use drugs do not become dependent on them. Nevertheless, people have to use the drug before they can become dependent, and the age at which they *begin* to use drugs is an important risk factor. For example, the prevalence rate for alcoholism among males who began drinking alcohol before the age of 14 is double that found among males who began drinking at age 18 (McGue et al., 2001). The same pattern is found among women; those who begin to use alcohol at an earlier age have a much higher risk of becoming dependent. It is not clear whether earlier initiation leads directly to increased risk of alcohol dependence or whether people who are already predisposed toward the development of drinking problems simply start using earlier.

Patterns of increased use can be alarming, particularly in adolescence. Consider, for example, evidence from the National Household Survey on Drug Abuse in the United States. In 2002, 12 percent of youths between 12 and 17 years of age used some kind of illicit drug within the 30 days prior to being interviewed. The highest rate of illicit drug use for this age group was reported in 1979 (16 percent). It went down to 5 percent in 1992 and is now back up, particularly for heroin, marijuana, and cocaine. You can retrieve recent results of this survey from the Internet Web site of the Substance Abuse and Mental Health Services Administration. The address is *www.samhsa.gov*.

Increases in the frequency of illicit drug use are reason for serious concern; however, most people who occasionally use alcohol and illicit drugs do not become addicted. Dependence almost always develops slowly after extended exposure to a drug. The average time between initial use of illicit drugs and the onset of symptoms of dependence is between 2 and 3 years (Anthony & Helzer, 1991). The distinction between people who eventually become addicted and those who use drugs without becoming addicted is an important consideration in the study of psychopathology.

Prevalence of Alcohol Abuse and Dependence

Approximately two out of every three males in Western countries drink alcohol regularly, at least on a social basis; less than 25 percent abstain

from drinking completely. Among all men and women who have ever used alcohol, roughly 20 percent will develop serious problems—abuse or dependence—at some point in their lives as a consequence of prolonged alcohol consumption (Anthony, Warner, & Kessler, 1994).

The Epidemiologic Catchment Area (ECA) study provides one detailed picture of the prevalence of alcoholism. The investigators found a lifetime prevalence rate of 13.8 percent for alcoholism (either alcohol abuse or dependence). The 12-month prevalence rate was 6.3 percent. Alcohol related disorders were the second most common type of mental disorder in the United States—second only to phobias—when men and women were considered together. These problems most often went untreated; only 15 percent of the men and women who were assigned a diagnosis of alcohol abuse or dependence had ever mentioned their symptoms to a doctor. More than half (54 percent) of these people had not experienced symptoms of alcoholism in the past year.

Gender Differences Approximately 60 percent of women in the United States drink alcohol at least occasionally, but, in comparison to men, relatively few develop alcoholism. Among people who chronically abuse alcohol, men outnumber women by a ratio of approximately 5 to 1 (Robins & Regier, 1991). Recent information suggests that this disparity may be narrower today than it was 20 years ago, especially among younger people. The National Comorbidity Survey (NCS) found a 12-month prevalence rate for alcohol dependence of 11 percent for men and 4 percent for women (Kessler et al., 1994). Although the rate of alcoholism among younger women appears to be increasing, prevalence is still much higher in

When it comes to abusing alcohol, men outnumber women 5 to 1, though this proportion may be lower than it was 20 years ago.

men, and the rates do not seem likely to converge (Greenfield & O'Leary, 2002). Persistent differences can probably be attributed to social and biological variables. American culture traditionally has held a negative view of intoxication among women. Social disapproval probably explains why women are more likely than men to drink in the privacy of their own homes, either alone or with another person. Women, therefore, may be less likely than men to drink heavily because the range of situations in which they are expected to drink, or in which they can drink without eliciting social disapproval, is narrower.

Biologically, there are also important gender differences in alcohol metabolism. A single standard dose of alcohol, measured in proportion to total body weight, will produce a higher peak blood alcohol level in women than in men. One explanation for this difference lies in the fact that men have a higher average content of body water than women do. A standard dose of alcohol will be less diluted in women because alcohol is distributed in total body water. This may help to explain the fact that women who drink heavily for many years are more vulnerable to liver disorders than are male drinkers.

Prevalence of Drug and Nicotine Dependence

The National Comorbidity Survey (NCS) surveyed more than 8,000 household residents in the United States between 1990 and 1992. Lifetime prevalence rates generated by this study for specific types of drug dependence are listed in Figure 11–3. The combined lifetime prevalence in the NCS for dependence on any type of controlled substance (those that are illegal or available only by prescription) was 7.5 percent. This is approximately half the rate for alcohol dependence. The NCS found a lifetime prevalence of 24 percent for nicotine dependence.

The percentage of adults in the United States who smoke tobacco has actually declined since 1964, when the U.S. Surgeon General's Report announced it had found a definite link between smoking and cancer and other diseases (see Critical Thinking *Matters*). The rate of decline has been greatest among men, who traditionally have smoked more than women. Among people between the ages of 18 and 25, however, smoking rates have increased from 35 percent in 1994 to 42 percent in 1998 (SAMHSA, 1999). Furthermore, although overall tobacco consumption has declined in industrialized countries, it has increased dramatically in the developing countries, where people may be less educated about the health risks associated with smoking (McKim, 2000).

Approximately 32 percent of those people who have ever used tobacco eventually meet the criteria for dependence (see Figure 11–3). This statistic might be considered an index of the addicting properties of a drug. In other words, if you use a drug repeatedly, will you develop symptoms of dependence? When viewed from this perspective, nicotine may be among the most addicting drugs used in our society. Comparable figures (percentage of users who develop dependence) for other drugs were heroin, 23 percent; cocaine, 17 percent; and alcohol, 15 percent. Among all psychoactive substances, the least addicting drugs appear to be the hallucinogens.

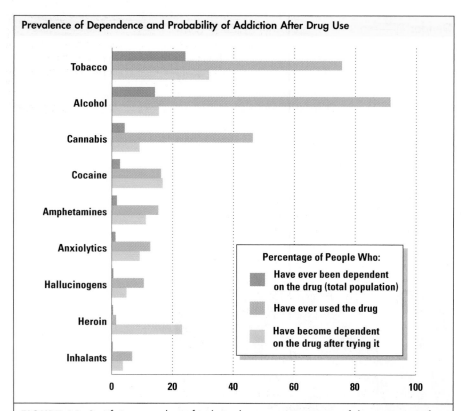

FIGURE 11–3: Lifetime prevalence for dependence on various types of drugs, percent of people who have ever used the drug, and the probability of becoming dependent among those who have used the drug.

Source: J.C. Anthony, L.A. Warner, & R.C. Kessler (1994). Comparative epidemiology of dependence on tobacco, alcohol, controlled substances, and inhalants: Basic findings from the National Comorbidity Survey. *Experimental and Clinical Psychology, 2,* 244–268.

critical thinking matters

SHOULD TOBACCO PRODUCTS BE ILLEGAL?

In 1996, the U.S. Food and Drug Administration (FDA) issued a regulation prohibiting the sale and distribution of tobacco products to children and adolescents. They remain legally available to adults. Previous efforts to limit smoking had focused more narrowly on restricting smoking in public places, eliminating cigarette advertisements on television, and increasing sales taxes. The new rule asserted that, as a drug, nicotine should be controlled by the government. The decisions behind this regulation raise a number of critical thinking issues with regard to substance use disorders. How does the FDA decide whether a product is a drug? Should the government control people's access to addicting drugs? If so, what is the best way to control access?

The FDA conducted an extensive investigation to examine the effects of tobacco products and to determine whether they were designed by their manufacturers to deliver nicotine to consumers. Independent research studies as well as documents from the tobacco industry's own laboratories pointed to the conclusion that *nicotine is addictive* (Dreyfuss, 1996). People who use tobacco products clearly develop symptoms of dependence, including tolerance, withdrawal, and a pattern of compulsive use. In fact, nicotine is one of the most addicting drugs, viewed in terms of the high proportion of people who become dependent if they use the drug for some period of time (see Figure 11–3).

After officially recognizing that nicotine is an addicting drug, the FDA could have banned tobacco products entirely (because they are not safe for human consumption). Another option would have been to require a complete elimination of nicotine from cigarettes. The FDA did not consider these options to be practical or politically viable. Because so many adults are already addicted to nicotine, extensive black markets would spring up immediately, similar to those involved with other illegal drugs. An outright ban on nicotine would fail, just as efforts to ban other drugs have failed (Husak, 2002; MacCoun, Reuter, & Wolf, 2001).

The FDA decided instead to approach the nicotine problem by invoking its authority to regulate medical devices (and treating cigarettes as a type of drug-delivery system). The tobacco regulations imposed by the FDA are *prevention* efforts designed to break the cycle of addiction to nicotine. They prohibit the sale of tobacco products to anyone under 18 years old and also severely restrict advertising (Cooper, 1994). Nicotine addiction almost always begins during adolescence. The FDA regulations are intended to reduce the rate at which young people are recruited to become new smokers and to minimize future health casualties from tobacco use.

This policy represents a moderate and thoughtful approach to the problem of nicotine dependence. It is a compromise between two extreme alternatives: allowing completely open access to a dangerous drug, or attempting to ban it completely. Preliminary evidence suggests that the FDA regulations regarding tobacco products have been modestly successful. Between 1997 and 2004, prevalence rates for current smoking among adults in the U.S. dropped from 25 percent to 21 percent (Schiller et al., 2005). Public policy will not be able to eliminate completely the use of harmful drugs by adults in our society. It can reduce the risk of dependence, however, by minimizing their use at an early age.

Risk for Addiction Across the Life Span

Older people do not drink as much alcohol as younger people. The proportion of people who abstain from drinking alcohol is only 22 percent for people in their thirties, goes up to 47 percent for people in their sixties, and is approximately 80 percent for people over 80 years of age. Prevalence rates for alcohol dependence are highest among young adults and lowest among the elderly. Most elderly alcohol abusers are people who have had drinking problems for many years (Gomberg, 1999).

The use of illegal drugs is relatively infrequent among the elderly, but there is a problem associated with their abuse of, and dependence on, prescription drugs and over-the-counter medications, especially hypnotics, sedatives, anxiolytics, and painkillers. The elderly use more legal drugs than do people in any other age group. One estimate suggested that 25 percent of all people over the age of 55 use psychoactive drugs of one kind or another (Koch & Knapp, 1987). The risk for substance dependence among the elderly is increased by frequent use of multiple psychoactive drugs combined with enhanced sensitivity to drug toxicity (caused by slowed metabolic breakdown of alcohol and other drugs).

The following case illustrates several issues that are associated with substance use disorders among the elderly, including the abuse of alcohol together with abuse of prescription medications, the presence of prominent symptoms of anxiety and depression, and the tendency to deny the extent of their use or abuse of drugs.

In what ways are drug problems different among the elderly?

♦♦♦

BRIEF CASE STUDY

Ms. E's Drinking

Ms. E is an 80-year-old woman who was brought in for an evaluation by her daughters because they noticed depressive symptoms, appetite disturbance, and memory deficits. She denied all problems related to her daughters' concerns. She had a depressed affect, mild psychomotor agitation, and decrements of recent and remote memory. She was disoriented to time. She verbalized statements of guilt and self-deprecation. She denied ever drinking alcohol, which was corroborated by the daughter with whom she lived but was refuted by her other daughter, who stated that Ms. E drank one or two glasses of brandy almost every day. She had been taking various barbiturates for "nerves" for over 30 years. The dosage she ingested gradually increased over the years, and she frequently took more medications than were prescribed. Because it was unclear if her symptoms were related to her barbiturate use, she reluctantly agreed to be slowly and gradually detoxified. She refused a dementia work-up. Once detoxification was complete, her affect and appetite were improved, but her cognitive deficits were unchanged. Several months later, she and her family dropped out of treatment. She was reportedly drinking brandy, wine, and "hard liquor" every afternoon and evening, with her hired caregiver mixing the drinks (Solomon et al., 1993).

♦♦♦

Diagnostic criteria for substance dependence and abuse are sometimes difficult to apply to the elderly, primarily because drug use has somewhat different consequences in their lives. Tolerance to many drugs is reduced among the elderly, and the symptoms of withdrawal may be more severe and prolonged. They are less likely to suffer occupational impairment because they are less frequently employed than younger people. The probability of social impairment may be reduced because elderly people are more likely to live apart from their families.

CAUSES

Our discussion of causal factors will focus primarily on alcohol dependence and abuse. We have chosen this approach because clinical scientists know more about alcohol and its abuse than about any of the other drugs. Twin studies also suggest that alcohol dependence and other forms of drug dependence share a common etiology (Kendler et al., 2003). Research on alcohol abuse illustrates the factors that are also important in the etiology of other forms of substance dependence.

Most contemporary investigators approach the development of alcoholism in terms of multiple systems (Sher et al., 2005). Biological factors obviously play an important role. The addicting properties of certain drugs are crucial: People become addicted to drugs like heroin, nicotine, and alcohol, but they do not become addicted to drugs like the antidepressants or to food additives like Nutrasweet. We must, therefore, understand how addicting drugs affect the brain in order to understand the process of dependence. At the same time, we need to understand the social and cultural factors that influence how and under what circumstances an individual first acquires and uses drugs. Our expectations about the effects of drugs are shaped by our parents, our peers, and the media. These are also important etiological considerations.

The etiology of alcoholism is best viewed within a developmental framework that views

"Before we begin, I think you should all know that I once smoked a reefer in 1935."

the problem in terms of various stages: (1) initiation and continuation, (2) escalation and transition to abuse, and (3) development of tolerance and withdrawal (Kandel & Yamaguchi, 1999; Leonard et al., 2000). In the following pages we review some of the social, psychological, and biological factors that explain why people begin to drink, how their drinking behaviors are reinforced, and how they develop tolerance after prolonged exposure.

Social Factors

People who don't drink obviously won't develop alcoholism, and culture can influence that decision. Some cultures prohibit or actively discourage alcohol consumption. Many Muslims, for example, believe that drinking alcohol is sinful. Other religions encourage the use of small amounts of alcohol in religious ceremonies—such as Jewish people drinking wine at Passover seders—while also showing disdain for those who drink to the point of intoxication (Westermeyer, 1999). This type of cultural constraint can decrease rates of substance dependence. In the ECA study, for example, Jews had significantly lower rates of alcohol abuse than Catholics and Protestants (Yeung & Greenwald, 1992).

Among those young people who choose to drink alcohol (or smoke cigarettes, or consume other addictive substances), which ones will eventually develop problems? The development of drug dependence requires continued use, and it is influenced by the manner in which the drug is consumed. In other words, with regard to alcohol, will the person's initial reaction to the drug be pleasant, or will he or she become sick and avoid alcoholic beverages in the future? If the person continues drinking, will he or she choose strong or weak drinks, with or without food, with others or alone, and so on?

Several studies have examined social factors that predict substance use among adolescents. Initial experimentation with drugs is most likely to occur among those individuals who are rebellious and extroverted and whose parents and peers model or encourage use (Chassin et al., 2003). The relative influence of parents and friends varies according to the gender and age of the adolescent as well as the drug in question.

Parents can influence their children's drinking behaviors in many ways. They can serve as models for using drugs to cope with stressful circumstances. They may also help promote attitudes and expectations regarding the benefits of drug consumption, or they may simply provide access to licit or illicit drugs (Jacob & Johnson, 1997; Lang & Stritzke, 1993). Adolescents with alcoholic parents are more likely to drink alcohol than those whose parents do not abuse alcohol. This increased risk seems to be due to several factors, including the fact that alcoholic parents monitor their children's behavior less closely, thereby providing more opportunities for illicit drinking. Parental monitoring is the aspect of parenting that appears to have the strongest effect on adolescent substance use; higher parental monitoring is associated with reduced risk of tobacco and alcohol use (Griffin et al., 2000). This phenomenon has been demonstrated across several ethnic groups and among adolescents from various countries (Rai et al., 2003; Ledoux et al., 2002).

The level of negative affect is also relatively high in the families of alcoholic parents. This unpleasant emotional climate, coupled with reduced parental monitoring, increases the probability that an adolescent will affiliate with peers who use drugs (Hussong & Chassin, 2002). Peer and sibling substance use are robust predictors of adolescent alcohol and drug use, even more than parental alcohol use (Windle, 2000).

The circumstances in which an adolescent is initially exposed to alcohol can influence the person's pattern of drinking. Drinking small amounts of wine with meals or during religious ceremonies may be less likely to lead to alcohol dependence than the sporadic consumption of hard liquor for the purpose of becoming intoxicated.

Biological Factors

Initial physiological reactions to alcohol can have a dramatic negative influence on a person's early drinking experiences. For example, millions of people are unable to tolerate even small amounts of alcohol. These people develop flushed skin, sometimes after only a single drink. They may also feel nauseated, and some experience an abnormal heartbeat. This phenomenon is most common among people of Asian ancestry and may affect 30 to 50 percent of this population. The adverse reaction is due to genetic variants in the ADH and ALDH genes, which are involved in the metabolism of alcohol, and are much more common in Asian populations than in other races (Dick & Foroud, 2003). Not coincidentally, the prevalence of alcoholism is unusually low among Asian populations. Research studies indicate a link between these two phenomena. For example, Japanese Americans who experience the fast-flushing response tend to drink less than those who do not flush (Wall & Ehlers, 1995; Yamashita, Koyama, & Ohmori, 1995). The basic evidence suggests that in addition to looking for factors that make some individuals especially vulnerable to the addicting effects of alcohol, it may also be important to identify protective factors that reduce the probability of substance dependence.

A person's initial use of addictive drugs is obviously one important step toward the development of substance dependence, but the fact remains that most people who drink alcohol do not develop alcoholism. What accounts for the next important phase of the disorder? Why do some people abuse the drug while others do not? In the following pages we outline several additional biological variables. We begin by examining genetic factors, and then we consider the neurochemical effects of the drugs themselves.

Genetics of Alcoholism

An extensive literature attests to the fact that patterns of alcohol consumption, as well as psychological and social problems associated with alcohol abuse, tend to run in families. The lifetime prevalence of alcoholism among the parents, siblings, and children of people with alcoholism is at least three to five times higher than the rate in the general population (Bierut et al., 1998; Merikangas et al., 1998b). Of course, this elevated risk among first-degree relatives could reflect the influence of either genetic or environmental factors, because families share both types of influence. Therefore we must look to the results of twin and adoption studies in an effort to disentangle these variables.

Twin Studies Several twin studies have examined patterns of alcohol consumption in nonalcoholic twins. The evidence indicates that both genetic factors and shared environmental factors influence the quantity and frequency of social drinking in normal men and women (Prescott et al., 1994).

Other studies have examined twin concordance rates when the proband meets diagnostic criteria for substance dependence. Here the focus is on severely disabling drinking problems rather than simply the consumption of alcohol. Several studies have found that concordance rates are higher among MZ than among DZ twin pairs. In some earlier studies, this finding was limited to male subjects. Recent data indicate a genetic influence on alcoholism for both men and women (McGue, 1999). For example, the psychologists Andrew Heath and Nick Martin analyzed data from a large sample of twins in Australia. They found concordance rates for alcohol dependence of 56 percent in male MZ twins and 33 percent in male DZ twins (Heath et al., 1997). Corresponding figures for MZ and DZ female twin pairs were 30 percent and 17 percent. Differences between MZ and DZ concordance rates were significant for both genders. The fact that concordance rates were higher for men than for women reflects the much higher prevalence rate for alcoholism among men. Heritability estimates were the same for both men and women, with approximately two-thirds of the variance in risk for alcoholism being produced by genetic factors.

Adoption Studies As discussed in Chapter 2, the strategy followed in an adoption study allows the investigator to separate relatively clearly the influence of genetic and environmental factors. The probands in this type of study are individuals who meet two criteria: (1) They had a biological parent who was alcoholic, and (2) they were adopted from their biological parents at an early age and raised by adoptive parents.

Two adoption studies were conducted in Sweden by Robert Cloninger and his colleagues (Cloninger, 1987; Sigvardsson, Bohman, & Cloninger, 1996). The results of these investigations are consistent with the data from twin studies and point toward the influence of genetic factors in the etiology of alcohol abuse and dependence. They also indicate, however, that the manner in which genetic and environmental events combine probably differs from one type of alcoholism to another. Alcohol dependence with an earlier age of onset, and alcohol dependence that is comorbid with antisocial personality disorder and/or other drug dependence appear to be more heritable forms of the disorder.

What can we conclude from the adoption studies? There are obviously some differences in both methods and results from one study to the next, but there are also consistent indications that genetic factors play some role in the etiology of alcohol abuse and dependence. McGue (1993) conducted a comprehensive review of the adoption study evidence and reached the following general conclusions:

- The offspring of alcoholic parents who are reared by nonalcoholic adoptive parents are more likely than people in the general population to develop drinking problems of their own. Thus the familial nature of alcoholism is at least partially determined by genes.
- Being reared by an alcoholic parent, in the absence of other etiological factors, does not appear to be a critical consideration in the development of the disorder.
- The etiology of alcoholism is probably heterogeneous in nature; that is, there are several pathways to the disorder.
- There is an association between antisocial personality traits, or "behavioral undercontrol," and alcohol abuse or dependence. The exact nature of this relation and the direction of effect have not been determined.

What exactly is inherited as the predisposition toward alcohol dependence? Some of the genes that influence the risk of developing alcohol dependence are genes involved in the metabolism of alcohol, such as the ADH and ALDH genes (discussed above). Other genes that alter the risk for alcohol dependence may be genes involved in personality traits (Slutske et al., 2002). For example, to the extent that genes influence novelty-seeking and sensation-seeking, these genes may also increase the person's risk for alcohol dependence because the person is more likely to participate in dangerous patterns of consumption (such as drinking several shots of liquor in rapid succession rather than sipping beer or wine).

Neuroanatomy and Neurochemistry All of the addicting drugs produce changes in the chemical processes by which messages are transmitted in the brain, including systems that involve catecholamines (for example, dopamine, norepinephrine, and serotonin), as well as the neuropeptides. In the following sections, we will outline some of the ways in which psychoactive drugs influence neural transmission and the areas of the brain in which these effects are most pronounced.

Dopamine and Reward Pathways Scientists who study the biological basis of addiction have devoted a considerable amount of their attention to understanding the rewarding or reinforcing properties of drugs (Koob, 2000; Self & Tamminga, 2004). People may become dependent on psychoactive drugs because they stimulate areas of the brain that are known as "reward pathways" (see Figure 11–4). One primary circuit in this pathway

What are the most important risk factors for alcoholism?

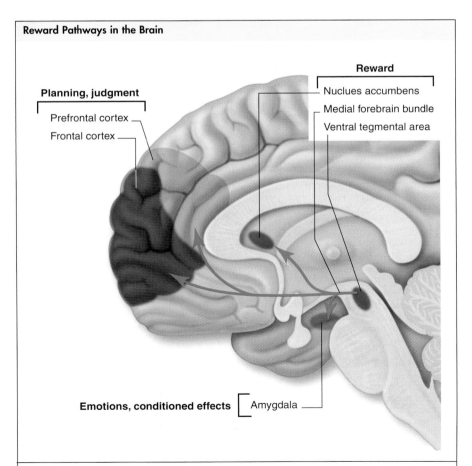

FIGURE 11–4: The limbic dopamine reward pathways include connections from the ventral tegmental area to the nucleus accumbens and the frontal cortex.

Source: After D.M. Tomkins & E.M. Sellers (2001). Addiction and the brain: The role of neurotransmitters in the cause and treatment of drug dependence. *Canadian Medical Association Journal, 164,* 817–821.

is the medial forebrain bundle, which connects the ventral tegmental area to the nucleus accumbens. Connections from these structures to the frontal and prefrontal cortex as well as areas of the limbic system, such as the amygdala, also moderate the influence of reward. For many years, scientists have known electrical stimulation of the medial forebrain bundle can serve as a powerful source of positive reinforcement for animals as

they perform an operant learning task (Olds & Milner, 1954). Natural rewards, such as food and sex, increase dopamine levels in certain crucial sections of this pathway, which is also known as the *mesolimbic dopamine pathway*.

Drugs of abuse have a dramatic effect on brain reward pathways. Some points at which different drugs influence the dopamine pathway between the ventral tegmental area and the nucleus accumbens are illustrated in Figure 11–5. For example, stimulants such as amphetamine and cocaine affect reward pathways by inhibiting the reuptake of dopamine into nerve terminals. Brain imaging studies with human participants have found that the administration of cocaine increases dopamine concentrations in limbic areas of the brain as well as the medial prefrontal cortex (Tomkins & Sellers, 2001). Furthermore, when people who are dependent on cocaine are exposed to cues that have previously signaled drug use, their medial prefrontal cortex becomes activated, suggesting that this area of the brain is involved in feelings of drug craving.

The effects of alcohol on reward pathways in the brain are more complex and less clearly understood than the effects of many other drugs (Julien, 2001). Alcohol clearly affects several different types of neurotransmitters. It may stimulate the mesolimbic dopamine pathway directly, or it may act indirectly by decreasing the activity of GABA neurons (which normally inhibit dopamine neurons). Interesting findings from genetic studies support the latter possibility. Several genes that affect GABA reception have recently been identified as influencing the risk for alcohol dependence (Covault et al., 2004; Radel et al., 2005).

Endogenous Opioid Peptides One of the most interesting and important advances in neuroscience research was the discovery of the endogenous opioids known as **endorphins** and enkephalins. These relatively short chains of amino acids, or *neuropeptides*, are naturally synthesized in the brain and are closely related to morphine in their pharmacological properties. Opioid peptides possess a chemical affinity for specific receptor sites, in the same way that a key fits into a specific lock. Several types of opioid peptides are distributed widely throughout the brain. They appear to be especially important in the activities associated with systems that control pain, emotion, stress, and reward, as well as such biological functions as

Neurochemical Mechanisms of Drug Action

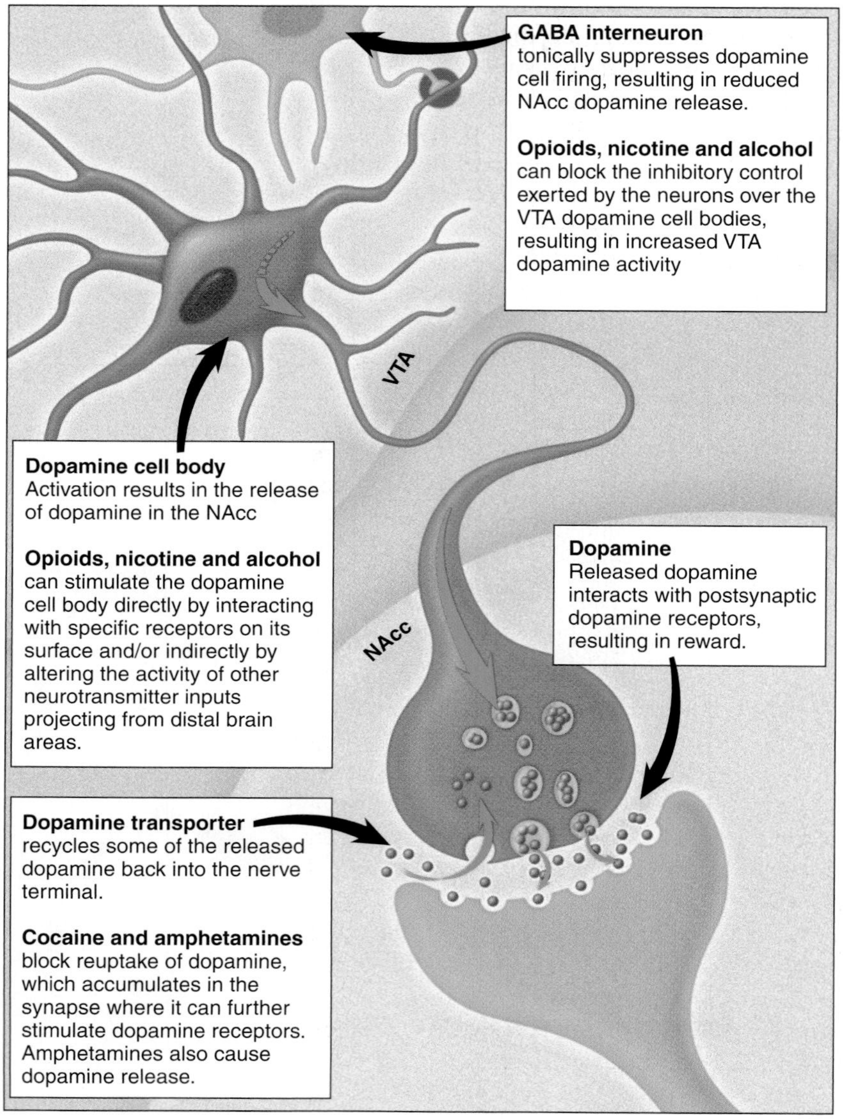

GABA interneuron
tonically suppresses dopamine cell firing, resulting in reduced NAcc dopamine release.

Opioids, nicotine and alcohol
can block the inhibitory control exerted by the neurons over the VTA dopamine cell bodies, resulting in increased VTA dopamine activity

Dopamine cell body
Activation results in the release of dopamine in the NAcc

Opioids, nicotine and alcohol
can stimulate the dopamine cell body directly by interacting with specific receptors on its surface and/or indirectly by altering the activity of other neurotransmitter inputs projecting from distal brain areas.

Dopamine
Released dopamine interacts with postsynaptic dopamine receptors, resulting in reward.

Dopamine transporter
recycles some of the released dopamine back into the nerve terminal.

Cocaine and amphetamines
block reuptake of dopamine, which accumulates in the synapse where it can further stimulate dopamine receptors. Amphetamines also cause dopamine release.

FIGURE 11–5: Effects of psychoactive drugs on dopamine activity in reward pathway from the ventral tegmental area (VTA) to the nucleus accumbens (NAcc).

Source: After D.M. Tomkins & E.M. Sellers (2001). Addiction and the brain: The role of neurotransmitters in the cause and treatment of drug dependence. *Canadian Medical Association Journal, 164,* 817–821.

feeding and growth (Froehlich, 1997; Julien, 2001).

Research studies have demonstrated many interesting features of the endorphins. Laboratory animals can develop tolerance to injections of endorphins, just as they develop tolerance to addicting drugs like morphine, and they also exhibit symptoms of withdrawal if the injections are suddenly discontinued. These studies confirm the pharmacological similarity between endogenous and exogenous opioids.

Some theorists associate alcoholism with exaggerated activation of the endogenous opioid system in response to alcohol stimulation (Gianoulakis, DeWaele, & Thavundayil, 1996). Several lines of evidence support this hypothesis. One is that opioid receptor antagonists (drugs that block the effects of opioid peptides) produce a decrease in alcohol self-administration in laboratory animals. Another important bit of information comes from drug trials with human participants: When alcoholic patients take naltrexone, an antagonist of endogenous opioids, they drink less alcohol and report that the subjective "high" associated with drinking is noticeably diminished (see the section on treatment with medication, later in this chapter). Finally, in both rodents and humans, a genetic predisposition toward increased consumption of alcohol is associated with high levels of opioid system response to the ingestion of alcohol (Froehlich, 1997). For all of these reasons, it seems likely that endogenous opioid peptides are somehow involved in mediating alcohol dependence.

Serotonin Involvement Although alcohol does not bind directly to any receptor sites in the brain, it does alter the permeability of neuronal membranes (Roberts & Koob, 1997; Valenzuela, 1997). Channels for potassium and chlorine ions are opened, and corresponding channels for sodium and calcium are closed, thus depressing the central nervous system. Concentrations of neurotransmitters, such as serotonin and dopamine, are initially increased. If the person continues to drink heavily over an extended period of time, the alcohol produces many effects that are opposite to those of short-term intoxication: The central nervous system becomes excited rather than depressed, and the ion channel events are reversed.

The theory that serotonin is involved in the etiology of alcoholism assumes that alcohol dependence is caused by a genetically determined deficiency in serotonin activity in certain areas of the limbic system of the brain (Lovinger, 1997; Wallis, Rezazadeh, & Lal, 1993). Some studies have reported that acute intoxication is accompanied by an increase in serotonin activity. When the person sobers up, serotonin activity is reduced to subnormal levels. The serotonin theory suggests that some people begin with a deficiency in serotonin, and the consumption of alcohol initially helps to correct for this deficiency. Unfortunately, prolonged consumption further depletes the system. Therefore the person initially drinks to feel good—alcohol stimulates activity in the reward systems of the brain—but after a while he or she must drink more to avoid feeling worse when serotonin levels are reduced below their initial point.

Evidence supporting the involvement of serotonin comes primarily from two kinds of investigation. First, animals that are bred to exhibit high and low preferences for alcohol exhibit differences in serotonin levels. Those with a high preference for alcohol have lower levels of serotonin in areas of the brain that regulate emotional responses (McBride et al., 1993). Second, drugs that enhance serotonin transmission (such as selective serotonin reuptake inhibitors or SSRIs; see Chapter 5) can decrease voluntary alcohol consumption in human subjects.

Psychological Factors

Genetic factors and neurochemistry undoubtedly account for many of the problems associated with addictive drugs, but as the systems perspective indicates, biological explanations are not incompatible with psychological ones. In fact, extensive research over the past several decades has found that the progression of substance dependence depends on an interaction between environmental and biological events. One time-honored perspective on the development of alcoholism is the tension-reduction hypothesis. At its most general level, this viewpoint holds that people drink alcohol in an effort to reduce the impact of a stressful environment.

The tension-reduction hypothesis became the focal point for scientific investigation when Conger (1956) adapted formal learning theory to the problem and proposed that alcohol consumption is reinforced by its ability to relieve unpleasant emotional states, especially fear and anxiety. As we will see in the following pages, the relation between stress and alcohol has turned out to be more complex than this theory suggests (Sayette, 1999b). Drug effects interact with the person's beliefs and attitudes, as well as with the social context in which the drugs are taken.

Expectations About Drug Effects   Placebo effects demonstrate that expectations are an important factor in any study of drug effects (see Chapter 3). During the 1970s and 1980s, several research studies sought to evaluate the influence of alcohol on various facets of behavior using the *balanced placebo design*. This procedure allows the investigator to separate the direct, biological effects of the drug from the subjects' expectations about how the drug should affect their behavior. The results indicated that expectations can account for many effects that have often been attributed to the drug itself. For example, subjects who believed that they had ingested alcohol but who had actually consumed only tonic water displayed exaggerated aggression and reported enhanced feelings of sexual arousal (Goldman, Brown, & Christiansen, 1987; Goldman et al., 1991; Hull & Bond, 1986). Much less is known about expectancies for drugs other than alcohol, but there is good reason to believe that these cognitive factors also influence the ways in which people respond to cannabis, nicotine, stimulants, anxiolytics, and sedatives (Brandon, Wetter, & Baker, 1996; S.A. Brown, 1993).

The results of experiments using the balanced placebo design stimulated considerable thought about the role that alcohol expectancies—expectations about alcohol or drug effects—may play in the etiology of drinking problems. These studies do not manipulate expectancies directly, however. They only lead subjects to believe that they have consumed alcohol when, in fact, they have not. The investigators infer that the subjects believed that alcohol would make them aggressive.

But is that really the case? Subsequent investigations began to examine alcohol expectancies directly (Goldman et al., 1999; Hittner, 1997). Investigators asked people, Why do you drink? What do you expect to happen after you have consumed a few beers or a couple of glasses of wine? Subjects' answers to these questions fit into six primary categories:

1. Alcohol transforms experiences in a positive way (for example: Drinking makes the future seem brighter).
2. Alcohol enhances social and physical pleasure (for example: Having a few drinks is a nice way to celebrate special occasions).
3. Alcohol enhances sexual performance and experience (for example: After a few drinks, I am more sexually responsive).
4. Alcohol increases power and aggression (for example: After a few drinks it is easier to pick a fight).
5. Alcohol increases social assertiveness (for example: Having a few drinks makes it easier to talk to people).
6. Alcohol reduces tension (for example: Alcohol enables me to fall asleep more easily).

These expectations may constitute one of the primary reasons for continued and increasingly heavy consumption of alcoholic beverages. In fact, expectancy patterns can help predict drinking behaviors. Longitudinal studies have found that adolescents who are just beginning to experiment with alcohol and who initially have the most positive expectations about the effects of alcohol go on to consume greater amounts of alcoholic beverages (Smith et al., 1995). This type of demonstration is important because it indicates that, in many cases, the expectations appear before the person begins to drink heavily. Therefore, they may play a role in the onset of the problem rather than being consequences of heavy drinking (see Research Methods).

Where do these expectations come from, and when do they develop? In some cases they may arise from personal experiences with

Common expectations about the effects of drinking alcohol include the notion that it enhances sexual arousal and experience.

STUDIES OF PEOPLE AT RISK FOR DISORDERS

We have used the term *risk* informally throughout this book to refer to a hazard—the possibility of suffering harm. In scientific research, a risk is a statement about the probability that a certain outcome will occur. For example, the NCS found that the risk that a person in the United States will develop alcoholism at some point in his or her life is about 14 in 100 (see Figure 11–3). The combined risk for all types of illegal and controlled substances (such as cannabis, cocaine, heroin, and barbiturates) is about 8 in 100. The concept of risk implies only probability, not certainty. Someone who is "at risk" may or may not suffer harm, depending on many other events and circumstances. For example, men are at greater risk than women for the development of alcoholism, but that does not mean that all men will become alcoholics.

Risk factors are variables that are associated with a higher probability of developing a disorder. Notice that this use of the term risk implies association, not causality. The concept of risk simply reflects a correlation between the risk factor and the disorder. Some risk factors are demographic variables, such as gender and race. Others are biological and psychological variables. In the case of alcoholism, and many other types of psychopathology, family

history of the disorder is an important risk factor. Expectancies about the effects of drugs represent another important risk factor for alcoholism. People who expect that alcohol will reduce tension or transform experiences in a positive way are more likely to drink frequently and heavily than those who have negative expectancies about the effects of alcohol.

In order to determine whether certain risk factors might play a *causal* role in the development of the disorder, it is often necessary to conduct longitudinal studies (see Research Methods in Chapter 8). The investigator collects information about each person before the onset of the disorder. He or she can therefore determine whether the risk factor is present before or only after the onset of symptoms. In other words, do people believe that alcohol reduces tension before they start to drink heavily, or do they develop this belief after they have been drinking heavily for some time? Longitudinal studies can be extremely expensive, and often they take several years to complete. They also require large numbers of participants because everyone in the study will not go on to develop the disorder in question.

Some of these shortcomings of longitudinal studies are especially relevant to research on substance abuse disorders. The risk for

developing such disorders is quite low in the general population. For example, even though alcoholism is one of the most prevalent forms of mental disorder, a longitudinal study that follows the development of 100 randomly selected people from childhood to middle age will find only about 14 alcoholic adults (based on NCS data). Thus, to collect a useful amount of data, researchers need to study a large sample, which can be very expensive.

Recognition of this problem led scientists to develop special methods to increase the productivity of longitudinal research. One important technique is the **high-risk research design.** In high-risk research, subjects are selected from the general population based on a well-documented risk factor (Sher & Gotham, 1999; Tarter & Vanyukov, 2001). A number of risk factors might be used to select subjects: positive family history for a given disorder, the presence of certain psychological characteristics, or perhaps a set of demographic variables such as age, gender, and/or race. High-risk research studies are designed to follow their participants over time, beginning before the onset of serious disorders. They hope to identify factors that increase or decrease the probability that people who are vulnerable to a disorder will eventually develop its active symptoms.

---

alcohol, but they can also be learned indirectly. Many adolescents hold strong beliefs about the effects of alcohol long before they take their first drink. These expectations may be influenced by parental and peer attitudes and by the portrayal of alcohol in the mass media (Brown et al., 1999). Follow-up studies have demonstrated that adolescents' expectations about the effects of alcohol are useful in predicting which individuals will later develop drinking problems (Jones, Corbin, & Fromme, 2001 Kilbey et al., 1998). Positive expectancies about alcohol, which are likely to encourage people to drink, are especially influential. Negative expectancies are associated with diminished use but seem to be less powerful.

Attention Allocation Scientists have studied the behavioral effects of alcohol extensively, especially its influence on anxiety, aggression, sexual

responsiveness, and mood. One of the puzzling results of this research is the inconsistency that has emerged from one study to the next. Some papers report that alcohol reduces tension; others conclude that it increases anxiety. Some investigators have found that drinking alcohol can increase self-esteem, whereas others have concluded that it can increase depression. Claude Steele, a psychologist at Stanford University, and Robert Josephs, a psychologist at the University of Texas, have proposed an attention-allocation model of alcohol effects that provides an explanation for these apparent inconsistencies (Steele & Josephs, 1988, 1990).

Steele and Josephs' theory is based on two general factors. First, when alcohol reaches the brain, it interferes with the capacity for controlled and effortful cognitive activities. Intoxicated people focus their attention, by necessity, on immediate internal and external cues and are less able

The attention-allocation model predicts that drinking alcohol will lead to drunken excess when strong cues pull for a particular response. In the photograph, a soccer fan in a sports bar reacts with rage after watching his national team lose an important game.

to consider subtle or complex aspects of a problem. Steele and Josephs (1990) call this process *alcohol myopia*—a marked tendency to engage in shortsighted information processing. The second component of the attention-allocation model involves the nature of the immediate environment. The impact of drinking on an intoxicated person's behavior will depend on the specific situation with which the person is confronted.

Steele and Josephs have used this model to study the effects of alcohol on several aspects of human behavior, including drunken excess—the tendency for social behavior to become more extreme under the influence of alcohol. The attention-allocation model predicts that alcohol myopia will lead to drunken excess only in situations in which strong cues are pulling for a particular response, but in which that response is also inhibited by higher level cognitive processing. Suppose, for example, that somebody insults you. If you are sober, you might be tempted to respond by punching or slapping the person, but you would also anticipate several negative consequences that might be associated with this choice of action. If you are intoxicated, however, you will be cognitively impaired and therefore less able to invoke these inhibitory cues. Therefore you are more likely to respond in an excessively aggressive fashion.

The attention-allocation theory is an intriguing explanation for the short-term effects of alcohol on human behavior. Of course, as with all theoretical models of psychopathology, the theory conflicts with certain facts. The most important point to be emphasized in considering this approach is that the short-term effects of alcohol on the behavior of nonalcoholic subjects is determined, at least in part, by the disruptive effects of alcohol consumption on cognitive processes (Sayettea, 1999).

Integrated Systems

Alcoholism and other forms of addiction clearly result from an interaction among several types of systems. Various social, psychological, and biological factors influence the person's behavior at each stage in the cycle, from initial use of the drug through the eventual onset of tolerance and withdrawal. Furthermore, it appears that different influences are important at different stages of use. The process seems to progress in the following way. Initial experimentation with drugs is influenced by the environment—the person's family, peers, school, and neighborhood (Rhee et al., 2003). Other people also influence the person's attitudes and expectations about the effects of drugs. Access to drugs, in addition to the patterns in which they are originally consumed, is determined, in part, by cultural factors.

For many people, drinking alcohol leads to short-term positive effects that reinforce continued consumption. The exact psychological mechanisms that are responsible for reinforcing heavy drinking may take several different forms. They may involve diminished self-awareness, stress reduction, or improved mood. These effects of alcohol on behavior and subjective experience are determined, in part, by the person's expectations about the way in which the drug will influence his or her feelings and behavior (Baer, 2002; Goldman, 1994).

Genetic factors play an important role in the etiology of alcoholism (Crabbe, 2002; Prescott & Kendler, 1999). After the person has begun to use alcohol, genetic factors become increasingly important in shaping patterns of use (Rose et al., 2001). There are most likely several different types of genetic influence, as illustrated by the results of the Swedish adoption studies. Genes interact strongly with environmental events for certain types of the disorder. A genetic predisposition to alcohol dependence probably causes the person to react to alcohol in an abnormal fashion. It is not clear whether those who are vulnerable to alcoholism are initially more or less sensitive than other people to the reinforcing effects of alcohol. Research studies have demonstrated both patterns of response (Sher, Grekin, & Williams, 2005).

The biological mechanisms responsible for abnormal reactions to alcohol seem to involve several interrelated neurotransmitter systems (Hyman & Malenka, 2001). Dopamine activity in the brain's reward pathway is stimulated by alcohol as well as other drugs of abuse. Another important consideration may be a deficiency in serotonin activity in certain areas of the limbic system. Drinking alcohol initially corrects this problem and increases serotonin activity, but the person eventually begins to feel worse after tolerance develops.

Drinking gradually becomes heavier and more frequent. The person becomes tolerant to the effects of alcohol and must drink larger quantities to achieve the same reinforcing effects. After he or she becomes addicted to alcohol, attempts to quit drinking are accompanied by painful withdrawal symptoms. Prolonged abuse can lead to permanent neurological impairment, as well as the disruption of many other organ systems.

TREATMENT

The treatment of alcoholism and other types of substance use disorders is an especially difficult task. Many people with substance use disorders do not acknowledge their difficulties, and only a relatively small number seek professional help. When they do enter treatment, it is typically with reluctance or on the insistence of friends, family members, or legal authorities. Compliance with treatment recommendations is often low, and dropout rates are high. The high rate of comorbidity with other forms of mental disorder presents an additional challenge, complicating the formulation of a treatment plan. Treatment outcome is likely to be least successful with those people who have comorbid conditions.

The goals of treatment for substance use disorders are a matter of controversy. Some clinicians believe that the only acceptable goal is total abstinence from drinking or drug use. Others have argued that, for some people, a more reasonable goal is the moderate use of legal drugs. Important questions have also been raised about the scope of improvements that might be expected from a successful treatment program. Is the goal simply to minimize or eliminate drug use, or should we expect that treatment will also address the social, occupational, and medical problems that are typically associated with drug problems? If these associated problems are the result of the person's prolonged abuse of alcohol

or other drugs, the problems may improve on their own if the person becomes abstinent. However, to the extent that family problems or interpersonal difficulties contribute to the person's use of drugs, it may be necessary to address these difficulties before the drug problem can be resolved (Lewis et al., 2004). Getting Help at the end of this chapter offers additional resources for those seeking help and information on recovering from substance abuse.

Detoxification

Alcoholism and related forms of drug abuse are chronic conditions. Treatment is typically accomplished in a sequence of stages, beginning with a brief period of **detoxification**—the removal of a drug on which a person has become dependent—for 3 to 6 weeks (Coombs, Howatt, & Coombs, 2005). This process is often extremely difficult, as the person experiences marked symptoms of withdrawal and gradually adjusts to the absence of the drug. For many types of CNS depressants, such as alcohol, hypnotics, and sedatives, detoxification is accomplished gradually. Stimulant drugs, in contrast, can be stopped abruptly (Schuckit, 1999a). During the detoxification period, medical professionals closely monitor the patient's vital signs to prevent seizures and delirium. Although detoxification usually takes place in a hospital, some evidence indicates that it can be accomplished with close supervision on an outpatient basis.

People who are going through alcohol detoxification are often given various types of medication, including benzodiazepines and anticonvulsants, primarily as a way of minimizing withdrawal symptoms (Kosten & O'Connor, 2003). This practice is controversial, in part because many people believe that it is illogical to use one form of drug, especially one that can be abused itself, to help someone recover from dependence on another drug.

Medications During Remission

Following the process of detoxification, treatment efforts are aimed at helping the person maintain a state of remission. The best outcomes are associated with stable, long term abstinence from drinking. Several forms of medication are used to help the person achieve this goal.

Disulfiram (Antabuse) is a drug that can block the chemical breakdown of alcohol. It was introduced as a treatment for alcoholism in Europe in 1948 and is still used fairly extensively (Fuller & Gordis, 2004). If a person who is taking disulfiram consumes even a small amount of alcohol, he or she will become violently ill. The symptoms include nausea, vomiting, profuse sweating, and increased heart rate and respiration rate. People who are taking disulfiram will stop drinking alcohol in order to avoid this extremely unpleasant reaction. Unfortunately, voluntary compliance with this form of treatment is poor. Many patients discontinue taking disulfiram, usually because they want to resume drinking or because they believe that they can manage their problems without the drug. Research studies report inconsistent results regarding outcome for patients who are treated with disulfiram (Mann, 2004). It may be most useful when used in combination with one of the other, more recently developed forms of medication for treating alcoholism (Hart et al., 2001).

Naltrexone (Revia) is an antagonist of endogenous opioids that has been found to be useful in the treatment of alcohol dependence following detoxification. Several research studies have demonstrated that patients who received naltrexone and psychotherapy are less likely to relapse than patients who receive psychotherapy plus a placebo (Carmen et al., 2004; Modesto-Lowe & Van Kirk, 2002). Among those who do drink some alcohol during recovery, people taking naltrexone are less likely to lose control and return to heavy drinking. Some clinical patients report that, if they drink while also taking naltrexone, they do not feel as "high" as they would without naltrexone. Naltrexone may dampen the person's craving by blocking alcohol's ability to stimulate the opioid system. In other words, it works by reducing the rewarding effects of alcohol rather than by inducing illness if the person drinks. The best effects for naltrexone are found with patients who are compliant with the medication (take it at least 80 percent of the time) and are also involved in a psychological treatment program.

How does AA differ from other approaches to treating alcoholism?

Another promising medication for treating alcoholism is acamprosate (Campral). An extensive body of evidence indicates that people taking acamprosate are able to reduce their average number of drinking days by 30 to 50 percent (Mann, Lehert, & Morgan, 2004). It also increases the proportion of people who are able to achieve total abstinence (approximately 22 percent among people taking acamprosate and 12 percent taking placebo after 12 months of treatment). Its mechanism of action is not entirely clear, but acamprosate appears to reduce symptoms of acute alcohol withdrawal. It is particularly effective with people who drink in order to neutralize symptoms of withdrawal and to reduce anxiety. Like naltrexone, acamprosate is intended to be used in conjunction with a psychological treatment program. The dropout rate is very high without these added features (Hart et al., 2001; Malcolm, 2003).

Psychiatrists also use SSRIs, such as fluoxetine, for the long term treatment of alcoholic patients. Outcome studies suggest that SSRIs have small and inconsistent effects in reducing drinking among those patients who are not also depressed. They do seem to be effective, however, for the treatment of people with a dual diagnosis of alcohol dependence and major depression (O'Brien & McKay, 2002). Among these patients, fluoxetine can reduce drinking levels as well as symptoms of depression.

Self-Help Groups: Alcoholics Anonymous

One of the most widely accepted forms of treatment for alcoholism is Alcoholics Anonymous (AA). Organized in 1935, this self-help program is maintained by alcohol abusers for the sole purpose of helping other people who abuse alcohol become and remain sober. Because it is established and active in virtually all communities in North America and Europe, as well as in many other parts of the world, AA is generally considered to be "the first line of attack against alcoholism" (Nathan, 1993). Surveys conducted by AA indicate that its membership increased considerably during the 1970s and 1980s. By the late 1990s, worldwide membership in AA was approximately 1.8 million people (Wallace, 1999). Many members of AA are also involved in other forms of treatment offered by various types of mental health professionals, but AA is not officially associated with any other form of treatment or professional organization. Similar self-help programs have been developed for people who are dependent on other drugs, such as opioids (Narcotics Anonymous) and cocaine (Cocaine Anonymous).

The viewpoint espoused by AA is fundamentally spiritual in nature (Kaskutas et al., 2003). AA is the original "12-step program." In the first step, the person must acknowledge that he or she is powerless over alcohol and unable to manage his or her drinking. The remaining steps involve spiritual and interpersonal matters such as accepting "a Power greater than ourselves" that can provide the person with direction; recognizing and accepting personal weaknesses; and making amends for previous errors, especially instances in which the person's drinking caused hardships for other people. One principal assumption is that people cannot recover on their own (Emrick, 1999).

The process of working through the 12 steps to recovery is facilitated by regular attendance at AA meetings, as often as every day of the first 90 days after the person stops drinking. Most people choose to attend less frequently if they are able to remain sober throughout this initial period. Meetings provide chronic alcohol abusers with an opportunity to meet and talk with other people who have similar problems, as well as something to do instead of having a drink. New members are encouraged to call older members for help at any time if they experience an urge to drink. There is enormous variability in the format and membership of local AA meetings (Montgomery, Miller, & Tonigan, 1993).

It is difficult to evaluate the effectiveness of AA, for a number of reasons. Long-term follow-up is difficult, and it is generally impossible to employ some of the traditional methods of outcome research, such as random assignment to groups and placebo controls. Early dropout rates are relatively high: About half of all the people who initially join AA leave in less than 3 months. On the other hand, survival rates (defined in terms of continued sobriety) are much higher for those people who remain in AA. About 80 percent of AA members who have remained sober for between 2 and 5 years will remain sober in the next year (Tonigan, Connors, & Miller, 2003).

Although AA does seem to help people, it is not clear how it helps, or why. Several mechanisms are possible (Owen et al., 2003). One explanation centers on the personal growth process that is described in the 12-step program, but the active ingredients may be more

Group therapy is an important part of most inpatient treatment programs. It offers an opportunity for patients to acknowledge and confront openly the severity of their problems.

social than spiritual. Membership in AA provides people with a stable social network that discourages rather than encourages the use of drugs. It also provides training in communication skills and cognitive coping strategies for stressful life events. Another possible explanation involves personality traits that are present before the person enters treatment. Those people with traits that are compatible with continued membership in a group like AA may be most likely to recover. People who exhibit antisocial traits of the type associated with Cloninger's Type 2 alcoholism, who also presumably have an earlier onset and more difficulty abstaining from drinking, may be least likely to benefit from AA.

Cognitive Behavior Therapy

Psychological approaches to substance use disorders have often focused on cognitive and behavioral responses that trigger episodes of drug abuse. In the case of alcoholism, heavy drinking has been viewed as a learned, maladaptive response that some people use to cope with difficult problems or to reduce anxiety. Cognitive behavior therapy teaches people to identify and respond more appropriately to circumstances that regularly precipitate drug abuse (Finney & Moos, 2002).

Coping Skills Training One element of cognitive behavior therapy involves training in the use of social skills, which might be used to resist pressures to drink heavily. It also includes problem-solving procedures, which can help the person both to identify situations that lead to heavy drinking and to formulate alternative courses of action. Anger management is one example. Some people drink in response to frustration. Through careful instruction and practice, people can learn to express negative emotions in constructive ways that will be understood by others. The focus in this type of treatment is on factors that initiate and maintain problem drinking rather than the act of drinking itself.

Cognitive events also play an important part in this approach to treatment. Expectations about the effects of alcohol are challenged, and more adaptive thoughts are rehearsed. Negative patterns of thinking about the self and events in the person's environment are also addressed because they are linked to unpleasant emotions that trigger problem drinking.

Relapse Prevention Most people who have been addicted to a drug will say that quitting is the easy part of treatment. The more difficult challenge is to maintain this change after it has been accomplished. Unfortunately, most people will slip up and return to drinking soon after they stop. The same thing can be said for people who stop smoking or using any other drug of abuse. These slips often lead to a full-scale return to excessive and uncontrolled use of the drug. Successful treatment, therefore, depends on making preparations for such incidents.

Alan Marlatt, a clinical psychologist at the University of Washington, and his colleagues have proposed a cognitive behavioral view of the relapse process (Marlatt, 1985; Marlatt, Blume, & Parks, 2001). This process applies to all forms of substance dependence, ranging from alcoholism to nicotine dependence (Shiffman et al., 1996). It has also been applied to other disorders associated with impulsive behavior, such as bulimia and inappropriate sexual behaviors (see Chapters 10 and 12). It places principal emphasis on events that take place after detoxification and the initial efforts at intensive treatment.

Alan Marlatt, Professor of Psychology at the University of Washington and a leading authority on psychological treatments for substance dependence, has promoted the use of relapse prevention methods.

The relapse prevention model addresses several important issues that confront the addict in trying to deal with the challenges of life without drugs. The model emphasizes increasing people's belief that they will be able to control their own behavior and events in their lives. The therapist also helps patients learn more adaptive coping responses, such as applied relaxation and social skills, that can be used in situations that formerly might have triggered drug use.

Another important feature of the relapse prevention model is concerned with the *abstinence violation effect,* which refers to the guilt and perceived loss of control that the person feels whenever he or she slips and finds himself or herself having a drink (or a cigarette or whatever drug is involved) after an extended period of abstinence. People typically blame themselves for failing to live up to their promise to quit. They also interpret the first drink or use of the drug as a signal that further efforts to control their drinking will be useless. The following brief case study describes one man's thoughts and feelings, shortly after he returned to the use of heroin. Just prior to this relapse, he had been actively involved in a treatment program and had stayed "clean" for several months.

BRIEF CASE STUDY
Relapse to Heroin Use

"It was like goin' home," he tells me later, "and mom's got your favorite dish on the stove, and you smell it, to the back of your tongue, way back. That's the rush of the dope. It's right there, and for like two, three minutes I'm floating. But it was just a quarter of a bag, a baby rush. So I get up and lay down in my bed, put on the (music) again. And I'm feeling dirty, man. I'm thinking, that wasn't nothing, it wasn't worth it. Two, three minutes of this hot euphoria and then I just nod off to sleep."

He slams his fist on his knee. "I can't believe how bad I (screwed) up," Mike wails through his tears. "Damn! I know what happened ain't nobody's fault but mine, and I'm eating myself up over it. I'm scared out of my mind. I mean, it's like I'm afraid of myself. I really see it now, there's so much (stuff) inside me from my past that I ain't worked out yet that I scare even me. So where do I go with that if they kick me out? How do I stay off the dope if I'm alone again?"

Mike looks up, his eyes wide, wet with tears.

"Maybe what they say is true, I'm already a junkie again. It's too late. But I did just one hit, that's all. And I can't be doing more dope, I know that. If I go on a real run of heroin this time, I won't come back, ever. I've seen it now—I *can* blow it, I *can* relapse, I can die. Damn! This is the time I need help more than ever, and this is when they're going to kick me out." (Shavelson, 2001, pp. 161 and 166)

Relapse prevention programs are aimed at exactly this type of conflict. They teach patients to expect that they may slip occasionally and to interpret these behaviors as a temporary "lapse" rather than a total "relapse."

Short-Term Motivational Therapy   Many people with substance use disorders do not seek or take full advantage of treatment opportunities because they fail to recognize the severity of their problems. Motivational interviewing is a nonconfrontational procedure that can be used to help people resolve their ambivalence about using drugs and make a definite commitment to change their behavior (Miller, 1995). It is based on the notion that in order to make a meaningful change, people must begin by recognizing the inconsistency between their current behavior and their long-term goals. For example, chronic heavy drinking is not compatible with academic or occupational success.

Motivational interviewing begins with a discussion of problems—issues reported by the patient as well as concerns that have been expressed by others such as friends and family members. The person is asked to reflect on feedback that is provided in a nonthreatening way. Rather than confronting the person, arguing about the reasons for drinking, or demanding action, the therapist responds empathically in an effort to avoid or minimize defensive reactions that will interfere with attempts to change.

The primary goal of this process is to increase the person's awareness of the nature of his or her substance use problems. Central features of motivational interviewing include a comprehensive assessment of the situation and personalized feedback. Emphasis is placed on ways in which the person sees his or her problems rather than assigning diagnostic labels, such as "alcoholism." Various options for creating change are discussed. The therapist and the patient work together to select the most appropriate method to follow. This stage of the interaction is designed to encourage the person's belief in his or her own ability to accomplish positive change.

Motivational interviewing may be most helpful to people whose substance abuse problems are not yet severe or chronic. It can be used as a stand-alone intervention or in combination with other approaches to treatment. If the person is not ready to abstain completely, short-term motivational therapy can be used to help the person reduce the frequency or intensity of alcohol consumption (Roberts & Marlatt, 1999).

Outcome Results and General Conclusions

Although many studies have evaluated the effects of alcohol treatment programs, two deserve special attention because of their large sample sizes and the rigorous methods that the investigators employed. One is known as Project MATCH because it was designed to test the potential value of matching certain kinds of clients to specific forms of treatment (Babor & Del Boca, 2003). In other words, would the outcomes associated with different forms of intervention be related to certain characteristics of the patients (such as the presence or absence of antisocial personality traits)?

The study evaluated three forms of psychological treatment: cognitive behavior therapy (12 sessions focused on coping skills and relapse prevention), 12-step facilitation therapy (12 sessions designed to help patients become engaged in AA), and motivational enhancement therapy (4 sessions over 12 weeks designed to increase commitment to change). Most of the people in all three groups attended at least some AA meetings in addition to their assigned form of treatment. More than 1,700 patients were randomly assigned to one of these three conditions. Outcome measures were collected for 3 years after the end of treatment.

Results indicated that all three forms of treatment led to major improvements in amount of drinking as well as other areas of life functioning (Miller & Longabaugh, 2003). Before treatment, patients in this study averaged 25 drinking days per month. After treatment, they averaged fewer than 6 days per month (across all forms of treatment). Patients who did drink decreased their average number of drinks from 15 to 3 drinks per day. Very few differences were found between the different treatment methods. The one exception favored 12-step facilitation therapy, in which 24 percent of patients were completely abstinent one year after treatment, compared to approximately 15 percent in the other two groups. Analyses that focused on the characteristics of individual clients suggested that there is relatively little reason to try to match certain kinds of patients to specific forms of treatment.

The second study involved a naturalistic evaluation of substance abuse treatment programs administered at 15 sites by the Department of Veterans Affairs (VA) (Finney, Moos, & Humphreys, 1999; Moos et al., 1999). The VA study compared programs that emphasized three approaches to the treatment of substance use disorders: 12-step programs, cognitive behavior therapy, and "eclectic therapy" (a combination of several approaches). The study included more than 3,000 patients. Most of these people had a diagnosis of alcohol dependence, but many also abused other types of drugs. Unlike Project MATCH, they were not randomly assigned to treatments. Despite these differences in methodology, results of the VA study were very similar to those obtained in Project MATCH. Patients in all three groups made significant improvements with regard to both patterns of substance use and levels of social and occupational functioning. People who participated in more treatment sessions had better outcomes than people who received less treatment. When differences were found between different forms of treatment, they tended to favor the 12-step programs. No support was found for the assumption that certain types of patients would do better in one form of treatment than in another.

Comprehensive reviews of these studies and the rest of the research literature regarding treatment of alcoholism and drug abuse point to several general conclusions (Donavan, 1999):

What factors predict better long-term outcome for treatment of alcoholism?

- People who enter treatment for various types of substance abuse and dependence typically show improvement in terms of reduced drug use that is likely to persist for several months following the end of treatment. Unfortunately, relapse is also relatively common.
- There is little evidence to suggest that one form of treatment (inpatient or outpatient, professional or self-help, individual or group) is more effective than another. When differences have been found, they tend to favor self-help groups, such as AA, particularly in terms of success in achieving abstinence.
- There is only limited support for the assumption that certain kinds of patients do better in one kind of treatment than another (the matching hypothesis).
- Increased amount of treatment and greater frequency of attendance in self-help meetings and aftercare counseling are associated with better outcomes.
- Among those people who are able to reduce their consumption of drugs, or abstain altogether, improvements following treatment are usually not limited to drug use alone but extend to the person's health in general as well as his or her social and occupational functioning.

Long-term outcome for the treatment of alcoholism is best predicted by the person's coping resources (social skills and problem-solving abilities), the availability of social support, and the level of stress in the environment. These considerations appear to be more important than the specific type of intervention that people receive. Those individuals who are in less stressful life situations, whose families are more cohesive and less supportive of continued drinking, and who are themselves better equipped with active coping skills are most likely to sustain their improvement over several years (Finney & Moos, 2002; Roberts & Marlatt, 1999).

getting help

If you have been looking for help in the area of substance dependence, you have probably noticed two things: (1) There are so many different sources of advice and information that the situation can quickly become quite confusing, and (2) the field is sharply divided on a number of crucial issues. Whose advice should you follow? Among all of the self-help books dealing with drugs and alcohol, one stands out on the basis of its strong link to the research literature as well as the extensive clinical experience of the author. Marc Schuckit's book, *Educating Yourself About Alcohol and Drugs: A People's Primer,* provides sensible answers to the questions asked by people who are wondering about their own, or someone else's, substance use problems.

Denial is a prominent feature of most substance use disorders. It is usually easier to dismiss suggestions that you have begun to use alcohol or drugs in a self-destructive pattern than it is to face the problem directly. Schuckit's book includes a perceptive chapter titled "Is there really a problem?" The bottom line is this: "If you repeatedly have returned to substance use even though that substance has caused a disruption in your life, you do have a problem." Subsequent chapters in Schuckit's book provide thoughtful and practical guidance on topics such as the symptoms of withdrawal, the process of detoxification, the relative merits of self-help groups, outpatient therapy, and hospitalization, and how to find a specific treatment program in your area.

The Internet also provides an enormous amount of information regarding substance use disorders. For information about problems associated with the use of alcohol and drugs, you might want to visit Web pages maintained by the National Institute on Alcohol Abuse and Alcoholism (*www.niaaa.nih.gov*) and the National Institute on Drug Abuse (*www.nida.nih.gov*). These Web sites are primarily concerned with information about federally funded research programs, but they also include answers to frequently asked questions, as well as treatment referral information.

Most people who enter treatment for substance use problems become involved, at least temporarily, with self-help groups such as Alcoholics Anonymous (AA) and Narcotics Anonymous (NA). Related groups, like Alanon and Alateen, are designed for the families and children of people who are dependent on alcohol. You can contact these groups through the Internet. The URL for Alcoholics Anonymous is *www.alcoholics-anonymous.org.* Many people believe, often passionately, that AA is the most beneficial program for helping people to recover from alcoholism. Others disagree. If you want to consider alternative points of view, visit the Web site maintained by Stanton Peele, who is one of AA's most persistent, enthusiastic, and articulate critics. The URL for his home page is *www.peele.net.* Peele challenges the biological reductionism that often dominates current views of alcoholism, and he promotes approaches to treatment that do not rely exclusively on total abstinence from drinking.

Evidence regarding the long-term outcome of serious substance use disorders can be discouraging, but it is important to remember that a substantial minority of people with these problems does manage to achieve an extended, stable recovery. The research literature does not point to one form of treatment as being clearly superior to another. Therefore, you should consider several alternatives to treatment and to select the one that makes most sense in terms of your own life and your own view of the world.

SUMMARY

DSM-IV-TR uses two terms to describe substance use disorders. **Substance dependence,** the more severe of the two forms, refers to a pattern of repeated self-administration that often results in **tolerance, withdrawal,** or compulsive drug-taking behavior. **Substance abuse** describes a more broadly conceived, less severe pattern of drug use that is defined in terms of interference with the person's ability to fulfill major role obligations at work or at home, recurrent use of a drug in dangerous situations, or repeated legal difficulties that are associated with drug use.

A **drug of abuse**—sometimes called a *psychoactive substance*—is a chemical substance that alters a person's mood, level of perception, or brain functioning. The list of chemicals on which people become dependent includes drugs that are legally available in the United States as well as many that are illegal. Although patterns of dependence are similar in some ways for all drugs, each type of drug also has some unique features.

Prolonged abuse of alcohol can have a devastating impact on social relationships and occupational functioning while disrupting the functions of several important organ systems. Alcohol dependence has more negative health consequences than does abuse of almost any drug, with the possible exception of nicotine.

Nicotine is one of the most harmful addicting drugs. Recognizing the serious long-term health consequences of exposure to nicotine, the U.S. Food and Drug Administration has prohibited the sale and distribution of tobacco products to children and adolescents. This policy attempts to prevent the development of nicotine addiction rather than trying to ban use of the drug completely.

The **psychomotor stimulants,** such as amphetamine and cocaine, activate the sympathetic nervous system and induce a positive mood state. High doses of amphetamines and cocaine can lead to the onset of psychosis. The most devastating effects of stimulant drugs center around the disruption of occupational and social roles.

Opiates have properties similar to those of opium and can induce a state of dreamlike euphoria. Tolerance develops quickly to opiates. After repeated use, their positive emotional effects are replaced by long-term negative changes in mood and emotion. Many of the severe health consequences of opiate use are the result of the lifestyle of the addict rather than the drug itself.

Barbiturates and **benzodiazepines** can be used, as prescribed by a physician, to decrease anxiety (tranquilizers) or help people sleep (hypnotics). They can also lead to a state of intoxication that is identical to that associated with alcohol. People who abruptly stop taking high doses of benzodiazepines may experience withdrawal symptoms, including a return of the original anxiety symptoms. Tolerance and withdrawal can develop after using barbiturates for several weeks.

Marijuana and **hashish** can induce a pervasive sense of well-being and happiness. People do not seem to develop tolerance to THC (the active ingredient in marijuana and hashish) unless they are exposed to high doses over an extended period of time. Withdrawal symptoms are unlikely to develop among people who smoke marijuana occasionally.

Hallucinogens induce vivid visual images that are usually pleasant but occasionally frightening. Unlike other drugs of abuse, hallucinogens are used sporadically rather than continuously. Most people do not increase their use of hallucinogens over time, and withdrawal symptoms are not observed.

It is impossible to specify a typical course for substance dependence. The specific pattern varies from one person to the next. In the case of alcoholism, the only thing that seems certain is that periods of heavy use alternate with periods of relative abstinence. Among alcoholic men in one long-term follow-up study, the proportion who became completely abstinent went up slowly but consistently over a period of many years. Relapse to alcohol abuse was unlikely among men who were able to remain abstinent for at least 6 years.

Alcohol dependence and abuse are the most common forms of mental disorder among men, with a lifetime prevalence of 13.8 percent in the ECA study. Among people with alcohol use disorders, men outnumber women by a ratio of approximately 5 to 1. Prevalence rates for alcohol dependence are highest among young adults and lowest among the elderly. According to the NCS, the combined lifetime prevalence for dependence on any type of controlled substance (those that are illegal or available only by prescription) was 7.5 percent.

Research on the etiology of alcoholism illustrates the ways in which various systems interact to produce and maintain drug dependence. The etiology of alcoholism is probably heterogeneous in nature. There are several pathways to the disorder. Social factors are particularly influential in the early phases of substance use. Initial experimentation with drugs is most likely to occur among those adolescents whose parents and peers model or encourage drug use. The culture in which a person lives influences the types of drugs that are used, the purposes for which they are used, and the expectations that people hold for the ways in which drugs will affect their experiences and behavior.

Considerable attention has been paid to the role of biological factors in the etiology of alcoholism, particularly the influence of genetic factors and neurochemical processes. Twin studies indicate that genetic factors influence patterns of social drinking as well as the onset of alcohol dependence. Adoption studies indicate that the offspring of alcoholic parents who are raised by nonalcoholic parents are more likely than people in the general population to develop drinking problems of their own. Genetic factors may be more influential in the development of alcoholism among men than among women.

The influence of genetic factors may vary in different subtypes of alcoholism. The Swedish adoption studies illustrate this possibility, focusing on the proposed distinction between Type 1 and Type 2 alcoholism. The combination of a genetic predisposition to alcoholism and environmental circumstances that encourage heavy drinking may lead to the onset of Type 1 alcoholism (late onset, no antisocial personality). In the case of Type 2 alcoholism (early onset, accompanied by antisocial personality), a genetic contribution increases risk for the disorder regardless of the type of environment in which the person is raised.

All of the psychoactive drugs cause increased dopamine activity in the reward pathways of the brain. Alcohol may stimulate the mesolimbic dopamine pathway directly, or it may act indirectly by inhibiting GABA neurons. Another focus of neurochemical research has been the role of endogenous opioids known as **endorphins.** Some theorists have argued that alcoholism is associated with excessive production of endorphins. A third neurochemical hypothesis suggests that alcohol dependence is caused by a genetically determined deficiency in serotonin activity in certain limbic areas of the brain.

Psychological explanations for the etiology of substance use disorders have often focused on the ability of drugs to relieve unpleasant emotional states. Expectations about drug effects have an important influence on the ways in which people respond to alcohol and other drugs. People who believe that alcohol enhances pleasure, reduces tension, and increases social performance are more likely than other people to drink frequently and heavily. The attention allocation theory is based on the recognition that alcohol reduces a person's capacity for cognitive activity. This process helps to explain the short-term effects of alcohol on mood and behavior, which may be reinforcing for some people.

Treatment of substance use disorders is an especially challenging and difficult task, in light of the fact that many people with these problems do not recognize or acknowledge their own difficulties. Recovery begins with a process of detoxification. Self-help programs, such as Alcoholics Anonymous, are the most widely used and probably one of the most beneficial forms of treatment.

KEY TERMS

barbiturates 356
benzodiazepines 356
detoxification 375
drug of abuse 346
endorphins 370

hallucinogens 357
hashish 356
high-risk research
   design 373
marijuana 356

opiates 354
polysubstance abuse 346
psychological
   dependence 348

psychomotor
   stimulants 352
substance abuse 345

substance dependence 345
tolerance 349
withdrawal 349

Go to www.prenhall.com/oltmanns for online quizzes, interactive flash cards, PowerPoint presentations, and chapter reviews.

13

Schizophrenic Disorders

◆◆

Schizophrenia is a severe form of abnormal behavior that encompasses what most of us have come to know as "madness." People with schizophrenia exhibit many different kinds of psychotic symptoms, indicating that the person has lost touch with reality. They may hear voices that aren't there or make comments that are difficult, if not impossible, to understand. Their behavior may be guided by absurd ideas and beliefs. For example, a person might believe that spaceships from another planet are beaming thoughts into his brain and controlling his behavior. Some people with schizophrenia recover fairly quickly, whereas others deteriorate progressively after the initial onset of symptoms. It is a disorder with "many different faces" (Andreasen, 2001). Because of the diversity of symptoms and outcomes shown by these patients, many clinicians believe that schizophrenia, or "the group of schizophrenias," may actually include several forms of disorder that have different causes. Others contend that schizophrenia is a single pathological process and that variations from one patient to the next in symptoms and course of the disorder reflect differences in the expression or severity of this process.

OVERVIEW

Many of the disorders that we have discussed in this book strike us as being familiar, at least in form if not in severity. For example, depression and anxiety are experiences with which we can easily empathize. Short-lived versions of these emotions help to shape our responses to daily events. Some clinical scientists speculate that mood and anxiety disorders may be viewed as evolved adaptations or mechanisms that can serve a useful purpose, but the symptoms of schizophrenia represent a different kind of problem. It is much harder for us to understand when someone hears voices that aren't there or speaks sentences that are meaningless. These symptoms seem to stem from a fundamental breakdown in basic cognitive functions that govern the way the person perceives and thinks about the world (McGuire & Troisi, 1998; Tsuang, 2001).

The most common symptoms of schizophrenia include changes in the way a person thinks, feels, and relates to other people and the outside environment. No single symptom or specific set of symptoms is characteristic of all schizophrenic patients. All of the individual symptoms of schizophrenia can also be associated with other psychological and medical conditions. Schizophrenia is officially defined by various combinations of psychotic symptoms in the absence of other forms of disturbance, such as mood disorders (especially manic episodes),

Painting by a young schizophrenic patient, illustrating his hallucinations. He saw monsters, like the one painted here, crawling on the floor. He also believed that the chairs next of his bed had turned into devils. Patient's description of the picture: "I was very sick at the time I painted this picture. The head represents my fragmented personality and a feeling of being helpless, hopeless, and off balance and of being in a cocoon of unreality. The bright colored rain and outlines represent the level of intensity of myself. The bright colors provided insulation and protected me. The colors felt like microwaves passing through my control center."

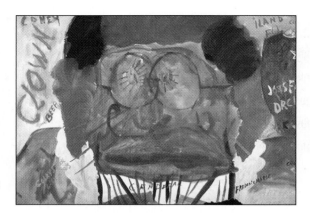

substance dependence, delirium, or dementia (see Chapter 14).

Schizophrenia is a devastating disorder for both the patients and their families. It can disrupt many aspects of the person's life, well beyond the experience of psychotic symptoms. The impact of this disorder is felt in many different ways. For people who develop schizophrenia, it often has a dramatic and lasting impact on their quality of life, both in terms of their own subjective satisfaction and their ability to complete an education, hold a job, and develop social relationships with other people. Approximately 10 percent of schizophrenic patients commit suicide (Andreasen, 2000).

For family members of patients with schizophrenia, the consequences can also be cruel. They must come to grips with the fact that their son or daughter, or brother or sister, has developed a severe disorder that may change his or her life forever. One woman whose daughter, then in her mid-thirties, had exhibited symptoms of schizophrenia for 17 years, described her feelings in the following way: "Nothing in (our daughter's) growing up years could have prepared us for the shock and devastation of seeing this normal, happy child become totally incapacitated by schizophrenia" (Smith, 1991, p. 691).

Schizophrenia also has an enormous impact on society. Among mental disorders, it is the second leading cause of disease burden (see Table 1–3 on page 21). Most people who develop the disorder do not recover completely, and many become homeless because long-term institutional care is not available (see Chapter 18). In the United States the financial costs associated with schizophrenia are greater than those incurred by all forms of cancer (Thaker & Carpenter, 2001).

In the following case studies we describe the experiences of two people who exhibited symptoms of schizophrenia. DSM-IV-TR divides schizophrenic disorders into several subtypes, based primarily on the type of symptoms that the patient exhibits. Our first case illustrates the paranoid subtype of schizophrenia, which is characterized by a preoccupation with one or more delusions or by frequent auditory hallucinations, most often persecutory.

CASE STUDY A New Mother's Paranoid Schizophrenia

Ann was 21 years old the first time that she was admitted to a psychiatric hospital. She had completed business college and had worked as a receptionist until she became pregnant with her son, who was born 6 months prior to her admission. She and her husband lived in a small apartment with his 5-year-old daughter from a previous marriage. This was her first psychotic episode.

The first signs of Ann's disturbance appeared during her pregnancy, when she accused her husband of having an affair with her sister. The accusation was based on a conversation that Ann had overheard on a bus. Two women (who were neighbors in Ann's apartment building) had been discussing an affair that some woman's husband was having.

Ann believed that this might have been their way of telling her about her husband's infidelity. Although her husband and her sister denied any romantic interest in each other, Ann clung to her suspicions and began to monitor her husband's activities closely. She also avoided talking with her neighbors and friends.

Before this period of time, Ann had been an outgoing and energetic person. Now she seemed listless and apathetic and would often spend days without leaving their apartment. Her husband at first attributed this change in her behavior to the pregnancy, believing that she would "snap out of it" after the baby was born. Unfortunately, Ann became even more socially isolated following the birth of her son.

She seldom left her bedroom and would spend hours alone, mumbling softly to herself.

Ann's behavior deteriorated markedly 2 weeks prior to her hospital admission, when she noticed that some photographs of herself and her baby were missing. She told her husband that they had been stolen and were being used to cast a voodoo spell on her. Ann became increasingly preoccupied with this belief in subsequent days. She called her mother repeatedly, insisting that something would have to be done to recover the missing photographs. Her friends and family tried to reassure Ann that the photographs had probably been misplaced or accidentally discarded, but she was totally unwilling to consider alternative explanations.

Ann finally announced to everyone who would listen that someone was trying to kill her and the children.

Believing that all the food in the house had been poisoned, she refused to eat and would not feed the children.

She became increasingly suspicious, hostile, and combative. Her husband and parents found it impossible to reason with her. She was no longer able to care for herself or the children. The family sought advice from their family physician, who recommended that they contact a psychiatrist. After meeting with Ann briefly, the psychiatrist recommended that she be hospitalized for a short period of time.

After admission, Ann argued heatedly with the hospital staff, denying that she was mentally disturbed and insisting that she must be released so that she could protect her children from the conspiracy. She had no insight into the nature of her problems.

The onset of schizophrenia typically occurs during adolescence or early adulthood. The period of risk for the development of a first episode is considered to be between the ages of 15 and 35. The number of new cases drops off slowly after that, with very few people experiencing an initial episode after the age of 55 (Gottesman, 1991).

The problems of most patients can be divided into three phases of variable and unpredictable duration: prodromal, active, and residual. Symptoms such as hallucinations, delusions, and disorganized speech are characteristic of the active phase of the disorder. The **prodromal phase** precedes the active phase and is marked by an obvious deterioration in role functioning as a student, employee, or homemaker. The person's friends and relatives often view the beginning of the prodromal phase as a change in his or her personality. Prodromal signs and symptoms are similar to those associated with schizotypal personality disorder (see Chapter 9). They include peculiar behaviors (such as talking to one's self in public), unusual perceptual experiences, outbursts of anger, increased tension, and restlessness. Social withdrawal, indecisiveness, and lack of willpower are often seen during the prodromal phase (Lencz et al., 2003).

The **residual phase** follows the active phase of the disorder and is defined by signs and symptoms that are similar in many respects to those seen during the prodromal phase. At this point, the most dramatic symptoms of psychosis have improved, but the person continues to be impaired in various ways. Negative symptoms, such as impoverished expression of emotions, may remain pronounced during the residual phase (McGlashan, 1998).

After the onset of schizophrenia, many people do not return to expected levels of social and occupational adjustment. Some prefer social isolation and avoid contact with other people. The man in our second case illustrates this pattern. He is also an example of the disorganized type of schizophrenia. Patients who fit criteria for this category say things that are difficult to understand, behave in a disorganized way, and fail to express expected emotions.

CASE STUDY Edward's Disorganized Schizophrenia

Edward was 39 years old and had lived at home with his parents since dropping out of school after the tenth grade. Edward worked on and off as a helper in his father's roofing business prior to his first psychotic episode at the age of 26. After that time, he was socially isolated and unable to hold any kind of job. He was hospitalized in psychiatric facilities 10 times in the next 14 years. When he was not in the hospital, most of his time at home was spent watching television or sitting alone in his room.

The tenth episode of psychosis became evident when Edward told his mother that he had seen people arguing violently on the sidewalk in front of their house. He believed that this incident was the beginning of World War II. His mother tried to persuade him that he had witnessed an ordinary, though perhaps heated, disagreement between two neighbors, but Edward could not be convinced. He continued to mumble about the fight and became increasingly agitated over the next few days. When he wasn't pacing back and forth from his bedroom to the living room, he could usually be found staring out the front window. Several days after witnessing the argument, he took curtains from several windows in the house and burned them in the street at 2 A.M. A neighbor happened to see what Edward was doing and called the police. When they arrived, they found Edward wandering in a snow-covered vacant lot, talking incoherently to himself. Recognizing that Edward was psychotic, the police took him to the psychiatric hospital.

Although his appearance was somewhat disheveled, Edward was alert and cooperative. He knew the current date and recognized that he was in a psychiatric hospital. Some of his speech was incoherent, and his answers to questions posed by the hospital staff were frequently irrelevant. For example, the following exchange occurred during a structured diagnostic interview. The psychologist asked Edward whether he had any special powers or abilities that other people do not have. He responded by saying that he didn't know because he didn't date women. Puzzled by this tangential response, the psychologist asked him to explain what he meant. Edward responded by asking his own question, "If you had a star in the middle of your head, would you swallow marbles?"

Edward's expressive gestures were severely restricted, and he sat in a relatively motionless position. Although he said that he was frightened by the recent events that he reported to his mother, his face did not betray any signs of emotion. He mumbled slowly in a monotonous tone of voice that was difficult to understand. He said that he could hear God's voice telling him that his father was "the Master of the universe" and he claimed that he had "seen the shadow of the Master."

Other voices seemed to argue with one another about Edward's special calling and whether he was worthy of this divine power.

The voices told him to prepare for God's return to earth. At times Edward said that he was a Nazi soldier and that he was born in Germany in 1886. He also spoke incoherently about corpses frozen in Greenland and maintained that he was "only half a person."

SYMPTOMS

In this section we describe in greater detail various types of symptoms that are commonly observed among schizophrenic patients and that are currently emphasized by official diagnostic systems, such as DSM-IV-TR. All of these symptoms can fluctuate in severity over time. Some patients exhibit persistent psychotic symptoms. Others experience symptoms during acute episodes and are better adjusted between episodes.

The symptoms of schizophrenia can be divided into three dimensions: positive symptoms, negative symptoms, and disorganization (Andreasen et al., 1995; Lenzenweger, 1999). **Positive symptoms,** also called *psychotic symptoms,* include hallucinations and delusions. In contrast, **negative symptoms** include characteristics such as lack of initiative, social withdrawal, and deficits in emotional responding. Some additional symptoms of schizophrenia, such as incoherent or disorganized speech, do not fit easily into either the positive or negative types. Verbal communication problems and bizarre behavior represent this third dimension, which is sometimes called disorganization. Note that these symptom dimensions overlap and combine in various ways within individual patients.

Positive Symptoms

The term *positive symptoms* of schizophrenia does not imply that these symptoms are beneficial or adaptive. Rather, it suggests that they are characterized by the presence of an aberrant response (such as hearing a voice that is not really there). Negative symptoms, on the other hand, are characterized by the absence of a particular response (such as emotion, speech, or willpower).

Hallucinations Our senses provide us with basic information that is vital to our notions of who we are, what we are doing, and what others think of us. Many people with schizophrenia experience perplexing and often frightening changes in perception. The most obvious perceptual symptoms are **hallucinations,** or sensory experiences that are not caused by actual external stimuli. Although hallucinations can occur in any of the senses, those experienced by schizophrenic patients are most often auditory. Many patients hear voices that comment on their behavior or give them instructions. Others hear voices that seem to argue with one another. Edward heard

Many of the symptoms of schizophrenia, including hallucinations and delusions, can be extremely distressing.

the voice of God talking to him. Like Edward, most patients find such voices to be frightening (Delespaul et al., 2002). In some cases, however, hallucinations can be comforting or pleasing to the patient.

Hallucinations should be distinguished from the transient mistaken perceptions that most people experience from time to time (Ohayon, 2000; Slade & Bentall, 1988). Have you ever turned around after thinking you heard someone call your name, to find that no one was there? You probably dismissed the experience as "just your imagination." Hallucinations, in contrast, strike the person as being real, in spite of the fact that they have no basis in reality. They are also persistent over time. Patients who experience auditory hallucinations often hear the voice (or voices) speaking to them throughout the day and for many days at a time.

Delusional Beliefs Many schizophrenic patients express **delusions,** or idiosyncratic beliefs that are rigidly held in spite of their preposterous nature (Maher, 2001; Stanton & David, 2000). Delusions have sometimes been defined as false beliefs based on incorrect inferences about reality. This definition has a number of problems, including the difficulty of establishing the ultimate truth of many situations. Ann's accusation that her husband was having an affair, for example, could easily become a choice between her word and his. This suspicion would not, on its own, be considered a delusion. The judgment that her beliefs were delusional depended to a large extent on their expansion to more absurd concerns about stolen photographs, voodoo spells, and alleged plots to kill her children.

Several additional characteristics are important in identifying delusions (Applebaum et al., 1999). In the most obvious cases, delusional patients express and defend their beliefs with utmost conviction, even when presented with contradictory evidence. For example, Ann's belief that the stolen photographs were being used to cast a spell on her was totally fixed and resistant to contradiction or reconsideration. Preoccupation is another defining characteristic of delusional beliefs. During periods of acute psychosis, many patients like Ann find it difficult, if not impossible, to avoid thinking or talking about these beliefs. Finally, delusional patients typically are unable to consider the perspective that other people hold with regard to their beliefs. Ann, for example, was unable to

appreciate the fact that other people considered her paranoid beliefs to be ridiculous.

Although delusional beliefs can take many forms, they are typically personal. They are not shared by other members of the person's family or cultural group. Common delusions include the belief that thoughts are being inserted into the patient's head, that other people are reading the patient's thoughts, or that the patient is being controlled by mysterious, external forces (Frith & Dolan, 2000; Gutierrez-Lobos et al., 2001). Many delusions focus on grandiose or paranoid content. For example, Edward expressed the grandiose belief that his father was the Master of the universe. Ann clung persistently to the paranoid belief that someone was trying to kill her and her children.

In actual clinical practice, delusions are complex and difficult to define (Lesser & O'Donohue, 1999; Oltmanns, 1988). Their content is sometimes bizarre and confusing, as in the case of Edward's insistence that he had witnessed the beginning of World War II. Delusions are often fragmented, especially among severely disturbed patients. In other words, delusions are not always coherent belief systems that are consistently expressed by the patient. At various times, for example, Edward talked about being a Nazi soldier and half a person. Connections among these fragmented ideas are difficult to understand.

What is the difference between hallucinations and delusions?

The subjective experiences of people who struggle with schizophrenia are an important source of knowledge about this disorder, particularly delusional beliefs. Some of the most fundamental elements of psychosis involve private events that cannot be observed directly by others. Fortunately, many articulate patients have provided compelling accounts of their own internal struggles. The following paragraphs were written by a patient who was being treated for schizophrenia. She describes experiences that are part of an elaborate delusional belief system.

Negative Symptoms

Negative symptoms of schizophrenia are defined in terms of responses or functions that appear to be missing from the person's behavior. In that sense, they may initially be more subtle or difficult to recognize than the positive symptoms of this disorder. Negative symptoms tend to be more stable over time than positive symptoms, which fluctuate in severity as the person moves in and out of active phases of psychosis (Earnst & Kring, 1997).

Affective and Emotional Disturbances   One of the most common symptoms of schizophrenia involves a flattening or restriction of the person's nonverbal display of emotional responses. This symptom, called **blunted affect,** or *affective flattening,* was clearly present in Edward's case. Blunted patients fail to exhibit signs of emotion or feeling. They are neither happy nor sad, and they appear to be completely indifferent to their surroundings. The faces of blunted patients are apathetic and expressionless. Their voices lack the typical fluctuations in volume and pitch that other people use to signal changes in their mood. Events in their environment hold little consequence for them. They may demonstrate a complete lack of concern for themselves and for others (Dworkin et al., 1998).

Another type of emotional deficit is called **anhedonia,** which refers to the inability to experience pleasure. Whereas blunted affect refers to the lack of outward expression, anhedonia is a lack of positive subjective feelings. People who experience anhedonia typically lose interest in recreational activities and social relationships, which they do not find enjoyable. They may also be unable to experience pleasure from physical sensations, such as taste and touch.

Longitudinal studies indicate that anhedonia associated with both social and physical experiences is an enduring feature of the disorder for many people with schizophrenia (Blanchard, Horan, & Brown, 2001; Herbener & Harrow, 2002). For some people, it may also be an early marker, signaling the onset of the prodromal phase of the disorder (Kwapil, 1998). Like other symptoms of schizophrenia, anhedonia is not unique to this disorder; it is also found among people who are severely depressed (Romney & Candido, 2001).

Apathy, Avolition, and Alogia   One of the most important and seriously debilitating aspects of schizophrenia is a malfunction of interpersonal relationships (Meehl, 1993). Many people with schizophrenia become socially withdrawn. In

---

FIRST PERSON ACCOUNT OF DELUSIONAL BELIEFS

"At the beginning of my last year at (the university), 'feelings' began to descend on me. I felt distinctly different from my usual self. I would sit for hours on end staring at nothing, and I became fascinated with drawing weird, disconnected monsters. I carefully hid my drawings, because I was certain I was being watched. Eventually I became aware of a magical force outside myself that was compelling me in certain directions. The force gained power as time went on, and soon it made me take long walks at 2 or 3 o'clock in the morning down dark alleys in my high-crime neighborhood. I had no power to disobey the force. During my walks I felt as though I was in a different, magical, four-dimensional universe. I understood that the force wanted me to take those walks so that I might be killed.

"I do not clearly understand the relationship between the force and the Alien Beings (alas, such a name!), but my universe soon became populated with them. The Alien Beings were from outer space, and of all the people in the world, only I was aware of them. The Alien Beings soon took over my body and removed me from it. They took me to a faraway place of beaches and sunlight and placed an Alien in my body to act like me. At this point I had the distinct impression that I did not really exist, because I could not make contact with my kidnapped self. I also saw that the Aliens were starting to take over other people as well, removing them from their bodies and putting Aliens in their place. Of course, the other people were unaware of what was happening; I was the only person in the world who had the power to know it. At this point I determined that the Aliens were involved in a huge conspiracy against the world.

"The Alien Beings were gaining strength and had given me a complex set of rules. The rules were very specific and governed every aspect of my behavior. One of the rules was that I could not tell anyone else about the Aliens or the rules, or else the Aliens would kill me. Another of the rules was that I had to become utterly, completely mad. So now I was living in a world of great fear.

"I had a number of other symptoms as well. I felt as though I had been pushed deep within myself, and I had little or no reaction to events or emotions around me. Almost daily the world became unreal to me. Everything outside of me seemed to fade into the distance; everything was miles away from me. I came to feel that I had the power to influence the behavior of animals; that I could, for instance, make dogs bark simply by hooking up rays of thought from my mind to theirs. Conversely, I felt that certain people had the capacity to read my mind. I became very frightened of those people and tried my best to avoid them. Whenever I saw a group of two or three people, I was sure they were talking about me. Paranoia is a very painful emotion! But when I saw crowds of people (as in a shopping mall), I felt an acute longing to wander among them, singing hymns and nursery rhymes" (Payne, 1992, pp. 726–727).

many cases, social isolation develops before the onset of symptoms, such as hallucinations and delusions. It can be one of the earliest signs that something is wrong. This was certainly true in Ann's case. She became socially isolated from her family and friends many weeks before she started to talk openly about the stolen pictures and the plot to kill her children. Social withdrawal appears to be both a symptom of the disorder and a strategy that is actively employed by some patients to deal with their other symptoms. They may, for example, attempt to minimize interactions with other people in order to reduce levels of stimulation that can exacerbate perceptual and cognitive disorganization (Walker, Davis, & Baum, 1993).

The withdrawal seen among many schizophrenic patients is accompanied by indecisiveness, ambivalence, and a loss of willpower. This symptom is known as **avolition** (lack of volition or will). A person who suffers from avolition becomes apathetic and ceases to work toward personal goals or to function independently. He or she might sit listlessly in a chair all day, not washing or combing his or her hair for weeks.

Another negative symptom involves a form of speech disturbance called **alogia,** which refers to impoverished thinking. Literally translated, it means "speechlessness." In one form of alogia, known as *poverty of speech,* patients show remarkable reductions in the amount of speech. They simply don't have anything to say. In another

form, referred to as thought blocking, the patient's train of speech is interrupted before a thought or idea has been completed.

Disorganization

Some symptoms of schizophrenia do not fit easily into either the positive or negative type. Thinking disturbances and bizarre behavior represent a third symptom dimension, which is sometimes called disorganization (Grube, Bilder, & Goldman, 1998; Peralta & Cuesta, 1999; van Os et al., 1996).

Thinking Disturbances One important set of schizophrenic symptoms, known as **disorganized speech,** involves the tendency of some patients to say things that don't make sense. Signs of disorganized speech include making irrelevant responses to questions, expressing disconnected ideas, and using words in peculiar ways (Berenbaum & Barch, 1995). This symptom is also called *thought disorder,* because clinicians have assumed that the failure to communicate successfully reflects a disturbance in the thought patterns that govern verbal discourse. The woman described in the following case exhibited signs of disorganized speech.

◆◆

CASE STUDY Marsha's Disorganized Speech and Bizarre Behavior

Marsha was a 32-year-old graduate student in political science. She had never been treated for psychological problems.

Marsha called Dr. Higgins, a clinical psychologist who taught at the university, to ask if she could speak with him about her twin sister's experience with schizophrenia.

When she arrived at his office, she was neatly dressed and had a Bible tucked tightly under her arm. The next 3 hours were filled with a rambling discussion of Marsha's experiences during the past 10 years. She talked about her education, her experience as a high school teacher before returning to graduate school, her relationships with her parents, and

most of all her concern for her identical twin sister, Alice, who had spent 6 of the last 10 years in psychiatric hospitals.

Marsha's emotional expression vacillated dramatically throughout the course of this conversation, which was punctuated by silly giggles and heavy sighs. Her voice would be loud and emphatic one moment as she talked about her stimulating ideas and special talents. At other moments, she would whisper in a barely audible voice or sob quietly as she described the desperation, fear, and frustration that she had experienced watching the progression of her sister's disorder. She said that she had been feeling very uptight in recent months, afraid that she might be "going crazy" like her sister. She had been scared to death to go home because her parents might sense that something was wrong

with her. Her behavior was frequently inconsistent with the content of her speech. As she described her intense fears, for example, Marsha occasionally giggled uncontrollably.

Dr. Higgins also found Marsha's train of thought difficult to follow. Her speech rambled illogically from one topic to the next, and her answers to his questions were frequently tangential. For example, when Dr. Higgins asked what she meant by her repeated use of the phrase "the ideal can become real," Marsha replied, "Well, after serving the Word of Christ in California for 3 years, making a public spectacle of myself, someone apparently called my parents and said I had a problem. I said I can't take this anymore and went home. I perceived that Mom was just unbelievably nice to me. I began to think that my face was changing.

Something about my forehead resembled the pain of Christ. I served Christ, but my power was not lasting."

At the end of this 3-hour interview, Dr. Higgins was convinced that Marsha should be referred to the mental health center for outpatient treatment. He explained his concerns to Marsha, but she refused to follow his advice, insisting that she did not want to receive the medication with which her sister had been treated. She agreed to return to Dr. Higgins's office in 3 days for another interview, but she did not keep that appointment.

Two weeks later, Marsha called Dr. Higgins to ask if he would talk with her immediately. It was very difficult to understand what she was saying, but she seemed to be repeating in a shrill voice "I'm losing my mind." The door to his office was closed when she arrived, but he could hear her shuffling awkwardly down the hallway, breathing heavily. He opened his door and found Marsha standing in a rigid posture, arms stiffly at her sides. Her eyes were opened wide, and she was staring vacantly at the nameplate on his door. In contrast to her prim

and neat appearance at their first meeting, Marsha's hair and clothes were now in disarray. She walked stiffly into the office without bending her knees and sat, with some difficulty, in the chair next to Dr. Higgins's desk. Her facial expression was rigidly fixed. Although her eyes were open and she appeared to hear his voice, Marsha did not respond to any of Dr. Higgins's questions. Recognizing that Marsha was experiencing an acute psychotic episode, Dr. Higgins and one of the secretaries took her to the emergency room at the local hospital.

◆◆

Marsha's speech provides one typical example of disorganized speech. She was not entirely incoherent, but parts of her speech were difficult to follow. Connections between sentences were sometimes arbitrary, and her answers to the interviewer's questions were occasionally irrelevant.

The following excerpt from an interview with another patient illustrates a more extreme form of disorganized speech.

> **Interviewer:** Have you been nervous or tense lately?
> **Patient:** No, I got a head of lettuce.
> **Interviewer:** You got a head of lettuce? I don't understand.
> **Patient:** Well, it's just a head of lettuce.
> **Interviewer:** Tell me about lettuce. What do you mean?
> **Patient:** Well, . . . lettuce is a transformation of a dead cougar that suffered a relapse on the lion's toe. And he swallowed the lion and something happened. The . . . see, the . . . Gloria and Tommy, they're two heads and they're not whales. But they escaped with herds of vomit, and things like that. (Neale & Oltmanns, 1980, p. 102)

When speech becomes this disrupted, it is considered incoherent. Notice that this patient did not string words together in a random fashion. His speech followed grammatical rules. He was placing nouns and verbs together in an appropriate order, but they didn't make any sense. His speech conveyed little, if any, meaning, and that is the hallmark of disorganized speech.

Several types of verbal communication disruption contribute to clinical judgments about disorganized speech (Docherty et al., 1996; Kerns

& Berenbaum, 2002). Common features of disorganized speech in schizophrenia include shifting topics too abruptly, called *loose associations* or *derailment*; replying to a question with an irrelevant response, called *tangentiality*; or persistently repeating the same word or phrase over and over again, called *perseveration*. We all say things from time to time that fit these descriptions. It is not the occasional presence of a single feature but, rather, the accumulation of a large number of such features that defines the presence of disorganized speech.

Bizarre Behavior   Schizophrenic patients may exhibit various forms of unusual motor behavior, such as the rigidity displayed by Marsha when she appeared for her second interview with Dr. Higgins. *Catatonia* most often refers to immobility and marked muscular rigidity, but it can also refer to excitement and overactivity. For example, some patients engage in apparently purposeless pacing or repetitious movements, such as rubbing their hands together in a special pattern for hours at a time. Many catatonic patients exhibit reduced or awkward spontaneous movements. In more extreme forms, patients may assume unusual postures or remain in rigid standing or sitting positions for long periods of time. For example, some patients will lie flat on their backs in a stiff position with their heads raised slightly off the floor as though they were resting on a pillow. Catatonic patients typically resist attempts to alter their position, even though maintaining their awkward postures would normally be extremely uncomfortable or painful.

Catatonic posturing is often associated with a *stuporous state*, or generally reduced responsiveness. The person seems to be unaware of his or her surroundings. For example, during her acute psychotic episode, Marsha refused to answer questions or to make eye contact with others. Unlike people with other stuporous conditions, however, catatonic patients seem to maintain a clear state of consciousness, and it is likely that Marsha could hear and understand everything that Dr. Higgins said to her. Many patients report after the end of a catatonic episode that they were perfectly aware of events that were taking place around them, in spite of their failure to respond appropriately.

Another kind of bizarre behavior involves affective responses that are obviously inconsistent with the person's situation. This symptom is particularly difficult to describe in words. The most remarkable features of **inappropriate affect** are incongruity and lack of adaptability in emotional expression. For example, when Marsha described the private terror that she felt in the presence of her family, she giggled in a silly fashion. The content of Marsha's speech was inconsistent with her facial expression, her gestures, and her voice quality.

DIAGNOSIS

The broad array of symptoms outlined in the previous section have all been described as being part of schizophrenic disorders. The specific organization of symptoms has been a matter of some controversy for many years. Schizophrenic disorders have been defined in many different ways. In the following pages we briefly review some of the more prominent trends that led to the DSM-IV-TR description of these disorders.

Brief Historical Perspective

Descriptions of schizophrenic symptoms can be traced far back in history, but they were not considered to be symptoms of a single disorder until late in the nineteenth century (Gottesman, 1991). At that time, Emil Kraepelin, a German psychiatrist, suggested that several types of problems that previously had been classified as distinct forms of disorder should be grouped together under a single diagnostic category called *dementia praecox*. This term referred to psychoses that ended in severe intellectual deterioration (dementia) and that had an early or premature (praecox) onset, usually during adolescence. Kraepelin argued that these patients could be distinguished from those suffering from other disorders (most

notably manic–depressive psychosis) largely on the basis of changes that occurred as the disorder progressed over time, primarily those changes involving the integrity of mental functions.

In 1911, Eugen Bleuler (1857–1939), a Swiss psychiatrist and a contemporary of Kraepelin, published an influential monograph in which he agreed with most of Kraepelin's suggestions about this disorder. He did not believe, however, that the disorder always ended in profound deterioration or that it always began in late adolescence. Kraepelin's term *dementia praecox* was, therefore, unacceptable to him. Bleuler suggested a new name for the disorder—*schizophrenia*. This term referred to the *splitting of mental associations*, which Bleuler believed to be the fundamental disturbance in schizophrenia. One unfortunate consequence of this choice of terms has been the confusion among laypeople of schizophrenia with dissociative identity disorder (also known as multiple personality), a severe form of dissociative disorder (see Chapter 7). The two disorders actually have very little in common.

Many other suggestions have been made in subsequent years regarding the description and diagnosis of schizophrenia (Gottesman, 1991; Neale & Oltmanns, 1980). Some clinicians have favored a broader definition, whereas others have argued for a more narrow approach.

DSM-IV-TR

The current U.S. approach to the diagnosis of schizophrenic disorders gives primary consideration to three types of symptoms: positive

These dementia praecox patients, treated by Emil Kraeplin in the late nineteenth century, display "waxy flexibility," a feature of catatonic motor behavior. "They were put without difficulty in the peculiar positions and kept them, some with a sly laugh, others with rigid seriousness."

The Swiss psychiatrist Eugen Bleuler coined the term *schizophrenia* in his 1911 monograph on the disorder.

TABLE 13–1 DSM-IV-TR Diagnostic Criteria for Schizophrenia

A. Characteristic Symptoms: Two (or more) of the following, each present for a significant portion of time during a 1-month period (or less if successfully treated):

1. Delusions
2. Hallucinations
3. Disorganized speech (such as frequent derailment or incoherence)
4. Grossly disorganized or catatonic behavior
5. Negative symptoms, such as affective flattening, alogia, or avolition

(*Note:* Only one A symptom is required if delusions are bizarre or hallucinations consist of a voice keeping up a running commentary on the person's behavior or thoughts, or two or more voices conversing with each other.)

B. Social/Occupational Dysfunction: For a significant portion of the time since the onset of the disturbance, one or more major areas of functioning such as work, interpersonal relations, or self-care is markedly below the level achieved prior to the onset.

C. Duration: Continuous signs of the disturbance persist for at least 6 months. This 6-month period must include at least 1 month of symptoms that meet criterion A (active phase symptoms), and may include periods of prodromal or residual symptoms. During these prodromal or residual periods, the signs of the disturbance may be manifested by only negative symptoms or two or more symptoms listed in Criterion A present in an attenuated form (such as odd beliefs, unusual perceptual experiences).

Reprinted with permission from the *Diagnostic and Statistical Manual of Mental Disorders,* Fourth Edition, Text Revision. Copyright © 2000 by the American Psychiatric Association.

(psychotic) symptoms, negative symptoms, and disorganized speech and behavior. The DSM-IV-TR definition includes a more restricted range of symptoms than Bleuler's description of the disorder, which placed less emphasis on the presence of persistent psychotic symptoms such as hallucinations and delusions. The inclusion of negative symptoms does represent, however, a remnant of Bleuler's influence.

DSM-IV-TR lists several specific criteria for schizophrenia (see Table 13–1). The first requirement (Criterion A) is that the patient must exhibit two (or more) active symptoms for at least 1 month. Notice that only one of the characteristic symptoms is required if that symptom is a bizarre delusion or hallucination that fits Schneider's description of first-rank symptoms. Negative symptoms, such as blunted affect, avolition, and social withdrawal, play a relatively prominent role in the DSM-IV-TR definition of schizophrenia, although some concern has been expressed about the reliability with which they are measured. The work group that developed DSM-IV-TR considered negative symptoms vital both to determining the causes of the disorder and to treating it successfully (Andreasen & Carpenter, 1993).

The DSM-IV-TR definition also takes into account social and occupational functioning as well as the duration of the disorder (Criteria B and C). These criteria reflect the influence of Kraepelin, who argued that the disorder is accompanied by marked impairment in functioning as well as a chronic, deteriorating course. The DSM-IV-TR definition requires evidence of a decline in the person's social or occupational functioning as well as the presence of disturbed behavior over a continuous period of at least 6 months. Active phase symptoms do not need to be present for this entire period. The total duration of disturbance is determined by adding together continuous time during which the person has exhibited prodromal, active, and residual symptoms of schizophrenia. If the person displays psychotic symptoms for at least 1 month but less than 6 months, the diagnosis would be schizophreniform disorder. The diagnosis would be changed to schizophrenic disorder if the person's problems persisted beyond the 6-month limit.

The final consideration in arriving at a diagnosis of schizophrenia involves the exclusion of related conditions, especially mood disorders. According to DSM-IV-TR, active phase symptoms of schizophrenia must appear in the absence of a major depressive or manic episode. If symptoms of depression or mania are present, their duration must be brief relative to the duration of the active and residual symptoms of schizophrenia.

Subtypes

Schizophrenia is a heterogeneous disorder with many different clinical manifestations and levels of severity. The title of Bleuler's classic text referred to "the group of schizophrenias" in an effort to draw attention to the varied presentations of the disorder. It is not clear, however, how best to think about the different forms of schizophrenia. Many clinicians and investigators believe that schizophrenia is a general term for a group of disorders, each of which may be caused by a completely different set of factors. Other clinicians believe that the numerous symptoms of schizophrenia are most likely varying manifestations of the same underlying condition (Gottesman, 1991). Given the current state of evidence, it is not possible to choose between these conceptual options. Nevertheless, most investigators agree that we should at least consider the possibility that there are distinct forms.

DSM-IV-TR recognizes five subtypes of schizophrenia. The subtypes are used to describe the clinical state of the patient during the most recent examination. Only one subtype can be assigned at any point in time. The five subtypes are arranged in a hierarchy so that patients who exhibit symptoms of different subtypes can be diagnosed. The catatonic type is at the top of the hierarchy. Patients who fit this description are diagnosed as catatonic even if they show additional symptoms that are characteristic of other subtypes. The remaining subtypes, in descending order, are the disorganized subtype, the paranoid subtype, the undifferentiated subtype, and the residual subtype (see Critical Thinking *Matters*).

The **catatonic type** is characterized by symptoms of motor immobility (including rigidity and posturing) or excessive and purposeless motor activity. In some cases, the person may be resistant to all instructions or refuse to speak, for no apparent reason. Catatonic patients may also show a decreased awareness of their environment and a lack of movement and activity. If her disorder lasted more than 6 months, Marsha would probably have received a diagnosis of schizophrenic disorder, catatonic type, on the basis of her prominent motor symptoms and stuporous behavior.

The **disorganized type** of schizophrenia is characterized by disorganized speech, disorganized behavior, and flat or inappropriate affect. All three features must be present to make this diagnosis. Social impairment is usually quite marked in these patients. The patient's speech is frequently incoherent, and if delusions or hallucinations are present, their content is usually not well organized. Consider, for example, the delusions expressed by Edward. At various times, he talked about Nazi soldiers and World War II, frozen corpses in Greenland, being "half a person," and having special powers because he was

Why do clinical scientists say that schizophrenia is a "heterogeneous" disorder?

critical thinking m a t t e r s

ARE SYMPTOM-BASED SUBTYPES OF SCHIZOPHRENIA USEFUL?

The validity of the traditional subtypes has been debated for many years. The evidence on which they are based is quite weak. Clinicians who favor continued use of subtype diagnoses claim that these categories are *moderately* stable over time (Fenton, 2000). There is also some evidence indicating that patients who fit descriptions of the catatonic and paranoid subtypes have a somewhat better prognosis, whereas those in the disorganized subtype may have—on average—a worse prognosis (McGlashan & Fenton, 1991). If we think critically, this is *not* strong support for the inclusion of these subtypes in the official diagnostic manual.

Critics point to a number of serious problems. Traditional subtypes do not strongly predict either the course of the disorder or response to treatment. The subtypes also have relatively poor diagnostic reliability and are frequently unstable over time. Patients who fit a traditional subcategory during one psychotic episode frequently qualify for a different subtype diagnosis during a subsequent episode. Based on this evidence, it seems reasonable to ask: "How does it help the clinician or the

patient to assign a subtype diagnosis such as disorganized type or undifferentiated type?"

Perhaps the most important consideration with regard to the validity of subtypes involves the genetic evidence. Studies of extended families suggest that the subtypes are not etiologically distinct syndromes (Cardno et al., 1998; Kendler et al., 1994). If several members of a family—or two members of a monozygotic twin pair—have developed symptoms of schizophrenia, they will not necessarily exhibit symptoms of the same subtype. That fact argues strongly against the notion that the subtypes are qualitatively different disorders.

Manfred Bleuler, a Swiss psychiatrist and the son of Eugen Bleuler, treated and observed more than 200 schizophrenic patients over a period of many years. His experience led him to believe that distinctions among subtypes become blurred over time. His data and much of the other research evidence support the hypothesis that the traditional subtypes based on obvious symptoms are a reflection of varying stages of a single disorder or varying levels of severity of the disorder (Gottesman, 1991).

This is perhaps the greatest irony in research on schizophrenia. For more than 100 years, clinicians and investigators have agreed that the disorder is extremely heterogenous. The diagnostic category that we now recognize as schizophrenia may well be composed of many different kinds of mental disorder. This common opinion stands in contrast to the harsh fact that no one has been able to identify truly meaningful subtypes. Don't take the official system too literally. Be skeptical. At best, the diagnostic subtypes for schizophrenia are place-holders, serving primarily to remind us that the disorder is heterogeneous in nature. We desperately need more knowledge in this area. We need better research that will help us find more meaningful subtypes based on sophisticated measurement procedures that may involve genetic factors, cognitive performance, treatment response, or some other facet of the disorder that has not yet been studied. One thing that does seem to be clear is that it has not been particularly useful to focus on symptoms as the basis for reducing the heterogeneity of the complex disorder.

People with paranoid delusions are constantly alert to evidence suggesting that they are being victimized. This constant search often leads them to misinterpret others' comments and behaviors.

the son of God. These fragmented and bizarre ideas were clearly delusional, but they were not woven into a coherent framework.

The most prominent symptoms in the **paranoid type** are systematic delusions with persecutory or grandiose content. Preoccupation with frequent auditory hallucinations can also be associated with the paranoid type. Ann would have received a diagnosis of schizophrenic disorder, paranoid type, because of her preoccupation with the systematic delusion about the photographs that had been stolen and the attempt to harm her children. Patients who exhibit disorganized speech, disorganized behavior, flat or inappropriate affect, or catatonic behavior are excluded from a diagnosis of paranoid schizophrenia and would fall into one of the other subtypes.

Two additional subtypes are described in DSM-IV-TR, presumably to cover those patients who do not fit one of the traditional types. The **undifferentiated type** of schizophrenia includes schizophrenic patients who display prominent psychotic symptoms and either meet the criteria for several subtypes or otherwise do not meet the criteria for the catatonic, disorganized, or paranoid types. They often exhibit some disorganized symptoms together with hallucinations and/or delusions.

The **residual type** includes patients who no longer meet the criteria for active phase symptoms but nevertheless demonstrate continued signs of negative symptoms or attenuated forms of delusions, hallucinations, or disorganized speech. They are in "partial remission."

Related Psychotic Disorders

The U.S. concept of schizophrenia is relatively narrow. The boundaries of the disorder have been refined by excluding patients with certain types of psychotic symptoms from a diagnosis of schizophrenic disorder. Immediately after its description of schizophrenia, DSM-IV-TR lists three additional disorders that are characterized by prominent psychotic symptoms.

Schizoaffective disorder is an ambiguous and somewhat controversial category (Averill et al., 2004). It describes the symptoms of patients who fall on the boundary between schizophrenia and mood disorder with psychotic features. This diagnosis applies only to the description of a particular episode of disturbance; it does not describe the overall lifetime course of the person's disorder. Schizoaffective disorder is defined by an episode in which the symptoms of schizophrenia partially overlap with a major depressive episode or a manic episode. The key to making this diagnosis is the presence of delusions or hallucinations for at least 2 weeks in the absence of prominent mood symptoms. If the delusions and hallucinations are present only during a depressive episode, for example, the diagnosis would be major depressive episode with psychotic features.

People with **delusional disorder** do not meet the full symptomatic criteria for schizophrenia, but they are preoccupied for at least 1 month with delusions that are not bizarre. These are beliefs about situations that could occur in real life, such as being followed or poisoned. Ann's delusion, for example, might have fit this description. She believed that someone was trying to kill her and her children and that someone was trying to cast a voodoo spell on them. Ann would not be assigned a diagnosis of delusional disorder, however, because she also displayed negative symptoms, such as avolition. The presence of hallucinations, disorganized speech, catatonic behavior, or negative symptoms rules out a diagnosis of delusional disorder. The definition of delusional disorder also holds that the person's behavior is not bizarre and that social and occupational functioning are not impaired except for those areas that are directly affected by the delusional belief.

Brief psychotic disorder is a category that includes those people who exhibit psychotic symptoms—delusions, hallucinations, disorganized speech, or grossly disorganized or catatonic behavior—for at least 1 day but no more than 1 month. An episode of this sort is typically accompanied by confusion and emotional turmoil, often (but not necessarily) following a markedly stressful event. After the symptoms are resolved, the person returns to the same level of functioning that had been achieved prior to the psychotic episode. The long-term outcome is good for most patients who experience a brief episode of psychosis (Susser et al., 1998). This diagnosis is not assigned if the symptoms are better explained by a mood disorder, schizophrenia, or substance abuse. This category is used infrequently, and very little research has been conducted with people who have this disorder.

Course and Outcome

Schizophrenia is a severe, progressive disorder that most often begins in adolescence and typically has a poor outcome. In fact, Kraepelin considered the deteriorating course to be one of the principal defining features of the disorder. Recent evidence suggests that this view may be unnecessarily pessimistic (Hafner et al., 2003; Riecher-Roessler & Roessler, 1998). Many patients experience a good outcome. For example, Manfred Bleuler (1978) studied a sample of 208 schizophrenic patients who had been admitted to his hospital in Switzerland during 1942 and 1943. After a follow-up period of 23 years, 53 percent of the patients were either recovered or significantly improved.

In order to describe more completely the various patterns that patients followed over time, Bleuler identified two types of onset (sudden or gradual), two types of course (undulating or simple), and two types of outcome (recovered/mild impairment or moderate/severe impairment). When combined, these elements form eight basic patterns for the onset and course of schizophrenic disorders, as illustrated in Figure 13–1.

A long-term follow-up study of schizophrenia, reported by the Swiss psychiatrist Luc Ciompi (1980), provided useful information about the proportion of patients whose disorder fits into the types of onset, course, and outcome that Bleuler proposed. Ciompi found that approximately half of the 228 patients in his study suffered an acute onset of symptoms during their initial episode. Again, during the intermediate stages of the disorder, half of the patients followed an undulating course, whereas the others exhibited relatively stable symptoms. By the time the patients had reached the end state of their disorder, half had recovered (or showed only mild residual symptoms), whereas the other half continued to experience moderate or severe impairment. The proportions of patients in Ciompi's study who fit different combinations of onset, course, and outcome are indicated in Figure 13–1.

Follow-up studies of schizophrenic patients have found that the description of outcome can be a complicated process. Many factors must be taken into consideration other than whether the person is still in the hospital. Is the person still exhibiting symptoms of the disorder? Does he or she have any other problems, such as depression or anxiety? Is the person employed? Does she have any friends? How does he get along with other people? The evidence indicates that different dimensions of outcome, such as social adjustment,

Video Case:

SCHIZOAFFECTIVE DISORDER

JOSH

"When I was first in the hospital, I thought I was in the middle of a massacre . . ."

On your CD-ROM menu, select "Schizophrenia and Other Psychotic Disorders" and click on "Schizoaffective Disorder: Josh." In addition to describing bizarre delusional beliefs, Josh has also experienced several symptoms of bipolar mood disorder, such as racing thoughts and grandiosity.

The life of John Forbes Nash, a mathematician, was portrayed in the film *A Beautiful Mind*. Nash won the Nobel Prize for Economics in 1994. His thesis, written at the age of 21, revolutionized the field of game theory. He has recovered from paranoid schizophrenia, after experiencing psychotic symptoms for more than 20 years.

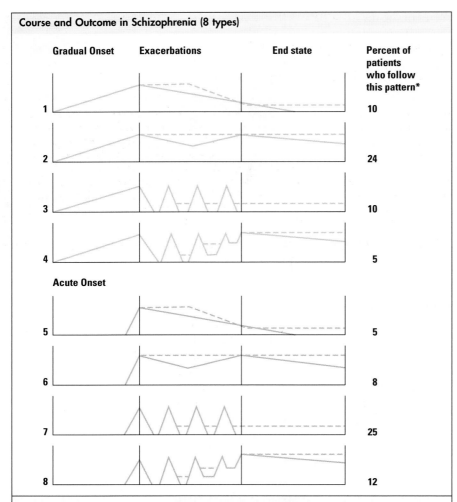

Course and Outcome in Schizophrenia (8 types)

Gradual Onset	Exacerbations	End state	Percent of patients who follow this pattern*
1			10
2			24
3			10
4			5

Acute Onset

5			5
6			8
7			25
8			12

FIGURE 13–1: Patterns identified in long-term follow-up studies. The horizontal axis represents time and the vertical axis represents severity of disturbance. Dotted lines represent slight variations on the overall pattern.

*Data from Ciompi, 1980.

Source: C.M. Harding, 1988, Course types in schizophrenia: An analysis of European and American studies, *Schizophrenia Bulletin, 14,* 633–643. Copyright © 1988. Reprinted by permission of Oxford University Press.

occupational functioning, and symptom severity, are only loosely correlated. As in most situations where psychologists attempt to predict future behavior, the outcome data regarding schizophrenia suggest that the best predictor of future social adjustment is previous social adjustment. Similarly, the best predictor of symptom severity at follow-up is severity of psychotic symptoms at initial assessment (Carpenter & Strauss, 1991; Strauss & Carpenter, 1978, 1981).

How should long-term outcome be measured in schizophrenia?

The long-term emotional impact of this disorder on parents and families has been described by a woman whose daughter, then in her mid-thirties, had exhibited symptoms of schizophrenia for 17 years. Her statement also indicates that even the most severely disturbed patients may eventually show signs of improvement (see First Person Account: A Mother's Observations).

FREQUENCY

One of the most informative ways of examining the frequency of schizophrenia is to consider the *lifetime morbidity risk*—that is, the proportion of a specific population that will be affected by the disorder at some time during their lives. Most studies in Europe and the United States have reported lifetime morbid risk figures of approximately 1 percent. In other words, approximately 1 out of every 100 people will experience or display schizophrenic symptoms at some time during their lives. Of course, prevalence rates depend on the diagnostic criteria that are used to define schizophrenia in any particular study, as well as the methods that are used to identify cases in the general population. Investigators who have employed more narrow or restrictive criteria for the disorder typically report lower morbid risk figures (Haefner & Heiden, 1997; Jones & Cannon, 1998).

Data from the Epidemiologic Catchment Area (ECA) study are consistent with figures reported in several other studies (Keith, Regier, & Rae, 1991). Using DSM-III criteria for the disorder, the investigators found a lifetime prevalence of 1.3 percent for schizophrenia and 0.2 percent for schizophreniform disorder. The mean age of onset was 20 years, and 71 percent of the people who met criteria for schizophrenia had experienced their first symptoms by the age of 25. For those persons who no longer exhibited active symptoms at the time of the interview, the mean duration of the disorder was 15 years.

Gender Differences

Most epidemiological studies have reported that across the life span men and women are equally likely to be affected by schizophrenia (Keith, Regier, & Rae, 1991). This conclusion has been challenged by a few studies (e.g., Iacono & Beiser, 1992) which suggest that among new cases of schizophrenia, men may outnumber women by a ratio of at least 2:1. This pattern seems to depend on the breadth of the diagnostic criteria that are employed to identify cases of the disorder, as studies that use broader, more

FIRST PERSON ACCOUNT: A MOTHER'S OBSERVATIONS

"The saddest thing of all is to realize that the stories of family life and previous achievements that were a part of the past lives of each of these people are no longer important to them. Nothing in (our daughter's) growing up years could have prepared us for the shock and devastation of seeing this normal, happy child become totally incapacitated by schizophrenia. Coming to grips with the thought of your child living in a mental hospital, possibly for many years, leaves you with a gnawing sense of helplessness that never really dissipates.

"In the past year, a new Cindy has emerged. Where once there was a rather unfriendly, often unpleasant girl, there is now an amiable, more responsive person. Cindy smiles more these days, something a person with schizophrenia doesn't do very often. For years her face was a solemn mask, and she could neither give nor receive affection. She knew something terrible had happened to her and could not understand why no one would rescue her from the hell in her head. In the past few months she has become quite loving, and the smiles that now light her face light mine as well" (Smith, 1991, pp. 690–691).

---

inclusive sets of diagnostic criteria are more likely to find equivalent rates of schizophrenia in men and women (Cannon et al., 1998).

The controversy surrounding gender differences in incidence may reflect, at least in part, gender differences in more specific aspects of schizophrenia. There are some interesting and widely recognized differences between male and female patients with regard to patterns of onset, symptoms, and course of the disorder. For example, the average age at which schizophrenic males begin to exhibit overt symptoms is younger by about 4 or 5 years than the average age at which schizophrenic women first experience problems (Tamminga, 1997). A summary of proposed gender differences in schizophrenia is presented in Table 13–2. Male patients are more likely than female patients to exhibit negative symptoms, and they are also more likely to follow a chronic, deteriorating course (Moriarty et al., 2001).

Gender differences in the age of onset and symptomatic expression of schizophrenia can be interpreted in several ways. The alternatives fall into two types of hypotheses. One approach assumes that schizophrenia is a single disorder and that its expression varies in men and women. A common, genetically determined vulnerability to schizophrenia might be expressed differently in men than in women. Mediating factors that might account for this difference could be biological differences between men and women—perhaps involving certain hormones—or different environmental demands, such as the timing and form of stresses associated with typical male and female sex roles. An alternative approach suggests that there are two qualitatively distinct subtypes of schizophrenia: one with an early onset that affects men more often than women, and another with a later onset that affects women more often than men. Both approaches fit the general diathesis-stress model. The available evidence does not allow us to favor one of these explanations over the other (Haefner et al., 1998).

Cross-Cultural Comparisons

Schizophrenia has been observed in virtually every culture that has been subjected to careful scrutiny. Of course, the formal term *schizophrenia* is not used in all societies, but the symptoms of the disorder are nevertheless present.

TABLE 13–2	Typical Gender Differences in Schizophrenia	
VARIABLE	**MEN**	**WOMEN**
Age of onset	Earlier (18–25)	Later (25–35)
Premorbid functioning; adjustment	Poor social functioning; more schizotypal traits	Good social functioning; fewer schizotypal traits
Typical symptoms	More negative symptoms; more withdrawn and passive	More hallucinations and paranoia; more emotional and impulsive
Course	More often chronic; poorer response to treatment	Less often chronic; better response to treatment

Source: Based on J.M. Goldstein, 1995, The impact of gender on understanding the epidemiology of schizophrenia. In M.V. Seeman (Ed.), *Gender and Psychopathology*, pp. 159–199. Washington, DC: American Psychiatric Press.

Schizophrenia affects people in all cultures. This Chinese man, whose symptoms include delusions and disorganized speech, lives with his adoptive parents and does not receive adequate treatment. One consequence of economic reforms in China has been reduced access to quality care for patients with chronic mental disorders.

Two large-scale epidemiological studies, conducted by teams of scientists working for the World Health Organization (WHO), indicate that the incidence of schizophrenia is relatively constant across different cultural settings. The International Pilot Study of Schizophrenia (IPSS) began in the 1960s and was conducted in nine countries in Europe, North America, South America, Africa, and Asia. It included 1,200 patients who were followed for 5 years after their initial hospitalization. The Collaborative Study on the Determinants of Outcome of Severe Mental Disorders (DOS) was conducted a few years later in six of the same countries that had participated in the IPSS, plus four others. The DOS study included more than 1,500 patients. Both the IPSS and DOS projects examined rural and urban areas in both Western and non-Western countries. For purposes of cultural comparison, the countries were divided into those that were "developing" and those that were already "developed" on the basis of prevailing socioeconomic conditions. All the interviewers were trained in the use of a single, standardized interview schedule, and all employed the same sets of diagnostic criteria.

The IPSS results indicated that patients who exhibited characteristic signs and symptoms of schizophrenia were found in all of the study sites. Comparisons of patients across research centers revealed more similarities than differences in clinical symptoms at the time of entry into the study, which was always an active phase of disorder that required psychiatric treatment. Using a relatively narrow set of diagnostic

criteria, scientists found that the incidence of schizophrenia did not differ significantly among the research centers. The IPSS investigators also found that clinical and social outcomes at 2- and 5-year follow-up were significantly better for schizophrenic patients in developing countries than in developed countries, such as the United States, England, and Russia (Leff et al., 1992). The DOS study confirmed those results (Craig et al., 1997; Jablensky et al., 1992).

Taken together, the WHO studies provide compelling support for the conclusion that schizophrenia occurs with similar frequency and presents with similar symptoms in different cultures. Most experts believe that the more favorable clinical outcome that was observed in India and Nigeria is a product of the greater tolerance and acceptance extended to people with psychotic symptoms in developing countries. This conclusion is consistent with evidence regarding the relationship between frequency of relapse and patterns of family communication, which we consider later in this chapter in the section on expressed emotion. These cross-cultural data certainly testify to the important influence of culture in shaping the experience and expression of psychotic symptoms (Thakker & Ward, 1998).

CAUSES

Having considered the defining characteristics of schizophrenia, ways in which it has been classified, and some basic information regarding its distribution within the general population, we now review the evidence regarding factors that might contribute to the development of the disorder, as well as its course and outcome.

Biological Factors

Many of the early investigators who originally defined schizophrenia at the beginning of the twentieth century believed that the disorder was the product of a biological dysfunction. At that time very little was known about human genetics or the biochemistry of the brain. Research in the areas of molecular genetics and the neurosciences has progressed at an explosive rate in the past decade. Much of what we know today about the biological substrates of schizophrenia has emerged from advances that have taken place in other sciences.

Genetics The role of genetic factors has been studied more extensively with regard to schizophrenia than with any other type of mental disorder. The existing data are based on sophisticated methods that have been refined over many years. The cumulative weight of this evidence points clearly toward some type of genetic influence in the transmission of this disorder (Gottesman & Reilly, 2003).

Family Studies Figure 13–2 illustrates the lifetime risk for schizophrenia for various types of relatives of a person with schizophrenia. Irving Gottesman, a psychologist at the University of Virginia, created this figure by pooling data from 40 European studies that were published between 1920 and 1987 (Gottesman, 1991). All of the studies employed conservative diagnostic criteria for the disorder.

Consider the data for first-degree relatives and second-degree relatives. On average, *siblings* and children share 50 percent of their genes with the schizophrenic proband; nieces, nephews, and cousins share only 25 percent. The lifetime morbid risk for schizophrenia is much greater among first-degree relatives than it is among second-degree relatives. The risk in the second-degree relatives is greater than the 1 percent figure that is typically reported for people in the general population. As the degree of genetic similarity increases between an individual and a schizophrenic patient, the risk to that person increases. The family history data are consistent with the hypothesis that the transmission of schizophrenia is influenced by genetic factors. They do not prove the point, however, because family studies do not separate genetic and environmental events (see Chapter 2).

Twin Studies Several twin studies have examined concordance rates for schizophrenia. The results of these studies are also summarized in Figure 13–2. The average concordance rate for MZ twins is 48 percent, whereas the comparable figure for DZ twins is 17 percent. One study from Finland, published after Gottesman computed average rates for his figure, found a concordance rate of 46 percent among MZ twins and only 9 percent among DZ twins (Cannon et al., 1998). Although the specific rates vary somewhat from study to study, all of the published reports have found that MZ twins are significantly more likely than DZ twins to be concordant for schizophrenia. This pattern suggests strongly that genetic factors play an important role in the development of the disorder.

It should also be pointed out, however, that none of the twin studies of schizophrenia has found a concordance rate that even approaches 100 percent, which would be expected if genetic factors were entirely responsible for schizophrenia. Thus the twin studies also provide compelling evidence for the importance of environmental events. Some people, like Marsha in the case presented earlier, apparently inherit a predisposition to the development of schizophrenia. Among that select group of vulnerable individuals, certain environmental events must determine whether a given person will eventually exhibit the full-blown symptoms of the disorder.

Adoption Studies Studies of children who were adopted away from their biological parents and reared by foster families provide this type of clear distinction between genetic and environmental influence. The first adoption study of schizophrenia was reported by Leonard Heston (1966), a psychiatrist at the University of Washington. He began by identifying records for a group of 49 children who were born between 1915 and 1945 while their mothers were hospitalized for schizophrenia. All the children were apparently normal at birth and were separated from their mothers

Irving Gottesman, Sherell J. Aston Professor Emeritus of Psychology at the University of Virginia, is one of the world's leading experts on genetic factors and schizophrenia.

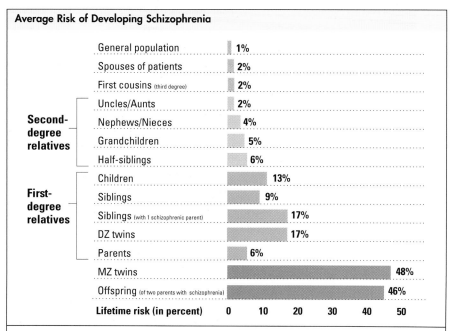

FIGURE 13–2: Average risk of schizophrenia among biological relatives of a schizophrenic proband.

Source: I.I. Gottesman, 1991, *Schizophrenia Genesis: The Origins of Madness*, p. 96. New York: Freeman. Copyright © 1991 by Irving I. Gottesman. Reprinted by permission of W. H. Freeman and Company.

within 3 days of birth. To rule out possible exposure to the environment associated with the mother's psychosis, any child who had been in contact with maternal relatives was excluded from the study. A control group of children was selected using the admission records of foundling homes where many of the target children had originally been placed. These children were matched to the patients' children on a number of variables, including age, sex, type of eventual placement, and amount of time spent in institutions.

Heston was able to locate and interview most of the offspring, the majority of whom were then in their mid-thirties. Five of the adult offspring of schizophrenic mothers received a diagnosis of schizophrenia. Correcting for the fact that most of the participants were still within the period of risk for the disorder, this resulted in a lifetime morbidity risk for schizophrenia of 16.6 percent in the target group, which is almost exactly the rate observed among children of schizophrenic parents who were raised by their biological parents (see Figure 13–2). In contrast, none of the adult offspring in the control group received a diagnosis of schizophrenia. Because the only difference between the two groups was the genetic relationship between the target offspring and their schizophrenic biological mothers, Heston's data indicate that genetic factors play a role in the development of the disorder. Several other adoption studies have been concerned with schizophrenia, and all reach the same conclusion as Heston's original report (see Gottesman, 1991, and Kendler & Diehl, 1993, for reviews of this literature).

The Spectrum of Schizophrenic Disorders

Results from adoption and twin studies have also provided interesting clues regarding the boundaries of the concept of schizophrenia. Several types of psychotic disorders and personality disorders resemble schizophrenia in one way or another, including schizoaffective disorder, delusional disorder, and schizotypal personality disorder (discussed in Chapter 9). Are these conditions a reflection of the same genetically determined predisposition as schizophrenia, or are they etiologically distinct disorders? If they are genetically related, then investigators should find that the biological relatives of schizophrenic adoptees are more likely to exhibit these conditions as well as schizophrenia.

Why are some personality disorders considered to be schizophrenia spectrum disorders?

Figure 9–2 presents one set of data from this type of study. The overall pattern of results suggests that vulnerability to schizophrenia is sometimes expressed as schizophrenia-like personality traits and other types of psychosis that are not specifically included in the DSM-IV-TR definition of schizophrenia (Kendler & Gardner, 1997).

Linkage Studies The combined results from twin and adoption studies indicate that genetic factors are involved in the transmission of schizophrenia. This conclusion does not imply, however, that the manner in which schizophrenia develops is well understood. We know little beyond the fact that genetic factors are involved in some way. The mode of transmission has not been identified. Some clinical scientists believe that a single dominant gene is involved. Others believe that schizophrenia is a polygenic characteristic, which means that it is the product of a reasonably large number of genes rather than a single gene (see Chapter 2).

One of the most exciting areas of research on genetics and schizophrenia focuses on the search for genetic linkage (see Research Methods in Chapter 14 for an explanation of this process). Studies of this type are designed to identify the location of a specific gene that is responsible for the disorder (or some important component of the disorder).

Linkage analysis has not been able to identify a *specific gene* for schizophrenia, but it has implicated *regions* on a small number of chromosomes that may contribute to the etiology of the disorder. For example, reports of positive linkage on regions of chromosomes 6, 8, 13, and 22 have been verified by more than one laboratory (Badner & Gershon, 2002; Kato et al., 2002). These findings clearly narrow the search. We must remember, however, that the identification of chromosome regions is only one step in the direction of finding specific genes. The region that has been implicated on the short arm of chromosome 6 probably contains between 2,000 and 4,000 genes. Supporters of linkage analysis contend that the absence of more definitive discoveries is not surprising when we consider the complexity of this process and the magnitude of the search. They feel that the search for a particular gene that causes schizophrenia will simply take more time (Waterworth, Bassett, & Brzustowicz, 2002).

One specific gene that has attracted considerable research attention in recent years is associated with the production of catechol-O-methyltransferase (COMT), which is an enzyme that is involved in breaking down the neurotransmitter dopamine. The COMT gene is located on chromosome 22, a region that has been linked to schizophrenia. People who possess a specific form of the COMT gene (called the Val allele) seem to have a small but consistently increased risk for schizophrenia (Glatt, Faraone, & Tsuang, 2003). Scientists believe that this gene may increase risk for schizophrenia by affecting dopamine transmission in the prefrontal cortex of the brain, with the net effect being impaired cognitive ability (Weickert et al., 2004) (see later section on working memory and vulnerability to schizophrenia).

Pregnancy and Birth Complications   People with schizophrenia are more likely than the general population to have been exposed to various problems during their mother's pregnancy and to have suffered birth injuries. Problems during pregnancy include the mother's contracting various types of diseases and infections. Birth complications include extended labor, breech delivery, forceps delivery, and the umbilical cord wrapped around the baby's neck. These events may be harmful, in part, because they impair circulation or otherwise reduce the availability of oxygen to developing brain regions. Birth records indicate that the mothers of people who later develop schizophrenia experienced more complications at the time of labor and delivery (Cannon, Jones, & Murray, 2002; McNeil & Cantor-Graae, 1999).

It is not clear whether the effects of pregnancy and birth complications interact with genetic factors. They may produce neurodevelopmental abnormalities that result in schizophrenia regardless of family history for the disorder. Conversely, a fetus that is genetically predisposed to schizophrenia may be more susceptible to brain injury following certain kinds of obstetric difficulties (Walker et al., 2004).

Dietary factors may also play a role in the etiology of the disorder. Severe maternal malnutrition in the early months of pregnancy leads to an increased risk of schizophrenia among the offspring. This conclusion is based on a study of medical and psychiatric records of people who were born in the western part of the Netherlands between 1944 and 1946 (Susser et al., 1996). The German blockade of ports and other supply routes in this area led to a severe famine at the end of World War II. People who were conceived during the worst months of the famine were twice as likely to develop schizophrenia as were people whose mothers became pregnant at other times, including the early months of the famine. These results suggest that prenatal nutritional deficiencies may disrupt normal development of the fetal nervous system (Hulshoff et al., 2000).

Viral Infections   Some speculation has focused on the potential role that viral infections may play in the etiology of schizophrenia (Brown et al., 2001; Munk-Jorgensen, 2001). One indirect line of support for this hypothesis comes from studies indicating that people who develop schizophrenia are somewhat more likely than other people to have been born during the winter months (McGrath & Welham, 1999; Narita et al., 2000). Some clinicians interpret this pattern to mean that, during their pregnancies, the mothers were more likely to develop viral infections, which are more prevalent during the winter. Exposure to infection presumably interferes with brain development in the fetus. This possibility has received considerable attention in the research literature and remains an important topic of debate. Research support for the hypothesis remains inconsistent (Westergaard et al., 1999).

Neuropathology   One important step toward understanding the etiology of schizophrenia would be to identify its neurological underpinnings. If people with schizophrenia suffer from a form of neurological dysfunction, shouldn't it be possible to observe differences between the structure of their brains and those of other people? This is a challenging task. Scientists have invented methods to create images of the living human brain (see Chapter 4). Some of these procedures provide static pictures of various brain structures at rest, just as an X ray provides a photographic image of a bone or some other organ of the body. More recently, sophisticated methods have enabled us to create functional images of the brain while a person is performing different tasks. Studies using these techniques have produced evidence indicating that a number of brain areas are involved in schizophrenia (Davidson & Heinrichs, 2003). You may want to review the description of brain structures in Chapter 2 (Figure 2–4) before reading the next sections of this chapter.

Structural Brain Imaging   Many investigations of brain structure in people with schizophrenia have employed magnetic resonance imaging (MRI; see

Chapter 4 for an explanation of this process). The disorder is not associated with abnormalities in one specific brain region or in one particular type of nerve cell. Rather, it seems to affect many different regions of the brain and the ways in which they connect or communicate with each other (Niznikiewicz, Kubicki, & Shenton, 2003). Most MRI studies have reported a decrease in total volume of brain tissue among schizophrenic patients. Another consistent finding is that some people with schizophrenia have mildly to moderately enlarged lateral ventricles, the cavities on each side of the brain that are filled with cerebrospinal fluid.

These differences seem to reflect a natural part of the disorder rather than a side effect of treatment with antipsychotic medication. In fact, some studies have found enlarged ventricles in young schizophrenic patients before they have been exposed to any form of treatment (Lieberman et al., 2001). Some studies have also found enlarged ventricles prior to the onset of symptoms. Significantly, these differences do not appear to become more marked as time goes on. The structural changes seem to occur early in the development of the disorder and therefore may play a role in the onset of symptoms (Cannon, 1998; Weinberger & McClure, 2002).

The temporal lobes have also been studied extensively using MRI scans. Several studies have reported decreased size of the hippocampus, the parahippocampus, the amygdala, and the thalamus, all of which are parts of the limbic system (Altshuler et al., 2000; Copolov et al., 2000). These areas of the brain (see Figure 13–3) play a crucial role in the regulation of emotion as well as the integration of cognition and emotion. Decreased size of these structures in the limbic area of the temporal lobes may be especially noticeable on the left side of the brain, which plays an important role in the control of language. Schizophrenic patients who exhibit the greatest degree of disorganized speech may be most likely to show a decrease in the size of left temporal lobe structures (Shenton, 1996).

Many questions remain to be answered regarding the relation between structural brain abnormalities and schizophrenia. Does the pattern reflect a generalized deterioration of the brain, or is it the result of a defect in specific brain sites? We don't know. Is the presence of enlarged ventricles and cortical atrophy consistently found in some subset of schizophrenic patients? Some investigators have reported an association between this type of neuropathology and other factors, such as negative symptoms, poor response to medication, and absence of family history of the disorder. These are all interesting possibilities, but none has been firmly established.

Functional Brain Imaging   In addition to static pictures of brain structures, clinical scientists use techniques that provide dynamic images of brain functions. One dynamic brain imaging technique, known as positron emission tomography (PET), can reflect changes in brain activity as the person responds to various task demands. Visual stimulation will produce increased cerebral blood flow in the visual cortex; people performing a simple motor task exhibit increased flow in the motor cortex. Functional MRI is another tool that can be used to observe brain activity. The results of studies using these techniques suggest dysfunction in various neural circuits, including some regions of the prefrontal cortex (see Figure 13–4) and several regions in the temporal lobes (Barch

Structures of the Brain Implicated in Schizophrenia

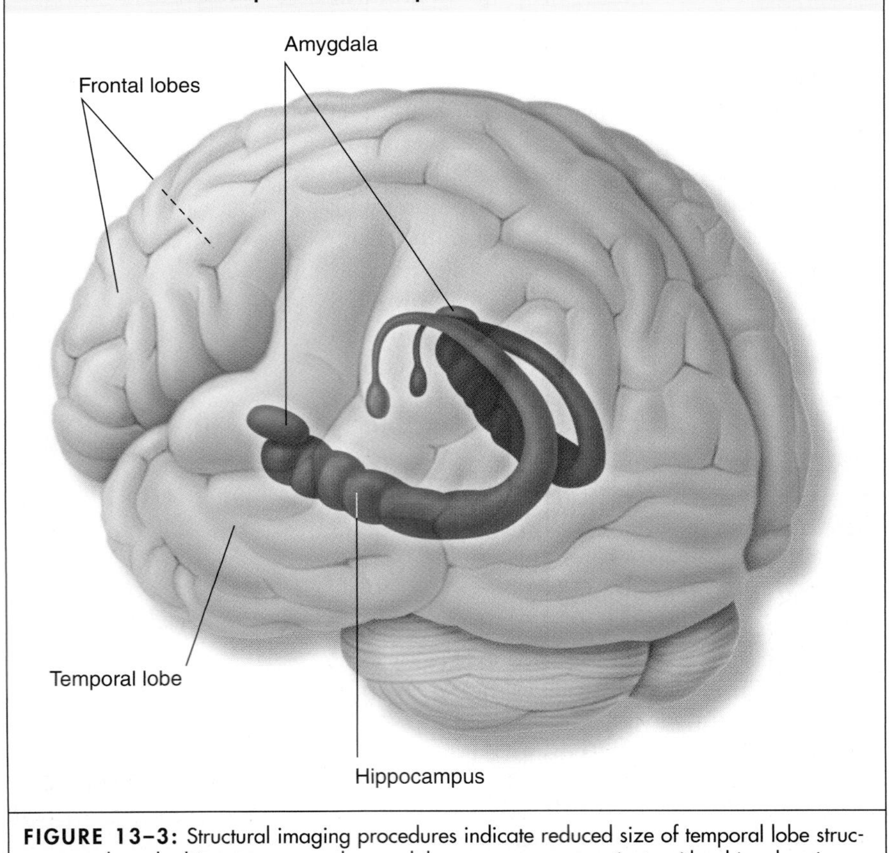

Amygdala

Frontal lobes

Temporal lobe

Hippocampus

FIGURE 13–3: Structural imaging procedures indicate reduced size of temporal lobe structures, such as the hippocampus and amygdalae, among some patients with schizophrenia.

et al., 2001; Harrison, 1999). The problems seem to involve activities within, as well as integration between, a variety of functional circuits rather than a localized abnormality in one region of the brain.

The role of neurological abnormalities in schizophrenia has been highlighted by a study of identical twins conducted by investigators at the National Institute of Mental Health (NIMH). Participants included 27 pairs of twins discordant for schizophrenia and 13 pairs that were concordant for the disorder. Changes in brain structure, measured by MRI, and changes in brain function, measured by cerebral blood flow, were prominent in the twins who had developed schizophrenia. Their well co-twins also exhibited more neurological impairment than a group of normal control participants, but these abnormalities were less marked than those found in the probands. Among discordant monozygotic pairs, the schizophrenic twin typically had the smaller hippocampus and smaller amygdala. The schizophrenic twins always showed reduced frontal lobe activity compared with their unaffected co-twins. Results for enlarged ventricles were less consistent. In general, neurological dysfunction seemed to be associated with the overall severity of the disorder rather than being indicative of an etiologically distinct subgroup of patients (Torrey et al., 1994).

General Conclusions The primary conclusion that can be drawn from existing brain imaging studies is that schizophrenia is associated with diffuse patterns of neuropathology. The most consistent findings point toward structural as well as functional irregularities in the frontal cortex and limbic areas of the temporal lobes, which play an important role in cognitive and emotional processes. The neural network connecting limbic areas with the frontal cortex may be fundamentally disordered in schizophrenia.

Speculation regarding disruptions in neural circuitry must also be tempered with caution. Evidence of neuropathology does not seem to be unique to schizophrenic patients. Many patients with other psychiatric and neurological disorders show similar changes in brain structure and function. Furthermore, a specific brain lesion has not been identified, and it is unlikely that one will be found. As Paul Meehl (1990) suggested, it is unlikely that a disorder as complex as schizophrenia will be traced to a single site in the brain. The various symptoms and cognitive

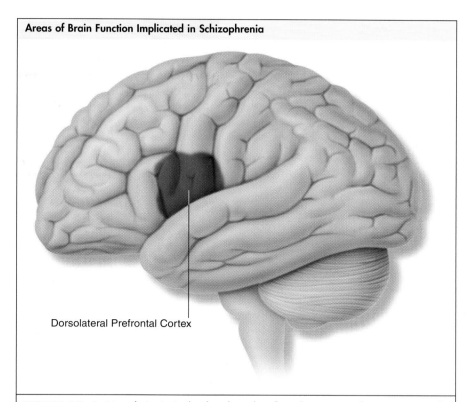

Areas of Brain Function Implicated in Schizophrenia

Dorsolateral Prefrontal Cortex

FIGURE 13–4: Neural circuits in the dorsolateral prefrontal cortex may function improperly in schizophrenia.

deficits that have been observed in schizophrenic patients may be linked to a host of subtle disruptions in neurological functions (Andreasen, 2001; Green, 2001).

It should also be emphasized that brain imaging procedures are not diagnostically meaningful tests for mental disorders. For example, an MRI showing enlarged ventricles does not prove that a patient has schizophrenia. Brain imaging procedures have identified interesting group differences, but they do not predict the presence of schizophrenia for individuals. The group differences that have been observed are very subtle in comparison to the levels of neuropathology found in disorders such as Alzheimer's disease and Huntington's disease (see Chapter 14). Some schizophrenic patients do not show abnormalities in brain structure or function.

A dramatic example of this point was found in the NIMH study of discordant MZ twins. In one pair, the well twin was a successful businessman who had never had any problems with mental disorder. His twin brother had been severely impaired with schizophrenia for 20 years. The

Why can't we use brain imaging to diagnose schizophrenia?

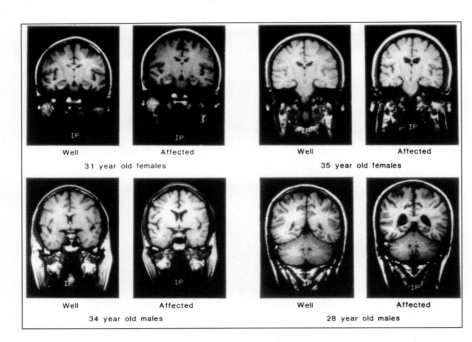

Well · Affected
31 year old females

Well · Affected
35 year old females

Well · Affected
34 year old males

Well · Affected
28 year old males

MRI scans from 4 identical twin pairs discordant for schizophrenia showing varying degrees of increased ventricular size in the twin with the disorder compared to the twin who is well.

well twin had ventricles that were five times larger than those of the schizophrenic twin. Thus we should approach all these hypotheses with caution and skepticism.

Neurochemistry   The neurological underpinnings of schizophrenia may not take the form of changes in the size or organization of brain structures. They may be even more subtle, involving alterations in the chemical communications among neurons within particular brain circuits.

The Dopamine Hypothesis   Scientists have proposed various neurochemical theories to account for the etiology of schizophrenia. The most influential theory, known as the *dopamine hypothesis*, focuses on the function of specific dopamine pathways in the limbic area of the brain. The original version of the dopamine hypothesis proposed that the symptoms of schizophrenia are the product of excessive levels of dopaminergic activity. This hypothesis grew out of attempts to understand how antipsychotic drugs improve the adjustment of many schizophrenic patients. Animals who receive doses of antipsychotic drugs show a marked increase in the production of dopamine. In 1963, Arvid Carlsson, a Swedish pharmacologist, suggested that antipsychotic drugs block postsynaptic dopamine receptors. The presynaptic neuron recognizes the presence of this blockade and increases its release of dopamine in a futile attempt to override it (Carlsson & Lindqvist, 1963).

If the dopamine system is dysfunctional in schizophrenic patients, what is the specific form

of this problem? One possibility is that certain neural pathways have an elevated sensitivity to dopamine because of increased numbers of postsynaptic dopamine receptors. The potency of various types of antipsychotic drugs is specifically related to their ability to block one type of dopamine receptor, known as receptors. Autopsy studies of schizophrenic patients' brains have found that some patients have an excessive number of receptors in the striatum (Roberts et al., 1996). The etiological significance of this finding is not clear because treatment with antipsychotic drugs produces an increase in the number of receptors. The density of dopamine receptors can be measured in the brains of living patients using PET. One laboratory has reported that untreated, first-episode schizophrenic patients have significantly more receptors when compared to a group of normal volunteers, but other studies have failed to replicate this result (Farde et al., 1995).

Interactions of Multiple Neurotransmitters   A dysregulation and exaggerated response of certain dopamine pathways is certainly involved in schizophrenia, at least for some patients. On the other hand, experts now agree that several other neurotransmitters also play an important role. A neurochemical model focused narrowly on dopamine fails to explain many different aspects of the disorder, including the following: Some patients do not respond positively to drugs that block dopamine receptors; the effects of antipsychotic drugs require several days to become effective, but dopamine blockage begins immediately; research studies that examined the by-products of dopamine in cerebrospinal fluid were inconclusive at best.

Current neurochemical hypotheses regarding schizophrenia focus on a broad array of neurotransmitters (Carlsson et al., 2001). Special interest has been focused on serotonin pathways since the introduction of a new class of antipsychotic drugs such as clozapine (Clozaril) that are useful in treating patients who were resistant to standard antipsychotic drugs. (See the section on treatment.) These "atypical" antipsychotics produce a strong blockade of serotonin receptors and only a weak blockade of D_2 receptors. Several studies have found decreased serotonin receptor density in cortical areas of schizophrenic patients (Harrison, 1999). This pattern leads to speculation that the neurochemical substrates of schizophrenia may involve a complex interaction between serotonin and dopamine pathways in the brain (Kapur & Remington, 1996).

Brain imaging studies that point to problems in the prefrontal cortex have also drawn attention to glutamate and GABA (gamma-aminobutyric acid), the two principal neurotransmitters in the cerebral cortex (Wassef et al., 2003; Weinberger, 1997). Glutamate is an excitatory neurotransmitter, and GABA is an inhibitory neurotransmitter. As in the case of serotonin, hypotheses regarding the role of glutamate and GABA focus on their interactions with dopamine pathways, especially those connecting temporal lobe structures with the prefrontal and limbic cortexes.

Social Factors

There is little question that biological factors play an important role in the etiology of schizophrenia, but twin studies also provide compelling evidence for the importance of environmental events. The disorder is expressed in its full-blown form only when vulnerable individuals experience some type of environmental event, which might include anything from nutritional variables to stressful life events (Howes et al., 2004; Walker et al., 2004). What sorts of nongenetic events interact with genetic factors and other biological factors to produce schizophrenia? Specific answers are not available at the present time. We can, however, review some of the hypotheses that have been proposed and studied.

Social Class   One general indicator of a person's status within a community's hierarchy of prestige and influence is social class. People from different social classes are presumably exposed to different levels of environmental stress, with those people in the lowest class being subjected to the most hardships. More than 50 years ago, social scientists working in Chicago found that the highest prevalence of schizophrenia was found in neighborhoods of the lowest socioeconomic status (Faris & Dunham, 1939). Many research studies have subsequently confirmed this finding in several other geographic areas (Boydell & Murray, 2003). The evidence supporting an inverse relationship between social class and schizophrenia is substantial.

There are two ways to interpret the relationship between social class and schizophrenia.

One holds that harmful events associated with membership in the lowest social classes, which might include many factors ranging from stress and social isolation to poor nutrition, play a causal role in the development of the disorder. This is often called the *social causation* hypothesis. It is also possible, however, that low social class is an outcome rather than a cause of schizophrenia. Those people who develop schizophrenia may be less able than others to complete a higher level education or to hold a well-paying job. Their cognitive and social impairments may cause downward social mobility. In other words, regardless of the social class of their family of origin, many schizophrenic patients may gradually drift into the lowest social classes. This view is sometimes called the *social selection hypothesis*.

Research studies have found evidence supporting both views. The social selection hypothesis is supported by studies that have compared the occupational roles of male schizophrenic patients with those of their fathers. The patients are frequently less successful than their fathers, whereas the opposite pattern is typical of men who do not have schizophrenia (Jones et al., 1993).

It is also true, however, that a disproportionately high percentage of the fathers of schizophrenic patients were from the lowest social class (Harrison et al., 2001). This finding is consistent with the social causation hypothesis. Additional support for the social causation hypothesis has been found using different research strategies. For example, a unique study considered the relation between economic conditions (employment rates) and rates of psychiatric hospitalization in the state of New York between 1852 and 1967 (Brenner, 1973). Throughout this extended period of time, increases in the rate of unemployment were followed closely, usually within a year, by sharp increases in the number of patients admitted to mental hospitals. The strongest relationship was found for schizophrenia and bipolar mood disorders.

In general, the evidence regarding socioeconomic status and schizophrenia indicates that the disorder is, to a certain extent, influenced by social factors. Adverse social and economic circumstances may increase the probability that persons who are genetically predisposed to the disorder will develop its clinical symptoms (van Os & McGuffin, 2003; Schiffman et al., 2001).

Psychological Factors

Most of the attention devoted to psychological factors and schizophrenia has focused on patterns of behavior and communication within families. Research evidence indicates that family interactions and communication problems are not primarily responsible for the initial appearance of symptoms. They may help to trigger the onset of the disorder among those who were already genetically predisposed to its development, and they also influence the course of the disorder after the symptoms have appeared.

In order to place current thinking about these issues in historical perspective, consider the sort of causal pathways that were imagined by therapists in the 1960s. One influential hypothesis was concerned with the relationship between thought disorder in schizophrenic patients and communication problems exhibited by their parents (Wynne & Singer, 1963). According to this theory, the parents of schizophrenic patients are often unable to communicate clearly. This deficiency results in disrupted conversations and confusion on the part of their children. The child is caught between parents who are locked in conflict and subsequently fails to develop either a secure identity or conventional forms of thinking and speaking. Over an extended period of time, these problems presumably lead to the onset of schizophrenic symptoms. Hypotheses of this kind were tested extensively during the 1960s and 1970s, and the results were negative (Goldstein, 1988; Miklowitz, 1995; Neale &

Oltmanns, 1980). Disturbed patterns of communication among family members do not cause people to develop schizophrenia. This knowledge is important to parents of schizophrenic patients. They experience enough emotional anguish without also being made to feel that something they did or said was the primary cause of their child's problems.

Expressed Emotion The family environment does have a significant impact on the course (as opposed to the etiology) of schizophrenia. Studies that point to this conclusion do not address the original onset of symptoms. Instead, they are concerned with the adjustment of patients who have already been treated for schizophrenic symptoms.

This effect was discovered by people who were interested in the adjustment of patients who were discharged after being treated in a psychiatric hospital. Men with schizophrenia were much more likely to return to the hospital within the next 9 months if they went to live with their wives or parents than if they went to live in other lodgings or with their siblings. The patients who relapsed seemed to react negatively to some feature of their close relationship with their wives or mothers.

Subsequent research confirmed this initial impression (Brown, Birley, & Wing, 1972; Vaughn & Leff, 1976). Relatives of schizophrenic patients were interviewed prior to the patients' discharge from the hospital, and many of the relatives made statements that reflected negative or intrusive attitudes toward the patient. These statements were used to create a measure of **expressed emotion (EE).** For example, many of the relatives expressed hostility toward the patient or repeatedly criticized the patient's behavior. The following comments, made by the stepfather of a young man with schizophrenia, illustrate generalized, hostile criticisms of the patient's behavior. These comments would be considered to be high in expressed emotion.

> **Interviewer:** What seemed different about Stephen's behavior?
> **Stepfather:** Everything and anything. In other words, he's the type of person, you don't tell him, he tells you.
> **Interviewer:** You say that he spent time in a juvenile facility?
> **Stepfather:** Yeah. This kid is a genuine con artist, believe me. I spent time in the service

Criticism and hostility can increase the risk of relapse for some patients with schizophrenia. Conversely, warmth and family support can serve as a protective factor.

and I've been around con artists. This kid is a first-class, genuine con artist, bar none. (Leff & Vaughn, 1985, p. 42)

Other family members appeared to be overprotective or too closely identified with the patient. These phenomena are also rated as being high in expressed emotion. Of course, a certain amount of worrying and concern should be expected from a parent whose child has developed a severe disorder such as schizophrenia. In the assessment of expressed emotion, relatives were considered to be emotionally overinvolved if they reported responses such as extreme anxiety or exaggerated forms of self-sacrifice. For example, the following exchange illustrates emotional overinvolvement (high EE) by the mother of a 24-year-old male patient who had his first onset of the disorder when he was 22:

> **Mother:** He talked to me a lot—because I was his therapist—the person he shared with more than anybody else. He involves me, ruminates with me, because I allow him to do it.
> **Interviewer:** How frequently?
> **Mother:** He would do it constantly. He would do it as much as I would be there with him.
> **Interviewer:** Once or twice a week?
> **Mother:** No, it happened daily. All the time I was with him, particularly in the last four or five months. He would talk to me for hours at a time, worrying and sharing how bad he felt, reporting to me every change in mood or feeling from 5-minute to 5-minute period. (Leff & Vaughn, 1985, p. 51).

Patients who returned to live in a home with at least one member who was high in EE were more likely than patients from low EE families to relapse in the first 9 months after discharge.

This result has been replicated many times. Approximately half of schizophrenic patients live in families that would be rated as being high in EE. Average relapse rates—defined primarily in terms of the proportion of patients who show a definite return of positive symptoms in the first year following hospital discharge—are 52 percent for patients in high EE families and 22 percent for patients in low EE families. Among the various types of comments that can contribute to a high EE rating, criticism is usually

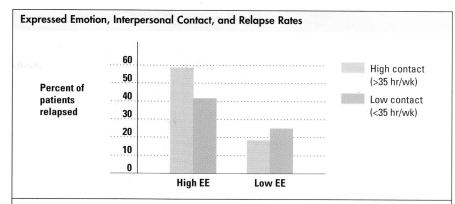

FIGURE 13–5: Close contact increases the risk of relapse for schizophrenic patients living with a high-EE relative. In low-EE families, increased contact has a protective effect.
Source: P. Beggington and L. Kuipers, 1994, The predictive utility of expressed emotion in schizophrenia: An aggregate analysis. *Psychological Medicine, 24,* 707–718. Copyright © 1994. Reprinted by permission of Cambridge University Press.

most strongly related to patients' relapse (Hooley & Gotlib, 2000).

Close contact with relatives increases the risk of relapse for schizophrenic patients living with a high EE relative. The opposite pattern is seen in low EE families, where increased contact with relatives seems to have a protective influence. The relationship between family contact and patients' relapse rates is illustrated in Figure 13–5. This figure is based on a reanalysis of data from 25 studies, with a combined sample of more than 800 patients (Bebbington & Kuipers, 1994). Patients who spent more than 35 hours per week in face-to-face contact with a high EE relative were placed in the "high-contact" category; less than 35 hours per week was considered "low contact." These data indicate that the effect of close contact with relatives depends on the emotional climate of the family.

High EE seems to be related, at least in part, to relatives' knowledge and beliefs about their family member's problems. Relatives find it easier to accept the most obvious positive symptoms as being the product of a mental disorder (Brewin et al., 1991). They show less tolerance toward negative symptoms, such as avolition and social withdrawal, perhaps because the patient may appear to be simply lazy or unmotivated.

Understanding Family Attitudes The influence of expressed emotion is not unique to schizophrenia. Patients with mood disorders, eating disorders, panic disorder with agoraphobia, and obsessive–compulsive disorder are also more likely to relapse following discharge if they are living with a high EE relative (Wearden et al., 2000). In fact, EE is an even better predictor of outcome for mood disorders and eating disorders than it is for schizophrenia (Butzlaff & Hooley, 1998). The extension of this phenomenon to other disorders should not be taken to mean that it is unimportant or that the social context of the family is irrelevant to our understanding of the maintenance of schizophrenia (see Research Methods). It may indicate, however, that this aspect of the etiological model is shared with other forms of psychopathology. The specific nature of the person's symptoms may hinge on the genetic predisposition.

How can expressed emotion explain cross-cultural differences in the course of schizophrenia?

Cross-cultural evidence suggests that high EE may be more common in Western or developed countries than in non-Western or developing countries (Hashemi & Cochrane, 1999; Lefley, 1992). This observation might help explain why the long-term course of schizophrenia is typically less severe in developing countries. Some speculation has focused on family members' attitudes and beliefs: People in developing countries may be more tolerant of eccentric behavior among their extended family members. These attitudes may create environments similar to those found in low EE homes in the West. An alternative view places greater emphasis on the culturally determined relationships between patients and other members of their families (Jenkins, 1993; Jenkins & Karno, 1992). Studies of Mexican-American families suggest that

research
methods

COMPARISON GROUPS: WHAT IS NORMAL?

Research studies in the field of psychopathology typically involve comparisons among two or more groups of participants. One group, sometimes called "cases," includes people who already meet the diagnostic criteria for a particular mental disorder, such as schizophrenia. Comparison groups are composed of people who do not have the disorder in question. This approach is sometimes called the case control design because it depends on a contrast between cases and control participants. If the investigators find a significant difference between groups, they have demonstrated that the dependent variable is correlated with the disorder (see Research Methods in Chapter 2). They hope to conclude that they have identified a variable that is relevant to understanding the etiology of this condition. Causal inferences are risky, however, in correlational research. Our willingness to accept these conclusions hinges in large part on whether the investigators selected an appropriate comparison group.

People conducting correlational research, then, must make every effort to identify and test a group of people who are just like the cases except that they do not have the disorder in question (Gehlbach, 1988). This typically means that the people in both groups should be similar with regard to such obvious factors as age, gender, and socioeconomic background. If the investigators find differences between people who have the disorder and those who do not, they want to attribute those differences to the disorder itself. Two main types of comparison groups are used in psychopathology research: people with no history of mental disorder, sometimes called "normal participants," and people who have some other form of mental disorder, sometimes called "patient controls."

Selecting normal comparison groups is not as simple as it might seem. In fact, researchers must make several basic decisions (Kendler, 1990). Does "normal" mean that the person has never had the disorder in question, or does it mean a complete absence of any type of psychopathology? Should people be included as normal control participants if they have a family history of the disorder, even though they do not have the disorder themselves?

A second research strategy involves comparing patients with one type of disorder to those who have another form of psychopathology. Investigators usually employ this strategy to determine whether the variable in question is specifically related to the disorder that they are studying. Are enlarged lateral ventricles or family communication problems unique to people with schizophrenia? Lack of specificity may raise questions about whether this variable is related to the cause of the disorder. It might suggest that this particular variable is, instead, a general consequence of factors such as hospitalization, which the patient control group has also experienced.

Many of the etiological variables that we have discussed in this chapter are not unique to schizophrenia. Expressed emotion predicts relapse among patients with mood disorders as well as among those with schizophrenia. Should this result be taken to mean that EE does not play an important role in the etiology of schizophrenia? Not necessarily. The answer to this question depends on the specific causal model that is being considered (Garber & Hollon, 1991). All forms of psychopathology depend on the interaction of multiple factors spanning biological, social, and psychological systems. Some of these may be specific to the disorder being studied, and others may be general. The development of schizophrenia may depend on a specific genetically determined predisposition. The environmental events that are responsible for eventually causing vulnerable people to express this disorder might be nonspecific. The course of schizophrenia is clearly influenced by the social context in which the patient lives. The fact that similar factors influence people with mood disorders should not be taken to mean that EE is not an important factor in the complex chain of events that explain the etiology and maintenance of schizophrenia.

For all these reasons, the selection of meaningful comparison groups can be a complex and difficult process. There are no perfect solutions to these issues. The research strategy chosen in any particular study will depend on the specific questions that the investigators are trying to answer.

prosocial aspects of interactions between patients and their families can enhance family cohesion and decrease the stigma associated with serious mental disorders. In some cultures, family warmth serves as a protective factor and reduces the probability of patients' relapse (Lopez et al., 1999).

We must be cautious to avoid a narrow view of this phenomenon. The concept of expressed emotion raises extremely sensitive issues for family members, who have too frequently been blamed for the problems of people with schizophrenia. Expressed emotion is not the only factor that can influence the course of a schizophrenic disorder. Some patients relapse in spite of an understanding, tolerant family environment. Furthermore, research studies have shown that the relationship between patients' behavior and relatives' expressed emotion is a transactional or reciprocal process. In other words, patients influence their relatives' attitudes at the same time that relatives' attitudes influence patients' adjustment. Persistent negative attitudes on the part of relatives appear to be perpetuated by a negative cycle of interactions in which patients play an active role (Goldstein et al., 1997).

Integration and Multiple Pathways

A useful etiological model for schizophrenia must include the interaction of genetic factors and environmental events. The heterogeneous nature of the disorder, in terms of symptoms as well as course, also suggests that schizophrenia should be explained in terms of multiple pathways. Some forms of the disorder may be the product of a strong genetic predisposition acting in combination with relatively common psychosocial experiences, such as stressful life events or disrupted communication patterns. For other people, relatively unusual circumstances, such as severe malnutrition during pregnancy, may be responsible for neurodevelopmental abnormalities that eventually lead to the onset of psychotic symptoms in the absence of genetic vulnerability.

Paul Meehl proposed a theory of schizophrenia that provides a useful guide to understanding this complex disorder. According to Meehl (1962, 1990, 1993), individuals who are predisposed to schizophrenia inherit a subtle neurological defect of unknown form. Meehl referred to this condition as **schizotaxia.** As a result of the interaction between this defect and inevitable learning experiences, schizotaxic individuals develop odd or eccentric behaviors, which he called *schizotypic signs*. Most prominent among these behaviors are "associative loosening," which is similar to the cognitive symptoms emphasized by Bleuler, and "aversive drift," in which the individual withdraws from interpersonal relationships because they are associated with negative affect. These are relatively subtle behaviors in comparison to the full-blown symptoms of psychosis. Only a small proportion of schizotypic persons will eventually become overtly schizophrenic.

Various kinds of environmental events have been linked to the etiology of schizophrenia. Some may operate in interaction with the genotype for schizophrenia; others may be sufficient to produce the disorder on their own. Considerable speculation has focused recently on biological factors, such as viral infections and nutritional deficiencies. Psychosocial factors, such as adverse economic circumstances, may also be involved. These events may be particularly harmful to people who are genetically predisposed to the disorder.

The Search for Markers of Vulnerability

Some people apparently inherit a predisposition to schizophrenia. Obviously, it would be useful to be able to identify those people. Genetic linkage studies may provide the answer, if one gene (or a small set of genes) is found to be responsible for the disorder. But that possibility is open to question. The search for more precise information about the development of the disorder may hinge on our ability to identify vulnerability markers, which have also been called *endophenotypes* (Gottesman & Gould, 2003). An endophenotype is a component or trait that lies somewhere on the pathway between the genotype, which lays the foundation for the disorder, and full-blown symptoms of the disorder. It can be measured with precise laboratory procedures of many kinds, but it cannot be seen by the unaided eye.

If we are looking for signs of vulnerability—or endophenotypes—that can be detected among individuals who are genetically predisposed to schizophrenia, where should we look? What form will these signs take? Is it possible to detect signs of vulnerability among individuals who approach the threshold for developing schizophrenia spectrum disorders but have not exhibited any kind of overt symptoms? This issue has attracted considerable attention, but we don't have firm answers to these questions.

According to Meehl's theoretical model, people who are vulnerable to schizophrenia might be identified by developing measures that could detect the underlying biological dysfunction (schizotaxia) or by developing sensitive measures of their subtle eccentricities of behavior (schizotypal traits). The range of possible markers is, therefore, quite large.

Assume that we have selected a specific measure, such as a biochemical assay or a psychological test, and we are interested in knowing whether it might be useful in identifying people who are vulnerable to schizophrenia. What criteria should a **vulnerability marker** fulfill? First, the proposed marker must distinguish between people who already have schizophrenia and those who do not. Second, it should be a stable characteristic over time. Third, the proposed measure of vulnerability should identify more people among the biological relatives of schizophrenic patients than among people in the general population. For example, it should be found among the discordant MZ twins of schizophrenic patients, even if they don't exhibit any symptoms of schizophrenia. Finally, the proposed measure of vulnerability should be able to predict the future development of schizophrenia among those who have not yet experienced a psychotic episode (Adler et al., 1999; Iacono, 1998).

Although reliable measures of vulnerability have not been identified, they are being actively pursued by many investigators with a wide variety of measurement procedures. In the following pages we will outline some of the psychological procedures that have been shown to be among the most promising.

Working Memory Impairment Many investigators have pursued the search for signs of vulnerability by looking at measures of cognitive performance in which schizophrenic patients differ from other people. Some of these studies have focused on cognitive tasks that evaluate information processing, working memory, and attention/vigilance (Green et al., 2004; Hoff & Kremen, 2002).

Considerable emphasis has been focused on one aspect of cognitive functioning known as *working memory*, or the ability to maintain and manipulate information for a short period of time. Working memory can be broken down into several more specific processes. Some of these involve memory buffers that provide short-term storage for visual and verbal information. The most important processes in working memory involve a *central executive component* that is responsible for the manipulation and transformation of data that is held in the storage buffers. Many studies have reported that people with schizophrenia are impaired in their ability to perform laboratory tasks that depend on this central executive component of working memory (Barch, 2005).

One important set of results regarding working memory impairment is based on use of the NBack task. In this task, the participant is presented with a series of items (such as numbers of symbols). He or she is asked to remember the sequence of items as they are being presented. Whenever the participant notices that the current item is the same as the item that was presented "N" trials previously (with N being a number from 0 to 3), he or she is supposed to press a button. The NBack task is one of the most frequently used measures of working memory, especially in studies that use functional neuroimaging in schizophrenia.

The identification of deficits in working memory is particularly interesting with regard to schizophrenia because it links to other evidence regarding brain functions and this disorder. Processes that are associated with central executive processing are associated with brain activity located in the dorsolateral area of the prefrontal cortex (see Figure 13–4) which seems to be dysfunctional in schizophrenia. Neurochemical hypotheses regarding schizophrenia are also relevant in this regard because the dopamine neurotransmitter system plays a crucial role in supporting activities involved in working memory (Goldman-Rakic et al., 2000).

Working memory problems seem to be a stable characteristic of patients with schizophrenia; they do not fluctuate over time (Cannon et al., 2002). Furthermore, these cognitive deficits are found with increased prevalence among the unaffected first-degree relatives of schizophrenic persons, including discordant MZ twins (Sitskoom et al., 2004). Finally, children who later receive a diagnosis of schizophrenia are more likely to have been impaired on tests of verbal working memory than are their siblings who do not develop the disorder. Therefore, measures of working memory fulfill several of the criteria for an index of vulnerability. The research indicates that problems in working memory may be useful signs of vulnerability to schizophrenia (Barch, 2005).

Eye-Tracking Dysfunction Another promising line of work involves impairments in eye movements—specifically, difficulty in tracking the motion of a pendulum or a similarly oscillating stimulus while the person's head is held motionless. When people with schizophrenia are asked to track a moving target, like an oscillating pendulum, with their eyes, a substantial number of them show dysfunctions in smooth-pursuit eye movement (Holzman, 2000; Levy & Holzman, 1997). Instead of reproducing the motion of the pendulum in a series of smooth waves, their tracking records show frequent interruptions of smooth-pursuit movements by numerous rapid movements. Examples of normal tracking records and those of schizophrenic patients are presented in Figure 13–6. Only about 8 percent of normal people exhibit the eye-tracking dysfunctions illustrated in part (c) of Figure 13–6, although some studies have reported higher figures.

Approximately 50 percent of the first-degree relatives of schizophrenic persons show similar smooth-pursuit impairments (Avila et al., 2002; Curtis, Calkins, & Iacono, 2001). The overall pattern of results seen in people with schizophrenia and their families suggests that poor tracking performance may be associated with the predisposition to schizophrenia. That conclusion becomes even more interesting in light of evidence from additional studies suggesting that tracking ability is stable over time, influenced by genetic factors, and found among people who exhibit features associated with schizotypal personality disorder (Gooding, Miller, & Kwapil, 2000; Iacono & Clementz, 1993).

It is not yet possible to identify people who are specifically predisposed to the development of schizophrenia, but research studies have identified potential vulnerability markers. The real test, of course, will center around predictive validity. Can any of these measures, such as smooth-pursuit eye-tracking impairment or attentional dysfunction, predict the later appearance of schizophrenia in people whose scores indicate possible vulnerability? High-risk studies will be useful in providing this type of evidence.

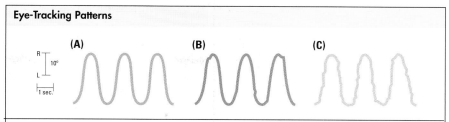

Eye-Tracking Patterns

FIGURE 13–6: This illustration contrasts smooth-pursuit eye-tracking patterns of normal subjects with those of schizophrenic patients. Part (A) shows the actual target. Part (B) illustrates the pattern for people without schizophrenia, and part (C) shows the pattern for people with schizophrenia.

Source: From D.L. Levy et al., Eye-tracking dysfunction and schizophrenia: A critical perspective, *Schizophrenia Bulletin, 19,* 462.

TREATMENT

Schizophrenia is a complex disorder that often must be treated over an extended period of time. Clinicians must be concerned about the treatment of acute psychotic episodes as well as the prevention of future episodes. A multifaceted approach to treatment is typically required. Antipsychotic medication is the primary mode of treatment for this disorder. Because many patients remain impaired between episodes, long-term care must often involve the provision of housing and social support. People with impaired occupational and social skills need special types of training. The treatment of schizophrenia requires attention on all of these fronts and is necessarily concerned with the cooperative efforts of many types of professionals (Lehman et al., 2004). Schizophrenia also takes its toll on families. The Getting Help section at the end of this chapter discusses some of the resources available for patients and families.

Antipsychotic Medication

The many different forms of medication that are used to treat patients with schizophrenia can be divided into two broad categories. The first generation of drugs began to be introduced in the 1950s, and a second generation swept into practice in the 1990s. Both kinds of medication are in standard use today, and both waves of discovery introduced significant improvements in care for patients with schizophrenia.

The first generation of antipsychotic drugs— also called classical or traditional antipsychotics— was discovered accidentally in the early 1950s by a French neurosurgeon who used them as a supplement to anesthesia. They were not effective for the purpose he intended, but they did have a calming effect on the patients. This experience prompted psychiatrists to use the same drugs with their patients. Early reports of success in treating chronic psychotic patients quickly led to the widespread use of these drugs, such as chlorpromazine (Thorazine), in psychiatric hospitals throughout Europe and the United States (Shen, 1999). The discovery of these drugs quickly changed the way in which schizophrenia was treated. Large numbers of patients who had previously been institutionalized could be discharged to community care (but see Chapter 18 on the effects of deinstitutionalization).

Several related types of drugs were developed in subsequent years. They are called **antipsychotic drugs** because they have a relatively specific effect—to reduce the severity of, and sometimes eliminate, psychotic symptoms. Classical antipsychotics are also known as *neuroleptic* drugs because they also induce side effects that resemble the motor symptoms of Parkinson's disease (see Chapter 14). Beneficial effects are sometimes noticed within a week after the patient begins taking antipsychotic medication, but it often takes several weeks before improvement is seen. Positive symptoms, such as hallucinations, respond better to antipsychotic medication than negative symptoms, such as alogia and blunted affect (Kane, 1999). This differential effect is not entirely clear-cut, however. For example, some patients who are socially withdrawn become less isolated when taking antipsychotic medication. Among the classical or typical antipsychotics, there is no convincing evidence to indicate that one is more effective than another (Bradford, Stroup, & Lieberman, 2002).

Double-blind, placebo-controlled studies have confirmed the effectiveness of antipsychotic medication in the treatment of patients who are acutely disturbed. Literally thousands of studies have addressed this issue over a period of more than 40 years (Marder et al., 1993). These studies provide substantial support for the effectiveness of antipsychotic medication. Most studies find that about half of the patients who receive medication are rated as being much improved after 4 to 6 weeks of treatment. Further improvements may continue beyond that point for some patients. In contrast, patients treated with placebos exhibit much smaller rates of improvement, and many of them actually deteriorate.

Unfortunately, a substantial minority of schizophrenic patients, perhaps 25 percent, do not improve on classical antipsychotic drugs (Conley & Kelly, 2001). Another 30 to 40 percent might be considered partial responders: Their condition improves, but they do not show a full remission of symptoms. Investigators have not been able to identify reliable differences between patients who improve on medication and those who do not. Some experts have suggested that treatment-resistant patients may have more prominent negative symptoms, greater disorganization, and more evidence of neurological abnormalities (Hellewell, 1999; McMahon et al., 2002).

Maintenance Medication   After patients recover from acute psychotic episodes, there is a high probability that they will have another episode. The relapse rate may be as high as 65 to 70 percent in the first year after hospital discharge if patients discontinue medication. Continued treatment with antipsychotic drugs can reduce this rate to approximately 40 percent (Hogarty, 1993; Kane, 2001b). Therefore the great majority of schizophrenic patients continue to take medication after they recover from psychotic episodes, although usually at lower dosages. The need for maintenance medication is less clearly defined among patients who have had only one episode of schizophrenia. The relapse rate for these patients is lower than among those who have had multiple episodes.

Figure 13–7 illustrates general relapse rates for schizophrenic outpatients. The estimated rates presented in this figure were generated by analyzing data from several outcome studies (Weiden & Olfson, 1995). They apply to outpatients who have experienced more than one episode, have responded positively to classical antipsychotic drugs, and are not receiving active psychosocial treatments (discussed later in the chapter). The best-case scenario represents expected relapse rates for patients who are receiving an optimal dose of medication and who continue taking the medication on a regular basis. Under these circumstances, slightly more than half of schizophrenic outpatients will relapse and require rehospitalization within 2 years of discharge. The real-world scenario in Figure 13–7 indicates that actual relapse rates are even higher because some patients stop taking medication, often to avoid unpleasant side effects (Glick & Berg, 2002).

Motor Side Effects   Antipsychotic drugs produce several unpleasant side effects. They come in varying degrees and affect different patients in different ways. In the case of classical or first-generation antipsychotic drugs, the most obvious and troublesome are called *extrapyramidal symptoms* (EPS) because they are mediated by the extrapyramidal neural pathways that connect the brain to the motor neurons in the spinal cord. These symptoms include an assortment of neurological disturbances, such as muscular rigidity, tremors, restless agitation, peculiar involuntary postures, and motor inertia. EPS may diminish spontaneously after 3 or 4 months of continuous treatment. Additional drugs, such as benztropine (Cogentin), can be used to minimize the severity of EPS during the first few months of treatment. Unfortunately, some patients exhibit persistent signs of EPS in spite of these efforts (Kane, 2001a).

Prolonged treatment with classical antipsychotic drugs frequently leads to the development of *tardive dyskinesia* (TD). This syndrome consists of abnormal involuntary movements of the mouth and face, such as tongue protrusion, chewing, and lip puckering, as well as spasmodic movements of the limbs and trunk of the body. The latter include writhing movements of the fingers and toes and jiggling of the legs, as well as jerking movements of the head and pelvis. Taken as a whole, this problem is distressing to patients and their families. The TD syndrome is induced by antipsychotic treatment, and it is irreversible in some patients, even after the medication has been discontinued. In fact, in some patients, TD becomes worse if antipsychotic medication is withdrawn (Lauterbach et al., 2001; Walters et al., 1997).

Atypical Antipsychotics

The second generation of antipsychotic medications began to be introduced in the 1990s and stimulated what some people have called a "second revolution" in the care of patients with schizophrenia. These drugs have come to be known as **atypical antipsychotics** because they are less likely than the classical antipsychotics to produce unpleasant motor side effects (Kapur & Remington, 2001). Clinical trials indicate that atypical antipsychotics are at least as effective as the first-generation drugs for the treatment of positive symptoms of schizophrenia, and they are generally more effective than classical antipsychotics in the treatment of negative symptoms (Leucht et al., 2002; Volavka et al., 2002).

The best known of the atypical drugs, clozapine (Clozaril), has been used extensively

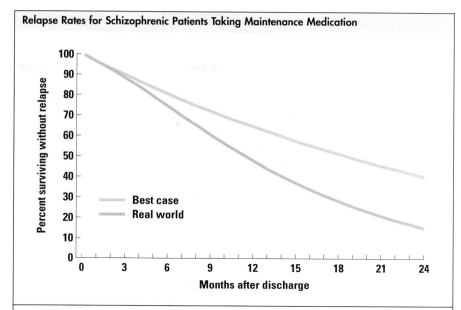

Relapse Rates for Schizophrenic Patients Taking Maintenance Medication

FIGURE 13–7: Estimated relapse rates for patients receiving optimal doses of standard neuroleptic medication while not receiving active psychosocial treatments. Real world: Assumes some noncompliance with medication. Best case: Assumes complete compliance with medication.

Source: P.J. Weiden and M. Olfson, 1995, Cost of relapse in schizophrenia, *Schizophrenia Bulletin, 21*, 425. Copyright © 1995. Reprinted by permission of Oxford University Press.

throughout Europe since the 1970s. Its use was delayed for several years in the United States because the drug can produce a lethal blood condition known as agranulocytosis in about 1 percent of patients. It was approved for use by the U.S. Food and Drug Administration (FDA) in 1990, with the requirement that patients receive weekly monitoring of their white blood cell levels. The second generation of antipsychotic medications also includes risperidone (Risperdal), olanzapine (Zyprexa), quetiapine (Seroquel), and several other drugs that have recently become available or are waiting for approval by the FDA. Some of these drugs are listed in Table 13–3.

Patients are more compliant with medication and less likely to drop out of treatment when taking one of the atypical antipsychotic drugs because of their decreased motor side effects. It should be noted, however, that atypical antipsychotics also produce side effects, and some of them are serious. For example, many of the second-generation antipsychotics lead to weight gain and obesity. These problems increase the person's risk for additional medical problems, such as diabetes, hypertension, and coronary artery disease.

At least 30 percent of schizophrenic patients who were previously treatment-resistant improve

TABLE 13-3   Examples of Medications Used to Treat Schizophrenic Disorders

| | | MODES OF ACTION | | | |
| | | SELECTED SIDE EFFECTS | | (SELECTED RECEPTORS) | |
DRUG CLASS	GENERIC NAME (TRADE NAME)	EPS	WEIGHT GAIN	D$_2$	5HT$_{2A}$
First-generation antipsychotics	chlorpromazine (Thorazine)	++	+	++	+
	haloperidol (Haldol)	++++	+	++++	+
Atypical antipsychotics	clozapine (Clozaril)	+/−	++++	++	++++
	risperidone (Risperdal)	++	++	+++	+++++
	olanzapine (Zyprexa)	+	++++	+++	++++
	quetiapine (Seroquel)	+/−	++	++	+++
	amisulpride (Solian)*	+	++	++++	−

D$_2$ = dopamine receptors; 5HT$_{2a}$ = serotonin receptors.

*Amisulpride is not yet available in the United States, but it has been used for more than 10 years in France (Leucht et al., 2002).

Source: S. Kapur and G. Remington, 2001, Atypical antipsychotics: new directions and new challenges in the treatment of schizophrenia, *Annual Review of Medicine, 52,* 503–517.

after taking atypical antipsychotic drugs (Chakos et al., 2001; Kapur & Remington, 2001). Treatment resistance is usually defined as failure to improve on at least three different types of classical antipsychotic medication after 6 weeks on moderate to high doses. Most of the research evidence regarding the efficacy of atypical antipsychotic medication with treatment-resistant patients is based on the use of clozapine because it has been available longer than the other drugs. Future studies will determine whether medications such as olanzapine and risperidone are also more effective than traditional antipsychotics with such patients.

Are newer antipsychotic medications more effective than older drugs?

All antipsychotic medications—both traditional and atypical forms—act by blocking dopamine receptors in the cortical and limbic areas of the brain (Factor, 2002). They also affect a number of other neurotransmitters, including serotonin, norepinephrine, and acetylcholine. Table 13–3 includes a comparison of two traditional and five atypical antipsychotic drugs in terms of their ability to block specific types of dopamine and serotonin receptors. Most atypical antipsychotics produce a broader range of neurochemical actions in the brain than do the standard neuroleptic drugs, which act primarily on dopamine receptors. Clozapine and olanzapine, for example, produce a relatively strong blockade of serotonin receptors and a relatively weaker blockade of dopamine receptors (Richelson, 1999). This increased affinity of some atypical drugs for serotonin receptors might explain why they can have a beneficial effect on symptoms of schizophrenia without producing marked motor side effects (EPS). This hypothesis is contradicted, however, by the modes of action associated with a newer form of atypical drug, amisulpride, which does not affect serotonin receptors (Leucht et al., 2002). Neurochemical differences between traditional and atypical antipsychotic drugs are not clearly understood and are currently the topic of interesting debate (Seeman, 2002).

Further progress in the pharmacological treatment of schizophrenia will undoubtedly produce new drugs that have varying mechanisms of neurochemical action. The rate of progress in this field is very rapid. You can obtain regularly updated reviews of evidence regarding the treatment of schizophrenia from the Cochrane Library at its Web site: www.cochrane.org.

Psychosocial Treatment

Several forms of psychological treatment have proved to be effective for schizophrenic patients. These procedures address a wide range of problems that are associated with the disorder. In contrast to pharmacological approaches, psychological approaches place relatively little emphasis on the treatment of acute psychotic episodes. Instead, they concentrate on long-term strategies (Kopelowicz, Liberman, & Zarate, 2002).

Family-Oriented Aftercare Studies of expressed emotion have inspired the development of innovative family-based treatment programs. Family treatment programs attempt to improve the coping skills of family members, recognizing the burdens that people often endure while caring for a family member with a chronic mental disorder. Patients are maintained on antipsychotic medication on an outpatient basis throughout this process. There are several different approaches to this type of family intervention. Most include an educational component that is designed to help family members understand and accept the nature of the disorder (see Getting Help). One goal of this procedure is to eliminate unrealistic expectations for the patient, which may lead to harsh criticism. Behavioral family management also places considerable emphasis on the improvement of communication and problem-solving skills, which may enhance the family members' ability to work together and thereby minimize conflict.

Several empirical studies have evaluated the effects of family interventions. Most have found reductions in relapse rates for people receiving family treatment. In the first year of treatment, relapse rates for patients who receive family treatment plus medication are typically below 20 percent, compared with 40 or 50 percent for those receiving medication alone (Pilling et al., 2002a). Relapse rates increase in the next year for both groups. Family-based treatment programs can delay relapse, but they do not necessarily prevent relapse in the long run. The beneficial effects of treatment may be lost shortly after treatment ends (Hogarty, 1993), and intensive family programs may not be cost-effective (Bellack et al., 2000; Schooler et al., 1997). In the case of a disorder such as schizophrenia, which is often chronic, difficult decisions have to be made about priorities and the availability of services. Family-based programs can have a positive effect, but we need to find more efficient and more effective ways to integrate this aspect of treatment into an overall treatment program.

Social Skills Training Many patients who avoid relapse and are able to remain in the community continue to be impaired in terms of residual

symptoms. They also experience problems in social and occupational functioning. For these patients, drug therapy must be supplemented by psychosocial programs that address residual aspects of the disorder. The need to address these problems directly is supported by evidence that shows that deficits in social skills are relatively stable in schizophrenic patients and relatively independent of other aspects of the disorder, including both positive and negative symptoms (Mueser et al., 1991).

Social skills training (SST) is a structured, educational approach to these problems that involves modeling, role playing, and the provision of social reinforcement for appropriate behaviors (Heinssen, Liberman, & Kopelwicz, 2000). A general description of this type of approach to treatment is provided in Chapter 3. Controlled-outcome studies indicate that, in combination with neuroleptic medication, SST leads to improved performance on measures of social adjustment. It is not clear, however, that SST has any beneficial effects on relapse rates (Pilling et al., 2002b). That result may not be surprising in light of evidence regarding the course of this disorder, which suggests that various aspects of outcome, including symptom severity and social adjustment, tend to be relatively independent.

Cognitive Therapy One area of treatment that has received much greater emphasis in recent years is the use of various forms of cognitive therapy

Patients and families respond in many creative ways to the presence of mental disorder. Brandon Staglin (left) has struggled with schizophrenia for several years. His parents founded an annual Music Festival for Mental Health, which has raised millions of dollars for mental health charities and research.

Many people have made remarkable achievements in spite of suffering from schizophrenia. Tom Harrell has been named jazz trumpeter of the year three times by *Downbeat Magazine*. He hears disturbing auditory hallucinations, but they disappear when he is playing music.

for schizophrenia (Pilling et al., 2002b; Rathod & Turkington, 2005). In some cases, these interventions have focused on the use of standard cognitive therapy procedures that are designed to help patients evaluate, test, and correct distorted ways of thinking about themselves and their social environments. Other forms of cognitive treatment have become more specialized and are aimed specifically at cognitive deficits that are particularly evident in schizophrenia.

One example of a specialized treatment program is cognitive enhancement therapy (CET) for schizophrenia (Hogarty et al., 2004). This is a comprehensive, integrated program aimed at the improvement of cognitive abilities, including those that are concerned with performance on laboratory tasks (such as attention, working memory, and problem solving) as well as social cognition (such as recognizing the perspectives of other people and appraising social contexts). It is designed for use with people who are also taking antipsychotic medication and have already recovered from active symptoms of psychosis but nevertheless continue to exhibit signs of cognitive disability. Patients spend many hours practicing computerized cognitive exercises. Several weeks after beginning cognitive training exercises, they also participate in an extended series of small group exercises (interpreting verbal messages, recognizing others' emotions, maintaining conversations, and so on). One large-scale 2-year outcome study compared patients who received cognitive enhancement therapy with patients in a control group who received enhanced supportive therapy.

Those who received CET showed more improvement with regard to performance on measures of cognitive performance, social cognition, and overall social adjustment. Thus, in the context of on-going treatment with antipsychotic medication, cognitive therapy can be beneficial for patients with schizophrenia.

Assertive Community Treatment   The treatment of a chronic disorder such as schizophrenia clearly requires an extensive range of comprehensive services that should be fully integrated and continuously available. *Assertive community treatment* (ACT) is a psychosocial intervention that is delivered by an interdisciplinary team of clinicians (Greenley, 1995; Stein & Santos, 1998). They provide a combination of psychological treatments—including education, support, skills training, and rehabilitation—as well as medication. Services are provided on a regular basis throughout the week and during crisis periods (any time of day and any day of the week). The program represents an intensive effort to maintain seriously disordered patients in the community and to minimize the need for hospitalization. It differs from more traditional outpatient services in its assertive approach to the provision of services: Members of an ACT team go to the consumer rather than expecting the consumer to come to them.

Outcome studies indicate that ACT programs can effectively reduce the number of days that patients spend in psychiatric hospitals, while improving their level of functioning (Phillips et al., 2001; Thornicroft & Susser, 2001). One study found that only 18 percent of the people in the ACT group were hospitalized during the first year of treatment compared to 89 percent of the people in the control group. ACT is an intensive form of treatment that requires a well-organized and extensive network of professional services. In spite of the expense that is required to maintain this kind of program, empirical studies indicate that it is more cost-effective than traditional services provided by community mental health centers (Lehman et al., 1999). Reduction in costs of inpatient care offsets the expense of the ACT program.

Institutional Programs   Although schizophrenic persons can be treated with medication on an outpatient basis, various types of institutional care continue to be important. Most patients experience recurrent phases of active psychosis. Brief periods of hospitalization (usually 2 or 3 weeks) are often beneficial during these times.

Some patients are chronically disturbed and require long-term institutional treatment. Social learning programs, sometimes called *token economies*, can be useful for these patients. In these programs specific behavioral contingencies are put into place for all of the patients on a hospital ward. The goal is to increase the frequency of desired behaviors, such as appropriate grooming and participation in social activities, and to decrease the frequency of undesirable behaviors, such as violence or incoherent speech. Staff members monitor patients' behavior throughout the day. Each occurrence of a desired behavior is praised and reinforced by the presentation of a token, which can be exchanged for food or privileges, such as time to watch television. Inappropriate behaviors are typically ignored, but occasional punishment, such as loss of privileges, is used if necessary.

Gordon Paul, a clinical psychologist at the University of Houston, and his colleagues conducted an extensive evaluation of behavioral treatment with chronic schizophrenic patients (Paul & Lentz, 1977). They compared two inpatient programs in the treatment of severely disturbed patients who had been continuously hospitalized for many years. One program followed a carefully designed and closely supervised social learning model, and the other followed a more traditional approach. These experimental treatments were compared to a group of similar patients who continued to reside in their original hospital wards. The patients' adjustment was evaluated at 6-month intervals over a period of approximately 6 years.

Both groups of patients who received treatment showed significant improvement, especially during the first 6 months of the study. This finding highlights the possibility for improvement, even among chronically disturbed patients. Patients in the social learning program showed even more improvement than those in the traditional group, especially with regard to social functioning and self-care. These benefits were maintained throughout the duration of the treatment program. Perhaps most impressive was the fact that by the end of the first 4 years of active treatment, 11 percent of the patients in the social learning program were discharged to independent living in the community without being readmitted to the hospital. In contrast, none of the patients in the standard hospital comparison group was released to independent living. This study indicates that carefully structured inpatient programs, especially those that follow behavioral principles, can have important positive effects for chronic schizophrenic patients.

Gordon Paul, Distinguished Professor of Psychology at the University of Houston, has developed behavioral assessment and treatment procedures for psychotic patients. His research indicates that social learning programs can lead to significant improvement in the adjustment of seriously disturbed patients.

getting help

Schizophrenia can be a devastating condition for patients and their families. Fortunately, the past 2 decades have seen many important advances in treatment for this disorder. Perhaps no other disorder requires such an extensive array of services, ranging from medication and short-term inpatient care to long-term residential facilities and psychosocial help for family members. An extremely useful book, *Coping with Schizophrenia: A Guide for Families,* written by Kim Mueser and Susan Gingrich, offers sound advice on a variety of crucial topics. For example, the authors discuss various forms of antipsychotic drugs, their side effects, their use in preventing relapse, and ways to respond to a patient's reluctance to continue taking necessary medication. They outline available community resources that help patients and their families deal with acute episodes, as well as the long-term challenges of residual symptoms, occupational difficulties, and housing needs.

Another excellent resource is *The Family Face of Schizophrenia,* by Patricia Backlar, who is a mental health ethicist and also the mother of a son who suffers from schizophrenia. This book includes a series of seven stories about people who have struggled with this disorder and the often confusing and sometimes inadequate array of mental health services that are available in many communities. Each story is followed by a commentary that includes advice for patients and their families (e.g., how to obtain insurance benefits for treatment, how to find a missing mentally ill family member, how to cope with suicidal risks, and how to navigate legal issues that can arise in caring for someone with a serious mental disorder). Anyone who must cope with a psychotic disorder will benefit from reading these books carefully.

The National Alliance for the Mentally Ill (NAMI) is an extremely influential grass-roots support and advocacy organization that has worked tirelessly to improve the quality of life for patients and their families. It has more than 1,000 state and local affiliates throughout the 50 states. Among various items on its public policy agenda, NAMI is committed to increasing access to community-based services such as housing and rehabilitation for people with severe mental disorders. The address for its Web site is www.nami.org. It is a comprehensive source of information regarding all aspects of severe mental disorders (especially schizophrenia and mood disorders), including referral to various types of support groups and professional service providers. The NAMI Web page includes "Helpline Online," which can provide direct answers to questions about severe mental disorders, as well as NAMI's own *Consumer and Family Guide to Schizophrenia Treatment.*

SUMMARY

People who meet the diagnostic criteria for **schizophrenia** exhibit many types of symptoms that represent impairments across a broad array of cognitive, perceptual, and interpersonal functions. These symptoms can be roughly divided into three types. **Positive symptoms** include **hallucinations** and **delusions. Negative symptoms** include **blunted affect, alogia, avolition,** and social withdrawal. Symptoms of disorganization include verbal communication problems and bizarre behavior.

The onset of schizophrenia is typically during adolescence or early adulthood. The disorder can follow different patterns over time. Some people recover fairly quickly from schizophrenia, whereas others deteriorate progressively after the initial onset of symptoms.

The disorder was originally defined by Emil Kraepelin, who emphasized the progressive course of the disorder in distinguishing it from manic–depressive psychosis. Eugen Bleuler coined the term schizophrenia, proposing that disturbances in speech and emotion are the fundamental symptoms of the disorder. Many clinicians believe that schizophrenia actually includes several types of disorder with different causes. Others believe that it is a single pathological process with variations in symptomatic expression and course.

The negative symptoms of schizophrenia have been given increased emphasis in DSM-IV-TR. The manual requires evidence of a decline in the person's social or occupational functioning, as well as the presence of disturbed behavior over a continuous period of at least 6 months. DSM-IV-TR recognizes several subtypes of schizophrenia, such as **paranoid, catatonic,** and **disorganized types,** that are based on prominent symptoms. These subtypes have relatively poor diagnostic reliability and are frequently unstable over time.

The lifetime prevalence of schizophrenia is approximately 1 or 2 percent in virtually all areas of the world. Men and women are equally likely to be affected, although the onset of the disorder appears at an earlier age in males. Male patients are more likely than female patients to exhibit negative symptoms, and they are also more likely to follow a chronic, deteriorating course. Two large cross-cultural studies found patients who exhibited characteristic signs and symptoms of schizophrenia in all of the study sites. Comparisons of patients across centers revealed more similarities than differences in clinical symptoms.

Genetic factors clearly play a role in the development of schizophrenia. Risk for developing the disorder is between 10 and 15 percent among first-degree relatives of schizophrenic patients. Concordance rates are approximately 48 percent in MZ twins compared to only 17 percent in DZ pairs. Adoption studies have found that approximately 15 percent of the offspring of a schizophrenic parent will eventually develop the disorder themselves, even if they are separated from their biological parent at an early age and are raised by adoptive families. Twin and adoption studies also indicate that the disorder has variable expressions, sometimes called the schizophrenia spectrum. Related disorders include schizotypal personality disorder and **schizoaffective disorder.** Linkage studies have not found consistent evidence for a specific gene of major influence.

Advances in brain imaging technology have allowed extensive study of structural and functional brain abnormalities in schizophrenia. A specific brain lesion has not been identified, and it is unlikely that a disorder as complex as schizophrenia will be traced to a single site in the brain. Structural images of schizophrenic patients' brains reveal enlarged ventricles as well as decreased size of parts of the limbic system. Studies of brain metabolism and blood flow have identified functional changes in the frontal lobes, temporal lobes, and basal ganglia in many persons with schizophrenia. Current evidence points toward a subtle and diffuse type of neuropathology in schizophrenia.

The discovery of antipsychotic medication stimulated interest in the role of neurochemical factors in the etiology of schizophrenia. The dopamine hypothesis provided the major unifying theme in this area for many years, but it is now considered too simple to account for the existing evidence. Current neurochemical hypotheses regarding schizophrenia focus on a broad array of neurotransmitters, with special emphasis on serotonin.

The importance of environmental events in the etiology of schizophrenia is evident in the results of twin studies, which show that concordance rates in MZ twins do not approach 100 percent. Several social and psychological factors have been shown to be related to the disorder. Social class is inversely related to the prevalence of schizophrenia. In some cases, low levels of socioeconomic achievement represent a consequence of the disorder. Several kinds of research studies have also found, however, that social factors appear to make a causal contribution to the disorder. Disturbed patterns of family communication have been presumed to be related to the etiology of schizophrenia for many years. There is no evidence to indicate that the behavior of family members contributes to the original onset of schizophrenic symptoms. Recent efforts on this topic have examined the relation between the social context of the family and the long-term course of the disorder. Patients from families that are high in **expressed emotion** are more likely to relapse than those from low EE families. Expressed emotion is the product of an ongoing interaction between patients and their families, with patterns of influence flowing in both directions.

The evidence regarding etiology supports a diathesis-stress model. It should be possible to develop **vulnerability markers** that can identify individuals who possess the genetic predisposition to the disorder. Promising research in this area is concerned with a broad range of possibilities, including smooth-pursuit eye-tracking movements and laboratory measures of working memory.

The central aspect of treatment for schizophrenia is antipsychotic medication. These drugs help to resolve acute psychotic episodes. They can also delay relapse and improve the level of patients' functioning between episodes. Unfortunately, they often produce troublesome side effects, and a substantial minority of schizophrenic patients are resistant to classic types of antipsychotic medication. The **atypical antipsychotics** are able to help some patients who do not respond to other drugs, and they produce fewer unpleasant motor side effects.

Various types of psychosocial treatment also provide important benefits to schizophrenic patients and their families. Prominent among these are family-based treatment for patients who have been stabilized on medication following discharge from the hospital. Social skills training can also be useful in improving the level of patients' role functioning.

KEY TERMS

alogia 427
anhedonia 426
antipsychotic drugs 450
atypical
    antipsychotics 451
avolition 427

blunted affect 426
brief psychotic
    disorder 432
catatonic type 431
delusions 425
delusional disorder 432

disorganized speech 427
disorganized type 431
expressed
    emotion (EE) 444
hallucinations 424
inappropriate affect 429

negative symptoms 424
paranoid type 432
positive symptoms 424
prodromal phase 423
residual phase 423
residual type 432

schizoaffective
    disorder 432
schizophrenia 421
schizotaxia 447
undifferentiated type 432
vulnerability marker 448

Go to www.prenhall.com/oltmanns for online quizzes, interactive flash cards, PowerPoint presentations, and chapter reviews.

16

Psychological Disorders
of Childhood

◆◆◆

Have you ever fallen to the floor, kicking, screaming, and crying because you did not get your way? Almost certainly. Of course, this is not normal behavior for 20-year-old college students. However, temper tantrums are normal, though sometimes obnoxious, behavior for 2-year-old children. Similarly, terrible fears of monsters are developmentally normal at the age of 4, but not at the age of 14. In evaluating whether a child's behavior is normal or abnormal, the first question we must ask is: How old is the child?

OVERVIEW

Viewing abnormal behavior within the context of normal development is important to understanding *all* abnormal behavior. However, a **developmental psychopathology** approach is absolutely essential to disorders of childhood, because children change rapidly during the first 20 years of life. Psychologists become concerned only when a child's behavior deviates substantially from **developmental norms,** behavior that is typical for children of a given age.

Children and adolescents may suffer from most of the disorders we have covered in earlier chapters. For example, children sometimes develop mood disorders, anxiety disorders, or (rarely) schizophrenia. With the exception of mental retardation and pervasive developmental disorders, however, all of the problems we have discussed in earlier chapters are more prevalent among adults than children.

Psychological problems that commonly begin during childhood are listed in the DSM-IV-TR category Disorders Usually First Diagnosed in Infancy, Childhood, or Adolescence. Other than mental retardation and pervasive developmental disorders (see Chapter 15), the most important disorders in this category are the various externalizing

disorders. **Externalizing disorders** create difficulties for the child's external world. They are characterized by children's failure to control their behavior according to the expectations of parents, peers, teachers, and/or legal authorities—for example, as a result of hyperactive behavior or conduct problems. Externalizing disorders are the most commonly diagnosed childhood disorders and account for about half of all children in treatment (Kazdin, 1995). For these reasons, we focus much of this chapter on them.

Internalizing disorders are psychological problems that primarily affect the child's internal world—for example, excessive anxiety or sadness. DSM-IV-TR does not list internalizing disorders as separate psychological disorders of childhood; rather, the manual notes that children may qualify for many "adult" diagnoses, such as anxiety or mood disorders. However, we think it is essential to take a developmental psychopathology approach and highlight children's unique experience of anxiety and depression. Children do not interpret events or express emotions in the same manner as adults; emotional experience changes rapidly with age; and the family, peer, and school contexts typically affect children more dramatically than they affect adults. In our view,

Temper tantrums are a normal, if trying, part of child development during the "terrible twos" (and beyond). Awareness of such developmental norms is essential to evaluating abnormal behavior in children.

childhood disorders is necessarily limited, not only by their sheer number but also by questions we have about the appropriateness of some diagnostic categories (Taylor & Rutter, 2002).

EXTERNALIZING DISORDERS

Few children or adolescents identify themselves as having an externalizing disorder. Instead, some adult, often a parent or teacher, decides that a child has a behavior problem. In some cases, children are unable to recognize or admit to their difficult behavior. In other cases, however, the problem may be as much the adult's as the child's (Yeh & Weisz, 2001). For example, a stressed parent may have trouble coping with normal misbehavior. This makes the assessment of externalizing disorders challenging, as illustrated in the following case study.

children's mood and anxiety disorders are not simply miniature versions of adult diagnoses.

In this chapter, we also introduce many of the 26 *additional* childhood diagnoses included in DSM-IV-TR. Our coverage of these other

CASE STUDY   Bad Boy, Troubled Boy, or All Boy?

Jeremy W. was 8 years old when his mother brought him to a clinical psychologist on the recommendations of his second-grade teacher and a school counselor. Mrs. W. came to the psychologist reluctantly, because she was not sure if she agreed with the suggestions of the school personnel. In fact, Mrs. W. wasn't sure if she agreed with her husband about what was going on with Jeremy.

According to Mrs. W., Jeremy was constantly in trouble at school. His teacher reprimanded Jeremy daily for disrupting the class, not paying attention, and failing to finish his work. The teacher felt that her attempts at discipline had little effect. Sometimes Jeremy would listen for a while, but soon he was pestering another child, talking out of turn, or simply staring off into space. Lately, Jeremy had begun to talk back when he was disciplined, and his teacher had sent him to the principal's office several times in the past month.

The psychologist confirmed this information in a telephone call to the school. The teacher also noted that Jeremy had no close friends, and that other kids thought of him as a "pain."

The teacher had referred Jeremy to a school psychologist, who gave him several academic tests. According to an individualized intelligence test, Jeremy had an IQ of 108. However, his achievement test scores indicated

performance at a first-grade level, almost a year behind his current grade. The school psychologist suspected that Jeremy had a learning disorder, but thought that his behavior problems also were interfering with his learning. She concluded that Jeremy should remain in his regular classroom for the present. As a first step, she recommended therapy for Jeremy and perhaps for his parents. After treatment, she would reevaluate him for possible placement in a "resource room," a special class for students with learning problems.

Mrs. W. was frightened by the suggestion that Jeremy might be "emotionally disturbed" or "learning disordered." According to his mother, Jeremy could be difficult to manage at home, but she had never considered the possibility that he needed psychological help. Jeremy had always been a handful, but in her view, he had never been a bad child. Instead, Mrs. W. thought that Jeremy expressed himself better through actions than words. In this respect, he was the opposite of his 11-year-old sister, who was an A and B student. Mrs. W. was not convinced that Jeremy's teacher was the best person to work with him, but she did agree that he was having problems in school. In her mind, Jeremy was developing low self-esteem, and many of his actions were attempts to get attention.

According to Mrs. W., Jeremy's father spent very little time with him. Mr. W. worked long hours on his construction job, and he often was off with his friends on weekends. Mrs. W. said that her husband was of little help even when he was home. He would tell his wife that it was her job to take care of the kids—he needed his rest. With tears in her eyes, Mrs. W. said that she needed a rest, too.

In any case, Mrs. W. said her husband was not concerned about Jeremy's behavior or his schoolwork. Instead, he thought that Jeremy was just "all boy" and not much of a student—just like Mr. W. was as a child. He refused to take time off from work to see the psychologist.

In confidence, Mrs. W. said that she, too, saw a lot of his father in Jeremy—too much of him, in fact. She got no support from her husband in disciplining Jeremy or in encouraging him in his schoolwork.

She blamed her husband for Jeremy's problems, and she was secretly furious with him.

She knew that Jeremy had to do well in school in order to live a better life, and she felt like a failure as a mother. She was willing to try anything to help Jeremy, but she doubted that there was anything she could do without her husband's support.

Is Jeremy a disobedient child, as his teacher thinks? A learning-disordered child, as suggested by the school psychologist? Suffering from low self-esteem, as his mother fears? Or is he simply "all boy," as his father claims? What about Jeremy? How does he feel about himself, his family, his schoolwork, and his friendships at school?

Mental health professionals who treat children are constantly vexed by such difficult questions, and treatment often begins with an attempt to achieve consensus about the nature of a child's problem (Hawley & Weisz, 2003). Psychologists want to reach an accurate diagnosis, but another goal is to get adults working together. In Jeremy's case, Mr. and Mrs. W. may need to present a united front to Jeremy, and to do so they may need to resolve issues in their marriage. Because of such conflicts, many psychologists prefer to see children in *family therapy* rather than treat children alone. Many psychologists also work to establish better communication and cooperation between parents and teachers.

Of course, Jeremy is at least part of the problem. If we can trust his teacher's report—and experienced child clinical psychologists do trust teachers—Jeremy clearly has some type of externalizing problem. Perhaps Jeremy's behavior is simply a reaction to his parents' conflicts, and he will get better if they work out their differences. Or perhaps Jeremy is a troubled child who is causing some of these conflicts, not just reacting to them. Mr. and Mrs. W. both felt that Jeremy and his father were a lot alike. Could Jeremy have learned or inherited some of his father's characteristics?

Symptoms of Externalizing Disorders

Children with externalizing disorders often break rules, are angry and aggressive, impulsive, overactive, and inattentive. These troublesome actions tend to occur together; however, different clusters of problems have different implications for the etiology, treatment, and course of children's externalizing disorders.

Rule Violations   Many externalizing symptoms involve violations of age-appropriate social rules, including disobeying parents or teachers, violating social or peer group norms (e.g., annoying others), and perhaps violating the law. All children break at least some social rules, of course,

Calvin and Hobbes   by Bill Watterson

CALVIN AND HOBBES, "What Are We Going to Do, Hobbes?" (April 14, 1980) © 1980 by Watterson. Distributed by UNIVERSAL PRESS SYNDICATE, and reprinted with their permission. All rights reserved.

and we often admire an innocent and clever rule breaker. For example, we see Calvin of the Calvin and Hobbes cartoons as devilish, but he is not really "bad," and we certainly do not view him as "sick."

Serious Rule Breaking   Some misconduct is normal, perhaps even healthy, for children. However, the rule violations in externalizing disorders are not trivial and are far from "cute." Many schoolteachers lament that they spend far too much time disciplining children, a circumstance that also is unfair to the well-behaved youngsters in the classroom. Even more serious, the Federal Bureau of Investigation reported that 30.9 percent of arrests for index offenses—major crimes including murder, forcible rape, and robbery—were of young people under the age of 21 in 2003 (FBI, 2004). Other evidence indicates that the worst 5 percent of juvenile offenders account for about half of all juvenile arrests (Farrington, Ohlin, & Wilson, 1986). With all our fears about youth violence, you should know, however, that the rate of violent crime among juveniles is falling, and in 2002, it was lower than any year since 1980 (Snyder, 2004; see Figure 16–1).

Several factors influence how we evaluate the seriousness of children's rule violations. Externalizing behavior is a far greater concern when it is frequent, intense, lasting, and pervasive. That is, externalizing behavior is more problematic when it is part of a *syndrome*, or cluster of problems, than when it is a *symptom* that occurs in isolation. The existence of an externalizing syndrome has been demonstrated consistently by statistical analysis (factor analysis) of checklists on which parents or teachers rate children's psychological symptoms. Moreover, agreement among adult raters typically is fairly high for the externalizing dimension (Duhig et al., 2000).

What are some differences between normal misbehavior and externalizing problems?

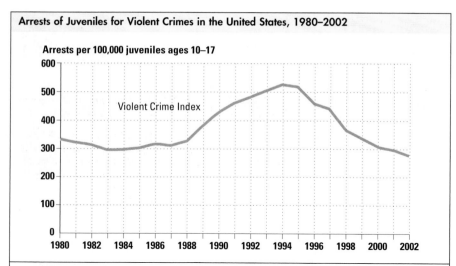

Arrests of Juveniles for Violent Crimes in the United States, 1980–2002

Arrests per 100,000 juveniles ages 10–17

Violent Crime Index

FIGURE 16–1: Despite widespread fears, youth violence in the U.S. has fallen for close to a decade.

Source: H.N. Snyder, September, 2002. Juvenile arrests 2002. *Juvenile Justice Bulletin,* 1–12.

Children's Age and Rule Violations   Children of different ages are likely to violate very different rules (Lahey et al., 2000). A preschooler with an externalizing problem may be disobedient to his parents and aggressive with other children. During the school years, he is more likely to be disruptive in the classroom, uncooperative on the playground, or defiant at home. By adolescence, the problem teenager may be failing in school, ignoring all discipline at home, hanging out with delinquent peers, and violating the law.

Children's age is important to consider in relation to the timing as well as the nature of rule violations. All children break rules, but children with externalizing problems violate rules at a younger age than is developmentally normal (Loeber, 1988). For example, most young people experiment with smoking, alcohol, or sexuality, but children with externalizing disorders do so at a notably younger age.

Adolescent Limited or Life Course Persistent?   Teenagers often violate the rules laid down by parents, teachers, and society as a means of asserting their independence and perhaps of conforming to the rules of their peer group. Because of this, psychologists distinguish between externalizing behavior that is *adolescent-limited*—that ends along with the teen years—and *life-course-persistent* antisocial behavior that continues into adult life (Moffitt, 1993). In fact, externalizing problems that begin *before* adolescence are more likely to persist over the individual's life course than are

problems that begin *during* adolescence. Psychologists can predict adult antisocial behavior more accurately from information obtained during childhood than from information obtained during adolescence (Moffitt, 1993).

Can adolescent-limited and life-course-persistent antisocial behavior be distinguished in other ways? Many investigators are searching for symptoms among young people that will predict adult antisocial behavior, particularly *antisocial personality disorder.* For example, callousness and lack of emotional response may be early indicators of this lifelong pattern of rule violations (Frick, Bodin, & Barry, 2000). Young people with antisocial tendencies do not readily recognize sadness and fear in other people's facial expressions (Blair et al., 2001).

Negativity, Anger, and Aggression   Children with externalizing problems often are negative, angry, and aggressive. Younger children may be stubborn and uncooperative, while adolescents are more likely to be hostile and physically injure others. In addition to their harmful effects, these symptoms shed light on the child's motivations. We chuckle at the innocent adventures of a Calvin, but we judge externalizing behavior harshly when children's *intent* is selfish and they show little *remorse.* You might wonder about Jeremy W.'s private motivations, and judge him differently based on whether he is an angry child who cares little about being "bad" or an impulsive child who wants to but just cannot consistently be "good."

Impulsivity   Impulsive children act before they think. They fail to wait for their turn, blurt out answers in class, and annoy and disrupt others. Impulsivity in infancy predicts subsequent impulsivity, inattention, and overactivity (Olson, Schilling, & Bates, 1999), but impulsive children generally are *trying* to behave. They struggle with *executive functioning,* the internal direction of behavior. Impulsive children seem unable to control their behavior according to the demands of many situations.

Hyperactivity   Hyperactivity involves squirming, fidgeting, and restless behavior. Hyperactive children are in constant motion, and they often have trouble sitting still, even during leisure activities like watching television. Hyperactivity is found across situations, even during sleep, but it is more obvious in structured settings than in unstructured ones (Barkley, 1998). Hyperactive behavior is particularly noticeable in the classroom.

Because of this, reports from teachers are critical in identifying hyperactive behavior.

Attention Deficits Attention deficits are characterized by distractibility, frequent shifts from one uncompleted activity to another, careless mistakes, poor organization or effort, and general "spaciness" (for example, not listening well). As with impulsivity, inattention is not intentional or oppositional; rather, it reflects an inability to maintain a focus despite an apparent desire to do so. A particular attention problem is "staying on task," or what is called *sustained attention* (Barkley, 1998). The *continuous performance* test is a commonly used laboratory measure of sustained attention. The task requires children to monitor and respond to numbers or letters presented on a computer screen, and distinguishes children with and without ADHD (Epstein et al., 2003).

Diagnosis of Externalizing Disorders

The DSM-IV-TR divides externalizing disorders into three major types. Attention-deficit/hyperactivity disorder (ADHD) is the problem that you may have heard called "hyperactivity" or perhaps "ADD." Oppositional defiant disorder (ODD) includes a wide range of problem behavior generally found among school-aged children. Conduct disorder (CD) is a lot like what you may think of as juvenile delinquency, because CD involves rule violations that also are violations of the law.

Brief Historical Perspective Hyperactivity was distinguished from ordinary misbehavior about 100 years ago by British physician George Still (1902), who speculated that the overactivity of some children he treated might be due to biological "defects." Since then, professionals have debated whether the misbehavior of school-aged children should be divided into two types. Children with what we now call ADHD are assumed to have a biological problem best treated with medication. Children with what we now call ODD are seen as having a psychological problem requiring psychological treatment (Schachar & Tannock, 2002).

Interest in what DSM-IV-TR calls conduct disorder also is about 100 years old but has a very different origin. At the end of the nineteenth century, juvenile crime was distinguished from adult criminal behavior for the first time in American law. The law adopted a compassionate view of juvenile delinquency, seeing the problem as a product of a troubled upbringing. As a result, the state adopted a parental role in trying to help wayward youth, not just punish them. Thus, the criminal behavior of juveniles came to be seen as a psychological problem, not just a legal one.

Attention-Deficit/Hyperactivity Disorder Attention-deficit/hyperactivity disorder (ADHD) is characterized by **hyperactivity,** attention deficit, and impulsivity. According to DSM-IV-TR, at least some symptoms must begin before the age of 7, they must persist for at least 6 months, and there must be evidence of consistency in symptoms across situations. The manual takes a quantitative "checklist" approach to counting symptoms, implying that the underlying problem is dimensional even though the diagnosis is categorical (see Table 16–1).

The symptoms of hyperactivity and attention deficit each have been viewed as being the core characteristics of ADHD. In fact, DSM-II called the disorder *hyperkinesis,* a synonym for "hyperactivity," whereas DSM-III referred to it as *attention-deficit disorder,* or *ADD.* Now, much theorizing focuses on impulsivity as the core characteristic (Barkley, 1998; Nigg, 2001; Olson et al., 1999). We are not concerned whether "attention deficit" or "hyperactivity"—or "impulsivity"—

Video Case
ADHD

JIMMY

"I think without it (medicine) I would be dreaming the whole entire day."

On your CD-ROM menu, select "ADHD" and click on "Jimmy—ADHD." As you watch the video, remember that Jimmy did *not* take his psychostimulant before the interview and note his rapid speech as well as his "fidgetiness."

Boys arguing on a school playground. Some anger is normative, but persistent hostility and aggression often are symptoms of externalizing disorders.

TABLE 16–1	DSM-IV-TR Diagnostic Criteria for Attention-Deficit/Hyperactivity Disorder

A. Either (I) or (II):

(I) Inattention: Six (or more) of the following symptoms of inattention have persisted for at least 6 months to a degree that is maladaptive and inconsistent with developmental level:

1. Often fails to give close attention to details or makes careless mistakes in schoolwork, work, or other activities.
2. Often has difficulty sustaining attention in tasks or play activities.
3. Often does not seem to listen when spoken to directly.
4. Often does not follow through on instructions and fails to finish schoolwork, chores, or duties in the workplace.
5. Often has difficulty organizing tasks and activities.
6. Often avoids, dislikes, or is reluctant to engage in tasks that require sustained mental effort.
7. Often loses things necessary for tasks or activities.
8. Is often easily distracted by extraneous stimuli.
9. Is often forgetful of daily activities.

(II) Hyperactivity and Impulsivity: Six (or more) of the following symptoms of hyperactivity-impulsivity have persisted for at least 6 months to a degree that is maladaptive and inconsistent with developmental level:

Hyperactivity

1. Often fidgets with hands or feet or squirms in seat.
2. Often leaves seat in classroom or in other situations in which remaining seated is expected.
3. Often runs about or climbs excessively in situations in which it is inappropriate.
4. Often has difficulty playing or engaging in leisure activities quietly.
5. Is often "on the go" or often acts as if "driven by a motor."
6. Often talks excessively.

Impulsivity

1. Often blurts out answers before questions have been completed.
2. Often has difficulty awaiting turn.
3. Often interrupts or intrudes on others.

B. Some hyperactive-impulsive or inattentive symptoms that caused impairment were present before age 7 years.

C. Some impairment from the symptoms is present in two or more settings.

D. There must be clear evidence of clinically significant impairment in social, academic, or occupational functioning.

Code Based on Type

Combined Type: Criteria for I and II are met for past 6 months.

Predominantly Inattentive Type: Criteria for I are met but Criteria for II are not met for past 6 months.

Predominantly Hyperactive-Impulsive Type: Criteria for II are met but Criteria for I are not met for past 6 months.

Reprinted with permission from the *Diagnostic and Statistical Manual of Mental Disorders,* Fourth Edition, Text Revision. Copyright © 2000 by the American Psychiatric Association.

gets top billing as the label for a problem with ever-changing names. Rather, we are concerned about two facts: First, contrary to what has been asserted by some professionals, hyperactivity is not merely a consequence of inattention, or vice versa (Barkley, 1998). Each is an independent symptom. Second, some children have problems primarily with only one of the two symptoms, as is evident in the subtypes of ADHD listed in DSM-IV-TR (see Table 16–1).

Oppositional Defiant Disorder Oppositional **defiant disorder (ODD)** is defined by a pattern of negative, hostile, and defiant behavior. The symptoms must last for at least 6 months, and, as with other diagnoses, they must cause clinically significant impairment in life functioning. As you can see from Table 16–2, the rule violations in ODD typically involve minor transgressions, such as refusing to obey adult requests, arguing, and acting angry. Such misbehavior is a cause for concern among school-aged children, and it often foreshadows the development of much more serious antisocial behavior during adolescence and adult life. However, these types of rule violations fit within developmental norms for adolescents, who are typically somewhat rebellious. Thus, a problem with the DSM-IV-TR diagnostic criteria for ODD—and for virtually every childhood disorder—is that the diagnostic criteria need to reflect developmental norms more fully.

ADHD Versus ODD Professionals have long debated whether ADHD and ODD are the same or separate disorders. Some experts argued that the two conditions are distinct not only in symptomatology but also in terms of etiology and effective treatment. Others asserted that the distinction between ADHD and ODD is false and is wrongly used to justify treating troubled children with medication. Testing these widely opposing viewpoints was hampered by the fact that a differential diagnosis between ADHD and ODD could not be made with a high level of reliability (Hinshaw, 1994).

This debate has subsided considerably in recent years. The current consensus is that the two disorders are separate but frequently comorbid (Waschbusch, 2002; see Figure 16–2). Approximately half of all children with one disorder also have the other problem (Schachar & Tannock, 2002). Because researchers have only recently recognized the comorbidity, past research often is difficult to interpret. For example, are the long-term problems in school or with substance abuse among externalizing children due to ADHD,

ODD, or the overlap between the two conditions? Emerging research suggests that future antisocial behavior among children with externalizing problems is attributable more to comorbid conduct disorders than ADHD. For example, ODD/CD but not ADHD predicts adult antisocial personality disorder (Lahey et al., 2005).

Comorbidity   Not only are ADHD and ODD highly comorbid, but, as illustrated in Figure 16–2, about 25 percent of children with each problem also have a learning disorder. To a lesser extent, ADHD also is comorbid with internalizing disorders such as depression and anxiety (Schachar & Tannock, 2002). Comorbid internalizing disorders are particularly common among girls with ADHD (Rucklidge & Tannock, 2001).

Subtypes of ADHD   The subtyping of ADHD into the predominantly inattentive, predominantly hyperactive-impulsive, or combined types is another sometimes controversial distinction. The predominantly inattentive subtype generally is accepted as an important diagnosis. Some children have difficulty with inattention and information processing, but they exhibit little or no hyperactivity (Milich, Balentine, & Lynam, 2001). Their struggles focus primarily on issues related to learning rather than behavior control. Some parents and professionals still use the DSM-III term ADD for this subtype of ADHD, because they find it to be less stigmatizing.

There is less support for the predominantly hyperactive-impulsive subtype. Preschool children generally are classified in the predominantly hyperactive-impulsive group, while school-aged children fall into the combined type. This implies that the two subtypes actually involve the same problems but are developmentally related. Problems with hyperactivity and impulsivity are evident during the preschool years, but attention deficits begin (or are first noticed) during the early school years (Hart et al., 1995).

Conduct Disorder   Conduct disorder (CD) is defined primarily by a persistent and repetitive pattern of serious rule violations, most of which are illegal as well as antisocial—for example, assault or robbery (see Table 16–3). CD often is developmentally related to ODD. Oppositional defiant disorder is diagnosed primarily among school-aged children and often develops into a more serious conduct disorder during preadolescence or adolescence (Loeber, Lahey, & Thomas, 1991). DSM-IV-TR distinguishes the age of onset

TABLE 16–2	DSM-IV-TR Diagnostic Criteria for Oppositional Defiant Disorder

A. **A pattern of negativistic, hostile, and defiant behavior lasting at least 6 months, during which four (or more) of the following are present:**
   1. Often loses temper.
   2. Often argues with adults.
   3. Often actively defies or refuses to comply with adults' requests or rules.
   4. Often deliberately annoys people.
   5. Often blames others for his or her mistakes or misbehavior.
   6. Is often touchy or easily annoyed by others.
   7. Is often angry and resentful.
   8. Is often spiteful and vindictive.

B. **The disturbance in behavior causes clinically significant impairment in social, academic, or occupational functioning.**

Note: Consider a criterion only if the behavior occurs more frequently than is typically observed in individuals of comparable age and developmental level.

Reprinted with permission from the *Diagnostic and Statistical Manual of Mental Disorders,* Fourth Edition, Text Revision. Copyright © 2000 by the American Psychiatric Association.

in defining conduct disorders—a distinction between adolescent-limited versus life-course patterns of antisocial behavior.

You may think of what DSM-IV-TR calls conduct disorder as being roughly equivalent to juvenile delinquency. Most of the symptoms of conduct disorder do indeed involve *index offenses*—crimes against people or property that are illegal at any age. A few diagnostic criteria are comparable to **status offenses**—acts that are illegal only because of the youth's status as a minor. Examples are running away from home and truancy from school. However, **juvenile delinquency** is a *legal*

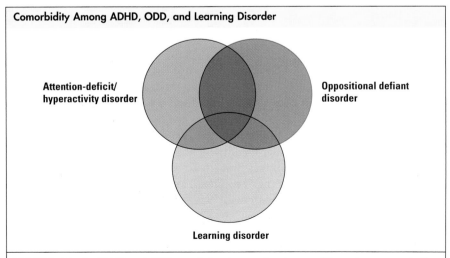

Comorbidity Among ADHD, ODD, and Learning Disorder

Attention-deficit/ hyperactivity disorder

Oppositional defiant disorder

Learning disorder

FIGURE 16–2: ADHD and ODD are distinct but overlapping conditions. As many as half of all children with one disorder also suffer from the other problem. To a lesser extent, ADHD and ODD also overlap with learning disorders.

TABLE 16–3   DSM-IV-TR Diagnostic Criteria for Conduct Disorder

A. A repetitive and persistent pattern of behavior in which the basic rights of others or major age-appropriate societal norms or rules are violated, as manifested by the presence of three (or more) of the following criteria in the past 12 months, with at least one criterion present in the past 6 months:

Aggression to People and Animals

1. Often bullies, threatens, or intimidates others.
2. Often initiates physical fights.
3. Has used a weapon that can cause serious physical harm to others.
4. Has been physically cruel to people.
5. Has been physically cruel to animals.
6. Has stolen while confronting a victim.
7. Has forced someone into sexual activity.

Destruction of Property

8. Has deliberately engaged in fire setting with the intention of causing serious damage.
9. Has deliberately destroyed others' property.

Deceitfulness or Theft

10. Has broken into someone else's house, building, or car.
11. Often lies to obtain goods or favors to avoid obligations.
12. Has stolen items of nontrivial value without confronting a victim.

Serious Violations of Rules

13. Often stays out at night despite parental prohibitions, beginning before age 13 years.
14. Has run away from home overnight at least twice while living in parental or parental surrogate home.
15. Is often truant from school, beginning before age 13 years.

B. The disturbance in behavior causes clinically significant impairment in social, academic, or occupational functioning.

***Code* Type Based on Age at Onset**

Conduct Disorder Childhood-Onset Type: Onset of at least one criterion characteristic of Conduct Disorder prior to age 10 years.

Conduct Disorder Adolescent-Onset Type: Absence of any criteria characteristic of Conduct Disorder prior to age 10 years.

Reprinted with permission from the *Diagnostic and Statistical Manual of Mental Disorders,* Fourth Edition, Text Revision. Copyright © 2000 by the American Psychiatric Association.

Michael Rutter, a British psychiatrist, is an international authority on child psychopathology. Rutter was knighted by the queen of England in recognition of his many contributions.

classification, not a mental health term. Adolescents who repeatedly break the law have conduct disorders whether or not they are arrested and convicted. Technically, however, youths are not delinquent until a judge finds them guilty. In the United States, juvenile court judges may base a finding of delinquency on either criminal or status offenses, although adjudication for status offenses is increasingly rare.

Frequency of Externalizing Disorders

The National Academy of Sciences (1989) concluded that at least 12 percent of the 63 million children living in the United States suffer from a

mental disorder, and the majority of these are externalizing disorders. The panel found that a minimum of $1.5 billion was spent annually for the direct mental health treatment of children—and this figure *excluded* the additional costs of treating children's emotional problems in general medical settings, schools, welfare agencies, and juvenile courts. Clearly, children's mental health is a major national problem (see Research Methods).

Between 3 and 5 percent of children in the United States are estimated to have ADHD at any point in time. Estimates in Europe are generally much lower, about 1 to 2 percent of children, but this is due to more conservative diagnostic practices in Europe, not to differences in children's behavior (Schachar & Tannock, 2002). Anywhere from 5 to 15 percent of youth in the United States may have ODD and/or CD.

After the first few years of life, from two to ten times as many boys as girls have an externalizing disorder (Keenan & Shaw, 1997; National Academy of Sciences, 1989). Except for the normative increase during adolescence, the prevalence of externalizing behavior generally declines with age, although it declines at much earlier ages for girls than for boys (Keenan & Shaw, 1997). In fact, the prevalence of life-course persistent antisocial behavior is far lower among girls than boys, even more so than for other externalizing problems (Earls & Mezzacappa, 2002).

Family Risk Factors   Externalizing disorders are associated with various indicators of family adversity, a fact highlighted by British psychiatrist Michael Rutter, an international authority on the epidemiology of child psychopathology. Rutter's (1989) Family Adversity Index includes six family predictors of behavior problems among children: (1) low income, (2) overcrowding in the home, (3) maternal depression, (4) paternal antisocial behavior, (5) conflict between the parents, and (6) removal of the child from the home. Rutter found that the risk for externalizing problems did not increase substantially when only one family risk factor was present. However, the risk increased fourfold when two family adversity factors were present. The risk for children's antisocial behavior increased even further with three or more sources of family adversity.

Other epidemiological findings underscore the relationship between children's externalizing problems and social disadvantage (Earls & Mezzacappa, 2002). For example, psychological disorders are found in more than 20 percent of

SAMPLES: HOW TO SELECT THE PEOPLE WE STUDY

Psychologists typically do not use a **representative sample**—a sample that accurately represents some larger group of people. Instead, mental health researchers commonly obtain *convenience samples*—groups of people who are easily recruited and studied. For many purposes, convenience samples work just fine. For example, we can study the effectiveness of medication for treating ADHD without using a representative sample. For other purposes, however, obtaining representative samples is essential. For example, researchers find that many children in clinical settings come from single-parent families, and to some psychologists, it seems that virtually every child from a single-parent family has psychological problems. When representative samples are studied,

however, researchers find that most children from single-parent families do *not* have psychological problems. Most children, and most single parent families, are *resilient;* they cope successfully with the stress of single parenting (Emery, 1999). Psychologists need to be cautious in *generalizing* from convenience or clinical samples, because these groups definitely are unrepresentative of the population of children or families. After all, pediatricians would assume that almost every child has an ear infection if they generalized from *their* clinical samples!

How do scientists select representative samples that allow them to generalize accurately to a larger population? First, the researcher must identify the *population* of interest, the entire group of people to whom the researcher wants

to generalize—for example, children under the age of 18 living in the United States. Second, the researcher must *randomly select* research participants from the population and obtain a large enough sample to ensure that the results are statistically reliable. This allows researchers to make generalizations that sometimes seem remarkable, such as when the outcome of a political election is accurately predicted by polling a relatively small number of voters.

Errors can occur in either step of the process of selecting a representative sample. One of the most famous errors occurred in 1948, when newspaper headlines heralded Thomas E. Dewey's election over Harry S Truman in the U.S. presidential election. Actually, Truman won the election handily. Where did the pollsters go wrong? They made a mistake in identifying the population of voters. The researchers sampled randomly from the U.S. population, but Democrats actually went to the polls more heavily to vote for Truman than more complacent Republicans did for Dewey. (This is one reason why election pollsters now do exit surveys.) The polls also were conducted a week or more before the election, and late voter sentiment swung from Dewey to Truman.

Political scientists have become much more sophisticated in their sampling strategies since 1948. A fortunate trend in psychology is a new collaboration with sociologists in studying normal and abnormal behavior. Many large scale surveys now follow a representative sample of children or families over time and include many measures of psychological well being. Psychological scientists increasingly are using these samples to make sure that the same pattern of findings obtained in intensive studies of small convenience samples are found in representative samples of the population.

children living in inner city neighborhoods (National Academy of Sciences, 1989) and are associated with divorce and single parenting.

Causes of Externalizing Disorders

Externalizing problems can develop when various normal influences on troublesome behavior go awry. Some children are especially difficult from birth; some parents fail to control their children's selfish behavior; peers, the media, and troubled family life can encourage rather than

inhibit children's misbehavior; some children never develop internal control over their behavior; others get into trouble trying to cope with early pubertal development and the expectations and social reactions it brings about (Ellis, 2004).

Biological Factors   All children require some external limits in order to learn to control their selfish and aggressive behavior. If you doubt this, we suggest that you visit a preschool where children frequently need to be reminded to share, to cooperate, to be nice, and not to hit, push, scratch, or bite. The natural behavior we observe in children also can be

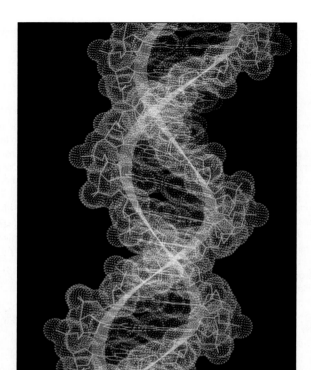

Although the genetic influence on ADHD is strong, many genes are involved. Therefore, the decision about where to divide normal from abnormal inattention or overactivity can be widely debated—and it is.

Why is it important to recognize that inherited ADHD behavior is on a continuum with normal behavior?

wonderful—preschoolers freely make friends, exchange favors, and show empathy when others are hurt. Still, all children need some discipline (together with a lot of love), although different children may need more or less guidance, as any parent of two children will attest.

Temperament **Temperament,** inborn behavioral characteristics including activity level, emotionality, and sociability, is one important way in which children differ (Buss, 1991). Temperament can be classified in various ways, but Thomas and Chess's (1977) grouping into easy, difficult, and slow-to-warm-up is a longstanding grouping. *Easy* children quickly form social relationships and follow discipline; *difficult* children challenge parental authority; *slow-to-warm-up* children tend to be shy and withdrawn. Research on infants and toddlers indicates that a difficult temperament is a risk factor for later externalizing disorders (Shaw, Keenan, & Vondra, 1994; Shaw et al., 1997).

Neuropsychological Abnormalities Neuropsychological research suggests other biological contributions to externalizing disorders, particularly to ADHD. Brain damage can produce overactivity and inattention, but *hard signs* of brain damage, such as an abnormal CT scan, are found in less than 5 percent of cases of ADHD (Rutter,

1983). Neurological *soft signs*, such as delays in fine motor coordination (as may be evident in poor penmanship), also are more frequent among children with ADHD. However, many children with ADHD do not show soft signs, while many normal children do (Barkley, 1998). Thus their implications are unclear.

Minor anomalies in physical appearance, delays in reaching developmental milestones, and a history of mothers' pregnancy and birth complications also appear more commonly among children with ADHD than normal children. Still, researchers have yet to discover a specific marker of biological vulnerability. One candidate is impairment in the prefrontal cortical-striatal network, an area of the brain that may control executive functions including attention, inhibition, and emotion regulation (Barkley, 1998). Some neuropsychological evidence also indicates impaired executive functioning in ADHD children and their relatives, but only for a subset of cases in this heterogeneous disorder (Nigg et al., 2004).

Genetics and ADHD Several studies show that genetic factors strongly contribute to ADHD. For example, a study of almost 4,000 Australian twins found concordance rates among MZ twins of roughly 80 percent, whereas DZ twins had concordance rates of approximately 40 percent (Levy et al., 1997). These rates are close to what one would expect for a *purely* genetic disorder (where the concordances would be 100 percent for MZ and 50 percent for DZ twins). In fact, genetic factors explained 90 percent of the variance in ADHD symptoms, a much higher proportion than for most behavior disorders (Plomin et al., 2001). Such evidence has spurred a search for specific genes that may cause ADHD. For example, recent evidence has linked ADHD with separate dopamine receptor (DRD4) and transporter (DAT1) genes.

Strong evidence on genetic contributions does *not* mean that ADHD is an "either you have it or you don't" disorder, that is, a problem qualitatively different from normal. You cannot be "a little bit pregnant," but you *can* be "a little bit ADHD." In fact, genetic analysis of the large Australian twin study supported a dimensional rather than a categorical conceptualization of ADHD (Levy et al., 1997). Children with ADHD do have real problems, but psychologists are vexed by the question of where to draw the line dividing "normal" overactivity (or inattention) from "abnormal" ADHD. This question and the dimensional nature of ADHD is particularly important to consider (as we do shortly) in relation to the categorical decision of whether or not to medicate a child—and whether medications for ADHD are overused in the U.S. today.

Gene–Environment Interactions and Conduct Problems Genes contribute less to ODD and especially CD than to ADHD (Burt et al., 2001; Rhee & Waldman, 2002; Rutter et al., 1999). Genetic influence is stronger for early than late onset antisocial behavior (Taylor, Iacono, & McGue, 2000), a finding consistent with the stronger relation between childhood and adult antisocial behavior compared to adolescent externalizing. Presumably, genes play a similar role in both early onset ODD and adult antisocial behavior, while the many environmental contributions to adolescent antisocial behavior obscure genetic effects (Gottesman & Goldsmith, 1994).

If genes contribute to ODD or CD, an essential question is: What is the inherited mechanism? Hyperactivity or inattention may be directly inherited, but rule violations surely are not (Earls & Mezzacappa, 2002). No one has suggested that there is a "crime gene," let alone an "argue with your teacher gene"!

Part of what is inherited may be a tendency to react more negatively to adverse environments. Researchers recently found that the effect of childhood maltreatment on adolescent conduct problems differs depending on the gene producing monoamine oxidase activity (MAOA). (The MAOA gene encodes an enzyme that metabolizes neurotransmitters and renders them inactive.) In a large sample of males followed from birth into adulthood, child maltreatment predicted significantly more adolescent conduct problems if the boys were genetically predisposed to low rather than high MAOA activity (Caspi et al., 2002; see Figure 16–3). Other recent research also shows that genes can contribute to externalizing problems by increasing susceptibility to family dysfunction (Button et al., 2005), and that physical maltreatment increases the risk for externalizing disorders even when controlling for genetic influences (Jaffee et al., 2005). Genes can alter susceptibility to adversity, but difficult experiences *are* critical to causing externalizing disorders.

Social Factors **Socialization** is the process of shaping children's behavior and attitudes to conform to the expectations of parents, teachers, and society as a whole. Many psychologists believe

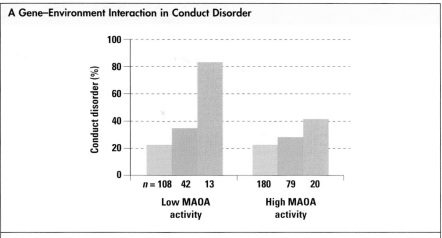

FIGURE 16-3: Child maltreatment increases the risk for conduct disorder, but the effect depends on an interaction with the MAOA gene (which encodes an enzyme that metabolizes neurotransmitters and renders them inactive).

Source: A. Caspi, et al. (2002), Role of genotype in the cycle of violence in maltreated children. *Science, 297,* 851–854. Copyright © 2002 by American Association for the Advancement of Science. Reprinted by permission of the publisher.

that parental explanation, example, and appropriate discipline are most important in socializing children, but other influences cannot be ignored. Peer groups exert strong if sometimes subtle conformity pressures that increase as children grow older. School and television also are powerful socialization agents.

Parenting Styles Parental discipline is sometimes mistakenly viewed as the opposite of loving children, but warm parent–child relationships make discipline both less necessary and more effective (Shaw & Bell, 1993). In fact, **authoritative parenting,** parenting that is both loving and firm, is most effective in rearing well-adjusted children. Warmth and control are so important that developmental psychologists classify parenting into four styles based on these dimensions (see Figure 16–4). In contrast to authoritative parents, *authoritarian* parents lack warmth, and their strict discipline is often harsh and autocratic. Children of authoritarian parents generally are compliant, but they also may be anxious. *Indulgent* parents are the opposite of authoritarian parents: affectionate but lax in discipline. Their children tend to be impulsive and noncompliant, but not extremely antisocial. Finally, *neglectful* parents are unconcerned either with their children's emotional needs or with their needs for discipline. Children with serious conduct problems often have neglectful parents (Maccoby & Martin, 1983).

Coercion More specific problems in parenting also contribute to children's externalizing problems. One

A Classification of Parenting Styles	Accepting, Responsive, Child-centered	Rejecting, Unresponsive, Parent-centered
Demanding, controlling	Authoritative	Authoritarian
Undemanding, low in control attempts	Indulgent	Neglectful

FIGURE 16–4: Four styles of parenting, based on dimensions of parental warmth and discipline efforts.

Source: E.E. Maccoby and J.A. Martin, 1983, Socialization in the context of the family: Parent-child interaction. In E.M. Hetherington (Ed.), *Socialization, Personality, and Social Development,* Vol. 4, Handbook of Child Psychology, pp. 1–101. New York: Wiley.

How do parental love and discipline combine in different parenting styles and in determining the motivation for children's coercive behavior?

of the most important is psychologist Gerald Patterson's (1982) concept of **coercion,** which occurs when parents *positively* reinforce a child's misbehavior by giving in to the child's demands. The child, in turn, *negatively* reinforces the parents by ending his or her obnoxious behavior as soon as the parents capitulate. Thus coercion describes a system of interaction in which parents and children reciprocally reinforce child misbehavior and parent capitulation. The concept is illustrated in the following brief case study.

BRIEF CASE STUDY

Ms. B's Son

Ms. B. finally admitted that she had lost all control of her 4-year-old son, Billy. Ms. B. was a single parent who was exhausted by her routine of working from 8 to 5:30 every day and managing Billy and the household in the evenings and on weekends. She had no parenting or financial support from Billy's father or anyone else, and Ms. B. was worn down. When it came time to discipline Billy, she usually gave in—either because this was the easiest thing to do or because she felt too guilty to say no.

Ms. B. described many difficult interactions with Billy. One example stood out in the mind of the psychologist she consulted. Ms. B. often stopped at the grocery store with Billy after work, and he inevitably gave her trouble. Dealing with the candy aisle was a particular problem. Billy would ask for some candy when they first approached the aisle. Ms. B. told him no, but in an increasingly loud voice Billy protested, "I WANT CANDY!" Ms. B. would attempt to stick to her guns, but

Clinical psychologist Gerald Patterson is a leader in studying children's aggression from a social learning perspective.

soon she was embarrassed by the disapproving looks on the faces of other mothers. Feeling both resentful and resigned, she would grab a bag of M&Ms and give it to Billy. This gave her a few minutes of peace and quiet while she completed her shopping.

Clearly, Ms. B. rewarded Billy for his misbehavior. Billy also (negatively) reinforced his mother by quieting down when she gave in to his demands. Because both parties were reinforced, the coercive interaction should continue over time (Patterson, 1982).

The coercion concept has direct, practical implications. Parents need to break the pattern of interaction by ignoring the misbehavior (extinction), punishing it, or rewarding more positive actions (Herbert, 2002). In Billy's case, the psychologist recommended the use of **time-out,** the technique of briefly isolating a child following misbehavior. The next time Billy acted up in the grocery store, Ms. B. left her shopping cart, and she and Billy sat in the car until he quieted down. She then completed her shopping. Several trips to the car were needed the first day, but Billy's behavior improved as a result. He quickly was earning rewards for being good— not for being bad—while shopping.

Love and Discipline Children's noncompliance may not always stem from a lack of discipline. Sometimes children misbehave as a way of getting attention rather than as a way of getting what they want. Consider the concept of *negative attention*, the idea that attempts at punishment sometimes accidentally reinforce children's misbehavior. Imagine, for example, the teacher who scolds the "class clown" for misbehaving. In some circumstances, the scolding increases rather than decreases the child's misbehavior; that is, the attempt at punishment actually serves as a reinforcement. Rather than trying to find a truly effective punishment, we think it is essential to understand *why* negative attention is reinforcing. Many children are reinforced by negative attention because they are not getting enough positive attention—enough love. If so, increasing parental affection should be a better way of treating their externalizing behavior than increasing parental discipline (Emery, 1992).

Conflict and Inconsistent Discipline Inconsistent discipline also is linked with children's externalizing problems (Patterson, DeBaryshe, & Ramsey, 1989). Inconsistency can involve frequent changes in the style and standards of one parent, or two parents may be inconsistent in their rules and expectations. Inconsistency often becomes a problem when parents have conflicts in their own relationship—when they are unhappily married or are divorced (Emery, 1982; Repetti, Taylor, & Seeman, 2002). Some angry parents even deliberately undermine each other.

Yet another problem occurs when parents' actions are inconsistent with their words. For example, consider the contradiction inherent in angry and harsh physical punishment (Gershoff, 2002). On one hand, such discipline tells children to follow the rules. On the other hand, harsh physical punishment teaches children that anger and aggression are acceptable means of solving problems. Parents socialize children by modeling appropriate behavior as well as by disciplining them, and children often do what their parents do, not what they say.

Peers, Neighborhoods, Television, and Society

Peer groups also can encourage delinquent and antisocial behavior (Dishion, McCord, & Poulin, 1999), and among adolescents, peer influences may be stronger than parental ones (Walden et al., 2004). In fact, socialized delinquency, in which criminal acts occur in the company of others, may be an important subtype of externalizing disorders (Kazdin, 1995).

Neighborhood and society also contribute to externalizing problems. Television violence is rampant, as is violence in computer games, and research shows that aggressive children both prefer and become more aggressive in response to video violence (Anderson et al., 2003). Youth who witness violence in their communities also are more likely to be violent themselves (Shahinfar, Kupersmidt, & Matza, 2001), and in general, children who grow up in poor, inner city neighborhoods are more likely to have externalizing problems (Shaw et al., 1994; Stouthamer-Loeber et al., 2002).

Cross-cultural evidence points to other influences on externalizing behavior. Robbery, sexual offenses, assault, and burglary are far more common in the United States than in Canada, Europe, or Japan, and juveniles account for many of these crimes. Some politicians argue that this is because the United States is "soft on crime," but far *more* people are imprisoned in the United States than in Canada, Europe, or Japan (see Figure 16–5). Other aspects of U.S. culture, such as higher poverty rates and lack of gun control, apparently

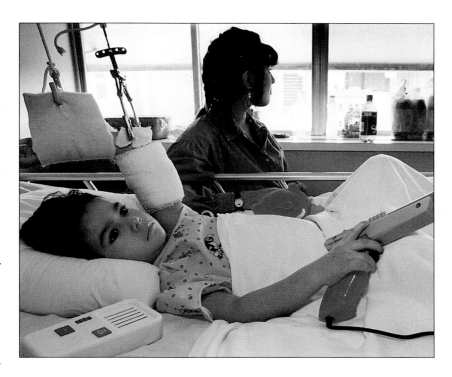

Societal influences on children's behavior are pervasive. This 3-year-old boy suffered a gunshot wound during a drive-by shooting. Still, the boy plays with a toy pistol while recuperating in his hospital bed.

explain our high rates of youth violence (Costello et al., 2003; Jones & Krisberg, 1994).

Social Factors in ADHD

There are no theories of how social factors play a unique role in the development of ADHD (Hinshaw, 1994). Mothers of children with ADHD are more critical, demanding, and controlling compared to the mothers of normal children (Mash & Johnston, 1982). However, research shows that problems primarily are a *reaction* to the children's troubles, not a cause of them. In a clever study design, children are randomly given either a medication that improves ADHD symptoms or a placebo. Research shows that children with ADHD become more attentive and compliant while medicated, and their mothers' behavior "improves" as well— mothers become less negative and less controlling (Danforth, Barkley, & Stokes, 1991). Because no one knows who got the medication or the placebo, the differences must be due to the medicine's effects on the children—and the children's effects on their mothers. Children with ADHD make social interactions more difficult.

This does not mean that good parenting is unimportant. Ineffective parenting surely intensifies ADHD symptoms (Hinshaw et al., 2000), and maternal warmth and understanding may help to prevent ADHD (Tully et al., 2005). Family and social adversity also contribute to ODD and its comorbidity with ADHD (Burt et al., 2001).

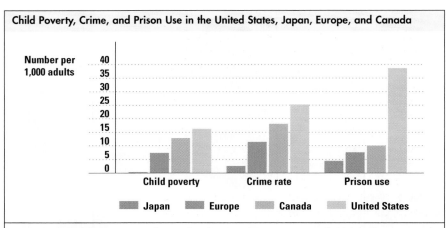

FIGURE 16–5: Prison use indicates that the United States is not "soft on crime" in comparison to other countries. Other factors, such as the higher rate of poverty, may explain the high crime rate in the United States.

Source: United Nations Interregional Crime and Justice Research Institute.

Note: Figure included here was reprinted in M.A. Jones and B. Krisberg, 1994, *Images and reality: Juvenile crime, youth violence, and public policy.* San Francisco: National Council on Crime and Delinquency.

Psychological Factors *Self-control,* the internal regulation of behavior, is the ultimate goal of socialization. Not surprisingly, several investigators have found problems with self-control among children with externalizing disorders. *Low self-esteem,* feelings of low worth, also is sometimes blamed as a cause of externalizing problems, but research shows, perhaps surprisingly, that children with ADHD *overestimate* rather than undervalue their competence (Hoza et al., 2004).

One area of research on self-control focuses on *delay of gratification*—the adaptive ability to defer smaller but immediate rewards for larger, long-term benefits. An example of delay of gratification is studying for an exam rather than going out with friends. In general, children with externalizing problems are less able to delay gratification and are more oriented to the present than are other children. They opt for immediate rewards rather than for long-term goals, a maladaptive characteristic for achieving educational and career goals (Nigg, 2001).

Children with externalizing problems also may fail to exert self-control because they misinterpret the intentions of others, particularly in ambiguous social situations. Studies by psychologist Ken Dodge and his colleagues indicate that aggressive children overinterpret the aggressive intentions of their peers (Dodge et al., 2003). That is, children with externalizing problems view other children as threatening to them. As a result, some of their aggression may be an attempt to "get you before you get me." Psychologist Seth Pollak and his colleagues show one way that such biases may develop. Physically abused children attend to angry facial cues longer than normal children (Pollak & Tolley-Schell, 2003), a reaction that may be adaptive in a threatening family but maladaptive in other relationships.

A related psychological issue concerns the "conscience" of children with externalizing problems. Psychologist Lawrence Kohlberg (1985) created a hierarchy of moral reasoning showing that children use increasingly abstract and sophisticated moral principles as they grow older. For example, a young boy may say that the reason he behaves well is because "Mommy will get mad." An older boy may explain that the reason he behaves well is because "You need to follow the rules." A teenager might explain that he behaves well because "It is the right thing to do."

According to Kohlberg, higher moral principles are based on values regarding appropriate conduct rather than on the immediate consequences of misbehavior. He hypothesized that these more sophisticated guidelines, in turn, lead to more prosocial behavior. In support of his theorizing, some evidence indicates that aggressive children follow the hedonic principles commonly used by children at younger ages (Kohlberg, 1985).

Integration and Alternative Pathways How can we integrate evidence on the diverse contributions to the development of externalizing? Two conclusions seem clear. First, externalizing disorders have many causes, not one. Second, biological, psychological, and social factors clearly interact in causing externalizing disorders. Temperament theorists note, for example, that the *goodness of fit* between a child's temperament and the family environment may be of greatest importance to healthy psychological development (Shaw & Bell, 1993). The combination of a difficult temperament and family adversity may result in ODD and eventually conduct disorder, while a temperamentally "easy" child might turn out well-behaved despite growing up in difficult family circumstances (Kasen et al., 1996). In fact, impulsive youth have unusually high rates of juvenile offending when they grow up in poor versus better off neighborhoods. However, whether the neighborhood is poor or better off has no effect on offending for nonimpulsive youth (Lynam et al., 2000).

Treatment of Externalizing Disorders

Numerous treatments have been developed for children's externalizing disorders, but unfortunately the problems are difficult to change (Kazdin, 1997). The most promising treatments include psychostimulants for ADHD, behavioral family therapy for ODD, and intensive programs for treating conduct disorders and delinquent youth.

Psychostimulants and ADHD Psychostimulants such as *Ritalin* are medications that increase central nervous system activity, and in appropriate dosages, the medications increase alertness, arousal, and attention. Psychostimulants produce immediate and noticeable improvements in the behavior of about 75 percent of children with ADHD. Before considering their effects further, we first must consider a long-held, and mistaken, view about psychostimulants and ADHD.

The "Paradoxical Effect" Paradox Psychostimulants heighten energy and alertness, and they lead to restless, even frenetic, behavior when abused. These effects are accurately conveyed by a street name for the drugs, "speed." The U.S. psychiatrist Charles Bradley (1937) was one of the first to observe that these medications seem to have a "paradoxical effect" on overactive children: The drug slows them down. For many years, professionals believed that this was proof of abnormal brain functioning in ADHD. The real irony, however, is that the idea of a paradoxical effect was wrong.

One reason for the enduring "paradoxical effect" paradox is that it was deemed unethical to experiment with psychostimulants on normal children, even though the medication was given regularly to millions of "abnormal" children. A group of researchers at the National Institute of Mental Health eventually found a clever way to address the ethical problem. They obtained permission from colleagues in the medical and mental health communities to study the effects of psychostimulants on their exceptionally competent children. The researchers found that the psychostimulants affected the normal children in the same way that they affected overactive children. The medication improved attention and decreased motor activity (Rapoport et al., 1978). In fact, psychostimulants have the same effects on *adults* when taken in comparably small dosages. There is no paradoxical effect of psychostimulants on children with ADHD.

Usage and Effects The most commonly prescribed psychostimulants are known by the trade names of Ritalin (the most commonly used psychostimulant), Dexedrine, Cylert, and Adderall. Each has the effect of increasing alertness and arousal. Psychostimulants usually are prescribed by pediatricians, who typically are consulted following a child's difficulties in the early years of school. The fact that behavior problems in school are the main concern about children with ADHD is demonstrated in how psychostimulants are prescribed. A pill is taken in the morning before school, and because the effects of most psychostimulants last only 3 or 4 hours, another pill is taken at the lunch hour. A third pill may or may not be taken after school, but the medication typically is not taken on weekends or during school vacations because of concerns about side effects.

Children take psychostimulants for years, not days or weeks. Traditionally, medication was discontinued in early adolescence, because it was believed that the problem was "outgrown" by that age. However, research shows that, while hyperactivity usually improves during the teen years, problems with inattention and impulsivity often continue (Schachar & Tannock, 2002). Thus psychostimulants now are taken through the teen years, and perhaps into adulthood, as interest has grown in "adult ADHD," inattention, impulsivity, and to a lesser extent, overactivity in adults (Barkley, 1998).

Numerous double-blind, placebo-controlled studies show that psychostimulants indisputably improve children's attentiveness and decrease their hyperactivity (Barkley, 1998; Pelham et al., 1993). In the largest treatment study to date, 579 children with ADHD were randomly assigned to one of four treatments:

Ritalin clearly helps the symptoms of ADHD. However, the line dividing normal from abnormal inattention and hyperactivity is necessarily arbitrary, and some question whether we medicate too many schoolchildren. In the U.S., 3% of school-aged children are medicated, far more than elsewhere in the world.

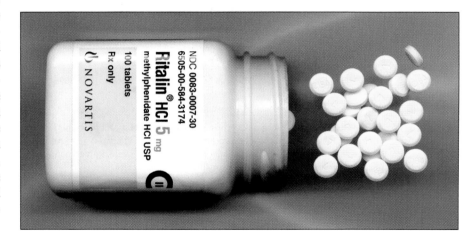

(1) controlled medication management, (2) intensive behavior therapy, (3) the two treatments combined, or (4) uncontrolled community care (which typically included medication). A 14-month follow-up assessment showed that the controlled medication and combined treatments produced significantly more improvements in ADHD symptoms than the alternatives. Intensive behavior therapy (part of the combined treatment) added only a slight improvement over medication for ADHD symptoms (see Figure 16–6) but may have modestly helped comorbid aggressive behavior (MTA Cooperative Group, 1999; Swanson et al., 2001) and perhaps was especially helpful for minority children and families (Arnold et al., 2003).

More aggressive behavior therapies, including summer treatment programs, may produce more notable benefits (Pelham et al., 2002). Still, this evidence establishes psychostimulant medication as the first-line treatment for ADHD. However, the findings also indicate that improvements are needed in standard community medication management, which was much less effective than carefully controlled medication use. Unfortunately, standard community practice often involves little ongoing monitoring of ADHD children.

Although psychostimulants improve hyperactivity and impulsivity, their effects on attention and learning are less certain. Children on medication complete more reading, spelling, and arithmetic assignments with somewhat improved accuracy (Pelham et al., 1985), but their grades and achievement test scores improve little if at all (Henker & Whalen, 1989). This pattern of improvement in behavior but not in learning was observed again in the large-scale MTA Cooperative Study (1999).

Research on **dose–response effects,** the response to different dosages of medication, was once thought to explain the different effects on behavior and learning. Sprague and Sleator (1977) found that a low dosage of psychostimulants produced gains in learning, but the medication *interfered* with learning at higher dosages. Higher dosages produced more improvements in behavior, however, suggesting that some children received too much medication, because medication typically is increased gradually or *titrated* based on improvements in behavior.

Subsequent evidence on dose–response effects is mixed, and it now appears that different children respond uniquely to different dosages (Tannock, Schachar, & Logan, 1995). Thus, it remains unclear why improved attention and behavior in the classroom do not translate into improved grades and achievement. An even more troubling and puzzling fact is that psychostimulants have not been found to lead to *long-term* improvements in behavior, learning, or any other areas of functioning (Barkley, 1998; Schachar & Tannock, 2002; see Table 16–4). Follow-up studies from the MTA Cooperative Study should help to clarify whether this is due to failure to continue medication.

Side Effects   The side effects of psychostimulants can be troubling. Some side effects are minor, such as decreased appetite, increased heart rate, and sleeping difficulties. (These effects are minor for the child's health, but not to parents who want their children to eat right and go to bed!) Other problems are more serious, such as an increase in motor tics in a small percentage of cases. Evidence that psychostimulants can slow physical growth is also an important concern. Children maintained on psychostimulants fall somewhat behind expected gains in height and weight, although rebounds in growth occur when the medication is stopped. This is one reason why the medication often is discontinued when children are out of school. Still, careful monitoring of cases is necessary because of possible individual differences in growth effects (Campbell, Green, & Deutsch, 1985).

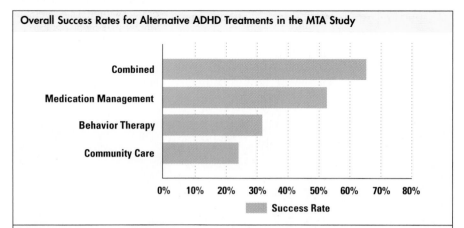

FIGURE 16–6: Carefully monitored use of psychostimulants produces notable benefits for ADHD. Adding behavior therapy to medication produces a small but significant increase in success rates. Behavior therapy alone and community care—typically involving medication prescribed with little follow-up—produce much lower rates of improvement.

Source: Based on J.M. Swanson et al., 2001. Clinical relevance of the primary findings of the MTA: Success rates based on severity of ADHD and ODD symptoms at the end of treatment. *Journal of the American Academy of Child and Adolescent Psychiatry, 40,* 168–179. Copyright © 2001. Reprinted by permission of Lippincott, Williams & Wilkins.

Another side effect that concerns some psychologists is that parents, teachers, and children may credit the pills, not the child, for the improved behavior (Whalen et al., 1991). When they are having an "off" day, for example, many children with ADHD are asked, "Did you take your pill today?" However, research indicates that ADHD children on psychostimulants do not credit "the pill"; they make internal attributions for their positive behavior (Pelham et al., 2002).

Are Psychostimulants Overused? Despite evidence on the effectiveness of psychostimulants, parents and professionals face a basic question: Should we use medication to correct children's misbehavior? Every year 1.5 million children in the United States—almost 3 percent of the school-age population—are treated with psychostimulants for ADHD (Safer, Zito, & Fine, 1996). This startling number generates considerable controversy, as do these facts: (1) Physician visits for psychostimulants increased 500 *percent* between 1988 and 1994 (Pincus et al., 1998); (2) The use of psychostimulants *tripled* among preschoolers during the 1990s (Zito et al., 2000); (3) Psychostimulants are used three to ten times more often in the United States as in Europe, Canada, and Australia (Heyman & Santosh, 2002; Schachar & Tannock, 2002); and (4) the U.S. consumes 90 percent of the psychostimulants produced in the world (LeFever et al., 2003).

Are psychostimulants for ADHD overused in the United States? As we have noted, ADHD is a dimensional, not a categorical, problem. Should mental health professionals in the United States raise the threshold for making the diagnosis? Pills also can be overused as a "quick fix" not only for troubled children but for troubled schools. Many public schools are underfunded, overcrowded, and inadequately staffed. Moreover, competitive parents sometimes demand psychostimulants for their basically well-functioning children so they can "get an edge" with heightened attention and alertness. Do we need to look at the bigger picture of children's lives more often instead of looking to a pill for a quick fix?

Psychostimulants are an inexpensive and effective treatment for ADHD, especially in comparison with the alternatives (see Critical Thinking *Matters* on page 542). Still, the benefits of medication are limited, various side effects are a source of concern, and, most importantly, there is no bright line between normal and

TABLE 16–4	Short-Term and Long-Term Effects of Psychostimulants on ADHD	
	HYPERACTIVITY/IMPULSIVITY	INATTENTION/LEARNING
Short-term	Dramatic improvements; less active and more focused; fewer social problems	More work completed, but no change in grades or standardized test scores
Long-term	No demonstrated benefit	No demonstrated benefit

abnormal behavior in diagnosing ADHD. Thus, it is reasonable to ask whether we are overdiagnosing ADHD and overmedicating schoolchildren.

Other Medications for ADHD Over the last decade, physicians tried antidepressants with many children with ADHD who do not respond to psychostimulants. Although depression and ADHD often co-occur, this is not the rationale for the treatment. Rather, antidepressants may affect ADHD symptoms directly for unknown reasons. However, antidepressants clearly are a second-line treatment for ADHD. Their use is justified only following the failure of psychostimulants (DeVane & Sallee, 1996; Spencer, Biederman, & Wilens, 1998).

Another medication, *clonidine*, may be used in combination with psychostimulants in as

Do you think psychostimulants are overused?

Psychostimulants are effective treatments of ADHD, but concern is rising that medication may be given too quickly to too many children.

critical thinking matters

ADHD'S FALSE CAUSES AND CURES

No one is more desperate for answers than a parent of a child with an emotional or behavior disorder. "We don't know what causes this" and "There is no cure" are *not* the kind of answers concerned parents want to hear. Unfortunately, these sorts of answers often are the most honest and scientifically accurate ones (which is why we are such strong advocates for more research—to give us better answers). However, the absence of scientific information does not prevent many self-appointed experts from answering parents' questions—with partial truths, dubious theories, or pure fantasy. Myths abound for almost every mental disorder, but if someone gave a prize for the most (and most audacious) misleading information and outright quackery about a psychological disorder, ADHD might just be the winner.

Self-proclaimed "experts" have blamed the cause of ADHD on everything from fluorescent lights (the lights were installed in schools during a time of increasing rates of ADHD) to sugar (a favorite among teachers and parents—after all, children get "hyper" around Halloween) to a failure to learn to crawl properly before learning to walk (somehow out-of-sequence locomotion is supposed to disrupt developing brain circuitry, a theory we never understood, nor do we wish to try). We hope we do not need to say this, but just in case: There is no evidence to support any of these theories, or treatments based on them. We know, for example, that sugar can cause cavities, but increasing dietary sugar does not produce hyperactivity nor does decreasing sugar cure it (Milich et al., 1986). Today, a number of "experts" (but no scientific studies) blame the MMR vaccine for causing ADHD along with autism, learning disorders, and who knows what else (see Critical Thinking

Matters in Chapter 2). Some critics claim that drug companies and the National Institute of Mental Health are conspiring to cover up evidence about this linkage. We give these worries the same credibility as theories that the government is covering up evidence of extraterrestrials visiting Earth.

A theory popular in the 1970s—that food additives, particularly *salicylates*, which are commonly found in processed foods, cause ADHD—is instructive. Physician Benjamin Feingold (1975) offered this theory in his immodestly titled book, *Why Your Child Is Hyperactive*, and recommended a natural-foods diet (the Feingold diet) as a cure. Hundreds of thousands of parents embraced the Feingold diet, and the theory became so popular that Congress considered banning salicylates. (Do a Web search, and you will still find advocates for the Feingold diet.) Actually,

Too much sugar can cause stomachaches and cavities, but too much sugar does not cause ADHD.

many parents of children with ADHD reported improvement in their children's symptoms as a result of the Feingold diet, even in some (flawed) research. In the end, the benefits proved to be nothing more than a placebo effect. The parents *believed* the diet would work, so it did in their minds, but according to carefully controlled research, not in their children's behavior (Conners, 1980).

Other cures, whether promised by well-meaning or unscrupulous experts, also do not work. Among the treatments that do *not* work for ADHD are food supplements (amino acids and megavitamins are two often recommended "treatments"); play therapy (the therapist plays with the child and interprets the play analogous to the way an analyst interprets free association); eye movement desensitization and reprocessing (see Chapter 7); neurofeedback (where patients watch EEG readings and try to alter their brain waves); sensorimotor integration therapy (which may include exercises like watching a pencil as you touch your nose with it); acupuncture (the ancient Chinese procedure); or various homeopathic remedies, including *pycnogenol* (an organically based substance which advocates claim is as effective as Ritalin—and also helps to cure tennis elbow!). Again, *none of these treatments work* (Waschbusch & Hill, 2004). Fortunately, there are some treatments for ADHD that do work, although not as well as we (and parents) might hope.

Critical thinking is one thing that will work for you, if you learn to use it. Sure: Watch science fiction movies and suspend belief for a couple of hours. But when it comes to real life problems, critical thinking *matters*—and you have many opportunities to use it in considering the causes and cures of ADHD.

many as 20 percent of cases. Despite this frequent practice, the use of clonidine is controversial. The medication's primary use is for high blood pressure in adults, and only limited research supports its effectiveness for ADHD. Most controversial, there are isolated reports of sudden death among treated children (Hazell & Stuart, 2003).

Behavioral Family Therapy for ODD   Behavioral **family therapy (BFT)** is a treatment based on

learning theory principles that teaches parents to be very clear and specific about their expectations for children's behavior, to monitor children's actions closely, and to systematically reward positive behavior while ignoring or mildly punishing misbehavior. BFT is sometimes used as an adjunct or alternative to medication in treating ADHD, although it offers limited benefits for ADHD symptoms (MTA Cooperative Study, 1999). However, BFT is more promising as a treatment of ODD (Brestan & Eyberg, 1998).

BFT typically begins with *parent training.* Parents are taught to identify specific problematic behaviors such as fighting with siblings, list preferred alternative behaviors like speaking nicely, and set consequences for appropriate and inappropriate behavior. Parents may also make a "star chart" for recording children's progress and perhaps develop a "daily report card" that the child will carry home from school as a way of coordinating discipline in both settings (Scott, 2002).

Other aspects of parent training may include teaching parents about punishment strategies, such as the time-out technique. Conventional wisdom holds that punishment should be firm but not angry, and that rewards should far outweigh punishments as a strategy of discipline. Some experts believe that parent training should directly emphasize increasing warmth as well as discipline in parent–child relationships (Cavell, 2001). From this perspective, the goal of parent training is to teach parents to be authoritative.

Research supports the short-term effectiveness of BFT (Patterson, 1982), and parent training can be effectively delivered in groups (Webster-Stratton, 1994) or even through the popular media (Sanders, Montgomery, & Brechman-Toussaint, 2000). However, evidence on long-term effectiveness is less certain, and benefits generally are limited to children under the age of 12 (Kazdin, 1997). In considering the challenges for BFT, you should recall that the parents of children with externalizing problems often live in adverse circumstances that make it difficult to alter their parenting (Emery, Fincham, & Cummings, 1992). Parents can be effective in changing children's behavior, but psychologists need to develop more ways to help parents who live in difficult circumstances (Scott, 2002). In fact, outcome in BFT is worse when parents are unhappily married, depressed, substance abusers, or harsh and critical with their children (Beauchaine, Webster-Stratton, & Reid, 2005). BFT is more effective when treatment includes efforts to help parents cope with their stress (Kazdin & Whitley, 2003).

Some behavioral therapies also include direct training of children as well as parents. *Problem-solving skills training (PSST)* is one commonly used technique in which children are taught to slow down, evaluate a problem, and consider alternative solutions before acting. Some evidence indicates that the combination of PSST and parent training leads to more improvement

than either therapy alone in the treatment of the problems found in ODD (Kazdin, Siegel, & Bass, 1992). As with behavioral family therapy, however, PSST offers only minimal help to children with ADHD.

Treatment of Conduct Disorders and Juvenile Delinquency Numerous programs have been developed to treat conduct disorders and juvenile delinquency. In fact, exciting claims about the effectiveness of new programs for difficult youth are commonly reported in the popular media. You should be cautious about these new approaches. Research indicates that conduct disorders among adolescents are even more resistant to treatment than are externalizing problems among younger children (Kazdin, 1995, 1997).

Some BFT approaches have shown promise in treating young people with family or legal problems (Alexander & Parsons, 1982). These treatments are based on principles similar to those in programs for younger children, except that *negotiation*—actively involving young people in setting rules—is central to BFT with adolescents. An obvious reason for the negotiation strategy is that parents have less direct control over adolescents than over younger children. Because of diminishing parental control, many mental health professionals also advocate treating externalizing problems prior to adolescence.

Multisystemic Therapy *Multisystemic therapy* (MST) is another intervention with conduct disorders that has received considerable attention (Henggeler & Borduin, 1990). In recognition of the diverse causes of externalizing behavior, MST

Research shows that treatments that involve parents are most effective for children with externalizing disorders.

A boot camp for juvenile offenders. Boot camps have been advocated widely as treatments for juvenile delinquency in recent years, but like other temporarily fashionable treatments, boot camps unfortunately do not reduce recidivism.

combines family treatment with coordinated interventions in other important contexts of the troubled child's life, including peer groups, schools, and neighborhoods. Several studies now document that MST therapy improves family relationships, and to a lesser extent, delinquent behavior and troubled peer relationships (Curtis, Ronan, & Borduin, 2004). A recent 13-year follow-up study found significantly lower **recidivism,** or repeat offending, among seriously troubled youth treated with MST versus individual therapy, but recidivism remained high for both groups: 50 percent following MST versus 81 percent for individual therapy (Schaeffer & Borduin, 2005). The data point to the importance of coordinating efforts to help troubled youth in

the various contexts of their lives—and to the frequent failure to prevent recidivism even following such extensive efforts.

Residential Programs and Juvenile Courts   Many adolescents with serious conduct problems or especially troubled families are treated in residential programs outside the home. One of the most actively researched residential programs is *Achievement Place,* a group home that operates according to highly structured behavior therapy principles. Achievement Place homes, like many similar residential programs, are very effective in improving aggression and noncompliance while the adolescent is living in the treatment setting. For this reason, professionals working in residential or inpatient settings are wise to adopt similar behavioral strategies. Unfortunately, the programs do not prevent recidivism once the adolescent leaves the residential placement (Bailey, 2002; Kazdin, 1995). Delinquent adolescents typically return to family, peer, and school environments that do not consistently reward prosocial behavior or monitor and punish antisocial behavior.

Of course, many delinquent youths are treated in the juvenile justice system, where *rehabilitation* is supposed to be the goal. The philosophy of the juvenile justice system in the United States is based on the principle of *parens patriae*—the state as parent. In theory, juvenile courts are supposed to help troubled youth, not to punish them. This lofty goal is belied by research indicating that *diversion*—keeping problem youths out of the juvenile justice system—is an effective "treatment" (Davidson et al., 1987). The juvenile justice system often creates delinquency instead of curing it, and recidivism is lower when delinquents are diverted away from the courts.

The struggles involved in treating conduct disorders have led some to question the *parens patriae* philosophy of the juvenile justice system, and statistics indicate that punishment rather than rehabilitation is becoming more common (Bailey, 2002). More minors are being transferred out of the juvenile justice system and tried as adults, and more youth are placed into custody (see Figure 16–7). In 1995, 108,746 youth under the age of 18 were being held in custody in the United States, an increase of 47 percent since 1983 (Sickmund, Snyder, & Poe-Yamagata, 1997).

Realism, Not Pessimism   Antisocial behavior is incredibly costly for children, families, and society, and we see the difficulties in treating problem

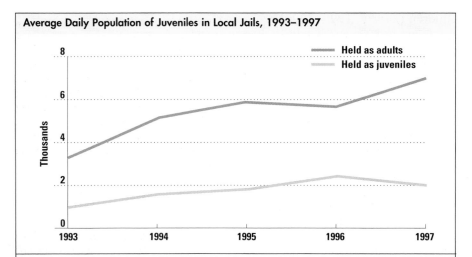

Average Daily Population of Juveniles in Local Jails, 1993–1997

FIGURE 16–7: More juveniles are being held together with adults in local jails. An increasing number of these youth are being held as adults—and awaiting trial as adults.
Source: Based on D.K. Gillard, 1999. *Prison and jail inmates at midyear 1998.* Washington, DC: U.S. Department of Justice.

youth as a challenge, not a defeat. Individually, therapists need to establish good relationships with troubled (and often difficult) children and youth, an important predictor of treatment outcome for externalizing problems (Shirk & Karver, 2003), and to coordinate efforts across the different contexts of youths' lives (Schaeffer & Borduin, 2005). Another key effort is preventing externalizing disorders from developing by easing the family adversity that creates them (Earls & Mezzacappa, 2002). Teaching new ways of coping with adversities that cannot be readily changed is another promising approach (Lochman & Wells, 2004). We need to be realistic about the limited effectiveness of treatment, but if we do not want troubled youth to give up on themselves, we can not give up on trying to help them.

Course and Outcome   Parents often want to know: Do children "outgrow" externalizing disorders? For ADHD, hyperactivity generally declines during adolescence, while attention deficits and impulsivity are more likely to continue. The continuity of symptoms into adult life for about half of children with ADHD is evident in the growing interest in adult ADHD (Mannuzza et al., 1998). Importantly, the prognosis of ADHD depends substantially on whether there is comorbid ODD or CD. If so, youth are more likely to develop problems with substance

abuse, criminality, and other forms of antisocial behavior (Hinshaw, 1994). In fact, roughly half of all children with ODD or CD continue to have problems with antisocial behavior into adulthood (Hinshaw, 1994; Kazdin, 1995). However, antisocial behavior that begins during adolescence is more likely to be transient than antisocial behavior that begins during childhood (Moffit, 1993).

The continuity of externalizing disorders clearly underscores the need for prevention and early intervention. If we can do better in helping troubled children and their families, we will succeed in preventing antisocial behavior not only during childhood but into adult life (Conduct Problems Prevention Research Group, 1999).

INTERNALIZING AND OTHER DISORDERS

Teachers cannot ignore disruptive children in the classroom, but they may overlook anxious or depressed children who sit quietly and unhappily alone. The negative effect of externalizing disorders is an important reason why we have focused on these problems, but like schoolteachers, we do not want to overlook children whose troubles are *not* disruptive. We begin with a case study.

◆◆

CASE STUDY   Turning the Tables on Tormentors

Mark was 12 years old when his mother brought him to see a new psychologist. Both Mark and his mother agreed that he had been depressed for well over a year, and 9 months of "play therapy" resulted in little or no improvement. Mark felt sad most of the time, cried often, and felt helpless and hopeless about the future. He had withdrawn from his usual activities, and his straight As had fallen to Bs, Cs, and even a few Ds—despite an IQ of 145. Teasing was a particular problem, one that brought Mark to tears during the first appointment. A group of boys at his school constantly tormented Mark, calling him the "little professor." As in the office, their teasing frequently brought Mark to the point of tears.

Mark's family was well functioning, and there was no family history of depression. Mark's mother was a homemaker, and his father made an adequate living as a police officer. His parents were happily married, and

his two younger brothers were doing well. Mark's mother attributed many of his problems to his unusual intelligence and to the fact that Mark had played with few children during the first years of his life. The family lived in an apartment in an unsafe neighborhood before the birth of his brothers.

The new treatment followed a cognitive behavior therapy approach, but began with a careful period of building rapport. Establishing a good therapeutic relationship was very important to Mark who was socially isolated and unhappy with his previous therapy. Treatment eventually focused on skills training and behavioral activation. Mark was encouraged to rejoin various activities and to initiate relationships with his peers. His parents were told to treat Mark normally. In particular, they were encouraged to hold the same high (but not demanding) expectations for Mark's schoolwork as they did for their other sons.

A special emphasis of treatment was how Mark could deal with his tormentors. As a step, the therapist began to tease Mark playfully at times and to encourage teasing back in return. This was viewed both as a way of teaching Mark some skills and of desensitizing him to teasing, which is normative if often vicious among 12-year-old boys. Given the strong therapeutic relationship that had developed, Mark quickly learned not only to accept this game but to relish it. With his high IQ,

he soon became devastatingly clever in his banter.

The benefits clearly generalized outside of the therapy session. Mark no longer cried when he was teased; instead, he learned retorts that set his tormentors on their heels. In fact, Mark did not limit his self-defense to words. He punched one particularly mean boy in the nose one day—a response that was *not* encouraged in therapy but one that did not upset his father, the police officer (or, privately, the therapist).

Over the course of about 3 months of therapy, Mark's mood improved considerably.

He started getting As again, he was re-engaged in various activities, and the teasing was no longer an issue. He remained himself—a quiet, intelligent, and introspective boy—but he had learned to have more rational expectations for himself, the importance of staying involved, and how to handle his tormentors.

◆◆◆

The case of Mark shows that children do suffer from "adult" disorders such as depression. Yet the diagnosis is not always so clear. Imagine, for example, if Mark were 6 years old. Although he might act and look sad, he certainly would be less able to express or reflect on his feelings at this young age or feel hopeless about the future. Moreover, his parents would have difficulty interpreting his crying, withdrawal, and falling grades without a good awareness of how Mark himself felt. Even if 6-year-old Mark could tell them that he was sad, the meaning of his words would be difficult to interpret. At young ages, children do not have the same ability to experience and express their thoughts and emotions as adults.

Symptoms of Internalizing Disorders

Children's internalizing symptoms include sadness, fears, and somatic complaints, as well as other indicators of mood and anxiety disorders—for example, feeling worthless or tense. DSM-IV-TR does not have a separate category for children's internalizing disorders, but the manual does identify some unique ways in which children experience the symptoms. When diagnosing major depressive episodes among children and adolescents, for example, the clinician is allowed to substitute "irritable mood" for "depressed mood." Children sometimes act angry when they are feeling sad, and they may try to hide their true emotions, especially when talking to adults.

The diagnosis of phobia offers another example. In contrast to adults, children are not

required to recognize that their fears are excessive or unreasonable, because children often have limited insight into their problems. In fact, children may lack the cognitive capacity to experience some of the internalizing symptoms found among adults with the same disorder. Self-awareness emerges across the course of development, and it is not until adolescence that children fully develop the cognitive abilities necessary for "adult" insight.

Children's capacity to experience and recognize emotions emerges over the course of development, as does their ability to express—and to mask—their own feelings. Unfortunately, the DSM-IV-TR offers only a few, scattered developmental considerations in diagnostic criteria. This is due in large part to the fact that the course of children's normal emotional development is not well charted. It is much more difficult for adults to evaluate children's inner experiences than it is to observe their externalizing behavior.

Depressive Symptoms The assessment of depression in children can be particularly difficult. For example, in one study of children hospitalized for depression, clinicians found a correlation of *zero* between children's and parents' ratings on identical measures of the children's depression (Kazdin, French, & Unis, 1983). What the adults said about the children was completely unrelated to what the children said about themselves. In another study, children's ratings of their own depression were associated with their own ratings of internal distress—feelings of hopelessness, low self-esteem, internal attributions for negative events, and external locus of control. In contrast, parents' ratings of children's depression were associated with their ratings of externalizing behavior, not children's internal distress (Kazdin, 1989). Finally, and perhaps of greatest concern, parents systematically underestimate the extent of depression reported by their children and adolescents (Kazdin & Petti, 1982; Rutter, 1989).

Given parents' and children's widely differing perceptions, psychologists are rightly concerned about a child's depression if *either* a parent or a child notes problems. In assessing

Calvin and Hobbes
by Bill Watterson

children's internalizing problems, mental health professionals must obtain information from *multiple informants*—parents, teachers, and the children themselves (Harrington, 2002).

When assessing children directly, child clinical psychologists are sensitive to different signs that may be indicative of depression at different ages: unresponsiveness to caregivers under the age of 2; sad expressions and social withdrawal in preschoolers; somatic complaints in young school-aged children; more direct admission of sad feelings or marked irritability in older school-aged children or early adolescents; and full-blown depression, including suicide risk, among adolescents.

Depression in children and adolescents often is comorbid both with externalizing problems and with anxiety. Depression in children also may differ from depression in adolescents, not only in how it is expressed but also in its lower prevalence, equal frequency among boys and girls, stronger relation with family dysfunction, and less persistent course (Harrington, 2002).

Children's Fears and Anxiety   *Anxiety* is a general and diffuse emotional reaction that often is linked with anticipation of future and perhaps unrealistic threats. In contrast, *fear* is an emotional reaction to real and immediate danger. As with depression, children often have trouble identifying their anxiety, but they are more aware of their fears, which are immediate and have a clear environmental referent. Also, adults can observe much of children's fearful behavior for the same reasons. Thus research on the development of children's fears is more advanced than it is for their anxiety.

Three findings from fear research are important to note. First, children develop different fears for the first time at different ages, and the onset of new fears may be sudden and have no apparent cause in the child's environment. For example, infants typically develop a fear of strangers in the months just before their first birthday; preschoolers develop fears of monsters and the dark between the ages of 2 and 4; and children between ages 5 and 8 often develop fears related to school. (To cite one curious example, if you ever dreamed of going to school in your underwear or partially dressed, you are not alone. Such dreams are surprisingly common among school-aged children.) In short, many fears, even those that seem odd or arise

Depression becomes much more common during adolescence, especially among teenage girls.

suddenly, are developmentally normal, a conclusion that can be reassuring to parents and perhaps to children. A second finding is that some fears, particularly fears of uncontrollable events such of disasters, are both common and relatively stable across different ages. Third, many other fears, especially specific ones like fears of monsters or normal worries about death, become less frequent as children grow older (King et al., 1989). Apparently, children "outgrow" many of their fears, probably by gradually confronting them in everyday life.

Separation Anxiety Disorder and School Refusal
The special case of separation anxiety illustrates the importance of development on children's fear. **Separation anxiety** is distress expressed following separation from an attachment figure, typically a parent or caregiver. This normal fear develops strongly around a baby's eighth month of life. An infant who easily tolerated separations in the past may suddenly start to cling, cry, and scream whenever a parent tries to leave, even for a brief separation. Separation anxiety peaks around 15 months and lessens over time. Toddlers and preschoolers typically continue to experience distress upon separation, however, particularly when left in an unfamiliar circumstance.

Although normal at younger ages, separation anxiety can become a serious problem if children fail to "outgrow" it (Silverman & Dick-Niederhauser, 2004). DSM-IV-TR contains a diagnosis for **separation anxiety disorder,** which is defined by symptoms such as persistent and excessive worry for the safety of an

How do children's fears change during the course of normal development?

Separation anxiety is a normal fear that typically develops just before a baby's first birthday. Toddlers and preschoolers continue to show a degree of distress even during routine separations from their attachment figures.

attachment figure, fears of getting lost or being kidnapped, nightmares with separation themes, and refusal to be alone. For a child to be diagnosed with this disorder, he or she must exhibit three or more of these symptoms for at least 4 weeks.

Separation anxiety disorder is especially problematic when it interferes with school attendance. **School refusal,** also known as *school phobia,* is characterized by an extreme reluctance to go to school, and is accompanied by various symptoms of anxiety, such as stomachaches and headaches. Some children are literally school phobic—they are afraid of school or specific aspects of attending school. But in many cases, school refusal can be traced to separation anxiety disorder (Last & Strauss, 1990). In such cases, the parent, as well as the child, may have difficulty separating. Whatever its origins, school refusal is a serious problem that has been reported to account for more than two-thirds of referrals to an anxiety disorders clinic for children.

Troubled Peer Relationships   Children with internalizing or externalizing problems often have troubled peer relationships. Children who are aggressive and disobedient or shy and withdrawn often are not well liked by their peers. However, different patterns of difficulties relating to peer relationships have been found among children with internalizing and externalizing problems.

The peer sociometric method often is used to assess children's relationships. *Peer sociometrics* evaluate children's relationships by obtaining information on who is "liked most" and who is "liked least" from a large group of children who know one another (for example, children in a classroom). Statistical procedures are then used to group children into one of five categories based on the ratings of their peers (Coie & Kupersmidt, 1983; Newcomb, Bukowski, & Pattee, 1993):

- *Popular* children receive many "liked most" and few "liked least" ratings.
- *Average* children also receive few "liked least" ratings, but they receive fewer "liked most" ratings than popular children.
- *Neglected* children receive few of either type of rating.
- *Rejected* children receive many "liked least" ratings and few "liked most" nominations.
- *Controversial* children receive many positive and many negative ratings from their peers.

Rejected children are considerably more likely to have externalizing problems in comparison to the other four peer status groups (Patterson, Kupersmidt, & Griesler, 1990), and peer rejection predicts the development of increased aggression (Dodge et al., 2003). Children with ADHD may be rejected because their symptoms impede social relationships (Greene et al., 2001; Hoza et al., 2005), whereas rejected children with ODD and CD are likely to have a few close friends—friends who, unfortunately, also engage in antisocial behavior (Olweus, 1984).

Neglected children also have more troubles than popular, average, and controversial children. Not surprisingly, neglected children are likely to have internalizing symptoms such as loneliness (Asher & Wheeler, 1985). An optimistic finding is the neglected status is not particularly stable over time and across situations (Coie & Kupersmidt, 1983; Newcomb, Bukowski, & Pattee, 1993). Apparently, children who are left out of one social group often succeed in finding friends as they grow older or move to a new school or participate in new activities.

Specific Developmental Deviations   A number of troubling symptoms of children's psychological disorders are best understood as specific developmental deviations, significant departures from age-appropriate norms in some specific area of functioning. In fact, some developmental deviations are considered disorders in their own right. Specific deviations in reading (*dyslexia*), writing (*dysgraphia*), or arithmetic (*dyscalulia*) are considered to be learning disorders if the deviation is substantial (see What Are Learning Disorders?). Similarly, once a child is past the age when most children toilet appropriately, delays in developing bladder or bowel control are considered to be abnormal. Of course, we can only determine if a child is delayed if we have good development norms.

Diagnosis of Internalizing and Other Disorders

Brief Historical Perspective   In 1896, the psychologist Lightner Witmer (1867–1956), of the University of Pennsylvania, established the first psychological clinic for children in the United States. Despite the early origins of child clinical psychology, children were largely ignored in early classifications of mental disorders (Garber, 1984). DSM-I (1952) contained only two separate diagnoses for children, and DSM-II (1968) listed only seven childhood disorders. DSM-III (1980) recognized

WHAT ARE LEARNING DISORDERS?

The DSM-IV-TR category of **learning disorders (LD)**—educators use the term *learning disabilities*—includes a collection of diverse problems where students perform substantially below academic ability in a specific area of learning. Researchers and practitioners operationally define learning disorders in many different ways (and often administer extensive diagnostic testing), but all attempts have serious problems with reliability and validity (Swanson, Harris, & Graham, 2003). The most common approach, the "discrepancy definition," is under attack by experts who say it fails to identify LD children correctly, but there is no agreed-upon alternative (Swanson et al., 2003). Discrepancy definitions compare scores on intelligence tests, which measure academic aptitude, with scores on *academic achievement tests*, which measure academic performance. A learning disorder commonly is defined as a difference of one or two standard deviations between aptitude and achievement in a specific area of learning—reading, writing, or mathematics. Thus, a diagnosis of learning disorder (dyslexia) would follow if a child scored a standard deviation above the mean on the verbal portion of an intelligence test (an IQ of 115) but a standard deviation below the mean in reading.

School professionals almost always identify children with learning disorders, followed by some form of school-based academic remediation. Thus mental health professionals typically work with children with learning disorders only when the problems co-occur with other psychological disorders. There is substantial comorbidity between learning disabilities and both ADHD and ODD (Barkley, 1998), but we can wonder why learning disorders are listed in the DSM (a listing of *mental* disorders) when the problems are so clearly academic in nature.

Learning disorders have been said to involve disruptions in a number of psychological processes, including perception, attention, language processing, and executive function. Typically, their cause is viewed as biological. Neuroimaging research on reading disorders identifies activity differences particularly in the temporal-parietal region of the left hemisphere of the brain (Miller et al., 2003; Tallal, 2003). (Recall that language abilities are lateralized in the left hemisphere.) Behavior genetic research shows that learning disorders, like normal reading abilities, are moderately heritable, and genetic linkage analysis suggests possible loci on chromosomes 1, 2, 6, 15, and 18 (Thomson & Raskind, 2003). However, no research to date has identified a specific psychological, neurological, or genetic cause of any learning disorder (Mash & Wolfe, 2005; Snowling, 2002; Swanson et al., 2003).

Tremendous efforts have gone into attempts to remediate learning disorders. In 1975, the U.S. Congress passed the Education for All Handicapped Children Act (now called the Individuals with Disabilities Education Act, or IDEA), a law mandating that local school systems provide special resources for educating handicapped children, including children with learning disorders. The federal legislation dramatically increased the number of children identified as having a learning disorder rising from less than 2 percent in 1976–1977 to over 4 percent in 2002–2003 (Office of Special Education Programs, 2003). However, some commentators wonder whether this reflects overly broad definitions of learning disorders (Lyon, 1996). And it is not clear that the identification of more students has led to more effective education. Interventions attempts include intensive tutoring, individually or in small groups (including teacher-based direct instruction and student-based cooperative learning); behavior therapy programs in which academic success is systematically rewarded; psychostimulant medication; counseling for related problems (for example, low self–esteem); and various special efforts such as training in visual–motor skills. Unfortunately, no treatment has demonstrated consistent success (Lyon, 1996; Swanson et al., 2003).

Perhaps 5 percent of all schoolchildren in the United States do not achieve at a level consistent with their abilities (Lyon, 1996). Learning disorders are "real" in the sense that these children seem to have the ability and motivation to perform better in school, yet they do not. Nevertheless, the identification of this discrepancy between ability and performance has not solved the puzzle of learning disorders. Controversy and uncertainty remain about their definition, cause, and treatment.

TABLE 16–5	DSM-IV-TR Disorders Usually First Diagnosed in Infancy, Childhood, or Adolescence

Attention-Deficit and Disruptive Behavior Disorders

Attention-deficit/hyperactivity disorder
   Combined type
   Predominantly inattentive type
   Predominantly hyperactive-impulsive type
Conduct disorder
Oppositional defiant disorder

Learning Disorders

Reading disorder
Mathematics disorder
Disorder of written expression

Motor Skills Disorder

Developmental coordination disorder

Communication Disorders

Expressive language disorder
Mixed receptive-expressive language disorder
Phonological disorder
Stuttering

Feeding and Eating Disorders of Infancy or Early Childhood

Pica
Rumination disorder
Feeding disorder of infancy or early childhood

Tic Disorders

Tourette's disorder
Chronic motor or vocal tic disorder
Transient tic disorder

Elimination Disorders

Encopresis
   With constipation and overflow incontinence
   Without constipation and overflow incontinence
Enuresis

Other Disorders of Infancy, Childhood, and Adolescence

Separation anxiety disorder
Selective mutism
Reactive attachment disorder of infancy or early childhood
Stereotypic movement disorder

Note: This listing does not include mental retardation or pervasive developmental disorders, which we discussed in Chapter 15. It also does not include "Not Otherwise Specified" (NOS) subtypes of the diagnoses. NOS subtypes exist for many of the disorders listed here, and they are used when a child meets many but not all of the diagnostic criteria for the specific disorder.

Reprinted with permission from the *Diagnostic and Statistical Manual of Mental Disorders,* Fourth Edition, Text Revision. Copyright © 2000 by the American Psychiatric Association.

a much wider range of childhood disorders, and in fact, contained a proliferation of diagnostic categories, 40 in all. Although laudable, the new effort was overly ambitious. Many of the new diagnoses were severely criticized and subsequently were dropped.

Contemporary Classification   Table 16–5 summarizes the childhood disorders contained in DSM-IV-TR. Many of these diagnoses may be unfamiliar to you, in part because some of them are rare and unusual problems. We can consider most of these disorders only briefly.

Pica and Rumination Disorder   Pica is the persistent eating of nonnutritive substances, such as paint or dirt. Many infants and toddlers put nonnutritive substances in their mouths, but the feeding disorder pica is rarely diagnosed, except among mentally retarded children. *Rumination disorder,* the repeated regurgitation and rechewing of food, is another infrequent feeding disorder. Rumination disorder is found primarily among infants, and it can be a serious problem that causes very low weight gain and can even lead to death.

Tourette's Disorder and Stereotypic Movement Disorder   *Tourette's disorder* is a rare problem (4 to 5 cases per 10,000 people) that is characterized by repeated motor and verbal tics. The tics can be voluntarily suppressed only for brief periods of time, and they can interfere substantially with life functioning. Other tic disorder classifications reflect the facts that children may develop verbal or motor tics in isolation, and that children's tics often last for only a brief period of time (see Table 16–5). *Stereotypic movement disorder* is self-stimulation or self-injurious behavior that is serious enough to require treatment, as may occur in mental retardation or pervasive developmental disorder.

Selective Mutism and Reactive Attachment Disorder   *Selective mutism* involves the consistent failure to speak in certain social situations (for example, in school) while speech is unrestricted in other situations (for example, at home). Selective mutism is found among less than 1 percent of the children treated for mental health disorders. *Reactive attachment disorder* is another rarely diagnosed problem, although it may be more prevalent than we would hope. Reactive attachment disorder is characterized by severely disturbed and developmentally inappropriate social relationships. Children may resist comfort and cuddling, for example, or they may "freeze" and watch others from a safe distance. Reactive attachment disorder is caused by parenting that is so grossly neglectful that the infant or preschooler fails to develop a selective attachment relationship. (In Chapter 18, we discuss the topics of child abuse and neglect, social problems that, unfortunately, are not rare.)

Enuresis and Encopresis   **Encopresis** and **enuresis** are common problems. The terms refer, respectively, to inappropriately controlled defecation and urination. According to DSM-IV-TR, enuresis may be considered abnormal beginning at age 5, as most children have developed bladder control by this age. Bedwetting is found among approximately 5 percent of 5-year-olds, 2 to 3 percent of 10-year-olds, and 1 percent of 18-year-olds. Encopresis, a much less common problem, may be diagnosed beginning at age 4. Encopresis is found among approximately 1 percent of all 5-year-olds and fewer older children.

Encopresis and enuresis typically are causes of, not reactions to, psychological distress. The symptoms that sometimes accompany enuresis or encopresis—for example, shyness or social anxiety—generally disappear once children learn to control their bowels and bladders. Encopresis and especially enuresis can be effectively treated with various biofeedback devices. The best-known is the *bell and pad*, a device that awakens children by setting off an alarm as they begin to wet the bed during the night. Research indicates that the bell and pad is about 75 percent effective in treating bedwetting among young school-aged children (Houts, 1991).

Overinclusive Listing of Disorders   Some of the disorders listed in Table 16–5 are unfamiliar because of their questionable status as "mental disorders." Beginning with DSM-III, the manual became overinclusive in its listing of childhood disorders, and included too many "disorders" that are not in fact mental disorders (Garmezy, 1978). Many "disorders" have been dropped, but there seem to be other "childhood disorders" that are *not* disorders.

"Developmental coordination disorder" is perhaps the most obvious example. The manual defines this problem as: "Performance in daily activities that require motor coordination is substantially below that expected given the person's chronological age and measured intelligence" (p. 58). In poking fun at such diagnostic overzealousness, two pediatricians proposed a new diagnostic category they called "sports deficit disorder." The major diagnostic criterion for this "disorder" is always being the last one chosen for a sports team (Burke & McGee, 1990).

The "learning disorders" and "communication disorders" are more controversial examples of possible overinclusion in DSM-IV-TR. Educators call these childhood problems *learning disabilities* and *speech and hearing problems*, respectively. Learning disabilities and speech and hearing problems are common and serious difficulties experienced by children, but we question their status as mental disorders. We view both problems as involving primarily educational concerns.

Contextual Classifications?   As a final note, we remind you that children's behavior is intimately linked with the family, school, and peer contexts. Because of this, some experts have suggested that diagnosing individual children is misleading and misguided. Instead, children's psychological problems could be classified within the context of key relationships, particularly the family (Group for the Advancement of Psychiatry, 1995). As you saw in the case of Jeremy, parents, teachers, and peers often are part of a child's "individual" problem. Given current research and theory, we have followed the traditional approach to classification. However, future research should attempt to classify children's problem behavior contextually in an attempt to improve upon the individual approach used in the DSM.

Frequency of Internalizing Disorders

The prevalence of externalizing disorders generally decreases as children grow older, but the opposite is true for internalizing disorders. Depression increases dramatically during preadolescence and adolescence, especially among girls (Garber et al., 2002; Hankin et al., 1998; see Figure 16–8). According to one startling estimate, 35 percent of young women and 19 percent of young men experience at least one major depressive episode by the age of 19 (Lewinsohn, Rhode, & Seeley, 1998). Anxiety disorders also are very common, and may occur among as many as 5 to 10 percent of all young people (Klein & Pine, 2002). One national study estimated that 3.7 percent of boys and 6.3 percent of girls suffered from PTSD during the past 6 months (Kilpatrick et al., 2003). Precise estimates of the prevalence of both anxiety and depression are controversial,

In what ways might DSM-IV-TR include too many childhood disorders?

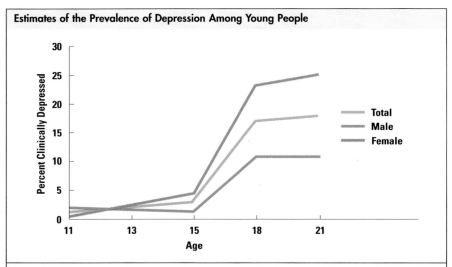

FIGURE 16–8: The prevalence of depression increases rapidly during adolescence, particularly among girls.

Source: Adapted from B.L. Hankin, et al., 1998. Development of depression from preadolescence to young adulthood: Emerging gender differences in a 10-year longitudinal study. *Journal of Abnormal Psychology, 107,* 128–140.

however, because of limited data and uncertainties about the best methods for diagnosing children and adolescents (Harrington, 2002). Much lower rates of clinically significant anxiety and depression certainly are suggested by the relatively small numbers of young people in treatment for internalizing problems.

The fact that boys have more externalizing disorders while girls have more internalizing problems leads to an interesting pattern in child treatment referrals across different ages. Parents, teachers, and other adults seek treatment for children with externalizing problems, especially during the school-aged years. Thus, among children under 12 years old, boys are much more likely to be treated than girls. The increase in depression among girls begins to balance the gender ratio of treatment referrals during the teenage years (Lewinsohn et al., 1994), and by early adult life, more females than males are identified with psychological problems.

Suicide   As we have noted, adults need to be sensitive to children's internal distress, as evidence on the epidemiology of suicide underscores in a dramatic fashion. Suicide is the third leading cause of death among teenagers, trailing only automobile accidents and natural causes. Suicide is extremely rare among children under the age of 10 (Shaffer & Gutstein, 2002). Teenage suicide is of special concern because adolescent suicide rates tripled in the 1960s and 1970s (see Figure 16–9). Fortunately, suicide rates have declined by about 20 percent in recent years (Shaffer & Gutstein, 2002).

In comparison to adult suicide attempts, suicide attempts among adolescents are more impulsive, are more likely to follow a family conflict, and are more often motivated by anger rather than depression (Shaffer & Gutstein, 2002). *Cluster suicides* also can occur among teenagers. When one teenager commits suicide, his or her peers are at an increased risk for suicide attempts. The risk sometimes stems from suicide pacts; also, the death may make suicide seem more acceptable to teenagers. Some adolescents may view a peer's suicide as understandable, even romantic.

Causes of Internalizing Disorders

Most research on the causes of mood and anxiety disorders among children is based on the same theories of etiology we have discussed in relation to adults (Puig-Antich, 1986). Evidence simply is lacking or inadequate on the development of many other psychological problems of childhood. Thus, our discussion of the etiology of these problems must be limited.

Biological Factors   Except for some research documenting genetic influences on childhood onset obsessive–compulsive disorder (March, Leonard,

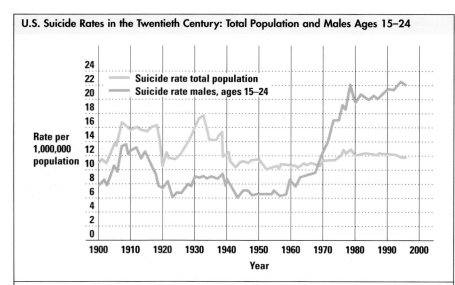

FIGURE 16–9: Teen suicide rates tripled during the 1960s and 1970s but have fallen in recent years.

Source: H. Hendin, 1995, *Suicide in America,* p. 53. New York: Norton. Copyright © 1995, 1989 by Herbert Hendin, M.D. Used by permission of W. W. Norton & Company, Inc. and Georges Borchardt, Inc., on behalf of the author.

& Swedo, 1995), few behavior genetic studies have been conducted on children's internalizing disorders. Moreover, existing research once again calls attention to the problems in classifying and assessing anxiety and depression among children. In the few studies completed to date, widely different estimates of genetic contributions are obtained based on children's versus parents' reports (Rutter et al., 1998).

Jerome Kagan and colleagues (Kagan & Snidman, 1991) have conducted some important basic research that suggests a more general, biological predisposition to anxiousness. These psychologists have identified a temperamental style that they call *inhibited to the unfamiliar*. Infants with this temperamental style cry easily and often in response to novel toys, people, or circumstances, and their psychophysiological responses (e.g., heart rate acceleration) also indicate their fearfulness. About 10 percent of babies consistently show inhibition to unfamiliar circumstances during the first 2 years of life (Kagan & Snidman, 1991). Research shows that children who are inhibited to the unfamiliar are more likely to develop anxiety disorders as they grow older (Schwartz et al., 1999; Klein & Pine, 2002). A recent prevention study found that the rate anxiety disorders can be significantly reduced by parent education that discourages overprotectiveness (a common reaction to inhibited children) and encourages gradually exposing children to the sources of their fear (Rapee et al., 2005).

Social Factors: A Focus on Attachments The major task of social development during the first year of life is the formation of a close bond, an *attachment*, between an infant and his or her caregivers. Extending the theories of John Bowlby (1969, 1973, 1980), the Canadian-American psychologist Mary Ainsworth (1913–1999) developed methods to test various propositions based on *attachment theory*, a set of proposals about the normal development of attachments and the adverse consequences of troubled attachment relationships. Troubled attachments may include the failure to develop a selective attachment early in life; the development of an insecure attachment; or multiple, prolonged separations from (or the permanent loss of) an attachment figure.

Reactive Attachment Disorder Extreme parental neglect deprives infants of the opportunity to form a selective attachment. Such neglect can cause *reactive attachment disorder*, or what attachment researchers sometimes call *anaclitic depression*—the

Mourners at the wake of three teenagers who committed suicide together.

lack of social responsiveness found among infants who do not have a consistent attachment figure (Sroufe & Fleeson, 1986). Research on the consequences of extreme neglect for children is strongly buttressed by evidence from animal analogue research. Nonhuman primates who are raised in isolation without a parent or a substitute attachment figure have dramatically troubled social relationships (Suomi & Harlow, 1972).

Insecure Attachments Attachment theory also predicts that variations in the quality of early attachments are associated with children's psychological adjustment. Attachment quality can be broadly divided into secure (healthy) and anxious attachments. Infants with *secure attachments* separate easily and explore away from their attachment figures, but they quickly seek comfort from their attachment figures when they are threatened or distressed. Infants with **anxious attachments** are fearful about exploration and are not easily comforted by their attachment figures, who respond inadequately or inconsistently to the child's needs (Carlson & Sroufe, 1995). Anxious attachments are further subcategorized into (1) *anxious avoidant attachments*, where the infant is generally unwary of strange situations and shows little preference for the attachment figure over others as a source of comfort; (2) *anxious resistant*

Canadian-American psychologist Mary Ainsworth (1913–1999) was an internationally renowned expert on infant-caregiver attachments. Her empirical studies grounded and expanded attachment theory.

attachments, where the infant is wary of exploration, not easily soothed by the attachment figure, and angry or ambivalent about contact; and (3) *disorganized attachments*, where the infant responds inconsistently because of conflicting feelings toward an inconsistent caregiver who is the potential source of either reassurance or fear (Carlson & Sroufe, 1995).

A number of longitudinal studies have demonstrated that anxious attachments during infancy foreshadow difficulties in children's social and emotional adjustment throughout childhood. However, an insecure attachment does not seem to result in the development of any particular emotional disorder. Rather, insecure attachments predict a number of internalizing and social difficulties, including lower self-esteem, less competence in peer interaction, and increased dependency on others (Carlson & Sroufe, 1995; Cassidy, 1988; Sroufe & Fleeson, 1986). Stable, anxious attachments during infancy also predict externalizing behavior at 3 years of age (Shaw & Vondra, 1995). Thus, anxious attachments appear to be a general rather than a specific risk factor for children's psychological problems.

Separation and Loss   Separation or loss is another threat to attachment, one that clearly causes distress among children, in the short run. Children move through a four stage process akin to grief when they are separated from or lose an attachment figure. The process includes (1) numbed responsiveness, (2) yearning and protest, (3) disorganization and despair, and ultimately (4), reorganization and detachment or loss of interest in the former attachment figure (Bowlby, 1979). However, there is considerable controversy about the consequences of separation, loss, and detachment. Bowlby (1973) asserted that detachment causes dependence, which, in turn, increases the risk for depression as the child's needs go unfulfilled in subsequent relationships. Critics suggest, however, that what Bowlby called detachment is really an indication of children's adjustment to the new circumstances (Rutter, 1981). This interpretation highlights children's **resilience**—their ability to "bounce back" from adversity (Masten, 2001). The resilience interpretation of children's coping with loss is consistent with research that fails to find a relationship between childhood loss and depression during adult life (Harrington & Harrison, 1999).

Psychological Factors   As with children's conduct, the regulation of children's emotions also progresses from external to internal control across the course of development. For example, attachment relationships offer security and soothe anxiety for infants and toddlers. As they grow older, however, children develop *internal working models* or expectations about relationships as extensions of their early attachment experiences (Carlson & Sroufe, 1995). **Emotion regulation** is a more general process as children learn to identify, evaluate, and control their feelings based on the reactions, attitudes, and advice of their parents and others in their social world. Anxious mothers, for example, are more anxious, less warm, more controlling, and perhaps more critical with their children, a style of interaction that can both create and fail to soothe children's fears and worries (Moore et al., 2004).

Our understanding of children's emotional development is far from complete, and only scattered research has linked troubles with emotion regulation to children's internalizing disorders. One exciting area of investigation focuses on the interactions of children and their depressed mothers (Goodman & Gotlib, 1999). *Role reversal*, where children care for the parent rather than vice versa, may be a particular problem in these interactions. Children may attempt, and inevitably fail, to improve a parent's mood, leaving them feeling excessively guilty and responsible. Researchers have found excessive guilt among 5- to 6-year-old children of depressed mothers, as well as defensiveness against guilt among 7- to 9-year-olds (Zahn-Waxler et al., 1990). Other research shows increased depression among adolescent girls who respond to parental depression either by trying to be helpful or by becoming depressed themselves (Davis et al., 2000) and increased distress in response to detailed and frequent maternal disclosures (Koerner et al., 2004).

Treatment of Internalizing Disorders

Relatively few treatments for anxiety or mood disorders have been developed or studied specifically as they apply to children. For example, medications known to alleviate depression in adults—SSRIs, tricyclics, and venlafaxine (Effexor, an atypical antidepressant) have rarely been studied among children and adolescents, and may be no more effective than placebos in treating their depression (Harrington, 2002; see Table 16–6). In fact, a recent review of published and *unpublished* data concluded the benefits of

TABLE 16–6 The Effectiveness of Biological Treatments for Adolescent Depression			
INTERVENTION	**STRENGTH OF RECOMMENDATION**	**QUALITY OF EVIDENCE**	**COMMENTS**
Serotonin-specific reuptake inhibitors	✓	B	Three randomized controlled trials
Tricyclic antidepressants	✗✗	A–	Second line in older adolescents
Venlafaxine	✗✓	B–	One randomized controlled trial
Electroconvulsive therapy	✗✓	D	Very severe cases

Recommendation: ✓✓✓ (good supporting evidence) through ✓✗ (uncertain evidence) to ✗✗✗ (good evidence to reject).

Quality: A (five independent, systematic randomized trials with consistent results) through C (systematic open studies) to E (opinion of respected authority).

Biological treatments for depression in children and adolescents have been studied rarely, and existing evidence provides little support for their effectiveness.

Source: R. Harrington, 2002, Affective disorders. In M. Rutter & E. Taylor (Eds.), *Child and Adolescent Psychiatry,* 4th ed., p. 472. Oxford: Blackwell. Copyright © 2002. Reprinted by permission of Blackwell Publishing Ltd.

antidepressants for children and adolescents have been overestimated (and perhaps overstated by drug companies), and only fluoxetine (Prozac) has demonstrated effectiveness (Whittington et al., 2004). The lack of research is particularly troubling, since antidepressants are second only to psychostimulants as the most commonly prescribed psychotropic drugs for children and adolescents (Zito et al., 2000).

Even more important concerns come from the possibility that antidepressants increase suicidal risk in adolescents, a worry substantial enough that the FDA required manufacturers to place a "black box" warning on the medications in 2004. Prescriptions to children and adolescents declined 10% in the year surrounding the controversy, which remains unresolved scientifically (*Washington Post,* February 2, 2005). One benefit of this furor is that treatments for troubled children are likely to be studied more on children in the future, instead of simply assuming that what works for adults will work for children too.

Researchers already have begun to correct the neglect of treatment research on children's internalizing disorders. Some forms of cognitive behavior therapy and interpersonal therapy show promise for treating children's depression (Harrington, 2002), and cognitive behavior therapy and family therapy have produced positive results in treating children's anxiety (Barrett, Dadds, & Rapee, 1996; Beidel, Turner, & Morris, 2000; Kendall, 1994; Silverman et al., 1999), including substantial benefits 6 to 7 years after treatment (Barrett et al., 2001; Kendall et al., 2004). Imipramine in combination with cognitive behavior therapy may be more effective in treating school refusal than therapy alone (Bernstein et al., 2000), and Luvox helps mixed anxiety in children (RUPP Anxiety Group, 2001). Perhaps the most clearly established finding is that both clomipramine and SSRIs are helpful in treating children with obsessive–compulsive disorders (Rapoport & Swedo, 2002), although exposure and response prevention, perhaps in combination with medication, is the treatment of choice for children with OCD, as it is for adults (Marsh et al., 2004).

Recent advances are promising, but research is sorely needed on developmentally appropriate interventions with carefully diagnosed samples of children with internalizing disorders (Weisz

What does research say about the effectiveness and potential dangers of treating depressed children with medication?

In hearings held by the U.S. Food and Drug Administration in 2005, this mother blamed the suicide of her 12-year-old girl on antidepressant medication.

& Hawley, 2002). Two recent reviews of the literature found that no treatment of childhood depression met accepted criteria as "well-established" (Kaslow & Thompson, 1998), and only one treatment was "well-established" as effective for anxiety disorders (Ollendick & King, 1998). It *is* easy to overlook children with internalizing problems.

Course and Outcome   Until recently, psychologists believed that children "outgrew" internalizing problems. Prospective research demonstrates, however, that some internalizing disorders persist over time. Specific fears tend to be relatively short-lived, but more complex disorders, such as depression (Harrington et al., 1990; Kovacs et al., 1984) and obsessive–compulsive disorder (March, Leonard, & Swedo, 1995), are likely to continue from childhood into adolescence and adult life. Childhood depression also predicts a six-fold increase in the risk for suicide in young adults (Harrington, 2002). Thus the prognosis is not optimistic for a child who has a full-blown mood or anxiety disorder, and the need to develop more effective treatments is pressing.

---

getting help

After reading this chapter, you might be wondering about your own mental health during your childhood. If so, your first reaction, as always, should be to caution yourself about the "medical student's syndrome": the tendency to diagnose yourself with every new disorder as you learn about it. Most psychological disorders are on a continuum with normal behavior, and most of us struggle at some time or other with a short attention span, restlessness, difficulty in learning, or moodiness. Still, we urge you to consider getting help if you are deeply concerned that you may have ADHD, a learning disorder, or long-hidden depression. Or perhaps you are struggling to come to grips with a very difficult childhood experience, anything from your parents' divorce to abuse. A first step could be to contact your college's mental health or counseling center, if you have one. Or you may want to begin by talking with an advisor, professor, or dean at your school. Many schools also have evaluation centers that offer testing for learning disabilities or other academic-related problems.

Instead of wondering about yourself, you may be more concerned about a younger brother or sister, or perhaps a child you are working with as a volunteer. If so, you may want to begin your search for information and help at the Web site of the National Institute of Child Health and Human Development. An excellent book for parents or teachers or student volunteers working with children with attention-deficit/hyperactivity disorder is Russell Barkley's *Taking Charge of ADHD.* For dealing with children who have ODD or other behavior problems, or simply for help with managing children, Rex Forehand and Nicholas Long's book, *Parenting the Strong-Willed Child* offers a lot of sound, practical advice. Martin Seligman's engaging book, *The Optimistic Child,* focuses on the prevention of depression in children. Katharine Manassis' *Keys to Parenting Your Anxious Child* offers helpful advice about dealing with children who are anxious generally and not necessarily suffering from an anxiety disorder.

Playing a game with a child is something else you may want to consider, especially for a child you know well or with whom you are working. The Feelings Company sells therapeutic games online; simply looking through the games may give you some creative ideas for making up your own. For example, you could make up cards with different feeling words (sad, mad, scared), facial expressions, or leading questions (When was the last time you felt really, really sad?). You could make the game on your own or together with the child.

What if you know a child or an adolescent who you think might need professional help? If the young person has confided in you, that's a great start. You can do a lot by being a caring friend or sibling and a good role model. But you also want to encourage a child with an internalizing problem to confide in a parent—if not about the details of the problems, at least about the child's interest in getting help. Or you may know a parent who is looking to find help for a child with an externalizing disorder. In either case, asking for names from a teacher or school counselor is a good place to start. In fact, the child's school may be able to—or required to—provide free services for a troubled student. Another option is the child's pediatrician, who can prescribe psychostimulants if appropriate, or make a referral to a mental health professional for therapy or perhaps a more specialized medication evaluation.

SUMMARY

Psychological problems that arise more commonly among children than adults are listed in the DSM-IV-TR category "Disorders Usually First Diagnosed in Infancy, Childhood, or Adolescence." **Externalizing disorders** create difficulties for the child's external world, where children fail to control their behavior according to the expectations of others. **Attention-deficit/hyperactivity disorder (ADHD)** is particularly noticeable in school and is characterized by inattention, overactivity, and impulsivity. **Oppositional defiant disorder (ODD)** is characterized by negative, hostile, and defiant behavior and is also common among school-aged children. **Conduct disorder (CD)** is similar to ODD, except the rule violations are much more serious and it is more common among adolescents than younger children.

Internalizing disorders primarily affect the child's internal world, for example, excessive anxiety or sadness. DSM-IV-TR does not include a list of internalizing disorders but instead notes that children may qualify for many "adult" diagnoses, such as anxiety or mood disorders. DSM-IV-TR does include 26 additional childhood disorders, such as **learning disorder** and **separation anxiety disorder.** Some of these disorders are relatively rare; other categories are questionable in terms of their status as "mental disorders."

At least 12 percent of the 63 million children living in the United States suffer from a mental disorder. Boys are more likely to have externalizing problems during childhood, but girls have more internalizing in adolescence and early adult life. Family adversity is an important risk factor for externalizing problems. Teen suicide rates surged until recently, but have declined over the last few years.

Parents are most effective when they are **authoritative:** loving and firm in disciplining their children. **Coercion** is a parenting problem that occurs when parents reinforce children's misbehavior by giving in to their demands. Conflict and inconsistent discipline are other parenting problems that may arise when parents are unhappily married or divorced. Other social factors that contribute to externalizing problems include television violence, deviant peer groups, poverty, and societal attitudes. The etiology of internalizing disorders in children has been studied inadequately, but may involve problems with attachments.

Biological factors in ADHD include **temperament,** neuropsychological abnormalities, and especially genetics. Genetics also contribute to ODD and CD, and may also affect children's reactions to difficult life experiences. Lack of self-control, a tendency to overattribute aggressive intentions to others, and less developed moral reasoning are some of the psychological characteristics related to externalizing disorders. Insecure working models of attachment or problems with emotion regulation may foreshadow the development of internalizing problems.

The most promising treatments for externalizing disorders include **psychostimulants** for attention-deficit/hyperactivity disorder, **behavioral family therapy** for oppositional defiant disorder, and multisystemic family therapy for conduct disorders and **juvenile delinquency.** Few treatments for anxiety or mood disorders (including widely used antidepressants) have been developed or tested specifically for children, but recent research shows that cognitive behavior therapy and perhaps some medications can help children's anxiety disorders. The continuity of both externalizing and internalizing disorders from childhood to adult life is one reason psychologists need to develop more effective treatments for troubled children.

KEY TERMS

Go to www.prenhall.com/oltmanns for online quizzes, interactive flash cards, PowerPoint presentations, and chapter reviews.

17

Adjustment Disorders and Life-Cycle Transitions

© Jane Sterrett

Glossary

Abnormal psychology The application of psychological science to the study of mental disorders. Includes investigation of the causes and treatment of psychopathological conditions.

Abstinence violation effect The guilt and perceived loss of control that the person feels whenever he or she slips and finds himself or herself returning to drug use after an extended period of abstinence.

Acquired immune deficiency syndrome (AIDS) A disease caused by the human immunodeficiency virus (HIV) that attacks the immune system and leaves the patient susceptible to unusual infections.

Actuarial interpretation Analysis of test results based on an explicit set of rules derived from empirical research.

Acute stress disorder (ASD) A new category of mental disorder in DSM-IV that is defined as a reaction occurring within 4 weeks following a traumatic event and is characterized by dissociative symptoms, reexperiencing, avoidance, and marked anxiety or arousal. Contrasts with posttraumatic stress disorder, which either lasts longer or has a delayed onset.

Adjustment disorder A DSM-IV classification designating the development of clinically significant symptoms in response to stress in which the symptoms are not severe enough to warrant classification as another mental disorder.

Affect The pattern of observable behaviors that are associated with subjective feelings. People express affect through changes in their facial expressions, the pitch of their voices, and their hand and body movements.

Ageism A number of misconceptions and prejudices about aging and older adults.

Agnosia ("perception without meaning") The inability to identify objects. The person's sensory functions are unimpaired, but he or she is unable to recognize the source of stimulation.

Agoraphobia An exaggerated fear of being in situations from which escape might be difficult. Literally means "fear of the marketplace," and is sometimes described as fear of public spaces.

Allegiance effect A characterization of psychotherapy outcome research such that investigators commonly find the most effective treatment is the one to which they hold a theoretical allegiance.

Alogia A form of speech disturbance found in schizophrenia. Can include reductions in the amount of speech (poverty of speech) or speech that does not convey meaningful information (poverty of content of speech).

Alzheimer's disease A form of dementia in which cognitive impairment appears gradually and deterioration is progressive. A definite diagnosis of Alzheimer's desease requires the observation of two specific types of brain lesions: neurofibrillary tangles and senile plaques.

Amenorrhea The absence of at least three consecutive menstrual cycles; a defining symptom of anorexia nervosa in females.

Amnestic disorder A form of cognitive disorder characterized by memory impairments that are more limited or circumscribed than those seen in dementia or delirium.

Amniocentesis The extraction of fluid from the amniotic sac in order to test for chromosomal and genetic defects in the developing fetus.

Amyloid plaques A central core of homogeneous protein material know as beta-amyloid found in large numbers in the cerebral cortex of patients with Alzheimer's disease, but they are not unique to that condition.

Analogue study A research procedure in which the investigator studies behaviors that resemble mental disorders or isolated features of mental disorders. Usually employed in situations in which the investigator hopes to gain greater experimental control over the independent variable.

Androgyny The possession of both "female" and "male" gender-role characteristics.

Anhedonia The inability to experience pleasure. In contrast to blunted affect, which refers to the lack of outward expression, anhedonia is a lack of positive subjective feelings.

Anorexia nervosa A type of eating disorder characterized by the refusal to maintain a minimally normal body weight along with other symptoms related to body image.

Anterograde amnesia The inability to learn or remember new material after a particular point in time.

Antisocial personality disorder A pervasive and persistent disregard for, and frequent violation of, the rights of other people. Also known as *psychopathy*. In DSM-IV, it is defined in terms of a persistent pattern of irresponsible and antisocial behavior that begins during childhood or adolescence and continues into the adult years.

Anxiety A diffuse emotional reaction that is out of proportion to threats from the environment. Rather than being directed toward the person's present, anxiety is typically associated with the anticipation of future problems.

Anxious attachment An insecure relationship in which an infant or child shows ambivalence about seeking reassurance or security from an attachment figure.

Aphasia The loss or impairment of previously acquired abilities in language comprehension or production that cannot be explained by sensory or motor defects or by diffuse brain dysfunction.

Apraxia The loss of a previously acquired ability to perform purposeful movements in response to verbal commands. The problem cannot be explained by muscle weakness or simple incoordination.

Asperger's disorder A subtype of pervasive developmental disorder (new in DSM-IV) that is identical to autism (oddities in social interaction, stereotyped behavior) with the exception that there is no clinically significant delay in language.

Assessment The process of gathering and organizing information about a person's behavior.

Attachments Selective bonds that develop between infants and their caregivers, usually their parents, and are theorized to be related to later development. Analogous to the process of imprinting, which has been observed in many animals.

Attention deficit Inattention characterized by distractibility, frequent shifts from one uncompleted activity to another, careless mistakes, and/or poor organization or effort. A key symptom of attention-deficit/hyperactivity disorder.

Attention-deficit/hyperactivity disorder A psychological disorder of childhood characterized by hyperactivity, inattention, and impulsivity. Typically has an onset by the early school years.

Attribution Perceived causes; people's beliefs about cause–effect relations.

Atypical antipsychotic A type of medication that is beneficial for psychotic patients but does not produce extrapyramidal motor side effects and may not be with increased risk of tardive dyskinesia.

Authoritative parenting A style of parenting that is both loving and firm and is often used by parents of well-adjusted children.

Autism Literally, "absorption in one's own mental activity." Formally, a severe pervasive developmental disorder characterized by profound problems in social interaction, communication, and stereotyped behavior, interests, and activities (see also *autistic disorder*).

Autistic disorder A severe form of pervasive developmental disorder characterized by oddities in social interaction (autistic aloneness), communication impairments, and stereotyped behavior, interests, and activities.

Autonomic nervous system The division of the peripheral nervous system that regulates the functions of various bodily organs such as the heart and stomach. The actions of the autonomic nervous system are largely involuntary, and it has two branches, the sympathetic and parasympathetic nervous systems.

Aversion therapy A classical conditioning technique for attempting to eliminate unwanted behavior by pairing an unpleasant (aversive) stimulus with the behavior—for example, inducing nausea when alcohol is consumed.

Avoidant personality disorder An enduring pattern of thinking and behavior that is characterized by pervasive social discomfort, fear of negative evaluation, and timidity. People with this disorder tend to be socially isolated outside of family circles. They want to be liked by others, but they are easily hurt by even minimal signs of disapproval from other people.

Avolition (lack of volition or will) A negative symptom of schizophrenia involving a loss of willpower, indecisiveness, and ambivalence. The person becomes apathetic and ceases to engage in purposeful actions.

Balanced placebo design A research design that combines the placebo and antiplacebo methods. It can be used to assess the effect of alcohol, the effect of expectations, and the interaction of alcohol by expectation.

Barbiturates Drugs that depress activities of the central nervous system; mostly for sedation.

Base rates Population frequencies. Relative base rates set statistical limits on the degree to which two variables can be associated with each other.

Battered woman syndrome A controversial classification of the common psychological effects of spousal abuse. Includes a tension-building phase leading up to violence, the battering incident itself, and a stage of loving contrition, during which the batterer apologizes. According to some experts, this induces learned helplessness in battered women.

Behavioral coding system (also known as a *formal observation schedule*) An observational assessment procedure that focuses on the frequency of specific behavioral events.

Behavioral family therapy (BFT) A form of family treatment that may include several variations, but always trains parents to use operant conditioning as a way of improving child discipline.

Behavioral gerontology A subspecialty within behavioral medicine developed specifically for studying and treating the behavioral components of illness among older adults.

Behavioral marital therapy A variation on couples therapy that emphasizes the partners' moment-to-moment interaction, particularly their exchange of positive and negative behaviors, their style of communication, and their strategies for solving problems.

Behavioral medicine A multidisciplinary field concerned with studying and treating the behavioral components of physical illness.

Behavior genetics The study of broad genetic contributions to the development of normal and abnormal behavior.

Behaviorism The belief within scientific psychology that observable behaviors, not unobservable cognitive or emotional states, are the appropriate focus of psychological study.

Benzodiazepines Group of drugs that have potent hypnotic, sedative, and anxiolytic action (also called antianxiety drugs).

Bereavement Grieving in response to the death of a loved one.

Beta-amyloid Protein material that forms the core of senile plaques, a type of brain lesion found in patients with Alzheimer's disease.

Binge eating Eating an amount of food in a fixed period of time that is clearly larger than most people would eat under similar circumstances. One part of the eating disorder of bulimia nervosa.

Binge eating disorder A controversial diagnosis defined by repeated episodes of binge eating but in the absence of compensatory behavior; included in an appendix of DSM-IV.

Biofeedback Behavioral medicine treatment that uses laboratory equipment to monitor physiological processes (that generally occur outside of conscious awareness) and provide feedback about them. Hypothesized to help patients to gain conscious control over problematic physiological processes such as hypertension.

Biological reductionism The assumption that biological explanations are more useful than psychological explanations because they deal with smaller units—with brain chemistry, for example, instead of emotional experience.

Biopsychosocial model A view of the etiology of mental disorders which assumes that disorders can best be understood in terms of the interaction of biological, psychological, and social systems.

Bipolar mood disorder A form of mood disorder in which the person experiences episodes of mania as well as episodes of depression.

Blunted affect A flattening or restriction of the person's nonverbal display of emotional responses. Blunted patients fail to exhibit signs of emotion or feeling.

Body dysmorphic disorder A type of somatoform disorder characterized by constant preoccupation with some imagined defect in physical appearance.

Body image A cognitive and affective evaluation of one's weight and shape, often a critical one.

Borderline personality disorder An enduring pattern of thinking and behavior whose essential feature is a pervasive instability in mood, self-image, and interpersonal relationships. Manifestations of this disorder include frantic efforts to avoid real or imagined abandonment. People who fit this description frequently hold opinions of significant others that vacillate between unrealistically positive and negative extremes.

Boundaries Rules defining a relationship, particularly the rules that separate a third person from an individual or another relationship. For example,

the boundary of the marital relationship is defined, in part, by the limited discussion of intimate topics outside the relationship.

Brief psychotic disorder A diagnostic category in DSM-IV that includes people who exhibit psychotic symptoms for at least 1 day but no more than 1 month. After the symptoms are resolved, the person returns to the same level of functioning that had been achieved prior to the psychotic episode.

Bulimia nervosa A type of eating disorder characterized by repeated episodes of binge eating followed by inappropriate compensatory behaviors (such as self-induced vomiting) together with other symptoms related to eating and body image.

Cardiovascular disease (CVD) A group of disorders that affect the heart and circulatory system. Hypertension (high blood pressure) and coronary heart disease are the most important forms of CVD.

Cardiovascular reactivity A measure of the intensity of an individual's cardiovascular reactions to stress in the laboratory; a predictor of future cardiovascular disease.

Case study A careful description and analysis of the problems experienced by one person.

Catatonia Motor symptoms that can include either immobility and marked muscular rigidity or excitement and overactivity.

Catatonic type A subtype of schizophrenia that is characterized by symptoms of motor immobility (including rigidity and posturing) or excessive and purposeless motor activity.

Categorical approach to classification A view of classification based on the assumption that there are qualitative differences between normal and abnormal behavior as well as between one form of abnormal behavior and other forms of abnormal behavior.

Central nervous system The major communication system in the body, comprising the brain and the spinal cord.

Cerebral cortex The uneven surface of the brain that lies just underneath the skull and controls and integrates sophisticated memory, sensory, and motor functions.

Cerebral hemispheres The two major structures of the forebrain and the site of most sensory, emotional, and cognitive processes. The functions of the cerebral hemispheres are lateralized. In general, the left cerebral hemisphere is involved in language and related functions, and the right side is involved in spatial organization and analysis.

Child abuse A legal decision that a parent or other responsible adult has inflicted damage or offered inadequate care to a child; may include physical abuse, sexual abuse, neglect, and psychological abuse.

Child custody A legal decision, especially common in separation and divorce, that involves determining where children will reside and how parents will share legal rights and responsibilities for child rearing.

Chorea Unusual, involuntary muscle movements associated with disorders such as Huntington's disease.

Chromosomes Chainlike structures found in the nucleus of cells that carry genes and information about heredity. Humans normally have 23 pairs of chromosomes.

Civil commitment The involuntary hospitalization of the mentally ill; the decision typically is justified based on dangerousness to self or others (or inability to care for self).

Classical conditioning Pavlov's form of learning through association. A conditioned response eventually is elicited by a conditioned stimulus after repeated pairings with an unconditioned stimulus (which produces an unconditioned response).

Classification system A system for grouping together objects or organisms that share certain properties in common. In psychopathology, the set of categories in DSM-IV that describes mental disorders.

Client-centered therapy Carl Rogers's humanistic therapy that follows the client's lead. Therapists offer warmth, empathy, and genuineness, but clients solve their own problems.

Clinical depression A syndrome of depression in which a depressed mood is accompanied by several other symptoms, such as fatigue, loss of energy, difficulty in sleeping, and changes in appetite. Clinical depression also involves a variety of changes in thinking and overt behavior.

Clinical psychology The profession and academic discipline that is concerned with the application of psychological science to the assessment and treatment of mental disorders.

Coercion A pattern of interaction in which unwitting parents positively reinforce children's misbehavior (by giving in to their demands), and children negatively reinforce parents' capitulation (by ending their obnoxious behavior).

Cognitive behavior therapy The expansion of the scope of behavior therapy to include cognition and research on human information processing. Includes various general techniques, such as Beck's cognitive therapy and Ellis's RET.

Cognitive therapy A psychotherapy technique and important part of cognitive behavior therapy that was developed by Aaron Beck specifically as a treatment. Beck's cognitive therapy involves challenging negative cognitive distortions through a technique called collaborative empiricism.

Cohort A group whose members share some feature in common, particularly their date of birth.

Cohort effect Differences that distinguish one cohort from another. Cohorts share some feature in common, especially their date of birth, and cohort effects often distinguish people born in one time period (e.g., the 1960s) from those born in another.

Comorbidity The simultaneous manifestation of more than one disorder.

Competence Defendants' ability to understand legal proceedings and act rationally in relation to them. Competence evaluations can take place at different points in the legal process, but competence to stand trial (the ability to participate in one's own defense) is particularly important.

Compulsion A repetitive, ritualistic behavior that is aimed at the reduction of anxiety and distress or the prevention of some dreaded event. Compulsions are considered by the person to be senseless or irrational. The person feels compelled to perform the compulsion; he or she attempts to resist but cannot.

Concordance Agreement. In behavior genetic studies, concordance occurs when a relative has the same disorder as a proband (index case); for example, when twin pairs either both have the same disorder or both are free from the disorder.

Conduct disorder (CD) A psychological disorder of childhood that is defined primarily by behavior that is illegal as well as antisocial.

Confidentiality The ethical obligation not to reveal private communications in psychotherapy and in other professional contacts between mental health professionals and their clients.

Construct validity The overall strength of the network of relations that have been observed among variables that are used to define a construct. The extent to which the construct possesses some systematic meaning.

Contingency management A form of operant behavior therapy that focuses on directly changing rewards and punishments in order to increase desired and decrease undesired behavior. A contingency is the relationship between a behavior and its consequences; contingency management involves changing this relationship.

Control group The group of participants in an experiment that receives no treatment or perhaps a placebo treatment. Participants in the control group are compared with participants in the experimental group (who are given an active treatment).

Controlled drinking A controversial goal for some alcohol abusers. This concept refers to moderate consumption of alcohol in a pattern that avoids drinking to the point of intoxication.

Conversion disorder A type of somatoform disorder characterized by physical symptoms that often mimic those found in neurological diseases, such as blindness, numbing, or paralysis. The symptoms often make no anatomic sense.

Coping An attempt to adapt to stress by changing the stressor or by altering one's thinking or emotional response.

Coronary heart disease (CHD) A group of diseases of the heart that includes angina pectoris (chest pains) and myocardial infarction (heart attack).

Correlational study A scientific research method in which the relation between two factors (their co-relation) is studied in a systematic fashion. Has the advantage of practicality, as correlations between many variables can be studied in the real world, but also has the disadvantage that "correlation does not mean causation."

Correlation coefficient A number that always ranges between −1.00 and +1.00 and indicates the strength and direction of the relation between two variables. A higher absolute value indicates a stronger relation, while a correlation coefficient of 0 indicates no relation. The sign indicates the direction of the correlation.

Cortisol A corticosteroid secreted by the adrenal cortex. Cortisol is known as the "stress hormone" because its release is so closely linked with stress.

Countertransference The therapist's own feelings toward the client, particularly as described in psychoanalysis.

Couples therapy Partners who are involved in an intimate relationship are seen together in psychotherapy; sometimes called *marital therapy* or *marriage counseling*. Improving communication and negotiation are common goals.

Creutzfeldt-Jakob disease A type of dementia caused by a specific viral infection.

Criminal responsibility A legal concept that holds a person responsible for committing a crime if he or she (a) has been proven to have committed the act and (b) was legally sane at the time.

Critical incident stress debriefing An early intervention following trauma involving a single 1- to 5-hour group meeting offered within one to three days following a disaster. CISD is used frequently, although data supporting its effectiveness are limited.

Cross-cultural psychology The scientific study of ways that human behavior and mental processes are influenced by social and cultural factors.

Cross-sectional study A research design in which subjects are studied only at one point in time. (Contrast with *longitudinal study*.)

Culture-bound syndrome Patterns of erratic or unusual thinking and behavior that have been identified in diverse societes around the world and do not fit easily into the other diagnostic categories that are listed in the main body of DSM-IV-TR.

Cultural-familial retardation Typically mild mental retardation that runs in families and is linked with poverty. Thought to be the most common cause of mental retardation. There is controversy about the relative roles of genes or psychosocial disadvantage.

Culture The shared way of life of a group or people; a complex system of accumulated knowledge that helps the people in a particular society adapt to their environment.

Cybernetics A communication and control process that uses feedback loops in order to adjust progress toward a goal, for example, the operation of a thermostat.

Cyclothymia A chronic, less severe form of bipolar disorder. The bipolar equivalent of dysthymia.

Defense mechanisms Unconscious processes that service the ego and reduce conscious anxiety by distorting anxiety-producing memories, emotions, and impulses—for example, projection, displacement, or rationalization.

Deinstitutionalization The movement to treat the mentally ill and mentally retarded in communities rather than in large mental hospitals.

Delirium A confusional state that develops over a short period of time and is often associated with agitation and hyperactivity. The primary symptom is clouding of consciousness or reduced awareness of one's surroundings.

Delusion An obviously false and idiosyncratic belief that is rigidly held in spite of its preposterous nature.

Delusional disorder Describes persons who do not meet the full symptomatic criteria for schizophrenia, but who are preoccupied for at least 1 month with delusions that are not bizarre.

Dementia A gradually worsening loss of memory and related cognitive functions, including the use of language as well as reasoning and decision making.

Dependent personality disorder An enduring pattern of dependent and submissive behavior. These people are exceedingly dependent on other people for advice and reassurance. Often unable to make everyday decisions on their own, they feel anxious and helpless when they are alone.

Dependent variable The outcome that is hypothesized to vary according to manipulations in the independent variable in an experiment.

Depersonalization disorder A type of dissociative disorder characterized by severe and persistent feelings of being detached from oneself (depersonalization experiences). For example, the repeated and profound sensation of floating above your body and observing yourself act.

Depressed mood Depressed feelings such as of disappointment and despair, but which are not yet necessarily part of a clinical syndrome.

Depression Can refer to a *symptom* (subjective feelings of sadness), a *mood* (sustained and pervasive feelings of despair), or to a clinical *syndrome* (in which the presence of a depressed mood is accompanied by several additional symptoms, such as fatigue, loss of energy, sleeping difficulties, and appetite changes).

Determinism The philosophical assumption (made by all psychologists except humanistic psychologists) that behavior is a potentially predictable consequence of biological, psychological, and social factors. Contrasts with the assumption that behavior is the product of free will.

Detoxification The process of short-term medical care (medication, rest, diets, fluids, and so on) during removal of a drug upon which a person has become dependent. The aim is to minimize withdrawal symptoms.

Developmental deviation Significant departures from age-appropriate norms in some specific area of functioning. Some developmental deviations are considered disorders in their own right.

Developmental norms Behavior that is typical for children of a given age.

Developmental psychopathology A new approach to abnormal psychology that emphasizes the importance of normal development to understanding abnormal behavior.

Developmental stage A distinct period of development focused on certain central "tasks" and marked by boundaries defined by changing age or social expectations.

Diagnosis The process of determining the nature of a person's disorder. In the case of psychopathology, deciding that a person fits into a particular diagnostic category, such as schizophrenia or major depressive disorder.

Diathesis A predisposition to disorder. Also known as *vulnerability*. A diathesis only causes abnormal behavior when it is combined with a stress or challenging experience.

Dimensional approach to classification A view of classification based on the assumption that behavior is distributed on a continuum from normal to abnormal. Also includes the assumption that differences between one type of behavior and another are quantitative rather than qualitative in nature.

Disorganized speech (also known as *formal thought disorder*) Severe disruptions of verbal communication, involving the form of the person's speech.

Disorganized type A subtype of schizophrenia (formerly known as *hebephrenia*) that is characterized by disorganized speech, disorganized behavior, and flat or inappropriate affect. If delusions or hallucinations are present, their content is not well organized.

Dissociation The separation of mental processes such as memory or consciousness that normally are integrated. Normal dissociative experiences include fleeting feelings of unreality and *déjà vu* experiences—the feeling that an event has happened before. Extreme dissociative experiences characterize dissociative disorders.

Dissociative amnesia A type of dissociative disorder characterized by the sudden inability to recall extensive and important personal information. The onset often is sudden and may occur in response to trauma or extreme stress.

Dissociative disorders A category of psychological disorders characterized by persistent, maladaptive disruptions in the integration of memory, consciousness, or identity. Examples include dissociative fugue and dissociative identity disorder (multiple personality).

Dissociative fugue A rare dissociative disorder characterized by sudden, unplanned travel, the inability to remember details about the past, and confusion about identity or the assumption of a new identity. The onset typically follows a traumatic event.

Dissociative identity disorder (DID) An unusual dissociative disorder characterized by the existence of two or more distinct personalities in a single individual (also known as *multiple personality disorder*). At least two personalities repeatedly take control over the person's behavior, and some personalities have limited or no memory of the other.

Distorted body image A perceptual inaccuracy in evaluating body size and shape that sometimes is found in anorexia nervosa.

Diversion A practice of directing problem youth away from the juvenile justice system and into some alternative treatment or program. For example, a juvenile offender may be referred to counseling instead of having a hearing held in court.

Divorce mediation A procedure in which former partners attempt to resolve child custody or other disputes that arise from a divorce with the help of an impartial third party (a mediator).

Dizygotic (DZ) twins Fraternal twins produced from separate fertilized eggs. Like all siblings, DZ twins share an average of 50 percent of their genes.

Dominance The hierarchical ordering of a social group into more and less powerful members. Dominance rankings are indexed by the availability of uncontested privileges.

Dose-response effects Different treatment responses to different dosages of a medication.

Double blind, placebo-controlled study A study in which neither the therapist nor the patient knows whether the patient receives the real treatment (for example, a medication) or a placebo.

Down syndrome A chromosomal disorder that is the most common known biological cause of mental retardation. It is caused by an extra chromosome (usually on the 21st pair) and associated with a characteristic physical appearance.

Drug of abuse (also called a *psychoactive substance*) A chemical substance that alters a person's mood, level of perception, or brain functioning.

Dualism The philosophical view that the mind and body are separate. Dates to the writings of the philosopher René Descartes, who attempted to balance the dominant religious views of his times with emerging scientific reasoning. Descartes argued that many human functions have biological explanations, but some human experiences have no somatic representation. Thus, he argued for a distinction—a dualism—between mind and body.

Dyskinesia Involuntary movements, such as tics, chorea, or tremors, that are often associated with certain types of dementia.

Dyspareunia Persistent genital pain during or after sexual intercourse. The problem can occur in either men or women.

Dysphoria Unpleasant mood, often associated with depression.

Dysthymia One of the mood disorders; a form of mild depression characterized by a chronic course (the person is seldom without symptoms).

Eating disorders A category of psychological disorders characterized by severe disturbances in eating behavior, specifically anorexia nervosa and bulimia nervosa.

Eclectic The term used to describe the therapeutic approach of a group of mental health professionals who do not identify themselves with a specific paradigm, but instead use different treatments for different disorders.

Ego One of Freud's three central personality structures. In Freudian theory, the ego must deal with reality as it attempts to fulfill id impulses as well as superego demands. The ego operates on the reality principle, and much of the ego resides in conscious awareness.

Ego analysis Originated in the work of different therapists trained in Freudian psychoanalysis, but who focus much more on the ego than on the id.

Ego analysts are concerned with the patient's dealings with the external world.

Electroconvulsive therapy (ECT) A treatment that involves the deliberate induction of a convulsion by passing electricity through one or both hemispheres of the brain. Modern ECT uses restraints, medication, and carefully controlled electrical stimulation to minimize adverse consequences. Can be an effective treatment for severe depression, especially following the failure of other approaches.

Emotion A state of arousal that is defined by subjective feeling states, such as sadness, anger, and disgust. Emotions are often accompanied by physiological changes, such as in heart rate and respiration rate.

Emotion-focused coping Internally oriented coping in an attempt to alter one's emotional or cognitive responses to a stressor.

Emotional processing A process of facing and coming to accept powerful emotions following trauma. Emotional processing involves confronting fear, diminishing its intensity, and coming to some new understanding of the trauma and its consequences.

Emotion regulation The process of learning to control powerful emotions according to the demands of a situation. Children learn to regulate their emotions initially through interactions with their parents and others in their social world, and eventually children learn to regulate their own emotions.

Empathy Emotional understanding. Empathy involves understanding others' unique feelings and perspectives. Highlighted by Rogers but basic to most forms of psychotherapy.

Encopresis Inappropriately controlled defecation among children old enough to maintain control of their bowels.

Endocrine system A collection of glands found at various locations throughout the body, including the ovaries or testes and the pituitary, thyroid, and adrenal glands. Releases hormones that sometimes act as neuromodulators and affect responses to stress. Also important in physical growth and development.

Endorphin The term is a contraction formed from the words *endogenous* (meaning "within") and *morphine*. Endorphins are relatively short chains of amino acids, or neuropeptides, that are naturally synthesized in the brain and are closely related to morphine (an opioid) in terms of their pharmacological properties.

Enmeshed family Families whose members are overly involved in one another's lives.

Enuresis Inappropriately controlled urination (during sleep or while awake) among children old enough to maintain control of their bladder.

Epidemiology The scientific study of the frequency and distribution of disorders within a population.

Equifinality A concept from systems theory that states that the same outcome (e.g., a psychological disorder) may have different causes. That is, there

may be not one cause but multiple pathways that lead to a given outcome (disorder).

Erectile dysfunction Difficulty experienced by a man in obtaining an erection that is sufficient to accomplish intercourse or maintaining an erection long enough to satisfy himself or his partner during intercourse.

Essential hypertension A form of high blood pressure in which the hypertension is the principal disorder, as opposed to hypertension that is secondary to a known illness such as a kidney disorder.

Estrogen The female sex hormone.

Etiology The causes or origins of a disorder.

Euphoria An exaggerated feeling of physical and emotional well-being, typically associated with manic episodes in bipolar mood disorder.

Exhibitionism One of the paraphilias, characterized by distress over, or acting on, urges to expose one's genitals to an unsuspecting stranger.

Experiment A powerful scientific method that allows researchers to determine cause-and-effect relations. Key elements include random assignment, the manipulation of the independent variable, and careful measurement of the dependent variable.

Experimental group The group of participants in an experiment that receives a treatment that is hypothesized to cause some measured effect. Participants in the experimental group are compared with untreated participants in a control group.

Experimental hypothesis A new prediction made by an investigator to be tested in an experiment.

Experimental method The powerful scientific method that allows researchers to determine cause and effect by randomly assigning participants to experimental and control groups. In an experiment, researchers systematically manipulate independent variables and observe their effects on dependent variables.

Expert witness An individual stipulated as an expert on some subject matter who, because of his or her expertise, is allowed to testify about matters of opinion and not just matters of fact. For example, mental health professionals may serve as expert witnesses concerning a defendant's sanity.

Expressed emotion (EE) A concept that refers to a collection of negative or intrusive attitudes sometimes displayed by relatives of patients who are being treated for a disorder. If at least one of a patient's relatives is hostile, critical, or emotionally overinvolved, the family environment typically is considered high in expressed emotion.

Externalizing disorders An empirically derived category of disruptive child behavior problems that create problems for the external world (for example, attention-deficit/hyperactivity disorder).

External validity Whether the findings of an experiment generalize to other people, places, and circumstances, particularly real-life situations.

Extinction The gradual elimination of a response when learning conditions change. In classical conditioning, extinction occurs when a conditioned stimulus no longer is paired with an unconditioned

stimulus. In operant conditioning, extinction occurs when the contingent is removed between behavior and its consequences.

Factitious disorder A feigned condition that, unlike malingering, is motivated by a desire to assume the sick role, not by a desire for external gain.

Family life cycle The developmental course of family relationships throughout life; most family life cycle theories mark stages and transitions with major changes in family relationships and membership.

Family therapy Treatment that might include two, three, or more family members in the psychotherapy sessions. Improving communication and negotiation are common goals, although family therapy also may be used to help well members adjust to a family member's illness.

Fear An unpleasant emotional reaction experienced in the face of real, immediate danger. It builds quickly in intensity and helps to organize the person's responses to threats from the environment.

Fetal alcohol syndrome A disorder caused by heavy maternal alcohol consumption and repeated exposure of the developing fetus to alcohol. Infants have retarded physical development, a small head, narrow eyes, cardiac defects, and cognitive impairments. Intellectual functioning ranges from mild mental retardation to intelligence with learning disabilities.

Fetishism The use of nonliving objects as a focus of sexual arousal.

Fight or flight response A response to a threat in which psychophysiological reactions mobilize the body to take action against danger.

Fixation The psychodynamic concept that psychological development is arrested at a particular age or stage. The person stops growing emotionally.

Flashbacks Reexperienced memories of past events, particularly as occurs in posttraumatic stress disorder or following use of hallucinogenic drugs.

Flooding A treatment for fears and phobias that involves exposure to the feared stimulus at full intensity. Works through extinction.

Fragile-X syndrome The second most common known biological cause of mental retardation. Transmitted genetically and indicated by a weakening or break on one arm of the X sex chromosome.

Free association A basic technique in Freudian psychoanalysis in which patients are encouraged to speak freely about whatever thoughts cross their mind; presumed to give insight into the unconscious.

Free will The capacity to make choices and freely act upon them. A philosophical counterpoint to determinism, which is the scientific assumption that behavior is a predictable consequence of internal and external events. Humanistic psychology and the American legal system assume people act out of free will.

Frotteurism One of the paraphilias, characterized by recurrent, intense sexual urges involving touching and rubbing against a nonconsenting person; it often takes place in crowded trains, buses, and elevators.

Gender identity A person's sense of himself or herself as being either male or female.

Gender identity disorder A strong and persistent identification with the opposite sex coupled with a sense of discomfort with one's anatomic sex.

Gender roles Roles associated with social expectations about gendered behavior, for example, "masculine" or "feminine" activities.

General adaptation syndrome (GAS) Selye's three stages in reaction to stress: alarm, resistance, and exhaustion.

Generalization Making accurate statements that extend beyond a specific sample to a larger population.

Generalized anxiety disorder One of the anxiety disorders, which is characterized by excessive and uncontrollable worry about a number of events or activities (such as work or school performance) and associated with symptoms of arousal (such as restlessness, muscle tension, and sleep disturbance).

General paresis (general paralysis) A set of severe symptoms including dementia, delusions of grandeur, and paralysis caused by the sexually transmitted disease syphilis. Discovery of the cause of general paresis spurred the biological model of mental illness.

Genes Ultramicroscopic units of DNA that carry information about heredity. Located on the chromosomes.

Genetic linkage A close association between two genes, typically the genetic locus associated with a disorder or a trait and the locus for a known gene. Two loci are said to be linked when they are sufficiently close together on the same chromosome.

Genotype An individual's actual genetic structure, most of which cannot be observed directly at this time.

Gerontology The multidisciplinary study of aging and older adults.

Gestalt therapy A variation of the humanistic approach to psychotherapy that underscores affective awareness and expression, genuineness, and experiencing the moment (living in the "here and now").

Grief The emotional and social process of coping with a separation or a loss, often described as proceeding in stages.

Group therapy The treatment of three or more people in a group setting, often using group relationships as a central part of therapy.

Hallucination A perceptual experience in the absence of external stimulation, such as hearing voices that aren't really there.

Hallucinogens Drugs that produce hallucinations.

Harmful dysfunction A concept used in one approach to the definition of mental disorder. A condition can be considered a mental disorder if it causes some harm to the person and if the condition results from the inability of some mental mechanism to perform its natural function.

Hashish The dried resin from the top of the female cannabis plant. Ingestion of hashish leads to a feeling of being "high" (see *marijuana*).

Health behavior A wide range of activities that are essential to promoting good health, including positive actions such as proper diet and the avoidance of negative activities such as cigarette smoking.

Health psychologist A psychologist who specializes in reducing negative health behavior (e.g., smoking) and promoting positive health behavior (e.g., exercise). Health psychology is a part of the interdisciplinary field of behavioral medicine.

Heritability The variability in a behavioral characteristic that is accounted for by genetic factors.

Heritability ratio A statistic for computing the proportion of variance in a behavioral characteristic that is accounted for by genetic factors in a given study or series of studies.

High-risk research design A longitudinal study of persons who are selected from the general population based on some identified risk factor that has a fairly high risk ratio.

Histrionic personality disorder An enduring pattern of thinking and behavior that is characterized by excessive emotionality and attention-seeking behavior. People with this disorder are self-centered, vain, and demanding. Their emotions tend to be shallow and may vacillate erratically.

Human Immunodeficiency Virus (HIV) The virus that causes AIDS and attacks the immune system, leaving the patient susceptible to infection, neurological complications, and cancers that rarely affect those with normal immune function.

Holism The assumption that the whole is more than the sum of its parts. A central tenet of systems theory, and counterpoint to reductionism.

Homeostasis The tendency to maintain a steady state. A familiar concept in biology that also is widely applicable in psychology.

Hopelessness theory A theory regarding the role of cognitive events in the etiology of depression; depression is associated with the expectation that very desirable events probably will not occur and that aversive events probably will occur regardless of what the person does.

Hormones Chemical substances that are released into the bloodstream by glands in the endocrine system. Hormones affect the functioning of distant body systems and sometimes act as neuromodulators.

Humanistic psychotherapy An approach that assumes that the most essential human quality is the ability to make choices and freely act on them (free will). Promoted as a "third force" to counteract the deterministic views of psychodynamic and the behavioral approaches to psychotherapy.

Huntington's disease A primary, differentiated dementia characterized by the presence of unusual involuntary muscle movements. Many Hunting-ton's patients also exhibit a variety of personality changes and symptoms of mental disorders, including primarily depression and anxiety.

Hyperactivity A symptom of attention-deficit/hyperactivity disorder (ADHD), often manifested as squirming, fidgeting, or restless behavior. Found across but particularly notable in structured settings.

Hypertension High blood pressure.

Hypnosis An altered state of consciousness during which hypnotized subjects are particularly susceptible to suggestion. There is considerable debate as to whether hypnosis is a unique state of consciousness or merely a form of relaxation.

Hypoactive sexual desire Diminished desire for sexual activity and reduced frequency of sexual fantasies.

Hypochondriasis A type of somatoform disorder characterized by a person's preoccupying fear or belief that he or she is suffering from a physical illness.

Hypomania An episode of increased energy that is not sufficiently severe to qualify as a full-blown manic episode.

Hypothalamus A part of the limbic system that plays a role in sensation, but more importantly it controls basic biological urges, such as eating, drinking, and activity, as well as much of the functioning of the autonomic nervous system.

Hypothesis A prediction about the expected findings in a scientific study.

Hypothetical construct A theoretical device that refers to events or states that reside within a person and are proposed to help understand or explain a person's behavior.

Hysteria An outdated but influential diagnostic category that included both somatoform and dissociative disorders. Attempts to treat hysteria had a major effect on Charcot, Freud, and Janet, among others. In Greek, *hysteria* means "uterus," a reflection of ancient speculation that hysteria was restricted to women and caused by frustrated sexual desires.

Iatrogenesis A creation of a disorder by an attempt to treat it.

Id One of Freud's three central personality structures. In Freudian theory, the id is present at birth and is the source of basic drives and motivations. The id houses biological drives (such as hunger), as well as Freud's two key psychological drives, sex and aggression. Operates according to the pleasure principle.

Identification A process wherein children not only imitate adults but also want to be like them and adopt their values. In Freudian theory, identification is to the Oedipal and Electra conflicts. In developmental psychology, a similar but broader concept than modeling.

Identity Erikson's term for the broad definition of self; in his view, identity is the product of the adolescent's struggle to answer the question "Who am I?"

Identity crisis Erikson's period of basic uncertainty about self during late adolescence and early adult life. A consequence of the psychosocial stage of identity versus role confusion.

Implicit memory Implicit memory is indicated by changes in behavior apparently based on a memory of a prior event but with nonconscious remembering of the event. *Explicit memory* is the conscious recollection of a past event.

Impulse control disorder A disorder characterized by failure to resist an impulse or a temptation to perform some pleasurable or tension-releasing act that is harmful to oneself or others; examples are pathological gambling, setting fires, and stealing.

Inappropriate affect A form of emotional disturbance seen in schizophrenia. The central features of inappropriate affect are incongruity and lack of adaptability in emotional expression.

Incest Sexual activity between close blood relatives, such as father-daughter, mother-son, or siblings.

Incidence The number of new cases of a disorder that appear in a population during a specific period of time.

Independent variable The variable in an experiment that is controlled and deliberately manipulated by the experimenter (for example, whether or not a subject receives a treatment). Affects the dependent variable.

Infarct The area of dead tissue produced by a stroke.

Informed consent A legal and ethical safeguard concerning risks in research and in treatment. Includes (a) accurate information about potential risks and benefits, (b) competence on the part of subjects/patients to understand them, and (c) the ability of subjects/patients to participate voluntarily.

Inhibited sexual arousal Difficulty experienced by a woman in achieving or maintaining genital responses, such as lubrication and swelling, that are necessary to complete sexual intercourse.

Insanity A legal term referring to a defendant's state of mind at the time of committing a crime. An insane individual is not held legally responsible for his or her actions because of a mental disease or defect.

Insanity defense An attempt to prove that a person with a mental illness did not meet the legal criteria for sanity at the time of committing a crime. The inability to tell right from wrong and an "irresistible impulse" are the two most common contemporary grounds for the defense.

Insight Self-understanding; the extent to which a person recognizes the nature (or understands the potential causes) of his or her disorder. In psychoanalysis, insight is the ultimate goal, specifically, to bring formerly unconscious material into conscious awareness.

Intelligence quotient (IQ) A measure of intellectual ability that typically has a mean of 100 and a standard deviation of 15. An individual's IQ is determined by comparisons with norms for same-aged peers.

Internalizing disorders An empirically derived category of psychological problems of childhood that affect the child more than the external world (for example, depression).

Internal validity Whether changes in the dependent variable can be accurately attributed to changes in the independent variable in an experiment, that is, there are no experimental confounds.

Interpretation A tool in psychotherapy and psychoanalysis in which the therapist suggests new meanings about a client's accounts of his or her past and present life.

Introceptive awareness Recognition of internal cues, including various emotional states as well as hunger.

In vivo desensitization A treatment for overcoming fears and phobias that involves gradual exposure to feared stimuli in real life while simultaneously maintaining a state of relaxation. Contrast with *systematic desensitization*.

Juvenile delinquency A legal term that refers to a minor who has violated the law and been judged responsible for the lawbreaking.

Kappa A statistical index of reliability (diagnostic agreement between clinicians) that reflects the proportion of agreement that occurred above and beyond that which would have occurred by chance.

Korsakoff's syndrome An amnestic disorder sometimes associated with chronic alcoholism. Memory is impaired but other cognitive functions are not.

Labeling theory A perspective on mental disorders that is primarily concerned with the social context in which abnormal behavior occurs. Labeling theory is more interested in social factors that determine whether or not a person will be given a psychiatric diagnosis than in psychological or biological reasons for the behaviors.

La belle indifference A flippant lack of concern about physical symptoms that may accompany somatoform disorders.

Lateralization The specialized functioning of each cerebral hemisphere. In general, the left hemisphere is involved in language and related functions, and the right side is involved in spatial organization and analysis.

Lead poisoning Ingestion of toxic levels of lead (mainly through environmental pollutants) that can cause brain damage and a number of adverse behavioral and cognitive impairments, including mental retardation.

Learned helplessness theory A theory that holds that depressed people do not recognize a contingency between their behavior and outcomes in their environments.

Learning disorders A heterogenous group of educational problems characterized by academic performance that is notably below academic aptitude.

Life-cycle transitions Movements from one social or psychological "stage" of adult development into a new one; often characterized by interpersonal, emotional, and identity conflict.

Life-span development The study of continuities and changes in behavior, affect, and cognition from infancy through the last years of life.

Limbic system A variety of brain structures, including the thalamus and hypothalamus, that are central to the regulation of emotion and basic learning processes.

Linkage A process used to locate the position of a gene on a particular chromosome. Two genetic loci are said to be linked if they are close together on the same chromosome.

Longitudinal study A type of research design in which subjects are studied over a period of time (contrasts with the cross-sectional approach of studying subjects only at one point in time). Longitudinal studies attempt to establish whether hypothesized causes precede their putative effects in time.

Mainstreaming The educational philosophy that mentally retarded children should be taught, as much as possible, in regular classrooms rather than in "special" classes.

Malingering Pretending to have a psychological disorder in order to achieve some external gain such as insurance money or avoidance of work.

Mania A disturbance in mood characterized by such symptoms as elation, inflated self-esteem, hyperactivity, and accelerated speaking and thinking. An exaggerated feeling of physical and emotional well-being.

Marijuana The dried leaves and flowers of the female cannabis plant. "Getting high" on marijuana refers to a pervasive sense of well-being and happiness.

Mean The arithmetic average of a distribution of scores; the sum of scores divided by the number of observations.

Median The midpoint of a frequency distribution; half of all subjects fall above and half fall below the median.

Medulla The part of the hindbrain that controls various body functions involved in sustaining life, including heart rate, blood pressure, and respiration.

Melancholia A particularly severe type of depression. In DSM-IV, melancholia is described in terms of a number of specific features, such as loss of pleasure in activities and lack of reactivity to events in the person's environment that are normally pleasurable.

Menopause The cessation of menstruation and the associated physical and psychological changes that occur among middle-aged women (the so-called "change of life").

Mental retardation Substantial limitations in present functioning characterized by significantly subaverage intellectual functioning (IQ of 70 to 75 or below), concurrent limitations in adaptive skills, and an onset before age 18.

Meta-analysis A statistical technique that allows the results from different studies to be combined in a standardized way.

Midbrain Part of the brain between the hindbrain and forebrain that is involved in the control of some motor activities, especially those related to fighting and sex.

Minimal brain damage (MBD) Damage to the brain too slight to be detected with objective instruments but sometimes inferred from behavior. Was once held to be the cause of attention-deficit/hyperactivity disorder but now widely rejected.

Mode The most frequent score in a frequency distribution.

Modeling A social learning concept describing the process of learning through imitation. Contrasts with the broader concept of identification.

Monoamine oxidase inhibitors A group of antidepressant drugs that inhibit the enzyme monoamine oxidase (MAO) in the brain and raise the levels of neurotransmitters, such as norepinephrine, dopamine, and serotonin.

Monozygotic (MZ) twins Identical twins produced from a single fertilized egg; thus MZ twins have identical genotypes.

Mood A pervasive and sustained emotional response that, in its extreme, can color the person's perception of the world.

Mood disorders A broad category of psychopathology that includes depressive disorders and bipolar disorders. These conditions are defined in terms of episodes in which the person's behavior is dominated by either clinical depression or mania.

Moral treatment A historically important movement in the treatment of the mentally ill that led to improved hospital conditions. This movement was based on the belief that the mentally ill deserve adequate care and that good care would promote their recovery.

Moratorium A period of allowing oneself to be uncertain or confused about identity. Erikson advocated a moratorium as an important step in the formation of an enduring identity.

Multiple personality disorder An unusual dissociative disorder characterized by the existence of two or more distinct personalities in a single individual (called *dissociative identity disorder* in DSM-IV).

Munchausen-by-Proxy Syndrome (MBPS) A unique, rare, but potentially very harmful form of physical child abuse in which a parent feigns, exaggerates, or induces illness in a child.

Myocardial infarction (MI) Commonly known as a heart attack, this most deadly form of coronary heart disease is caused by oxygen deprivation to the heart and results in the death of at least some heart tissue.

Narcissistic personality disorder An enduring pattern of thinking and behavior that is characterized by pervasive grandiosity. Narcissistic people are preoccupied with their own achievements and abilities.

Nature–nurture controversy The debate that pits genetic and biological factors against life experience as causes of abnormal behavior.

Negative symptoms (of schizophrenia) Include flat or blunted affect, avolition, alogia, and anhedonia.

Neurofibrillary tangles A type of brain lesion found in the cerebral cortex and the hippocampus in patients with Alzheimer's disease. A pattern of disorganized neurofibrils, which provide structural support for the neurons and help transport chemicals that are used in the production of neurotransmitters.

Neuroleptic A type of antipsychotic medication that also induces side effects that resemble the motor symptoms of Parkinson's disease.

Neurologist A physician who deals primarily with diseases of the brain and nervous system.

Neuron The nerve cells that form the basic building blocks of the brain. Each neuron is composed of the soma or cell body, the dendrites, the axon, and the terminal buttons.

Neuropsychological assessment Assessment procedures focused on the examination of performance on psychological tests to indicate whether a person has a brain disorder. An example is the Halstead-Reitan Neuropsychological Test Battery.

Neuropsychologist A psychologist who has particular expertise in the assessment of specific types of cognitive impairment, including those associated with dementia and amnestic disorders.

Neurosis A traditional term, often associated with psychoanalytic theory, that describes maladaptive behavior resulting from the ego's failure to control anxiety resulting from unconscious conflicts. In DSM-I and DSM-II, neurotic disorders were defined as those in which anxiety is the chief characteristic. Anxiety presumably could be felt and expressed directly, or it could be controlled unconsciously by defense mechanisms.

Neurotransmitters Chemical substances that are released into the synapse between two neurons and carry signals from the terminal button of one neuron to the receptors of another.

Nonshared environment The component of a sibling's environment inside or outside the family that is unique to that sibling, for example, being a favorite child or one's best friend. Contrasts with the shared environment, family experiences that are common across siblings.

Normal distribution A frequency distribution represented by a bell-shaped curve—the normal curve—that is important for making statistical inferences. Many psychological characteristics (e.g., intelligence) are assumed to follow the normal distribution.

Normalization The philosophy that mentally retarded or mentally ill people are entitled to live as much as possible like other members of the society. Often with deinstitutionalization in providing custodial care and mainstreaming in education.

Null hypothesis The prediction that an experimental hypothesis is not true. Scientists must assume that the null hypothesis holds until research contradicts it.

Obesity Excess body fat, a circumstance that roughly corresponds with a body weight 20 percent above the expected weight.

Obsession A repetitive, unwanted, intrusive cognitive event that may take the form of thoughts,

images, or impulses. Obsessions intrude suddenly into consciousness and lead to an increase in subjective anxiety.

Obsessive–compulsive personality disorder An enduring pattern of thinking and behavior that is characterized by perfectionism and inflexibility. These people are preoccupied with rules and efficiency. They are excessively conscientious, moralistic, and judgmental.

Operant conditioning A learning theory asserting that behavior is a function of its consequences. Specifically, behavior increases if it is rewarded, and it decreases if it is punished.

Operational definition A procedure that is used to measure a theoretical construct.

Opiates (sometimes called *opioids*) Drugs that have properties similar to opium. The main active ingredients in opium are morphine and codeine.

Oppositional defiant disorder A psychological disorder of childhood characterized by persistent but relatively minor transgressions, such as refusing to obey adult requests, arguing, and acting angry.

Optimism A general and effective style of coping with stress involving a positive attitude when a stressor cannot be changed.

Orgasmic disorder A sexual disorder in which the person has recurrent difficulties reaching orgasm after a normal sexual arousal.

Outpatient Commitment Outpatient commitment generally requires the same dangerousness standards as inpatient commitment, but the patient is court-ordered to comply with treatment in the community (e.g., making regular office visits, taking medication). Outpatient commitment is permitted by 39 states, and because it involves less infringement on civil liberties, commitment criteria may be applied less stringently for outpatient versus inpatient commitment.

Pain disorder A type of somatoform disorder characterized by preoccupation with pain, and complaints are motivated at least in part by psychological factors.

Panic attack A sudden, overwhelming experience of terror or fright. While anxiety involves a blend of several negative emotions, panic is more focused.

Panic disorder A form of anxiety disorder in which a person experiences recurrent, unexpected panic attacks. At least one of the attacks must have been followed by a period of one month or more in which the person has either persistent concern about having additional attacks, worry about the implications of the attack or its consequences, or a significant change in behavior related to the attacks. Panic disorder is divided into two subtypes, depending on the presence or absence of agoraphobia.

Paradigm A set of assumptions both about the substance of a theory and about how scientists should collect data and test theoretical propositions. The term was applied to the progress of science by Thomas Kuhn, an influential historian and philosopher.

Paranoid personality disorder An enduring pattern of thinking and behavior characterized by a pervasive tendency to be inappropriately suspicious of other people's motives and behaviors. People who fit the description for this disorder expect that other people are trying to harm them, and they take extraordinary precautions to avoid being exploited or injured.

Paranoid type A subtype of schizophrenia that is characterized by systematic delusions with persecutory or grandiose content. Preoccupation with frequent auditory hallucinations can also be associated with the paranoid type.

Paraphilias Forms of sexual disorder that involve sexual arousal in association with unusual objects and situations, such as inanimate objects, sexual contacts with children, exhibiting their genitals to strangers, and inflicting pain on another person.

Parkinson's disease A disorder of the motor system that is caused by a degeneration of a specific area of the brain stem known as the *substantia nigra* and loss of the neurotransmitter dopamine, which is produced by cells in this area.

Pedophilia One of the paraphilias, characterized by marked distress over, or acting on urges involving, sexual activity with a prepubescent child.

Peer sociometrics A method of assessing children's social relationships and categorizing children's social standing by obtaining information on who is "liked most" and who is "liked least" from a group of children who know each other.

Peripheral nervous system Nerves that stem from the central nervous system and connect to the body's muscles, sensory systems, and organs. Divided into two subdivisions, the somatic and the autonomic nervous systems.

Personality The combination of persistent traits or characteristics that, taken as a whole, describe a person's behavior. In DSM-IV, personality is defined as "enduring patterns of perceiving, relating to, and thinking about the environment and oneself, which are exhibited in a wide range of important social and personal contexts."

Personality disorder Inflexible and maladaptive patterns of personality that begin by early adulthood and result in either social or occupational problems or distress to the individual.

Personality inventory Sometimes called an *objective personality test*, it consists of a series of straightforward statements that the person is required to rate or endorse as being either true or false in relation to himself or herself.

Pervasive developmental disorders A category of unusual psychological problems that begin early in life and involve severe impairments in a number of areas of functioning. Autistic disorder is one example.

Phenomenology The study of events and symptoms (including subjective experiences) in their own right rather than in terms of inferred causes.

Phenotype The observed expression of a given genotype or genetic structure, for example, eye color.

Phenylketonuria (PKU) A cause of mental retardation transmitted by the pairing of recessive genes that results in the deficiency of the enzyme that metabolizes phenylalanine. Infants have normal intelligence at birth, but the ingestion of foods containing phenylalanine causes phenylketonuria and produces brain damage. Can be prevented with a phenylalanine-free diet.

Phobia A persistent and irrational narrowly defined fear that is associated with a specific object or situation.

Pick's disease A form of primary dementia that is associated with atrophy of the frontal and temporal lobes of the brain. Very similar to Alzheimer's disease in terms of both behavioral symptoms and cognitive impairment.

Placebo control group A group of subjects given a treatment with no known specific ingredients for the purpose of comparison with alternative treatments that are thought to contain specific, therapeutic benefits.

Placebo effect The improvement in a condition produced by a placebo (sometimes a substantial change). An overriding goal of scientific research is to identify treatments that exceed placebo effects.

Polygenic Caused by more than one gene. Characteristics become normally distributed as more genes are involved in the phenotypic expression of a trait.

Polysubstance abuse (also known as *multidrug abuse*) A disorder characterized by the abuse of at least three different psychoactive drugs (not including nicotine or caffeine). No single substance predominates in the pattern of abuse.

Polythetic class A category that is defined in terms of a set of criteria that are neither necessary nor sufficient. Each member of the category must possess a certain minimal number of the defining features, but none of the features has to be found in each member of the category.

Pons Part of the hindbrain that serves various functions in regulating stages of sleep.

Population The entire group of people about whom a researcher wants to generalize.

Positive symptoms (of schizophrenia) Include hallucinations, delusions, disorganized speech, inappropriate affect, and disorganized behavior.

Posttraumatic stress disorder (PTSD) A psychological disorder characterized by recurring symptoms of numbing, reexperiencing, and hyperarousal following exposure to a traumatic stressor.

Prefrontal lobotomy A psychosurgery technique introduced in 1935 by Egas Moniz in which the two hemispheres of the brain are severed. Moniz won a Nobel Prize for the treatment, which now is discredited.

Premature ejaculation A type of sexual disorder, in which a man is unable to delay ejaculation long enough to accomplish intercourse.

Premorbid history A pattern of behavior that precedes the onset of an illness. Adjustment prior to the disorder.

Preparedness theory The notion that organisms are biologically prepared, on the basis of neural pathways in their central nervous systems, to learn certain types of associations (also known as *biological constraints on learning*).

Prevalence An epidemiological term that refers to the total number of cases that are present within a given population during a particular period of time.

Primary appraisal The cognitive evaluation of the challenge, threat, or harm posed by a stressful life event.

Primary prevention An attempt to prevent new cases of disorder by improving the environment; promotes health, not just the treatment of illness.

Primary sleep disorder A condition where a sleeping difficulty is the principal complaint. In DSM-IV, either a dyssomnia—a difficulty in the amount, quality, or timing of sleep, or a parasomnia—an abnormal event that occurs during sleep; for example, nightmares.

Probands Index cases. In behavior genetic studies, probands are family members who have a disorder, and the relatives of the index cases are examined for concordance.

Problem-focused coping Externally oriented coping in an attempt to change or otherwise control a stressor.

Prodromal phase Precedes the active phase of schizophrenia and is marked by an obvious deterioration in role functioning. Prodromal signs and symptoms are less dramatic than those seen during the active phase of the disorder.

Professional responsibilities A professional's obligation to follow the ethical standards of his or her profession and to uphold the laws of the states in which he or she practices, for example, confidentiality.

Prognosis Predictions about the future course of a disorder with or without treatment.

Projective tests Personality tests, such as the Rorschach inkblot test, in which the person is asked to interpret a series of ambiguous stimuli.

Prospective design A research design in which people are studied longitudinally and forward in time. Supposed causes of future outcomes are assessed in the present, and subjects are then followed to see if the hypothesized effects develop over time.

Psychiatry The branch of medicine that is concerned with the study and treatment of mental disorders.

Psychoactive substance A drug that alters a person's mood, level of perception, or brain functioning.

Psychoanalysis Freud's orthodox form of psychotherapy that is practiced rarely today because of its time, expense, and questionable effectiveness in treating mental disorders. Freud viewed the task of psychoanalysis as promoting insight by uncovering the unconscious conflicts and motivations that cause psychological difficulties.

Psychoanalytic theory A paradigm for conceptualizing abnormal behavior based on the concepts and writings of Sigmund Freud. Highlights uncon-scious processes and conflicts as causing abnormal behavior and emphasizes psychoanalysis as the treatment of choice.

Psychodynamic A variation on the Freudian approach that searches for unconscious conflicts and motivations, but does not adhere to Freud lit-erally as in psychoanalysis.

Psychodynamic psychotherapy An "uncovering" form of psychotherapy in which the therapist typ-ically is more engaged and directive; the process is considerably less lengthy than in psychoanalysis.

Psychological dependence A term used to describe forceful, subjective urges to use drugs, often as a means of relieving negative mood states. Contrasts with the term "physiological depend-ence," which involves symptoms of tolerance and withdrawal.

Psychology The science, profession, and academic discipline concerned with the study of mental processes and behavior in humans and animals.

Psychometric approach A method of classifica-tion that forms diagnostic categories from statisti-cal analysis of symptom checklists. Particularly used in classifying and internalizing disorders of child-hood.

Psychomotor retardation A generalized slowing of physical and emotional reactions. The slowing of movements and speech; frequently seen in de-pression.

Psychomotor stimulants Drugs such as amphet-amine and cocaine that produce their effect by sim-ulating the effects of certain neurotransmitters, specifically norepinephrine, dopamine, and sero-tonin.

Psychoneuroimmunology (PNI) Research on the effects of stress on the functioning of the immune system.

Psychopathology The manifestations of (and the study of the causes of) mental disorders. Generally used as another term to describe abnormal be-havior.

Psychopathy Another term for *antisocial personality disorder*. Usually associated with Cleckley's defini-tion of that concept, which included features such as disregard for the truth, lack of empathy, and inability to learn from experience.

Psychopharmacology The study of the effects of psychoactive drugs on behavior. Clinical psy-chopharmacology involves the expert use of drugs in the treatment of mental disorders.

Psychophysiology The study of changes in the functioning of the body that result from psycho-logical experiences.

Psychosis A term that refers to several types of severe mental disorder in which the person is out of contact with reality. Hallucinations and delu-sions are examples of psychotic symptoms.

Psychosomatic disorder A term indicating that a physical disease is a product both of the psyche (mind) and the soma (body).

Psychostimulants Medications that heighten energy and alertness when taken in small dosages,

but lead to restless, even frenetic, behavior when misused. Often used in the treatment of attention-deficit/hyperactivity disorder.

Psychosurgery A controversial treatment that involves the surgical destruction of specific regions of the brain. Modern psychosurgery involves rela-tively little destruction of brain tissue, unlike the discredited prefrontal lobotomy.

Psychotherapy The use of psychological tech-niques in an attempt to produce change in the con-text of a special, helping relationship.

Psychotropic medications Chemical substances that when taken internally affect a person's psy-chological state.

Purging An intentional act designed to eliminate consumed food from the body. Self-induced vom-iting is the most common form.

Random assignment Any of several methods of ensuring that each subject has a statistically equal chance of being exposed to any level of an inde-pendent variable.

Random selection A method of selecting samples from a larger population that ensures that each sub-ject has a statistically equal chance of being selected.

Rape Acts involving nonconsensual sexual pene-tration obtained by physical force, by threat of bod-ily harm, or when the victim is incapable of giving consent by virtue of mental illness, mental retar-dation, or intoxication.

Rating scale An assessment tool in which the observer is asked to make judgments that place the person somewhere along a dimension.

Rational–emotive therapy (RET) A cognitive behavior therapy technique designed to challenge irrational beliefs about oneself and the world. Developed by Albert Ellis as a treatment for anxiety, depression, and related problems.

Reaction range A behavior genetic concept for conceptualizing the joint influence of genes and environment; specifically, that heredity determines the upper and lower limits of a trait and experi-ence determines the extent to which people fulfill their genetic potential.

Reactivity The influence of an observer's presence on the behavior of the person who is being observed.

Receptors Sites on the dendrites or soma of a neu-ron that are sensitive to certain neurotransmitters.

Recidivism Repeat offending in violating the law.

Reciprocal causality The concept of causality as bidirectional (or circular). Interaction is a process of mutual influence, not separable causes and effects.

Reciprocity The social exchange of cooperation and conflict. Family members with happy rela-tionships reciprocate positive actions; family mem-bers with troubled relationships reciprocate negative ones.

Recovered memories Dramatic recollections of long-forgotten traumatic experiences; a contro-versial topic because the "memories" often are

impossible to validate and many such memories may be created rather than recovered.

Reductionism The scientific perspective that the whole is the sum of its parts, and that the task of scientists is to divide the world into its smaller and smaller components.

Regression A return or retreat to an earlier stage or style of coping or behaving.

Relapse The reappearance of active symptoms fol-lowing a period of remission (such as a return to heavy drinking by an alcoholic after a period of sustained sobriety).

Reliability The consistency of measurements, including diagnostic decisions. One index of reli-ability is agreement among clinicians.

Remission A stage of disorder characterized by the absence of symptoms (i.e., symptoms that were previously present are now gone).

Representative sample A sample that accurately represents the larger population of an identified group (e.g., a representative sample of all children in the United States).

Residual phase Follows the active phase of a dis-order such as schizophrenia. At this point, psy-chotic symptoms have improved, but the person continues to be impaired in various ways. Nega-tive symptoms may be more pronounced during the residual phase.

Residual type A subtype of schizophrenia that includes patients who no longer meet the criteria for active phase symptoms but nevertheless demon-strate continued signs of negative symptoms or attenuated forms of delusions, hallucinations, or disorganized speech.

Resilience The ability to "bounce back" from adversity despite life stress and emotional distress.

Retrograde amnesia The loss of memory for events prior to the onset of an illness or the expe-rience of a traumatic event.

Retrospective reports Recollections about past experiences that are often questioned in terms of reliability and validity.

Reuptake The process of recapturing some neu-rotransmitters in the synapse before they reach the receptors of another cell and returning the chem-ical substances to the terminal button. The neuro-transmitter then is reused in subsequent neural transmission.

Reverse causality Indicates that causation could be operating in the opposite direction: Y could be causing X instead of X causing Y. A threat to inter-pretation in correlational studies, and a basic rea-son why correlation does not mean causation.

Risk A statement about the probability that a cer-tain outcome will occur.

Risk factor A variable that is associated with a higher probability of developing a disorder.

Role playing Improvisational play acting that may be used in therapy to teach clients alternative ways of acting in problematic situations.

Savant performance An exceptional ability in a highly specialized area of functioning typically involving artistic, musical, or mathematical skills.

Schema A general cognitive pattern that guides the way a person perceives and interprets events in his or her environment.

Schizoaffective disorder A disorder defined by a period of disturbance during which the symptoms of schizophrenia partially overlap with a major depressive episode or a manic episode.

Schizoid personality disorder An enduring pattern of thinking and behavior characterized by pervasive indifference to other people, coupled with a diminished range of emotional experience and expression. People who fit this description prefer social isolation to interactions with friends or family.

Schizophrenia A type of (or group of) psychotic disorders characterized by positive and negative symptoms and associated with a deterioration in role functioning. The term was originally coined by Eugen Bleuler to describe the *splitting of mental associations*, which he believed to be the fundamental disturbance in schizophrenia (previously known as *dementia praecox*).

Schizophrenic spectrum A group of disorders that, on the basis of family history and adoption study data, are presumed to be genetically related to schizophrenia. These disorders may include schizotypal personality disorder, schizoaffective disorder, and delusional disorder.

Schizophreniform disorder A condition characterized by the same symptoms as schizophrenia, in which the patient has exhibited symptoms for less than the 6-month period required by DSM-IV for a diagnosis of schizophrenia.

Schizotaxia According to Paul Meehl's theoretical model for schizophrenia, a subtle neurological defect of unknown form that is inherited by all individuals who are predisposed to schizophrenia.

Schizotypal personality disorder An enduring pattern of discomfort with other people coupled with peculiar thinking and behavior. The latter symptoms take the form of perceptual and cognitive disturbances. Considered by some experts to be part of the schizophrenic spectrum.

School refusal (*school phobia*) Extreme reluctance to go to school, accompanied by various symptoms of anxiety such as stomachaches and headaches. May be a fear of school or an expression of separation anxiety disorder.

Seasonal affective disorder A type of mood disorder (either unipolar or bipolar) in which there has been a regular temporal relation between onset (or disappearance) of the person's episodes and a particular time of the year. For example, the person might become depressed in the winter.

Secondary appraisal The assessment of one's abilities and resources for coping with a stressful life event.

Secondary gain The psychoanalytic concept that conversion (or other somatoform) symptoms can help a patient avoid responsibility or receive attention (reinforcement).

Secondary prevention Focuses on the early detection of emotional problems (for instance, "at-risk" groups) in an attempt to prevent problems from becoming more serious and difficult to treat.

Selective serotonin reuptake inhibitors (SSRIs) A group of antidepressant drugs that inhibit the reuptake of serotonin into the presynaptic nerve endings and therefore promote neurotransmission in serotonin pathways.

Self-control Appropriate behavior guided by internal (rather than external) rules.

Senile plaques A type of brain lesion found in Alzheimer's disease that consists of a central core of homogeneous protein material known as *amyloid* surrounded by clumps of debris left over from destroyed neurons.

Sensate focus A procedure for the treatment of sexual dysfunction that involves a series of simple exercises in which the couple spends time in a quiet, relaxed setting, learning to touch each other.

Separation anxiety A normal fear that begins to develop around 8 months and peaks around 15 months. The infant expresses distress following separation from an attachment figure, typically a parent or other close caregiver.

Separation anxiety disorder A psychological disorder of childhood characterized by persistent and excessive worry for the safety of an attachment figure and related fears such as getting lost, being kidnapped, nightmares, and refusal to be alone. Distinct from normal separation anxiety, which typically develops shortly before an infant's first birthday.

Sexual aversion disorder A form of sexual dysfunction in which a person has an extreme aversion to, and avoids, genital sexual contact with a partner.

Sexual dysfunctions Forms of sexual disorder that involve inhibitions of sexual desire or interference with the physiological responses leading to orgasm.

Sexual masochism A form of paraphilia in which sexual arousal is associated with the act of being humiliated, beaten, bound, or otherwise made to suffer.

Sexual sadism A form of paraphilia in which sexual arousal is associated with desires to inflict physical or psychological suffering, including humiliation, on another person.

Shared environment The component of the family environment that offers the same or highly similar experiences to all siblings, for example, socioeconomic status. Stands in contrast to the non-shared environment, experiences inside and outside the family that are unique to one sibling.

Social clocks Age-related goals people set for themselves and later use to evaluate life achievements.

Socialization The process of shaping children's behavior and attitudes to conform to the expectations of parents, teachers, and society.

Social phobia A type of phobic disorder in which the person is persistently fearful of social situations that might expose him or her to scrutiny by others, such as fear of public speaking.

Social skills training A behavior therapy technique in which clients are taught new skills that are desirable and likely to be rewarded in the everyday world.

Social support The emotional and practical assistance received from others.

Social work A profession whose primary concern is how human needs can be met within society.

Somatic symptoms Symptoms of mood disorders that are related to basic physiological or bodily functions, including fatigue, aches and pains, and serious changes in appetite and sleep patterns.

Somatization disorder A type of somatoform disorder characterized by multiple, somatic complaints in the absence of organic impairments.

Somatoform disorders A category of psychological disorders characterized by unusual physical symptoms that occur in the absence of a known physical pathology. Examples include hypochondriasis and conversion disorder. Somatoform disorders are somatic in form only, thus their name (note the distinction from psychosomatic disorders, which do involve real physical pathology).

Standard deviation A measure of dispersion of scores around the mean. Technically, the square root of the variance.

Standard scores A standardized frequency distribution in which each score is subtracted from the mean and the difference is divided by the standard deviation.

State-dependent learning Learning that occurs in one state of affect or consciousness is best recalled in the same state of affect or consciousness.

Statistically significant A statistical statement that a research result has a low probability of having occurred by chance alone. By convention, a result is said to be statistically significant if the probability is 5% or less that it was obtained by chance. This probability is often written as $p < .05$.

Status offense An act that is illegal only because of a youth's status as a minor, for example, running away from home, truancy from school.

Stigma A negative stamp or label that sets the person apart from others, connects the person to undesirable features, and leads others to reject the person.

Stress An event that creates physiological or psychological strain for the individual. Stress has been defined differently by various scientists.

Stress management A treatment used in behavioral medicine and health psychology to teach more effective coping skills, reduce adverse reactions to stress, and improve health behavior.

Substance abuse The less severe form of substance use disorder listed in DSM-IV. Describes a pattern of drug use that is defined in terms of interference with the person's ability to fulfill major role obligations, the recurrent use of a drug in dangerous situations, or the experience of repeated legal difficulties that are associated with drug use.

Substance dependence The more severe form of substance use disorder listed in DSM-IV. Refers to a pattern of repeated self-administration that results in tolerance, withdrawal, or compulsive drug-taking behavior.

Superego One of Freud's three central personality structures, roughly equivalent to the "conscience." In Freudian theory, the superego contains societal standards of behavior, particularly rules that children learn from identifying with their parents. The superego attempts to control id impulses.

Synapse A small gap filled with fluid that lies between the axon of one neuron and a dendrite or soma of another neuron.

Syndrome A group of symptoms that appear together and are assumed to represent a specific type of disorder.

Systematic desensitization A treatment for overcoming fears and phobias developed by Joseph Wolpe. Involves learning relaxation skills, developing a fear hierarchy, and systematic exposure to imagined, feared events while simultaneously maintaining relaxation.

Systems theory An innovation in the philosophy of conceptualizing and conducting science that emphasizes interdependence, cybernetics, and especially holism—the idea that the whole is more than the sum of its parts. Often traced to the biologist and philosopher Ludwig von Bertalanffy.

Temperament Characteristic styles of relating to the world that are often conceptualized as inborn traits. Generally emphasizes the "how" as opposed to the "what" of behavior.

Tend and befriend An alternative response to stress hypothesized to be more common among females. Tending involves caring for offspring in a way that protects them from harm, and also alters the offspring's neuroendocrine responses in a healthful manner. Befriending is responding to threat with social affiliation, thereby reducing the risk of physical danger and encouraging the exchange of resources.

Tertiary prevention Involves treatment for a disorder, but also attempts to address some of the adverse consequences of mental illness (such as unemployment).

Thalamus A part of the limbic system that is involved in receiving and integrating sensory information both from the sense organs and from higher brain structures.

Therapeutic alliance The emotional bond of confidence and trust between a therapist and client believed to facilitate therapy.

Third variable An unmeasured factor that may account for a correlation observed between any two variables. A threat to interpretation in correlational studies, and a basic reason why correlation does not mean causation.

Threshold model A perspective on etiology that holds that people can exhibit characteristics of a disorder without experiencing any adverse impact on their adjustment until they pass a critical threshold. Beyond that level, there is presumably a dramatic increase in the number of problems that are encountered.

Time-out A discipline technique that involves briefly isolating a child as a punishment for misbehavior.

Token economy A type of contingency management program that has been adopted in many institutional settings. Desired and undesired behaviors are identified, contingencies are defined, behavior is monitored, and rewards or punishments are given according to the rules of the economy.

Tolerance The process through which the nervous system becomes less sensitive to the effects of a psychoactive substance. As a result, the person needs to consume increased quantities of the drug to achieve the same subjective effect.

Transference In psychoanalysis, the process whereby patients transfer feelings about a key figure in their lives onto the analyst. In psychotherapy, the client's feelings toward the therapist.

Transsexualism A severe form of gender identity disorder in adults.

Transvestic fetishism A form of paraphilia in which sexual pleasure is derived from dressing in the clothing of the opposite gender.

Trauma desensitization A treatment for post-traumatic stress disorder where the client is first taught to relax, and while maintaining a state of relaxation, he or she relives the traumatic event through discussions or fantasies.

Traumatic stress A catastrophic event that involves real or perceived threat to life or physical well-being.

Tricyclics A group of antidepressant drugs that block the uptake of neurotransmitters, such as norepinephrine and dopamine, from the synapse.

Two-factor theory A combination of classical conditioning and operant conditioning that is hypothesized to explain the acquisition and maintenance of fear. Fears are acquired through classical conditioning and maintained through operant conditioning (the reduction in anxiety that stems from avoidance).

Type A behavior pattern A characterological response to challenge that is competitive, hostile, urgent, impatient, and achievement-striving. Linked to an increased risk for coronary heart disease.

Undifferentiated type A subtype of schizophrenia that includes patients who display prominent psychotic symptoms and either meet the criteria for several subtypes or otherwise do not meet the criteria for the catatonic, paranoid, or disorganized types.

Unipolar mood disorder A form of mood disorder in which the person experiences episodes of depression but has never experienced an episode of mania or hypomania.

Vaginismus A form of sexual dysfunction in which the outer muscles of the vagina snap tightly shut when penetration is attempted, thus preventing insertion of any object.

Validity The meaning or systematic importance of a construct or a measurement.

Variance A measure of dispersion of scores around the mean. Technically, the average squared difference from the mean (see also *standard deviation*).

Vascular dementia (also known as *multi-infarct dementia*) A type of dementia associated with vascular disease. The cognitive symptoms of vascular dementia are the same as those for Alzheimer's disease, but a gradual onset is not required.

Ventricles Four connected chambers in the brain filled with cerebrospinal fluid. The ventricles are enlarged in some psychological and neurological disorders.

Victimization A pattern of responses often observed among victims of violent crimes, particularly rape, that includes fear, guilt, self-blame, powerlessness, and lowered self-esteem.

Voyeurism A form of paraphilia (also known as *peeping*) in which a person becomes sexually aroused by observing unsuspecting people (usually strangers) while they are undressing or engaging in sexual activities.

Vulnerability marker A specific measure, such as a biochemical assay or a psychological test, that might be useful in identifying people who are vulnerable to a disorder such as schizophrenia.

Weight set point Fixed weights or small ranges of weight around which the body regulates weight, for example, by increasing or decreasing metabolism.

Withdrawal The constellation of symptoms that are experienced shortly after a person stops taking a drug after heavy or prolonged use.

Worry A relatively uncontrollable sequence of negative, emotional thoughts and images that are concerned with possible future threats or danger.

References

Abel, G.G., Becker, J.V., Mittelman, M., Cunningham-Rathner, J., et al. (1987). Self-reported sex crimes of nonincarcerated paraphiliacs. *Journal of Interpersonal Violence*, 2, pp. 3–25.

Abel, G.G., & Gouleau, J.L. (1990). Male sex offenders. In M.E. Thase, B.A. Edelstein, & M. Hersen (Eds.), *Handbook of Outpatient Treatment of Adults: Nonpsychotic Mental Disorders*, pp. 271–290. New York: Plenum.

Abel, G.G., & Osborn, C. (1992). The paraphilias: The extent and nature of sexually deviant and criminal behavior. *Psychotic Clinics of North America*, 15, pp. 675–687.

Abraído-Lanza, A.F., Vásquez, E. & Echeverría, S.E. (2004). En las manos de Dios [in God's hands]: Religious and other forms of coping among Latinos with arthritis. *Journal of Consulting and Clinical Psychology*, 72, pp. 91–102.

Abramowitz, J. S. (1998). Does cognitive-behavioral therapy cure obsessive-compulsive disorder? A meta-analytic evaluation of clinical significance. *Behavior Therapy*, 29, pp. 339–355.

Abramowitz, J.S. (1997). Effectiveness of psychological and parmacological treatments for obsessive-compulsive disorder: A quantitative review. *Journal of Consulting and Clinical Psychology*, 65, pp. 44–52.

Abramowitz, J.S., Tolin, D.F., & Street, G.P. (2001). Paradoxical effects of thought suppression: A meta-analysis of controlled studies. *Clinical Psychology Review*, 21, pp. 683–703.

Abrams, R. (2002). *Electroconvulsive Therapy* (4th ed.). New York: Oxford University Press.

Abramson, L.Y., Metalsky, G.I., & Alloy, L.B. (1989). Hopelessness depression: A theory-based subtype of depression. *Psychological Review*, 96, pp. 358–372.

Abramson, L.Y., Alloy, L.B., Hankin, B.L., Haeffel, G.J., MacCoon, D.G., & Gibb, B.E. (2002). Cognitive vulnerability-stress models of depression in a self-regulatory and psychobiological context. In I.H. Gotlib and C.L. Hammen (Eds.) *Handbook of Depression*, pp. 268–294. New York: Guilford.

Ackerman, M.D., & Carey, M.P. (1995). Psychology's role in the assessment of erectile dysfunction: Historical precedents, current knowledge, and methods. *Journal of Consulting and Clinical Psychology*, 63, pp. 862–876.

Adams, G.R., & Adams, C.M. (1989). Developmental issues. In L.K.G. Hsu & M. Hersen (Eds.), *Recent Developments in Adolescent Psychiatry*, pp. 13–30. New York: Wiley.

Adams, G.R., Abraham, K.G., & Markstrom, C.A. (1987). The relation among identity development, self-consciousness and self-focusing during middle and late adolescence. *Developmental Psychology*, 23, pp. 292–297.

Adams, G.R., Ryan, J.H., Hoffman, J.J., Dobson, W.R., & Nielsen, E.C. (1985). Ego identity status, conformity behavior and personality in late adolescence. *Journal of Personality and Social Psychology*, 47, pp. 1091–1104.

Addis, M.E., & Mahalik, J.R. (2003). Men, masculinity, and the contexts of help seeking. *American Psychologist*, 58, pp. 5–14.

Adler, L.E., Freedman, R., Ross, R.G., Olincy, A., & Waldo, M.C. (1999). Elementary phenotypes in the neurobiological and genetic study of schizophrenia. *Biological Psychiatry*, 46, pp. 8–18.

Adler, R. (2001). Psychoneuroimmunology. *Current Directions in Psychological Science*, 10, pp. 94–98.

Agras, W.S. (1987). *Eating Disorders: Management of Obesity, Bulimia, and Anorexia Nervosa*. Elmsford, NY: Pergamon.

Agras, W.S., Rossiter, E.M., Arnow, B., et al. (1992). Pharmacologic and cognitive-behavioral treatment for bulimia nervosa. *American Journal of Psychiatry*, 149, pp. 82–87.

Agras, W.S., Walsh, B.T., Fairburn, C.G., Wilson, G.T., & Kraemer, H.C. (2002). A multicenter comparison of cognitive-behavioral therapy and interpersonal psychotherapy for bulimia nervosa. *Archives of General Psychiatry*, 57, pp. 459–466.

Ainsworth, M.D.S. (1989). Attachments beyond infancy. *American Psychologist*, 44, pp. 709–716.

Akagi, H., & House, A. (2001) Epidemiology of Conversion Hysteria. In P. Halligan, C. Bass & J. Marshall (Eds.), *Contemporary Approaches to the Study of Hysteria*, pp. 73–86. Oxford: Oxford University Press.

Akiskal, H.S. (1992). Borderline: An adjective still in search of a noun. In D. Silver & M. Rosenbluth (Eds.), *Handbook of Borderline Disorders*, pp. 155–176. Madison, CT: International Universities Press.

Akyuz, G., Dogan, O., Sar, V., Yargic, L.I., & Tutkun, H. (1999). Frequency of dissociative identity disorder in the general population in Turkey. *Comprehensive Psychiatry*, 40, pp. 151–159.

Al-Sawaf, M, & Al-Issa, I. (2000). Sex and sexual dysfunction in an Arab-Islamic society. In I. Al-Issa (Ed.), *Mental Illness in the Islamic World*, pp. 295–311. International Universities Press.

Alarcon, R.D., Foulks, E.F., & Vakkur, M. (1998). *Personality Disorders and Culture: Clinical and Conceptual Interactions*. New York: Wiley.

Aldridge-Morris, R. (1989). *Multiple Personality: An Exercise in Deception*. Hillsdale, NJ: Erlbaum.

Alexander, F. (1950). *Psychosomatic Medicine: Its Principles and Applications*. New York: Norton.

Alexander, F., French, T.M., & Pollock, G.H. (1968). *Psychosomatic Specificity*. Chicago: University of Chicago Press.

Alexander, J.F., & Parsons, B.V. (1982). *Functional Family Therapy*. Monterey, CA: Brooks/Cole.

Alexander, J.F., Holtzworth-Munroe, A., & Jameson, P.B. (1994). The process and outcome of marital and family therapy: Research, review, and evaluation. In A.E. Bergin & S.L. Garfield (Eds.), *Handbook of Psychotherapy and Behavior Change*, 4th ed., pp. 595–630. New York: Wiley.

Alexander, J.F., Newell, R.M., Robbins, M.S., & Turner, C.W. (1995). Observational coding in family therapy process research. *Journal of Family Psychology*, 9, pp. 355–365.

Allen, J.P., et al. (2002). Attachment and autonomy as predictors of the development of social skills and delinquency during midadolescence. *Journal of Consulting and Clinical Psychology*, 70, pp. 56–66.

Alloy, L.B., Abramson, L.Y., & Francis, E.L. (1999). Do negative cognitive styles confer vulnerability to depression? *Current Directions in Psychological Science*, 8, pp. 128–132.

Alloy, L.B., Reilly-Harrington, N., Fresco, D.M., Whitehouse, W.G., & Zechmeister, J.S. (1999). Cognitive styles and life events in subsyndromal unipolar and bipolar disorders. *Journal of Cognitive Psychotherapy*, 13, pp. 21–40.

Alloy, L.B., Abramson, L.Y., Gibb, B.E., Crossfield, A.G., Pieracci, A.M., Spasojevic, J., & Steinberg, J.A. (2004). Developmental antecedents of cognitive vulnerability to depression: Review of findings from the cognitive vulnerability to depression project. *Journal of Cognitive Psychotherapy*, 18, pp. 115–133.

Altshuler, L.L., Bartzokis, G., Grieder, T., Curran, J., Jimenez, T., Leight, K., Wilkins, J., Gerner, R., & Mintz, J. (2000). An MRI study of temporal lobe structures in men with bipolar disorder or schizophrenia. *Biological Psychiatry*, 48, pp. 147–162.

America's Children: Key National Indicators of Well-Being (1999). Federal Interagency Forum on Child and Family Statistics. Washington: U.S. Government Printing Office.

American Association on Mental Retardation (2002). *Mental Retardation: Definition, Classification, and Systems of Supports* (10th ed.). Washington, D.C.: AAMR.

American Bar Association (1995). *Mental Disability Law*, 5th ed. Washington, DC.

American Cancer Society (1994). *Cancer Facts and Figures, 1993*. New York.

American Psychiatric Association (1980). *Psychiatric Glossary*. Washington, DC: American Psychiatric Press.

American Psychiatric Association (1983). American Psychiatric Association statement on the insanity defense. *American Journal of Psychiatry*, 140, pp. 681–688.

American Psychiatric Association (1994). *Diagnostic and Statistical Manual of Mental Disorders*, 1st ed. 1952; 2nd ed. 1968; 3rd ed. 1980; rev. 3rd ed. 1987; 4th ed. 1994. Washington, DC.

American Psychiatric Association. (2000). *Diagnostic and Statistical Manual of Mental Disorders* (DSM-IV-TR, 4th edition, text revision). Washington, D.C.

American Psychological Association (1995). *Violence in the Family*. Washington, DC.

Anda, R., Williamson, D., Jones, D., Macera, C., Eaker, E., Glasman, A., & Marks, J. (1993). Depressed affect, hopelessness, and the risk of ischemic heart disease. *Epidemiology*, 4, pp. 285–294.

Andersen, A.E. (1995). Eating disorders in males. In K.D. Brownell & C.G. Fairburn (Eds.), *Eating Disorders and Obesity: A Comprehensive Handbook*, pp. 177–182. New York: Guilford.

Andersen, B.L., & Cyranowski, J.M. (1995). Women's sexuality: Behaviors, responses, and individual differences. *Journal of Consulting and Clinical Psychology*, 63, pp. 891–906.

Anderson, A.E. (2002). Eating disorders in males. In C.G. Fairburn & K.D. Brownell (Eds.). *Eating Disorders and Obesity*, 2nd ed., pp. 188–192. New York: Guilford.

Anderson, B.L., Kiecolt-Glaser, J.K., & Glaser, R. (1994). A biobehavioral model of cancer stress and disease course. *American Psychologist*, 49, pp. 389–404.

Anderson, C.A., Berkowitz, L., Donnerstein, E., Huesmann, L.R., Johnson, J.D., Linz, D., Malamuth, N.M., & Wartella, E. (2003). The influence of media violence on youth. *Psychological Science in the Public Interest,* 4(3), 81–110.

Anderson, N.B., & McNeilly, M. (1991). Age, gender, and ethnicity as variables in psychophysiological assessment: Sociodemographics in context. *Psychological Assessment,* 3, pp. 376–384.

Andrade, L., Caraveo-Anduaga, J.J., Berglund, P., Bijl, R.V., Graaf, R., Vollebergh, W., Dragomirecka, E., Kohn, R., Keller, M., Kessler, R.C., Kawakami, N. Kilic, C., Offord, D., Ustun, T.B., Wittchen, H. (2003). The epidemiology of major depressive episodes: Results from the International Consortium of Psychiatric Epidemiology (ICPE) Surveys. *International Journal of Methods in Psychiatric Research,* 12, pp. 3–21.

Andreasen, N.C. (2000). Schizophrenia: The fundamental questions. *Brain Research Reviews,* 31, pp. 106–112.

Andreasen, N.C. (2001). *Brave New Brain: Conquering Mental Illness in the Era of the Genome.* New York: Oxford University Press.

Andreasen, N.C., & Carpenter, W.T., Jr. (1993). Diagnosis and classification of schizophrenia. *Schizophrenia Bulletin,* 19, pp. 199–214.

Andreasen, N.C., Arndt, S., Alliger, R., Miller, D., & Flaum, M. (1995). Symptoms of schizophrenia: Methods, meanings, and mechanisms. *Archives of General Psychiatry,* 52, pp. 341–351.

Andrews, G., MacMahon, S.W., Austin, A., & Byrne, D.G. (1984). Hypertension: Comparison of drug and nondrug treatments. *British Medical Journal,* 284, pp. 1523–1530.

Andrews, G., Slade, T., & Peters, L. (1999). Classification in psychiatry: ICD-10 versus DSM-IV. *British Journal of Psychiatry,* 174, pp. 3–5.

Angst, J., Sellaro, R., & Angst, F. (1998). Long-term outcome and mortality of treated versus untreated bipolar and depressed patients: A preliminary report. *International Journal of Psychiatry in Clinical Practice,* 2, pp. 115–119.

Angst, J., Sellaro, R., & Merikangas, K.R. (2000). Depressive spectrum diagnoses. *Comprehensive Psychiatry,* 41, pp. 39–47.

Anthony, J.C., & Helzer, J.E. (1991). Syndromes of drug abuse and dependence. In L.N. Robins & D.A. Regier (Eds.), *Psychiatric Disorders in America: The Epidemiologic Catchment Area Study,* pp. 116–154. New York: Free Press.

Anthony, J.C., Warner, L.A., & Kessler, R.C. (1994). Comparative epidemiology of dependence on tobacco, alcohol, controlled substances, and inhalants: Basic findings from the National Comorbidity Survey. *Experimental and Clinical Psychopharmacology,* 2, pp. 1–24.

Antonucci, T.C. (2001). Social relations. In J.E. Birren & K.W. Schaie (Eds.), *Handbook of the Psychology of Aging,* 5th ed., pp. 427–453. San Diego: Academic Press.

Appelbaum, P.S. (1994). *Almost a Revolution: Mental Health Law and the Limits of Change.* New York: Oxford University Press.

Appels, M.C.M., Sitskoorn, M.M., Vollema, M.G., & Kahn, R.S. (2004). Elevated levels of schizotypal features in parents of patients with a family history of schizophrenia spectrum disorders. *Schizophrenia Bulletin,* 30, pp. 781–790.

Applebaum, P.S., Robbins, P.C., & Roth, L.H. (1999). Dimensional approach to delusions: Comparison across types and diagnoses. *American Journal of Psychiatry,* 156, pp. 1938–1943.

Apter, J.T., & Allen, L.A. (1999). Buspirone: Future directions. *Journal of Clinical Psychopharmacology,* 19, pp. 86–93.

Archer, R.P. (1992). Review of the Minnesota Multiphasic Personality Inventory-2. In J.J. Kramer & J.C. Conoley (Eds.), *The Eleventh Mental Measurements Yearbook.* Lincoln: University of Nebraska Press.

Arnett, J.J. (1999). Adolescent storm and stress, reconsidered. *American Psychologist,* 54, pp. 317–326.

Arnold, L.E., Elliot, M., Sachs, L., Bird, H., Kraemer, H.C., Wells, K.C., Abikoff, H.B., Comarda, A., Conners, C.K., Elliott, G.R., Greenhill, L.L., Hechtman, L., Hindshaw, S.P., Hoza, B., Jensen, P.S., March, J.S., Newcorn, J.H., Pelham, W.E., Severe, J.B., Swanson, J.M., Vitiello, B., & Wigal, T. (2003). Effects of ethnicity on treatment attendance, stimulant response/dose, and 14-month outcome in ADHD. *Journal of Consulting and Clinical Psychology,* 71(4), pp. 713–727.

Asher, S.R., & Wheeler, V.A. (1985). Children's loneliness: A comparison of rejected and neglected peer status. *Journal of Consulting and Clinical Psychology,* 53, pp. 500–505.

Asperger, H. (1944/1991). "Autistic psychopathy" in childhood. In U. Frith (Ed. and Trans.), *Autism and Asperger Syndrome,* pp. 37–92. Cambridge: Cambridge University Press. (Original published in 1944.)

Astin, M.C., Ogland-Hand, S.M., Coleman, E.M., & Foy, D.W. (1995). Posttraumatic stress disorder and childhood abuse in battered women: Comparisons with maritally distressed women. *Journal of Consulting and Clinical Psychology,* 63, pp. 308–312.

Attie, I., & Brooks-Gunn, J. (1989). Development of eating problems in adolescent girls: A longitudinal study. *Developmental Psychology,* 25, pp. 70–79.

Averill, P.M., Reas, D.L., Shack, A., Shah, N.N., Cowan, K., Krajewski, K., Kopecky, C., & Guynn, R.W. (2004). Is schizoaffective disorder a stable diagnostic category? A retrospective examination. *Psychiatric Quarterly,* 75, pp. 215–227.

Avila, M.T., McMahon, R.P., Elliott, A.R., & Thaker, G.K. (2002). Neurophysiological markers of vulnerability to schizophrenia: Sensitivity and specificity of specific quantitative eye movement measures. *Journal of Abnormal Psychology,* 111, pp. 259–267.

Ayres, J.J.B. (1998). Fear conditioning and avoidance. In W.T. O'Donohue (Ed.), *Learning and Behavior Therapy,* pp. 122–145. Needham Heights, MA: Allyn and Bacon.

Babior, S., & Goldman, C. (1996). *Overcoming Panic, Anxiety, and Phobias: New Strategies for Free Yourself from Worry and Fear.* Duluth, MN: Whole Person Associates.

Babor, T.F., & Del Boca, F.K. (Eds.) (2002). *Treatment Matching in Alcoholism.* New York: Cambridge University Press.

Bach, A.K., Brown, T.A., & Barlow, D.H. (1999). The effects of false negative feedback on efficacy expectancies and sexual arousal in sexually functional males. *Behavior Therapy,* 30, pp. 79–95.

Bachar, K., & Koss, M.P. (2001). From prevalence to prevention: Closing the gap between what we know about rape and what we do. In C.M. Renzetti and J.L. Edleson (Eds.), *Sourcebook on Violence Against Women,* pp. 117–142. Thousand Oaks: CA: Sage.

Badner, J.A., & Gershon, E.S. (2002). Meta-analysis of whole-genome linkage scans of bipolar disorder and schizophrenia. *Molecular Psychiatry,* 7, pp. 405–411.

Baer, J.S. (2002). Student factors: Understanding individual variation in college drinking. *Journal of Studies on Alcohol, Supp.* 14, pp. 40–53.

Bailey, A., Le Couteur, A., Gottesman, I., Bolton, P., Simonoff, E., Yuzda, E., & Rutter, M. (1995). Autism as a strongly genetic disorder: Evidence from a British twin study. *Psychological Medicine,* 25, pp. 63–77.

Bailey, S. (2002). Treatment of delinquents. In M. Rutter & E. Taylor (Eds.), *Child and Adolescent Psychiatry,* 4th ed., pp. 1019–1037. Oxford, UK: Blackwell.

Baker, J.D., Capron, E.W., & Azorlosa, J. (1996). Family environment characteristics of persons with histrionic and dependent personality disorders. *Journal of Personality Disorders,* 10, pp. 82–87.

Ballard, C.G., O'Brien, J.T., Swann, A.G., Thompson, P., Neill, D., & McKeith, I.G. (2001). The natural history of psychosis and depression in dementia with Lewy bodies and Alzheimer's disease: Persistence and new cases over 1 year of follow-up. *Journal of Clinical Psychiatry,* 62, pp. 46–49.

Ballenger, J.C. (2001). Overview of different pharmacotherapies for attaining remission in generalized anxiety disorder. *Journal of Clinical Psychiatry,* 62 (suppl. 19), pp. 11–19.

Ballenger, J.C., Burrows, G.D., DuPont, R.L., Lesser, I.M., Noyes, R., et al. (1988). Alprazolam in panic disorder and agoraphobia: Results from a multicenter trial. I. Efficacy in short term treatment. *Archives of General Psychiatry,* 45, pp. 413–422.

Ballenger, J.C., et al. (2000). Consensus statement on posttraumatic stress disorder from the International Consensus on Depression and Anxiety. *Journal of Clinical Psychiatry,* 61, pp. 60–66.

Balon, R. (1998). Pharmacological treatment of paraphilias with a focus on antidepressants. *Journal of Sex and Marital Therapy,* 24, pp. 241–254.

Baltes, P.B. (1993). The aging mind: Potential and limits. *Gerontologist,* 33, pp. 580–594.

Baltes, P.B. (1997). On the incomplete architecture of human ontogeny. Selection, optimization, and compensation as foundation of developmental theory. *American Psychologist,* 52, pp. 366–380.

Banki, C.M. (1995). Prophylactic potential of selective reuptake inhibitors in suicidal patients. *International Clinical Psychopharmacology,* 9 (suppl. 4), pp. 61–65.

Bankier, B., Aigner, M., & Bach, M. (2001). Alexithymia in DSM-IV disorder: Comparative evaluation of somatoform disorder, panic disorder, obsessive-compulsive disorder, and depression. *Psychosomatics,* 42, pp. 235–240.

Barbaree, H.E., & Seto, M.C. (1997). Pedophilia: Assessment and treatment. In D.R. Laws & W.T. O'Donohue (Eds.), *Handbook of Sexual Deviance: Theory and Application.* New York: Guilford.

Barbaree, H.E., Seto, M.C., Serin, R.C., Amos, N.L., & Preston, D.L. (1994). Comparisons between sexual and nonsexual rapist subtypes: Sexual arousal to rape, offense precursors, and offense characteristics. *Criminal Justice and Behavior,* 21, pp. 95–114.

Barbaresi, W.J., Katusic, S.K., Colligan, R.C., Weaver, A.L., Jacobsen, S.J. (2005). The incidence of autism in Olmsted County, Minnesota, 1976–1997: Results from a population-based study. *Archives of Pediatric & Adolescent Medicine,* 159, pp. 37–44.

Barch, D.M. (2005). The cognitive neuroscience of schizophrenia. *Annual Review of Clinical Psychology,* 1, pp. 321–353.

Barch, D.M., Carter, C.S., Braver, T.S., Sabb, F.W., MacDonald, A., Noll, D.C., & Cohen, J.D. (2001). Selective deficits in prefrontal cortex function in medication-naïve patients with schizophrenia. *Archives of General Psychiatry,* 58, pp. 280–288.

Barkley, R.A. (1995). *Taking Charge of ADHD.* New York: Guilford.

Barkley, R.A. (1998). *Attention-Deficit/Hyperactivity Disorder,* 2nd ed. New York: Guilford.

Barlow, D.H. (1997). Cognitive-behavioral therapy for panic disorder: Current status. *Journal of Clinical Psychiatry,* 58 (suppl. 2), pp. 32–37.

Barlow, D.H. (2001). *Anxiety and its Disorders* (2nd edition). New York: Guilford.

Barlow, D.H. (2001). *Clinical Handbook of Psychological Disorders* (3rd ed.). New York: Guilford.

Barlow, D.H., & Campbell, L.A. (2000). Mixed anxiety-depression and its implications for models of mood and anxiety disorders. *Comprehensive Psychiatry,* 41 (Suppl. 1), pp. 55–60.

Barlow, D.H., Brown, T.A., & Craske, M.G. (1994). Definitions of panic attacks and panic disorder in the DSM-IV: Implications for research. *Journal of Abnormal Psychology,* 103, pp. 553–564.

Barlow, D.H., Pincus, D.B., Heinrichs, N., & Choate, M.L. (2003). Anxiety disorders. In George Stricker and

Thomas Widiger (Eds.), *Handbook of Psychology: Clinical Psychology*, Vol. 8, pp. 119–147. New York: Wiley.

Barlow, D.H., Raffa, S.D., & Cohen, E.M. (2002). Psychosocial treatments for panic disorders, phobias, and generalized anxiety disorder. In P.E. Nathan & J.M. Gorman (Eds.), *A Guide to Treatments That Work*, 2nd ed., pp. 301–336. New York: Oxford.

Barnes, G.M., & Farrell, M.P. (1992). Parental support and control as predictors of adolescent drinking, delinquency, and related problem behaviors. *Journal of Marriage and the Family*, 54, pp. 763–776.

Barnier, A.J. (2002). Posthypnotic amnesia for autobiographical episodes: A laboratory model of functional amnesia? *Psychological Science*, 13, pp. 232–237.

Baroff, G.S. (1986). *Mental Retardation: Nature, Cause, and Management*, 2nd ed. Washington, DC: Hemisphere.

Baroff, G.S., & Olley (1999). *Mental Retardation*, 3rd ed. Philadelphia: Brunner/Mazel.

Baron-Cohen, S., Leslie, A.M., & Frith, U. (1985). Does the autistic child have a "theory of mind"? *Cognition*, 21, pp. 37–46.

Baron-Cohen, S., Tager-Flusberg, H., & Cohen, D.J. (Eds.) (1993). *Understanding Other Minds*. Oxford: Oxford University Press.

Barrett, J.E; Williams, J.W. Jr; Oxman, T.E; Frank, E.; Katon, W.; Sullivan, M.; Hegel, M.T; Cornell, J.E; Sengupta, A.S. (2001). Treatment of dysthymia and minor depression in primary care: A randomized trial in patients aged 18 to 59 years. *Journal of Family Practice*, 50, pp. 405–412.

Barrett, M.S., & Berman, J.S. (2001). Is psychotherapy more effective when therapists disclose information about themselves? *Journal of Consulting and Clinical Psychology*, 69, pp. 597–603.

Barrett, P.M. et al., (2001). Cognitive-behavioral treatment of anxiety disorders in children: Longterm (6-year) follow-up. *Journal of Consulting and Clinical Psychology*, 69, pp. 135–141.

Barrett, P.M., Dadds, M.R., & Rapee, R.M. (1996). Family treatment of childhood anxiety: A controlled trial. *Journal of Consulting and Clinical Psychology*, 64, pp. 333–342.

Baskin, T.W., Tierney, S.C., Minami, T., & Wampold, B.E. (2003). Establishing specificity in psychotherapy: A meta-analysis of structural equivalence of placebo controls. *Journal of Consulting and Clinical Psychology*, 71, pp. 973–979.

Basoglu, M., Mineka, S., Paker, M., Aker, T., Livanou, M., & Gok, S. (1997). Psychological preparedness for trauma as a protective factor in survivors of torture. *Psychological Medicine*, 27, pp. 1421–1433.

Bass, C., Peveler, R., & House, A. (2001). Somatoform disorders: Severe psychiatric illnesses neglected by psychiatrists. *British Journal of Psychiatry*, 179, pp. 11–14.

Bass, E., & Davis, L. (1988). *The Courage to Heal*. New York: Harper & Row.

Basson, R. (2001). Human sex-response cycles. *Journal of Sex and Marital Therapy*, 27, pp. 33–43.

Basson, R., Berman, J., Burnett, A., Derogatis, L., Ferguson, D., Fourcroy, J., Goldstein, I., Graziottin, Al, Heiman, J., Laan, E., Leiblum, S., Padma-Nathan, H., Rosen, R., Segraves, K., Segraves, R.T., Shabsigh, R., Sipski, M., Wagner, G., & Whipple, B. (2000). Report of the international consensus development conference on female sexual dysfunction: Definitions and classification. *Journal of Urology*, 163, pp. 888–896.

Bastiani, A.M., Rao, R., Weltzin, T., & Kaye, W.H. (1995). Perfectionism in anorexia nervosa. *International Journal of Eating Disorders*, 17, pp. 147–152.

Bastien C.H. et al., (2004). Cognitive-behavioral therapy for insomnia: Comparison of individual therapy, group therapy, and telephone consultations. *Journal of Consulting and Clinical Psychology*, 72, pp. 653–659.

Bates, J.E., Wachs, T.D., & Emde, R.N. (1994). Toward practical uses for biological concepts of tempera- ment. In J.E. Bates & T.D. Wachs (Eds.), *Temperament: Individual Differences at the Interface of Biology and Behavior*, pp. 275–306. Washington, DC: American Psychological Association.

Battaglia, M., & Torgersen, S. (1996). Schizotypal disorder: At the crossroads of genetics and nosology. *Acta Psychiatrica Scandinavica*, 94, pp. 303–310.

Baucom, D.H., Epstein, N., & LaTaillade, J.J. (2002). Cognitive-behavioral couple therapy. In A. Gurman & N. Jacobson (Eds.), *Clinical Handbook of Couple Therapy*, 3rd ed., pp. 26–58. New York: Guilford.

Baucom, D.H., Notarius, C.I., Burnett, C.K., & Haefner, P. (1990). Gender differences and sex-role identity in marriage. In F.D. Fincham & T.N. Bradbury (Eds.), *The Psychology of Marriage: Basic Issues and Applications*, pp. 150–171. New York: Guilford.

Bauer, M.S., & Mitchner, L. (2004). What is a "mood stabilizer?" An evidence-based response. *American Journal of Psychiatry*, 161, pp. 3–18.

Bauer, R.M., & Demery, J.A. (2003). Agnosia. In K.M. Heilman and E. Valenstein (Eds.), *Clinical Neuropsychology*, 4th ed., pp. 236–295. London: Oxford University Press.

Baum, A., Davidson, L.M., Singer, J.E., & Street, S.W. (1987). Stress as a psychophysiological response. In A. Baum & J.E. Singer (Eds.), *Handbook of Psychology and Health Stress*, vol. 5, pp. 1–24. Hillsdale, NJ: Erlbaum.

Bauman, M.L. (1996). Neuroanatomic observations of the brain in pervasive developmental disorders. *Journal of Autism and Developmental Disorders*, 26, pp. 199–203.

Baumeister, R.F. (1990). Suicide as escape from self. *Psychological Review*, 97, pp. 90–113.

Baumeister, R.F. (1997). Identity, self-concept, and self-esteem: The self lost and found. In R. Hogan, J. Johnson, & S. Briggs (Eds.), *Handbook of Personality Psychology*, pp. 681–710. San Diego, CA: Academic Press.

Baumeister, R.F., & Butler, J.L. (1997). Sexual masochism. In D.R. Laws & W.T. O'Donohue (Eds.), *Handbook of Sexual Deviance: Theory and Application*. New York: Guilford.

Baumeister, R.F., Campbell, J.D., Krueger, J.L., & Vohs, K.D. (2003). Does high self-esteem cause better performance, interpersonal success, happiness, or healthier lifestyles? *Psychological Science in the Public Interest*, 4, pp. 1–44.

Bay-Cheng, L.Y., et al. (2002). Linking femininity, weight concern, and mental health among Latina, Black and White women. *Psychology of Women Quarterly*, 26, pp. 36–45.

Beach, S.R.H., Sandeen, E.E., & O'Leary, K.D. (1990). *Depression in Marriage: A Model for Etiology and Treatment*. New York: Guilford.

Beauchaine, T.P., Webster-Stratton, C., & Reid, M.J. (2005). Mediators, moderators, and predictors of 1-year outcomes among children treated for early-onset conduct problems: A latent growth curve analysis. *Journal of Consulting and Clinical Psychology*, 73, pp. 371–388.

Bebbington, P., & Kuipers, L. (1994). The predictive utility of expressed emotion in schizophrenia: An aggregate analysis. *Psychological Medicine*, 24, pp. 707–718.

Bechtoldt, H., Norcross, J.C., Wyckoff, L.A., Pokrywa, M.L., & Campbell, L.F. (2001). Theoretical orientations and employment settings of clinical and counseling psychologists: A comparative study. *The Clinical Psychologist*, 54, pp. 3–6.

Beck, A.T. (1967). *Depression: Clinical, Experimental, and Theoretical Aspects*. New York: Harper & Row.

Beck, A.T. (1974). The development of depression. In R.J. Friedman & M.M. Katz (Eds.), *The Psychology of Depression: Contemporary Theory and Research*, pp. 3–20. New York: Winston-Wiley.

Beck, A.T., & Emery, G. (1985). *Anxiety Disorders and Phobias: A Cognitive Perspective*. New York: Basic Books.

Beck, A.T., Freeman, A., & Davis, D.D. (2004). *Cognitive Therapy of Personality Disorders*, 2nd ed. New York: Guilford.

Beck, A.T., Rush, A.J., Shaw, B.F., & Emery, G. (1979). *Cognitive Therapy of Depression*. New York: Guilford.

Beck, J.G. (1995). Hypoactive sexual desire disorder: An overview. *Journal of Consulting and Clinical Psychology*, 63, pp. 919–927.

Becker, D., & Lamb, S. (1994). Sex bias in the diagnosis of borderline personality disorder and posttraumatic stress disorder. *Professional Psychology: Research and Practice*, 25, pp. 55–61.

Becker, J.V., Alpert, J.L., BigFoot, D.S., Bonner, B.L., Geddie, L.F., Henggeler, S.W., Kaufman, K.L., & Walker, C.E. (1995). Empirical research on child abuse treatment: Report by the Child Abuse and Neglect Treatment Working Group, American Psychological Association. *Journal of Clinical Child Psychology*, 24, pp. 23–46.

Beidel, D.C., Turner, S.M., & Cooley, M.R. (1993). Assessing reliable and clinically significant change in social phobia: Validity of the social phobia and anxiety inventory. *Behaviour Research and Therapy*, 31, pp. 331–337.

Beidel, D.C., Turner, S.M., & Morris, T.L. (2000). Behavioral treatment of childhood social phobia. *Journal of Consulting and Clinical Psychology*, 68, pp. 1072–1080.

Belkin, L. (2005). Can you catch obsessive-compulsive disorder? *New York Times Magazine*. May 22, 2005, pp. 65–69.

Bellack, A.S., Haas, G.L., Schooler, N.R., & Flory, J.D. (2000). Effects of behavioural family management on family communication and patient outcomes in schizophrenia. *British Journal of Psychiatry*, 177, pp. 434–439.

Bender, L. (1947). Childhood schizophrenia, clinical study of one hundred schizophrenic children. *American Journal of Orthopsychiatry*, 17, pp. 40–56.

Benjamin, L.S. (1996). *Interpersonal Diagnosis and Treatment of Personality Disorders*, 2nd ed. New York: Guilford.

Bennett, F.C., & Sherman, R. (1983). Management of childhood "hyperactivity" by primary care physicians. *Journal of Developmental and Behavioral Pediatrics*, 4, pp. 88–93.

Berenbaum, H., & Barch, D. (1995). The categorization of thought disorder. *Journal of Psycholinguistic Research*, 24, pp. 349–376.

Berman, A.L., & Jobes, D.A. (1994). Treatment of the suicidal adolescent. In A.A. Leenaars, J.T. Maltsberger, & R.A. Neimeyer (Eds.), *Treatment of Suicidal People*, pp. 89–100. Washington, DC: Taylor & Francis.

Berman, J.R., Berman, L.A., Werbin, T.J., Flaherty, E.E., Leahy, N.M., & Goldstein, I. (1999). Clinical evaluation of female sexual function: Effects of age and estrogen status on subjective and physiologic sexual responses. *International Journal of Impotence Research*, 11 (suppl. 1), pp. 31–38.

Bernard, S.H. (2002). Services for children and adolescents with severe learning disabilities (mental retardation). In M. Rutter & E. Taylor (Eds.), *Child and Adolescent Psychiatry*, 4th ed., pp. 1114–1127. Oxford: Blackwell.

Bernlef, J. (1988). *Out of Mind*. London: Faber.

Bernstein, D.A., & Borkovec, T.D. (1973). *Progressive Relaxation Training: A Manual for the Helping Professions*. Champaign, IL: Research Press.

Bernstein, D.P., Cohen, P., Velez, C.N., Schwab-Stone, M., Siever, L.J., & Shinsato, L. (1993). Prevalence and stability of the DSM-III-R personality disorders in a community-based survey of adolescents. *American Journal of Psychiatry*, 150, pp. 1237–1243.

Bernstein, D.P., Useda, D., & Siever, L.J. (1995). Paranoid personality disorder. In W.J. Livesley (Ed.), *The DSM-IV Personality Disorders*, pp. 45–57. New York: Guilford.

Berrios, G.E. (1992). Research into the history of psychiatry. In C. Freeman & P. Tyrer (Eds.), *Research Methods in Psychiatry: A Beginner's Guide*, 2nd ed. London: Gaskell.

Bersoff, D.N. (1999). *Ethical Conflicts in Psychology*, 2nd ed. Washington: American Psychological Association.

Bertelson, A., Harvald, B., & Hauge, M. (1977). A Danish twin study of manic-depressive disorders. *British Journal of Psychiatry*, 130, pp. 330–351.

Besharov, D.J. (1992). A balanced approach to reporting child abuse. *Child, Youth, and Family Services Quarterly*, 15, pp. 5–7.

Bettelheim, B. (1967). *The Empty Fortress*. New York: Free Press.

Beumont, P.J.V., Garner, D.M., & Touyz, S.W. (1994). Diagnoses of eating or dieting disorders: What may we learn from past mistakes? *International Journal of Eating Disorders*, 16, pp. 349–362.

Bieling, P.J., Beck, A.T., & Brown, G.K. (2000). The sociotropy-autonomy scale: Structure and implications. *Cognitive Therapy and Research*, 24, pp. 763–780.

Bierut, L.J.; Heath, A.C; Bucholz, K.K; Dinwiddie, S.H; Madden, P.A.F; Statham, D.J; Dunne, M.P; Martin, N.G. (1999). Major depressive disorder in a community-based twin sample: Are there different genetic and environmental contributions for men and women? *Archives of General Psychiatry*, 56, pp. 557–563.

Bierut, L.M., Dinwiddie, S.H., Begleiter, H., Crowe, R.R., Hesselbrock, V., Nurnberger, J.I., Porjesz, B., Schuckit, M.A., & Reich, T. (1998). Familial transmission of substance dependence: Alcohol, marijuana, cocaine, and habitual smoking. *Archives of General Psychiatry*, 55, pp. 982–988.

Binik, Y.M. (2005). Should dyspareunia be retained as a sexual dysfunction in DSM-V? *Archives of Sexual Behavior*, 34, pp. 11–21.

Binik, Y.M., Reissing, E., Pukall, C., Flory, N., Payne, K.A., & Khalife, S. (2002). The female sexual pain disorders: Genital pain or sexual dysfunction? *Archives of Sexual Behavior*, 31, pp. 425–431.

Black, D.W., Kehrberg, L.D., Flumerfelt, D.L., & Schlosser, S.S. (1997). Characteristics of 36 subjects reporting compulsive sexual behavior. *American Journal of Psychiatry*, 154, pp. 243–250.

Black, D.W., Noyes, R., Goldstein, R.B., & Blum, N. (1992). A family study of obsessive-compulsive disorder. *Archives of General Psychiatry*, 49, pp. 362–368.

Black, P.H., & Garbutt, L.D. (2002). Stress, inflammation and cardiovascular disease *Journal of Psychosomatic Research*, 52, pp. 1–23

Blair, R.J.R., et al. (2001). A selective impairment in the processing of sad and fearful expressions in children with psychopathic tendencies. *Journal of Abnormal Child Psychology*, 29, pp. 491–498.

Blanchard, E.B. (Ed.) (1992). Special issue on behavioral medicine. *Journal of Consulting and Clinical Psychology*, 60.

Blanchard, E.B. (1994). Behavioral medicine and health psychology. In A.E. Bergin & S.L. Garfield (Eds.), *Handbook of Psychotherapy and Behavior Change*, 4th ed., pp. 701–733. New York: Wiley.

Blanchard, J.J., Horan, W.P., & Brown, S.A. (2001). Diagnostic differences in social anhedonia: a longitudinal study of schizophrenia and major depressive disorder. *Journal of Abnormal Psychology*, 110, pp. 363–371.

Blanchard, R. (1989). The classification and labeling of nonhomosexual gender dysphorias. *Archives of Sexual Behavior*, 18, pp. 315–334.

Blashfield, R.K., & McElroy, R.A. (1987). The 1985 literature on the personality disorders. *Comprehensive Psychiatry*, 28, pp. 536–546.

Blazer, D.G. (1997). Generalized anxiety disorder and panic disorder in the elderly: A review. *Harvard Review of Psychiatry*, 5, pp. 18–27.

Blazer, D.G. (2004). The epidemiology of depressive disorders in late life. In S.P. Roose and H.A. Sackheim (Eds.), *Late-Life Depression*, pp. 3–11. New York: NYU Press.

Blennow, K., & Cowburn, R.F. (1996). The neurochemistry of Alzheimer's disease. *Acta Neurologica Scandinavia Suppl.* 168, pp. 77–86.

Bleuler, M. (1978). *The Schizophrenic Disorders: Long-Term Patient and Family Studies*. New Haven, CT: Yale University Press.

Bliss, E.L. (1986). *Multiple Personality, Allied Disorders, and Hypnosis*. New York: Oxford University Press.

Blundell, J.E. (1995). The psychobiological approach to appetite and weight control. In K.D. Brownell & C.G. Fairburn (Eds.), *Eating Disorders and Obesity: A Comprehensive Handbook*, pp. 13–20. New York: Guilford.

Blustein, D.L., Juntunen, CL., Worthington, R.L. (2000). The school-to-work transition: Adjustment challenges of the forgotten half. In S.D. Brown & R.W. Lent (Eds.), *Handbook of Counseling Psychology*, 3rd ed, pp. 435–470. New York: Wiley.

Bogg, T. & Roberts, B.W. (2004). Conscientiousness and health-related behaviors: A meta-analysis of the leading behavioral contributors to mortality. *Psychological Bulletin*, 130, pp. 887–919.

Bohus, M., Haaf, B., Simms, T., Limberger, M.F., Schmahl, C., Unckel, C., Lieb, K., & Linehan, M.M. (2004). Effectiveness of inpatient dialectical behavioral therapy for borderline personality disorder: A controlled trial. *Behaviour Research & Therapy*, 42, pp. 487–499.

Boland, R., & Keller, M.B. (2001). Chronic and recurrent depression: Pharmacotherapy and psychotherapy combinations. In J.F. Greden (Ed.), *Treatment of Recurrent Depression*. *Review of Psychiatry*, 20, pp. 59–80. Washington, D.C.: American Psychiatric Association.

Bolla, K.I., Cadet, J., & London, E.D. (1998). The neuropsychiatry of chronic cocaine abuse. *Journal of Neuropsychiatry and Clinical Neurosciences*, 10, pp. 280–289.

Bonanno, G.A. (2004). Loss, trauma, and human resilience: Have we underestimated the human capacity to thrive after extremely aversive events? *American Psychologist*, 59, pp. 20–28.

Bonanno, G.A., Papa, A., Lelande, K., Westphal, M., & Coifman, K. (2004). The importance of being flexible: The ability to both enhance and suppress emotional expression predicts long-term adjustment. *Psychological Science*, 15, pp. 482–487.

Bonanno, G.A., Papa, A., Lalande, K., Zhang, N., & Noll, J.G. (2005). Grief processing and deliberate grief avoidance: A prospective comparison of bereaved spouses and parents in the United States and the People's Republic of China. *Journal of Consulting and Clinical Psychology*, 73, pp. 86–98.

Booth, A., et al. (2000). Biosocial perspectives on the family. *Journal of Marriage and the Family*, 62, pp. 1018–1034.

Booth-Kewley, S., & Friedman, H.S. (1987). Psychological predictors of heart disease: A quantitative review. *Psychological Bulletin*, 101, pp. 343–362.

Bootzin, R.R. (2000). Cognitive-behavioral treatment of insomnia: Knitting up the ravell'd sleave of care. In D.T. Kenny et al. (Eds.), *Stress and Health*. Sydney, AU: Harwood Academic Press.

Borduin, C.M., Mann, B.J., Cone, L.T., Henggeler, S.W., Fucci, B.R., Blaske, D.M., & Williams, R.A. (1995). Multisystemic treatment of serious juvenile offenders: Long-term prevention of criminality and violence. *Journal of Consulting and Clinical Psychology*, 63, pp. 569–578.

Borkovec, T.D., Alcaine, O.M., & Behar, E. (2004). Avoidance theory of worry and generalized anxiety disorder. In R.G. Heimberg and C.L. Turk (Eds), *Generalized Anxiety Disorder: Advances in Research and Practice*, pp. 77–108. New York: Guilford.

Borkovec, T.D., Newman, M.G., Pincus, A.L., & Lytle, R. (2002). A component analysis of cognitive-behavioral therapy for generalized anxiety disorder and the role of interpersonal problems. *Journal of Consulting and Clinical Psychology*, 70, pp. 288–298.

Bornstein, R.F. (1996). Dependency. In C.G. Costello (Ed.), *Personality Characteristics of the Personality Disordered*, pp. 120–145. New York: Wiley-Interscience.

Bornstein, R.F. (1998). Dependency in the personality disorders: Intensity, insight, expression, and defense. *Journal of Clinical Psychology*, 54, pp. 175–189.

Bosma, H.A., & Kunnen, E.S. (2001). Determinants and mechanisms in ego identity development: A review and synthesis. *Developmental Review*, 21, pp. 39–66.

Bouchard, C. (2002). Genetic influences on body weight. In C.G. Fairburn & K.D. Brownell (Eds.), *Eating Disorders and Obesity*, 2nd ed., pp. 16–21. New York: Guilford.

Bourin, M., Baker, G.B., & Bradwejn, J. (1998). Neurobiology of panic disorder. *Journal of Psychosomatic Research*, 44, pp. 163–180.

Bouton, M.E., Mineka, S., & Barlow, D. (2001). A modern learning theory perspective on the etiology of panic disorder. *Psychological Review*, 108, pp. 4–32.

Bower, G.H. (1990). Awareness, the unconscious, and repression: An experimental psychologist's perspective. In J.L. Singer (Ed.), *Repression and Dissociation*, pp. 209–232. Chicago: University of Chicago Press.

Bower, H. (2001). The gender identity disorder in the DSM-IV classification: A critical evaluation. *Australian & New Zealand Journal of Psychiatry*, 35, pp. 1–8.

Bowker, G.C., & Star, S.L. (1999). *Sorting Things Out: Classification and Its Consequences*. Cambridge, MA: MIT Press.

Bowlby, J. (1969). *Attachment*. New York: Basic Books.

Bowlby, J. (1973). *Separation: Anxiety and Anger*. New York: Basic Books.

Bowlby, J. (1979). *The Making and Breaking of Affectional Bonds*. London: Tavistock.

Bowlby, J. (1980). *Loss: Sadness and Depression*. New York: Basic Books.

Boydell, J., & Murray, R. (2003). Urbanization, migration and risk of schizophrenia. In R.M. Murray and P.B. Jones (Eds), *The Epidemiology of Schizophrenia*, pp. 49–67. New York: Cambridge University Press.

Bradbury, T.N., & Fincham, F.D. (1990). Attributions in marriage: Review and critique. *Psychological Bulletin*, 107, pp. 3–33.

Bradbury, T.N., Fincham, F.D., & Beach, S.R.H. (2000). Research on the nature and determinants of marital satisfaction: A decade in review. *Journal of Marriage and the Family*, 62, pp. 964–980.

Bradford, D., Stroup. S., & Lieberman, J. (2002). Pharmacological treatments for schizophrenia. In P.E. Nathan and J.M. Gorman (Eds.), *A Guide to Treatments That Work*, 2nd ed., pp. 169–199. London, England: Oxford University Press.

Bradford, J. (1997). Medical interventions in sexual deviance. In D.R. Laws & W.T. O'Donohue (Eds.), *Handbook of Sexual Deviance: Theory and Application*. New York: Guilford.

Bradford, J.M.W. (2001). The neurobiology, neuropharmacology, and pharmacological treatment of the paraphilias and compulsive sexual behaviour. *Canadian Journal of Psychiatry*, 46, pp. 26–34.

Bradford, J.M.W., & Pawlak, A. (1993). Double-blind placebo cross-over study of cyproterone acetate in the treatment of paraphilias. *Archives of Sexual Behavior*, 22, pp. 383–402.

Bradley, C. (1937). The behavior of children receiving benzedrine. *American Journal of Psychiatry*, 94, pp. 577–585.

Bradley, S.J., & Zucker, K.J. (1997). Gender identity disorder: A review of the past 10 years. *Journal of the*

American Academy of Child and Adolescent Psychiatry, 36, pp. 872–880.

Brady, K.T., Back, S.E., & Coffey, S.F. (2004). Substance abuse and posttraumatic stress disorder. *Current Directions in Psychological Science*, 13, pp. 206–209.

Brandon, T.H., Wetter, D.W., & Baker, T.B. (1996). Affect, expectancies, urges, and smoking: Do they conform to models of drug motivation and relapse? *Experimental and Clinical Psychopharmacology*, 4, pp. 29–36.

Braun, B.G. (1989). Psychotherapy of the survivor of incest with a dissociative disorder. *Psychiatric Clinics of North America*, 12, pp. 307–324.

Braun, D.L., Sunday, S.R., & Halmi, K.A. (1994). Psychiatric comorbidity in patients with eating disorders. *Psychological Medicine*, 24, pp. 859–867.

Braun, P., Kochansky, G., Shapiro, R., et al. (1981). Overview: Deinstitutionalization of psychiatric patients: A critical review of outcome studies. *American Journal of Psychiatry*, 138, pp. 736–749.

Breggin, P.R. (2004). Recent U.S., Canadian and British regulatory agency actions concerning antidepressant-induced harm to self and others: A review and analysis. *International Journal of Risk and Safety in Medicine*, 16, pp. 247–259.

Bregman, J.D., Dykens, E., Watson, M., Ort, S.I., & Leckman, J.F. (1987). Fragile-X syndrome: Variability of phenotypic expression. *Journal of the American Academy of Child and Adolescent Psychiatry*, 26, pp. 463–471.

Breitner, J.C.S., Gatz, M., Bergem, A.L.M., Christian, J.C., Mortimer, J.A., McClearn, G.E., Heston, L.L., Welsh, K.A., Anthony, J.C., Folstein, M.F., & Radebaugh, T.S. (1993). Use of twin cohorts for research in Alzheimer's disease. *Neurology*, 43, pp. 261–267.

Bremmer, J.D. (2005). *Brain Imaging Handbook*. New York: Norton.

Brenner, M.H. (1973). *Mental Illness and the Economy*. Cambridge, MA: Harvard University Press.

Brent, D.A. (2004). Antidepressants and pediatric depression—The risk of doing nothing. *New England Journal of Medicine*, 351, pp. 1598–1601.

Brent, D.A., & Bridge, J. (2003). Firearms availability and suicide: Evidence, interventions, and future directions. *American Behavioral Scientist*, 46, pp. 1192–1210.

Breslau, N., Davis, G.C., & Andreski, P. (1995). Risk factors for PTSD-related traumatic events: A prospective analysis. *American Journal of Psychiatry*, 152, pp. 529–535.

Breslau, N., Davis, G.C., Andreski, P., and Peterson, E. (1991). Traumatic events and posttraumatic stress disorder in an urban population of young adults. *Archives of General Psychiatry*, 48, pp. 216–222.

Breslau, N., Kessler, R.C., Chilcoat, H.D., Schultz, L.R., Davis, G.C., & Andreski, P. (1998). Trauma and post traumatic stress disorder in the community: The 1996 Detroit Area Survey of Trauma. *Archives of General Psychiatry*, 55, pp. 626–632.

Brestan, E.V., & Eyberg, S.M. (1998). Effective psychosocial treatments of conduct-disordered children and adolescents: 29 years, 82 studies, and 5,272 kids. *Journal of Clinical Child Psychology*, 27, pp. 180–189.

Brewerton, T.D., Lydiard, R.B., Herzog, D.B., Brotman, A.W., O'Neil, P.M., & Ballenger, J. (1995). Comorbidity of Axis I psychiatric disorders in bulimia nervosa. *Journal of Clinical Psychiatry*, 56, pp. 77–80.

Brewin, C.R., Andrews, B., & Gotlib, I.H. (1993). Psychopathology and early experience: A reappraisal of retrospective reports. *Psychological Bulletin*, 113, pp. 82–98.

Brewin, C.R., MacCarthy, B., Duda, K., et al. (1991). Attributions and expressed emotion in the relatives of patients with schizophrenia. *Journal of Abnormal Psychology*, 100, pp. 546–554.

Brody, E.M., Saperstein, A.R., & Lawton, M.P. (1989). A multi-service respite program for caregivers of Alzheimer's patients. *Journal of Gerontological Social Work*, 14, pp. 41–75.

Bromley, D.B. (1990). *Behavioral Gerontology: Central Issues in the Psychology of Ageing*. New York: Wiley.

Brown, A.S. A review of the déjà vu experience. (2003). *Psychological Bulletin*, 129, pp. 394–413.

Brown, A.S., Cohen, P., Harkavy-Friedman, J., Babulas, V., Malaspina, D., Gorman, J.M., & Susser, E.S. (2001). Prenatal rubella, premorbid abnormalities, and adult schizophrenia. *Biological Psychiatry*, 49, pp. 473–486.

Brown, G.W. (1998). Genetic and population perspectives on life events and depression. *Social Psychiatry and Psychiatric Epidemiology*, 33, pp. 363–372.

Brown, G.W. (2002). Social roles, context and evolution in the origins of depression. *Journal of Health and Social Behavior*, 43, pp. 255–276.

Brown, G.W., Bifulco, A., & Harris, T.O. (1987). Life events, vulnerability and onset of depression: Some refinements. *British Journal of Psychiatry*, 150, pp. 30–42.

Brown, G.W., Birley, J.L.T., & Wing, J.K. (1972). Influence of family life on the course of schizophrenic disorders: A replication. *British Journal of Psychiatry*, 121, pp. 241–258.

Brown, G.W., & Harris, T.O. (1978). *Social Origins of Depression: A Study of Psychiatric Disorder in Women*. London: Tavistock.

Brown, G.W., & Harris, T.O. (1993). Aetiology of anxiety and depressive disorders in an inner-city population. 1. Early adversity. *Psychological Medicine*, 23, pp. 143–154.

Brown, P. (1994). Toward a psychobiological model of dissociation and post-traumatic stress disorder. In S.J. Lynn & J.W. Rhue (Eds.), *Dissociation: Clinical and Theoretical Perspectives*, pp. 94–122. New York: Guilford.

Brown, R. (1990). Limitations on expert testimony on the battered women syndrome in homicide cases: The return of the ultimate issue rule. *Arizona Law Review*, 32, pp. 665–689.

Brown, R.J. (2004). Psychological mechanisms of medically unexplained syndromes: An integrative conceptual model. *Psychological Bulletin*, 130, pp. 793–812.

Brown, S.A. (1993). Drug effect expectancies and addictive behavior change. *Experimental and Clinical Psychopharmacology*, 1, pp. 55–67.

Brown, S.A., Tate, S.R., Vik, P.W., Haas, A.L., & Aarons, G.A. (1999). Modeling of alcohol use mediates the effect of family history of alcoholism on adolescent alcohol expectancies. *Experimental and Clinical Psychopharmacology*, 7, pp. 20–27.

Brown, S.L., Nesse, R.M., Vinokur, A.D., Smith, D.M. (2003). Providing social support may be more beneficial than receiving it: Results from a prospective study of mortality. *Psychological Science*, 14, pp. 320–327.

Brown, T.A., & Barlow, D.H. (1992). Comorbidity among anxiety disorders: Implications for treatment and DSM-IV. *Journal of Consulting and Clinical Psychology*, 60, pp. 835–844.

Brown, T.A., Barlow, D.H., & Liebowitz, M.R. (1994). The empirical basis of generalized anxiety disorder. *American Journal of Psychiatry*, 151, pp. 1272–1280.

Brown, T.A., Chorpita, B.F., & Barlow, D.H. (1998). Structural relationships among dimensions of the DSM-IV anxiety and mood disorders and dimensions of negative affect, positive affect, and autonomic arousal. *Journal of Abnormal Psychology*, 107, pp. 179–192.

Browning, C.R., & Laumann, E.O. (1997). Sexual contact between children and adults: A life course perspective. *American Sociological Review*, 62, pp. 540–560.

Brownell, K.D. (1995). Definition and classification of obesity. In K.D. Brownell & C.G. Fairburn (Eds.), *Eating Disorders and Obesity: A Comprehensive Handbook*, pp. 386–390. New York: Guilford.

Brownell, K.D., & Fairburn, C.G. (Eds.) (1995). *Eating Disorders and Obesity: A Comprehensive Handbook*. New York: Guilford.

Brownell, K.D., & Rodin, J. (1994). The dieting maelstrom: Is it possible and advisable to lose weight? *American Psychologist*, 49, pp. 781–791.

Bruch, H. (1982). Anorexia nervosa: Therapy and theory. *American Journal of Psychiatry*, 132, pp. 1531–1538.

Bryant, R.A., & Harve A.G. 2000. *Acute Stress Disorder: A Handbook of Theory Assessment and Treatment*. Washington: American Psychological Association.

Bryant, R.A., Moulds, M.L., Guthrie, R.M., Dang, S.T. & Nixon, R.D.V. (2003). Imaginal exposure alone and imaginal exposure with cognitive restructuring in treatment of posttraumatic stress disorder. *Journal of Consulting and Clinical Psychology*, 71, pp. 706–712.

Bryant, R.A., Moulds, M.L., Guthrie, R.M., & Nixon, R.D.V. (2005). The additive benefit of hypnosis and cognitive behavior therapy in treating acute stress disorder. *Journal of Consulting and Clinical Psychology*.

Bryne, S.M. (2002). Sport, occupation, and eating disorders. In C.G. Fairburn & K.D. Brownell (Eds.), *Eating Disorders and Obesity*, 2nd ed., pp. 256–259. New York: Guilford.

Bryson, S.E. (1996). Epidemiology of autism. *Journal of Autism and Developmental Disorders*, 26, pp. 165–167.

Bucholz, K.K. (1999). Nosology and epidemiology of addictive disorders and their comorbidity. *Psychiatric Clinics of North America*, 22, pp. 221–240.

Bucholz, K.K., Heath, A.C., Reich, T., Hesselbrock, V.M., et al. (1996). Can we subtype alcoholism? A latent class analysis of data from relatives of alcoholics in a multicenter family study of alcoholism. *Alcoholism: Clinical and Experimental Research*, 20, pp. 1462–1471.

Buck, R. (1999). The biological affects: A typology. *Psychological Review*, 106, pp. 301–336.

Buka, S.L., & Gilman, S.E. (2002). Psychopathology and the life course. In J.E. Helzer and J.J. Hudziak (Eds.), *Defining Psychopathology in the 21st Century*, pp. 129–142. Washington, D.C.: American Psychiatric Press.

Bulik, C.M., Wade, T.D., & Kendler, K.S. (2000). Characteristics of monozygotic twins discordant for bulimia nervosa. *International Journal of Eating Disorders*, 19, pp. 1–10.

Bullock, R. (2002). New drugs for Alzheimer's disease and other dementias. *British Journal of Psychiatry*, 180, pp. 135–147.

Bullough, B., & Bullough, V. (1997). Are transvestites necessarily heterosexual? *Archives of Sexual Behavior*, 26, pp. 1–11.

Burke, B.L., & McGee, D.P. (1990). Sports deficit disorder. *Pediatrics*, 85, p. 1118.

Burke, C. (1995). Foreword. In L. Nadel & D. Rosenthal (Eds.), *Down Syndrome: Living and Learning in the Community*, p. ix. New York: Wiley.

Burns, D.D. (1999). *Feeling Good: The New Mood Therapy* (revised edition). Wholecare.

Burt, S.A., Krueger, R.F., McGue, M., & Iancono, W.G. (2001). Sources of covariation among attention-deficit/hyperactivity disorder, oppositional defiant disorder, and conduct disorder: The importance of shared environment. *Journal of Abnormal Psychology*, 110, pp. 516–525.

Buss, A. (1991). The EAS theory of temperament. In J. Strelau & A. Angleitner (Eds.), *Explorations in Temperament*. New York: Plenum.

Buss, D.M. (1999). Human nature and individual differences. In L.A. Pervin and O.P. John (Eds.), *Handbook of Personality: Theory and Research*, 2nd ed., pp. 31–56. New York: Guilford.

Butcher, J.N., & Williams, C.L. (2000). *Essentials of MMPI-2 and MMPI-A Interpretation*, 2nd ed. Minneapolis, MN: University of Minnesota Press.

Butler, S.M., Ashford, J.W., & Snowdon, D.A. (1996). Age, education, and changes in the Mini-Mental State Exam scores of older women: Findings from the Nun Study. *Journal of the American Geriatrics Society*, 44, pp. 675–681.

Button, T.M.M., Scourfield, J., Martin, N., Purcell, S., & McGuffin, P. (2005). Family dysfunction interacts with genes in the causation of antisocial symptoms. *Behavior Genetics*, 35(2), pp. 115–120.

Butzlaff, R.L., & Hooley, J.M. (1998). Expressed emotion and psychiatric relapse. *Archives of General Psychiatry*, 55, pp. 547–552.

Bystritsky, A., Pontillo, D., Powers, M., Sabb, F.W., Craske, M.G., & Bookheimer, S.Y. (2001). Functional MRI changes during panic anticipation and imagery exposure. *NeuroReport*, 12, pp. 3953–3957.

Cacioppo, J.T., Bernston, G.G., Sheridan, J.F., & McClintock, M.K. (2000). Multilevel integrative analyses of human behavior: Social neuroscience and the complementing nature of social and biological approaches. *Psychological Bulletin*, 126, pp. 829–843.

Cadòret, R.J., Yates, W.R.,Troughton, E.,Woodworth, G., & Stewart, M.A. (1995). Genetic-environmental interaction in the genesis of aggressivity and conduct disorders. *Archives of General Psychiatry*, 52, pp. 916–924.

Cadieux, R.J. (1996). Azapirones: An alternative to benzodiazepines for anxiety. *American Family Physician*, 53, pp. 2349–2353.

Cairns, R.B., & Green, J.A. (1979). How to assess personality and social patterns: Observations or ratings? In R.B. Cairns (Ed.), *The Analysis of Social Interactions: Methods, Issues, and Illustrations*. Hillsdale, NJ: Erlbaum.

Cale, E.M., & Lilienfeld, S.O. (2002). Histrionic personality disorder and antisocial personality disorder: Sex-differentiated manifestations of psychopathy? *Journal of Personality Disorders*, 16, pp. 52–72.

Calev, A., Guadino, E.A., Squires, N.K., & Zervas, I.M. (1995). ECT and memory cognition: A review. *British Journal of Clinical Psychology*, 34, pp. 505–515.

Callahan, L.A., Steadman, H.J., McGreevy, M.A., & Robbins, P.C. (1991). The volume and characteristics of insanity defense pleas: An eight-state study. *Bulletin of the American Academy of Psychiatry and the Law*, 19, pp. 331–338.

Cameron, H.M., & McGoogan, E. (1981). A prospective study of 1152 hospital autopsies. II. Analysis of inaccuracies in clinical diagnoses and their significance. *Journal of Pathology*, 133, pp. 285–300.

Campbell, E. (1990). The psychopath and the definition of "mental disease of defect" under the Model Penal Code test of insanity: A question of psychology or a question of law? *Nebraska Law Review*, 69, pp. 190–229.

Campbell, M., Green, W.H., & Deutsch, S.I. (1985). *Child and Adolescent Psychopharmacology*. Beverly Hills, CA: Sage.

Campbell, R., Sefl, T., Barnes, H.E., Ahrens, C.E., Wasco, S.M., & Zaragoza-Diesfeld, Y. (1999). Community services for rape survivors: Enhancing psychological well-being or increasing trauma? *Journal of Consulting and Clinical Psychology*, 67, pp. 847–858.

Canino, G.L., Bird, H.R., et al. (1987). Prevalence of specific psychiatric disorders in Puerto Rico. *Archives of General Psychiatry*, 44, pp. 727–735.

Cannon, M., Jones, P.B., & Murray, R.M. (2002). Obstetric complications and schizophrenia: Historical and meta-analytic review. *American Journal of Psychiatry*, 159, pp. 1080–1092.

Cannon, T.D. (1998). Neurodevelopmental influences in the genesis and epigenesis of schizophrenia: An overview. *Applied and Preventive Psychology*, 7, pp. 47–62.

Cannon, T.D., Kaprio, J., Loennqvist, J., Huttunen, M., & Koskenvuo, M. (1998). The genetic epidemiology of schizophrenia in a Finnish twin cohort: A population-based modeling study. *Archives of General Psychiatry*, 55, pp. 67–74.

Cannon, T.D., Mednick, S.A., & Parnas, J. (1990). Antecedents of predominantly negative and predominantly positive-symptom schizophrenia in a high-risk population. *Archives of General Psychiatry*, 47, pp. 622–632.

Cannon, T.D., van Erp, T.G., Glahn, D.C. (2002). Elucidating continuities and discontinuities between schizotypy and schizophrenia in the nervous system. *Schizophrenia Research*, 54, pp. 151–156.

Cannon, W.B. (1935). Stress and strains of homeostasis. *American Journal of Medical Science*, 189, pp. 1–14.

Cantwell, D.P., Baker, L., & Rutter, M. (1979). Families of autistic and dysphasic children. I. Family life and interactions patterns. *Archives of General Psychiatry*, 36, pp. 682–687.

Caplan, P.J. (1995). *They Say You're Crazy: How the World's Most Powerful Psychiatrists Decide Who's Normal*. Reading: MA: Addison-Wesley.

Cappeliez, P., O'Rourke, N., & Chaudhury, H. (2005). Functions of reminiscence and mental health in later life. *Aging & Mental Health*, 9, pp. 95–301.

Capron, C., & Duyme, M. (1989). Assessment of effects of socioeconomic status on IQ in a full cross-fostering study. *Nature*, 340, pp. 552–554.

Cardno, A.G., Jones, L.A., Murphy, K.C., Sanders, R.D., Asherson, P., Owen, M.J., & McGuffin, P. (1998). Sibling pairs with schizophrenia or schizoaffective disorder: Associations of subtypes, symptoms and demographic variables. *Psychological Medicine*, 28, pp. 815–823.

Carey, G., & Gottesman, I.I. (1996). Genetics and antisocial behavior: Substance versus sound bytes. *Politics and the Life Sciences*, March, pp. 88–90.

Carlat, D.J., Camargo, C.A., & Herzog, D.B. (1997). Eating disorders in males: A report on 135 patients. *American Journal of Psychiatry*, 154, pp. 1127–1132.

Carlson, E.A., & Sroufe, A. (1995). Contribution of attachment theory to developmental psychopathology. In D. Cicchetti & D.J. Cohen (Eds.), *Developmental Psychopathology*, vol. 1, pp. 581–617. New York: Wiley.

Carlsson, A., & Lindqvist, M. (1963). Effect of chlorpromazine and haloperidol on the formation of 3-methoxytyramine and normetanephrine in mouse brain. *Acta Pharmacology*, 20, p. 140.

Carlsson, A., Waters, N., Holm-Waters, S., Tedroff, J., Nilsson, M., & Carlsson, M.L. (2001). Interactions between monoamines, glutamate, and GABA in schizophrenia: New evidence. *Annual Review of Pharmacology and Toxicology*, 41, pp. 237–260.

Carmen, B., Angeles, M., Munoz, A., & Amate, J. (2004). Efficacy and safety of naltrexone and acamprosate in the treatment of alcohol dependence: A systematic review. *Addiction*, 99, pp. 811–823.

Carmin, C.N., Pollard, C.A., & Gillock, K.L. (1999). Assessment of anxiety disorders in the elderly. In P.A. Lichtenberg (Ed.), *Handbook of Assessment in Clinical Gerontology*, pp. 59–90. New York: Wiley.

Carney, R.M., Freeland, K.E., Rich, M.W., & Jaffe, A.S. (1995). Depression as a risk factor for cardiac events in established coronary heart disease: A review of possible mechanisms. *Annals of Behavioral Medicine*, 17, pp. 142–149.

Carpenter, W.T., & Strauss, J.S. (1991). The prediction of outcome in schizophrenia. IV. Eleven-year follow-up of the Washington IPSS cohort. *Journal of Nervous and Mental Disease*, 179, pp. 517–525.

Carr. E.G. (1982). *How to Teach Sign Language to Developmentally Disabled Children*. Lawrence, KS: H & H Enterprises.

Carroll, R.A. (1999). Outcomes of treatment for gender dysphoria. *Journal of Sex Education and Therapy*, 24, pp. 128–136.

Carstensen, L.L., Isaacowitz, D.M., & Charles, S.T. (1999). Taking time seriously: A theory of socioemotional selectivity. *American Psychologist*, 54, pp. 165–181.

Carter, J.C., & Fairburn, C.G. (1998). Cognitive-behavioral self-help for binge eating disorder: A controlled effectiveness study. *Journal of Consulting and Clinical Psychology*, 66, pp. 616–623.

Carter, R. (1999) *Mapping the Mind*. Berkeley, CA: University of California Press.

Carver, C.S., &. Scheier, M.F. (1999). Optimism. In C.R. Snyder (Ed.), *Coping: The Psychology of What Works*, pp. 182–204. New York: Oxford University Press.

Casey, P. (2001). Multiple personality disorder. *Primary Care Psychiatry*, 7, pp. 7–11.

Cash, T.F., & Henry, P.E. (1995). Women's body images: The results of a national survey in the U.S.A. *Sex Roles*, 33, pp. 19–28.

Cash, T.F., Morrow, J.A., Hrabosky, J.I., & Perry, A.A. (2004). How has body image changed? A cross-sectional investigation of college women and men from 1983–2001. *Journal of Consulting and Clinical Psychology*, 72, pp. 1081–1089.

Caspi, A., Henry, B., McGee, R.O., Moffitt, T.E., et al. (1995). Temperamental origins of child and adolescent behavior problems: From age three to fifteen. *Child Development*, 66, pp. 55–68.

Caspi, A., & Moffitt, T.E. (1995). The continuity of maladaptive behavior: From description to understanding in the study of antisocial behavior. In D. Cicchetti & D.J. Cohen (Eds.), *Developmental Psychopathology*, vol. 1, pp. 472–511. New York: Wiley.

Caspi, A., & Roberts, B.W. (1999). Personality continuity and change across the life course. In L.A. Pervin & O.P. John (Eds.), *Handbook of Personality: Theory and Research*, 2nd ed., pp. 300–326. New York: Guilford.

Caspi, A. Sugden, K., Moffitt, T.E., Taylor, A., Craig, I.W., Harrington, H., McClay, J., Mill, J., Martin, J., Braithwaite, A., & Poulton, R. (2003). Influence of life stress on depression: Moderation by a polymorphism in the 5-HTT gene. *Science*, 301, pp. 386–389.

Caspi, A., McClay, J., Moffitt, T.E., Mill, J., Martin, J., Craig, I.W., Taylor, A., & Poulton, R. (2002). Role of genotype in the cycle of violence in maltreated children. *Science*, 297, pp. 851–854.

Cassidy, J. (1988). Child-mother attachment and the self in six-year-olds. *Child Development*, 59, pp. 121–134.

Cassidy, J., & Mohr, J.J. (2001). Unsolvable fear, trauma, and psychopathology: Theory, research, and clinical considerations related to disorganized attachment, across the life span. *Clinical Psychology: Science and Practice*, 8, pp. 275–298.

Cattarin, J.A., & Thompson, J.K. (1994). A three-year longitudinal study of body image, eating disturbance, and general psychological functioning in adolescent females. *Eating Disorders: Journal of Treatment and Prevention*, 2, pp. 114–125.

Cavell, T.A. (2001). Updating our approach to parent training. I: The case against targeting noncompliance. *Clinical Psychology: Science and Practice*, 8, pp. 299–318.

Celio, A.A., Winzelberg, A.J., Wilfley, D.E., Eppstein-Herald, D., Springer, E.A., Dev, P., & Taylor, C.B. (2000). Reducing risk ractors for eating disorders: Comparison of an internet and a clasroom-delivered psychoeducational program. *Journal of Consulting and Clinical Psychology*, 68, pp. 650–657.

Centers for Disease Control and Prevention (1999b). Data presented at the 1999 National HIV Prevention Conference, Atlanta, August 29–September 1.

Centers for Disease Control and Prevention (2000). National Center for HIV, STD, and TB Prevention. Special data run.

Chakos, M., Lieberman, J., Hoffman, E., Bradford, D., & Sheitman, B. (2001). Effectiveness of second-generation antipsychotics in patients with treatment-resistant schizophrenia: a review and meta-analysis of randomized trials. *American Journal of Psychiatry*, 158, pp. 518–526.

Chakrabarti, S., & Fombonne, E. (2001). Pervasive developmental disorders in preschool children. *Journal of the American Medical Association 285*, pp. 3093–3099.

Chamberlain, P., & Reid, J.B. (1998). Comparison of two community alternatives to incarceration for chronic juvenile offenders. *Journal of Consulting and Clinical Psychology, 66*, pp. 624–633.

Chambless, D.L., & Ollendick, T.H. (2000). Empirically supported psychological interventions. Controversies and evidence. *Annual Review of Psychology, 52*, pp. 685–716.

Chambless, D.L., et al. (2002). Marital interaction of agoraphobic women: A controlled, behavioral observation study. *Journal of Abnormal Psychology, 111*, pp. 502–512.

Charman, T. (2002). The prevalence of autism spectrum disorders: Recent evidence and future challenges. *European Child & Adolescent Psychiatry, 11*, pp. 249–256.

Chassin, L., Ritter, J., Trim, R.S., & King, K.M. (2003). Adolescent substance use disorders. In E.J. Mash and R.A. Barkley (Eds.), *Child Psychopathology*, 2nd ed., pp. 199–230. New York: Guilford.

Chen, R.T., & DeStefano, R. (1998). Vaccine adverse events: Causal or coincidental? *Lancet, 351*, pp. 611–612.

Cherlin, A.J. (1992). *Marriage, Divorce, Remarriage,* 2nd ed. Cambridge, MA: Harvard University Press.

Chesselet, M., & Delfs, J.M. (1996). Basal ganglia and movement disorders: An update. *Trends in Neurosciences, 19*, pp. 417–423.

Chiu, H.F.K., Lam, L.C.W., Chi, I., Leung, T., Li, S.W., Law, W.T., Chung, D.W.S., Fung, H.H.L, Kan, P.S., Lum, C.M., Ng, J., & Lau, J. (1998). Prevalence of dementia in Chinese elderly in Hong Kong. *Neurology, 50*, pp. 1002–1009.

Chorpita, B.F., Brown, T.A., & Barlow, D.H. (1998). Diagnostic reliability of the DSM-III-R anxiety disorders: Mediating effects of patient and diagnostician characteristics. *Behavior Modification, 22*, pp. 307–320.

Christensen, A., Atkins, D.C., Berns, S., Wheeler, J., Baucom, D.H., & Simpson, L.E. (2004). Traditional versus integrative behavioral couple therapy for significantly and chronically distressed married couples. *Journal of Consulting and Clinical Psychology, 72*, pp. 176–191.

Christensen, H. (2001). *Australian and New Zealand Journal of Psychiatry 35*, pp. 768–775.

Cicchetti, D., & Beegly, M. (1990). *Children with Down Syndrome: A Developmental Perspective.* New York: Cambridge University Press.

Ciompi, L. (1980). Catamnestic long-term study on the course of life and aging of schizophrenics. *Schizophrenia Bulletin, 6*, pp. 606–618.

Cipparone, R.C. (1987). The defense of battered women who kill. *University of Pennsylvania Law Review, 135*, pp. 427–452.

Claar, R.L. & Blumenthal, J.A. (2003). The value of stress-management interventions in life-threatening medical conditions. *Current Directions in Psychological Science, 12*, pp. 133–137.

Clark, D.A., Beck, A.T., & Alford, B.A. (1999). *Scientific Foundations of Cognitive Theory and Therapy of Depression.* New York: Wiley.

Clark, D.C., & Goebel-Fabbri, A.E. (1999). Lifetime risk of suicide in major affective disorders. In D.G. Jacobs et al. (Eds.), *The Harvard Medical School Guide to Suicide Assessment and Intervention*, pp. 270–286. San Francisco: Jossey-Bass.

Clark, D.M. (1986b). Cognitive therapy for anxiety. *Behavioral Psychotherapy, 14*, pp. 283–294.

Clark, D.M., Salkovskis, P.M., Hackmann, A., Wells, A., Fennell, M., Ludgate, J., Ahmad, S., Richards, H.C., & Gelder, M. (1998). Two psychological treatments for hypochondriasis: A randomised controlled trial. *British Journal of Psychiatry, 173*, pp. 218–225.

Clark, D.M., Salkovskis, P.M., Hackmann, A., Wells, A., Ludgate, J., & Gelder, M. (1999). Brief cognitive therapy for panic disorder: A randomized controlled trial. *Journal of Consulting and Clinical Psychology, 67*, pp. 583–589.

Clark, L.A. (1999). Dimensional approaches to personality disorder assessment and diagnosis. In C.R. Cloninger (Ed.), *Personality and Psychopathology*, pp. 219–244. Washington, D.C.: American Psychiatric Press.

Clark, L.A., Livesley, W.J., & Morey, L. (1997). Personality disorder assessment: The challenge of construct validity. *Journal of Personality Disorders, 11*, pp. 205–231.

Clark, L.A., & Watson, D. (1991). Tripartite model of anxiety and depression: Psychometric evidence and taxonomic implications. *Journal of Abnormal Psychology, 100*, pp. 316–336.

Clark, R., Anderson, N.B., Clark, V.R., & Williams, D.R. (1999). Racism as a stressor for African Americans: A biopsychosocial model. *American Psychologist, 54*, pp. 805–816.

Clarke, J.W. (1990). *On Being Mad or Merely Angry.* Princeton, NJ: Princeton University Press.

Clarkin, J.F., Foelsch, P.A., Levy, K.N., Hull. J.W., Delaney, J.C., & Kernberg, O.F., (2001). The development of a psychodynamic treatment for patients with borderline personality disorder: A preliminary study of behavioral change. *Journal of Personality Disorders, 15*, pp. 487–495.

Clayton, A.H., & West, S.G. (2003). The effects of antidepressants on human sexuality. *Primary Psychiatry, 10*, pp. 62–70.

Cleckley, H. (1976). *The Mask of Sanity,* 5th ed. St. Louis: Mosby.

Clifton, A., Turkheimer, E., & Oltmanns, T.F. (2004). Contrasting perspectives on personality problems: Descriptions from the self and others. *Personality and Individual Differences, 36*, pp. 1499–1514.

Cloninger, C.R. (1987). Neurogenetic adaptive mechanisms in alcoholism. *Science, 236*, pp. 410–416.

Cloninger, C.R., Sigvardsson, S., & Bohman, M. (1996). Type I and type II alcoholism: An update. *Alcohol Health and Research World, 20*, pp. 18–23.

Cohen, A.N., Hammen, C., Henry, R.M., & Daley, S.E. (2004). Effects of stress and social support on recurrence in bipolar disorder. *Journal of Affective Disorders, 82*, pp. 143–147.

Cohen, L.J., & Galynker, I.I. (2002). Clinical features of pedophilia and implications for treatment. *Journal of Psychiatric Practice, 8*, pp. 276–289.

Cohen, S., Kaplan, J.R., Cunnick, J.E., Manuck, S.B., & Rabin, B.S. (1992). Chronic social stress, affiliation, and cellular immune response in nonhuman primates. *Psychological Science, 3*, pp. 301–304.

Cohen, S., & Williamson. G.M. (1991). Stress and infectious disease in humans. *Psychological Bulletin, 109*, pp. 5–24.

Cohen-Kettenis, P.T., & Gooren, L.J. (1999). Transsexualism: A review of etiology, diagnosis and treatment. *Journal of Psychosomatic Research, 46*, pp. 315–333.

Cohler, B.J., & Nakamura, J.E. (1996). In J. Sadavoy, L.W. Lazarus, L.F. Jarvik, & G.T. Grossberg (Eds.), *Comprehensive Review of Geriatric Psychiatry II*, pp. 153–194. Washington, DC: American Psychiatric Press.

Coie, J., & Kupersmidt, J., (1983). A behavioral analysis of emerging social status in boys' groups. *Child Development, 54*, pp. 1400–1416.

Colcombe, S., & Kramer, A.F. (2003). Fitness effects on the cognitive function of older adults: A meta-analytic study. *Psychological Science, 14*, pp. 125–130.

Cole, M.G., McCusker, J., Dendukuri, N., & Han, L. (2002). Symptoms of delirium among elderly medical inpatients with or without dementia. *Journal of Neuropsychiatry and Clinical Neuroscience 14*, pp. 167–175.

Cole, W. (1992). Incest perpetrators: Their assessment and treatment, *Psychiatric Clinics of North America, 15*, pp. 689–670.

Coleman, P.G. (2005). Uses of reminiscence: Functions and benefits. *Aging & Mental Health, 9*, pp. 291–294.

Collaer, M.L., & Hines, M. (1995). Human behavioral sex differences: A role for gonadal hormones during early development. *Psychological Bulletin, 118*, pp. 55–107.

Comas-Diaz, L. (2000). An ethnopolitical approach to working with people of color. *American Psychologist, 55*, pp. 1319–1325.

Compton, W.M., Helzer, J.E., Hwu, H.G., Yeh, E.K., McEvoy, L., Tipp, J.E., & Spitznagel, E.L. (1991). New methods in cross-cultural psychiatry: Psychiatric illness in Taiwan and the United States. *American Journal of Psychiatry, 148*, pp. 1697–1704.

Conduct Problems Prevention Research Group (1999). Initial impact of the Fast Track prevention trial for conduct problems: II. Classroom effects. *Journal of Consulting and Clinical Psychology, 67*, pp. 648–657.

Conger, J.J. (1956). Alcoholism: Theory, problem, and challenge. II. Reinforcement theory and the dynamics of alcoholism. *Quarterly Journal of Studies on Alcohol, 17*, pp. 296–305.

Conley, R.R., & Kelly, D.L. (2001). Management of treatment resistance in schizophrenia. *Biological Psychiatry, 50*, pp. 898–911.

Conners, C.K. (1980). Artificial colors and the diet of disruptive behavior: Current status of research. In R.M. Knights & D.J. Bakker (Eds.), *Treatment of Hyperactive and Learning Disabled Children.* Baltimore: University Park Press.

Consumer Reports (1995, November). Mental health: Does therapy help? pp. 734–739.

Connor, T.J., Kelly, J.P., & Leonard, B.E. (1997). Forced swim test-induced neurochemical, endocrine, and immune changes in the rat. *Pharmacology Biochemistry and Behavior, 58*, pp. 961–967.

Constable, N. (2004). *This Is Cocaine (Addiction).* New York: Sanctuary Publishing.

Contrada, R.J. et al., (2001). Ethnicity-related sources of stress and their effects on wellbeing. *Current Directions in Psychological Science 9*, pp. 136–139.

Cook, J.M., Riggs, D.S., Thompson, R., Coyne, J.C., & Sheikh, J.I. (2004). Posttraumatic stress disorder and current relationship functioning among World War II ex-prisoners of war. *Journal of Family Psychology, 18*, pp. 36–45.

Cook, M., & Mineka, S. (1991). Selective associations in the origins of phobic fears and their implications for behavior therapy. In P.R. Martin (Ed.), *Handbook of Behavior Therapy and Psychological Science: An Integrative Approach*, pp. 413–434. New York: Pergamon.

Coombs, R.H., Howatt, W.A., & Coombs, K. (2005). Addiction recovery tools. In R.H. Coombs (Ed.), *Addiction Counseling Review*, pp. 425–446. Mahwah, NJ: Erlbaum.

Coons, P. (1986). The prevalence of multiple personality disorder. *Newsletter of the International Society for the Study of Multiple Personality and Dissociation, 4*, pp. 6–8.

Coons, P., & Milstein, V. (1988). Psychogenic amnesia: A clinical investigation of 25 consecutive cases. Unpublished data cited in D. Spiegel & E. Cardena (1991). Disintegrated experience: The dissociative disorders revisited. *Journal of Abnormal Psychology, 100*, pp. 366–378.

Coons, P.M., & Bowman, E.S. (2001). Ten-year follow-up study of patients with dissociative identity disorder. *Journal of Trauma and Dissociation, 2*, pp. 73–89.

Cooper, M.H. (1994). Regulating tobacco: Can the FDA break America's smoking habit? *CQ Research, 4*, pp. 843–858.

Cooper, P.J. (1995). Eating disorders and their relationship to mood and anxiety disorders. In K.D. Brownell & C.G. Fairburn (Eds.), *Eating Disorders and Obesity: A Comprehensive Handbook*, pp. 159–164. New York: Guilford.

Coovert, D.L., Kinder, B.N., & Thompson, J.K. (1989). The psychosexual aspects of anorexia nervosa and bulimia nervosa: A review of the literature. *Clinical Psychology Review*, 9, pp. 169–180.

Copolov, D., Velakoulis, D., McGorry, P., Mallard, C., Yung, A., Rees, S., Jackson, G., Rehm, A., Brewer, W., & Pantelis, C. (2000). Neurobiological findings in early phase schizophrenia. *Brain Research Reviews*, 31, pp. 157–165.

Corbitt, E.M. (2002). Narcissism from the perspective of the five-factor model. In P.T. Costa, Jr., & T.A. Widiger (Eds.), *Personality Disorders and the Five-Factor Model of Personality*, 2nd ed., pp. 293–298. Washington, D.C.: American Psychological Association.

Cordova, J.V., Jacobson, N.S., Gottman, J.M., Rushe, R., & Cox, G. (1993). Negative reciprocity and communication in couples with a violent husband. *Journal of Abnormal Psychology*, 102, pp. 559–564.

Corse, C.D., Manuck, S.B., Cantwell, J.D., Giordani, B., & Matthews, K.A. (1982). Coronary-prone behavior pattern and cardiovascular response in persons with and without coronary heart disease. *Psychosomatic Medicine*, 44, pp. 449–459.

Coryell, W., Solomon, D., Turvey, C., Keller, M., Leon, A.C., Endicott, J., Schettler, P., Judd, L., & Mueller, T. (2003). The long-term course of rapid-cycling bipolar disorder. *Archives of General Psychiatry*, 60, pp. 914–920.

Coser, L.A. (1977). *Masters of Sociological Thought: Ideas in Historical and Social Context*. San Diego: Harcourt Brace Jovanovich.

Costello, E.J., Compton, S.N., Keeler, G., & Angold, A. (2003). Relationships between poverty and psychopathology: A natural experiment. *JAMA*, 290(15), pp. 2023–2029.

Courchesne, E., et al. (2001). Unusual brain growth patterns in early life in patients with autistic disorder: An MRI study. *Neurology*, 57, pp. 245–254.

Couture, S.M., & Penn, D.L. (2003). Interpersonal contact and the stigma of mental illness. A review of the literature. *Journal of Mental Health*, 12, pp. 291–305.

Covault, J., Gelernter, J., Hesselbrock, V., Nellissery, M., & Kranzler, H.R. (2004). Allelic and haplotypic association of GABRA2 with alcohol dependence. *American Journal of Medical Genetics (Neuropsychiatric Genetics)*, 129B, pp. 104–109.

Cowan, C.P., & Cowan, P.A. (1992). *When Partners Become Parents*. New York: Basic Books.

Cox, B.J., Enns, M.W., Walker, J.R., Kjernisted, K., & Pidlubny, S.R. (2001). Psychological vulnerabilities in patients with major depression vs panic disorder. *Behaviour Research and Therapy*, 39, pp. 567–573.

Coyne, J.C. (1999). Thinking interactionally about depression: A radical restatement. In T. Joiner & J.C. Coyne (Eds.), *The Interactional Nature of Depression*, pp. 365–392. Washington, DC: American Psychological Association.

Coyne, J.C., Thompson, R., & Palmer, S.C. (2002). Marital quality, coping with conflict, marital complaints, and affection in couples with a depressed wife. *Journal of Family Psychology*, 16, pp. 26–37.

Crabbe, J.C. (2002). Genetic contributions to addiction. *Annual Review of Psychology*, 53, pp. 435–462.

Craig, T.J., Siegel, C., Hopper, K., Lin, S., et al. (1997). Outcome in schizophrenia and related disorders compared between developing and developed countries: A recursive partitioning re-analysis of the WHO. *British Journal of Psychiatry*, 170, pp. 229–233.

Craighead, W.E., & Miklowitz, D.J. (2000). Psychosocial interventions for bipolar disorder. *Journal of Clinical Psychiatry*, 61 (suppl 13), pp. 58–64.

Cramer, P. (2000). Defense mechanisms in psychology today: Further processes for adaptation. *American Psychologist*, 55, pp. 637–646.

Craske, M.G., & Rowe, M.K. (1997). Nocturnal panic. *Clinical Psychology: Science and Practice*, 4, pp. 153–174.

Crawford, T.N., Cohen, P., & Brook, J.S. (2001). Dramatic-erratic personality disorder symptoms: I. Continuity from early adolescence into adulthood. *Journal of Personality Disorders*, 15, pp. 319–335.

Crick, N.R., & Dodge, K.A. (1994). A review and reformulation of social information-processing mechanisms in children's social adjustment. *Psychological Bulletin*, 115, pp. 74–101.

Crimlisk, H., Bhatia, K., Cope, H., et al. (1998) Slater revisited: 6-year follow-up study of patients with medically unexplained motor symptoms. *British Medical Journal*, 316, pp. 582–586.

Crits-Christoph, P. (1998). Psychosocial treatments for personality disorders. In P.E. Nathan & J.M. Gorman (Eds.), *A Guide to Treatments that Work*, pp. 544–553. New York: Oxford University Press.

Cronbach, L.J., & Meehl, P.E. (1955). Construct validity in psychological tests. *Psychological Bulletin*, 52, pp. 281–302.

Cross-National Collaborative Panic Study. Second Phase Investigators. (1992). Drug treatment of panic disorder: Comparative efficacy of alprazolam, imipramine, and placebo. *British Journal of Psychiatry*, 160, pp. 191–202.

Crowley, T.J., Milkulich, S.K., MacDonald, M., Young, S.E., & Zerbe, G.O. (1998). Substance-dependent, conduct-disordered adolescent males: Severity of diagnosis predicts 2-year outcome. *Drug & Alcohol Dependence*, 49, pp. 225–237.

Csikszentmihalyi, M., & Larson, R. *Being Adolescent*. New York: Basic Books.

Cuckle, H. (2001). Time for a total shift to first trimester screening for Down syndrome. *The Lancet*, 358, pp. 1658–1659.

Cummings, E.M., & Davies, P. (1994). *Children and Marital Conflict*. New York: Guilford.

Cummings, J.L., & Cole, G. (2002). Alzheimer disease. *Journal of the American Medical Association*, 287, pp. 2335–2338.

Cummings, J.L., Vinters, H.V., Cole, G.M., & Khachaturian, Z.S. (1998). Alzheimer's disease: Etiologies, pathophysiology, cognitive reserve, and treatment opportunities. *Neurology*, 51 (suppl. 1), pp. S2–17.

Curtis, C.E., Calkins, M.E., & Iacono, W.G. (2001). Saccadic disinhibition in schizophrenia patients and their first-degree biological relatives. *Experimental Brain Research*, 137, pp. 228–236.

Curtis, N.M., Ronan, K.R., & Borduin, C.M. (2004). Multisystemic treatment: A meta-analysis of outcome studies. *Journal of Family Psychology*, 18(3), pp. 411–419.

D'Emilio, J., & Freedman, E.B. (1988). *Intimate Matters: A History of Sexuality in America*. New York: Harper & Row.

D'Onofrio, B., Turkheimer, E., Emery, R., Slutske, W., Heath, A., Madden, P., & Martin, N. (In press). A genetically informed study of marital instability and its association with offspring psychopathology. *Journal of Abnormal Psychology*.

Daly, M.P. (1999). Diagnosis and management of Alzheimer disease. *Journal of the American Board of Family Practice*, 12, pp. 375–385.

Danforth, J.S., Barkley, R.A., & Stokes, T.F. (1991). Observations of parent-child interactions with hyperactive children: Research and clinical implications. *Clinical Psychology Review*, 11, pp. 703–727.

Davidson, J.R., DuPont, R.L., Hedges, D., & Haskins, J.T. (1999). Efficacy, safety, and tolerability of venlafaxine extended release and buspirone in outpatients with generalized anxiety disorder. *Journal of Clinical Psychiatry*, 60, pp. 528–535.

Davidson, J.R.T. (2001). Pharmacotherapy of generalized anxiety disorder. *Journal of Clinical Psychiatry*, 62 (suppl. 11), pp. 46–50.

Davidson, L.L., & Heinrichs, R.W. (2003). Quantification of frontal and temporal lobe brain-imaging findings in schizophrenia: A meta-analysis. *Psychiatry Research: Neuroimaging*, 122, pp. 69–87.

Davidson, P.R., & Parker, K.C.H. (2001). Eye movement desensitization and reprocessing (EMDR): A meta-analysis. *Journal of Consulting and Clinical Psychology*, 69, pp. 305–316.

Davidson, R.J., Pizzagalli, D., Nitschke, J.B., & Putnam, K. (2002). Depression: Perspectives from affective neuroscience. *Annual Review of Psychology*, 53, pp. 545–574.

Davidson, W.S., Redner, R., Blakely, C.H., Mitchell, C.M., & Emshoff, J.G. (1987). Diversion of juvenile offenders: An experimental comparison. *Journal of Consulting and Clinical Psychology*, 55, pp. 68–75.

Davila, J. (2001). Refining the association between excessive reassurance seeking and depressive symptoms: The role of related interpersonal constructs. *Journal of Social and Clinical Psychology*, 20, pp. 538–559.

Davis, B., Sheeber, L., Hops, H., & Tildesley, E. (2000). Adolescent responses to depressive parental behaviors in problem-solving interactions: Implications for depressive symptoms. *Journal of Abnormal Child Psychology*, 28, pp. 541–465.

Davis, D., & Herdt, G. (1997). Cultural issues and sexual disorders. In T.A. Widiger, A.J. Frances, H.A. Pincus, R. Ross, M.B. First, & W. Davis (Eds.), *DSM-IV Sourcebook*, Vol. 3, pp. 951–958. Washington, D.C.: American Psychiatric Press.

Davis, D.L. (1998). The sexual and gender identity disorders. *Transcultural Psychiatry*, 35, pp. 401–412.

Davis, G.C., & Akiskal, H.S. (1986). Descriptive, biological, and theoretical aspects of borderline personality disorder. *Hospital and Community Psychiatry*, 37, pp. 685–692.

Dawson, D.A. (2000). Drinking patterns among individuals with and without DSM-IV alcohol use disorders. *Journal of Studies on Alcohol*, 61, pp. 111–125.

De Silva, P., & Rachman, S. (2004). *Obsessive–Compulsive Disorders: The Facts*, 3rd ed. Oxford: Oxford University Press.

Deblinger, E., McLeer, S.V., Atkins, M.S., Ralphe, D., & Foa, E. (1989). Post-traumatic stress in sexually abused, physically abused, and nonabused children. *Child Abuse and Neglect*, 13, pp. 403–408.

Delespaul, P., deVries, M., & van Os, J. (2002). Determinants of occurrence and recovery from hallucinations in daily life. *Social Psychiatry and Psychiatric Epidemiology*, 37, pp. 97–104.

D'Emilio, J., & Freedman, E.B. (1988). *Intimate Matters: A History of Sexuality in America*. New York: Harper & Row.

DePaulo, J.R., & Horvitz, L.A. (2002). *Understanding Depression: What We Know and What You Can Do About it*. New York: Wiley.

Dershowitz, A.M. (1994). *The Abuse Excuse and Other Copouts, Sob Stories, and Evasions of Responsibility*. Boston: Little-Brown.

DeRubeis, R.J., Gelfand, L.A., Tang, TZ, & Simons, A.D. (1999). Medications versus cognitive behavior therapy for severely depressed outpatients: Mega-analysis of four randomized comparisons. *American Journal of Psychiatry*, 156, pp. 1007–1013.

Devanand, D.P., & Levy, S.T. (1995). Neuroleptic treatment of agitation and psychosis in dementia. *Journal of Geriatric Psychiatry and Neurology*, 8, (suppl. 1), pp. S18–S27.

DeVane, C.L., & Sallee, F.R. (1996). Serotonin selective reuptake inhibitors in child and adolescent psychopharmacology: A review of published evidence. *Journal of Clinical Psychiatry, 57,* pp. 55–66.

Dick, D.M., & Foroud, T. (2003). Candidate genes for alcohol dependence: A review of genetic evidence from human studies. *Alcoholism: Clinical and Experimental Research, 5,* pp. 868–879.

Dick, D.M., Jones, K., Saccone, N., Hinrichs, A.L., Wang, J.C., Goate, A. et al. (2006). Endophenotypes successfully lead to gene identification: Results from the collaborative study on the genetics of alcoholism. *Behavior Genetics, 36.*

Dickens, C. (1842/1970). *American Notes and Pictures from Italy.* New York: Oxford University Press.

Dickens, W.T., & Flynn, J.R. (2001). Heritability estimates versus large environmental effects: The IQ paradox resolved. *Psychological Review, 108,* pp. 346–369.

Dickerson, S.S. & Kemeny, M.E. (2004). Acute stressors and cortisol responses: A theoretical integration and synthesis of laboratory research. *Psychological Bulletin, 130,* pp. 355–391.

Dickson, D.W. (2001). Neuropathology of Alzheimer's disease and other dementias. *Clinics in Geriatric Medicine, 17,* pp. 209–228.

Digman, J.M. (2002). Historical antecedents of the five-factor model. In P.T. Costa, Jr., & T.A. Widiger (Eds.), *Personality Disorders and the Five-Factor Model of Personality,* 2nd ed., pp. 17–22. Washington, D.C.: American Psychological Association.

Dinan, T.G. (2000). Antidepressants and violence: Cause for concern or media hype? *Human Psychopharmacology: Clinical and experimental, 15,* pp. iii–iv.

Dishion, T.J, McCord, J., & Poulin, F. (1999). When interventions harm: Peer groups and problem behavior. *American Psychologist, 54,* pp. 755–764.

Dishion, T.J., French, D.C., & Patterson, G.R. (1995). The development and ecology of antisocial behavior. In D. Cicchetti & D.J. Cohen (Eds.), *Developmental Psychopathology,* vol. 1, pp. 421–471. New York: Wiley.

Ditton, P.M. (1999). *Mental Health and Treatment of Inmates and Probationers.* Washington, DC: Bureau of Justice Statistics.

Docherty, N.M., DeRosa, M., & Andreasen, N.C. (1996). Communication disturbances in schizophrenia and mania. *Archives of General Psychiatry, 53,* pp. 358–364.

Dodge, K.A., Lansford, J.E., Burks, V.S., Bates, J.E., Pettit, G.S., Fontaine, R., & Price, J.M. (2003). Peer rejection and social information-processing factors in the development of aggressive behavior problems in children. *Child Development, 74*(2), pp. 374–393.

Dohrenwend, B.P., Link, B.G., Kern, R., Shrout, P.E., & Markowitz, J. (1990). Measuring life events: The problem of variability within event categories. *Stress Medicine, 6,* pp. 179–187.

Dolan-Sewell, R.T., Krueger, R.F., & Shea, M.T. (2001). Co-occurrence with syndrome disorders. In W.J. Livesley (Ed.), *Handbook of Personality Disorders: Theory, Research, and Treatment,* pp. 84–104. New York: Guilford.

Donahey, K.M., & Carroll, R.A. (1993). Gender differences in factors associated with hypoactive sexual desire. *Journal of Sex and Marital Therapy, 19,* pp. 25–40.

Donavan, D.M. (1999). Efficacy and effectiveness: Complementary findings from two multisite trials evaluating outcomes of alcohol treatments differing in theoretical orientations. *Alcoholism: Clinical and Experimental Research, 23,* pp. 564–572.

Doss, B.D. (2004). Changing the way we study change in psychotherapy. *Clinical Psychology: Science and Practice, 11,* pp. 368–386.

Dotti, M.T., et al. (2002). A Rett syndrome MECP2 mutation that causes mental retardation in men. *Neurology, 58,* pp. 226–230.

Dougherty, D.D., & Rauch, S.L. (Eds.) (2001). *Psychiatric Neuroimaging Research: Contemporary Strategies.* Washington, D.C.: American Psychiatric Publishing.

Douglas, V.I. (1983). Attention and cognitive problems. In M. Rutter (Ed.), *Developmental Neuropsychiatry,* pp. 280–329. New York: Guilford.

Draguns, J.G. & Tanaka-Matsumi, J. (2003). Assessment of psychopathology across and within cultures: Issues and findings. *Behaviour Research & Therapy, 41,* pp. 755–776.

Drevets, W.C. (2002). Neuroimaging studies of mood disorders. In J.E. Helzer and J.J. Hudziak (Eds.), *Defining Psychopathology in the 21st Century: DSM-IV and Beyond,* pp. 71–106. Washington, D.C.: American Psychiatric Press.

Drevets, W.C., & Raichle, M.E. (1998). Reciprocal suppression of regional cerebral blood flow during emotional versus higher cognitive processes: Implications for interactions between emotion and cognition. *Cognition and Emotion, 12,* pp. 353–385.

Dreyfuss, R. (1996). Tobacco, enemy number 1. *Mother Jones, 21,* pp. 42–48.

Drobes, D.J., Stritzke, W.G.K., & Coffey, S.F. (2000). Psychophysiological factors. In M. Hersen and A.S. Bellack (Eds.), *Psychopathology in Adulthood,* 2nd ed., pp. 112–130. Needham Heights, MA: Allyn & Bacon.

Duhig, A.M., Renk, K., Epstein, M.K., & Phares, V. (2000). Interparental agreement on internalizing, externalizing, and total behavior problems: A meta-analysis. *Clinical Psychology: Science and Practice, 7,* pp. 435–453.

Dunkin, J.J., & Anderson-Hanley, C. (1998). Dementia caregiver burden: A review of the literature and guidelines for assessment and intervention. *Neurology, 51* (suppl. 1), pp. 53–59.

Dunmore, E., Clark, D.M., & Ehlers, A. (2001). A prospective investigation of the role of cognitive factors in persistent Posttraumatic Stress Disorder (PTSD) after physical and sexual assault. *Behaviour Research and Therapy, 39,* pp. 1063–1084.

Durham, M.L., & LaFond, J.Q. (1988). A search for the missing premise of involuntary therapeutic commitment: Effective treatment of the mentally ill. *Rutgers Law Review, 40,* pp. 303–368.

Durkheim, E. (1897/1951). *Suicide: A Study in Sociology.* New York: Free Press.

Dusseldorp, E., van Elderen, T., Maes, S., Meulman, J., & Kraaij, V. (1999). A meta-analysis of psychoeducational programs for coronary heart disease patients. *Health Psychology, 18,* pp. 506–519.

Dworkin, R.H., Oster, H., Clark, S.C., & White, S.R. (1998). Affective expression and affective experience in schizophrenia. In M.F. Lenzenweger & R.H. Dworkin (Eds.), *Origins and Development of Schizophrenia: Advances in Experimental Psychopathology,* pp. 385–424. Washington, DC: American Psychological Association.

Dyk, P.H., & Adams, G.R. (1990). Identity and intimacy: An initial investigation of three theoretical models using cross-lag panel correlations. *Journal of Youth and Adolescence, 19,* pp. 91–110.

Earls, F., & Mezzacappa, E. (2002). Conduct and oppositional disorders. In M. Rutter & E. Taylor (Eds.), *Child and Adolescent Psychiatry,* 4th ed., pp. 419–436. Oxford, UK: Blackwell.

Earnst, K.S., & Kring, A.M. (1997). Construct validity of negative symptoms: An empirical and conceptual review. *Clinical Psychology Review, 17,* pp. 167–190.

Eberlin, M., McConnachie, G., Igel, S., & Volpe, L. (1993). Facilitated communication: A failure to replicate the phenomenon. *Journal of Autism and Developmental Disorders, 23,* pp. 507–530.

Eddy K.T., Keel, P.K., Dorer, D.J., Delinsky, S.S., Franko, D.L., & Herzog, D.B. (2002). Longitudinal compari-

son of anorexia nervosa subtypes. *International Journal of Eating Disorders, 31,* pp. 191–201.

Edenberg, H.J., Dick, D.M., Xuei, X., Tian, H., Almasy, L., Bauer, L.O., et al. (2004). Variations in GABRA2, encoding the a2 subunit of the GABA-A receptor are associated with alcohol dependence and with brain oscillations. *American Journal of Human Genetics, 74,* pp. 705–714.

Edwards, W., & Hensley, C. (2001). Contextualizing sex offender management legislation and policy: Evaluating the problem of latent consequences in community notification laws. *International Journal of Offender Therapy and Comparative Criminology, 45,* pp. 83–101.

Egeland, J.D., & Sussex, J.N. (1985). Suicide and family loading for affective disorders. *Journal of the American Medical Association, 254,* pp. 915–918.

Ehlers, A., & Clark, D.M. (2000). A cognitive model of persistent posttraumatic stress disorder. *Behavior Research and Therapy, 38,* pp. 319–345.

Ehlers, A., Mayou, R.A., & Bryant, B. (1998). Psychological predictors of chronic posttraumatic stress disorders after motor vehicle accidents. *Journal of Abnormal Psychology, 107,* pp. 508–519.

Eich, E., Macaulay, D., Lowenstein, R.J., & Dihle, P.H. (1997). Memory, amnesia, and dissociative identity disorder. *Psychological Science, 8,* pp. 417–422.

Eifert, G.H., Zvolensky, M.J., & Lejuez, C.W. (2000). Heart-focused anxiety and chest pain: A conceptual and clinical review. *Clinical Psychology: Science and Practice, 7,* pp. 403–417.

Eisenberg, N., Shepard, S.A., Fabes, R.A., Murphy, B.C., & Guthrie, I.K. (1998). Shyness and children's emotionality, regulation, and coping: Contemporaneous, longitudinal, and across-context relations. *Child Development 69,* pp. 767–790.

Ellason, J.W., & Ross, C.A. (1997). Two-year follow-up of inpatients with dissociative identity disorder. *American Journal of Psychiatry, 154,* pp. 832–839.

Ellis, A. (1962). *Reason and Emotion in Psychotherapy.* New York: Lyle Stuart.

Ellis, A. (1999). Early theories and practices of rational-emotive behavior therapy and how they have been augmented and revised during the last three decades. *Journal of Rational-Emotive and Cognitive Behavior Therapy, 17,* pp. 69–93.

Ellis, B.J. (2004). Timing of pubertal maturation in girls: An integrated life history approach. *Psychological Bulletin, 130*(6), pp. 920–958.

Emery, R.E. (1982). Interparental conflict and the children of discord and divorce. *Psychological Bulletin, 92,* pp. 310–330.

Emery, R.E. (1992). Family conflict and its developmental implications: A conceptual analysis of deep meanings and systemic processes. In C.U. Shantz & W.W. Hartup (Eds.), *Conflict in Child and Adolescent Development,* pp. 270–298. London: Cambridge University Press.

Emery, R.E. (1994). *Renegotiating Family Relationships: Divorce, Child Custody, and Mediation.* New York: Guilford.

Emery, R.E. (1999). *Marriage, Divorce, and Children's Adjustment.* Thousand Oaks, CA: Sage.

Emery, R.E. (1999a). *Marriage, Divorce, and Children's Adjustment,* 2nd ed. Thousand Oaks, CA: Sage.

Emery, R.E. (1999b). Changing the rules for determining child custody in divorce cases. *Clinical Psychology: Science and Practice, 6,* pp. 323–327.

Emery, R.E., & Laumann-Billings, L. (1998). An overview of the nature, causes, and consequences of abuse family relationships: Toward differentiating maltreatment and violence. *American Psychologist, 53,* pp. 121–135.

Emery, R.E., & Laumann-Billings, L. (2002). In M. Rutter & E. Taylor (Eds.), *Child and Adolescent Psychiatry,* 4th ed., pp. 325–339. Oxford, UK: Blackwell.

Emery, R.E., & Rogers, K.C. (1990). The role of behavior therapists in child custody cases. In M. Hersen & R.M. Eisler (Eds.), *Progress in Behavior Modification*, pp. 60–89. Beverly Hills: Sage.

Emery, R.E., Fincham, F.D., & Cummings, E.M. (1992). Parenting in context: Systemic thinking about parental conflict and its influence on children. *Journal of Consulting and Clinical Psychology, 60*, pp. 909–912.

Emery, R.E., Laumann-Billings, L., Waldron, M., Sbarra, D.A., and Dillon, P. (2001). Child custody mediation and litigation: Custody, contact, and co-parenting 12 years after initial dispute resolution. *Journal of Consulting and Clinical Psychology, 69*, pp. 323–332.

Emery, R.E., Matthews, S., & Kitzmann, K. (1994). Child custody mediation and litigation: Parents' satisfaction and functioning a year after settlement. *Journal of Consulting and Clinical Psychology, 62*, pp. 124–129.

Emery, R.E., Otto, R.K., & O'Donohue, W. (In press). A Critical Assessment of Child Custody Evaluations: Weak Science in a Flawed System. *Psychological Science in the Public Interest*.

Emery, R.E., Sbarra, D.S., & Grover, T. (2005). Divorce mediation: Research and reflections. *Family Court Review, 43*, pp. 22–37.

Emery, R.E., Waldron, M.C., Kitzmann, K.M., & Aaron, J. (1999). Delinquent behavior, future divorce or nonmarital childbearing, and externalizing behavior among offspring: A 14 year prospective study. *Journal of Family Psychology, 13*, pp. 1–12.

Emmons, R.A. (1997). Motives and goals. In R. Hogan, J. Johnson, & S. Briggs (Eds.), *Handbook of Personality Psychology*, pp. 486–512. San Diego, CA: Academic Press.

Emrick, C.D. (1999). Alcoholics anonymous and other 12-step groups. In M. Galanter & H.D. Kleber (Eds.), *Textbook of Substance Abuse Treatment*, 2nd ed., pp. 403–411. Washington, DC: American Psychiatric Press.

Eng, W., Heimberg, R.G., Hart, T.A., Schneier, F.R., & Liebowitz, M.R. (2001). Attachment in individuals with social anxiety disorder: The relationship among adult attachment styles, social anxiety, and depression. *Emotion, 1*, pp. 365–380.

Ennis, B., & Emery, R. (1978). *The Rights of Mental Patients*. New York: Avon.

ENRICHD Investigators (2003). Effects of treating depression and low percieved social support on clinical events after myocardial infarction. *Journal of the American Medical Association, 289*, p. 3106.

Epstein, J.N., Erkanli, A., Conners, C.K., Klaric, J., Costello, J.E., & Angold, A. (2003). Relations between continuous performance test performance measures and ADHD behaviors. *Journal of Abnormal Child Psychology, 31*(5), pp. 543–554.

Epstein, S. (1994). Integration of the cognitive and the psychodynamic unconscious. *American Psychologist, 49*, pp. 709–724.

Erdelyi, M.H. (1990). Repression, reconstruction, and defense: History and integration of the psychoanalytic and experimental frameworks. In J.L. Singer (Ed.), *Repression and Dissociation*, pp. 1–32. Chicago: University of Chicago Press.

Erikson, E.H. (1950). *Childhood and Society*. New York: Norton (revised edition 1963), Harmondsworth: Penguin.

Erikson, E.H. (1959, 1980). *Identity and the Life Cycle*. New York: Norton.

Erikson, E.H. (1968). *Identity: Youth and Crisis*. New York: Norton.

Erlenmeyer-Kimling, L., Squires-Wheeler, E., Adamo, U.H., Bassett, A.S., Cornblatt, B.A., Kestenbaum, C.J., Rock, D., Roberts, S.A., & Gottesman, I.I. (1995). The New York high-risk project: Psychoses and cluster: A personality disorders in offspring of schizophrenic parents at 23 years of follow-up. *Archives of General Psychiatry, 52*, pp. 857–865.

Ernulf, K.E., & Innala, S.M. (1995). Sexual bondage: A review and unobtrusive investigation. *Archives of Sexual Behavior, 24*, pp. 631–655.

Eron, L.D. (1982). Parent-child interaction, television violence, and aggression in children. *American Psychologist, 37*, pp. 197–211.

Esterling, B.A., L'Abate, L., Murray, E.J., & Pennebaker, J.W. (1999). Empirical foundations for writing in prevention and psychotherapy: Mental and physical health outcomes. *Clinical Psychology Review, 19*, pp. 79–96.

Eubanks-Carter, C., Burckell, L.A., & Goldfried, M.R. (2005). Enhancing therapeutic effectiveness with lesbian, gay, and bisexual clients. *Clinical Psychology: Science and Practice, 12*, pp. 1–18.

Evans, D.L., Leserman, J., Perkins, D.O., et al. (1997). Severe life stress as a predictor of early disease progression in HIV infection. *American Journal of Psychiatry, 154*, pp. 630–634.

Evans, G.W. (2004). The environment of childhood poverty. *American Psychologist, 59*, pp. 7–92.

Ewing, C. (1991). Preventive detention and execution: The constitutionality of punishing future crimes. *Law and Human Behavior, 15*, pp. v139–163.

Ewing, S.E., Falk, W.E., & Otto, M.W. (1996). The recalcitrant patient: Treating disorders of personality. In M.H. Pollack & M.W. Otto (Eds.), *Challenges in Clinical Practice: Pharmacologic and Psychosocial Strategies*, pp. 355–379. New York: Guilford.

Exner, J.E., Jr. (1993). *The Rorschach: A Comprehensive System, Vol. 1: Basic Foundations*, 3rd ed. New York: Wiley.

Exner, J.E., Jr. (1999). The Rorschach: Measurement concepts and issues of validity. In S.E. Embretson, & S.L. Hershberger (Eds.), *The New Rules of Measurement: What Every Psychologist and Educator Should Know*, pp. 159–183. Mahwah, NJ: Erlbaum.

Factor, S.A. (2002). Pharmacology of atypical antipsychotics. *Clinical Neuropharmacology, 25*, pp. 153–157.

Fadda, R., & Rosetti, Z.L. (1998). Chronic ethanol consumption: From neuroadaptation to neurodegeneration. *Progress in Neurology, 56*, pp. 385–431.

Fagan, P.J., Wise, T.N., Schmidt, C.W., & Berlin, F.S. (2002). Pedophilia. *Journal of the American Medical Association, 288*, pp. 2458–2465.

Faigman, D.L., & Monahan, J. (2005). Psychological evidence at the dawn of the law's scientific age. *Annual Review of Psychology, 56*, pp. 631–659.

Faigman, D.L., Kaye, D.H., Saks, M.J., & Sanders, J. (1997). *Modern Scientific Evidence: The Law and Science of Expert Testimony*. St. Paul, MN: West.

Fairburn, C.G. (1996). *Overcoming Binge Eating*. New York: Guilford.

Fairburn, C.G. (2002). Cognitive-behavioral therapy for bulimia nervosa. In C.G. Fairburn & K.D. Brownell (Eds.), *Eating Disorders and Obesity*, 2nd ed., pp. 302–307. New York: Guilford.

Fairburn, C.G., & Beglin, S.J. (1990). Studies of the epidemiology of bulimia nervosa. *American Journal of Psychiatry, 147*, pp. 401–480.

Fairburn, C.G., & Brownell, K.D. (Eds.), *Eating Disorders and Obesity*, 2nd ed. New York: Guilford.

Fairburn, C.G., & Wilson, G.T. (Eds.) (1993). *Binge Eating: Nature, Assessment, and Treatment*. New York: Guilford.

Fairburn, C.G., Hay, P.J., & Welch, S.L. (1993). Binge eating and bulimia nervosa: Distribution and determinants. In C.G. Fairburn & G.T. Wilson (Eds.), *Binge Eating: Nature, Assessment, and Treatment*, pp. 123–143. New York: Guilford.

Fairburn, C.G., Jones, R., Peveler, R.C., Carr, S.J., Solomon, R.A., O'Connor, M.E., Burton, J., & Hope, R.A. (1991). Three psychological treatments for bulimia nervosa. *Archives of General Psychiatry, 48*, pp. 463–469.

Fairburn, C.G., Jones, R., Peveler, R.C., Hope, R.A., & O'Connor, M. (1993). Psychotherapy and bulimia nervosa: Longer-term effects of interpersonal psychotherapy, behavior therapy, and cognitive behavior therapy. *Archives of General Psychiatry, 50*, pp. 419–428.

Fairburn, C.G., Stice, E., Cooper, Z., Doll, H.A., Norman, P.A. & O'Connor, M.E. (2003). Understanding persistence in bulimia nervosa: A 5-year naturalistic study. *Journal of Consulting and Clinical Psychology, 71*, pp. 103–109.

Fairburn, C.G., Welch, S.L., Doll, H.A., Davies, B.A., & O'Connor, M.E. (1997). Risk factors for bulimia nervosa: A community-based case-control study. *Archives of General Psychiatry, 54*, pp. 509–517.

Falk, A.J. (1999). Sex offenders, mental illness, and criminal responsibility: The constitutional boundaries of civil commitment after *Kansas v. Hendricks American Journal of Law and Medicine, 25*, pp. 117–147.

Fallon, P., Katzman, M.A., & Wooley, S.C. (1994). *Feminist Perspectives on Eating Disorders*. New York: Guilford.

Fann, J.R. (2000). The epidemiology of delirium: A review of studies and methodological issues. *Seminars in Clinical Neuropsychiatry, 5*, pp. 64–74.

Farah, M.J., O'Reilly, R.C., & Vecera, S.P. (1993). Dissociated overt and covert recognition as an emergent property of a lesioned neural network. *Psychological Review, 100*, pp. 571–588.

Faraone, S.V. (2003). Report from the 4th international meeting of the attention deficit hyperactivity disorder molecular genetics network. *American Journal of Medical Genetics, 121B*, pp. 55–59.

Faraone, S.V., Tsuang, M.T., & Tsuang, D.W. (1999). *Genetics of Mental Disorders*. New York: Guilford.

Farde, L., Nordstrom, A., Karlsson, P., Halldin, C., & Sedvall, G. (1995). Positron emission tomography studies on dopamine receptors in schizophrenia. *Clinical Neuropharmacology, 18* (suppl. 1), pp. S121–S129.

Faris, R.E.L., & Dunham, H.W. (1939). *Mental Disorders in Urban Areas: An Ecological Study of Schizophrenia and other Psychoses*. Chicago: University of Chicago Press.

Farmer, A.E., & Griffiths, H. (1992). Labeling and illness in primary care: Comparing factors influencing general practitioners' and psychiatrists' decisions regarding patient referral to mental illness services. *Psychological Medicine, 22*, pp. 717–723.

Farmer, A.E., McGuffin, P., & Gottesman, I.I. (1987). Twin concordance for DSM-III schizophrenia: Scrutinizing the validity of the definition. *Archives of General Psychiatry, 44*, pp. 634–641.

Farquhar, J.W., Macoby, N., Wood, P.D., et al. (1977). Community education for cardiovascular health. *Lancet, i*, pp. 1192–1195.

Farrer, L.A., Cupples, A., Haines, J.L., Hyman, B., Kukull, W.A., Mayeux, R., Myers, R.H., Pericek-Vance, M.A., Risch, N., & van Duijn, C.M. (1997). Effects of age, sex, and ethnicity on the association between apolipoprotein E genotype and Alzheimer disease: A meta-analysis. *Journal of the American Medical Association. 278*, pp. 1349–1356.

Farrington, D., Ohlin, L., & Wilson, J.Q. (1986). *Understanding and Controlling Crime*. New York: Springer.

Faust, D., & Ziskin, J. (1988). The expert witness in psychology and psychiatry. *Science, 241*, pp. 31–35.

Fawzy, F.I., Fawzy, N.W., Hyun, C.S., Gutherie, D., Fahey, J.L., & Morton, D. (1993). Malignant melanoma. Effects of an early structured psychiatric intervention, coping, and affective state on recurrence and survival six years later. *Archives of General Psychiatry, 50*, pp. 681–689.

Federal Bureau of Investigation (2004). *Uniform Crime Reports*. Washington, DC.

Federal Bureau of Investigation. (1999). *Uniform Crime Reports, 1998*. Washington, DC: U.S. Department of Justice.

Federoff, I.C., & Taylor, S. (2001). Psychological and pharmacological treatments of social phobia: A meta-analysis. *Journal of Clinical Psychopharmacology, 21,* pp. 311–324.

Fedoroff, J.P. (2003). The paraphilic world. In S.B. Levine and C.B. Risen (Eds.), *Handbook of Clinical Sexuality for Mental Health Professionals,* pp. 333–356. New York: Brunner-Routledge.

Feingold, A., & Mazzella, R. (1998). Gender differences in body image are increasing. *Psychological Science, 9,* pp. 190–195.

Feingold, B.F. (1975). *Why Your Child Is Hyperactive.* New York: Random House.

Fenton, W.S. (2000). Heterogeneity, subtypes, and longitudinal course in schizophrenia. *Psychiatric Annals, 30,* pp. 638–644.

Fernandez, H. (1998). *Heroin.* Center City, MN: Hazeldon.

Ferster, C.B. (1961). Positive reinforcement and behavioral deficits of autistic children. *Child Development, 32,* pp. 437–456.

Figley, C.R. (1978). *Stress Disorders Among Vietnam Veterans.* New York: Brunner/Mazel.

Fingarette, H. (1988). *Heavy Drinking: The Myth of Alcoholism as a Disease.* Berkeley: University of California Press.

Fink, H.A., MacDonald, R., Rutks, I.R., Nelson, D.B., and Wilt, T.J. (2002). Sildenafil for male erectile dysfunction: a systematic review and meta-analysis. *Archives of Internal Medicine, 162,* pp. 1349–1360.

Fink, M. (2001). Convulsive therapy: A review of the first 55 years. *Journal of Affective Disorders, 63,* pp. 1–15.

Finney, J.W., & Moos, R.H. (2002). Psychosocial treatments for alcohol use disorders. In P.E. Nathan & J.M. Gorman (Eds.), *A Guide to Treatments That Work,* 2nd ed., pp. 157–168. New York: Oxford.

Finney, J.W., Moos, R.H., & Humphreys, K. (1999). A comparative evaluation of substance abuse treatment. II. Linking proximal outcomes of 12-step and cognitive-behavioral treatment to substance use outcomes. *Alcoholism: Clinical and Experimental Research, 23,* pp. 537–544.

Finney, J.W., Moos, R.H., & Timko, C. (1999). The course of treated and untreated substance use disorders: Remission and resolution, relapse and mortality. In B.S. McCrady & E.E. Epstein (Eds.), *Addictions: A Comprehensive Guidebook,* pp. 30–49. New York: Oxford University Press.

First, M.B., Bell, C.C., Cuthbert, B., Krystal, J.H., Malison, R., Offord, D.R., Reiss, D., Shea, M.T., Widiger, T., & Wisner, K.L. (2002). Personality disorders and relational disorders. In D.J. Kupfer, M.B. First, and D.A. Regier (Eds.), *A Research Agenda for DSM-V,* pp. 123–199. Washington, D.C.: American Psychiatric Association.

Fischer, C., Bozanovic-Sosic, R., & Norris, M. (2004). Review of delusions in dementia. *American Journal of Alzheimer's Disease & Other Dementias, 19,* pp. 19–23.

Fischer, M., Barkley, R.A., Smallish, L., & Fletcher, K. (2002). Young adult follow-up of hyperactive children: Self-reported psychiatric disorders, comorbidity, and the role of childhood conduct problems and teen CD. *Journal of Abnormal Child Psychology, 30*(5), pp. 463–475.

Fishbain, D.A., Cutler, R.B, Rosomoff, H.L., Rosomoff, R., Steele, R. (1998). Do antidepressants have an analgesic effect in psychogenic pain and somatoform pain disorder? A meta-analysis. *Psychosomatic Medicine, 60,* pp. 503–509.

Fisher, P.J., & Breakey, W.R. (1991). The epidemiology of alcohol, drug, and mental disorders among homeless persons. *American Psychologist, 46,* pp. 1115–1128.

Fitch, S.A., & Adams, G.R. (1983). Ego-identity and intimacy status: Replication and extension. *Developmental Psychology, 19,* pp. 839–845.

Fitch, W.L., Petrella, R.C., & Wallace, J. (1987). Legal ethics and the use of mental health experts in criminal cases. *Behavioral Sciences and the Law, 5,* pp. 105–117.

Fitzpatrick, A.L., Kuller, L.H., Ives, D.G., Lopez, O.L., Jagust, W., Breitner, J.C.S., Jones, B., Lyketsos, C., & Dulberg, C. (2004). Incidence and prevalence of dementia in the cardiovascular health study. *Journal of the American Geriatrics Society, 52,* pp. 195–204.

Flanagan, J.C. (1982). *New Insights to Improve the Quality of Life at Age 70.* Palo Alto, CA: American Institutes for Research.

Flint, A.J. (1994). Epidemiology and comorbidity of anxiety disorders in the elderly. *American Journal of Psychiatry, 151,* pp. 640–649.

Foa, E.B. & Street, G.P. (2001). Women and traumatic events. *Journal of Clinical Psychiatry, 62* pp. 29–34.

Foa, E.B., & Riggs, D.S. (1995). Post traumatic stress disorder following assault: Theoretical considerations and empirical findings. *Current Directions in Psychological Science, 5,* pp. 61–65.

Foa, E.B., & Wilson, R. (2001). *Stop Obsessing: How to Overcome Your Obsessions and Compulsions* (revised edition). New York: Bantom Doubleday.

Foa, E.B., Dancu, C.V., Hembree, E.A., Jaycox, L.H., Meadows, E.A., & Street, G.P. (1999). A comparison of exposure therapy, stress inoculation training, and their combination for reducing post-traumatic stress disorder in female assault victims. *Journal of Consulting and Clinical Psychology, 67,* pp. 194–200.

Foa, E.B., Zoellner, L.A., Feeny, N.C., Hembree, E.A., & Alvarez-Conrad, J. (2002). Does imaginal exposure exacerbate PTSD symptoms? *Journal of Consulting and Clinical Psychology, 70,* pp. 1022–1028.

Folkman, S., & Moskowitz, J.T. (2000). Stress, positive emotion, and coping. *Current Directions in Psychological Science, 9,* pp. 115–118.

Foot, P. (1990). Ethics and the death penalty: Participation of forensic psychiatrists in capital trials. In R. Rosner & R. Weinstock (Eds.), *Ethical Practice in Psychiatry and the Law,* pp. 202–217. New York: Plenum.

Fordyce, W.E. (1976). *Behavioral Methods for Chronic Pain and Illness.* St. Louis: Mosby.

Forehand, R., & Long, N. (2002). *Parenting the Strong-willed Child.* New York: McGraw-Hill.

Foreman, M.C., Wakefield, B., Culp, K., & Milisen, K. (2001). Delirium in elderly patients: An overview of the state of the science. *Journal of Gerontological Nursing, 27,* pp. 12–20.

Fornari, V., Wlodarczyk-Bisaga, K., Matthews, M., Sandberg, D., Mandel, F.S., & Katz, J.L. (1999). Perception of family functioning and depressive symptomatology in individuals with anorexia nervosa or bulimia nervosa. *Comprehensive Psychiatry, 40,* pp. 434–444.

Forrest, K.A. (2001). Toward an etiology of dissociative identity disorder: A neurodevelopmental approach. *Consciousness and Cognition, 10,* pp. 259–293.

Fortgang, E. (1999). Is pot bad for you? Six questions answered. *Rolling Stone, 807,* pp. 53–54.

Foster, S.L., & Cone, J.D. (1986). Design and use of direct observation procedures. In A.R. Ciminero, K.S. Calhoun, & H.E. Adams (Eds.), *Handbook of Behavioral Assessment,* 2nd ed. New York: Wiley.

Foster, S.L., & Cone, J.D. (1995). Validity issues in clinical assessment. *Psychological Assessment, 7,* pp. 248–260.

Fox, P.J., Kelly, S.E., & Tobin, S.L. (1999). Defining dementia: Social and historical background of Alzheimer disease. *Genetic Testing, 3,* pp. 13–19.

Fozard, J.L., & Gordon-Salant, S. (2001). Changes in vision and hearing with aging. In J.E. Birren & K.W. Schaie (Eds.), *Handbook of the Psychology of Aging,* 5th ed., pp. 241–266. San Diego: Academic Press.

Frances, A., First, M.B., & Pincus, H.A. (1995). *DSM-IV Guidebook.* Washington, DC: American Psychiatric Press.

Frank, E., & Thase, M.E. (1999). Natural history and preventative treatment of recurrent mood disorders. *Annual Review of Medicine, 50,* pp. 453–468.

Frank, E., Swartz, H.A., & Kupfer, D.J. (2000). Interpersonal and social rhythm therapy: Managing the chaos of bipolar disorder. *Biological Psychiatry, 48,* pp. 593–604.

Franklin, J.A., & Andrews, G. (1989). Stress and the onset of agoraphobia. *Australian Psychologist, 24,* pp. 203–219.

Franklin, M.E., & Foa, E.B. (2002). Cognitive behavioral treatments for obsessive compulsive disorder. In P.E. Nathan and J.M. Gorman (Eds.), *A Guide to Treatments That Work,* 2nd ed. London, England: Oxford University Press.

Frasure-Smith, N. & Lespérance, F. (2005). Depression and coronary heart disease: Complex synergism of mind, body, and environment. *Current Directions in Psychological Science, 14,* pp. 39–43.

Frasure-Smith, N., & Prince, R. (1985). Long-term follow-up of the ischemic heart disease life stress monitoring program. *Psychosomatic Medicine, 51,* pp. 485–513.

Freud, S. (1917/1961). Mourning and melancholia. In J. Strachey (Ed. and Trans.), *The Standard Edition of the Complete Psychological Works of Sigmund Freud,* vol. 14. London: Hogarth Press.

Freud, S. (1924/1962). The aetiology of hysteria. In J. Strachey (Ed. and Trans.), *The Standard Edition of the Complete Psychological Works of Sigmund Freud,* vol. 3, pp. 191–221. London: Hogarth Press.

Freund, A.M., & Baltes, P.B. (2002). Life-management strategies of selection, optimization, and compensation: Measurement by self-report and construct validity. *Journal of Personality and Social Psychology, 82,* pp. 642–662.

Freund, K., & Blanchard, R. (1993). Erotic target location errors in male gender dysphorics, paedophiles, and fetishists. *British Journal of Psychiatry, 162,* pp. 558–563.

Freund, K., & Seto, M.C. (1998). Preferential rape in the theory of courtship disorder. *Archives of Sexual Behavior, 27,* pp. 433–445.

Frick, P.J., Bodin, S.D., & Barry, C.T. (2000). Psychopathic traits and conduct problems in community and clinic-referred samples of children: Further development of the psychopathy screening device. *Psychological Assessment, 12,* pp. 382–393.

Friedman, M., & Rosenman, R.H. (1959). Association of specific overt behavior pattern with blood and cardiovascular findings: Blood cholesterol level, blood clotting time, incidence of arcus senilis and clinical coronary artery disease. *Journal of the American Medical Association, 169,* pp. 1286–1296.

Friedman, M., Thoresen, C.D., Gill, J.J., et al. (1986). Alteration of Type A behavior and its effect on cardiac recurrences in post-myocardial infarction patients: Summary results of the recurrent coronary prevention project. *American Heart Journal, 112,* pp. 653–665.

Friedman, R.A., & Kocsis, J.H. (1996). Pharmacotherapy for chronic depression. *Psychiatric Clinics of North America, 19,* pp. 121–132.

Fries, J.F. (1990). Medical perspectives upon successful aging. In P.B. Baltes & M.M. Baltes (Eds.), *Successful Aging: Perspectives from the Behavioral Sciences,* pp. 35–49. Cambridge: Cambridge University Press.

Frith, C., & Dolan, R.J. (2000). The role of memory in the delusions associated with schizophrenia. In D.L. Schacter and E. Scarry (Eds.), *Memory, Brain, and Belief,* pp. 115–135. Cambridge, MA: Harvard University Press.

Frith, U. (2003). *Autism: Explaining the Enigma,* 2nd ed. Oxford, England: Blackwell.

Froehlich, J.C. (1997). Opioid peptides. *Alcohol Health and Research World, 21,* pp. 144–148.

Frueh, B.C., Turner, S.M., & Beidel, D.C. (1995). Exposure therapy for combat-related PTSD: A critical review. *Clinical Psychology Review,* 15, pp. 799–817.

Fuller, R.K., & Gordis, E. (2004). Does disulfiram have a role in alcoholism treatment today? *Addiction,* 99, pp. 115–135. 21–24.

Funtowicz, M.N., & Widiger, T.A. (1999). Sex bias in the diagnosis of personality disorders: An evaluation of DSM-IV criteria. *Journal of Abnormal Psychology,* 108, pp. 195–201.

Furstenberg, F.F. (2000). The sociology of adolescence and youth in the 1990s: A critical commentary. *Journal of Marriage and the Family,* 62, pp. 896–910.

Fyer, A.J., Mannuzza, S., Chapman, T.F., Liebowitz, M.R., & Klein, D.F. (1993). A direct interview family study of social phobia. *Archives of General Psychiatry,* 50, pp. 286–293.

Gabbard, G.O. (2000). Psychodynamic psychotherapy of borderline personality disorder: A contemporary approach. *Bulletin of the Menninger Clinic,* 65, pp. 41–57.

Gabbard, G.O. (2001). Musings on the report of the international consensus development conference on female sexual dysfunction: Definitions and classification. *Journal of Sex and Marital Therapy,* 27, pp. 145–147.

Gadde, K.M., & Krishman, R.R. (1997). Recent advances in the pharmacologic treatment of bipolar illness. *Psychiatric Annals,* 27, pp. 496–506.

Galea, S., Ahern, J., Resnick, H., Kilpatrick, D., Bucuvalas, M., Gold, J., & Vlahov, D. (2002). Psychological sequelae of the September 11 terrorist attacks. *New England Journal of Medicine,* 346, pp. 982–987.

Galea, S., Boscarino, J., Resnick, H., & Vlahov, D. (2003). Mental health in New York City after September 11 terrorist attacks: Results from two population surveys. In R.W. Manderscheid & M.J. Henderson (Eds.), *Mental Health, United States, 2002.* Washington: U.S. Government Printing Office.

Gallagher-Thompson, D., & Osgood, N.J. (1997). Suicide in later life. *Behavior Therapy,* 28, pp. 23–41.

Garb, H. (1998). *Studying the Clinician: Judgment Research and Psychological Assessment.* Washington, D.C.: American Psychological Association.

Garber, H.I. (1988). *The Milwaukee Project: Preventing Mental Retardation in Children at Risk.* Washington, DC: American Association on Mental Retardation.

Garber, J. (1984). Classification of childhood psychopathology: A developmental perspective. *Child Development,* 55, pp. 30–48.

Garber, J., & Hollon, S.D. (1991). What can specificity designs say about causality in psychopathology research? *Psychological Bulletin,* 110, pp. 129–136.

Garber, J., Keiley, M.K., & Martin, N.C. (2002). Developmental trajectories of adolescents' depressive symptoms: Predictors of change. *Journal of Consulting and Clinical Psychology,* 70(1), pp. 79–95.

Garfinkel, P.E., & Garner, D.M. (1982). *Anorexia Nervosa: A Multidimensional Perspective.* New York: Basic Books.

Garfinkel, P.E., Kennedy, S.H., & Kaplan, A.S. (1995). Views on classification and diagnosis of eating disorders. *Canadian Journal of Psychiatry,* 40, pp. 445–456.

Garfinkel, P.E., Lin, B., & Goering, P. (1996). Purging and nonpurging forms of bulimia nervosa in a community sample. *International Journal of Eating Disorders.*

Garland, A.F., & Zigler, E. (1993). Adolescent suicide prevention: Current research and social policy implications. *American Psychologist,* 48, pp. 169–182.

Garmezy, N. (1978). DSM-III: Never mind the psychologists; Is it good for the children? *Clinical Psychologist,* 31, pp. 1–6.

Garner, D.M., & Bemis, K.M. (1982). A cognitive-behavioral approach to anorexia nervosa. *Cognitive Therapy and Research,* 6, pp. 123–150.

Garner, D.M., & Needleman, L.D. (1996). Stepped-care and decision-tree models for treating eating disor-

ders. In J.K.Thompson, *Body Image, Eating Disorders, and Obesity,* pp. 225–252. Washington, DC: American Psychological Association.

Garner, D.M., Garfinkel, P.E., Schwartz, D., & Thompson, M. (1980). Cultural expectations of thinness in women. *Psychological Reports,* 47, pp. 483–491.

Garner, D.M., Garner, M.V., & Rosen, L.W. (1993). Anorexia nervosa "restrictors" who purge: Implications for subtyping anorexia nervosa. *International Journal of Eating Disorders,* 13, pp. 171–185.

Garner, D.M., Olmstead, M.P., & Polivy, J. (1983). The Eating Disorder Inventory: A measure of cognitive-behavioral dimensions of anorexia nervosa and bulimia. In P.L. Darby, P.E. Garfinkel, D.M. Garner, & D.V. Coscina (Eds.), *Anorexia Nervosa: Recent Developments in Research,* pp. 173–184. New York: Liss.

Garssen, B., de Ruiter, C., & Van Dyck, R. (1992). Breathing retraining: A rational placebo? *Clinical Psychology Review,* 12, pp. 141–153.

Garza-Trevino, E. (1994). Neurobiological factors in aggressive behavior. *Hospital and Community Psychiatry,* 45, pp. 690–699.

Gatz, M., & Smyer, M.A. (2001). Mental health and aging at the outset of the twenty-first century. In J.E. Birren & K.W. Schaie (Eds.), *Handbook of the Psychology of Aging,* 5th ed., pp. 523–544. San Diego: Academic Press.

Gaulin, S.J.C., & McBurney, D.H. (2001). *Psychology: An Evolutionary Approach.* Upper Saddle River, NJ: Prentice-Hall.

Geddes, J.R., Burgess, S., Hawton, K., Jamison, K., & Goodwin, G.M. (2004). Long-term lithium therapy for bipolar disorder: Systematic review and meta-analysis of randomized controlled studies. *American Journal of Psychiatry,* 161, pp. 217–222.

Gehlbach, S.H. (1988). *Interpreting the Medical Literature: Practical Epidemiology for Clinics,* 2nd ed. New York: Macmillan.

Geller, J.L., McDermeit, M., & Brown, J. (1997). Pyromania? What does it mean? *Journal of Forensic Sciences,* 42, pp. 1052–1057.

Gershoff, E.T. (2002). Corporal punishment by parents and associated child behaviors and experience: A meta-analytic and theoretical review. *Psychological Bulletin,* 128, pp. 539–579.

Ghaemi, S.N., Lenox, M.S., & Baldessarini, R.J. (2001). Effectiveness and safety of long-term antidepressant treatment in bipolar disorder. *Journal of Clinical Psychiatry,* 62, pp. 565–569.

Gianoulakis, C., DeWaele, J.P., & Thavundayil, J. (1996). Implications of the endogenous opioid system in excessive ethanol consumption. *Alcohol,* 13, pp. 19–23.

Gibbs, N.A., & Oltmanns, T.F. (1995). The relation between obsessive-compulsive personality traits and subtypes of compulsive behavior. *Journal of Anxiety Disorders,* 9, pp. 397–410.

Gibbs, N.A., South, S.C., & Oltmanns, T.F. (2002). Attentional coping style in obsessive-compulsive personality disorder: A test of the intolerance of uncertainty hypothesis. *Personality and Individual Differences,* 33, pp. 1205–1222.

Gilbert, P. (2001). Evolutionary approaches to psychopathology: The role of natural defences. *Australian and New Zealand Journal of Psychiatry,* 35, pp. 17–27.

Gilbertson, M.W. et al. (2002). Smaller hippocampal predicts pathologic vulnerability to psychological trauma. *Nature Neuroscience,* 5, pp. 1242–1247.

Gillberg, C. (1988). The role of the endogenous opioids in autism and possible relationships to clinical features. In L. Wing (Ed.), *Aspects of Autism: Biological Research,* pp. 31–37. London: Gaskell.

Gillberg, C., & Schaumann, H. (1982). Social class and infantile autism. *Journal of Autism and Developmental Disorders,* 12, pp. 223–228.

Gillberg, C., Rastam, M., & Gillberg, C. (1995). Anorexia nervosa 6 years after onset. I. Personality disorders. *Comprehensive Psychiatry,* 36, pp. 61–69.

Gilligan, C. (1982). *In a Different Voice.* Cambridge, MA: Harvard University Press.

Gladis, M.M.; Gosch, E.A.; Dishuk, N.M.; Crits-Christoph, P. (1999). Quality of life: Expanding the scope of clinical significance. *Journal of Consulting and Clinical Psychology,* 6, pp. 320–331.

Glaser, D. (2002). Child sexual abuse. In M. Rutter & E. Taylor (Eds.), *Child and Adolescent Psychiatry,* 4th ed., pp. 340–358. Oxford, UK: Blackwell.

Glatt, S.J., Faraone, S.V., & Tsuang, M.T. (2003). Association between a functional catechol o-methyl-transferase gene polymorphism and schizophrenia: Meta-analysis of case-control and family-based studies. *American Journal of Psychiatry,* 160, pp. 469–476.

Gleaves, D.H. (1996). The sociocognitive model of dissociative identity disorder: A reexamination of the evidence. *Psychological Bulletin,* 120, pp. 42–59.

Gleaves, D.H., Smith, S.M., Butler, L.D., & Spiegel, D. (2004). False and recovered memories in the laboratory and clinic: A review of experiment and clinical evidence. *Clinical Psychology: Science & Practice,* 11, pp. 3–28.

Glick, I.D., & Berg, P.H. (2002). Time to study discontinuation, relapse, and compliance with atypical or conventional antipsychotics in schizophrenia and related disorders. *International Clinical Psychopharmacology,* 17, pp. 65–68.

Goddard, A.W., & Charney, D.S. (1997). Toward an integrated neurobiology of panic disorder. *Journal of Clinical Psychiatry,* 58, (suppl. 2), pp. 4–11.

Gold, M.S., Tabrah, H., Frost-Pineda, K. (2001). Psychopharmacology of MDMA (Ecstasy). *Psychiatric Annals,* 31, pp. 675–681.

Gold, S.N., & Heffner, C.L. (1998). Sexual addiction: Many conceptions, minimal data. *Clinical Psychology Review,* 18, pp. 367–381.

Goldberg, J., True, W.R., Eisen, S.A., & Henderson, W.G. (1990). A twin study of the effects of the Vietnam War on posttraumatic stress disorder. *Journal of the American Medical Association,* 263, pp. 2725–2729.

Goldberg, J.F., & Truman, C.J. (2003). Antidepressant-induced mania: An overview of current controversies. *Bipolar Disorders,* 5, pp. 407–420.

Goldberg, T.E., & Weinberger, D.R. (1995). A case against subtyping in schizophrenia. *Schizophrenia Research,* 17, pp. 147–152.

Goldfried, M.R., & Davison, G.C. (1994). *Clinical Behavior Therapy,* 2nd ed. New York: Wiley-Interscience.

Goldman, M.S. (1994). The alcohol expectancy concept: Applications to assessment, prevention, and treatment of alcohol abuse. *Applied and Preventive Psychology,* 3, pp. 131–144.

Goldman, M.S., Brown, S.A., & Christiansen, B.A. (1987). Expectancy theory: Thinking about drinking. In H.T. Blane & K.E. Leonard (Eds.), *Psychological Theories of Drinking and Alcoholism,* pp. 181–226. New York: Guilford.

Goldman, M.S., Brown, S.A., Christiansen, B.A., & Smith, G.T. (1991). Alcoholism and memory: Broadening the scope of alcohol-expectancy research. *Psychological Bulletin,* 110, pp. 137–146.

Goldman, M.S., Darkes, J., & Del Boca, F.K. (1999). Expectancy mediation of biopsychosocial risk for alcohol use and alcoholism. In I. Kirsch (Ed.), *How Expectancies Shape Experience,* pp. 233–262. Washington, DC: American Psychological Association.

Goldman-Rakic, P.S., Muly, E.C., & Williams, G.V. (2000). D1 receptors in prefrontal cells and circuits. *Brain Research Review,* 31, pp. 295–301.

Goldsmith, S.K. (2001). *Risk Factors for Suicide.* Washington, D.C.: National Academy Press.

Goldstein, A.J., & Chambless, D.L. (1978). A reanalysis of agoraphobia. *Behavior Therapy*, 9, pp. 47–59.

Goldstein, G. (2003). Delirium, dementia, and amnestic and other cognitive disorders. In M. Hersen and S.M. Turner (Eds.), *Adult Psychopathology and Diagnosis*, 4th ed., pp. 153–191. New York: Wiley.

Goldstein, I. (2004). Epidemiology of erectile dysfunction. *Sexuality & Disability*, 22, pp. 113–120.

Goldstein, J.J., Rosenfarb, I., Woo, S., & Nuechterlein, K. (1997). Transactional processes which can function as risk or protective factors in the family treatment of schizophrenia. In H.D. Brenner and W. Boeker (Eds.), *Towards a Comprehensive Therapy for Schizophrenia*, pp. 147–157. Kirkland, WA: Hogrefe & Huber.

Goldstein, M.J. (1988). The family and psychopathology. *Annual Review of Psychology*, 39, pp. 283–299.

Golwyn, D.H., & Sevlie, C.P. (1992). Paraphilias, nonparaphilic sexual addictions, and social phobia. *Journal of Clinical Psychiatry*, 53, p. 330.

Gomberg, E.S.L. (1999). Substance abuse in the elderly. In P.J. Ott, R.E. Tarter, & R.T. Ammerman (Eds.), *Sourcebook on Substance Abuse: Etiology, Epidemiology, Assessment, and Treatment*, pp. 113–125. Boston: Allyn & Bacon.

Good, B., & Kleinman, A. (1985). Culture and anxiety: Cross-cultural evidence for the patterning of anxiety disorders. In A.H. Tuma & J. Maser (Eds.), *Anxiety and the Anxiety Disorders*. Hillsdale, NJ: Erlbaum.

Gooding, D.G., Miller, M.D., & Kwapil, T.R. (2000). Smooth pursuit eye tracking and visual fixation in psychosis-prone individuals. *Psychiatry Research*, 93, pp. 41–54.

Goodman, G.S., Ghetti, S., Quas, J.A., Edelstein, R.S., Alexander, K.W., Redlich, A.D., Cordon, I.M., & Jones, D.P.H. (2003). A prospective study of memory for child sexual abuse: New findings relevant to the repressed-memory controversy. *Psychological Science*, 14, pp. 113–118.

Goodman, L.A., Koss, M.P., & Russo, N.F. (1993). Violence against women: Physical and mental health effects. Part I. Research findings. *Applied and Preventive Psychology*, 2, pp. 79–89.

Goodman, L.A., Koss, M.P., Fitzgerald, L.F., Russo, N.F., & Keita, G.P. (1993). Male violence against women: Current research and future directions. *American Psychologist*, 48, pp. 1054–1058.

Goodman, S.H., & Gotlib, I.H. (1999). Risk for psychopathology in the children of depressed mothers: A developmental model for understanding mechanisms of transmission. *Psychological Review*, 106(3), pp. 458–490.

Goodman, T.A. (1985). From Tarasoff to Hopper: The evolution of the therapist's duty to protect third parties. *Behavioral Sciences and the Law*, 3, pp. 195–225.

Goodman, W.K., Price, L.H., Rasmussen, S.A., Mazure, C., Fleischman, R.L., Hill, C.L., Heninger, G.R., & Charmey, D.S. (1989). The Yale-Brown Obsessive-Compulsive Scale. 1. Development, use, and reliability. *Archives of General Psychiatry*, 46, pp. 1006–1011.

Goodwin, D.W. (1991). The genetics of alcoholism. In P.R. McHugh & V.A. McKusick (Eds.), *Genes, Brain, and Behavior*. New York: Raven Press.

Goodwin, P. J. et al., (2001). The Effect of Group Psychosocial Support on Survival in Metastatic Breast Cancer. *New England Journal of Medicine*, 345, pp. 1719–1726.

Gordis, L. (2004). *Epidemiology* (3rd ed.). Philadelphia, PA: Elsevier Saunders.

Gosselin, C.C., & Wilson, G.D. (1980). *Sexual Variations*. London: Faber & Faber.

Gotlib, I.H., & Hammen, C. (1992). *Psychological Aspects of Depression: Toward a Cognitive-Interpersonal Integration*. New York: Wiley.

Gotlib, I.H., & Neubauer, D.L. (2000). Information-processing approaches to the study of cognitive biases in depression. In S.L. Johnson and A.M. Hayes (Eds.), *Stress, Coping, and Depression*, pp. 117–143. Mahwah, NJ: Erlbaum.

Gottesman, I.G. (1963). Genetic aspects of intelligent behavior. In N. Ellis (Ed.), *The Handbook of Mental Deficiency: Psychological Theory and Research*, pp. 253–296. New York: McGraw-Hill.

Gottesman, I.I. & Hanson, D.R. (in press). Human development: Biological and genetic processes. *Annual Review of Psychology*.

Gottesman, I.I. (1987). The psychotic hinterlands or, the fringes of lunacy. *British Medical Bulletin*, 43, pp. 1–13.

Gottesman, I.I. (1991). *Schizophrenia Genesis: The Origins of Madness*. New York: Freeman.

Gottesman, I.I., & Goldsmith, H.H. (1994). Developmental psychopathology of antisocial behavior: Inserting genes into its ontogenesis and epigenesis. In C.A. Nelson (Ed.), *Threats to Optimal Development: Integrating Biological, Psychological, and Social Risk Factors*, pp. 69–104. Hillsdale, NJ: Erlbaum.

Gottesman, I.I., & Gould, T.D. (2003). The endophenotype concept in psychiatry: Etymology and strategic intentions. *American Journal of Psychiatry*, 160, pp. 636–645.

Gottesman, I.I., & Hanson, D.R. (2005). Human development: Biological and genetic processes. *Annual Review of Psychology*, 56, pp. 10.1–10.24.

Gottesman, I.I., & Reilly, J.L. (2003). Strengthening the evidence for genetic factors in schizophrenia. In M.F. Lenzenweger and J.M. Hooley (Eds.), *Principles of Experimental Psychopathology*, pp. 31–44. Washington, D.C.: American Psychological Association.

Gottman, J., Notarius, C., Gonso, J., & Markman, H. (1976). *A Couple's Guide to Communication*. Champaign, IL: Research Press.

Gottman, J.M. (1985). Observational measures of behavior therapy outcome: A reply to Jacobsen. *Behavioral Assessment*, 7, pp. 317–321.

Gottman, J.M. (1994). *Why Marriages Succeed or Fail*. New York: Simon & Schuster.

Gottman, J.M. (1999). *The Marriage Clinic: A Scientifically Based Marital Therapy*. New York: W. Norton & Co.

Gottman, J.M., & Katz, L.F. (1989). Effects of marital discord on young children's peer interaction and health. *Developmental Psychology*, 25, pp. 373–381.

Gottman, J.M., & Levenson, R.W. (1986). Assessing the role of emotion in marriage. *Behavioral Assessment*, 8, pp. 31–48.

Gottman, J.M., & Levenson, R.W. (1988). The social psychophysiology of marriage. In P. Noller & M.A. Fitzpatrick (Eds.), *Perspectives on Marital Interaction*, pp. 182–200. Clevedon, England: Multilingual Matters.

Gottman, J.M., & Notarious, C.I. (2000). Decade review: Observing marital interaction. *Journal of Marriage and the Family*, 62, pp. 927–947.

Gove, W.R. (1990). Labeling theory's explanation of mental illness: An update of recent evidence. In M. Nagler (Ed.), *Perspectives on Disability*. Palo Alto, CA: Health Markets Research.

Grant, B.F., Stinson, F.S., Dawson, D.A., Chou, P., Dufour, M.C., Compton, W., Pickering, R.P., & Kaplan, K. (2004). Prevalence and co-occurrence of substance use disorders and independent mood and anxiety disorders: Results from the national epidemiologic survey on alcohol and related conditions. *Archives of General Psychiatry*, 61, pp. 807–816.

Grant, B.F., Stinson, F.S., Dawson, D.A., Chou, S.P., & Ruan, W.J. (2005). Co-occurrence of DSM-IV personality disorders in the United States: Results from the National Epidemiologic Survey on Alcohol and Related Conditions. *Comprehensive Psychiatry*, 46, pp. 1–5.

Grant, William T., Foundation. (1988). *The Forgotten Half: Pathways to Success for America's Youth and Young Families*. Washington, DC: Youth and America's Future: William T. Grant Foundation Commission on Work, Family and Citizenship.

Grasel, E. (1997). Temporary institutional respite in dementia cases: Who utilizes this form of respite care and what effect does it have? *International Psychogeriatrics*, 9, pp. 437–448.

Gratzer, T., & Bradford, J.M.W. (1995). Offender and offense characteristics of sexual sadists: A comparative study. *Journal of Forensic Sciences*, 40, pp. 450–455.

Graves, A.B., et al. (1999). Cognitive decline and Japanese culture in a cohort of older Japanese-Americans in King County, WA: The Kame Project. *Journals of Gerontology Series B-Psychological Sciences and Social Sciences*, 54B, pp. S154–S161.

Greaves, G.B. (1980). Multiple personality disorder: 165 years after Mary Reynolds. *Journal of Nervous and Mental Disease*, 168, pp. 577–596.

Green, B.L., Epstein, S.A., Krupnick, J.L., & Rowland, J.H. (1997). Trauma and medical illness: Assessing trauma-related disorders in medical settings. In J.P. Wilson & T.M. Keane (Eds.), *Assessing Psychological Trauma and PTSD*. New York: Guilford.

Green, M.F. (2001). *Schizophrenia Revealed: From Neurons to Social Interactions*. New York: Norton.

Green, M.F., Nuechterlein, K.H., Gold, J.M., Barch, D.M., Cohen, J., Essock, S., Fenton, W.S., Frese, F., Goldberg, T.E., Heaton, R.K., Keefe, R.S.E., Kern, R.S., Kraemer, H., Stover, E., Weinberger, D.R., Zalcman, S., & Marder, S.R. (2004). Approaching a consensus cognitive battery for clinical trials in schizophrenia: The NIMH-MATRICS conference to select cognitive domains and test criteria. *Biological Psychiatry*, 56, pp. 301–307.

Greenberg, R.P., Bornstein, R.F., Zborowski, M.J., Fisher, S., & Greenberg, M.D. (1994). A meta-analysis of fluoxetine outcome in the treatment of depression. *Journal of Nervous and Mental Disease*, 182, pp. 547–551.

Greene, R.L. (2000). *The MMPI-2: An Interpretive Manual* (2nd Ed.). Needham Heights, MA: Allyn & Bacon.

Greene, R.W. et al., (2001). Social impairment in girls with ADHD: Patterns, gender comparisons, and correlates. *Journal of the American Academy of Child and Adolescent Psychiatry*, 40, pp. 704–710.

Greenfield, S.F., & O'Leary, G. (2002). Sex differences in substance use disorders. In F. Lewis-Hall and T.S. Williams (Eds.), *Psychiatric Illness in Women: Emerging Treatments and Research*, pp. 467–533. Washington, DC: American Psychiatric Press.

Greenley, J.R. (1995). Madison, Wisconsin, United States: Creation and implementation of the Program of Assertive Community Treatment (PACT). In R. Schulz & J.R. Greenley (Eds.), *Innovating in Community Mental Health: International Perspectives*, pp. 83–96. Westport, CT: Praeger.

Griffin, K.W., Botvin, G.J., Scheier, L.M., Diaz, T., & Miller, N.L. (2000). Parenting practices as predictors of substance use, delinquency, and aggression among urband minority youth: Moderating effects of family structure and gender. *Psychology of Addictive Behaviors*, 14, pp. 174–184.

Griffin, M.G., Resick, P.A., & Mechanic, M.B. (1997). Objective assessment of peritraumatic dissociation: Psychophysiological indicators. *American Journal of Psychiatry*, 154, pp. 1081–1088.

Grilo, C.M., Shea, M.T., Sanislow, C.A., Skodol, A.E., Gunderson, J.G., Stout, R.L., Pagano, M.E., Yen, S., Morey, L.C., Zanarini, M.C., & McGlashan, T.H. (2004). Two-year stability and change of schizotypal, borderline, avoidant, and obsessive-compulsive personality disorders. *Journal of Consulting and Clinical Psychology*, 72, pp. 767–775.

Grisso, T., & Appelbaum, P.S. (1992). Is it unethical to offer predictions of future violence? *Law and Human Behavior*, 16, pp. 621–633.

Grossman, H.J. (1983). *Classification in Mental Retardation.*Washington, DC: American Association on Mental Deficiency.

Grotevant, H.D., & Carlson, C.I. (1989). *Family Assessment: A Guide to Methods and Measures.* New York: Guilford.

Group for the Advancement of Psychiatry (1966). *Psychopathological Disorders of Childhood: Theoretical Considerations and a Proposed Classification.* Report 62. New York: Mental Health Memorials Center.

Group for the Advancement of Psychiatry. (1995). A model for the classification and diagnosis of relational disorders. *Psychiatric Services,* 46, pp. 926–931.

Grove, A.S. (1996). *Only the Paranoid Survive: How to exploit the crisis points that challenge every company.* New York: Doubleday.

Grube, B.S., Bilder, R.M., & Goldman, R.S. (1998). Meta-analysis of symptom factors in schizophrenia. *Schizophrenia Research,* 31, pp. 113–120.

Grych, J.H., & Fincham, F.D. (1990). Marital conflict and children's adjustment: A cognitive-contextual framework. *Psychological Bulletin,* 101, pp. 267–290.

Guarnaccia, P.J. (1997). A cross-cultural perspective on anxiety disorders. In S. Friedman (Ed.), *Cultural Issues in the Treatment of Anxiety,* pp. 3–20. New York: Guilford.

Guarnaccia, P.J., & Rogler, L.H. (1999). Research on culture-bound syndromes: New Directions. *American Journal of Psychiatry,* 156, pp. 1322–1327.

Gunderson, J. (1984). *Borderline Personality Disorder.* Washington, DC: American Psychiatric Press.

Gunderson, J.G. (1994). Building structure for the borderline construct. *Acta Psychiatrica Scandinavica,* 89 (suppl. 379), pp. 12–18.

Gureje, O., Simon, G.E., Ustun, T.B., & Goldberg, D.P. (1997). Somatization in cross-cultural perspective: A world health organization study in primary care. *American Journal of Psychiatry,* 154, pp. 989–995.

Gurman, A., & Jacobson, N. (Eds.), *Clinical Handbook of Couple Therapy* (Prd ed.). New York: Guilford.

Gurman, A.S., & Jacobson, N.S. (2002). *Clinical handbook of couple therapy* (3rd ed.). New York: Guilford.

Gusella, J.F., Wexler, N.S., Conneally, P.M., Naylor, S.L., Anderson, M.A., Tanzi, R.E., Watkins, P.C., Ottina, K., Wallace, M.R., Sakaguchi, A.Y., Young, A.B., et al. (1983). A polymorphic DNA marker genetically linked to Huntington's disease. *Nature,* 306, pp. 234–238.

Gutheil, T.G. (1986). The right to refuse treatment: Paradox, pendulum and the quality of care. *Behavioral Sciences and the Law,* 4, pp. 265–277.

Gutierrez-Lobos, K., Schmid-Siegel, B., Bankier, B., & Walter, H. (2001). Delusions in first-admitted patients: Gender, themes, and diagnoses. *Psychopathology,* 34, pp. 1–7.

Guzder, J., Paris, J., Zelkowitz, P., & Marchessault, K. (1996). Risk factors for borderline psychology in children. *Journal of the American Academy of Child and Adolescent Psychiatry,* 35, pp. 26–33.

Haefner, H., & Heiden, W. (1997). Epidemiology of schizophrenia. *Canadian Journal of Psychiatry,* 42, pp. 139–151.

Haefner, H., Heiden, W., Behrens, S., Gattaz, W.F., Hambrecht, M., Loeffler, W., Maurer, K., Munk-Jorgensen, P., Nowotny, B., Riecher-Roessler, A., & Stein, A. (1998). Causes and consequences of the gender difference in age at onset of schizophrenia. *Schizophrenia Bulletin,* 24, pp. 99–113.

Hafner, H., Maurer, K., Loffler, W., an der Heiden, W., Hambrecht, M., & Schultze-Lutter, F. (2003). Modeling the early course of schizophrenia. *Schizophrenia Bulletin,* 29, pp. 325–340.

Hage, J.J. (1995). Medical requirements and consequences of sex reassignment surgery. *Medicine, Science and the Law,* 35, pp. 17–24.

Hahlweg, K., Fiegenbaum, W., Frank, M., Schroeder, B., & Witzleben, I. (2001). Short- and long-term effec-

tiveness of an empirically supported treatment for agoraphobia. *Journal of Consulting and Clinical Psychology,* 69, pp. 375–382.

Hahlweg, K., Markman, H.J., Thurmaier, F., Engl, J., & Eckert, V. (1998). Prevention of martial distress: Results of a German prospective longitudinal study. *Journal of Family Psychology,* 12, pp. 543–556.

Hall, G.C.N. (2001). Psychotherapy research with ethnic minorities: Empirical, ethical, and conceptual issues. *Journal of Consulting and Clinical Psychology,* 69, pp. 502–510.

Halligan, S.L., Michael, T., Clark, D.M., & Ehlers, A. (2003). Posttraumatic stress disorder following assault: The role of cognitive processing, trauma memory, and appraisals. *Journal of Consulting and Clinical Psychology,* 71, pp. 419–431.

Halliwell, E. & Dittmar, H. (2004). Does size matter? The impact of model's body size on women's body-focused anxiety and advertising effectiveness. *Journal of Social & Clinical Psychology,* 23, pp. 104–122.

Halmi, K.A. (1997). Models to conceptualize risk factors for bulimia nervosa. *Archives of General Psychiatry,* 54, pp. 507–509.

Hammen, C. (2002). Context of stress in families of children with depressed parents. In S.H. Goodman and I.H. Gotlib (Eds.), *Children of Depressed Parents: Mechanisms of Risk and Implications for Treatment,* pp. 175–199. Washington, D.C.: American Psychological Association.

Hammen, C. (2005). Stress and Depression. *Annual Review of Clinical Psychology,* 55, pp. 11.1–11.27.

Hankin, B.L. et al. (1998). Development of depression from preadolescence to young adulthood: Emerging gender differences in a 10-year longitudinal study. *Journal of Abnormal Pyschology,* 107, pp. 128–140.

Hankin, B.L., & Abramson, L.Y. (2001). Development of gender differences in depression: An elaborated cognitive vulnerability-transactional stress theory. *Psychological Bulletin,* 127, pp. 773–796.

Hansen, N.B., Lambert, M.J., & Forman, E.M. (2002). The psychotherapy dose–response effect and its implications for treatment service delivery. *Clinical Psychology: Science and Practice,* 9, pp. 329–343.

Happe, F. (1995). *Autism.* Cambridge, MA: Harvard University Press.

Hardin, S., & Schooley, B. (2002). A story of Pick's disease: A rare form of dementia. *Journal of Neuroscience Nursing,* 34, pp. 117–122.

Harding, C.M. (1988). Course types in schizophrenia: An analysis of European and American studies. *Schizophrenia Bulletin,* 14, pp. 633–643.

Hare, R.D. (1993). *Without Conscience: The Disturbing World of the Psychopaths Among us.* New York: Pocket Books.

Harkness, K.L., & Wildes, J.E. (2002). Childhood adversity and anxiety versus dysthymia co-morbidity in major depression. *Psychological Medicine,* 32, pp. 1239–1249.

Harkness, K.L., Monroe, S.M., Simons, A.D., & Thase, M. (1999). The generation of life events in recurrent and non-recurrent depression. *Psychological Medicine,* 29, pp. 135–144.

Harpur, T.J., & Hare, R.D. (1994). Assessment of psychopathy as a function of age. *Journal of Abnormal Psychology,* 103, pp. 604–609.

Harrington, R. (2002). Affective disorders. In M. Rutter & E. Taylor (Eds.), *Child and Adolescent Psychiatry,* 4th ed., pp. 463–485. Oxford, UK: Blackwell.

Harrington, R., Fudge, H., Rutter, M., Pickles, A., & Hill, J. (1990). Adult outcomes of childhood and adolescent depression. I. Psychiatric status. *Archives of General Psychiatry,* 47, pp. 465–473.

Harrington, R.C., & Harrison, L. (1999). Unproven assumptions about the impact of bereavement on children. *Journal of the Royal Society of Medicine,* 92, pp. 230–233.

Harris, J.R. (1995). Where is the child's environment? A group socialization theory of development. *Psychological Review,* 102, pp. 458–489.

Harrison, G., Gunnell, D., Glazebrook, C., Page, K., & Kwiecinski, R. (2001). Association between schizophrenia and social inequality at birth: Case control study. *British Journal of Psychiatry,* 179, pp. 346–350.

Harrison, P.J. (1999). The neuropathology of schizophrenia: A critical review of the data and their interpretation. *Brain,* 122, pp. 593–624.

Hart, A.B., Craighead, W.E., & Craighead, L.W. (2001). Predicting recurrence of major depressive disorder in young adults: A prospective study. *Journal of Abnormal Psychology,* 110, pp. 633–643.

Hart, C., McCance-Katz, E.F., & Kosten, T.R. (2001). Pharmacotherapies used in common substance use disorders. In F.M. Tims and C.G. Leukefeld (Eds.), *Relapse and Recovery in Addictions,* pp. 303–333. New Haven, CT: Yale University Press.

Hart, E.L., Lahey, B.B., Loeber, R., Applegate, B., & Frick, P.J. (1995). Developmental change in attention-deficit hyperactivity disorder in boys: A four-year longitudinal study. *Journal of Abnormal Child Psychology,* 23, pp. 729–750.

Hart, S.D., & Hare, R.D. (1997). Psychopathy: Assessment and association with criminal conduct. In D.M. Stoff, J. Breiling, & J. Maser (Eds.), *Handbook of Antisocial Behavior,* pp. 22–35. New York: Wiley.

Harvey, A.G., & Bryant, R.A. (1998). The relationship between acute stress disorder and posttraumatic stress disorder: A prospective evaluation of motor vehicle accident survivors. *Journal of Consulting and Clinical Psychology,* 66, pp. 507–512.

Harvey, A.G., & Bryant, R.A. (1999). The relationship between acute stress disorder and posttraumatic stress disorder: A 2-year prospective evaluation. *Journal of Consulting and Clinical Psychology,* 67, pp. 985–988.

Harvey, A.G., & Bryant, R.A. (2002). Acute stress disorder: A synthesis and critique. *Psychological Bulletin,* 128, pp. 886–902.

Harvey, A.G., Bryant, R.A., & Dang, S.T. (1998). Autobiographical memory in acute stress disorder. *Journal of Consulting and Clinical Psychology,* 66, pp. 500–506.

Harvey, R.J. (1996). Review: Delusions in dementia. *Age and Ageing,* 25, pp. 405–409.

Hashemi, A.J., & Cochrane, R. (1999). Expressed emotion and schizophrenia: A review of studies across cultures. *International Review of Psychiatry,* 11, pp. 219–224.

Hasin, D., Paykin, A., Endicott, J., & Grant, B. (1999). The validity of DSM-IV alcohol abuse: Drunk drivers versus all others. *Journal of Studies on Alcohol,* 60, pp. 746–755.

Haskett, R.F. (1993). The HPA axis and depressive disorders. In J. John Mann & David J. Kupfer (Eds.), *Biology of Depressive Disorders,* Part A: A systems perspective, pp. 171–188. New York: Plenum.

Haslam, N. (2003). Categorical versus dimensional models of mental disorder: The taxometric evidence. *Australian & New Zealand Journal of Psychiatry,* 3, pp. 696–704.

Haugaard, J.J., & Reppucci, N.D. (1988). *The Sexual Abuse of Children.* San Francisco: Jossey-Bass.

Hawley, K.M., & Weisz, J.R. (2003). Child, parent, and therapist (dis)agreement on target problems in outpatient therapy: The therapist's dilemma and its implications. *Journal of Consulting and Clinical Psychology,* 71(1), pp. 62–70.

Hayes, S.C., Nelson, R.O., & Jarrett, R.B. (1987). The treatment utility of assessment: A functional approach to evaluating assessment quality. *American Psychologist,* 42, pp. 963–974.

Haynes, S.G., & Feinleib, M. (1980). Women, work, and coronary heart disease: Prospective findings from the

Framingham heart study. *American Journal of Public Health*, 70, pp. 133–141.

Hazell, P.L., & Stuart, J.E. (2003). A randomized controlled trial of clonidine added to psychostimulant medication for hyperactive and aggressive children. *Journal of the American Academy of Child and Adolescent Psychiatry*, 42(8), pp. 886–894.

Heath, A.C., Bucholz, I.I., Madden, P.A.F., Dinwiddie, S.H., Slutske, W.S., Bierut, L.J., Statham, D.J., Dunne, M.P., Whitfield, J.B., & Martin, N.G. (1997). Genetic and environmental contributions to alcohol dependence risk in a national twin sample: Consistency of findings in women and men. *Psychological Medicine*, 27, pp. 1381–1396.

Heath, D.B. (1999). Culture. In P.J. Ott, R.E. Tarter, & R.T. Ammerman (Eds.), *Sourcebook on Substance Abuse: Etiology, Epidemiology, Assessment, and Treatment*, pp. 175–183. Boston: Allyn & Bacon.

Heatherton, T.F., & Polivy, J. (1992). Chronic dieting and eating disorders: A spiral model. In J. Crowther, S.E. Hobfall, M.A.P. Stephens, & D.L. Tennenbaum (Eds.), *The Etiology of Bulimia: The Individual and Familial Context*, pp. 135–155. Washington, D.C.: Hemisphere.

Heavey, C.L., Christensen, A., & Malamuth, N.M. (1995). The longitudinal impact of demand and withdrawal during marital conflict. *Journal of Consulting and Clinical Psychology*, 63, pp. 797–801.

Heber, R. (1959). A manual on terminology and classification in mental retardation. *American Journal on Mental Deficiency*, 64 (Monograph Supplement).

Heiman, J.R. (1998). Psychophysiological models of female sexual response. *International Journal of Impotence Research*, 10 (suppl. 2), pp. 94–97.

Heiman, J.R., & LoPiccolo, J. (1988). *Becoming Orgasmic: A Sexual and Personal Growth Program for Women*. Fireside.

Heinberg, L.J., Thompson, J.K., & Matzon, J.L. (2001). Body image dissatisfaction as a motivator for healthy lifestyle change: Is some distress beneficial? In R.H. Striegel-Moore & L. Smolak (Eds.), *Eating Disorders: Innovative Directions in Research and Practice*, pp. 215–232. Washington: American Psychological Association.

Heinberg, L.J., Thompson, J.K., & Stormer, S. (1995). Development and validation of the sociocultural attitudes towards appearance questionnaire. *International Journal of Eating Disorders*, 17, pp. 81–89.

Heinssen, R.K., Liberman, R.P., & Kopelowicz, A. (2000). Psychosocial skills training for schizophrenia: Lessons from the laboratory. *Schizophrenia Bulletin* 26, pp. 21–46.

Helgeland, M.I., & Torgersen, S. (2004). Developmental antecedents of borderline personality disorder. *Comprehensive Psychiatry*, 45, pp. 138–147.

Hellewell, J.S.E. (1999). Treatment-resistant schizophrenia: Reviewing the options and identifying the way forward. *Journal of Clinical Psychiatry*, 60 (suppl. 23), pp. 14–19.

Helmes, E., & Reddon, J.R. (1993). A perspective on developments in assessing psychopathology: A critical review of the MMPI and MMPI-2. *Psychological Bulletin*, 113, pp. 453–471.

Helzer, J.E., Robins, L.N., & McEvoy, L. (1987). Posttraumatic stress disorder in the general population: Findings of the Epidemiologic Catchment Area Survey. *New England Journal of Medicine*, 317, pp. 1630–1634.

Hempel, C.G. (1961). Introduction to problems of taxonomy. In J. Zubin (Ed.), *Field Studies in the Mental Disorders*. New York: Grune & Stratton.

Hendin, H. (1995). *Suicide in America*. New York: Norton.

Hendricks, C.L. (1993–94). The trend toward mandatory mediation in custody and visitation disputes of minor children: An overview. *Journal of Family Law*, 32, pp. 491–510.

Hendrie, H.C. (1998). Epidemiology of dementia and Alzheimer's disease. *American Journal of Geriatric Psychiatry*, 6 (suppl. 1), pp. 3–18.

Hendrie, H.C., Osuntokun, B.O., Hall, K.S., et al. (1995). Prevalence of Alzheimer's disease and dementia in two communities: Nigerian Africans and African Americans. *American Journal of Psychiatry*, 152, pp. 1485–1492.

Henggeler, S.W. (1994). *Treatment Manual for Family Preservation Using Multisystemic Therapy*. Charleston: Medical University of South Carolina.

Henggeler, S.W., & Borduin, C.M. (1990). *Family Therapy and Beyond: A Multisystemic Approach to Treating the Behavior Problems of Children and Adolescents*. Pacific Grove, CA: Brooks/Cole.

Henker, B., & Whalen, C.K. (1989). Hyperactivity and attention deficits. *American Psychologist*, 44, pp. 216–223.

Herbener, E.S., & Harrow, M. (2002). The course of anhedonia during 10 years of schizophrenic illness. *Journal of Abnormal Psychology*, 111, pp. 237–248.

Herbert, M. (2002). Behavioural therapies. In M. Rutter & E. Taylor (Eds.), *Child and Adolescent Psychiatry*, 4th ed., pp. 900–920. Oxford, UK: Blackwell.

Herman, C.P., & Polivy, J. (1988). Excess and restraint in bulimia. In K. Pirke, W. Vandereycken, & D. Ploog (Eds.), *The Psychobiology of Bulimia*, pp. 33–41. Munich: Springer-Verlag.

Hermann, D.H.J. (1990). Autonomy, self determination, the right of involuntarily committed persons to refuse treatment, and the use of substituted judgment in medication decisions involving incompetent persons. *International Journal of Law and Psychiatry*, 13, pp. 361–385.

Hernandez, D.J. (1993). *America's Children: Resources from Family, Government, and the Economy*. New York: Russell Sage.

Herpertz, S.C., Werth, U., Lucas, G., Qunaibi, M., Schuerkens, A., Kunert, H., Freese, R., Flesch. M., Mueller-lsberner, R., Osterheider, M., & Sass, H. (2001). Emotion in criminal offenders with psychopathy and borderline personality disorders. *Archives of General Psychiatry*, 58, pp. 737–745.

Herzog, D.B. & Delinsky, S.S. (2001). Classification of eating disorders. In R.H. Striegel-Moore & L. Smolak (Eds.), *Eating Disorders: Innovative Directions in Research and Practice*, pp. 31–50. Washington: American Psychological Association.

Herzog, D.B., Dorer, D.J., Keel, P.K., Selwyn, S.E., Ekeblad, E.R., Flores, A.T., Greenwood, D.N., Burwell, R.A., & Keller, M.B. (1999). Recovery and relapse in anorexia and bulimia nervosa: A 75-year follow-up study. *Journal of the American Academy of Child & Adolescent Psychiatry*, 38, pp. 829–837.

Hess, T.M. (2005). Memory and aging in context. *Psychological Bulletin*, 131, pp. 383–406.

Heston, L.L. (1966). Psychiatric disorders in foster home reared children of schizophrenic mothers. *British Journal of Psychiatry*, 112, pp. 819–825.

Heston, L.L., & White, J.A. (1991). *The Vanishing Mind: A Practical Guide to Alzheimer's Disease and Other Dementias*. New York: Freeman.

Hettema, J.M., Neale, M.C., & Kendler, K.S. (2001). A review and meta-analysis of the genetic epidemiology of anxiety disorders. *American Journal of Psychiatry*, 158, pp. 1568–1578.

Hettema, J.M., Prescott, C.A., Myers, J.M., Neale, M.C., & Kendler, K.S. (2005). The structure of genetic and environmental risk factors for anxiety disorders in men and women. *Archives of General Psychiatry*, 62, pp. 182–189.

Heyman, I., & Santosh, P. (2002). Pharmacological and other physical treatments. In M. Rutter & E. Taylor (Eds.), *Child and Adolescent Psychiatry*, 4th ed., pp. 998–1018. Oxford, UK: Blackwell.

Hill, A., Briken, P., Kraus, C., Strohm, K., & Berner, W. (2003). Differential pharmacological treatment of paraphilias and sex offenders. *International Journal of Offender Therapy*, 47, pp. 407–421.

Hill, J., & Holmbeck, G. (1986). Attachment and autonomy during adolescence. In G. Whitehurst (Ed.), *Annals of Child Development*, Vol. 3, pp. 145–189. Greenwich, CT: JAI.

Hill, M.A. (1992). Light, circadian rhythms, and mood disorders: A review. *Annals of Clinical Psychiatry*, 4, pp. 131–146.

Hilliard, R.B., & Spitzer, R.L. (2002). Change in criterion for paraphilias in DSM-IV-TR. *American Journal of Psychiatry*, 159, p. 1249.

Hillman, J.L. (2000). *Clinical Perspectives on Elderly Sexuality*. New York: Kluwer Academic/Plenum.

Hinshaw et al. (2000). Family processes and treatment outcome in the MTA: Negative/ineffective parenting practices in relations to multimodal treatment. *Journal of Abnormal Child Psychology*, 28, pp. 555–568.

Hinshaw, S.P. (1994). *Attention Deficits and Hyperactivity in Children*. Thousand Oaks, CA: Sage.

Hirschfeld, R.M.A. (2001). Antidepressants in the United States: Current status and future needs. In M.M. Weissman (Ed.), *Treatment of Depression: Bridging the 21st Century*, pp. 123–134. Washington, D.C.: American Psychiatric Press.

Hirschfeld, R.M.A., Shea, M.T., & Weise, R. (1995). Dependent personality disorder. In W.J. Livesley (Ed.), *The DSM-IV Personality Disorders*, pp. 239–256. New York: Guilford.

Hittner, J.B. (1997). Alcohol-related expectancies: Construct overview and implications for primary and secondary prevention. *Journal of Primary Prevention*, 17, pp. 297–314.

Hlastala, S.A., Frank, E., Kowalski, J., Tu, X.M., Anderson, B., & Kupfer, D.J. (2000). Stressful life events, bipolar disorder, and the "kindling model." *Journal of Abnormal Psychology*, 109, pp. 777–786.

Ho, D.Y. (1994). Introduction to cross-cultural psychology. In L.L. Adler & U.P. Gielen (Eds.), *Cross-Cultural Topics in Psychology*, pp. 3–14. Westport, CT: Praeger.

Hoek, H.W. (1995). The distribution of eating disorders. In K.D. Brownell & C.G. Fairburn (Eds.), *Eating Disorders and Obesity: A Comprehensive Handbook*, pp. 207–211. New York: Guilford.

Hoek, H.W. (2002). Distribution of eating disorders. In C.G. Fairburn & K.D. Brownell (Eds.), *Eating Disorders and Obesity*, 2nd ed., pp. 233–237. New York: Guilford.

Hoenig, J. (1985). Etiology of transsexualism. In B.W. Steiner (Ed.), *Gender Dysphoria: Development, Research, Management*, pp. 33–74. New York: Plenum.

Hoff, A.L., & Kremen, W.S. (2002). Is there a cognitive phenotype for schizophrenia? The nature and course of the disturbance in cognition. *Current Opinion in Psychiatry*, 15, pp. 43–48.

Hoffman, P.B., & Foust, L.L. (1977). Least restrictive treatment of the mentally ill: A doctrine in search of its senses. *San Diego Law Review*, 14, pp. 1100–1154.

Hofmann, S.G., Heinrichs, N., & Moscovitch, D.A. (2004). The nature and expression of social phobia: Toward a new classification. *Clinical Psychology Review*, 24, pp. 769–797.

Hofmann, S.G., Moscovitch, D.A., & Heinrichs, N. (2004). Evolutionary mechanisms of fear and anxiety. In P. Gilbert (Ed.), *Evolutionary Theory and Cognitive Therapy*, pp. 119–136. New York: Springer.

Hogan, D.R. (1990). Sexual dysfunctions: A historical perspective. In C.E. Walker (Ed.), *History of Clinical Psychology*, pp. 279–309. Pacific Grove, CA: Brooks/Cole.

Hogarty, G.E. (1993). Prevention of relapse in chronic schizophrenic patients. *Journal of Clinical Psychiatry*, 54 (suppl.), pp. 18–23.

Hogarty, G.E., Flesher, S., Ulrich, R., Carter, M., Greenwald, D., Pogue-Geile, M., Kechavan, M., Cooley, S., DiBarry, A.L., Garrett, A., Parepally, H., & Zoretich, R. (2004). Cognitive enhancement therapy for schizophrenia: Effects of a 2-year randomized trial on cognition and behavior. *Archives of General Psychiatry*, 61, pp. 866–876.

Holland, J. (2001). *Ecstasy: The Complete Guide: A Comprehensive Look at the Risks and Benefits of MDMA*. Inner Traditions.

Hollander, E., & Rosen, J. (2000). Impulsivity. *Journal of Psychopharmacology*, 14 (suppl. 1), pp. S39–S44.

Hollon, S.D., Shelton, R.C., & Davis, D.D. (1993). Cognitive therapy for depression: Conceptual issues and clinical efficacy. *Journal of Consulting and Clinical Psychology*, 61, pp. 270–275.

Hollon, S.D., Thase, M.E., & Markowitz, J.C. (2002). Treatment and prevention of depression. *Psychological Science in the Public Interest*, 3, pp. 39–77.

Holmes, C. (2002). Genotype and phenotype in Alzheimer's disease. *British Journal of Psychiatry*, 180, pp. 131–134.

Holmes, T.H., & Rahe, R.H. (1967). The Social Readjustment Rating Scale. *Journal of Psychosomatic Research*, 11, pp. 213–218.

Holsinger, T., Steffens, D.C., Phillips, C., Helms, M.J., Havlik, R.J., Breitner, J.C.S., Guralnik, J.M., & Plassman, B.L. (2002). Head injury in early adulthood and the lifetime risk of depression. *Archives of General Psychiatry*, 59, pp. 17–22.

Holtzworth-Munroe, A. Meehan, J.C., Herron, K., Rehman, U., & Stuart, G.L. (2000). Testing the Holtzworth-Munroe and Stuart (1994). Batterer Typology. *Journal of Consulting and Clinical Psychology*, 68, pp. 1000–1019.

Holzman, P.S. (2000). Eye movements and the search for the essence of schizophrenia. *Brain Research Reviews*, 31, pp. 350–356.

Homewood, J., & Bond, N.W. (1999). Thiamin deficiency and Korsakoff's syndrome: Failure to find memory impairments following nonalcoholic Wernicke's encephalopathy. *Alcohol*, 19, pp. 75–84.

Hooley, J.M., & Gotlib, I.H. (2000). A diathesis-stress conceptualization of expressed emotion and clinical outcome. *Applied and Preventive Psychology* 9, pp. 135–151.

Horevitz, R., & Loewenstein, R.J. (1994). The rational treatment of multiple personality disorder. In S.J. Lynn & J.W. Rhue (Eds.), *Dissociation: Clinical and Theoretical Perspectives*, pp. 289–316. New York: Guilford.

Horley, J. (2001). Frotteurism: A term in search of an underlying disorder. *Journal of Sexual Aggression*, 7, pp. 51–55.

Horn, J.M., Loehlin, J.C., & Willerman, L. (1979). Intellectual resemblance among adoptive and biological relatives: The Texas Adoption Project. *Behavior Genetics*, 9, pp. 177–205.

Horney, K. (1939). *New Ways in Psychoanalysis*. New York: International Universities Press.

Horowitz, L.M. (2004). Dependent and avoidant personality disorders. In L.M. Horowitz (Ed.), *Interpersonal Foundations of Psychopathology*, pp. 103–129. Washington, D.C.: American Psychological Association.

Horowitz, M.J., Siegel, B., Holen, A., Bonanno, G.A., Milbrath, C., & Stinson, C.H. (1997). Diagnostic criteria for complicated grief disorder. *American Journal of Psychiatry*, 154, pp. 904–910.

Horwath, E., Cohen, R.S., & Weissman, M.M. (2002). Epidemiology of depressive and anxiety disorders. In Ming T. Tsuang and Mauricio Tohen (Eds), *Textbook in Psychiatric Epidemiology*, 2nd ed., pp. 389–426. New York: Wiley-Liss.

Horwitz, A.V. (2002). *Creating Mental Illness*. Chicago: University of Chicago Press.

Houezec, J.L. (1998). Pharmacokinetics and pharmacodynamics of nicotine. In J. Snel & M.M. Lorist (Eds.), *Nicotine, Caffeine and Social Drinking: Behaviour and Brain Function*, pp. 3–20. Amsterdam: Harwood.

Houts, A.C. (1991). Nocturnal enuresis as a biobehavioral problem. *Behavior Therapy*, 22, pp. 133–151.

Houts, A.C. (2001). The diagnostic and statistical manual's new white coat and circularity of plausible dysfunctions: response to Wakefield. *Behaviour Research and Therapy*, 39, pp. 315–345.

Howe, M.L. (2003). Memories from the cradle. *Current Directions in Psychological Science*, 12, pp. 62–65.

Howes, O.D., McDonald, C., Cannon, M., Arseneault, L., Boydell, J., & Murray, R.M.(2004). Pathways to schizophrenia: The impact of environmental factors. *International Journal of Neuropsychopharmacology*, 7 (suppl. 1), pp. S7–S13.

Hoza, B. et al. (2005). What aspects of peer relationships are impaired in children with attention-deficit/hyperactivity disorder? *Journal of Consulting and Clinical Psychology*, 73, pp. 411–423.

Hsu, L.K.G. (1990). *Eating Disorders*. New York: Guilford.

Hsu, L.K.G. (1995). Outcome of bulimia nervosa. In K.D. Brownell & C.G. Fairburn (Eds.), *Eating Disorders and Obesity: A Comprehensive Handbook*, pp. 238–244. New York: Guilford.

Hucker, S.J. (1997). Impulsivity in DSM-IV impulse-control disorders. In C.D. Webster & M.A. Jackson (Eds.), *Impulsivity: Theory, Assessment, and Treatment*, pp. 195–211. New York: Guilford.

Hucker, S.J. (1997). Sexual sadism: Theory and psychopathology. In D.R. Laws & W.T. O'Donohue (Eds.), *Handbook of Sexual Deviance: Theory and Application*. New York: Guilford.

Huettel, S.A., Song, A.W., & McCarthy, G. (2004). *Functional Magnetic Resonance Imaging*. Sunderland, MA: Sinauer.

Hughes, C.C. (1998). The glossary of culture-bound syndromes in DSM-IV: A critique, *Transcultural Psychiatry*, 35, pp. 413–421.

Hull, J.G., & Bond, C.F., Jr. (1986). Social and behavioral consequences of alcohol consumption and expectancy: A meta-analysis. *Psychological Bulletin*, 99, pp. 347–360.

Hulshoff, H.E., Hoek, H.W., Susser, E., Brown, A.S., Dingemans, A., Schnack, H.G., van Haren, N.E.M., Ramos, L.M.P., Wied, C.C.G., & Kahn, R.S. (2000). Prenatal exposure to famine and brain morphology in schizophrenia. *American Journal of Psychiatry*, 157, pp. 1170–1172.

Human Capital Initiative. (1996). *Doing the Right Thing: A Research Plan for Healthy Living*. Washington, DC: American Psychological Society.

Humphrey, L.L. (1987). Comparison of bulimic-anorexic and nondistressed families using structural analysis of social behavior. *Journal of the American Academy of Child and Adolescent Psychiatry*, 26, pp. 248–255.

Hunsley, J., & Bailey, M.J. (2001). Whither the Rorschach? An analysis of the evidence. *Psychological Assessment*, 13, pp. 472–485.

Huntington's Disease Collaborative Research Group (1993). A novel gene containing a trinucleotide repeat that is expanded and unstable on Huntington's disease chromosomes. *Cell*, 72, pp. 971–983.

Hurt, S.W., Reznikoff, M., & Clarkin, J.F. (1991). *Psychological Assessment, Psychiatric Diagnosis, and Treatment Planning*. New York: Brunner/Mazel.

Husain, S.S., Kevan, I.M., Linnell, R., & Scott, A.I.F. (2004). Electroconvulsive therapy in depressive illness that has not responded to drug treatment. *Journal of Affective Disorders*, 83, pp. 121–126.

Husak, D.N. (2002). *Legalize This: The Case for Decriminalizing Drugs*. New York: Verso.

Hussong, A.M., & Chassin, L. (2002). Parent alcoholism and the leaving home transition. *Development and Psychopathology*, 14, pp. 139–157.

Hviid, A., Stellfeld, M., Wohlfahrt, J., & Melbye, M. (2003). Association between thimerosal-containing vaccine and autism. *Journal of the American Medical Association*, 290, pp. 1763–1766.

Hyman, S.E., & Malenka, R.C. (2001). Addiction and the brain: The neurobiology of compulsion and its persistence. *Nature Reviews Neuroscience*, 2, pp. 695–703.

Hyman, S.E., & Moldin, S.O. (2001). Genetic science and depression: Implications for research and treatment. In M.M. Weissman (Ed.), *Treatment of Depression: Bridging the 21st Century*, pp. 83–103. Washington, D.C.: American Psychiatric Press.

Iacono, W.G. (1998). Identifying psychophysiological risk for psychopathology: Examples from substance abuse and schizophrenia research. *Psychophysiology*, 35, pp. 621–637.

Iacono, W.G., & Beiser, M. (1992). Are males more likely than females to develop schizophrenia? *American Journal of Psychiatry*, 149, pp. 1070–1074.

Iacono, W.G., & Clementz, B.A. (1993). A strategy for elucidating genetic influences on complex psychopathological syndromes. In L.J. Chapman, J.P. Chapman, & D. Fowles (Eds.), *Progress in Experimental Personality and Psychopathology Research*, pp. 11–65. New York: Springer.

Imperato-McGinley, J., Guerrero, L., Gautier, T., & Peterson, R.E. (1974). Steroid 5a-reductase deficiency in man: An inherited form of male pseudohermaphroditism. *Science*, 186, pp. 1213–1215.

Ingram, J.L., Stodgell, C.J., Hyman, S.L., Figlewicz, D.A., Weitkamp, L.R., & Rodier, P.M. (2000). Discovery of allelic variants of HOXA1 and HOXB1: Genetic susceptibility to autism spectrum disorders. *Teratology*, 62, pp. 396–409.

Ingram, R.E., & Ritter, J. (2000). Vulnerability to depression: Cognitive reactivity and parental bonding in high-risk individuals. *Journal of Abnormal Psychology*, 109, pp. 588–596.

Inouye, S.K., Schlesinger, M.J., & Lydon, T.J. (1999). Delirium: A symptom of how hospital care is failing older persons and a window to improve quality of hospital care. *American Journal of Medicine*, 106, pp. 565–573.

Insel, K.C., & Badger, T.A. (2002). Deciphering the 4 D's: cognitive decline, delirium, depression and dementia—a review. *Journal of Advanced Nursing*, 38, pp. 360–368.

Izard, C. et al. (2001). Emotion knowledge as a predictor of social behavior and academic competence in children at risk. *Psychological Science*, 12, pp. 18–25.

Jablensky, A. (1985). Approaches to the definition and classification of anxiety and related disorders in European psychiatry. In A.H. Tuma & J. Maser (Eds.), *Anxiety and the Anxiety Disorders*. Hillsdale, NJ: Erlbaum.

Jablensky, A. (1999). The nature of psychiatric classification: Issues beyond ICD-10 and DSM-IV. *Australian and New Zealand Journal of Psychiatry*, 33, pp. 137–144.

Jablensky, A. (2000). Epidemiology of schizophrenia: The global burden of disease and disability. *European Archives of Psychiatry and Clinical Neuroscience*, 250, pp. 274–285.

Jablensky, A., Sartorius, N., Ernberg, G., Anker, M., Korten, A., Cooper, J.E., Day, R., & Bertelsen, A. (1992). Schizophrenia: Manifestations, incidence and course in different cultures: A World Health Organization ten-country study. *Psychological Medicine, Monograph Suppl.*, 20, pp. 1–97.

Jacob, T., & Johnson, S. (1997). Parenting influences on the development of alcohol abuse and dependence. *Alcohol Health and Research World*, 21, pp. 204–209.

Jacobi, C., Hayward, C., de Zwaan, M., Kraemer, H.C., & Agras, W.S. (2004). Coming to terms with risk factors for eating disorders: Application of risk terminology and suggestions for a general taxonomy. *Psychological Bulletin*, 130, pp. 19–65.

Jacobson, E. (1938). *Progressive Relaxation*. Chicago: University of Chicago Press.

Jacobson, J.W., Mulick, J.A., & Schwartz, A.A. (1995). A history of facilitated communication: Science, pseudoscience, and antiscience. *American Psychologist*, 50, pp. 750–765.

Jacobson, N.S., & Christensen, A. (1996). *Integrative Couple Therapy: Promoting Acceptance and Change*. New York: Norton.

Jacobson, N.S., & Truax, P. (1991). Clinical significance: A statistical approach to defining meaningful change in psychotherapy research. *Journal of Consulting and Clinical Psychology*, 59, pp. 12–19.

Jacobson, N.S., Holtzworth-Munroe, A., & Schmaling, K.B. (1989). Marital therapy and spouse involvement in the treatment of depression, agoraphobia, and alcoholism. *Journal of Consulting and Clinical Psychology*, 57, pp. 5–10.

Jacobson, S.A. (1997). Delirium in the elderly. *Psychiatric Clinics of North America*, 20, pp. 91–110.

Jaffe, J.H. (1995). Pharmacological treatment of opioid dependence: Current techniques and new findings. *Psychiatric Annals*, 25, pp. 369–375.

Jaffe, J.H., & Jaffe, A.R. (1999). Neurobiology of opiates/opioids. In M. Galanter & H.D. Kleber (Eds.), *Textbook of Substance Abuse Treatment*, 2nd ed., pp. 11–20. Washington, DC: American Psychiatric Press.

Jaffee, S.R., Caspi, A., Moffitt, T.E., & Taylor, A. (2004). Physical maltreatment victim to antisocial child: Evidence of an environmentally mediated process. *Journal of Abnormal Psychology*, 113(1), pp. 44–55.

Jamison, K.R. (1995). *An Unquiet Mind: A Memoir of Moods and Madness*. New York: Knopf.

Jamison, K.R. (1999). *Night Falls Fast: Understanding Suicide*. New York: Knopf.

Janet, P. (1914/1915). Psychoanalysis. *Journal of Abnormal Psychology*, 1–35, pp. 187–253.

Janssen, E.Vissenberg, M.,Visser, S., & Everaerd,W. (1997). An in vivo comparison of two circumferential penile strain gauges: The introduction of a new calibration method. *Psychophysiology*, 34, pp. 717–720.

Jefferson, J.W. (1997). Antidepressants in panic disorder. *Journal of Clinical Psychiatry*, 58 (suppl 2), pp. 20–24.

Jenkins, C.D. (1988). Epidemiology of cardiovascular diseases. *Journal of Consulting and Clinical Psychology*, 56, pp. 324–332.

Jenkins, J.H. (1993).Too close for comfort: Schizophrenia and emotional overinvolvement among Mexican families. In A.D. Gaines (Ed.), *Ethnopsychiatry*, pp. 203–221. Albany: State University of New York Press.

Jenkins, J.H., & Karno, M. (1992). The meaning of expressed emotion:Theoretical issues raised by cross-cultural research. *American Journal of Psychiatry*, 149, pp. 9–21.

Jiang,W., Babyak, M., Krantz, D.S.,Waugh, R.A., et al. (1996). Mental stress-induced myocardial ischemia and cardiac events. *Journal of the American Medical Association*, 275, pp. 1651–1656.

Johnson, C.C., Rybicki, B.A., Brown, G., D'Hondt, E., Herpolsheimer, B., Roth, D., & Jackson, C.E. (1997). Cognitive impairment in the Amish: A four county survey. *International Journal of Epidemiology*, 26, pp. 387–394.

Johnson, J.G., Cohen, P., Brown, J., Smailes, E.M., & Bernstein, D.P. (1999). Childhood maltreatment increases risk for personality disorders during early adulthood. *Archives of General Psychiatry*, 56, pp. 600–606.

Johnson, J.G., Cohen, P., Skodol, A.E., Oldham, J.M., Kasen, S., & Brook, J.S. (1999). Personality disorders in adolescence and risk of major mental disorders and suicidality during adulthood. *Archives of General Psychiatry*, 56, pp. 805–811.

Johnson, P. (1989). Hemingway: Portrait of the artist as an intellectual. *Commentary*, 87, pp. 49–59.

Johnson, S.L., Sandrow, D., Meyter, B., Winters, R., Miller, I., Solomon, D., & Keitner, G. (2000). Increases in manic symptoms after life events involving goal attainment. *Journal of Abnormal Psychology*, 109, pp. 721–727.

Johnson, S.L., & Kizer, A. (2002). Bipolar and unipolar depression: A comparison of clinical phenomenology and psychosocial predictors. In I.H. Gotlib and C.L. Hammen (Eds.), *Handbook of Depression*, pp. 141–165. New York: Guilford.

Johnson, S.L., & Miller, I. (1997). Negative life events and time to recovery from episodes of bipolar disorder. *Journal of Abnormal Psychology*, 106, pp. 449–457.

Johnson, S.L., Winett, C.A., Meyer, B., Greenhouse, W.J., & Miller, I. (1999). Social support and the course of bipolar disorder. *Journal of Abnormal Psychology*, 108, pp. 558–566.

Johnston, D.W. (1985). Psychological interventions in cardiovascular disease. *Journal of Psychosomatic Research*, 29, pp. 447–456.

Johnston, D.W. (1989). Prevention of cardiovascular disease by psychological methods. *British Journal of Psychiatry*, 154, pp. 183–194.

Joiner, R.E., & Metalsky, G.I. (1995). A prospective test of an integrative interpersonal theory of depression: A naturalistic study of college roommates. *Journal of Personality and Social Psychology*, 69, pp. 778–788.

Joiner, T.E., Jr., (2002). Depression in its interpersonal context. In I.H. Gotlib and C.L. Hammen (Eds.), *Handbook of Depression*, pp. 295–313. New York: Guilford.

Joiner, T.E., Jr., Brown, J.S., & Wingate, L.R. (2005). The psychology and neurobiology of suicidal behavior. *Annual Review of Psychology*, 56, pp. 287–314.

Jones, B.T., Corbin, W., & Fromme, K. (2001). A review of expectancy theory and alcohol consumption. *Addiction*, 96, pp. 57–72.

Jones, D.M. (1985). Bulimia: A false self identity. *Clinical Social Work*, 13, pp. 305–316.

Jones, J.C., & Barlow, D.H. (1990).The etiology of posttraumatic stress disorder. *Clinical Psychology Review*, 10, pp. 299–328.

Jones, J.H. (1997). *Alfred C. Kinsey: A Public/Private Life*. New York: Norton.

Jones, M.A., & Krisberg, B. (1994). *Images and Reality: Juvenile Crime,Youth Violence, and Public Policy*. San Francisco: National Council on Crime and Delinquency.

Jones, P., & Cannon, M. (1998). The new epidemiology of schizophrenia. *Psychiatric Clinics of North America*, 21, pp. 1–25.

Jones, P.B., Bebbington, P., Foerster, A., Lewis, S.W., et al. (1993). Premorbid social underachievement in schizophrenia: Results from the Camberwell Collaborative Psychosis Study. *British Journal of Psychiatry*, 162, pp. 65–71.

Jones, R. T., & Ollendick, T.H. (In press). The impact of residential fire on children and their families. In A. La Greca, W. Silverman, E. Vernberg, & M. Roberts (Eds.), *Helping Children Cope with Disasters: Integrating Research and Practice*. Washington, DC: APA Books.

Jones, R.R., Reid, J.B., & Patterson, G.R. (1975). Naturalistic observation in clinical assessment. In P. McReynolds (Ed.), *Advances in Psychological Assessment*, vol. 3. San Francisco: Jossey-Bass.

Jones, S. (2004). Psychotherapy of bipolar disorder: A review. *Journal of Affective Disorders*, 80, pp. 101–114.

Jordan, J.V. (2004). Personality disorder or relational disconnection? In J.J. Magnavita (Ed.), *Handbook of Personality Disorders:Theory and Practice*, pp. 120–134. New York: Wiley.

Jorm, A.F. (2001). History of depression as a risk factor for dementia: An updated review. *Australian and New Zealand Journal of Psychiatry*, 35, pp. 776–781.

Josephs, L. (1994). Psychoanalytic and related interpretations. In B.B.Wolman & G. Stricker (Eds.), *Anxiety and Related Disorders:A Handbook*, pp. 11–29. New York:Wiley-Interscience.

Julien, R.M. (2001). *A Primer of Drug Action: A Concise, Nontechnical Guide to the Actions Uses and Side Effects of Psychoactive Drugs* (9th edition). New York: Worth.

Junginger, J. (1997). Fetishism. In D.R. Laws & W.T. O'Donohue (Eds.), *Handbook of Sexual Deviance:Theory and Application*. New York: Guilford.

Just, N., & Alloy, L.B. (1997).The response styles theory of depression:Tests and an extension of the theory. *Journal of Abnormal Psychology*, 106, pp. 221–229.

Kübler-Ross, E. (1969). *On Death and Dying*. New York: Macmillian.

Kafka, M.P. (2001). The paraphilia-related disorders: A proposal for a unified classification of nonparaphilic hypersexuality disorders. *Sexual Addiction and Compulsivity*, 8, pp. 227–239.

Kagan, J. (1998). *Three Seductive Ideas*. Cambridge, MA: Harvard University Press.

Kagan, J., & Snidman, N. (1991).Temperamental factors in human development. *American Psychologist*, 46, pp. 856–862.

Kahneman, Daniel (2003). A perspective on judgment and choice: Mapping bounded rationality. *American Psychologist*. 58, pp. 697–720.

Kallman, W.M., & Feuerstein, M.J. (1986). Psychophysiological procedures. In A.R. Ciminero, K.S. Calhoun, & H.E. Adams (Eds.), *Handbook of Behavioral Assessment*, 2nd ed., pp. 325–350. New York: Wiley-Interscience.

Kamarck,T., & Jennings, J.R. (1991). Biobehavioral factors in sudden cardiac death. *Psychological Bulletin*, 109, pp. 42–75.

Kanaya, T., Scullin, M.H., & Ceci, S.J. (2003). The Flynn effect and U.S. policies: The impact of rising IQ scores on American society via mental retardation diagnoses. *American Psychologist*, 58(10), pp. 778–790.

Kandel, D.B., & Yamaguchi, K. (1999). Developmental stages of involvement in substance use. In P.J. Ott, R.E. Tarter, & R.T. Ammerman (Eds.), *Sourcebook on Substance Abuse: Etiology, Epidemiology, Assessment, and Treatment*, pp. 50–74. Boston: Allyn & Bacon.

Kane, J. M. (2001b). Long-term therapeutic management in schizophrenia. In A. Breier, and P.V. Tran (Eds.), *Current Issues in the Psychopharmacology of Schizophrenia*, pp. 430–446. Philadelphia, PA: Lippincott.

Kane, J.M. (1999). Pharmacologic treatment of schizophrenia. *Biological Psychiatry*, 46, pp. 1396–1408.

Kane, J.M. (2001a). Extrapyramidal side effects are unacceptable. *European Neuropsychopharmacology*, 11 (Suppl. 4), pp. S397–S403.

Kaneko, K. (2001). Penetration disorder: Dyspareunia exists on the extension of vaginismus. *Journal of Sex and Marital Therapy*, 27, pp. 153–155.

Kanner, L. (1943). Autistic disturbances of affective contact. *Nervous Child*, 2, pp. 217–250.

Kaplan, H.S. (1974). *The New Sex Therapy: Active Treatment of Sexual Dysfunctions*. New York: Brunner/Mazel.

Kaplan, L.J. (1989). *Female Perversions:The temptations of Emma Bovary*. New York: Doubleday.

Kapur, S., & Remington, G. (1996). Serotonin-dopamine interaction and its relevance to schizophrenia. *American Journal of Psychiatry*, 153, pp. 466–476.

Kapur, S., & Remington, G. (2001). Antypical antipsychotics: New directions and new challenges in the treatment of schizophrenia. *Annual Review of Medicine*, 52, pp. 503–517.

Karasek, R.A., Theorell, T.G., Schwartz, J., Pieper, C., & Alfredsson, L. (1982). Job, psychological factors and coronary heart disease: Swedish prospective findings and U.S. prevalence findings using a new occupational inference method. *Advances in Cardiology,* 29, pp. 62–67.

Karney, B.R., & Bradbury, T.N. (1995). The longitudinal course of marital quality and stability: A review of theory, method, and research. *Psychological Bulletin,* 118, pp. 3–34.

Karno, M., & Golding, J.M. (1991). Obsessive-compulsive disorder. In L.N. Robins & D.A. Regier (Eds.), *Psychiatric Disorders in America: The Epidemiologic Catchment Area Study.* New York: Free Press.

Karon, J.M., et al. (1996). Prevalence of HIV infection in the United States, 1984 to 1992. *Journal of the American Medical Association,* 276, pp. 126–131.

Karras, A., & Otis, D.B. (1987). A comparison of inpatients in an urban state hospital in 1975 and 1982. *Hospital and Community Psychiatry,* 38, pp. 963–967.

Kasen, S., Cohen, P., Brook, J.S., & Hartmark, C. (1996). A multiple-risk interaction model: Effects of temperament and divorce on psychiatric disorders in children. *Journal of Abnormal Child Psychology,* 24, pp. 121–150.

Kaskutas, L.A., Turk, N., Bond, J., & Weisner, C. (2003). The role of religion, spirituality and Alcoholics Anonymous in sustained sobriety. *Alcoholism Treatment Quarterly,* 21, pp. 1–16.

Kaslow, N.J., & Thompson, M.P. (1998). Applying the criteria for empirically supported treatments to studies of psychosocial interventions for child and adolescent depression. *Journal of Clinical Child Psychology,* 27, pp. 146–155.

Kasvikis, Y.G., Tsakiris, F., Marks, I.M., Basogulu, M., & Noshirvani, H.V. (1986). Past history of anorexia nervosa in women with obsessive-compulsive disorders. *International Journal of Eating Disorders,* 5, pp. 1069–1075.

Katschnig, H., & Amering, M. (1990). Panic attacks and panic disorder in cross-cultural perspective. In J.C. Ballenger (Ed.), *Clinical Aspects of Panic Disorder.* New York: Wiley.

Katschnig, H., & Amering, M. (1998). The long-term course of panic disorder and its predictors. *Journal of Clinical Psychopharmacology,* 18 (suppl. 2), pp. 6–11.

Katz, R., & McGuffin, P. (1993). The genetics of affective disorders. In D. Fowles (Ed.), *Progress in Experimental Personality and Psychopathology Research.* New York: Springer.

Katz, R.J., DeVeaugh-Geiss, J., & Landau, P. (1990). Clomipramine in obsessive-compulsive disorder. *Biological Psychiatry,* 28, pp. 401–414.

Katzman, R. (1976). The prevalence and malignancy of Alzheimer's disease. *Archives of Neurology,* 33, pp. 217–218.

Katzman, R. (1993). Education and the prevalence of dementia and Alzheimer's disease. *Neurology,* 43, pp. 13–20.

Kaufman, G., & Elder, G.H., Jr. (2003). Grandparenting and age identity. *Journal of Aging Studies,* 17, pp. 269–282.

Kaufman, J., Aikins, D., & Krystal, J. (2004). Neuroimaging studies in PTSD. In J.P. Wilson & T.M. Keane (Eds.), *Assessing Psychological Trauma and PTSD,* 2nd ed. New York: Guilford.

Kaye, D.W.K. (1995). The epidemiology of age-related neurological disease and dementia. *Reviews in Clinical Gerontology,* 5, pp. 39–56.

Kaye, W.H., Weltzin, T.E., Hsu, L.K.G., McConahan, C.W., & Bolton, B. (1993). Amount of calories retained after binge eating and vomiting. *American Journal of Psychiatry,* 150, pp. 969–971.

Kaysen, S. (2001). *The Camera My Mother Gave Me.* New York: Knopf.

Kazdin, A.E. (1989). Identifying depression in children: A comparison of alternative selection criteria. *Journal of Abnormal Child Psychology,* 17, pp. 437–455.

Kazdin, A.E. (1994a). Methodology, design, and evaluation in psychotherapy research. In A.E. Bergin and S.L.

Garfield (Eds.), *Handbook of Psychotherapy and Behavior Change,* 4th ed., pp. 19–71, New York: Wiley.

Kazdin, A.E. (1994b). Psychotherapy for children and adolescents. In A.E. Bergin & S.L. Garfield (Eds.), *Handbook of Psychotherapy and Behavior Change,* 4th ed., pp. 543–594. New York: Wiley.

Kazdin, A.E. (1995). *Conduct Disorders in Childhood and Adolescence,* 2nd ed. Thousand Oaks, CA: Sage.

Kazdin, A.E. (1997). Parent management training: Evidence, outcomes, and issues. *Journal of the American Academy of Child and Adolescent Psychiatry,* 36, pp. 1349–1365.

Kazdin, A.E., & Petti, T.A. (1982). Self-report and interview measures of childhood and adolescent depression. *Journal of Child Psychology and Psychiatry,* 23, pp. 437–457.

Kazdin, A.E., & Whitley, M.K. (2003). Treatment of parental stress to enhance therapeutic change among children referred for aggressive and antisocial behavior. *Journal of Consulting and Clinical Psychology,* 71(3), pp. 504–515.

Kazdin, A.E., French, N.H., & Unis, A.S. (1983). Child, mother, and father evaluations of depression in psychiatric inpatient children. *Journal of Abnormal Child Psychology,* 11, pp. 167–180.

Kazdin, A.E., Siegel, T.C., & Bass, D. (1992). Cognitive problem-solving skills training and parent management training in the treatment of antisocial behavior in children. *Journal of Consulting and Clinical Psychology,* 60, pp. 753–747.

Keane, T.M., Zimering, R.T., & Caddell, J.M. (1985). A behavioral formulation of posttraumatic stress disorder in Vietnam veterans. *Behavior Therapist,* 8, pp. 9–12.

Keefe, F.J., Lumley, M., Anderson, T., Lynch, T., & Carson, K.L. (2001). Pain and emotion: New research directions. *Journal of Clinical Psychology,* 57, pp. 587–607.

Keel, P.K., et al. (2000). Predictive validity of bulimia nervosa as a diagnostic category. *American Journal of Psychiatry,* 157, pp. 136–138.

Keel, P.K. et al. (In press). Predictors of treatment utilization among women with anorexia and bulimia nervosa. *American Journal of Psychiatry.*

Keel, P.K., & Klump, K.L. (2003). Are eating disorders culture-bound syndromes? Implications for conceptualizing their etiology. *Psychological Bulletin,* 129, pp. 747–769.

Keel, P.K., & Mitchell, J.E. (1997). Outcome in bulimia nervosa. *American Journal of Psychiatry,* 154, pp. 313–321.

Keel, P.K., Mitchell, J.E., Davis, T.L., & Crow, S.J. (2002). Long-term impact of treatment in women diagnosed with bulimia nervosa. *International Journal of Eating Disorders,* 31, pp. 151–158.

Keenan, K., & Shaw, D. (1997) Developmental and social influences on young girls' early problem behavior. *Psychological Bulletin,* 121, pp. 95–113.

Keesey, R.E. (1995). A set-point model of body weight regulation. In K.D. Brownell & C.G. Fairburn (Eds.), *Eating Disorders and Obesity: A Comprehensive Handbook,* pp. 46–50. New York: Guilford.

Keith, S.J., Regier, D.A., & Rae, D.S. (1991). Schizophrenic disorders. In L.N. Robins & D.A. Regier (Eds.), *Psychiatric Disorders in America: The Epidemiologic Catchment Area Study,* pp. 33–52. New York: Free Press.

Keller, J., Hicks, B.D., & Miller, G.A. (2000). Psychophysiology in the study of psychopathology. In J.T. Cacioppo, L.G. Tassinary, and G.G. Berntson (Eds.), *Handbook of Psychophysiology,* 2nd ed., pp. 719–750. New York: Cambridge University Press.

Keller, M.B. (2003). The lifelong course of social anxiety disorder: A clinical perspective. *Acta Psychiatrica Scandinavica,* 108 (suppl. 417), pp. 85–94.

Kellner, C.H. (1997). Left unilateral ECT: Still a viable option. *Convulsive Therapy,* 13, pp. 65–67.

Kellner, R. (1985). Functional somatic symptoms in hypochondriasis. *Archives of General Psychiatry,* 42, pp. 821–833.

Kelly, M.P., Strassberg, D.S., & Turner, C.M. (2004). Communication and associated relationship issues in female anorgasmia. *Journal of Sex & Marital Therapy,* 30, pp. 263–276.

Kelly, T., Soloff, P.H., Cornelius, J., George, A., Lis, J.A., & Ulrich, R. (1992). Can we study (treat) borderline patients? Attrition from research and open treatment. *Journal of Personality Disorders,* 6, pp. 417–433.

Kempe, C.H., Silverman, F., Steele, B., Droegueller, W., & Silver, H. (1962). The battered child syndrome. *Journal of the American Medical Association,* 181, pp. 17–24.

Kendall, P.C. (1994). Treating anxiety disorders in children: Results of a randomized clinical trial. *Journal of Consulting and Clinical Psychology,* 62, pp. 100–110.

Kendall, P.C., Safford, S., Flannery-Schroeder, E., & Webb, A. (2004). Child anxiety treatment: Outcomes in adolescence and impact on substance use and depression at 7.4-year follow-up. *Journal of Consulting and Clinical Psychology,* 72(2), pp. 276–287.

Kendell, R.E. (1989). Clinical validity. *Psychological Medicine,* 19, pp. 45–55.

Kendell, R.E. (2002) The distinction between personality disorder and mental illness. *British Journal of Psychiatry,* 180, pp. 110–115.

Kendell, R.E. (2002). Five criteria for an improved taxonomy of mental disorders. In J.E. Helzer and J.J. Hudziak (Eds.), *Defining Psychopathology in the 21st Century,* pp. 3–17. Washington, D.C.: American Psychiatric Press.

Kendler, K.S. (1990). The super-normal control group in psychiatric genetics: Possible artifactual evidence for coaggregation. *Psychiatric Genetics,* 1, pp. 45–53.

Kendler, K.S., & Diehl, S.R. (1993). The genetics of schizophrenia: A current, genetic-epidemiologic perspective. *Schizophrenia Bulletin,* 19, pp. 261–285.

Kendler, K.S., & Gardner, C.O. (1997). The risk for psychiatric disorders in relatives of schizophrenic and control probands: A comparison of three independent studies. *Psychological Medicine,* 27, pp. 411–419.

Kendler, K.S., Hettema, J.M., Butera, F., Gardner, C.O., & Prescott, D.A. (2003). Life event dimensions of loss, humiliation, entrapment, and danger in the prediction of onsets of major depression and generalized anxiety. *Archives of General Psychiatry,* 60, pp. 789–796.

Kendler, K.S., Karkowski, L.M., & Prescott, C.A. (1999). Causal relationship between stressful life events and the onset of major depression. *American Journal of Psychiatry,* 156, pp. 837–848.

Kendler, K.S., MacLean, C., Neale, M., Kessler, R., Heath, A., & Eaves, L. (1991). The genetic epidemiology of bulimia nervosa. *American Journal of Psychiatry,* 148, pp. 1627–1637.

Kendler, K.S., McGuire, M., Gruenberg, A.M., & Walsh, D. (1994). Outcome and family study of the subtypes of schizophrenia in the west of Ireland. *American Journal of Psychiatry,* 151, pp. 849–856.

Kendler, K.S., McGuire, M., Gruenberg, A.M., O'Hare, A., Spellman, M., & Walsh, D. (1993). The Roscommon Family Study. III. Schizophrenia-related personality disorders in relatives. *Archives of General Psychiatry,* 50, pp. 781–788.

Kendler, K.S., Neale, M.C., Kessler, R.C., Heath, A.C., & Eaves, L.J. (1992a). Generalized anxiety disorder in women: A population-based twin study. *Archives of General Psychiatry,* 49, pp. 267–272.

Kendler, K.S., Neale, M.C., Kessler, R.C., Heath, A.C., & Eaves, L.J. (1992b). The genetic epidemiology of phobias in women: The interrelationship of agoraphobia, social phobia, situational phobia, and simple phobia. *Archives of General Psychiatry,* 49, pp. 273–281.

Kendler, K.S., Prescott, C., Myers, J., & Neale, M. C. (2003). The structure of genetic and environmental risk factors for common psychiatric and substance use disorders in men and women. *Archives of General Psychiatry*, 60, pp. 929–937.

Kendler, K.S., Walters, E.E., Neale, M.C., Kessler, R.C., Heath, A.C., & Eaves, L.J. (1995). The structure of the genetic and environmental risk factors for six major psychiatric disorders in women. *Archives of General Psychiatry*, 52, pp. 374–383.

Kernberg, O.F. (1967). Borderline personality organization. *Journal of the American Psychoanalytic Association*, 15, pp. 641–685.

Kernberg, O.F. (1975). *Borderline Conditions and Pathological Narcissism*. New York: Aronson.

Kerns, J.G., & Berenbaum, H. (2002). Cognitive impairments associated with formal thought disorder in people with schizophrenia. *Journal of Abnormal Psychology*, 111, pp. 211–224.

Kessler, R.C, Keller, M.B; Wittchen, H. (2001). The epidemiology of generalized anxiety disorder. *Psychiatric Clinics of North America*, 24, pp. 19–39.

Kessler, R.C. (1995). The national comorbidity survey: Preliminary results and future directions. *International Journal of Methods in Psychiatric Research*, 5, pp. 139–151.

Kessler, R.C. (2002). Epidemiology of depression. In I.H. Gotlib and C.L. Hammen (Eds.), *Handbook Of depression*. New York: Guilford.

Kessler, R.C., & Zhao, S. (1999). The prevalence of mental disorder. In A.V. Horwitz and T.L. Scheid (Eds.), *A Handbook for the Study of Mental Health: Social Contexts, Theories, and Systems*, pp. 58–78. Cambridge, UK: Cambridge University Press.

Kessler, R.C., Gillis-Light, J., Magee, W.J., Kendler, K.S., & Eaves, L.J. (1997). Childhood adversity and adult psychopathology. In I.H. Gotlib & B.Wheaton (Eds.), *Stress and Adversity over the Life Course: Trajectories and turning Points*, pp. 29–49. New York: Cambridge University Press.

Kessler, R.C., McGonagle, K.A., Zhao, S., Nelson, C.R., Highes, M., Eshleman, S., Wittchen, H., & Kendler, K.S. (1994). Lifetime and 12-month prevalence of DSM-III-R psychiatric disorders in the United States: Results from the National Comorbidity Survey. *Archives of General Psychiatry*, 51, pp. 8–19.

Kessler, R.C., Sonnega, A., Bromet, E., Hughes, M., & Nelson, C.B. (1995). Posttraumatic stress disorder in the National Comorbidity Survey. *Archives of General Psychiatry*, 52, pp. 1048–1060.

Kessler, R.C., Stang, P.E., Wittchen, H., Ustun, T.B., Roy-Burne, P.P., & Walters, E. (1998). Lifetime panic-depression comorbidity in the National Co-morbidity Survey. *Archives of General Psychiatry*, 55, pp. 801–808.

Keteyian, A. (1986). The straight-arrow addict: Compulsive gambling of A. Schlichter. *Sports Illustrated*, March 10, pp. 74–77.

Kettl, P.A. (1993). 10 basic rules for managing dementia. *Patient Care*, 27, pp. 79–86.

Keys, A., Brozek, J., Henschel, A., Mickelsen, O., & Taylor, H.L. (1950). *The Biology of Human Starvation*, 2 vols. Minneapolis: University of Minnesota Press.

Kiecolt-Glaser, J.K. (1999). Stress, personal relationships, and immune function: Health implications. *Brain, Behavior, and Immunity*, 13, pp. 61–72.

Kiecolt-Glaser, J.K., & Newton, T.L. (2001). Marriage and health: His and hers. *Psychological Bulletin*, 127, pp. 472–503.

Kiecolt-Glaser, J.K., Bane, C., Glaser, R., & Malarkey, W.B. (2003). Love, marriage, and divorce: Newlyweds' stress hormones foreshadow relationship changes. *Journal of Consulting and Clinical Psychology*, 71, pp. 176–188.

Kiecolt-Glaser, J.K., Malarkey, W.B., Chee, M., Newton, T., Cacioppo, J.T., Mao, H., & Glaser, R. (1993). Negative behavior during marital conflict is associated with immunological down-regulation. *Psychosomatic Medicine*, 55, pp. 395–409.

Kiesler, C. (1982). Mental hospitals and alternative care: Coninstitutionalization as potential public policy for mental patients. *American Psychologist*, 37, pp. 349–360.

Kihlstrom, J.F. (1998a). Exhumed memory. In S.J. Lynn & K.M. McConkey (Eds.), *Truth in Memory*, pp. 3–31. New York: Guilford.

Kihlstrom, J.F. (1998b). Dissociations and dissociation theory in hypnosis: A comment on Kirch and Lynn (1998). *Psychological Bulletin*, 123, pp. 186–191.

Kihlstrom, J.F. (2002). To honor Kraepelin: From symptoms to pathology in the diagnosis of mental illness. In Larry E. Beutler and Mary L. Malik (Eds.), *Rethinking the DSM: A Psychological Perspective*, pp. 279–303. Washington, D.C.: American Psychological Association.

Kihlstrom, J.F. (2005). Dissociative disorders. *Annual Reviews in Clinical Psychology*, 1, pp. 10.1–10.27.

Kihlstrom, J.F., & Hastie, R. (1997). Mental representations of persons and personality. In R. Hogan, J. Johnson, & S. Briggs (Eds.), *Handbook of Personality Psychology*, pp. 712–735. San Diego, CA: Academic Press.

Kihlstrom, J.F., Glisky, M.L., & Angiulo, M.J. (1994). Dissociative tendencies and dissociative disorders. *Journal of Abnormal Psychology*, 103, pp. 117–124.

Kilbey, M.M., Downey, K., & Breslau, N. (1998). Predicting the emergence and persistence of alcohol dependence in young adults: The role of expectancy and other risk factors. *Experimental and Clinical Psychopharmacology*, 6, pp. 149–156.

Kilmann, P.R., et al. (1982). The treatment of sexual paraphilias: A review of the outcome research. *Journal of Sex Research*, 18, pp. 193–252.

Kilpatrick, D.G., & Acierno, R. (2003). Mental health needs of crime victims: Epidemiology and outcomes. *Journal of Traumatic Stress*, 16, pp. 119–132.

Kilpatrick, D.G., Edmunds, C.N., & Seymour, A.K. (1992). *Rape in America: A Report to the Nation*. Arlington, VA: National Victim Center.

Kilpatrick, D.G., Ruggiero, K.J., Acierno, R., Saunders, B.E., Resnick, H.S., & Best, C.L. (2003). Violence and risk of PTSD, major depression, substance abuse/dependence, and comorbidity: Results from the national survey of adolescents. *Journal of Consulting and Clinical Psychology*, 71, pp. 692–700.

Kilpatrick, D.G., Saunders, B.E., Amick-McMullan, A., Best, C.L., Veronen, L.J., & Resnick, H.S. (1989). Victim and crime factors associated with the development of crime-related posttraumatic stress disorder. *Behavior Therapy*, 20, pp. 199–214.

Kim, J.E., & Moen, P. (2001). Is retirement good or bad for subjective well-being? *Current Directions in Psychological Science*. 10, pp. 83–86.

Kimble, G.A. (1989). Psychology from the standpoint of a generalist. *American Psychologist*, 44, pp. 491–499.

King, B.M. (1996). *Human Sexuality Today*. Upper Saddle River, NJ: Prentice Hall.

King, N.J., Ollier, K., Iacuone, R., Schuster, S., Bays, K., Gullone, E., & Ollendick, T.H. (1989). Fears of children and adolescents: A cross-sectional Australian study using the Revised-Fear Survey Schedule for Children. *Journal of Child Psychology and Psychiatry*, 30, pp. 775–784.

King, R.A., Segman, R.H., & Anderson, G.M. (1994). Serotonin and suicidality: The impact of acute fluoxetine administration. I. Serotonin and suicide. *Israel Journal of Psychiatry and Related Sciences*, 31, pp. 271–279.

Kingsberg, S.A., & Janata, J.W. (2003). The sexual aversions. In S.B. Levine and C.B. Risen (Eds.), *Handbook of Clinical Sexuality for Mental Health Professionals*, pp. 153–165. New York: Brunner-Routledge.

Kinsey, A.C., Pomeroy, W.B., & Martin, C.E. (1948). *Sexual Behavior in the Human Male*. Philadelphia: Saunders.

Kirk, S.A., & Kutchins, H. (1992). *The Selling of DSM: The Rhetoric of Science in Psychiatry*. New York: Aldine.

Kirmayer, L.J. (2001). Cultural variations in the clinical presentation of depression and anxiety: Implications for diagnosis and treatment. *Journal of Clinical Psychiatry*, 62 (Suppl 13), pp. 22–28.

Kirmayer, L.J., Robbins, J.M., & Paris, J. (1994). Somatoform disorders: Personality and the social matrix of somatic distress. *Journal of Abnormal Psychology*, 103, pp. 125–136.

Kirsch, I., & Lynn, S.J. (1995). The altered state of hypnosis: Changes in the theoretical landscape. *American Psychologist*, 50, pp. 846–858.

Kirsch, I., & Lynn, S.J. (1998). Dissociation theories of hypnosis. *Psychological Bulletin*, 123, pp. 100–115.

Klein, D.F. (1981). Anxiety reconceptualized. In D.F. Klein & J. Rabkin (Eds.), *Anxiety: New Research and Changing Concepts*, pp. 235–263. New York: Raven Press.

Klein, D.F. (1996). Preventing hung juries about therapy studies. *Journal of Consulting and Clinical Psychology*, 64, pp. 81–87.

Klein, D.F. (1999). Harmful dysfunction, disorder, disease, illness, and evolution. *Journal of Abnormal Psychology*, 108, pp. 421–429.

Klein, D.F., & Klein, H.M. (1989). The definition and psychopharmacology of spontaneous panic and phobia. In P. Tyrer (Ed.), *Psychopharmacology of Anxiety*. New York: Oxford University Press.

Klein, D.N. (2003). Patients' versus informants' reports of personality disorders in predicting 7 1/2 year outcome in outpatients with depressive disorders. *Psychological Assessment*, 15, pp. 216–222.

Klein, R.G., & Pine, D.S. (2002). Anxiety disorders. In M. Rutter & E. Taylor (Eds.), *Child and Adolescent Psychiatry*, 4th ed., pp. 486–509. Oxford, UK: Blackwell.

Kleinman, A. (1988). *Rethinking Psychiatry: From Cultural Category to Personal Experience*. New York: Free Press.

Kleinman, A. (2004). Culture and depression. *New England Journal of Medicine*, 352, pp. 951–953.

Klerman, G. (1990b). The psychiatric patient's right to effective treatment: Implications of Osheroff vs. Chestnut Lodge. *American Journal of Psychiatry*, 147, pp. 409–418.

Klerman, G.L. (1990a). History and development of modern concepts of anxiety and panic. In J. Ballenger (Ed.), *Clinical Aspects of Panic Disorder*, pp. 3–12. New York: Wiley.

Klerman, G.L., Weissman, M.M., Rounsaville, B.J., & Chevron, E.S. (1984). *Interpersonal Psychotherapy of Depression*. New York: Basic Books.

Kluft, R.P. (1987). An update on multiple personality disorder. *Hospital and Community Psychiatry*, 38, pp. 363–373.

Klump, K.L., McGue, M., & Iacono, W.G. (2000). Age differences in genetic and environmental influences on eating attitudes and behaviors in preadolescent and adolescent female twins. *Journal of Abnormal Psychology*, 109, pp. 239–251.

Kluznik, J.C., Speed, N., Van Valkenburg, C., & Magraw, R. (1986). Forty-year follow-up of United States prisoners of war. *American Journal of Psychiatry*, 143, pp. 1443–1446.

Knight, R.A. (1999). Validation of a typology for rapists. *Journal of Interpersonal Violence*, 14, pp. 303–330.

Knight, R.A., Prentky, R.A., & Cerce, D.D. (1994). The development, reliability, and validity of an inventory for the multidimensional assessment of sex and aggression. *Criminal Justice and Behavior*, 21, pp. 72–94.

Koch, H., & Knapp, D.E. (1987). Highlights of drug utilization in office practice. National Ambulatory Medical Survey, 1885. *Advance Data from Vital and Health Statistics*, No. 134, U.S. Department of Health and Human Services Publication No. (PHS) 87–1250.

Koegel, R.L., Koegel, L.K., & McNerney, E.K. (2001). Pivotal areas intervention for autism. *Journal of Clinical Child Psychology*, 30, pp. 19–32.

Koenen, K.C., Stellman, J.M., Stellman, S.D., & Sommer, J.F. (2003). Risk factors for course of posttraumatic stress disorder among Vietnam veterans: A 14-year follow-up of American Legionnaires. *Journal of Consulting and Clinical Psychology*, 71, pp. 980–986.

Koenig, H.G., & Blazer, D.G. (1990). Depression and other affective disorders. In C.K. Cassel, D.E. Riesenberg, L.B. Sorenson, & J.R.Walsh (Eds.), *Geriatric Medicine*, 2nd ed., pp. 473–489. New York: Springer.

Koenigsberg, H.W., Reynolds, D., Goodman, M., New, A.S., Mitropoulou, V., Trestman, R.L., Silverman, J., & Siever, L.J. (2003). Risperidone in the treatment of schizotypal personality disorder. *Journal of Clinical Psychiatry*, 64, pp. 628–634.

Koerner, S.S., Wallace, S., Lehman, S.J., Lee, S.A., & Escalante, K.A. (2004). Sensitive mother-to-adolescent disclosures after divorce: Is the experience of sons different from that of daughters? *Journal of Family Psychology*, 18(1), pp. 46–57.

Kohlberg, L. (1985). *The Psychology of Moral Development*. San Francisco: Harper & Row.

Koluchova, J. (1972). Severe deprivation in twins: A case study of marked IQ change after age 7. *Journal of Child Psychology and Psychiatry*, 13, pp. 107–114.

Kontakos, N., & Stokes, J. (1999). Parkinson's disease—Recent developments and new directions. *Chronic Diseases in Canada*, 20, pp. 58–76.

Koob, G.F. (2000). Neurobiology of addiction: Toward the development of new therapies. *Annals of the New York Academy of Sciences*, 909, pp. 170–185.

Koons, C.R., Robins, C.J., Tweed, J.L., Lynch, T.R., Gonzales. A.M., Morse, J.Q., Bishop, G.K., Butterfield, M.I., & Bastian, L.A. (2001). Efficacy of dialectical behavior therapy in women veterans with borderline personality disorder. *Behavior Therapy*, 32, pp. 371–390.

Kop, W.J. (1999). Chronic and acute psychological risk factors for liar clinical manifestations of coronary artery disease. *Psychosomatic Medicine*, 61, pp. 476–487

Kopelman, M.D. (1995). The Korsakoff syndrome. *British Journal of Psychiatry*, 166, pp. 154–173.

Kopelowicz, A., Liberman, R.P., & Zarate, R. (2002). Psychosocial treatments for schizophrenia. In P.E. Nathan and J.M. Gorman (Eds.). *A Guide to Treatments that Work*, (2nd ed.) pp. 201–228. London, England: Oxford University Press.

Koran, L.J. (1975). The reliability of clinical methods, data and judgments. *New England Journal of Medicine*, 293, pp. 642–646, 695–701.

Koranyi, E.K. (1989). Physiology of stress reviewed. In S. Cheren (Ed.), *Psychosomatic Medicine: Theory, Physiology, and Practice*, Vol. 1, pp. 241–278. Madison, CT: International Universities Press.

Koskenvuo, M., Kaprio, J., Rose, R.J., Kesaniemi, A., Sarna, S., Heikkila, K., & Langinvainio, H. (1988). Hostility as a risk factor for mortality and ischemic heart disease in men. *Psychosomatic Medicine*, 50, pp. 330–340.

Koski, L, Iacoboni, M., & Mazziotta, J.C. (2002). Deconstructing apraxia: Understanding disorders of intentional movement after stroke. *Current Opinion in Neurology*, 15, pp. 71–77.

Koss, M.P., Tromp, S., & Tharan, M. (1995). Traumatic memories: Empirical foundations, forensic, and clinical implications. *Clinical Psychology: Science and Practice*, 2, pp. 111–132.

Kosten, T.R., & O'Connor, P.G. (2003). Management of drug and alcohol withdrawal. *New England Journal of Medicine*, 348, pp. 1786–1795.

Kovacs, M., Feinberg, T.L., Crouse-Novak, M.A., Paulaukas, S., Pollock, M., & Finkelstein, R. (1984). Depressive disorders in childhood. II. A longitudinal study of the risk for a subsequent major depression. *Archives of General Psychiatry*, 41, pp. 643–649.

Kowalski, K.M. (1998). The dangers of alcohol. *Current Health*, 24, pp. 6–13.

Kozak, M.J., Liebowitz, M.R., & Foa, E.G. (2000). Cognitive behavior therapy and pharmacotherapy for obsessive-compulsive disorder: The NIMH-sponsored collaborative study. In W.K. Goodman & M.V. Rudorfer (Eds.), *Obsessive-Compulsive Disorder: Contemporary Issues in Treatment*, pp. 501–530. Mahwah, NJ: Erlbaum.

Kozlowski, L.T., Henningfield, J.E., & Brigham, J. (2001). *Cigarettes, Nicotine, and Health: A Biobehavioral Approach*. Thousand Oaks, CA: Sage Publications.

Kraepelin, E. (1921). *Manic-Depressive Insanity and Paranoia*. Edinburgh: Livingstone.

Krakow, B. et al. (2001). Imagery rehearsal therapy for chronic nightmares in sexual assault survivors with posttraumatic stress disorder: A randomized clinical trial. *Journal of the American Medical Association*, 286, pp. 537–545.

Krantz, D.S., Contrada, R.J., Hill, D.R., & Friedler, E. (1988). Environmental stress and biobehavioral antecedents of coronary heart disease. *Journal of Consulting and Clinical Psychology*, 56, pp. 333–341.

Krantz, D.S., Gabbay, F.H., Hedges, S.M., Leach, S.G., Gottdiener, J.S., & Rozanski, A. (1993). Mental and physical triggers of silent myocardial ischemia: Ambulatory studies using self-monitoring diary methodology. *Annals of Behavioral Medicine*, 15, pp. 33–40.

Kroenke, K., & Swindle, R. (2000). Cognitive behavioural therapy for somatization and symptom syndromes: a critical review of controlled clinical trials. *Psychotherapy and Psychosomatics*, 69, pp. 205–215

Kroenke, K., Spitzer, R.L., deGruy, F.V., Hahn, S.R., Linzer, M., Williams, J.B.W., Brody, D., & Davies, M. (1997). Multisomatoform disorder: An alternative to undifferentiated somatoform disorder for the somatizing patient in primary care. *Archives of General Psychiatry*, 54, pp. 352–358.

Kroenke, K., West, S.L., Gilsenan, A., Eckert, G.J., Dolor, R., Stang, P. Zhou, X., Hays, R., & Weinberger, M. (2001). Similar effectiveness of paroxetine, fluoxetine, and sertraline in primary care: A randomized trial. *Journal of the American Medical Association*, 286, pp. 2947–2955.

Krueger, R.B., & Kaplan, M.S. (1997). Frotteurism: Assessment and treatment, In D.R. Laws and W. O'Donohue (Eds.), *Sexual Deviance: Theory, Assessment, and Treatment*. New York: Guilford.

Krueger, R.F. (1999). Personality traits in late adolescence predict mental disorders in early adulthood: A prospective-epidemiological study. *Journal of Personality*, 67, pp. 39–65.

Krueger, R.F. (2002). Psychometric perspectives on comorbidity. In J.E. Helzer and J.J. Hudziak (Eds.), *Defining Psychopathology in the 21st Century*, pp. 41–54. Washington, D.C.: American Psychiatric Press.

Kuban, M., Barbaree, H.E., & Blanchard, R. (1999). A comparison of volume and circumference phallometry: Response magnitude and method agreement. *Archives of Sexual Behavior*, 28, pp. 345–359.

Kübler-Ross, E. (1969). *On Death and Dying*, New York: Macmillian.

Kubzansky, L.D., Sparrow, D., Vokonas, P., & Kawachi, I. (2001). Is the glass half empty or half full? A prospective study of optimism and coronary heart disease in the normative aging study. *Psychosomatic Medicine*, 63, pp. 910–916.

Kuehner, C. (2003). Gender differences in unipolar depression: An update of epidemiological findings and possible explanations. *Acta Psychiatrica Scandinavica*, 108, pp. 163–174.

Kukull, W.A., & Bowen, J.D. (2002). Dementia epidemiology. *Medical Clinics of North America*, 86, pp. 573–590.

Kupfer, D.J., & Frank, E. (2001). The interaction of drug- and psychotherapy in the longterm treatment of depression. *Journal of Affective Disorders*, 62, pp. 131–137.

Kupfer, D.J., Chengappa, K.N.R., Gelenberg, A.J., Hirschfeld, R.M.A., Goldberg, J.F., Sachs, G.S., Grochocinski, V.J. Houck, P.R., & Kolar, A.B. (2001). Citalopram as adjunctive therapy in bipolar depression. *Journal of Clinical Psychiatry*. 62, pp. 985–990.

Kurlan, R. (2004). The PANDAS hypothesis: Losing its bite? *Movement Disorders*, 19, pp. 371–374.

Kurlan, R., & Kaplan, E.L. (2004). The pediatric autoimmune neuropsychiatric disorders associated with streptococcal infection (PANDAS) etiology for tics and obsessive-compulsive symptoms: Hypothesis or entity? *Pediatrics*, 113, pp. 883–886.

Kushner, M.G., Sher, K.J., & Erickson, D.J. (1999). Prospective analysis of the relation between DSM-III anxiety disorders and alcohol use disorders. *American Journal of Psychiatry*, 156, pp. 723–732.

Kwapil, T.R. (1998). Social anhedonia as a predictor of the development of schizophrenia-spectrum disorders. *Journal of Abnormal Psychology*, 107, pp. 558–565.

L'Abate, L., & Bagarozzi, D.A. (1993). *Sourcebook of Marriage and Family Evaluation*. New York: Brunner/Mazel.

Lacey, J.I. (1967). Somatic response patterning and stress: Some revisions of activation theory. In M.H. Appley & R.Trumball (Eds.), *Psychological Stress*. New York: McGraw-Hill.

LaCroix, A.Z., & Haynes, S.G. (1987). Gender differences in the stressfulness of workplace roles: A focus on work and health. In R. Barnett, G. Baruch, & L. Biener (Eds.), *Gender and Stress*, pp. 96–121. New York: Free Press.

Ladwig, K., Marten-Mittag, B.; Erazo, N., & Guendel, H. (2001). Identifying somatization disorder in a population-based health examination survey: Psychosocial burden and gender differences. *Psychosomatics*, 42, pp. 511–518.

Lahey, B.B., et al. (1994). DSM-IV field trials for attention deficit/hyperactivity disorder in children and adolescents. *Journal of the American Academy of Child and Adolescent Psychiatry*, 151, pp. 1673–1685.

Lahey, B.B., Loeber, R., Burke, J.D., & Applegate, B. (2005). Predicting future antisocial personality disorder in males from a clinical assessment in childhood. *Journal of Consulting and Clinical Psychology*, 73, pp. 389–399.

Lahti, R.A., Roberts, R.C., Conley, R.R., Cochrane, E.V., et al. (1996). D₂ type receptors in postmortem human brain sections from normal and schizophrenic subjects. *Neuroreport: An International Journal for the Rapid Communication of Research in Neuroscience*, 7(12), pp. 1945–1948.

Lamberg, L. (1998). New drug for erectile dysfunction boon for many, "viagravation" for some. *Journal of the American Medical Association*, 280, pp. 867–869.

Lancet (1991). Editorial. Phenylketonuria grows up, 337, pp. 1256–1257.

Lang, A.R., & Stritzke, W.G.K. (1993). Children and alcohol. In M. Galanter, H. Begleiter, R. Deitrich, et al. (Eds.), *Recent Developments in Alcoholism*. Vol. 11. *Ten Years of Progress*, pp. 73–85. New York: Plenum.

Lang, C.T., & Daro, D. (1996). *Current trends in Child Abuse Reporting and Fatalities: The Results of the 1995 Annual State Survey*. Working paper 808. Washington, DC: National Committee on the Prevention of Child Abuse.

Langevin, R. (1992). Biological factors contributing to paraphilic behavior. *Psychiatric Annals*, 22, pp. 307–314.

Langlais, P.J. (1995). Alcohol-related thiamine deficiency. *Alcohol Health and Research World*, 19, pp. 113–122.

Lara, M.E., & Klein, D.N. (1999). Psychosocial processes underlying the maintenance and persistence of depression: Implications for understanding chronic depression. *Clinical Psychology Review*, 19, pp. 553–570.

Larsen, R.J., & Buss, D.J. (2002). *Personality Psychology*. New York: McGraw-Hill.

Larson, R., Csikszentmihalyi, M., & Graef, R. (1980). Mood variability and the psychosocial adjustment of adolescents. *Journal of Youth and Adolescence*, 9, pp. 469–490.

Last, C.G., & Strauss, C.C. (1990). School refusal in anxiety-disordered children and adolescents. *Journal of the American Academy of Child and Adolescent Psychiatry*, 29, pp. 31–35.

Laumann, E.O., Gagnon, J.H., Michael, R.T., & Michaels, S. (1994). *The Social Organization of Sexuality: Sexual Practices in the United States*, Chicago: University of Chicago Press.

Laumann, E.O., Paik, A., & Rosen, R. (1999). Sexual dysfunction in the United States: Prevalence and predictors. *Journal of the American Medical Association*, 281, pp. 537–544.

Laumann-Billings, L. &. Emery, R.E. (2000). Distress among young adults from divorced families. *Journal of Family Psychology*, 14, pp. 671–687.

Lauterbach, E.C., Carter, W.G., Rathke, K.M., Thomas, B.H., Shillcutt, S.D., Vogel, R.L., Moore, N.C., Mimbs, J.W., & Nelson, W.H. (2001). Tardive dyskinesia-Diagnostic issues, sybsyndromes, and concurrent movement disorders. *Schizophrenia Bulletin* 27, pp. 601–614.

Lavori, P.W., Klerman, G.L., Keller, M.B., Reich, T., Rice, J., & Endicott, J. (1987). Age-period-cohort analysis of secular trends in onset of major depression: Findings in siblings of patients with major affective disorder. *Journal of Psychiatric Research*, 21, pp. 23–35.

Lawton, M.P. (1989). Environmental approaches to research and treatment of Alzheimer's disease. In E. Light & B.D. Lebowitz (Eds.), *Alzheimer's Disease Treatment and Family Stress: Directions for Research*, U.S. Department of Health and Human Services, Publication No. (ADM) 89-1569, pp. 340–362.

Lawton, M.P. (2001). Quality of life and the end of life. In J.E. Birren & K. W. Schaie (Eds.), *Handbook of the Psychology of Aging*, 5th ed., pp. 592–616. San Diego: Academic Press.

Lazarus, R. S. (2000). Toward better research on stress and coping. *American Psychologist* 55, pp. 665–673.

Lazarus, R.S. (1966). *Psychological Stress and the Coping Process*, New York: McGraw-Hill.

Lazarus, R.S., & Folkman, S. (1984). *Stress, Appraisal, and Coping*, New York: Springer.

Lazoritz, S. (1990). What ever happened to Mary Ellen? *Child Abuse and Neglect*, 14, pp. 143–149.

Ledoux, J.E., & Gorman, J.M. (2001). A call to action: Overcoming anxiety through active coping. *American Journal of Psychiatry*, 158, pp. 1953–1955.

Ledoux, S., Miller, P., Choquet, M., & Plant, M. (2002). Family structure, parent-child relationships, and alcohol and other drug use among teenagers in France and the United Kingdom. *Alcohol & Alcoholism*, 37, pp. 52–60.

LeDoux. J.E. (2000). Emotion circuits in the brain. *Annual Review of Neuroscience*, 23, pp. 155–184.

Leenaars, A.A. (2004). Altruistic suicide: A few reflections. *Archives of Suicide Research*, 8, pp. 1–7.

Leesfield, I.H. (1987). Negligence of mental health professionals. *Trial*, 23, pp. 57–61.

LeFever, G.B. et al., (2003). ADHD among American schoolchildren: Evidence of overdiagnosis and over-medication. *The Scientific Review of Mental Health Practice*, 2.

Leff, J. (1992). Transcultural aspects. In E.S. Paykel (Ed.), *Handbook of Affective Disorders*, 2nd ed., pp. 539–550. New York: Guilford.

Leff, J., & Vaughn, C. (1985). *Expressed Emotion in Families: Its Significance for Mental Illness*, New York: Guilford.

Leff, J., Sartorius, N., Jablensky, A., Korten, A., & Ernberg, G. (1992). The International Pilot Study of Schizophrenia: Five-year follow-up findings. *Psychological Medicine*, 22, pp. 131–145.

Leff, J.P. (1988). *Psychiatry Around the Globe: A Transcultural View*, London: Royal College of Psychiatrists.

Lefley, H.P. (1992). Expressed emotion: Conceptual, clinical, and social policy issues. *Hospital and Community Psychiatry*, 43, pp. 591–598.

Lehman, A.F., Dixon, L.B., Hoch, J.S., DeForge, B., Kernan, E., & Frank, R. (1999). Cost-effectiveness of assertive community treatment for homeless persons with severe mental illness. *British Journal of Psychiatry*, 174, pp. 346–352.

Lehman, A.F., Kreyenbuhl, J., Buchanan, R.W., Dickerson, F.B., Dixon, L.B., Goldberg, R., Green-Paden, L.D., Tenhula, W.N., Boerescu, D., Tek, D., Sandson, N., & Steinwachs, D.M. (2004). The schizophrenia patient outcomes research team (PORT): Updated treatment recommendations. *Schizophrenia Bulletin*, 30, pp. 193–217.

Lehrer, P., & Carr, R. (1997). Progressive relaxation. In W.T. Roth & I.D. Yalom (Eds.), *Treating Anxiety Disorders*, pp. 83–116. San Francisco: Jossey-Bass.

Leiblum, S. R. (1995). Relinquishing virginity: The treatment of a complex case of vaginismus. In R.C. Rosen & S.R. Leiblum (Eds.), *Case Studies in Sex Therapy*, pp. 250–263. New York, NY: Guilford.

Leiblum, S.R. (1999). What every urologist should know about female sexual dysfunction. *International Journal of Impotence Research*, 11 (suppl. 1), pp. 39–40.

Leiblum, S.R. (2001). Critical overview of the new consensus-based definitions and classification of female sexual dysfunction. *Journal of Sex and Marital Therapy*, 27, pp. 159–168.

Leland, J. (1996). The fear of heroin is shooting up. *Newsweek*, August 26, pp. 55–56.

Lencz, T., Smith, C.W., Auther, A.M., Correll, C.U., & Cornblatt, B.A. (2003). The assessment of prodromal schizophrenia: Unresolved issues and future directions. *Schizophrenia Bulletin*, 29, pp. 717–728.

Lenzenweger, M.F. (1999). Schizophrenia: Refining the phenotype, resolving endophenotypes. *Behaviour Research and Therapy*, 37, pp. 281–295.

Leon, G., Fulkerson, J.A., Perry, C.L., & Cudeck, R. (1993). Personality and behavioral vulnerabilities associated with risk status for eating disorders in adolescent girls. *Journal of Abnormal Psychology*, 102, pp. 438–444.

Leon, G.R., Fulkerson, J.A., Perry, C.L., & Early-Zald, M.B. (1995). Prospective analysis of personality and behavioral vulnerabilities and gender influences in the later development of disordered eating. *Journal of Abnormal Psychology*, 104, pp. 140–149.

Leonard, H.L., Swedo, S.E., Lenane, M.C., Rettew, D.C., Hamburger, S.D., Bartko, J.J., & Rapoport, J.L. (1993). A 2- to 7-year follow-up study of 54 obsessive-compulsive children and adolescents. *Archives of General Psychiatry*, 50, pp. 429–439.

Leonard, K.E., Eiden, R.D., Wong, M.M., Zucker, R.A., Puttler, L.I., Fitzgerald, H.E., Hussong, A., Chassin, L., & Mudar, P. (2000). Developmental perspectives on risk and vulnerability in alcoholic families. *Alcoholism: Clinical and Experimental Research*, 24, pp. 238–240.

Leonard, L.M., & Follette, V.M. (2002). Sexual functioning in women reporting a history of child sexual abuse: Review of the empirical literature and clinical implications. *Annual Review of Sex Research*, 13, pp. 346–388.

Lepine, J.P. (2002). The epidemiology of anxiety disorders: Prevalence and societal costs. *Journal of Clinical Psychiatry*, 63 (suppl 14), pp. 4–8.

Lerner, A.J. (1999). Women and Alzheimer's disease. *Journal of Clinical Endocrinology and Metabolism*, 84, pp. 1830–1834.

Leserman, J., Jackson, E.D., Petitto, J.M., Golden, R.N., Silva, S.G., Perkins, D.O., Cai, J., Folds, J.D., & Evans, D.L. (1999). Progression to AIDS: The effects of stress, depressive symptoms, and social support. *Psychosomatic Medicine*, 61, pp. 397–406.

Leshner, A.I. (1997). Addiction is a brain disease, and it matters. *Science*, 278, pp. 45–47.

Lesser, J., & O'Donohue, W. (1999). What is a delusion? Epistemological dimensions. *Journal of Abnormal Psychology*, 108, pp. 687–694.

Lester, D. (2002). The effectiveness of suicide prevention and crisis intervention services. In D. Lester (Ed.), *Crisis Intervention and Counseling by Telephone*, 2nd ed., pp. 289–298. Springfield, IL: Charles C Thomas.

Leucht, S., Pitschel-Walz, G., Engel, R.R., & Kissling, W. (2002). Amisulpride, an unusual "atypical' antipsychotic: A meta-analysis of randomized controlled trials. *American Journal of Psychiatry*, 159, pp. 180–190.

LeVay, S. (1993). *The Sexual Brain*, Cambridge, MA: MIT Press.

LeVay, S., & Valente, S.M. (2003). *Human Sexuality*. Sunderland, MA: Sinauer Associates.

Levenson, M.R. (1992). Rethinking psychopathy. *Theory and Psychology*, 2, pp. 51–71.

Levenson, R.W., Carstensen, L.L., & Gottman, J.M. (1994). The influence of age and gender on affect, physiology, and their interrelations: A study of long-term marriages. *Journal of Personality and Social Psychology*, 67, pp. 56–68.

Leventhal, A.M., & Rehm, L.P. (2005). The empirical status of melancholia: Implications for psychology. *Clinical Psychology Review*, 25, pp. 25–44.

Leventhal, H., et al. (2001). Heath risk behaviors and aging. In J.E. Birren & K.W. Schaie (Eds.), *Handbook of the Psychology of Aging*, 5th ed., pp. 186–214. San Diego: Academic Press.

Leventhal, T., & Brooks-Gunn, J. (2000). The neighborhoods they live in: The effects of neighborhood residence on child and adolescent outcomes. *Psychological Bulletin*, 126, pp. 309–337.

Levine, H.G. (1978). The discovery of addiction: Changing conceptions of habitual drunkenness in America. *Journal of Studies on Alcohol*, 39, pp. 143–174.

Levine, S.B. (1995). What is clinical sexuality? *Psychiatric Clinics of North America*, 18, pp. 1–6.

Levine, S.B., Risen, C.B., & Althof, S.E. (1990). Essay on the diagnosis and nature of paraphilia. *Journal of Sex and Marital Therapy*, 16, pp. 89–102.

Levinson, B. (1999). Erectile dysfunction and culture in South Africa. *Journal of Sex and Marital Therapy*, 25, pp. 267–270.

Levinson, D.J. (1986). A conception of adult development. *American Psychologist*, 41, pp. 3–13.

Levitan, R.D., Rector, N.A., Sheldon, T., & Goering, P. (2003). Childhood adversities associated with major depression and/or anxiety disorders in a community sample of Ontario: Issues of co-morbidity and specificity. *Depression & Anxiety*, 17, pp. 34–42.

Levitt, E.E., Moser, C., & Jamison, K.V. (1994). The prevalence and some attributes of females in the sadomasochistic subculture: A second report. *Archives of Sexual Behavior*, 23, pp. 465–474.

Levy, D.L., & Holzman, P.S. (1997). Eye tracking dysfunction and schizophrenia: An overview with special reference to the genetics of schizophrenia. *International Review of Psychiatry*, 9, pp. 365–371.

Levy, F., Hay, D.A., McStephen, M., Wood, C., & Waldman, I. (1997). Attention-deficit/hyperactivity disorder: A category or a continuum? Genetic analysis of a large-scale twin study. *Journal of the American Academy of Child and Adolescent Psychiatry, 36*, pp. 737–744.

Lewinsohn, P.M., Roberts, R.E., Seely, J.R., Rohde, P., Gotlib, I.H., & Hops, H. (1994). Adolescent psychopathology. II. Psychosocial risk factors for depression. *Journal of Abnormal Psychology, 103*, pp. 302–315.

Lewinsohn, P.M., Rohde, P., & Seeley, J.R. (1998). Major depressive disorder in older adolescents: Prevalence, risk factors, and clinical implications. *Clinical Psychology Review, 18*, pp. 765–794.

Lewis, M.H. (1996). Psychopharmacology of autism spectrum. *Journal of Autism and Developmental Disorders, 26*, pp. 231–235.

Lewis, V., Allen-Byrd, L., & Rouhbakhsh, P. (2004). Understanding successful family recovery in treating alcoholism. *Journal of Systemic Therapies, 23*, p. 39.

Ley, R. (1999). The modification of breathing behavior: Pavlovian and operant control in emotion and cognition. *Behavior Modification, 23*, pp. 441–479.

Leys, D., Pasquier, F., & Parnetti, L. (1998). Epidemiology of vascular dementia. *Haemostasis, 28*, pp. 134–150.

Li, S. (2003). Biocultural orchestration of developmental plasticity across levels: The interplay of biology and culture in shaping the mind and behavior across the life span. *Psychological Bulletin, 129*, pp. 171–194.

Lidz, C.W., Hoge, S.K., Gardner, W., Bennett, N.S., Monahan, J., Mulvey, E.P., & Roth, L.H. (1995). Perceived coercion in mental hospital admission: Pressures and process. *Archives of General Psychiatry, 52*, pp. 1034–1039.

Lidz, C.W., Mulvey, E.P., & Gardner, W. (1993). The accuracy of predictions of violence to others. *Journal of the American Medical Association 269*, pp. 1007–1011.

Lieberman, J., Chakos, M., Wu, H., Alvir, J., Hoffman, E., Robinson, D., & Bilder R. (2001). Longitudinal study of brain morphology in first episode schizophrenia. *Biological Psychiatry, 49*, pp. 487–499.

Lilienfeld, S.O. (1992). The association between antisocial personality and somatization disorders: A review and integration of theoretical models. *Clinical Psychology Review, 12*, pp. 641–662.

Lilienfeld, S.O. (1994). Conceptual problems in the assessment of psychopathy. *Clinical Psychology Review, 14*, pp. 17–38.

Lilienfeld, S.O., Lyn, S.J., Kirsch, I., Chaves, J.F., Sarbin, T.R., Ganaway, G.K., & Powell, R.A. (1999). Dissociative identity disorder and the sociocognitive model: Recalling lessons of the past. *Psychological Bulletin, 125*, pp. 507–523.

Lilienfeld, S.O., Lynn, S.J., & Lohr, J.M. (2003). *Science and Pseudoscience in Clinical Psychology.* New York: Guilford.

Lindenberger, U., & Baltes, P.B. (1997). Intellectual functioning in old and very old age: Cross-sectional results from the Berlin Aging Study. *Psychology and Aging, 12*, pp. 410–432.

Lindsay, D.S., Hagen, L., Read, J.D., Wade, K.A., & Garry, M. (2004). True photographs and false memories. *Psychological Science, 15*, pp. 149–154.

Linehan, M.M. (1993). *Cognitive-Behavioral Treatment of Borderline Personality Disorder,* New York: Guilford.

Linehan, M.M., Cochran, B.N., & Kehrer, C.A. (2001). Dialectical behavior therapy for borderline personality disorder. In D.H. Barlow (Ed.), *Clinical Handbook of Psychological Disorders: A Step By Step Treatment Manual,* 3rd ed., pp. 470–522. New York: Guilford.

Linehan, M.M., Kanter, J.W., & Comtois, K.A. (1999). Dialectical behavior therapy for borderline personality disorder: Efficacy, specificity, and cost effectiveness. In D.S. Janowsky (Ed.), *Psychotherapy Indications and Outcomes,* pp. 93–118. Washington, DC: American Psychiatric Press.

Linehan, M.M., Tutek, D.A., Heard, H.L., & Armstrong, H.E. (1994). Interpersonal outcome of cognitive-behavioral treatment for chronically suicidal borderline patients. *American Journal of Psychiatry, 151*, pp. 1771–1776.

Link, B., Cullen, F., & Andrews, H. (1990, August). Violent and illegal behavior of current and former mental patients compared to community controls. Paper presented at the meeting of the Society for the Study of Social Problems.

Link, B.G., & Phelan, J.C. (1999). The labeling theory of mental disorder (II): The consequences of labeling. In A.V. Horwitz and T.L. Scheid (Eds.), *A Handbook for the Study of Mental Health: Social Contexts Theories and Systems,* pp. 361–376. New York: Cambridge University Press.

Link, B.G., Struening, E., Rahav, M., Phelan, J.C., & Nuttbrock, L. (1997). On stigma and its consequences: Evidence from a longitudinal study of men with dual diagnoses of mental illness and substance abuse. *Journal of Health and Social Behavior, 38*, pp. 177–190.

Links, P.S., Heslegrave, R., & Villella, J. (1998). Psychopharmacological management of personality disorders: An outcome-focused model. In K.R. Silk (Ed.), *Biology of Personality Disorders,* pp. 93–127. Washington, DC: American Psychiatric Press.

Linley, P.A. & Joseph, S. (2005). The human capacity for growth through adversity. *American Psychologist, 60*, pp. 262–264.

Linney, Y.M., Murray, R.M., Peters, E.R., MacDonald, A.M., Rijskijk, F., & Sham, P. (2003). A quantitative genetic analysis of schizotypal personality traits. *Psychological Medicine, 33*, pp. 803–816.

Lipowski, Z.J. (1988). Somatization: The concept and its clinical applications. *American Journal of Psychiatry, 145*, pp. 1358–1368.

Lisanby, S.H., Maddox, J.H., Prudic, J., Devanand, D.P., & Sackheim, H.A. (2000). The effects of electroconvulsive therapy on memory of autobiographical and public events. *Archives of General Psychiatry, 57*, pp. 581–590.

Litz, B.T. (2005). Has resilience to severe trauma been underestimated? *American Psychologist, 60*, p. 262.

Litz, B.T. (Ed.) (2004). *Early Intervention for Trauma and Traumatic Loss.* New York: Guilford.

Livesley, W.J. (1995). Commentary on dependent personality disorder. In W.J. Livesley (Ed.), *The DSM-IV Personality Disorders,* pp. 257–260. New York: Guilford.

Lochman, J.E., & Wells, K.C. (2004). The coping power program for preadolescent aggressive boys and their parents: Outcome effects at the 1-year follow-up. *Journal of Consulting and Clinical Psychology, 72*(4), pp. 571–578.

Loeb, T.B., Williams, J.K., Carmona, J.V., Rivkin, I., Wyatt, G.E., Chin, D., & Asuan-O'Brien, A. (2002). Child sexual abuse: Associations with the sexual functioning of adolescents and adults. *Annual Review of Sex Research, 13*, pp. 307–345.

Loeber, R. (1988). Natural histories of conduct problems, delinquency, and associated substance use: Evidence for developmental progression. In B.B. Lahey & A.E. Kazdin (Eds.), *Advances in Clinical Child Psychology,* vol. 11, pp. 73–118. New York: Plenum.

Loeber, R., Lahey, B.B., & Thomas, C. (1991). Diagnostic conundrum of oppositional defiant disorder and conduct disorder. *Journal of Abnormal Psychology, 100*, pp. 379–390.

Loftus, E., & Ketcham, K. (1994). *The Myth of Repressed Memory,* New York: St. Martin's Press.

Loftus, E.F. (1993). The reality of repressed memories. *American Psychologist, 48*, pp. 518–537.

Loftus, E.F. (2003). Make-believe memories. *American Psychologist, 58*, pp. 867–871.

Loftus, E.F. (2004). Memories of things unseen. *Current Directions in Psychological Science, 13*, pp. 145–147.

Loftus, E.F., & Klinger, M.R. (1992). Is the unconscious smart or dumb? *American Psychologist, 47*, pp. pp. 761–765.

Lohr, J.M., Kleinknecht, R.A., Conley, A.T., Dal Cerro, S., Schmidt, J., & Sonntag, M.E. (1992). A methodological critique of the current status of eye movement desensitization (EMD). *Behavior Therapy and Experimental Psychiatry, 23*, pp. 159–167.

Lombardo, P.A. (2001). Carrie Buck's pedigree. *Journal of Laboratories in Clinical Medicine. 138*, pp. 278–282.

Longino, C.F., & Mittelmark, M.B. (1996). In J. Sadavoy, L.W. Lazarus, L.F. Jarvik, & G.T. Grossberg (Eds.), *Comprehensive Review of Geriatric Psychiatry—II*, pp. 135–152. Washington, DC: American Psychiatric Press.

Lonner, W.J., & Malpass, R.S. (1994). When psychology and culture meet: An introduction to cross-cultural psychology. In W.J. Lonner & R.S. Malpass (Eds.), *Psychology and Culture,* pp. 1–12. Boston: Allyn & Bacon.

Looper, K.J, Kirmayer, L.J. (2001). Hypochondriacal concerns in a community population. *Psychological Medicine 31*, pp. 577–584.

Looper, K.J, & Kirmayer, L.J. (2002). Behavioral medicine approaches to somatoform disorders. *Journal of Consulting and Clinical Psychology, 70*, pp. 810–827.

Lopez, A.D., & Murray, C.J.L. (1998). The global burden of disease, 1990–2020. *Nature Medicine, 4*, pp. 1241–1243.

Lopez, S.R., & Guarnaccia, P.J. (2000). Cultural psychopathology: Uncovering the social world of mental illness. *Annual Review of Psychology, 51*, pp. 571–598.

Lopez, S.R., Nelson, K., Snyder, K., & Mintz, J. (1999). Attributions and affective reactions of family members and course of schizophrenia. *Journal of Abnormal Psychology, 108*, pp. 307–314.

Lord, C., & Bailey, A. (2002). Autism spectrum disorders. In M. Rutter & E. Taylor (Eds.), *Child and Adolescent Psychiatry,* 4th ed., pp. 636–663. Oxford: Blackwell.

Lotter, V. (1966). Epidemiology of autistic conditions in young children. *Social Psychiatry, 1*, pp. 124–137.

Lovaas, O.I. (1987). Behavioral treatment and normal educational and intellectual functioning in young autistic children. *Journal of Consulting and Clinical Psychology, 55*, pp. 3–9.

Lovaas, O.I., Schreibman, L., Koegel, R.L., & Rehm, R. (1971). Selective responding by autistic children to multiple sensory input. *Journal of Abnormal Psychology, 77*, pp. 211–222.

Lovinger, D.M. (1997). Serotonin's role in alcohol's effects on the brain. *Alcohol Health and Research World, 21*, pp. 114–120.

Low, P.W., Jeffries, J.C., & Bonnie, R.J. (1986). *The Trial of John W. Hinckley, Jr.: A Case Study in the Insanity Defense,* Mineola, NY: Foundation Press.

Lubs, H.A. (1969). A marker X chromosome. *American Journal of Human Genetics, 21*, pp. 231–244.

Lucas, A.R., Crowson, C.S., O'Fallon, W.M., & Melton, L.J. (1999). The ups and downs of anorexia nervosa. *International Journal of Eating Disorders, 26*, pp. 397–405.

Luszcz, M.A., & Bryan, J. (1999). Toward understanding age-related memory loss in late adulthood. *Gerontology, 45*, pp. 2–9.

Lyketsos, C.G., Garrett, E., Liang, K., & Anthony, J.C. (1999). Cannabis use and cognitive decline in persons under 65 years of age. *American Journal of Epidemiology, 149*, pp. 794–781.

Lykken, D.T. (1957). A study of anxiety in the sociopathic personality. *Journal of Abnormal and Social Psychology, 55*, pp. 6–10.

Lynam, D.R. et al. (2000). The interaction between impulsivity and neighborhood context on offending: The effects of impulsivity are stronger in poor neighborhoods. *Journal of Abnormal Psychology, 109*, pp. 563–574.

Lynam, D.R., & Widiger, T.A. (2001). Using the five-factor model to represent the DSM-IV personality disorders: An expert consensus approach. *Journal of Abnormal Psychology, 110,* pp. 401–412.

Lynn, S.J., & McConkey, K.M. (1998). *Truth in Memory,* New York: Guilford.

Lyon, G.R. (1996). Learning disabilities. *Future of Children,* 6, pp. 54–76.

Lyons, M.J. (1995). Epidemiology of personality disorders. In M.T.Tsuang, M.Tohen, & G.E.P. Zahner (Eds.), *Textbook in Psychiatric Epidemiology,* pp. 407–436. New York: Wiley.

Maccoby, E.E., & Martin, J.A. (1983). Socialization in the context of the family: Parent-child interaction. In E.M. Hetherington (Ed.), *Socialization, Personality, and Social Development,* Vol. 4, *Handbook of Child Psychology,* pp. 1–101. New York: Wiley.

Maccoby, E.E., & Mnookin, R.H. (1992). *Dividing the Child: Social and Legal Dilemmas of Custody,* Cambridge, MA: Harvard University Press.

MacCoun, R.J., Reuter, P., & Wolf, C. (2001). *Drug War Heresies: Learning from Other Vices, Times, and Places (RAND Studies in Policy Analysis).* New York: Cambridge University Press.

MacDonald, G., & Leary, M.R. (2005). Why does social exclusion hurt? The relationship between social and physical pain. *Psychological Bulletin, 131,* pp. 202–223.

Mack, A.H., Forman, L., Brown, R., & Frances, A. (1994). A brief history of psychiatric classification: From the ancients to DSM-IV. *Psychiatric Clinics of North America, 17,* pp. 515–523.

Mackay, R.D. (1988). Post-Hinckley insanity in the U.S.A. *Criminal Law Review,* pp. 88–96.

MacLeod, C., Rutherford, E., Campbell, L., Ebsworthy, G., & Holker, L. (2002). Selective attention and emotional vulnerability: Assessing the causal basis of their association through the experimental manipulation of attentional bias. *Journal of Abnormal Psychology, 111,* pp. 107–123.

MacMillan, D.L., Gresham, F.M., & Siperstein, G.N. (1995). Heightened concerns over the 1992 AAMR definition: Advocacy versus precision. *American Journal on Mental Retardation, 100,* pp. 87–97.

Magai. C. (2001). Emotions over the life span. In J.E. Birren & K.W. Schaie (Eds.), *Handbook of the Psychology of Aging,* 5th ed., pp. 399–426. San Diego: Academic Press.

Magenis, R.E., Overton, K.M., Chamberlin, J., Brady, T., & Lovrien, E. (1977). Parental origin of the extra chromosome in Down's syndrome. *Human Genetics, 37,* pp. 7–16.

Mahe, V., & Balogh, A. (2000). Long-term pharmacological treatment of generalized anxiety disorder. *International Clinical Psychopharmacology, 15,* pp. 99–105.

Maher, B.A. (2001). Delusions. In P.B. Sutker and H.E. Adams (Eds.), *Comprehensive Handbook of Psychopathology,* 3rd ed., pp. 309–339. New York: Kluwer Academic/ Plenum.

Maier, S. & Watkins, L.R. (1998). Cytokines for psychologists: Implications of bidirectional immune-to-brain communication for understanding behavior, mood, and cognition. *Psychological Review, 105,* pp. 83–107.

Maier, S.F., Watkins, L.R., & Fleshner, M. (1994). Psychoneuroimmunology: The interface between behavior, brain, and immunity. *American Psychologist, 49,* pp. 1004–1017.

Malcolm, J.G. (1987). Treatment choices and informed consent in psychiatry: Implications of the Osheroff case for the profession. *Journal of Psychiatry and the Law, 15,* pp. 9–81.

Malcolm, R. (2003). Pharmacologic treatments manage alcohol withdrawal, relapse prevention. *Psychiatric Annals, 33,* pp. 593–601.

Maldonado, J.R., Butler, L.D., & Spiegel, D. (2001). Treatments for dissociative disorders. In P.E. Nathan & J.M. Gorman (Eds.), *A Guide to Treatments That Work,* pp. 463–469. London: Oxford University Press.

Maletzky, B.M. (2002). The paraphilias: Research and treatment. In P.E. Nathan and J.M. Gorman (Eds.), *A Guide to Treatments That Work,* 2nd ed., pp. 525–557. London: Oxford University Press.

Manassis, K. (1996). *Keys to Parenting Your Anxious Child.* New York: Barron's.

Manicavasagar, V., Silove, D., & Hadzi-Pavolvic, D. (1998). Subpopulations of early separation anxiety: Relevance to risk of adult anxiety disorders. *Journal of Affective Disorders,* 48, pp. 181–190.

Manley, G., & Koehler, J. (2001). Sexual behavior disorders: Proposed new classification in the DSM-V. *Sexual Addiction & Compulsivity,* 8, pp. 253–265.

Mann, K. (2004). Pharmacotherapy of alcohol dependence: A review of the clinical data. *CNS Drugs,* 18, pp. 485–504.

Mann, K., Lehert, P., & Morgan, M.Y. (2004). The efficacy of acamprosate in the maintenance of abstinence in alcohol-dependent individuals: Results of a meta-analysis. *Alcoholism: Clinical & Experimental Research,* 28, pp. 51–63.

Mannuzza, S. et al. (1998). Adult psychiatric status of hyperactive boys grown up. *American Journal of Psychiatry,* 155, pp. 493–498.

Mannuzza, S., Schneier, F.R., Chapman, T.F., Liebowitz, M.R., Klein, D.F., & Fyer, A.J. (1995). Generalized social phobia: Reliability and validity. *Archives of General Psychiatry,* 52, pp. 230–237.

Manson, S.M., & Kleinman, A. (1998). DSM-IV, culture and mood disorders: A critical reflection on recent progress. *Transcultural Psychiatry,* 35, pp. 377–386.

March, J.S. et al., (2004). Obsessive–compulsive disorder. In T.L. Morris & J.S. March (Eds.), *Anxiety Disorders in Children and Adolescents,* 2nd ed., pp. 212–240. New York: Guilford.

March, J.S., Leonard, H.L., & Swedo, S.E. (1995). Obsessive-compulsive disorder. In J.S. March (Ed.), *Anxiety Disorders in Children and Adolescents,* pp. 251–275. New York: Guilford.

Marcia, J.E. (1966). Development and validation of ego-identity status. *Journal of Personality and Social Psychology, 24,* pp. 551–558.

Marcia, J.E. (1994). The empirical study of ego identity. In H.A. Bosma, T.L.G. Graafsma, H.D. Grotevant, & D.J. de Levita (Eds.), *Identity and Development,* pp. 67–80. Thousand Oaks, CA: Sage.

Marder, K.,Tang, M., Cote, L., & Stern,Y. (1995). The frequency and associated risk factors for dementia in patients with Parkinson's disease. *Archives of Neurology,* 52, pp. 695–701.

Marder, S.R., Ames, D., Wirshing, W.C., & Van Putten, T. (1993). Schizophrenia. *Psychiatric Clinics of North America,* 16, pp. 567–587.

Margolin, G., Christensen, A., & John, R.S. (1996). The continuance and spillover of everyday tensions in distressed and nondistressed families. *Journal of Family Psychology,* 10, pp. 304–321.

Margraf, J., Taylor, C.B., Ehlers, A., Roth, W.T., & Agras, W.S. (1987). Panic attacks in the natural environment. *Journal of Nervous and Mental Disease,* 175, pp. 558–565.

Markman, H.J., Floyd, F.J., Stanley, S.M., & Storaasli, R.D. (1988). Prevention of marital distress: A longitudinal investigation. *Journal of Consulting and Clinical Psychology,* 56, pp. 210–217.

Markman, H.J., Leber, B.D., Cordova, A.D., & St. Peters, M. (1995). Behavioral observation and family psychology: Strange bedfellows or happy marriage? *Journal of Family Psychology,* 9, pp. 371–379.

Markman, H.J., Renick, M.J., Floyd, F.J., Stanley, S.M., & Clements, M. (1993). Preventing marital distress throught communication and conflict management training: A 4- and 5-year follow-up. *Journal of Consulting and Clinical Psychology,* 61, pp. 70–77.

Marks, I. (1997). Behaviour therapy for obsessive-compulsive disorder: A decade of progress. *Canadian Journal of Psychiatry,* 42, pp. 1021–1027.

Marks, I.M., & Nesse, R.M. (1994). Fear and fitness: An evolutionary analysis of anxiety disorders. *Ethology and Sociobiology,* 15, pp. 247–261.

Marks, I.M., Swinson, R.P., Basoglu, M., Kuch, K., Noshirvani, H., O'Sullivan, G., Lelliott, P.T., Kirby, M., McNamee, G., Sengun, S., & Wickwire, K. (1993). Alprazolam and exposure alone and combined in panic disorder with agoraphobia: A controlled study in London and Toronto. *British Journal of Psychiatry,* 162, pp. 776–787.

Marks, P.A., Seeman, W., & Haller, D.L. (1974). *The actuarial Use of the MMPI with Adolescents and Adults,* New York: Oxford University Press.

Marlatt, G.A. (1985). Relapse prevention: Theoretical rationale and overview of the model. In G.A. Marlatt & J.R. Gordon (Eds.), *Relapse Prevention,* New York: Guilford.

Marlatt, G.A., Baer, J.S., Donovan, D.M., & Kivlahan, D.R. (1988). Addictive behaviors: Etiology and treatment. *Annual Review of Psychology,* 39, pp. 223–252.

Marlatt, G.A., Blume, A.W., & Parks, G.A. (2001). Integrating harm reduction therapy and traditional substance abuse treatment. *Journal of Psychoactive Drugs,* 33, pp. 13–21.

Marques, J.K. (1999). How to answer the question "Does sexual offender treatment work?" *Journal of Interpersonal Violence,* 14, pp. 437–451.

Marques, J.K., Day, D.M., Nelson, C., & West, M.A. (1993). Findings and recommendations from California's experimental treatment program. In G.C.N. Hall, R. Hirschman, J.R. Graham, & M.S. Zaragoza (Eds.), *Sexual Aggression: Issues in Etiology, Assessment, and Treatment,* pp. 197–214. Washington, DC: Hemisphere.

Marshall, W.L. (1989). Intimacy, loneliness, and sexual offenders. *Behaviour Research and Therapy,* 27, pp. 491–503.

Marshall, W.L., Bryce, P., Hudson, S.M., Ward, T., & Moth, B. (1996). The enhancement of intimacy and the reduction of loneliness among child molesters. *Journal of Family Violence,* 11, pp. 219–236.

Marshall, W.L., Eccles, A., & Barbaree, H.E. (1991). The treatment of exhibitionists: A focus on sexual deviance versus cognitive and relationship features. *Behaviour Research and Therapy,* 29, pp. 129–135.

Martin, G. (1998). Media influence to suicide: The search for solutions. *Archives of Suicide Research,* 4, pp. 51–66.

Martin, R.L., Roberts, W.V., & Clayton, P.J. (1980). Psychiatric status after hysterectomy: A one-year prospective follow-up. *Journal of the American Medical Association,* 244, pp. 350–353.

Marwit, S.J. (1996). Reliability of diagnosing complicated grief: A preliminary investigation. *Journal of Consulting and Clinical Psychology,* 64, pp. 563–568.

Masand, P.S., & Gupta, S. (1999). Selective serotonin-reuptake inhibitors: An update. *Harvard Review of Psychiatry,* 7, pp. 69–84.

Mash, E.J., & Johnston, C. (1982). A comparison of the mother-child interactions of younger and older hyperactive and normal children. *Child Development,* 53, pp. 1371–1381.

Mash, E.J., & Wolfe, D.A. (2005). *Abnormal Child Psychology,* 3rd ed. Belmont, CA: Thomson Wadsworth.

Maslow, A.H. (1954). *Motivation and Personality.* New York: Harper & Row.

Maslow, A.H. (1970). *Motivation and Personality,* 2nd ed. New York: Harper & Row.

Mason, J.W. (1975). A historical view of the "stress" field. II. *Journal of Human Stress,* 1, pp. 12–16.

Masten, A.S. (2001). Ordinary magic: Resilience processes in development. *American Psychologist,* 56, pp. 227–238.

Masters, W.H., & Johnson, V.E. (1966). *Human Sexual Response.* Boston: Little, Brown and company.

Masters, W.H., & Johnson, V.E. (1970). *Human Sexual Inadequacy.* Boston: Little, Brown and Company.

Mate-Kole, C., Freschi, M., & Robin, A. (1988). Aspects of psychiatric symptoms at different stages in the treatment of transsexualism. *British Journal of Psychiatry*, 152, pp. 550–553.

Mathews, A. (1990). Why worry: The cognitive function of anxiety. *Behaviour Research and Therapy*, 28, pp. 455–468.

Mathews, A., & Mackintosh, B. (2000). Induced emotional interpretation bias and anxiety. *Journal of Abnormal Psychology*, 109, pp. 602–615.

Mathis, J. (2001). Community integration of individuals with disabilities: An update on Olmstead implementation. *Journal of Poverty Law and Policy*, 23, pp. 395–410.

Matson, J.L., & Frame, C.L. (1986). *Psychopathology Among Mentally Retarded Children and Adolescents*. Beverly Hills, CA: Sage.

Mattia, J.I., & Zimmerman, M. (2001). Epidemiology. In W.J. Livesley (Ed.), *Handbook of Personality Disorders: Theory, Research, and Treatment*, pp. 107–123. New York: Guilford.

Mavissakalian, M.R., & Ryan, M.T. (1998). Rational treatment of panic disorder with antidepressants. *Annals of Clinical Psychiatry*, 10, pp. 185–195.

Mayes, S.D., Calhoun, S.L., & Crites, D.L. (2001). Does DSM-IV Asperger's Disorder Exist? *Journal of Abnormal Child Psychology*, 29, pp. 263–271.

Mayeux, R., & Ottman, R. (1998). Alzheimer's disease genetics: Home runs and strikeouts. *Annals of Neurology*, 44, pp. 716–719.

Mayeux, R., & Sano, M. (1999). Treatment of Alzheimer's disease. *New England Journal of Medicine*, 341, pp. 1670–1679.

Mazure, C.M., Bruce, M.L., Maciejewski, P.K., & Jacobs, S.C. (2000). Adverse life events and cognitive-personality characteristics in the prediction of major depression and antidepressant response. *American Journal of Psychiatry*, 157, pp. 896–903.

McAllister-Williams, R.H. (2002). Mood disorders. In E. Perry and H. Ashton (Eds), *Neurochemistry of Consciousness: Neurotransmitters in the Mind*, pp. 293–307. Amsterdam, Netherlands: Benjamins Publishing.

McAnulty, R.D., & Adams, H.E. (1992). Validity and ethics of penile circumference measures of sexual arousal: A reply to McConaghy. *Archives of Sexual Behavior*, 21, pp. 177–195.

McBride, W.J., Murphy, J.M., Yoshimoto, K., Lumeng, L., & Li, T.K. (1993). Serotonin mechanisms in alcohol-drinking behavior. *Drug Development Research*, 30, pp. 170–177.

McCabe, M.P. (2001). Evaluation of a cognitive behavior therapy program for people with sexual dysfunction. *Journal of Sex and Marital Therapy*, 27, pp. 259–271.

McCabe, M.P., & Wauchope, M. (2005). Behavioral characteristics of men accused of rape: Evidence for different types of rapists. *Archives of Sexual Behavior*, 34, pp. 241–253.

McCabe, P.M. et al. (2002). Social environment influences the progression of atherosclerosis in the Watanabe heritable hyperlipidemic rabbit. *Circulation*, 105, pp. 354–359.

McCann, U.D., Rossiter, E.M., King, R.J., & Agras, W.S. (1991). Nonpurging bulimia: A distinct subtype of bulimia nervosa. *International Journal of Eating Disorders*, 10, pp. 679–687.

McCarroll, J.E., Ursano, R.J., Fullerton, C.S., Liu, X., & Lundy, A. (2002). Somatic symptoms in Gulf War mortuary workers. *Psychosomatic Medicine*, 64, pp. 29–33.

McCarthy, B.W. (1989). Cognitive-behavioral strategies and techniques in the treatment of early ejaculation. In S.R. Leiblum & R.C. Rosen (Eds.), *Principles and Practice of Sex Therapy*, 2nd ed. New York: Guilford.

McCarthy, B.W. (1998). Integrating Viagra into cognitive-behavioral couples sex therapy. *Journal of Sex Education and Therapy*, 23, pp. 302–308.

McCarthy, B.W. (1998). Sex therapy workshops: The Indian experience. *Journal of Sex Education and Therapy*, 23, pp. 309–311.

McCarthy, B.W. (2004). An integrative cognitive-behavioral approach to understanding, assessing, and treating female sexual dysfunction. *Journal of Family Psychotherapy*, 15, pp. 19–35.

McConaghy, N. (1999b). Methodological issues concerning evaluation of treatment for sexual offenders: Randomization, treatment dropouts, untreated controls, and within-treatment studies. *Sexual Abuse: Journal of Research and Treatment*, 11, pp. 183–193.

McConaghy, N. (2005). Sexual dysfunctions and disorders. In J.E. Maddux and B.A. Winstead (Eds.), *Psychopathology: Foundations for a Contemporary Understanding*, pp. 255–280. Mahwah, N.J.: Erlbaum.

McCullough, J.P., Jr., Klein, D.N., Borian, F.E., Howland, R.H., Riso, L.P., Keller, M.B., & Banks, P.L.C. (2003). Group comparisons of DSM-IV subtypes of chronic depression: Validity of the distinctions, Part 2. *Journal of Abnormal Psychology*, 112, pp. 614–622.

McDougle, C.J., Price, L.H., & Volkmar, F.R. (1994). Recent advances in the pharmacotherapy of autism and related conditions. *Child and Adolescent Psychiatric Clinics of North America*, 3, pp. 71–89.

McElroy, S.L. (1999). Recognition and treatment of intermittent explosive disorder and explosivity. *Journal of Clinical Psychiatry Monograph Series*, 17, pp. 8–11.

McFall, R.M. (2001). New manifesto.

McFall, R.M., & McDonel, E.C. (1986). The continuing search for units of analysis in psychology: Beyond persons, situations, and their interactions. In R.O. Nelson & S.C. Hayes (Eds.), *Conceptual Foundations of Behavioral Assessment*, pp. 201–241. New York: Guilford.

McFarlane, W.R., Dixon, L., Lukens, E., & Lucksted, A. (2003). Family psychoeducation and schizophrenia: A review of the literature. *Journal of Marital and Family Therapy*, 29, pp. 223–245.

McGeer, P.L., & McGeer, E.G. (1996). Anti-inflammatory drugs in the fight against Alzheimer's disease. *Annals of the New York Academy of Sciences*, 777, pp. 213–220.

McGlashan, T.H. (1998). The profiles of clinical deterioration in schizophrenia. *Journal of Psychiatric Research*, 32, pp. 133–141.

McGlashan, T.H., & Fenton, W.S. (1991). Classical subtypes for schizophrenia: Literature review for DSM-IV. *Schizophrenia Bulletin*, 17, pp. 609–623.

McGrath, J.J., & Welham, J.L. (1999). Season of birth and schizophrenia: A systematic review and meta-analysis of data from the Southern Hemisphere. *Schizophrenia Research*, 35, pp. 237–242.

McGue, M. (1993). From proteins to cognitions: The behavioral genetics of alcoholism. In R. Plomin & G.E. McClearn (Eds.), *Nature, Nurture, and Psychology*. Washington, DC: American Psychological Association.

McGue, M. (1999). The behavioral genetics of alcoholism. *Current Directions in Psychological Science*, 8, pp. 109–115.

McGue, M., & Lykken, D.T. (1992). Genetic influence on risk of divorce. *Psychological Science*, 3, pp. 368–373.

McGuffin, P., & Thapar, A. (1998). Genetics and antisocial personality disorder. In T. Millon and E. Simonsen (Eds.), *Psychopathy: Antisocial, Criminal, and Violent Behavior*, pp. 215–230. New York: Guilford.

McGuffin, P., Katz, R., Watkins, S., & Rutherford, J. (1996). A hospital-based twin register of the heritability of DSM-IV unipolar depression. *Archives of General Psychiatry*, 53, pp. 129–136.

McGuffin, P., Rijsdijk, F., Andrew, M., Sham, P., Katz, R., & Cardno, A. (2003). The heritability of bipolar affective disorder and the genetic relationship to unipolar depression. *Archives of General Psychiatry*, 60, pp. 497–502.

McGuire, M.T., & Troisi, A. (1998a). *Darwinian Psichiatry*. New York: Oxford University Press.

McGuire, M.T., & Troisi, A. (1998b). Prevalence differences in depression among males and females: Are there evolutionary explanations? *British Journal of Medical Psychology*, 71, pp. 479–491.

McKeith, I.G. (2002). Dementia with Lewy bodies. *British Journal of Psychiatry*, 180, pp. 144–147.

McKenna, M.C., Zevon, M.A., Corn, B., & Rounds, J. (1999). Psychosocial factors and the development of breast cancer: A meta-analysis. *Health Psychology*, 18, pp. 520–531.

McKey, R.H., Condelli, L., Granson, H., Barrett, B., McConkey, C., & Plantz, M. (1985, June). *The Impact of Head Start on Children, Families, and Communities*. Final Report of the Head Start Evaluation, Synthesis and Utilization Project. Washington, DC: CSR.

McKim, W. (2000). *Drugs and Behavior: An Introduction to Behavioral Pharmacology*, 4th ed. Upper Saddle River, NJ: Prentice Hall.

McLemore, C.W., & Benjamin, L.A. (1979). Whatever happened to interpersonal diagnosis? A psychosocial alternative to DSM-III. *American Psychologist*, 34, pp. 17–34.

McMahon, F.J., Simpson, S.G., McInnis, M.G., Badner, J.A., MacKinnon, D.F., & DePaulo, J.R. (2001). Linkage of bipolar disorder to chromosome 18q and the validity of bipolar II disorder. *Archives of General Psychiatry*, 58, pp. 1025–1031.

McMahon, R.P., Kelly, D.L., Kreyenbuhl, J., Kirkpatrick, B., Love, R.C., & Conley, R.R. (2002). Novel factor-based symptom scores in treatment resistant schizophrenia: Implications for clinical trials. *Neuropsychopharmacology*, 26, pp. 537–545.

McNally, R.J. (1994). Cognitive bias in panic disorder. *Current Directions in Psychological Science*, 3, pp. 129–132.

McNally, R.J. (1998). Information-processing abnormalities in anxiety disorders: Implications for cognitive neuroscience. *Cognition and Emotion*, 12, pp. 479–495.

McNally, R.J. (2003). Recovering memories of trauma: A view from the laboratory. *Current Directions in Psychological Science*, 12, pp. 32–35.

McNally, R.J., Bryant, R.A., & Ehlers, A. (2003). Does early psychological intervention promote recovery from posttraumatic stress? *Psychological Science in the Public Interest*, 4, pp. 45–79.

McNeil, T.F., & Cantor-Graae, E. (1999). Does preexisting abnormality cause labor-delivery complications in fetuses who will develop schizophrenia? *Schizophrenia Bulletin*, 25, pp. 425–435.

Meana, M., & Binik, Y.M. (1994). Painful coitus: A review of female dyspareunia. *Journal of Nervous and Mental Disease*, 182, pp. 264–272.

Meaney, M.J. (2001). Nature, nurture, and the disunity of knowledge. *Annals of the New York Academy of Sciences*, 935, pp. 50–61.

Medine, J. (1999). *What You Need to Know About Alzheimer's*. Oakland, CA: New Harbinger.

Mednick, S.A., & Schulsinger, F. (1968). Some premorbid characteristics related to breakdown in children with schizophrenic mothers. *Journal of Psychiatric Research* (suppl. 1), pp. 6, 354–362.

Meehl, P.E. (1962). Schizotaxia, schizotypy, schizophrenia. *American Psychologist*, 17, pp. 827–838.

Meehl, P.E. (1990). Toward an integrated theory of schizotaxia, schizotypy, and schizophrenia. *Journal of Personality Disorders*, 4, pp. 1–99.

Meehl, P.E. (1993). The origins of some of my conjectures concerning schizophrenia. In L.J. Chapman, J.P. Chapman, & D. Fowles (Eds.), *Progress in Experimental Personality and Psychopathology Research*, pp. 1–11. New York: Springer.

Meehl, P.E., & Rosen, A. (1955). Antecedent probability and the efficiency of psychometric signs, patterns, or cutting scores. *Psychological Bulletin*, 52, pp. 194–216.

Mejeur, J. (1999). There's more to TEA-21 than .08. *State Legislatures*, 25, p. 33.

Melman, A., & Tiefer, L. (1992). Surgery for erectile disorders: Operative procedures and psychological issues. In R.C. Rosen & S.R. Leiblum (Eds.), *Erectile Disorders: Assessment and Treatment*, pp. 255–282. New York: Guilford.

Melton, G.B., & Limber, S. (1989). Psychologists' involvement in cases of child maltreatment: Limits of roles and expertise. *American Psychologist*, 44, pp. 1225–1233.

Melton, G.B., Petrila, J., Poythress, N.G., & Slobogin, C. (1997). *Psychological Evaluations for the Courts*, 2nd ed. New York: Guilford.

Mendlewicz, J., Souery, D., & Rivelli, S.K. (1999). Short-term and long-term treatment for bipolar patients: Beyond the guidelines. *Journal of Affective Disorders*, 55, pp. 79–85.

Merckelbach, H., Muris, P., & Schouten, E. (1996). Pathways to fear in spider phobic children. *Behaviour Research and Therapy*, 34, pp. 935–938.

Merikangas, K.R., Avenevoli, S., Acharyya, S., Zhang, H., & Angst, J. (2002). The spectrum of social phobia in the Zurich cohort study of young adults. *Biological Psychiatry*, 51, pp. 81–91.

Merikangas, K.R., Stolar, M., Stevens, D.E., Goulet, J., Preisig, M.A., Fenton, B., Zhang, H., O'Malley, S.S., & Rounsaville, B.J. (1998b). Familial transmission of substance use disorders. *Archives of General Psychiatry*, 55, pp. 973–979.

Merkin, D. (1996). Unlikely obsession: confronting a taboo. *The New Yorker*, February 26 and March 4, pp. 98–115.

Mersky, H. (1992). The manufacture of personalities: The production of multiple personality disorder. *British Journal of Psychiatry*, 160, pp. 327–340.

Mervielde, I., DeClercq, B., DeFruyt, F., & Van Leeuwen, K. (2005). Temperament, personality, and developmental psychopathology as childhood antecedents of personality disorders. *Journal of Personality Disorders*, 19, pp. 171–201.

Meston, C.M., Trapnell, P.D., & Gorzalka, B.B. (1996). Ethnic and gender differences in sexuality: Variations in sexual behavior between Asian and non-Asian university students. *Archives of Sexual Behavior*, 25, pp. 33–72.

Metalsky, G.I., Joiner, T.E., Hardin, T.S., & Abramson, L.Y. (1993). Depressive reactions to failure in a naturalistic setting: A test of the hopelessness and self-esteem theories of depression. *Journal of Abnormal Psychology*, 102, pp. 101–109.

Metz, M.E., & Epstein, N. (2002). Assessing the role of relationship conflict in sexual dysfunction. *Journal of Sex and Marital Therapy*, 28, pp. 139–164.

Metz, M.E., & Pryor, J.L. (2000). Premature ejaculation: A psychophysiological approach for assessment and management. *Journal of Sex and Marital Therapy*, 26, pp. 293–320.

Metzl, J.M. (2004). Voyeur nation? Changing definitions of voyeurism, 1950–2004. *Harvard Review of Psychiatry*, 12, pp. 127–131.

Meuret, A.E., Ritz, T., Wilhelm, F.H., & Roth, W.T. (2005). Voluntary hyperventilation in the treatment of panic disorder. *Clinical Psychology Review*, 25, pp. 285–306.

Meyer, G.J., & Archer, R.P. (2001). The hard science of Rorschach research: What do we know and where do we go? *Psychological Assessment*, 13, pp. 486–502.

Meyer, I.H. (2003). Prejudice, social stress, and mental health in lesbian, gay, and bisexual populations: Conceptual issues and research evidence. *Psychological Bulletin*, 129, pp. 674–697.

Meyers, B.S. (1998). Depression and dementia: Comorbidities, identification, and treatment. *Journal of Geriatric Psychiatry and Neurology*, 11, pp. 201–205.

Mezzich, J.E., Berganza, C.E., & Ruiperez, M.A. (2001). Culture in DSM-IV, ICD-10, and evolving diagnostic systems. *Psychiatric Clinics of North America*, 24, pp. 407–419.

Michelini, S., Cassano, G.B., Frare, F., & Perugi, G. (1996). Long-term use of benzodiazepines: Tolerance, dependence and clinical problems in anxiety and mood disorders. *Pharmacopsychiatry*, 29, pp. 127–134.

Mickelson, K.D., Kessler, R.C., & Shaver, P.R. (1997). Adult attachment in a nationally representative sample. *Journal of Personality and Social Psychology*, 73, pp. 1092–1106.

Migliorelli, R., Teson, A., Sabe, L., Petracchi, M., Leiguarda, R., & Starkstein, S.E. (1995). Prevalence and correlates of dysthymia and major depression among patients with Alzheimer's disease. *American Journal of Psychiatry*, 152, pp. 37–45.

Miklowitz, D.J. (1995). The evolution of family-based psychopathology. In R.H. Mikesell, D. Losterman, & S.H. McDaniel (Eds.), *Integrating Family Therapy: Handbook of Family Psychology and Systems Theory*, pp. 183–197. Washington, DC: American Psychological Association.

Miklowitz, D.J. (2002). *The Bipolar Disorder Survival Guide: What You and Your Family Need to Know*. New York: Guilford.

Miklowitz, D.J., Goldstein, M.J., & Nuechterlein, K.H. (1995). Verbal interactions in the families of schizophrenic and bipolar affective patients. *Journal of Abnormal Psychology*, 104, pp. 268–276.

Milich, R., Balentine, A.C., & Lynam, D.R. (2001). ADHD combined type and ADHD predominantly inattentive type are distinct and unrelated disorders. *Clinical Psychology: Science and Practice*, 8, pp. 463–488.

Milich, R., Wolraich, M., & Lindgren, S. (1986). Sugar and hyperactivity: A critical review of empirical findings. *Clinical Psychology Review*, 6, pp. 493–513.

Miller, C.J., Sanchez, J., & Hynd, G.W. (2003). Neurological correlates of reading disabilities. In H.L. Swanson, K.R. Harris, & S. Graham (Eds.), *Handbook of Learning Disabilities*, pp. 242–255. New York: Guilford.

Miller, G.A., & Keller, J. (2000). Psychology and neuroscience: Making peace. *Current Directions in Psychological Science*, 9, pp. 212–215.

Miller, M.W., Kaloupek, D.G., Dillon, A.L., & Keane, T.M. (2004). Externalizing and internalizing subtypes of combat-related PTSD: A replication and extension using the PSY-5 scales. *Journal of Abnormal Psychology*, 113, pp. 636–645.

Miller, T.Q., Smith, T.W., Turner, C.W., Guijarro, M.L., & Hallet, A.J. (1996). A meta-analytic review of research on hostility and physical health. *Psychological Bulletin*, 119, pp. 322–348.

Miller, T.Q., Turner, C.W., Tindale, R.S., Posavac, E.J., & Dugoni, B.L. (1991). Reasons for the trend toward null findings in research on Type A behavior. *Psychological Bulletin*, 110, pp. 469–485.

Miller, T.W. (1989). *Stressful Life Events*. Madison, CT: International Universities Press.

Miller, W.R. (1995). Increasing motivation for change. In R.K. Hester & W.R. Miller (Eds.), *Handbook of Alcoholism Treatment Approaches*, 2nd ed., pp. 89–104. Boston: Allyn & Bacon.

Miller, W.R., & Longabaugh, R. (2003). Summary and conclusions. In T.F. Babor and F.K. Del Boca (Eds.), *Treatment Matching in Alcoholism*, pp. 207–221. New York: Cambridge University Press.

Miller-Johnson, S., Emery, R.E., Marvin, R.S., Clarke, W., Lovinger, R., & Martin, M. (1994). Parent-child relationships and the management of insulin-dependent diabetes mellitus. *Journal of Consulting and Clinical Psychology*, 62, pp. 603–610.

Millon, T., & Martinez, A. (1995). Avoidant personality disorder. In W.J. Livesley (Ed.), *The DSM-IV Personality Disorders*, pp. 218–233. New York: Guilford.

Mineka S., & Zinbarg R. (1998). Experimental approaches to the anxiety and mood disorders. In J.G. Adair and D. Belanger (Eds.), *Advances in Psychological Science Vol. 1: Social, Personal, and Cultural Aspects*, pp. 429–454. Hove, England: Psychology Press/Erlbaum (UK) Taylor & Francis.

Mineka, S., & Cook, M. (1993). Mechanisms involved in the observational conditioning of fear. *Journal of Experimental Psychology: General*, 122, pp. 23–38.

Mineka, S., & Ohman, A. (2002). Born to fear: non-associative vs associative factors in the etiology of phobias. *Behaviour Research and Therapy*, 40, pp. 173–184.

Mineka, S., & Thomas, C. (1999). Mechanisms of change in exposure therapy for anxiety disorders. In T. Dalgleish & M.J. Power (Eds.), *Handbook of Cognition and Emotion*, pp. 747–764. Chichester, England: Wiley.

Mineka, S., & Zinbarg, R. (1991). Animal models of psychopathology. In C.E. Walker (Ed.), *Clinical Psychology*, pp. 51–86. New York: Plenum Press.

Mineka, S., Watson, D., & Clark, L.A. (1998). Comorbidity of anxiety and unipolar mood disorders. *Annual Review of Psychology*, 49, pp. 377–412.

Minino, A.M., & Smith, B.L. (2001). Deaths: Preliminary data for 2000. *National Vital and Statistics Report*, 49, #12. Hyattsville, MD: National Center for Health Statistics.

Minton, H.L. (2002). *Departing from Deviance: A History of Homosexual Rights and Emancipatory Science in America*. Chicago, IL: University of Chicago Press.

Minuchin, S., Rosman, B.L., & Baker, L. (1978). *Psychosomatic Families*. Cambridge, MA: Harvard University Press.

Mitchell, J. (1982). When disaster strikes. . . The critical incident stress debriefing process. *Journal of Emergency Medical Services*, 8, pp. 36–39.

Mitchell, J., & Dyregrov, A. (1993). Traumatic stress in disaster workers and emergency personnel. In J.P. Wilson & B. Raphael (Eds.), *International Handbook of Traumatic Stress Syndromes*, pp. 905–914. New York: Plenum.

Mitchell, J.E., Pyle, R.L., Eckert, E.D., Hatsukami, D., Pomeroy, C., & Zimmerman, R. (1990). A comparison study of antidepressants and structured intensive group psychotherapy in the treatment of bulimia nervosa. *Archives of General Psychiatry*, 47, pp. 149–157.

Mitchell, J.E., Raymond, N., & Specker, S. (1993). A review of controlled trials of pharmacotherapy and psychotherapy in the treatment of bulimia nervosa. *International Journal of Eating Disorders*, 14, pp. 229–247.

Mittelman, M.S., Ferris, S.H., Shulman, E., Steinberg, G., Ambinder, A., & Mackell, J. (1997). Effects of a multicomponent support program on spouse-caregivers of Alzheimer's disease patients: Results of a treatment/control study. In L. Heston (Ed.), *Progress in Alzheimer's Disease and Similar Conditions*. Washington, DC: American Psychiatric Press.

Mnookin, R.H. (1975). Child-custody adjudication: Judicial functions in the face of indeterminancy. *Law and Contemporary Problems*, 88, pp. 226–293.

Mnookin, R.H. (1985). *In the Interest of Children: Advocacy, Law Reform, and Public Policy*. New York: Freeman.

Modesto-Lowe, V. & Van Kirk, J. (2002). Clinical uses of naltrexone: A review of the evidence. *Experimental & Clinical Psychopharmacology*, 10, pp. 213–227.

Moffitt, T.E. (1993). Adolescence-limited and life-course-persistent antisocial behavior: A developmental taxonomy. *Psychological Review*, 100, pp. 674–701.

Moffitt, T.E. (1997). Adolescence-limited and life-course-persistent offending: A complementary pair of developmental theories. In T.P. Thornberry (Ed.),

Developmental Theories of Crime and Delinquency. Advances in Criminological Theory, Vol. 7, pp. 11–54. New Brunswick, NJ: Transaction.

Moldavsky, M., Dorit, L., & Lerman-Sagie, T. (2001). Behavioral phenotypes in genetic syndromes: A reference guide for psychiatrists. Journal of the American Academy of Child and Adolescent Psychiatry, 40, pp. 749–761.

Moldin, S.O. (2003). Neurobiology of autism: The new frontier. Genes, Brain and Behavior, 2, pp. 253–254.

Monahan, J. (1981). The Clinical Prediction of Violent Behavior. Rockville, MD: National Institute of Mental Health.

Monahan, J. (1992). Mental disorder and violent behavior: Perceptions and evidence. American Psychologist, 47, pp. 511–521.

Monahan, J. (1993). Limiting therapist exposure to Tarasoff liability: Guidelines for risk containment. American Psychologist, 48, pp. 242–250.

Monahan, J. et al. (2001a). Mandated community treatment: Beyond outpatient commitment. Psychiatric Services, 52, pp. 1198–1205.

Monahan, J. et al. (2001b). Rethinking Risk Assessment. New York: Oxford.

Monahan, J., Redlich, A.D., Swanson, J., Robbins, P.C., Applebaum, P.S., Petrila, J., Steadman, H.J., Swartz, M., Angell, B., & McNiel, D.E. (2005). Use of leverage to improve adherence to psychiatric treatment in the community. Psychiatric Services, 56, pp. 37–44.

Money, J. (1984). Paraphilias: Phenomenology and classification. American Journal of Psychotherapy, 38, pp. 164–179.

Monroe, S.M., & Harkness, K.L. (2005). Life stress, the "kindling" hypothesis, and the recurrence of depression: Considerations from a life stress perspective. Psychological Review, 112, pp. 417–445.

Monroe, S.M., & Simons, A.D. (1991). Diathesis-stress theories in the context of life stress research: Implications for the depressive disorders. Psychological Bulletin, 110, pp. 406–425.

Montgomery, H.A., Miller, W.R., & Tonigan, J.S. (1993). Differences among AA groups: Implications for research. Journal of Studies on Alcohol, 54, pp. 502–504.

Moore, M. (1975). Some myths about "mental illness." Inquiry, 18, pp. 233–240.

Moore, P.S., Whaley, S.E., Sigman, M. (2004). Interactions between mothers and children: Impacts of maternal and child anxiety. Journal of Abnormal Psychology, 113(3), pp. 471–476.

Moos, R.H. (1990). Conceptual and empirical approaches to developing family-based assessment procedures: Resolving the case of the Family Environment Scale. Family Process, 29, pp. 199–208.

Moos, R.H., Finney, J.W., Ouimette, P.C., & Suchinsky, R.T. (1999). A comparative evaluation of substance abuse treatment. I. Treatment orientation, amount of care, and 1-year outcomes. Alcoholism: Clinical and Experimental Research, 23, pp. 529–536.

Moran, P. (1999). The epidemiology of antisocial personality disorder. Social Psychiatry and Psychiatric Epidemiology, 34, pp. 231–242.

Morgan, C.D., & Baade, L.E. (1997). Neuropsychological testing and assessment scales for dementia of the Alzheimer's type. Psychiatric Clinics of North America, 20, pp. 25–43.

Morgentaler, A. (2003). The Viagra Myth: The Surprising Impact on Love and Relationships. New York: Jossey-Bass.

Moriarty, P.J., Lieber, D., Bennett, A., White, L., Parrella, M., Harvey, P.D., & Davis, K.L. (2001). Gender differences in poor outcome patients with lifelong schizophrenia. Schizophrenia Bulletin, 27, pp. 103–113.

Morokoff, P.J. (1989). Sex bias and POD. American Psychologist, pp. 73–75.

Morris, J. (1995). Dementia and cognitive changes in Huntington's disease. In W.J. Weiner & A.E. Lang (Eds.), Behavioral Neurology of Movement Disorders. Advances in Neurology, vol. 65, pp. 187–200. New York: Raven Press.

Morris, J.C. (2003). Dementia update 2003. Alzheimer Disease & Associated Disorders, 17, pp. 245–258.

Morrison, J., & Herbstein, J. (1988). Secondary affective disorder in women with somatization disorder. Comprehensive Psychiatry, 29, pp. 433–440.

Morse, K.L. (1990). A uniform testimonial privilege for mental health professionals, Ohio State Law Journal, 51, pp. 741–757.

Moscicki, E.K. (1995). Epidemiology of suicidal behavior. Suicide and Life-Threatening Behavior, 25, pp. 22–35.

Moser, C. (2001). Paraphilia: A critique of a confused concept. In P.J. Kleinplatz (Ed.), New Directions in Sex Therapy: Innovations and Alternatives, pp. 91–108. Philadelphia, PA: Brunner-Routledge.

Moskovitz, R.A. (1996). Lost in the Mirror: An Inside Look at Borderline Personality Disorder. Dallas, TX: Taylor Publishing.

MTA Cooperative Group. (1999). A 14-month randomized clinical trial of treatment strategies for attention-deficit/hyperactivity disorder. Archives of General Psychiatry, 56, pp. 1073–1086.

Mueser, K.T., & Gingerich, S. (1994). Coping with Schizophrenia: A Guide for Families. Oakland, CA: New Harbinger.

Mueser, K.T., Bellack, A.S., Douglas, M.S., & Morrison, R.L. (1991). Prevalence and stability of social skill deficits in schizophrenia. Schizophrenia Research, 5, pp. 167–176.

Mulder, R.T. (2002). Personality pathology and treatment outcome in major depression: A review. American Journal of Psychiatry, 159, pp. 359–371.

Multiple Risk Factor Intervention Trial Research Group (1982). Multiple Risk Factor Intervention Trial: Risk factor changes and mortality results, Journal of the American Medical Association, 248, pp. 1465–1477.

Munk-Jorgensen, P., & Ewald, H. (2001). Epidemiology in neurological research: Exemplified by the influenza-schizophrenia theory. British Journal of Psychiatry, 178 (suppl. 40), pp. s30–s32.

Muris, P., Merckelbach, H., & Clavan, M. (1997). Abnormal and normal compulsions. Behaviour Research and Therapy, 35, pp. 249–252.

Murphy, W.D. (1997). Exhibitionism: Psychopathology and theory. In D.R. Laws & W.T. O'Donohue (Eds.), Handbook of Sexual Deviance: Theory and Application, New York: Guilford.

Murray, C.J.L., & Lopez, A.D. (1997). Global mortality, disability, and the contribution of risk factors: Global Burden of Disease Study. Lancet, 349, pp. 1436–1442.

Myers, J.E.B. (1983–84). Involuntary civil commitment of the mentally ill: A system in need of change. Villanova Law Review, 29, pp. 367–433.

Narding, P., & Janzing, J.G.E. (2003). The neuropsychiatric manifestations of Huntington's disease. Current Opinion in Psychiatry, 16, pp. 337–340.

Narita, K., Sasaki, T., Akaho, R., Okazaki, YI, Kusumi, I. et al. (2000). Human leukocyte antigen and season of birth in Japanese patients with schizophrenia. American Journal of Psychiatry, 157, pp. 1173–1175.

Narrow, W.E., Rae, D.S., Robins, L.N., & Regier, D.A. (2002). Revised prevalence estimates of mental disorders in the United States. Archives of General Psychiatry, 59, pp. 115–123.

Nathan, P.E. (1993). Alcoholism: Psychopathology, etiology, and treatment. In P.B. Sutker & H.E. Adams (Eds.), Comprehensive Handbook of Psychopathology, 2nd ed., pp. 451–476. New York: Plenum.

Nathan, P.E., & Gorman, J.M. (Eds.), A Guide to Treatments That Work (2nd ed) New York: Oxford.

Nathan, P.E., & Langenbucher, J. (2003). Diagnosis and classification. In G. Stricker, T.A. Widiger, et al. (Eds), Handbook of Psychology: Clinical Psychology (Volume 8), pp. 3–26. New York: Wiley.

Nathan, P.E., Stuart, S.P., & Dolan, S.L. (2000). Research on psychotherapy efficacy and effectiveness: Between Scylla and Charybdis? Psychological Bulletin, 126, pp. 964–981.

National Academy of Sciences, Institute of Medicine (1989). Research on Children & Adolescents with Mental, Behavioral, and Developmental Disorders. Washington, DC: National Academy Press.

National Institute of Mental Health. (1990). Somatization Disorder in the Medical Setting. Rockville, MD: NIMH.

National Institutes of Health (2000). Phenylketonuria (PKU): Screening and Management. NIH Consensus Statement, 17, pp. 1–33.

National Victim Center. (1992). Crime and Victimization in America: Statistical Overview. Arlington, VA.

Neale, J.M., & Oltmanns, T.F. (1980). Schizophrenia. New York: Wiley.

Nehlig, A. (1999). Are we dependent upon coffee and caffeine? A review on human and animal data. Neuroscience and Biobehavioral Reviews, 23, pp. 563–576.

Neisser, U., & Harsch, N. (1992). Phantom flashbulbs: False recollections of hearing the news about Challenger. In E. Winograd & U. Neisser (Eds.), Affect and Accuracy in Recall: Studies of "flashbulb" Memories, pp. 9–31. New York: Cambridge University Press.

Nemeroff, C.B. (1998). Psychopharmacology of affective disorders in the 21st century. Biological Psychiatry, 44, pp. 517–525.

Nemeroff, C.B. (1998). The neurobiology of depression. Scientific American, 278, pp. 42–49.

Nesse, R.M. (1999). Proximate and evolutionary studies of anxiety, stress and depression: Synergy at the interface. Neuroscience and Biobehavioral Reviews, 23, pp. 895–903.

Nestadt, G., Romanoski, A.J., Brown, C.H., Chahal, R., Merchant, A., Folstein, M.F., Gruenberg, E.M., & McHugh, P.R. (1991). DSM-III compulsive personality disorder: An epidemiological study. Psychological Medicine, 21, pp. 461–471.

Nestadt, G., Romanoski, A.J., Chahal, R., Merchant, A., Folstein, J.F., Gruenberg, E.M., & McHugh, P.R. (1990). An epidemiological study of histrionic personality disorder. Psychological Medicine, 20, pp. 413–422.

Nestler, E.J. (1998). Antidepressant treatments in the 21st century. Biological Psychiatry, 44, pp. 526–533.

Neuhaus, I.M., & Rosenthal, N.E. (1997). Light therapy as a treatment modality for affective disorders. In A. Honig and H.M. van Praag (Eds.), Depression: Neurobiological, Psychopathological and therapeutic Advances, pp. 591–605. New York: Wiley.

Neuner, F., Schauer, M., Klaschik, C., Karunakara, U., & Elbert, T. (2004). A comparison of narrative exposure therapy, supportive counseling, and psychoeducation for treating posttraumatic stress disorder in an African refugee settlement. Journal of Consulting and Clinical Psychology, 72, pp. 579–587.

Newcomb, A.F., Bukowski, W.M., & Pattee, L. (1993). Children's peer relations: A meta-analytic review of popular, rejected, neglected, controversial, and average sociometric status. Psychological Bulletin, 113, pp. 99–128.

Newhouse, P.A. (1997). Alzheimer's disease and the cholinergic system: An introduction to clinical pharmacological research. In L. Heston (Ed.), Progress in Alzheimer's Disease and Similar Conditions. Washington, DC: American Psychiatric Press.

Newman, J.P., & Wallace, J.F. (1993). Psychopathy and cognition. In K.S. Dobson & P.C. Kendall (Eds.), Psychopathology and Cognition, pp. 293–349. San Diego, CA: Academic Press.

Newman, J.P., Schmitt, W.A., & Voss, W.D. (1997). The impact of motivationally neutral cues on psychopathic individuals: Assessing the generality of the response modulation hypothesis. *Journal of Abnormal Psychology, 106*, pp. 563–575.

Newport, D.J., & Nemeroff, C.B. (2000). Neurobiology of posttraumatic stress disorder. *Cognitive Neuroscience, 10*, pp. 211–218.

Newschaffer, C.J., Falb, M.D., & Gurney, J.G. (2005). National autism prevalence trends from United States Special Education Data. *Pediatrics, 115*(3), pp. e277–e282.

Newsom, C., & Hovanitz, C.A. (in press). Autistic spectrum disorders. In E.J. Mash & R.A. Barkely (Eds.), *Treatment of Childhood Disorders*, 3rd ed. New York: Guilford Press.

Niebuhr, R. (1951). To be abased and to abound. *Messenger*, February 13, p. 7.

Nietzel, M.T., Bernstein, D.A., & Milich, R. (1994). *Introduction to Clinical Psychology*, 4th ed. Englewood Cliffs, NJ: Prentice Hall.

Nigg, J.T. (2001). Is ADHD a disinhibitory disorder? *Psychological Bulletin, 127*, pp. 571–598.

Nigg, J.T., & Goldsmith, H.H. (1994). Genetics of personality disorders: Perspectives from personality and psychopathology research. *Psychological Bulletin, 115*, pp. 346–380.

Nigg, J.T., Blaskey, L.G., Stawicki, J.A., & Sachek, J. (2004). Evaluating the endophenotype model of ADHD neuropsychological deficit: Results for parents and siblings of children with ADHD combined and inattentive subtypes. *Journal of Abnormal Psychology, 113*(4), pp. 614–625.

Ninan, P.T. (1999). The functional anatomy, neurochemistry, and pharmacology of anxiety. *Journal of Clinical Psychiatry, 60* (suppl. 22), pp. 12–17.

Ninan, P.T., & Dunlop, B.W. (2005). Neurobiology and etiology of panic disorder. *Journal of Clinical Psychiatry, 66* (suppl. 4), pp. 3–7.

Niznikiewicz, M.A., Kubicki, M., & Shenton, M.E. (2003). Recent structural and functional imaging findings in schizophrenia. *Current Opinion in Psychiatry, 16*, pp. 123–147.

Nolen-Hoeksema, S. (1994). An interactive model for the emergence of gender differences in depressive in adolescence. *Journal of Research on Adolescence, 4*, pp. 519–534.

Nolen-Hoeksema, S. (2000). The role of rumination in depressive disorders and mixed anxiety/depressive symptoms. *Journal of Abnormal Psychology, 109*, pp. 504–511.

Nolen-Hoeksema, S. (2002). Gender differences in depression. In I.H. Gotlib and C.L. Hammen (Eds.), *Handbook of Depression*. New York: Guilford.

Norcross, J.C. (2002). *Psychotherapy Relationships That Work.* New York: Oxford.

Norcross, J.C., & Hill, C.E. (2004). Empirically supported therapy relationships. *The Clinical Psychologist, 57*, pp. 19–25.

Nordstrom, P., Samuelsson, M., Asberg, M., Traskman-Bendz, L., et al. (1994). CSF-5-HIAA predicts suicide risk after attempted suicide. *Suicide and Life Threatening Behavior, 24*, pp. 1–9.

Norris, F.H., Murphy, A.D., Baker, C.K., Perilla, J.L., Rodriguez, F.G., & Rodriguez, J.J. (2003). Epidemiology of trauma and posttraumatic stress disorder in Mexico. *Journal of Abnormal Psychology, 112*, pp. 646–656.

North, C.S. et al. (2002). Psychiatric disorders in rescue workers after the Oklahoma City bombing. *American Journal of Psychiatry, 159*, pp. 857–859.

Noyes, R., Garvey, M.J., & Cook, B.L. (1989). Follow-up study of patients with panic disorder and agoraphobia with panic attacks treated with tricyclic antidepressants. *Journal of Affective Disorders, 16*, pp. 249–257.

Noyes, R., Jr., Clarkson, C., Crowe, R.R., Yates, W.R., & McChesney, C.M. (1987). A family study of general-ized anxiety disorder. *American Journal of Psychiatry, 144*, pp. 1019–1024.

Nuechterlein, K.H., Asarnow, R.F., Subotnik, K.L., Fogelson, D.L., Payne, D.L., Kendler, K.S., Neale, M.C., Jacobson, K.C., & Mintz, J. (2002). The structure of schizotypy: Relationships between neurocognitive and personality disorder features in relatives of schizophrenic patients in the UCLA family study. *Schizophrenia Research 54*, pp. 121–130.

Nunes, E.V., Frank, K.A., & Kornfeld, J. (1987). Psychologic treatment for the Type A behavior pattern and for coronary heart disease: A meta-analysis of the literature. *Psychosomatic Medicine, 48*, pp. 159–173.

Nutt, D.J. (2001). Neurobiological mechanisms in generalized anxiety disorder. *Journal of Clinical Psychiatry, 62* (suppl. 11), pp. 22–27.

O'Brien, C.P., & McKay, J. (2002). Pharmacological treatments for substance use disorders. In P.E. Nathan and J.M. Gorman (Eds.), *A Guide to Treatments That Work*, 2nd ed., pp. 125–156. London: Oxford University Press.

O'Connor, G.T., Buring, J.E., Yusuf, S., Goldhaber, S.Z., Olmstead, E.M., Paffenbarger, R.S., & Hennekens, C.H. (1989). An overview of randomized trials of rehabilitation with exercise after myocardial infarction. *Circulation, 80*, pp. 234–244.

O'Donohue, W., & Bradley, A.R. (1999). Conceptual and empirical issues in child custody evaluations. *Clinical Psychology: Sciences and Practice, 6*, pp. 310–322.

O'Donohue, W.T., Swingen, D.N., Dopke, C.A., & Regev, L.G. (1999). Psychotherapy for male sexual dysfunction: A review. *Clinical Psychology Review, 19*, pp. 591–630.

O'Donovan, M.C., Williams, N.M., & Owen, M.J. (2003). Recent advances in the genetics of schizophrenia. *Human Molecular Genetics, 12* Spec No 2, pp. R125–133.

O'Meara, E.S., Kukull, W.A., Sheppard, L., Bowen, J.D., McCormick, W.C., Teri, L., Pfanschmidt, M., Thompson, J.D., Schellenberg, G.D., & Larson, E.B. (1997). Head injury and risk of Alzheimer's disease by apolipoprotein E genotype. *American Journal of Epidemiology, 146*, pp. 373–384.

O'Sullivan, R.L., Mansueto, C.S., Lerner, E.A., & Miguel, E.C. (2000). Characterization of trichotillomania: A phenomenological model with clinical relevance to obsessive-compulsive spectrum disorders. *Psychiatric Clinics of North America, 23*, pp. 587–604.

Oakley, R. (2004). How the mind hurts and heals the body. *American Psychologist, 59*, pp. 29–40.

Oei, T.P.S., Lim, B., & Hennessy, B. (1990). Psychological dysfunction in battle: Combat stress reactions and posttraumatic stress disorder. *Clinical Psychology Review, 10*, pp. 355–388.

Office of Special Education Programs (2003). *Implementation of the Individuals with Disabilities Act: 25th Annual Report to Congress.* Washington, DC: U.S. Office of Education.

Ohayon, M.M. (2000). Prevalence of hallucinations and their pathological associations in the general population. *Psychiatry Research, 97*, pp. 153–164.

Ohman, A., & Mineka, S. (2001). Fears, phobias, and preparedness: Toward an evolved module of fear and fear learning. *Psychological Review, 108*, pp. 483–522.

Ohman, A., & Mineka, S. (2003): The malicious serpent: Snakes as a prototypical stimulus for an evolved module of fear. *Current Directions in Psychological Science, 12*, pp. 5–9.

Öhman, A. (1996). Preferential preattentive processing of threat in anxiety: Preparedness and attentional biases. In R.M. Rapee (Ed.), *Current Controversies in the Anxiety Disorders*, pp. 253–290. New York: Guilford.

Olds, J., & Milner, P. (1954). Positive reinforcement produced by electrical stimulation of septal area and other regions of rat brain. *Journal of Comparative and Physiological Psychology, 47*, pp. 419–427.

Ollendick, T.H., & King, N.J. (1998). Empirically supported treatments for children with phobic and anxiety disorders: Current status. *Journal of Clinical Child Psychology, 27*, pp. 156–167.

Olmstead, M.P., Kaplan, A.S., & Rockert, W. (1994). Rate and prediction of relapse in bulimia nervosa. *American Journal of Psychiatry, 151*, pp. 738–743.

Olson, S.L., Schilling, E.M., & Bates, J.E. (1999). Measurement of impulsivity: Construct coherence, longitudinal stability, and relationship with externalizing problems in middle childhood and adolescence. *Journal of Abnormal Child Psychology, 27*(2), pp. 151–165.

Olsson, S., & Moller, A.R. (2003). On the incidence and sex ratio of transsexualism in Sweden, 1972–2002. *Archives of Sexual Behavior, 32*, pp. 381–386.

Oltmanns, T.F. (1988). Defining delusional beliefs. In T.F. Oltmanns & B.A. Maher (Eds.), *Delusional Beliefs.* New York: Wiley.

Oltmanns, T.F., & Gibbs, N. (1995). Emotional responsiveness and obsessive-compulsive behavior. *Cognition and Emotion, 25*, pp. 563–578.

Oltmanns, T.F., & Turkheimer, E. (2006). Perceptions of self and others regarding pathological personality traits. In R. Krueger and J. Tackett (Eds.), *Personality and Psychopathology: Building Bridges.* New York: Guilford.

Oltmanns, T.F., Melley, A.H., & Turkheimer, E. (2002). Impaired social functioning and symptoms of personality disorders in a non-clinical population. *Journal of Personality Disorders, 16*, pp. 438–453.

Olweus, D. (1984). Aggressors and their victims: Bullying at school. In N. Frude & H. Gault (Eds.), *Disruptive Behavior in Schools*, pp. 57–76. New York: Wiley.

Onaivi, E.S. (2002). *Biology of Marijuana: From Gene to Behavior.* London: Taylor & Francis.

Oosterwegel, A., & Wicklund, R.A. (1995). *The Self in European and North American Culture: Development and Processes.* Boston: Kluwer.

Oren, D.A., & Rosenthal, N.E. (1992). Seasonal affective disorders. In E.S., Paykel (Ed.), *Handbook of Affective Disorders*, 2nd ed., pp. 551–568, New York: Guilford.

Orne, M.T., Dingers, D.F., & Orne, E.C. (1984). On the differential diagnosis of multiple personality in the forensic context. *International Journal of Clinical and Experimental Hypnosis, 32*, pp. 118–169.

Osman, A.K., & Al-Sawaf, M.H. (1995). Cross-cultural aspects of sexual anxieties and the associated dysfunction. *Journal of Sex Education and Therapy, 21*, pp. 174–181.

Osterling, J.A., Dawson, G., & Munson, J.A. (2002). Early recognition of 1-year-old infants with autism spectrum disorder versus mental retardation. *Development and Psychopathology, 14*, pp. 239–251.

Otto, J.W., Smits, J.A.J., & Reese, H.E. (2004). Cognitive-behavioral therapy for the treatment of anxiety disorders. *Journal of Clinical Psychiatry, 65* (suppl. 5), pp. 34–41.

Otto, J.W., Smits, J.A.J., & Reese, H.E. (2005). Combined psychotherapy and pharmacotherapy for mood and anxiety disorders in adults: Review and analysis. *Clinical Psychology: Science and Practice, 12*, pp. 72–86.

Otto, M.W., Smits, J.A.J., & Reese, H.E. (2005). Combined psychotherapy and phramcotherapy for mood and anxiety disorders in adults: Review and analysis. *Clinical Psychology: Science and Practice, 12*, pp. 72–86.

Otto, M.W., Wilhelm, S., Cohen, L.S., Harlow, B.L. (2001). Prevalence of hody dysmorphic disorder in a community sample of women. *American Journal of Psychiatry, 158*, pp. 2061–2063.

Otto, R.K., Poythress, N.G., Nicholson, R.A., Edens, J.F., Monahan, J., Bonnie, R.J., Hoge, S.K., & Eisenberg, M. (1998). Psychometric properties of the MacArthur Competence Assessment Tool—Criminal Adjudication. *Psychological Assessment, 10*, pp. 435–443.

Owen, P.L., Slaymaker, V., Torigan, J.S., McCrady, B.S., Epstein, E.E., Kaskutas, L.A., Humphreys, K., & Miller, W.R. (2003). Participation in Alcoholics Anonymous: Intended and unintended change mechanisms. *Alcoholism: Clinical & Experimental Research*, 27, pp. 524–532.

Owen, P.R. & Laurel-Seller, E. (2000). Weight and shape ideals: Thin is dangerously in. *Journal of Applied Social Psychology*, 30, pp. 979–990.

Ozer, E.J., & Weiss, D.S. (2004). Who develops posttraumatic stress disorder? *Current Directions in Psychological Science*, 13, pp. 169–172.

Ozer, E.J., Best, S.R., Lipsey, T.L., & Weiss, D.S. (2003). Predictors of posttraumatic stress disorder and symptoms in adults: A meta-analysis. *Psychological Bulletin*, 129, pp. 52–73.

Padilla, A.M. (2001). Issues in culturally appropriate assessment. In L.A. Suzuki, J.G. Ponterotto, and P.J. Metter (Eds.). *Handbook of Multicultural Assessment: Clinical Psychological, and Educational Applications* (2nd ed.). San Francisco, CA: Jossey-Bass.

Paikoff, R.L., & Brooks-Gunn, J. (1991). Do parent-child relationships change during puberty? *Psychological Bulletin*, 110, pp. 47–66.

Pally, R. (2002). The neurobiology of borderline personality disorder: The synergy of "nature and nurture." *Journal of Psychiatric Practice*, 8, pp. 133–142.

Palmer, R.L. (1995). Sexual abuse and eating disorders. In K.D. Brownell & C.G. Fairburn (Eds.), *Eating Disorders and Obesity: A Comprehensive Handbook*, pp. 230–233. New York: Guilford.

Panksepp, J. (2005). Why does separation distress hurt? Comment on MacDonald and Leary. *Psychological Bulletin*, 131, pp. 224–230.

Pantle, M., Pasewark, R., & Steadman, H. (1980). Comparing institutionalization periods and subsequent arrests of insanity acquittees and convicted felons. *Journal of Psychiatry and the Law*, 8, pp. 305–316.

Pargament, K.I. & Park, C.L. (1995). Merely a defense? The variety of religious means and ends. *Journal of Social Issues*, 51, pp. 13–32.

Park, D.C., Nisbett, R., & Hedden, T. (1999). Aging, culture, and cognition. *Journal of Gerontology*, Ser. B, pp. p75–p84.

Parker, G., Roussos, J., Mitchell, P., Wilhelm, K., et al. (1997). Distinguishing psychotic depression from melancholia. *Journal of Affective Disorders*, 42, pp. 155–167.

Parker, J.G., & Asher, S.R. (1987). Peer relations and later personality adjustment: Are low-accepted children at risk? *Psychological Bulletin*, 102, pp. 357–389.

Parker, R.A., & Aldwin, C.M. (1997). Do aspects of gender identity change from early to middle adulthood? Disentangling age, cohort and period effects. In J.E. Lachman and J.B. James (Eds.), *Multiple Paths of Midlife Development*, pp. 67–107. Chicago: University of Chicago Press.

Parks, F.M. (2003). The role of African American folk beliefs in the modern therapeutic process. *Clinical Psychology: Science and Practice*, 10, pp. 456–467.

Parnas, J., Cannon T.D., Jacobsen, B., Schulsinger, H., Schulsinger, F., & Mednick, S.A. (1993). Lifetime DSM-III-R diagnostic outcomes in the offspring of schizophrenic mothers: Results from the Copenhagen high-risk study. *Archives of General Psychiatry*, 50, pp. 707–714.

Parry-Jones, B. (1994). Merycism or rumination disorder: A historical investigation and current assessment. *British Journal of Psychiatry*, 165, pp. 303–314.

Partonen, T., & Magnusson, A. (Eds). (2001). *Seasonal Affective Disorder: Practice and Research*. New York: Oxford University Press.

Pasupathi, M. (2001). The social construction of the personal past and its implications for adult development. *Psychological Bulletin*, 127, pp. 651–672.

Pasupathi, M., Carstensen, L.L., & Tsai, J.L. (1995). Ageism in interpersonal settings. In B. Lott & D. Maluso (Eds.), *The Social Psychology of Interpersonal Discrimination*, pp. 160–182. New York: Guilford.

Patrick, C.J., & Zempolich, K.A. (1998). Emotion and aggression in the psychopathic personality. *Aggression and Violent Behavior*, 3, pp. 303–338.

Patterson, C.J., Kupersmidt, J.B., & Griesler, P.C. (1990). Children's perceptions of self and of relationships with others as a function of sociometric status. *Child Development*, 61, pp. 1335–1349.

Patterson, C.M., & Newman, J.P. (1993). Reflectivity and learning from aversive events: Toward a psychological mechanism for the syndromes of disinhibition. *Psychological Review*, 100, pp. 716–736.

Patterson, D.R. (2004). Treating pain with hypnosis. *Current Directions in Psychological Science*, 13, pp. 252–255.

Patterson, G.R. (1982). *Coercive Family Process*. Eugene, OR: Castalia.

Patterson, G.R. (Ed.) (1990). *Depression and Aggression in Family Interaction*. Hillsdale, NJ: Erlbaum.

Patterson, G.R., & Fleischman, M.J. (1979). Maintenance of treatment effects: Some considerations concerning family systems and follow-up data. *Behavior Therapy*, 10, pp. 168–185.

Patterson, G.R., DeBaryshe, B.D., & Ramsey, E. (1989). A developmental perspective on antisocial behavior. *American Psychologist*, 44, pp. 329–325.

Patton, J.R., Beirne-Smith, M., & Payne, J.S. (1990). *Mental Retardation*, 3rd ed. Columbus, OH: Merrill.

Paul, G.L., & Lentz, R.J. (1977). *Psychosocial Treatment of Chronic Mental Patients: Milieu Versus Social-Learning Programs*. Cambridge, MA: Harvard University Press.

Paul, R., Garrett, K., & Cohen, R. (2003). Vascular dementia: A diagnostic conundrum for the clinical neuropsychologist. *Applied Neuropsychology*, 10, pp. 129–136.

Pauli, P., & Alpers, G.W. (2002). Memory bias in patients with hypochondriasis and somatoform pain disorder. *Journal of Psychosomatic Research*, 52, pp. 45–53.

Payne, R.L. (1992). First person account: My schizophrenia. *Schizophrenia Bulletin*, 18, pp. 725–728.

Pedersen, N.L., & Gatz, M. (1991). Twin studies as a tool for bridging the gap between genetics and epidemiology of dementia: The study of dementia in Swedish twins [abstract]. *Gerontologist*, 31, p. 333.

Pedersen, N.L., Gatz, M., Berg, S., & Johansson, B. (2004). How heritable is Alzheimer's disease late in life? Findings from Swedish twins. *Annals of Neurology*, 55, pp. 180–185.

Pelham, W.E., Carlson, C., Sams, S.E., Vallano, G., Dixon, M.J., & Hoza, B. (1993). Separate and combined effects of methylphenidate and behavior modification with attention deficit-hyperactivity disorder in the classroom. *Journal of Consulting and Clinical Psychology*, 61, pp. 506–515.

Pelham, W.E., et al. (1985). Methylphenidate and children with attention deficit disorder: Dose effects on classroom academic and social behavior. *Archives of General Psychiatry*, 42, pp. 948–952.

Pelham, W.E., et al. (2000). Behavioral versus behavioral and pharmacological treatment in ADHD children attending a summer treatment program. *Journal of Abnormal Child Psychology*, 28, pp. 507–525.

Pelham, W.E., et al. (2002). Effects of methylphenidate and expectancy on children with ADHD: Behavior, academic performance, and attributions in a summer treatment program and regular classroom settings. *Journal of Consulting and Clinical Psychology*, 70, pp. 320–335.

Pennebaker, J.W. (1990). *Opening up: The Healing Power of Confiding in others*. New York: Morrow.

Pennebaker, J.W., Kiecolt-Glaser, J., & Glaser, R. (1988). Disclosure of traumas and immune function: Health implications for psychotherapy. *Journal of Consulting and Clinical Psychology*, 56, pp. 239–245.

Pennix, B., Van Tilburg, T., Kriegsman, D., Deeg, D., Boeke, A., & Van Eijk, J. (1997). Effects of social support and personal coping resources on mortality in older age: The Longitudinal Aging Study of Amsterdam. *American Journal of Epidemiology*, 146, pp. 510–519.

Peralta, V., & Cuesta, M.J. (1999). Dimensional structure of psychotic symptoms: An item-level analysis of SAPS and SANS symptoms in psychotic disorders. *Schizophrenia Research*, 38, pp. 13–26.

Perris, C. (1992). Bipolar-unipolar distinction. In E.S. Paykel (Ed.), *Handbook of Affective Disorders*, 2nd ed., pp. 57–75. New York: Guilford.

Perry, C., & Laurence, J. (1984). Mental processing outside of awareness: The contributions of Freud and Janet. In K.S. Bowers & D. Meichenbaum (Eds.), *The Unconscious Reconsidered*, pp. 9–48. New York: Wiley.

Pescosolido, B. et al. (1999). The public's view of the competence, dangerousness, and need for legal coercion among persons with mental illness. *American Journal of Public Health*, 89, pp. 1339–1345.

Pescosolido, B.A., & Georgianna, S. (1989). Durkheim, suicide, and religion: Toward a network theory of suicide. *American Sociological Review*, 54, pp. 33–48.

Peters, K.D., Kochanek, K.D., and Murphy, S.L. (1998). Deaths: Final data for 1996. *National Vital Statistics Reports*, vol. 47, no. 9. Hyattsville, MD: National Center for Health Statistics.

Petrie, K.J., Booth, R.J., Pennebaker, J.W., Davison, K.P., & Thomas, M.G. (1995). Disclosure of trauma and immune response to a hepatitis B vaccination program. *Journal of Consulting and Clinical Psychology*, 63, pp. 787–792.

Pfohl, B., Blum, N., & Zimmerman, M. (1995). *Structured Interview for DSM-IV Personality (SIDP-IV)*. Iowa City: University of Iowa.

Pfohl, B., Coryell, W., Zimmerman, M., & Stangl, D. (1986). DSM-III personality disorders: Diagnostic overlap and internal consistency of individual DSM-III-criteria. *Comprehensive Psychiatry*, 27, pp. 21–34.

Phelan, J.C., & Link, B.G. (1999). The labeling theory of mental disorder (I): The role of social contingencies in the application of psychiatric labels. In A.V. Horwitz and T.L. Scheid (Eds.), *A Handbook for the Study of Mental Health: Social Contexts, Theories, and Systems*, pp. 139–150. New York: Cambridge University Press.

Phillips, K.A. (1991). Body dysmorphic disorder: The distress of imagined ugliness. *American Journal of Psychiatry*, 148, pp. 1138–1149.

Phillips, K.A., Albertini, R.S., & Rasmussen, S.A. (2002). A randomized placebo-controlled trial of fluoxetine in body dysmorphic disorder. *Archives of General Psychiatry*, 59, pp. 381–388.

Phillips, K.A., Grant, J., Siniscalchi, J., Albertini, R.S. (2001). Surgical and nonpsychiatric medical treatment of patients with body dysmorphic disorder. *Psychosomatics*, 42, pp. 504–510.

Phillips, S.D., Burns, B.J., Edgar, E.R., Mueser, K.T., Linkins, K.W., Rosenheck, R.A., Drake, R.E., & McDonel Herr, E.C. (2001). Moving assertive community treatment into standard practice. *Psychiatric Services*, 52, pp. 771–779.

Piasecki, T., Fiore, M.C., & Baker, T.B. (1998). Profiles in discouragement: Two studies of variability in the time course of smoking withdrawal symptoms. *Journal of Abnormal Psychology*, 107, pp. 238–251.

Pilling, S, Bebbington, P., Kuipers, E., Garety, P., Geddes, J. Orbach, G., & Morgan, C. (2002b). Psychological treatments in schizophrenia: II. Meta-analyses of family intervention and cognitive behavior therapy. *Psychological Medicine*, 32, pp. 763–782.

Pilling, S., Bebbington, P., Kuipers, E., Garety, P., Geddes, J., Martindale, B., Orbach, G., & Morgan, C. (2002a).

Psychological treatments in schizophrenia: II. Meta-analyses of randomized controlled trials of social skills training and cognitive remediation. *Psychological Medicine*, 32, pp. 783–791.

Pincus, H.A., Tanielian, T.L., Marcus, S.C., Olfson, M., Zarin, D.A.,Thompson, J., & Zito, J.M. (1998). Prescribing trends in psychotropic medications: Primary care, psychiatry, and other medical specialties. *Journal of the American Medical Association*, 279, pp. 526–531.

Pincus, T., & Morley, S. (2001). Cognitive-processing bias in chronic pain: A review and integration. *Psychological Bulletin*, 127, pp. 599–617.

Pinker, S. (1997). *How the Mind Works*. New York: Norton.

Pinto, C., Dhavale, H.S., Nair, S., Patil, B., & Dewan, M. (2000). Borderline personality disorder exists in India. *Journal of Nervous and Mental Disease*, 188, pp. 386–388.

Piper, A. (1994). Multiple personality disorder. *British Journal of Psychiatry*, 164, pp. 600–612.

Pitman, R.K. (1997). Overview of biological themes in PTSD. In R. Yehuda & A.C. McFarlane (Eds.), *Psychobiology of Posttraumatic Stress Disorder*. New York: New York Academy of Sciences.

Pitts, F.N., Jr., & McClure, J.N., Jr. (1967). Lactate metabolism in anxiety neurosis. *New England Journal of Medicine*, 277, pp. 1329–1336.

Plassman, B.L., & Breitner, J.C.S. (1997). The genetics of dementia in late life. *Psychiatric Clinics of North America*, 20, pp. 59–76.

Plaut, S.M. (1995). *Sex Therapy Following Treatment By an Exploitive Therapist*, pp. 264–278. In R.C. Rosen and S.R. Leiblum (Eds.), *Case Studies in Sex Therapy*. New York: Guilford.

Plomin, R., & Crabbe, J. (2000). *Psychological Bulletin*, 126, pp. 806–828.

Plomin, R., & Daniels, D. (1987). Why are children in the same family so different from one another? *Behavioral and Brain Sciences*, 10, pp. 1–60.

Plomin, R., Owen, M.J., & McGuffin, P. (1994). The genetic bases of complex human behaviors. *Science*, 264, pp. 1733–1739.

Plotsky, P.M., Owens, M.J., & Nemeroff, C.B. (1998). Psychoneuroendocrinology of depression: Hypothalamic-pituitary-adrenal axis. *Psychiatric Clinics of North America*, 21, pp. 293–307.

Pokony, A. (1983). Prediction of suicide in psychiatric patients: A prospective study. *Archives of General Psychiatry*, 40, pp. 249–257.

Polaschek, D.L. (1997). New Zealand rapists: An examination of subtypes. In G.M. Habermann (Ed.), *Looking Back and Moving Forward: 50 Years of New Zealand Psychology*, pp 224–231.Wellington, New Zealand: New Zealand Psychological Society.

Polivy, J., & Herman, C.P. (2002). Causes of eating disorders. *Annual Review of Psychology*, 53, pp. 187–213.

Pollack, M.H. (2001). Comorbidity, neurobiology, and pharmacotherapy of social anxiety disorder. *Journal of Clinical Psychiatry*, 62 (suppl. 12), pp. 24–29.

Pollak, S.D. & Tolley-Schell, S.A. Selective attention to facial emotion in physically abused children. (2003). *Journal of Abnormal Psychology*, 112(3), pp. 323–338.

Polleux, F., & Lauder, J.M. (2004). Toward a developmental neurobiology of autism. *Mental Retardation and Developmental Disabilities Research Reviews*, 10, pp. 303–317.

Pomeroy, C. (1996). Anorexia nervosa, bulimia nervosa, and binge eating disorder: The assessment of physical status. In J.K. Thompson, *Body Image, Eating Disorders, and Obesity*, pp. 177–204. Washington, DC: American Psychological Association.

Poole, D.A., Lindsay, D.S., Memon, A., & Bull, R. (1995). Psychotherapy and the recovery of memories of childhood sexual abuse: U.S. and British practitioners' opinions, practices, and experiences. *Journal of Consulting and Clinical Psychology*, 63, pp. 426–437.

Pope, H.G., & Yurgelun-Todd, D. (1996). The residual cognitive effects of heavy marijuana use in college students. *Journal of the American Medical Association*, 275, pp. 521–527.

Posner, M.I., & DiGirolamo, G.J. (2000). Cognitive neuroscience: Origins and promise. *Psychological Bulletin*, 126, p. 873.

Potter, N.N. (2004). Perplexing issues in personality disorders. *Current Opinion in Psychiatry*, 17, pp. 487–492.

Poulton, R., & Menzies, R.G. (2002). Non-associative fear acquisition: A review of the evidence from retrospective and longitudinal research. *Behaviour Research and Therapy*, 40, pp. 127–149.

Prentky, R.A. (1997). Arousal reduction in sexual offenders: A review of antiandrogen interventions. *Sexual Abuse: Journal of Research and Treatment*, 9, pp. 335–347.

Prescott, C.A., & Kendler, K.S. (1999). Genetic and environmental contributions to alcohol abuse and dependence in a population-based sample of male twins. *American Journal of Psychiatry*, 156, pp. 34–40.

Prescott, C.A., Hewitt, J.K., Heath, A.C., Truett, K.R., Neale, M.C., & Eaves, L.J. (1994). Environmental and genetic influences on alcohol use in a volunteer sample of older twins. *Journal of Studies on Alcohol*, 55, pp. 18–32.

Presnell, K. & Stice, E. (2003). An experimental test of the effect of weight-loss dieting on bulimic pathology: Tipping the scales in a different direction. *Journal of Abnormal Psychology*, 112, pp. 166–170.

Presta, S., Marazziti, D., Dell'Osso, L., Pfanner, C., Pallanti, S., & Cassano, G.B. (2002). Kleptomania: Clinical features and comorbidity in an Italian sample. *Comprehensive Psychiatry*, 43, pp. 7–12.

Price, J.S., Gardner, R., Jr., & Erickson, M. (2004). Can depression, anxiety and somatization be understood as appeasement displays? *Journal of Affective Disorders*, 79, pp. 1–11.

Prigerson, H.G., Maciejewski, P.K., & Rosenheck, R.A. (2002). Population attributable fractions of psychiatric disorders and behavioral outcomes associated with combat exposure among U.S. men. *American Journal of Public Health*, 92, pp. 59–63.

Prince, M., Acosta, D., Chiu, H., Scazufca, M., & Varghese, M. (2003). Dementia diagnosis in developing countries: A cross-cultural validation study. *Lancet*, 361, pp. 909–917.

Pryor, J.P. (2002). Pharmacotherapy of erectile dysfunction. *Sexual & Relationship Therapy*, 17, pp. 389–400.

Pryse-Phillips, W. (1999). Do we have drugs for dementia? *Archives of Neurology*, 56, pp. 735–737.

Puig-Antich, J. (1986). Psychobiological markers: Effects of age and puberty. In M. Rutter, C. Izard, & P. Read (Eds.), *Depression in Young People*, pp. 341–382. New York: Guilford.

Pujol, J., Soriano-Mas, C., Alonso, P., Cardoner, N., Menchon, J.M., Deus, J., & Vallejo, J. (2004). Mapping structural brain alterations in obsessive-compulsive disorder. *Archives of General Psychiatry*, 61, pp. 720–730.

Purdon, C. (2004). Empirical investigations of thought suppression in OCD. *Journal of Behavior Therapy & Experimental Psychiatry*, 35, pp. 121–136.

Putnam, F.W., Curoff, J.J., et al. (1986). The clinical phenomenology of multiple personality disorder: Review of 100 recent cases. *Journal of Clinical Psychiatry*, 47, pp. 285–293.

Quadagno, D., Sly, D.F., Harrison, D.F., Eberstein, I.W., & Soler, H.R. (1998). Ethnic differences in sexual decisions and sexual behavior. *Archives of Sexual Behavior*, 27, pp. 57–75.

Quay, H.C. (1993).The psychobiology and undersocialized aggressive conduct disorder: A theoretical perspective. *Development and Psychopathology*, 5, pp. 165–180.

Rabins, P.V. (1997). Caring for persons with dementing illnesses: A current perspective. In L. Heston (Ed.), *Progress in Alzheimer's Disease and Similar Conditions*. Washington, DC: American Psychiatric Press.

Rachman, S. (1991). *Fear and Courage*, 2nd ed. San Francisco: Freeman.

Rachman, S. (2002). *Anxiety*, 2nd ed. New York: Psychology Press (Taylor and Francis Group).

Rachman, S., & de Silva, P. (1978). Abnormal and normal obsessions. *Behaviour Research and Therapy*, 16, pp. 233–248.

Rachman, S.J., & Hodgson, R.J. (1980). *Obsessions and Compulsions*. Englewood Cliffs, NJ: Prentice Hall.

Radel, M., Vallejo, R.L., Iwata, N., Aragon, R., Long, J.C., Virkkunen, M., et al. (2005). Haplotype-based localization of an alcohol dependence gene to the 5q34 gamma-aminobutyric acid type A gene cluster. *Archives of General Psychiatry*, 62, pp. 47–55.

Rai, A., Stanton, B., Wu, Y., Xiaoming, L., Galbraith, J., Cottrell, L., et al. (2003). Relative influences of perceived parental monitoring and perceived peer involvement on adolescent risk behaviors: An analysis of six cross-sectional data sets. *Journal of Adolescent Health*, 33, pp. 108–118.

Raichle, M.E. (2001). Bold insights. *Nature*, 412, pp. 128–130.

Raine, A., Moffit, T.E., Caspi, A., Loeber, R., Southamer-Loeber, M., & Lynam, D. (2005). Neurocognitive impairments in boys on the life-course persistent antisocial path. *Journal of Abnormal Psychology*, 114(1), pp. 38–49.

Ramey, C.T., & Bryant, D. (1982). Evidence for primary prevention of developmental retardation. *Journal of the Division of Early Childhood*, 5, pp. 73–78.

Rangaswamy, M., Porjesz, B., Chorlian, D. B., Wang, K., Jones, K. A., Kuperman, S., et al. (2004). Resting EEG in offspring of male alcoholics: beta frequencies. *International Journal of Psychophysiology*, 51, pp. 239–251.

Rapee, R.M. (1995). Psychological factors influencing the affective response to biological challenge procedures in panic disorder. *Journal of Anxiety Disorders*, 9, pp. 59–74.

Rapee, R.M. et al., (2005). Prevention and early intervention of anxiety disorders in inhibited preschool children. *Journal of Consulting and Clinical Psychology*, 73, pp. 488–497.

Raphael, B., Wilson, J., Meldrum L., & McFarlane, A.C. (1996). Acute preventive interventions. In B.A. van der Kolk, A.C. McFarlane, & L.Weisaeth (Eds.), *Traumatic Stress*, pp. 463–479. New York: Guilford.

Rapoport, J., & Swedo, S. (2002). Obsessive-compulsive disorders. In M. Rutier & E. Taylor (Eds.), *Child and Adolescent Psychiatry*, 4th ed., pp. 571–592. Oxford, UK: Blackwell.

Rapoport, J.L., Buchsbaum, M.S., Zahn, T.P., Weingartner, H., Ludlow, C., & Mikkelsen, E.J. (1978). Dextroamphetamine: Cognitive and behavioral effects in normal prepubertal boys. *Science*, 199, pp. 560–563.

Raskind, M.A. (1998). The clinical interface of depression and dementia. *Journal of Clinical Psychiatry*, 59 (suppl. 10), pp. 9–12.

Raskind, M.A., & Peskind, E.R. (1997). Neurotransmitter abnormalities and the psychopharmacology of Alzheimer's disease. In L. Heston (Ed.), *Progress in Alzheimer's Disease and Similar Conditions*. Washington, DC: American Psychiatric Press.

Rastam, M., Gillberg, C., & Gillberg, C. (1995). Anorexia nervosa 6 years after onset. Part II. Cormorbid psychiatric problems. *Comprehensive Psychiatry*, 36, pp. 70–76.

Rathod, S., & Turkington, D. (2005). Cognitive-behaviour therapy for schizophrenia: A review. *Current Opinion in Psychiatry*, 18, pp. 159–163.

Read, J. (1995). Female sexual dysfunction. *International Review of Psychiatry*, 7, pp. 175–182.

Regier, D.A., & Narrow, W.E. (2002). Defining clinically significant psychopathology with epidemiologic data. In J.E. Helzer & J.J. Hudziak (Eds.), *Defining Psychopathology in the 21st Century: DSM-V and beyond*, pp. 19–30. Washington, D.C.: American Psychiatric Publishing.

Reich, J. (1996). The morbidity of DSM-III-R dependent personality disorder. *Journal of Nervous and Mental Disease*, 184, pp. 22–26.

Reid, W.H., & Gacono, C. (2000). Treatment of antisocial personality, psychopathy, and other characterologic antisocial syndromes. *Behavioral Sciences and the Law*, 18, pp. 647–662.

Reis, H.T., Collins, W.A., & Berscheid, E. (2000). The relationship context of human behavior and development. *Psychological Bulletin*, 6, pp. 844–872.

Reisner, R., Slobogin, C., & Rai, A. (1999). *Law and the Mental Health System. Civil and Criminal Aspects*, 3rd ed. St. Paul, MN: West.

Reisner, R., Slobogin, C., & Rai, A. (2004). *Law and the mental health system*, 4th ed. St. Paul, MN: West.

Reiss, A.L., Feinstein, C., & Rosenbaum, K.N. (1986). Autism and genetic disorders. *Schizophrenia Bulletin*, 12, pp. 724–738.

Reissing, E.D., Binik, Y.M., Khalife, S., Cohen, D., & Amsel, R. (2004). Vaginal spasm, pain, and behavior: An empirical investigation of the diagnosis of vaginismus. *Archives of Sexual Behavior*, 33, pp. 5–17.

Repetti, R.L., Taylor, S.E., & Seeman, T.E. (2002). Risky families. Family social environments and the mental and physical health of offspring. *Psychological Bulletin*, 128, pp. 330–366.

Research Units on Pediatric Psychopharmacology (RUPP) Anxiety Group (2001) *New England Journal of Medicine*, 344, pp. 1279–1285.

Resick, P.A., & Calhoun, K.S. (2001). Posttraumatic stress disorder. In D. Barlow (Ed.), *Clinical Handbook of Psychological Disorders*, 3rd ed. New York: Guilford.

Resick, P.A., Nishith, P., Weaver, T.L., Astin, M.C., & Feuer, C.A. (2002). *Journal of Consulting and Clinical Psychology*, 70, pp. 867–879.

Reynolds, C.F., et al. (1999). Nortriptyline and interpersonal psychotherapy as maintenance therapies for recurrent major depression. *Journal of the American Medical Association*, 281, pp. 39–45.

Rhee, S.H., & Waldman, I.D. (2002). Genetic and environmental influences on antisocial behavior: A meta-analysis of twin and adoption studies. *Psychological Bulletin*, 128, pp. 490–529.

Rhee, S.H., & Waldman, I.D. (2002). Genetic and environmental influences on antisocial behavior: A meta-analysis of twin and adoption studies. *Psychological Bulletin*, 128(3), pp. 490–529.

Rhee, S.H., Hewitt, J.K., Young, S.E., Corley, R.P., Crowley, T.J., & Stallings, M.C. (2003). Genetic and environmental influences on substance initiation, use, and problem use in adolescents. *Archives of General Psychiatry*, 60, pp. 1256–1264.

Ricciardelli, L.A., & McCabe, M.P. (2004). A biopsychosocial model of disordered eating and the pursuit of muscularity in adolescent boys. *Psychological Bulletin*, 130, pp. 179–205.

Riccio, C.A., Reynolds, C.R., Lowe, P., & Moore, J.J. (2002). The continuous performance test: A window on the neural substrates for attention? *Archives of Clinical Neuropsychology*, 17, pp. 235–272.

Rice, M.E., & Harris, G.T. (1997). The treatment of adult offenders. In D.M. Stoff, J. Breiling, & J. Maser (Eds.), *Handbook of Antisocial Behavior*, pp. 425–435. New York: Wiley.

Richardson, K. (2000). *Developmental Psychology: How Nature and Nurture Interact*. Mahwah, NJ: Lawrence Erlbaum.

Richardson, S. (1996). The besieged brain: Immune cells in brain may further progression of Alzheimer's disease. *Discover*, 17, pp. 30–32.

Richelson, E. (1999). Receptor pharmacology of neuroleptics: Relation to clinical effects. *Journal of Clinical Psychiatry*, 60 (suppl. 10), pp. 5–14.

Richters, J.E., & Hinshaw, S.P. (1999). The abduction of disorder in psychiatry. *Journal of Abnormal Psychology*, 108, pp. 438–445.

Rieber, R.W. (1999). Hypnosis, false memory and multiple personality: A trinity of affinity. *History of Psychiatry*, 10, pp. 3–11.

Riecher-Roessler, A., & Roessler, W. (1998). The course of schizophrenic psychoses: What do we really know? A selective review from an epidemiological perspective. *European Archives of Psychiatry and Clinical Neuroscience*, 248, pp. 189–202.

Rief, W., Hiller, W., & Margraf, J. (1998). Cognitive aspects of hypochondriasis and the somatization syndrome. *Journal of Abnormal Psychology*, 107, pp. 587–595.

Rind, B., Tromovitch, P., & Bauserman, R. (1998). A meta-analytic examination of assumed properties of child sexual abuse using college samples. *Psychological Bulletin*, 124, pp. 22–53.

Rivas-Vazquez, R.A., Saffa-Biller, D., Ruiz, I., Blais, M.A., & Rivas-Vazquez, A. (2004). Current issues in anxiety and depression: Comorbid, mixed, and subthreshold disorders. *Professional Psychology: Research and Practice*, 35, pp. 74–83.

Roberts, A.J., & Koob, G.F. (1997). The neurobiology of addiction: An overview. *Alcohol Health and Research World*, 21, pp. 101–106.

Roberts, J., & Rowland, M. (1981). *Hypertension in Adults 25–74 Years of Age: United States, 1971–75*. Vital and Health Statistics Series 11, No. 221., DHEW Publication No. PHS 81–1671. Washington, DC: U.S. Government Printing Office.

Roberts, L.J., & Marlatt, G.A. (1999). Harm reduction. In P.J. Ott, R.E. Tarter, & R.T. Ammerman (Eds.), *Sourcebook on Substance Abuse: Etiology, Epidemiology, Assessment, and Treatment*, pp. 389–398. Boston: Allyn & Bacon.

Robin, A.L., Siegel, P.T., Moye, A.W., Gilroy, M., Dennis, A.B., & Sikand, A. (1999). A controlled comparison of family versus individual therapy for adolescents with anorexia nervosa. *Journal of the American Academy of Child & Adolescent Psychiatry*, 38, pp. 1482–1489.

Robiner, W.N., Bearman, D.L., Berman, M, Grove, W.M., Colon, E., Armstrong, J., Mareck, S., & Tanenbaum, R.L. (2003). Prescriptive authority for psychologists: Despite deficits in education and knowledge? *Journal of Clinical Psychology in Medical Settings*, 10, pp. 211–212.

Robins, C.J., & Chapman, A.L. (2004). Dialectical behavior therapy: Current status, recent developments, and future directions. *Journal of Personality Disorders*, 18, pp. 73–89.

Robins, E., & Guze, S. (1989). Establishment of diagnostic validity in psychiatric illness. In L.N. Robins & J.E. Barrett (Eds.), *The Validity of Psychiatric Diagnosis*. pp. 177–197. New York: Raven Press.

Robins, L.N. (1966). *Deviant Children Grown up: A Sociological and Psychiatric Study of Sociopathic Personality*. Baltimore: Williams & Wilkins.

Robins, L.N., & Regier, D.A. (1991). *Psychiatric Disorders in America: The Epidemiologic Catchment Area Study*. New York: Free Press.

Robins, L.N., Tipp, J., & Przybeck, T. (1991). Antisocial personality. In L.N. Robins & D.A. Regier (Eds.), *Psychiatric Disorders in America: The Epidemiologic Catchment Area Study*, pp. 258–290. New York: Free Press.

Robinson, N.M., Zigler, E., & Gallagher, J.J. (2000). Two tails of the normal curve: Similarities and differences in the study of mental retardation and giftedness. *American Psychologist*, 55, pp. 1413–1424.

Robinson, P. (1976). *The Modernization of Sex: Havelock Ellis, Alfred Kinsey, William Masters and Virginia Johnson*. New York: Harper & Row.

Roemer, L., & Borkovec, T.D. (1993). Worry: Unwanted cognitive activity that controls unwanted somatic experience. In D.M. Wegner & J.W. Pennebaker (Eds.), *Handbook of Mental Control*. Englewood Cliffs, NJ: Prentice Hall.

Rogers, M.P., Weinshenker, N.J., Warshaw, M.G., et al. (1996). Prevalence of somatoform disorders in a large sample of patients with anxiety disorders. *Psychosomatics*, 37, pp. 17–22.

Rogers, S., Wehner, E.A., & Hagerman, R. (2001). The behavioral phenotype in fragile X: Symptoms of autism in very young children with fragile X syndrome, idiopathic autism, and other developmental.

Rohrbaugh, M.J., Shoham, V., Coyne, J.C., Cranford, J.A., Sonnega, J.S., & Nicklas, J.M. (2004). Beyond the "self" in self-efficacy: Spouse confidence predicts patient survival following heart failure. *Journal of Family Psychology*, 18, pp. 184–193.

Roisman, G.I. (2005). Conceptual clarifications in the study of resilience. *American Psychologist*, 60, pp. 264–265.

Rojas-Fernandez, C.H., & MacKnight, C. (1999). Dementia with Lewy bodies: Review and pharmacotherapeutic implications. *Pharmacotherapy*, 19, pp. 795–803.

Rojas-Fernandez, C.H., Lanctot, K.L., Allen, D.D., & MacKnight, C. (2001). Pharmacotherapy of behavioral and psychological symptoms of dementia: Time for a different paradigm? *Pharmacotherapy*, 21, pp. 74–102.

Roman, G.C. (2002). Vascular dementia revisited: Diagnosis, pathogenesis, treatment, and prevention. *Medical Clinics of North America*, 86, pp. 477–499.

Romney, D.M., & Candido, C.L. (2001). Anhedonia in depression and schizophrenia: A reexamination. *Journal of Nervous and Mental Disease*, 189, pp. 735–740.

Ronningstam, E., & Gunderson, J. (1991). Differentiating borderline personality disorder from narcissistic personality disorder. *Journal of Personality Disorders*, 5, pp. 225–232.

Rose, R. J., Dick, D. M., Viken, R. J., & Kaprio, J. (2001). Gene–environment interaction in patterns of adolescent drinking: Regional residency moderates longitudinal influences on alcohol use. *Alcoholism: Clinical and Experimental Research*, 25, pp. 637–643.

Rose, R.J., Viken, R.J., Dick, D.M., Bates, J., Pulkkinen, L., & Kaprio, J. (2003). It does take a village: Nonfamilial environments and children's behavior. *Psychological Science*, 14, pp. 273–277.

Rosen, J.C., Reiter, J., & Orosan, P. (1995). Cognitive-behavioral body image therapy for body dysmorphic disorder. *Journal of Consulting and Clinical Psychology*, 63, pp. 263–269.

Rosen, R.C. (2000). Medical and psychological interventions for erectile dysfunction: Toward a combined treatment approach. In edited book. *Principles and Practice of Sex Therapy*, pp. 276–304.

Rosen, R.C., & Leiblum, S.R. (1995). Treatment of sexual disorders in the 1990s: An integrated approach. *Journal of Consulting and Clinical Psychology*, 63, pp. 877–890.

Rosen, R.C., & McKenna, K.E. (2002). PDE-5 inhibition and sexual response: Pharmacological mechanisms and clinical outcomes. *Annual Review of Sex Research*, 13, pp. 36–88.

Rosenfeld, B. (2004). *Assisted Suicide and the Right to Die*. Washington: American Psychological Association.

Rosenstein, L.D. (1998). Differential diagnosis of the major progressive dementias and depression in middle and later adulthood: A summary of the literature of the early 1990s. *Neuropsychology Review*, 8, pp. 109–167.

Rosenthal, D. (Ed.) (1963). *The Genain Quadruplets*. New York: Basic Books.

Rosenthal, N.E. (1998). *Winter Blues: Seasonal Affective Disorder.* New York: Guilford.

Rosler, A., & Witztum, E. (1998). Treatment of men with paraphilia with a long-acting analogue of gonadotripin-releasing hormone. *New England Journal of Medicine,* 338, pp. 416–422.

Ross, C.A. (1991). Epidemiology of multiple personality disorder and dissociation. *Psychiatric Clinics of North America,* 14, pp. 503–516.

Ross, C.A. (1997). *Dissociative Identity Disorder: Diagnosis, Clinical Features, and Treatment of Multiple Personality.* New York: Wiley.

Ross, C.A., Duffy, C.M., & Ellason, J.W. (2002). Prevalence, reliability, and validity of dissociative disorders in an inpatient setting. *Journal of Trauma and Dissociation,* 3, pp. 7–17.

Ross, C.A., Norton, G.R., & Wozney, K. (1989). Multiple personality disorder: An analysis of 236 cases. *Canadian Journal of Psychiatry,* 34, pp. 413–418.

Ross, G.W., & Bowen, J.D. (2002). The diagnosis and differential diagnosis of dementia. *Medical Clinics of North America,* 86, pp. 455–476.

Ross, J., & Carter, R. (1995). *Triumph over Fear.* New York: Bantam Books.

Rossor, M.N. (2001). Pick's disease: A clinical overview. *Neurology,* 56 (suppl. 4), pp. S3–S5.

Roth, D., & Bean, J. (1986). New perspectives on homelessness: Findings from a statewide epidemiological study. *Hospital and Community Psychiatry,* 37, pp. 712–723.

Roth, W.T., Wilhelm, F.H., & Pettit, D. (2005). Are current theories of panic falsifiable? *Psychological Bulletin,* 131, pp. 171–192.

Rothbaum, B.O., & Foa, E.B. (1996). Cognitive behavioral therapy for posttraumatic stress disorder. In B.A. van der Kolk, A.C., McFarlane, & L. Weisaeth (Eds.), *Traumatic Stress,* pp. 491–509. New York: Guilford.

Roy-Byrne, P.P., & Cowley, D.S. (2002). Pharmacological treatments for panic disorder, generalized anxiety disorder, specific phobia, and social anxiety disorder. In P.E. Nathan and J.M. Gorman (Eds.), *A Guide to Treatments That Work,* 2nd ed., pp. 337–365. London, England: Oxford University Press.

Rozanski, A., Blumenthal, J.A., & Kaplan, J. (1999). Impact of psychological factors on the pathogenesis of cardiovascular disease and implications for therapy. *Circulation,* 99, pp. 2192–2217.

Rubonis, A.V., & Bickman, L. (1991). Psychological impairment in the wake of disaster: The disaster-psychopathology relationship. *Psychological Bulletin,* 109, pp. 384–399.

Rucklidge, J.J., & Tannock, R. (2001). Psychiatric, psychosocial, and cognitive functioning of female adolescents with ADHD. *Journal of the American Academy of Child and Adolescent Psychiatry,* 40, pp. 530–540.

Rueter, M.A., Scaramella, L., Wallace, L.E., & Conger, R.D. (1999). First onset of depressive or anxiety disorders predicted by the longitudinal course of internalizing symptoms and parent-adolescent disagreements. *Archives of General Psychiatry,* 56, pp. 726–732.

Ruitenberg, A., Ott, AL, van Swieten, J.C., Hofman, A., & Breteler, M.M.B. (2001). Incidence of dementia: Does gender make a difference? *Neurobiology of Aging,* 22, pp. 575–580.

Ruscio, A.M., Borkovec, T.D., & Ruscio, J. (2001). A taxometric investigation of the latent structure of worry. *Journal of Abnormal Psychology,* 110, pp. 413–422.

Russel, C.J. & Keel, P.K. (2002). Homosexuality as a specific risk factor for eating disorders in men. *International Journal of Eating Disorders,* 31, pp. 300–306.

Russell, D.E.H. (1984). *Sexual Exploitation: Rape, Child Sexual Abuse, and Workplace Harassment.* Beverly Hills, CA: Sage.

Russell, G.F.M. (1979). Bulimia nervosa: An ominous variant of anorexia nervosa. *Psychological Medicine,* 9, pp. 429–448.

Russell, G.F.M., Szmukler, G.I., Dare, C., & Eisler, I. (1987). An evaluation of family therapy in anorexia nervosa and bulimia nervosa. *Archives of General Psychiatry,* 44, pp. 1047–1056.

Rutherford, J., McGuffin, P., Katz, R.J., & Murray, R.M. (1993). Genetic influences on eating attitudes in a normal female twin population. *Psychological Medicine,* 23, pp. 425–436.

Rutter, M. (1970). Autistic children: Infancy to adulthood. *Seminars in Psychiatry,* 2, pp. 435–450.

Rutter, M. (1983). Introduction: Concepts of brain dysfunction syndromes. In M. Rutter (Ed.), *Developmental Neuropsychiatry,* pp. 1–14. New York: Guilford Press.

Rutter, M. (1989). Isle of Wight revisited: Twenty-five years of child psychiatric epidemiology. *Journal of the American Academy of Child & Adolescent Psychiatry,* 28, pp. 633–653.

Rutter, M. (1996). Autism research: Prospects and priorities. *Journal of Autism and Developmental Disorders,* 26, pp. 257–275.

Rutter, M. (2005). Incidence of autism spectrum disorders: Changes over time and their meaning. *ACTA Paediatrica,* 94(1), pp. 2–15.

Rutter, M., & Rutter, M. (1993). *Developing Minds.* New York: Basic Books.

Rutter, M., Greenfield, D., & Lockyer, L. (1967). A five- to fifteen-year follow-up study of infantile psychosis. II. Social and behavioral outcome. *British Journal of Psychiatry,* 113, pp. 1187–1199.

Rutter, M., Pickles, A., Murray, R., & Eaves, L. (2001). Testing hypotheses on specific environmental causal effects on behavior. *Psychological Bulletin,* 127, pp. 291–324.

Rutter, M., Silberg, J., O'Connor, T., & Simonoff, E. (1998). Genetics and child psychiatry. II Empirical research findings. *Journal of Child Psychology and Psychiatry,* 40, pp. 19–55.

Rutter, M.L. (1981). *Maternal Deprivation Reassessed,* 2nd ed. London: Penguin.

Rutter, M.L. (1997). Nature-nurture integration: The example of antisocial behavior. *American Psychologist,* 52, pp. 390–398.

Ryan, C.S. (1996). Battered children who kill: Developing an appropriate legal response. *Notre Dame Journal of Law, Ethics, and Public Policy,* 10, pp. 301–339.

Ryff, C.D., Kwan, C.M.L., & Singer, B.H. (2001). Personality and aging: Flourishing agendas and future challenges. In J.E. Birren & K.W. Schaie (Eds.), *Handbook of the Psychology of Aging,* 5th ed., pp. 477–499. San Diego: Academic Press.

Saavedra, J.E., Messich, J.E., Salloum, I.M., & Kirisci, L. (2001). Predictive validity of the physical disorders axis of the DSM multiaxial diagnostic system. *Journal of Nervous and Mental Disease,* 189, pp. 435–441.

Sacks, O. (1985). *The Man Who Mistook His Wife for a Hat and Other Clinical Tales.* New York: Summit.

Safer, D.J., Zito, J.M., & Fine, E. (1996). Increased methylphenidate usage for attention deficit disorder in the 1990s. *Pediatrics,* 98, pp. 1084–1088.

Saffran, E.M. (2000). Aphasia and the relationship of language and brain. *Seminars in Neurology,* 20, pp. 409–418.

Salekin, R.T. (2002). Psychopathy and therapeutic pessimism Clinical lore or clinical reality? *Clinical Psychology Review,* 22, pp. 79–112.

Salkovskis, P.M. (1999). Understanding and treating obsessive-compulsive disorder. *Behaviour Research and Therapy,* 37 (suppl.), pp. 29–52.

Salkovskis, P.M., & Harrison, J. (1984). Abnormal and normal obsessions—A replication. *Behaviour Research and Therapy,* 22, pp. 549–552.

Salthouse, T.A. (1999). Pressing issues in cognitive aging. In N. Schwarz and D.C. Park (Eds.), *Cognition, Aging, and Self-Reports,* pp. 185–198. Hove, England: Psychology Press/Erlbaum.

Salthouse, T.A. (2004). What and when of cognitive aging. *Current Directions in Psychological Science,* 13, pp. 140–144.

Samuels, J., Eaton, W.W., Bienvenu, O.J., Brown, C., Costa, P.T., & Nestadt, G. (2002). Prevalence and correlates of personality disorders in a community sample. *British Journal of Psychiatry,* 180, pp. 536–542.

Sanderlin, T.K. (2001). Anger management counseling with the antisocial personality. *Annals of the American Psychotherapy Association,* 4, pp. 9–11.

Sanders, M.R., Montgomery, D.T., & Brechman-Toussaint, M.L. (2000), The mass media and the prevention of child behavior problems: The evaluation of a television series to promote better child and parenting outcomes. *Journal of Child Psychology and Psychiatry,* 41, pp. 939–948.

Sanderson, W.C., & McGinn, L.K. (2001). Cognitive-behavioral therapy of depression. In M.M. Weissman (Ed.), *Treatment of Depression: Bridging the 21st Century,* pp. 249–279. Washington, D.C.: American Psychiatric Press.

Sanderson, W.C., Rapee, R.M., & Barlow, D.H. (1989). The influence of an illusion of control on panic attacks induced via inhalation of 5.5% carbon dioxide-enriched air. *Archives of General Psychiatry,* 46, pp. 157–162.

Sapolsky, R. (2003). Taming stress. *Scientific American,* 286, pp. 86–95.

Sapolsky, R.M. (1992). Neuroendocrinology of the stress response. In J.B. Becker, S.M. Breedlove, & D. Crews (Eds.), *Behavioral Endocrinology,* pp. 288–324. Cambridge, MA: MIT Press.

Sartor, C.E., & Youniss, J. (2002). The relationship between positive parental involvement and identity achievement during adolescence. *Adolescence,* 37, pp. 221–234.

Sartorius, N., Kaelber, C.T., Cooper, J.E., Roper, M.T., Rae, D.S., Gulbinat, W., Ustun, B., & Regier, D.A. (1993). Progress toward achieving a common language in psychiatry: Results from the field trial of the clinical guidelines accompanying the WHO classification of mental and behavioral disorders in ICD-10. *Archives of General Psychiatry,* 50, pp. 115–124.

Sayer, N.A., Sackeim, H.A., Moeller, J.R., Prudic, J., Devanand, D.P., Coleman, E.A., & Kiersky, J.E. (1993). The relations between observer-rating and self-report of depressive symptomatology. *Psychological Assessment,* 5, pp. 350–360.

Sayette, M.A. (1999b). Does drinking reduce Stress? *Alcohol Research and Health,* 23, pp. 250–255.

Sayette, M.A., Shiffman, S., Tiffany, S.T., Niaura, R.S., Martin, C.S., & Shadel, W.G. (2000). The measurement of drug craving. *Addiction,* 95 (supplement 2), pp. S189–S210.

Sbarra, D.S. & Emery, R.E. (2005). The emotional sequelae of non-marital relationship dissolution: Descriptive evidence from a 28-day prospective study. *Personal Relationships,* 12, pp. 213–232.

Scarr, S., & McCartney, K. (1983). How people make their own environments: A theory of genotype-environment effects. *Child Development,* 54, pp. 424–435.

Scepkowski, L.A., Wiegel, M., Bach, A.K., Weisberg, R.B., Brown, T.A., & Barlow, D.H. (2004). Attributions for sexual situations in men with and without erectile disorder: Evidence from a sex-specific attributional style measure. *Archives of Sexual Behavior,* 33, pp. 559–569.

Schachar, R., & Tannock, R. (2002). Syndromes of hyperactivity and attention deficit. In M. Rutter & E. Taylor (Eds.), *Child and Adolescent Psychiatry,* 4th ed., pp. 399–418. Oxford, UK: Blackwell.

Schacter, D.L. (1987). Implicit memory: History and current status. *Journal of Experimental Psychology: Learning, Memory, and Cognition,* 13, pp. 501–518.

Schaeffer, C.M. & Borduin, C.M. (2005). Long-term follow-up to a randomized clinical trial of multisystemic therapy with serious and violent juvenile offenders. *Journal of Consulting and Clinical Psychology*, 73, pp. 445–453.

Scharko, A.M. (2004). Selective serotonin reuptake inhibitor-induced sexual dysfunction in adolescents: A review. *Journal of the American Academy of Child & Adolescent Psychiatry*, 43, pp. 1071–1079.

Schatzberg, A.F. (1999). Antidepressant effectiveness in severe depression and melancholia. *Journal of Clinical Psychiatry*, 60, pp. 14–22.

Scheel, K.R. (2000). The empirical basis of dialectical behavior therapy: Summary, critique, and implications. *Clinical Psychology Science and Practice*, 7, pp. 68–86.

Scheerenberger, R.C. (1982). Public residential services, 1981: Status and trends. *Mental Retardation*, 20, pp. 210–215.

Schell, T.L., Marshall, G.N., & Jaycox, L.H. (2004). All symptoms are not created equal: The prominent role of hyperarousal in the natural course of posttraumatic psychological distress. *Journal of Abnormal Psychology*, 113, pp. 189–197.

Schiavi, R.C., & Segraves, R.T. (1995). The biology of sexual function. *Psychiatric Clinics of North America*, 18, pp. 7–23.

Schiavi, R.C., Stimmel, B.B., Mandeli, J., & White, D. (1995). Chronic alcoholism and male sexual function. *American Journal of Psychiatry*, p.152.

Schiff, M., Duyme, M., Dumaret, A., & Tomkiewicz, S. (1982). How much could we boost scholastic achievement and IQ scores? A direct answer from a French adoption study. *Cognition*, 12, pp. 165–196.

Schiffman, J., Abrahamson, A., Cannon, T., LaBrie, J., Parnas, J., Schulsinger, F., & Mednick, S. (2001). Early rearing factors in schizophrenia. *International Journal of Mental Health*, 30, pp. 3–16.

Schiller, J.S., Martinez, M., Hao, C., Barnes, P. Early release of selected estimates based on data from the January–September 2004 National Health Interview Survey. National Center for Health Statistics. http://www.cdc.gov/nchs/nhis.htm, March 2005.

Schmitt, D.P. (2004). Evaluating evidence of psychological adaptation: How do we know one when we see one? *Psychological Science*, 15, pp. 643–651.

Schneider, J.P., & Irons, R. (1996). Differential diagnosis of addictive sexual disorders using the DSM-IV. *Sexual Addiction and Compulsivity*, 3, pp. 7–21.

Schneiderman, N., Chesney, M.A., & Krantz, D.S. (1989). Biobehavioral aspects of cardiovascular disease: Progress and prospects. *Health Psychology*, 8, pp. 649–676.

Schneiderman, N., Ironson, G., & Siegel, S.D. (2004). Stress and health: Psychological, behavioral, and biological determinants. *Annual Review of Clinical Psychology*, 1, pp. 19.1–19.22.

Schneidman, E.S. (1996). *The Suicidal Mind*. New York: Oxford University Press.

Schneller, J. (1988). Terror on the A-train: Anatomy of a panic attack. *Mademoiselle*, 94, pp. 148–159.

Schooler, N.R., Keith, S.J., Severe, J.B. et al. (1997). Relapse and rehospitalization during maintenance treatment of schizophrenia: The effects of dose reduction and family treatment. *Archives of General Psychiatry*, 54, pp. 453–463.

Schopler, E.M., Andrews, C.E., & Strupp, K. (1979). Do autistic children come from upper-middle-class parents? *Journal of Autism and Developmental Disorders*, 9, pp. 139–152.

Schopp, R.F., Sturgis, B.J., & Sullivan, M. (1994). Battered woman syndrome, expert testimony, and the distinction between justification and excuse. *University of Illinois Law Review*, 54, pp. 45–113.

Schott, R.L. (1995). The childhood and family dynamics of tranvestites. *Archives of Sexual Behavior*, 24, pp. 309–328.

Schotti, J.R., Evans, I.M., Meyer, L.H., & Walker, P. (1991). A meta-analysis of intervention research with problem behavior: Treatment validity and standards of practice. *American Journal on Mental Retardation*, 96, pp. 233–256.

Schreibman, L. (1988). *Autism*. Beverly Hills, CA: Sage.

Schuckit, J.A., & Monteiro, J.G. (1988). Alcoholism, anxiety and depression. *British Journal of Addiction*, 83, pp. 1373–1380.

Schuckit, M. (1998). *Educating Yourself About alcohol and Drugs: A People's Primer*. New York: Plenum.

Schuckit, M. (1999). *Drug and Alcohol Abuse*. Norwell, MA: Kluwer.

Schuckit, M., & Smith, T.L. (1997). Assessing the risk for alcoholism among sons of alcoholics. *Journal of Studies on Alcohol*, 58, pp. 141–145.

Schuckit, M.A. (2000). *Drug and Alcohol Abuse: A Clinical Guide to Diagnosis and Treatment* (5th edition). New York: Kluwer Academic/Plenum.

Schuckit, M.A., Daeppen, J., Danko, G.P. Tripp, M.L., Smith, T.L., Li, T.K., Hesselbrock, V.M., & Bucholz, K.K. (1998a). Clinical implications for four drugs of the DSM-IV distinction between substance dependence with and without a physiological component. *American Journal of Psychiatry*, 156, pp. 41–49.

Schuckit, M.A., Smith, T.L., Daeppen, J., Eng, M., Li, T.K., Hesselbrock, V.M., Nurnberger, J.I., & Bucholz, K.K. (1998b). Clinical relevance of the distinction between alcohol dependence with and without a physiological component. *American Journal of Psychiatry*, 155, pp. 733–740.

Schuckit, M.A., Smith, T.L., Danko, G.P., Reich, T., Bucholz, K.K., & Bierut, L.J. (2002). Similarities in the clinical characteristics related to alcohol dependence in two populations. *American Journal on Addictions*, 11, pp. 1–9.

Schuepbach, W.M.M., Adler., R.H., Sabbioni, M.E.E. (2002). Accuracy of clinical diagnosis of psychogenic disorders' in the presence of physical symptoms suggesting a general medical condition: A 5-year follow-up in 162 patients. *Psychotherapy and Psychosomatics*, 71, pp. 11–17.

Schulberg, H.C., Katon, W.J., Simon, G.E., & Rush, A.J. (1999). Best clinical practice: Guidelines for managing major depression in primary medical care. *Journal of Clinical Psychiatry*, 60 (suppl 7), pp. 19–26.

Schuyler, D. (1991). *A Practical Guide to Cognitive Therapy*. New York: Norton.

Schwartz, C.E., Covino, N., Morgenstaler, A., & DeWolf, W. (2000). Quality of life after penile prosthesis placed at radical prostatectomy. *Psychology & Health*, 15, pp. 651–661.

Schwartz, C.E., Snidman, N., & Kagan, J. (1999). Adolescent social anxiety as an outcome of inhibited temperament in childhood. *Journal of the American Academy of Child and Adolescent Psychiatry*, 38, pp. 1008–1015.

Schwartz, G.E. (1989). Dysregulation theory and disease: Toward a general model for psychosomatic medicine. In S. Cheren (Ed.), *Psychosomatic Medicine: Theory, Physiology, and Practice*, vol. 1, pp. 91–118. Madison, CT: International Universities Press.

Scott, S. (2002). Parent training programs. In M. Rutter & E. Taylor (Eds.), *Child and Adolescent Psychiatry*, 4th ed., pp. 949–967. Oxford, UK: Blackwell.

Scroppo, J.C., Drob, S.L., Weinberger, J.L., & Eagle, P. (1998). Identifying dissociative identity disorder: A self-report and projective study. *Journal of Abnormal Psychology*, 107, pp. 272–284.

Scurfield, R.M. (1985). Posttrauma stress assessment and treatment: Overview and formulations. In C.R.

Figley (Ed.), *Trauma and Its Wake*, pp. 219–259. New York: Brunner/Mazel.

Searles, J.S. (1988). The role of genetics in the pathogenesis of alcoholism. *Journal of Abnormal Psychology*, 97, pp. 153–167.

Searles, J.S. (1990). Methodological limitations of research on the genetics of alcoholism. In C.R. Cloninger & H. Begleiter (Eds.), *Genetics and Biology of Alcoholism*, pp. 89–100. Cold Spring Harbor, NY: Cold Spring Harbor Laboratory Press.

Sechrest, L., Stickle, T.R., & Stewart, M. (1998). The role of assessment in clinical psychology. In A. Bellack, Hersen, & Reynolds, C.R. (Eds.), *Comprehensive Clinical Psychology: Vol. 4. Assessment*, pp. 2–28. New York: Pergamon.

Seeman, P. (2002). Atypical antipsychotics: Mechanisms of action. *Canadian Journal of Psychiatry*, 47, pp. 27–38.

Segal, D.L. (1997). Structured interviewing and DSM classification. In S.M. Turner and M. Hersen (Eds.), *Adult Psychopathology and Diagnosis*, 3rd ed., pp. 24–57. New York: Wiley.

Segerstrom, S.C. & Miller, G.E. (2004). Psychological stress and the human immune system: A meta-analytic study of 30 years of inquiry. *Psychological Bulletin*, 130, pp. 601–630.

Segraves, R.T., & Blindt, Segraves, K. (2001). Female sexual disorders. In N.L. Stotland and D.E. Stewart (Eds.), *Psychological Aspects of Women's Health Care: The Interface Between Psychiatry and Obstetrics and Gynecology*, 2nd ed., pp. 379–400. Washington, D.C.: American Psychiatric Press.

Segraves, T., & Althof, S. (2002). Psychotherapy and pharmacotherapy for sexual dysfunctions. In P.E. Nathan and J.M. Gorman (Eds.), *A Guide to Treatments That Work*, 2nd ed., pp. 497–524. London, England: Oxford University Press.

Segrin, C., & Abramson, L.Y. (1994). Negative reactions to depressive behaviors: A communication theories analysis. *Journal of Abnormal Psychology*, 103, pp. 655–668.

Seidman, B.T., Marshall, W.L., Hudson, S.M., & Robertson, P.J. (1994). An examination of intimacy and loneliness in sex offenders. *Journal of Interpersonal Violence*, 9, pp. 518–534.

Seivewright, H., Tyrer, P., & Johnson, T. (2002). Change in personality status in neurotic disorders. *Lancet*, 359, pp. 2253–2254.

Self, D., & Tamminga, C.A. (2004). Drug dependence and addiction: Neural substrates. *American Journal of Psychiatry*, 161, p. 223.

Selfe, L. (1977). *Nadia: A Case of Extraordinary Drawing Ability in an Autistic Child*. London: Academic Press.

Seligman, M.E. (1996). *The Optimistic Child: A Proven Program to Safeguard Children Against Depression and Build Lifelong Resistance*. New York: Harper Collins.

Seligman, M.P. (1995). *What You Can Change, and What You Can't: The Complete Guide to Successful Self-Improvement*. Fawcett Books.

Selye, H. (1956). *The Stress of Life*. New York: McGraw-Hill.

Serdula, M.K., Collins, M.E., Williamson, D.F., Anda, R.F., Pamuk, E.R., & Byers, T.E. (1993). Weight control practices of U.S. adolescents and adults. *Annals of Internal Medicine*, 119, pp. 667–671.

Seto, M.C., & Barbaree, H.E. (2000). Paraphilias. In V.B. Van Hasselt and M. Horsen (Eds.). *Aggression and Violence: An Introductory text*. Boston: Allyn and Bacon.

Seyfried, L.S., & Marcus, S.M. (2003). Postpartum mood disorders. *International Review of Psychiatry*, 15, pp. 231–242.

Shadish, W.R., & Baldwin, S.A. (2005). Effects of behavioral marital therapy: A meta-analysis of randomized controlled trials. *Journal of Consulting and Clinical Psychology*, 73, pp. 6–14.

Shadish, W.R., Matt, G.E., Navarro, A.N., & Phillips, G. (2000). The effects of psychological therapies under clinically representative conditions: A meta-analysis. *Psychological Bulletin, 126*, pp. 512–529.

Shaffer, D., & Gutstein, J. (2002). Suicide and attempted suicide. In M. Rutter & E. Taylor (Eds.), *Child and Adolescent Psychiatry*, 4th ed., pp. 529–554. Oxford, UK: Blackwell.

Shaffer, H.J., Hall, M.N., & Bilt, J.V. (1999). Estimating the prevalence of disordered gambling behavior in the United States and Canada: A research synthesis. *American Journal of Public Health, 89*, pp. 1369–1376.

Shahinfar, A., Kupersmidt, J.B., & Matza, L.S. (2001). The relation between exposure to violence and social information processing among incarcerated adolescents. *Journal of Abnormal Psychology, 110*, pp. 136–141.

Shakib, S., Mouttapa, M., Johnson, C. A., Ritt-Olson, A., Trinidad, D. R., Gallaher, P.E., et al. (2003). Ethnic variation in parenting characteristics and adolescent smoking. *Journal of Adolescent Health, 33*, pp. 88–97.

Shalev, A., & Munitz, H. (1986). Conversion without hysteria: A case report and review of the literature. *British Journal of Psychiatry, 148*, pp. 198–203.

Shalev, A.Y. (1996). Stress versus traumatic stress: From acute homeostatic reactions to chronic psychopathology. In B.A. van der Kolk, A.C. McFarlane, & L. Weisaeth (Eds.), *Traumatic Stress*, pp. 77–101. New York: Guilford.

Shalev, A.Y. (In press). Historical concepts and present patterns: Stress management and debriefing. In J.P. Wilson & B. Raphael (Eds.), *Stress Debriefing: Theory, Practice, and Challenge*. Cambridge, England: Cambridge University Press.

Shalev, A.Y., Peri, T., Caneti, L., & Schreiber, S. (1996). Predictors of PTSD in injured trauma survivors. *American Journal of Psychiatry, 53*, pp. 219–224.

Shankman, S.A., & Klein, D.N. (2003). The relation between depression and anxiety: An evaluation of the tripartite, approach-withdrawal and valence-arousal models. *Clinical Psychology Review, 23*, pp. 605–637.

Shapiro, D. (1965). *Neurotic Styles*. New York: Basic Books.

Shapiro, F. (1995). *Eye Movement Desensitization and Reprocessing*. New York: Guilford.

Sharpe, L. (2002). A reformulated cognitive-behavioral model of problem gambling: A biopsychosocial perspective. *Clinical Psychology Review, 22*, pp. 1–25.

Shatte, A.J., Reivich, K., Gillham, J.E., & Seligman, M.E.P. (1999). Learned optimism in children. In C.R. Snyder (Ed.), *Coping: The Psychology of What Works*, pp. 165–181. New York: Oxford University Press.

Shavelson, L. (2001). *Hooked: Five Addicts Challenge Our Misguided Drug Rehab System*. New York: New Press.

Shaw, D.S., & Bell, R.Q. (1993). Developmental theories of parental contributors to antisocial behavior. *Journal of Abnormal Child Psychology, 21*, pp. 493–518.

Shaw, D.S., & Vondra, J.I. (1995). Infant attachment security and maternal predictors of early behavior problems: A longitudinal study of low-income families. *Journal of Abnormal Child Psychology, 23*, pp. 335–357.

Shaw, D.S., Keenan, K., & Vondra, J.I. (1994). Developmental precursors of externalizing behavior: Ages 1 to 3. *Developmental Psychology, 30*, pp. 355–364.

Shaw, D.S., Vondra, J.I., Hommerding, K.D., Keenan K., & Dunn, M. (1994). Chronic family adversity and early child behavior problems: A longitudinal study of low income families. *Journal of Child Psychology and Psychiatry, 35*, pp. 1109–1122.

Shaw, D.S., Winslow, E.B., Owens, E.B., Vondra, J.I., Cohn, J.F., & Bell, R.Q. (1997). The development of early externalizing problems among children from low-income families: A transformational perspective. *Journal of Abnormal Child Psychology, 26*, pp. 95–107.

Shear, M.K. (1996). Factors in the etiology and pathogenesis of panic disorder: Revisiting the attachment-separation paradigm. *American Journal of Psychiatry, 153* (festschrift suppl.), pp. 125–135.

Shearer, D.E., & Shearer, M.S. (1976). The Portage Project: A model for early childhood intervention. In T.D. Tjossem (Ed.), *Intervention Strategies for High Risk Infants and Young Children*. Baltimore: University Park Press.

Shedler, J., Mayman, M., & Manis, M. (1993). The illusion of mental health. *American Psychologist, 48*, pp. 1117–1131.

Sheffield, A. (1998). *How You Can Survive When They're Depressed: Living and Coping with Depression Fallout*. New York: Three Rivers Press.

Shen, W.W. (1999). A history of antipsychotic drug development. *Comprehensive Psychiatry, 40*, pp. 407–417.

Shenton, M.E. (1996). Temporal lobe structural abnormalities in schizophrenia: A selective review and presentation of new magnetic resonance findings. In S. Matthysse & D.L. Levy (Eds.), *Psychopathology: The Evolving Science of Mental Disorder*, pp. 51–99. New York: Cambridge University Press.

Sher, K.J. (1991). *Children of Alcoholics: A Critical Appraisal of Theory and Research*. Chicago: University of Chicago Press.

Sher, K.J. (1993). Children of alcoholics and the intergenerational transmission of alcoholism: A biopsychosocial perspective. In J.S. Baer, G.A. Marlatt, & R.J. McMahon (Eds.), *Addictive Behaviors Across the Life Span: Prevention, Treatment, and Policy Issues*. pp. 3–33. Newbury Park, CA: Sage.

Sher, K.J., & Gotham, H.J. (1999). Pathological alcohol involvement: A developmental disorder of young adulthood. *Development and Psychopathology, 11*, pp. 933–956.

Sher, K.J., Grekin, E.R., & Williams, N.A. (2005). The development of alcohol use disorders. *Annual Review of Clinical Psychology, 1*, pp. 493–523.

Shiffman, S., Paty, J.A., Gnys, M., Kassel, J.A., et al. (1996). *Journal of Consulting and Clinical Psychology, 64*, pp. 366–379.

Shirk, S.R., & Karver, M. (2003). Prediction of treatment outcome from relationship variable in child and adolescent therapy: A meta-analytic review. *Journal of Consulting and Clinical Psychology, 71*(3), pp. 452–464.

Short, A.B., & Schopler, E. (1988). Factors relating to age of onset in autism. *Journal of Autism and Developmental Disorders, 18*, pp. 207–216.

Shorter, E. (1992). *From Paralysis to Fatigue: A History of Psychosomatic Illness in the Modern Era*. New York: Free Press.

Shorter, E., & Tyrer, P. (2003). Separation of anxiety and depressive disorders: Blind alley in psychopharmacology and classification of disease. *British Medical Journal, 327*, pp. 158–160.

Shoulson, I. (1990). Huntington's disease: Cognitive and psychiatric features. *Neuropsychiatry, Neuropsychology, and Behavioral Neurology, 3*, pp. 15–22.

Showalter, E. (1997). *Hystories: Hysterical Epidemics and Modern Medicine*. New York: Columbia University Press.

Sickmund, M., Snyder, H., and Poe-Yamagata, E. (1997). *Juvenile Offenders and Victims: 1997 Update on Violence*. Washington, DC: Office of Juvenile Justice and Delinquency Prevention.

Siegel, J.M., & Kuykendall, D.H. (1990). Loss, widowhood, and psychological distress among the elderly. *Journal of Consulting and Clinical Psychology, 58*, pp. 519–524.

Siegel, S. (2001). Pavlovian conditioning and drug overdose: When tolerance fails. *Addiction Research and Theory, 9*, pp. 503–513.

Siever, L.J., Bernstein, D.P., & Silverman, J.M. (1995). Schizotypal personality disorder. In W.J. Livesley, (Ed.), *The DSM-IV Personality Disorders*, pp. 71–90. New York: Guilford.

Sigvardsson, S., Bohman, M., & Cloninger, C.R. (1996). Replication of the Stockholm adoption study of alcoholism: Confirmatory cross-fostering analysis. *Archives of General Psychiatry, 53*, pp. 681–687.

Silverman, W.K., & Dick-Niederhauser, A. (2004). Separation anxiety disorder. In T.L. Morris & J.S. March (Eds.), *Anxiety Disorders in Children and Adolescents*, 2nd ed., pp. 164–188. New York: Guilford.

Silverman, W.K., et al. (1999). Contingency management, self-control, and education support in the treatment of childhood phobic disorders. A randomized clinical trial. *Journal of Consulting and Clinical Psychology, 67*, pp. 675–687.

Simard, M., van Reekum, R., & Cohen, T. (2000). A review of the cognitive and behavioral symptoms in dementia with Lewy bodies. *Journal of Neuropsychiatry and Clinical Neuroscience, 12*, pp. 425–450.

Simon, G.E. (2002). Management of somatoform and factitious disorders. In P.E. Nathan & J.M. Gorman (Eds.), *A Guide to Treatments That Work*, 2nd ed., pp. 447–461. New York: Oxford.

Singer, H.S., & Loiselle, C. (2003). PANDAS: A commentary. *Journal of Psychosomatic Research, 55*, pp. 31–39.

Singer, M.T., & Lalich, J. (1996). *"Crazy" therapies*. San Francisco: Jossey-Bass.

Singh, N.N., Guernsey, T.F., & Ellis, C.R. (1992). Drug therapy for persons with developmental disabilities: Legislation and litigation. *Clinical Psychology Review, 12*, pp. 665–679.

Sitskoom, M.M., Aleman, A., Ebisch, S.J.H., Appels, M.C.M., & Kahn, R.S. (2004). Cognitive deficits in relatives of patients with schizophrenia: A meta-analysis. *Schizophrenia Research, 71*, pp. 285–295.

Sizemore, C.C. (1989). *A Mind of Her Own*. New York: Morrow.

Sizemore, C.C., & Pittillo, E.S. (1977). *I'm Eve!* New York: Doubleday.

Skilling, T.A., Harris, G.T., Rice, M.E., & Quinsey, V.L. (2002). Identifying persistently antisocial offenders using the Hare Psychopathy Checklist and DSM antisocial personality disorder criteria. *Psychological Assessment, 14*, pp. 27–38.

Skodak, M., & Skeels, H. (1949). A final follow-up study of one hundred adopted children. *Journal of Genetic Psychology, 75*, pp. 85–125.

Skodol, A.E., & Bender, D.S. (2003). Why are women diagnosed borderline more than men? *Psychiatric Quarterly, 74*, pp. 349–360.

Skodol, A.E., Dohrenwend, B.P., Link, B.G., & Shrout, P.E. (1990). The nature of stress: Problems of measurement. In J.D. Noshpit & K.D. Coddington (Eds.), *Stressors and the Adjustment Disorders*, pp. 3–20. New York: Wiley.

Skodol, A.E., Siever, L.J., Livesley, W.J., Gunderson, J.G., Pfohl, B., & Widiger, T.A. (2002). The borderline diagnosis II: Biology, genetics, and clinical course. *Biological Psychiatry, 51*, pp. 951–963.

Skoog, G., & Skoog, I. (1999). A 40-year follow-up of patients with obsessive-compulsive disorder. *Archives of General Psychiatry, 56*, pp. 121–127.

Skre, I., Onstad, S.I., Edvardsen, J., Torgersen, S., & Kringlen, E. (1994). A family study of anxiety disorders: Familial transmission and relationship to mood disorder and psychoactive substance use disorder. *Acta Psychiatrica Scandinavica, 90*, pp. 366–374.

Slade, P.D., & Bentall, R.P. (1988). *Sensory Deception: A Scientific Analysis of Hallucination*. Baltimore: Johns Hopkins University Press.

Slade, P.D., & Russell, G.F.M. (1973). Awareness of body dimensions in anorexia nervosa and bulimia nervosa: Cross-sectional and longitudinal studies. *Psychological Medicine, 3*, pp. 188–199.

Slater, E. (1965). Diagnosis of hysteria. *British Medical Journal, 1*, pp. 1395–1399.

Sloan, D.M. & Marx, B.P. (2004). A closer examination of the structured written disclosure procedure. *Journal of Consulting and Clinical Psychology, 72*, pp. 165–175.

Slutske, W.S., Eisen, S., True, W.R., Lyons, M.J., Goldberg, J., & Tsuang, M. (2000). Common genetic vulnerability for pathological gambling and alcohol dependence in men. *Archives of General Psychiatry*, 57, pp. 666–673.

Slutske, W.S., Eisen, S., Xian, H., True, W.R., Lyons, M.J., Goldberg, J., & Tsuang, M. (2001). A twin study of the association between pathological gambling and antisocial personality disorder. *Journal of Abnormal Psychology*, 110, pp. 297–308.

Slutske, W.S., Heath, A.C., Madden, P.A.F., Bucholz, K.K., Statham, D.J., & Martin, N.G. (2002). Personality and the genetic risk for alcohol dependence. *Journal of Abnormal Psychology*, 111, pp. 124–133.

Small, S.A., Tsai, W.Y., DeLaPaz, R., Mayeux, R., & Stern, Y. (2002). Imaging hippocampal function across the human life span: Is memory decline normal or not? *Annals of Neurology*, 51, pp. 290–295.

Smalley, S.L., & Collins, F. (1996). Brief report: Genetic, prenatal, and immunologic factors. *Journal of Autism and Developmental Disorders*, 26, pp. 195–197.

Smalley, S.L., Asarnow, R.F., & Spence, M.A. (1988). Autism and genetics: A decade of research. *Archives of General Psychiatry*, 45, pp. 953–961.

Smetana, J.G. (1989). Adolescents' and parents' reasoning about actual family conflict. *Child Development*, 60, pp. 1052–1067.

Smith, A.L., & Weissman, M.M. (1992). Epidemiology. In E.S. Paykel (Ed.), *Handbook of Affective Disorders*, 2nd ed., pp. 111–130. New York: Guilford.

Smith, E. (1991). First person account: Living with schizophrenia. *Schizophrenia Bulletin*, 17, pp. 689–691.

Smith, G., & Hall, M. (1982). Evaluating Michigan's guilty but mentally ill verdict: An empirical study. *University of Michigan Journal of Law Reform*, 16, pp. 77–114.

Smith, G.R., Monson, R.A., & Ray, D.C. (1986). Psychiatric consultation in somatization disorder: A randomized controlled study. *New England Journal of Medicine*, 314, pp. 1407–1413.

Smith, G.T., Goldman, M.S., Greenbaum, P.E., & Christiansen, A. (1995). Expectancy for social facilitation from drinking: The divergent paths of high-expectancy and low-expectancy adolescents. *Journal of Abnormal Psychology*, 104, pp. 32–40.

Smith, R.C., Gardiner, J.C., Lyles, J.S., Sirbu, C., Dwamena, F.C., Hodges, A., Collins, C., Lein, C., Given, C.W., Given, B., & Goddeeris, J. (2005). Exploration of DSM-IV criteria in primary care patients with medically unexplained symptoms. *Psychosomatic Medicine*, 67, pp. 123–129.

Smith, S.R., & Meyer, R.G. (1985). Child abuse reporting laws and psychotherapy: A time for reconsideration. *International Journal of Law and Psychiatry*, 7, pp. 351–366.

Smith, T., Groen, AD., & Wynn, J.W. Randomized trial of intensive early intervention for children with pervasive developmental disorder. *American Journal of Mental Retardation*, 105, pp. 269–285.

Smith, T.W. & Ruiz, J.M. (2002). Psychosocial influences on the development and course of coronary heart disease: Current status and implications for research and practice. *Journal of Consulting and Clinical Psychology*, 70, pp. 548–568.

Smith, Y.L.S., van Goozen, S.H.M., & Cohen-Kettenis, P.T. (2001). Adolescents with gender identity disorder who were accepted or rejected for sex reassignment surgery: A prospective follow-up study. *Journal of the American Academy of Child and Adolescent Psychiatry*, 40, pp. 472–481.

Smith-Gamble, V., Baiyewu, O, Perkins, A.J., Gureje, O., Hall, K.S., Ogunniyi, A., Hui, S.L., & Hendrie, H.C. (2002). Informant reports of changes in personality predict dementia in a population-based study of elderly African Americans and Yoruba. *American Journal of Geriatric Psychiatry*, 10, pp. 724–732.

Smyth, J.M., Stone, A.A., Hurewitz, A., & Kaell, A. (1999). Effects of writing about stressful experiences on symptom reduction in patients with asthma or rheumatoid arthritis: A randomized trial. *Journal of the American Medical Association*, 281, pp. 1304–1309.

Snowden, J.S., Neary, D., & Mann, D.A. (2002). Frontotemporal dementia. *British Journal of Psychiatry*, 180, pp. 140–143.

Snowling, M.J. (2002). Reading and other learning difficulties. In M. Rutter & E. Taylor (Eds.), *Child and Adolescent Psychiatry*, 4th ed., pp. 682–696. Oxford, UK: Blackwell.

Snyder, C.R. (Ed.) (1999). *Coping: The Psychology of What Works*, pp. 182–204. New York: Oxford University Press.

Snyder, D.K. (1999). Affective reconstruction in the context of a pluralistic approach to couple therapy. *Clinical Psychology: Science and Practice*, 6, pp. 348–365.

Snyder, H.N. (September 2002). Juvenile arrests 2002. *Juvenile Justice Bulletin*, pp. 1–12.

Sobell, L.C., & Sobell, M.B. (2003). Using motivational interviewing techniques to talk with clients about their alcohol use. *Cognitive & Behavioral Practice*, 10, pp. 214–221.

Solomon, A. (2001). *The Noonday Demon: An Atlas of Depression*. New York: Scribner.

Solomon, K., Manepalli, J., Ireland, G.A., & Mahon, G.M. (1993). Alcoholism and prescription drug abuse in the elderly: St. Louis University grand rounds. *Journal of the American Geriatrics Society*, 41, pp. 57–69.

Somerfield, M.R., & McCrae, R.R. (2000). Stress and coping research: Methodological challenges, theoretical advances, and clinical applications. *American Psychologist*, 55, pp. 620–625.

Song, C., & Leonard, BE (2000). *Fundamentals of Psychoneuroimmunology*. New York: Wiley.

Sonino, N., & Fava, G.A. (2001). Psychiatric disorders associated with Cushing's syndrome: Epidemiology, pathophysiology and treatment. *Cns Drugs*, 15, pp. 361–373.

Souery, D., Oswald, P., Linkowski, P., & Mendlewicz, J. (2003). Molecular genetics in the analysis of suicide. *Annals of Medicine*, 35, pp. 191–196.

Souery, D., Rivelli, S.K., & Mendlewicz, J. (2001). Molecular genetic and family studies in affective disorders: State of the art. *Journal of Affective Disorders*, 62, pp. 45–55.

Southall, D.P., Plunkett, M.C., Banks, M.W., Falkov, A.F., & Samuels, M.P (1997). Covert video recordings of life-threatening child abuse: Lessons for child protection. *Pediatrics*, 100, pp. 735–774.

Spanos, N.P. (1994). Multiple identity enactments and multiple personality disorder: A sociocognitive perspective. *Psychological Bulletin*, 116, pp. 143–165.

Spanos, N.P., Weekes, J.R., & Bertrand, L.D. (1985). Multiple personality: A social psychological perspective. *Journal of Abnormal Psychology*, 94, pp. 362–376.

Spanos, N.P., Weekes, J.R., Menary, E., & Bertrand, L.D. (1986). Hypnotic interview and age regression procedures in the elicitation of multiple personality symptoms: A simulation study. *Psychiatry*, 49, pp. 298–311.

Spencer, T.J., Biederman, J., & Wilens, T. (1998). Pharmacotherapy of ADHD with antidepressants. In R.A. Barkley (Ed.), *Attention-Deficit/Hyperactivity Disorder*, 2nd ed., pp. 552–563. New York: Guilford.

Spiegel, D., & Cardena, E. (1991). Disintegrated experience: The dissociative disorders revisited. *Journal of Abnormal Psychology*, 100, pp. 366–378.

Spiegel, D.A., & Bruce, T.J. (1997). Benzodiazepines and exposure-based cognitive behavior therapies for panic disorder: Conclusions from combined treatment trials. *American Journal of Psychiatry*, 154, pp. 773–781.

Spitzer, R.L., First, M.B., Williams, J.B.W., Kendler, K., Pincus, H.A., & Tucker, G. (1992). Now is the time to retire the term "organic mental disorders." *American Journal of Psychiatry*, 149, pp. 240–244.

Sprague, R.L., & Sleator, E.K. (1977). Methlphenidate in hyperkinetic children: Differences in doses effects learning and social behavior. *Science*, 198, pp. 1274–1276.

Sramek, J.J., & Cutler, N.R. (1999). Recent developments in the drug treatment of Alzheimer's disease. *Drugs and Aging*, 14, pp. 359–373.

Sroufe, L.A., & Fleeson, J. (1986). Attachment and the construction of relationships. In W.W. Hartup & Z. Rubin (Eds.), *Relationships and Development*, pp. 51–72. Hillsdale, NJ: Erlbaum.

Stack, S. (2004). Emile Durkheim and altruistic suicide. *Archives of Suicide Research*, 8, pp. 9–22.

Stanton, A.L. et al. (2000). Emotional expressive coping predicts psychological and physical adjustment to breast cancer. *Journal of Consulting and Clinical Psychology*, 68, pp. 875–882.

Stanton, B., & David, A. (2000). First-person accounts of delusions. *Psychiatric Bulletin*, 24, pp. 333–336.

Starr, P. (1982). *The Social Transformation of American Medicine*. New York: Basic Books.

Stayton, W.R. (1996). Sexual and gender identity disorders in a relational perspective. In F.W. Kaslow (Ed.), *Handbook of Relational Diagnosis and Dysfunctional Family Patterns*, pp. 357–370. New York: Wiley.

Steadman, H. et al. (1993). *Before and After Hinckley. Evaluating Insanity Defense Reform*. New York: Guilford.

Steadman, H., Pantle, R., & Pasewark, S. (1983). Factors associated with a successful insanity defense. *American Journal of Psychiatry*, 140, pp. 401–405.

Steadman, H.J., Mulvey, E.P., Monahan, J., Robbins, P.C., Appelbaum, P.S., Grisso, T., Roth, L.H., & Silver, E. (1998). Violence by people discharged from acute psychiatric inpatient facilities and by others in the same neighborhoods. *Archives of General Psychiatry*, 55, pp. 393–401.

Steele, C.M., & Josephs, R.A. (1988). Drinking your troubles away. II. An attention-allocation model of alcohol's effect on psychological stress. *Journal of Abnormal Psychology*, 97, pp. 196–205.

Steele, C.M., & Josephs, R.A. (1990). Alcohol myopia: Its prized and dangerous effects. *American Psychologist*, 45, pp. 921–933.

Steffenburg, S., Gillberg, C., Hellgren, L., Andersson, L., Gillberg, I., Jakobsson, G., & Bohman, M. (1989). A twin study of autism in Denmark, Finland, Iceland, Norway and Sweden. *Journal of Child Psychology and Psychiatry*, 30, pp. 405–416.

Steggall, M.J., Gann, S.Y., & Chinegwundoh, F.I. (2004). Sexual dysfunction screening: The advantages of a culturally sensitive joint assessment clinic. *Sexual & Relationship Therapy*, 19, pp. 179–189.

Steiger, H., Gauvin, L., Jabalpurwala, S., Seguin, J.R., & Stotland, S. (1999) Hypersensitivity to social interactions in bulimic syndromes: Relationship to binge eating. *Journal of Consulting & Clinical Psychology*, 67, pp. 765–775.

Stein, D.J. (2000). Neurobiology of the obsessive-compulsive spectrum disorders. *Biological Psychiatry*, 47, pp. 296–304.

Stein, D.J., Westenberg, H.G.M., & Liebowitz, M.R. (2002). Social anxiety disorder and generalized anxiety disorder: Serotonergic and dopaminergic neurocircuitry. *Journal of Clinical Psychiatry*, 63 (suppl. 6), pp. 12–19.

Stein, L.I., & Santos, A.B. (1998). *Assertive Community Treatment of Persons with Severe Mental Illness*. New York: Norton.

Steinhausen, H. (1996). The course and outcome of anorexia nervosa. In K.D. Brownell & C.G. Fairburn (Eds.), *Eating Disorders and Obesity: A Comprehensive Handbook*, pp. 234–237. New York: Guilford.

Steketee, G. (1993). Social support and treatment outcome of obsessive-compulsive disorder at 9-month follow-up. *Behavioral Psychotherapy*, 21, pp. 81–95.

Stern, Y., Gurland, B., Tatemichi, T.K., et al. (1994). Influence of education and occupation on the incidence of Alzheimer's disease. *JAMA*, 271, pp. 1004–1010.

Stern, Y., Tang, M., Albert, M.S., Brandt, J., Jacobs, D.M., Bell, K., Marder, K., Sano, M., Devanand, D., Albert, S.M., Bylsma, F., & Tsai, W. (1997). Predicting time to nursing home care and death in individuals with Alzheimer disease. *Journal of the American Medical Association*, 277, pp. 806–812.

Stevens, S.E., Hynan, M.T., & Allen, M. (2000). A meta-analysis of common factor and specific treatment effects across the outcome domains of the phase model of psychotherapy. *Clinical Psychology: Science and Practice*, 7, pp. 273–290.

Stevens, V.J. et al. (2001). Long-Term Weight Loss and Changes in Blood Pressure: Results of the Trials of Hypertension Prevention, Phase II. *Annals of Internal Medicine*, 134, pp. 1–11.

Stewart, A.J., & Ostrove, J.M. (1998). Women's personality in middle age: Gender, history, and midcourse corrections. *American Psychologist*, 53, pp. 1185–1194.

Stewart, J.T. (1995). Management of behavior problems in the demented patient. *American Family Physician*, 52, pp. 231–240.

Stewart, S., & Podd, J. (2004). The placebo effect: Dissolving the expectancy versus conditioning debate. *Psychological Bulletin*, 130, pp. 324–340.

Stice, E. & Fairburn, C.G. (2003). Dietary and dietary-depressive subtypes of bulimia nervosa show differential symptom presentation, social impairment, comorbidity, and course of illness. *Journal of Consulting and Clinical Psychology*, 71, pp. 1090–1094.

Stice, E. (2001). A prospective test of the dual-pathway model of bulimic pathology: Mediating effects of dieting and negative affect. *Journal of Abnormal Psychology*, 110, pp. 124–135.

Stice, E. (2002). Risk and maintenance factors for eating pathology: A meta-analytic review. *Psychological Bulletin*, 128, pp. 825–848.

Stice, E., & Agras, W.S. (1999). Subtyping bulimic women along dietary restraint and negative affect dimensions. *Journal of Consulting & Clinical Psychology*, 67, pp. 460–469.

Stice, E., & Shaw, H. (2004). Eating disorder prevention programs: A meta-analytic review. *Psychological Bulletin*, 130, pp. 206–227.

Stice, E., Schupak-Neuberg, E., Shaw, H.E., & Stein, R.I. (1994). Relation of media exposure to eating disorder symptomatology: An examination of mediating mechanisms. *Journal of Abnormal Psychology*, 103, pp. 836–840.

Stice, E., Spangler, D., & Agras, W.S. (2001) Exposure to media-portrayed thin-ideal images adversely affects vulnerable girls: A longitudinal experiment. *Journal of Social & Clinical Psychology*, 20, pp. 270–288.

Still, G.F. (1902). The Coulstonian Lectures on some abnormal physical conditions in children. *Lancet*, 1, pp. 1008–1012, 1077–1082, 1163–1168.

Stirman, S.W., DeRubeis, R.J., Crits-Christoph, P., & Brody, P.E. (2003). Are samples in randomized controlled trials of psychotherapy representative of community outpatients? A new methodology and initial findings. *Journal of Consulting and Clinical Psychology*, 71, pp. 963–972.

Stockard, J., & O'Brien, R.M. (2002). Cohort effects on suicide rates: International variations. *American Sociological Review*, 67, pp. 854–872.

Stockmeier, C.A. (2003). Involvement of serotonin in depression: Evidence from postmortem and imaging studies of serotonin receptors and the serotonin transporter. *Journal of Psychiatric Research*, 37, pp. 357–373.

Stokols, D. (1992). Establishing and maintaining healthy environments: Toward a social ecology of health promotion. *American Psychologist*, 47, pp. 6–22.

Stoller, R.J. (1991). *Pain and Passion: A Psychoanalyst Explores the World of S & M*. New York: Plenum.

Stone, M.H. (1993). Long-term outcome in personality disorders. *British Journal of Psychiatry*, 162, pp. 299–313.

Stone, M.H. (2001). Natural history and long-term outcome. In W.J. Livesley (Ed.), *Handbook of Personality Disorders: Theory Research, and Treatment*, pp. 259–273. New York: Guilford.

Storandt, M., Grant, E.A., Miller, J.P., & Morris, J.C. (in press). Progression in mild cognitive impairment: A comparison of diagnostic criteria. *Journal of the American Medical Association*.

Stouthamer-Loeber, M., Loeber, R., Wei, E., Farrington, D.P., & Wilkstrom, P.H. (2002). Risk and promotive effects in the explanation of persistent serious delinquency in boys. *Journal of Consulting and Clinical Psychology*, 70(1), pp. 111–123.

Strauss, J.S., & Carpenter, W.T., Jr. (1981). *Schizophrenia*. New York: Plenum.

Strauss, J.S., & Carpenter, W.T. (1978). The prognosis of schizophrenia: Rationale for a multidimensional concept. *Schizophrenia Bulletin*, 4, pp. 56–67.

Striegel-Moore, R.H. (1995). A feminist perspective on the etiology of eating disorders. In K.D. Brownell & C.G. Fairburn (Eds.), *Eating Disorders and Obesity: A Comprehensive Handbook*, pp. 224–229. New York: Guilford.

Striegel-Moore, R.H., Silberstein, L.R., & Rodin, J. (1993). The social self in bulimia nervosa: Public self-consciousness, social anxiety, and perceived fraudulence. *Journal of Abnormal Psychology*, 102, pp. 297–303.

Striegel-Moore, RH., & Smolak, L. (2001). *Eating Disorders: Innovative Directions in Research and Practice*. Washington: American Psychological Association.

Strober, M. (1995). Family-genetic perspectives on anorexia nervosa and bulimia nervosa. In K.D. Brownell & C.G. Fairburn (Eds.), *Eating Disorders and Obesity: A Comprehensive Handbook*, pp. 212–218. New York: Guilford.

Strober, M., & Bulik, C.M. (2002). Genetic epidemiology of eating disorders. *Eating Disorders and Obesity*, 2nd ed., pp. 238–242. New York: Guilford.

Stroebe, M., Stroebe, W., Schut, H., Zech, E., & van den Bout, J. (2002). Does disclosure of emotions facilitate recovery from bereavement? Evidence from two prospective studies. *Journal of Consulting and Clinical Psychology*, 70, pp. 169–178.

Strunk, D.R., & DeRubeis, R.J. (2001). Cognitive therapy for depression: A review of its efficacy. *Journal of Cognitive Psychotherapy*, 15, pp. 289–297.

Substance Abuse and Mental Health Services Administration (1999). *Report of the 1998 National Household Survey on Drug Abuse*. www.samhsa.gov.

Sullivan, E.V., Lane, B., Deshmukh. A., Rosenbloom, M.J., Desmond, J.E., Lim, K.O., & Pfefferbaum, A. (1999). In vivo mammillary body volume deficits in amnesic and nonamnesic alcoholics. *Alcoholism: Clinical and Experimental Research*, 23, pp. 1629–1636.

Sullivan, K.T., & Bradbury, T.N. (1996). Preventing marital dysfunction: The primacy of secondary strategies. *Behavior Therapist*, 19, pp. 33–36.

Sullivan, P.F., Neale, M.C., & Kendler, K.S. (2000). Genetic epidemiology of major depression: Review and meta-analysis. *American Journal of Psychiatry*, 157, pp. 1552–1562.

Suomi, S.J., & Harlow, H.F. (1972). Social rehabilitation of isolate-reared monkeys. *Developmental Psychology*, 6, pp. 487–496.

Surgeon General, (2001). *Mental Health: Culture. Race, and Ethnicity*. Washington: Department of Health and Human Services.

Susser, E., Neugebauer, R., Hoek, H.W., Brown, A.S., et al. (1996). Schizophrenia after prenatal famine: Further evidence. *Archives of General Psychiatry*, 53, pp. 25–31.

Susser, E., Varma, V.K., Mattoo, S.K., Finnerty, M., Mojtabi, R., Tripathi, B.M., Mistra, A.K., & Wig, N.N. (1998). Long-term course of acute brief psychosis in a developing country setting. *British Journal of Psychiatry*, 173, pp. 226–230.

Sussman, N., & Ginsberg, D. (1998). Rethinking side effects of the selective serotonin reuptake inhibitors: Sexual dysfunction and weight gain. *Psychiatric Annals*, 28, pp. 89–97.

Sutker, P.B., Davis, J.M., Uddo, M., & Ditta, S.R. (1995). War zone stress, personal resources, and PTSD in Persian Gulf War returnees. *Journal of Abnormal Psychology*, 104, pp. 444–452.

Swaab, D.F., & Gofman, M.A. (1995). Sexual differentiation of the human hypothalamus in relation to gender and sexual orientation. *Trends in Neurosciences*, 18, pp. 264–270.

Swanson, H.L, Harris, K.R., & Graham S. (Eds.), *Handbook of Learning Disabilities*. New York: Guilford.

Swanson, J.M. et al. (2001). Clinical relevance of the primary findings of the MTA: Success rates based on severity of ADHD and ODD symptoms at the end of treatment. *Journal of the American Academy of Child and Adolescent Psychiatry*, 40, pp. 168–179.

Swanson, J.M., & Wigal, T. (2004). Self-perceptions of competence in children with ADHD and comparison children. *Journal of Consulting and Clinical Psychology*, 72(3), pp. 382–391.

Swartz, M.S. et al. (2001). Randomized controlled trial of outpatient commitment in North Carolina. *Psychiatric Services*, 52, pp. 325–329.

Swartz, M.S., Hughes, D., Blazer, D.G., & George, L.K. (1987). Somatization disorder in the community: A study of diagnostic concordance among three diagnostic systems. *Journal of Nervous and Mental Disorder*, 175, pp. 26–33.

Swedo, S.E., & Grant, P.J. (2005). Annotation: PANDAS: A model for human autoimmune disease. *Journal of Child Psychology & Psychiatry*, 46, pp. 227–234.

Swedo, S.E., Leonard, H.L., Garvey, M., Mittleman, B., Allen, A.J., Perlmutter, S., Dow, S., Zamkoff, J., Dubbert, B., & Lougee, L. (1998). Pediatric autoimmune neuropsychiatric disorders associated with streptococcal infections: Clinical description of the first 50 cases. *American Journal of Psychiatry*, 155, pp. 264–271.

Swendsen, J.D, & Merikangas, K.R. (2000). The comorbidity of depression and substance use disorders. *Clinical Psychology Review*, 20, pp. 173–189.

Swoboda, H., Amering, M., Windhaber, J., & Katschnig, H. (2003). The long-term course of panic disorder—an 11 year follow-up. *Journal of Anxiety Disorders*, 17, pp. 223–232.

Symonds, T., Roblin, D., Hart, K., & Althof, S. (2003). How does premature ejaculation impact a man's life? *Journal of Sex & Marital Therapy*, 29, pp. 361–370.

Szasz, T. (1963). *Law, Liberty, and Psychiatry: An Inquiry into the Social Uses of Mental Health Practices*. New York: Macmillan.

Szasz, T. (1970). *Ideology and Insanity: Essays on the Psychiatric Dehumanization of Man*. New York: Doubleday.

Szechtman, H. & Woody, E. (2004). Obsessive-compulsive disorder as a disturbance of security motivation. *Psychological Review*, 111, pp. 111–127.

Szechtman, H., & Woody, E. (2004). Obsessive-compulsive disorder as a disturbance of security motivation. *Psychological Review*, 111, pp. 111–127.

Tabakoff, B., & Hoffman, P.L. (1999). Neurobiology of alcohol. In M. Galanter & H.D. Kleber (Eds.), *Textbook of Substance Abuse Treatment*, 2nd ed., pp. 3–10. Washington, DC: American Psychiatric Press.

Tager-Flusberg, H. (1996). Current theory and research on language and communication in autism. *Journal of Autism and Developmental Disorders*, 26, pp. 169–171.

Tallal, P. (2003). Language learning disabilities: Integrating research approaches. *Current Directions in Psychological Science*, 12, pp. 206–211.

Tamminga, C.A. (1997). Gender and schizophrenia. *Journal of Clinical Psychiatry*, 58 (suppl. 15), pp. 33–37.

Tannock, R., Schachar, R., & Logan, G. (1995). Methylphenidate and cognitive flexibility: Dissociated dose effects in hyperactive children. *Journal of Abnormal Child Psychology*, 23, pp. 235–266.

Tardiff, K., Marzuk, P.M., & Leon, A.C. (2002). Role of antidepressants in murder and suicide. *American Journal of Psychiatry*, 159, pp. 1248–1249.

Tarrier, N., & Barrowclough, C. (1995). Family interventions in schizophrenia and their long-term outcomes. *International Journal of Mental Health*, 24, pp. 38–53.

Tarter, R.E., & Vanyukov, M.M. (2001). Theoretical and operational framework for research into the etiology of substance use disorders. *Journal of Child and Adolescent Substance Abuse*, 10, pp. 1–12.

Taschentke, T.M. (2001). Pharmacology and behavioral pharmacology of the mesocortical dopamine system. *Progress in Neurobiology*, 63, pp. 241–320.

Taylor, C.B., & Luce, K.H. (2003). Computer- and Internet-based psychotherapy interventions. *Current Directions in Psychological Science*, 12, pp. 18–22.

Taylor, E., & Rutter, M. (2002). Classification: Conceptual issues and substantive findings. In M. Rutter & E. Taylor (Eds.), *Child and Adolescent Psychiatry*, 4th ed., pp. 3–17. Oxford, UK: Blackwell.

Taylor, J., Iacono, W.G., & McGue, M. (2000). Evidence for a genetic etiology of early-onset delinquency. *Journal of Abnormal Psychology*, 109, pp. 634–643.

Taylor, R.L., Richards, S.B., & Brady, M.P. (2005). *Mental Retardation: Historical Perspectives, Current Practices, and Future Directions*. New York: Pearson Education.

Taylor, S.E. (1990). Health psychology: The science and the field. *American Psychologist*, 45, pp. 40–50.

Taylor, S.E. (1995). *Health Psychology*, 3rd ed. New York: McGraw-Hill.

Taylor, S.E., Klein, L.C., Lewis, B.P., Gruenewald, T.L., Gurung, R.A.R., & Updegraff, J.A. (2000). Biobehavioral responses to stress in females: Tend-and-befriend, not fight-or-flight. *Psychological Bulletin*, 107, pp. 411–429.

Taylor, S.E., Lerner, J.S., Sherman, D.K., Sage, R.M., & McDowell, N.K. (2003). Portrait of the self-enhancer: Well adjusted and well liked or maladjusted and friendless? *Journal of Personality & Social Psychology*, 84, pp. 165–176.

Tellegen, A. (1985). Structures of mood and personality and their relevance to assessing anxiety, with an emphasis on self-report. In A.H. Tuma & J.D. Maser (Eds.), *Anxiety and the Anxiety Disorders*, pp. 681–706. Hillsdale, NJ: Erlbaum.

Teplin, L.A., Abram, K.M., & McClelland, G.M. (1994). Does psychiatric disorder predict violent crime among released jail detainees? A six-year longitudinal study. *American Psychologist*, 49, pp. 335–342.

Teri, L., Gibbons, L.E., McCurry, S.M., Logsdon, R.G., Buchner, D.M., Barlow, W.E. Kukull, W.A., LaCroix, A.Z., McCormick, W., & Larson, E.B. (2003). Exercise plus behavioral management in patients with Alzheimer's disease: A randomized controlled trial. *Journal of the American Medical Association*, 290, pp. 2015–2022.

Tesman, J.R., & Hills, A. (1994). Developmental effects of lead exposure in children. *Social Policy Report: Society for Research in Child Development*, 8 (3), pp. 1–16.

Thaker, G.K. Carpenter W.T. (2001). Advances in schizophrenia. *Nature Medicine*, 7, pp. 667–71.

Thakker, J., & Ward, T. (1998). Culture and classification: The cross-cultural application of the DSM-IV. *Clinical Psychology Review*, 18, pp. 501–529.

Thapar, A., Gottesman, I.I., Owen, M.J., O'Donovan, M.C., & McGuffin, P. (1994). The genetics of mental retardation. *British Journal of Psychiatry*, 164, pp. 747–758.

Thase, M. (1988). The relationship between Down syndrome and Alzheimer's disease. In L. Nadel (Ed.), *The Psychobiology of Down Syndrome*. Cambridge, MA: MIT Press.

Thase, M.E. (2003). Achieving remission and managing relapse in depression. *Journal of Clinical Psychiatry*, 64 (suppl 118), pp. 3–7.

Thase, M.E., Ripu, J., & Howland, R.H. (2002). Biological aspects of depression. In I.H. Gotlib and C.L. Hammen (Eds.), *Handbook of Depression*. New York: Guilford.

Thigpen, C.H., & Cleckley, H.M. (1957). *The Three Faces of Eve*. New York: McGraw-Hill.

Thomas, A., & Chess, S. (1977). *Temperament and Development*. New York: Brunner/Mazel.

Thomas, J., Turkheimer, E., & Oltmanns, T.F. (2000). Psychometric analysis of racial differences on the Maudsley Obsessional Compulsive Inventory. *Assessment*, 7, pp. 247–258.

Thomas, K.M., Drevets, W.C., Dahl, R.E., Ryan, N.D., Birmaher, B., Eccard, C.H., Axelson, D., Whalen, P.J., & Casey, B.J. (2001). Amygdala response to fearful faces in anxious and depressed children. *Archives of General Psychiatry*, 58, pp. 1057–1063.

Thomas, V.H., Melchert, T.P., & Banken, J.A. (1999). Substance dependence and personality disorders: Comorbidity and treatment outcome in an inpatient treatment population. *Journal of Studies on Alcohol*, 60, pp. 271–277.

Thompson, J.K. (1996). *Body Image, Eating Disorders, and Obesity*. Washington, DC: American Psychological Association.

Thompson-Brenner, H., Glass, S., & Westen, D. (2003). A multidimensional meta-analysis of psychotherapy for bulimia nervosa. *Clinical Psychology*, 10, pp. 269–287.

Thomson, J.B. & Raskind, W.H. (2003). Genetic influences on reading and writing disabilities. In H.L. Swanson, K.R. Harris, & S. Graham (Eds.), *Handbook of Learning Disabilities*, pp. 256–270. New York: Guilford.

Thoresen, C.E., & Powell, L.H. (1992). Type A behavior pattern: New perspectives on theory, assessment, and intervention. *Journal of Consulting and Clinical Psychology*, 60, pp. 595–604.

Thornicroft, G., & Sartorius, N. (1993). The course and outcome of depression in different cultures: 10-year follow-up of the WHO Collaborative Study on the Assessment of Depressive Disorders. *Psychological Medicine*, 23, pp. 1023–1032.

Thornicroft, G., & Susser, E. (2001). Evidence-based psychotherapeutic interventions in the community care of schizophrenia. *British Journal of Psychiatry*, 178, pp. 2–4.

Tiefer, L. (1999). Challenging sexual naturalism, the shibboleth of sex research and popular sexology. In D. Bernstein (Ed.), *Gender and Motivation. Nebraska Symposium on Motivation*, Vol 45, pp. 143–172. Lincoln, NE: University of Nebraska Press.

Tiefer, L. (2001). The "consensus" conference on female sexual dysfunction: Conflicts of interest and hidden agendas. *Journal of Sex and Marital Therapy*, 27, pp. 227–236.

Tiefer, L., & Kring, B (1995). Gender and the organization of sexual behavior. *Psychiatric Clinics of North America*, 18, pp. 25–37.

Toffel, H. (1996). Crazy women, unharmed men, and evil children: Confronting the myths about battered people who kill their abusers, and the argument for extending battering syndrome self-defenses to all victims of domestic violence. *Southern California Law Review*, 70, pp. 337–380.

Tomkins, D.M., & Sellers, E.M. (2001). Addiction and the brain: The role of neurotransmitters in the cause and treatment of drug dependence. *Canadian Medical Association Journal*. 164, pp. 817–821.

Tonigan, J.S., Connors, G.J., & Miller, W.R. (2003). Participation and involvement in Alcoholics Anonymous. In T.F. Babor and F.K. Del Boca (Eds.), *Treatment Matching in Alcoholism*, pp. 184–204. New York: Cambridge University Press.

Torgersen, S. (1986). Genetic factors in moderately severe and mild affective disorders. *Archives of General Psychiatry*, 43, pp. 222–226.

Torgersen, S. (1994). Genetics in borderline conditions. *Acta Psychiatrica Scandinavica*, 89 (suppl. 379), pp. 19–25.

Torgersen, S., Kringlen, E., & Cramer, V. (2001). The prevalence of personality disorders in a community sample. *Archives of General Psychiatry*, 58, pp. 590–596.

Torrey, E.F. (1988). *Nowhere to Go: The Tragic Odyssey of the Homeless Mentally Ill*. New York: Harper & Row.

Torrey, E.F. (1997). *Out of the Shadows*. New York: Wiley.

Torrey, E.F., Bowler, A.E., Taylor, E.H., & Gottesman, I.I. (1994). *Schizophrenia and Manic-Depressive Disorder: The Biological Roots of Mental Illness as Revealed By the Landmark Study of Identical Twins*. New York: Basic Books.

Trials of the Hypertension Prevention Collaborative Research Group. (1992). The effects of nonpharmacologic interventions on blood pressure of persons with high normal levels: Results of the Trials of Hypertension Prevention, Phase I, *JAMA*, 267, pp. 1213–1220.

Triandis, H.C. (1994). Culture and social behavior. In W.J. Lonner & R.S. Malpass (Eds.), *Psychology and Culture*, pp. 169–174. Boston: Allyn & Bacon.

True, W.R., Rice, J., Eisen, S.A., Heath, A.C., Goldberg, J., Lyons, M.J., & Nowak, J. (1993). A twin study of genetic and environmental contributions to liability for posttraumatic stress symptoms. *Archives of General Psychiatry*, 50, pp. 257–264.

Trull, T.J. (1995). Borderline personality disorder features in nonclinical young adults. 1. Identification and validation. *Psychological Assessment*, 7, pp. 33–41.

Trull, T.J., & McCrae, R.R. (2002). A five-factor perspective on personality disorder research. In P.T. Costa, Jr., & T.A. Widiger (Eds.), *Personality Disorders and the Five-Factor Model of Personality*, 2nd ed., pp. 45–58. Washington, D.C.: American Psychological Association.

Tsai, J.L., & Chentsova-Dutton, Y. (2002). Understanding depression across cultures. In I.H. Gotlib and C.L. Hammen (Eds.), *Handbook of Depression*. New York: Guilford.

Tsai, J.L., Butcher, J.N., Munoz, R.F., & Vitousek, K. (2001). Culture, ethnicity, and psychopathology. In P.B. Sutker and H.E. Adams (Eds.), *Comprehensive Handbook of Psychopathology*, 3rd ed., pp. 105–127. New York, NY: Kluwer Academic/Plenum Publishers.

Tsai, L.Y. (1996). Comorbid psychiatric disorders of autistic disorder. *Journal of Autism and Developmental Disorders*, 26, pp. 159–163.

Tsuang, M.T. (2001). Defining alternative phenotypes for genetic studies: What can we learn from studies of schizophrenia? *American Journal of Medical Genetics*, 105, pp. 8–10.

Tsuang, M.T., Simpson, J.C., & Fleming, J.A. (1992). Epidemiology of suicide, *International Review of Psychiatry*, 4, pp. 117–129.

Tsuang, M.T., Stone, W.S., Tarbox, S.I., & Faraone, S.V. (2003). In sights from neuroscience for the concepts of schizotaxia and the diagnosis of schizophrenia. In K.A. Phillips and M.B. First (Eds.), *Advancing DSM: Dilemmas in Psychiatric Diagnosis*, pp. 105–127. Washington, D.C.: American Psychiatric Association.

Tully, L.A., Arseneault, L., Caspi, A., Moffitt, T.E., & Morgan, J. (2004). Does maternal warmth moderate the effects of birth weight on twins' attention-deficit/hyperactivity disorder (ADHD) symptoms and low IQ? *Journal of Consulting and Clinical Psychology*, 72(2), pp. 218–226.

Tune, L. (2002). Treatments for dementia. Pp. 87–124. In P.E. Nathan and J.M. Gorman (Eds.), *A Guide to Treatments That Work*, 2nd ed. London, England: Oxford University Press

Turkat, I.D., & Carlson, C.R. (1984). Data-based versus symptomatic formulation of treatment: The case of a dependent personality. *Journal of Behavior Therapy and Experimental Psychiatry*, 15, pp. 153–160.

Turkheimer, E. (1991). Individual and group differences in adoption studies of IQ. *Psychological Bulletin*, 110, pp. 392–405.

Turkheimer, E., & Waldron, M. (2000). Nonshared environment: A theoretical, methodological and quantitative review. *Psychological Bulletin*, 126, pp. 78–108.

Turvey, C.L., Coryell, W.H., Solomon, D.A., Leon, A.C., Endicott, J., Keller, M.B., & Akiskal, H. (1999). Long-term prognosis of bipolar I disorder. *Acta Psychiatrica Scandinavica*, 99, pp. 110–119.

Tyrer, P. (2001). The case for cothymia: Mixed anxiety and depression as a single diagnosis. *British Journal of Psychiatry*, 179, pp. 191–193.

Tyrer, P., Seivewright, H., & Johnson, T. (2004). The Nottingham study of neurotic disorder: Predictors of 12-year outcome of dysthymic, panic and generalized anxiety disorder. *Psychological Medicine*, 34, pp. 1385–1394.

U.S. Census Bureau (1996). Sixty-five plus in the United States. *Current Population Reports*, pp. 23–190. Washington, DC: U.S. Government Printing Office.

U.S. Census Bureau (2002). "Historical poverty tables;" published February 13, <http://www.census.gov/_hhes/poverty/histpov/hstpov4.html3>

U.S. Department of Health and Human Services, Administration on Children, Youth and Families (2001). *Child Maltreatment 1999: Reports From the States to the National Child Abuse and Neglect Data Systems—National Statistics on Child Abuse and Neglect*. Washington, DC: U.S. Government Printing Office.

U.S. Department of Health and Human Services, Administration on Children, Youth and Families (2002). *Child Maltreatment 2000: Reports from the States to the National Child Abuse and Neglect Data Systems—National Statistics on Child Abuse and Neglect*. Washington, DC: U.S. Government Printing Office.

U.S. Department of Health and Human Services, Administration on Children, Youth and Families (2003). *Child Maltreatment 2001: Reports from the States to the National Child Abuse and Neglect Data Systems—National Statistics on Child Abuse and Neglect*. Washington, DC: U.S. Government Printing Office.

U.S. Department of Health and Human Services, Administration on Children, Youth and Families (2004). *Child Maltreatment 2002: Reports from the States to the National Child Abuse and Neglect Data Systems—National Statistics on Child Abuse and Neglect*. Washington, DC: U.S. Government Printing Office.

U.S. Department of Health and Human Services, Administration on Children, Youth and Families (2005). *Child Maltreatment 2003: Reports from the States to the National Child Abuse and Neglect Data Systems—National Statistics on Child Abuse and Neglect*. Washington, DC: U.S. Government Printing Office.

U.S. Department of Health and Human Services. (1993). *AIDS Research: An NIMH Blueprint for the Second Decade*. NIH Publication No. 93–3563.Washington, DC: U.S. Government Printing Office.

U.S. Department of Justice, Bureau of Justice Statistics, (1999). *Special Report: Mental Health and Treatment of Inmates and Probationers*. Washington, D.C.: NCJ.

Uchino, B.N., Cacioppo, J.T., & Kiecolt-Glaser, J.K. (1996). The relationship between social support and physiological processes: A review with emphasis underlying mechanisms and implications for health. *Psychological Bulletin*, 119, pp. 488–531.

Updegraff, J.A., & Taylor, S.E. (2000). From vulnerability to growth: Positive and negative effects of stressful life events. In J.H. Harvey and E.D. Miller (Eds.), *Loss and Trauma: General and Close Relationship Perspectives*, pp. 3–28. Philadelphia, PA: Brunner-Routledge.

Uttal, W.R. (2001). *The New Phrenology:The Limits of Localizing Cognitive Processes in the Brain*. Cambridge, MA: MIT Press.

Vaillant, G. (2003). A 60-year follow-up of alcoholic men. *Addiction*. 98, pp. 1043–1051.

Vaillant, G.E. (1994). Evidence that the Type 1/Type 2 dichotomy in alcoholism must be re-examined. *Addiction*, 89, pp. 1049–1057.

Vaillant, G.E. (1995). *The Natural History of Alcoholism Revisited*. Cambridge, MA: Harvard University Press.

Vaillant, G.E. (1996). A long-term follow-up of male alcohol abuse. *Archives of General Psychiatry*, 53, pp. 243–249.

Valenstein, E.S. (1973). *Brain Control*. New York: Wiley.

Valenstein, E.S. (1986). *Great and Desperate Cures*. New York: Basic Books.

Valente, J. (1996). A long road to daylight: Football player's gambling problems. *People Weekly*, January 15, p. 811.

Valenzuela, C.F. (1997). Alcohol and neurotransmitter interactions. *Alcohol Health and Research World*, 21, pp. 144–148.

Vallenstein, E.S. (1998). *Blaming the Brain*. New York: Free Press.

van den Heuvel, O.A., van de Wetering, B.J.M. Veltman, D.J., & Pauls, D.L. (2000). *Journal of Clinical Psychiatry*, 61, pp. 756–766.

van der Kolk, B.A. (1996). The psychobiology of PTSD. In B.A. van der Kolk, A.C. McFarlane, & L. Weisaeth (Eds.), *Traumatic Stress*, pp. 214–241. New York: Guilford.

van der Kolk, B.A., & McFarlane, A.C. (1996). The black hole of trauma. In B.A. van der Kolk, A.C. McFarlane, & L. Weisaeth (Eds.), *Traumatic Stress*, pp. 3–23. New York: Guilford.

Van Heeringen, C., & Marusic, A. (2003). Understanding the suicidal brain. *British Journal of Psychiatry*, 183, pp. 282–284.

Van Ommeren, M., de Jong, J., Sharma, B., Komproe, I., Thapa, S.B., & Cardena, E. (2001). Psychiatric disorders among tortured Bhutanese refugees in Nepal. *Archives of General Psychiatry*, 58, pp. 475–482.

Van Os, J. & McGuffin, P.M. (2003). Can the social environment cause schizophrenia? *British Journal of Psychiatry*, 182, pp. 291–292.

Van Os, J., Fahy, T.A., Jones, P., Harvey, I., Sham, P., Lewis, S., Bebbington, P.,Toone, B.,Williams, M., & Murray, R. (1996). Psychopathological syndromes in the functional psychoses: Associations with course and outcome. *Psychological Medicine*, 26, pp. 161–176.

Vandereycken, W. (1995). The families of patients with an eating disorder. In K.D. Brownell & C.G. Fairburn (Eds.), *Eating Disorders and Obesity: A Comprehensive Handbook*, pp. 219–223. New York: Guilford.

Vandereycken, W. (2002). Families of patients with eating disorders. In C.G. Fairburn & K.D. Brownell (Eds.), *Eating Disorders and Obesity*, 2nd ed., pp. 215–22. New York: Guilford.

Vasey, M.W., & Borkovec,T.D. (1992). A catastrophizing assessment of worrisome thoughts. *Cognitive Therapy and Research*, 16, pp. 505–520.

Vaughn, C.E., & Leff, J.P. (1976).The influence of family and social factors on the course of psychiatric illness: A comparison of schizophrenic and depressed neurotic patients. *British Journal of Psychiatry*, 129, pp. 125–137.

Verheul, R., van den Bosch, L.M.C., Koeter, M.W.J., de Ridder, M.A.J., Stijnen, T., & van den Brink, W. (2003). Dialectical behaviour therapy for women with borderline personality disorder: 12-month, randomized clinical trial in The Netherlands. *British Journal of Psychiatry*, 182, pp. 135–140.

Vertue, F.M. (2003). From adaptive emotion to dysfunction: An attachment perspective on social anxiety disorder. *Personality & Social Psychology Review*, 7, pp. 170–191.

Viken, R.J., Treat, T.A., Nosofsky, R.M., McFall, R.M., & Palmeri, T.J. (2002). Modeling individual differences in perceptual and attentional processes related to bulimic symptoms. *Journal of Abnormal Psychology*, 111, pp. 598–609.

Visintainer, M.A., Seligman, M.E.P., & Volpicelli, J.R. (1982).Tumor rejection in rats after inescapable or escapable electric shock. *Science*, 216, pp. 437–439.

Vitousek, K.B. (2002). Cognitive-behavioral therapy for anorexia nervosa. In C.G. Fairburn & K.D. Brownell (Eds.), *Eating Disorders and Obesity*, 2nd ed., pp. 308–313. New York: Guilford.

Vohs, K.D., Bardone, A.M., Joiner, T.E., & Abramson, L.Y. (1999). Perfectionism, perceived weight status, and self-esteem interact to predict bulimic symptoms: A model of bulimic symptom development. *Journal of Abnormal Psychology*, 108, pp. 695–700.

Volavka, J., Czobor, P., Sheitman, B., Lindenmayer, J., Citrome, L., McEvoy, J.P., Cooper, T.B., Chakos, M., & Lieberman, J.A. (2002). Clozapine, olanzapine, risperidone, and haloperidol in the treatment of patients with chronic schizophrenia and schizoaffective disorder. *American Journal of Psychiatry*, 159, pp. 255–262.

Volicer, L., McKee, A., & Hewitt, S. (2001). Dementia. *Neurologic Clinics*, 19, pp. 867–885.

Volkmar, F., & Dykens, E. (2002). Mental retardation. In M. Rutter & E.Taylor (Eds.), *Child and Adolescent Psychiatry*, 4th ed., pp. 697–710. Oxford: Blackwell.

Volkmar, F., Chawarska, K., & Klin, A. (2005). Autism in infancy and early childhood. *Annual Review of Psychology*, 56, pp. 315–336.

Volkmar, F.R., Klin, A., Siegel, B., et al. (1994). Field trial for autistic disorder in DSM-IV. *American Journal of Psychiatry*, 151, pp. 1361–1367.

Wagner,W., Zaborny, B.A., & Gray, T.E. (1994). Fluvoxamine: A review of its safety profile in worldwide studies. *International Clinical Psychopharmacology*, 9, pp. 223–227.

Wahl, R.L. (Ed.) (2002). *Principles and Practice of Position Emission Tomography*. Philadelphia: Lippincott, Williams and Wilkins.

Waite, L.J., & Gallagher, M. (2000). *The Case for Marriage*. New York: Doubleday.

Wakefield et al., (1998) Ileal lymphoid nodular hyperplasia, non-specific colitis, and regressive developmental disorder in children. *Lancet*, 351, pp. 637–641.

Wakefield, J.C. (1999). The measurement of mental disorder. In A.V. Horwitz and T.L. Scheid (Eds.), *A Handbook for the Study of Mental Health: Social Contexts,Theories, and Systems*. Cambridge, UK, Cambridge University Press.

Wald, M.S., Carlsmith, J.M., & Leiderman, P.H. (1988). *Protecting Abused and Neglected Children*. Stanford, CA: Stanford University Press.

Walden, B., McGue, M., Iacono, W.G., Burt, S.A., & Elkins, I. (2004). Identifying shared environmental contributions to early substance use: The respective roles of peers and parents. *Journal of Abnormal Psychology*, 113(3), pp. 440–450.

Walden, J., Normann, C., Langosch, J., Berger, M., & Grunze, H. (1998). Differential treatment of bipolar disorder with old and new antiepileptic drugs. *Neuropsychobiology*, 38, pp. 181–184.

Waldinger, M.D. (2003). Rapid ejaculation. In S.B. Levine and C.B. Risen (Eds.), *Handbook of Clinical Sexuality for Mental Health Professionals*, pp. 257–274. New York: Brunner-Routledge.

Walker, E., Davis, D., & Baum, K. (1993). Social withdrawal. In C.G. Costello (Ed.), *Symptoms of Schizophrenia*, pp. 227–260. New York: Wiley.

Walker, E., Kestler, L., Bollini, A., & Hochman, K.M. (2004). Schizophrenia: Etiology and course. *Annual Review of Psychology*, 55, pp. 401–430.

Walker, L. (1979). *The Battered Woman*. New York: Harper & Row.

Walker, L. (1989). Psychology and violence against women. *American Psychologist*, 44, pp. 695–702.

Wall, T.L., & Ehlers, C.L. (1995). Genetic influences affecting alcohol use among Asians. *Alcohol Health and Research World*, 19, pp. 184–189.

Wallace, J. (1999). The twelve-step recovery approach. In P.J. Ott, R.E. Tarter, & R.T. Ammerman (Eds.), *Sourcebook on Substance Abuse: Etiology, Epidemiology, Assessment, and Treatment*, pp. 293–302. Boston: Allyn & Bacon.

Waller, N.G., & Ross, C.A. (1997). The prevalence and biometric structure of pathological dissociation in the general population: Taxometric and behavior genetic findings. *Journal of Abnormal Psychology*, 106, pp. 499–510.

Wallis, C.J., Rezazadeh, S.M., & Lal, H. (1993). Role of serotonin in ethanol abuse. *Drug Development and Research*, 30, pp. 178–188.

Walsh, B.T. (1995). Pharmacotherapy of eating disorders. In K.D. Brownell & C.G. Fairburn (Eds.), *Eating Disorders and Obesity: A Comprehensive Handbook*, pp. 313–317. New York: Guilford.

Walsh, B.T. et al., (2004). Treatment of bulimia nervosa in a primary care setting. *American Journal of Psychiatry*, 161, pp. 556–561.

Walsh, T., Wilson, G.T., Loeb, K.L., et al. (1997). Medication and psychotherapy in the treatment of bulimia nervosa. *American Journal of Psychiatry*, 154, pp. 523–531.

Walters, G.D. (1999). *The Addiction Concept: Working Hypothesis or Self-Fulfilling Prophesy?* Boston: Allyn & Bacon.

Walters, V.L., Tognolini, R.Z., Rueda, H.M., Rueda, R.M., & Torres, R.G. (1997). New strategies for old problems: Tardive dyskinesia. *Schizophrenia Research*, 28, pp. 231–246.

Wandersman, A., & Florin, P. (2003). Community interventions and effective prevention. *American Psychologist*, 2003, pp. 441–448.

Wang, C.T., & Harding, K. (1999). *Current Trends in Child Abuse Reporting and Fatalities: The Results of the 1998 Annual Fifty Sate Survey*. Chicago: National Center on Child Abuse Prevention Research.

Wang, P.S., Simon, G., & Kessler, R.C. (2003). The economic burden of depression and the cost-effectiveness of treatment. *International Journal of Methods in Psychiatric Research*, 12, pp. 22–33.

Waraich, P., Goldner, E.M., Somers, J.M., & Hsu, L. (2004). Prevalence and incidence studies of mood disorders: A systematic review of the literature. *Canadian Journal of Psychiatry*, 49, pp. 124–138.

Warnock, J.K. (2002). Female hypoactive sexual desire disorder: Epidemiology, diagnosis and treatment. *CNS Drugs*, 16, pp. 745–753.

Warren, S.T., & Ashley, C.T. (1995). Triplet repeat expansion mutations: The example of fragile X syndrome. *Annual Review of Neuroscience*, 18, pp. 77–99.

Waschbusch, D.A. & Hill, G.P. (2004). Empirically supported, promising, and unsupported treatments for children with Attention-Deficit/Hyperactivity Disorder. In S.O. Lilienfeld et al. (Eds.), *Science and Pseudoscience in Clinical Psychology*, pp. 333–362. New York: Guilford.

Waschbusch, D.A. (2002). A meta-analytic examination of comorbid hyperactive-impulsive-attention problems and conduct problems. *Psychological Bulletin*, 128(1), pp. 118–150.

Wassef, A., Baker, J., & Kochan, L.D. (2003). GABA and schizophrenia: A review of basic science and clinical studies. *Journal of Clinical Psychopharmacology*, 23, pp. 601–640.

Waterman, A.S., & Archer, S. (1990). A life-span perspective on identity formation: Development in form, function, and process. In P.B. Baltes, D.L. Featherman, & R.M. Lerner (Eds.), *Life-Span Development and Behavior*, Vol. 10, pp. 29–57. Hillsdale, NJ: Erlbaum.

Waterman, A.S., & Goldman, J.A. (1976). A longitudinal study of changes in ego identity development at a liberal arts college. *Journal of Youth and Adolescence*.

Waterman, G., Geary, P., & Waterman, C. (1974). Longitudinal study of changes in ego identity status from the freshman to the senior year at college. *Developmental Psychology*, 10, pp. 387–392.

Waters, E., Hay, D., & Richters, J. (1986). Infant-parent attachment and the origins of prosocial and antisocial behavior. In D. Olweus, J. Block, & M. Radke-Yarrow (Eds.), *Development of Antisocial and Prosocial Behavior: Research, Theories, and Issues*, pp. 97–126. Orlando, FL: Academic Press.

Waterworth, D.M., Bassett, A.S., & Brzustowicz, L.M. (2002). Recent advances in the genetics of schizophrenia. *Cellular and Molecular Life Sciences*, 59, pp. 331–348.

Watkins, J.G. (1984). The Bianchi (L.A. Hillsdale Strangler) case: Sociopath or multiple personality. *International Journal of Clinical and Experimental Hypnosis*, 32, pp. 67–101.

Watson, D., & Clark, L.A. (1990). *The Positive and Negative Affect Schedule-Expanded Form*. Unpublished manuscript. Southern Methodist University.

Watson, D., Clark, L.A., Weber, K., Assenheimer, J.S., Strauss, M.E., & McCormick, R.A. (1995). Testing a tripartite model. II. Exploring the symptom structure of anxiety and depression in student, adult, and patient samples. *Journal of Abnormal Psychology*, 104, pp. 15–25.

Watson, J.B., & Rayner, R. (1920). Conditioned emotional reactions. *Journal of Experimental Psychology*, 3, pp. 1–14.

Watts, C., & Zimmerman, C. (2002). Violence against women: Global scope and magnitude. *Lancet*, 359, pp. 1232–1237.

Wearden, A.J., Tarrier, N., Barrowclough, C., Zastowny, T.R., & Rahill, A.A. (2000). A review of expressed emotion research in health care. *Clinical Psychology Review*, 20, pp. 633–666.

Webster-Stratton, C. (1994). Advancing videotape parent training: A comparison study. *Journal of Consulting and Clinical Psychology*, 62, pp. 583–593.

Wegner, D.M. (1994). Ironic processes of mental control. *Psychological Review*, 101, pp. 34–52.

Wehr, T.A. (1989). Seasonal affective disorder: A historical overview. In N.E. Rosenthal, & M.C. Blehar. (Eds.), *Seasonal Affective Disorders and Phototherapy*. New York: Guilford.

Weickert, T.W., Goldberg, T.E., Mishara, A., Apud, J.A. Kolachana, B.S., Egan, M.F., & Weinberger, D.R. (2004). Catechol-o-methyltransferase Val 108/158 Met genotype predicts working memory respose to antipsychotic medications. *Biological Psychiatry*, 56, pp. 677–682.

Weiden, P.J., & Olfson, M. (1995). Cost of relapse in schizophrenia. *Schizophrenia Bulletin*, 21, pp. 419–429.

Weinberger, D.R. (1997). The biological basis of schizophrenia: New directions. *Journal of Clinical Psychiatry*, 58, (suppl. 10), pp. 22–27.

Weinberger, D.R., & McClure, R.K. (2002). Neurotoxicity, neuroplasticity, and magnetic resonance imaging morphometry: What is happening in the schizophrenic brain? *Archives of General Psychiatry*, 59, pp. 553–558.

Weiner, H., & Fawzy, F.I. (1989). An integrative model of health, disease, and illness. In S. Cheren (Ed.), *Psychosomatic Medicine: Theory, Physiology, and Practice*, vol. 1, pp. 9–44. Madison, CT: International Universities Press.

Weiner, I.B. (2000). Using the Rorschach properly in practice and research. *Journal of Clinical Psychology*, 56, pp. 435–438.

Weiss, J.M., Cierpial, M.A., & West, C.H.K. (1998). Selective breeding of rats for high and low motor activity in a swim test: Toward a new animal model of depression. *Pharmacology Biochemistry and Behavior*, 61, pp. 49–66.

Weissman, M.M. (1993). The epidemiology of personality disorders: A 1990 update. *Journal of Personality Disorders*, (suppl.), pp. 44–62.

Weissman, M.M., Bruce, M.L., Leaf, P.J., Florio, L.P., & Holzer, C. (1991). Affective disorders. In L.N. Robins & D.A. Regier (Eds.), *Psychiatric Disorders in America: The Epidemiologic Catchment Area Study*, pp. 53–80. New York: Free Press.

Weissman, M.M., Markowitz, J.C., & Klerman, G.L. (2000). *Comprehensive Guide to Interpersonal Psychotherapy*. New York: Basic Books.

Weisz, J.R., & Hawley, K.M. (2002). Developmental factors in the treatment of adolescents. *Journal of Consulting and Clinical Psychology*, 70, pp. 21–43.

Weithorn, L.A. (1988). Mental hospitalization of troublesome youth: An analysis of skyrocketing admission rates. *Stanford Law Review*, 40, pp. 773–838.

Welsh, R.S. (2003). Prescription privileges: Pro or con. *Clinical Psychology: Science & Practice*, 10, pp. 371–372.

Welte, J., Barnes, G., Wieczorek, W., Tidwell, M., & Parker, J. (2001). Alcohol and gambling pathology among U.S. adults: Prevalence, demographic patterns and comorbidity. *Journal of Studies on Alcohol* 62, pp. 706–712.

Werner, J.S., & Smith, R.S. (1982). *Vulnerable but Invincible: A Longitudinal Study of Resilient Children and Youth*. New York: McGraw-Hill.

Wesson, V.A., & Levitt, A.J. (1998). Light therapy for seasonal affective disorder. In R.W. Lam (Ed.), *Seasonal Affective Disorder and Beyond: Light Treatment for SAD and Non-SAD Conditions*, pp. 45–89. Washington, D.C.: American Psychiatric Press.

Westen, D., & Arkowitz-Westen, L. (1998). Limitations of Axis II in diagnosing personality pathology in clinical practice. *American Journal of Psychiatry*, 155, pp. 1767–1771.

Westen, D., & Morrison, K. (2001). A multidimensional meta-analysis of treatments for depression, panic, and generalized anxiety disorder: An empirical examination of the status of empirically supported therapies. *Journal of Consulting and Clinical Psychology*, 69, pp. 875–899

Westen, D., & Weinberger, J. (2004). When clinical description becomes statistical prediction. *American Psychologist*, 59, pp. 595–613.

Westergaard, T., Mortensen, P.B., Pedersen, C.B., Wohlfahrt, J., & Melbye, M. (1999). Exposure to prenatal and childhood infections and the risk of schizophrenia. *Archives of General Psychiatry*, 56, pp. 993–998.

Westermeyer, J. (1999). Cross-cultural aspects of substance abuse. In M. Galanter & H.D. Kleber (Eds.), *Textbook of Substance Abuse Treatment*, 2nd ed., pp. 75–88. Washington, DC: American Psychiatric Press.

Weston, D. (1998). The scientific legacy of Sigmund Freud: Toward a psychodynamically informed psychological science. *Psychological Bulletin, 124*, pp. 333–371.

Weston, D., Novotny, C.M., & Thompson-Brenner, H. (2004). The empirical status of empirically supported psychotherapies: Assumptions, findings, and reporting in controlled clinical trials. *Psychological Bulletin, 130*, pp. 631–663.

Whalen, C., Henker, B., Hinshaw, S., Heller, T., & Huber-Dressler, A. (1991). Messages of medication: Effects of actual versus informed medication status on hyperactive boy's expectancies and self-evaluation. *Journal of Consulting and Clinical Psychology, 59*, pp. 602–606.

Whaley, A.L. (1998). Cross-cultural perspective on paranoia: A focus on the black American experience. *Psychiatric Quarterly, 69*, pp. 325–343.

Whisman, M.A., Sheldon, C.T., & Goering, P. (2000). Psychiatric disorders and dissatisfaction with social relationships: Does type of relationship matter? *Journal of Abnormal Psychology, 109*, pp. 803–808.

Whittington, C.J., et al., (2004). Selective serotonin reuptake inhibitors in childhood depression: Systematic review of published versus unpublished data. *Lancet, 363*, pp. 1341–1345.

Whybrow, P.C. (1997). *A Mood Apart: The Thinker's Guide to Emotion and Its Disorders.* New York: HarperCollins.

Wicks-Nelson, R., & Israel, A.C. (2000). *Behavior Disorders of Childhood*, 4th ed. Upper Saddle River, NJ: Prentice Hall.

Widiger, T.A. (2001). Social anxiety, social phobia, and avoidant personality. In W.R. Crozier and L.E. Alden (Eds.), *International Handbook of Social Anxiety; Concepts, Research, and Interventions Relating to the Self and Shyness*, pp. 336–356. New York: Wiley.

Widiger, T.A., & Clark, L.A. (2000). Toward DSM-V and the classification of psychopathology. *Psychological Bulletin, 126*, pp. 946–963.

Widiger, T.A., & Simonsen, E. (2005). Alternative dimensional models of personality disorder: Finding a common ground. *Journal of Personality Disorders, 19*, pp. 110–130.

Widiger, T.A., Costa, P.T., Jr., & McCrae, R.M. (2002). A proposal for Axis II: Diagnosing personality disorders using the five-factor model. In P.T. Costa, Jr., & T.A, Widiger (Eds.), *Personality Disorders and the Five-Factor Model of Personality*, 2nd ed., pp. 431–456. Washington, D.C.: American Psychological Association.

Widiger, T.A., Trull, T.J., Clarkin, J.F., Sanderson, C., & Costa, P.T., Jr. (2002). A description of the DSM-IV personality disorders with the five-factor model of personality. In P.T. Costa, Jr., & T.A. Widiger (Eds.), *Personality Disorders and the Five-Factor Model of Personality*, 2nd ed., pp. 89–102. Washington, D.C.: American Psychological Association.

Widiger, T.A. (1998). Sex biases in the diagnosis of personality disorders. *Journal of Personality Disorders, 12*, pp. 95–118.

Widiger, T.A., & Trull, T.J. (1993). Borderline and narcissistic personality disorders. In P.B. Sutker & H.E. Adams (Eds.), *Comprehensive Handbook of Psychopathology*, 2nd ed., pp. 371–394. New York: Plenum.

Widiger, T.A., Cadoret, R., Hare, R., Robins, L., et al. (1996). DSM-IV antisocial personality disorder field trial. *Journal of Abnormal Psychology, 105*, pp. 3–16.

Wiederman, M.W. (1997). Pretending orgasm during sexual intercourse: Correlates in a sample of young adult women. *Journal of Sex and Marital Therapy, 23*, pp. 131–139.

Wiederman, M.W. (2003). Paraphilia and fetishism. *Family Journal-Counseling & Therapy for Couples & Families, 11*, pp. 315–321.

Wiegel, M., Wlncze, J.P., & Barlow, D.H. (2002). Sexual dysfunction. In M.M. Antony and D.H. Barlow (Eds.), *Handbook of Assessment and Treatment Planning for Psychological Disorders*, pp. 481–522. New York: Guilford.

Wiehe, V.R., & Richards, A.L. (1995). *Intimate Betrayal: Understanding and Responding to the Trauma of Acquaintance Rape.* Thousand Oaks, CA: Sage.

Wierzbicki, M. (1993). *Issues in Clinical Psychology: Subjective Versus Objective Approaches.* Boston: Allyn & Bacon.

Wildes, J.E., Emery, R.E., & Simons, A.D. (2001). The roles of ethnicity and culture in the development of eating disturbance and body dissatisfaction: A meta-analytic review. *Clinical Psychology Review, 21*, pp. 521–551.

Wileman, S.M., Eagles, J.M., Andrew, J.E., Howie, F.L., Cameron, I.M., McCormack, K., & Naji, S.A. (2001). Light therapy for seasonal affective disorder in primary care: Randomised controlled trial. *British Journal of Psychiatry, 178*, pp. 311–316.

Williams, J.M.B., Mathews, A., & MacLeod, C. (1996). The emotional stroop task and psychopathology. *Psychological Bulletin, 120*, pp. 3–24.

Williams, K.E., Chambless, D.L., & Ahrens, A. (1997). Are emotions frightening? An extension of the fear of fear construct. *Behaviour Research and Therapy, 35*, pp. 239–248.

Williams, L.M. (1994). Recall of childhood trauma: A prospective study of women's memories of child sexual abuse. *Journal of Consulting and Clinical Psychology, 62*, pp. 1167–1176.

Williams, L.M., & Finkelhor, D. (1990). The characteristics of incestuous fathers: A review of recent studies. In W.L. Marshall, D.R. Laws, & H.E. Barbaree (Eds.), *Handbook of Sexual Assault: Issues, Theories, and Treatment of the Offender*, p. 231. New York: Plenum.

Williams, N., & Leiblum, S.L. (2002). Sexual dysfunction. In G.M. Wlngood and R.J. DiClemente (Eds.), *Handbook of Women's Sexual and Reproductive Health*, pp. 303–328. New York: Kluwer Academic.

Williams, R.B., Barefoot, J.C., Califf, R.M., Haney, T.L., Saunders, W.B., et al. (1992). Prognostic importance of social and economic resources among medically treated patients with angiographically documented coronary artery disease. *Journal of the American Medical Association, 267*, pp. 520–524.

Wilson, G.T., Loeb, K.L., Walsh, B.T., Labouvie, E., Petkova, E., Liu, X., & Waternaux, C. (1999). Psychological versus pharmacological treatments of bulimia nervosa: Predictors and processes of change. *Journal of Consulting & Clinical Psychology, 67*, pp. 451–459.

Wilson, T.D. (2002). *Strangers to Ourselves: Discovering the Adaptive Unconscious.* New York: Belknap.

Wimberly, S.R. et al. (2005). Perceived partner reactions to diagnosis and treatment of breast cancer: Impact on psychosocial and psychosexual adjustment. *Journal of Consulting and Clinical Psychology, 73*, pp. 300–311.

Wincze, J.P. (1989). Assessment and treatment of atypical sexual behavior. In S.R. Lieblum & R.C. Rosen (Eds.), *Principles and Practice of Sex Therapy*, 2nd ed., pp. 382–404. New York: Guilford.

Windle, M. (2000). Parental, sibling, and peer influences on adolescent substance use and alcohol problems. *Applied Developmental Science, 4*, pp. 98–110.

Wing, L. (1988). Autism: Possible clues to the underlying pathology. 1. Clinical facts. In L.Wing (Ed.), *Aspects of Autism: Biological Research*, pp. 11–18. London, Gaskell.

Wing, L., & Potter, D. (2002). The epidemiology of autistic spectrum disorders: Is the prevalence rising? *Mental Retardation and Developmental Disabilities Research Reviews, 8*(3), pp. 151–161.

Winograd, E., & Killinger, W.A. (1983). Relating age at encoding in early childhood to adult recall: Development of flashbulb memories. *Journal of Experimental Psychology: General, 112*, pp. 413–422.

Winokur, G., Coryell, W., Keller, M., Endicott, J., & Leon, A. (1995). A family study of manic-depressive (bipolar I) disease. *Archives of General Psychiatry, 52*, pp. 367–373.

Winslow, B.W., & Carter, P. (1999). Patterns of burden in wives who care for husbands with dementia. *Nursing Clinics of North America, 34*, pp. 275–287.

Winter, D.G., John, O.P., Stewart, A.J., Klohnen, E.C., & Duncan, L.E. (1998). Traits and motives: Toward an integration of two traditions in personality research. *Psychological Review, 105*, pp. 230–250.

Winters, K.C., Latimer, W., & Stinchfield, R.D. (1999). The DSM-IV criteria for adolescent alcohol and cannabis use disorders. *Journal of Studies on Alcohol, 60*, pp. 337–344.

Wiseman, C.V., Gray, J.J., Mosimann, J.E., & Ahrens, A.H. (1992). Cultural expectations of thinness in women: An update. *International Journal of Eating Disorders, 11*, pp. 85–89.

Wittchen, H., & Hoyer, J. (2001). Generalized anxiety disorder: Nature and course. *Journal of Clinical Psychiatry, 62* (suppl. 11), pp. 15–19.

Wittchen, H., Holsboer, F., & Jacobi, F. (2001). Met and unmet needs in the management of depressive disorder in the community and primary care: The size and breadth of the problem. *Journal of Clinical Psychiatry, 62* (suppl. 26), pp. 23–28.

Wittchen, H., Knauper, B., & Kessler, R.C. (1994). Lifetime risk of depression. *British Journal of Psychiatry, 165* (suppl. 26), pp. 16–22.

Wittchen, H., Schuster, P., & Lieb, R. (2001). Comorbidity and mixed anxiety-depressive disorder: Clinical curiosity or pathophysiological need? *Human Psychopharmacology, 16* (suppl. 1), pp. S21–S30.

Witvliet, C., Ludwig, T.W., & Vander Laan, K.L. (2001). Granting forgiveness or harboring grduges: Implications for emotion, physiology, and health. *Psychological Science, 12*, pp. 117–124.

Wolfe, D. (1987). *Child Abuse: Implications for Child Development and Psychopathology.* Beverly Hills, CA: Sage.

Wolff, M., Alsobrook, J.P., & Pauls, D.L. (2000). Genetic aspects of obsessive-compulsive disorder. *Psychiatric Clinics of North America, 23*, pp. 535–544.

Wolpe, J. (1958). *Psychotherapy and Reciprocal Inhibition.* Stanford, CA: Stanford University Press.

Wong, P.T., & Watt, L.M. (1991). What types of reminiscence are associated with successful aging? *Psychology and Aging, 6*, pp. 272–279.

Wood, J.M., Lilienfeld, S.O., Nezworski, M.T., & Garb, H.N. (2001). Coming to grips with negative evidence for the comprehensive system for the Rorschach. *Journal of Personality Assessment, 77*, pp. 48–70.

Wood, J.M., Nezworski, M.T., Lilienfeld, S.O., & Garb, H.N. (2003). *What's Wrong with the Rorschach?* San Francisco: Jossey-Bass.

Woodside, D. B., Garfinkel, P.E., Lin, E., Goering, P., & Kaplan, A.S. (2001). Comparisons of men with full or partial eating disorders, men without eating disorders, and women with eating disorders in the community. *American Journal of Psychiatry, 158*, pp. 570–574.

Woody, E., & Sadler, P. (1998). On reintegrating dissociated theories: Comment on Kirsch and Lynn (1998). *Psychological Bulletin, 123*, pp. 192–197.

Woody, S.R., Steketee, G., & Chambless, D.L. (1995). Reliability and validity of the Yale-Brown obsessive-compulsive scale. *Behaviour Research and Therapy, 33*, pp. 597–605.

Worden, J.W. (1986). *Grief Counseling and Grief Therapy: A Handbook for the Mental Health Practitioner.* New York: Springer.

Wortman, C.B., & Silver, R.C. (2001). The myths of coping with loss revisited. In M.S. Stroebe et al. (Eds.), *Handbook of Bereavement Research*, pp. 405–429. Washington, D.C.: American Psychological Association.

Wouda, J.C., Hartman, P.M., Bakker, R.M., Bakker, J.O., van de Wiel, H.B.M., & Weijmar Schultz, W.C.M. (1998). Vaginal plethysmography in women with dyspareunia. *Journal of Sex Research, 35*, pp. 141–147.

Wrosch, C. Schulz, R., & Heekhausen, J. (2004). Health stresses and depressive symptomatology in the elderly: A control-process approach. *Current Directions in Psychological Science, 13*, pp. 17–20.

Wynne, L.C., & Singer, M.T. (1963). Thought disorder and family relations of schizophrenics. II. A classification of forms of thinking. *Archives of General Psychiatry, 9,* pp. 199–206.

Yamashita, I., Koyama, T., & Ohmori, T. (1995). Ethnic differences in alcohol metabolism and physiological responses to alcohol: Implications in alcohol abuse. In B. Tabakoff & P.L. Hoffman (Eds.), *Biological Aspects of Alcoholism,* pp. 49–61. Seattle, WA: Hogrefe & Huber.

Yang, J., McCrae, R.R., Costa, P.T., Yao, S., Dai, X, Cai, T., & Gao, B. (2000). The cross-cultural generalizability of Axis-II constructs: An evaluation of two personality disorder assessment instruments in the People's Republic of China. *Journal of Personality Disorders, 14,* pp. 249–263.

Yartz, A.R., & Hawk, L.W. (2001). Psychophysiological assessment of anxiety: Tales from the heart. In M.M. Antony, S.M. Orsillo, et al. (Eds), *Practitioner's Guide to Empirically Based Measures of Anxiety,* pp. 25–30. Dordrecht: Netherlandshers.

Yates, A. (1990). Current perspectives on the eating disorders. II. Treatment, outcome, and research directions. *Journal of the American Academy of Child and Adolescent Psychiatry, 29,* pp. 1–9.

Yates, W.R., Cadoret, R.J., & Troughton, E.P. (1999). The Iowa adoption studies: Methods and results. In M.C. LaBuda & E.L. Grigorenko (Eds.), *On the Way to Individuality: Current Methodological Issues in Behavioral Genetics,* pp. 95–125. Huntington. NY: Nova Science Publishers.

Yeh, M., & Weisz, J.R. (2001). Why are we here at the clinic? Parent-child (dis)agreement on referral problems at outpatient treatment entry. *Journal of Consulting and Clinical Psychology, 69,* pp. 1018–1025.

Yehuda, R. (2002). Current concepts: Posttraumatic stress disorder. *New England Journal of Medicine, 346,* pp. 108–114.

Yehuda, R., & McFarlane, A.C. (1995). Conflict between current knowledge about posttraumatic stress disorder and its original conceptual basis. *American Journal of Psychiatry, 152,* pp. 1705–1713.

Yeung, P.P., & Greenwald, S. (1992). Jewish Americans and mental health: Results of the NIMH Epidemiologic Catchment Area study. *Social Psychiatry and Psychiatric Epidemiology, 27,* pp. 292–297.

Yonkers, K.A., Bruce, S.E., Dyck, I.R., & Keller, M.B. (2003). Chronicity, relapse, and illness—course of panic disorder, social phobia, and generalized anxiety disorder: Findings in men and women from 8 years of follow-up. *Depression & Anxiety, 17,* pp. 173–179.

Yonkers, K.A., Zlotnick, C., Allsworth, J., Warshow, M., Shea, T., & Keller, M.B. (1998). Is the course of panic disorder the same in women and men? *American Journal of Psychiatry, 155,* pp. 596–602.

Younglove, J.A., & Vitello, C.J. (2003). Community notification provisions of "Megan's Law" from a therapeutic jurisprudence perspective: A case study. *American Journal of Forensic Psychology, 21,* pp. 25–38.

Yudofsky, S.C. (2005). *Fatal Flaws: Navigating Destructive Relationships with People with Disorders of Personality and Character.* Washington, D.C.: American Psychiatric Publishing.

Zahn-Waxler, C., Kochanska, G., Krupnick, J., & McKnew, D. (1990). Patterns of guilt in children depressed and well mothers. *Developmental Psychology, 26,* pp. 51–59.

Zanarini, M.C., & Frankenburg, F.R. (2001). Olanzapine treatment of female borderline personality disorder patients: A double-blind, placebo-controlled pilot study. *Journal of Clinical Psychiatry, 62,* pp. 849–854.

Zanarini, M.C., Frankenburg, F.R., Hennen, J., Reich, D.B., & Sink, K.R. (2005). Psychosocial functioning of borderline patients and Axis II comparison subjects followed prospectively for six years. *Journal of Personality Disorders, 19,* pp. 19–29.

Zarate, C.A., & Tohen, M. (1996). Epidemiology of mood disorders throughout the life cycle. In Shulman, K.I., & Tohen, M. (Eds.), *Mood Disorders Across the Lifespan.* New York: Wiley.

Zarit, S.H., Zarit, J.M., & Rosenberg-Thompson, S. (1990). A special treatment unit for Alzheimer's disease: Medical, behavioral, and environmental features. *Clinical Gerontologist, 9,* pp. 47–63.

Zautra, A.J., Johnson, L.M., & Davis, M.C. (2005). Positive affect as a source of resilience for women in chronic pain. *Journal of Consulting and Clinical Psychology, 73,* pp. 212–220.

Zebb, B.J., & Beck, J.G. (1998). Worry versus anxiety: Is there really a difference? *Behavior Modification, 22,* pp. 45–61.

Zigler, E. (1967). Familial mental retardation: A continuing dilemma. *Science, 155,* pp. 292–298.

Zigler, E., & Hodapp, R.M. (1986). *Understanding Mental Retardation.* New York: Cambridge University Press.

Zigler, E., & Styfco, S.J. (1993). Using research and theory to justify and inform Head Start expansion. *Social Policy Report for the Society Research in Child Development, 7* (2), pp. 1–20.

Zilbergeld, B. (1995). The critical and demanding partner in sex therapy pp. 311–330. In R.C. Rosen and S.R. Leiblum (Eds.), *Case Studies in Sex Therapy.* New York: Guilford.

Zilbergeld, B. (1999). *The New Male Sexuality* (revised edition). New York: Bantam Doubleday Dell.

Zill, N. (1978). *Divorce, Marital Happiness, and the Mental Health of Children: Findings from the FCD National Survey of Children.* Paper presented at the NIMH workshop on divorce and children. Bethesda, MD.

Zill, N., & Schoenborn, C.A. (1990). Developmental, learning, and emotional problems: Health of our nation's children. United States, 1988. *Advance Data from Vital and Health Statistics,* no. 190. Hyattsville, MD: National Center for Health Statistics.

Zito, J.M., Safer, D.J., dos Reis, S., Gardner, J.F., Boles, M., & Lynch, F. (2000). Trends in the prescribing of psychotropic medications to preschoolers. *Journal of the American Medical Association, 283,* pp. 1025–1030.

Zoccolillo, M., & Cloninger, C.R. (1986). Somatization disorder: Psychologic symptoms, social disability, and diagnosis. *Comprehensive Psychiatry, 27,* pp. 65–73.

Zoellner, L.A., Foa, E.B., Bartholomew, D.B., & Przeworski, A. (2000). Are trauma victims susceptible to "false memories"? *Journal of Abnormal Psychology, 109,* pp. 517–524.

Zohar, J., Sasson, Y., Chopra, M., Amital, D., & Iancu, I. (2000). Pharmacological treatment of obsessive-compulsive disorder: A review. In M. Maj and N. Sartorius (Eds.), *Obsessive-Compulsive Disorder,* pp. 43–92. New York: Wiley.

Zucker K.J. (2000) Gender identity disorder. In A.J. Sameroff, M. Lewis, & S.M. Miller (Eds.), *Handbook of Developmental Psychopathology,* 2nd ed., pp. 671–686. New York: Kluwer Academic.

Zucker, K.J., & Blanchard, R. (1997). Tranvestic fetishism: Psychopathology and theory. In D.R. Laws & W.T. O'Donohue (Eds.), *Handbook of Sexual Deviance: Theory and Application.* New York: Guilford.

Zuckerman, M. (1999). *Vulnerability to Psychopathology: A Biosocial Model.* Washington: American Psychological Association Press.

Credits
Photographs/Cartoons

Name Index

Subject Index

LICENSE AGREEMENT AND LIMITED WARRANTY

READ THE FOLLOWING TERMS AND CONDITIONS CAREFULLY BEFORE OPENING THIS DISK PACKAGE. THIS LEGAL DOCUMENT IS AN AGREEMENT BETWEEN YOU AND PRENTICE-HALL, INC. (THE "COMPANY"). BY OPENING THIS SEALED DISK PACKAGE, YOU ARE AGREEING TO BE BOUND BY THESE TERMS AND CONDITIONS. IF YOU DO NOT AGREE WITH THESE TERMS AND CONDITIONS, DO NOT OPEN THE DISK PACKAGE. PROMPTLY RETURN THE UNOPENED DISK PACKAGE AND ALL ACCOMPANYING ITEMS TO THE PLACE YOU OBTAINED THEM FOR A FULL REFUND OF ANY SUMS YOU HAVE PAID.

1. **GRANT OF LICENSE:** In consideration of your payment of the license fee, which is part of the price you paid for this product, and your agreement to abide by the terms and conditions of this Agreement, the Company grants to you a nonexclusive right to use and display the copy of the enclosed software program (hereinafter the "SOFTWARE") on a single computer (i.e., with a single CPU) at a single location so long as you comply with the terms of this Agreement. The Company reserves all rights not expressly granted to you under this Agreement.

2. **OWNERSHIP OF SOFTWARE:** You own only the magnetic or physical media (the enclosed disks) on which the SOFTWARE is recorded or fixed, but the Company retains all the rights, title, and ownership to the SOFTWARE recorded on the original disk copy(ies) and all subsequent copies of the SOFTWARE, regardless of the form or media on which the original or other copies may exist. This license is not a sale of the original SOFTWARE or any copy to you.

3. **COPY RESTRICTIONS:** This SOFTWARE and the accompanying printed materials and user manual (the "Documentation") are the subject of copyright. You may not copy the Documentation or the SOFTWARE, except that you may make a single copy of the SOFTWARE for backup or archival purposes only. You may be held legally responsible for any copying or copyright infringement which is caused or encouraged by your failure to abide by the terms of this restriction.

4. **USE RESTRICTIONS:** You may not network the SOFTWARE or otherwise use it on more than one computer or computer terminal at the same time. You may physically transfer the SOFTWARE from one computer to another provided that the SOFTWARE is used on only one computer at a time. You may not distribute copies of the SOFTWARE or Documentation to others. You may not reverse engineer, disassemble, decompile, modify, adapt, translate, or create derivative works based on the SOFTWARE or the Documentation without the prior written consent of the Company.

5. **TRANSFER RESTRICTIONS:** The enclosed SOFTWARE is licensed only to you and may not be transferred to any one else without the prior written consent of the Company. Any unauthorized transfer of the SOFTWARE shall result in the immediate termination of this Agreement.

6. **TERMINATION:** This license is effective until terminated. This license will terminate automatically without notice from the Company and become null and void if you fail to comply with any provisions or limitations of this license. Upon termination, you shall destroy the Documentation and all copies of the SOFTWARE. All provisions of this Agreement as to warranties, limitation of liability, remedies or damages, and our ownership rights shall survive termination.

7. **MISCELLANEOUS:** This Agreement shall be construed in accordance with the laws of the United States of America and the State of New York and shall benefit the Company, its affiliates, and assignees.

8. **LIMITED WARRANTY AND DISCLAIMER OF WARRANTY:** The Company warrants that the SOFTWARE, when properly used in accordance with the Documentation, will operate in substantial conformity with the description of the SOFTWARE set forth in the Documentation. The Company does not warrant that the SOFTWARE will meet your requirements or that the operation of the SOFTWARE will be uninterrupted or error-free. The Company warrants that the media on which the SOFTWARE is delivered shall be free from defects in materials and workmanship under normal use for a period of thirty (30) days from the date of your purchase. Your only remedy and the Company's only obligation under these limited warranties is, at the Company's option, return of the warranted item for a refund of any amounts paid by you or replacement of the item. Any replacement of SOFTWARE or media under the warranties shall not extend the original warranty period. The limited warranty set forth above shall not apply to any SOFTWARE which the Company determines in good faith has been subject to misuse, neglect, improper installation, repair, alteration, or damage by you. EXCEPT FOR THE EXPRESSED WARRANTIES SET FORTH ABOVE, THE COMPANY DISCLAIMS ALL WARRANTIES, EXPRESS OR IMPLIED, INCLUDING WITHOUT LIMITATION, THE IMPLIED WARRANTIES OF MERCHANTABILITY AND FITNESS FOR A PARTICULAR PURPOSE. EXCEPT FOR THE EXPRESS WARRANTY SET FORTH ABOVE, THE COMPANY DOES NOT WARRANT, GUARANTEE, OR MAKE ANY REPRESENTATION REGARDING THE USE OR THE RESULTS OF THE USE OF THE SOFTWARE IN TERMS OF ITS CORRECTNESS, ACCURACY, RELIABILITY, CURRENTNESS, OR OTHERWISE.

IN NO EVENT, SHALL THE COMPANY OR ITS EMPLOYEES, AGENTS, SUPPLIERS, OR CONTRACTORS BE LIABLE FOR ANY INCIDENTAL, INDIRECT, SPECIAL, OR CONSEQUENTIAL DAMAGES ARISING OUT OF OR IN CONNECTION WITH THE LICENSE GRANTED UNDER THIS AGREEMENT, OR FOR LOSS OF USE, LOSS OF DATA, LOSS OF INCOME OR PROFIT, OR OTHER LOSSES, SUSTAINED AS A RESULT OF INJURY TO ANY PERSON, OR LOSS OF OR DAMAGE TO PROPERTY, OR CLAIMS OF THIRD PARTIES, EVEN IF THE COMPANY OR AN AUTHORIZED REPRESENTATIVE OF THE COMPANY HAS BEEN ADVISED OF THE POSSIBILITY OF SUCH DAMAGES. IN NO EVENT SHALL LIABILITY OF THE COMPANY FOR DAMAGES WITH RESPECT TO THE SOFTWARE EXCEED THE AMOUNTS ACTUALLY PAID BY YOU, IF ANY, FOR THE SOFTWARE.

SOME JURISDICTIONS DO NOT ALLOW THE LIMITATION OF IMPLIED WARRANTIES OR LIABILITY FOR INCIDENTAL, INDIRECT, SPECIAL, OR CONSEQUENTIAL DAMAGES, SO THE ABOVE LIMITATIONS MAY NOT ALWAYS APPLY. THE WARRANTIES IN THIS AGREEMENT GIVE YOU SPECIFIC LEGAL RIGHTS AND YOU MAY ALSO HAVE OTHER RIGHTS WHICH VARY IN ACCORDANCE WITH LOCAL LAW.

ACKNOWLEDGMENT

YOU ACKNOWLEDGE THAT YOU HAVE READ THIS AGREEMENT, UNDERSTAND IT, AND AGREE TO BE BOUND BY ITS TERMS AND CONDITIONS. YOU ALSO AGREE THAT THIS AGREEMENT IS THE COMPLETE AND EXCLUSIVE STATEMENT OF THE AGREEMENT BETWEEN YOU AND THE COMPANY AND SUPERSEDES ALL PROPOSALS OR PRIOR AGREEMENTS, ORAL, OR WRITTEN, AND ANY OTHER COMMUNICATIONS BETWEEN YOU AND THE COMPANY OR ANY REPRESENTATIVE OF THE COMPANY RELATING TO THE SUBJECT MATTER OF THIS AGREEMENT.

Should you have any questions concerning this Agreement or if you wish to contact the Company for any reason, please contact in writing at the address below or call the at the telephone number provided.

PTR Customer Service
Prentice Hall PTR
One Lake Street
Upper Saddle River, New Jersey 07458

Telephone: 201-236-7105

DSM-IV-TR Classification

NOS: Not otherwise specified

If criteria are currently met, one of the following severity specifiers may be noted after the diagnosis:

Mild
Moderate
Severe

If criteria are no longer met, one of the following specifiers may be noted:

In Partial Remission
In Full Remission
Prior History

Disorders Usually First Diagnosed in Infancy, Childhood, or Adolescence

Mental Retardation

Note: These are coded on Axis II.
Mild Mental Retardation
Moderate Mental Retardation
Severe Mental Retardation
Profound Mental Retardation
Mental Retardation, Severity Unspecified

Learning Disorders

Reading Disorder
Mathematics Disorder
Disorder of Written Expression
Learning Disorder NOS

Motor Skills Disorder

Developmental Coordination Disorder

Communication Disorders

Expressive Language Disorder
Mixed Receptive-Expressive Language Disorder
Phonological Disorder
Stuttering
Communication Disorder NOS

Pervasive Developmental Disorders

Autistic Disorder
Rett's Disorder
Childhood Disintegrative Disorder
Asperger's Disorder
Pervasive Developmental Disorder NOS

Attention-Deficit and Disruptive Behavior Disorders

Attention-Deficit/Hyperactivity Disorder
Attention-Deficit/Hyperactivity Disorder NOS
Conduct Disorder
Oppositional Defiant Disorder
Disruptive Behavior Disorder NOS

Feeding and Eating Disorders of Infancy or Early Childhood

ca
ination Disorder
q Disorder of Infancy or Early Childhood

ers
order
or Vocal Tic Disorder
rder

a General Medical

Other Disorders of Infancy, Childhood, or Adolescence

Separation Anxiety Disorder
Selective Mutism
Reactive Attachment Disorder of Infancy or Early Childhood
Stereotypic Movement Disorder
Disorder of Infancy, Childhood, or Adolescence NOS

Delirium, Dementia, and Amnestic and Other Cognitive Disorders

Delirium

Delirium Due to . . . [Indicate the General Medical Condition]
Substance Intoxication Delirium
Substance Withdrawal Delirium
Delirium Due to Multiple Etiologies
Delirium NOS

Dementia

Dementia of the Alzheimer's Type, with Early Onset
Dementia of the Alzheimer's Type, with Late Onset
Vascular Dementia
Dementia Due to HIV Disease
Dementia Due to Head Trauma
Dementia Due to Parkinson's Disease
Dementia Due to Huntington's Disease
Dementia Due to Pick's Disease
Dementia Due to Creutzfeldt-Jakob Disease
Dementia Due to . . . [Indicate the General Medical Condition not listed above]
Substance-Induced Persisting Dementia
Dementia Due to Multiple Etiologies
Dementia NOS

Amnestic Disorders

Amnestic Disorder Due to . . . [Indicate the General Medical Condition]
Specify if: Transient/Chronic
Substance-Induced Persisting Amnestic Disorder
Amnestic Disorder NOS

Substance-Related Disorders

Alcohol Use Disorders

Alcohol Dependence
Alcohol Abuse

Alcohol-Induced Disorders

Alcohol Intoxication
Alcohol Withdrawal
Alcohol Intoxication Delirium
Alcohol-Induced Persisting Amnestic Disorder
Alcohol-Induced Psychotic Disorder

Amphetamine Use Disorders

Amphetamine Dependence
Amphetamine Abuse

Amphetamine-Induced Disorders

Amphetamine Intoxication
Amphetamine Withdrawal
Amphetamine Intoxication Delirium
Amphetamine-Induced Psychotic Disorder

Caffeine-Induced Disorders

Caffeine Intoxication
Caffeine-Induced Anxiety Disorder
Caffeine-Induced Sleep Disorder

Cannabis Use Disorders

Cannabis Dependence
Cannabis Abuse

Cannabis-Induced Disorders

Cannabis Intoxication
Cannabis Intoxication Delirium
Cannabis-Induced Psychotic Disorder
Cannabis-Induced Anxiety Disorder

Cocaine Use Disorders

Cocaine Dependence
Cocaine Abuse

Cocaine-Induced Disorders

Cocaine Intoxication
Cocaine Withdrawal
Cocaine Intoxication Delirium
Cocaine-Induced Psychotic Disorder

Hallucinogen Use Disorders

Hallucinogen Dependence
Hallucinogen Abuse

Hallucinogen-Induced Disorders

Hallucinogen Intoxication
Hallucinogen Persisting Disorder (Flashbacks)
Hallucinogen Intoxication Delirium
Hallucinogen-Induced Psychotic Disorder

Inhalant Use Disorders

Inhalant Dependence
Inhalant Abuse

Inhalant-Induced Disorders

Inhalant Intoxication
Inhalant Intoxication Delirium
Inhalant-Induced Persisting Dementia
Inhalant-Induced Psychotic Disorder

Nicotine Use Disorder

Nicotine Dependence

Nicotine-Induced Disorder

Nicotine Withdrawal

Opioid Use Disorders

Opioid Dependence
Opioid Abuse

Opioid-Induced Disorders

Opioid Intoxication
Specify if: With Perceptual Disturbances
Opioid Withdrawal
Opioid Intoxication Delirium
Opioid-Induced Psychotic Disorder

Phencyclidine Use Disorders

Phencyclidine Dependence
Phencyclidine Abuse

Phencyclidine-Induced Disorders

Phencyclidine Intoxication
Specify if: With Perceptual Disturbances
Phencyclidine-Induced Psychotic Disorder

Sedative, Hypnotic, or Anxiolytic Use Disorders

Sedative, Hypnotic, or Anxiolytic Dependence
Sedative, Hypnotic, or Anxiolytic Abuse

Sedative-, Hypnotic-, or Anxiolytic-Induced Disorders

Sedative, Hypnotic, or Anxiolytic Intoxication
Sedative, Hypnotic, or Anxiolytic Withdrawal
Specify if: With Perceptual Disturbances